DreamCreators Corp
11818 S.E. Mill Plain Blvd. Suite 311 F
Vancouver, WA 98684
Phone 360-260-9797

Teacher's Edition

Integrated Mathematics 2

Authors

Senior Authors
Rheta N. Rubenstein
Timothy V. Craine
Thomas R. Butts

Kerry Cantrell
Linda Dritsas
Valarie A. Elswick
Joseph Kavanaugh
Sara N. Munshin
Stuart J. Murphy
Anthony Piccolino
Salvador Quezada
Jocelyn Coleman Walton

McDougal Littell
A HOUGHTON MIFFLIN COMPANY
Evanston, Illinois • Boston • Dallas

Authors

Senior Authors

Rheta N. Rubenstein Associate Professor of Education, University of Michigan at Dearborn, Dearborn, Michigan

Timothy V. Craine Assistant Professor of Mathematical Sciences and Department Chair, Central Connecticut State University, New Britain, Connecticut

Thomas R. Butts Professor of Mathematics Education, University of Texas at Dallas, Dallas, Texas

Kerry Cantrell Mathematics Teacher and Divisional Technology Coordinator, Marshfield High School, Marshfield, Missouri

Linda Dritsas Mathematics Coordinator, Fresno Unified School District, Fresno, California

Valarie A. Elswick Mathematics Consultant and former Mathematics Teacher, Roy C. Ketcham Senior High School, Wappingers Falls, New York

Joseph Kavanaugh Academic Head of Mathematics, Scotia-Glenville Central School District, Scotia, New York

Sara N. Munshin Middle School Mathematics Specialist, Los Angeles Unified School District, Los Angeles, California

Stuart J. Murphy Visual Learning Specialist, Evanston, Illinois

Anthony Piccolino Associate Professor of Mathematics, Montclair State University, Upper Montclair, New Jersey

Salvador Quezada Mathematics Teacher, Theodore Roosevelt High School, Los Angeles, California

Jocelyn Coleman Walton Educational Consultant, Mathematics K-12, and former Mathematics Supervisor, Plainfield High School, Plainfield, New Jersey

The authors wish to thank **Jane Pflughaupt**, Mathematics Teacher, Pioneer High School, San Jose, California, **John Fourcroy**, Mathematics Teacher, Lindhurst High School, Marysville, California, and **Anita G. Morris**, Coordinator of Mathematics, Anne Arundel County Public Schools, Annapolis, Maryland, for their contributions to this Teacher's Edition.

ISBN: 0-618-07398-1

1 2 3 4 5 6 7 8 9 10—DWO—04 03 02 01 00

Contents of the Teacher's Edition

PHILOSOPHY
of Integrated Mathematics

Goals of the Course

Integrated Mathematics has been written to prepare your students for success in college, and in their careers and daily lives in the 21st century, by helping them develop their abilities to:

➤ **Explore and solve mathematical problems**

➤ **Think critically**

➤ **Work cooperatively with others**

➤ **Communicate ideas clearly**

Underlying Concept

This program is built on the idea that students develop better conceptual understanding of mathematics and stronger problem solving skills when they:

➤ **See the connections among different branches of mathematics**

➤ **Are actively involved in the learning process**

➤ **Study mathematics that is meaningful**

➤ **Continually build on prior learning because topics are spiraled**

Accessible and Inviting Mathematics

Integrated Mathematics was designed to make mathematics accessible and inviting. It opens the door to mathematics for more students by incorporating a variety of different teaching strategies, including:

➤ **Visual and hands-on approaches**

➤ **Real-life applications**

➤ **Exploratory activities and projects**

➤ **Use of technology**

➤ **Group work**

➤ **Open-ended problem solving**

A Manageable Program

Integrated Mathematics makes it easy for you to manage these teaching strategies by incorporating them directly into the textbook — at the places where you would use them in teaching. In addition, ongoing assessment that matches the instruction is included throughout the course.

Basis of the Curriculum

This program is based on the recommendations of the National Council of Teachers of Mathematics and other curriculum groups that emphasize problem solving, critical thinking, communication, and connections among mathematical topics and connections between mathematics and other subject areas.

Mathematical Content

Over a three-year period, *Integrated Mathematics* teaches the same mathematical topics as a contemporary Algebra 1/Geometry/Algebra 2 sequence. The difference is in the organization of the content. Instead of being divided into separate courses, algebra and geometry are taught in each of the three years. In addition, topics from logical reasoning, measurement, probability, statistics, discrete mathematics, and functions are interwoven throughout each year.

Integrated Mathematics 2 builds on the mathematical topics and problem solving techniques introduced in *Integrated Mathematics 1*. The Topic Spiraling chart on page xiii of the textbook shows how mathematical concepts are spiraled over the three years of the program.

Advantages of an Integrated Approach

With an integrated approach, your students can:

➤ **Learn more mathematics**

➤ **Solve problems that are more realistic and more interesting**

➤ **Have better retention of what they have learned**

Field Testing

Preliminary versions of *Integrated Mathematics* were tried out by hundreds of teachers and thousands of students in many different types of classrooms nationwide. Their comments and suggestions have guided the development of this book. Here is what some teachers who piloted the book have said:

"The kids look forward to the Explorations and working together in groups. This course has made a real difference in their attitude toward math."

"I heard one father make the comment that if all teachers would use this approach — trying to show connections and trying to show group efforts toward a final project or final result — his job in industry would be far easier."

"I've noticed a real difference in students' critical thinking skills. And they are better able to conceptualize the algebraic and geometric concepts and how they relate to each other."

Contents

What Students Are Saying   xiv

Course Preview   xvi

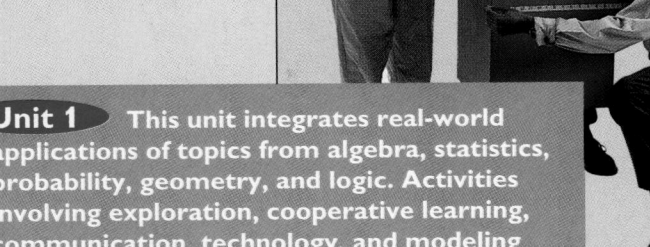

Unit 1 This unit integrates real-world applications of topics from algebra, statistics, probability, geometry, and logic. Activities involving exploration, cooperative learning, communication, technology, and modeling help students become actively involved.

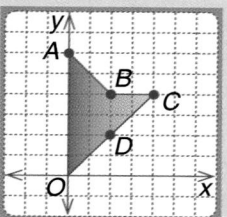

Unit 3   Linear Systems and Matrices

Unit 2 The focus of this unit is modeling a variety of situations using equations, functions, graphs, and tables. Connections to driver education, music, earth science, literature, physics, and other topics are explored.

Unit 3 This unit connects the key ideas of linear systems to technology, graphing, matrices, and transformations. The new techniques for analyzing real-world applications presented in this unit highlight the power of mathematics.

Table of Contents

Unit 4   Quadratic Functions and Graphs

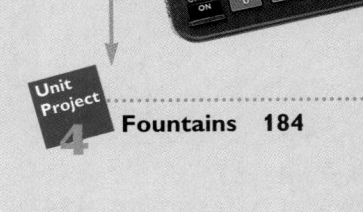

Unit Project 4   Fountains   184

Unit 4 Students explore quadratic functions and equations in this unit. Technology, manipulatives, and visual displays facilitate understanding of concepts.

Unit 5 In this unit, students use coordinate geometry and matrices to explore properties of polygons and characteristics of transformations. Applications of these topics to literature, biology, sports, history, and geology highlight their usefulness.

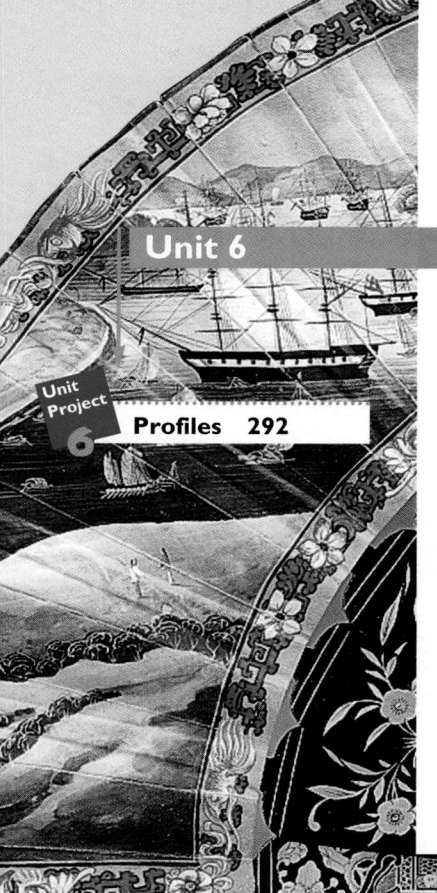

Table of Contents

Unit 6 This unit presents many topics from discrete mathematics, including probability, permutations, combinations, binomial experiments, and the binomial theorem. To aid learning, many concepts are presented both visually and verbally.

Unit 7 — Logic and Proof

Unit 7   This unit extends the study of reasoning begun in Units 1 and 5. Algebraic and geometric proofs presented in real-life contexts enable students to reach conclusions about the world around them.

Unit 8 | Similar and Congruent Triangles

Unit 8 Building on the foundation of proof presented in Unit 7, this unit develops many important concepts from geometry. Practical applications relating to perspective, ancient and contemporary tools, and architecture underscore the importance of geometry in everyday life.

Unit 9 This unit extends the study of polynomial functions and equations begun in Unit 4. Graphics calculators provide an important means of exploring graphs and understanding the connection between functions and equations. Many interesting and relevant applications are included.

Unit 10 The focus of this unit is three-dimensional coordinate geometry. Activities involving manipulatives, technology, applications, research, and cooperative learning are incorporated throughout.

Integrated Mathematics Topic Spiraling

This chart shows how mathematical strands are spiraled over the three years of the *Integrated Mathematics* program.

	Course 1	Course 2	Course 3
Algebra	Linear equations Linear inequalities Multiplying binomials Factoring expressions	Quadratic equations Linear systems Rational equations Complex numbers	Polynomial functions Exponential functions Logarithmic functions Parametric equations
Geometry	Angles, polygons, circles Perimeter, circumference Area, surface area Volume Trigonometric ratios	Similar and congruent figures Geometric proofs Coordinate geometry Transformational geometry Special right triangles	Inscribed figures Transforming graphs Vectors Triangle trigonometry Circular trigonometry

Statistics, Probability	Analyzing data and
	  displaying data
	Experimental and
	  theoretical probability
	Geometric probability
		Sampling methods
		Simulation
		Binomial distributions
			Variability
			Standard deviation
			z-scores

Logical Reasoning	Conjectures Counterexamples If-then statements	Inductive and deductive reasoning Valid and invalid reasoning Postulates and proof	Identities Contrapositive and inverse Comparing proof methods
Discrete Math	Discrete quantities Matrices to display data Lattices	Matrix operations Transformation matrices Counting techniques	Sequences and series Recursion Limits

Teachers today are being asked to teach more mathematics, and better mathematics, to more students.

How is this possible?

Integrated Approach

Integrated Mathematics interweaves mathematical topics and contemporary teaching strategies throughout the course. Key mathematical strands are spiraled through the units — and integrated within individual sections.

FUNCTIONS

Throughout this course, *function* is a unifying idea that ties together topics from algebra, geometry, statistics, and discrete mathematics.

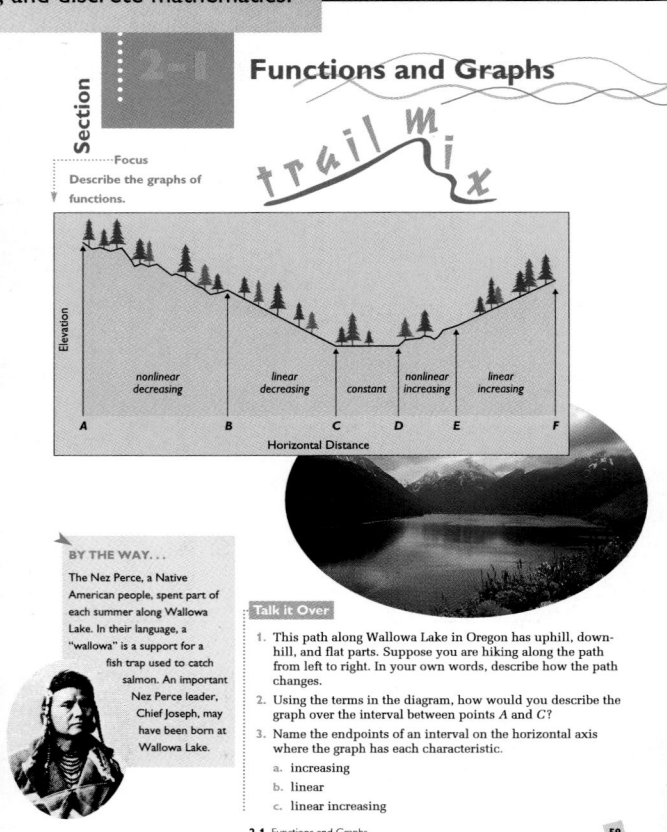

Section 2-1

Functions and Graphs

trail mix

Focus
Describe the graphs of functions.

BY THE WAY...

The Nez Perce, a Native American people, spent part of each summer along Wallowa Lake. In their language, a "wallowa" is a support for a fish trap used to catch salmon. An important Nez Perce leader, Chief Joseph, may have been born at Wallowa Lake.

Talk it Over

1. This path along Wallowa Lake in Oregon has uphill, down-hill, and flat parts. Suppose you are hiking along the path from left to right. In your own words, describe how the path changes.

2. Using the terms in the diagram, how would you describe the graph over the interval between points *A* and *C*?

3. Name the endpoints of an interval on the horizontal axis where the graph has each characteristic.
   a. increasing
   b. linear
   c. linear increasing

2-1 Functions and Graphs

59

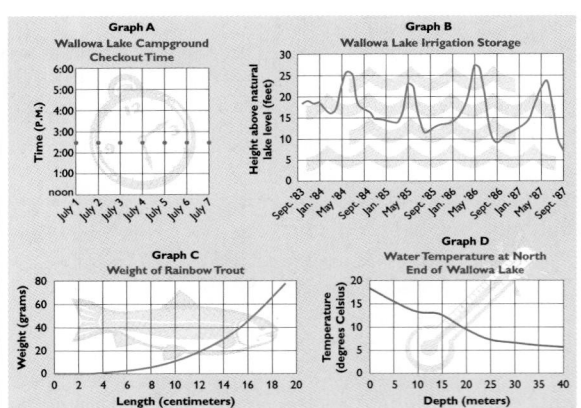

4. Use graphs A–D.
   a. The graph of a straight line is **linear.** Which graphs are linear throughout? Which are nonlinear throughout?
   b. Which graphs are increasing throughout? Which are decreasing throughout? Which are constant throughout?
   c. Which graphs show discrete data? continuous data?

5. From graph A, what can you say about the checkout time for Wallowa Lake Campground during the first week of July?

6. Can you use graph B to predict the water level for October 1987? Why or why not?

7. From graph C, estimate the weight of a rainbow trout that is 18 cm long.

8. From graph D, can you tell if the temperature changes at the same rate from the surface down to a depth of 40 m? Explain.

9. Graphs can have different characteristics over different intervals. Using this idea and the terms in the diagram on page 59, describe the characteristics of graph D.

10. Remember that a **function** is a relationship in which there is *only one* value of the *dependent variable* for each value of the *control,* or *independent, variable.* Do you think graphs A–D are graphs of functions? Why or why not?

Student Resources Toolbox
p. 649 *Graphs, Equations, and Inequalities*

60

DATA ANALYSIS

In coordinate graphing, concepts from algebra and geometry are combined to provide tools for analyzing and displaying real-world data.

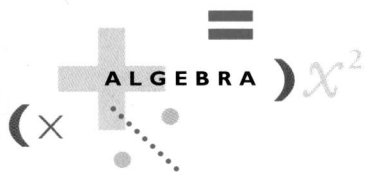

ALGEBRA

Functions, equations, graphs: linear, quadratic, cubic, exponential, polynomial, rational 2-2, 2-3, 2-5, 2-7, Unit 4, Unit 9

Solving systems 3-1, 3-2, 3-3, 3-4, 3-8, 4-7, 9-6

Modeling problem situations 2-2, 2-7, 3-1, 3-2, 4-1, 4-3, 4-7, 9-1, 9-5, 9-6

Mathematical operations: exponents, factoring, powers of binomials, complex numbers, radicals 2-6, 4-3, 4-4, 4-6, 6-9, 8-7, 8-8, 9-2, 9-3, 9-4, 9-5

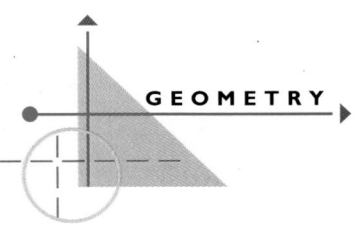

GEOMETRY

Logical reasoning and proof 1-5, 1-6, 1-7, 5-1, 5-6, Unit 7, Unit 8

Properties and applications of plane and space figures 1-5, 1-6, 2-4, Unit 5, 7-2, 7-4, 7-7, 7-8, Unit 8, 9-4, Unit 10

Coordinate geometry 2-2, 2-3, 2-5, 2-7, 3-1, 3-3, 4-1, 4-2, 5-2–5-6, 7-1, 8-6, 9-4, 10-4, 10-5, 10-6

Transformations 3-6, 4-2, 5-4, 8-6, 10-2

STATISTICS & PROBABILITY

Surveys, sampling, simulation 1-1, 1-2, 1-3, 1-4

Probability of events 6-3, 6-4, 9-5

Binomial experiments 6-7, 6-8

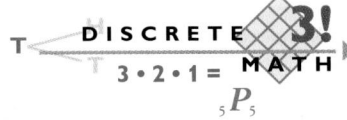

DISCRETE MATH

$3 \cdot 2 \cdot 1 = {}_5P_5$

Matrix operations and applications 3-5, 3-6, 3-7, 3-8

Transformation matrices 3-6, 5-4

Counting strategies, permutations, combinations 1-6, 6-1, 6-2, 6-5, 6-6, 6-9

TOPIC INTEGRATION

Topic spiraling enables students to continually build on prior learning. The list at the right illustrates how major topic strands are integrated into the sections of the book.

ALGEBRA AND GEOMETRY

The basic concepts of functions and their graphs introduced in this unit provide a strong foundation for the rest of the course.

Growth and Decay

Graphs of functions can be examples of *growth*, *decay*, or a *constant* depending on whether the value of the dependent variable continually increases, decreases, or remains the same when the value of the control variable increases.

TYPES OF GRAPHS

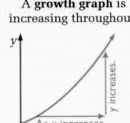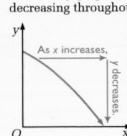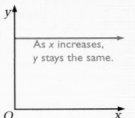

A **growth graph** is increasing throughout.

A **decay graph** is decreasing throughout.

A **constant graph** is linear and horizontal.

As x increases, y increases.

As x increases, y decreases.

As x increases, y stays the same.

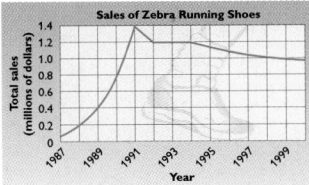

Sales of Zebra Running Shoes

Sample 1

a. Use the terms *linear* or *nonlinear* and *increasing*, *decreasing*, or *constant* to describe the graph.

b. Is this a *growth graph*, a *decay graph*, or *neither*? Explain your choice.

c. **Writing** Based on the graph, do you think Zebra Company stock is a good investment? Why or why not?

Sample Response

a. Between 1987 and 1991: nonlinear and increasing.
Between 1991 and 1992: linear and decreasing.
Between 1992 and 1994: constant.
Between 1994 and 2000: nonlinear and decreasing.

b. Neither, because the graph is sometimes increasing, sometimes decreasing, and sometimes constant.

c. Zebra Company stock does not look like a good investment. The graph shows that sales were not increasing over the last nine years shown.

▸ Now you are ready for:
Exs. 1–17 on pp. 63–64

61

LOGICAL REASONING

The discussion and writing questions help students develop their reasoning skills. Logical reasoning, both formal and informal, is an important focus of this course.

I want *all* my students to have the mathematical and problem solving skills they need. But some students just don't seem interested in learning math.

How can I get them involved?

Active Learning

Integrated Mathematics makes it easy for you to get your students actively involved because projects, explorations, activities, and discussion questions are built right into the book.

EXPLORATIONS

The Explorations get students involved in investigating math. They build strong conceptual understanding by helping students move from the concrete to the abstract.

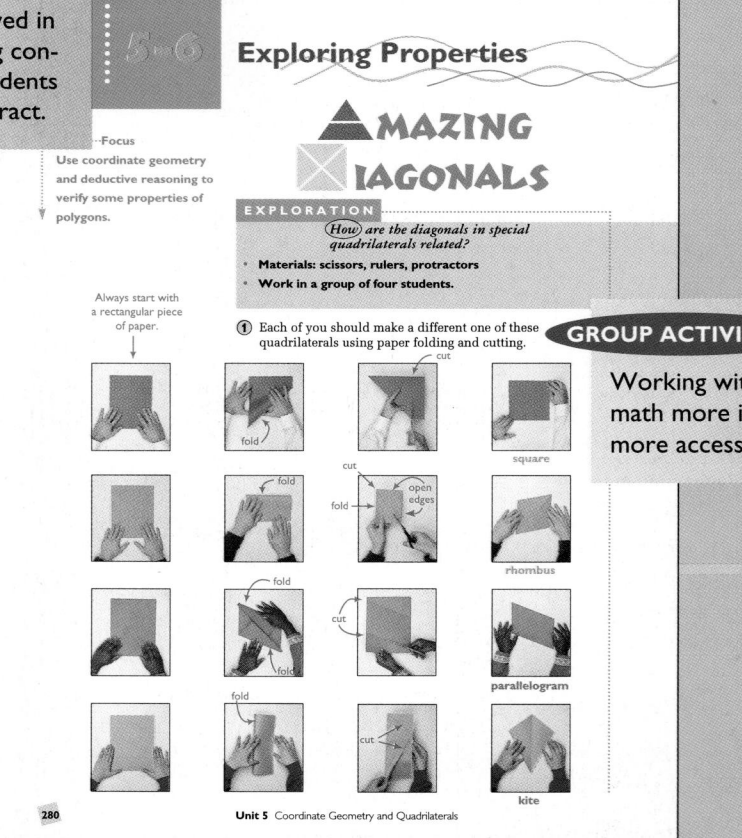

5-6

Exploring Properties

▲MAZING ⊠IAGONALS

Focus
Use coordinate geometry and deductive reasoning to verify some properties of polygons.

EXPLORATION

How are the diagonals in special quadrilaterals related?

• **Materials: scissors, rulers, protractors**
• **Work in a group of four students.**

Always start with a rectangular piece of paper.

① Each of you should make a different one of these quadrilaterals using paper folding and cutting.

square

rhombus

parallelogram

kite

280   **Unit 5** Coordinate Geometry and Quadrilaterals

GROUP ACTIVITIES

Working with others can make math more interesting and more accessible for students.

Each unit begins with a Unit Project. These projects give your students a chance to work on the types of open-ended, long-range problems that prepare them for future careers.

The Unit Projects
➤ put the mathematics in context
➤ unify related mathematical topics
➤ give all students an opportunity to participate and contribute

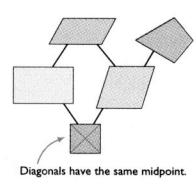

② The **diagonal** of a polygon is a segment joining two non-consecutive vertices. Show that the square has each of these properties. Use a ruler and a protractor if necessary.
  a. The diagonals have the same midpoint.
  b. The diagonals are perpendicular to each other.
  c. The diagonals are equal in measure.

③ Decide whether each of the other quadrilaterals you made in step 1 has any or all of the properties listed in step 2. The person who made the square should explore the properties of a rectangle.

④ Organize your results from step 3 in a quadrilateral chart like the one at the left.

Diagonals have the same midpoint.
Diagonals are perpendicular.
Diagonals are equal in measure.

Verifying Properties with Coordinates

In the Exploration, you used inductive reasoning to support your findings. You can also use coordinates and deductive reasoning to prove conjectures.

Sample 1

Use the coordinates of a rectangle in standard position to show that the diagonals of every rectangle have each property.
a. The diagonals are equal in measure.
b. The diagonals have the same midpoint.

Sample Response

a. Use the distance formula. Find the length of each diagonal and compare.
$$OR = \sqrt{(a-0)^2 + (c-0)^2} = \sqrt{a^2 + c^2}$$
$$SQ = \sqrt{(a-0)^2 + (0-c)^2} = \sqrt{a^2 + c^2}$$
These are equal, so the diagonals are equal in measure.

b. Use t

The

The

▶ N
Exs. 1-5

Properties of diagonals are investigated by inductive and deductive reasoning, and by synthetic and coordinate methods.

Shared Properties

Coordinate geometry can be used to show that the diagonals of special quadrilaterals have the properties you have been exploring. Here is a summary of those properties.

X⌒ab

DIAGONALS OF SPECIAL QUADRILATERALS

In a *parallelogram*, the diagonals have the same midpoint.

In a *kite*, the diagonals are perpendicular to each other.

In a *rectangle*, the diagonals are equal in measure.
The diagonals are equal in measure.

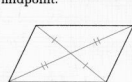
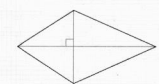
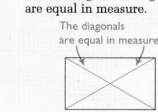

parallelogram

kite

rhombus

Every special quadrilateral shares the properties of the family of quadrilaterals to which it belongs. For example, a rhombus is a kite and a parallelogram. As you saw in the Exploration, its diagonals are perpendicular and have the same midpoint.

Here is another property of special quadrilaterals that is explored in Exercise 4.

X⌒ab

OPPOSITE SIDES OF A PARALLELOGRAM

In a *parallelogram*, opposite sides are equal in measure.

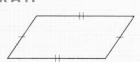

Talk it Over

Use the quadrilateral chart that you made in the Exploration. Name all special quadrilaterals that have each property.
  1. The diagonals have the same midpoint.
  2. The diagonals are perpendicular to each other.
  3. The diagonals are equal in measure.
  4. Opposite sides are equal in measure.

Unit 5 Coordinate Geometry and Quadrilaterals

The Talk it Over questions give students a chance to communicate their understanding.

The Working on the Unit Project exercises in each section help students build the knowledge and the skills they need to complete the project.

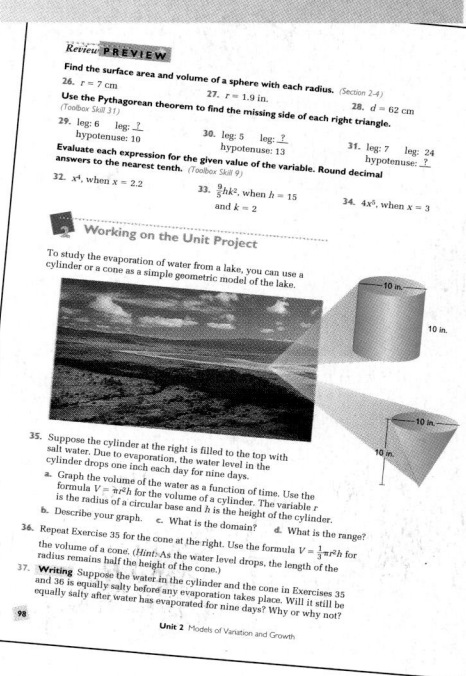

Review **PREVIEW**

Find the surface area and volume of a sphere with each radius. *(Section 2-4)*
26. $r = 7$ cm
27. $r = 1.9$ in.
28. $d = 62$ cm

Use the Pythagorean theorem to find the missing side of each right triangle. *(Toolbox Skill 31)*
29. leg: 6 leg: ? hypotenuse: 10
30. leg: 5 leg: ? hypotenuse: 13
31. leg: 7 leg: 24 hypotenuse: ?

Evaluate each expression for the given value of the variable. Round decimal answers to the nearest tenth. *(Toolbox Skill 9)*
32. x^4, when $x = 2.2$
33. $\frac{9}{5}hk^2$, when $h = 15$ and $k = 2$
34. $4x^5$, when $x = 3$

Working on the Unit Project

To study the evaporation of water from a lake, you can use a cylinder or a cone as a simple geometric model of the lake.

35. Suppose the cylinder at the right is filled to the top with salt water. Due to evaporation, the water level in the cylinder drops one inch each day for nine days.
  a. Graph the volume of the water as a function of time. Use the formula $V = \pi r^2 h$ for the volume of a cylinder. The variable r is the radius of a circular base and h is the height of the cylinder.
  b. Describe your graph. c. What is the domain? d. What is the range?

36. Repeat Exercise 35 for the cone at the right. Use the formula $V = \frac{1}{3}\pi r^2 h$ for the volume of a cone. (*Hint:* As the water level drops, the length of the radius remains half the height of the cone.)

37. **Writing** Suppose the water in the cylinder and the cone in Exercises 35 and 36 is equally salty before any evaporation takes place. Will it still be equally salty after water has evaporated for nine days? Why or why not?

98

Unit 2 Models of Variation and Growth

T17

I'm tired of my students asking, "When am I ever going to use this?" I want them to realize that mathematics is useful and powerful.

How can I convince them?

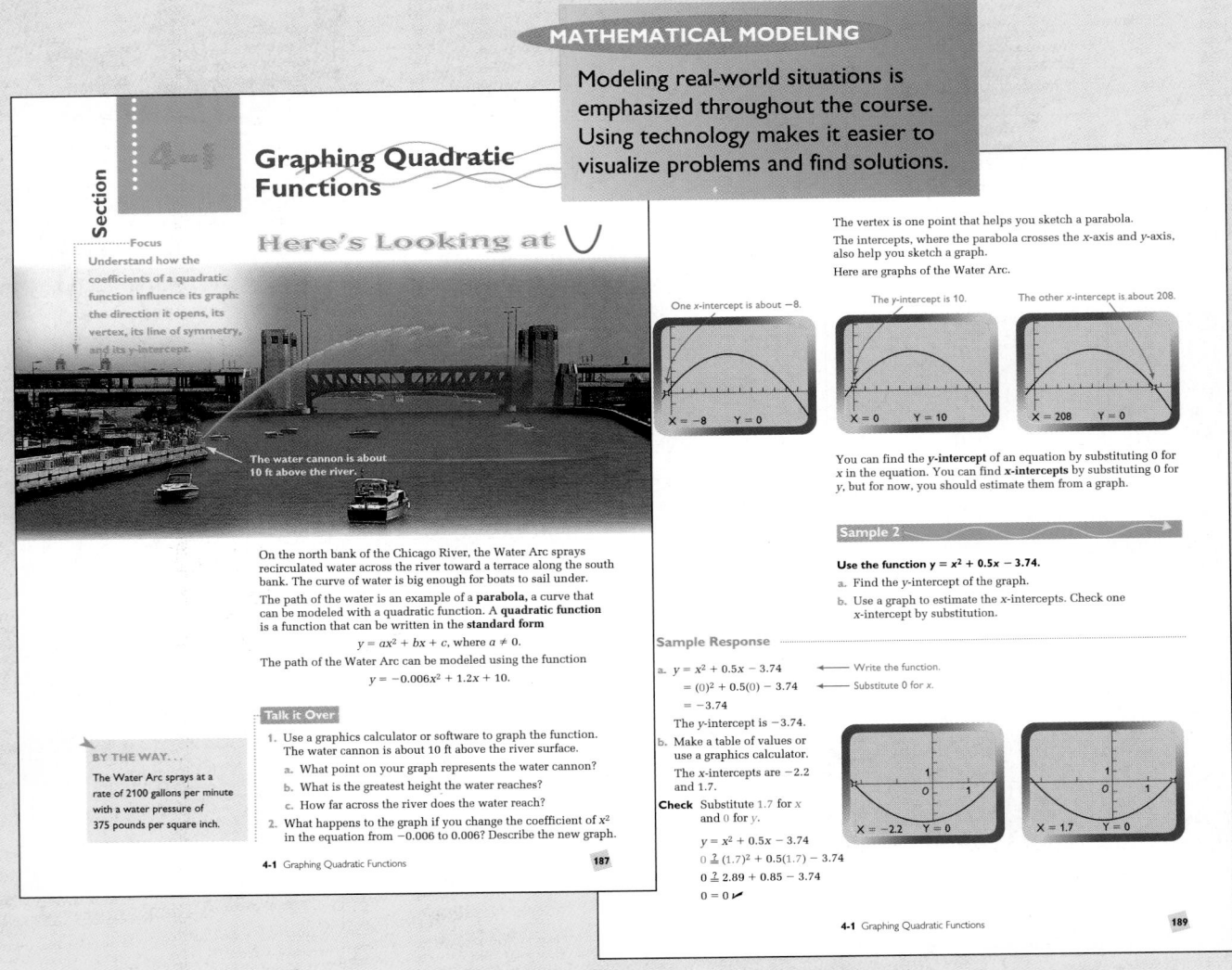

Meaningful Mathematics

Integrated Mathematics focuses on important concepts in mathematics and shows how they can be applied to solve a wide variety of types of problems in daily life and in careers.

MATHEMATICAL MODELING

Modeling real-world situations is emphasized throughout the course. Using technology makes it easier to visualize problems and find solutions.

Section 4-1

Graphing Quadratic Functions

Here's Looking at ∨

Focus
Understand how the coefficients of a quadratic function influence its graph: the direction it opens, its vertex, its line of symmetry, and its y-intercept.

The water cannon is about 10 ft above the river.

On the north bank of the Chicago River, the Water Arc sprays recirculated water across the river toward a terrace along the south bank. The curve of water is big enough for boats to sail under.

The path of the water is an example of a **parabola**, a curve that can be modeled with a quadratic function. A **quadratic function** is a function that can be written in the **standard form**

$$y = ax^2 + bx + c, \text{ where } a \neq 0.$$

The path of the Water Arc can be modeled using the function

$$y = -0.006x^2 + 1.2x + 10.$$

Talk it Over

BY THE WAY...

The Water Arc sprays at a rate of 2100 gallons per minute with a water pressure of 375 pounds per square inch.

1. Use a graphics calculator or software to graph the function. The water cannon is about 10 ft above the river surface.
   a. What point on your graph represents the water cannon?
   b. What is the greatest height the water reaches?
   c. How far across the river does the water reach?
2. What happens to the graph if you change the coefficient of x^2 in the equation from −0.006 to 0.006? Describe the new graph.

4-1 Graphing Quadratic Functions   **187**

The vertex is one point that helps you sketch a parabola. The intercepts, where the parabola crosses the x-axis and y-axis, also help you sketch a graph.

Here are graphs of the Water Arc.

One x-intercept is about −8.

X = −8   Y = 0

The y-intercept is 10.

X = 0   Y = 10

The other x-intercept is about 208.

X = 208   Y = 0

You can find the **y-intercept** of an equation by substituting 0 for x in the equation. You can find **x-intercepts** by substituting 0 for y, but for now, you should estimate them from a graph.

Sample 2

Use the function $y = x^2 + 0.5x - 3.74$.

a. Find the y-intercept of the graph.
b. Use a graph to estimate the x-intercepts. Check one x-intercept by substitution.

Sample Response

a. $y = x^2 + 0.5x - 3.74$ ⟵ Write the function.
   $= (0)^2 + 0.5(0) - 3.74$ ⟵ Substitute 0 for x.
   $= -3.74$
   The y-intercept is −3.74.

b. Make a table of values or use a graphics calculator. The x-intercepts are −2.2 and 1.7.

Check Substitute 1.7 for x and 0 for y.

X = −2.2   Y = 0

X = 1.7   Y = 0

$y = x^2 + 0.5x - 3.74$
$0 \overset{?}{=} (1.7)^2 + 0.5(1.7) - 3.74$
$0 \overset{?}{=} 2.89 + 0.85 - 3.74$
$0 = 0$ ✔

4-1 Graphing Quadratic Functions   **189**

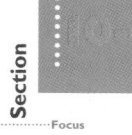

Cautions in Using Statistics

Section

In Line
WITH THE FACTS

▸ Focus
Learn to raise questions about surveys.

Survey: Rights of Citizens
Do you think that in-line skaters should be able to move freely throughout the city?

Survey: High-Speed Dangers
Should in-line skaters be allowed to endanger the safety of pedestrians by skating on sidewalks?

Talk it Over

1. Compare the two survey questions. How are they different?
2. Suppose the two questions were given to unbiased samples of people. What resu
3. Create another version of this question. the response would be?
4. How could the question be written to a the results?

HIGH–INTEREST APPLICATIONS

Students appreciate the impact that mathematics has on their lives when they see a wide range of applications.

Points That Fit Conditions

Section

It's Around Here Somewhere

▸ Focus
Describe or draw a set of points that meet one or more conditions.

On January 17, 1994, a large earthquake struck the western United States. The earthquake recording station at Topopah Spring, Nevada, recorded that the *epicenter* was located about 370 km away. The epicenter of a quake is the place on the surface of Earth above the focus of the quake.

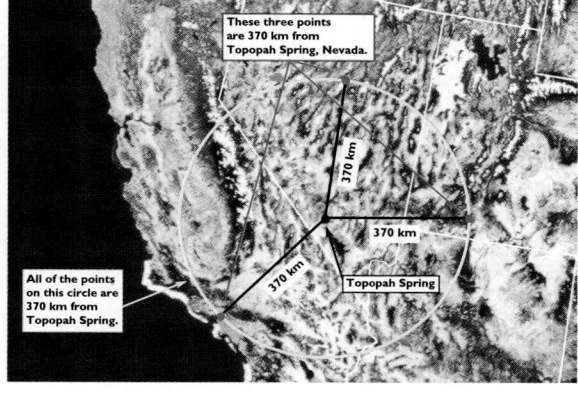

These three points are 370 km from Topopah Spring, Nevada.

370 km

370 km

370 km

Topopah Spring

All of the points on this circle are 370 km from Topopah Spring.

Earthquake stations record only the distance to the epicenter, not the direction. The location of the epicenter could be any point on a circle with radius 370 km centered at the recording station.

571

---

connection to **BIOLOGY**

A system of classifying living things by phylum, class, order, family, genus, and species was developed by Carolus Linnaeus in 1758. This chart shows a portion of one of the eleven phyla, the Chordates. Mammals are one of seven classes of Chordates.

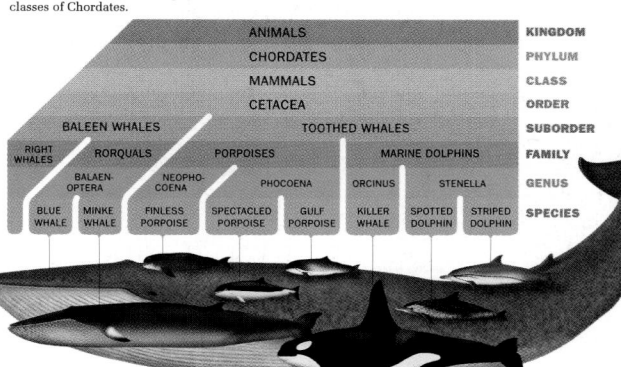

ANIMALS	KINGDOM
CHORDATES	PHYLUM
MAMMALS	CLASS
CETACEA	ORDER
BALEEN WHALES / TOOTHED WHALES	SUBORDER
RIGHT WHALES / RORQUALS / PORPOISES / MARINE DOLPHINS	FAMILY
BALAEN-OPTERA / NEOPHO-COENA / PHOCOENA / ORCINUS / STENELLA	GENUS
BLUE WHALE / MINKE WHALE / FINLESS PORPOISE / SPECTACLED PORPOISE / GULF PORPOISE / KILLER WHALE / SPOTTED DOLPHIN / STRIPED DOLPHIN	SPECIES

Use the chart for Exercises 18–28.

18. Which species are part of the Porpoise family?
19. Name all the groups that a spotted dolphin belongs to.
20. How is a killer whale like a minke whale?
21. In *Moby Dick*, the author uses the word *Cetacea* to refer to the whale. Why do you think he chose this word?
22. According to the chart, how are members of the Rorqual family different from members of the Porpoise family?

For Exercises 23–28, tell whether each statement is *True* or *False*.

23. All Baleen whales are Mammals.
24. If an animal is a killer whale, then it is a Marine dolphin.
25. Every blue whale is a member of the Right whale family.
26. If an animal is a spectacled porpoise, then it is a member of the Toothed whales suborder.
27. Every striped dolphin is a member of the *Orcinus* genus.
28. All blue whales are minke whales.

BY THE WAY...

Blue whales, the largest animals on Earth, have *baleen* plates instead of teeth. The plates are made out of the same type of material as human fingernails. In a single day, a blue whale is likely to eat up to eight TONS of krill!

248   **Unit 5** Coordinate Geometry and Quadrilaterals

INTERDISCIPLINARY PROBLEMS

These theme exercises connect mathematics to other subjects areas. They illustrate the power of mathematics as a problem solving tool.

I've heard that math educators need to make some changes.
I'd like to try new teaching strategies, but I'm not sure how
to get started.

How can I make change work for me?

Teaching

Flexibility

The *Integrated Mathematics* program provides teaching flexibility that enables
you to incorporate the changes that are right for you and your students — at
a pace that is comfortable for you. This program makes it easy for you to try
new approaches and accommodate different learning styles.

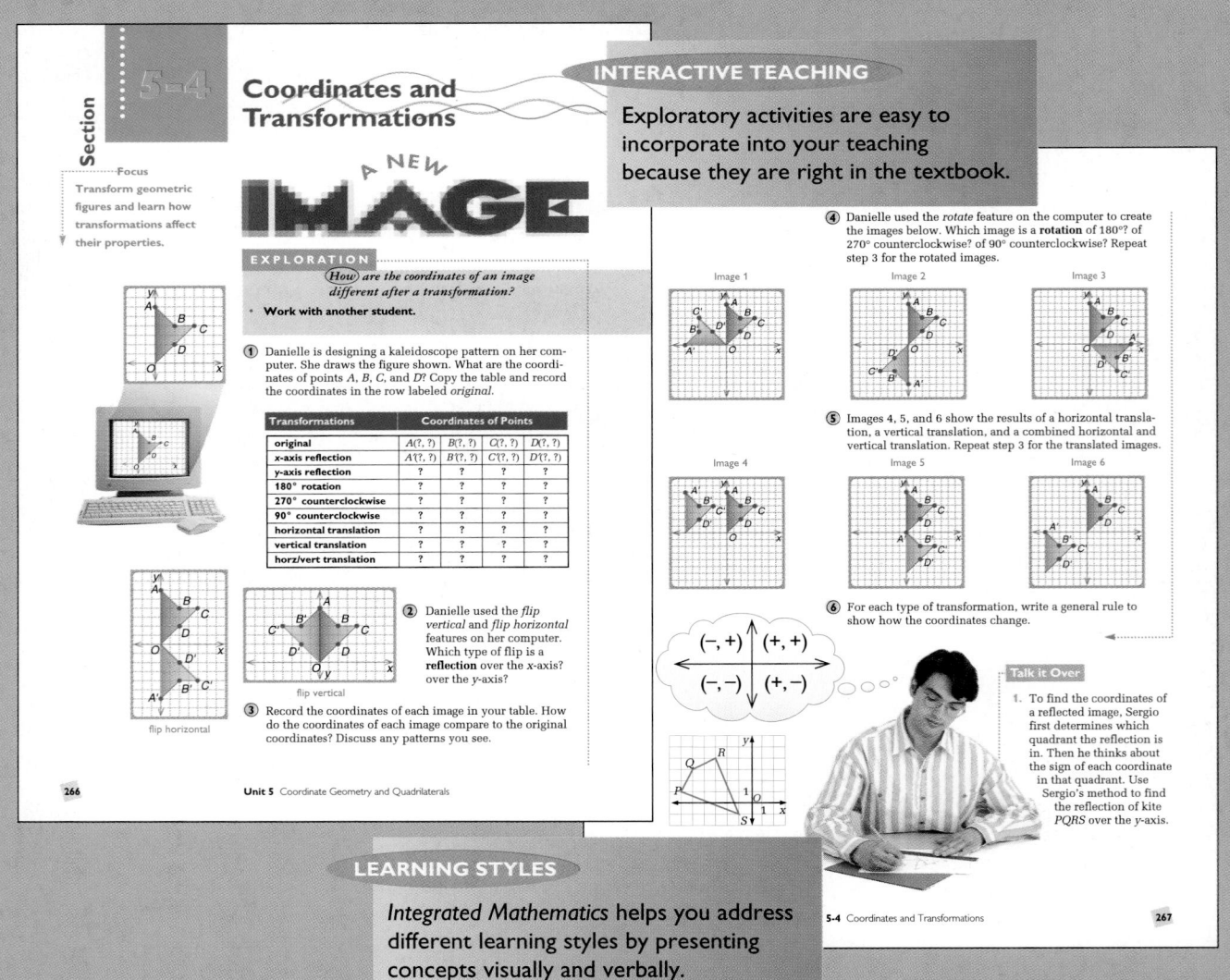

INTERACTIVE TEACHING

Exploratory activities are easy to
incorporate into your teaching
because they are right in the textbook.

LEARNING STYLES

Integrated Mathematics helps you address
different learning styles by presenting
concepts visually and verbally.

For Exercises 9–14, use quadrilateral QRST. Tell what type of transformation is described. Then copy QRST and sketch its image.

9. The figure is shifted 2 units right and 5 units down.

10. Each point on the image has the opposite x-coordinate and the opposite y-coordinate of the corresponding point on the original.

11. The coordinates of the image are three times the corresponding coordinates of the original.

12. Each point on the image has the same x-coordinate as the original point, but the opposite y-coordinate.

13. Each x-coordinate of the image is 4 more than the corresponding x-coordinate of the original. The y-coordinates are the same in both figures.

14. Each coordinate of the image is two thirds of the corresponding original coordinate.

connection to EARTH SCIENCE

15. Geologists believe that all of the world's continents were once connected into one super-continent that is called *Pangaea*. These computer images show the possible path of the continents when the Atlantic Ocean formed.

   a. What types of transformations describe the movement of the continents?

   b. **Open-ended** Describe where you think the continent that you live on will be 100 million years from now.

200 million years ago

100 million years ago

Present

Exercises continued

---

c. The slope of $\overline{HG}$ =

The slope of $\overline{H'G'}$ =

The slopes are the same.

Now you are ready for:
Exs. 16–44 on pp. 272–273

Look Back

Which of the four transformations chan___ segment? Which changes the length of ___

5-4 Exercises and Problems

Name the transformation that was used to create each design.

Original Figure   1. 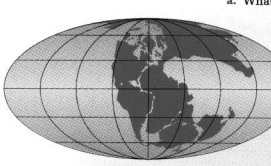   2.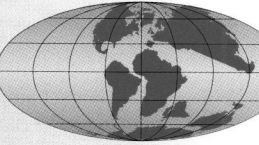

Stamps or coins with errors can be collectors' items. Describe the transformation(s) that may have occurred to cause these errors.

3. 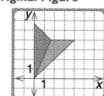   4. 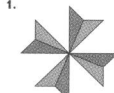   5.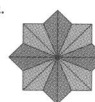

For Exercises 6–8:

a. Tell what kind of transformation is shown.

b. Write a rule to describe what must be done to the coordinates of the original figure to get the coordinates of the image.

6.    7.    8.

270   **Unit 5** Coordinate Geometry and Quadrilaterals

COMPLETE TEACHING SUPPORT

In the Teacher's Edition, each section has a planning list that tells you the materials you will need and the other resources that are available to help you present, extend, or reinforce the section.

PLANNING

Objectives and Strands
See pages 240A and 240B.

Spiral Learning
See page 240B.

Materials List
➤ Graph paper

Recommended Pacing
Section 5-4 is a two-day lesson.

Day 1
Pages 266–267: Exploration through Talk it Over 1, *Exercises 1–15*

Day 2
Pages 268–270: Sample 1 through Look Back, *Exercises 16–44*

Toolbox References
➤ **Toolbox Skill 12:** Simplifying Expressions with Radicals

Extra Practice
See pages 622–623.

Warm-Up Exercises
Warm-Up Transparency 5-4

Support Materials
➤ Practice 37
➤ Enrichment 33 in the Activity Bank
➤ Study Guide 5-4
➤ Problem Set 10
➤ Diagram Masters 2, 17 in the Explorations Lab Manual
Overhead Visual 5
➤ Using TI-81 and TI-82 Calculators: Transformations Using Matrices and Draw Feature
➤ Quiz 5-4
➤ Alternative Assessment 3

VARIED PRACTICE AND EXTENSIONS

The wide variety of exercises, problems, and activities in the textbook and in the support materials allows you to tailor the course to the needs of your students and your teaching preferences.

Practice Bank

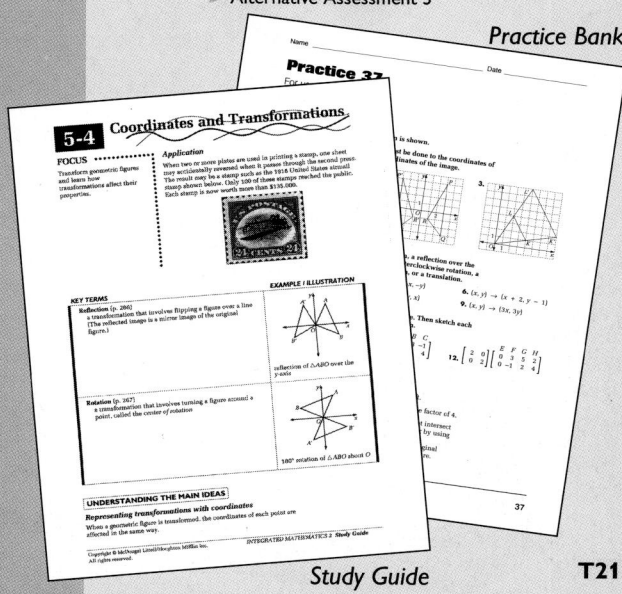

Study Guide

T21

A Complete Program

Teaching Support

The *Integrated Mathematics* program supports the full range of teaching and learning needs.

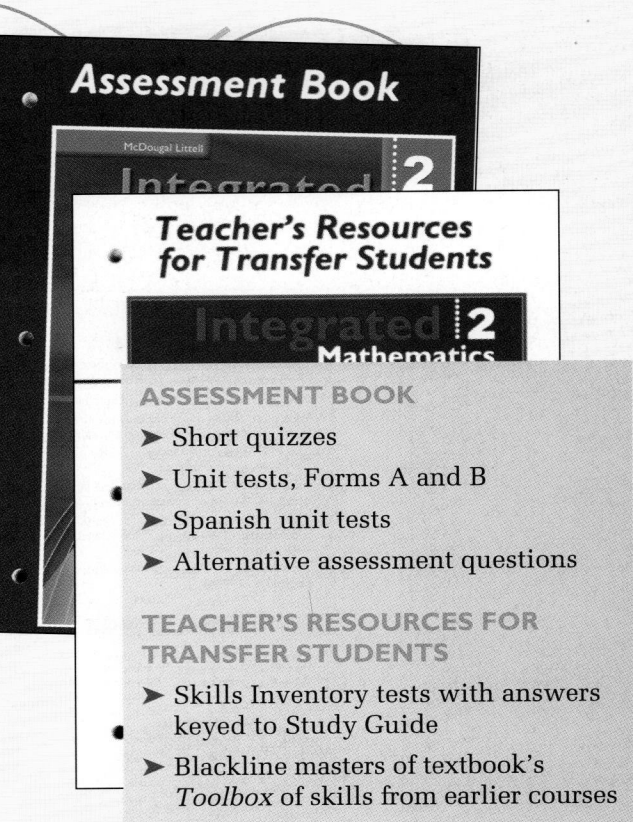

ASSESSMENT BOOK
➤ Short quizzes
➤ Unit tests, Forms A and B
➤ Spanish unit tests
➤ Alternative assessment questions

TEACHER'S RESOURCES FOR TRANSFER STUDENTS
➤ Skills Inventory tests with answers keyed to Study Guide
➤ Blackline masters of textbook's *Toolbox* of skills from earlier courses

TEACHER'S EDITION
➤ Student pages with answers and teaching commentary, planning information, assignment guide
➤ **Solution Key** with solutions to all problems also available

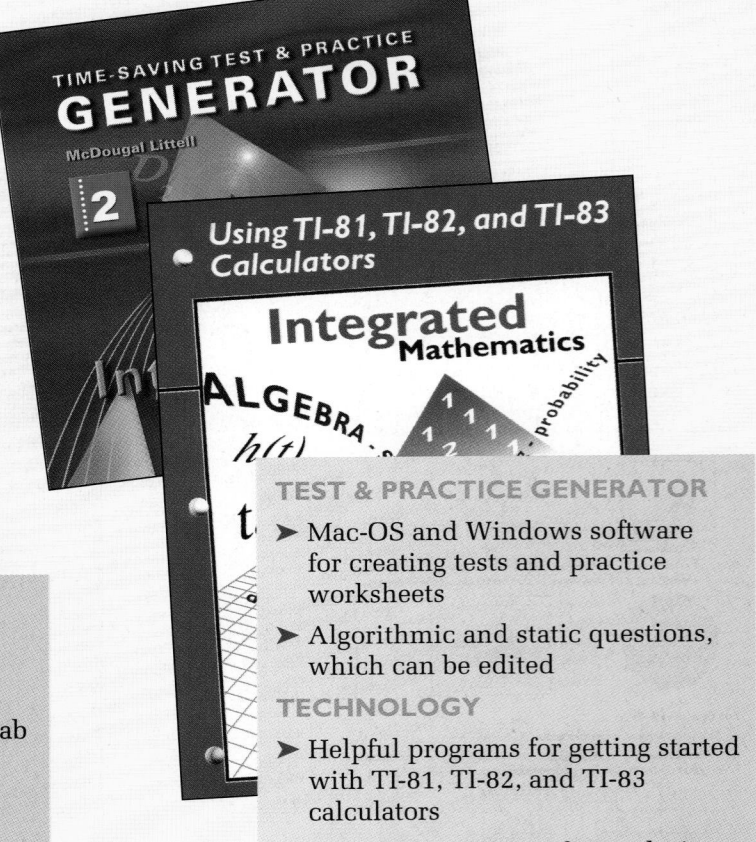

TEST & PRACTICE GENERATOR
➤ Mac-OS and Windows software for creating tests and practice worksheets
➤ Algorithmic and static questions, which can be edited

TECHNOLOGY
➤ Helpful programs for getting started with TI-81, TI-82, and TI-83 calculators
➤ Calculator activities for exploring mathematical ideas

TEACHER'S RESOURCES
➤ Assessment Book
➤ Teacher's Resources for Transfer Students
➤ Warm-Up Exercises transparencies
➤ Using TI-81, TI-82, and TI-83 Calculators
➤ Multi-Language Glossary
➤ Study Guides
➤ Project Book
➤ Explorations Lab Manual
➤ Skills Bank
➤ Problem Bank
➤ Activity Bank
➤ Practice Bank

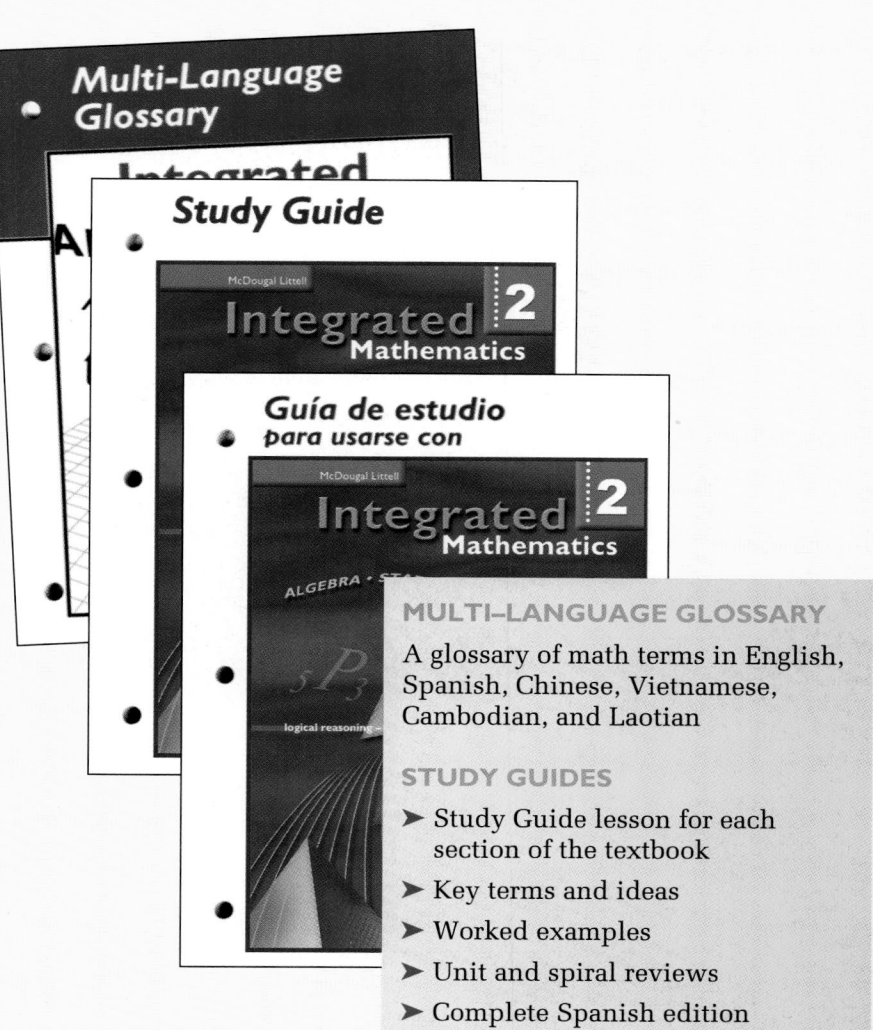

MULTI–LANGUAGE GLOSSARY

A glossary of math terms in English, Spanish, Chinese, Vietnamese, Cambodian, and Laotian

STUDY GUIDES

➤ Study Guide lesson for each section of the textbook
➤ Key terms and ideas
➤ Worked examples
➤ Unit and spiral reviews
➤ Complete Spanish edition

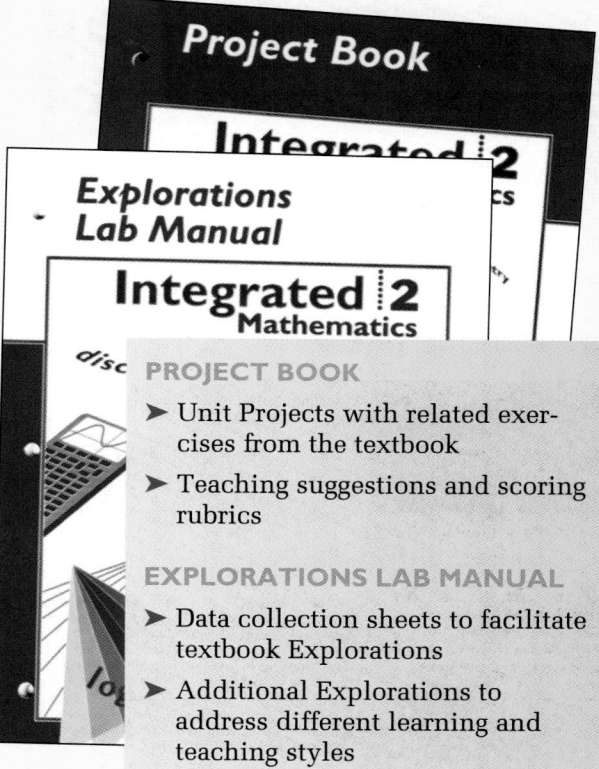

PROJECT BOOK

➤ Unit Projects with related exercises from the textbook
➤ Teaching suggestions and scoring rubrics

EXPLORATIONS LAB MANUAL

➤ Data collection sheets to facilitate textbook Explorations
➤ Additional Explorations to address different learning and teaching styles

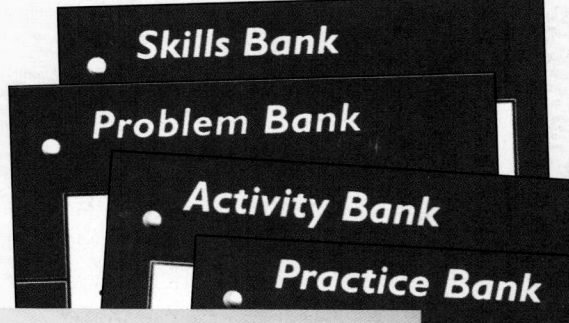

SKILLS BANK

➤ Lessons that extend the curriculum and provide practice with skills
➤ Teaching notes and assessment for each lesson

PROBLEM BANK

➤ Additional problems for each section
➤ Unifying Problems for each unit

ACTIVITY BANK

➤ Family involvement activities for each unit
➤ Enrichment activities for each section

PRACTICE BANK

➤ Practice exercises and problems for each textbook section
➤ Cumulative reviews for each unit

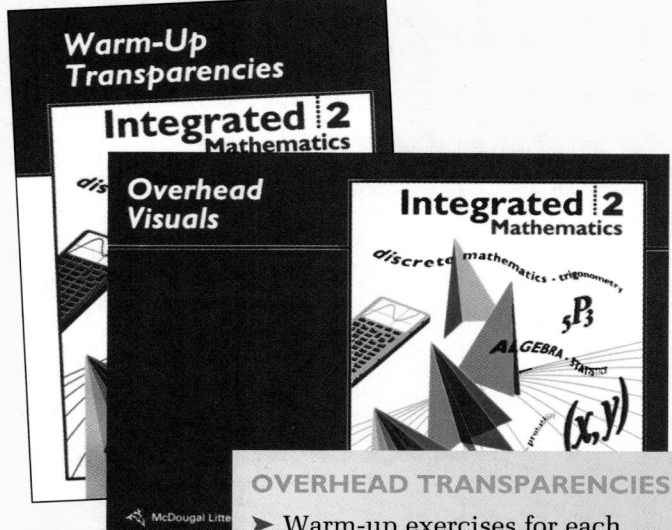

OVERHEAD TRANSPARENCIES

➤ Warm-up exercises for each section
➤ Multi-color overhead visuals with teaching suggestions

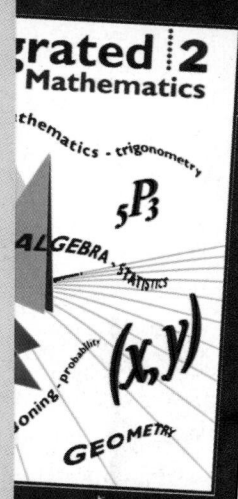

Special Planning Pages for Every Unit

4 Quadratic Functions and Graphs

OVERVIEW

Internet Resources
Visit our Web site
www.mcdougallittell.com for
additional resources when teaching
this unit.

➤ Unit 4 discusses quadratic functions and equations, including graphing and translating graphs of quadratic functions. Quadratic equations are solved by taking the square root of both sides of the equation, by factoring, and by using the quadratic formula. Students examine the discriminant of the quadratic formula to determine the nature of the roots, which leads to a discussion of complex numbers and operations on them. Quadratic systems of equations are introduced.

➤ The theme of the Unit Project is designing a water fountain. Students study a variety of situations in which water is sprayed into an arc. The path of the water is modeled by an equation, and students take measurements to write equations from their own experiments.

➤ Connections to oceanography, games, wave lengths, cliff diving, fire fighting, acrobatics, basketball, baseball, and water slides are integrated into the teaching materials and exercises.

➤ Graphics calculators are used in Sections 4-1 and 4-6 to graph quadratic functions, in Section 4-2 to explore translations of parabolas, in Sections 4-3 and 4-4 to solve quadratic equations, and in Section 4-7 to solve quadratic systems. Computer software, such as Plotter Plus, can be used in Sections 4-1 and 4-2 to explore the properties of parabolas.

➤ Problem-solving strategies used in Unit 4 include using formulas, graphs, transformations, patterns, technology, manipulatives, and mathematical models.

Unit Objectives

Section	Objectives	NCTM Standards
4-1	• Understand how the coefficients of a quadratic function influence its graph: the direction it opens, its vertex, its line of symmetry, and its y-intercept.	1, 2, 3, 4, 5, 6, 8
4-2	• Explore translations of parabolas.	1, 2, 3, 4, 5, 6, 8
4-3	• Solve simple quadratic equations by graphing and undoing.	1, 2, 4, 5, 6, 8
4-4	• Solve quadratic equations by factoring.	1, 2, 5
4-5	• Use the quadratic formula to solve quadratic equations.	1, 2, 5
4-6	• Use the discriminant to find the number of real solutions of a quadratic equation.	1, 2, 3, 4, 5
	• Add, subtract, and multiply complex numbers.	
4-7	• Solve problems involving quadratic systems.	1, 2, 4, 5, 8

Skills Bank To extend the curriculum and provide practice with skills, you may wish to assign the following topics from the **Skills Bank** ancillary: completing the square (for use after Section 4-4) and division of complex numbers (for use after Section 4-6).

184A

Topic Integration

➤ **Topic Spiraling** gives connections to past and future learning.

➤ **Integrating the Strands** shows the integration of mathematical strands throughout the unit.

Unit Overview

➤ **Overview** provides a summary of the mathematical topics, applications, and problem solving strategies for each unit.

➤ **Unit Objectives** gives objectives and NCTM Standards for each section.

Section	Connections to Prior and Future Concepts
4-1	**Section 4-1** presents quadratic functions and their graphs. The coefficients of a quadratic function are examined to determine the characteristics of the related parabola. Parabolas were explored in Unit 10 of Book 1, and are used in Units 2, 4, and 9 of Book 2, and in Unit 2 of Book 3.
4-2	**Section 4-2** explores translations of a parabola. This topic was first introduced in Section 10-2 of Book 1. Standard form, from Section 10-7 of Book 1, is reviewed as a means of finding the coordinates of the vertex of a parabola. This skill is important in Unit 2 of Book 3 for solving optimization problems.
4-3	**Section 4-3** introduces solving a quadratic equation by taking the square root of both sides of the equation. Students can find extra practice on taking square roots in the Toolbox.
4-4	**Section 4-4** uses algebra tiles to illustrate factoring. Special quadratics, whose factors follow specific patterns, are introduced. Factors for quadratic expressions were explored in Unit 10 of Book 1 and will be used again in Unit 2 of Book 3. Factoring quadratic expressions leads to solving quadratic equations by factoring.
4-5	**Section 4-5** reviews the quadratic formula, first developed in Section 10-8 of Book 1. This skill is used in Unit 9 of Book 2 and Unit 2 of Book 3. Solving a quadratic equation by completing the square, an extension of Section 4-3 of Book 2, is found in the exercise set.
4-6	**Section 4-6** uses the discriminant of the quadratic formula to determine the number and nature of the solutions of a quadratic equation. This discussion leads to the development of the set of complex numbers. Students are introduced to operations on the complex numbers.
4-7	**Section 4-7** introduces solving a system of quadratic equations. Students find the point(s) of intersection of two parabolas by graphical and algebraic methods. The algebraic method is the substitution method, which is used in all three books for solving systems of linear equations.

Integrating the Strands

Strands	Sections
Number	4-5
Algebra	4-1, 4-2, 4-3, 4-4, 4-5, 4-6, 4-7
Functions	4-1, 4-2, 4-3, 4-4, 4-5, 4-6, 4-7
Geometry	4-2, 4-5, 4-7
Statistics and Probability	4-6
Discrete Mathematics	4-5
Logic and Language	4-1, 4-2, 4-3, 4-4, 4-5, 4-6, 4-7

184B

Quadratic Functions and Graphs

Section Planning Guide

➤ Essential exercises and problems are indicated in boldface.
➤ Ongoing work on the Unit Project is indicated in color.
➤ Exercises and problems that require student research, group work, manipulatives, or graphing technology are indicated in the column headed "Other."

Section	Materials	Pacing	Standard Assignment	Extended Assignment	Other
4-1	graphing technology	Day 1	2, 3, **4–17**	1–3, **4–17**, 18–20	
		Day 2	**21–28**, 29–36, 37–40	**21–28**, 29–36, 37–40	38, 40
4-2	graphics calculator, tracing paper, tape measure, water hose	Day 1	**1–9**	1–9, 10	11
		Day 2	**13–18**, 21–28, 29	12, **13–18**, 19–28, 29	29
4-3	graphics calculator	Day 1	**2–24**, 25, 26, 31–38, 39	1, **2–24**, 25–38, 39	
4-4	algebra tiles, graphics calculator	Day 1	**4–15**, 18	1–3, **4–15**, 16, 18	17
		Day 2	**20–35**, 36, 38–44, 45	19, **20–35**, 36, 38–44, 45	37
4-5	graphics calculator	Day 1	**5–14**, 17–19	1, 2, 4, **5–14**, 15, 17–19	3, 16
		Day 2	**24–35**, 39, 44–51, 52	20–23, **24–35**, 36–51, 52	52
4-6	graphics calculator	Day 1	**3–15**	1, 2, **3–15**, 16–18	
		Day 2	**20–43**, 46–52, 53	19, **20–43**, 44, 46–52, 53	45
4-7	graphics calculator	Day 1	**2–18**, 22–29, 30	1, **2–18**, 19–29, 30	
Review		Day 1	**Unit Review**	**Unit Review**	
Test		Day 2	**Unit Test**	**Unit Test**	

Yearly Pacing	Unit 4 Total	Units 1–4 Total	Remaining	Total
	16 days (2 for Unit Project)	65 days	95 days	160 days

Support Materials

➤ See **Project Book** for notes on Unit 4 Project: Design a Fountain.
➤ "UPP" and "disk" refer to **Using Plotter Plus** booklet and **Plotter Plus** disk.
➤ "TI-81/82" refers to **Using TI-81 and TI-82 Calculators** booklet.
➤ Warm-up exercises for each section are available on **Warm-Up Transparencies**.
➤ "FI," "PC," "GI," "MA," and "Stats!" refer, respectively, to the McDougal Littell Mathpack software Activity Books for **Function Investigator, Probability Constructor, Geometry Inventor, Matrix Analyzer, and Stats!.**

Section	Study Guide	Practice Bank	Problem Bank	Activity Bank	Explorations Lab Manual	Assessment Book	Visuals	Technology
4-1	4-1	Practice 26	Set 7	Enrich 23		Quiz 4-1		TI-81/82, p. 40 Parabola Plotter (disk)
4-2	4-2	Practice 27	Set 7	Enrich 24	Master 2	Quiz 4-2		
4-3	4-3	Practice 28	Set 7	Enrich 25		Quiz 4-3		
4-4	4-4	Practice 29	Set 7	Enrich 26	Masters 2–4	Quiz 4-4 Test 13	Folder 4	
4-5	4-5	Practice 30	Set 8	Enrich 27		Quiz 4-5		
4-6	4-6	Practice 31	Set 8	Enrich 28	Add. Expl. 6	Quiz 4-6		
4-7	4-7	Practice 32	Set 8	Enrich 29		Quiz 4-7 Test 14		
Unit 4	Unit Review	Practice 33	Unifying Problem 4	Family Involve 4		Tests 15, 16		

184C

Teaching Information

➤ **Section Planning Guide** gives materials, pacing, and suggested assignments for each section.

➤ **Support Materials** lists all support materials for each section.

Teacher's Resources

➤ **Unit Tests** shows reduced facsimiles of Unit Tests, Forms A and B.

➤ **Outside Resources** lists books, periodicals, manipulatives and activities, software, and videos.

Facsimiles of the *Practice* masters appear in the side columns next to the section that they accompany.

UNIT TESTS

Spanish versions of these tests are on pages 130–133 of the **Assessment Book.**

Form A

Form B

Software Support

McDougal Littell Mathpack
Function Investigator

Plotter Plus
Macintosh and MS-DOS
(worksheets included)

Outside Resources

Books/Periodicals

Owens, John F. "Families of Parabolas." *Mathematics Teacher* (September 1992): pp. 477–479.

Activities/Manipulatives

Howden, Hilde. *Algebra Tiles for the Overhead Projector.* Cuisinaire Co, 1985.

Laycock, Mary and Reuben Schadler. *Algebra in the Concrete.* Hayward, CA: Activities Resource Co., 1987.

Software

Goodson, B. *Artillery.* San Mateo, CA: CUF, 1981. (Apple Shareware Game to match project.)

Logal Company. *Physics Explorer Series: One Body.* Pleasantville, NY: Sunburst, 1994. Macintosh and Windows.

Videos

Futures with Jaime Escalante. Program No. 12: Sports Performance. PBS, 1990.

Videodisk: "Projectile Motion." *Science: Forces & Energy;* (Side A). Macmillan/ McGraw-Hill, 1993.

184D

A Teaching Plan for Every Section

Planning

A column referencing
- **Objectives and Strands**
- **Spiral Learning**
- **Materials List**
- **Recommended Pacing**
- **Toolbox References**
- **Extra Practice**
- **Warm-Up Exercises**
- **Support Materials**

Section 4-2 — Translating Parabolas

SLIDE—OVER

Focus
Explore translations of parabolas.

EXPLORATION

How do changes in the equation affect the graph of a parabola?

- Materials: graphics calculators
- Work with another student.

① Graph $y = x^2$, $y = 2x^2$, $y = 5x^2$, and $y = 12x^2$ on the same axes. What happens to the graph of $y = x^2$ when the coefficient of x^2 is greater than 1?

② Graph $y = x^2$, $y = \frac{1}{2}x^2$, $y = \frac{1}{4}x^2$, and $y = \frac{1}{10}x^2$ on the same axes. What happens to the graph of $y = x^2$ when the coefficient of x^2 is between 0 and 1?

③ How do you think the graphs in steps 1 and 2 will change when the coefficient of x^2 is negative? Check your answer by graphing some examples.

④ Graph $y = 5x^2$, $y = 5x^2 + 3$, and $y = 5x^2 - 3$ on the same axes. How does the graph of $y = 5x^2$ change when you add 3 to $5x^2$? when you subtract 3 from $5x^2$?

⑤ Predict what the graph of $y = 5x^2 - 7$ looks like. Check your answer by graphing.

⑥ Graph each function on the same axes as $y = 2x^2$. Describe how the graph of each function is different from the graph of $y = 2x^2$.
  a. $y = 2(x + 2)^2$ b. $y = 2(x - 3)^2$ c. $y = 2(x - 6)^2$

⑦ What relationship do you see between the equations in step 6, parts (a)–(c), and their graphs?

⑧ Use what you discovered in steps 4 and 6 to predict what the graph of $y = (x - 7)^2 + 4$ will look like. Sketch your prediction on a piece of paper. Then check your prediction by graphing.

⑨ Describe how the graph of $y = 2(x + 3)^2 - 1$ is different from the graph of $y = x^2$.

4-2 Translating Parabolas

Answers to Exploration

1. The innermost parabola is the graph of $y = 12x^2$; the outermost parabola is the graph of $y = x^2$.

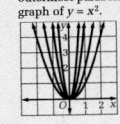

2. See answers in back of book.

Descriptions may vary. An example is given. For coefficients of x^2 greater than 1, the parabola becomes steeper and narrower.

3. Answers may vary. An example is given. When the coefficient of x^2 is negative, the parabola opens down. The graph of $y = -ax^2$ is the image of the graph of $y = ax^2$ under a reflection over the horizontal axis.

4–9. See answers in back of book.

193

TEACHING

Exploration

The goal of the Exploration is to have students investigate how changes in a quadratic equation affect the graph of a parabola. Students explore changes in the shape and position of the graph. Changes in shape are explored in steps 1 and 2. Step 3 considers reflections of the graphs used in steps 1 and 2. Steps 4–9 explore changes in position.

Using Technology

For the Exploration, optimal graph screens for the graphs are as follows:

Step 1: $-2 \le x \le 2$ and $-1 \le y \le 2$;

Step 2: $-10 \le x \le 10$ and $-5 \le y \le 10$;

Step 4: $-2 \le x \le 2$ and $-5 \le y \le 10$;

Step 6: $-5 \le x \le 8$ and $-5 \le y \le 10$.

Students can also use the *Function Investigator* software to graph the functions.

Teaching Tip

A translation changes a graph's position by moving the graph up or down, to the left or right, or some combination of an up-down movement with a left-right movement. The graph of $y = (x + 3)^2 + 2$ is a translation of $y = x^2$ three (3) units to the left and two (2) units up.

Additional Sample

S1 Tell how to translate the graph of $y = 0.3x^2$ in order to produce the graph of each function.

a. $y = 0.3x^2 + 4$
  Translate the graph of $y = 0.3x^2$ up 4 units.

b. $y = 0.3(x - 2)^2$
  Translate the graph of $y = 0.3x^2$ to the right 2 units.

c. $y = 0.3(x + 6)^2 - 5$
  Translate the graph of $y = 0.3x^2$ to the left 6 units and down 5 units.

194

The graph of $y = (x + 3)^2 + 2$ is a tra... $y = x^2$. A translation changes only a ... not change a graph's size or shape o... graph opens.

Talk it Over

Tell whether the graph of each func...

1. $y = x^2 + 6$ 2. $y = 3x^2$

4. Describe the information you ca... parabola from its equation.

Sample 1

Tell how to translate the graph of y ... produce the graph of each function.

a. $y = -0.5x^2 - 2$ b. $y = -0.5(x + ...

Sample Response

a. $y = -0.5x^2 - 2$

Translate the graph of $y = -0.5x^2$ 2 units down.

(0, −2)

b. $y = -0.5(x + 4)^2$

Translate the graph of $y = -0.5x^2$ 4 units to the *left*.

(−4, 0)

➤ Now you are ready for... Exs. 1–11 on pp. 196–197

194

Unit 4 Quadratic Functions and Graphs

Answers to Talk it Over

1. Yes.
2. No.
3. Yes.
4. Answers may vary. An example is given. You can tell if the graph has the same shape or position as a parabola with a simpler equation. You can determine the coordinates of the vertex and tell whether the

parabola opens up or down.

5. (0, 0); (0, 3); The vertex is translated 3 units up.

6. In equation (a), the vertex is translated down 2 units; in equation (b), the vertex is translated 4 units to the left; in equation (c), the vertex is translated 1 unit to the right and 3 units up.

---

5. What is the vertex of the graph of $y = 4x^2$? What is the vertex of the graph of $y = 4x^2 + 3$? Describe the change in the position of the vertex when 3 is added to $4x^2$.

6. For each parabola in Sample 1, describe the translation of the vertex.

PLANNING

Objectives and Strands
See pages 184A and 184B.

Spiral Learning
See page 184B.

Materials List
- Graphics calculator
- Graph paper
- Tracing paper
- Tape measure
- Water hose

Recommended Pacing
Section 4-2 is a two-day lesson.

Day 1
Pages 193–194: Exploration through Talk it Over 6, *Exercises 1–11*

Day 2
Pages 195–196: Top of page 195 through Look Back, *Exercises 12–29*

Extra Practice
See pages 620–621.

Warm-Up Exercises
- Warm-Up Transparency 4-2

Support Materials
- Practice 27
- Enrichment 24 in the Activity Bank
- Study Guide 4-2
- Problem Set 7
- Diagram Master 2 in the Explorations Lab Manual
- McDougal Littell Mathpack software: *Function Investigator*
- Function Investigator with Matrix Analyzer Activity Book: Function Investigator Activities 12–15
- Using IBM/Mac Plotter Plus Disk: Parabola Quiz
- Quiz 4-2
- Alternative Assessment 2

193

Answers

Answers to Explorations, Talk it Over questions, Look Back questions, and Exercises and Problems are conveniently located at the bottom of each page.

In addition to the section side-column notes, a **Quick Quiz** is provided at each Checkpoint in the student book, as well as at the end of each unit.

Notes on
- ➤ **Explorations**
- ➤ **Talk it Over questions**
- ➤ **Additional Samples**
- ➤ **Teaching Tips**
- ➤ **Error Analysis**
- ➤ **Problem Solving**
- ➤ **Using Technology**
- ➤ **Using Manipulatives**
- ➤ **Communication**
- ➤ **Cooperative Learning**
- ➤ **Reasoning**
- ➤ **Mathematical Procedures**
- ➤ **Students Acquiring English**
- ➤ **Multicultural Information**
- ➤ **Visual Thinking**
- ➤ **Look Back questions**

---

10. Make a concept map to describe the ways the graph of $y = 3x^2$ can be translated. Give examples of at least two functions for each type of translation. Use functions that show vertical translations, horizontal translations, or both vertical and horizontal translations.

11. a. **Using Manipulatives** Make a coordinate grid on graph paper. Place tracing paper on top of the graph paper.

Graph $y = \frac{2}{5}x^2$ on your tracing paper.

b. Move the tracing paper so that the parabola is translated up 6 units. What is the y-intercept? the line of symmetry? Rewrite the equation $y = \frac{2}{5}x^2$ to show the translation.

c. Repeat part (b) but translate the original parabola 4 units to the left.

d. Repeat part (b) but translate the original parabola 2 units down and 3 units to the right.

e. Repeat part (b) but reflect the original parabola over the x-axis.

12. **Writing** Jack says that the y-intercept of the graph of $y = 3(x + 1)^2 - 8$ is -8. Lindsey rewrites the function in standard form and says the y-intercept of the graph is -5. Who do you think is right? Why?

For the graph of each function:
a. Find the coordinates of the vertex.
b. Find the y-intercept.

13. $y = (x + 6)^2$
14. $y = (x + 3)^2 - 4$
15. $y = (x - 5)^2 + 2$
16. $y = 2(x + 4)^2 - 18$
17. $y = 5(x - 1)^2 + 11$
18. $y = -4(x - 2)^2 + 9$

19. The equation for the area of a circle is written $A = \pi r^2$.
a. When you rewrite $A = \pi r^2$ using x for the radius and y for the area, you get $y = \pi x^2$. Graph the function $y = \pi x^2$. (Use $\pi \approx 3.14$.)
b. What is a reasonable domain for this function?

4-2 Translating Parabolas   **197**

Suggested Assignment

Day 1
Standard 1–9
Extended 1–10

Day 2
Standard 13–18, 21–29
Extended 12–29

Integrating the Strands
Algebra Exs. 1–29
Functions Exs. 1–25, 29
Geometry Exs. 19, 20
Logic and Language Exs. 1, 10, 12

Communication: Reading
For Ex. 1, discuss also the effect that changing the value of a has on the graph of $y = ax^2$ (Exploration steps 1 and 2). For $a > 1$, increasing values of a make the shape of the parabola more narrow. For $a < 1$, decreasing values of a make the shape wider. If the sign of a changes (step 3), then the direction in which the graph of $y = ax^2$ opens is changed from up to down or down to up.

Communication: Discussion
The use of concept maps in Ex. 10 can stimulate a discussion among students as they compare their maps and examples. These activities would provide an excellent summary of the ideas associated with translating the graph of a parabola.

Assessment: Task
For Ex. 20, students should be able to analyze the quadratic equation function $y = \pi(x^2 - 4)$ and describe the coordinates of the vertex. What portion of the graph should be considered, remembering that this is the area as a function of the radius? Do both x-intercepts have physical meaning? Why? If the radius of the larger circle is double the radius of the smaller circle, what is the shaded region? Students should analyze the geometric sketch and correlate the findings on the graphics calculator with their analysis.

197

Talk it Over

For question 8, students can also tell that the two functions are equivalent by referring back to Method 1 of Sample 2. The expansion of $y = 3(x - 4)^2 + 1$ yields the equivalent equation $y = 3x^2 - 24x + 49$.

Using Technology

You can use the TI-81/82/83 to help write a function of the form $y = ax^2 + bx + c$ in the form $y = a(x + h)^2 + k$. Consider $y = 5x^2 + 7x + 1$. Graph the function on the standard graph screen. Locate the vertex by finding the minimum point. With the TI-82 or TI-83, you can do this quickly by using 3:minimum from the CALCULATE menu. With the TI-81, you will get similar coordinates for the minimum point by zooming and tracing. The results indicate that the vertex is at $(-0.7, -1.45)$. The vertex $(0, 0)$ of the "parent" function $y = 5x^2$ seems to have been translated 0.7 units to the left and 1.45 units down. You can verify algebraically that $y = 5x^2 + 7x + 1$ is equivalent to $y = 5(x + 0.7)^2 + (-1.45)$. Alternatively, graph both functions. The graphs coincide.

Look Back

The movements of the graph of the function $y = x^2$ can be summarized by using the single function $y = a(x + h)^2 + k$.
If $h > 0$, $y = x^2$ moves left h units.
If $h < 0$, $y = x^2$ moves right h units.
If $k > 0$, $y = x^2$ moves up k units.
If $k < 0$, $y = x^2$ moves down k units.

Using Technology

Function Investigator Activities 12–15 in the *Function Investigator with Matrix Analyzer Activity Book* can be used to further explore how changing the equation of a quadratic function changes its graph.

196

Talk it Over

7. In Method 1 of Sample 2, does it ~~ute~~ the 3 before you expand $(x - \ldots$

8. Graph $y = 3(x - 4)^2 + 1$ and $y = \ldots$ same set of axes. What do the gra~~ functions?~~

Look Back

In the Exploration, you discovered t~~ function $y = x^2$ can move its graph u~~ Describe a way to remember the effe~~ the function has on the graph.~~

➤ Now you are ready for:
Exs. 12–29 on pp. 197–198

4-2 ### Exercises and Problems

1. **Reading** Which of the parabolas in the Exploration are translations of the graph of $y = x^2$?

2. Without graphing, list the functions in order from the one with the narrowest graph to the one with the widest graph.

$y = \frac{2}{3}x^2 + 1$ $y = 12x^2 - 5$ $y = 0.01x^2$ $y = 5x^2 + 8$

3. Without graphing, list the functions in order beginning with the one whose graph has the vertex farthest to the left.

$y = \frac{2}{3}(x + 1)^2$ $y = 12(x - 5)^2$ $y = 0.01(x - 3)^2$ $y = 5(x + 8)^2$

For Exercises 4–7, tell how to translate the graph of $y = -3x^2$ in order to produce the graph of each function.

4. $y = -3(x + 7)^2$
5. $y = -3(x - 2)^2 + 3$
6. $y = -3(x - 1)^2 - 2$
7. $y = -3(x + 2)^2 + 5$

Each graph is a translation of $y = \frac{1}{3}x^2$. Write a function for each graph.

8.

9.

196   **Unit 4** Quadratic Functions and Graphs

Answers to Exercises and Problems

1. the graph in step 8, $y = (x - 7)^2 + 4$

2. $y = 12x^2 - 5$, $y = 5x^2 + 8$, $y = \frac{2}{3}x^2 + 1$, $y = 0.01x^2$

3. $y = 5(x + 8)^2$, $y = \frac{2}{3}(x + 1)^2$, $y = 0.01(x - 3)^2$, $y = 12(x - 5)^2$

4. Move the graph 7 units to the left.

5. Move the graph 2 units to the right and 3 units up.

6. Move the graph 1 unit to the right and 2 units down.

7. Move the graph 2 units to the left and 5 units up.

8. $y = \frac{1}{3}(x - 2)^2$

9. $y = \frac{1}{3}(x + 4)^2 - 3$

10. See answers in back of book.

11. a. Check students' graphs.
b. 6; $x = 0$; $y = \frac{2}{5}x^2 + 6$

c. 6.4; $x = -4$; $y = \frac{2}{5}(x + 4)^2$

d. 1.6; $x = 3$; $y = \frac{2}{5}(x - 3)^2 - 2$

e. 0; $x = 0$; $y = -\frac{2}{5}x^2$

12. Lindsey is right; when $x = 0$, $3(x + 1)^2 - 8 = 3(0 + 1)^2 - 8 = 3 - 8 = -5$. Jack found the y-intercept of $y = 3x^2 - 8$.

13–19. See answers in back of book.

197

Answers to Talk it Over

7. Yes. Explanations may vary. An example is given. According to the order of operations, the power should be simplified first. Then the expression can be multiplied by 3. If you distribute the 3 first and then simplify the power, you actually multiply each term by 3^2 or 9.

8. The equations have the same graph; they are equivalent equations.

Answers to Look Back

Answers may vary. An example is given. The equation $y = (x + a)^2$ has a horizontal translation of a units left or right (left if a is positive); the equation $y = x^2 + b$ has a vertical translation of b units up or down (up if b is positive).

Notes on
- ➤ **Suggested Assignments**
- ➤ **Integrating the Strands**
- ➤ **Problem Solving**
- ➤ **Using Technology**
- ➤ **Using Manipulatives**
- ➤ **Cooperative Learning**
- ➤ **Reasoning**
- ➤ **Multicultural Information**
- ➤ **Unit Projects**
- ➤ **Careers**
- ➤ **Applications**
- ➤ **Research**
- ➤ **Visual Thinking**
- ➤ **Interdisciplinary Problems**
- ➤ **Assessment**

Pacing and Making Assignments

Pacing Chart

A yearly Pacing Chart and daily assignments are provided for two levels of courses—a standard course and an extended course. Both levels provide for 160 days, including days for using the Unit Openers, completing the Unit Project, and review and testing. The Pacing Chart below shows the number of days allotted for each unit of both courses. Semester and trimester divisions are indicated by a red rule and blue rules, respectively.

Unit	1	2	3	4	5	6	7	8	9	10
Standard Course	14	18	17	16	14	18	16	19	15	13
Extended Course	14	18	17	16	14	18	16	19	15	13

trimester   semester   trimester

Standard Course

The standard course is intended for students who enter with typical mathematical and problem solving skills. The course covers all ten units. The daily assignments include all the essential exercises and problems plus a number of other exercises that focus on higher-order thinking skills.

Extended Course

The extended course is intended for students who enter with strong mathematical and problem solving skills and who are able to understand new concepts quickly. The course covers all ten units. The daily assignments include all the essential exercises plus many other exercises that focus on higher-order thinking skills. It is recommended that these students be assigned some of the exercises that are listed in the Other column of the Section Planning Guide.

Helping Transfer Students

You may have students who enter your *Integrated Mathematics 2* class at the beginning of the year, or during the year, without having studied all of the mathematical topics covered in an *Integrated Mathematics 1* course. The supplementary publication *Teacher's Resources for Transfer Students* for *Integrated Mathematics 2* was developed to make it easier for you to help your transfer students catch up. This publication contains diagnostic Skills Inventory tests, blackline masters of the textbook's *Toolbox* of skills assumed from previous courses, and blackline masters of selected sections from the *Study Guide* for *Integrated Mathematics 1*. The Skills Inventories help you identify the concepts and skills that transfer students need to learn, and the *Toolbox* and *Study Guide* masters offer students a way to learn them.

Section Planning Guide

The Section Planning Guide for each unit is located on the interleaved pages preceding the unit. A part of the Section Planning Guide for Unit 4 is shown here. A key describing the exercises and problems for the assignments is given in each Section Planning Guide.

Section Planning Guide

➤ Essential exercises and problems are indicated in boldface.
➤ Ongoing work on the Unit Project is indicated in color.
➤ Exercises and problems that require student research, group work, manipulatives, or graphing technology are indicated in the column headed "Other."

Section	Materials	Pacing	Standard Assignment	Extended Assignment	Other
4-1	graphing technology	Day 1	2, 3, **4–17**	1–3, **4–17**, 18–20	
		Day 2	**21–28**, 29–36, 37–40	**21–28**, 29–36, 37–40	38, 40
4-2	graphics calculator, tracing paper, tape measure, water hose	Day 1	**1–9**	**1–9**, 10	11
		Day 2	**13–18**, 21–28, 29	12, **13–18**, 19–28, 29	29
4-3	graphics calculator	Day 1	**2–24**, 25, 26, 31–38, 39	1, **2–24**, 25–38, 39	
4-4	algebra tiles, graphics calculator	Day 1	**4–15**, 18	1–3, **4–15**, 16, 18	17
		Day 2	**20–35**, 36, 38–44, 45	19, **20–35**, 36, 38–44, 45	37
4-5	graphics calculator	Day 1	**5–14**, **17–19**	1, 2, 4, **5–14**, 15, **17–19**	3, 16
		Day 2	**24–35**, 39, 44–51, 52	20–23, **24–35**, 36–51, 52	52

Essential Exercises and Problems

These exercises and problems, indicated in boldface, are essential to understanding and applying the mathematical concepts presented in each section. They are listed in both the Standard and Extended Assignments and should be completed by all students.

Working on the Unit Project Exercises

These exercises provide students with ongoing work on the Unit Project. They are listed in color in both the Standard and Extended Assignments. Some of these exercises may involve group work, graphing technology, or manipulatives and may require time in class for completion. Others may involve student research and may require extended time outside of class for completion.

"Other" Exercises

These exercises require group work, use of technology, use of manipulatives, or student research. They have been placed in the "Other" category to alert you to the fact that those involving group work, technology, or manipulatives may require time in class for completion and those involving student research may require extended time outside of class for completion.

Support Materials

The extensive support materials available for *Integrated Mathematics 2* can provide an additional source for assignments that fit the needs of particular classes and teaching preferences. In particular, the *Practice Bank, Problem Bank, Study Guide,* and *Skills Bank* can be used for this purpose. The Support Materials Charts on the "C" interleaved pages list ancillary materials for each section. References to the *Skills Bank* are on the "A" interleaved pages.

Effective Learning and Teaching

by **Gerlena R. Clark**
Mathematics Consultant
Jefferson City Missouri

"All students can learn mathematics."

The Challenge

American businesses want their future employees to be able to work with others, to solve problems, to read and understand the principles of mathematics, and to communicate ideas. The primary question for teachers today is: How do I help students build a foundation of skills and information while simultaneously encouraging them to use their creative and intellectual abilities to solve real-world problems?

Recent research on how students learn suggests some strategies for accomplishing the challenging goal of preparing students for their lives as adults in the 21st century. These strategies are based on the assumption that:

> All students can learn mathematics if mathematics is taught in the way that students learn.

How Do Students Learn Mathematics?

Learning in the traditional manner is not sufficient in a world that demands attitudes that are conducive to creativity, as well as specific knowledge and skills. In the past students were expected to acquire facts through drill, practice, and memorization. The teacher was the giver of knowledge through lecturing and demonstrating.

Now we know that:

> Students must be actively involved in the learning process.

> Students learn best through dialogue, discussion, and interaction with others.

> Students benefit from reviewing, critiquing, and revising another's work as well as their own.

> What students learn is connected to how they learn.

> Students learn by experiencing tasks that are as closely aligned to real life as possible.

> Students learn by making connections to what they already know about the task and the real world.

We may summarize these statements by defining:

> **knowledge** as the result of individuals constructing meaning for themselves, by creating rules and hypotheses to explain what they've experienced.

> **intelligence** as a function of experiences. The brain learns best through first-hand experiences.

How Does This Learning Take Place in the Classroom?

If we put what we know about learning into action, what will be happening in the classroom?

In the classroom, students should:

- work with objects to represent mathematical models
- work in cooperative groups, or in pairs, as the task dictates
- write results, or outline strategies
- discuss mathematical ideas
- ask and answer each other's questions

In the classroom, the teacher should:

- allow time for students to think through problem formation and solution
- maintain an atmosphere of freedom for students' expressions
- encourage mathematical arguments with questions such as, Do you agree or disagree? Why?
- not focus on the "correct" answer, but allow discussion on alternative answers and solution procedures
- avoid paraphrasing what students say; ask students to clarify their own thinking
- model expected behavior for working in a group and for solving problems
- ask questions that will allow students to go beyond one-dimensional responses
- encourage students to go to each other for assistance
- encourage students to revise their written responses
- allow students to self-assess as well as assist in the assessment of others

Meeting the Challenge

All of this implies a change in the way students learn and in the way teachers teach. Making this change may not be simple or easy at first, but it will become simpler and easier with time. And the result—students who know and use mathematics, who are mathematically empowered—will be of benefit to all.

In *Integrated Mathematics 2*
See student pages 4, 59, and 206 and side-column commentary on pages 10, 225, and 252.

Cooperative Learning

by *Judith Collison*
Assistant Professor, Critical and Creative Thinking
University of Massachusetts/Boston

"Group work can decrease or eliminate math anxiety."

Benefits of Cooperative Learning

The NCTM *Curriculum and Evaluation Standards* stress the importance of developing skills of collaboration in mathematics teaching and learning. Developing skills of group participation is an important goal of all education, but it is especially useful in mathematics. Research has shown that group work in math classes has decreased or eliminated math anxiety; increased motivation, flexibility, confidence, self-esteem, curiosity, and perseverance; improved ability to solve problems and to communicate mathematically; and resulted in more positive attitudes towards mathematics.

When and how should cooperative strategies be used?

Teachers should use collaboration to create a sense of community and trust among students, as well as to create a deeper and more personal understanding of mathematics.

Cooperative forms are natural for problems that seem too big, too time-consuming, or too complex to be tackled by one person, and problems that require multiple perspectives, ability levels, or discussions.

Adequate preparations are key to the success of cooperative group work. The teacher needs to decide how to configure the groups, what type of group work will be used, how the problem will be divided among or within the groups, and how the work of the groups and of individual group members will be assessed.

Before students embark on their assignment, the teacher should verify that all groups and group members understand all instructions and expectations.

How should groups be formed?

The teacher selects the method by which group membership is determined. The composition of the group may be decided by the teacher or the students, according to some criteria, or randomly.

Types of group structure

Most typical cooperative structures include students working in *pairs,* in *small groups* made up of three or more members, or as a *whole class.* The teacher needs to choose the structure most useful for the activity or problem at hand. The following descriptions of the various types of cooperative structures are adapted from Neil Davidson's *Cooperative Learning in Mathematics: A Handbook for Teachers* (Addison-Wesley, 1990).

INTERVIEW (2-4 participants in each group) Most useful for getting students acquainted with each other in order to begin forming a sense of community. Members of the group ask each other questions dealing with either personal information or with applications of mathematics to their lives. They then share the information with the larger group or with the whole class.

Teacher's Choice
(by ability, social, psychological, or random grouping)

HOMOGENEOUS	HETEROGENEOUS	RANDOM
ability level	mixed levels	counting off
talents/interests	complementary talents/	according to height
learning style	interests	arbitrary numbering
social group	combination of learning	e.g., phone or social
psychological group	styles	security numbers
	diverse ethnic represen-	
	tation	

Student's Choice

SELF-SELECTION
Students choose their own working partners.

MODIFIED SELF-SELECTION
Students list first, second, and third choices, and the teacher constructs groups based on these preferences.

THINK-PAIR-SHARE Useful for developing communication about concepts and procedures, and practice in problem solving. Students think about the problem alone, then discuss possible solutions with their partners and agree on the correct solution. They share their conclusions with the rest of the class. Having students work in pairs is probably the best cooperative format when using computers in problem solving.

PEER PRACTICE AND DRILL There are several versions of this format. It provides opportunities to practice the mastery of skills or concepts.

a. Partner drill Students take turns asking their partners questions.

b. Flashcards Each student makes up flash cards with questions for a partner. The student presenting the cards should have the correct answer(s) for each question asked.

c. Teams-Games-Tournaments In every round, individual students from each team compete with each other. The team's score is determined by members of each team.

d. Peer-pair-problem solving (also called "pairs check") Each of the students in the pair has a unique role. One is the "solver" or "performer," the other is the "checker" or "coach." The "solver" works on solving the problem. The "checker" observes, gives hints, points out errors, and gives positive feedback and encouragement to the partner. The "checker" can only give suggestions, not part or all of the solution. Roles are reversed for the next problem to be solved.

JIGSAW Most useful for solving large or complex problems or doing an extended class project. The task is divided into several component parts, approaches, or topics.

a. Each group member is assigned to work on a different aspect of the problem. For example, if a problem requires students to make measurements, check and tabulate data, and report on results, a "measurer," "checker," "tabulator," and "reporter" may be designated.

b. Each group works on a different part of the problem or project. Each group's effort becomes part of the unified effort of the whole class, as pieces of a jigsaw puzzle fit together to form a larger, complete picture.

ROUNDTABLE This method is not highly interactive, but is excellent for brainstorming, for generating enthusiasm, and for generating a large number of answers to problems with multiple solutions. Each group has one piece of paper. After the teacher poses the question or problem, students write a solution or suggestion on the paper, then pass the paper to the next student. Within a given time frame, the paper continues to be circulated among the group (or the whole class). A student may choose to pass a round without penalty.

WHOLE CLASS AS A GROUP The whole class as a group may decide on classroom procedures, divide work among the groups, decide on topics for class projects, brainstorm, present the results of their project to the school or the community, go over homework, review materials, or play mathematical games.

Is cooperative learning always an appropriate methodology?

Clearly, it is not always appropriate to use cooperative learning strategies in a mathematics class, nor should group work be the only strategy used. Students need to be engaged in a combination of individual and collaborative efforts. In addition to developing a common vocabulary and shared understanding of concepts, students need to develop a personal voice and a personal understanding of the ideas.

In *Integrated Mathematics 2* See student pages 105, 249, and 406 and side-column commentary on pages 36, 211, and 278.

Enhancing Mathematics Learning Using Graphing Technology

by **Bill Leonard**
Mathematics Instructor
Shawnee Mission West High School; Shawnee Mission, Kansas

"Graphing technology helps students make connections between logic, symbols, and visualization."

Benefits of Graphing Technology

Developments in graphing software and graphics calculators have had a great impact on the teaching and learning of mathematics and have allowed teachers and students opportunities that were unavailable before. Teachers can present the same problem situation algebraically and geometrically within the same lesson. Students can visualize problems much more easily than in the past, and can attempt to solve problems that in the past might have been too complicated to deal with using only paper and pencil and algorithms.

Graphing technology can be used to facilitate students' many different individual learning styles, including verbal/linguistic, visual/spatial, logical, and kinesthetic. Graphing technology works as well with students whose learning style is interpersonal as with those who learn best working on their own.

Perhaps the greatest strength of graphing technology is its facility in helping students to make connections between logic, symbols, and visualization.

Features that Enhance Different Learning Styles

The relationship between two lines that have equal slope but different y-intercepts can quickly be seen by graphing the equations of two or more such lines using graphing software or a graphics calculator. The image on the screen helps all students, and especially visual learners, conclude that lines with equal slope but different y-intercepts are parallel. The effect of changes in the y-intercept for a line with given slope is also apparent, which helps make the slope-intercept form of an equation, $y = mx + b$, more meaningful. While an example such as this is particulary beneficial to the visual learner, the hands-on approach is also helpful to the kinesthetic learner.

Lines with the Same Slope

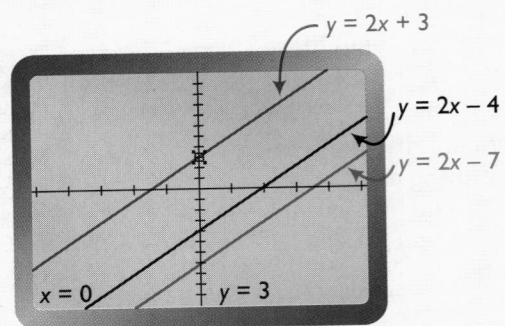

$y = 2x + 3$
$y = 2x - 4$
$y = 2x - 7$
$x = 0$ $y = 3$

Reflections

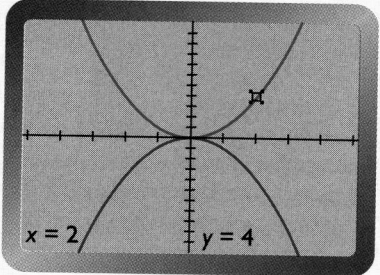

x = 2   y = 4

The relationship between changes in a quadratic equation and resulting translations of the graph can also be viewed quickly using graphing technology. The examples at the left and below demonstrate how graphing technology can be used to show how changes in an equation affect its graph. For example, when the graphs of $y_1 = x^2$ and $y_2 = -x^2$ are displayed on the same screen, students can see that the effect of multiplying the coefficient of x^2 by -1 is to reflect the graph of the original equation in the x-axis. When 3 is added to the equation, the graph is translated up 3 units. When 3 is added to the x-term before squaring, the graph is shifted 3 units left.

Vertical Shift

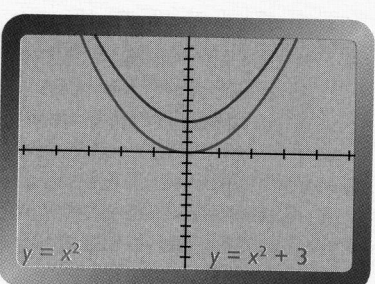

$y = x^2$ $y = x^2 + 3$

Horizontal Shift

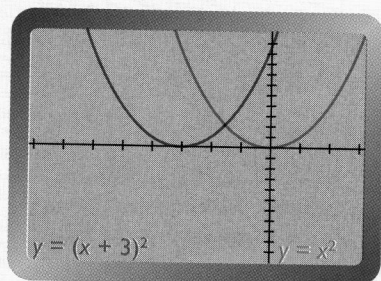

$y = (x + 3)^2$ $y = x^2$

Solving a quadratic equation graphically by hand may be time-consuming, but, worse, may produce a graph from which it is extremely difficult to estimate solutions. However, using a graphics calculator or software produces the graph quickly. The student can use the TRACE and ZOOM features to estimate solutions quickly and accurately.

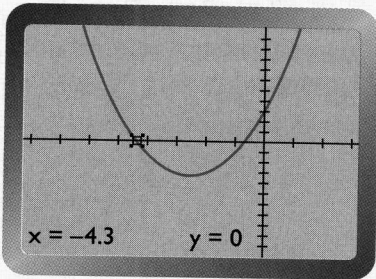

x = −4.3   y = 0

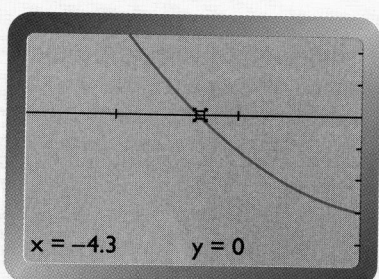

x = −4.3   y = 0

Meeting the Needs of Students for the Year 2000 and Beyond

In *Integrated Mathematics 2*
See student pages 78, 95, and 193 and side-column commentary on pages 19, 36, and 188.

As technology continues to become more and more a part of everyday life, students need to develop a familiarity and ease with using technology. They also need to recognize that math can be used to model and solve real-life problems. Graphics software and graphics calculators are successful tools for enabling students to achieve both of these goals. What may be just as important, they are fun to use!

Using Manipulatives to Develop Understanding

by **Valarie A. Elswick**
Mathematics Teacher
Roy C. Ketcham Senior High School; Wappingers Falls, New York

"Using manipulatives encourages active participation."

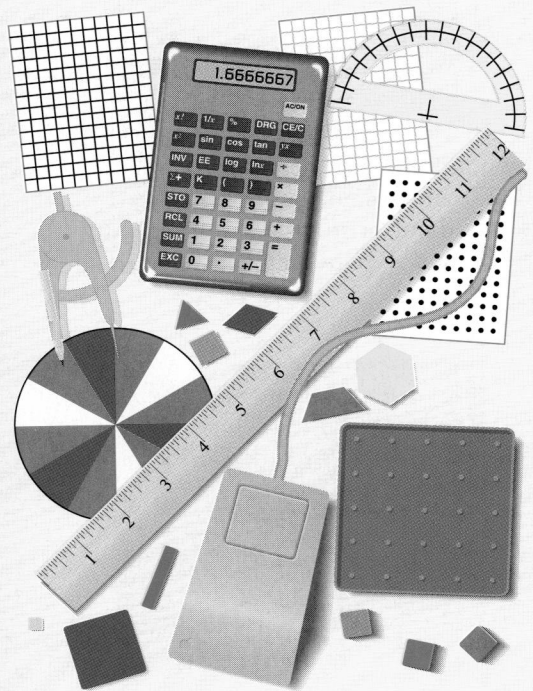

Incorporating Manipulatives

Are the materials shown at the left available to you and your students?

These are some of the many different types of manipulatives that can be found in mathematics classes around the country. Many mathematics teachers today are learning to incorporate manipulatives into their lessons to improve student comprehension. At all levels of mathematics instruction, the use of manipulatives can help students build conceptual understanding and nurture their learning of abstract ideas.

Student Goals

Manipulatives can help students understand specific topics and procedures. Over a period of time manipulatives can also help students achieve some broader goals. For example, manipulative activities help instill in students a sense of confidence in their ability to think and communicate mathematically, especially when group work is involved. While working with manipulatives, students have the opportunity to take chances, make several tries, and reach appropriate decisions in selecting strategies and techniques. The potential exists for students to take intellectual risks by raising questions, formulating conjectures, and presenting solutions.

Using manipulatives encourages active participation by all students. Students can be asked to investigate, explore, predict, test, develop, describe orally and in a written format, discuss in a group or with the whole class, justify, solve, and use and apply ideas.

The Teacher's Role

Preparing the Activity

Using manipulatives in a lesson can be very exciting and motivating. It can also challenge teachers to develop lesson plans that keep students actively involved and prevent inappropriate use of the manipulatives. Advance planning and preparation are essential for successful use of manipulatives.

➤ Thought should be given to selecting the best manipulative for the learning objective.

➤ Materials should be organized for easy use and distribution to the class.

➤ An evaluation process appropriate to the activity should be selected.

Facilitating the Activity

Before beginning a manipulative activity, students need to have an understanding of the procedure and directions for getting the materials and beginning their work. They might be asked to reflect on the mathematics involved and directed to communicate their thoughts in a verbal or written format at the end of the activity. Once the activity begins, the teacher should move among the students, listening to the discussions and exchanges of ideas. As the activity continues, the teacher may need to answer questions or redirect the focus.

Making Connections

Using manipulatives enables students to make connections between mathematical topics, such as algebra and geometry. Algebra tiles and tangrams are two types of manipulatives that can be used to connect algebra and geometry, both symbolically and visually, as these examples illustrate.

Factoring Polynomials Using Algebra Tiles

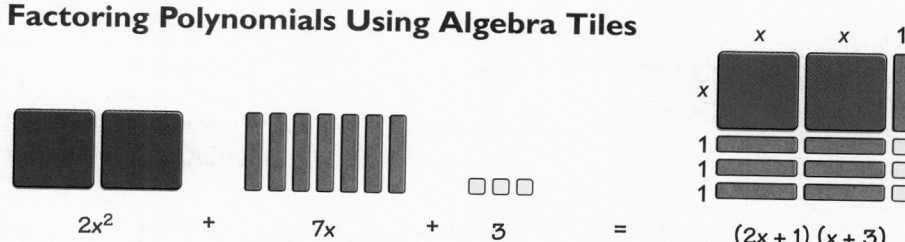

$$2x^2 \quad + \quad 7x \quad + \quad 3 \quad = \quad (2x + 1)(x + 3)$$

Exploring Quadrilaterals with Tangrams

Using a standard seven-piece tangram puzzle, is it possible to make a parallelogram with one piece, two pieces, three pieces, and so on up to seven pieces? Some of the possibilities are shown here. You might consider a similar question for squares and trapezoids.

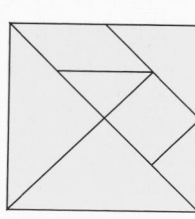

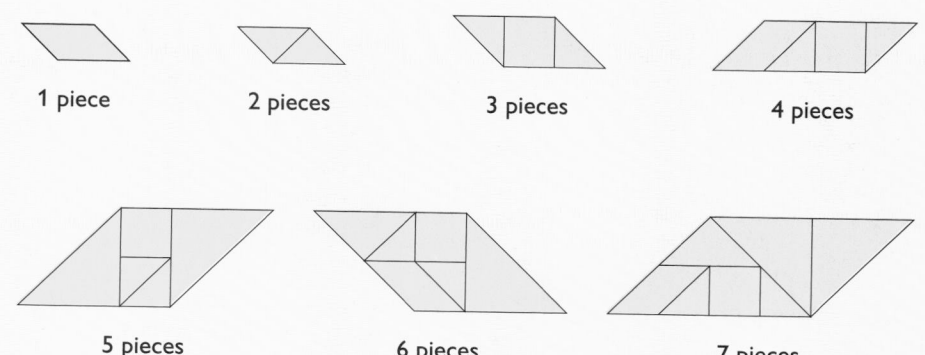

1 piece   2 pieces   3 pieces   4 pieces

5 pieces   6 pieces   7 pieces

Summary of Benefits

In *Integrated Mathematics 2* See student pages 75, 137, and 415 and side-column commentary on pages 17, 218, and 420.

Working with manipulatives can help students overcome language barriers, improve their listening and speaking skills, and increase their receptivity to a variety of concepts and approaches. Manipulatives motivate students by involving them in the learning process. Manipulatives also develop students' confidence in their ability to solve problems and to reason and communicate mathematically.

Writing in Mathematics

by **Joan C. Countryman**
Head of School
Lincoln School; Providence, Rhode Island

> ## "When students write they learn that mathematics is a human endeavor."

"Does your answer make sense?"

The student had come in for extra help and we were going over the homework problems. In the silence, I looked up, expecting some sort of defense for his solution to the exercise, but as our eyes met I realized that my question had startled him.

"Is it supposed to make sense?"

For too many students, studying mathematics has nothing to do with making sense. Practicing the steps, learning the rules, passing tests, adding, subtracting, multiplying, dividing—these are the activities of math class. If you get the right answer, the one in the back of the book, or the one your friend got, you can move on to the next task. If not, you must retrace your steps, find the mistake, do the calculations once more.

My student's quizzical look reminded me that, for some math students, none of it makes sense. I needed to find a way to help the young people enrolled in my classes build connections between what they already knew and what I wanted them to learn. I wanted to help them learn to stop and think about what we were doing in class. Why does the graph rise here and fall there? What does x represent in this example? Are squares of numbers always bigger than the numbers? Why not multiply and divide in this case?

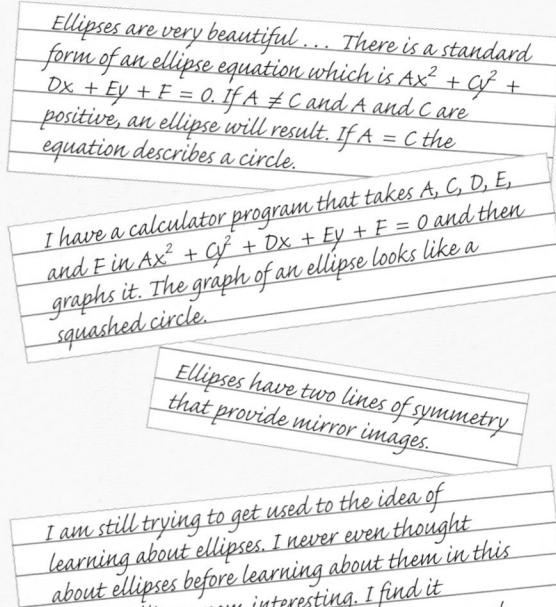

Ellipses are very beautiful ... There is a standard form of an ellipse equation which is $Ax^2 + Cy^2 + Dx + Ey + F = 0$. If $A \neq C$ and A and C are positive, an ellipse will result. If $A = C$ the equation describes a circle.

I have a calculator program that takes A, C, D, E, and F in $Ax^2 + Cy^2 + Dx + Ey + F = 0$ and then graphs it. The graph of an ellipse looks like a squashed circle.

Ellipses have two lines of symmetry that provide mirror images.

I am still trying to get used to the idea of learning about ellipses. I never even thought about ellipses before learning about them in this course. Ellipses seem interesting. I find it extremely interesting to learn about how much one equation can do for you.

I started asking my students to write about their work in mathematics because I thought that writing might help them move beyond a mechanical approach to learning, an approach that they found annoying but familiar. I wanted to help them discover the questions that are central to the discipline, the questions that mathematicians might pose. I also wanted them to think about themselves as learners. Over the years, I have found that one way to help students clarify, express, and reflect on their work in mathematics is to ask them to write to learn.

When I talk about writing in math I mean writing in its broadest sense. I ask students to take notes, make lists, record their observations and feelings, as well as to write essays, term papers, and stories. Having students write supports an active approach to teaching and learning. I expect my students to construct meaning. In order to make sense of the material, they must connect new information to what they already know. Writing helps them to learn to ask their own questions, and to explore some of the questions that I pose.

Many teachers use the writing process across the grades to help students construct mathematical knowledge. The examples at the left are from the math journals of tenth graders. The students recorded their observations about ellipses during a unit on analytic geometry. These brief comments, written at the end of class, provided insight for the teacher about how the students understood their work in conics.

Keeping journals and writing word problems are just two of many activities that math teachers might require of their students. Autobiographies, the stories of their growth as math students, written in the first weeks of a math course, can serve to inform teachers about students' initial perceptions of mathematics and their own learning styles. Letters to parents or friends provide current accounts of coursework. Study guides, test questions, and lesson summaries can serve as excellent reviews. One way to get started is simply to ask students to write a comment, on the back of the homework, about the exercises they have completed. Which was the most difficult? Which provided the most insight on the material? Which ones were easy to complete?

Advocates of writing across the curriculum are not suggesting that all teachers assign essays and correct them as an English teacher might. Instead we imagine that teachers might ask students to think and write as essayists, scientists, historians, and mathematicians do, posing questions, and solving problems by writing and reflecting on the material of the discipline.

Most useful to us as teachers is the writing that provides insights on how our students think about their work. The following example is from a mathematics student who was also studying physics. For the teacher, the student's comments revealed the depth of his thinking about mathematical concepts of real phenomena.

> Since I have been very interested and involved in physics, I wanted to find a topic for my final paper that would in some way investigate some of the principles we were studying in physics. I also wanted to study empirically one of these topics, that is, to take my own data, and develop equations based not on a textbook but on my own data-taking and analysis. For these reasons, I decided to examine the behavior of different balls as they bounce, specifically to establish a relationship between the height from which a ball is dropped and the height that it then bounces. While I worked on this project, I also became interested in the time over which a ball continues to bounce, and I added my investigations in this area to my paper.

My hope is that one day students and teachers will write to learn freely. Pages of notes, stories, plays, lists, poems, sketches, and journal entries about math, language, literature, science, and history will help students make sense of the world in which they live. Teachers of all subjects will serve as coaches and experts about the learning process, knowledgeable about students—who they are, what they can do, what they know, and what they need to know.

What might students learn when they write about math? What can we as teachers learn from their writing? First, when students write they learn that mathematics is a human endeavor, one that comes not from the sky, but from the work of human minds. In fact, when students write some of the mathematics comes from their own minds. Second, when reading students' writing, teachers discover that learners, like mathematicians, must construct the mathematics for themselves. If we give them time to do this, they will succeed in constructing their understanding of the material. Finally, students and teachers will learn that meaning lies not in the words and symbols themselves, but in the ways that we use those words and symbols to make sense of information.

In **Integrated Mathematics 2**
See student pages 32, 254, and 391 and side-column commentary on pages 27, 285, and 396.

Developing Good Problem Solvers

by **Martha E. Wilson**
Preparatory Mathematics Specialist
Mathematical Sciences Teaching and Learning Center
University of Delaware; Newark, Delaware

> "Teaching itself is a complex problem solving process."

The Goal of Mathematics Instruction

Mathematics educators have agreed for some time that problem solving is a very important, if not the most important, goal of mathematics instruction. Students who learn mathematics through drill in routine operations lose interest in the subject and miss the opportunity for intellectual development. Stimulating them to solve appropriately challenging problems, and helping them to solve those problems, provides students with interest in and tools for independent thinking.

Research in mathematics education has not been able to identify any one single way of teaching that is "best" for developing problem solving skills in mathematics for all students in all situations. There are, however, examples of good problem solving that point to actions that teachers might take to help students develop those skills.

Cooperative Learning

The National Council of Teachers of Mathematics *Curriculum and Evaluation Standards* and *Professional Standards for Teaching Mathematics* both call for a classroom where students have an opportunity to explore and investigate ideas, develop conjectures, and verify hypotheses. Cooperative learning in mathematics is often recommended as one way to help students because:

➤ they become active participants in the classroom

➤ they may be encouraged to discuss and communicate their ideas about mathematics in an environment that is less threatening than in whole-class discussions

➤ when groups of students struggle with an interesting problem, the outcome for many students is a new and refreshing view of doing mathematics

Whole-Group Instruction

Research also suggests that an active, problem solving approach to learning can be accomplished in whole-group instruction, where the teacher directs the activities of the entire class. Students can become actively involved when the teacher selects and presents an interesting idea or problem and then leads students to a discovery of concepts and connections through a series of questions. Questions should develop a train of thought in logical sequence and should include these types:

➤ some moderately challenging, to stimulate thinking

➤ some factual, to bring out important facts or information

➤ some requiring considerable thought and formulation of a conclusion

The Teacher's Role

The role of the teacher in preparing for either model of instruction becomes one of organizing for learning by selecting an engaging task or problem. An understanding of the background knowledge and interests of the students and thoughtful planning of future lessons is necessary for the design of this task. Good tasks prompt an interest in investigation whether they are presented for group work or for whole-class discussion.

Example

Not this: Given $y = \frac{1}{2}x^2 + 17x - 3$, find the coordinates of the vertex of the parabola.

But this: Write equations for two parabolas whose graphs will "trap" the point (2,3). Sketch your results or get a printout and label the graphs. (One possibility is shown below.)

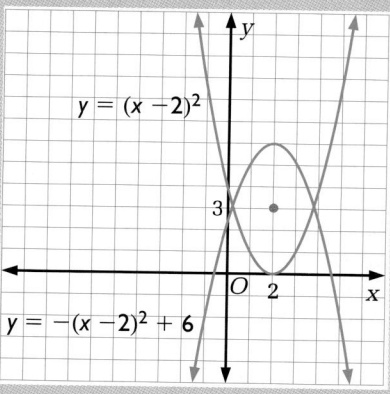

Selecting Good Tasks

A task should be:

➤ set in a context that will engage the interest of students

➤ complex and difficult enough to challenge students' thinking, but not so difficult that they will give up quickly

➤ solvable by more than one method, so that a subsequent discussion can point out connections and the possibility of multiple approaches

In discussions, the teacher must prepare to ask the questions that lead to clear and concise mathematical conclusions and emphasize the connections that can be made.

Teachers as Problem Solvers

Research on teaching and learning mathematics is still incomplete, and there is no indication that teaching mathematics must be done in a single prescribed way in order for students to become good mathematical problem solvers. Teachers may choose among a variety of styles, including teacher presentation, large-group activities, small-group cooperative learning, and combinations of these. As researchers have investigated several modes of teaching in search for the one that produces good problem solvers, they seem to have found that teaching itself is a complex problem solving process.

In *Integrated Mathematics 2*
See student pages 40, 296, and 305 and side-column commentary on pages 212, 219, and 405.

Ongoing **ASSESSMENT**

38. **Writing** A basketball player shoots at a basket that is 10 ft from the floor. The function in the photo gives the distance from the ball to the floor, in feet.

a. Explain how the equation $10 = -16t^2 + 20t + 6$ or $0 = -16t^2 + 20t - 4$ can help you find when the ball is at basket level.

b. Solve $0 = -16t^2 + 20t - 4$ by factoring. Which solution represents the time that the ball passes through the basket?

c. Explain how the equation $0 = -16t^2 + 20t + 6$ can help you find when the ball hits the ground.

d. Solve $0 = -16t^2 + 20t + 6$ by factoring. Which solution makes sense as the time the ball hits the ground?

From *Integrated Mathematics 2*, page 212

Teaching Students Acquiring English

by **Cesar Larriva**
Doctoral Student, Department of Education
Stanford University; Stanford, California

"The strategies for teaching students with limited English proficiency work well for all students."

Challenge

The educational backgrounds of LEP (limited English proficient) students in general are as varied as the nationalities they represent. Some students have received top-quality public or private education in their native countries while others have barely attended school. The students' first (native) language proficiency can also vary considerably and has a strong influence on student academic success in the second language setting. The LEP student generally comes from a culture where education is valued, and the school and the teacher are highly respected. These students are generally very motivated by their desire to succeed.

They are also motivated by their desire to please the teacher and by peer pressure from other LEP students, which is largely achievement oriented.

The wide range of mathematics skills, English proficiency, and first language proficiency of LEP students within a classroom makes it challenging to meet the needs of all students. Meeting this challenge therefore requires special strategies.

Sheltering Techniques

Sheltering techniques are an important tool. Sheltered English instruction is a method of delivering subject matter (e.g., mathematics) instruction to LEP students using English as the medium for instruction. A language can be learned only if it is presented as comprehensible input. Information is comprehensible when the vocabulary and language used are familiar to the learner and the information is presented in a meaningful context.

In sheltered English instruction, the delivery of the message is simplified (sheltered), but subject matter remains challenging; material is not "watered down." Instruction in the sheltered English classroom is adjusted to ensure student comprehension. Input can be made more comprehensible by the following techniques.

Teacher's Speech

Language is simplified by avoiding compound sentences, by favoring simple grammatical structures such as the present tense, by limiting the vocabulary, and by avoiding use of idioms. A phrase such as "I want you to stay on top of things here" should be used only if its meaning is discussed first. Content is emphasized over grammatical accuracy. Student oral and written responses are evaluated based on content not grammatical accuracy. Important ideas are repeated several times for emphasis.

Providing Clues

Effort should constantly be made to provide contextual clues. These may be graphical representations such as photographs or graphs. The clues may be in written form, such as the posting of important vocabulary on a chalk or bulletin board; a written vocabulary word can be pointed to as the teacher uses it in the sentence during lecture. Clues may be physical, such as real objects and scaled models.

Acceptance

The classroom culture is supportive, motivational, and non-threatening so that the student's defense mechanism (which hinders participation) is low. LEP students experience a pre-speech stage or silent period during which active listening and learning occur without language production. Students will produce language when ready and should be encouraged but not pushed.

Manipulatives

Concepts are contextualized and communication is facilitated through the use of hands-on activities and manipulatives, such as algebra tiles. A great deal of emphasis is placed on making the abstract more concrete. For example, students can physically act out or model a problem. The diagram shows students physically plotting a linear equation on a tennis court or a school yard on which coordinate axes have been drawn using chalk.

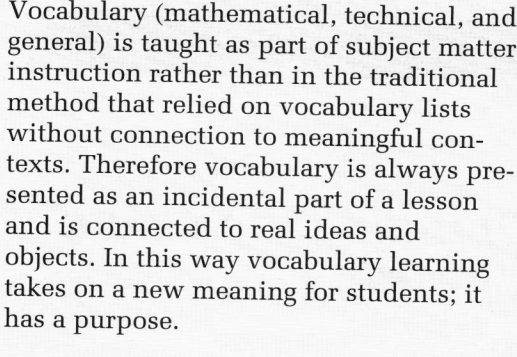

Students physically model the function $y = x + 2$.

Any technique like this that facilitates communication by decreasing the reliance on language is beneficial.

Prior Experience

Provide sufficient preparation and background when introducing a new topic. A lesson on probability using playing cards, for example, will definitely require an explanation of the playing cards themselves, since many LEP students have never seen these cards that are so familiar to us. New concepts should be presented in a context that is meaningful to the student.

It is important to recognize that LEP students have a wealth of prior skills and experience to draw upon. Many also have highly developed informal math skills. It is our job to help students utilize their prior knowledge. Since thinking skills transfer from one language to another, problems involving experiences such as travel, money, and school life can trigger students' interest and motivation. Classroom activities should encourage students to draw upon these.

Cooperative Learning

Related to the goal of encouraging LEP student participation is the goal of creating a positive feeling toward mathematics and the mathematics classroom. Maintaining a friendly non-threatening, supportive environment is an essential aspect of encouraging participation and thus learning. Additionally, fostering a feeling of community is essential in a classroom for students to acquire lasting knowledge. The community should generate and sustain a mathematics culture.

Cooperative learning groups play an important role in promoting the exchange of values and providing a forum for participation in the mathematics culture. The culture values and rewards inquiry, effort, and risk taking. It is the responsibility of the teacher to facilitate the development of such a culture within the classroom. Student conversational interaction is encouraged through cooperative learning activities. I am careful to seat LEP students next to others who can translate and/or provide support. Small groups provide a safer environment since many students are reluctant to ask questions or offer answers in a large class setting. Students pool their talents and strengths (e.g. language, computational, and problem solving abilities) to piece together solutions to problems.

The teacher should allow for a reasonable noise level since a class of 30 or 40 engaged in cooperative learning can generate considerable noise. Classroom management skills become important in maintaining the balance between the organized group debates which develop, and anarchy.

Language Development

Vocabulary (mathematical, technical, and general) is taught as part of subject matter instruction rather than in the traditional method that relied on vocabulary lists without connection to meaningful contexts. Therefore vocabulary is always presented as an incidental part of a lesson and is connected to real ideas and objects. In this way vocabulary learning takes on a new meaning for students; it has a purpose.

Students' language development is central to success for LEP students in the mathematics classroom and thus deserves added attention. Collaborative problem solving is an effective way to foster written and verbal communication between students. The student discussions create opportunities for students to hear themselves and other students using the language of mathematics. Students must be given opportunities to write and speak mathematically with each other as well as the teacher. Additional methods of promoting language development include the use of investigations and projects in collaborative group settings. Assigning portfolios and journal writing is also useful. Do not avoid assigning problems that require writing. Instead, use these problems as vehicles for students to develop oral and written language skills in cooperative group settings.

Effective Teaching

The instructional approaches recommended thus far for teaching mathematics to limited English proficient students are in fact nothing more than good teaching techniques that work well for all students. It is therefore possible to accommodate the needs of limited English proficient students and native English speakers concurrently without compromising the learning of either.

In *Integrated Mathematics 2*
See student pages 16, 243, and 297 and side-column commentary on pages 14, 282, and 398.

Visual Learning Strategies

by **Stuart J. Murphy**
Visual Learning Specialist
Evanston, Illinois

"Linking the visual and the verbal is a powerful teaching tool."

Our Visual Environment

There is no question that we are living in an intensely visual environment. Whether from television and videos, or magazines and books, information regularly comes to us in a variety of formats. In addition to text, these formats include charts and graphs, maps and diagrams, photographs and illustrations, symbols and cartoons.

Even the way in which text is presented has become more varied to include a greater use of highlighted phrases, headlines, call-outs, and captions. The need to absorb more information—in more formats—has never been greater.

With this need come many learning opportunities. There is growing evidence that comprehension increases when verbal information is augmented by high-quality visual displays.

Linking the visual and the verbal is a powerful teaching tool. Such a link interests and motivates learners, provides more information, and reaches a broader audience than either method alone.

Visual Learning in Mathematics

In the study of mathematics, visual learning strategies play an especially important role. Understanding symbols—and the use of symbols within the concise language of mathematics—is critical to the ability to comprehend and express mathematical ideas.

Icons and symbols also play an important role in the use of technology in mathematical instruction. Calculators and computers use a carefully constructed symbolic language to provide direction and convey meaning to users.

Visual presentations help us to model mathematical ideas, to see patterns, and to understand relationships. Indeed, a basic understanding of many important mathematical concepts—concepts such as comparison, scale, dimension, translation, and perspective—depends upon the ability of the student to visualize.

A better understanding of how information is conveyed visually can also help us as we work with students who are visual/spatial learners, students who have limited English proficiency, and students who come from a variety of socio-economic and cultural backgrounds. In fact, using visual learning strategies can help us increase the learning potential of all students.

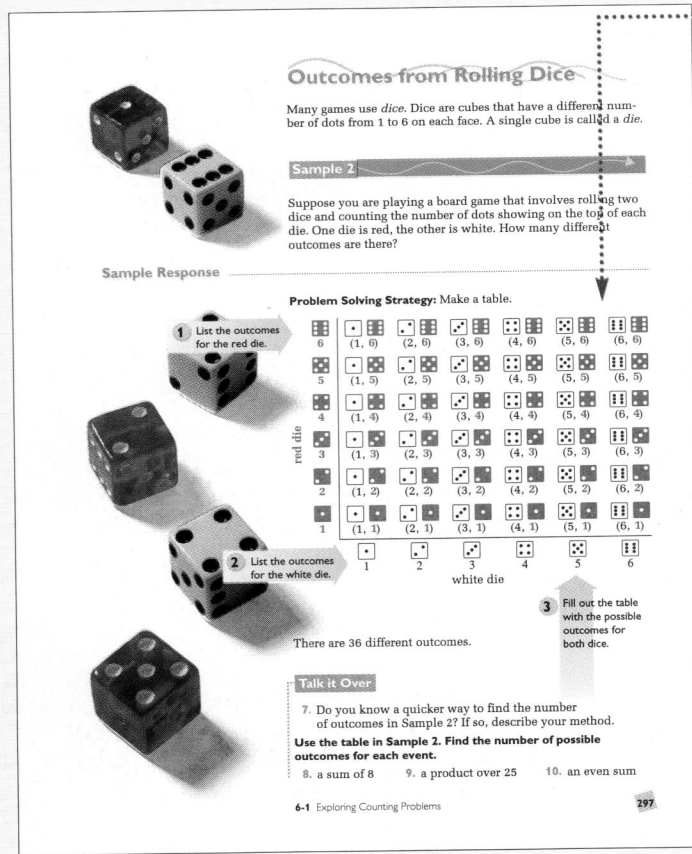

Outcomes from Rolling Dice

Many games use *dice*. Dice are cubes that have a different number of dots from 1 to 6 on each face. A single cube is called a *die*.

Sample 2

Suppose you are playing a board game that involves rolling two dice and counting the number of dots showing on the top of each die. One die is red, the other is white. How many different outcomes are there?

Sample Response

Problem Solving Strategy: Make a table.

1. List the outcomes for the red die.
2. List the outcomes for the white die.
3. Fill out the table with the possible outcomes for both dice.

There are 36 different outcomes.

Talk it Over

7. Do you know a quicker way to find the number of outcomes in Sample 2? If so, describe your method.

Use the table in Sample 2. Find the number of possible outcomes for each event.

8. a sum of 8   9. a product over 25   10. an even sum

6-1 Exploring Counting Problems   297

Photographs help students connect mathematical ideas to other lands and cultures.

Integrated Mathematics includes a carefully planned visual learning strand to help students develop visual learning skills. Pages are designed to allow easy access to the material being presented and to provide multiple points of entry, including images, titles, diagrams, and call-outs.

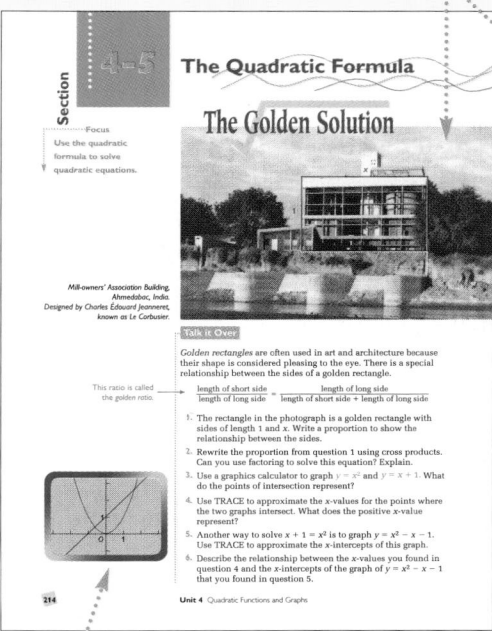

Special callouts explain mathematical concepts and thinking processes.

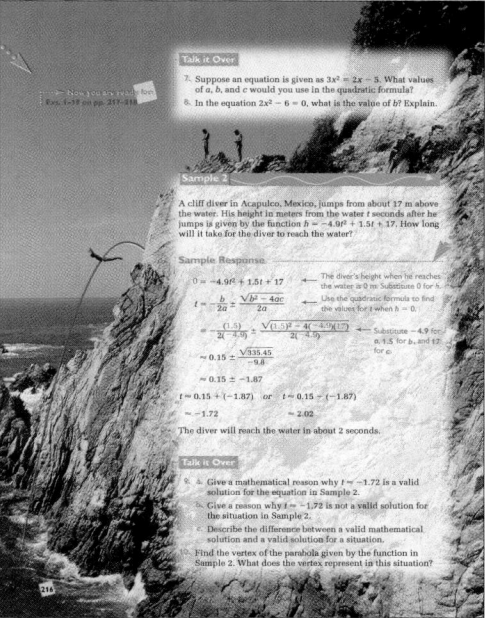

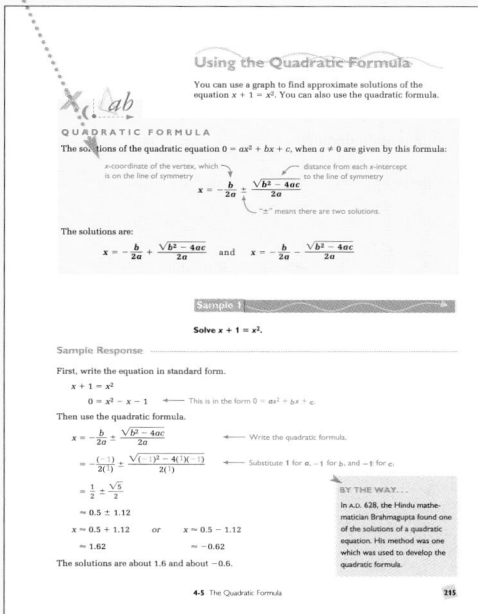

Screen displays provide guidance for students with calculators and visual models for those without calculators.

Strategies for Developing Visual Skills

Here are some visual learning strategies that you can use on an ongoing basis.

➤ Display visual materials to interest, excite, and motivate students.

➤ Emphasize photos within the text that demonstrate real applications of mathematical concepts and ask students to consider and discuss other examples.

➤ Explain—or have students explain—the diagrams within a lesson.

➤ Develop—or have students develop—ways to visualize abstract concepts.

➤ When students are having trouble understanding a concept, try to explain the concept without using words.

➤ Encourage students to:
  • draw and sketch as part of their note-taking and journal practice
  • take photographs or clip photos from magazines to connect related ideas
  • demonstrate their thinking by mapping out the steps or acting out the process
  • show their understanding by drawing a concept map
  • construct charts, graphs, and diagrams to explain concepts

Using these strategies and the images that have been provided in *Integrated Mathematics* will help your students develop their visual learning skills—help them to link visual to verbal, process to concept, and learning to life.

In **Integrated Mathematics 2**
See student pages 199, 339, and 351 and side-column commentary on pages 7, 160, and 314.

Assessment Methods

by **Karen S. Norwood**
Assistant Professor, Department of Mathematics and Science Education
North Carolina State University; Raleigh, North Carolina

> "*Assessment needs to be embedded in the instructional process.*"

Investigate the shape and the dimensions of the pen with the largest area that can be constructed with 36 feet of fencing.

Explain which is larger:

π^6 or 6π

Do not use your calculator.

Write a paragraph explaining how the sine and the cosine ratios are alike and how they are different.

Demonstration
Tell the class everything you know about the graphs of

A $y = x^2 + 2x + 1$

and

B $y = -x^2 + 2$

Use a graphics calculator or computer software if you wish.

Assessment Goals

The purpose of assessment in mathematics is to improve and evaluate learning and teaching. In the teaching-learning process, it is imperative that assessment be used to broaden and inform, rather than restrict, the process. Assessment needs to be embedded in the instructional process, instead of being apart from it. This view was well stated in the NCTM's *Curriculum and Evaluation Standards for School Mathematics.* "In an instructional environment that demands a deeper understanding of mathematics, testing instruments that call for only the identification of single correct responses no longer suffice. Instead, our instruments must reflect the scope and intent of our instructional program to have students solve problems, reason, and communicate."

Traditional paper-and-pencil tests are incomplete measures of achievement. In fact, no single type of assessment can serve all the information needs of an educational institution. Using alternative assessment methods provides a more equitable measure of a student's mathematical progress, has less potential for bias, and encourages respect for diversity by modeling appreciation for varied approaches to a problem. The goals of alternative assessment are to:

➤ find out what the students already know

➤ evaluate the depth of the students' conceptual understanding and their ability to transfer this understanding to new and different situations

➤ evaluate the students' ability to communicate their understanding mathematically, make mathematical connections, and reason mathematically

➤ plan the mathematics instruction in order to achieve the objectives

➤ report individual student progress and show growth in mathematical maturity

➤ analyze the overall effectiveness of the mathematical instruction

When using alternative assessment, it is important to start slowly, so as not to become overwhelmed. Journal writing is a good place to start. Once you become comfortable with this technique, try to add another alternative assessment strategy to your repertoire. Don't try to use alternative assessment alone; involve colleagues, parents, and administrators.

Scoring

There are several ways to score alternative assessment assignments. One of the most simple methods is to divide papers into piles labeled "satisfactory" and "unsatisfactory." Then assign a grade from 0 to 3 based on the following criteria. Satisfactory papers are given a grade of 3 if the student gives a clear explanation with appropriate diagrams or graphs, and a score of 2 if the student's work is complete and shows understanding but contains computational errors or minor flaws in explanation. Unsatisfactory papers are given a 1 if the work is incomplete and contains serious conceptual errors along with flagrant computational errors. A score of 0 is given if little or no effort was made to complete the assignment.

Some people prefer to use a scale of 1 to 4, where 4 indicates excellent and 1 indicates unacceptable work. Five- and six-point scales are also used.

Alternative Assessment Formats

Several types of alternative assessment items are appropriate to the mathematics classroom.

JOURNALS Regular use of a journal encourages students to express complex mathematical concepts in words. Writing helps to make students aware of what they do and don't understand, what they can and cannot do. Reading a journal gives the teacher insight into the student's understanding.

RESEARCH PROJECTS Group or individual research projects allow students to investigate topics that encompass many mathematical concepts and their real-world applications. Examples of such projects are the Unit Projects in this book.

DEMONSTRATION/PERFORMANCE ASSESSMENT Teachers can assess their students' comprehension of a mathematical concept by asking them to explain the concept in their own words using such items as compasses, graph paper, calculators, and computers.

PROBLEM SOLVING Problem solving is considered to be the link between facts and algorithms and the real-life problem situations that we all face. Problem-solving activities include non-routine problems where the strategy necessary to solve the problem is not immediately apparent, and analysis and synthesis of previously learned knowledge are required.

PORTFOLIOS As artists and writers use portfolios to show off their best work, mathematics students can use portfolios to document their growth and the development of their mathematical power. Portfolios can be used to assess a student's mathematical reasoning, understanding, attitudes, and ability to communicate mathematically.

Both the teacher and the student should have input into selecting what will be included in a portfolio. For example, the teacher might determine how many pieces are to be included and the categories from which they will come. The student might be allowed to choose the pieces. The portfolio should include a table of contents and a cover letter. Each included work should be labeled with the date, a description of the task or problem, and the identity of the person who selected the work. A self-assessment should also be included.

The contents of a portfolio might include:

➤ open-ended questions, problems, and tasks, in which the student is asked to formulate hypotheses, explain a mathematical situation, make a generalization, and so on, either orally or in writing

➤ research projects

➤ presentations, discussions, and debates

➤ journal entries

➤ cooperative learning activities

➤ math logs: problems assigned by the teacher which require that the student not only show computations, but validate the solution

➤ problem solving

➤ investigations

➤ models and simulations

➤ interviews: students talk, individually or in groups, while the teacher listens and asks questions. The teacher may encourage students to further elaborate in an interview by using phrases such as, "I am interested in your thinking," or "I understand it better now, but..."

➤ photographs of items the student may have produced that are too bulky to fit in a portfolio

➤ work dealing with the same mathematical idea sampled at different times

➤ copies of awards or prizes

Ongoing **ASSESSMENT**

16. **Open-ended** A mouse goes through this maze. Assume that the mouse always heads toward the cheese. Also assume that at every intersection with a choice, the probability that the mouse will turn is equal to the probability that the mouse will go straight.

Use simulation to estimate the probability that the mouse will go through the corner marked *A* on the maze to get to the cheese. Describe your method.

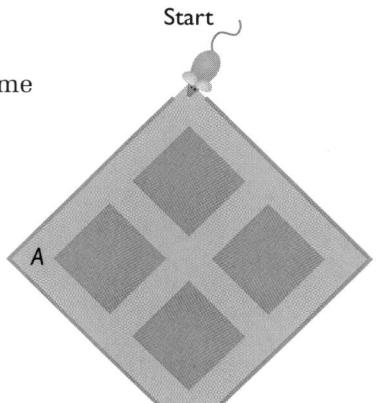
Start

A

Finish

From *Integrated Mathematics 2*, page 15

In *Integrated Mathematics 2*
See student pages 66, 73, and 318 and side-column commentary on pages 141, 301, and 438.

Preparing for College Entrance Examinations

by **Anita G. Morris**
Coordinator of Mathematics
Anne Arundel County Public Schools
Annapolis, Maryland

"Students need to acquire a solid base of knowledge in mathematics."

Purpose of College Entrance Examinations

College entrance examinations are intended to measure how well students will do in their first year in college. Test makers are very careful to state that the results of these tests are only predictors of success; they are not meant to measure a student's aptitude for academic work, knowledge, or intelligence. As education changes and the goals of colleges evolve to emphasize thinking rather than rote memorization, the format of college entrance exams will change to reflect a new emphasis on the ability to apply information and skills. The overall purpose of these tests, however, will remain the same.

Three-Tiered Approach to Test Preparation

The mathematics portion of college entrance exams, such as the SAT 1, generally tests three major areas in mathematics: arithmetic, algebra, and geometry. Student success on these tests rests on:

➤ acquiring a knowledge base in mathematics
➤ practicing general test-taking strategies
➤ practicing strategies specific to the mathematical items on the test

Acquiring a Knowledge Base in Mathematics

It is essential that students enroll in mathematics courses that will provide them with a substantive knowledge of arithmetic, algebra, and geometry. Advanced mathematics and formal geometry proofs are usually not included on college entrance exams; however, students should be encouraged to take as many mathematics courses in high school as possible. This not only prepares them for entrance exams but also better prepares them for success in college.

Practicing General Test-Taking Strategies

Test Structure and Format

Students should become familiar with the structure and format of the college entrance exam they will be taking, including such information as the instructions for each question type, the number of questions in each section, the types of questions in each section, the timing of each section, scoring, and deductions for wrong answers.

Key Concepts

Arithmetic

Simple computation

Operations with whole numbers, integers, and rational numbers

Number properties

Averages

Percents

Rates

Number lines

Ratio/proportion

Algebra

Verbal to algebraic translation

Substitution

Simplifying algebraic expressions

Factoring

Solving equations/inequalities

Exponents

Square roots

Quadratic equations

Algebraic symbol problems

Geometry

Parallel and perpendicular lines

Angles in geometric figures

Properties of triangles (right, isosceles, equilateral, 30-60-90)

Pythagorean theorem

Similarity

Properties of polygons, circles

Perimeter, circumference, area, and volume

Simple coordinate geometry

Attractive Distractors

Unlocking the test involves thinking like the test makers. Answer choices for multiple-choice sections will include incorrect answers that are based on common student errors. These are called "attractive distractors." Students should be aware of these distractors and not assume that because their answer appears among the answer choices that it is correct.

Deductions for Wrong Answers

Students may not have taken tests before on which credit is deducted for wrong answers. Test makers include these deductions to eliminate random guessing on multiple-choice items. A common procedure is the following: If there are five answer choices for a question, 1/4 of a point is deducted for a wrong answer; if there are four answer choices, 1/3 of a point is deducted for a wrong answer; 0 points are deducted for omitted answers. It has been found that if one can narrow the answer choices to two or three, taking an "educated guess" at an answer will increase one's scores substantially over the long run.

Difficulty of Questions and Timing

Some entrance exams are constructed so that the questions increase in difficulty over a section. It is extremely important for students to know whether the same number of points is awarded for answering easy questions as for answering hard questions. If so, on a timed test it is to students' advantage to concentrate on answering as many easy and medium questions as possible. They should avoid using a majority of testing time in answering difficult questions. Timing is essential in becoming a successful test taker.

Simulated Test Practice

Short-term test preparation should include simulated test practices, where students concentrate on general test-taking strategies, including:

➤ knowing the test structure

➤ knowing the format of each question type

➤ knowing the test directions

➤ knowing how to pace themselves

➤ learning when to guess

➤ concentrating on easy questions

Practicing Strategies Specific to Mathematical Items

Mathematical Topics

Within the three broad categories of arithmetic, algebra, and geometry, there are key concepts with which students should be familiar. The table at the left categorizes concepts that are often required. In addition, concepts of simple probability, logic, statistics, and other topics may be included on the test. Simply knowing these concepts will not assure success; students must be comfortable

Multiple Choice

If $3(x - 2) = 27$, then $x - 2$ is:

(A) 3

(B) 5

(C) 6

(D) 9

(E) 11

The correct answer is (D).

Quantitative Comparison

Column A	Column B
3^{12}	$3^{13} - 3^{12}$

Adding 3^{12} to both columns allows you to compare:

$2(3^{12})$	3^{13}
$2(3^{12})$	$3(3^{12})$

The answer is (B).

Student-Produced Response

If the lengths of two sides of a triangle are 4 cm and 7 cm, what is a possible value for the length of the third side?

Any value between 11 and 3 would be correct. If a student chose $9\frac{1}{2}$ as the solution, the correct gridded answer would be:

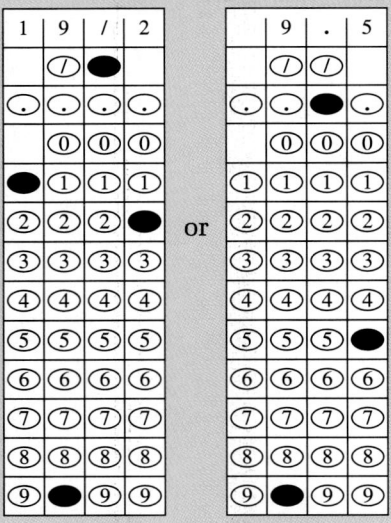

with applying them in a problem solving situation. Students should look over the list of required skills for the test they will be taking and categorize them as ones they know, ones they need to review, or ones that are difficult. Testing simulations, using actual items from previous tests, will help them decide where to concentrate their efforts. A long-term goal in test preparation should be increasing their ability to solve problems that apply these skills. This type of preparation will have the greatest effect on increasing their test scores and assuring their success in college.

Types of Questions

It is important that students be familiar with the question types typically found on college entrance exams. These include: five-choice Multiple-Choice questions, four-choice Quantitative Comparison questions, and Student-Produced Responses. An example of a Multiple-Choice question is shown at the left. In Quantitative Comparison questions, students are presented two quantities, one in Column A and one in Column B. They must determine whether the quantity in Column A is greater (choice A), the quantity in Column B is greater (choice B), the quantities are equal (choice C), or you cannot determine which is greater from the information given (choice D). An (E) response will not be scored. A typical Quantitative Comparison question appears at the left.

Student-Produced Responses require students to fill in the correct answer, rather than choose from a group of choices. Specific instructions for entering answers in the grid are provided by the test makers. A sample of this type of question, and two possible gridded answers for it, are shown at the left. With this type of question, only gridded answers are scored; handwritten answers at the top of the grid are not considered.

The Use of Calculators

Some college entrance exams now allow students to use calculators. However, calculators with a word processing unit, paper tape, or a typewriter keyboard are generally not allowed. Also forbidden are calculators that make noise or require a power outlet. Students are advised to bring a calculator with which they are familiar. It is particularly important that they know how their calculator handles order of operations. Students should not try to answer every question with the calculator. First, they should decide how to solve the problem; then if the calculator will help with the computation, they should use it. The test may be constructed so that every question can be answered without the use of a calculator, but appropriate calculator usage can give them an edge.

Integrated Mathematics **2**

Mathematics

Authors

Senior Authors

Rheta N. Rubenstein
Timothy V. Craine
Thomas R. Butts

Kerry Cantrell
Linda Dritsas
Valarie A. Elswick
Joseph Kavanaugh
Sara N. Munshin
Stuart J. Murphy
Anthony Piccolino
Salvador Quezada
Jocelyn Coleman Walton

McDougal Littell
A HOUGHTON MIFFLIN COMPANY
Evanston, Illinois • Boston • Dallas

Authors

Senior Authors

Rheta N. Rubenstein   Associate Professor of Education, University of Michigan at Dearborn, Dearborn, Michigan

Timothy V. Craine   Assistant Professor of Mathematical Sciences and Department Chair, Central Connecticut State University, New Britain, Connecticut

Thomas R. Butts   Professor of Mathematics Education, University of Texas at Dallas, Dallas, Texas

Kerry Cantrell   Mathematics Teacher and Divisional Technology Coordinator, Marshfield High School, Marshfield, Missouri

Linda Dritsas   Mathematics Coordinator, Fresno Unified School District, Fresno, California

Valarie A. Elswick   Mathematics Consultant and former Mathematics Teacher, Roy C. Ketcham Senior High School, Wappingers Falls, New York

Joseph Kavanaugh   Academic Head of Mathematics, Scotia-Glenville Central School District, Scotia, New York

Sara N. Munshin   Middle School Mathematics Specialist, Los Angeles Unified School District, Los Angeles, California

Stuart J. Murphy   Visual Learning Specialist, Evanston, Illinois

Anthony Piccolino   Associate Professor of Mathematics, Montclair State University, Upper Montclair, New Jersey

Salvador Quezada   Mathematics Teacher, Theodore Roosevelt High School, Los Angeles, California

Jocelyn Coleman Walton   Educational Consultant, Mathematics K-12, and former Mathematics Supervisor, Plainfield High School, Plainfield, New Jersey

All authors contributed to the planning and writing of the series. In addition to writing, the Senior Authors played a special role in establishing the philosophy of the program, planning the content and organization of topics, and guiding the work of the other authors.

Field Testing   The authors give special thanks to the teachers and students in classrooms nationwide who used a preliminary version of this book. Their suggestions made an important contribution to its development.

ISBN: 0-618-07397-3   1 2 3 4 5 6 7 8 9 10–VJM–04 03 02 01 00

Welcome

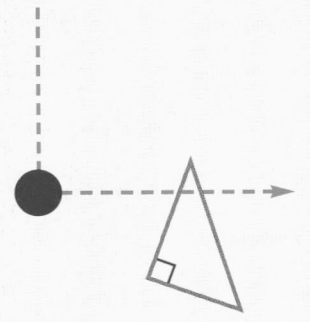

to Integrated Mathematics 2!

Building on Experience

Integrated Mathematics 2 builds on the mathematical topics and problem solving techniques in *Integrated Mathematics 1*. The Topic Spiraling chart on page xiii shows how mathematical concepts are spiraled over the three years of the *Integrated Mathematics* program, so that you continually build on what you have learned.

Mathematical Strands

You can learn more with *Integrated Mathematics* because the mathematical topics are integrated. Over a three-year period, this program teaches all the essential topics in a contemporary Algebra 1/Geometry/Algebra 2 sequence, plus many other interesting topics.

➤ Algebra and Geometry are taught in each of the three years.

➤ Topics from Logical Reasoning, Measurement, Probability, Statistics, Discrete Mathematics, and Functions are interwoven throughout.

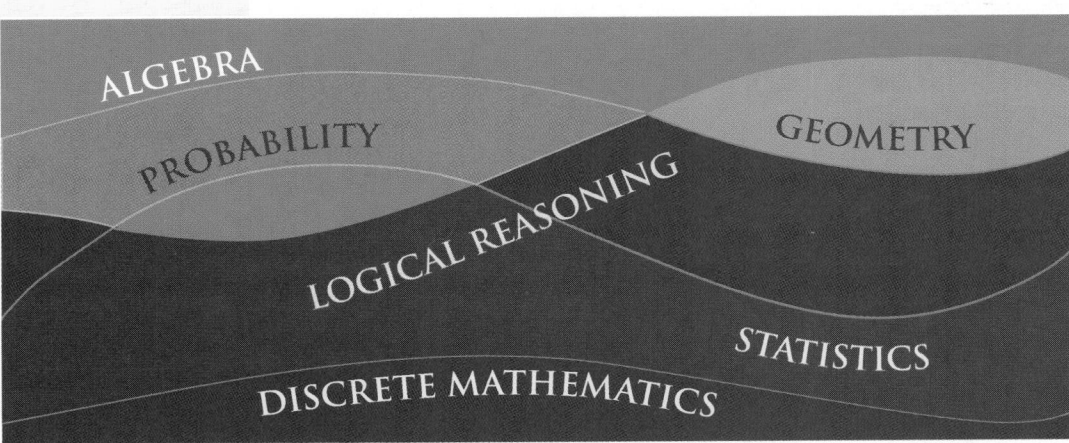

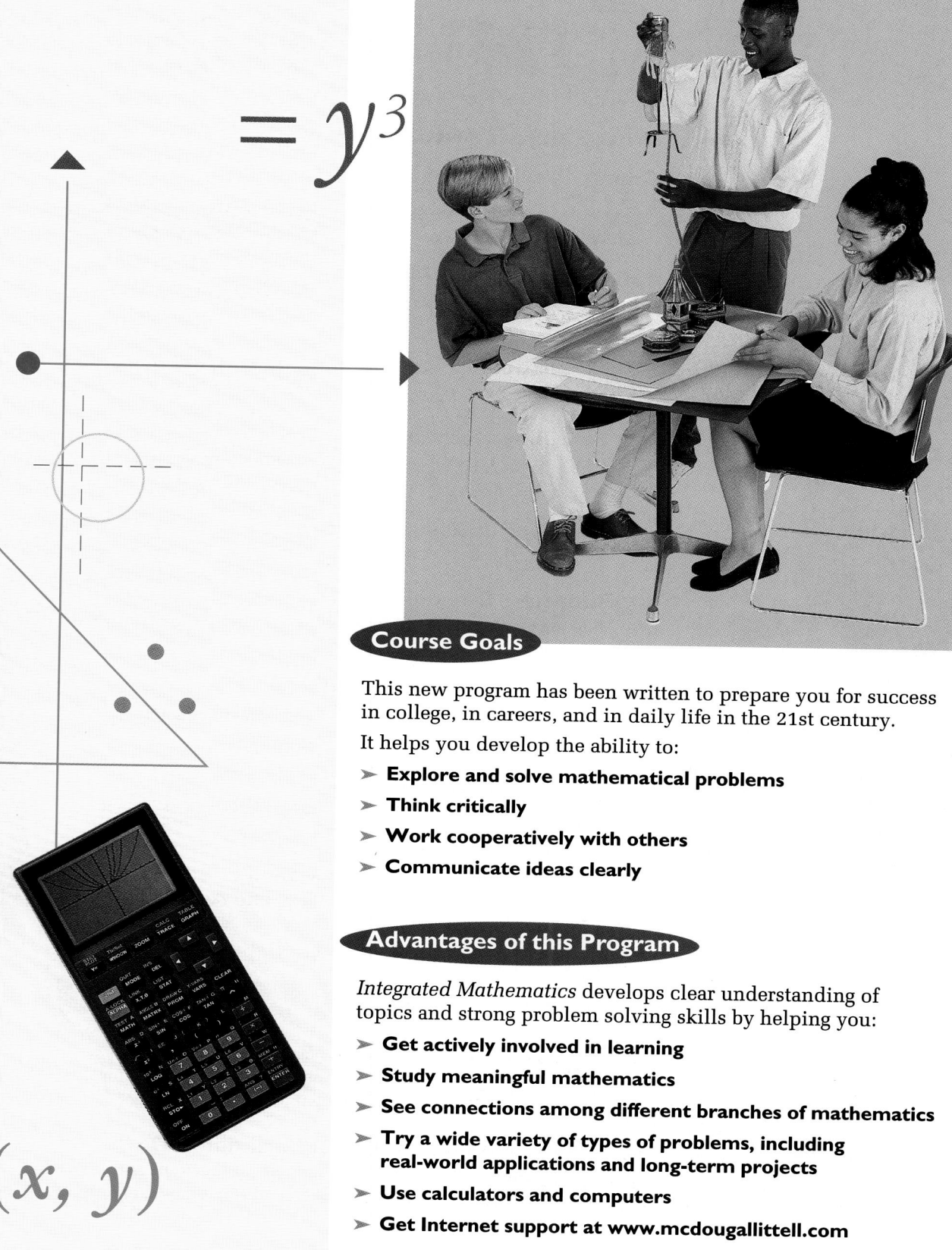

$= y^3$

(x, y)

Course Goals

This new program has been written to prepare you for success in college, in careers, and in daily life in the 21st century.

It helps you develop the ability to:

➤ **Explore and solve mathematical problems**

➤ **Think critically**

➤ **Work cooperatively with others**

➤ **Communicate ideas clearly**

Advantages of this Program

Integrated Mathematics develops clear understanding of topics and strong problem solving skills by helping you:

➤ **Get actively involved in learning**

➤ **Study meaningful mathematics**

➤ **See connections among different branches of mathematics**

➤ **Try a wide variety of types of problems, including real-world applications and long-term projects**

➤ **Use calculators and computers**

➤ **Get Internet support at www.mcdougallittell.com**

v

Contents

Unit 3   Linear Systems and Matrices

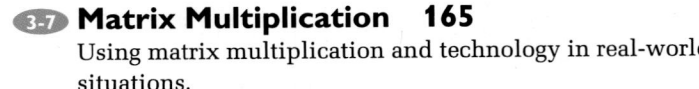

Unit 4 — Quadratic Functions and Graphs

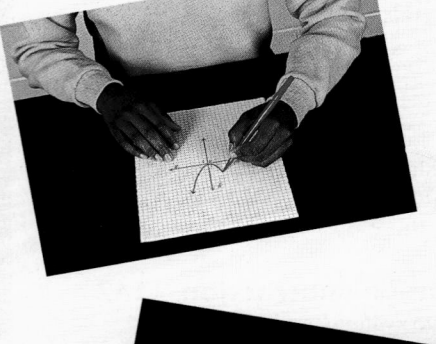

Table of Contents

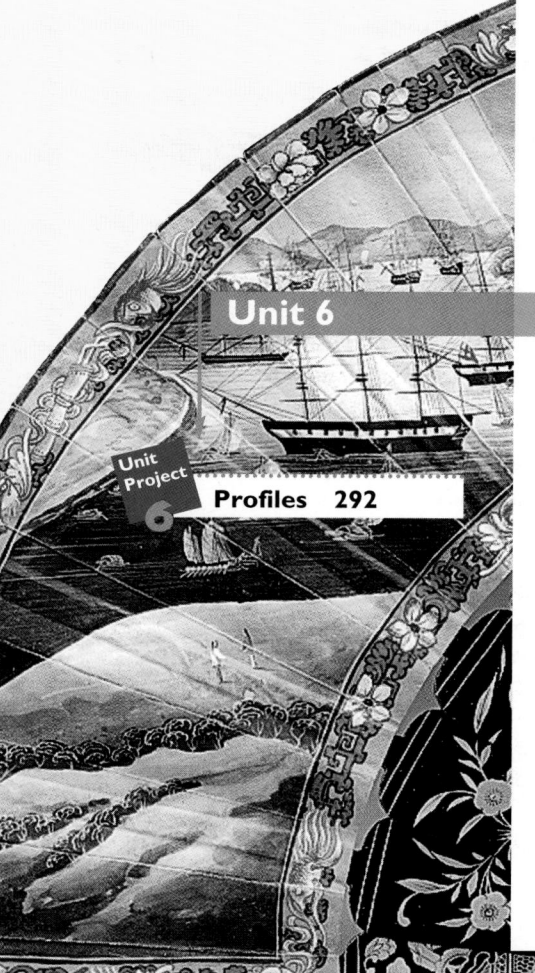

Unit 7   Logic and Proof

Unit 8   Similar and Congruent Triangles

Integrated Mathematics   Topic Spiraling

This chart shows how mathematical strands are spiraled over the three years of the *Integrated Mathematics* program.

	Course 1	Course 2	Course 3
Algebra	Linear equations Linear inequalities Multiplying binomials Factoring expressions	Quadratic equations Linear systems Rational equations Complex numbers	Polynomial functions Exponential functions Logarithmic functions Parametric equations
Geometry	Angles, polygons, circles Perimeter, circumference Area, surface area Volume Trigonometric ratios	Similar and congruent figures Geometric proofs Coordinate geometry Transformational geometry Special right triangles	Inscribed figures Transforming graphs Vectors Triangle trigonometry Circular trigonometry

Statistics, Probability	Analyzing data and
	  displaying data
	Experimental and
	  theoretical probability
	Geometric probability
		Sampling methods
		Simulation
		Binomial distributions
			Variability
			Standard deviation
			z-scores

Logical Reasoning	Conjectures Counterexamples If-then statements	Inductive and deductive reasoning Valid and invalid reasoning Postulates and proof	Identities Contrapositive and inverse Comparing proof methods
Discrete Math	Discrete quantities Matrices to display data Lattices	Matrix operations Transformation matrices Counting techniques	Sequences and series Recursion Limits

Table of Contents

xiii

What Students are Saying...

Who has the **BEST IDEAS** about how mathematics should be taught? **Students** and **teachers**, of course! That is why preliminary versions of this book were tried out by thousands of students and their teachers in CLASSROOMS NATIONWIDE. The suggestions from these students and teachers have been incorporated into this book.

Here is what some of the students who have already studied this course have said.

Our class liked the Explorations, especially collecting data and using calculators and computers to make predictions. We learned a lot by working together.

$$\frac{k}{x}$$

I feel more comfortable with mathematics since being in this course. I am willing to try harder problems because I feel confident.

$\angle C$

This year started off with interesting, new topics. We didn't have to spend a lot of time on boring review. Once we got into the course, I realized how much I remembered from last year.

xiv

Get Involved

This course may be different from ones you have taken before. In this course you will be

➤ **TALKING** about mathematics

➤ working *together* to explore ideas

➤ gathering **DATA**

➤ looking for **patterns**

➤ making and testing **predictions**

➤ using *calculators* or **computers**.

Your ideas and viewpoints are important. Sharing them with others will help everyone learn more. So don't hold back. Jump right in and get involved.

Guide to Your Course

The next ten pages will give you an overview of the organization of your book and a preview of what you will be learning in the course. They will help you get off to a good start.

Your Ideas are Important!

2^x

$m \parallel n$

This course showed me that math really does relate to everyday life — in sports, music, jobs, health, nature, and lots of other places.

I used to just sit back and listen in math class. Now I get involved. I think and talk and write about math.

Before I started Integrated Mathematics, I could hardly wait to take my last math class. Now I'm looking forward to math next year.

Unit Projects

Each unit begins with a project that sets the stage for the mathematics in the unit. The project gives you a chance to **apply** what you are *learning* right away. As you study the unit, you will gather the **INFORMATION** and develop the **SKILLS** to complete the project. The first three pages of each unit help you get started.

Project Theme

Each project has a theme, like mysteries, that relates the mathematics of the unit to daily life and to careers.

unit 7

Logic and Proof

Mysteries

How good a detective are you? What clues can you find in this picture that could help you determine WHODUNIT? For instance, what day and time did the crime likely take place? Can you tell whether the writer was left-handed or right-handed? What do you think the message on the paper means? Does it look as if anything was removed from the desk?

whoDUNit?

Mystery stories have been popular in many countries for centuries. Among the mystery writers whose books have served as the basis for TV programs or movies are British author Agatha Christie and French author Maurice Leblanc. In their stories the mystery is solved by the police or by detectives like Jane Marple and Arsène Lupin.

362

Unit Project 7

Write a Mystery Story

Your project is to write a mystery story. To structure your story, you will need an outline that contains all the clues you give the reader. Your outline should show how the clues fit together to point to the solution of your mystery. As you outline your story, use two of the techniques of logical argument presented in the unit.

Also include in your story a travel itinerary and applications of at least two of the postulates and theorems about angles and parallel lines that you study in the unit.

When all the groups have completed their stories, have the members of another group read your group's story. Ask them to evaluate it according to the following criteria.

? Does the reader want to continue reading in order to solve the mystery?

? Does the reader have enough clues to solve the mystery?

? Does solving the mystery challenge, surprise, or inform the reader?

In **real life** not all mysteries are solved by amateur, police, or private detectives. Specialists in many fields use logic and reasoning to solve mysteries.

archaeology
Archaeologists dig for evidence of the existence of a mythic empire like the Toltec empire in central Mexico.

art history
Art historians are able to date paintings by determining the elements contained in the paint.

law enforcement
Forensic, or legal, scientists analyze the DNA in samples of blood or hair to determine if they came from a suspect in the case.

363

Unit Projects

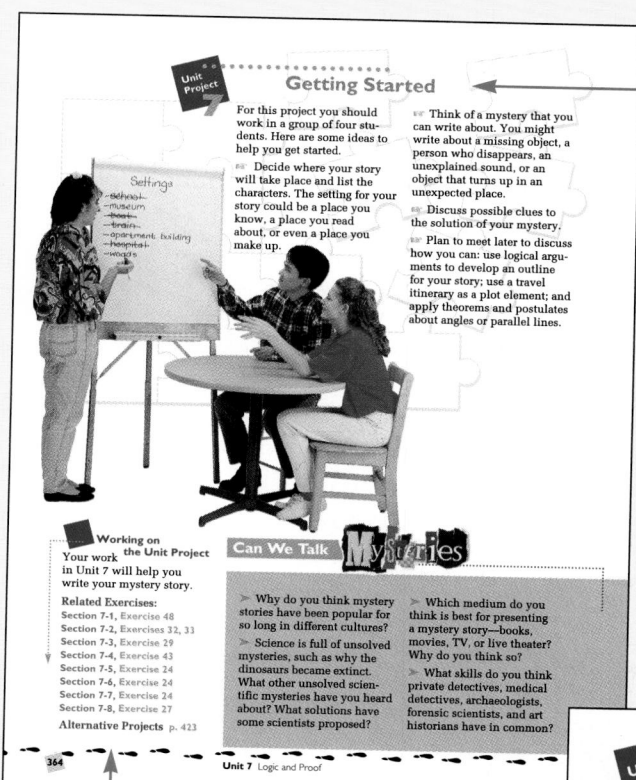

Unit Project 7

Getting Started

For this project you should work in a group of four students. Here are some ideas to help you get started.

☞ Decide where your story will take place and list the characters. The setting for your story could be a place you know, a place you read about, or even a place you make up.

☞ Think of a mystery that you can write about. You might write about a missing object, a person who disappears, an unexplained sound, or an object that turns up in an unexpected place.

☞ Discuss possible clues to the solution of your mystery.

☞ Plan to meet later to discuss how you can: use logical arguments to develop an outline for your story; use a travel itinerary as a plot element; and apply theorems and postulates about angles or parallel lines.

Working on the Unit Project

Your work in Unit 7 will help you write your mystery story.

Related Exercises:
Section 7-1, Exercise 48
Section 7-2, Exercises 32, 33
Section 7-3, Exercise 29
Section 7-4, Exercise 43
Section 7-5, Exercise 24
Section 7-6, Exercise 24
Section 7-7, Exercise 24
Section 7-8, Exercise 27

Alternative Projects p. 423

Can We Talk — Mysteries

➤ Why do you think mystery stories have been popular for so long in different cultures?

➤ Science is full of unsolved mysteries, such as why the dinosaurs became extinct. What other unsolved scientific mysteries have you heard about? What solutions have some scientists proposed?

➤ Which medium do you think is best for presenting a mystery story—books, movies, TV, or live theater? Why do you think so?

➤ What skills do you think private detectives, medical detectives, archaeologists, forensic scientists, and art historians have in common?

364   **Unit 7** Logic and Proof

Starting the Project

At the beginning of each unit, there is a description of the project, hints for getting started, and questions to get you thinking and talking about the project.

Working on the Unit Project

In each section of the unit, there are exercises to help you complete your work on the project.

Completing the Unit Project

After you complete the unit, you can finish the project and present your results. Then you are ready to look back over what you learned.

Unit Project 7

Completing the Unit Project

Complete your mystery story. Your finished project should include these things:

➤ an outline that contains valid logical arguments leading to the solution of your mystery. Include at least two types of logical argument.

➤ an interesting mystery story with a plot that involves a travel itinerary and applications of at least two of the geometry postulates and theorems from this unit

➤ a written report of readers' reactions to your story

Look Back
How could you revise your story to make it more interesting? to make the mystery more challenging to solve?

Alternative Projects

Project 1: Testing the Validity of Arguments in the News Media

Collect examples of implications in advertisements, newspaper or magazine editorials, and news stories presenting various points of view on a controversial issue. Analyze the implications in the advertisements, editorials, and news stories. Identify arguments based on these implications. (If there are none, write some of your own.) Determine whether or not the arguments are valid. Discuss your reasoning.

Project 2: Analyzing a Mystery Story

Read a mystery story or watch a mystery movie or TV program. List the clues that are given to the reader or viewer. Identify the important premises and implications in the story. Write an outline of the story in the form of a series of valid arguments.

Unit 7 Completing the Unit Project   **423**

Unit Projects

Section Organization

The organization of material within sections is patterned after the way that you learn: Ideas are introduced. You **EXPLORE** them, **think** about them, and TALK about them with other students. You check that you UNDERSTAND them by working through some sample problems. Before going on, you pause and **look back** at what you have learned.

Focus This is what you will be doing in the lesson.

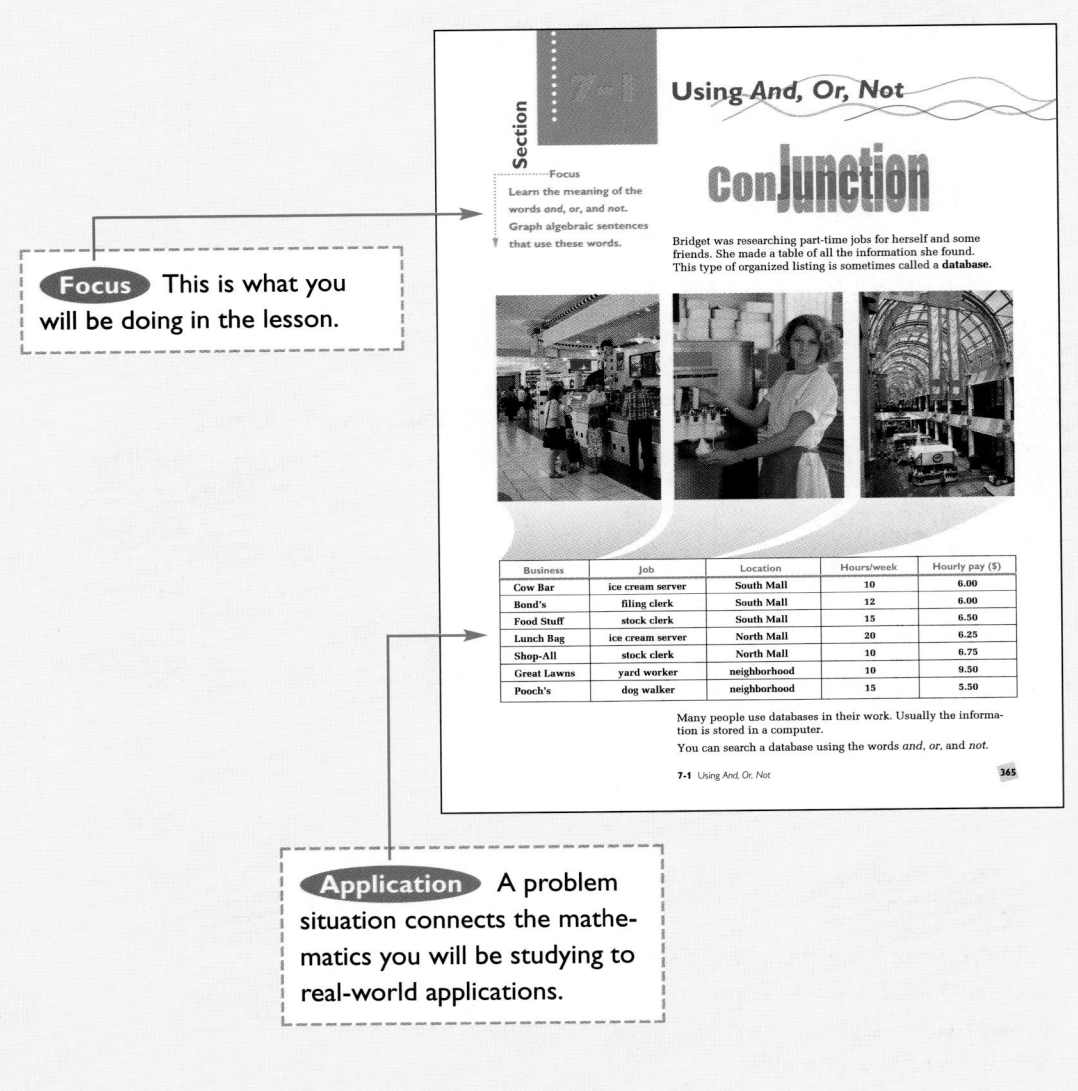

Application A problem situation connects the mathematics you will be studying to real-world applications.

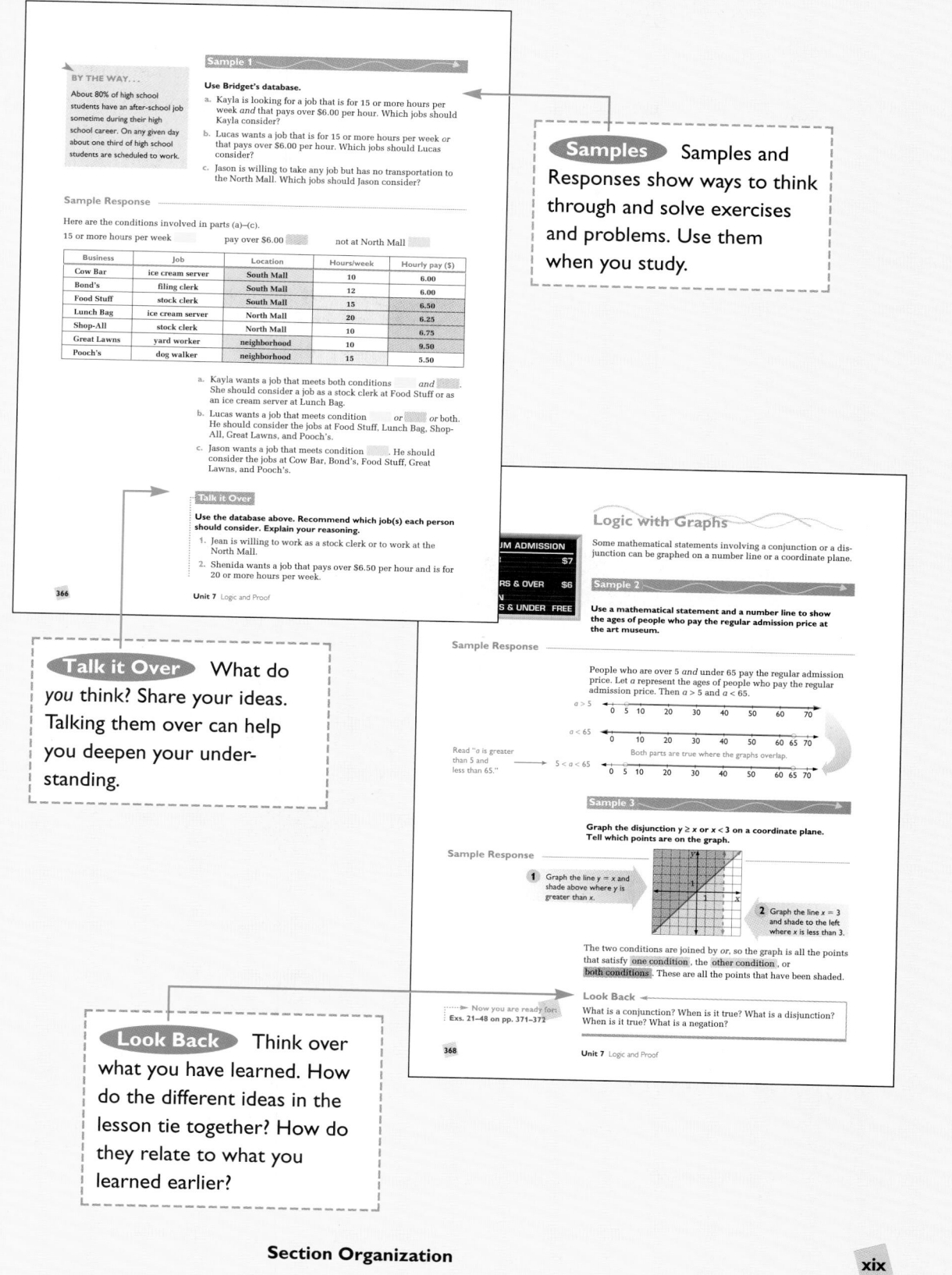

BY THE WAY...

About 80% of high school students have an after-school job sometime during their high school career. On any given day about one third of high school students are scheduled to work.

Sample 1

Use Bridget's database.

a. Kayla is looking for a job that is for 15 or more hours per week *and* that pays over $6.00 per hour. Which jobs should Kayla consider?

b. Lucas wants a job that is for 15 or more hours per week *or* that pays over $6.00 per hour. Which jobs should Lucas consider?

c. Jason is willing to take any job but has no transportation to the North Mall. Which jobs should Jason consider?

Sample Response

Here are the conditions involved in parts (a)–(c).

15 or more hours per week   pay over $6.00   not at North Mall

Business	Job	Location	Hours/week	Hourly pay ($)
Cow Bar	ice cream server	South Mall	10	6.00
Bond's	filing clerk	South Mall	12	6.00
Food Stuff	stock clerk	South Mall	15	6.50
Lunch Bag	ice cream server	North Mall	20	6.25
Shop-All	stock clerk	North Mall	10	6.75
Great Lawns	yard worker	neighborhood	10	9.50
Pooch's	dog walker	neighborhood	15	5.50

a. Kayla wants a job that meets both conditions   and   . She should consider a job as a stock clerk at Food Stuff or as an ice cream server at Lunch Bag.

b. Lucas wants a job that meets condition   or   or both. He should consider the jobs at Food Stuff, Lunch Bag, Shop-All, Great Lawns, and Pooch's.

c. Jason wants a job that meets condition   . He should consider the jobs at Cow Bar, Bond's, Food Stuff, Great Lawns, and Pooch's.

Talk it Over

Use the database above. Recommend which job(s) each person should consider. Explain your reasoning.

1. Jean is willing to work as a stock clerk or to work at the North Mall.

2. Shenida wants a job that pays over $6.50 per hour and is for 20 or more hours per week.

366   **Unit 7** Logic and Proof

Samples Samples and Responses show ways to think through and solve exercises and problems. Use them when you study.

Talk it Over What do *you* think? Share your ideas. Talking them over can help you deepen your understanding.

Look Back Think over what you have learned. How do the different ideas in the lesson tie together? How do they relate to what you learned earlier?

UM ADMISSION
$7
RS & OVER $6
N
S & UNDER FREE

Logic with Graphs

Some mathematical statements involving a conjunction or a disjunction can be graphed on a number line or a coordinate plane.

Sample 2

Use a mathematical statement and a number line to show the ages of people who pay the regular admission price at the art museum.

Sample Response

People who are over 5 *and* under 65 pay the regular admission price. Let a represent the ages of people who pay the regular admission price. Then $a > 5$ and $a < 65$.

$a > 5$

$a < 65$

Read "a is greater than 5 and less than 65." $5 < a < 65$

Both parts are true where the graphs overlap.

Sample 3

Graph the disjunction $y \geq x$ or $x < 3$ on a coordinate plane. Tell which points are on the graph.

Sample Response

1 Graph the line $y = x$ and shade above where y is greater than x.

2 Graph the line $x = 3$ and shade to the left where x is less than 3.

The two conditions are joined by *or*, so the graph is all the points that satisfy one condition , the other condition , or both conditions . These are all the points that have been shaded.

Now you are ready for:
Exs. 21–48 on pp. 371–372

Look Back

What is a conjunction? When is it true? What is a disjunction? When is it true? What is a negation?

368   **Unit 7** Logic and Proof

Section Organization

Exercises and Problems

Each section has a wide variety of exercises and problems. Some **practice** and **EXTEND** the concepts and skills you have learned. Others apply the concepts to everyday situations and **explore connections** to other subject areas and to careers. The problems help you sharpen your **THINKING** and **problem solving skills**.

Reading After you read the section, try the Reading exercise. It helps you check that you understand what you have read.

Connections to... Mathematics is a part of many different subject areas, including history, literature, science, music, driver education.

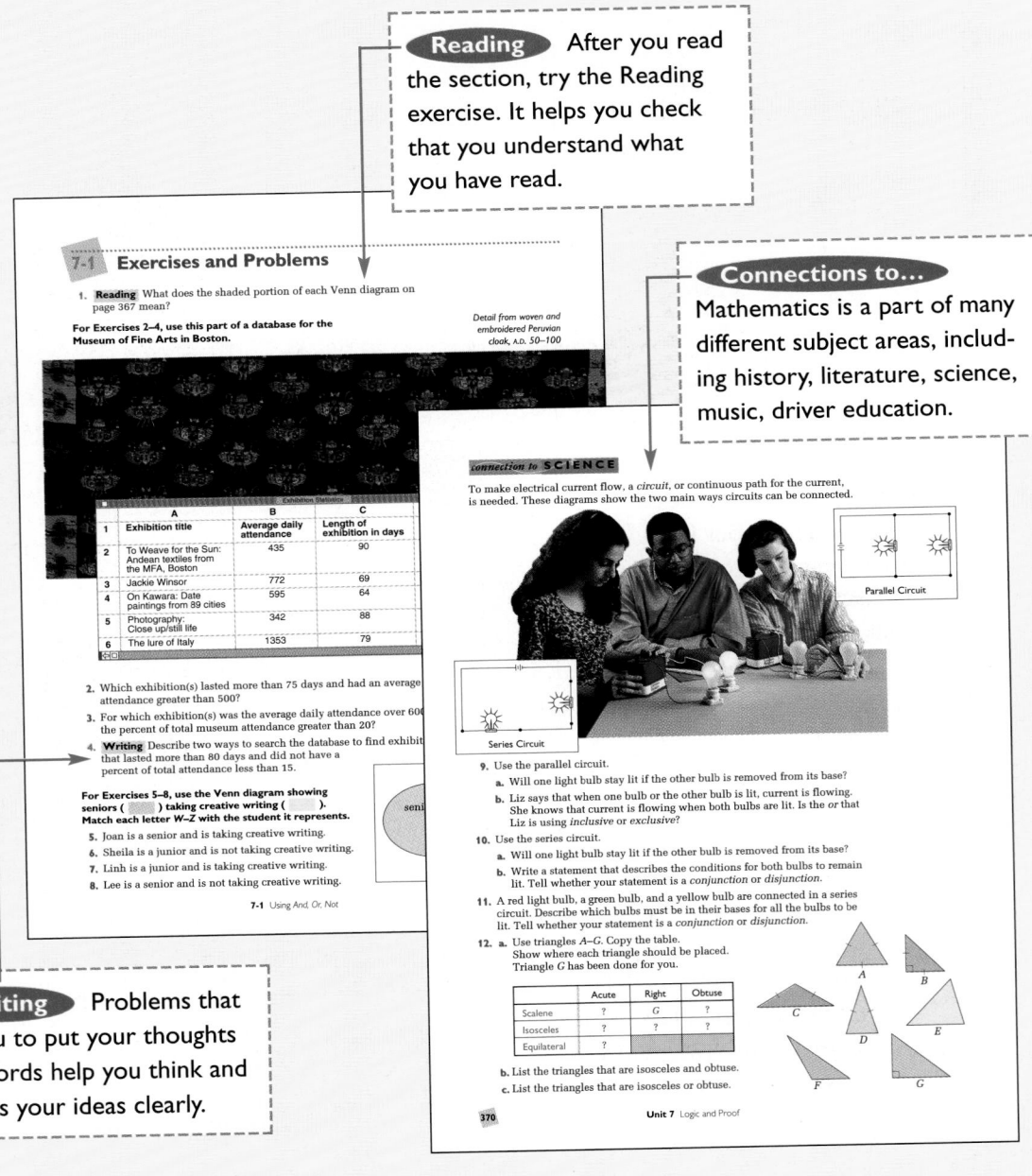

Writing Problems that ask you to put your thoughts into words help you think and express your ideas clearly.

Exercises and Problems

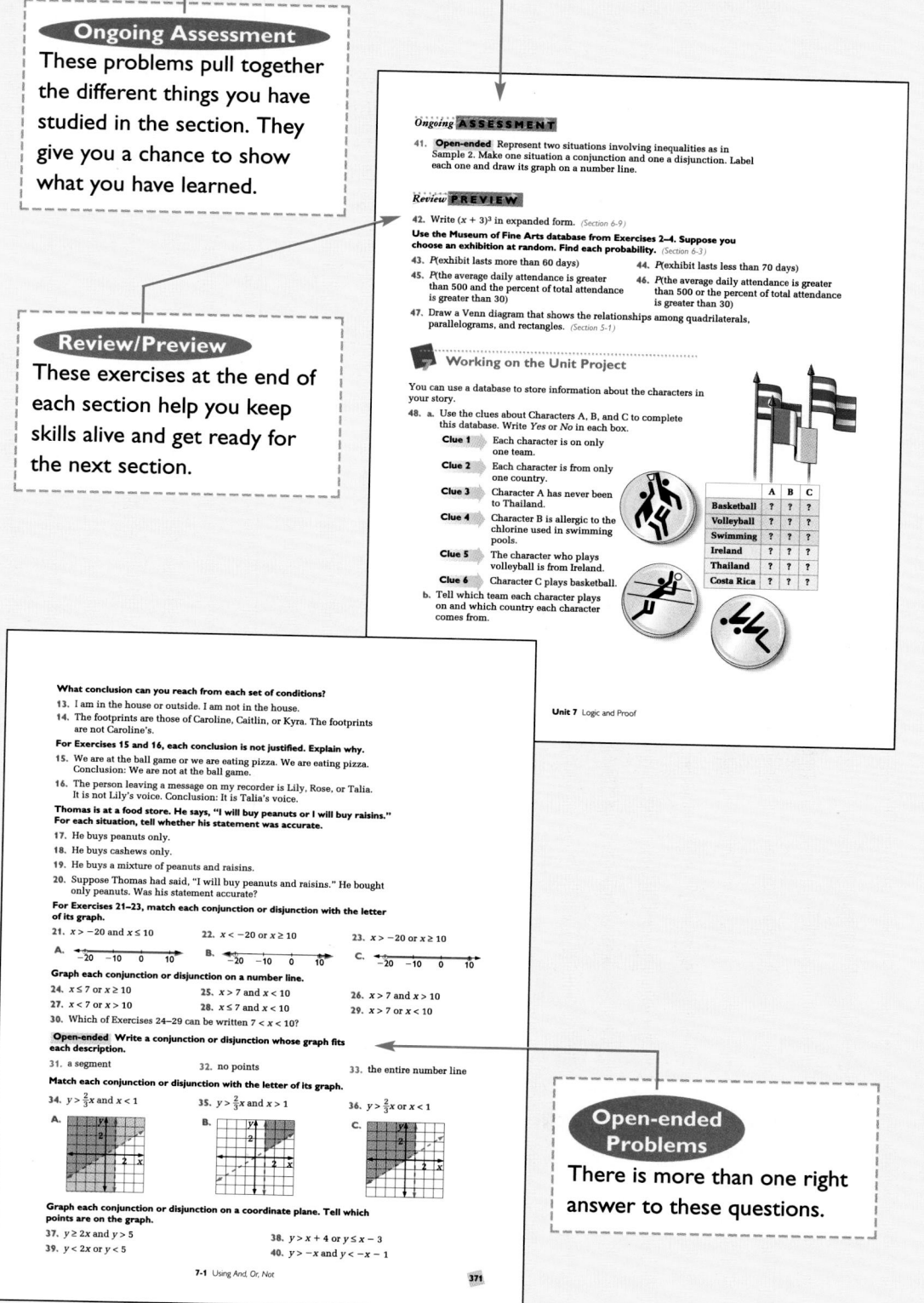

Ongoing ASSESSMENT

41. **Open-ended** Represent two situations involving inequalities as in Sample 2. Make one situation a conjunction and one a disjunction. Label each one and draw its graph on a number line.

Review PREVIEW

42. Write $(x + 3)^3$ in expanded form. *(Section 6-9)*

Use the Museum of Fine Arts database from Exercises 2–4. Suppose you choose an exhibition at random. Find each probability. *(Section 6-3)*

43. P(exhibit lasts more than 60 days)

44. P(exhibit lasts less than 70 days)

45. P(the average daily attendance is greater than 500 and the percent of total attendance is greater than 30)

46. P(the average daily attendance is greater than 500 or the percent of total attendance is greater than 30)

47. Draw a Venn diagram that shows the relationships among quadrilaterals, parallelograms, and rectangles. *(Section 5-1)*

Working on the Unit Project

You can use a database to store information about the characters in your story.

48. a. Use the clues about Characters A, B, and C to complete this database. Write *Yes* or *No* in each box.

Clue 1 Each character is on only one team.

Clue 2 Each character is from only one country.

Clue 3 Character A has never been to Thailand.

Clue 4 Character B is allergic to the chlorine used in swimming pools.

Clue 5 The character who plays volleyball is from Ireland.

Clue 6 Character C plays basketball.

	A	B	C
Basketball	?	?	?
Volleyball	?	?	?
Swimming	?	?	?
Ireland	?	?	?
Thailand	?	?	?
Costa Rica	?	?	?

b. Tell which team each character plays on and which country each character comes from.

Unit 7 Logic and Proof

What conclusion can you reach from each set of conditions?

13. I am in the house or outside. I am not in the house.

14. The footprints are those of Caroline, Caitlin, or Kyra. The footprints are not Caroline's.

For Exercises 15 and 16, each conclusion is not justified. Explain why.

15. We are at the ball game or we are eating pizza. We are eating pizza. Conclusion: We are not at the ball game.

16. The person leaving a message on my recorder is Lily, Rose, or Talia. It is not Lily's voice. Conclusion: It is Talia's voice.

Thomas is at a food store. He says, "I will buy peanuts or I will buy raisins." For each situation, tell whether his statement was accurate.

17. He buys peanuts only.

18. He buys cashews only.

19. He buys a mixture of peanuts and raisins.

20. Suppose Thomas had said, "I will buy peanuts and raisins." He bought only peanuts. Was his statement accurate?

For Exercises 21–23, match each conjunction or disjunction with the letter of its graph.

21. $x > -20$ and $x \le 10$

22. $x < -20$ or $x \ge 10$

23. $x > -20$ or $x \ge 10$

A. [number line: -20 -10 0 10]   B. [number line: -20 -10 0 10]   C. [number line: -20 -10 0 10]

Graph each conjunction or disjunction on a number line.

24. $x \le 5$ or $x \ge 10$

25. $x > 7$ and $x < 10$

26. $x > 7$ and $x > 10$

27. $x < 7$ or $x > 10$

28. $x \le 7$ and $x < 10$

29. $x > 7$ or $x < 10$

30. Which of Exercises 24–29 can be written $7 < x < 10$?

Open-ended Write a conjunction or disjunction whose graph fits each description.

31. a segment

32. no points

33. the entire number line

Match each conjunction or disjunction with the letter of its graph.

34. $y > \frac{2}{3}x$ and $x < 1$

35. $y > \frac{2}{3}x$ and $x > 1$

36. $y > \frac{2}{3}x$ or $x < 1$

A. [graph]   B. [graph]   C. [graph]

Graph each conjunction or disjunction on a coordinate plane. Tell which points are on the graph.

37. $y \ge 2x$ and $y > 5$

38. $y > x + 4$ or $y \le x - 3$

39. $y < 2x$ or $y < 5$

40. $y > -x$ and $y < -x - 1$

7-1 Using And, Or, Not

371

Exercises and Problems

Explorations

Explorations are an important part of this course. They will help you discover, understand, and connect mathematical ideas. In the Explorations, you will be gathering **data**, looking for **patterns**, and making **generalizations**. You will be working with others and sharing your ideas.

Exploration Goal This is the question you will be investigating in the Exploration.

Extending the Exploration
The text and the Talk it Over questions extend what you have discovered in the Exploration.

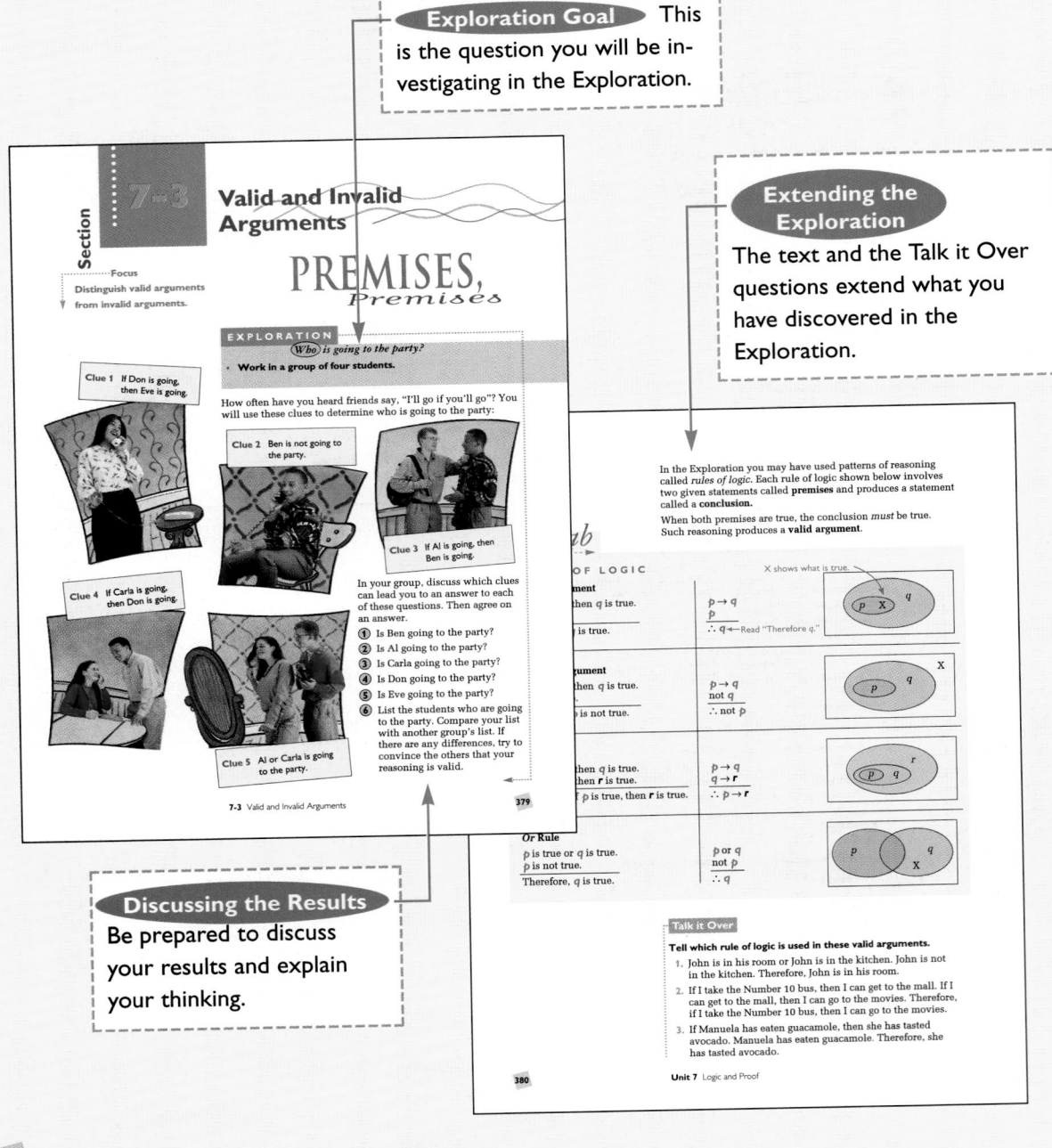

Discussing the Results
Be prepared to discuss your results and explain your thinking.

Review and Assessment

With this book you review and **ASSESS YOUR PROGRESS** as you go along. In each unit there are one or two Checkpoints for self-assessment, plus a thorough Unit Review and Assessment at the end.

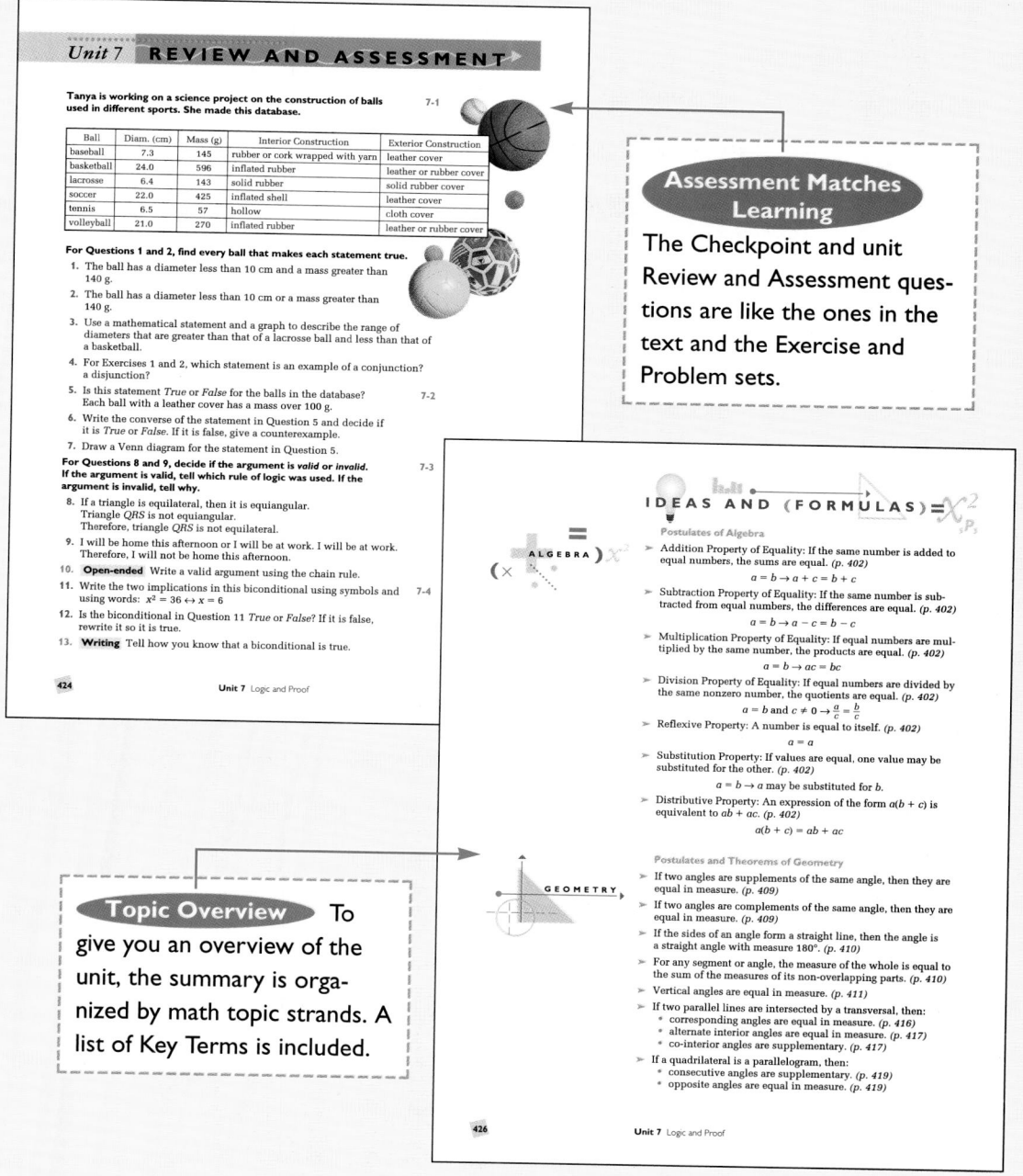

Unit 7 REVIEW AND ASSESSMENT

Tanya is working on a science project on the construction of balls used in different sports. She made this database.

7-1

Ball	Diam. (cm)	Mass (g)	Interior Construction	Exterior Construction
baseball	7.3	145	rubber or cork wrapped with yarn	leather cover
basketball	24.0	596	inflated rubber	leather or rubber cover
lacrosse	6.4	143	solid rubber	solid rubber cover
soccer	22.0	425	inflated shell	leather cover
tennis	6.5	57	hollow	cloth cover
volleyball	21.0	270	inflated rubber	leather or rubber cover

For Questions 1 and 2, find every ball that makes each statement true.

1. The ball has a diameter less than 10 cm and a mass greater than 140 g.

2. The ball has a diameter less than 10 cm or a mass greater than 140 g.

3. Use a mathematical statement and a graph to describe the range of diameters that are greater than that of a lacrosse ball and less than that of a basketball.

4. For Exercises 1 and 2, which statement is an example of a conjunction? a disjunction?

5. Is this statement *True* or *False* for the balls in the database? Each ball with a leather cover has a mass over 100 g.

7-2

6. Write the converse of the statement in Question 5 and decide if it is *True* or *False*. If it is false, give a counterexample.

7. Draw a Venn diagram for the statement in Question 5.

For Questions 8 and 9, decide if the argument is *valid or invalid*. If the argument is valid, tell which rule of logic was used. If the argument is invalid, tell why.

7-3

8. If a triangle is equilateral, then it is equiangular. Triangle *QRS* is not equiangular. Therefore, triangle *QRS* is not equilateral.

9. I will be home this afternoon or I will be at work. I will be at work. Therefore, I will not be home this afternoon.

10. **Open-ended** Write a valid argument using the chain rule.

11. Write the two implications in this biconditional using symbols and using words: $x^2 = 36 \leftrightarrow x = 6$

7-4

12. Is the biconditional in Question 11 *True* or *False*? If it is false, rewrite it so it is true.

13. **Writing** Tell how you know that a biconditional is true.

424 Unit 7 Logic and Proof

Assessment Matches Learning

The Checkpoint and unit Review and Assessment questions are like the ones in the text and the Exercise and Problem sets.

Topic Overview To give you an overview of the unit, the summary is organized by math topic strands. A list of Key Terms is included.

IDEAS AND (FORMULAS) = x^2

ALGEBRA

Postulates of Algebra

▸ Addition Property of Equality: If the same number is added to equal numbers, the sums are equal. *(p. 402)*
$$a = b \rightarrow a + c = b + c$$

▸ Subtraction Property of Equality: If the same number is subtracted from equal numbers, the differences are equal. *(p. 402)*
$$a = b \rightarrow a - c = b - c$$

▸ Multiplication Property of Equality: If equal numbers are multiplied by the same number, the products are equal. *(p. 402)*
$$a = b \rightarrow ac = bc$$

▸ Division Property of Equality: If equal numbers are divided by the same nonzero number, the quotients are equal. *(p. 402)*
$$a = b \text{ and } c \neq 0 \rightarrow \frac{a}{c} = \frac{b}{c}$$

▸ Reflexive Property: A number is equal to itself. *(p. 402)*
$$a = a$$

▸ Substitution Property: If values are equal, one value may be substituted for the other. *(p. 402)*
$$a = b \rightarrow a \text{ may be substituted for } b.$$

▸ Distributive Property: An expression of the form $a(b + c)$ is equivalent to $ab + ac$. *(p. 402)*
$$a(b + c) = ab + ac$$

Postulates and Theorems of Geometry

GEOMETRY

▸ If two angles are supplements of the same angle, then they are equal in measure. *(p. 409)*

▸ If two angles are complements of the same angle, then they are equal in measure. *(p. 409)*

▸ If the sides of an angle form a straight line, then the angle is a straight angle with measure 180°. *(p. 410)*

▸ For any segment or angle, the measure of the whole is equal to the sum of the measures of its non-overlapping parts. *(p. 410)*

▸ Vertical angles are equal in measure. *(p. 411)*

▸ If two parallel lines are intersected by a transversal, then:
  * corresponding angles are equal in measure. *(p. 416)*
  * alternate interior angles are equal in measure. *(p. 417)*
  * co-interior angles are supplementary. *(p. 417)*

▸ If a quadrilateral is a parallelogram, then:
  * consecutive angles are supplementary. *(p. 419)*
  * opposite angles are equal in measure. *(p. 419)*

426 Unit 7 Logic and Proof

Review and Assessment

Technology

In this course you will see many different ways that
CALCULATORS and **COMPUTERS** can make
exploring ideas and solving problems easier.

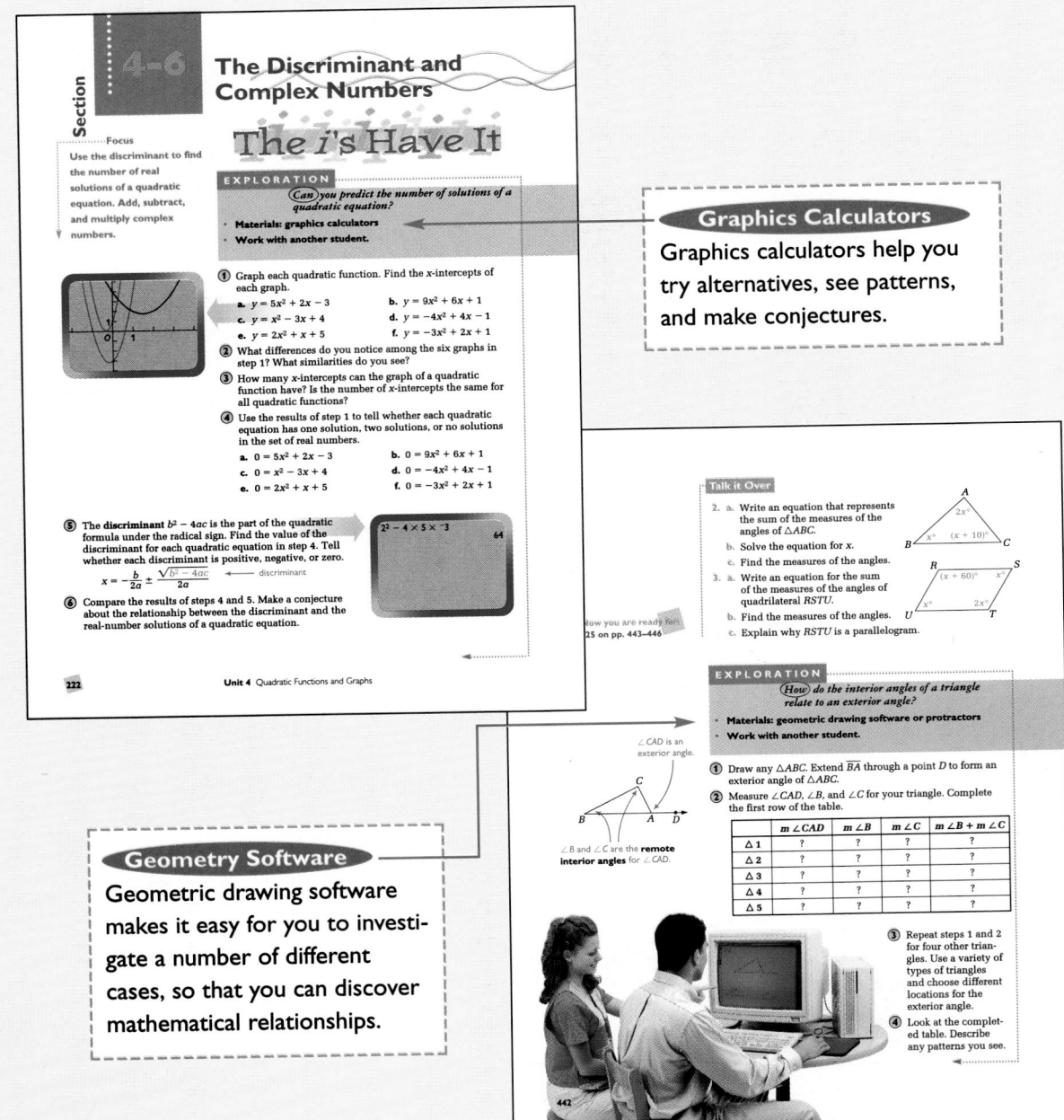

Graphics Calculators

Graphics calculators help you try alternatives, see patterns, and make conjectures.

Geometry Software

Geometric drawing software makes it easy for you to investigate a number of different cases, so that you can discover mathematical relationships.

xxiv

Technology

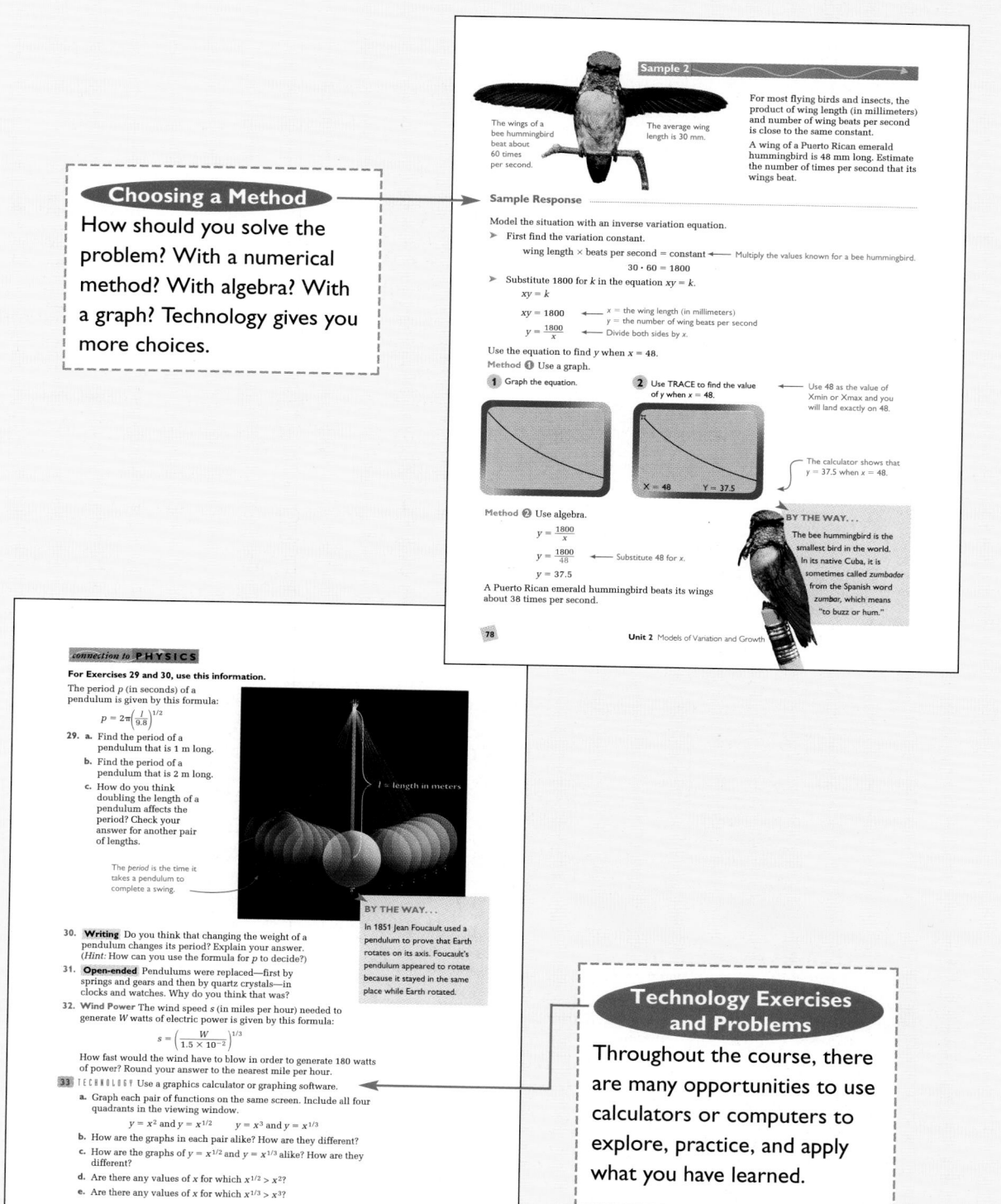

Choosing a Method

How should you solve the problem? With a numerical method? With algebra? With a graph? Technology gives you more choices.

Sample 2

The wings of a bee hummingbird beat about 60 times per second.

The average wing length is 30 mm.

For most flying birds and insects, the product of wing length (in millimeters) and number of wing beats per second is close to the same constant.

A wing of a Puerto Rican emerald hummingbird is 48 mm long. Estimate the number of times per second that its wings beat.

Sample Response

Model the situation with an inverse variation equation.

➤ First find the variation constant.

wing length × beats per second = constant ← Multiply the values known for a bee hummingbird.

$$30 \cdot 60 = 1800$$

➤ Substitute 1800 for k in the equation $xy = k$.

$$xy = k$$
$$xy = 1800$$ ← x = the wing length (in millimeters) / y = the number of wing beats per second
$$y = \frac{1800}{x}$$ ← Divide both sides by x.

Use the equation to find y when $x = 48$.

Method ❶ Use a graph.

1 Graph the equation.

2 Use TRACE to find the value of y when $x = 48$. ← Use 48 as the value of Xmin or Xmax and you will land exactly on 48.

X = 48   Y = 37.5

The calculator shows that $y = 37.5$ when $x = 48$.

Method ❷ Use algebra.

$$y = \frac{1800}{x}$$
$$y = \frac{1800}{48}$$ ← Substitute 48 for x.
$$y = 37.5$$

A Puerto Rican emerald hummingbird beats its wings about 38 times per second.

BY THE WAY...
The bee hummingbird is the smallest bird in the world. In its native Cuba, it is sometimes called *zumbador* from the Spanish word *zumbar*, which means "to buzz or hum."

78   **Unit 2** Models of Variation and Growth

---

connection to PHYSICS

For Exercises 29 and 30, use this information.

The period p (in seconds) of a pendulum is given by this formula:

$$p = 2\pi\left(\frac{l}{9.8}\right)^{1/2}$$

29. a. Find the period of a pendulum that is 1 m long.
   b. Find the period of a pendulum that is 2 m long.
   c. How do you think doubling the length of a pendulum affects the period? Check your answer for another pair of lengths.

l = length in meters

The *period* is the time it takes a pendulum to complete a swing.

30. **Writing** Do you think that changing the weight of a pendulum changes its period? Explain your answer. (*Hint:* How can you use the formula for p to decide?)

31. **Open-ended** Pendulums were replaced—first by springs and gears and then by quartz crystals—in clocks and watches. Why do you think that was?

32. **Wind Power** The wind speed s (in miles per hour) needed to generate W watts of electric power is given by this formula:

$$s = \left(\frac{W}{1.5 \times 10^{-2}}\right)^{1/3}$$

How fast would the wind have to blow in order to generate 180 watts of power? Round your answer to the nearest mile per hour.

33. TECHNOLOGY Use a graphics calculator or graphing software.

   a. Graph each pair of functions on the same screen. Include all four quadrants in the viewing window.

   $y = x^2$ and $y = x^{1/2}$ $y = x^3$ and $y = x^{1/3}$

   b. How are the graphs in each pair alike? How are they different?
   c. How are the graphs of $y = x^{1/2}$ and $y = x^{1/3}$ alike? How are they different?
   d. Are there any values of x for which $x^{1/2} > x^2$?
   e. Are there any values of x for which $x^{1/3} > x^3$?

BY THE WAY...
In 1851 Jean Foucault used a pendulum to prove that Earth rotates on its axis. Foucault's pendulum appeared to rotate because it stayed in the same place while Earth rotated.

2-6 Using Powers   103

Technology Exercises and Problems

Throughout the course, there are many opportunities to use calculators or computers to explore, practice, and apply what you have learned.

Technology

Sampling and Reasoning

OVERVIEW

➤ In **Unit 1,** students extend their previous experience with statistics by studying surveys, samples, and sampling techniques, while they continue to explore and develop reasoning skills. The **Student Resources Toolbox** on pages 632–664 provides a convenient review of key topics from previous courses.

➤ Students are given opportunities to predict results from surveys and samples, use different methods for selecting a sample, simulate the results of a survey, and use inductive and deductive reasoning.

➤ Recycling is the theme of the Unit Project. The goal of the project is for students to write, conduct, interpret, and use the results of a survey and a sampling of trash as the basis for a plan to reduce the amount of trash produced by students in the school.

➤ Connections to wildlife, history, basketball, literature, and emergency medical procedures are some of the topics included in the teaching materials and the exercises.

➤ Graphics calculators are used in Section 1-3 to help choose a random sample and in Section 1-5 to graph a linear function and a quadratic function to estimate the point where the two graphs intersect. In Section 1-6, combinations of linear and quadratic equations are graphed as part of an activity involving Venn diagrams and if-then statements.

➤ Problem-solving strategies used in Unit 1 include using proportions, simulation, inductive reasoning, tables, and deductive reasoning.

Unit Objectives

Section	Objectives	NCTM Standards
1-1	• Know how a survey of part of a population can be used to predict results for the entire population.	1, 2, 4, 5, 10, 11
1-2	• Use an experiment to simulate the results of a survey.	1, 2, 4, 5, 10, 11
1-3	• Learn about different ways to select a sample.	1, 2, 4, 5, 10, 11
1-4	• Learn to raise questions about surveys.	1, 2, 4, 5, 10, 11
1-5	• Apply inductive reasoning to many situations. • Learn that inductive reasoning does not always lead to a good conclusion.	1, 2, 3, 4, 5, 7
1-6	• Write if-then statements in other ways and draw simple conclusions from them. • Learn the difference between inductive and deductive reasoning. • Apply deductive reasoning to many situations.	1, 2, 3, 4, 5, 7
1-7	• Recognize errors in mathematical and logical reasoning.	1, 2, 3, 4, 5, 6, 7, 12

Section	Connections to Prior and Future Concepts
1-1	**Section 1-1** covers the use of a sample's responses to predict the results of a population's responses. The need for the use of a sample is emphasized. Students use proportions to predict the results for a population. Predicting from samples is covered in Book 1, Section 6-4. Methods of choosing samples will be developed in Book 2, Section 1-3.
1-2	**Section 1-2** introduces experimentation to simulate survey results. Students are given opportunities to simulate situations in which conducting the actual experiment in order to obtain responses would be difficult. Simulation is extended in Unit 7 of Book 3. Measures of central tendency are reviewed in the Student Resources Toolbox.
1-3	**Section 1-3** covers different types of sampling methods and the relative value of each type as to how well it represents the population. Students use random numbers as a means of creating multiple random samples. Sampling methods were first introduced in Book 1, Section 6-4. Variability and patterns in samples continue the topic in Book 3.
1-4	**Section 1-4** stresses the importance of the wording of questions and responses on a survey. Students learn that good wording is important to avoid influencing responses. Students analyze graphs for misuse in representation of data.
1-5	**Section 1-5** explores using inductive reasoning to make conjectures. This is an important first step in understanding the nature of proof, which is covered more thoroughly in Book 2, Units 7 and 8, and Book 3, Unit 3. Counterexamples are used to disprove a conjecture.
1-6	**Section 1-6** explores if-then statements. Venn diagrams are used to show the truth value of a statement. The methods of inductive and deductive reasoning are compared. If-then statements were introduced in Book 1, Section 9-3, and are used in logical arguments throughout Units 7 and 8 of Book 2 and Unit 3 of Book 3.
1-7	**Section 1-7** explores errors in reasoning, including the converse error. The topic of errors in reasoning is further developed in Unit 3 of Book 3.

Integrating the Strands

Strands	Sections
Number	1-1, 1-5, 1-6, 1-7
Algebra	1-1, 1-2, 1-3, 1-4, 1-5, 1-6, 1-7
Functions	1-7
Geometry	1-1, 1-4, 1-5, 1-6, 1-7
Statistics and Probability	1-1, 1-2, 1-3, 1-4
Discrete Mathematics	1-7
Logic and Language	1-1, 1-2, 1-3, 1-5, 1-6, 1-7

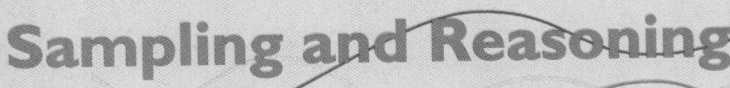
Section Planning Guide

> ➤ Essential exercises and problems are indicated in boldface.
> ➤ Ongoing work on the Unit Project is indicated in color.
> ➤ Exercises and problems that require student research, group work, manipulatives, or graphing technology are indicated in the column headed "Other."

Section	Materials	Pacing	Standard Assignment	Extended Assignment	Other
1-1		Day 1	**1–9, 12, 14**, 17–25, 26	**1–9, 12**, 13, **14**, 15–25, 26	10, 11, 26
1-2	spinner, paper clip, die, coin	Day 1 Day 2	**1–10** **12, 13, 15**, 16–24, 25	**1–10** **12, 13, 15**, 16–24, 25	6, 11 12, 14, 15
1-3	scientific or graphics calculator, glossary or telephone book	Day 1 Day 2	**1–10** **11–15, 18–20**, 22–27, 28	**1–10** **11–15**, 17, **18–20**, 22–27, 28	16, 21
1-4		Day 1	**1–13**, 14, 16, 17–23, 24–26	**1–13**, 14, 16, 17–23, 24–26	4b, 15, 16c, 17
1-5	protractor, graphing technology, rubber gloves, trash bag	Day 1	1, **2–23**, 26–30, 31, 32	1, **2–23**, 26–30, 31, 32	19, 24, 25, 31
1-6	graphing technology	Day 1 Day 2	1, **2–12, 14–20** **21–34**, 35, 37–43, 44	1, **2–12, 14–20** **21–34**, 35, 37–43, 44	13 36
1-7		Day 1	1, **2–10**, 14–17, 23–32, 33	1, **2–10**, 11, 14–18, 20–32, 33	12, 13, 19
Review Test		**Day 1** **Day 2**	**Unit Review** **Unit Test**	**Unit Review** **Unit Test**	

Yearly Pacing	Unit 1 Total	Remaining	Total
	14 days (2 for Unit Project)	146 days	160 days

Support Materials

> ➤ See **Project Book** for notes on Unit 1 Project: Disposal Proposal.
> ➤ "UPP" and "disk" refer to **Using Plotter Plus** booklet and **Plotter Plus** disk.
> ➤ "TI-81/82" refers to **Using TI-81 and TI-82 Calculators** booklet.
> ➤ Warm-up exercises for each section are available on **Warm-Up Transparencies.**
> ➤ "FI," "PC," "GI," "MA," and "Stats!" refer, respectively, to the McDougal Littell Mathpack software Activity Books for **Function Investigator, Probability Constructor, Geometry Inventor, Matrix Analyzer,** and **Stats!.**

Section	Study Guide	Practice Bank	Problem Bank	Activity Bank	Explorations Lab Manual	Assessment Book	Visuals	Technology
1-1	1-1	Practice 1	Set 1	Enrich 1	Add. Expl. 1	Quiz 1-1		FI Act. 23
1-2	1-2	Practice 2	Set 1	Enrich 2	Masters 8, 9	Quiz 1-2	Folder 1	
1-3	1-3	Practice 3	Set 1	Enrich 3	Master 5	Quiz 1-3		
1-4	1-4	Practice 4	Set 1	Enrich 4	Master 1	Quiz 1-4 Test 1		Stats! Acts. 1–7
1-5	1-5	Practice 5	Set 2	Enrich 5	Master 2	Quiz 1-5		
1-6	1-6	Practice 6	Set 2	Enrich 6	Add. Expl. 2 Masters 2, 10–12	Quiz 1-6		
1-7	1-7	Practice 7	Set 2	Enrich 7	Masters 1, 2	Quiz 1-7 Test 2		
Unit 1	Unit Review	Practice 8	Unifying Problem 1	Family Involve 1		Tests 3, 4		

UNIT TESTS

Spanish versions of these tests are on pages 118–121 of the **Assessment Book**.

Form A

Name _____ Date _____ Score _____

Test 3

Test on Unit 1 (Form A)

Directions: Write the answers in the spaces provided.

Match each sample of students with a sampling method.
A. random   B. convenience   C. systematic   D. cluster

1. students wearing black shoes today
2. every third student on the class lists
3. students with summer birthdays
4. the first 10 students who enter the office

For Questions 5–7, tell whether each method would produce a random sample of a school population of 1000 students. Write *Yes* or *No.*

5. All the students attending a 9th grade conferencing session are selected.
6. One student from each third-period class in the school is selected.
7. All the students in the National Honor Society are selected.
8. **Writing** Compare and contrast convenience sampling and systematic sampling.
   Sample answer: A convenience sample is one that is obtained in a manner that is easy for the researcher. A systematic sample is obtained using an ordered list of the population from which members are selected systematically.
9. A recent survey indicated that "most teens watch television an average of three hours per day." What are two questions you might ask about the survey?
   Sample answer: 1) Was the survey taken during the school year or during the summer? 2) Are the teens watching educational television?
10. In math class Shawnda has earned B's on each of her first six tests. She predicts she will make a B on the next test. Do you agree with her prediction? Why or why not?
   Answers may vary. Check students' answers.

Answers
1. A
2. C
3. D
4. B
5. No
6. Yes
7. No
8. *See question.*
9. *See question.*
10. *See question.*

3

Name _____ Date _____ Score _____

Test 3 *(continued)*

Directions: Write the answers in the spaces provided.

11. Use deductive reasoning to show that the difference of two even numbers is even.
   Let $2x$ and $2y$ represent any two even numbers. Their difference is $2x - 2y$, or $2(x - y)$. Since 2 is a factor of this difference, $2x - 2y$ is even.

For Questions 12–14, tell whether each statement about sports participants is *True* or *False*. Use the Venn diagram at the right.

12. If a student plays baseball, the student also plays volleyball.
13. If a student plays football, the student does not play volleyball.
14. Some students play both football and baseball.

For Questions 15 and 16:
a. Tell whether each statement is *True* or *False*. If it is false, give a counterexample.
b. Write the converse of each statement.
c. Tell whether the converse of each statement is *True* or *False*. If it is false, give a counterexample.

15. If a triangle has two congruent sides, then the triangle is isosceles.
   a. True. b. If a triangle is isosceles, then it has two congruent sides. c. True.
16. If $3x$ is an integer, then x is a rational number.
   a. True. b. If x is a rational number, then $3x$ is an integer.
   c. False; $x = \frac{1}{4}$.
17. **Open-ended** Make up an if-then statement whose converse is always true. Write the statement and its converse.
   Sample answer: statement: If a quadrilateral has four congruent sides, then it is a rhombus. converse: If a quadrilateral is a rhombus, then it has four congruent sides.

Answers
11. *See question.*
12. False
13. True
14. True
15. *See question.*
16. *See question.*
17. *See question.*

4

Form B

Name _____ Date _____ Score _____

Test 4

Test on Unit 1 (Form B)

Directions: Write the answers in the spaces provided.

Match each sample of students with a sampling method.
A. random   B. convenience   C. systematic   D. cluster

1. the first 5 students who enter the cafeteria
2. one student from each classroom
3. the third row of students from each classroom
4. the student closest to the door in each classroom

For Questions 5–7, tell whether each method would produce a random sample of a school population of 1000 students. Write *Yes* or *No.*

5. One student from each letter of the alphabet (by last name) is selected.
6. All the student body officers are selected.
7. All the students on the football team are selected.
8. **Writing** Compare and contrast random sampling and cluster sampling.
   Sample answer: In random sampling, each member of the population is equally likely to be selected, and the sample members are independently chosen. In cluster sampling, groups of members of the population are selected; this is not a random sample, since the members of the group are not chosen independently.
9. A recent survey indicated that "most adults work at least 20 hours per week at a paying job." What are two questions you might ask about the survey?
   Sample answer: 1) What group of people were surveyed? 2) Was the survey taken during a regular work week or during a holiday?
10. In each of the last six football games Eric has scored a touchdown. He predicts that he will score a touchdown in the next game. Do you agree with his prediction? Why or why not?
   Answers may vary. Check students' answers.

Answers
1. B
2. A
3. D
4. C
5. Yes
6. No
7. No
8. *See question.*
9. *See question.*
10. *See question.*

5

Name _____ Date _____ Score _____

Test 4 *(continued)*

Directions: Write the answers in the spaces provided.

11. Use deductive reasoning to show that the product of two even numbers is even.
   Let $2x$ and $2y$ represent any two even numbers. Their product is $(2x)(2y)$, or $4xy$. Since 2 is a factor of 4 and thus of $4xy$, $(2x)(2y)$ is even.

For Questions 12–14, tell whether each statement about music listeners is *True* or *False*. Use the Venn diagram at the right.

12. Some people like hip-hop and rock and roll.
13. If a person does not like oldies, then the person likes hip-hop and rock and roll.
14. If a person likes hip-hop, the person also likes oldies.

For Questions 15 and 16:
a. Tell whether each statement is *True* or *False*. If it is false, give a counterexample.
b. Write the converse of each statement.
c. Tell whether the converse of each statement is *True* or *False*. If it is false, give a counterexample.

15. If a triangle has three congruent sides, then the triangle is equilateral.
   a. True. b. If a triangle is equilateral, then it has three congruent sides. c. True.
16. If x is a rational number, then $5x$ is an integer.
   a. False; $x = \frac{1}{2}$. b. If $5x$ is an integer, then x is a rational number.
   c. True.
17. **Open-ended** Create a Venn diagram with three parts. Label the parts of your diagram and write a sentence describing the situation.
   Sample answer:

   Students who take a music or drama class do not take an art class.

Answers
11. *See question.*
12. True
13. False
14. False
15. *See question.*
16. *See question.*
17. *See question.*

6

Software Support

McDougal Littell Mathpack

Function Investigator
Probability Constructor
Stats!

Outside Resources

Books/Periodicals

California Department of Education and California Energy Commission. *Compendium for Integrated Waste Management.* 1994

Jacobs, Harold R. *Mathematics: A Human Endeavor.* (Ch. 1: Mathematical Ways of Thinking, and Ch. 9: An Introduction to Statistics) San Francisco, CA: W.H. Freeman and Company, 1982.

Software

O'Brien, Thomas. *Blockers and Finders.* Pleasantville, NY: Sunburst, 1986. Apple, Macintosh, and IBM.

Owirko-Godycki, R. Jerzy. *Enchanted Forest.* Pleasantville, NY: Sunburst, 1985. Apple (attribute puzzles).

Videos

Futures with Jaime Escalante. Program No. 1: Statistics. PBS, 1990.

Mathematical Eye. Program No. 5. Logic and Problem Solving. Journal Films, 1988.

Math Works. Programs No. 12 and No. 21: Statistics. Agency for Instructional Technology, 1985.

Sturdevant, Thomas. *Real World Problem Solvers: The Garbage Dump Dilemma.* Pleasantville, NY: HRM Video, 1992.

Organizations

California Integrated Waste Management, 6311 F St., Sacramento, CA 95819 Phone (916) 255-2448

1D

PROJECT GOALS

➤ Students develop a recycling proposal to reduce and dispose of trash produced at school.

➤ Students conduct a survey among the students at school using a particular sample size and sampling method.

➤ Students plan an event or a special display to persuade all students in their school to recycle as much as possible. ....●

PROJECT PLANNING

Materials List

➤ Rubber gloves
➤ Trash bags
➤ Graph paper

Project Teams

Have students work on the project in groups of four. One way for the individuals in the group to distribute the work is as follows:

1. Surveyor: coordinates development and refinement of survey questions, selection of sample size and sampling method, conducts the survey, and summarizes the results of the survey.

2. Analyzer: coordinates activities leading to selection and analysis of a classroom trash sample, and leading to a prediction of trash amounts for the entire school.

3. Writer/Illustrator: writes the disposal proposal, including questions, charts, and graphs, based on the results of the survey, the trash analysis, and the recommendations of the group to reduce, reuse, and recycle.

4. Communicator: arranges for and coordinates the activities necessary for the presentation of the groups' disposal proposal to the entire school.

unit 1

Like buried time capsules, the landfills of America wait to be dug up by future generations of archaeologists. That newspaper tossed into the trash 12 years ago is still quite readable today. Those uneaten hot dogs and ears of corn from a family picnic are still with us many years later.

reduce

Corn buried 1971

People all over the world are looking for ways to REUSE nonconsumable items rather than throw them away, to REDUCE the amount of trash produced and RECYCLE more of it.

Associations that support recycling have sprung up in Canada, Brazil, and Europe. Japan recycles about a third of its trash. In the United States, the number of curbside recycling programs jumped from about 1000 to over 9000 between 1989 and 1998!

discard

Landfills admit no light, no air, and very little moisture, so trash decomposes slowly.➤

What happens to worn-out tires?

reuse

In Ecuador, used tires become market baskets.➤

General Rubric for Unit Projects

Each unit project can be evaluated in many possible ways. The following rubric is just one way to evaluate these open-ended projects. It is based on a 4-point scale.

4 The student fully achieves all mathematical and project goals. The presentation demonstrates clear thinking and explanation.

3 The student substantially achieves the mathematical and project goals. The main thrust of the project and the mathematics behind it is understood, but there may be some minor misunderstanding of content, errors in computation, or weakness in presentation.

2 The student partially achieves the mathematical and project goals. A limited grasp of the main mathematical ideas or project requirements is demonstrated. Some of the work may be incomplete, misdirected, or unclear.

1 The student makes little progress toward accomplishing the goals of the project because of lack of understanding or lack of effort.

Unit Project

Disposal Proposal

Your project is to develop a proposal for reducing the amount of trash produced by the students in your school. First, you will need to survey students about their attitudes toward recycling and reuse. Then you will obtain a sample of the trash from a classroom and analyze its contents.

In this unit, you will learn about surveys, sampling, and reasoning. You will use your findings from the survey and sample analysis to make a

display or plan an event to persuade students to throw away less and recycle and reuse more. You may build a three-dimensional model for a display case, make a series of posters, organize an assembly program, present a humorous skit, or make an announcement over the public-address system.

Your presentation should include your survey questions, a summary of the results, and a graph showing the contents of the classroom trash sample.

A glass recycling station in Portugal ➤

products

Take a **pile of trash**—car tires, used plastic foam cups, old canvas, empty milk jugs, cardboard boxes, old file folders. Add a dash of technology and you have ... brand-new shoes!

Recycling creates new products out of old. You can buy sweaters made from soft drink bottles and even sea-green stationery made from old paper money.

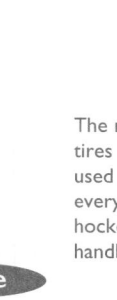

The rubber in tires can be used to make everything from hockey pucks to handbags.➤

recycle

create

▲This house was built out of used tires and aluminum cans.

1

Suggested Rubric for Unit Project

4 Students have used their surveys, sampling, and valid arguments correctly. They have incorporated a copy of their survey and its results into their disposal proposal. The summary is clearly written and supports their recommendations. The format chosen is effective, and the arguments used are persuasive.

3 Students' survey questions, sampling method, and sample size can be improved. The writ-

ten summary of the survey results and the graph are included in the proposal but show some minor deficiencies. The findings and recommendations in the form of a skit, poster, or a display convince students but are not fully persuasive.

2 Students' survey questions need major revisions. The summary of the survey results is not well written and shows a lack of serious thought. The mathematics of sampling and

reasoning that underlies the project is not well understood.

1 Students do not know how to apply the mathematics of sampling and reasoning to get started correctly. The findings and recommendations are not supported by the survey results, and the final proposal is inadequate. The group should be encouraged to speak with the teacher as soon as possible to review their work and to make a new start on the project.

How Recycling Helps

Recycling can help to improve the quality of peoples' lives on Earth today and in the future. The resources of planet Earth are not limitless. As the population of Earth continues to grow, there is a greater demand for its resources. Forests are vanishing and advanced technology is rapidly using up natural resources. Recycling paper and other trash not only helps to slow the depletion of Earth's resources, but it also reduces the amount of land that communities have to set aside for landfills. In heavily populated areas, the disposal of trash is becoming a serious problem that contributes to the degradation of land and water resources.

ALTERNATIVE PROJECTS

Project 1, page 52

Conclusions in Advertisements

Select and analyze several newspaper and magazine advertisements that make claims based on surveys. Include information about the sample size and sampling method, if the format of the advertisements could lead you to make reasoning errors, and the effectiveness of the ads.

Project 2, page 52

Simulating Survey Results

Pick an interesting topic to ask people about. Design a survey for the topic in which the results can be simulated using dice, coins, spinners, or random numbers. First conduct the simulation and note the results. Then conduct the personal survey. Write a report to compare and contrast the results of both activities.

Unit Project

Getting Started

For this project you should work in a group of four students. Here are some ideas to help you get started.

☞ Discuss what questions to ask on your reduce/reuse/recycle survey. Decide whether you will survey all the students in the school or only a sample. If you use a sample, plan to meet later to choose a sampling method and a sample size.

☞ Set a date and time for collecting a sample of classroom trash. Plan to wear rubber gloves and bring along trash bags for the trash you remove from wastebaskets.

☞ Think about how to get students' attention and convince them of the need to change. Plan to meet later to discuss how to use reasoning to construct good arguments that will help students understand the problem.

☞ Choose an effective format—written, visual, or dramatic—for communicating your findings and recommendations to all the students in your school.

Can We Talk RECYCLING

Working on the Unit Project

Your work in Unit 1 will help you develop a disposal proposal for your school.

Related Exercises:
Section 1-1, Exercise 26
Section 1-2, Exercise 25
Section 1-3, Exercise 28
Section 1-4, Exercises 24–26
Section 1-5, Exercises 31, 32
Section 1-6, Exercise 44
Section 1-7, Exercise 33

Alternative Projects p. 52

➤ Where do you think most of the trash comes from in your school? What type of trash do you think is the most common?

➤ Is recycling practiced in your city or town? If so, what types of materials are picked up at curbside and what types do you bring to a collection center?

➤ About 50% of the trash in an average landfill is paper. Do you think that half of any pile of trash is paper? Why or why not?

➤ What other products do you know about that are made of recycled materials? How do the prices and the quality of these products compare with those made from all new materials?

➤ What do you think archaeologists can learn about the lifestyle of a culture by examining its trash?

A recycling center in France ➤

Answers to Can We Talk?

➤ Answers may vary. An example is given. Most of the trash in our school comes from the cafeteria and the classrooms. The type of trash that is most common is paper.

➤ Answers may vary. An example is given. Yes, recycling is practiced in my city. Aluminum cans, glass, plastic bottles, and newspapers are picked up at curbside. Tin cans, yard waste, and telephone books can be brought to a collection center.

➤ Answers may vary. An example is given. No. A pile of trash from a factory or a laundromat may not be half paper.

➤ Answers may vary. Examples are given. Some glass and plastic containers are made from recycled materials. The prices of products are usually lower while the quality is as good as the quality of new products.

➤ Answers may vary. An example is given. Archaeologists can learn how people lived and some of their practices and customs. If archaeologists find cooking pots or utensils, they can get an idea of what people ate and how they prepared their food. If archaeologists find clothes or tools, they can get an idea of what people wore, how the clothes were made, and how things were fixed or built.

Surveys and Samples

PLANNING

Objectives and Strands
See pages 1A and 1B.

Spiral Learning
See page 1B.

Recommended Pacing
Section 1-1 is a one-day lesson.

Extra Practice
See pages 614–615.

Warm-Up Exercises
Warm-Up Transparency 1-1

Support Materials
➤ Practice 1
➤ Enrichment 1 in the Activity Bank
➤ Study Guide 1-1
➤ Problem Set 1
➤ Additional Exploration 1
➤ Function Investigator with Matrix Analyzer Activity Book: Function Investigator Activity 23
➤ Quiz 1-1
➤ Alternative Assessment 1

Focus
Know how a survey of part of a population can be used to predict results for the entire population.

In 1992 the United States Postal Service asked the public its opinion on this issue: Should a young Elvis or an older Elvis picture be used on a commemorative stamp?

A survey in a popular magazine showed pictures of the two stamps. Voters marked their choices on postcards. The young Elvis stamp was chosen by 851,200 people. The older Elvis stamp was chosen by 277,723 people.

There were about 250 million people living in the United States in 1992, but less than 2 million people voted on the Elvis stamp issue.

A complete group is a **population**. The population of the United States was about 250 million.

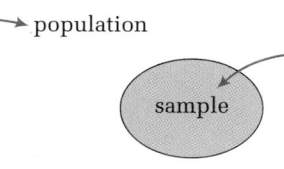

A part of a group is a **sample**. The sample that sent in an Elvis stamp ballot included 1,128,923 people.

According to a network news report, by the end of the first week of voting 300,000 ballots were received. 78% were for the young Elvis; 17% were for the older Elvis.

BY THE WAY...

The Postal Service printed 517 million Elvis stamps, about three times the usual amount, and projected $36 million in profit from them.

Talk it Over

1. What do you think the other 5% of the ballots showed at the end of the first week?

2. What percent of the final results were for the young Elvis? the older Elvis?

3. Were the results at the end of the first week a good indication of the final results? Explain your reasoning.

Answers to Talk it Over

1. Answers may vary. An example is given. People may have expressed no preference for either design or wanted both issued as stamps.

2. about 75%; about 25%

3. Answers may vary. An example is given. Yes; both indicate that the young Elvis stamp is preferred by most people.

Talk it Over

Questions 1–3 involve students in thinking about the details of the Elvis stamp survey and surveys in general. Question 1 leads students to realize that a certain amount of ballots or questionnaires (5% in this case) may show no preference. Questions 2 and 3 present the idea that, in some cases, early returns may be a good indicator of final results.

Multicultural Note

Since the middle of the nineteenth century, the nations of the world have issued more than 250,000 different postage stamps. The themes of most nations' stamps are not limited by their boundaries. For example, a number of countries that have produced stamps honoring the Olympic games have paid tribute to great athletes of other countries. In 1968, the Republic of Chad issued a stamp honoring U.S. swimmer and gold medal winner Deborah Meyer. Scientists whose discoveries have had far-reaching benefit have also been honored by numerous countries through the issuance of commemorative stamps. The African countries of Gabon and Comoro Islands issued stamps honoring the French scientist Louis Pasteur, 150 years after his birth.

Exploration

The goal of the Exploration is to have students conduct their own survey in order to explore what is involved in doing so. Students are also implicitly exploring a much more general question: Can the results of a sample (the class) be applied to the larger population (the school)?

Teaching Tip

Teaching strategies for effective learning and teaching are presented on page T30 in the front of this Teacher's Edition.

Every ten years, the United States government gathers data about the entire population of the country. This process is called a *census* because every member of the population is included.

A census is expensive and requires lots of planning. It is more common for people who collect information to take a survey of a sample of a population.

Many surveys ask questions that can be answered with either a "yes" or a "no."

EXPLORATION

What is typical for your class?

• **Work with the whole class.**

① Take a survey of your class. Use one yes-no question from the list at the left, or make up one of your own.

② Find the total number of people who answered "yes" to your survey question. Find the total who answered "no."

③ What percent of the answers were "yes"? What percent were "no"?

④ Do you think that your results accurately reflect the views of your school population? Explain why or why not.

Have you ever bought a commemorative stamp?

Have you ever participated in a nationwide survey?

Do you speak more than one language?

Do you think a college education is important for getting a good job?

Do you like to do homework?

Do you prefer the young Elvis stamp?
Yes 18
No

Answers to Exploration

1–4. Answers may vary.

Answers to Talk it Over

4. Answers may vary.

5–7. Answers may vary. Examples are given.

5. They are easy to compile and compare.

6. b; A larger sample can more accurately reflect the diversity in the student body.

Talk it Over

4. How might the results of your survey be different if you had taken the survey of a retirement community? of people at a video arcade?

5. Why do you think yes-no or multiple-choice questions are often used on surveys?

6. Suppose you want to predict how someone in your school might answer the question you used in the Exploration. Choose the letter of the sample size you think will give you the most representative response. Explain your choice.

   a. 20 people   b. 200 people   c. 2 people

7. What are some factors to consider when you are making a survey? Make a list.

Surveys (or polls) are used to predict such things as election results, the popularity of new products, or opinions of television shows. Based on the results, information is projected for the entire population.

Sample

Suppose everyone in the United States had to choose an Elvis stamp. Use the results of the Elvis stamp ballot to estimate the number who would select the young Elvis.

Sample Response

Problem Solving Strategy: Use a proportion.

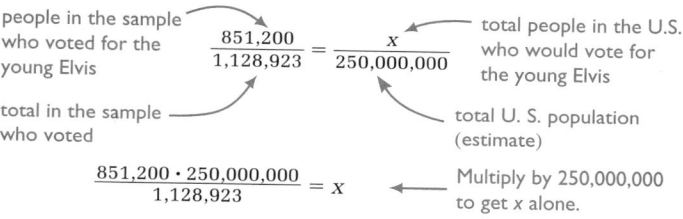

people in the sample who voted for the young Elvis

$$\frac{851,200}{1,128,923} = \frac{x}{250,000,000}$$

total people in the U.S. who would vote for the young Elvis

total in the sample who voted

total U. S. population (estimate)

$$\frac{851,200 \cdot 250,000,000}{1,128,923} = x$$

Multiply by 250,000,000 to get x alone.

$$188,498,241 \approx x$$

About 188,500,000 people would choose the young Elvis stamp.

75% of the voters chose the young Elvis.

Look Back

A city planner wants to know if a stoplight is needed at a street corner. What population should the planner consider? What is a sample that the planner might use? Write a short survey that the planner could give the people in that sample.

Answers to Talk it Over

7. (1) Can the information you are looking for be found by asking a yes-no or multiple-choice question? (2) How should you word the survey questions? (3) How should you interpret the results? (4) What size sample group would give you reasonable results? (5) How should you choose your sample group?

Answers to Look Back

Answers may vary. An example is given. The city planner should consider residents of the area and drivers and pedestrians who pass through the intersection. The planner might choose a sample by choosing some number n (depending on the population and traffic density) and questioning every nth household and every nth driver who passes through the intersection at different times throughout the day. Sample questions: "Should there be a traffic light at this intersection?"; "How often do you drive or walk through this intersection?"; "What direction are you heading?"; "Do you have an alternate route?"; "What time of day do you pass through the intersection?"

Talk it Over

Questions 4–7 lead students to consider some factors that could influence the outcome of their survey, such as age, format of questions, or size of the sample. Since the results of a survey are used to predict the views of an entire population, factors that influence the outcome in a particular way need to be eliminated.

Additional Sample

A survey was taken in a class of 36 students to determine which of three sports, baseball, basketball, or football, was the most popular to watch. Twelve students said they liked baseball best, 16 chose basketball, and 8 liked football the most. Estimate how many students in a school with a population of 1026 would choose each sport.

Baseball:

$$\frac{12}{36} = \frac{x}{1026}$$

$$\frac{12 \cdot 1026}{36} = x$$

$$342 = x$$

About 342 students would choose baseball.

Basketball:

$$\frac{16}{36} = \frac{x}{1026}$$

$$\frac{16 \cdot 1026}{36} = x$$

$$456 = x$$

About 456 students would choose basketball.

Football:

$$\frac{8}{36} = \frac{x}{1026}$$

$$\frac{8 \cdot 1026}{36} = x$$

$$228 = x$$

About 228 students would choose football.

Look Back

In answering the questions about the population and sample, students should be able to justify their answers using ideas they have learned in this section. Also, volunteers can suggest survey questions in order to construct a short survey for the people in the sample. A student can write the questions on the board for further evaluation and refinement.

Integrating the Strands
Number Ex. 16

Algebra Exs. 6, 18–21

Geometry Ex. 15

Statistics and Probability
Exs. 1–17, 22–26

Logic and Language Exs. 2, 3,
5, 14, 26

Reasoning

In Exs. 3–5, students have an opportunity to think again about the key ideas of a sample and a population. The two key factors that make it more reasonable to collect information by surveying a sample than to take a census are *time* and *cost*. It takes much less time and costs far less money to survey a sample than to contact each person in the entire population.

Teaching Tip

In Ex. 6, you may wish to point out that a margin of error of 3% can be written as ±3%. Thus, in this sample, the results can be expressed as 63% ± 3%.

Application

Exs. 6–9 apply the concepts of sample and population to various real-world situations. In all prior situations in this section up to Ex. 9, populations involved people only because students know the meaning of a population of *people.* In Ex. 9, however, the population involves birds and not people and thus implicitly generalizes this concept. In Ex. 9 and Exs. 15 and 16 on page 8, students see that a population can be something other than people, such as birds, geometric figures, or numbers. In mathematics, population is a technical term that can be applied to any group of living things, objects, or abstractions (such as numbers).

1-1 Exercises and Problems

1. **Reading** About what percent of the United States population voted for one Elvis stamp or the other?

2. **Reading** Complete each __?__ using a key word from this section. A part is to the whole as a __?__ is to the __?__.

For Exercises 3–5, use the survey results below.

3. Do the results show the views of a *sample* of consumers or of the entire *population* of consumers?

4. Why is it more reasonable to survey a sample of the population than to take a census to collect this information?

5. **a.** Write two multiple-choice questions that could have been used in this survey.

   b. Would you be able to find each average percent of increase shown based on the responses to your questions? Why or why not?

recycled plastic packaging: 6.1%

gasoline with $\frac{1}{3}$ less pollutants: 7.4%

detergents with $\frac{1}{3}$ less pollutants: 7.3%

recycled paper products: 6.0%

A survey of 1413 people has shown that consumers want to buy products that are safe for the environment, even if the products are more expensive. The diagram shows the average percent of increase consumers will pay.

6. **Opinion Polls** Suppose that 63% of the people in a sample said that they supported a plan to pay for a new school. Because sampling never gives perfect measures, the actual results could be different by up to 3% in either direction. This is called the *margin of error.*

   a. What is the largest percent of the population that might support the plan? What is the smallest percent?

   b. Write an inequality to describe the percent of the population that might support the plan.

   c. Graph the inequality from part (b) on a number line.

7. At a preview of a movie, 6 people out of 500 walk out. Suppose 600,000 people see the movie. Estimate the number of people who walk out.

8. In a 125-seat section of a baseball park, 38 people bought programs. The park holds 54,000 people. Estimate the total number of programs sold.

9. **Wildlife** In part of a shoreline reserve, there are 45 nesting adult sanderlings and 17 sanderling chicks. There are 120 nesting adult sanderlings in the reserve. Estimate the total number of sanderling chicks.

BY THE WAY...

Amy Gustafson is a chemical engineer whose work involves designing *biodegradable* plastics, such as the plastic film she is holding. The base for this clear, flexible, water-repelling film is corn starch.

Answers to Exercises and Problems

1. about 0.45%

2. sample; population

3. a sample

4. It would be impossible to question every consumer in the United States.

5. **a.** Answers may vary. Two examples are given. Choose one response to complete each question. (1) I would be willing to

   pay an average percent of increase of __?__ for recycled paper products. (a) 0% (b) 3% (c) 6% (d) 9% (2) Which percent shows how much more you would be willing to pay for a product made from recycled plastic packaging? (a) 2% or less (b) 4% (c) 6% (d) 8%

   b. No. My questions would give results for only two products, not all four.

6. **a.** 66%; 60%

   b. Let p be the percentage of the population that might support the plan; $60\% \leq p \leq 66\%$ or $0.60 \leq p \leq 0.66$

   c.
   0.58 0.60 0.62 0.64 0.66 0.68

10. a. **Research** Find out the number of students in your school.

   b. Use the results of the Exploration on page 4 to estimate the total number of students in your school who would answer "yes" to the question you used in the Exploration.

   c. **Group Activity** Ask the question of at least 10 students who are not in your mathematics class. Combine the data your class collects and estimate the total number of students in your school who would answer "yes" to the question.

   d. Compare your answers to parts (b) and (c). Suppose you asked another 20 students. How do you think the results would change?

11. a. **Research** Find the results of a survey in a magazine or a newspaper.

   b. Identify at least two reasons why a sample was used, rather than the entire population.

   c. Use the data in the survey to project the results for the population of the United States.

   d. Describe who could use the information from the survey and how they might use it.

connection to HISTORY

12. In the late 1700s, Thomas Paine estimated that one person in sixteen in England was over 50 years old. He concluded that 420,000 people were then over 50. What number does it appear that he was using for the population of England?

13. **Writing** England did not have a formal census until 1801, so Paine had to rely on rough estimates of the population.

   Write about how a historian might estimate the population of a country 200 years ago.

14. **Open-ended** The passage at the right is from *The Rights of Man*, by Thomas Paine. In it, he describes the method he used to estimate the number of people over 50 years old.

   Do you think this method gave Paine a good estimate of the number of people over 50 years old? Why or why not?

"To form some judgment of the number of those above fifty years of age, I have several times counted the persons I met in the streets of London, men, women, and children, and have generally found that the average is about one in sixteen or seventeen."

1-1 Surveys and Samples

7

Answers to Exercises and Problems

7. about 7200 people

8. about 16,416 programs

9. about 45 chicks

10. a–d. Answers may vary.

11. a–d. Answers may vary.

12. about 6,720,000 people

13. Answers may vary. An example is given. The historian could sample church enrollment or tax records for a number of different communities and estimate the entire population from these samples.

14. Answers may vary. An example is given. This method gave a good estimate because there were enough people to count and there should be a good cross-section of England's population in London.

Cooperative Learning

The activities in Ex. 10 can be done by having students work in small groups of 3 or 4. Allow some class time for students to combine their data and make their estimates. Each group can contribute its results to the class data in part (c). Detailed suggestions on cooperative learning techniques are presented on page T32 in the front of this Teacher's Edition.

Interdisciplinary Problems

Exs. 12–14 apply the concepts of sample and population to a historical situation in England. Of course, a good estimate of the number of people over 50 years old by Paine would depend entirely on his choosing a good sample. Also, a historian would have to be very careful in selecting a sample for use in estimating the population of a country 200 years ago.

Visual Thinking

Ideas for helping students develop their visual learning skills are provided on page T44 in the front of this Teacher's Edition and at strategic points throughout the side-column notes. Visual learning skills include:

1. Observation
2. Identification
3. Recognition
4. Recall
5. Interpretation
6. Exploration
7. Correlation
8. Generalization
9. Inference
10. Perception
11. Communication
12. Self-Expression

Each Visual Thinking note indicates the visual learning skills that are involved in the suggested activity.

Practice 1 For use with Section 1-1

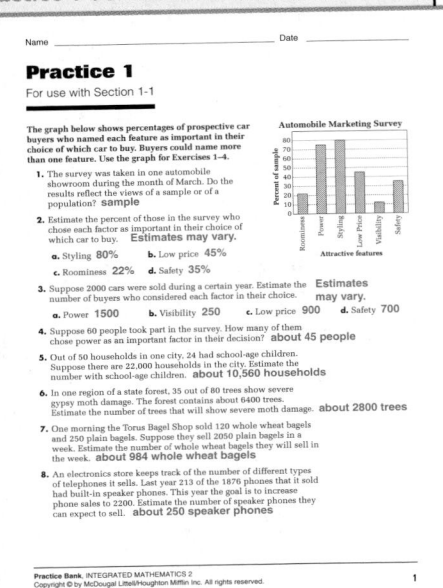

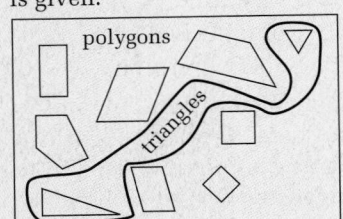

15. The diagram shows that part of the population of polygons is the sample of squares. Choose another sample from this population and draw a diagram that shows the sample and the population.

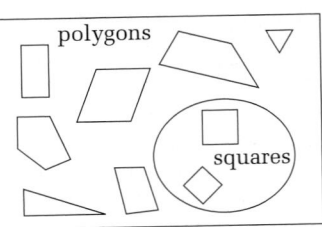

16. Suppose that the population is the set of all real numbers. A sample of that set might be the even integers.

   a. Name at least two other sets that could be samples of this population.

   b. Draw a diagram that shows the population, the set of even integers, and the samples that you described in part (a).

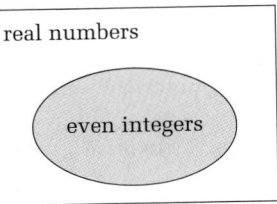

Ongoing ASSESSMENT

17. **Open-ended** Describe two situations where a sample might be used. Give the advantages and disadvantages of using a sample in each case.

Review PREVIEW

Solve. *(Toolbox Skill 13)*

18. $3x + 7 = 13$

19. $-8x - 1 = 3$

20. $14 - \frac{1}{2}x = 26$

21. Make a table of values to graph the equation $y = 0.25x - 2$. Find the slope and the intercepts of the graph. *(Toolbox Skills 20, 21, and 24)*

Assume that the needle on the spinner is equally likely to land on each section. Find each probability. *(Toolbox Skill 7)*

22. $P(2)$

23. $P(\text{odd})$

24. $P(\text{less than } 3)$

25. $P(8)$

Working on the Unit Project

26. **Group Activity** Write a first draft of your survey with a minimum of ten questions about reducing, reusing, and recycling trash at your school. Describe the student population that might participate in your survey. Tell whether you would take a census or take a survey of a sample of the population. Explain your choice.

Answers to Exercises and Problems

15. Answers may vary. An example is given.

16. Answers may vary. Examples are given.

16. a. the set of negative numbers; the numbers 3, 5, and 7

   b.

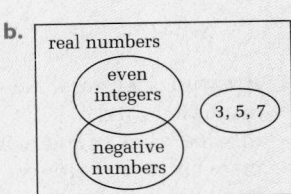

17. Answers may vary. Examples are given. You could use a sample to determine whether students in your school would prefer a new name for one of its sports teams or new school colors. One advantage of using a sample is that it is usually easier than questioning an entire population. One disadvantage is that you may not be sure that the sample you have chosen is truly representative of the entire population.

18. 2

19. $-\frac{1}{2}$

20. -24

21.

x	y
-8	-4
-4	-3
0	-2
4	-1
8	0

slope = 0.25;
x-intercept = 8;
y-intercept = −2

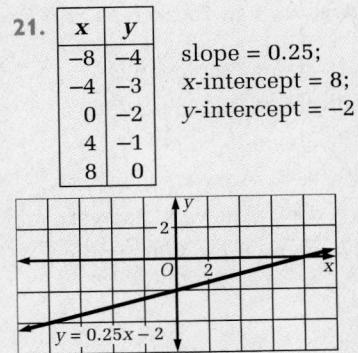

22–26. See answers in back of book.

Simulation

·····Focus
Use an experiment to simulate the results of a survey.

Give it a Spin

HOW TO MAKE A SPINNER

Draw a large circle with five equal sections labeled as shown.

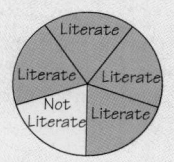

Make a pointer out of a paper clip.

Use a pencil to hold the pointer at the center of the circle.

EXPLORATION

How can you describe a sample without actually choosing it?

- **Materials:** spinner (look to the left), paper clip
- **Work in a group of four students.**

The 1870 census recorded that 80% of the total population of the United States, age 10 years or older, was literate (able to read and write in some language).

① a. What is 80% of 10 people? If you could choose 10 people at random from the population in 1870, how many literate people would you be likely to get?

b. What is 80% of 25 people? If you could choose 25 people at random from the population in 1870, how many literate people would you be likely to get?

② It is unlikely that exactly 80% of any sample will be literate, and it is difficult to find the records to do a historical survey of a sample of the United States population in 1870. However, you can use an experiment to find the number of people in a sample who are literate.

a. Make a spinner as described at the left.

b. Discuss with your group why the blue shaded sections represent 80% of the circle.

Continued on next page.

9

Answers to Exploration

1. **a.** 8 people; about 8
   b. 20 people; about 20
2. **a.** Check students' spinners.
   b. Four of the five sections are blue; $\frac{4}{5} = \frac{80}{100} = 80\%$.

PLANNING

Objectives and Strands
See pages 1A and 1B.

Spiral Learning
See page 1B.

Materials List
➤ Spinner
➤ Paper clip
➤ Die
➤ Coin

Recommended Pacing
Section 1-2 is a two-day lesson.
Day 1
Pages 9–10: Exploration through Talk it Over 3, *Exercises 1–11*
Day 2
Pages 11–12: Probability and Simulation through Look Back, *Exercises 12–25*

Toolbox References
➤ **Toolbox Skill 6:** Finding Experimental Probability
➤ **Toolbox Skill 7:** Finding Theoretical Probability
➤ **Toolbox Skill 4:** Finding Mean, Median, Mode, Range

Extra Practice
See pages 614–615.

Warm-Up Exercises
♀ Warm-Up Transparency 1-2

Support Materials
➤ Practice 2
➤ Enrichment 2 in the Activity Bank
➤ Study Guide 1-2
➤ Problem Set 1
➤ Diagram Masters 8, 9 in the Explorations Lab Manual
♀ Overhead Visual 1
➤ McDougal Littell Mathpack software: *Probability Constructor*
➤ Quiz 1-2
➤ Alternative Assessment 2

Exploration

The goal of the Exploration is to have students simulate results based upon statistical information. In step 1, a brief discussion of what it means to choose people at *random* may be appropriate. In step 4, students see again that a large sample gives a better estimate than a smaller sample. This idea was presented in the previous section and appears also in Talk it Over question 3.

Using Technology

Students can use the *Probability Constructor* software to simulate spinning the spinner in the Exploration. (For information about using the McDougal Littell Mathpack software, see the *Mathpack User's Guide*.)

Talk it Over

When discussing question 1, you might wish to review briefly the meaning of a theoretical probability and an experimental probability. To find the experimental probability of an event *E*, observe how often the event happens and calculate the ratio:

$P(E) =$
$\dfrac{\text{number of times event } E \text{ happens}}{\text{number of times experiment is done}}$

To find the theoretical probability, use this ratio:

$P(E) =$
$\dfrac{\text{number of favorable outcomes}}{\text{number of possible outcomes}}$

The answers to question 2 require that students think about the fact that a physical model must accurately reflect the probabilities of a particular situation if it is to be used in a simulation experiment.

Teaching Tip

Remind students that probabilities can be expressed in the form of a fraction, a decimal, or a percent. The following probabilities are equivalent: $\frac{1}{4}$, 0.25, and 25%.

---

3 Each student spins the spinner 25 times. Tally the results.

	Number of landings on a blue section	Number of landings on a yellow section	Total number of spins	Percent of total that landed on a blue section
Student 1	?	?	25	?
Student 2	?	?	25	?
Student 3	?	?	25	?
Student 4	?	?	25	?
Total	?	?	100	?

4 Tally the results for the entire class. Which is closer to 80%, the percent for your group or the percent for the whole class?

When you use an experiment based on a real-life situation to answer a question, you are using **simulation.** Each run of the experiment is called a **trial.** Simulation experiments may use physical models (like a spinner or a coin) or computer programs.

Simulation allows people to test new ideas, procedures, and equipment while saving time and money. For example, pilots may use flight simulators to learn about flying under dangerous conditions without actually putting themselves or their airplanes in danger.

Student Resources Toolbox
p. 637 *Probability*

heads

tails

▶ Now you are ready for:
Exs. 1–11 on pp. 12–13

Talk it Over

1. The theoretical probability that a person chosen at random from the population of 1870 is literate is 0.8. What is the experimental probability that you found in the Exploration?

2. Suppose that you guess the answer to a true-false question. The probabilities that you are right or wrong are equal. Decide whether you could use each of these methods to simulate whether or not you answer correctly.

   a. Toss a coin. You are correct if it lands with heads facing up.

   b. Use the spinner at the right. You are correct if the spinner lands on a shaded section.

   c. Roll a die. You are correct if the outcome is an even number.

3. Suppose you run 20 trials of an experiment. Would you expect the average of the results to be *more accurate* or *less accurate* than the average of the results of 200 trials?

Answers to Exploration ·······································

3. Results may vary. Results of one 25-trial experiment are shown.

Number of landings on a blue section	Number of landings on a yellow section	Total number of spins	Percent of total that landed on a blue section
18	7	25	72%

4. Answers may vary.

Answers to Talk it Over ·······

1. Answers may vary, but should be reasonably close to 0.8.

2. a. Yes; guessing on a true-false question involves two outcomes with equal probabilities, as does tossing a coin.

   b. No; spinning the spinner involves two outcomes with unequal probabilities.

Probability and Simulation

The simulation in the Exploration is based on an observation of a population. Some simulations are based on other facts.

There are two traffic lights on a school bus route. On the route to school the probability that the first light is red is $\frac{1}{3}$, and the average wait is 1 min. The probability that the second light is red is $\frac{1}{2}$, and the average wait is 2 min.

On average, how long will the school bus be stopped at a light?

Sample Response

Problem Solving Strategy: Use simulation.

Step 1 Make a **tree diagram** to show the possibilities at each light.

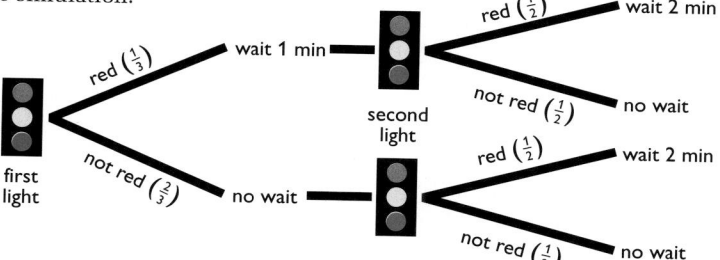

Step 2 For the first light, roll a die to simulate a $\frac{1}{3}$ probability. If the roll is 2 or 4, record a wait of 1 min. If not, record a wait of 0 min. For the second light, simulate a $\frac{1}{2}$ probability with another roll. If it is even, record a wait of 2 min. If not, record a wait of 0 min.

The results of the trials will vary. Some possible results are shown.

Trial	First light		Second light		Total wait in minutes
	Roll	Wait in minutes	Roll	Wait in minutes	
1	2	1	3	0	1
2	6	0	1	0	0
3	4	1	6	2	3
⋮	⋮	⋮	⋮	⋮	⋮
10	1	0	2	2	2
					13

Repeat the experiment several times.

Suppose you ran 10 trials and spent a total of 13 min waiting.

Step 3 Find the mean of the waiting times.

$$\frac{\text{total time spent waiting}}{\text{total number of trials}} = \frac{13}{10} = 1.3$$

Based on the table in step 2, the school bus will wait at the lights an average of 1.3 min each day on the route to school.

Answers to Talk it Over

c. Yes; the possible outcomes (an even number or an odd number) have equal probabilities.

3. less accurate

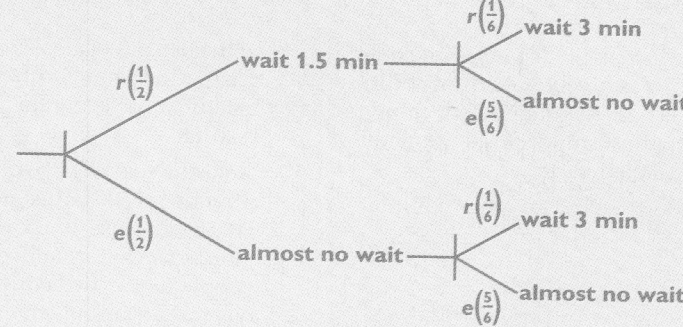

A grocery store and a drugstore each have a regular checkout aisle and an express checkout aisle for no more than three items. Travis goes to the grocery store first, and then to the drugstore and buys more than three items in each store. The probability of waiting in the first regular line is $\frac{1}{2}$ and the average wait time is 1.5 min. At the drugstore, the probability of waiting in the regular line is $\frac{1}{6}$ and the average wait time is 3 min. There is almost no wait time in either express line. On average, how long will Travis spend waiting in the regular lines?

Step 1. Make a tree diagram to show the possibilities at each checkout aisle. See diagram below.

Step 2. Simulate a probability of $\frac{1}{2}$ by tossing a coin. If heads, then the wait time is 1.5 min. If tails, there is no wait. Simulate the probability of $\frac{1}{6}$ with the roll of a die. If 1, then the wait time is 3 min. Otherwise, there is no wait time. Conduct at least 10 trials and record the results in a chart. Combine the grocery store time and the drugstore time to find the total time waiting. Some possible results are shown.

Trial	Grocery Store
1	coin: heads–1.5 min
2	coin: heads–1.5 min
3	coin: tails –no wait
⋮	
10	coin: tails–no wait

Trial	Drugstore
1	roll: 6–no wait
2	roll: 1–3 min
3	roll: 5–no wait
⋮	
10	roll: 1–3 min

Trial	Total time waiting
1	1.5 min
2	4.5 min
3	0.0 min
⋮	
10	3.0 min
	13.5 min

Step 3. Find the mean of the waiting times.

$$\frac{\text{total time waiting}}{\text{total number of trials}} = \frac{13.5}{10} = 1.35$$

Travis will spend an average of 1.35 min waiting in lines.

Talk it Over

Question 4 reviews the fact that the probability of an event happening plus the probability of the event not happening is always 1. This is true because the probability of an event that is certain is 1. The probability of an impossible event is 0.

Look Back

Students can use the physical models introduced earlier in this section to answer these questions, namely, a spinner, a coin, a die, or other models they may come up with that work for these probabilities.

APPLYING

Suggested Assignment

Day 1

Standard 1–10

Extended 1–10

Day 2

Standard 12, 13, 15–25

Extended 12, 13, 15–25

Integrating the Strands

Algebra Exs. 18–24

Statistics and Probability Exs. 1–17, 25

Logic and Language Exs. 1–5, 11–16

Using Technology

Students can use the *Probability Constructor* software to do Ex. 3(c).

---

4. In the Sample, the probability that the first light is red is $\frac{1}{3}$. Why does the probability that it is not red equal $\frac{2}{3}$?

5. In the Sample, a roll of 2 or 4 was used to represent a wait at the first stoplight. Would the experiment be different if a roll of 1 or 5 was used to represent a wait? Explain why or why not.

Look Back

How could you simulate a 50% probability with a physical model? a 25% probability? a $\frac{1}{6}$ probability?

► Now you are ready for: Exs. 12–25 on pp. 14–15

1-2 Exercises and Problems

1. How many trials of the experiment in the Exploration did each individual do? How many trials did each group do? Do you think that the results would have been more accurate if you had done fewer trials? more trials?

2. **Reading** Give two reasons to use simulation instead of a real-life experiment.

3. **a. History** Use the graph. About what percent of the people graduating from high school in 1900 were female?

   b. Use your answer to part (a). If you could choose 20 high school graduates at random from the high school graduates in 1900, how many females would you be likely to get?

   c. Use simulation to answer the question in part (b).

   d. Compare your answers to parts (b) and (c). Should you be surprised if the two answers are not the same? Why or why not?

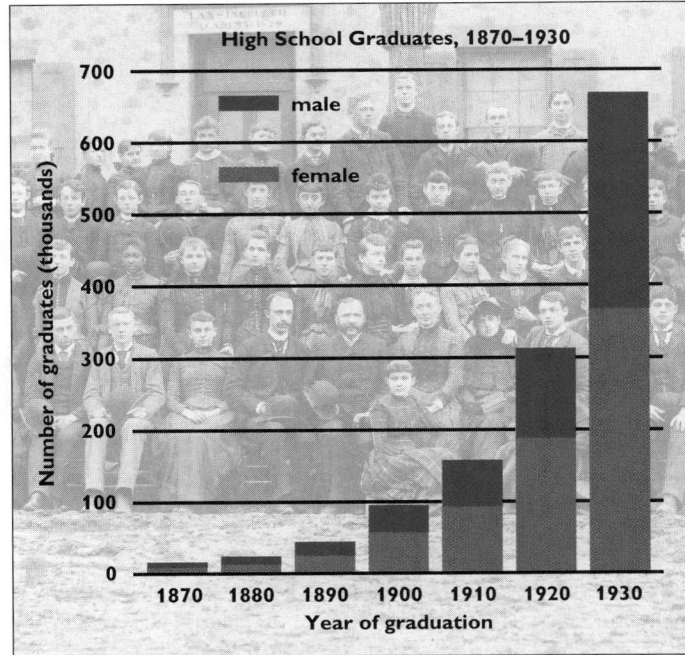

High School Graduates, 1870–1930
■ male
■ female
Number of graduates (thousands): 0, 100, 200, 300, 400, 500, 600, 700
Year of graduation: 1870 1880 1890 1900 1910 1920 1930

Unit 1 Sampling and Reasoning

---

4. There are only two possibilities: the light will be red or the light will not be red. The sum of the two probabilities is 1.

   $P(\text{red}) + P(\text{not red}) = 1$, so $P(\text{not red}) = 1 - P(\text{red}) = 1 - \frac{1}{3} = \frac{2}{3}$.

5. No; you simply need an event with the same probability of getting a red light at the first traffic light. You could use any two numbers between 1 and 6.

Answers may vary. An example is given. Each probability can be simulated by a spinner with the appropriate number of shaded sections.

1. 25 trials; 100 trials; The greater the number of trials, the more accurate the results.

2. Answers may vary. Examples are given. Using simulation can save time and money as well as allow people to practice dangerous tasks without actually putting themselves in danger. Simulation allows you to sample a population that you may not have direct access to on a regular basis.

3. **a.** Estimates may vary; about 60%.

   b. about 12

   c. Answers may vary.

   d. Answers may vary. An example is given. No. A sample of 20 is quite small.

Traffic Safety For Exercises 4–12, suppose that 60% of all people normally wear seat belts.

4. **Writing** Explain how the spinner at the right could be used to simulate how many people in a sample wear seat belts.

5. Suppose you want to know how many people out of 20 are likely to wear seat belts. Would 20 trials give you enough data? Why or why not?

6. a. **Using Manipulatives** Draw a large circle with five equal sections. Use the circle and a paper clip to make a spinner as shown.

   b. Spin the pointer 10 times and tally the results. Repeat this until you have 5 samples of 10 spins each.

Use the results of Exercise 6 to estimate the probability of each event.

7. Exactly 6 out of 10 people normally wear seat belts.

8. Out of 10 people, 6 or fewer normally wear seat belts.

9. Approximately 50–70% of the people in a sample of 10 people normally wear seat belts.

10. All the people in a sample normally wear seat belts.

11. **Group Activity** Work with the whole class.

Combined Results of Simulation About Wearing a Seat Belt

Number of seat belt wearers in sample	0	1	2	3	4	5	6	7	8	9	10
Number of samples	?	?	?	?	?	?	?	?	?	?	?

a. Combine your data from Exercise 6. In a table like the one above, tally the number of samples that have 0, 1, 2, 3, 4, 5, 6, 7, 8, 9, or 10 seat belt wearers.

b. What observations can you make about the data in the table? Is there a pattern in the data?

c. What is the greatest number of seat belt wearers in any sample?

d. What is the least number of seat belt wearers in any sample?

e. What is the mean of the number of seat belt wearers in the samples? Is this about what you would expect it to be? Explain why or why not.

f. What is the given probability that a person chosen at random normally wears a seat belt? What is the experimental probability found by your class?

Student Resources Toolbox
p. 635 *Data Displays and Measures*

Application

Exs. 4–12 present an application involving seat belt usage that allows students to use all the concepts presented in this section. Students are called upon to use their reasoning abilities to write explanations, make observations, and analyze and compare data. The observations and data are gained through the use of a number of manipulative activities that further strengthen students' understanding of simulations and how they are used.

Using Technology

For Ex. 11, students can use the *Stats!* software to sort the data and find the mean.

Assessment: Standard

In Ex. 11, part (e) can be used to assess students' understanding of how to compute the mean by using the data in the table. In part (f), students should be able to show that the theoretical probability is 60%.

Answers to Exercises and Problems

4. On each trial, if the spinner stops on a shaded section, record that as a person wearing a seat belt. If the spinner stops on an unshaded section, that indicates a person not wearing a seat belt.

5. No; that is much too small a sample.

6. Answers may vary. Results of one experiment are given. Trial 1:6; Trial 2:7; Trial 3:6; Trial 4:8; Trial 5:10

7–10. Answers may vary. Answers are based on the results from Ex. 6.

7. 0.4

8. 0.4

9. 0.6

10. 0.2

11. a. Answers may vary.

   b. The greatest number of samples should show 6 seat belt wearers.

   c. probably 10

   d. probably 0

   e. You would expect the mean to be 6 because of the given information that 60% of all Americans wear seat belts.

   f. The given probability is 60%; the experimental probability should be similar if enough trials were run.

13

12. Suppose that it is equally probable that a seat belt wearer is male or female. Use a coin and the spinner from Exercise 6. Let heads represent females and tails represent males.

Coin	Spinner	Result
heads	unshaded	female, no seat belt
heads	shaded	?
tails	unshaded	?
tails	shaded	?

   a. Copy and complete the table.

   b. **Using Manipulatives** Do 20 trials of an experiment to predict how many people out of 20 might be female seat belt wearers.

   c. Based on the given information, what is the probability that a person chosen at random will be a female seat belt wearer?

   d. Compare your answers to parts (b) and (c). Should you be surprised if the two answers are not the same? Why or why not?

13. In the parking lot of a shopping mall there is a 25% probability that a driver can find a parking spot close to the entrance. There is a 100% probability of finding a space farther away.

   Assume that a driver first looks for a space close to the entrance.

   It takes an average of 3 min to find a parking spot close to the entrance, but only an average of 1 min to find a spot farther away.

   a. Use simulation to estimate the average time needed to find a parking spot.

   b. The owner of the mall wants parking spots available in less than 2 min. How often did this occur in your simulation?

14. **Research** Find out how simulators are used in training pilots, drivers, surgeons, or for another use. Describe the factors that are simulated. Give some reasons why a simulator is used instead of real-life training.

15. You are going to take a ten-question true-false test. This is an unusual test. There are no test questions and the results are based on guessing.

   a. On a piece of paper, write the numbers from 1 to 10. For each question number write *True* or *False*.

   b. Flip a coin to find the answer for the first question. If the result is heads, your answer is correct. If the result is tails, your answer is incorrect. Continue this way for the ten questions and write the number you have correct at the top of the paper.

   c. **Group Activity** Record the results for the whole class. Make a chart or graph to show how the scores are distributed in your class.

   d. Suppose that 50% is a passing score on the test. Do you think that a true-false test is a good way to see if a student understands a topic? Explain why or why not.

Answers to Exercises and Problems

12. a.

Coin	Spinner	Result
heads	unshaded	female, no seat belt
heads	shaded	female, seat belt
tails	unshaded	male, no seat belt
tails	shaded	male, seat belt

   b. about 6 should be female seat belt wearers

   c. 30%

   d. No. Part (b) involves experimental probability and part (c) involves theoretical probability. Also, 20 trials may not be enough to give a correct indication.

13. a. Answers may vary. Examples are given. Make a spinner and divide it into fourths. Mark $\frac{1}{4}$ "park close" and the other $\frac{3}{4}$ "park far." Then do trials to estimate the average time.

   b. about 3 out of 4 times

14. Answers may vary. Examples are given. In pilot training, a trainee sits in a simulated cockpit with a computer screen in the place of the windshield. The pilot uses controls and the computer simulates an airplane's response. The computer simulates take-off and landing, normal flying conditions, and emergencies. Simulators allow people to train without risking danger to themselves or others or damage to expensive equipment.

16. **Open-ended** A mouse goes through this maze. Assume that the mouse always heads toward the cheese. Also assume that at every intersection with a choice, the probability that the mouse will turn is equal to the probability that the mouse will go straight.

Use simulation to estimate the probability that the mouse will go through the corner marked *A* on the maze to get to the cheese. Describe your method.

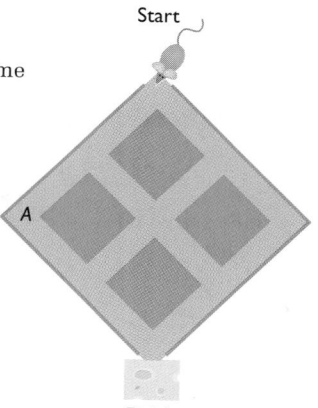

Start

A

Finish

Review PREVIEW

17. On a list of best-selling books, three out of twenty are mysteries. Estimate the number of mysteries in a catalog of 750 best-selling books. *(Section 1-1)*

Simplify. *(Toolbox Skill 10)*

18. $-x + 5y - 4x + 7$

19. $5a^2 + 8b - 4ab + 7a^2$

20. $10n - 8mn + 3mn - n$

Graph each inequality on a number line. *(Toolbox Skill 14)*

21. $x > 0$

22. $x < 2.5$

23. $x \geq -4$

24. $x \leq 4$

Working on the Unit Project

25. Suppose that 50% of the people in your school recycle newspapers and that 30% of the newspaper recyclers also recycle aluminum cans. Design a simulation to estimate about what percent of the people in your school are likely to recycle both newspapers and aluminum cans.

1-2 Simulation

15

Practice 2 For use with Section 1-2

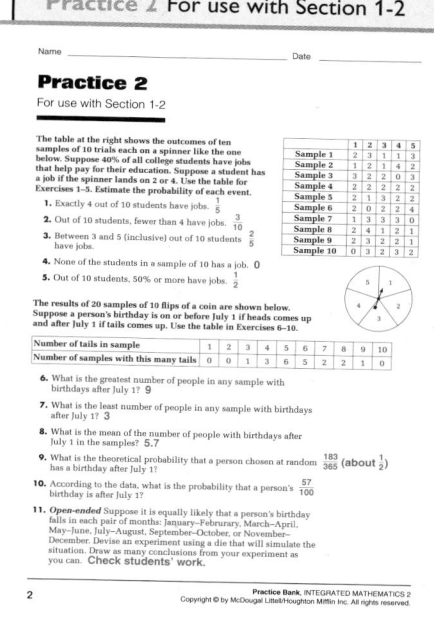

Answers to Exercises and Problems

15. **a–d.** Answers may vary. The results should show that a student would almost always pass under the given circumstances. Since a student has a good chance of passing without even knowing what the questions are, a true-false test is not a good way to see if a student understands a topic.

16. Answers may vary. An example is given. You can simulate the route by tossing a coin for each turn and choosing "heads" to indicate that the mouse goes straight and "tails" to indicate that it turns. The probability that the mouse goes through *A* is about $\frac{1}{4}$.

17. about 113 mysteries

18. $-5x + 5y + 7$

19. $12a^2 + 8b - 4ab$

20. $9n - 5mn$

21. [number line with open circle at 0, shaded to the right; marks at −1, 0, 1, 2, 3]

22. [number line with open circle at 2.5, shaded to the left; marks at −1, 0, 1, 2, 3]

23. [number line with closed circle at −4, shaded to the right; marks at −6, −4, −2, 0]

24. [number line with closed circle at 4, shaded to the left; marks at −2, 0, 2, 4, 6]

25. Answers may vary. An example is given. Use a coin where heads represents those who recycle newspapers and tails represents those who do not recycle newspapers. Use a spinner divided into 10 parts, three of which are shaded. Shaded parts represent those who recycle aluminum cans and unshaded parts represent those who do not recycle aluminum cans. Results should be about 15% who recycle both newspapers and aluminum cans.

Sampling Methods

Focus
Learn about different ways to select a sample.

Take Your PICK

A drama teacher plans to choose four students from the drama club to be in a publicity photo. How could the teacher choose the four students?

The teacher could put the names of all the students in a box, mix the names, and pull out four names without looking. This is an example of a random sample.

The teacher could choose the four students in the first row. This is an example of a convenience sample.

The teacher could mix the names of the girls and choose two. Then do the same for the boys. This is an example of a stratified random sample.

The teacher could choose a group of four students, such as the four students in the back left corner. This is an example of a cluster sample.

The teacher could choose every third student, beginning in the front row and counting left to right. This is an example of a systematic sample.

Types of Samples

 In a **random sample,** each member of the population has an equally likely chance of being selected. The members of the sample are chosen independently of each other.

 A sample that is chosen so that it is easy for the researcher is called a **convenience sample.**

 For a **stratified random sample,** the population is divided into subgroups, so that each population member is in only one subgroup. Then individuals are chosen randomly from each subgroup.

 A sample that consists of items in a group, such as a neighborhood or a household, is called a **cluster sample.** The group may be chosen at random. However, this is not a random sample because the items in the group are not chosen independently of each other.

 A **systematic sample** is obtained using an ordered list of the population, then selecting members systematically from the list. The point at which to start in the list is usually chosen at random.

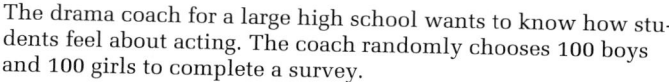
Sample 1

The drama coach for a large high school wants to know how students feel about acting. The coach randomly chooses 100 boys and 100 girls to complete a survey.

a. Classify the sample as *random, convenience, stratified random, cluster,* or *systematic.* Explain your choice.

b. Are any groups likely to be underrepresented? If so, which ones?

Sample Response

a. Stratified random; the subgroups are *boys* and *girls*, and students are chosen randomly from within each subgroup.

b. No group is likely to be underrepresented.

Random, stratified random, and systematic samples are generally preferred since they are usually representative of the population.

A sample that overrepresents or underrepresents part of the population is called **biased.** For example, the teacher discussed on page 16 could choose the four soccer players in the drama club. This is an example of a *biased cluster sample.*

1-3 Sampling Methods

Using Manipulatives

To better students' understanding of the five types of samples, you may wish to actually perform the sampling described on page 16 with your students.

Additional Sample

S1 The owner of a small business employing people in 5 departments of about equal size wants to know what her employees think about working more than 35 hours per week. She asks the people in the sales department what they think.

a. Classify the sample and explain your choice.

Cluster sample: only one subgroup of employees has been chosen.

b. Will the owner really know what her employees think? Why?

No; the sample is not representative of all employees.

Talk it Over

Questions 1–3 on page 18 lead students through the sampling process to help them understand when a sample is likely to reflect the population as a whole and when it is likely to be biased.

Mathematical Procedures

The type of sample usually preferred by people conducting surveys is a random sample because it is the one that is most representative of a population. It is also, however, the most challenging sample to construct because it must be free of bias. Random samples are usually generated by using a table of random numbers as given on Diagram Master 5 in the Explorations Lab Manual.

A random *process* is a chance physical process, such as a coin toss, where each head gives 1 and each tail gives 0. Random numbers use the digits from 0 to 9 and are generated by a random process. In other words, some physical process is used that can generate each of the digits 0 to 9 with a probability of $\frac{1}{10}$ occurring on each trial and with each trial being independent. When the random process is set in motion, thousands of digits are generated and written down in the order they occur. A table is then constructed using three digits.

Additional Sample

S2 Suppose you want to use a random number table to give a survey about listening to music to 35 juniors. You have a list of the names of the 190 juniors in your school. Describe how to use the list to obtain a random sample.

Assign to each student one of the three-digit numbers 001, 002, …, 190. Enter the random number table and examine successive three-digit numbers. Each three-digit number is either the number of a student in the list or it is not. If not, ignore the number and proceed to the next. If the random number belongs to a student, write it down. Proceed through the table until the numbers of 35 students have been written down.

▶ Now you are ready for: Exs. 1–10 on pp. 20–21

TECHNOLOGY NOTE

You can use the random number generator on a calculator to help you choose a random sample. The generator may be a second function on a scientific calculator. It may be on the MATH menu of a graphics calculator. ◀

Talk it Over

1. Kenesha Williams wants to estimate how many hours of sports each resident of her town watches on television each week. She surveyed people attending a baseball game in her town. What group is likely to be underrepresented in her sample?

2. A school district supervisor wants to know how students feel about cafeteria food. The supervisor randomly chooses a school in the district, then randomly chooses a classroom in the school, then gives a survey to the students in the classroom.

   a. What type of sample is this? Is it likely to be biased? Why or why not?

   b. Suppose the supervisor chooses 20 classrooms by this method. Is the overall sample likely to be biased? Why or why not?

3. A sports director sent an all-male team to represent the class at the Super Sports rally. The director said that this was a random sample. How is that possible?

Give an example of each type of sample.

4. systematic   5. convenience   6. cluster

Random Sampling

You can get only an estimate of how a population behaves or thinks by surveying a sample. For example, the exact percent of the population who watch a TV show could be found only by surveying every viewer.

One way you can get better and more representative results from a survey is to use larger random samples. Another way is to take a survey of several random samples rather than just one.

You do not have to pull names out of a box to select a random sample. When the population is large, it is easier to use other methods.

Sample 2

Suppose you want to give a survey about bicycle riding to 40 sophomores. You have a list of the names of the 200 sophomores in your school. Describe how to use the list to obtain a random sample.

Unit 1 Sampling and Reasoning

Answers to Talk it Over

1. people in town who watch sports on TV but who did not attend the game or people who neither watch sports on TV nor attended the game.

2. a. stratified random sample or cluster sample; Yes. Only one school and one classroom are represented, not all students from all grades in all schools.

   b. It would be better and less likely to be biased.

   There is the underlying assumption that all the food in all the buildings is identical. The method offers a better cross-section of the population. However, the use of the cafeteria must be equally distributed among the entire student population of the district.

3. The school or the class may be all male or the sports director could have chosen all males by chance.

4–6. Answers may vary. Examples are given.

4. Make a list of the social security numbers of all the members of the population, and then select every 50th number.

Number the sophomores from 1 to 200.

Generate random numbers from 1 to 200, and give the survey to the students whose numbers you generate.

Method ❶ Use a calculator.

Most scientific and graphics calculators will produce a random number between 0 and 1.

➤ Produce a random number on a calculator.

➤ Multiply the number by 201 to get a number between 0 and 201.

➤ Use the integer part of the number, which will be a number from 1 to 200 if you ignore values less than 1.

➤ Give the survey to the student whose number you have generated.

➤ Repeat this process until 40 students are chosen. Ignore duplicates.

Method ❷ Use a physical model.

You could use a random number table, but a telephone book provides a good approximation of a list of random numbers if you ignore the exchanges (the first three digits).

➤ Begin as described at the left.

➤ Then give the survey to the student whose number you have chosen. Ignore numbers over 200.

➤ Continue down the column, and into the next if necessary, until 40 students are chosen. Ignore duplicates.

Choose a position on a page, such as the third number from the top in a middle column.

Consider the last three digits as a number.

Look Back ◀

Do you think a random sample from your class could contain only girls? Do you think that this sample would represent your class as a whole? Explain why or why not.

········➤ **Now you are ready for:**
: **Exs. 11–28 on pp. 21–22**

1-3 Sampling Methods

Using Technology

Note: In this and subsequent Using Technology notes, "TI-83" refers to both the TI-83 and the TI-83 Plus unless the TI-83 Plus is explicitly mentioned.

If you press MATH ▶ on the TI-82 or TI-83, you will see a menu of special functions. Item 2 on the TI-82 and item 3 on the TI-83 is iPart, which gives the integer part of any decimal that you enter. For example, if you enter iPart 27.043 on the TI-82 or iPart (27.043) on the TI-83 and press ENTER, the calculator displays the result 27, the integer part of 27.043.

You can use iPart and the TABLE feature to generate a table of numbers such as those that are generated one by one by the procedure of Sample 2, Method 1. Suggestions for enhancing mathematics learning by using graphing technology are given on page T34 in the front of this Teacher's Edition.

Students can also use the random-number feature of the *Probability Constructor* software to obtain a random sample for Sample 2.

Application

In real-world applications that use random samples, usually involving hundreds or thousands of people, the use of physical objects, such as a telephone book, coins, cards, thrown dice, or drawing slips of paper, to create the sample is not practical. Random numbers provide a basis for mathematical experiments to simulate physical ones. There are published tables of random numbers that have as many as 1,000,000 digits.

Look Back

You may wish to have students suggest some ways to select a random sample from their class. Then use the methods suggested to select a few samples to see how they turn out.

Answers to Talk it Over ·····

5. Ask the first 20 people exiting a movie theater what they thought of the movie.

6. Ask the people in a corner of a restaurant to evaluate the food they ate for their meal.

Answers to Look Back ········

Answers may vary. An example is given. Even if the class is not all girls, it would be possible to choose at random and still choose all girls. Whether it represents the class as a whole might depend on what questions are asked or what characteristics of the students are under consideration.

APPLYING

Suggested Assignment

Day 1

Standard 1–10

Extended 1–10

Day 2

Standard 11–15, 18–20, 22–28

Extended 11–15, 17–20, 22–28

Integrating the Strands

Algebra Exs. 18–20, 24–26

Statistics and Probability Exs. 1–23, 27, 28

Logic and Language Exs. 1, 9, 11–15, 22

Communication: Reading and Writing

Students may make errors in classifying samples because the distinctions involved are not always obvious. Refer students to the descriptions given on pages 16 and 17 to help them remember how samples are classified and what the key differences among them are.

Students Acquiring English

The excerpt from *The Crystal Desert* will be challenging for most second-language learners. Suggest that they work with a peer tutor to read the excerpt together and then discuss the questions that appear below it.

Answers to
Exercises and Problems

1. **a.** Answers may vary. Examples: random, convenience, stratified random, cluster, systematic

   b. Descriptions may vary. An example is given. All of the methods involve choosing some smaller group to represent a larger group. The methods vary in how the members of the sample are related. The members may not be connected in any way or they may be connected by inclination or location, for example.

2. **a.** systematic

1-3 Exercises and Problems

1. **a.** **Reading** Name three different sampling methods.

   b. **Writing** Describe how the methods you listed in part (a) are alike. How are they different?

For each situation:

a. Classify each sample as *random, convenience, stratified random, cluster,* or *systematic*. **Explain your choice.**

b. Tell which groups, if any, are likely to be underrepresented.

2. For a sample of households, an environmental group dials the first number on every tenth page of the white pages in the telephone book.

3. A general interest magazine conducts a poll that asks teen readers questions about dating.

4. A college professor selects 100 high school students in a summer mathematics and science workshop as the sample for a study about high school students.

5. **Open-ended** A group of 30 students from your school is randomly selected to discuss future school events, such as dances. Eight of the students say they do not want to attend and are dropped from the sample.

connection to LITERATURE

In *The Crystal Desert*, David Campbell describes an underwater diving project in Antarctica. For the project he collected small shellfish called *amphipods*.

> Today I will descend to about fifteen meters to collect the tiny amphipods that skitter over the ocean floor and hide beneath the boulders that have been dropped by the icebergs passing overhead. … I want representative samples of both diseased and healthy animals. A baited trap would attract only those amphipods with strong appetites, which are necessarily the healthy ones. A trawl net or bottom grabber would favor the slow and sick animals that couldn't escape, biasing the sample toward the unhealthy ones. So I use a simple hand-held net, purchased in a tropical fish store in New York.

6. What types of samples does David Campbell want to avoid?

7. How do you think David Campbell will proceed with the net to get a representative sample?

8. Do you think that David Campbell will be able to predict the percent of the amphipod population that is healthy from his sample?

---

b. Those households where there is no telephone or those with unlisted or unpublished numbers will likely be underrepresented because they will not be considered.

3. **a.** cluster

   b. teenagers who do not read the magazine

4. **a.** convenience

   b. students who are less interested in math or science than the given group; If the 100 students are all from one school or one ethnic, religious, racial, or socio-economic group, all those not in that group would be underrepresented.

5. **a.** stratified random

   b. Students who do not attend school events are underrepresented

6. samples that are biased either toward healthy animals or toward diseased animals

7. Answers may vary. An example is given. He may choose several locations, collect samples from each, and compare the number of healthy amphipods to the total number.

9. **Writing** Suppose you surveyed the first 50 students who entered the school cafeteria at lunch. Would that sample be representative of all the people who use the cafeteria? Explain why or why not.

10. Which is more likely to give accurate results, a random sample of 50 students chosen from a class of 300, or a random sample of 50 students chosen from a class of 100? Why?

Use a glossary or dictionary as a population. Select 13 words to obtain each of these types of samples. Explain your method.

11. cluster sample

12. convenience sample

13. systematic sample

14. stratified random sample

15. Use a glossary as a population. Tell how you could select a random sample of 13 words from the glossary.

16. **Research** Use the stock market report in a daily newspaper. Select a random sample of 30 stocks.

17. Use the phone extensions shown or select 20 extensions randomly from a telephone book.

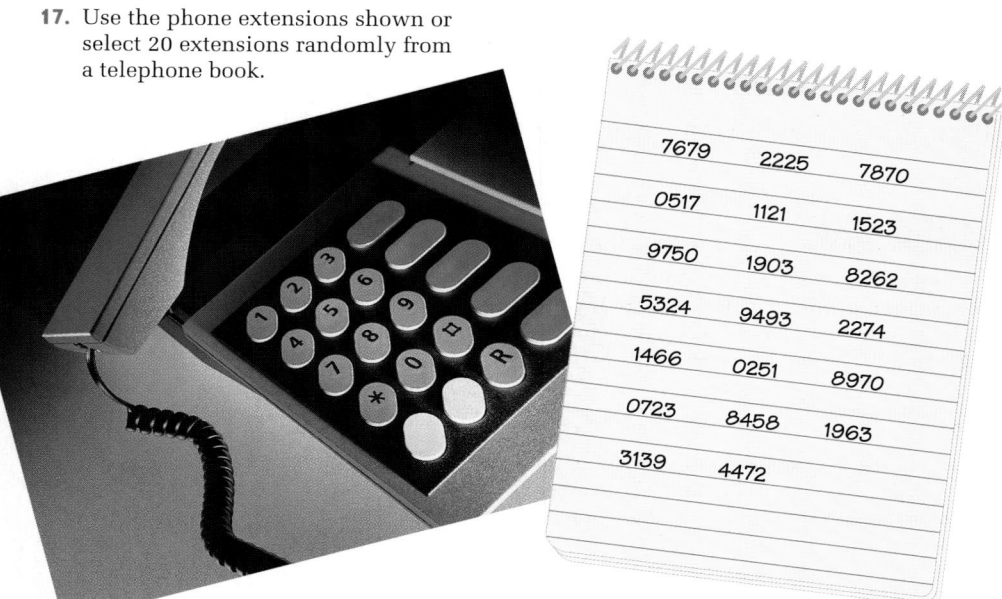

7679	2225	7870
0517	1121	1523
9750	1903	8262
5324	9493	2274
1466	0251	8970
0723	8458	1963
3139	4472	

a. Change each extension into an ordered pair. For example, the extension 4460 becomes the ordered pair (44, 60).

b. Graph the ordered pairs on a scatter plot.

c. Describe the scatter plot. Does it show a *positive correlation*, a *negative correlation*, or *no correlation*? Explain what type of correlation, if any, you would expect to see in the scatter plot.

d. Describe how you would expect the graph of a random sample of ordered pairs to look.

> **Student Resources Toolbox**
> **p. 632** *Data Displays and Measures*

Research

If possible, have several newspapers available in the classroom for use with Ex. 16. Students may not recognize the names of companies as they are listed in the stock market report. Ask them to list just the letters given in the paper. You may want to direct their attention to a particular exchange, for example, the NYSE, the NASDAQ, or the AMEX.

Using Technology

Students can use the random-number feature of the *Probability Constructor* software to obtain random samples for Exs. 16 and 17.

Visual Thinking

Ex. 17 provides an excellent opportunity for students to think about a random sample in visual terms as a plot of points having no correlation. This activity involves the visual skills of *identification* and *interpretation*.

Assessment: Group Activity

For Ex. 17, students should work in groups and compare the results of their scatter plots. By examining several scatter plots, they should conclude as a group that there is no correlation.

14. Use the alphabet to make 13 groups of two letters each by combining letters next to each other. Thus, A and B are one group, C and D are another group, E and F a third, and so on. Then randomly select a word from each group.

15. Answers may vary. An example is given. Assign each word in the glossary a number from 1 to n, where n is the number of words. Print each number on a piece of paper, mix the papers together in a bowl, and draw out 13 of them. Use the corresponding words in your sample.

16. Answers may vary.

17. See answers in back of book.

Answers to Exercises and Problems

8. Answers may vary. An example is given. Yes, he can probably make a reasonable prediction.

9. Answers may vary. An example is given. The sample is a convenience sample. Whether the sample is a random sample depends on how the lunch schedule is arranged at the school. The first 50 students may all be the same age or may all be in the same class. Also, teachers may also use the cafeteria and they would not be represented.

10. Since a greater part of the group is represented, the random sample of 50 chosen from a class of 100 would probably give more accurate results.

11–14. For each type of sample, an example of a method for choosing the sample from a 250-word glossary is described.

11. Open to a page. Choose the first 13 words on the page.

12. Choose the first 13 words on the first page.

13. Choose every tenth word.

Assessment: Portfolio

For Ex. 22, those students who respond with well-written and mathematically correct descriptions of a method to find a random sample may wish to include this work in their portfolio.

Working on the Unit Project

For Ex. 28, one student in each group should be appointed to summarize the choices and the reasons for them.

For Exercises 18–20, use the numbers −5, −4, −3, −2, −1, 0, 1, 2, 3, 4, and 5 as the population for x.

18. **a.** Solve $3x - 1 = x + 5$.

   b. Suppose you randomly choose a number from the population. What is the probability that it is a solution of the equation in part (a)?

19. **a.** Solve $x^2 = 1$.

   b. Suppose you randomly choose a number from the population. What is the probability that it is a solution of the equation in part (a)?

20. **a.** Solve $3x - 5 \geq -8$.

   b. Suppose you randomly choose a number from the population. What is the probability that it is a solution of the inequality in part (a)?

21. **Research** Find out how juries are selected in your area. Are any random sampling techniques used? Is a jury selected from the entire population, or are some groups not included?

Ongoing ASSESSMENT

22. **Writing** Describe a method that you could use to find a random sample of 25 books from your school library.

Review PREVIEW

23. Suppose that one eighth of all Americans live below the poverty level. Use simulation to answer this question: If you could choose 50 Americans at random, how many would likely be below the poverty level? Describe your method. *(Section 1-2)*

Simplify. *(Toolbox Skill 10)*

24. $(-6m)(12m)$

25. $(5w)(-2x)(3y)$

26. $9x - 2(x + 3)$

27. A recent poll of 200 people from a town of 10,000 found that 140 people approve of the mayor's performance. The actual results could be different by up to 3% in either direction. Estimate the interval for the number of people in the town who approve of the mayor's performance. *(Section 1-1)*

Working on the Unit Project

28. Consider the survey that you wrote for Exercise 26 in Section 1-1. Choose the sample size and the type of sample that you would like to use. Explain your choices.

Answers to Exercises and Problems

18. **a.** 3

   b. $\frac{1}{11} \approx 0.09$

19. **a.** −1, 1

   b. $\frac{2}{11} \approx 0.18$

20. **a.** −1, 0, 1, 2, 3, 4, 5, or $x \geq -1$

   b. $\frac{7}{11} \approx 0.64$

21. Answers may vary.

22. Answers may vary. An example is given. Find out how many books are in your library and assign a number to each book. Use a calculator or telephone directory to generate a random selection of numbers.

23. Answers may vary. An example is given. Make a spinner divided into 8 sections. Shade one section for "below poverty level" and leave the other sections unshaded. Spin 50 times to approximate about 6 people below the poverty level.

24. $-72m^2$

25. $-30wxy$

26. $7x - 6$

27. between 6700 and 7300 people

28. Answers may vary. Choose a manageable sample size, such as 25–50 people. The type of sample may vary but should be unbiased.

Cautions in Using Statistics

In Line
WITH THE FACTS

Survey:
Rights of Citizens

Do you think that in-line skaters should be able to move freely throughout the city?

Survey:
High-Speed Dangers

Should in-line skaters be allowed to endanger the safety of pedestrians by skating on sidewalks?

Talk it Over

1. Compare the two survey questions. How are they alike? How are they different?

2. Suppose the two questions were given to two different unbiased samples of people. What results would you expect?

3. Create another version of this question. What do you think the response would be?

4. How could the question be written to avoid influencing the results?

1-4 Cautions in Using Statistics   23

PLANNING

Objectives and Strands
See pages 1A and 1B.

Spiral Learning
See page 1B.

Materials List
➤ Graph paper

Recommended Pacing
Section 1-4 is a one-day lesson.

Extra Practice
See pages 614–615.

Warm-Up Exercises
Warm-Up Transparency 1-4

Support Materials
➤ Practice 4
➤ Enrichment 4 in the Activity Bank
➤ Study Guide 1-4
➤ Problem Set 1
➤ Diagram Master 1 in the Explorations Lab Manual
➤ McDougal Littell Mathpack software: *Stats!*
➤ *Stats!* Activity Book: Activities 1–7
➤ Quiz 1-4
➤ Test 1

Answers to Talk it Over

1–4. Answers may vary. Examples are given.

1. Both ask the same question. Both have an apparent built-in bias. The first raises the issue of personal civil rights, which might influence a positive response. The second raises the issue of public safety in a negative manner, perhaps influencing a negative response.

2. Because of the issues raised in the answer to question 1, more "yes" answers might be expected to the first survey, more "no" answers to the second.

3. Answers may vary.

4. The survey should raise no issues other than the question at hand: "Should the city permit in-line skating on the sidewalk?"

Talk it Over

Questions 1–3 help students to understand that the way in which a question is worded can bias the answers, and thus influence the outcome of a survey. For question 4, students have to write the question in a way that is free of bias. This kind of task requires some careful thinking and is not always easy to do.

Application

When writing survey questions, two major types of errors need to be avoided: bias and lack of precision. Bias has been addressed in Talk it Over questions 1–4. Lack of precision is addressed in questions 5 and 6.

Talk it Over

Questions 5 and 6 highlight the differences between vague meaning words such as *some* and *not very many* and specific use of numbers. Without using numbers, it is impossible to find the mean or median of a set of data because these statistics are defined by using mathematical operations.

Teaching Tip

Students should be able to understand why the first two *Cautions in Using Statistics* are important based upon what they have already learned. The other three will become more meaningful to students as they do the Samples and the Exercises and Problems.

Using Technology

You may wish to assign Activities 1–7 in the *Stats! Activity Book* to introduce students to the *Stats!* software and review basic concepts and skills of data analysis.

When you give a survey, asking unbiased questions is as important as choosing an unbiased sample. Even multiple-choice questions can be interpreted in different ways.

Talk it Over

Use the survey questions below.

5. Which set of choices is less precise? Why?

6. a. Could you find the mode of the answers to the question on the left? the mean? the median?

   b. Could you find the mode of the answers to the question on the right? the mean? the median?

> How many days per week should in-line skaters be allowed to skate on the street?
>
> a) every day
> b) some days
> c) not very many days
> d) no days

> How many days per week should in-line skaters be allowed to skate on the street?
>
> a) zero   e) four
> b) one   f) five
> c) two   g) six
> d) three   h) seven

CAUTIONS IN USING STATISTICS

These are some important factors to consider about surveys:

➤ how the questions are worded
➤ how the survey is distributed
➤ how the responses are collected
➤ how the results are presented
➤ how the results are interpreted

Answers to Talk it Over

5. The choices in the box on the left are less precise. The phrases "some" and "not very many" have no exact meaning.

6. a. Yes; No; No.

   b. Yes; Yes; Yes.

Sample 1

The managing editor of a fashion magazine wants to find out what parts of the magazine people like to read. The editor sends a survey to 800 subscribers. Three weeks later, 68 surveys have been returned.

Writing Describe some problems with this method of surveying.

Sample Response

By using only the subscribers as the population, the director will not find out what people who buy the magazine in stores think. Also, the sample contains only people who were interested enough to return the surveys, so people who have strong opinions or who have more time to read may be overrepresented.

Sample 2

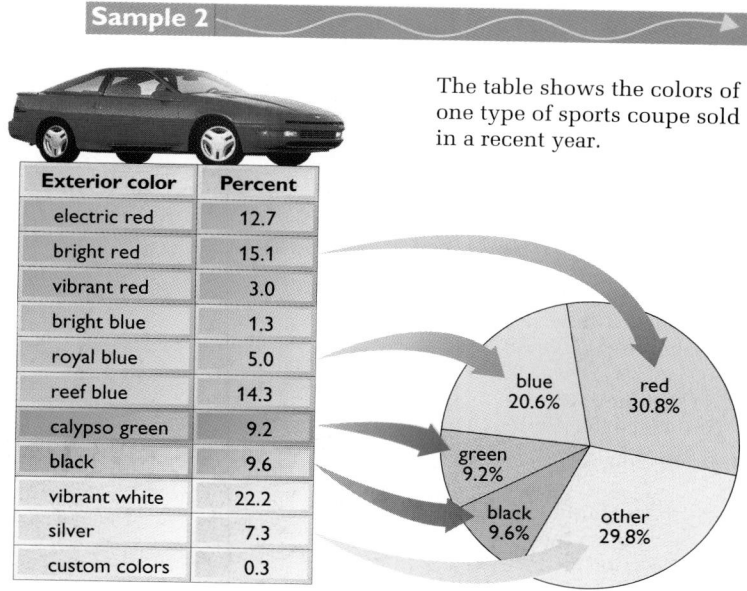

The table shows the colors of one type of sports coupe sold in a recent year.

Exterior color	Percent
electric red	12.7
bright red	15.1
vibrant red	3.0
bright blue	1.3
royal blue	5.0
reef blue	14.3
calypso green	9.2
black	9.6
vibrant white	22.2
silver	7.3
custom colors	0.3

The circle graph was used in a report of the data. Do you think that the graph presents a misleading picture of the data? Why or why not?

Sample Response

Yes. The graph leads you to think that blue may be the second most popular color of this model. The category called "Other" hides information that may give a different impression of the data.

1-4 Cautions in Using Statistics

Additional Samples

S1 An automobile manufacturer wants to find out from people who bought one of their new cars during the past year what they think about the quality of the car. They send a survey to every person who has bought the car during the past 12 months, including a self-addressed stamped envelope to return the survey. In the survey, they specify that only the principal driver of a family car should complete the survey. Four weeks later, 71% of the surveys have been returned. Describe your thoughts about this survey.

By using only those people who have bought the car, the manufacturer has distributed the survey to the right people. The return envelope will encourage people to return the survey. The 71% return rate indicates that the results will be reliable as does the fact that it is the principal driver who responds.

S2 Ask students to use the data for Sample 2 to suggest a type of graph that would present an accurate picture of the data.

a bar graph whose bars represent red, blue, green, black, white, silver, and other; The bars could be arranged in descending order of sales from left to right.

25

Mathematical Procedures

In any use of statistics, a person is concerned with the (1) collection of data, (2) its organization, (3) its analysis and interpretation, and (4) its presentation. The way in which data are presented is usually determined by the interpretation given to the data. In Sample 2, the analysis and interpretation of the data was faulty, leading to a poorly designed circle graph that gave an incorrect impression of the data.

Look Back

In considering these questions and providing three more, students need to keep in mind that the results of a survey should be free of bias, representative of the population, clear and precise, and interpreted and presented accurately. Without adhering strictly to these guidelines, survey results will often produce misleading information. ....●

APPLYING

Suggested Assignment

Standard 1–14, 16–26

Extended 1–14, 16–26

Integrating the Strands

Algebra Exs. 14, 22, 23

Geometry Exs. 19–21

Statistics and Probability Exs. 1–18, 24–26

Look Back ◄────

When you use data from a survey, you need to consider what might have influenced the results. Here are some questions to ask.

➤ How was the sample chosen?

➤ What was the population?

➤ What was the sample size?

In your own words, what are three more questions that you might have about a survey?

1-4 Exercises and Problems

For Exercises 1–6, use this survey.

1. Decide whether each question is worded so that it will not influence the response.

2. Could you find the median of the answers to the first question? to any of the questions?

3. Write at least four more questions that will help you find out if students are satisfied with your school. Make sure that your questions are worded so that they will not influence the results.

4. **a.** Decide how to choose a sample of people in your school and how you will give them the survey. Describe the method you chose.

   b. Research If possible, give the survey to the sample of people you have chosen.

5. What biases might be reflected in the results of the survey?

6. Suppose you give the survey during a final exam week. Explain how this might influence the results.

> *School Satisfaction Survey*
> (Please circle the appropriate response.)
>
> 1) How long have you been enrolled in this school district?
>   *a)* since I started school
>   *c)* 2–3 years
>   *b)* This is my first year.
>   *d)* 4 or more years
>
> 2) How many times have you been tardy to your classes this week?
>   *a)* 0
>   *c)* 2–3
>   *b)* 1
>   *d)* 4 or more
>
> 3) How many hours did you spend on homework during the last week?
>   *a)* less than 1
>   *c)* between 2 and 3
>   *b)* from 1 to 2
>   *d)* 3 or more
>
> 4) How satisfied are you with the choices of classes available to you?
>   *a)* All the classes I want are available.
>   *b)* Most of the time I am satisfied with the classes available.
>   *c)* There are many classes I would like to take, but cannot get into.
>   *d)* There are not enough _____ classes.
>   (Write the type of class in the blank.)

Unit 1 Sampling and Reasoning

Answers to Look Back

Answers may vary. Examples are given. Was each question asked in a way that would not influence the answer? Were the possible answers clear and precise? How were the results displayed? Were the displays slanted in any way to produce a desired survey result?

Answers to Exercises and Problems

1. Answers may vary. It is reasonable to say that none of the questions is worded in such a way as to influence a response.

2. No; No.

3–6. Answers may vary. Examples are given.

3. Other questions might cover availability of sports programs, clubs, social activities, school facilities, availability and quality of food services, grading practices, or interaction between students and teachers. Questions: (5) How do you feel about the time allowed for each class period? (a) too long (b) never enough time (c) just right (d) occasionally not enough time (6) How do you feel about school lunches? (a) would like more variety of foods (b) usually can find something I like (c) always find something I like (d) never eat school lunches (7) How many extracurricular activities do you participate in? (a) 0 (b) 1 (c) 2 (d) 3 or more (8) How many sports activities do you participate in? (a) 0 (b) 1 (c) 2 (d) 3 or more

7. **Reading** Describe how the wording of a survey question can lead to a biased sample. Give an example.

8. **Open-ended** Do you think it matters whether a survey is given in person, over the phone, or in written form? Which kind of survey would you prefer to take? Which kind of survey would you prefer to give? Explain.

Writing For Exercises 9–12, describe some problems with each method of surveying. Then write one question that you would like to ask the people who gave the survey.

9. **Market Research** A marketing firm selects a sample for a survey on toothpaste by calling numbers randomly chosen from a telephone book. People who do not want to participate are listed as "no opinion."

10. A teen magazine conducts a survey about the presidential candidates for the next election. The Republican and Democratic candidates are listed along with several popular singers and actors. More than 25,000 people respond to the survey.

11. Television rating sheets are sent to 10,000 viewers four times a year. At the end of a ten-week period, about 30-50% of the viewing diaries are returned and the results are studied.

12. A radio station surveys its audience by asking people to call the station between 9 A.M. and noon on a weekday.

13. **Basketball** The table shows the salaries of the players on a professional basketball team. Do you think that the graph presents a misleading picture of the data? Why or why not?

Annual Salaries (thousands of dollars)		
A	**B**	**C**
1	302	1289	2531
2	302	1595	2777
3	485	1980	4875
4	550	2000	5290
5	975		8355
6			9900

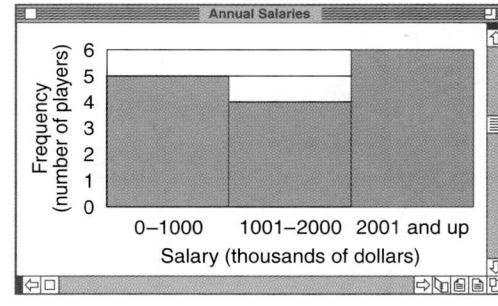

1-4 Cautions in Using Statistics

27

Answers to Exercises and Problems

4. **a.** Choose a sample size. Suppose there are 1000 students in the school and you want to survey 200 of them. Obtain an alphabetical enrollment list if possible. Select every fifth person on the list.

 b. Results may vary.

5. The sample may be biased (that is, it was not random-ly selected). Those interpreting the results may decide to ignore input from those in the sample who are in their first year at the school. The answers to Question 4 might be grouped into "satisfied" (those who selected "a") and "dissatisfied" (those who selected any other choice).

6. Students are apt to feel more pressure during final exam week, which might decrease their satisfaction in general with courses, teachers, facilities, and so on.

7. Answers may vary. An example is given. If the question suggests a response conveying dissatisfaction, you may be more likely to get that response. For

Reasoning

Ex. 8 focuses on having students consider how responses to a survey can be collected, which is one of the cautions listed in the box on page 24. As they formulate their answers to this question, students will come to have a better understanding of this caution.

Communication: Writing

As students respond to Exs. 9–12, they should consider which factors about surveys, given on page 24, are being violated. This approach will help students to focus upon the key ideas that lead to the problems with Exs. 9–12.

example, "Do you think the school requires too much homework?" would be biased.

8. Answers may vary. Examples are given. Yes. People may be less open in giving answers face-to-face than over the phone or in writing. It might be easier to misinterpret answers given orally than in writing. If a survey involves forms that must be returned, it may be difficult to get people to participate.

9–13. Answers may vary. Examples are given.

9. People who choose not to participate may have strong positive or negative opinions. Why not eliminate those choosing not to respond from the sample, rather than assigning them a response they did not make? How large a group was surveyed?

10. Most teen magazines aim at teenagers younger than 18, so the results would not be meaningful other than as opinion. The inclusion of singers and actors implies this is not a serious survey in any case. Why were the non-candidates included? What did you intend the results to show?

11. The sample is fairly small, considering results from at most 5000 viewers in a nation of 250 million people, most of whom watch television at some time. How were the 10,000 people selected? What sort of information is collected in the diaries and how is it used?

Answers continued on next page.

27

14. Sam has to graph the equation $y = x^2$ for his homework. He makes this table and draws this graph.

   a. Explain why Sam's graph is not accurate.

   b. Describe Sam's mistake in terms of what you know about sampling.

x	y
-1	1
0	0
1	1

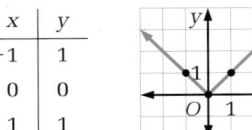

15. **Research** Find an example of a study whose results could be interpreted in more than one way. Describe possible biases or sampling errors in the study. Give an example of a different conclusion that could be drawn from the study.

16. The table below shows the number of bicycles produced in eight countries.

   a. Create a graph that gives a misleading picture of the data.

   b. Explain how your graph is misleading.

   c. **Research** Find the population of each country in the table in 1998. How many bicycles did each country produce per person?

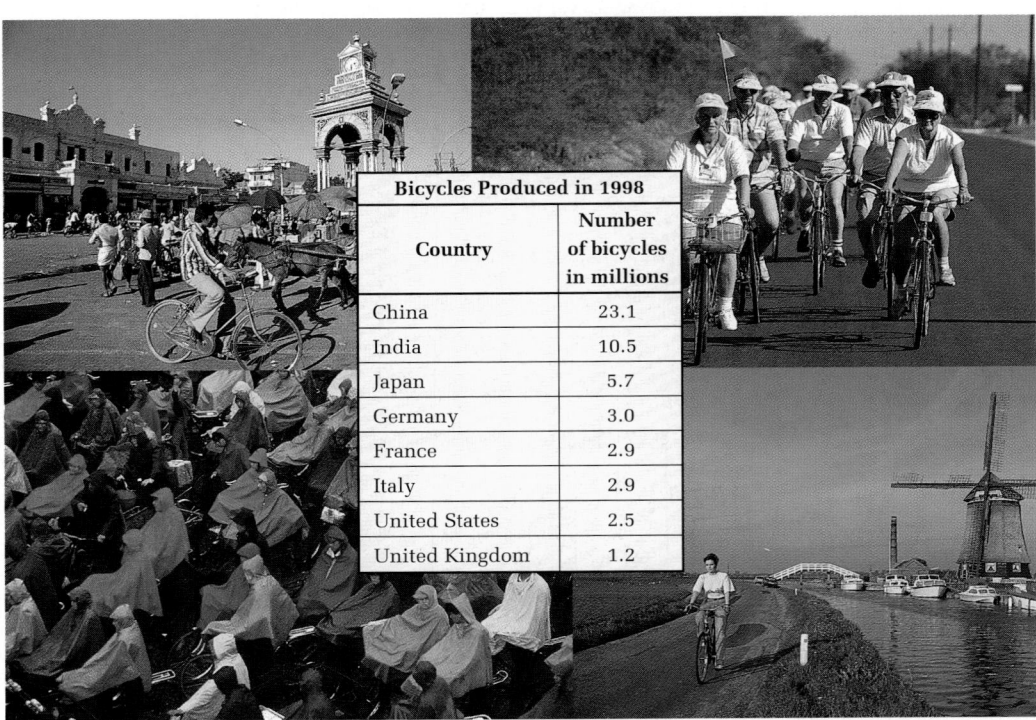

Bicycles Produced in 1998	
Country	Number of bicycles in millions
China	23.1
India	10.5
Japan	5.7
Germany	3.0
France	2.9
Italy	2.9
United States	2.5
United Kingdom	1.2

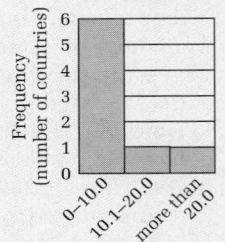

28   **Unit 1** Sampling and Reasoning

Answers to Exercises and Problems

12. Some listeners might be willing to call in but not be able to call during that time period. Why did you choose that time period? Did you intend to influence the outcome by limiting the response?

13. The graph does not give an accurate picture of team salaries. Three of the salaries under $1,000,000 are actually under $500,000. The graph would give a truer picture if the intervals were $0–$500,000, $500,001–$1,000,000, and so on.

14. a. Sam's graph is not accurate because, for example, it shows the point (2, 2) on the graph and $2^2 \neq 2$.

   b. Based on a small sample, Sam made incorrect assumptions about the population as a whole.

15. Answers may vary.

16. Answers may vary. Examples are given.

16. a.
Bicycles Produced in Selected Countries

Frequency (number of countries) vs. Number of bicycles produced (millions)

Categories: 0–10.0, 10.1–20.0, more than 20.0

   b. Of the six countries listed as having produced 0–10 million bicycles, five produced fewer than 3 million. The categories make the data seem less diverse than they actually are.

   c. Check populations and averages.

17. **Group Activity** Work with another student.

a. Each person should write a four-question survey on music likes and dislikes. You may want to look at music magazines for ideas. Then write a short description of how you could give the survey to a sample of students in your school.

b. Exchange surveys and descriptions and read each other's work. Discuss any factors that may influence the results of the survey.

c. Use your surveys to create eight questions that will not influence the results of the survey. Decide how you can give the survey to the sample.

d. If possible, give the survey to the sample and present the results in a table or graph.

e. After reviewing the results, describe what you would change in your questions or method.

Review **PREVIEW**

18. To give a survey to a grocery store's customers, the store manager randomly chooses one section of one aisle of the store and asks each person who buys something in that section to complete the survey. What type of sampling is this? *(Section 1-3)*

Find the missing length in each right triangle. *(Toolbox Skill 31)*

19.
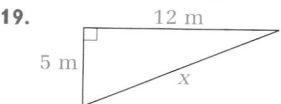
12 m
5 m
x

20.
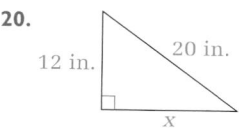
20 in.
12 in.
x

21.
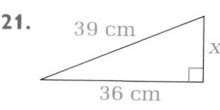
39 cm
x
36 cm

Decide which of the given numbers are solutions of each inequality.
(Toolbox Skill 14)

22. $12x + 4 \geq 10$; 0.25, 0.5, 1.75

23. $-3y - 14 < 4$; $-7, -6, 0$

Working on the Unit Project

24. Consider the survey that you wrote for Exercise 26 in Section 1-1. Might any of the questions you wrote influence the results of the survey? If so, rewrite the questions.

25. Consider the sample size and the type of sample that you chose for Exercise 28 in Section 1-3. Do you think your sample will give an accurate representation of the student population? If not, choose a larger or better type of sample.

26. Select the students to include in your sample. Give them your survey.

1-4 Cautions in Using Statistics

29

Assessment: Performance Task

For Ex. 16, students can also share their graphs with others, who can then try to explain why the graphs are misleading.

Working on the Unit Project

If a surveyor has been chosen by the group at the beginning of the project, he or she should conduct the survey.

Practice 4 For use with Section 1-4

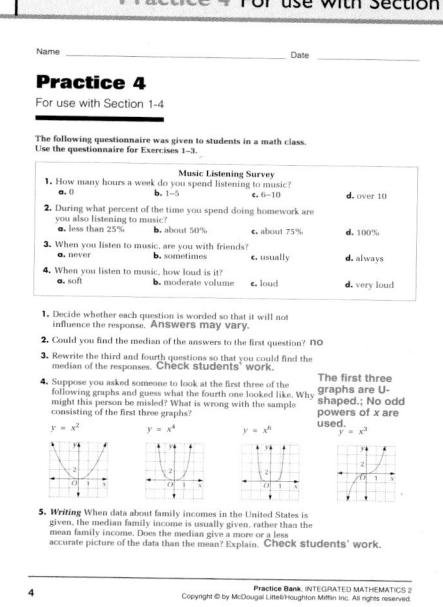

Answers to Exercises and Problems

17. **a–e.** Surveys and results may vary.

18. a cluster sample

19. 13 m

20. 16 in.

21. 15 cm

22. 0.5; 1.75

23. 0

24. Answers may vary. An example is given. A question such as, "Would you be willing to recycle even if you had to carry materials to a recycling center?" might make a person think, "That sounds like a lot of work. I would rather have materials collected."

25. Answers may vary.

26. Results may vary.

Unit 1 CHECKPOINT

1. **Writing** Suppose you want to convince your cafeteria manager to add a certain food to the cafeteria menu. How could you use a survey to convince the manager? What questions might be on the survey? Describe a sampling technique you could use.

2. At Huron High School, 45 of 180 students chosen at random play sports. There are 760 students in the entire school. Estimate the total number of students who play sports.   **1-1**

3. In a recent election, two thirds of the voters were at least 60 years old. Describe two different ways to simulate the percent of voters under 60.   **1-2**

For Exercises 4 and 5, classify the sample selected in each situation as *random, convenience, stratified random, cluster,* or *systematic*.   **1-3**

4. To win a door prize at a dance, each of the 170 students attending the dance writes his or her name on a piece of paper. The pieces are put in a box, mixed, and one name is drawn.

5. The owner of a sandwich shop studies sales of food sold between 1 P.M. and 2 P.M. and food sold between 6 P.M. and 7 P.M.

6. Before ordering new cake pans, the owner of a bakery surveys customers to find out whether circular or rectangular cakes are preferred at weddings. Here are two questions on the survey.   **1-4**

Which shape is more appealing?	Which shape tastes better?
a) circular, because it is traditional	a) circular, because each piece will have more frosting
b) rectangular, because the decorators can be more creative	b) rectangular, because some pieces will have extra frosting

 a. Explain why the questions are biased.

 b. Rewrite each question so it is not biased.

Answers to Checkpoint

1. Answers may vary. An example is given. A random sample chosen from the student population could be surveyed. Questions might include, "How often do you eat in the cafeteria? Would you buy this food if it were offered? Would having this food available make you more likely to use the cafeteria?"

2. about 190 students

3. Answers may vary. Examples are given. Use a spinner with $\frac{2}{3}$ representing "at least 60" and $\frac{1}{3}$ representing "under 60." Use a die. If 1 or 2 is rolled, let that represent "under 60." If 3, 4, 5, or 6 is rolled, let that represent "at least 60."

4. random

5. cluster

6. a. Both parts of both questions give information that may influence the answers.

 b. Which shape is more appealing? (a) circular (b) rectangular; Which shape tastes better? (a) circular (b) rectangular

Inductive Reasoning

Focus

Apply inductive reasoning to many situations. Learn that inductive reasoning does not always lead to a good conclusion.

Base It On
EXPERIENCE

Rosario looked in the mirror one morning and noticed a rash on her face. It occurred to her that she might be allergic to a new facial soap she had used the night before, but then she noticed the rash on her legs as well. She decided to go see her doctor.

BY THE WAY...

In 1990, Dr. Antonia Novello became the first woman and the first Hispanic to hold the position of Surgeon General. She chose a career in medicine after struggling with a serious health problem throughout her childhood and into her early twenties.

Dr. Gutierrez asked Rosario some questions, looked at her rash, and decided that Rosario was allergic to penicillin. Dr. Gutierrez made observations and used past experience to reach this diagnosis.

In mathematics, a guess based on past experience is called a **conjecture.** When you make a conjecture based on several observations, you are using **inductive reasoning.**

Inductive reasoning is used in other careers besides medicine. A mechanic could use inductive reasoning when repairing cars. A store owner uses inductive reasoning when deciding what to reorder based on what has sold well in the past.

Inductive reasoning is often used to solve problems in mathematics.

31

Objectives and Strands
See pages 1A and 1B.

Spiral Learning
See page 1B.

Materials List
➤ Protractor
➤ Graphics calculator, graphing software, or graph paper
➤ Rubber gloves
➤ Trash bag

Recommended Pacing
Section 1-5 is a one-day lesson.

Toolbox References
Toolbox Skill 20: Making a Table of Values to Graph

Extra Practice
See pages 614–615.

Warm-Up Exercises
Warm-Up Transparency 1-5

Support Materials
➤ Practice 5
➤ Enrichment 5 in the Activity Bank
➤ Study Guide 1-5
➤ Problem Set 2
➤ Diagram Master 2 in the Explorations Lab Manual
➤ McDougal Littell Mathpack software: *Function Investigator*
➤ Quiz 1-5
➤ Alternative Assessment 4

Additional Sample

S1 Do you think that the product of an odd number and an even number is odd or even? Explain your reasoning.

Use inductive reasoning.

Odd	Even	Product
3	2	6
5	4	20
7	6	42
9	8	72
13	12	156
31	50	1550

The product is always even.
Conjecture: I tried many pairs of odd and even numbers and the product was never odd. I think the product of an odd number and an even number is always even.

Reasoning

Students need to understand that in Sample 1, even though many more pairs of numbers could be checked (and the sum will always be even), there will always be many times more pairs that have not been checked. If hundreds or thousands or millions of pairs are checked, the pattern of always getting an even sum seems to lend overwhelming support to the truth of the conjecture. However, because of the unlimited number of odd numbers, no one can say with absolute certainty that some pair might show up that is not even. Thus, inductive reasoning can never establish the truth of a conjecture that involves an infinite set of mathematical objects such as numbers or geometric figures.

Talk it Over

Question 1 points out the critical fact that inductive reasoning cannot show that the sum of two odd numbers is always even because it is impossible to check all possible pairs of odd numbers.

Sample 1

Writing Do you think the sum of any two odd numbers is even or odd? Explain your reasoning.

Sample Response

Problem Solving Strategy: Use inductive reasoning.

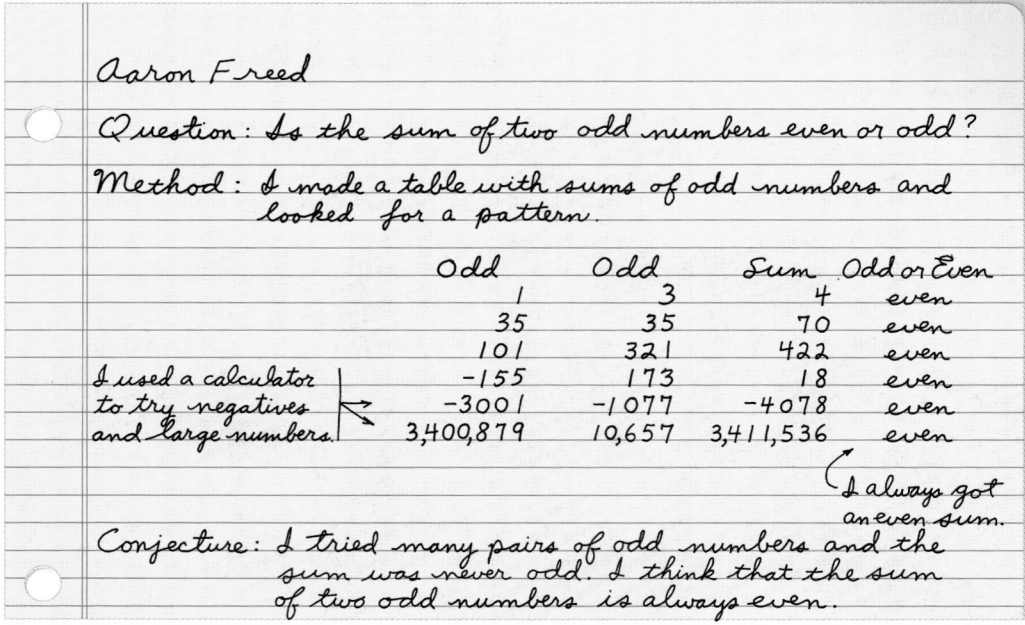

Aaron Freed

Question: Is the sum of two odd numbers even or odd?

Method: I made a table with sums of odd numbers and looked for a pattern.

Odd	Odd	Sum	Odd or Even
1	3	4	even
35	35	70	even
101	321	422	even
-155	173	18	even
-3001	-1077	-4078	even
3,400,879	10,657	3,411,536	even

I used a calculator to try negatives and large numbers.

I always got an even sum.

Conjecture: I tried many pairs of odd numbers and the sum was never odd. I think that the sum of two odd numbers is always even.

Talk it Over

1. In Sample 1, does inductive reasoning show that the sum of two odd numbers is always even? Explain.

2. Do you think the sum of any three odd numbers is *even* or *odd*? Explain your reasoning.

Sample 2

Make a conjecture about a relationship among the exterior angles of a polygon.

32   **Unit 1** Sampling and Reasoning

Answers to Talk it Over

1, 2. Answers and explanations may vary. Examples are given.

1. No; there are infinitely many odd numbers, and there is no way to test every possible pair of them to check that all the sums are even.

2. It is odd; the sum of two odd numbers is even, and when you add one more odd number to this even sum the result will be odd.

Problem Solving Strategy: Use inductive reasoning.

Draw several polygons. Measure the exterior angles and make a table.

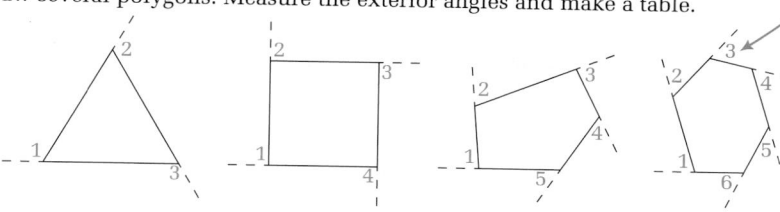

> An **exterior angle** of a polygon is an angle formed by extending a side of the polygon.

What do you know about angle measure relationships? You know that the measures of the interior angles of a triangle have a *sum* of 180°. Maybe there is a relationship among the sums of the external angle measures. Include a sum column in your table.

Polygon	∠1	∠2	∠3	∠4	∠5	∠6	Sum
triangle	120°	120°	120°	—	—	—	360°
square	90°	90°	90°	90°	—	—	360°
pentagon	85°	75°	85°	55°	60°	—	360°
hexagon	75°	60°	60°	60°	40°	65°	360°

Conjecture: The sum of the measures of the exterior angles of a polygon is 360°.

Talk it Over

3. Is it a good idea to test only regular polygons when you are making a conjecture? Why or why not? (*Note:* In a regular polygon, all the sides are the same length and all the angles are equal in measure.)

4. Is the conjecture in Sample 2 true for interior angles? Why or why not?

Shortcomings of Inductive Reasoning

Movie executives sometimes use inductive reasoning. Based on past experience, they predict which movies will be popular in the future. They are not always correct. For example, the sequel of a hit movie is not always as popular as the original.

You cannot *prove* that a conjecture is true just by using inductive reasoning. For example, in Samples 1 and 2 it would be impossible to test all the possibilities. However, you can *disprove* a conjecture by finding any example that does *not* work, a **counterexample.**

1-5 Inductive Reasoning

33

Additional Sample

S2 Make two conjectures about the diagonals of a rectangle.

Use inductive reasoning. Draw several rectangles. Make one a square. Measure the diagonals of each rectangle.

Conjecture: The diagonals of a rectangle are equal in length. The diagonals of a rectangle bisect each other.

Communication: Reading

Students need to understand the concept presented in the last paragraph on this page, mainly that inductive reasoning cannot be used to prove a conjecture. (This concept was first presented in Talk it Over question 1 on page 32.) Inductive reasoning can only be used to make conjectures.

Mathematical Procedures

A mathematical statement is either true or false; it cannot be true sometimes and false other times. Since a conjecture is a statement, it too must be either always true or false. The power of a counterexample is that it shows that a conjecture is not *always true* and therefore must be false.

Answers to Talk it Over

3, 4. Answers may vary. Examples are given.

3. No; the property you are testing might be unique to regular polygons. Also, if you test only regular polygons, your conjecture would apply only to them.

4. No; for example, you already know the sum of the measures of the interior angles of a triangle is 180°.

S3 Tell whether you think the inequality $\frac{1}{x} \geq \frac{1}{x^2}$ is *True* or *False.* If you think it is false, give a counter-example.

Use a table.

x	x^2	$\frac{1}{x} \overset{?}{\geq} \frac{1}{x^2}$
1	1	True
2	4	True
3	9	True
−1	1	False

The value of −1 gives a counterexample.

Conclusion: $\frac{1}{x} \geq \frac{1}{x^2}$ is false.

Using Technology

The TABLE feature of the TI-82 and TI-83 can be used to construct tables for use in finding counterexamples. Consider the inequality in Sample 3. Press [Y=] and enter Y1=X and Y2=X². On the TI-82, press [2nd] [TblSet] and set TblMin=0 and ΔTbl=0.2. On the TI-83, press [2nd] [TBLSET] and set TblStart=0 and ΔTbl=0.2. Then, on either calculator, press [2nd] [TABLE] to display tables of values for x and x^2. The values in the Y1-column are *greater* than the values in the Y2-column, from $x = 0.2$ to $x = 0.8$. All these values of x provide counterexamples which show that $x \leq x^2$ is *not* true for all values of x.

Talk it Over

Question 6 brings out the important idea that a conjecture about triangles in general should be based upon an examination of all the different kinds of triangles that exist. However, conjectures could also be made about a more limited set of triangles, for example, right triangles or isosceles triangles.

Tell whether you think the inequality $x \leq x^2$ is *True* or *False.* If you think it is false, give a counterexample.

Sample Response

Problem Solving Strategy: Use a table.

x	x^2	$x \overset{?}{\leq} x^2$
0	0	True
3	9	True
−8	64	True
−0.5	0.25	True
0.5	0.25	False

This is a counterexample: 0.5 is not less than 0.25. →

Conclusion: $x \leq x^2$ is false.

Watch Out!
For a statement to be considered *true*, it must be true in all cases.

Talk it Over

5. How many counterexamples are needed to disprove a conjecture?

6. Suppose you are using inductive reasoning to make a conjecture about triangles. What types of triangles should you test to check your conjecture?

7. Tell whether you think the inequality $|x| > x$ is *True* or *False.* If it is false, give a counterexample.

Look Back ◄

Can you use inductive reasoning to show that a conjecture is *always* true? *sometimes* true? *never* true? Why or why not?

1-5   Exercises and Problems

1. **Reading** What kinds of numbers should you test to support a conjecture about an algebraic statement?

Open-ended **For Exercises 2 and 3, make a conjecture about each situation.**

2. When Sarah visited Michelle, she played with Michelle's cat. After a while, Sarah's eyes began to itch and water. The next week Sarah visited another friend who also had a cat. On her way home, Sarah noticed that her eyes were very itchy and watery. Two days later, the neighbor's cat came and rubbed against Sarah. Again, her eyes began to itch and water.

Answers to Talk it Over

5. one

6. You should test acute, obtuse, and scalene triangles. You may also test right, isosceles, and equilateral triangles, so long as you do not consider them exclusively.

7. The inequality is false; any number $x \geq 0$ provides a counterexample.

Answers to Look Back

Except in finite cases, you cannot use inductive reasoning to prove that a conjecture is always true or never true, because you could not test every possibility. (An example of a finite case may be, "Every student in this school has a middle name." You could question every student in the school to test the conjecture and so could prove it true or false.) You can use inductive reasoning to show that a conjecture is sometimes true; in fact, that is the reason for using inductive reasoning.

3. In the cartoon Shing is wondering why he has been called to the principal's office. Should he be worried? Why or why not?

4. Julia was walking down a hallway in her school. She noticed that a boy was seated in the chair closest to the door in each of the five classrooms that she passed. She made this conjecture.

"In each classroom a boy is seated in the chair closest to the door."

a. Is her conjecture an example of inductive reasoning? Explain.

b. Do you think her conjecture is correct for the rest of the classrooms in the school? Why or why not?

5. When Marvin turned 25 years old, he bought a new red car. He had never gotten a speeding ticket before that time. During the first six months after buying the car, he got three speeding tickets.

a. What conjecture might Marvin make about red cars?

b. Are the officers who issued the tickets likely to make the same conjecture? Why or why not?

c. What observations might Marvin make to test his conjecture?

d. What about Marvin's behavior could have changed after he bought the car?

e. Do you think your conjecture in part (a) is valid? Why or why not?

Predict the next number in each pattern.

6. 4, 12, 36, 108, __?__

7. 1, 1, 2, 3, 5, 8, 13, __?__

8. $1 = 1^2$
$1 + 3 = 2^2$
$1 + 3 + 5 = 3^2$
$1 + 3 + 5 + 7 = \underline{\ ?\ }$

9. $1 \cdot 11 = 11$
$11 \cdot 11 = 121$
$111 \cdot 111 = 12321$
$1111 \cdot 1111 = \underline{\ ?\ }$

10. On a test, Morgan Philips asked her students to tell whether the diagonals of a quadrilateral are *always*, *sometimes*, or *never* equal in length. Here is a wrong answer that she received.

The diagonals of a quadrilateral are always equal in length.

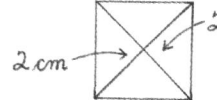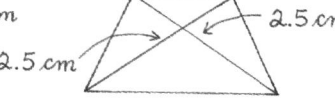

a. What other kinds of quadrilaterals might the student have tested?

b. What advice might you give the student?

1-5 Inductive Reasoning

Answers to Exercises and Problems

1. Answers may vary. An example is given. You should test positive and negative numbers, as well as small and large numbers. If appropriate, you may need to test other numbers as well, including 0, fractions, and decimals.

2, 3. Answers may vary. Examples are given.

2. A reasonable conjecture is that Sarah is allergic to cats.

3. A reasonable conjecture is that everyone called to the principal's office has been given some good news, so Shing should not be worried.

4. a. Yes; she made her conjecture based on several observations.

b. Answers may vary. Responses may be based on personal experience. There is no reason to make such an assumption in general.

5–10. See answers in back of book.

Look Back

These questions focus students' thinking on the meaning of inductive reasoning and the role it plays in establishing the truth of a conjecture. The key idea for students to understand is that conjectures are made by observing a limited number of true examples. The conjecture is a statement that the true examples illustrate a more general pattern that is always true. Therefore, inductive reasoning is a means of coming up with a conjecture, not a means of establishing truth. A conjecture that is never true would, in essence, be a wild guess made without observing any true examples.

APPLYING

Suggested Assignment
Standard 1–23, 26–32
Extended 1–23, 26–32

Integrating the Strands
Number Exs. 6–9, 11, 14, 25
Algebra Exs. 1, 15–18, 24, 29, 30
Geometry Exs. 10, 12, 13, 19, 25
Logic and Language Exs. 1–32

Communication: Discussion
Exs. 1–5 can be discussed in class as a whole group activity. Students can read each exercise silently, and when all have finished the reading, answers can be volunteered and discussed.

Reasoning
Exs. 6–19 provide students with an opportunity to apply their inductive reasoning skills to a mathematical task. For Exs. 11–14, students should use many examples to support and check their reasoning. For example, in Ex. 12, different types of triangles should be drawn before any conclusions are made.

Cooperative Learning

For Ex. 19, suggest that students start with a triangle, pentagon, and hexagon to explore the sum of the angle measures. Some students may have to use other polygons with more sides before coming up with the formula for the sum of the angle measures of a polygon.

Interdisciplinary Problems

Inductive reasoning is a powerful tool in solving real-world problems as shown in Exs. 20–23. Many times, only small bits of information are known about a new situation. These discrete facts can be studied to see if there is a pattern connecting them. If so, a conjecture can be made to organize the facts and generalize the pattern. This is the procedure that is usually followed in making scientific discoveries. Experiments provide data that are used to make conjectures, which are either supported by additional experiments or are verified mathematically.

Using Technology

Students can use the *Function Investigator* software or a graphics calculator to do Ex. 24, on page 37.

On the TI-82 and TI-83, the CALCULATE menu can be used to find the points where the two graphs intersect. Use the follow procedure after the calculator displays the graphs.

Press 2nd [CALC] and select 5:intersect. A blinking cursor will appear on the graph of the first equation. Use ◄ and ► to move the cursor as close as possible to the point of intersection whose coordinates you want to find. Press ENTER. The cursor moves to the second graph. Again, move it as close as you can to the point of intersection. Press ENTER twice. The coordinates of the point of intersection will then be displayed at the bottom of the screen. Depending on the equation, these coordinates may be only approximations.

36

---

11. **Writing** Do you think the product of any two odd numbers is *even* or *odd*? Explain.

12. **Writing** Suppose you extend a ray that bisects an angle of a triangle so that it passes through the opposite side. Do you think it will bisect the opposite side? Explain your reasoning.

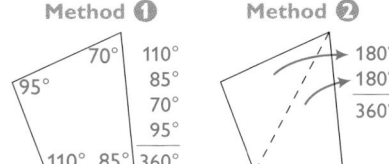

13. Suppose you draw a triangle with its vertices on a circle and with one side that is a diameter of the circle. Make a conjecture about the angle opposite the diameter.

14. Make a conjecture about the value of the product of any two numbers between 0 and 1.

For Exercises 15–18, tell whether you think each statement is *True* or *False*. If you think it is false, give a counterexample.

15. $-x < x$

16. $x \geq \dfrac{1}{x}$

17. $2(x + 3) > 2x + 1$

18. For any whole number n, $n^2 + n + 11$ is a prime number.

19. **Group Activity** Work with another student to explore the sum of the angle measures of a polygon. Each of you should use a different one of the two methods shown and try a few different polygons. How do the methods compare? What do you think is the formula for the sum of the angle measures of a polygon?

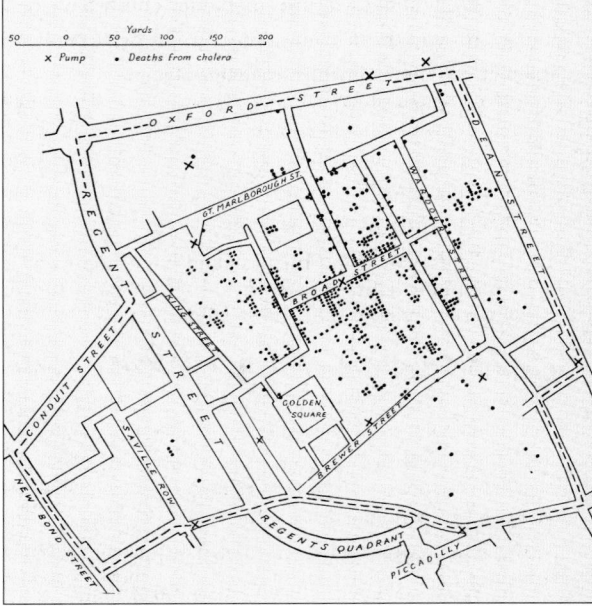

connection to HISTORY

There was a cholera epidemic in London in 1854. Dr. John Snow made a map to study the epidemic. Using the map and inductive reasoning, he was able to find the cause of the epidemic and take steps to end it.

For Exercises 20–23, use the map.

20. What do the dots on the map represent?

21. How many water pumps are shown on the map?

22. Based on the map, what do you think might have been the cause of the epidemic?

23. What do you think Dr. Snow did in order to end the epidemic?

36   **Unit 1** Sampling and Reasoning

Answers to Exercises and Problems

11–14. Each conjecture is based on inductive reasoning.

11. The product of two odd numbers is odd.

12. In general, an angle bisector of a triangle does not bisect the opposite side. (The angle bisector does bisect the opposite side for the vertex angle of an isosceles triangle or any angle of an equilateral triangle. Since these triangles are special cases, they should not be used exclusively to test the conjecture.)

13. If a triangle has its vertices on a circle and one side of the triangle is a diameter of the circle, the angle opposite the diameter is a right angle.

14. The product of any two numbers between 0 and 1 is also between 0 and 1.

15. False; any number $x \leq 0$ is a counterexample.

16. False; any number x with $0 < x < 1$, is a counterexample.

17. True.

18. False; one counterexample is $n = 10$ since $10^2 + 10 + 11 = 121 = 11^2$.

24 TECHNOLOGY Use a graphics calculator or graphing software.

Alternative Approach Use graph paper. Make a table of values and draw the graphs as indicated in part (a). Cover up all but the first quadrant for part (d).

a. Graph $y = -x + 2$ and $y = x^2$ together on the same axes. Use this viewing window: $-10 \le x \le 10$ and $-10 \le y \le 10$.

b. What is the shape of each graph?

c. Do the graphs intersect? If so, where?

d. Use a new viewing window: $0 \le x \le 10$ and $0 \le y \le 10$. How does this affect what appears on the graph?

e. What false conjecture might someone make by looking only at the viewing window used in part (d)?

Student Resources Toolbox
p. 649 *Graphs, Equations, and Inequalities*

TECHNOLOGY NOTE

You can use TRACE on your graphics calculator to estimate the point where two graphs intersect. ◄

Ongoing **ASSESSMENT**

25. **Group Activity** Work with another student.

a. Each of you should make two conjectures, one about even and odd numbers and another about equilateral triangles.

b. Use inductive reasoning to test each other's conjectures.

Review **PREVIEW**

26. A school tries to find out what parents think about school dances by calling the homes of students chosen at random. All the calls are made between 11 A.M. and 1 P.M. Describe a problem with this method of surveying. *(Section 1-4)*

Identify the dependent variable and the control variable in each situation. *(Toolbox Skill 19)*

27. Evy is writing his final essay for English class. The longer the test, the more paper he uses.

28. If she is making breakfast for all the people in her family, Dania uses more eggs.

Use the distributive property to complete each _?_. *(Toolbox Skill 10)*

29. _?_ $(m + n + 1) = 2m + 2n + 2$

30. _?_ $(2a - 3b + 1) = 10a - 15b + 5$

 Working on the Unit Project

31. **Research** You will need rubber gloves and a trash bag. Take a sample of the trash in one classroom. Can you use it to predict the amount of trash produced by the entire school in one day? Explain why or why not.

32. Use the results of your survey or some additional sampling to estimate the amount of materials students in your school reuse, recycle, or throw away each day.

1-5 Inductive Reasoning

37

Assessment: Standard

For Ex. 25, students should write down on paper their two conjectures and use diagrams if necessary. The test of each conjecture should also be in writing.

Working on the Unit Project

The individual in each group appointed as the analyzer should coordinate the activities leading to the collection of the samples of trash.

Practice 5 For use with Section 1-5

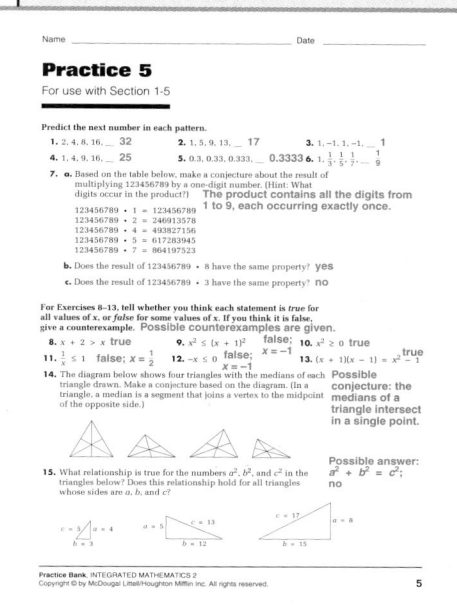

27. control variable: length of the test; dependent variable: amount of paper used

28. control variable: number of people for whom she is fixing breakfast; dependent variable: number of eggs used

29. 2

30. 5

31. Answers may vary. An example is given. It is not likely that a prediction based on the trash in one classroom during one class period would be accurate. Consider the difference between the trash produced during a class where a video or film is shown for the entire class period and an art class in which all the students are cutting out figures to make a collage.

32. Estimates may vary.

Answers to Exercises and Problems

19. Both methods combine angle measures to find the total sum of the angle measures of a polygon. Method 1 involves measuring, while method 2 uses the fact that the angles of a triangle total 180°; $180°(n - 2)$, where n is the number of sides of the polygon.

20. The dots represent locations of deaths from cholera.

21. 11

22. A reasonable conjecture is that lack of access to clean water might have caused the epidemic.

23. Based on the conjecture given, Dr. Snow might have increased access to clean water either by tem-

porarily bringing water into the area or by extending the water-pumping system.

24. See answers in back of book.

25. a, b. Conjectures and tests may vary.

26. Parents who work regular daytime jobs would be underrepresented.

Objectives and Strands
See pages 1A and 1B.

Spiral Learning
See page 1B.

Materials List
➤ Graphics calculator, graphing software, or graph paper

Recommended Pacing
Section 1-6 is a two-day lesson.

Day 1

Pages 38–39: Exploration through Talk it Over 8, *Exercises 1–20*

Day 2

Pages 39–41: Inductive versus Deductive through Look Back, *Exercises 21–44*

Toolbox References
➤ **Toolbox Skill 10:** Simplifying Algebraic Expressions

Extra Practice
See pages 614–615.

Warm-Up Exercises
Warm-Up Transparency 1-6

Support Materials
➤ Practice 6
➤ Enrichment 6 in the Activity Bank
➤ Study Guide 1-6
➤ Problem Set 2
➤ Additional Exploration 2
➤ Diagram Masters 2, 10–12 in the Explorations Lab Manual
➤ McDougal Littell Mathpack software: *Function Investigator*
➤ Quiz 1-6
➤ Alternative Assessment 5

Section 1-6

Deductive Reasoning

Play by the Rules ✓

Focus

Write if-then statements in other ways and draw simple conclusions from them. Learn the difference between inductive and deductive reasoning. Apply deductive reasoning to many situations.

EXPLORATION

(How) can you use your class to visualize if-then statements?

• **Divide the class into four teams.**

① In your team, decide on two rules for grouping the students in your class. Write your rules in this form.

If …, then you are in Group A.
If …, then you are in Group B.

② Are any students in your class in both groups? If so, how many?

③ Are any students in your class in neither group? If so, how many?

④ The diagrams shown are **Venn diagrams.** They are used to show relationships between groups. Decide which Venn diagram can be used to illustrate your rules and make a large copy of it.

⑤ Take turns with the other teams in your class. Have your classmates stand up. Without telling your team's rules, arrange your classmates into Groups A and B. Write each student's name on your Venn diagram. Have the other teams try to guess your rules.

Groups do not overlap

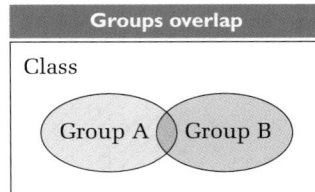

Groups overlap

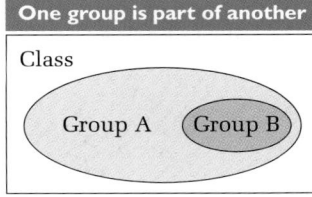

One group is part of another

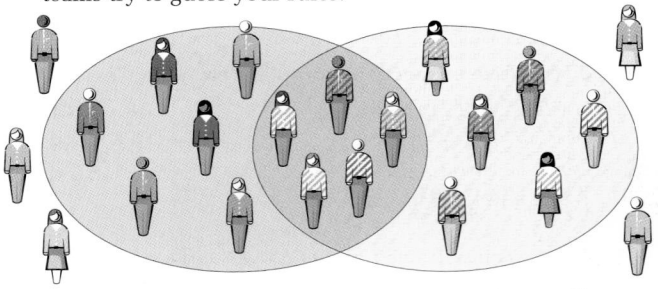

In the Exploration, you used *deductive reasoning* to decide which students belonged in each group. **Deductive reasoning** involves using facts, definitions, logic, and accepted rules and properties to reach conclusions.

Unit 1 Sampling and Reasoning

38

Answers to Exploration

1. Groupings may vary. One possible set of rules is "If you have brown eyes, then you are in Group A. If you have brown hair, then you are in Group B.

2, 3. Answers may vary. Examples are given based on the grouping described in step 1.

2. There would probably be students in both groups.

3. There might be students in neither group.

4, 5. Diagrams and guesses may vary.

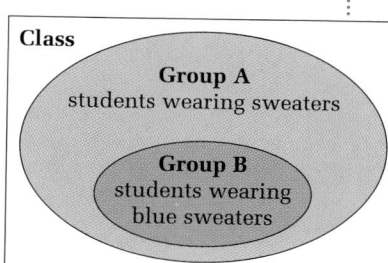

Class

Group A
students wearing sweaters

Group B
students wearing
blue sweaters

 **Now you are ready for:**
Exs. 1–20 on pp. 41–42

Talk it Over

Use the Venn diagram to tell whether each statement about the students in the class is *True* or *False*.

1. Janice is wearing a blue sweater. Janice is in Group B.

2. Lyle is wearing a blue sweater. Lyle is in Group A.

3. If a student is wearing a sweater, then the student is wearing a blue sweater.

4. If a student is not wearing a sweater, then the student is not wearing a blue sweater.

5. If a student is not wearing a blue sweater, then the student is not wearing a sweater.

6. Reword the statement in question 4 using the word *all*.

7. Reword the statement in question 4 using the word *every*.

8. The **converse** of an if-then statement is formed by interchanging the "if" and "then" parts. Which statements are converses of each other in questions 3–5?

Inductive versus Deductive

You use *inductive* reasoning to make conjectures based on a sample of cases. You use *deductive* reasoning to show that statements are true based on general rules.

Sample 1

Show that if two integers are odd, then their sum is even.

Sample Response

Problem Solving Strategy: Use deductive reasoning.

Step 1 Write variable expressions for any two odd integers.

Let m and n be any integers.

Then $2m$ is even and $2n$ is even.   ← Any integer that is 2 times another integer is even.

So, $2m + 1$ is odd and $2n + 1$ is odd.   ← Any integer that is 1 more than an even integer is odd.

Step 2 Add the two odd integers.

$(2m + 1) + (2n + 1) = 2m + 2n + 2$

$= 2(m + n + 1)$ ← Use the distributive property.

Step 3 Interpret the result.

$2(m + n + 1)$ is 2 times another integer, so it is even. Therefore the sum of any two odd integers is even.

1-6 Deductive Reasoning

39

Answers to Talk it Over

1. True.

2. True.

3. False.

4. True.

5. False.

6. All students who are not wearing a sweater are not wearing a blue sweater.

7. Every student who is not wearing a sweater is not wearing a blue sweater.

8. Statements 4 and 5 are converses of each other.

TEACHING

Exploration

The goal of the Exploration is to introduce students to the idea of deductive reasoning in a concrete way by using groups of students. The relationships between groups are given by student-made rules written in *If ..., then* form and are illustrated visually by using Venn diagrams.

Talk it Over

As students work through questions 1–5, they will see that the groups shown in the Venn diagram *force* a conclusion as to whether each statement is true or false. This is a key insight for students to have: given certain facts (those in the Venn diagram), clear-cut decisions can be made about the truth or falsity of other statements.

Mathematical Procedures

Talk it Over question 8 informs students how to create the converse of an *if-then* statement. Also, the question can be used to show that the converse of a true statement may be a false statement. (The converse of true statement 4 is statement 5, which is false.)

Additional Sample

S1 Show that the sum of an even integer and a odd integer is odd.

Use deductive reasoning.

Step 1. Write variable expressions for an odd integer and an even integer.

Let n be any integer. Then $2n$ is even and $2n + 1$ is odd.

Step 2. Add the two integers.

$2n + 2n + 1 = 4n + 1$

$= 2(2n) + 1$

Step 3. Interpret the result.

2 times an integer is even, so $2(2n)$ is even. 1 more than an even integer is odd. Therefore, $4n + 1$ is odd.

39

Talk it Over

Question 9 reviews the way in which an integer can be determined to be even or odd. These ideas were used in the Sample 1 response and will be presented again in Exs. 21 and 30–32.

Additional Sample

S2 Find the sum of the interior angle measures and the sum of the exterior angle measures of a polygon that has 100 sides.

Use deductive reasoning.

Step 1. Think about what facts you know about the angle measures of a polygon. The sum of the interior angle measures is $180(n-2)$ by Ex. 19 on page 36. The sum of the exterior angle measures is 360° by Sample 2.

Step 2. The sum of the interior angle measures is $180(n-2) = 180(100-2) = 180(98) = 17,640°$. The sum of the exterior angle measures is 360° by Sample 2.

Problem Solving

You can connect the ideas of conjecture, deductive reasoning, and problem solving by using Samples 1 and 2. Since a conjecture is a statement that is believed to be true (the statements given in the samples can serve as examples), the problem is to show that it is, in fact, a true statement. Deductive reasoning is the problem solving strategy that is used to show the statement is true or, in other words, deductive reasoning is used to solve the problem. Ideas and suggestions on how to develop good problem solvers are given on page T40 in the front of this Teacher's Edition.

9. Suppose a and b represent integers.

    a. How can you show that $2a + 4b + 6$ represents an even integer?

    b. How can you show that $2a + 4b + 7$ represents an odd integer?

In Sample 2 of Section 1-5 on pages 32–33, you saw how inductive reasoning was used to make a conjecture about the exterior angles of a polygon. Here you will see that the conjecture is true based on deductive reasoning.

Sample 2

Show that the sum of the exterior angle measures of any polygon is 360°.

Sample Response

Problem Solving Strategy: Use deductive reasoning.

Step 1 Think about what facts you know about the angles of a polygon.

You saw in Exercise 19 on page 36 that the sum of the *interior* angle measures of a polygon is $180(n-2)$, where n is the number of sides.

Step 2 See if there is a relationship between interior and exterior angle measures of a polygon. Use a diagram.

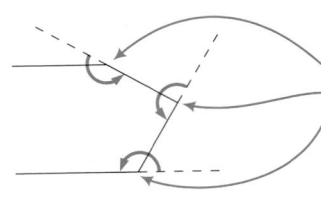

At each vertex, the sum of the interior and exterior angle measures is 180°.

There are n vertices in an n-gon. The sum of all the angle measures, interior plus exterior, is $180n$.

Step 3 Subtract the interior angle measures from the sum of all the angle measures.

$$\text{Sum of exterior angle measures} = 180n - 180(n-2)$$
$$= 180n - 180n + 360$$
$$= 360$$

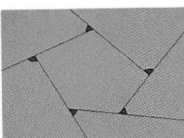  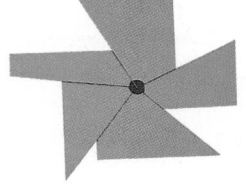

Answers to Talk it Over

9. **a.** $2a + 4b + 6 = 2(a + 2b + 3)$; Any integer that is the product of 2 and another integer is even.

    b. $2a + 4b + 7 = (2a + 4b + 6) + 1$; $2a + 4b + 6$ was shown to be even in part (a) and any integer that is 1 more than an even integer is odd.

Answers to Look Back

Answers may vary. Inductive reasoning results in a conjecture based on the observation of a number of examples. Deductive reasoning proves the conjecture to be true by using facts and accepted rules and properties.

Look Back ◄——

In Sample 2 of Section 1-5 on pages 32–33, you saw how inductive reasoning was used to make a conjecture about the sum of the exterior angle measures of a polygon. In Sample 2 of this section, you saw how deductive reasoning was used to show that the sum is always 360°. Compare the reasoning in the two cases.

┈┈► Now you are ready for:
Exs. 21–44 on pp. 43–44

1-6 Exercises and Problems

1. Use the two rules your group wrote for the Exploration on page 38.

   a. Rewrite each rule using the word *all*.

   b. Rewrite each rule using the word *every*.

   c. Write the converse of each rule.

The Venn diagram shows how students responded to a survey about using after-school time on five specific activities. For Exercises 2–9, tell whether each statement about the students in the survey is *True* or *False*.

listen to music
watch TV
work at a job
do volunteer work
watch movies

2. All students listen to music.

3. Some students watch TV.

4. If a student works at a job, then the student watches TV.

5. If a student watches TV, then the student does volunteer work.

6. Every student who watches movies watches TV.

7. Some students who watch movies do volunteer work.

8. Some students who do volunteer work also work at a job.

9. All students who do not watch TV do not do volunteer work.

10. Pick three statements from Exercises 2–9. Write the converse of each statement. Tell whether the converse is *True* or *False* about the students in the survey.

11. Write one statement about the Venn diagram that is true about *all* students, a second statement that is true about *some* students, and a third statement that is true for *no* students.

12. Draw a Venn diagram that shows the relationships among these groups: triangles, geometric figures, polygons, and three-dimensional figures.

1-6 Deductive Reasoning

41

Answers to Exercises and Problems ┈┈┈┈┈┈┈┈┈┈┈┈┈┈┈┈┈┈┈┈┈┈

1. Answers may vary. Examples are based on the rules "If you have brown eyes, then you are in Group A" and "If you have brown hair, then you are in Group B."

1. a. All people with brown eyes are in Group A. All people with brown hair are in Group B.

   b. Every person with brown eyes is in Group A. Every person with brown hair is in Group B.

   c. If you are in Group A, then you have brown eyes. If you are in Group B, then you have brown hair.

2. True.

3. True.

4. True.

5. False.

6. True.

7. True.

8. False.

9. True.

10–12. See answers in back of book.

Look Back

A written explanation for this Look Back would make a good journal entry. A brief class discussion prior to the journal entry might help students confirm that their comparison of the reasoning in the two samples is accurate. ┈┈┈┈┈●

APPLYING

Suggested Assignment

Day 1

Standard 1–12, 14–20

Extended 1–12, 14–20

Day 2

Standard 21–35, 37–44

Extended 21–35, 37–44

Integrating the Strands

Number Exs. 21, 30–32

Algebra Exs. 13, 20, 26, 27, 41–43

Geometry Exs. 19, 24, 25, 28, 29, 33, 34, 38–40

Logic and Language Exs. 1–37, 44

Error Analysis

Some students may have difficulty initially with the use of the words *all*, *some*, *every*, *no*, and the correct translation of an *if-then* sentence using one of these terms. Emphasize that *some* means *at least one* or *one or more*. *Every* has the same meaning as *all*, and *no* has the opposite meaning of *all*. An *if-then* sentence is always rewritten using *all* or *every*. Exs. 1–12 should help students to understand the meanings of these terms and how to use them correctly.

Using Technology

Students can use the *Function Investigator* software to graph the functions in Ex. 13.

Integrating the Strands

Exs. 17–34 and 36 all make use of deductive reasoning. The content of these exercises contain a variety of both mathematical and non-mathematical topics. The mathematics is from the strands of number, algebra, and geometry but could have included other strands as well. Deductive reasoning, being a *method of thinking*, can be applied to any field of study. When used in mathematics, however, it can serve to integrate concepts from different strands by using them as statements of fact in solving problems or writing proofs. For example, a mathematical proof may use deductive reasoning to link together concepts from number theory, algebra, geometry, and other strands as well.

Career Note

Emergency medical technicians (EMTs) are individuals trained to respond quickly to administer medical aid to people in need. They may work with an emergency response unit for a hospital or with other community-based response units. EMTs are trained to handle a wide variety of medical problems such as cold exposure, broken bones, bleeding, heart attacks, drowning, snake bites, and many others. Upon arriving at a scene, they need to analyze the emergency situation and decide upon a course of action. The procedures they follow involve a hands-on application of practical skills learned both in classroom training sessions and on-the-job training.

---

13 TECHNOLOGY Use a graphics calculator or graphing software.

Alternative Approach Work in a group of three students. Make tables and use graph paper. Each student should graph two different equations in part (a).

a. Graph each equation.

$$y = 3x - 4 \qquad y = x^2 \qquad y = -2x + 5$$
$$y = 3x^2 \qquad y = -5x \qquad y = x - 3$$

b. How could you group the equations in part (a) according to your graphs? Make a Venn diagram that shows your groupings. Label each loop with the name of its group.

c. Write two if-then statements that are true based on your diagram.

Career Emergency medical technicians (EMTs) follow established procedures when they respond to emergencies. A procedure is shown for responding to someone who has had exposure to the cold.

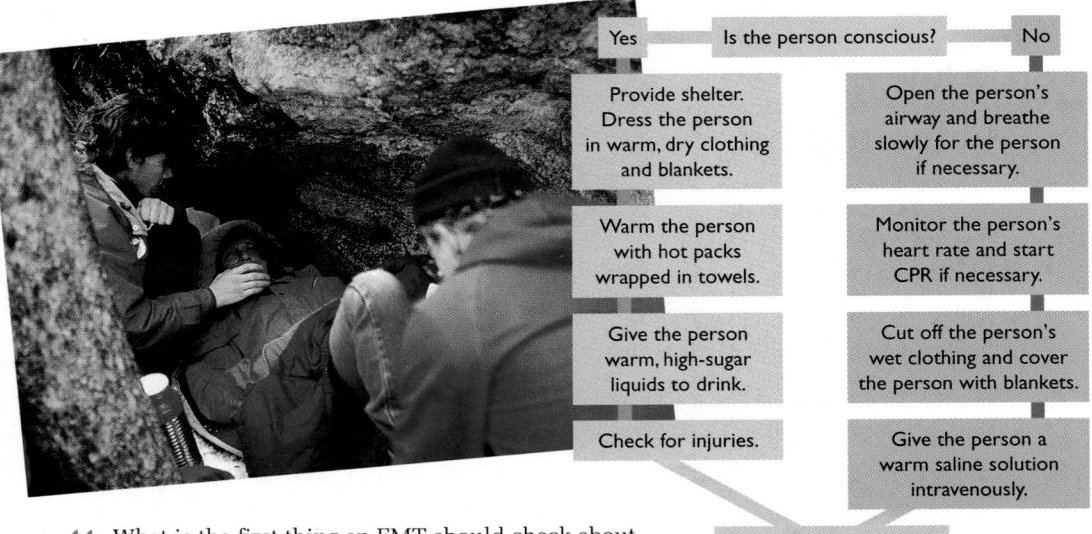

14. What is the first thing an EMT should check about a person who has had exposure to the cold?

15. What should an EMT do first if a person exposed to the cold is not conscious?

16. What are the two things an EMT should do for a person exposed to the cold whether or not the person is conscious?

For Exercises 17–20, use deductive reasoning to reach a conclusion.

17. Rachel is older than Michelle and Hector is younger than Michelle.

18. If a person is in Sacramento, then that person is in California. If a person is in California, then that person is in the United States.

19. If the base angles of a triangle are equal in measure, then the triangle is isosceles. If the triangle is isosceles, then the sides opposite the base angles are equal in measure.

20. $x = 3 + 2$ and $3 + 2 = 5$

Unit 1 Sampling and Reasoning

Answers to Exercises and Problems

13. See answers in back of book.

14. Is the person conscious?

15. Open the person's airway and breathe slowly for the person if necessary.

16. Cover the person with blankets; get the person to the hospital.

17. Rachel is older than Hector (or Hector is younger than Rachel).

18. If a person is in Sacramento, then that person is in the United States.

19. If the base angles of a triangle are equal in measure, then the sides opposite the base angles are equal in measure.

20. $x = 5$

21. a. No.

b. Yes; $2x$ is even because any integer that is the product of 2 and another integer is even.

c. Yes; $2x + 1$ is odd, because $2x$ is even and any integer that is 1 more than an even integer is odd.

21. Reading Suppose x represents an integer.

   a. Do you know whether x is even or odd? If so, which is it?

   b. Do you know whether $2x$ is even or odd? If so, which is it?

   c. Do you know whether $2x + 1$ is even or odd? If so, which is it?

Replace each _?_ with a phrase that makes a true statement.
(Note: You may have to first decide whether the converse is true.)

22. If Alta Perez is at school, then she will teach mathematics third period. Alta Perez is at school. Therefore, _?_.

23. If it is raining, then physical education class will be held indoors. It is raining. Therefore, _?_.

24. If a quadrilateral is a square, then its sides are equal in measure. In quadrilateral $ABCD$, $AB \neq CD$. Therefore, _?_.

25. All isosceles triangles have at least two sides equal in measure. No two sides of $\triangle PQR$ are equal in measure. Therefore, _?_.

26. If $3x + 5 = 14$, then $x = 3$. But, $x \neq 3$. Therefore, _?_.

27. If $5x - 7 > -17$, then $x > -2$. But, $x \leq -2$. Therefore, _?_.

28. If a triangle is equilateral, then all three sides are equal in measure. The three sides of $\triangle ABC$ are equal in measure. Therefore, _?_.

29. If a quadrilateral is a rectangle, then its four angles are right angles. The angles of quadrilateral $MNOP$ are right angles. Therefore, _?_.

Use deductive reasoning to show that each statement is true.

30. The difference of two odd numbers is even.

31. The product of two odd numbers is odd.

32. The product of an odd and an even number is even.

33. Vertical angles are equal in measure.

34. The sum of the measures of the acute angles of a right triangle is 90°.

Student Resources Toolbox
p. 641 *Algebraic Expressions*

35. Literature An old Sufi tale tells about an elephant that is put on exhibit in a darkened room. Those who go to the exhibit must rely on touch to describe the elephant.

   a. Tell whether each conclusion was reasonable based upon the observations. Write *Yes* or *No*.

   b. How might the observers have worked together to give a more consistent description?

   c. Writing Write a moral for this story using ideas and vocabulary from this unit.

A. water spout   B. fan
C. pillar   D. throne

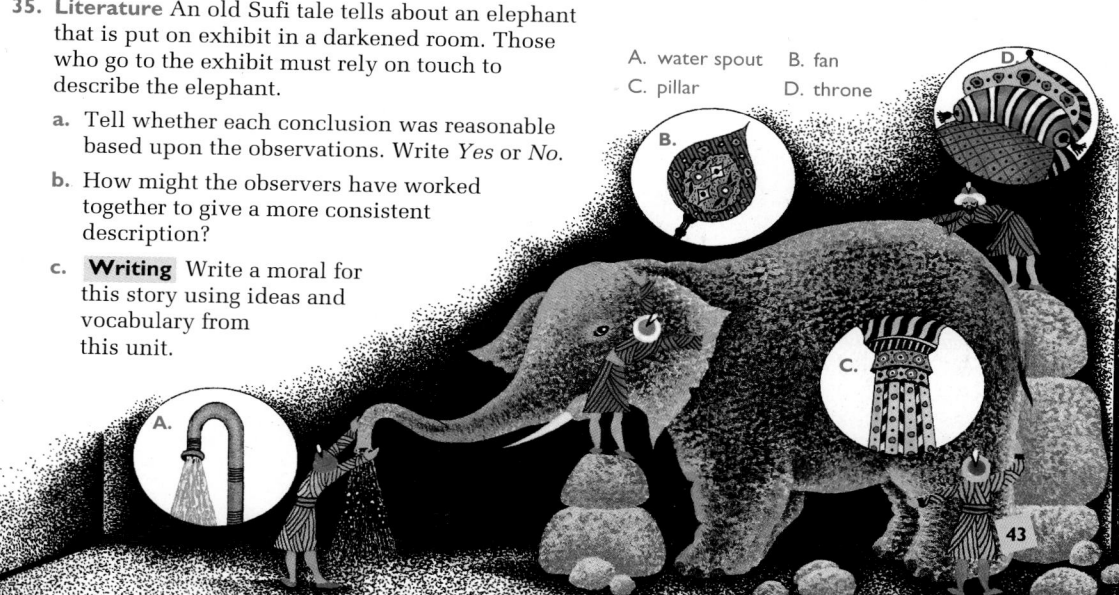

Answers to Exercises and Problems

22. she will be teaching mathematics third period

23. physical education class will be held indoors

24. $ABCD$ is a not a square

25. $\triangle PQR$ is not isosceles

26. $3x + 5 \neq 14$

27. $5x - 7 \leq -17$

28. $\triangle ABC$ is an equilateral triangle

29. quadrilateral $MNOP$ is a rectangle

30–32. Answers are based on the following facts. Any even number can be written as $2m$ for some integer m, and any odd number can be written as $2n + 1$ for some integer n. Also, any integer that is the product of 2 and anoth-er integer is even, and any integer that is 1 more than an even integer is odd.

30. Let $2x + 1$ and $2y + 1$ be two odd numbers. Then $2x + 1 - (2y + 1) = 2x - 2y = 2(x - y)$, which is even.

Problem Solving

If students have difficulty getting started with Exs. 30–32, suggest that they review their answers to Ex. 21 on this page and Sample 1 on page 39.

Assessment: Standard

For Exs. 30–34, students should be able to translate each statement into algebraic form and then interpret their answers.

31. Let $2x + 1$ and $2y + 1$ be two odd numbers. Then $(2x + 1)(2y + 1) = 4xy + 2x + 2y + 1 = 2(2xy + x + y) + 1$, which is odd.

32. Let $2x$ be any even number and $2y + 1$ be any odd number. Then $2x(2y + 1) = 4xy + 2x = 2(2xy + x)$, which is even.

33. Methods may vary. An example is given. Draw two intersecting lines and number the angles 1–4 in order so that $\angle 1$ and $\angle 3$ are vertical angles. $\angle 1$ and $\angle 2$ together form a straight angle, so $\angle 1 + \angle 2 = 180°$. But $\angle 2$ and $\angle 3$ together form a straight angle, so $\angle 2 + \angle 3 = 180°$, also. Then $\angle 1 + \angle 2 = \angle 2 + \angle 3$, and $\angle 1 = \angle 3$.

34. Methods may vary. An example is given. Let $\angle A$ and $\angle B$ be the acute angles of a right triangle. The sum of the measures of the angles of a triangle in 180°. Then $\angle A + \angle B + 90° = 180°$, and $\angle A + \angle B = 90°$.

35. a. A. Yes; B. Yes; C. Yes; D. Yes.

   b. Answers may vary. An example is given. The men could have pooled their observations, realized how different they were, and tried to analyze why. They could have traded places, tried to establish connections between the different parts, and tried to figure out the function of each part they had described. This might have lead to a better overall description.

   c. Answers may vary. An example is given. When using inductive reasoning, do not base your conjectures on information that is too limited. Be sure to use test cases that are as varied and as numerous as possible and reasonable.

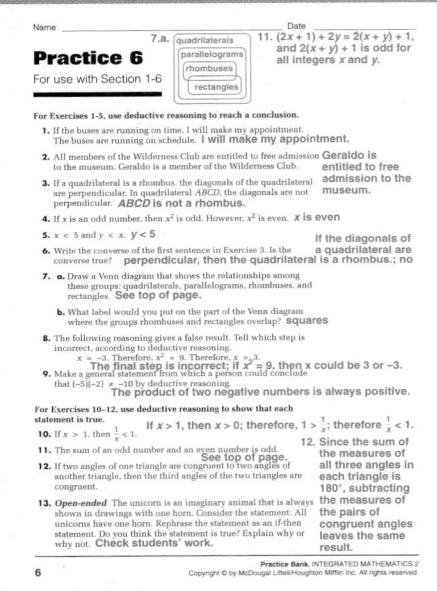
Ongoing ASSESSMENT

36. **Group Activity** Work with another student.

   a. Work together to solve this puzzle using deductive reasoning.

   Hana is thinking of a number. If you subtract the number of quarters in a dollar from the number, multiply by the number of days in a week, and add the number of weeks in a year, then the result is 17. What is the number?

   b. Each student should write a number puzzle like the one in part (a).

   c. Use deductive reasoning to solve each other's puzzle.

Review PREVIEW

37. Do you think that the inequality $-x \leq x^2$ is true? Use inductive reasoning to support your answer. *(Section 1-5)*

Identify each type of space figure and find its surface area. *(Toolbox Skill 28)*

38.

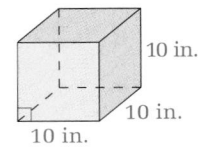
10 in.
10 in.
10 in.

39.

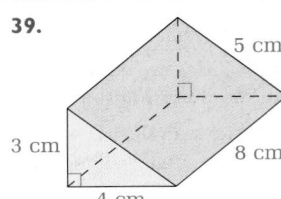
5 cm
3 cm
8 cm
4 cm

40.

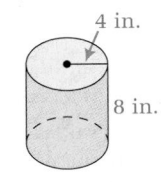
4 in.
8 in.

For Exercises 41–43: *(Toolbox Skills 21, 23, and 24)*

a. **Find the slope and the vertical intercept of each graph.**

b. **Write an equation for each line.**

41.

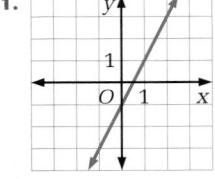

42.

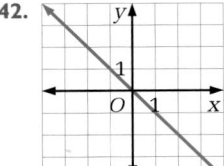

43.

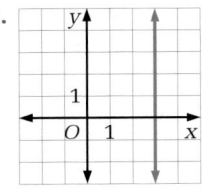

Working on the Unit Project

44. What conclusions can you reach from the results of your recycling survey? Are you using *inductive* or *deductive* reasoning when you reach those conclusions? Explain.

Answers to Exercises and Problems

36. a. −1

   b. Number puzzles may vary.

   c. Check students' work.

37. Answers may vary. An example is given. I think the inequality is true for all x. I will test some numbers.

x	$-x$	x^2	$-x \overset{?}{\leq} x^2$	
2	−2	4	$-2 \leq 4$	✓
0	0	0	$0 \leq 0$	✓
−2	2	4	$2 \leq 4$	✓
$-\frac{1}{2}$	$\frac{1}{2}$	$\frac{1}{4}$	$\frac{1}{2} \leq \frac{1}{4}$	No.

The inequality is not true for $x = -\frac{1}{2}$, so it is not true for all x.

38. cube; 600 in.^{2}

39. triangular prism; 108 cm^2

40. cylinder; 96π in.^{2}

41. a. slope = 2; vertical intercept = −1

   b. $y = 2x - 1$

42. a. slope = −1; vertical intercept = 0

   b. $y = -x$

43. a. Slope is undefined; there is no vertical intercept.

   b. $x = 3$

44. Conclusions may vary.

Errors in Reasoning

Read Between the Lines

Talk it Over

1. Which statement means "If you wish a thing done well, do it yourself"? Which means "If you overextend yourself, you will accomplish little"?

2. What does the "it" refer to on the recycling bumper sticker? What conclusion might you draw from the bumper sticker?

3. Suppose the statement "If you buy two of something, then you get another one free" is true. Is the converse of this statement true? Why or why not?

4. Give an example of a false statement that has a true converse.

Objectives and Strands
See pages 1A and 1B.

Spiral Learning
See page 1B.

Materials List
➤ Graph paper

Recommended Pacing
Section 1-7 is a one-day lesson.

Extra Practice
See pages 614–615.

Warm-Up Exercises
💡 Warm-Up Transparency 1-7

Support Materials
➤ Practice 7
➤ Enrichment 7 in the Activity Bank
➤ Study Guide 1-7
➤ Problem Set 2
➤ Diagram Masters 1, 2 in the Explorations Lab Manual
➤ Quiz 1-7
➤ Test 2
➤ Alternative Assessment 6

Answers to Talk it Over

1. Selbst getan ist wohl getan; Quien mucho abarca, poco aprieta.

2. "It" refers to Earth. Recycling helps preserve the natural resources of Earth.

3. No. The converse is "If you get another one free, then you buy two of something." The free item is conditional upon the purchase of the first two.

4. Answers may vary. An example is given. If I live in California, then I live in San Fancisco. Converse: If I live in San Francisco, then I live in California.

Talk it Over

Questions 3 and 4 make students aware of the fact that a statement and its converse need not have the same truth value.

Additional Samples

S1 If two angles are vertical angles, then they are equal in measure.

a. Write the converse of this statement. **If two angles are equal in measure, then they are vertical angles.**

b. Is the converse true? Why or why not? **The converse is not always true. Two angles with the same measure could be adjacent to each other. The picture below shows a counterexample.**

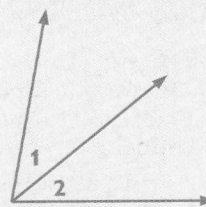

m ∠1 = 40°, *m* ∠2 = 40°

S2 Dana and Reema solved the equation $4x + 20 = x + 5$ and reached two different conclusions. Which conclusion is incorrect and why?

Dana's Method
$$4x + 20 = x + 5$$
$$4(x + 5) = x + 5$$
$$\frac{4(x + 5)}{(x + 5)} = \frac{x + 5}{(x + 5)}$$
$$4 = 1$$

Conclusion: The equation has no solution.

Sample continued on next page.

One common error in reasoning is to assume that the converse of a true statement is also true. It is a good idea to look at the converse and see if you can think of a counterexample.

Sample 1

If two triangles are congruent, then the corresponding angles are equal in measure.

a. Write the converse of this statement.

b. Is the converse true? Why or why not?

Sample Response

a. If the corresponding angles of two triangles are equal in measure, then the triangles are congruent.

b. The converse is not always true. It is only true when the corresponding sides of the triangles have the same length. A picture can show a counterexample.

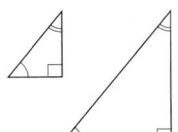

When you solve an equation, your steps are supported by valid mathematical reasoning. If one of your steps is invalid, you may reach an incorrect solution. An example of an invalid step is to divide by zero. Division by zero is *undefined*.

Sample 2

Writing Amalia and Cassandra used two different methods to solve $2x - 4 = 3x - 6$. One student reached an invalid conclusion. Which conclusion is wrong? Which step leads to the invalid conclusion?

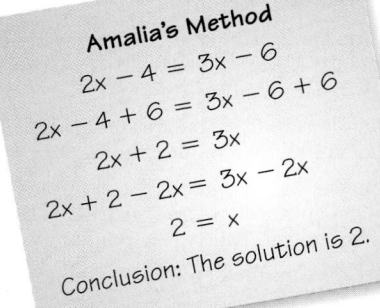

Amalia's Method
$$2x - 4 = 3x - 6$$
$$2x - 4 + 6 = 3x - 6 + 6$$
$$2x + 2 = 3x$$
$$2x + 2 - 2x = 3x - 2x$$
$$2 = x$$

Conclusion: The solution is 2.

Cassandra's Method
$$2x - 4 = 3x - 6$$
$$2(x - 2) = 3(x - 2)$$
$$\frac{2(x - 2)}{x - 2} = \frac{3(x - 2)}{x - 2}$$
$$2 = 3$$

Conclusion: The equation has no solution.

Cassandra's conclusion is wrong.

When Cassandra divided both sides of the equation by $x - 2$, she made the assumption that $x - 2$ was not 0. Before she can conclude that the equation has no solution, Cassandra needs to see whether the original equation has a solution when $x - 2 = 0$.

The statement $x - 2 = 0$ is true when $x = 2$. If Cassandra substitutes 2 for x in the original equation, the statement is true. The correct solution is 2.

Talk it Over

FirstGene Labs Accounting Report

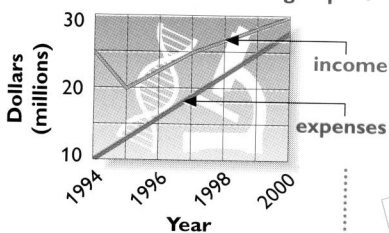

5. Substitute 2 for x in the original equation of Sample 2. What is the true statement you get?

6. The information in the graph is used to make a prediction about the future finances of FirstGene Labs. Nathan and Gavin each made a prediction.

Nathan's Prediction:
The future for this company is very good. The company made $5 million more in 2000 than it did in 1994. Its income continues to increase steadily.

Gavin's Prediction:
This business is heading for bankruptcy! The company's expenses are rising faster than its income. By 2002 the company will be spending more than it earns.

a. Which prediction do you think is more likely to be correct? Why?

b. A company's profit is its income minus its expenses. In what year did FirstGene Labs have the biggest profit? the smallest profit?

c. Based on your answers to part (b), which student's prediction do you support?

Look Back ◄

Darcy reads that if a figure is a square, then it is a quadrilateral. What is the converse of this statement? Is the converse true? Why or why not?

1-7 Errors in Reasoning

Reema's Method

$$4x + 20 = x + 5$$
$$4x + 20 - 20 = x + 5 - 20$$
$$4x = x - 15$$
$$4x - x = x - 15 - x$$
$$3x = -15$$
$$\frac{3x}{3} = -\frac{15}{3}$$
$$x = -5$$

Conclusion: The solution is -5.

Dana's conclusion is incorrect. He assumed that $x + 5$ does not equal zero when he divided both sides of the equation by $x + 5$. If $x + 5 = 0$, then $x = -5$ is a possible solution. If Dana substitutes -5 for x in the original equation, the statement is true. The correct solution is -5.

....

Mathematical Procedures

In Sample 2, students see that division by zero can lead to invalid conclusions because division by zero is undefined. In an algebraic situation, students need to avoid dividing both sides of an equation by a factor that could be equal to zero. The use of an invalid mathematical procedure, which is equivalent to using incorrect reasoning, can lead to incorrect results.

....

Talk it Over

Question 6 illustrates an error in reasoning based upon reading a graph. The key idea is to recognize the relationship between income and expenses.

....

Look Back

After students answer these questions, have them consider what other types of errors they encountered in this section. (dividing by zero; failure to interpret correctly all the information provided by a graph)

.............●

Answers to Talk it Over ·················

5. $0 = 0$

6. a. Gavin's prediction is more likely to be correct. The slope of the income line is less than the slope of the expenses line. If things continue as they are now, expenses will surpass income in about 2 years.

b. 1994; 2000

c. The reasonable answer is "Gavin's."

Answers to Look Back ·········:

If a figure is a quadrilateral, then it is a square. The converse is not true. A counterexample is a trapezoid, since it is a quadrilateral that is not a square.

APPLYING

Suggested Assignment

Standard 1–10, 14–17, 23–33

Extended 1–11, 14–18, 20–33

Integrating the Strands

Number Exs. 3, 4, 19

Algebra Exs. 3, 4, 11, 19, 29, 30

Functions Exs. 31, 32

Geometry Exs. 5–7, 27

Discrete Mathematics Ex. 19

Logic and Language Exs. 1–28, 33

Communication: Discussion

Exs. 2–11 provide students with an excellent opportunity to use logical reasoning, write converses, and create counterexamples. Having students explain their reasoning and give their counterexamples will make for an interesting and lively class discussion.

Answers to
Exercises and Problems

1. Nathan based his prediction solely on the income information. Gavin based his on the relationship between the income and expenses.

2–7. Counterexamples may vary.

2. a. True.

   b. If you live on the west coast, then you live in California.

   c. False; you might live in Oregon.

3. a. False; $|-3| > 0$ for $n = -3$.

   b. If $n > 0$, then $|n| > 0$ for all n.

   c. True.

4. a. True.

   b. If $x^2 > 0$, then $x > 0$ for all x.

   c. False; if $x = -2$, $(-2)^2 = 4 > 0$, but $-2 < 0$.

5. a. True.

   b. If a triangle is isosceles, then two sides of the triangle are congruent.

   c. True.

6. a. True.

   b. If a triangle is a right triangle, then the sum of two angles is 90°.

   c. True.

---

1. **Reading** In *Talk it Over* question 5, both students used the same graph to arrive at different conclusions. What information from the graph did Nathan use to make his prediction? What information from the graph did Gavin use?

For Exercises 2–7:

a. **Tell whether each statement is *True* or *False*. If it is false, give a counterexample.**

b. **Write the converse of each statement.**

c. **Tell whether the converse of each statement is *True* or *False*. If it is false, give a counterexample.**

2. If you live in California, then you live on the west coast.

3. If $|n| > 0$, then $n > 0$ for all n.

4. If $x > 0$, then $x^2 > 0$ for all x.

5. If two sides of a triangle are congruent, then the triangle is isosceles.

6. If the sum of two angles of a triangle is 90°, then the triangle is a right triangle.

7. If a figure is a square, then it has four equal sides.

For Exercises 8–10, tell whether each conclusion is valid. Write *Yes* or *No*. If not, give a counterexample.

8. If Sejal runs under 3 min, then she will win the race. Sejal won the race. Conclusion: She ran under 3 min.

9. If the girls' basketball team wins Friday's game, then they will be in the championships. The girls' basketball team is in the championships. Conclusion: They won Friday's game.

10. If Liu answers the phone, then she is home. Liu is home. Conclusion: She answers the phone.

11. Lewis tries to convince his friend that 1 = 2. He uses the steps below to show his reasoning. Explain the error in his reasoning.

Think about two equal positive numbers a and b. You can write $a = b$.

$$a = b$$
$$ab = b^2 \qquad \longleftarrow \text{Multiply both sides by } b.$$
$$ab - a^2 = b^2 - a^2 \qquad \longleftarrow \text{Subtract } a^2 \text{ from both sides.}$$
$$a(b - a) = (b + a)(b - a) \qquad \longleftarrow \text{Factor each side.}$$
$$a = (b + a) \qquad \longleftarrow \text{Divide both sides by } (b - a).$$
$$a = (a + a) \qquad \longleftarrow \text{Since } a = b, \text{ substitute } a \text{ for } b.$$
$$a = 2a$$
$$\frac{a}{a} = \frac{2a}{a} \qquad \longleftarrow \text{Divide both sides by } a.$$
$$1 = 2$$

BY THE WAY...

Apparently, sea lions can understand simple chains of logic. A sea lion named Rio was taught that the symbol for "mug" is equivalent to the symbol for "watch" and that the symbol for "watch" is equivalent to the symbol for "bomb." Rio then indicated that the symbol for "mug" is equivalent to the symbol for "bomb" 24 times out of 28 trials.

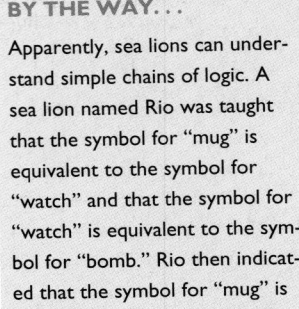
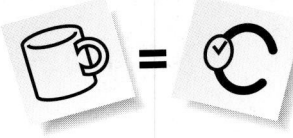
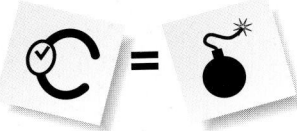
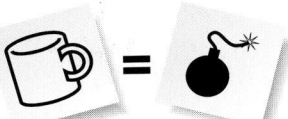

---

7. a. True.

   b. If a figure has four equal sides, then it is a square.

   c. False; it could be an octagon or a rhombus.

8. No; as long as Sejal's finish time was faster than all the other runners', it could have been less than, greater than, or equal to 3 minutes.

9. No; they might have lost Friday's game but other teams who had to win may also have lost, or been eliminated in some other way.

10. No; Liu may not hear the phone ring, or she may be unwilling or unable to answer it.

11. If $a = b$, then $b - a = 0$ and Lewis divided by 0 in step 4.

12. Answers may vary. Examples are given.

12. a. Smoking causes lung cancer, heart disease, emphysema, and may complicate pregnancy.

   b. Many cigarette advertisements picture healthy, active young people smoking cigarettes. The visual image and the written health warning are contradictory. One implies that smoking is a healthy, normal thing to do, the

---

12. a. Research Find an advertisement for cigarettes. What is the Surgeon General's warning?

  b. What type of images and people appear? Are the visual image and the written message contradictory? If so, how?

  c. Which image do you think the advertiser expects people to notice? How effective is the advertiser in promoting the product?

  d. Why do you think the advertisement may lead people to draw an incorrect conclusion?

13. Research Find an article about the effects of cigarette smoking on a person's health. Write about the main ideas of the article. Present some of the information in a graph.

For Exercises 14–18, use the three graphs.

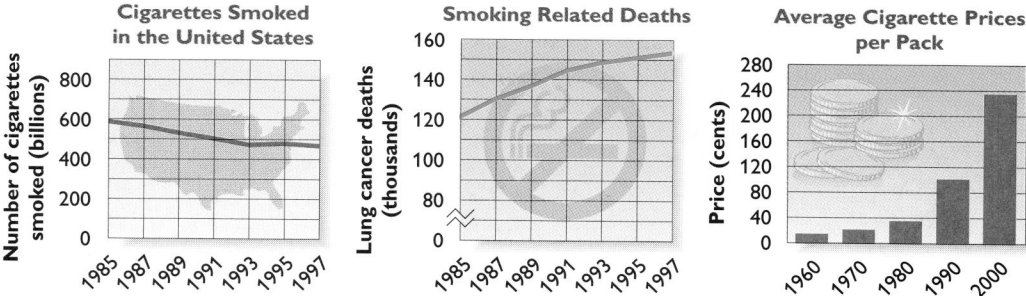

14. How might the two line graphs be misleading?

15. Give an example of an incorrect conclusion that someone might make from the graphs.

16. Writing Write a convincing argument to explain why the number of cigarettes smoked in a year has decreased.

17. Writing Write a convincing argument to explain why the number of smoking-related deaths has risen even though the number of cigarettes smoked in a year has decreased.

18. Writing Write at least three questions that you would like to ask the surveyor about the information in the graphs.

19. Computer Programming The first time Nituna ran her computer program, she had an error in line 40. She noticed that the program worked for a little while because the program printed $\frac{1}{2}$ and 2. Then she saw her error. Explain the error in line 40.

Program

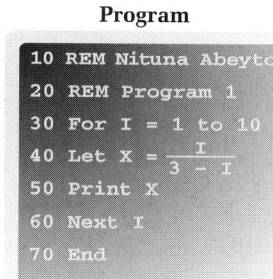

Output

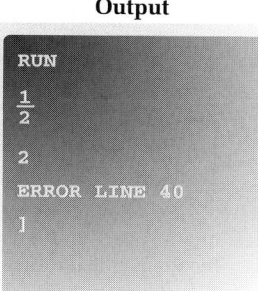

```
10 REM Nituna Abeyto
20 REM Program 1
30 For I = 1 to 10
40 Let X = I / (3 - I)
50 Print X
60 Next I
70 End
```

```
RUN
1
2
2
ERROR LINE 40
]
```

49

Communication: Writing

Exs. 12–18 require some research and a number of writing activities. Allow students sufficient time to complete this work. Students should submit their assignments for evaluation. Teaching strategies involving writing in mathematics are presented on page T38 in the front of this Teacher's Edition.

14–17. Answers may vary. Examples are given.

14. The graphs may give the impression that since the number of cigarettes smoked each year decreased but lung cancer deaths continued to increase, there must be little or no connection. This doesn't account for the time it takes for cancers to develop. The graph on the right has a break in the vertical axis which may make the number of smoking-related deaths seem much lower than it is. Also, the vertical axis is labeled "lung cancer deaths," while the graph is titled "Smoking-related deaths." This implies all smoking-related deaths are due to lung cancer. Many smoking-related deaths are due to heart disease, damage to the circulatory system, and to lung diseases other than cancer.

15. One example is given in Ex. 14. That is, the graphs may give the impression that since the number of cigarettes smoked each year decreased but lung cancer deaths continued to increase, there must be little or no connection. This doesn't account for the time it takes for cancers to develop.

16. The cost of cigarettes has risen sharply. Over the 10-year period from 1980 to 1991, the cost of cigarettes tripled and from 1990 to 2000 the cost doubled. From 1985 to 1997 the number of cigarettes smoked in a year has decreased about 20%. Another example is the negative publicity given to cigarette smoking in recent years.

17. Because cancers develop so slowly, you would not expect to see a sudden change. A drop in smoking this year might not be reflected in the number of smoking-related deaths for 10 to 20 years.

Answers to Exercises and Problems

other is a clear message that it is not.

  c. The advertisers clearly hope people notice the visual image and not the written one. Since the law compels the advertisers to make the written message noticeable, they cannot make it so small or so similar to the background that it can be easily overlooked.

However, since cigarette sales are substantial, the advertisers must be somewhat successful.

  d. People may look at the pictures and think, "These people look attractive and healthy and fit, and they are smoking. Perhaps it's not so bad after all." That is contrary to the scientific evidence.

13. The points covered in the article may include respiratory problems, heart and circulatory problems, shortened life span, low birth weight and premature birth in infants whose mothers smoked before they were born, and the dangers of second-hand smoke.

20. Since 1975, the number of cars in the world has increased and the number of rhinoceros in the world has decreased.

Can you conclude that the number of cars has increased *because* the number of rhinoceros has decreased? Explain why or why not.

connection to LITERATURE

The story of *The Phantom Tollbooth* by Norton Juster is about Milo, a young boy who travels with his dog, Tock, and his friend Humbug.

In the distance a beautiful island covered with palm trees and flowers beckoned invitingly from the sparkling water.

"Nothing can possibly go wrong now," cried the Humbug happily, and as soon as he'd said it he leaped from the car...and sailed all the way to the little island.

"And we'll have plenty of time," answered Tock, who hadn't noticed that the bug was missing—and he, too, suddenly leaped into the air and disappeared.

"It certainly couldn't be a nicer day," agreed Milo, who was too busy looking at the road to see that the others had gone. And in a split second he was gone also.

He landed next to Tock and the terrified Humbug on the tiny island...."Pardon me," said Milo to the first man who happened by; "can you tell me where I am?"

"To be sure," said Canby; "you're on the Island of Conclusions. Make yourself at home. You're apt to be here for some time."

"But how did we get here?" asked Milo, who was still a bit puzzled by being there at all.

"You jumped, of course," explained Canby. "That's the way most everyone gets here. It's really quite simple: every time you decide something without having a good reason, you jump to Conclusions whether you like it or not. It's such an easy trip to make that I've been here hundreds of times."

21. When the Humbug, Tock, and Milo see a beautiful island in the distance, each character makes a statement that causes him to jump to Conclusions. Explain why each character's statement is not necessarily true.

22. **Open-ended** Give an example of a situation from your life when someone jumped to the wrong conclusion. Describe how you think the person reached the conclusion.

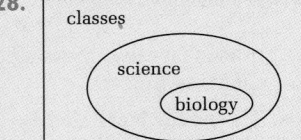

Traffic Safety For Exercises 23–26, use the graphs on states with bicycle helmet laws and bicycle fatalities.

23. What relationship do the graphs imply?

24. Is there a direct correlation between the number of states with bicycle helmet laws and the number of bicycle fatalities?

25. Do the graphs support the conclusion that the *cause* of the decrease in bicycle fatalities was the increase in states with bicycle helmet laws? Explain why or why not.

26. Besides bicycle helmet laws, what other factors might have contributed to the drop in bicycle fatalities?

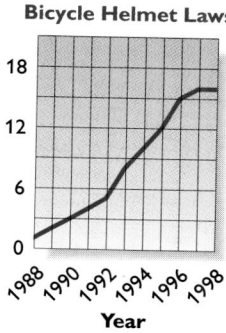

States with Bicycle Helmet Laws

Year

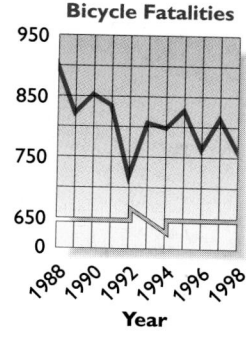

Bicycle Fatalities

Year

Ongoing **ASSESSMENT**

27. **Writing** Write a true if-then statement about the relationship among the sides of right triangle △*ABC*. Write the converse of your statement. Is the converse also true? Why or why not?

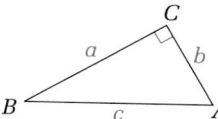

Review **PREVIEW**

28. Draw a Venn diagram that shows that if a student is in a biology class, then the student is in a science class. *(Section 1-6)*

For Exercises 29 and 30, copy each graph. Then shade the side that will give you the graph of the given inequality. *(Toolbox Skill 25)*

29. $x - 2y \geq -2$

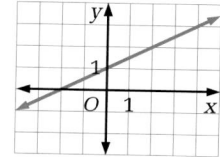

30. $x + 4y \leq 4$

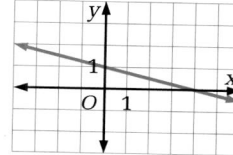

For Exercises 31 and 32, draw a graph of each situation. Tell whether each graph represents a function. Write Yes or No. *(Toolbox Skill 19)*

31. Doug Weber borrowed $12,000 from his mom for college. Each month he pays her $300.

32. Every week Jennika learns how to play two new songs on the piano.

Working on the Unit Project

33. Gather your survey and trash-sampling results. Come to a final decision about the form in which you will present your findings and recommendations. Start to think about the recommendations you will make.

1-7 Errors in Reasoning

Practice 7 For use with Section 1-7

Practice 7
For use with Section 1-7

Name _____ Date _____

For Exercises 1-7, do these things:
a. Tell whether or not each statement is true. If not, give a counterexample.
b. Write the converse of each statement.
c. Tell whether or not the converse of each statement is true. If not, give a counterexample.

1. If you are fifteen years old, then you go to school.
2. If $x > 0$, then $x^2 > 0$.
3. If it's raining, then the sidewalk is wet.
4. If $a^2 = 25$, then $a = 5$.
5. If the diagonals of a quadrilateral are congruent, then the quadrilateral is a rectangle.
6. If the Wolverines outscore their opponents, then they win the game.
7. If $ab = ac$, then $b = c$.

For Exercises 8–10, tell whether each conclusion is valid. Write Yes or No. If not, give a counterexample.

8. If Claudio scores above 90 on his next math test, his average will be an A. Claudio has an A average after the test. Conclusion: He scored above 90.
9. If Mei Hua finishes her homework, she will take part in the New Year celebration. Mei Hua finishes her homework. Conclusion: She takes part in the celebration.
10. If Giang has a sore throat, she will stay home from school. Giang stays home from school. Conclusion: She has a sore throat.
11. Dwayne read in a book that one could use cricket chirps to estimate the temperature in degrees Celsius. The book gave the formula $t = \frac{1}{8}n + 6$, where t is the Celsius temperature and n is the number of chirps per minute. Dwayne solved the equation for n and got $n = 5t - 30$. He used this equation and predicted that for a temperature of 100° C, a cricket would chirp 470 times per minute. Do you agree with his prediction? Explain your thinking.

1. true; If you go to school, then you are fifteen years old.; False, since you could be fourteen.
2. true; If $x^2 > 0$, then $x > 0$.; False, since x could be −1.
3. true; If the sidewalk is wet, then it is raining.; False, since someone could be cleaning the sidewalk with a hose.
4. False, since a could be −5.; If $a = 5$, then $a^2 = 25$.; true
5. False, since the quad. could be an isos. trap.; If a quad. is a rect., then the diagonals are congruent.; true
6. true; If the Wolverines win the game, then they outscore their opponents.; true
7. False, since you could have $a = 0$, $b = 1$, $c = 2$.; If $b = c$, then $ab = ac$.; true
8. no; He could have three 100's and then get an 87.
9. true
10. false; Perhaps she had a stomach virus.
11. Possible answer: no, because a cricket cannot live at a temperature as high as 100°C.

Answers to Exercises and Problems

29.
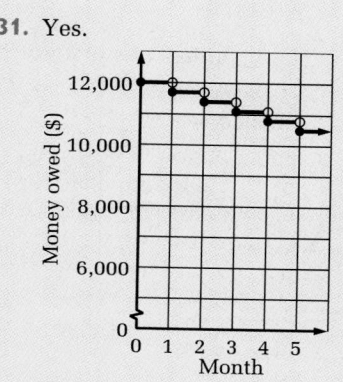

30.

31. Yes.

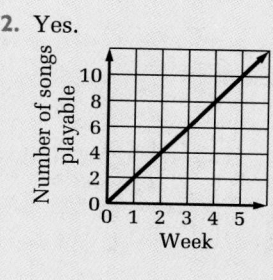

32. Yes.

33. Data should include an estimation of how much trash the school produces each day with graphs and tables as necessary to support the data.

Completing the Unit Project

Now you are ready to complete your disposal proposal.

Your completed disposal proposal should include these things:

➤ a copy of your survey of students' attitudes about trash disposal

➤ a written summary of the survey results

➤ a graph showing the contents of the classroom trash sample you analyzed

➤ your findings and recommendations in the form of a skit, a poster, a display, or a script for an assembly program or a public-address announcement designed to convince students to accept your disposal proposal

Look Back

How did the use of surveys and sampling help you prepare your proposal for reducing waste in your school?

Alternative Projects

 Project 1: Conclusions in Advertisements

Cut out newspaper and magazine advertisements that make claims based on surveys. Present your answers to these questions visually.

Do the ads tell you anything about their sampling methods? Would anything about the ads lead you to make errors in statistical reasoning or errors in deduction? Were the ads as effective after you analyzed them as they were when you first looked at them?

Project 2: Simulating Survey Results

Pick a topic that you find interesting and that you would like to ask people about. Design a survey for which you can simulate the results using dice, coins, number cubes, spinners, or random numbers. Use simulation to predict the results of the survey, and then conduct the survey. Write a report that compares the results of your simulation with the results of the survey.

52   **Unit 1** Completing the Unit Project

Answers to Unit 1 Review and Assessment

1. A survey is less expensive and requires less planning than a census.

2. about 1440

3. about 90 min; Use a spinner divided into quarters. Each quarter represents a student from each class.

4. No.

5. Yes.

6. No.

7. Yes.

8. Answers may vary. An example is given. A cluster sample consists of items in a group such as a neighborhood or household. Since the members of the group are not chosen independently of each other, they may share opinions and experiences to a greater extent than members of a

1. Why would a business use a sample instead of a census to learn about its customers' needs?

1-1

2. A radio station in Middletown surveyed 50 people and found that 18 of them prefer listening to classical music. Predict how many of the 4000 people in the town prefer classical music.

3. On average, a school counselor spends 10 min with each freshman, 6 min with each sophomore, 5 min with each junior, and 15 min with each senior during registration. The probability is equal that a freshman, sophomore, junior, or senior will come to the counselor's office.

1-2

Use simulation to estimate the total time that the counselor spends with 10 students chosen randomly. Describe the method that you used.

STUDENT	Class	Time spent
1	?	?
2	?	?
3	?	?
⋮	⋮	⋮

For Exercises 4–7, tell whether each method would produce a random sample of a school audience of 400 students. Write *Yes* or *No*.

1-3

4. The students in the back row are selected.

5. Select the students whose birth dates are multiples of four.

6. The 20 tallest students are selected.

7. Assign each girl in the audience a number from 1 through 200; assign each boy a number from 201 through 400. Use a random number table to select 20 numbers between 1 and 400 for the sample.

8. **Writing** Discuss three different sampling methods. Give examples of each method. Tell whether you think that each method might influence the results.

9. A manager at a television station wants to know audience reaction to its news show. The manager telephones viewers at home and surveys those who are 35–49 years old. Describe at least two problems with this method of surveying.

1-4

10. A report on music preferences concluded that "most students 18–21 years old that we surveyed listen to music more than four hours a day." What are two questions you might ask about the survey?

11. **Writing** Suppose you draw a segment that corresponds to a height of a triangle. An example is shown. Do you think it will always bisect the corresponding base? Explain your reasoning.

1-5

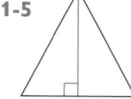

Answers to Unit 1 Review and Assessment

random sample. This certainly might influence the results.

9. Answers may vary. Examples are given. The manager is limiting the sample to those at home when the calls are made. Also, the audience includes many people outside that age group. Even if the manager has some rea-

son to limit responses to those in that group, he or she has no way of knowing if a person giving a response is actually between 35 and 49.

10. Answers may vary. Examples are given. How was the sample chosen? How was the survey worded? What were the actual responses?

11. No; it will bisect the base only if the triangle is isosceles. A counterexample is given.

· ·

Unit Support Materials

➤ Unit 1 Cumulative Practice 8

➤ Unit 1 Study Guide Review

➤ Unifying Problem 1 in the Problem Bank.

➤ Unit Tests 3 and 4

➤ Spanish versions of the Unit Tests are in the Assessment Book.

➤ Teacher's Resources for Transfer Students

· ·

Quick Quiz (1-5 through 1-7)

1. Predict the next number in the pattern. [1-5]
2, 5, 3, 10, 4, 15, ... **5**

2. Identify the type of reasoning used by a scientist who makes a conjecture based upon the results of an experiment. [1-6]
inductive reasoning

3. Draw a Venn diagram to show the relationships between all scalene, isosceles, and equilateral triangles. [1-6]

Triangle Relationships

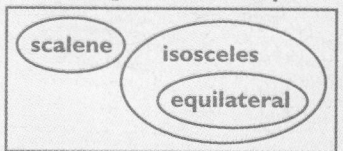

4. An advertisement shows prices slashed 15% and then another reduction of 10%, with a claim that the total savings is 25%. Is this claim correct? Explain why or why not. [1-7]
The claim is not correct. For example, if an item cost $10, reducing its cost by 15% gives a cost of $8.50. This amount, reduced by another 10% yields a final cost of $7.65. However, if the original cost of $10 is reduced by 25%, the final cost would be $7.50.

12. Do you think the sum of any two multiples of 4 is also a multiple of 4? Explain your reasoning.

13. On a bus trip home from school, Marvella noticed that two students got off at each of the first four bus stops. She predicts that two students will get off at every bus stop.

   a. Do you agree with her prediction? Why or why not?

   b. Suppose Marvella attends a school in which every student has a brother or sister also attending. Does this affect whether you agree or disagree with her prediction? Why or why not?

14. Use deductive reasoning to show that the sum of two even numbers is even.   **1-6**

For Questions 15–17, tell whether each statement about the singing groups is *True* or *False*.

15. If a student is in the Chorus, then the student is also in the Freshman Singers.

16. If a student is in the Freshman Singers, then the student is not in the Chorus.

17. No students are in both the Chorus and Madrigal Singers.

18. Reword the statement in Question 16 using the word *none*.

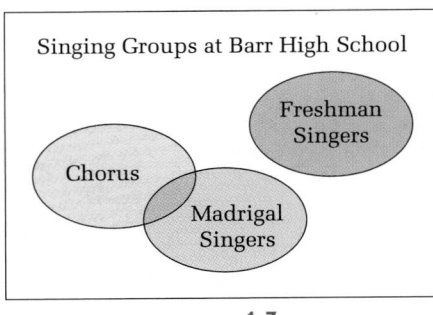

Singing Groups at Barr High School

Freshman Singers

Chorus

Madrigal Singers

1-7

For Questions 19–21:

a. Tell if each statement is *True* or *False*. If it is false, give a counterexample.

b. Write the converse of each statement.

c. Tell if the converse of each statement is *True* or *False*. If it is false, give a counterexample.

19. If you arrive after most people at the movie, you sit in the front row.

20. If two lines that intersect form right angles, the lines are perpendicular.

21. If $\frac{1}{x+1}$ is a rational number, then x is an integer.

22. **Open-ended** Make a conjecture about triangles. Explain your reasoning.

23. **Self-evaluation** Discuss how the ways that you might use data, statistics, or reasoning have changed. Do you accept most statements as true, or do you look for bias or errors in reasoning? Give examples.

24. **Group Activity** Your group will create an advertisement for a product, such as shampoo or an automobile.

   a. In your ad, make a claim based on a survey that could have been conducted before creating the product.

   b. What kind of sampling might be used for the survey in part (a)? (Remember, you want survey results that give a favorable impression.)

   c. What photographs might you feature in the ad?

   d. What if-then statements might you include in the ad?

54   **Unit 1** Sampling and Reasoning

Answers to Unit 1
Review and Assessment ⋯⋯⋯⋯⋯

12. Yes. Let $4m$ and $4n$ be two different numbers that are both multiples of 4. Then $4m + 4n = 4(m + n)$, which is a multiple of 4.

13. a. Answers may vary. An example is given. No; it is reasonable to assume that more than two students, or only one student, will get off at some bus stop.

   b. This would make her prediction more reasonable, since a brother and sister are likely to get off at the same stop.

14. Let $2m$ and $2n$ be any two even numbers. Then $2m + 2n = 2(m + n)$, which is even, since any integer that is the product of 2 and an integer is even.

15. False.

16. True.

17. False.

18. None of the students in the Freshmen Singers is in the chorus.

19–21. Counterexamples may vary.

19. a. Most likely answer: True.

   b. If you sit in the front row at a movie, you arrived after most people.

   c. False; you may simply like to sit close to the screen.

20. a. True.

   b. If two lines are perpendicular, they intersect to form right angles.

   c. True.

21. a. False; $\frac{2}{3}$ is a rational number and $\frac{2}{3} = \frac{1}{\frac{1}{2} + 1}$; $\frac{1}{2}$ is not an integer.

   b. If x is an integer, then $\frac{1}{x+1}$ is a rational number.

   c. False; -1 is an integer and $\frac{1}{-1+1} = \frac{1}{0}$ is not a rational number, it is undefined.

22. Answers may vary. An example is given. A triangle can have at most one right angle. (The sum of the measures of the angles of a triangle is 180°. If a triangle contained two right angles, the sum of the three angle measures would have to be 90° + 90° + x = 180° + x, which would be greater than 180°.)

23. Answers may vary. One possible response is, "I try not to accept data and statistics at face value, without asking how they were collected and interpreted." Examples may vary.

24. Answers may vary. Examples, based on a detangling shampoo, are given.

   a. We found that people are looking for a shampoo that will leave hair smooth and tangle-free without the bother of a conditioner.

   b. Shoppers with hair that is particularly long or curly or both would most likely agree they would like such a product.

54

IDEAS AND (FORMULAS) $= X^2$

ALGEBRA

➤ A proportion can be used to estimate population values from sample values. *(p. 5)*

➤ The expression $2n$ can be used to represent an even integer. $2n + 1$ represents an odd integer. *(p. 39)*

STATISTICS & PROBABILITY

➤ Censuses and surveys are used to collect information. Surveys cost less and involve only samples of a population. *(p. 4)*

➤ Simulations make it possible to answer questions about real-life situations that are otherwise difficult to explore. *(p. 10)*

➤ Rolling a die, spinning a spinner, and tossing a coin are common methods of simulating. *(p. 10)*

➤ There are many different types of samples: random, convenience, stratified random, cluster, and systematic. Random samples tend to be the most representative. *(pp. 16–17)*

➤ Larger samples give more reliable results. *(p. 18)*

➤ You can generate random numbers from a computer, a calculator, or a list of numbers such as telephone numbers. *(p. 19)*

➤ The way a survey is written and conducted affects the results. *(p. 24)*

LOGICAL REASONING

p ↔ q
if - then

➤ Inductive reasoning is based on several observations. *(p. 31)*

➤ You cannot *prove* a conjecture by inductive reasoning, but you can *disprove* one by finding a counterexample. *(p. 33)*

➤ You can use if-then statements to draw conclusions. *(p. 38)*

➤ You can use a Venn diagram to determine whether an if-then statement is true or false. *(p. 39)*

➤ You can use deductive reasoning to show that statements are always true based on facts, definitions, logic, and accepted rules and properties. *(pp. 38–39)*

➤ One common error in deduction is assuming that the converse of a true statement is also true. *(p. 46)*

➤ Division by zero is undefined and can lead to an error in reasoning. *(p. 46)*

Key Terms

- **population** (p. 3)
- **trial** (p. 10)
- **convenience sample** (p. 17)
- **systematic sample** (p. 17)
- **inductive reasoning** (p. 31)
- **Venn diagram** (p. 38)

- **sample** (p. 3)
- **tree diagram** (p. 11)
- **stratified random sample** (p. 17)
- **biased** (p. 17)
- **exterior angle** (p. 33)
- **deductive reasoning** (p. 38)

- **simulation** (p. 10)
- **random sample** (p. 17)
- **cluster sample** (p. 17)
- **conjecture** (p. 31)
- **counterexample** (p. 33)
- **converse** (p. 39)

Unit 1 Review and Assessment

55

Answers to Unit 1 Review and Assessment

c. Photographs might show models with silky, shiny hair that is softly styled.

d. "If you want silky, shiny hair with no tangles and without all the bother of a conditioner, then try our product."

Quick Quiz (1-1 through 1-4)

1. At a local factory, 46 out of 130 workers chosen at random take the bus to work. The factory employs 583 workers. Estimate the total number of workers who take the bus to work. [1-1]

$\frac{46}{130} = \frac{n}{583}$

$n < 206.29$

About 206 workers take the bus to work.

2. In a high school, one-fourth of the students are in ninth grade. Describe two different ways to simulate the percentage of ninth grade students in that high school. [1-2] **Answers may vary. Examples are given. (1) Use colored chips. One blue for ninth grade students and 3 red for students in the other grades. (2) Use a tetrahedron die, with the numbers one through four. Let only the number one stand for ninth grade students.**

3. Give an example of a cluster sample. [1-3] **Answers may vary. An example is given. In a school cafeteria, students are seated in groups of 6 at round tables. Pick one group of 6 students seated at one of the tables nearest the entrance to the cafeteria.**

4. This multiple choice survey question was given to people swimming at a lake one day in June. [1-4] "How often do you swim at this lake?"

(a) always
(b) many times a month
(c) a few times a month
(d) never

a. Explain why this question is biased. **The terms *many* and *a few* are not well defined and may be interpreted in different ways.**

b. Rewrite the question so it is not biased. **Answers may**

Models of Variation and Growth

OVERVIEW

➤ **Unit 2** reviews and extends direct and inverse variation functions, their characteristics, and their graphs, begun in Book 1. Growth and decay functions are introduced. The **Student Resources Toolbox** on pages 651–652 provides additional work with modeling direct variation functions.

➤ Students continue their study of zero and negative exponents. Direct variation is extended to include variation with the square and the cube. The volume and surface area formulas for a sphere are introduced.

➤ The Unit Project theme is the ecosystem of a salt lake. Students investigate functions relating the salt content, water volume, and wildlife of Mono Lake to time, physical changes, and each other.

➤ Connections to meteorology, fitness, biology, architecture, skydiving, and roller coasters are integrated into the teaching materials and exercises.

➤ Graphics calculators are used in Section 2-2 with activities involving the slope of a line and graphs of direct variation, in Section 2-5 with graphs of direct variation with powers, in Section 2-6 with fractional exponents, and in Section 2-7 with doubling and halving problems. Computer software, such as Plotter Plus, can be used in Section 2-2 to explore the properties of linear equations.

➤ Problem-solving strategies used in Unit 2 include using graphs, manipulatives, formulas, equations, tables, technology, and diagrams.

Unit Objectives

Section	Objectives	NCTM Standards
2-1	• Describe the graphs of functions.	1, 2, 3, 4, 5, 6, 8
2-2	• Review linear functions, slope of a line, and direct variation.	1, 2, 3, 4, 5, 6, 8
2-3	• Explore situations that involve constant products.	1, 2, 4, 5, 6, 8
2-4	• Find the surface area and volume of spheres. • Use the fact that all spheres are similar.	1, 2, 3, 4, 5, 7
2-5	• Model and apply relationships in which one quantity is proportional to the square or the cube of another quantity.	1, 2, 3, 4, 5, 6, 8
2-6	• Use negative, zero, and fractional exponents.	1, 2, 3, 4, 5, 8
2-7	• Explore situations in which quantities repeatedly double or split in half.	1, 2, 4, 5, 6, 8

Section	Connections to Prior and Future Concepts
2-1	**Section 2-1** presents topics concerning functions and their graphs, including linear versus nonlinear, increasing versus decreasing, and domain and range. The topic of functions was introduced in Section 4-6 of Book 1 and is used extensively throughout all three books. Page 649 in the Toolbox reviews the vertical-line test for functions.
2-2	**Section 2-2** presents linear models and direct variation. Writing the slope-intercept form of a linear equation is presented and then related to writing a direct variation equation. Pages 650–653 in the Toolbox provide review of these skills. Both of these skills, first introduced in Book 1, are used extensively throughout all three books.
2-3	**Section 2-3** introduces inverse variation functions. Students graph inverse variation functions and recognize when a graph, a set of data, or an equation is an example of inverse variation. The hyperbola was first seen in Section 4-7 of Book 1 and is visited again in Unit 2 of Book 3.
2-4	**Section 2-4** introduces formulas for the volume and surface area of a sphere. This extends the work begun in Unit 9 of Book 1, which covered prisms, pyramids, cylinders, and cones. The formulas in this section are used to introduce direct variation with powers in the next section.
2-5	**Section 2-5** connects the work on quadratic functions begun in Section 4-7 of Book 1 and extended in Sections 10-2 and 10-7 of Book 1 with graphing direct variation with the square. This skill is extended to graphing direct variation with the cube. Work with polynomial functions is developed further in Unit 9 of Book 2 and Unit 2 of Book 3.
2-6	**Section 2-6** presents zero and negative exponents which were introduced originally in Book 1. Fractional exponents are introduced. Skill with these exponents is needed throughout all three books. For example, they are used in exponential growth and decay, beginning in Section 2-7 of Book 2 and continued in Unit 9 of Book 2 and in Unit 5 of Book 3.
2-7	**Section 2-7** introduces exponential growth and decay. This topic extends the concept of linear growth and decay from Section 8-1 of Book 1, and will be covered more extensively in Unit 5 of Book 3.

Integrating the Strands ....

Strands	Sections
Number	2-6
Algebra	2-1, 2-2, 2-3, 2-4, 2-5, 2-6, 2-7
Functions	2-1, 2-2, 2-3, 2-5, 2-7
Geometry	2-1, 2-2, 2-3, 2-4, 2-5, 2-6, 2-7
Trigonometry	2-2
Statistics and Probability	2-1, 2-2, 2-4
Logic and Language	2-1, 2-2, 2-4, 2-5, 2-6

Section Planning Guide

➤ Essential exercises and problems are indicated in boldface.
➤ Ongoing work on the Unit Project is indicated in color.
➤ Exercises and problems that require student research, group work, manipulatives, or graphing technology are indicated in the column headed "Other."

Section	Materials	Pacing	Standard Assignment	Extended Assignment	Other
2-1		Day 1	**1, 2–11, 13–15**	1, **2–11, 13–15**, 16, 17	12
		Day 2	**18–21**, 22–29, 30–32	**18–21**, 22–29, 30–32	
2-2	graphics calculator	Day 1	**1–17, 20–26**	**1–17**, 19, **20–26**	18
		Day 2	27, 28, 30, 34–42, 43	27, 28, 29–32, 34–42, 43	33
2-3	36 small squares of paper, scissors, graphing technology, compass, centimeter ruler, salt, hot tap water, 5 clear glasses	Day 1	**1–5**	**1–5**, 6, 7	
		Day 2	**8–19**, 23–31, 32, 33	**8–19**, 20–31, 32, 33	
2-4	orange	Day 1	1, **2–15**, 16, 17	1, **2–15**, 16–19	
		Day 2	**20–29**, 30–32, 34–41, 42	**20–29**, 30–32, 34–41, 42	33, 42
2-5	graphing technology	Day 1	1, 2, **3–11**, 12, 13	1, 2, **3–11**, 12–14	
		Day 2	**15–23**, 25–34, 35–37	**15–23**, 24–34, 35–37	
2-6	graphing technology	Day 1	**1–10**, 11	**1–10**, 11	
		Day 2	**12–27**, 28, 34–42, 43	**12–27**, 28–32, 34–42, 43	33
2-7	newspaper, graphics calculator, 8.5 × 11 in. typing paper	Day 1	**1–10**	**1–10**, 11	
		Day 2	**16–19**, 21–32, 33	12–14, **16–19**, 21–32, 33	15, 20
Review Test		**Day 1**	**Unit Review**	**Unit Review**	
		Day 2	**Unit Test**	**Unit Test**	

Yearly Pacing	Unit 2 Total	Units 1–2 Total	Remaining	Total
	18 days (2 for Unit Project)	32 days	128 days	160 days

Support Materials

➤ See **Project Book** for notes on Unit 2 Project: Be a Park Guide.
➤ "UPP" and "disk" refer to **Using Plotter Plus** booklet and **Plotter Plus** disk.
➤ "TI-81/82" refers to **Using TI-81 and TI-82 Calculators** booklet.
➤ Warm-up exercises for each section are available on **Warm-Up Transparencies**.
➤ "FI" and "Stats!" refer, respectively, to the McDougal Littell Mathpack software Activity Books for **Function Investigator** and **Stats!**.

Section	Study Guide	Practice Bank	Problem Bank	Activity Bank	Explorations Lab Manual	Assessment Book	Visuals	Technology
2-1	2-1	Practice 9	Set 3	Enrich 8	Master 1	Quiz 2-1		Stats! Acts. 8 and 14
2-2	2-2	Practice 10	Set 3	Enrich 9	Add. Expl. 3 Master 2	Quiz 2-2	Folder 2	FI Acts. 3–5 Line Plotter (disk)
2-3	2-3	Practice 11	Set 3	Enrich 10	Add. Expl. 4 Masters 1, 13, 14	Quiz 2-3 Test 5	Folder 2	FI Act. 24 TI-81/82, p. 36 UPP, p. 38
2-4	2-4	Practice 12	Set 4	Enrich 11		Quiz 2-4		
2-5	2-5	Practice 13	Set 4	Enrich 12		Quiz 2-5		
2-6	2-6	Practice 14	Set 4	Enrich 13		Quiz 2-6		
2-7	2-7	Practice 15	Set 4	Enrich 14	Masters 1, 2, 15	Quiz 2-7 Test 6		TI-81/82, p. 37
Unit 2	Unit Rev.	Practice 16	Unif. Prob. 2	Fam. Inv. 2		Tests 7, 8		

UNIT TESTS

Form A

Spanish versions of these tests are on pages 122–125 of the **Assessment Book**.

Name _____ Date _____ Score _____

Test 7

Test on Unit 2 (Form A)

Directions: Write the answers in the spaces provided.

For Questions 1–4, use the graph at the right.

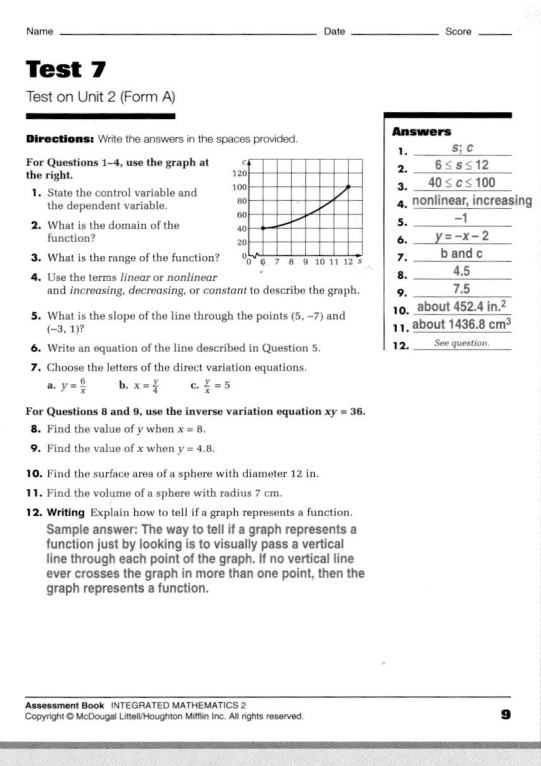

1. State the control variable and the dependent variable.

2. What is the domain of the function?

3. What is the range of the function?

4. Use the terms *linear* or *nonlinear* and *increasing, decreasing,* or *constant* to describe the graph.

5. What is the slope of the line through the points (5, −7) and (−3, 1)?

6. Write an equation of the line described in Question 5.

7. Choose the letters of the direct variation equations.

   a. $y = \frac{6}{x}$ b. $x = \frac{y}{4}$ c. $\frac{y}{x} = 5$

For Questions 8 and 9, use the inverse variation equation $xy = 36$.

8. Find the value of y when $x = 8$.

9. Find the value of x when $y = 4.8$.

10. Find the surface area of a sphere with diameter 12 in.

11. Find the volume of a sphere with radius 7 cm.

12. **Writing** Explain how to tell if a graph represents a function.

   Sample answer: The way to tell if a graph represents a function just by looking is to visually pass a vertical line through each point of the graph. If no vertical line ever crosses the graph in more than one point, then the graph represents a function.

Answers

1.	$s; c$
2.	$6 \le s \le 12$
3.	$40 \le c \le 100$
4.	nonlinear, increasing
5.	−1
6.	$y = -x - 2$
7.	b and c
8.	4.5
9.	7.5
10.	about 452.4 in.^{2}
11.	about 1436.8 cm^3
12.	*See question.*

9

Name _____ Date _____ Score _____

Test 7 *(continued)*

Directions: Write the answers in the spaces provided.

For Questions 13–15, the ratio of the radii of two spheres is 2:3.

13. What is the ratio of the surface areas of the two spheres?

14. What is the ratio of the volumes of the two spheres?

15. If the volume of the larger sphere is 54 in.^{3}, what is the volume of the smaller sphere?

For Questions 16 and 17, write each expression with positive exponents.

16. $\frac{7^0}{d^{-3}}$ 17. $(6w^{-3})(c^{-2})$

18. Rewrite the expression $\sqrt{7xy}$ using fractional exponents.

19. Rewrite the expression $-8(x^2)^{1/3}$ in radical form.

For Questions 20 and 21, use the equation $y = -3 \cdot 2^x$.

20. Find the value of y when $x = 11$.

21. Find the value of x when $y = -6$.

For Questions 22–24, use the fact that the half-life of a certain radioactive material is 4 days. An initial sample of the material has a mass of 2048 kg.

22. Write an exponential equation which models the decay of this material.

23. Find the amount of radioactive material left after 60 days.

24. After how many days will 256 kg of the material remain?

25. **Open-ended** Write an equation that represents direct variation with the cube. Give three ordered pairs that are solutions of your equation.

   Sample answer: $y = 3x^3$ (all answers should be of the form $y = kx^3$); (1, 3), (−2, −24), and (0, 0) are solutions.

Answers

13.	4:9
14.	8:27
15.	16 in.^{3}
16.	d^3
17.	$\frac{6}{c^2 w^3}$
18.	$(7xy)^{1/2}$
19.	$-8\sqrt[3]{x^2}$
20.	−6144
21.	1
22.	$y = 2048(\frac{1}{2})^x$
23.	0.0625 kg
24.	12 days
25.	*See question.*

Form B

Name _____ Date _____ Score _____

Test 8

Test on Unit 2 (Form B)

Directions: Write the answers in the spaces provided.

For Questions 1–4, use the graph at the right.

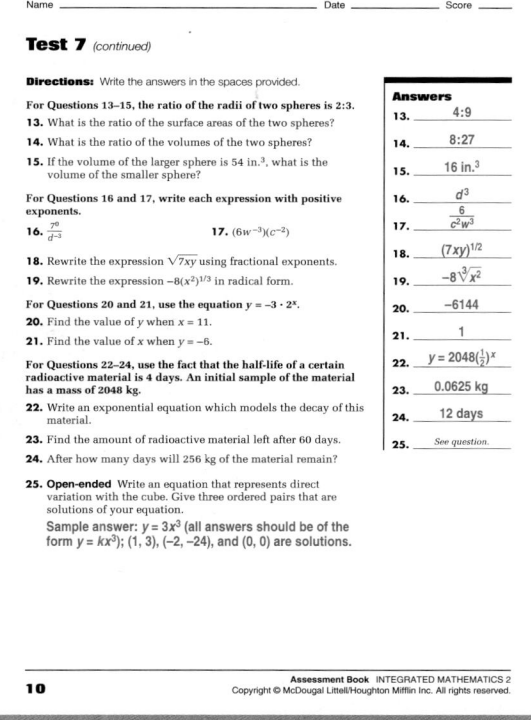

1. State the control variable and the dependent variable.

2. What is the domain of the function?

3. What is the range of the function?

4. Use the terms *linear* or *nonlinear* and *increasing, decreasing,* or *constant* to describe the graph.

5. What is the slope of the line through the points (5, 1) and (−7, −11)?

6. Write an equation of the line described in Question 5.

7. Choose the letters of the direct variation equations.

   a. $\frac{y}{x} = 2$ b. $y = \frac{8}{x}$ c. $x = \frac{y}{9}$

For Questions 8 and 9, use the inverse variation equation $xy = 28$.

8. Find the value of x when $y = 2.5$.

9. Find the value of y when $x = 5$.

10. Find the surface area of a sphere with radius 7 cm.

11. Find the volume of a sphere with diameter 22 cm.

12. **Writing** Explain how to tell if a graph represents a function.

   Sample answer: The way to tell if a graph represents a function just by looking is to visually pass a vertical line through each point of the graph. If no vertical line ever crosses the graph in more than one point, then the graph represents a function.

Answers

1.	$n; t$
2.	$1 \le n \le 6$
3.	$20 \le t \le 50$
4.	nonlinear, decreasing
5.	1
6.	$y = x - 4$
7.	a and c
8.	11.2
9.	5.6
10.	about 615.8 cm^2
11.	about 5575.3 cm^3
12.	*See question.*

11

Name _____ Date _____ Score _____

Test 8 *(continued)*

Directions: Write the answers in the spaces provided.

For Questions 13–15, the ratio of the radii of two spheres is 5:4.

13. What is the ratio of the surface areas of the two spheres?

14. What is the ratio of the volumes of the two spheres?

15. If the volume of the smaller sphere is 16 m^3, what is the volume of the larger sphere?

For Questions 16 and 17, write each expression with positive exponents.

16. $(8^0)(4d^{-5})$ 17. $\frac{6c^{-3}}{3c^{-2}}$

18. Rewrite the expression $\sqrt[3]{9h^2k}$ using fractional exponents.

19. Rewrite the expression $12x^{1/2}$ in radical form.

For Questions 20 and 21, use the equation $y = -7 \cdot 2^x$.

20. Find the value of y when $x = 9$.

21. Find the value of x when $y = -7$.

For Questions 22–24, use the fact that the half-life of a certain radioactive material is 6 days. An initial amount of the material has a mass of 512 kg.

22. Write an exponential equation which models the decay of this material.

23. Find the amount of radioactive material left after 72 days.

24. After how many days will 32 kg of the material remain?

25. **Open-ended** Write an equation that represents direct variation with the square. Give three ordered pairs that are solutions of your equation.

   Sample answer: $y = 2x^2$ (all answers should be of the form $y = kx^2$); (0, 0), (5, 50), and (−2, 8) are solutions.

Answers

13.	25:16
14.	125:64
15.	31.25 m^3
16.	$\frac{4}{d^5}$
17.	$\frac{2}{c}$
18.	$(9h^2k)^{1/3}$
19.	$12\sqrt{x}$
20.	−3584
21.	0
22.	$y = 512(\frac{1}{2})^x$
23.	0.125 kg
24.	24 days
25.	*See question.*

Software Support

McDougal Littell Mathpack

Function Investigator
Stats!

Plotter Plus

Macintosh and MS-DOS
(worksheets included)

Outside Resources

Books/Periodicals

Allen, R. F. *101 Ways to Teach about Exponential Growth and its Consequences.* Sebring, FL: Tri-County Teacher Education Center. (ERIC No. ED 225 856)

Jones, Graham. "Mathematical Modeling in a Feast of Rabbits." *Mathematics Teacher* (December 1993): pp. 770–773.

Activities/Manipulatives

Kincaid, Charlene, Deanna Mauldin, and Guy Mauldin. "Marble Sifter, a Half-Life Simulation." *Mathematics Teacher* (December 1993): pp. 748–750.

Software

Dugdale, Sharon and David Kibbey. *Graphing Equations and Green Globs.* Teacher's Guide. Edwards, Lois and Lisa Paul. Pleasantville, NY: Sunburst, 1985. Apple and IBM.

Videos

Southern Illinois University at Carbondale. *World Population Review,* 1990.

Organizations

Mono Lake Committee
P.O. Box 29
Lee Vining, CA 93541
Phone (619) 647-6386

PROJECT GOALS

➤ Students apply models of variation and growth to help them understand the ecosystem of a salt lake.

➤ As a park guide, students strive to educate, entertain, and satisfy the curiosity of visitors to Mono Lake.

➤ As a park guide, students point out the major features of the ecosystem, past, present, and future, and are prepared to answer visitors' questions.

PROJECT PLANNING

Materials List

➤ Note cards

Project Teams

Have students work on the project with another student. Students can work together to develop the material for their guide notes. They should discuss the special features of the ecosystem, the application of variation and growth models, and any questions they think visitors may ask about the Mono Lake environment.

Models of Variation and Growth

For the California gull, the best fast food place around is a place called Mono Lake. The air there is so thick with brine flies that all a gull needs to do to get a square meal is to open its beak. The number of brine flies has been estimated at 4000 per square foot of shore.

Mono Lake was named by the Yokut people, a group of Native Americans who lived west of the lake. *Mono* means "brine fly" in their language.

To the average visitor, the most attractive feature of Mono Lake may be the **tufa**, calcium carbonate formations that rise above the lake like castle towers.

MONO MEANS BRINE FLY

ECOSYSTEMS

calcium carbonate

56

Suggested Rubric for Unit Project

4 Students' note cards for their Mono Lake guided tour include the following five things: (1) a description of the major features of the Mono Lake ecosystem; (2) historical information about changes in the ecosystem; (3) predictions about the future of the ecosystem; (4) interesting details to enliven their tour; and (5) backup information for

answering visitors' questions. Students are able to explain correctly how mathematical models can be used to understand the ecosystem of a salt lake. They have also made use of some ideas from the Working on the Unit Project exercises in this unit.

3 Students' understanding of models of variation and growth is somewhat incomplete. This

partial understanding of the models that explain the ecosystem of a salt lake are reflected in their note cards for the guided tour. The information on the cards is adequate but will not offer visitors to the lake a fully educational or entertaining experience. Students have not anticipated some basic questions that visitors may ask.

Unit Project 2

Be a Park Guide

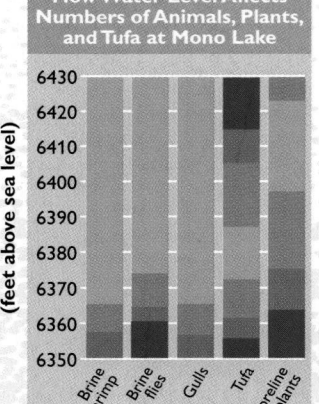

Limnologists from the University of California at Santa Barbara check oxygen and temperature levels in Mono Lake.

studies

How Water Level Affects Numbers of Animals, Plants, and Tufa at Mono Lake

Water level (feet above sea level): 6430, 6420, 6410, 6400, 6390, 6380, 6370, 6360, 6350

Categories: Brine shrimp, Brine flies, Gulls, Tufa, Shoreline plants

Legend:
- No change
- Slight drop
- Severe drop
- Complete elimination

In many salt lakes, the water level has dropped over time, bringing changes in the salt concentration. In this project, you will apply models of variation and growth to understand the ecosystem of a salt lake.

You will use what you learn to prepare to become a park guide at Mono Lake. Your role as a park guide is to educate, entertain, and satisfy the curiosity of visitors to Mono Lake. You should be ready to point out the major features of the ecosystem, describe how it has changed, predict how it may change in the future, and answer visitors' questions.

On a set of note cards you will record the points you plan to address in your guided tour. You can use the cards to rehearse your talk. The cards will also serve as a data bank for answering questions.

To scientists, called **limnologists**, who study the ecosystems of lakes and ponds, salt lakes have a special appeal. They are easier to model than fresh water ones because they support only a few types of plants and animals.

Mono Lake has no fish but supports huge numbers of brine shrimp, brine flies, and gulls and shore birds.

Another important salt lake lies in Africa, between Lake Victoria and Mt. Kilimanjaro in northern Tanzania. **Lake Natron** is the breeding ground for many of the world's flamingos.

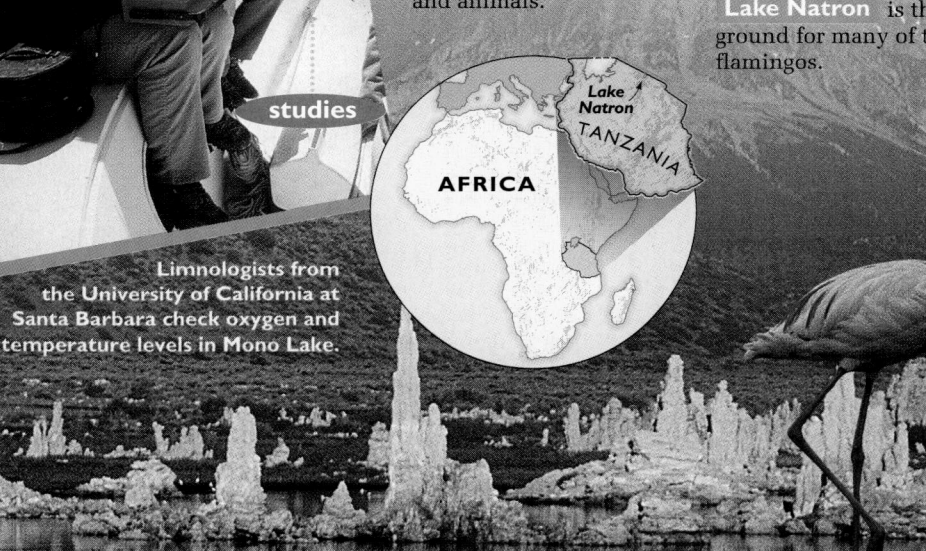

Lake Natron
TANZANIA
AFRICA

57

Suggested Rubric for Unit Project

2 Students' note cards are incomplete in two or more of the five things necessary for a first-rate guided tour of Mono Lake. They also demonstrate an incomplete understanding of such basic concepts of how a drop in the water level of a salt lake affects the saltiness of the water or other aspects of the ecosystem of a salt lake.

Based upon the information in the set of note cards, visitors to the lake would not be educated or entertained on their tour.

1 Students' note cards are inadequate. They will not prepare the students to become a park guide at Mono Lake. The mathematical concepts and models of variation and growth presented in this unit are not

understood. The group should be encouraged to speak with the teacher as soon as possible to review their work and to make a new start on the project.

National Parks

The National Park System of the United States started with the establishment of Yellowstone National Park in 1872. The park system includes spectacular scenic regions and superior recreational assets. There are also sites with special historic, prehistoric, and scientific characteristics. There are about 355 different sites with areas totaling over 80,117,313 acres.

ALTERNATIVE PROJECTS

Project 1, page 113

Tropical Rain Forest

Write a report about the ecosystem of a tropical rain forest, including how rain forests are affected by logging and how they affect the global climate. Use models of variation and growth to write the report.

Project 2, page 113

Population Growth

Obtain and analyze population data for your state for as many years as possible. A report should determine if there is a constant doubling period, contain a graph of the data, predict changes for the next 20 years, and compare the predictions with professional forecasts (if available).

Getting Started

For this project you should work with another student. Here are some ideas to help you get started.

☞ Discuss with your partner what features of the Mono Lake ecosystem you will point out and describe during a tour of Mono Lake.

☞ Plan to meet again later to discuss how you can apply models of variation and growth in your guided tour. At that time you may consider using some of the following ideas from the "Working on the Unit Project" exercises: how a drop in the water level of a salt lake affects the saltiness of the water, the size of bird populations, the aquatic life, and the formation of tufa.

☞ Think about what questions visitors to Mono Lake may ask.

Working on the Unit Project

Your work in Unit 2 will help you prepare to be a Mono Lake park guide.

Related Exercises:
Section 2-1, Exercises 30–32
Section 2-2, Exercise 43
Section 2-3, Exercises 32, 33
Section 2-4, Exercise 42
Section 2-5, Exercises 35–37
Section 2-6, Exercise 43
Section 2-7, Exercise 33

Alternative Projects p. 113

Can We Talk ECOSYSTEMS

➤ Why do you think no fish live in either Mono Lake or Lake Natron?

➤ What factors influence the water level of a lake? Which are natural causes and which are due to human activity?

➤ Which do you think is more important, providing water for people or protecting natural ecosystems?

➤ Some of the fresh water that used to run into Mono Lake is being used to provide drinking water for the population of Los Angeles. What kind of conservation steps can Los Angeles residents take to reduce their water usage?

➤ What effect do you think global warming might have on a salt lake?

Unit 2 Models of Variation and Growth

58

Answers to Can We Talk?

➤ Answers may vary. An example is given. Because fish cannot survive in such a high salt-content lake.

➤ Answers may vary. Examples are given. Temperature, ground composition of the surrounding area, rainfall, level of feeding rivers or streams, water consumption in the area. Most are natural causes but can be influenced by human activity. If many roads or buildings are built around the lake, the water level would rise due to run-off.

➤ Answers may vary. An example is given. Both are important because both are needed for survival. Finding a balance between the two so that people can have water without hurting the natural ecosystems would be the most beneficial for both.

➤ Answers may vary. Examples are given. Take baths instead of showers or shorten shower time, turn water off when brushing your teeth, mend or fix any leaky or dripping faucets, put a brick or heavy object in the toilet tank, only water your lawn very early in the morning to lessen evaporation or stop watering the lawn altogether.

➤ Answers may vary. An example is given. Global warming would probably speed up the evaporation of water from the lake since global warming decreases rainfall and raises the temperature of the air.

Functions and Graphs

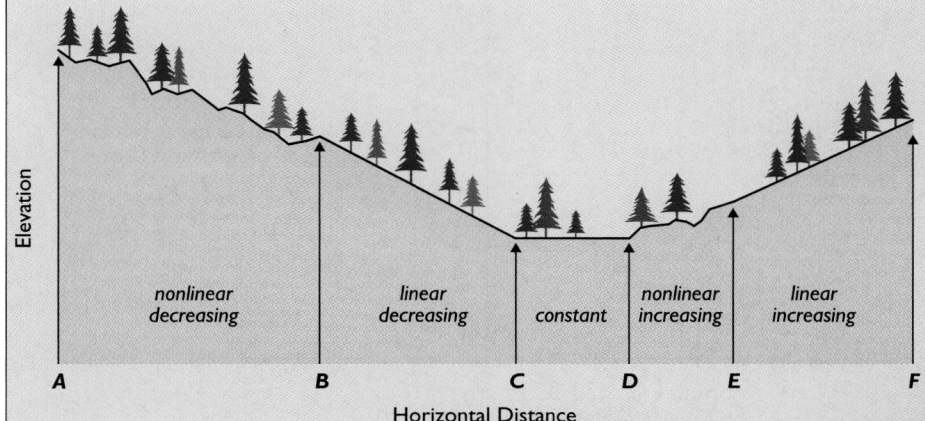

Focus
Describe the graphs of
functions.

Elevation

nonlinear
decreasing

linear
decreasing

constant

nonlinear
increasing

linear
increasing

A

B

C

D

E

F

Horizontal Distance

BY THE WAY...

The Nez Perce, a Native
American people, spent part of
each summer along Wallowa
Lake. In their language, a
"wallowa" is a support for a
fish trap used to catch
salmon. An important
Nez Perce leader,
Chief Joseph, may
have been born at
Wallowa Lake.

Talk it Over

1. This path along Wallowa Lake in Oregon has uphill, downhill, and flat parts. Suppose you are hiking along the path
from left to right. In your own words, describe how the path
changes.

2. Using the terms in the diagram, how would you describe the
graph over the interval between points *A* and *C*?

3. Name the endpoints of an interval on the horizontal axis
where the graph has each characteristic.

   a. increasing

   b. linear

   c. linear increasing

2-1 Functions and Graphs

Answers to Talk it Over

1. Answers may vary. An
example is given. The path
is downhill and bumpy at
first, then downhill and
straight until it becomes
flat and straight. The graph
then turns uphill and
bumpy until it then be-
comes uphill and straight
at the end.

2. Answers may vary. An
example is given. The
graph is nonlinear decreasing from point *A* to point
B, then linear decreasing
from point *B* to point *C*.

3. a. *D* and *E* or *E* and *F*

   b. *B* and *C, C and D,* or *E*
   and *F*

   c. *E* and *F*

PLANNING

Objectives and Strands
See pages 56A and 56B.

Spiral Learning
See page 56B.

Materials List
➤ Graph paper

Recommended Pacing
Section 2-1 is a two-day lesson.

Day 1

Pages 59–61: Talk it Over 1
through Sample 1, *Exercises 1–17*

Day 2

Page 62: Talk it Over 11 through
Look Back, *Exercises 18–32*

Toolbox References
➤ **Toolbox Skill 19:** Recognizing
Functions
➤ **Toolbox Skill 28:** Using
Formulas from Geometry

Extra Practice
See pages 616–617.

Warm-Up Exercises
Warm-Up Transparency 2-1

Support Materials
➤ Practice 9
➤ Enrichment 8 in the Activity Bank
➤ Study Guide 2-1
➤ Problem Set 3
➤ Diagram Master 1 in the
Explorations Lab Manual
➤ McDougal Littell Mathpack
software: *Stats!* and *Function
Investigator*
➤ *Stats!* Activity Book: Activities
8 and 14
➤ Quiz 2-1
➤ Alternative Assessment 1

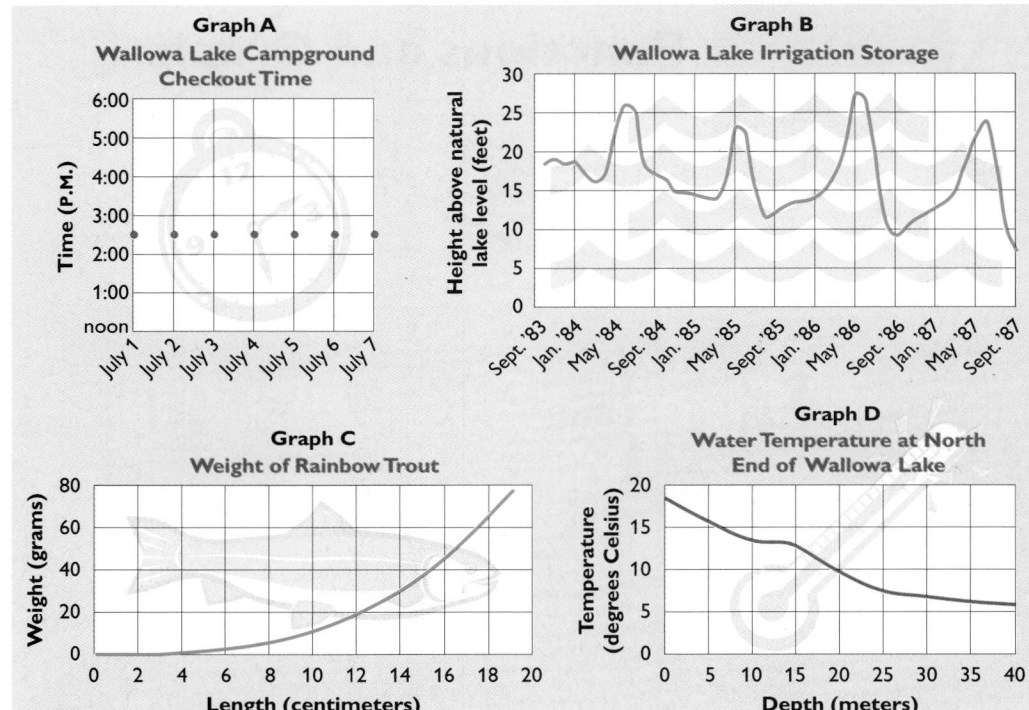

Graph A
Wallowa Lake Campground Checkout Time

Graph B
Wallowa Lake Irrigation Storage

Graph C
Weight of Rainbow Trout

Graph D
Water Temperature at North End of Wallowa Lake

Talk it Over

Questions 1–9 introduce students to a number of basic ideas involving the graphs of linear and nonlinear functions. They introduce vocabulary to describe graphs (questions 1–4), ask students to use graphs to predict values (questions 5–8), and also ask students to describe the characteristics of a graph over different intervals (question 9). Question 10 reviews the definition of a function.

Teaching Tip

When discussing Talk it Over question 10, remind students that the independent variable is always plotted along the x-axis. In other words, the first symbol in the ordered pairs that define a function is the independent variable. The second symbol in the ordered pairs is the dependent variable and is plotted along the y-axis.

Reasoning

The terms *independent* and *dependent* are not inherently difficult for students to understand. Yet it might help some students to think of the independent variable as the one that can be *arbitrarily* chosen (within the domain of the function). The dependent variable is *determined* by the arbitrarily chosen value of the independent variable.

4. Use graphs A–D.
   a. The graph of a straight line is **linear.** Which graphs are linear throughout? Which are nonlinear throughout?
   b. Which graphs are increasing throughout? Which are decreasing throughout? Which are constant throughout?
   c. Which graphs show discrete data? continuous data?

5. From graph A, what can you say about the checkout time for Wallowa Lake Campground during the first week of July?

6. Can you use graph B to predict the water level for October 1987? Why or why not?

7. From graph C, estimate the weight of a rainbow trout that is 18 cm long.

8. From graph D, can you tell if the temperature changes at the same rate from the surface down to a depth of 40 m? Explain.

9. Graphs can have different characteristics over different intervals. Using this idea and the terms in the diagram on page 59, describe the characteristics of graph D.

Student Resources Toolbox
p. 649 *Graphs, Equations, and Inequalities*

10. Remember that a **function** is a relationship in which there is *only* one value of the *dependent variable* for each value of the *control*, or *independent*, *variable*. Do you think graphs A–D are graphs of functions? Why or why not?

Answers to Talk it Over

4. a. A; B, C, D
   b. C; none; A
   c. A; B, C, D

5. The checkout time during the first week in July remained constant.

6. Answers may vary. An example is given. Yes. By looking at the water level change from September to October for the years 1983,

1984, 1985, and 1986, you can make a reasonable estimate of the water level for October 1987.

7. about 67 g

8. Yes. The steepness of the graph can tell you how fast the temperature is changing at each depth.

9. Answers may vary. An example is given. The

graph is linear and decreasing from a depth of 0 to 10 meters, constant from a depth of 10 to 13 meters, and nonlinear and decreasing from 13 to 40 meters.

10. Answers may vary. An example is given. Yes; no two points lie on the same vertical line (vertical-line test).

Growth and Decay

Graphs of functions can be examples of *growth*, *decay*, or a *constant* depending on whether the value of the dependent variable continually increases, decreases, or remains the same when the value of the control variable increases.

TYPES OF GRAPHS

A **growth graph** is increasing throughout.

A **decay graph** is decreasing throughout.

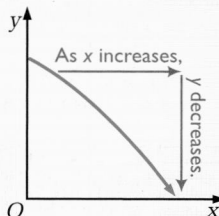

A **constant graph** is linear and horizontal.

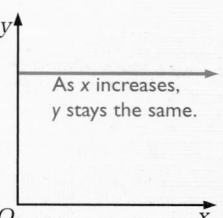

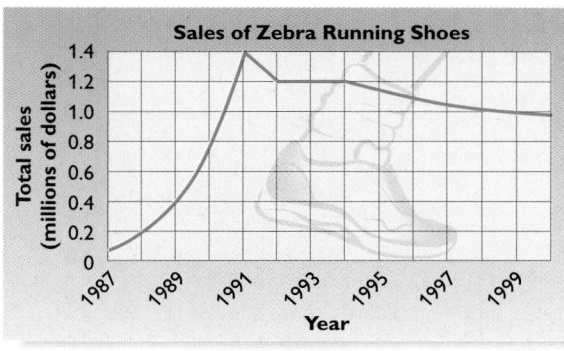

Sales of Zebra Running Shoes

Sample 1

a. Use the terms *linear* or *nonlinear* and *increasing, decreasing,* or *constant* to describe the graph.

b. Is this a *growth graph*, a *decay graph*, or *neither*? Explain your choice.

c. **Writing** Based on the graph, do you think Zebra Company stock is a good investment? Why or why not?

Sample Response

a. Between 1987 and 1991: nonlinear and increasing.
Between 1991 and 1992: linear and decreasing.
Between 1992 and 1994: constant.
Between 1994 and 2000: nonlinear and decreasing.

b. Neither, because the graph is sometimes increasing, sometimes decreasing, and sometimes constant.

c. Zebra Company stock does not look like a good investment. The graph shows that sales were not increasing over the last nine years shown.

▶ **Now you are ready for:**
Exs. 1–17 on pp. 63–64

2-1 Functions and Graphs

61

Exs. 1–17 on pp. 63–64

Students Acquiring English

In this section, and in fact throughout this unit, students must recall or learn many new terms that relate to functions and graphs. To ensure that this vocabulary does not block the progress of students acquiring English, you may want to have them work in small groups with students fluent in English.

Communication: Drawing

The drawings of the three types of graphs shown on this page show clearly that it is the change in the *dependent variable* that gives the graph its name. In all three graphs, the control variable or independent variable is increasing.

Additional Sample

S1

Lisa's Savings Accounts

a. Use the terms *linear* or *nonlinear* and *increasing, decreasing,* or *constant* to describe the graph. **nonlinear and increasing**

b. Is this a *growth graph*, a *decay graph*, or *neither*. Explain your choice. **growth graph; because for each new year, the total savings increases**

c. Suppose Lisa made a withdrawal from her savings account of $2000 in 1999 and a deposit of $5000 in 2000. Complete the graph for these two years. **See graph.**

Questions 11 and 12 prepare students to understand the concepts of the *domain* and *range* of a function.

Communication: Writing

It would be instructive to have students use the terms domain and range to rewrite the definition of a function given in Talk it Over question 10 on page 60. (A function is a relationship such that for each value in the domain of the function there is only one value in its range.)

Additional Sample

S2 Find the domain and range for the function represented by this graph.

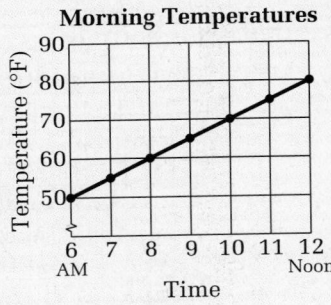

Morning Temperatures

The control variable is the time. The domain is the time from 6 A.M. to 12 noon. The dependent variable is temperature. The range is the temperature from 50°F to 80°F.

---

11. What is the least value of the control variable shown for the graph in Sample 1 on page 61? What is the greatest value?

12. Estimate the least value and the greatest value of the dependent variable in Sample 1.

For any function, the **domain** is all the values of the control variable for which the function is defined. The **range** is all the values of the dependent variable over the domain.

Sample 2

Find the domain and range for the function represented by this graph.

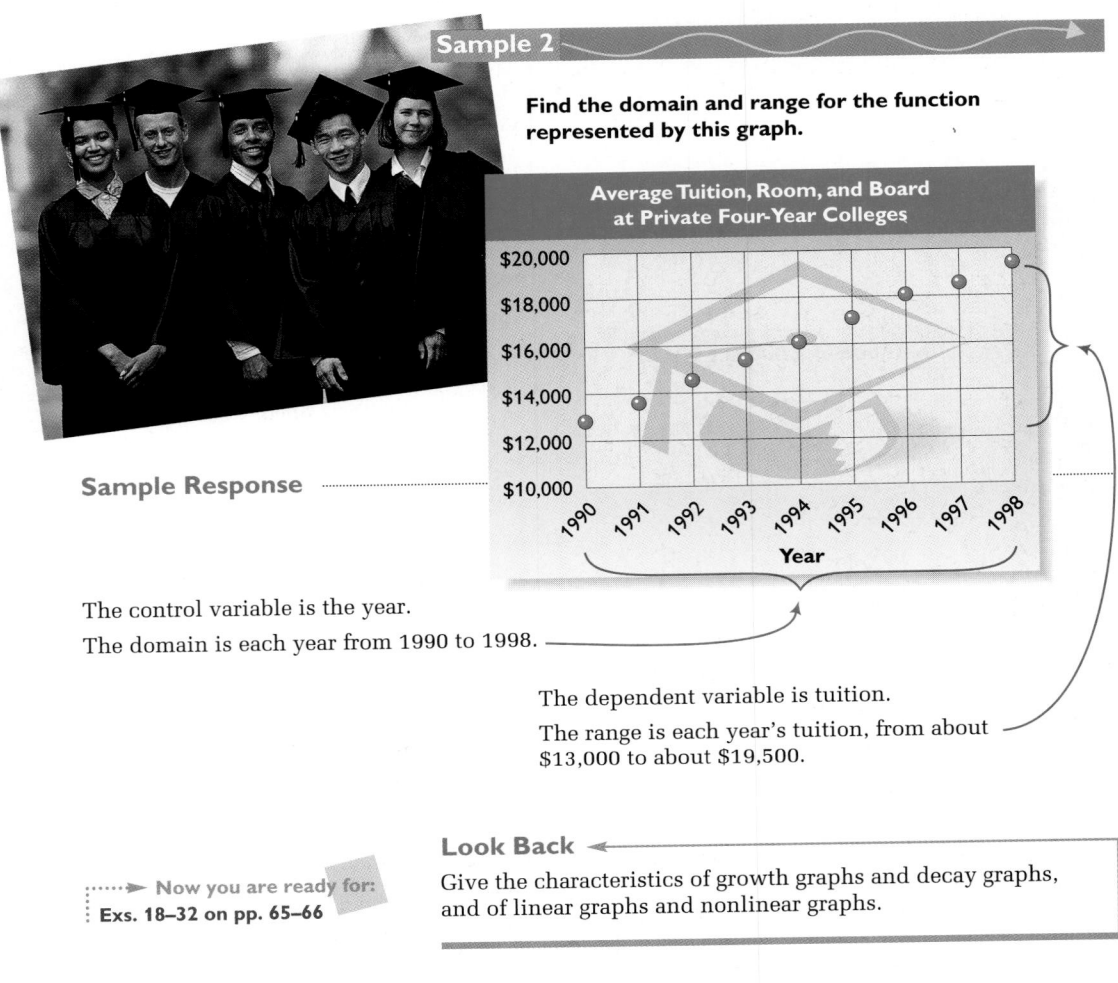

Sample Response

The control variable is the year.
The domain is each year from 1990 to 1998.

The dependent variable is tuition.
The range is each year's tuition, from about $13,000 to about $19,500.

Look Back

Give the characteristics of growth graphs and decay graphs, and of linear graphs and nonlinear graphs.

▸ **Now you are ready for:**
Exs. 18–32 on pp. 65–66

Answers to Talk it Over

11. 1987; 2000
12. $100,000; $1,400,000

Answers to Look Back

Answers may vary. Examples are given. In growth graphs and decay graphs, the direction of the change (that is, an increase or decrease in the dependent variable) does not change and both may be linear or nonlinear or both. Growth graphs show an increase in the dependent variable, while a decay graph shows a decrease in the dependent variable.

Linear and nonlinear graphs may show growth or decay. A linear graph is a line; a nonlinear graph is not. As the control variable increases or decreases by the same amount, the dependent variable changes by a constant amount or not at all in a linear graph, and by different amounts in a nonlinear graph.

Exercises and Problems

1. **Reading** Give the characteristics of a constant graph.

Use the terms _linear_ or _nonlinear_ and _increasing, decreasing,_ or _constant_ to describe each graph.

2.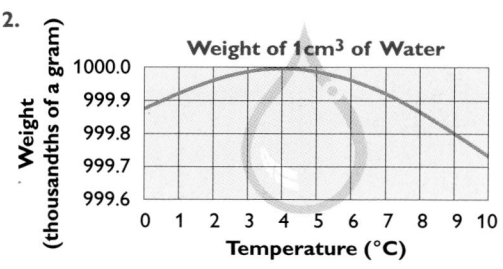

3.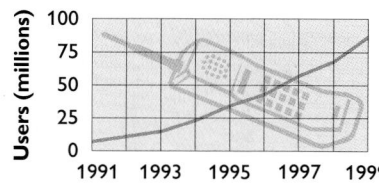

4.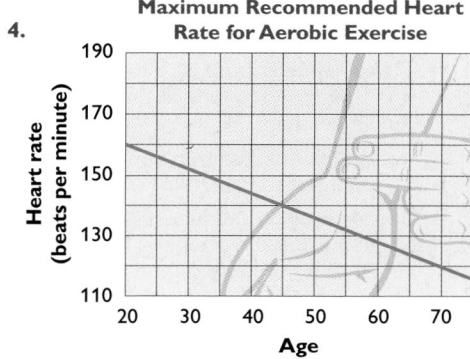

5.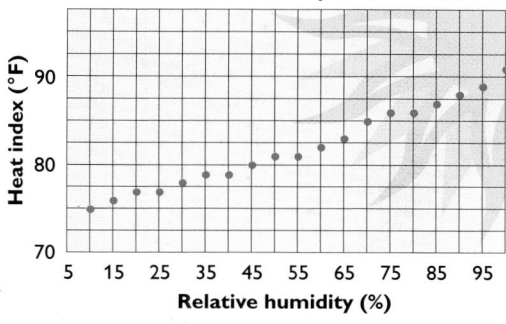

6. Which of the graphs in Exercises 2–5 are growth graphs? Explain your choices.

7. Is the graph of $x = 4$ a constant graph? Why or why not?

For Exercises 8–11, use the graphs in Exercises 2–5.

8. **Physics** At what temperature between 0°C and 10°C is water the heaviest?

9. **Writing** Inez Barco is planning to invest some money. Based on the graph, would you advise her to invest some money in cellular phone service? Why or why not?

10. **Fitness** Boris Aronsky checks his pulse during a high-intensity/low-impact aerobics class. He counts 27 beats in 10 seconds. Boris is 26 years old. Is Boris's heart rate above or below the suggested maximum?

11. **Meteorology** When the air temperature reaches 80°F, does it always feel like 80°F? Explain your answer. (_Note:_ The Heat Index is how hot it feels due to the combined effect of temperature and humidity.)

APPLYING

Suggested Assignment

Day 1

Standard 1–11, 13–15

Extended 1–11, 13–17

Day 2

Standard 18–32

Extended 18–32

Integrating the Strands

Algebra Exs. 1–32

Functions Exs. 1–25, 31, 32

Geometry Ex. 19

Statistics and Probability Exs. 27, 30

Logic and Language Ex. 26

Interdisciplinary Problems

Most of the Exercises and Problems on pages 63–66 involve functional relationships between two variables. Since the concept of a function is very general, it can be applied in any situation where one element is dependent upon another. As the exercises are discussed, students should be able to recognize the interdependence of the quantities involved. The various interdisciplinary problems from physics, business, fitness, meteorology, movies, and geometry illustrate both the notion of functionality itself and its applicability to different real-world situations.

Answers to Exercises and Problems

1. A constant graph is linear; the slope is 0. As x increases, y stays the same.

2. nonlinear and increasing on the interval from 0 to 4; nonlinear and decreasing on the interval from 4 to 10

3. nonlinear and increasing

4. linear and decreasing

5. linear and increasing on the interval from 10 to 20; constant on the interval from 20 to 25; linear and increasing on the interval from 25 to 35; constant on the interval from 35 to 40; linear and increasing on the interval from 40 to 50; constant on the interval from 50 to 55; nonlinear and increasing on the interval from 55 to 75; constant on the interval from 75 to 80; nonlinear and increasing on the interval from 80 to 100

6. Answers may vary. The graph in Ex. 3 is a growth graph because, over the whole graph, as the value of the control variable increases, the value of the dependent variable increases.

7. No; a constant graph is a horizontal line and its slope is 0. The graph of $x = 4$ is a vertical line and its slope is undefined.

8. 4°C

9. It would be reasonable to advise her to invest because according to the graph in Ex. 3, the use of cellular telephones has increased throughout the 1990s.

10. above

11. No; according to the graph in Ex. 5, the temperature can feel hotter or cooler, depending on the relative humidity.

12. a. Writing Describe how the graph of the height of a person might look over the person's lifetime.

    b. Research Find out what your height was at various ages from your day of birth through today. Graph the data. How well does your graph match your description in part (a)?

Tell whether each graph is an example of *linear growth, nonlinear growth, linear decay, nonlinear decay, a constant,* **or** *none of these.*

13. 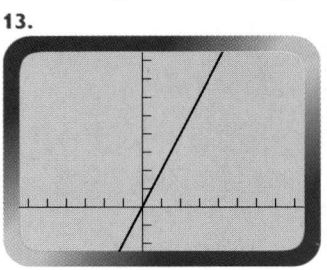   **14.** 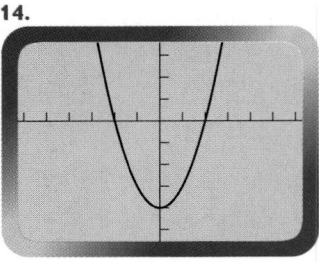   **15.**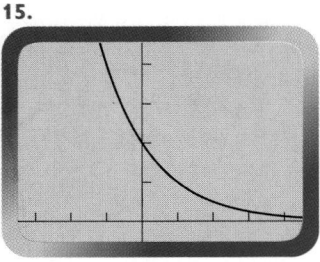

Career Some directors use graphs to analyze a movie as it is being filmed.

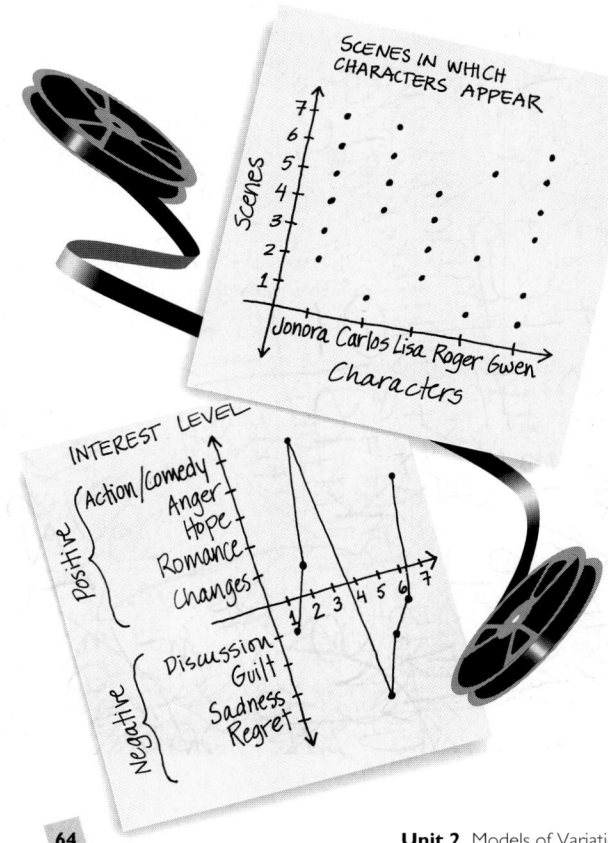

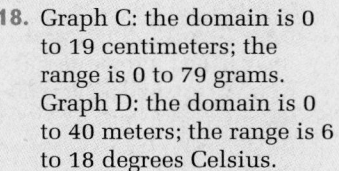

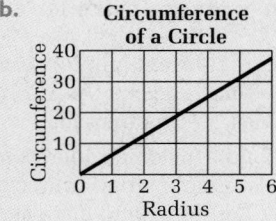

16. Open-ended Suppose a director made the first graph to look at the impact of the characters.

    a. Which character do you think has the least impact? Why?

    b. Writing What changes, if any, do you think the director should make in order to increase the impact of the character in part (a)?

17. Suppose a director made the second graph to chart a movie's emotional high points and low points. The numbers represent the scenes.

    a. How many strong "highs" are there? How many strong "lows"?

    b. Writing What changes, if any, do you think the director should make to increase the emotional impact of the movie?

Answers to
Exercises and Problems

12. a. Answers may vary. Over the first few years of life, the graph would probably be nonlinear and increasing, with the increase slowing in adolescence, at some point becoming linear and increasing. In late adolescence or early adulthood, the graph would become constant. In old age, the graph might become nonlinear and slightly decreasing before becoming constant again.

    b. Answers may vary.

13. linear growth

14. none

15. nonlinear decay

16. a. Answers may vary. An example is given. Carlos has the least impact since he appears in scenes 1, 4, 5, and 6, which are four of the five least interesting scenes.

    b. Answers may vary. An example is given. To increase the impact of Carlos, put him in scenes involving action, comedy, anger, or hope.

17. a. There are two strong "highs" and two strong "lows."

    b. Answers may vary. An example is given. Change scenes 1, 2, and 6 to involve stronger positive or negative emotions.

18. Graph C: the domain is 0 to 19 centimeters; the range is 0 to 79 grams. Graph D: the domain is 0 to 40 meters; the range is 6 to 18 degrees Celsius.

19. a. circumference of a circle

    b.

Circumference of a Circle

    c. linear and increasing

    d. a growth graph because the circumference increases as the radius increases

18. Find the domain and range for the functions represented by graphs C and D on page 60.

19. a. What does the formula $C = 2\pi r$ represent in the study of geometry?

    b. Graph the function. Use r for the control variable and C for the dependent variable. (*Note:* If you are using a graphics calculator, use x and y instead.)

    c. Use the terms *linear* or *nonlinear* and *increasing, decreasing,* or *constant* to describe your graph.

    d. Is the graph of $C = 2\pi r$ a *growth graph,* a *decay graph,* or *neither?* Explain your choice.

    e. **Writing** Does the domain of the function $C = 2\pi r$ include negative values? Does the range? Why or why not?

20. Repeat Exercise 19 with the formula $A = \pi r^2$.

Student Resources Toolbox
p. 657 *Formulas and Relationships*

connection to DRIVER'S EDUCATION

Under certain conditions the distance a car travels once the driver has decided to stop the car is given by the function in the photograph.

21. a. Graph the function. Use s for the control variable and d for the dependent variable.

    b. Use the terms *linear* or *nonlinear* and *increasing, decreasing,* or *constant* to describe your graph.

    c. Is your graph a *growth graph,* a *decay graph,* or *neither?* Explain your choice.

    d. How does the graph show that the stated relationship between stopping distance and speed is a function?

    e. Suppose the top speed for a car is 110 mi/h. Find the domain and range for the stated stopping distance relationship.

$d = 0.05s^2 + s$, where d is the stopping distance in feet and s is the speed of the car in miles per hour

2-1 Functions and Graphs

65

Reasoning

In Ex. 19, students work with a geometric formula that illustrates clearly the concept of dependence. The circumference of a circle is uniquely determined by its radius. As presented in Ex. 19, C is a function of r. However, since any change in the circumference of a circle produces a corresponding change in its radius, C could have been chosen as the control variable. Then r would be the dependent variable, and r would be a function of C. In astronomy, for example, it is possible to determine the circumference of a star by making certain measurements and calculations which do not involve using the formula $C = 2\pi r$ because r is unknown. By knowing the circumference of a star, astronomers can then determine its radius and diameter.

Using Technology

Students can use the *Function Investigator* software to graph the function in Ex. 19.

Application

The function $d = 0.05s^2 + s$ that is used to calculate the stopping distance of a car traveling at speed s illustrates not only that stopping distance is a function of speed, but also that many drivers do not leave enough distance between their cars and the ones in front of them when traveling at high speeds.

Answers to Exercises and Problems

  e. No; No; because the radius and the circumference cannot be negative.

20. a. area of a circle

    b.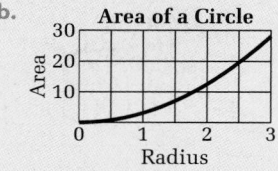
Area of a Circle

  c. nonlinear and increasing

  d. a growth graph because the area increases as the radius increases

  e. No; No; because a circle cannot have a negative radius or area.

21. a.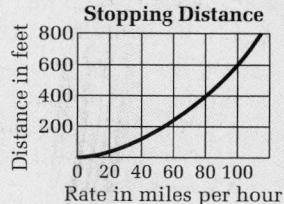
Stopping Distance

  b. nonlinear and increasing

  c. a growth graph because stopping distance increases with increasing speed

  d. For every speed, there is one stopping distance and the graph passes the vertical-line test.

  e. domain: $0 \le s \le 110$; range: $0 \le d \le 715$

Practice 9 For use with Section 2-1

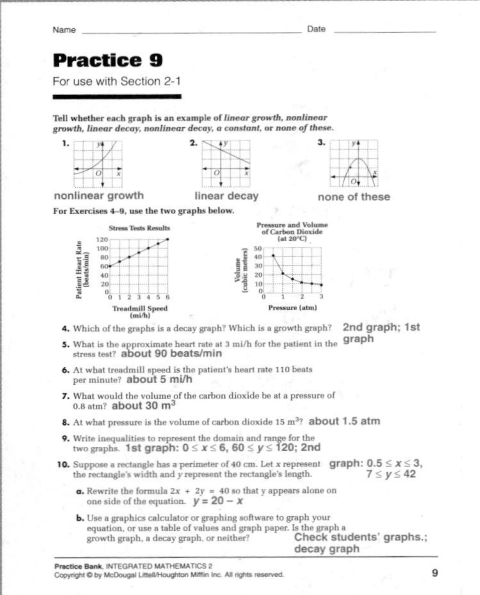

Open-ended Describe a situation that can be modeled by each type of graph. Sketch a graph for your situation.

22. linear graph   **23.** nonlinear graph   **24.** decay graph   **25.** constant graph

Review **PREVIEW**

26. Gabriel read this advertisement for a pain-relief medication. He was surprised to learn that three fourths of doctors recommend this medication. What is Gabriel's error in reasoning? *(Section 1-7)*

> "Three out of four doctors who use this medication recommend it."

27. Make a scatter plot of the data and draw a fitted line. *(Toolbox Skill 1)*

x	113	187	245	310	332	405	559	621
y	237	369	498	632	668	812	1120	1260

For Exercises 28 and 29, tell whether each statement is *True* or *False*.
(Toolbox Skill 21)

28. The slope of a horizontal line is 0.

29. The slope of a vertical line is negative.

Working on the Unit Project

30. a. Make a scatter plot of this data for Mono Lake. Graph salt content as a function of the water level in the lake.

   b. Describe the graph.

31. When the concentration of salt in a lake is greater than three percent by weight, the lake is a *salt lake.*

   a. Find the percent of salt by weight for each of the water levels of Mono Lake shown in the table. One liter of water weighs 1 kg, or 1000 g.

   b. Graph the concentration of salt as a function of water level.

   c. Describe the graph.

32. About 40 in. of water evaporates from Mono Lake each year.

   a. Sketch the graph of the changing water level due to evaporation as a function of time.

   b. Is the function an example of *linear growth, nonlinear growth, linear decay, nonlinear decay,* or a *constant*?

Water level (feet above sea level)	Salt content (grams per liter)
6417	51.3
6414	54.0
6410	56.3
6407	58.1
6403	60.2
6380	89.3
6378	86.8
6377	91.6
6376	89.3
6375	93.4
6373	97.7
6372	99.4

Unit 2 Models of Variation and Growth

Answers to Exercises and Problems

22–25. Answers may vary. Examples are given. Check students' graphs.

22. cost of filling a gas tank at a given cost per gallon as a function of number of gallons the tank holds

23. area of a square as a function of the length of a side

24. amount of loan remaining to be paid as a function of the number of months left in the payment period

25. average human body temperature as a function of age

26. The survey did not claim that three out of four doctors recommend the medication, only that three out of four doctors who use it recommend it. Gabriel did not consider that the sample was biased.

27.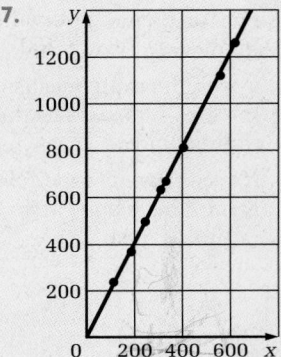

28–31. See answers in back of book.

32. a.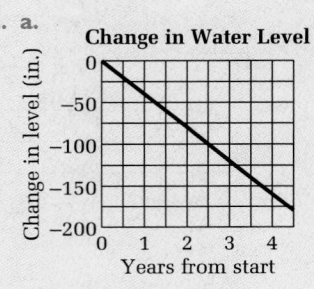

   b. linear decay

Linear Models and Direct Variation

On-line

Focus
Review linear functions, slope of a line, and direct variation.

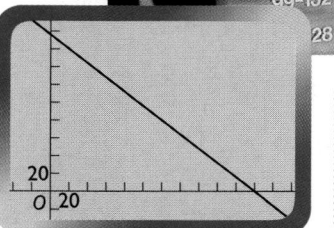

a	h
0	176
10	168
20	160
30	152
40	144

Exercise makes your heart beat faster. To keep your workout safe, you must make sure your heart does not beat too fast.

Health and fitness experts use this formula to find the *maximum target heart rate* during aerobic exercise:

$$h = -0.8a + 176$$

heart rate in → beats per minute

← age in years

This formula is a *mathematical model* of the relationship between age and maximum target heart rate during exercise. Functions, tables, graphs, equations, and inequalities that describe a situation are called **mathematical models.**

Talk it Over

1. How does the maximum target heart rate change with age?

2. How does the formula show that the maximum target heart rate is always under 176 beats per minute?

3. a. What is a reasonable domain for this function?
   b. Find the range for the function over this domain.

4. This table of values and this graph also model the relationship between age and maximum target heart rate.
   a. In the table, the value of a increases by 10. How does the value of h change?
   b. Is the graph *linear* or *nonlinear*?
   c. Is the graph *increasing, decreasing,* or *constant*?
   d. Is the graph a *growth graph*, a *decay graph*, or *neither*? Explain your choice.

2-2 Linear Models and Direct Variation   **67**

Answers to Talk it Over

1. Maximum heart rate declines with age.

2. $-0.8a$ is always a negative number since a must be positive, so at any age $-0.8a + 176$ is less than 176.

3. a. Answers may vary. An example is given.
   $0 \leq a \leq 80$

   b. Based upon the domain given in question 3(a), $112 \leq h \leq 176$.

4. a. decreases by 8
   b. linear
   c. decreasing
   d. decay graph; As a increases, h decreases.

PLANNING

Objectives and Strands
See pages 56A and 56B.

Spiral Learning
See page 56B.

Materials List
➤ Graph paper
➤ Graphics calculator
➤ Graphing software such as Plotter Plus

Recommended Pacing
Section 2-2 is a two-day lesson.
Day 1
Pages 67–69: Opening paragraph through Sample 1, *Exercises 1–26*
Day 2
Pages 69–70: Sample 2 through Look Back, *Exercises 27–43*

Toolbox References
➤ **Toolbox Skill 29:** Finding Sine, Cosine, and Tangent Ratios

Extra Practice
See pages 616–617.

Warm-Up Exercises
Warm-Up Transparency 2-2

Support Materials
➤ Practice 10
➤ Enrichment 9 in the Activity Bank
➤ Study Guide 2-2
➤ Problem Set 3
➤ Additional Exploration 3
➤ Diagram Master 2 in the Explorations Lab Manual
Overhead Visual 2
➤ McDougal Littell Mathpack software: *Function Investigator* and *Stats!*
➤ Function Investigator with Matrix Analyzer Activity Book: Function Investigator Activities 3–5
➤ Using IBM/Mac Plotter Plus Disk: Line Plotter
➤ Quiz 2-2
➤ Alternative Assessment 2

Teaching Tip

When discussing the idea of a mathematical model, you might ask students to suggest any physical models of things they are familiar with. Point out that manufacturing companies often make models of new products to use for tests and experiments. Ask students to suggest some advantages that a business might get from first working with a model. (A model is less expensive to make than the finished product and it can be manipulated to learn the defects and strengths of the product before making a full-scale version.) Relate the idea of manipulating a physical model (to learn how the finished product might work) to studying a mathematical model to understand the real-world situation it describes.

Talk it Over

Questions 1–4 give students an opportunity to explore the mathematical model for maximum target heart rate. Question 4 points out that graphs and tables can also be used as models.

Additional Sample

S1 Write an equation for the line through points $(-5, 3)$ and $(4, -6)$.

Step 1. **Find the slope.**
$$m = \frac{y_2 - y_1}{x_2 - x_1} = \frac{-6 - 3}{4 - (-5)} = \frac{-9}{9} = -1$$

Step 2. **Find the vertical intercept.**
$$y = mx + b$$
$$3 = -1(-5) + b$$
$$3 = 5 + b$$
$$-2 = b$$

Step 3. **Substitute the values you found for m and b.**
$$y = mx + b$$
$$y = (-1)x - 2$$
$$y = -x - 2$$

The target heart rate formula on page 67 is an example of a **linear function.** Its graph is a line. The function is written in **slope-intercept form.**

dependent variable — control variable

$$y = mx + b$$

slope — The **vertical intercept** is the value of the dependent variable when the control variable is 0.

$$h = -0.8a + 176$$

SLOPE OF A LINE

$$\text{slope} = \frac{\text{vertical change}}{\text{horizontal change}}$$

$$m = \frac{y_2 - y_1}{x_2 - x_1}$$

The slope of a horizontal line is 0.

The slope of a vertical line is undefined.

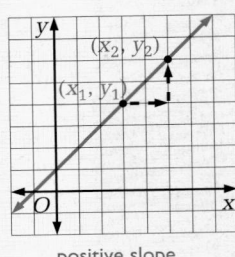

positive slope

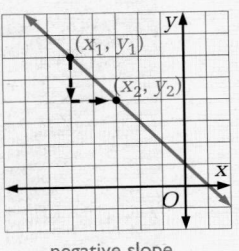

negative slope

There is exactly one line through any two points. You can use slope to find an equation for the line through any two points.

Sample 1

Write an equation for the line through the points (10, 7) and (−6, −1).

Sample Response

Use the slope-intercept form of the equation of a line.

Step 1 Find the slope.

$$m = \frac{y_2 - y_1}{x_2 - x_1} \longleftarrow \text{Write the slope formula.}$$

$$m = \frac{-1 - 7}{-6 - 10} \longleftarrow \begin{array}{l}\text{Substitute the coordinates of} \\ \text{(10, 7) and (−6, −1).}\end{array}$$

$$m = \frac{-8}{-16}$$

$$m = \frac{1}{2}$$

Unit 2 Models of Variation and Growth

Step 2 Find the vertical intercept.

$y = mx + b$ ← Write the slope-intercept form of the equation of a line.

$7 = \frac{1}{2} \cdot 10 + b$ ← Substitute the value of the **slope** and the **coordinates of a point.**

$7 = 5 + b$

$2 = b$

Step 3 Substitute the values you found for m and b.

$y = mx + b$

$y = \frac{1}{2}x + 2$

····▶ Now you are ready for:
Exs. 1–26 on pp. 70–72

Sample 2

Ashanthi is on a pledge-walk to raise money. She is an experienced walker who maintains a steady pace of 4 mi/h.

a. Write an equation that models the distance she walks.

b. Draw a graph that models the distance she walks.

Sample Response

a. Let D = the distance in miles.

Let t = the time in hours.

Distance = rate × time

$D = 4t$

b. Make a table of values or use a graphics calculator. Use y for the dependent variable and x for the control variable.

$y = 4x$	
x	**y**
0	0
1	4
2	8
3	12
4	16

← Time and distance are both nonnegative.

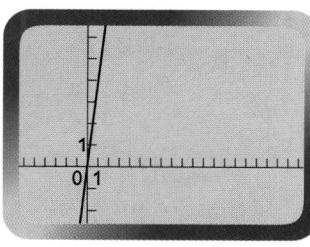

The part of the graph in the first quadrant models the distance she walks.

69

Using Technology

You can use the TI-81, TI-82, or TI-83 to find an equation for the line through two given points. To use the TI-82 or TI-83 and the points in Sample 1, press STAT and select ClrList from the EDIT menu to clear the lists L1 and L2 (see the manual for the TI-82 or TI-83 as needed). Next, press STAT and select Edit from the EDIT menu to enter 10 and −6 (the x-coordinates) in the L1 column and 7 and −1 (the y-coordinates) in the L2 column. Press STAT and select item 5:LinReg $(ax + b)$ from the CALC menu on the TI-82 or item 4:LinReg $(ax + b)$ from the CALC menu on the TI-83. After LinReg appears on the screen, press ENTER. The calculator will display the equation $y = ax + b$ and values identified as a, b, and r on the TI-82 and as a, b, r^2, and r on the TI-83. Use $a = 0.5$ and $b = 2$ to obtain the desired equation, $y = 0.5x + 2$. The procedure for the TI-81 is somewhat similar to that of the TI-82 and TI-83. For details, see the manual for the TI-81.

Additional Sample

S2 Eleanor uses 10 Calories of energy in warming up for her morning run. For every minute of running time, she uses 15 Calories.

a. Write an equation that models the total number of Calories (y) Eleanor uses in warming up and running for x minutes.
   $y = 10 + 15x$

b. Draw a graph that models her activities.
   Use a graphics calculator.

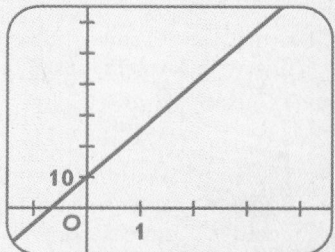

69

Talk it Over

Question 5 leads students to recognize that a direct variation equation in the form $y = kx$ is a special case of the linear equation $y = mx + b$, when $b = 0$. Questions 6–9 further strengthen this connection by having students analyze the direct variation equation of Sample 2.

Look Back

If students have difficulty answering these questions, suggest that they refer to Talk it Over questions 8 and 9, which deal with the same type of question but in a more specific sense.

APPLYING

Suggested Assignment

Day 1

Standard 1–17, 20–26

Extended 1–17, 19–26

Day 2

Standard 27, 28, 30, 34–43

Extended 27–32, 34–43

Integrating the Strands

Algebra Exs. 1–43

Functions Exs. 1–16, 18–36, 40–43

Geometry Ex. 32

Trigonometry Ex. 32

Statistics and Probability Ex. 43

Logic and Language Exs. 19, 26, 29, 43

In Sample 2 on page 69, the distance Ashanthi walks *varies directly with* the time she walks. The equation that models the distance is $D = 4t$. An equation in the general form

$$y = kx$$

is called a **direct variation** equation. The value of k $(k \neq 0)$ is called the **variation constant.**

BY THE WAY...

Hubble's Law is an important direct variation equation used by astronomers. The law states that the more distant galaxies are moving faster.

Talk it Over

5. Compare the equations $y = kx$ and $y = mx + b$. Explain why direct variation is a linear function.

6. What is the variation constant in the equation in Sample 2?

7. What is the vertical intercept of the graph in Sample 2?

8. In Sample 2 the slope of the graph is the walking rate, 4 mi/h. If Ashanthi walks at a rate of 3 mi/h instead, how does the graph change?

9. Suppose Ashanthi gets credit for the 2.5 mi she walks to the starting line of the pledge-walk. How does the graph change?

Look Back

How does the graph of a linear function change when the slope increases or decreases? when the vertical intercept increases or decreases?

▶ Now you are ready for:
Exs. 27–43 on pp. 72–74

2-2 Exercises and Problems

1. **Reading** What is the vertical intercept of the graph of the maximum target heart rate formula on page 67?

For each pair of points in Exercises 2–7:

a. **Find the slope of the line through the points.**

b. **Describe the line through the points as *increasing, decreasing,* or *constant.***

2.
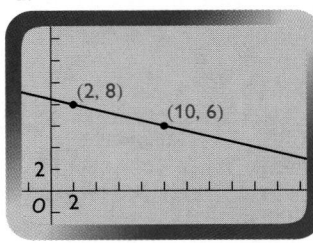

3.

4.
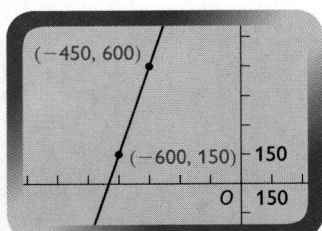

5. $(0, 6)$ and $(-2, 0)$

6. $(-7, 3)$ and $(5, -1)$

7. $(5, -12)$ and $(11, -12)$

Answers to Talk it Over

5. Direct variation is a linear function with y-intercept $b = 0$.

6. 4

7. 0

8. The graph would not be as steep. It would rise 3 units for every positive 1 increase in x.

9. The graph would have the same slope, but would be shifted up 2.5 units.

Answers to Look Back

As the slope changes, the steepness of the graph changes. The graph shifts up when the vertical intercept increases or down when the vertical intercept decreases.

Answers to Exercises and Problems

1. 176 beats/min

2. $-\frac{1}{4}$; decreasing

3. 0; constant

4. 3; increasing

5. 3; increasing

6. $-\frac{1}{3}$; decreasing

7. 0; constant

8. $y = 4x + 1$

9. $y = 3x - 2$

10. $y = \frac{1}{4}x + 3$

11. $y = -2x + 5$

12. $y = -4x - 7$

13. $y = \frac{2}{3}x - 9$

14. $(7.89, 3.97)$ and $(2.84, 2.71)$; 0.25

15. c; $58.32

16. $m = \frac{b-b}{a-0} = \frac{0}{a} = 0$

17. $m = \frac{d-0}{c-c} = \frac{d}{0} =$ undefined

For Exercises 8–13, write an equation for the line through each pair of points.

8. (0, 1) and (2, 9)
9. (1, 1) and (4, 10)
10. (8, 5) and (−4, 2)

11. (2, 1) and (4, −3)
12. (−1, −3) and (−3, 5)
13. (3, −7) and (0, −9)

14. The graphs show the coordinates of two points on the same line.

Round the coordinates to the nearest hundredth. Then find the slope of the line.

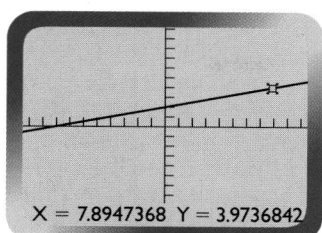 X = 7.8947368 Y = 3.9736842

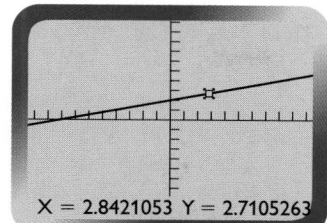 X = 2.8421053 Y = 2.7105263

15. Let c = the cost of a tune-up.

Let s = the number of spark plugs needed.

Choose the letter of the equation that models the price information shown in the advertisement. Then find the cost of tuning up a car that needs eight spark plugs.

a. $c = 40s + 2.29$
b. $s = 2.29c + 40$
c. $c = 2.29s + 40$
d. $s = 40c + 2.29$

Engine Tune-Up
$40.00 Labor
plus
$2.29 per Spark Plug

For Exercises 16 and 17, use the diagrams.

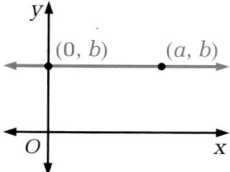
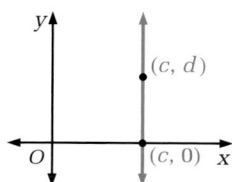

16. Show that the slope of a horizontal line is 0.

17. Show that the slope of a vertical line is undefined.

18 TECHNOLOGY Use a graphics calculator.

a. Enter the maximum target heart rate equation, $h = -0.8a + 176$.

b. Set the window to show the domain and range you found in question 3 on page 67. Graph the equation you entered.

c. Use TRACE to find the coordinates of two points on the line. Round the coordinates to the nearest thousandth.

d. Find the change in x and the change in y between your two points.

e. Use your answers to part (d) to find the slope of the line. Compare your answer to the value of m in the equation you entered.

f. Repeat parts (c)–(e) for two more pairs of points. Try two points that are far apart and two points that are close together. Do you get about the same value for the slope each time?

TECHNOLOGY NOTE

See the Technology Handbook, pp. 604–606.

2-2 Linear Models and Direct Variation

71

Answers to Exercises and Problems ·

18. Answers may vary.

a. Check students' work.

b. domain: $0 \le x \le 80$; range: $112 \le y \le 176$

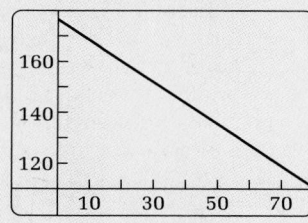

c. (20.211, 159.832) and (40.421, 143.663)

d. change in x: 20.210; change in y: −16.169

e. $m = -0.8$; The slope is the same by both methods for any two given points.

f. points (16, 163.2) and (64, 124.8) have slope −0.8; points (48, 137.6) and (47, 138.4) have slope −0.8; The slope stays the same for any two points.

71

19. **Writing** Here are two new forms of an equation of a line. Use them to answer the questions.

point-slope form: $y - y_1 = m(x - x_1)$

two-point form: $y - y_1 = \dfrac{y_2 - y_1}{x_2 - x_1}(x - x_1)$

a. Use the slope-intercept form, the point-slope form, and the two-point form to write an equation of the line through the points (5, 11) and (−10, −1). Which method do you prefer? Why?

b. Explain why the point-slope form is equivalent to the definition of slope. Why is "point-slope form" an appropriate name?

c. Explain how to combine the point-slope form with the definition of slope to write the two-point form. Why is "two-point form" an appropriate name?

For each equation:

a. **Identify the slope and the vertical intercept of the graph.**

b. **Graph the equation.**

c. **Use the term *increasing, decreasing,* or *constant* to describe the graph.**

20. $y = 2x - 3$ 21. $y = 7x$ 22. $y = -5x - 4$

23. $y = x + 3.7$ 24. $y = -4.2$ 25. $y = -\frac{3}{5}x + 2$

26. **Writing** Explain how you can use the slope of a line to tell if the line represents an *increasing,* a *decreasing,* or a *constant* function.

27. Choose the letters of the direct variation equations.

a. $y = 3x$ b. $y = x - 3$ c. $y = 3$ d. $\frac{y}{x} = 3$

28. Choose the letters of the graphs that show direct variation.

a.   b.   c.   d.

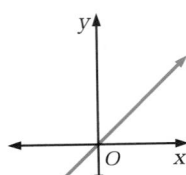 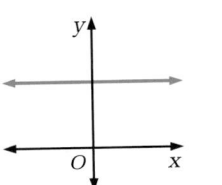 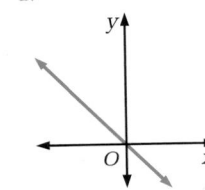

29. **Open-ended** Describe a real-world situation that fits a direct variation model.

30. Nora Ramond works as a service station attendant. She earns a weekly salary of $280.00 plus $10.50 per hour for overtime over 40 hours.

a. Write an equation that you can use to find Nora's weekly earnings.

b. What do you think is a reasonable domain for the function?

c. Find the range for the domain you gave in part (b).

d. Graph the function.

Answers to Exercises and Problems

19. a. slope-intercept form:

$y = \frac{4}{5}x + 7$; point-slope

form: $y - 11 = \frac{4}{5}(x - 5)$;

two-point form:

$y - 11 = \frac{-1 - 11}{-10 - 5}(x - 5)$

b. Answers may vary. An example is given. You can obtain the definition of slope by dividing the

point-slope form equation by $x - x_1$ and using a point (x, y) as the second point. "Point-slope form" is an appropriate name because you need one point and the slope to write a linear equation.

c. Answers may vary. An example is given. Substitute the definition of slope, namely $\frac{y_2 - y_1}{x_2 - x_1}$, for m in the point-slope form equation. "Two-point form" is an appropriate name because you need two points to write a linear equation.

20–25. See answers in back of book.

e. What is the vertical intercept of the graph? Explain the meaning of the vertical intercept in terms of the situation.

f. What is the slope of the graph? Explain the meaning of the slope in terms of the situation.

31. **Fitness Training** Damon Carson exercises on a cross-country skiing machine. One day he recorded the distances shown by the machine at various times.

a. Find the ratio $\frac{D}{t}$ for each pair of data values.

b. Is direct variation a good model for the data? If so, what is the variation constant?

c. Write an equation that models the situation.

d. Graph your equation.

e. Predict the distance the machine will show after 25 min.

f. How long will Damon Carson need to exercise for the machine to show a distance of 4.5 km?

Time t (minutes)	Distance D (kilometers)
3	0.435
5	0.725
10	1.450
12	1.740
17	2.465

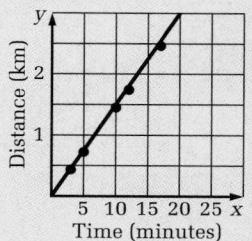

Student Resources Toolbox
p. 659 *Trigonometry*

32. $\overleftrightarrow{AB}$ crosses the x-axis at a 52° angle. The vertical intercept is 2.

a. Explain why the slope of $\overleftrightarrow{AB}$ has the same value as tan 52°.

b. Write an equation of $\overleftrightarrow{AB}$.

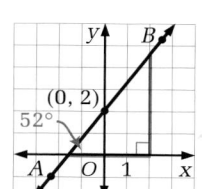

Ongoing **ASSESSMENT**

33. **Group Activity** Work in a group of three students.

TECHNOLOGY Use a graphics calculator.

a. Each of you should write equations of three lines that have vertical intercepts between −5 and 5. Be sure to include these three types of graphs: *growth, decay,* and *constant.* Do not show your list to anyone.

b. Choose one student to go first. That student graphs one of his or her equations on the calculator.

c. Another member of the group identifies the vertical intercept of the graph shown on the calculator and states which type of graph it is.

d. Continue around the group until each group member has entered all three of his or her equations.

e. Discuss any errors and how to avoid them.

2-2 Linear Models and Direct Variation

73

Assessment: Portfolio
Given an equation of a line in slope-intercept form, students should be able to state how the slope determines the function as increasing, decreasing, or constant and how the value of the y-intercept determines whether the function is a direct variation. The written results of this analysis should appear in students' portfolios.

Integrating the Strands
Ex. 32 integrates algebra, geometry, and trigonometry. Part (a) shows the connection between the slope of a line and the tangent of the angle with which the line intersects the x-axis.

30. e. 280; This represents the base amount Nora receives each week for working 40 hours.

f. 10.5; This represents the amount Nora receives for each hour of overtime she works each week.

31. a. rounded to the nearest hundredth: 0.15, 0.15, 0.15, 0.15, 0.15

b. Yes; 0.15.

c. $y = 0.15x$

d.

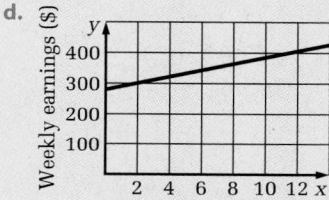

e. 3.75 km

f. 30 min

32. a. $\tan 52° = \frac{\text{opposite side}}{\text{adjacent side}}$; The opposite side can be found by calculating $y_2 - y_1$, and the adjacent side can be found by calculating $x_2 - x_1$. By substituting, $\tan 52° = \frac{y_2 - y_1}{x_2 - x_1}$ = slope of line AB.

b. $y = (\tan 52°)x + 2$

33. a–e. Group activity. Equations and discussions may vary.

Answers to Exercises and Problems ································

26. Increasing functions have a positive slope, decreasing functions have a negative slope, and constant functions have a slope of 0.

27. a and d

28. a and d

29. Answers may vary. An example is given. the amount of sales tax charged on cost of merchandise

30. a. $y = 10.5x + 280$

b. Answers may vary. An example is given. $0 \le x \le 12$

c. Answers may vary. An example is given based upon the answer in part (b). $280 \le y \le 406$

d.

73

Working on the Unit Project

Students can work Ex. 43 with their partner. They should keep a record of their answers to build a description of the major features of the Mono Lake ecosystem.

Review PREVIEW

Tell whether each graph is an example of *linear growth*, *nonlinear growth*, *linear decay*, *nonlinear decay*, a *constant*, or *none of these*. *(Section 2-1)*

34.

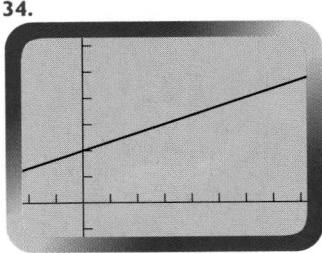

35.

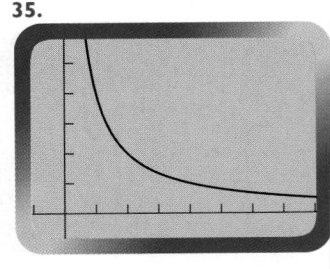

36.

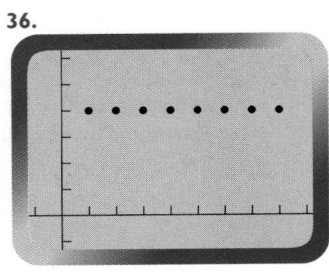

Solve. *(Toolbox Skill 13)*

37. $\frac{x}{4} - 4 = 8$

38. $7y = 3y - 56$

39. $2h = 5(h + 15)$

Solve for each indicated variable. *(Toolbox Skill 15)*

40. $A = lw$, for l

41. $V = Bh$, for h

42. $D = rt$, for r

Working on the Unit Project

43. The table shows one scientist's model of the rate at which water must flow into Mono Lake in order to keep the water level at the heights shown.

Inflow (cubic feet per second)	Water level (feet above sea level)
127	6390
110	6380
93	6370
76	6360
59	6350
42	6340
26	6330

a. Make a scatter plot of the data.

b. Draw a fitted line.

c. Is the function an example of *linear growth* or *linear decay*? Explain.

d. Is the function an example of direct variation? Explain.

e. Write an equation of the fitted line.

f. Use your equation from part (e) to predict the rate of inflow needed to maintain the water level at 6430 ft above sea level. At this water level, gulls will breed at the same high levels as they did in 1987.

 74   **Unit 2** Models of Variation and Growth

Practice 10 For use with Section 2-2

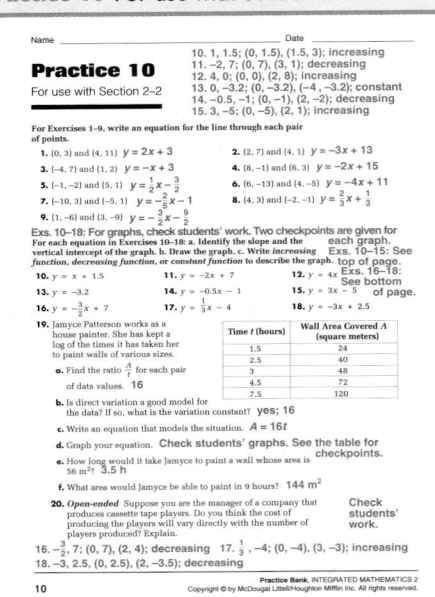

Name _____ Date _____

Practice 10
For use with Section 2–2

10. 1, 1.5; (0, 1.5), (1.5, 3); increasing
11. −2, 7; (0, 7), (3, 1); decreasing
12. 4, 0; (0, 0), (2, 8); increasing
13. 0, −3.2; (0, −3.2), (−4, −3.2); constant
14. −0.5, −1; (0, −1), (2, −2); decreasing
15. 3, −5; (0, −5), (2, 1); increasing

For Exercises 1–9, write an equation for the line through each pair of points.

1. (0, 3) and (4, 11) $y = 2x + 3$
2. (2, 7) and (4, 1) $y = -3x + 13$
3. (−4, 7) and (1, 2) $y = -x + 3$
4. (8, −1) and (6, 3) $y = -2x + 15$
5. (−1, −2) and (5, 1) $y = \frac{1}{2}x - \frac{3}{2}$
6. (6, −13) and (4, −5) $y = -4x + 11$
7. (−10, 3) and (−5, 1) $y = -\frac{2}{5}x - 1$
8. (4, 3) and (−2, −1) $y = \frac{2}{3}x + \frac{1}{3}$
9. (1, −6) and (3, −9) $y = -\frac{3}{2}x - \frac{9}{2}$

Exs. 10-18: For graphs, check students' work. Two checkpoints are given for each graph.
For each equation in Exercises 10-18: a. Identify the slope and the vertical intercept of the graph. b. Draw the graph. c. Write *increasing function, decreasing function,* or *constant function* to describe the graph.
Exs. 16–18: See top of page.
Exs. 10–15: See bottom of page.

10. $y = x + 1.5$
11. $y = -2x + 7$
12. $y = 4x$
13. $y = -3.2$
14. $y = -0.5x - 1$
15. $y = 3x - 5$
16. $y = -\frac{3}{2}x + 7$
17. $y = \frac{1}{3}x - 4$
18. $y = -3x + 2.5$

19. Jamyce Patterson works as a house painter. She has kept a log of the times it has taken her to paint walls of various sizes.

Time *t* (hours)	Wall Area Covered *A* (square meters)
1.5	24
2.5	40
3	48
4.5	72
7.5	120

a. Find the ratio $\frac{A}{t}$ for each pair of data values. 16
b. Is direct variation a good model for the data? If so, what is the variation constant? yes; 16
c. Write an equation that models the situation. $A = 16t$
d. Graph your equation. Check students' graphs. See the table for checkpoints.
e. How long would it take Jamyce to paint a wall whose area is 56 m²? 3.5 h
f. What area would Jamyce be able to paint in 9 hours? 144 m²

20. **Open-ended** Suppose you are the manager of a company that produces cassette tape players. Do you think the cost of producing the players will vary directly with the number of players produced? Explain. Check students' work.

16. $-\frac{3}{2}$, 7; (0, 7), (2, 4); decreasing   17. $\frac{1}{3}$, −4; (0, −4), (3, −3); increasing
18. −3, 2.5, (0, 2.5), (2, −3.5); decreasing

Practice Bank, INTEGRATED MATHEMATICS 2
Copyright © by McDougal Littell/Houghton Mifflin Inc. All rights reserved.

10

74

Answers to Exercises and Problems ·······················

34. linear growth

35. nonlinear decay

36. constant

37. 48   38. −14

39. −25

40. $l = \frac{A}{w}$

41. $h = \frac{V}{B}$

42. $r = \frac{D}{t}$

43. a, b.

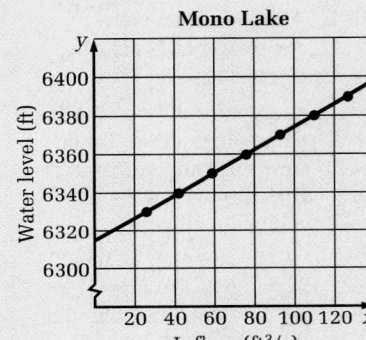

Mono Lake

c. linear growth

d. No; if inflow is 0, the water level would not be 0.

e. $y = 0.59x + 6315.1$

f. about 194.75 cubic feet per second

Inverse Variation

One's ↓Loss Is Another's Gain

Focus
Explore situations that involve constant products.

PLANNING

Objectives and Strands
See pages 56A and 56B.

Spiral Learning
See page 56B.

Materials List
➤ 36 small squares of paper
➤ Graph paper
➤ Scissors
➤ Graphics calculator or software
➤ Compass
➤ Centimeter ruler
➤ Salt
➤ Hot tap water
➤ 5 clear glasses

Recommended Pacing
Section 2-3 is a two-day lesson.
Day 1
Pages 75–77: Exploration through Talk it Over 8, *Exercises 1–7*
Day 2
Pages 78–79: Sample 2 through Look Back, *Exercises 8–33*

Extra Practice
See pages 616–617.

Warm-Up Exercises
Warm-Up Transparency 2-3

Support Materials
➤ Practice 11
➤ Enrichment 10 in the Activity Bank
➤ Study Guide 2-3
➤ Problem Set 3
➤ Additional Exploration 4
➤ Diagram Masters 1, 13, 14 in the Explorations Lab Manual
➤ Overhead Visual 2
➤ McDougal Littell Mathpack software: *Function Investigator* and *Stats!*
➤ Function Investigator with Matrix Analyzer Activity Book: Function Investigator Activity 24
➤ Using TI-81 and TI-82 Calculators: Inverse Variation
➤ Using Plotter Plus: Inverse Variation
➤ Quiz 2-3
➤ Test 5

EXPLORATION

What kinds of rectangles have an area of 36 square units?

• **Materials: 36 small squares of paper of the same size, graph paper, scissors**

• **Work with another student.**

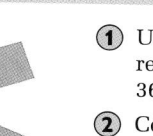

List both the 4 × 9 and the 9 × 4 rectangles.

width	length
4	9
9	4
⋮	⋮

① Use the squares to build as many rectangles as you can with area 36 square units.

② Copy and complete the table of the lengths and widths of your rectangles.

③ Make a scatter plot of the data in the table. Use width as the control variable.

④ Cut each square in half to form two rectangles. Make at least two new rectangles with area 36 square units. Add these to your table and your scatter plot.

⑤ Describe what happens to the lengths of rectangles with area 36 square units:

a. as the widths become very small

b. as the widths become very large

⑥ Describe the shape of the scatter plot.

2-3 Inverse Variation

75

Answers to Exploration

1. Lengths and widths of the possible rectangles with integer lengths and widths are shown in the table in step 2.

2, 3. See answers in back of book.

4. Possible additional points are $\left(\frac{1}{2}, 72\right)$, $\left(72, \frac{1}{2}\right)$, $\left(1\frac{1}{2}, 24\right)$, $\left(24, 1\frac{1}{2}\right)$, $\left(4\frac{1}{2}, 8\right)$, and $\left(8, 4\frac{1}{2}\right)$. If a curve is drawn through the points in the graph shown in step 3, these points will lie on the curve.

5. **a.** As the width becomes very small, the length becomes very large.

b. As the width becomes very large, the length becomes very small.

6. The points on the scatter plot appear to lie on a curve that gets closer and closer to the vertical axis without actually touching it, as x approaches but does not reach zero, and closer and closer to the horizontal axis without actually touching it as x gets large.

The goal of the Exploration is to have students explore a situation that involves a constant product. In working through steps 1–6, students learn that decreasing the width of a rectangle with a constant area increases its length and increasing the width decreases its length. The scatter plot of various widths and lengths assumes the shape of one branch of a hyperbola, which is introduced on page 77. As an alternative to using small squares of paper, students can also use graph paper to draw the rectangles.

Using Manipulatives

The manipulative activity of the Exploration allows students to experience in a concrete manner a situation in which an increase in one variable results in a decrease in the other variable. It also connects the new algebraic concept of inverse variation to the familiar geometric concept of area of a rectangle.

Additional Sample

S1 Is inverse variation a good model for the data in the table. Why or why not?

x	y
17.62	0.85
16.85	0.89
15.03	0.99
14.67	1.08
13.08	1.24

No; the products of the data in each row are not constant.

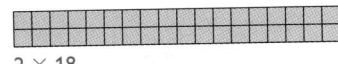

1 × 36

2 × 18

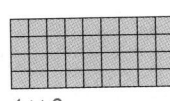

3 × 12

4 × 9

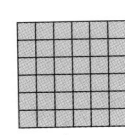

6 × 6

The area of the rectangles in the Exploration was constant while the length and width varied. When the width increased, the length decreased. When the width decreased, the length increased. This is an example of *inverse variation.*

$$lw = 36$$

When two quantities have a constant nonzero product, their relationship is called **inverse variation.**

You can say that the width *varies inversely with* the length of the rectangle. You can also say that the length varies inversely with the width of the rectangle.

Talk it Over

1. Suppose you want to graph all the possible dimensions for rectangles with area 36 square units. Should you connect the points on your scatter plot with straight lines or a curve? Explain your choice.

2. How is inverse variation different from direct variation? How is it like direct variation?

Sample 1

Is inverse variation a good model for the data in the table? If it is, write an equation that models the data.

x	y
25.2632	0.4750
25.8947	0.4634
26.5263	0.4524
27.1579	0.4419
27.7895	0.4318

Sample Response

Multiply the data in each row to see if the product is constant.

x	y	xy
25.2632	0.4750	12.00002
25.8947	0.4634	11.99960398
26.5263	0.4524	12.00049812
27.1579	0.4419	12.00107601
27.7895	0.4318	11.9995061

All the products are very close to 12.

Inverse variation is a good model for the data.

The equation $xy = 12$ models the data.

Unit 2 Models of Variation and Growth

Answers to Talk it Over

1. a curve; The points on the scatter plot indicate a curve would fit to connect the points.

2. Answers may vary. An example is given. The graph of an inverse variation is a curve and the graph of a direct variation is a line. In an inverse variation, the products of corresponding x- and y-values are constant. In a direct variation, the quotients are constant.

3. The data in Sample 1 are all positive. In which quadrant(s) does a scatter plot of the data appear?

4. Look at these other pairs of numbers that satisfy the equation in Sample 1: $(-12, -1)$, $(-6, -2)$, $(-4, -3)$, $(-1, -12)$, $(-2, -6)$, $(-3, -4)$. In which quadrant(s) does a scatter plot of these data appear?

The graph of inverse variation is a shape made of two curves, called a **hyperbola.** To graph inverse variation on a graphics calculator, you first rewrite the equation $xy = k$ as $y = \frac{k}{x}$.

INVERSE VARIATION

The equation has these forms
($k \neq 0$, $x \neq 0$):

$$xy = k \quad \text{or} \quad y = \frac{k}{x}$$

— variation constant

You read them as follows:

"y varies inversely with x,"
or
"y is proportional to $\frac{1}{x}$."

The graph is a hyperbola.

when k is positive
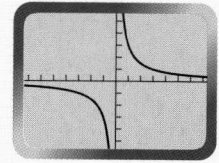

when k is negative
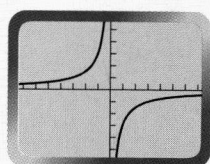

5. Explain why there are two curves in the graph of $xy = 12$.

6. Explain how to rewrite the equation $xy = k$ as $y = \frac{k}{x}$.

7. How does changing the sign of k affect the graph of $y = \frac{k}{x}$?

8. How do you think increasing the value of k changes the graph of $y = \frac{k}{x}$? To check your answer, graph $y = \frac{1}{x}$, $y = \frac{2}{x}$, and $y = \frac{4}{x}$ on the same calculator or computer screen.

▶ **Now you are ready for:**
Exs. 1–7 on pp. 79–80

2-3 Inverse Variation

77

Talk it Over

Questions 5–7 check students' understanding of why a hyperbola has two curves and how the sign of k affects the location of the curves. Question 8 asks students to think about how an increasing value of k affects the position of the curves within their quadrants.

Reasoning

Students should understand by examining the equation $y = \frac{k}{x}$ that as k increases or decreases, the graph of the hyperbola approaches the x-axis and y-axis more or less quickly but never actually touches them. When k decreases in value, the hyperbola gets closer to the x-axis and y-axis and thus approaches them more quickly. Ask students to think about what happens if k equals zero. (Then $xy = 0$, which implies that $x = 0$ or $y = 0$. In either case, there is no curve.)

Using Technology

To extend the section, students can use Function Investigator Activity 24 in the *Function Investigator with Matrix Analyzer Activity Book* to explore the extreme behavior of hyperbolas.

Answers to Talk it Over

3. the first quadrant

4. the third quadrant

5. For every ordered pair (x, y) for which $xy = 12$, it is also true that $(-x)(-y) = 12$. So, for every point of the graph in the first quadrant, there is a corresponding point in the third quadrant.

6. Divide both sides of the equation $xy = k$ by x.

7. The graph of $xy = -k$ is the image of $xy = k$ reflected over the vertical axis.

8. The smaller the value of k, the closer the curve lies to the axes. When k is larger, the curve lies farther out and its ends approach the axes more slowly.

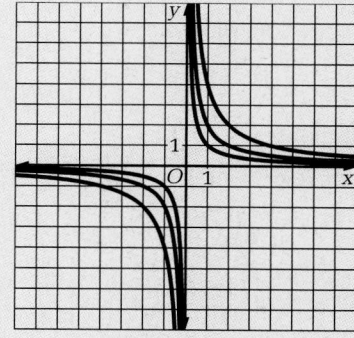

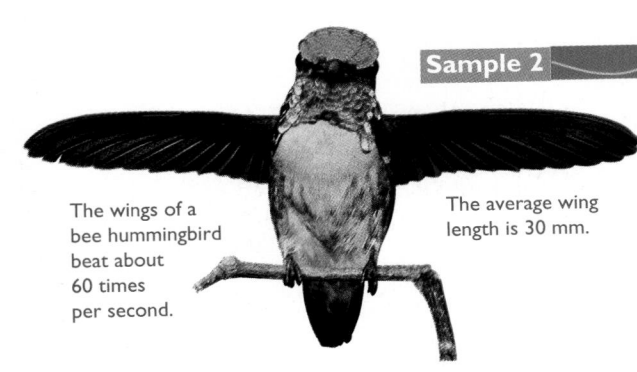

The wings of a bee hummingbird beat about 60 times per second.

The average wing length is 30 mm.

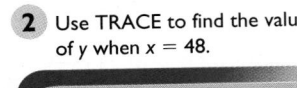

For most flying birds and insects, the product of wing length (in millimeters) and number of wing beats per second is close to the same constant.

A wing of a Puerto Rican emerald hummingbird is 48 mm long. Estimate the number of times per second that its wings beat.

Sample Response

Model the situation with an inverse variation equation.

➤ First find the variation constant.

wing length × beats per second = constant ◄——— Multiply the values known for a bee hummingbird.

$$30 \cdot 60 = 1800$$

➤ Substitute 1800 for *k* in the equation $xy = k$.

$xy = k$

$xy = 1800$ ◄——— *x* = the wing length (in millimeters)
y = the number of wing beats per second

$y = \dfrac{1800}{x}$ ◄——— Divide both sides by *x*.

Use the equation to find *y* when x = 48.

Method ❶ Use a graph.

1 Graph the equation.

2 Use TRACE to find the value of *y* when *x* = 48. ◄——— Use 48 as the value of Xmin or Xmax and you will land exactly on 48.

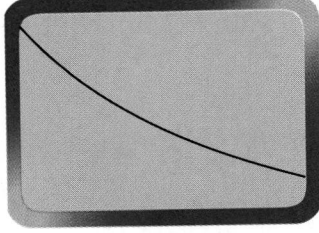

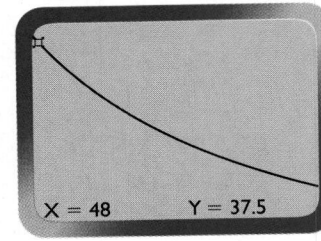

X = 48   Y = 37.5

The calculator shows that *y* = 37.5 when *x* = 48.

Method ❷ Use algebra.

$y = \dfrac{1800}{x}$

$y = \dfrac{1800}{48}$ ◄——— Substitute 48 for *x*.

$y = 37.5$

A Puerto Rican emerald hummingbird beats its wings about 38 times per second.

Look Back

Describe how you can tell when a set of data, a graph, or an equation is an example of inverse variation.

······▶ Now you are ready for:
Exs. 8–33 on pp. 80–82

2-3 Exercises and Problems

1. In the Exploration, in which quadrant(s) was your scatter plot?

2. **Reading** Suppose x and y are any two numbers.

   a. In which quadrants is the graph of $xy = 12$?

   b. In which quadrants is the graph of $xy = -12$?

3. Dividers separate a box for juice glasses into 48 square regions. The dimensions of the box are 4 glasses wide by 12 glasses long.

   a. Make a table of the dimensions of some other one-layer boxes that will hold 48 of the same type of juice glass.

   b. Write an equation that relates the width and length of each box.

Is inverse variation a good model for each set of data? Why or why not? If it is, write an equation that models the data.

4.

x	y
0.4228	4.9670
0.4438	4.7319
0.4648	4.5184
0.4858	4.3231
0.5067	4.1441
0.5277	3.9793

5.

x	y
1.7895	0.9762
2.0000	0.9093
2.2105	0.8023
2.4211	0.6598
2.6316	0.4541
2.8421	0.2950

6. a. Draw a circle with a diameter between 8 cm and 10 cm.

   b. Draw a *chord* of length 7 cm. (A *chord* is a segment with endpoints on the circle.) The chord divides the circle into two regions. Label the smaller region X and the larger region Y.

   c. Mark a dot 5 cm along the chord. Draw 5 different chords that pass through the dot.

   d. Measure to the nearest millimeter the part of each chord that lies in region X and the part of each chord that lies in region Y. Record these lengths in a table as x and y.

   e. Make a scatter plot of the data in your table. Describe it.

   f. Is your graph an example of inverse variation? If it is, what is the constant product?

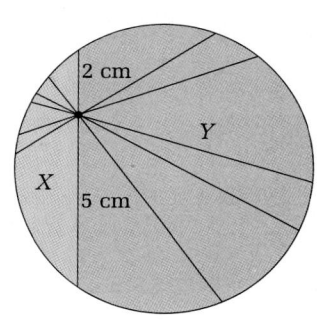

Suggested Assignment

Day 1

Standard 1–5

Extended 1–7

Day 2

Standard 8–19, 23–33

Extended 8–33

Integrating the Strands

Algebra Exs. 1–28, 32, 33

Functions Exs. 1–24, 32, 33

Geometry Exs. 6, 7, 14, 29–31

Assessment: Project

For Exs. 6 and 7, students should use the results of Ex. 6 to predict how the placement of the dot in Ex. 7 affects the results. They should test their predictions by placing the dot so that the ratio of the segments is 3:4. Ask them to change the length of the chord and repeat the experiment. Students should also be able to state that the products of the segments of the divided chord are equal.

x (mm)	y (mm)
13	77
15	67
20	50
25	40
45	22

e. The points on the scatter plot appear to lie on one branch of a hyperbola.

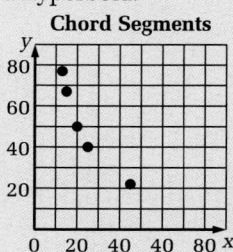

Chord Segments

f. Yes; 1000.

Answers to Exercises and Problems

1. quadrant I

2. a. quadrants I and III

   b. quadrants II and IV

3. a. Only one pair of dimensions is given for each pair of numbers; that is, a box w glasses wide and l glasses long is identical to one l glasses wide and w glasses long.

width	length
1	48
2	24
3	16
6	8

   b. If x is the width and y is the length, the equation $xy = 48$ relates the width and length of each box.

4. Yes; all the products are about 2.1. The equation $xy = 2.1$ models the data.

5. No; $xy \neq$ constant.

6. a–f. Answers may vary.

   a–c. Check students' drawings.

   d. Examples are given for a circle with diameter 10 cm.

7. **Writing** Repeat Exercise 6 but mark the dot halfway along the 7 cm chord. Make a conjecture about how the placement of the dot affects the results. Test your conjecture by marking the dot somewhere else along the 7 cm chord. Summarize your observations.

For Exercises 8–10, rewrite the equation in the form $y = \dfrac{k}{x}$.

8. $xy = 18$ **9.** $xy = -7$ **10.** $x = \dfrac{2}{y}$

For Exercises 11–13, find y when x = 6.

11. $y = \dfrac{72}{x}$ **12.** $x = \dfrac{51}{y}$ **13.** $xy = 3$

14. A rectangle has length 42 cm and width 22 cm. Find the length of another rectangle of equal area whose width is 12 cm.

15. Some college students want to share an apartment off campus. The rent will be $600 per month. The maximum number of tenants allowed is 6.

  a. **Writing** Explain why the relationship between each student's share of the monthly rent and the number of students is an example of inverse variation. Assume that each student pays the same amount.

  b. How many people would have to share the rent of the apartment to make the cost $120 per month?

16. When a seesaw is balanced, each person's weight varies inversely with the distance from the center support. If a person who weighs 90 lb sits at one end of a 12 ft seesaw, how far from the support must a 120 lb person sit in order to balance the seesaw?

For Exercises 17 and 18, use the equation in Sample 2 to estimate how many times the wings beat per second.

17. sphinx moth with wing length 20 mm

18. wandering albatross with wing length 1.5 m

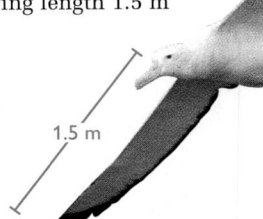

20 mm

1.5 m

BY THE WAY...

The wandering albatross has the largest wingspan of any living bird.

METHOD OF TRAVEL	Rate (miles per hour)	Time (hours)
backpacking	3	?
cross-country skiing	4	?
bicycling	10	?
car: slow & scenic	25	?
car: moderate	45	?
car: speed limit	55	?

19. Suppose you are planning a camping trip to a lake 12 mi away.

The equation $rt = 12$ describes the relationship between r, the rate of travel, and t, the time it takes to get to the lake.

  a. Rewrite the equation $rt = 12$ so you could enter it on a graphics calculator.

  b. Complete the table.

  c. What is a reasonable domain for the function? Why?

For Exercises 20 and 21, use this information.

The length of a sound wave, or wavelength, varies inversely with the frequency of the wave. The speed of sound is the variation constant. When the wavelength is in meters and the frequency is in number of waves per second, the speed of sound is given in meters per second.

20. a. The speed of sound in air is 343 m/s. Write an equation showing how frequency f and wavelength w are related when sound travels in air.

The frequency of A above middle C is 440 waves per second.

The frequency of A below middle C is 220 waves per second.

middle C

b. What is the wavelength in air of A above middle C?

c. What is the wavelength in air of A below middle C?

21. a. The speed of sound in water is 1497 m/s. Write an equation showing how frequency and wavelength are related when sound travels in water.

b. What is the wavelength in water of A above middle C?

c. What is the wavelength in water of A below middle C?

22. a. **Open-ended** Make a table of data for an inverse variation.

b. Write an equation that describes the data in your table. Identify the control variable and the dependent variable.

c. Draw a graph of your data.

Ongoing **ASSESSMENT**

23. **Open-ended** Suppose you are helping a friend with homework over the telephone. Describe how the graph of an inverse variation is like other types of graphs you have worked with and how it is different.

2-3 Inverse Variation

81

Assessment: Technology

For Ex. 19, students should enter the rewritten equation of $rt = 12$ into their graphics calculators. Check to see that they have set an appropriate range for the window. (This should be determined by the domain chosen.) Using the TRACE key and INTEGER function, students should be able to complete the table. Discuss how to convert the y-values on the calculator to minutes. Ask which part of the graph should be discounted? Why?

Communication: Discussion

You may wish to engage students in a discussion of those factors that affect the speed of sound in air. For example, temperature, humidity, and wind speed all affect the speed of sound in air. The value given in Ex. 20 is for still, dry air at room temperature (20°C).

For Ex. 21, the value given is for pure water near room temperature (20°C). Temperature and presence of dissolved minerals (including salt) affect the speed of sound in water.

Using Technology

Students can use the *Function Investigator* software to graph the equation they write for Ex. 22.

23. Answers may vary. An example is given. The graph of an inverse variation is a pair of curves. Most other graphs seen so far consist of a line or a single curve. The graph of an inverse variation also differs from the graph of a direct variation, which always passes through the origin. The graph of an inverse variation never intersects either axis. The graph is like the graph of a quadratic equation in that it is not a line and like a parabola in that there is a line of symmetry. For example, each portion of the graph of $xy = k$, where k is positive, is the image of the other portion reflected over the line $y = -x$.

Answers to Exercises and Problems

Number of people	Cost per person
10	30
12	25
15	20
16	18.75
20	15
25	12

b. $xy = 300$; The control variable is x, the number of people, and the dependent variable is y, the cost per person.

c.

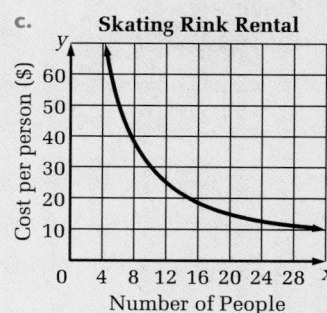

Skating Rink Rental

24. Choose the letters of the direct variation equations. *(Section 2-2)*

    a. $y = 6$ **b.** $y = 6x$ **c.** $y = 6x - 6$ **d.** $\frac{y}{x} = 6$

Graph each inequality. *(Toolbox Skill 25)*

25. $y \geq 4$ **26.** $x < 2$ **27.** $y \leq 3x + 2$ **28.** $y > \frac{1}{2}x - 1$

Find the volume of each figure. In Exercises 29 and 31, find the surface area also. *(Toolbox Skill 28)*

29.
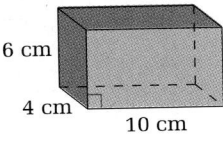
6 cm   4 cm   10 cm

30.
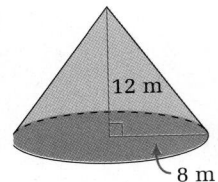
12 m   8 m

31.
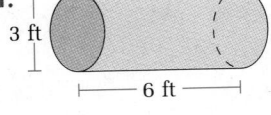
3 ft   6 ft

Working on the Unit Project

32. The graph shows scientists' predictions of the salt content of Mono Lake when the water level reaches the levels in the graph.

    a. Describe the graph.

    b. Does the graph show inverse variation? How do you know?

33. Over the next several days, you will do this experiment to learn how tufa form.

    a. Mix five different concentrations of salt water. Add 1–5 teaspoons of salt to a cup of hot tap water in clear glasses labeled 1–5.

1   2   3   4   5

    b. Each day observe the growth of the salt deposits on the bottoms of the glasses and record the water level. (Some evaporation will take place.)

    c. **Writing** Describe the relationship between the rate of growth of the salt deposits and the salt concentration.

    d. **Writing** Describe the relationship between the size of the salt deposits and the salt concentration.

Answers to Exercises and Problems

24. b and d

25.
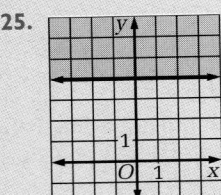

26.
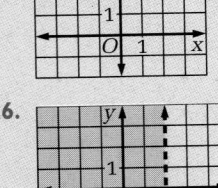

27.
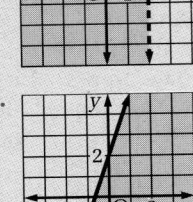

28.
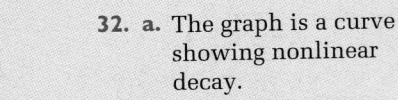

29. S.A. = 248 cm²; $V = 240$ cm³

30. $V \approx 804.25$ m³

31. S.A. ≈ 70.69 ft²; $V \approx 42.41$ ft³

32. a. The graph is a curve showing nonlinear decay.

    b. No. Answers may vary. An example is given. The points (6350, 150) and (6370, 100) are on the graph.
$6350 \cdot 150 = 952{,}500$ and $6370 \cdot 100 = 63{,}700$; the products are not equal.

33. a–d. Answers may vary. The rate of salt deposit growth and the size of the salt deposits will vary directly with the salt concentration; the higher the concentration, the faster the growth and the bigger the size.

Quick Quiz (2-1 through 2-3)
See page 117.

1. **Writing** Describe a situation that can be modeled by this graph. Describe the characteristics of the graph over four intervals. Copy the graph and add scales and labels on the axes.

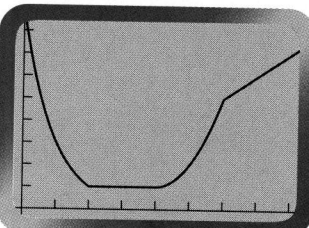

For Exercises 2–4, use the heart rate graph.

2-1

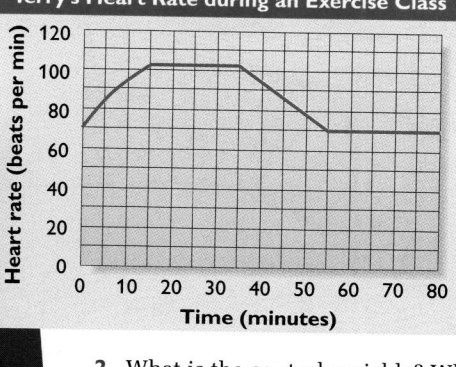

Terry's Heart Rate during an Exercise Class

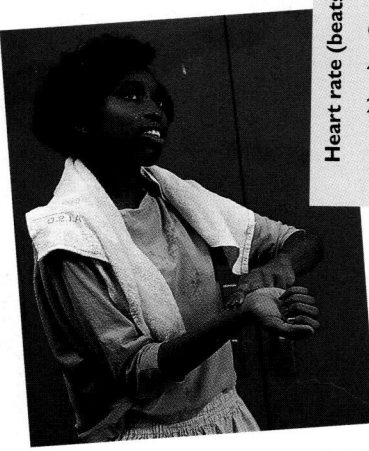

2. What is the control variable? What is the dependent variable?

3. What is the domain of the function? What is the range?

4. Use the terms *linear* or *nonlinear* and *increasing, decreasing,* or *constant* to describe the graph.

5. The coordinates of two points are (3, 21) and (−1, −11).
   2-2
   a. Find the slope of the line through the points.
   b. Find the vertical intercept of the line.
   c. Write an equation of the line.
   d. Find the value of x when $y = 7$.

6. Use the equation $xy = 10$.
   2-3
   a. Write the equation in the form $y = \dfrac{k}{x}$.
   b. Graph the equation over a domain of −10 to 10.
   c. Describe the graph.
   d. Find the value of y when $x = 2.5$.
   e. Find the value of x when $y = 8$.

2-3 Inverse Variation

83

Practice 11 For use with Section 2-3

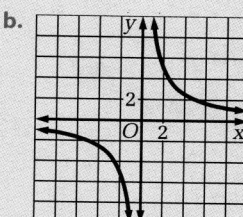

Name _____ Date _____

Practice 11
For use with Section 2-3

For Exercises 1–6, find y for each specified x-value.

1. $xy = 18$; $x = 4.5$ **4**　　2. $y = \frac{6}{x}$; $x = 9$ **$\frac{2}{3}$**　　3. $x = -\frac{75}{y}$; $x = 6$ **−12.5**

4. $y = \frac{80}{x}$; $x = 25$ **3.2**　　5. $xy = -17.5$; $x = 7$ **−2.5**　　6. $y = \frac{12}{x}$; $x = 16$ **0.75**

For Exercises 7–9, rewrite the equation in the form $y = \frac{k}{x}$.

7. $xy = -45$ $y = -\frac{45}{x}$　　8. $x = \frac{15}{y}$ $y = \frac{15}{x}$　　9. $2xy = 9$ $y = \frac{4.5}{x}$

10. Suppose you and a friend are standing on an ice-skating rink and you push off against each other. You will go in opposite directions, but the product of your speed and your weight will be the same as the product of your friend's speed and her weight.

   a. Suppose the common value of this product is 483, when the units are pounds and miles per hour. Let w = your weight in pounds, and let s = your speed in miles per hour. Write an equation that models the situation. Is this an example of inverse variation? $ws = 483$; **yes**

   b. Let's say you weigh 105 lb. How fast will you be traveling after you push off? **4.6 mi/h**

   c. Suppose your friend weighs 75 lb. How fast will she be going after you push off? **6.44 mi/h**

11. A batch of a photographic chemical called "fixer" will process prints with a total surface area of 2800 in.²

   a. Let n = the number of prints processed, and let a = the surface area of each print. Write an equation that models the situation. Is this an example of inverse variation? $na = 2800$; **yes**

   b. How many rectangular prints measuring 8 in. by 10 in. will the batch of fixer process? **35 prints**

   c. How many 5 in.-by-7 in. prints can be processed with the batch of fixer? **80 prints**

12. **Writing** Describe the shape of the graphs of $y = \frac{k}{x}$ and $y = -\frac{k}{x}$ (where $k \neq 0$) as you move along the x-axis, to the left or to the right, *away from* 0. Describe the relationship between the variables that each graph shows. For example, you might start, "As the value of x gets larger and larger ..." **Check students' work. Answers should take two cases into consideration: $k > 0$ and $k < 0$.**

Answers to Checkpoint

1. Answers may vary. An example is given. The graph represents the amount of money in a student's bank account over a series of months. The first drop is in August as the student buys back-to-school supplies and clothing. Then the amount in the account stays low as the student has no job for a few months and cuts back on expenditures. In December and January, the student gets a job at the mall during peak Christmas shopping and inventory times. He puts all money earned in the bank anticipating a big ski vacation in late winter.

2. time; heart rate

3. $0 \leq t \leq 80$; $70 \leq h \leq 105$

4. Over the interval $0 \leq t \leq 15$, the graph is nonlinear increasing. Over the interval $15 \leq t \leq 35$, the graph is constant. Over the interval $35 \leq t \leq 55$, the graph is linear decreasing. And over the interval $55 \leq t \leq 80$, the graph is constant.

5. a. 8　　　　b. −3
   c. $y = 8x - 3$　　d. 1.25

6. a. $y = \dfrac{10}{x}$

   b.

   c. The graph is a hyperbola.

   d. 4　　　　e. 1.25

Objectives and Strands
See pages 56A and 56B.

Spiral Learning
See page 56B.

Materials List
➤ Orange

Recommended Pacing
Section 2-4 is a two-day lesson.

Day 1

Pages 84–86: Talk it Over 1 through Talk it Over 8, *Exercises 1–19*

Day 2

Pages 86–87: Similar Spheres through Look Back, *Exercises 20–42*

Toolbox References
➤ **Toolbox Skill 16:** Solving Square and Cube Root Equations

Extra Practice
See pages 616–617.

Warm-Up Exercises
Warm-Up Transparency 2-4

Support Materials
➤ Practice 12

➤ Enrichment 11 in the Activity Bank

➤ Study Guide 2-4

➤ Problem Set 4

➤ McDougal Littell Mathpack software: *Stats!*

➤ Quiz 2-4

➤ Alternative Assessment 3

Section 2-4

Surface Area and Volume of Spheres

around and round

Focus
Find the surface area and volume of spheres, and use the fact that all spheres are similar.

Talk it Over

Suppose you have an orange that is almost perfectly round. Suppose you also have the materials shown here: string, a vegetable peeler, scissors, aluminum foil, and a ruler.

1. The *surface area* of the orange is the area of the skin of the orange. Suggest how to estimate the surface area of the orange in at least three ways—using string, using a peeler, and using the aluminum foil.

2. The *volume* of the orange is everything inside the skin. Suggest how to use any of the materials in question 1 to estimate the volume of the orange in at least two different ways.

3. How could you use any of the materials shown to measure the radius of an orange?

4. Imagine packing a round object into a cylinder that is just tall and just wide enough to contain it. What is the volume of this cylinder? (Remember that the formula for the volume of a cylinder is $V = \pi r^2 h$.) About how much of the cylinder is filled by the object?

An orange is shaped like a *sphere*. A **sphere** is a round space figure. The *radius of a sphere* is the distance from its center to its surface. The *diameter of a sphere* is twice the radius.

84   **Unit 2** Models of Variation and Growth

Answers to Talk it Over

1. Answers may vary. Examples are given. (1) Peel the orange carefully with the peeler, trying to make rectangular, triangular, or square pieces. Lay the pieces out and measure the area of each piece using the ruler. Add the areas to find the total surface area. (2) Wrap the string around the orange so that the entire surface is covered. Then arrange the string to form a rectangular region and calculate its area. (3) Wrap the orange with aluminum foil, cutting away the overlap. Unwrap the foil and use the ruler to measure the area of the foil that covered the orange. Find the area of this foil to find the surface area of the orange.

2. Answers may vary. Examples are given. (1) Cut six curved pieces off the orange so that you have a cube on the inside plus the six curved pieces. Measure the volume of the cube and estimate the volume of the six curved pieces. (2) Cut the orange into sections and carefully arrange the sections into a prism-like shape and find its volume.

SURFACE AREA AND VOLUME OF A SPHERE

Surface Area

S.A. $= 4\pi r^2$

↙ measured in square units

Volume

$V = \frac{4}{3}\pi r^3$

↙ measured in cubic units

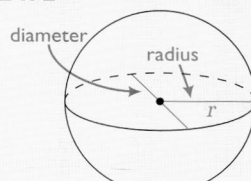

diameter, radius

r

The terms **radius** and **diameter** refer to the segments shown and to the lengths of those segments.

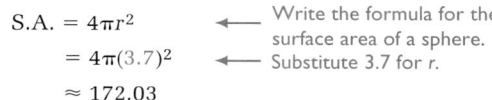

Sample 1

The radius of a field hockey ball is about 3.7 cm.

a. Find its surface area to the nearest square centimeter.

b. Find its volume to the nearest cubic centimeter.

Sample Response

a. **Problem Solving Strategy:** Use a formula.

S.A. $= 4\pi r^2$ ← Write the formula for the surface area of a sphere.

$= 4\pi(3.7)^2$ ← Substitute 3.7 for r.

≈ 172.03

The surface area of a field hockey ball is about 172 cm².

b. **Problem Solving Strategy:** Use a formula.

$V = \frac{4}{3}\pi r^3$ ← Write the formula for the volume of a sphere.

$= \frac{4}{3}\pi(3.7)^3$ ← Substitute 3.7 for r.

≈ 212.17

The volume of a field hockey ball is about 212 cm³.

For calculations involving π, give your answers to the nearest tenth unless told otherwise.

Talk it Over

5. Why is surface area measured in square units and volume measured in cubic units?

6. How close is the estimate you made in question 4 to the formula for the volume of a sphere?

7. How can you use the formula for the surface area of a sphere if you know the diameter instead of the radius?

2-4 Surface Area and Volume of Spheres

Answers to Talk it Over

3. Answers may vary. An example is given. Use the string to find the circumference, $C = 2\pi r$. Divide the circumference by 2π to find r.

4. $V = 2\pi r^3$; The sphere fills $\frac{2}{3}$ of the cylinder.

5. Surface area is two-dimensional and so is measured in square units. Volume is three-dimensional and so is measured in cubic units.

6. Answers may vary.

7. Diameter $d = 2r$, so use the formula S.A. $= 4\pi r^2 = 4\pi\left(\frac{d}{2}\right)^2 = \pi d^2$.

TEACHING

Talk it Over

Questions 1 and 2 introduce students to the concepts of surface area and volume of a sphere by using an orange as a physical model. In making their estimates of the surface area and volume of the orange, students need to recall that area is measured in square units and volume is measured in cubic units. For question 4, you might wish to remind students that the formula for the volume of a cylinder results from multiplying the area of a base (which is a circle having area πr^2) and the height.

Additional Sample

S1 The radius of a spherical melon is about 7.5 cm.

a. Find its surface area to the nearest square centimeter.
Use a formula.
S.A. $= 4\pi r^2$
$= 4\pi(7.5)^2$
≈ 706.86
The surface area of the melon is about 707 cm².

b. Find its volume to the nearest cubic centimeter.
Use a formula.
$V = \frac{4}{3}\pi r^3$
$= \frac{4}{3}\pi(7.5)^3$
≈ 1767.15
The volume of the melon is about 1767 cm³.

Reasoning

Students can use the formulas for the volume of a sphere and the volume of a cylinder to find the ratio of their volumes. This procedure would answer Talk it Over question 4 exactly.
$\left(\frac{4}{3}\pi r^3 \div \pi r^2 h = \frac{4r}{3h}\right.$
Since $h = 2r$, then $\frac{4r}{3h} = \frac{4r}{6r} = \frac{2}{3}.\left.\right)$

85

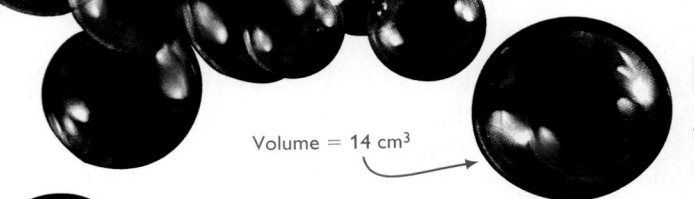

Additional Sample

S2 Find the diameter of a spherical tank whose volume is 1000 m³.

Use a formula.

$$V = \frac{4}{3}\pi r^3$$

$$1000 = \frac{4}{3}\pi r^3$$

$$1000 \approx 4.19r^3$$

$$238.66 \approx r^3$$

$$\sqrt[3]{238.66} \approx r$$

$$6.20 \approx r$$

The diameter of the tank is about 2 · 6.20 or 12.40 m.

Communication: Reading

Students should be aware of the fact that the ratios for the surface area and the volume of two spheres do not have any units in them. Remind students that rates contain units but ratios do not. This fact can be brought up again when the response to Sample 3 is discussed.

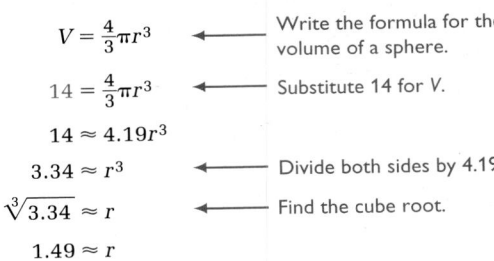

Volume = 14 cm³

Sample 2

What is the radius of this spherical bubble?

Sample Response

Problem Solving Strategy: Use a formula.

$$V = \frac{4}{3}\pi r^3 \qquad \longleftarrow \quad \text{Write the formula for the volume of a sphere.}$$

$$14 = \frac{4}{3}\pi r^3 \qquad \longleftarrow \quad \text{Substitute 14 for } V.$$

$$14 \approx 4.19r^3$$

$$3.34 \approx r^3 \qquad \longleftarrow \quad \text{Divide both sides by 4.19.}$$

$$\sqrt[3]{3.34} \approx r \qquad \longleftarrow \quad \text{Find the cube root.}$$

$$1.49 \approx r$$

The radius of the bubble is about 1.5 cm.

Student Resources Toolbox
p.647 *Solving Equations and inequalities*

Talk it Over

8. The surface area of a basketball is about 1810 cm².

   a. Describe how to find the radius of a basketball using the surface area information.

   b. How is solving this problem different from Sample 2?

······▶ Now you are ready for:
: **Exs. 1–19 on pp. 87–89**

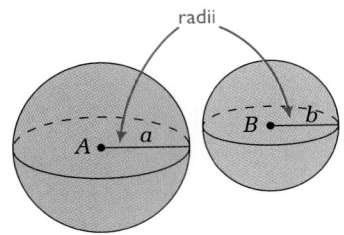

radii

Sphere A is similar to sphere B. (Spheres are named by their centers.)

Similar Spheres

All spheres have the same shape, so all spheres are similar. The ratio of the surface areas of two spheres is the ratio of the squares of the corresponding radii.

$$\frac{\text{surface area of sphere } A}{\text{surface area of sphere } B} = \frac{(\text{radius of sphere } A)^2}{(\text{radius of sphere } B)^2} = \frac{a^2}{b^2}$$

Also, the ratio of the volumes of two spheres is the ratio of the cubes of the corresponding radii.

$$\frac{\text{volume of sphere } A}{\text{volume of sphere } B} = \frac{(\text{radius of sphere } A)^3}{(\text{radius of sphere } B)^3} = \frac{a^3}{b^3}$$

Talk it Over

9. Is the ratio of the squares of the diameters of two spheres the same as the ratio of the squares of their radii? Why or why not?

10. Is the ratio of the cubes of the diameters of two spheres the same as the ratio of the cubes of their radii? Why or why not?

Unit 2 Models of Variation and Growth

Answers to Talk it Over ··························

8. **a.** Substitute 1810 for S.A. in the equation S.A. = $4\pi r^2$. Using 12.57 as an estimate for 4π, divide both sides of the equation by 12.57 to get $143.99 \approx r^2$. Take the square root of 143.99 to estimate $r \approx 12.0$ cm.

b. Answers may vary. An example is given. Sample 2 uses volume to find r and involves calculating a cube root. This problem uses surface area to find r and involves calculating a square root.

9. Yes. Using $d = 2r$,
$$\frac{(d_1)^2}{(d_2)^2} = \frac{(2r_1)^2}{(2r_2)^2} = \frac{4(r_1)^2}{4(r_2)^2} = \frac{(r_1)^2}{(r_2)^2}.$$

10. Yes. Using $d = 2r$,
$$\frac{(d_1)^3}{(d_2)^3} = \frac{(2r_1)^3}{(2r_2)^3} = \frac{8(r_1)^3}{8(r_2)^3} = \frac{(r_1)^3}{(r_2)^3}.$$

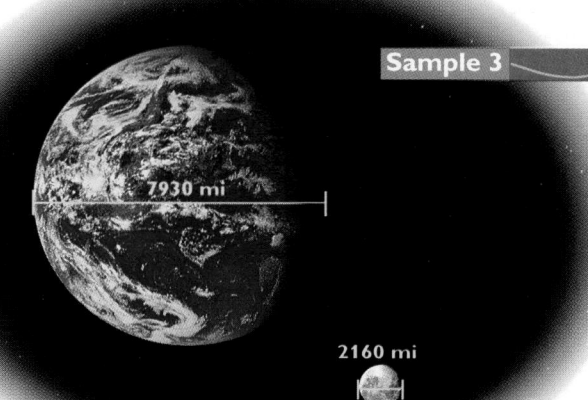
7930 mi

2160 mi

To the nearest 10 mi, the diameter of Earth is about 7930 mi. The diameter of the moon is about 2160 mi. Compare the volumes of Earth and the moon.

Sample Response

Assume that Earth and the moon are spheres. The ratio of their volumes is the ratio of the cubes of their diameters.

$$\frac{\text{volume of Earth}}{\text{volume of the moon}} = \frac{(\text{diameter of Earth})^3}{(\text{diameter of the moon})^3}$$

$$= \frac{7930^3}{2160^3}$$

$$\approx 50$$

The volume of Earth is about 50 times the volume of the moon.

Look Back

Use the formula for the surface area of a sphere to write the ratio of the surface areas of two spheres, one with radius a and the other with radius b. Write the ratio in simplified form. Is it what you expect? Do the same with the ratio of the volumes.

▶ Now you are ready for:
Exs. 20–42 on pp. 89–90

Additional Sample

S3 To the nearest 10 mi, the diameter of Earth is about 7930 mi. The diameter of the sun is about 864,950 mi. Compare the volumes of Earth and the sun.

$$\frac{\text{volume of the sun}}{\text{volume of Earth}} =$$

$$\frac{(\text{diameter of the sun})^3}{(\text{diameter of Earth})^3} = \frac{864,950^3}{7930^3}$$

$$\approx 1{,}297{,}637$$

The volume of the sun is about 1.3 million times the volume of Earth.

APPLYING

Suggested Assignment

Day 1
Standard 1–17
Extended 1–19
Day 2
Standard 20–32, 34–42
Extended 20–32, 34–42

Integrating the Strands
Algebra Exs. 34, 38–41
Geometry Exs. 1–33
Statistics and Probability Exs. 35–37
Logic and Language Ex 42

2-4 Exercises and Problems

1. **Reading** Look at the formulas for the surface area and the volume of a sphere on page 85. How are the formulas alike? How are they different? How are they like other formulas you know for area and volume?

Find the surface area and the volume of each sphere.

2.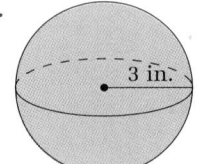
3 in.

3.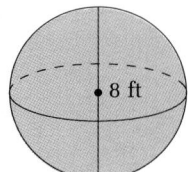
8 ft

4.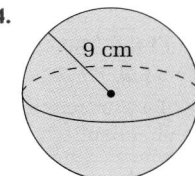
9 cm

5.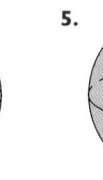
20 mi

Answers to Look Back

Using the formula for surface area, $\frac{4\pi a^2}{4\pi b^2} = \frac{a^2}{b^2}$; Yes. Using the formula for volume, $\frac{\frac{4}{3}\pi a^3}{\frac{4}{3}\pi b^3} = \frac{a^3}{b^3}$; Yes.

Answers to Exercises and Problems

1. Answers may vary. An example is given. They both use π and the measure of the radius r in the formula. The formula for surface area has a coefficient of 4 and is measured in square units, while the formula for volume has a coefficient of $\frac{4}{3}$ and is measured in cubic units. Other formulas for area are also measured in square units and other formulas for volume are also measured in cubic units.

2. S.A. = 36π in.^{2}; $V = 36\pi$ in.^{3}

3. S.A. = 64π ft^2; $V = \frac{256\pi}{3}$ ft^3

4. S.A. = 324π cm^2; $V = 972\pi$ cm^3

5. S.A. = 400π mi^2; $V = \frac{4000\pi}{3}$ mi^3

Sports **Complete the table.**

	Type of Ball	Diameter (cm)	Radius (cm)	Surface Area (cm²)	Volume (cm³)
6.	basketball	24.0	?	?	?
7.	soccer ball	22.0	?	?	?
8.	large softball	13.0	?	?	?
9.	tennis ball	6.5	?	?	?
10.	golf ball	4.3	?	?	?
11.	table tennis ball	3.7	?	?	?

Find the radius of each sphere with the given surface area or volume.

12. S.A. $= 36\pi$ in.²   **13.** $V = 36\pi$ cm³   **14.** $V = 288\pi$ ft³   **15.** S.A. $= 100\pi$ m²

BY THE WAY...

A few oil lamps can raise the temperature inside an igloo to 65°F above that of the outside air.

Architecture Round houses are built by people all over the world, from the frozen Arctic to sunny Polynesia to the windswept plains of Central Asia. Round houses are warmer in cold climates, are cooler in hot climates, and can withstand high winds.

16. The Inuit people of the Arctic use blocks of snow to build igloos in the shape of a *hemisphere,* or half a sphere. The thick snow walls and the round shape help to hold heat inside an igloo. Suppose an igloo is 15 ft in diameter.

   a. Find the amount of floor space in the igloo to the nearest square foot.

   b. Find the surface area of the igloo to the nearest square foot and its volume to the nearest cubic foot.

   c. Suppose you build a snow house with a square floor, flat walls, and a flat roof. Your house is as tall as the igloo and has the same amount of floor space. Find the surface area and volume of your snow house.

   d. What is the ratio of the surface areas of the igloo and your snow house? What is the ratio of their volumes?

   e. **Writing** Use the fact that heat loss is proportional to surface area to explain why hemispherical houses are built in the Arctic.

17. The traditional homes of the herders of the plains of Central Asia are called *yurts.* A Kirghiz or Turkic yurt has a felt covering over a round framework of willow poles. Curved poles form a domed roof.

   a. Find the surface area of a Turkic yurt with walls that are 7 ft high and a hemispherical dome with a diameter of 18 ft.

   b. Find the volume of the yurt in part (a).

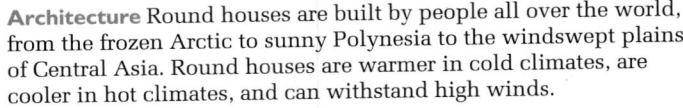

Answers to Exercises and Problems

6–11.

Type of Ball	Diameter (cm)	Radius (cm)	Surface Area (cm²)	Volume (cm³)
basketball	24.0	12.0	1809.6	7238.2
soccer ball	22.0	11.0	1520.5	5575.3
large softball	13.0	6.5	530.9	1150.3
tennis ball	6.5	3.25	132.7	143.8
golf ball	4.3	2.15	58.1	41.6
table tennis ball	3.7	1.85	43.0	26.5

12. 3 in.

13. 3 cm

14. 6 ft

15. 5 m

16. a. 177 ft²

   b. 353 ft²; 884 ft³

   c. 753 ft²; 1328 ft³

   d. about 7 to 15 or 0.47; about 2 to 3 or 0.67

e. Hemispherical houses have the smallest amount of surface area for a given volume so they have the least heat loss.

17. a. 904.8 ft²

   b. 3308.1 ft³

18. 88.4 cm²

19. about 2.4 in.²

18. The outside of a baseball is made of two congruent pieces of stitched leather. Find the area of one piece. The diameter of a baseball is about 7.5 cm.

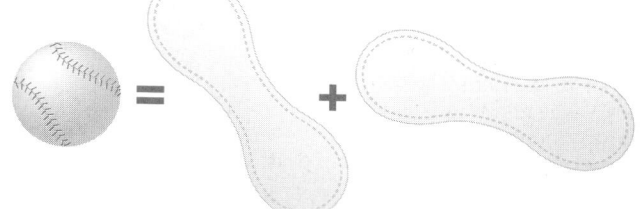

19. When a bubble gum bubble bursts, it leaves 9 in.^{2} of gum on Sara's face. Assume the bubble was a sphere whose surface area was twice the area of gum on Sara's face. Estimate the diameter of the bubble.

20. Sphere Q has radius 12 units. Sphere R has radius 8 units.

   a. What is the ratio of the diameters of the spheres?

   b. What is the ratio of the surface areas of the spheres?

   c. What is the ratio of the volumes of the spheres?

connection to **EARTH SCIENCE**

Career Geologists use a series of nested spheres to model the interior of Earth.

Writing Use the diagram to predict which layer in each pair has the greater volume. Explain how you made your choice.

21. the crust or the inner core

22. the upper mantle or the outer core

Complete the table. Round volumes to the nearest billion cubic kilometers.

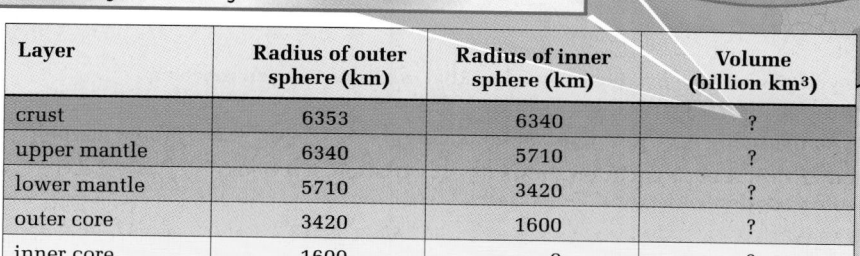

> volume of crust = volume of outer sphere − volume of inner sphere
> $$= \tfrac{4}{3}\pi(6353)^3 - \tfrac{4}{3}\pi(6340)^3 \approx 7,000,000,000$$

	Layer	Radius of outer sphere (km)	Radius of inner sphere (km)	Volume (billion km³)
23.	crust	6353	6340	?
24.	upper mantle	6340	5710	?
25.	lower mantle	5710	3420	?
26.	outer core	3420	1600	?
27.	inner core	1600	0	?

28. Compare your results in Exercises 23, 24, 26, and 27 with your predictions in Exercises 21 and 22. Do the results surprise you? Why or why not?

29. **Astronomy** Jupiter has a diameter of about 88,846 mi and Earth has a diameter of about 7926 mi.

   a. Find the ratio of their surface areas.   **b.** Find the ratio of their volumes.

Career Note

Geologists (Exs. 21–28) are scientists who study the surface and near-surface of Earth. They have divided Earth into three major zones. The *lithosphere* contains all solid matter from the surface to Earth's center. The *hydrosphere* contains all surface water areas. The *atmosphere* contains the gaseous envelope surrounding the surface.

Astronomers (Ex. 29) are scientist who study our own solar system as well as the stars, galaxies, and other objects in the universe. The objects of great interest to astronomers today are *black holes*. Black holes are thought to be dead stars that were once extraordinarily large (20 or more times greater than the sun). When these stars began to cool off, the force of their own gravity caused them to implode into very dense bodies toward which things can fall but out of which nothing can ever escape (and thus the name black hole).

Answers to Exercises and Problems

20. a. $\frac{3}{2}$

   b. $\frac{9}{4}$

   c. $\frac{27}{8}$

21. Answers may vary. An example is given: the inner core since the crust is just a very thin layer and the core is a fairly large sphere.

22. Answers may vary. An example is given: the upper mantle since it includes a greater amount of space between its inner and outer radii.

23. about 7 billion km³

24. about 288 billion km³

25. about 612 billion km³

26. about 150 billion km³

27. about 17 billion km³

28. Answers may vary. An example is given. No; my predictions were correct.

29. a. about $\frac{125.65}{1}$ or 125.65:1

   b. about $\frac{1408.48}{1}$ or 1408.48:1

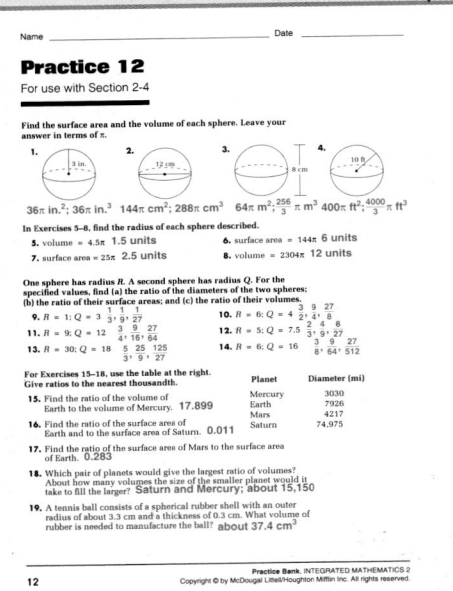
connection to LITERATURE

In *Journey to the Centre of the Earth*, written by Jules Verne and published in 1864, Axel reluctantly accompanies his uncle, Professor Lidenbrock, on a trip down a secret passage that leads to the center of Earth.

Today we know that the radius of Earth is about 3963 mi.

30. By Axel's reasoning, how long would it actually take Axel and his uncle to reach the center of Earth?

31. Find the ratio of the surface area of Earth to the surface area found with Axel's estimate of Earth's radius.

32. Find the ratio of the actual volume of Earth to the volume found with Axel's estimate of Earth's radius.

" ... I want to be able to draw a map of our journey, a sort of vertical section of the globe ... [said Professor Lidenbrock]."

"That will be very interesting, Uncle, but are your observations sufficiently precise .... ?"

"Yes. ... I estimate that we have come 213 miles ... and we are at a depth of 48 miles."

"Uncle," I said, "admitting that your calculations are correct, will you allow me to draw a vigorous conclusion from them?"

"Conclude away, my boy."

"... the radius of the earth is about ... 4,800 miles [and] we have done forty-eight ... And this at a cost of 213 miles diagonally ... In about twenty days ... If we keep on like that, it will take us ... nearly five and a half years, to reach the centre! ... Not counting the fact that ...we shall come out ... on the earth's circumference long before we reach the centre."

"To blazes with your calculations!" retorted my uncle angrily.

Ongoing ASSESSMENT

33. a. **Using Manipulatives** Find an orange that is close in shape to a sphere. Using any materials you have at home, estimate the surface area and the volume of the orange *without using the formulas.*

b. Use the formulas to see how close your estimates are to the actual surface area and volume of the orange.

c. **Writing** Describe the methods you used in part (a).

Review PREVIEW

34. Choose the letters of the inverse variation equations. *(Section 2-3)*

a. $y = 5x$ b. $y = \frac{x}{5}$ c. $5 = xy$ d. $y = \frac{5}{x}$

Suppose you choose one marble from a bag that contains 2 green marbles, 3 red marbles, and 3 blue marbles. Find each probability. *(Toolbox Skill 7)*

35. P(green marble)   36. P(red marble)   37. P(blue marble)

Tell whether or not each equation shows direct variation. If it does, identify the variation constant. *(Section 2-2)*

38. $y = 196x$ 39. $y = 1.4x + 27$ 40. $\frac{y}{x} = 13$ 41. $y = 35$

Working on the Unit Project

42. **Research** To learn more about the ecosystems of salt lakes, you may want to read selected chapters from these books:

➤ *East African Mountains and Lakes* by Leslie Brown

➤ *Planet Earth: Rivers and Lakes* by Lawrence Pringle and the Editors of Time-Life Books

Answers to Exercises and Problems

30. about 4 years and 7 months

31. $\frac{(3963)^2}{} \approx \frac{0.68}{1}$ or 0.68 : 1

32. $\frac{(3963)^3}{} \approx \frac{0.56}{1}$ or 0.56 : 1

33. a–c. Answers and descriptions may vary.

34. c and d

35. $\frac{1}{4} = 0.25$

36. $\frac{3}{8} = 0.375$

37. $\frac{3}{8} = 0.375$

38. Yes; variation constant 196.

39. No.

40. Yes; variation constant 13.

41. No.

42. Choices of books may vary.

Direct Variation with Powers

Focus

Model and apply relationships in which one quantity is proportional to the square or the cube of another quantity.

EXPLORATION

(How) *do the graphs of some formulas from geometry compare?*

- **Materials: graphics calculators or graphing software**
- **Work in a group of three students.**

As a group, decide which formula each of you will work with.

$$C = \pi d \qquad\qquad S.A. = 4\pi r^2 \qquad\qquad V = \frac{4}{3}\pi r^3$$

① Answer these questions about your formula.

  a. What does each of the variables mean?

  b. What is the control variable? the dependent variable?

② Replace the control variable in your formula with *x* and the dependent variable with *y*. Then graph your formula. Sketch the graph in your notebook.

③ Answer these questions about your graph.

  a. Is it *linear* or *nonlinear*?

  b. Is it a *constant graph*, a *growth graph*, a *decay graph*, or *none of these*?

  c. Does it pass through the point (0, 0)?

  d. Is it the graph of a function?

④ Answer these questions with the other members of your group.

  a. How are the formulas alike? How are they different?

  b. How are the graphs alike? How are they different?

Objectives and Strands
See pages 56A and 56B.

Spiral Learning
See page 56B.

Materials List
➤ Graphics calculator or graphing software

Recommended Pacing
Section 2-5 is a two-day lesson.
Day 1
Pages 91–93: Exploration through Sample 2, *Exercises 1–14*
Day 2
Pages 94–95: Direct Variation with the Cube through Look Back, *Exercises 15–37*

Extra Practice
See pages 616–617.

Warm-Up Exercises
Warm-Up Transparency 2-5

Support Materials
➤ Practice 13
➤ Enrichment 12 in the Activity Bank
➤ Study Guide 2-5
➤ Problem Set 4
➤ McDougal Littell Mathpack software: *Function Investigator*
➤ Quiz 2-5
➤ Alternative Assessment 4

Answers to Exploration

1. a. C = circumference; d = diameter; S.A. = surface area; r = radius; V = volume

  b. In $C = \pi d$, d is the control variable and C is the dependent variable; in S.A. = $4\pi r^2$, r is the control variable and S.A. is the dependent variable; in $V = \frac{4}{3}\pi r^3$, r is the

control variable and V is the dependent variable.

2, 3. See answers in back of book.

4. a. Answers may vary. Examples are given. They all contain π and all have two variables. The first is a linear equation, the second is a quadratic equation, and the third is a cubic equation.

  b. Answers may vary. Examples are given. They all go through the point (0, 0) and all are graphs of functions. The graph of circumference is a line, the graph of surface area is a parabola, and the graph of volume is an s-shaped curve.

TEACHING

Exploration

The goal of the Exploration is to have students explore the concept of direct variation with the square and the cube of the control variable. By graphing and comparing the surface area (square) and volume (cube) formulas with the circumference formula, students also see the similarities and differences among the three types of direct variation.

Using Technology

The *Function Investigator* software can be used to graph the functions in the Exploration.

Talk it Over

Questions 1 and 2 have students explore how changing the sign of the variation constant or its value affects the graph of $y = kx^2$.

Reasoning

You might wish to ask students what type of transformation would change the parabola shown when k is positive to the one shown when k is negative. (a reflection in the x-axis)

Additional Sample

S1 If the hang time of a basketball player is about 0.73 seconds, what is the leap height?

Use an equation.

$L = 4t^2$

$\approx 4(0.73)^2$

≈ 2.13 ft

Direct Variation with the Square

In the formula S.A. $= 4\pi r^2$, the dependent variable, the surface area, varies directly with the square of the control variable, the radius. The relationship between the variables is called **direct variation with the square**.

$$\text{S.A.} = 4\pi r^2 \quad \text{variation constant}$$

DIRECT VARIATION WITH THE SQUARE

The equation has this form:

$$y = k\mathbf{x}^2$$

variation constant ($k \neq 0$)

You read this as follows:

"y varies directly with x^2,"

or

"y is proportional to x^2."

The graph is a curve called a *parabola*.

when k is positive

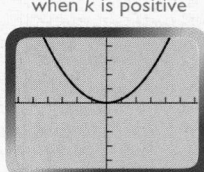

when k is negative

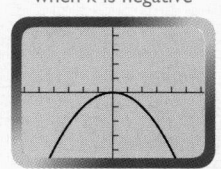

Talk it Over

1. How does changing the sign of k affect the graph of $y = kx^2$?

2. How do you think increasing the value of k changes the graph of $y = kx^2$? To check your answer, graph $y = \frac{1}{2}x^2$, $y = x^2$, and $y = 2x^2$ on the same screen.

Videotapes of basketball games show that some players leap as high as 3 ft.

Sample 1

BY THE WAY...

The great basketball player Michael Jordan appeared to have an impossibly long hang time because he released the ball *on the way down*, instead of at or before the peak of his leap.

The leap height of a basketball player varies directly with the square of the "hang time." When the leap height is in feet and the hang time is in seconds, the variation constant is 4.

What is the hang time for a leap height of 3 ft? Round your answer to the nearest hundredth of a second.

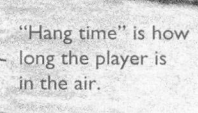

"Hang time" is how long the player is in the air.

Unit 2 Models of Variation and Growth

Answers to Talk it Over

1. Changing the sign of k reflects the graph of $y = kx^2$ over the horizontal or x-axis. When k is positive, the graph is a parabola that opens up; when k is negative, the graph is a parabola that opens down.

2. As k increases, the parabola becomes "narrower" or closer to the vertical or y-axis. Check students' graphs.

leap height

Sample Response

Problem Solving Strategy: Use an equation.

Let L = the leap height in feet.

Let t = the hang time in seconds.

$$L = 4t^2$$ ← L varies directly with t^2. The variation constant is 4.

$$3 = 4t^2$$ ← Substitute 3 for L.

$$0.75 = t^2$$ ← Divide both sides by 4.

$$\sqrt{0.75} = t$$ ← The hang time cannot be negative. Find the positive square root.

$$0.87 \approx t$$

The hang time is about 0.87 second.

The pole vault is a track and field event. From a running start, the athlete uses a springy pole to leap over a high crossbar.

Sample 2

The height reached by a pole-vaulter varies directly with the square of the speed of the athlete at the moment the pole is stuck in the ground. If one pole-vaulter reaches a height of 16 ft with a speed of 32 ft/s, how high does a second pole-vaulter leap with a speed of 35 ft/s? Round the answer to the nearest foot.

Sample Response

Problem Solving Strategy: Use an equation.

Step 1 Model the situation with an equation that represents direct variation with the square.

Let h = the height in feet.
Let s = the speed in feet per second.

$$h = ks^2$$

Step 2 Find the variation constant.

$$16 = k(32^2)$$ ← Substitute **16** for **h** and **32** for **s**.

$$0.016 \approx k$$ ← Divide both sides by 32^2.

Step 3 Find the height when the speed is 35 ft/s.

$$h \approx (0.016)(35^2)$$ ← Substitute **0.016** for **k** and **35** for **s**.

$$\approx 19.6$$

A pole-vaulter with a speed of 35 ft/s leaps about 20 ft.

⋯⋯► Now you are ready for:
Exs. 1–14 on pp. 96–97

Additional Sample

S2 How high can a pole-vaulter leap with a speed of 30 ft/s?

Use an equation.

$$h = ks^2$$

$$\approx (0.016)(30)^2$$

$$\approx 14.4 \text{ ft}$$

Research

Have students research past world or Olympic pole vault records. Students should then apply the formula given in Sample 2 to determine the pole-vaulter's speed for each record they have found.

94

In the formula $V = \frac{4}{3}\pi r^3$, the dependent variable, the volume, varies directly with the cube of the control variable, the radius. The relationship between the variables is called **direct variation with the cube**.

$$V = \frac{4}{3}\pi r^3 \qquad \text{variation constant}$$

DIRECT VARIATION WITH THE CUBE

The equation has this form:

$$y = kx^3$$

variation constant ($k \neq 0$)

You read this as follows:

"y varies directly with x^3," or "y is proportional to x^3."

The graph is a curve through the origin.

when k is positive

when k is negative

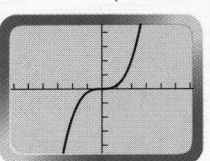 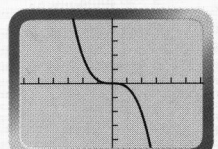

Additional Sample

S3 Suppose a wind is blowing at 35 mi/h. Find the number of watts of power generated by a windmill in this wind.

Use a formula.

$W = 0.015s^3$
$ = 0.015(35)^3$
$ = 643.13$

The number of watts of power generated is about 643.

Communication: Discussion

Electrical power is often expressed in kilowatts (1000 watts) or megawatts (1000 kilowatts). Using the By the Way, you might wish to ask students to determine the kilowatt and megawatt capacity India had in 1999. (1.08×10^6 kilowatts and 1.08×10^3 megawatts)

Multicultural Note

Although windmills may in the future produce significant amounts of energy for the people of India, at present they generate less than 1% of the nation's electrical energy. Coal- and petroleum-based facilities produce about 81% of India's electricity. Hydroelectric plants, located on the banks of India's powerful rivers, produce about 17% of the nation's electrical power. Nuclear plants generate approximately 2%. The leading industries in India are manufacturing and weaving cotton fabric. Other important industries include the production of jute, iron, and steel.

BY THE WAY...

India is a world leader in the use of wind power. At the end of 1999, India had the capacity to produce 1.08×10^9 watts with wind power.

Talk it Over

3. How does changing the sign of k affect the graph of $y = kx^3$?

4. How do you think increasing the value of k changes the graph of $y = kx^3$? To check your answer, graph $y = \frac{1}{2}x^3$, $y = x^3$, and $y = 2x^3$ on the same screen.

Sample 3

The number of watts of power generated by a windmill varies directly with the cube of the wind speed in miles per hour.

How fast must the wind be blowing for this windmill to produce 200 watts of power? For this windmill, the variation constant is 0.015. Round your answer to the nearest mile per hour.

Answers to Talk it Over

3. Changing the sign of k reflects the graph of $y = kx^3$ over the vertical or y-axis.

4. As k increases, the curve becomes "narrower" or closer to the vertical or y-axis. Check students' graphs.

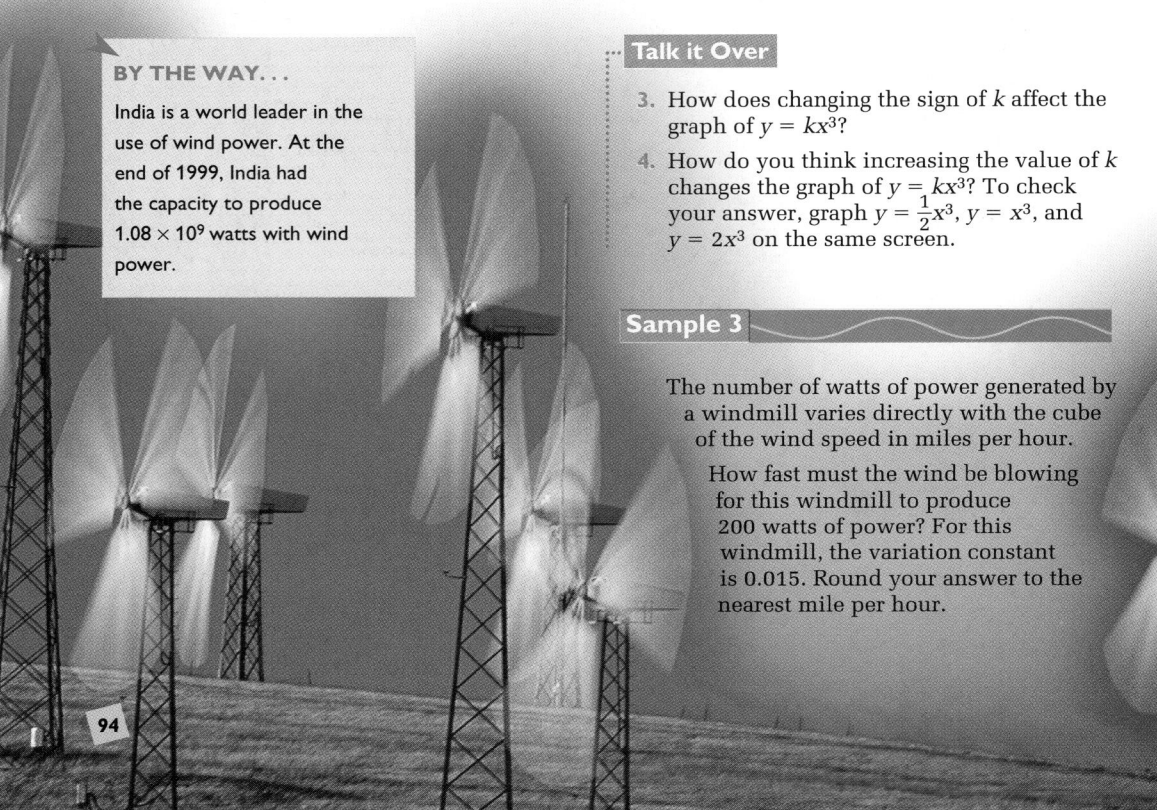

Sample Response

Problem Solving Strategy: Use a formula.

Let W = the power in watts.

Let s = the wind speed in miles per hour.

$W = 0.015s^3$ ◄——— W varies directly with s^3. The variation constant is 0.015.

Method ❶ Use algebra.

$$W = 0.015s^3$$
$$200 = 0.015s^3 \quad \text{◄——— Substitute 200 for } W.$$
$$13{,}333.33 \approx s^3 \quad \text{◄——— Divide both sides by 0.015.}$$
$$\sqrt[3]{13{,}333.33} \approx s \quad \text{◄——— Find the cube root.}$$
$$23.71 \approx s$$

The wind speed must be about 24 mi/h.

Method ❷ Use a graph.

Replace the control variable with x and the dependent variable with y.

1 Graph the function $y = 0.015x^3$.

2 Use TRACE to find the value of x when $y = 200$.

3 To get a more precise answer, reset the viewing window. Use TRACE again.

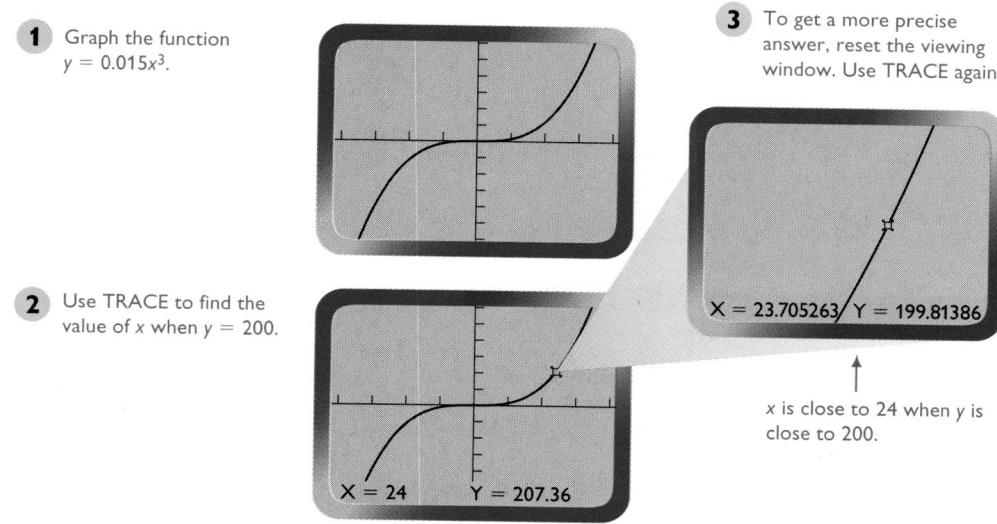

X = 23.705263 Y = 199.81386

X = 24   Y = 207.36

x is close to 24 when y is close to 200.

The wind speed must be about 24 mi/h.

Now you are ready for:
► Now you are ready for:
Exs. 15–37 on pp. 97–98

Look Back ◄————

How are the graphs and equations for direct variation, direct variation with the square, and direct variation with the cube alike? How are they different?

2-5 Direct Variation with Powers

Answers to Look Back ··

Answers may vary. Examples are given. All three kinds of equations are alike in that they are in the form $y = kz$, where k is a constant and z is a power of x, and each graph is contained entirely within two quadrants. The equations are different in that direct variation is linear, direct variation with the square is quadratic, and direct variation with the cube is cubic. The first graph is a line, the second is a parabola, and the third a somewhat s-shaped curve.

Using Technology

For Method 2 of the Sample Response, students can use the *Function Investigator* software or a graphics calculator.

Students who use a graphics calculator may need help in deciding on a good graph screen. One way to proceed on the TI-82 or TI-83 is the following. Enter the equation on the Y= list, press ZOOM, and select ZStandard. The calculator will display the graph on the standard graph screen $(-10 \le x \le 10, -10 \le y \le 10)$. Press TRACE and use ► until you get to the last coordinate readout for which Y is just below 200. Round the readouts *down* to 23 for X and 197 for Y. Write these down so you do not forget them. Press ► once and the readout for Y will be just a bit over 200. Round the readouts *up* to 24 for X and 203 for Y. Now press WINDOW and set the values for the viewing window to have Xmin = 23, Xmax = 24, Ymin = 197, and Ymax = 203. When you press GRAPH and use TRACE, you see that Y is almost exactly 200 when X is about 23.71.

A similar procedure works with the TI-81, though the coordinate readouts will be slightly different from those obtained with the TI-82 or TI-83 and you press RANGE instead of WINDOW.

························

Look Back

As students respond to these questions, it is important that they understand that all three types of variation are examples of functions. The function concept can help students to integrate their thinking about direct variation with powers.

·············

Suggested Assignment

Day 1

Standard 1–13

Extended 1–14

Day 2

Standard 15–23, 25–37

Extended 15–37

Integrating the Strands

Algebra Exs. 1–25, 32–37

Functions Exs. 1–25, 35–37

Geometry Exs. 2, 8, 10, 11, 22, 23, 26–31, 35–37

Logic and Language Exs. 3, 25, 37

Communication: Writing

For Ex. 3, you may need to remind students that a concept map is a visual summary that helps a person remember the connections between ideas. For examples of concept maps, see *Integrated Mathematics 1*, page 5, and pages 245, 320, and 339 of this textbook.

Interdisciplinary Problems

Exs. 9–14, 19–21, 24, and 35–37 illustrate the use of the concept of variation in various real-world situations. By working through these problems, students will become more familiar with direct variation with powers and should be able to apply the formulas $y = kx^2$ and $y = kx^3$ to solve variation problems.

2-5 Exercises and Problems

1. **Reading** In which quadrant(s) does the graph of $y = kx^2$ appear when k is positive? when k is negative?

2. Suppose you repeat the Exploration using the formulas for the perimeter of a square ($P = 4s$), the area of a square ($A = s^2$), and the volume of a cube ($V = s^3$). Without graphing, predict how your group's answers will compare.

3. Make a concept map for all the variation models presented in this unit.

For each equation in Exercises 4–7, find the values of x when $y = 15$. Round decimal answers to the nearest tenth.

4. $y = \pi x^2$ 5. $y = 4\pi x^2$ 6. $y = 4x^2$ 7. $y = 5.7x^2$

For Exercises 8 and 9, write an equation that models each situation. Use k to represent the variation constant.

8. The surface area, S.A., of a hemisphere varies directly with the square of the diameter, d.

9. The energy, E, of a moving car varies directly with the square of its speed, s.

10. The amount of material needed to cover a ball varies directly with the square of the radius. It takes about 172 cm^2 of material to cover a ball with a radius of 3.7 cm. What is the radius of a ball that needs 366 cm^2 of material to cover it?

11. The area of a square varies directly with the square of the diagonal. A square with a diagonal of 9 in. has an area of 40.5 in.^{2}. What is the area of a square with a diagonal of 14 in.?

connection to **DRIVER'S EDUCATION**

When a car goes around a curve on a flat road, the car will stay on the road only if the force between the car and the road is great enough. The force, in pounds, needed to accelerate a car around a curve varies directly with the square of the speed of the car in feet per second.

For Exercises 12 and 13, the value of the variation constant is 1.3.

12. Suppose that when the road is dry, the maximum force between the car and the road is 2250 lb. How fast can the car take the turn? Round your answer to the nearest mile per hour. (*Hint:* 1 ft/s ≈ 0.68 mi/h)

13. Suppose that when the road is wet, the maximum force between the car and the road is 1500 lb. How fast can the car take the turn? Round the answer to the nearest mile per hour.

Unit 2 Models of Variation and Growth

Answers to Exercises and Problems

1. When k is positive, the graph is in quadrants I and II; when k is negative, the graph is in quadrants III and IV.

2. P = perimeter; s = side; A = area; V = volume. In each equation, s is the control variable and P, A, and V are the dependent variables. The graph of $P = 4s$ is a straight line, the graph of $A = s^2$ is a parabola, and the graph of $V = s^3$ is an s-shaped curve. $P = 4s$ is a

linear growth graph that passes through (0, 0); $A = s^2$ is a nonlinear graph that passes through (0, 0); $V = s^3$ is a nonlinear growth graph that passes through (0, 0).

3. Answers may vary. An example is given.

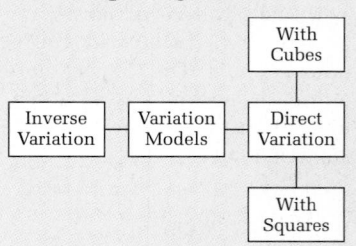

4. about 2.2; about −2.2

5. about 1.1; about −1.1

6. about 1.9; about −1.9

7. about 1.6; about −1.6

8. S.A. $= kd^2$

9. $E = ks^2$

10. about 5.4 cm

11. 98 in.^{2}

12. about 28 mi/h

13. about 23 mi/h

14. The distance an object falls varies directly with the square of the time the object is in the air. When distance is measured in feet and time is measured in seconds, the variation constant is 16.

    a. Write an equation for the distance an object falls as a function of time. Use d for distance and t for time.

    b. **Skydiving** A skydiver jumps from an airplane at an altitude of 15,000 ft. The parachute opens at an altitude of 3000 ft. Use your equation to calculate how long the skydiver has been in the air when the parachute opens.

For each equation in Exercises 15–18, find the value of x when $y = 15$. Round decimal answers to the nearest tenth.

15. $y = \frac{4}{3}\pi x^3$ **16.** $y = -x^3$ **17.** $y = 3.7x^3$ **18.** $y = -4x^3$

Wind Power For Exercises 19–21, use this information.

The power generated by a windmill is given by the equation $W = ks^3$, where W is power measured in watts and s is the wind speed in miles per hour.

19. One windmill has a variation constant of 0.013. How fast must the wind be blowing for the windmill to produce 170 watts of power?

20. How does the power output from a windmill change if the variation constant is increased?

21. How does the power output from a windmill change if the wind speed is halved?

For Exercises 22 and 23, use the formula for the volume of a sphere.

22. What is the radius of a sphere with volume 282 in.^{3}?

23. a. How does the volume of a sphere change when the radius doubles?

    b. How does the volume of a sphere change when the radius is halved?

24. **Biology** Suppose the height of an animal is h.

    a. The strength of an animal's bones varies directly with h^2. Model this relationship with an equation. Use s as the variation constant.

    b. The weight of an animal varies directly with h^3. Model this relationship with an equation. Use w as the variation constant.

    c. Explain why, as the height of the animal increases, its body weight increases much faster than the strength of its bones.

Ongoing **ASSESSMENT**

25. **Writing** Explain how to test a graph or data set of an unknown function to decide whether it shows direct variation, inverse variation, direct variation with the square, direct variation with the cube, or none of these.

BY THE WAY...

No gorilla could ever be as big as the movie monster King Kong. Its skeleton could not support its weight.

Answers to Exercises and Problems

14. a. $d = 16t^2$

    b. about 27.4 sec

15. about 1.5

16. about −2.5

17. about 1.6

18. about −1.6

19. about 23.6 mi/h

20. The power output is increased.

21. It is decreased to $\frac{1}{8}$ of the power generated by the original wind speed.

22. about 4.1 in.

23. a. It is multiplied by 8.

    b. It is divided by 8.

24. a. bone strength $B = sh^2$

    b. weight $M = wh^3$

    c. Answers may vary. An example is given. Using

the equations in parts (a) and (b), the weight will increase much quicker than bone strength because the weight is affected by h^3, and bone strength is affected by h^2.

25. Answer may vary. An example is given. You could test the graph by comparing its characteristics with those of the types of varia-

Working on the Unit Project

Exs. 35 and 36 help students to understand the process of evaporation of water from a lake. In their role as a park guide, students can use this knowledge to educate visitors to Mono Lake.

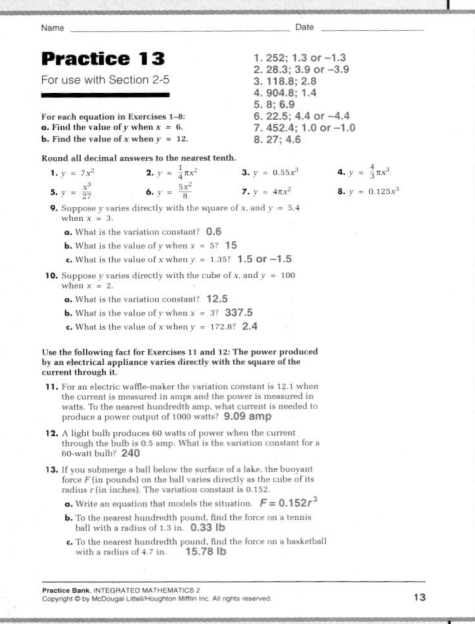
Answers to
Exercises and Problems

26. S.A. ≈ 615.8 cm²; V ≈ 1436.8 cm³

27. S.A. ≈ 45.4 in.²; V ≈ 28.7 in.³

28. S.A. ≈ 48,305.1 cm²;
    V ≈ 998,306.0 cm³

29. 8   30. 12

31. 25   32. 23.4

33. 108   34. 972

35. a. **Volume after Evaporation**

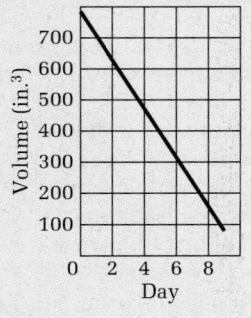

Find the surface area and volume of a sphere with each radius. *(Section 2-4)*

26. $r = 7$ cm   **27.** $r = 1.9$ in.   **28.** $d = 62$ cm

Use the Pythagorean theorem to find the missing side of each right triangle.
(Toolbox Skill 31)

29. leg: 6   leg: _?_
     hypotenuse: 10

30. leg: 5   leg: _?_
     hypotenuse: 13

31. leg: 7   leg: 24
     hypotenuse: _?_

Evaluate each expression for the given value of the variable. Round decimal answers to the nearest tenth. *(Toolbox Skill 9)*

32. x^4, when $x = 2.2$

33. $\frac{9}{5}hk^2$, when $h = 15$ and $k = 2$

34. $4x^5$, when $x = 3$

Working on the Unit Project

To study the evaporation of water from a lake, you can use a cylinder or a cone as a simple geometric model of the lake.

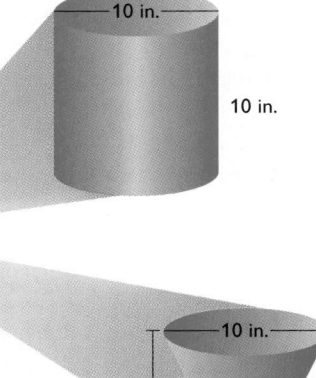

10 in.

10 in.

10 in.

10 in.

35. Suppose the cylinder at the right is filled to the top with salt water. Due to evaporation, the water level in the cylinder drops one inch each day for nine days.

   a. Graph the volume of the water as a function of time. Use the formula $V = \pi r^2 h$ for the volume of a cylinder. The variable r is the radius of a circular base and h is the height of the cylinder.

   b. Describe your graph.   **c.** What is the domain?   **d.** What is the range?

36. Repeat Exercise 35 for the cone at the right. Use the formula $V = \frac{1}{3}\pi r^2 h$ for the volume of a cone. (*Hint:* As the water level drops, the length of the radius remains half the height of the cone.)

37. **Writing** Suppose the water in the cylinder and the cone in Exercises 35 and 36 is equally salty before any evaporation takes place. Will it still be equally salty after water has evaporated for nine days? Why or why not?

98   **Unit 2** Models of Variation and Growth

---

b. Answers may vary. An example is given. The graph shows linear decay.

c. domain: $0 \le x \le 9$

d. range: $79 \le y \le 785$ or $25\pi \le y \le 250\pi$

36. a.
Volume after Evaporation

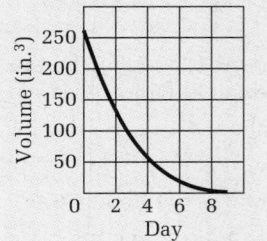

b. The graph shows non-linear decay.

c. $0 \le x \le 9$

d. $0.26 \le y \le 261.8$ or $\frac{\pi}{12} \le y \le \frac{250\pi}{3}$

37. No; the water in the cone will be much saltier. The cone and the cylinder will still contain the same amount of salt, but the ratio of the volume of water in the cylinder to the volume of water in the cone will have increased from 3 : 1 to 300 : 1.

Focus
Use negative, zero, and
fractional exponents.

Using Powers

The Powers *that be*

EXPLORATION

What definition of negative and zero
exponents does your calculator use?

• **Materials: scientific or graphics calculators**

• **Work with another student.**

Table 1		
2^{-1}	?	$\frac{1}{2}$
2^{-2}	?	$\frac{1}{4}$
2^{-3}	?	$\frac{1}{8}$
2^{-4}	?	$\frac{1}{16}$
2^{-5}	?	$\frac{1}{32}$

1 **a.** To complete the second column
of Table 1, use a calculator to
find the value of the expression
in the first column.

b. Use your calculator to show
that the decimals you wrote
in the second column are
equal to the fractions in the
third column.

c. What definition of x^{-n} do
you think your calculator
uses? Check that this
definition works for 8^{-1},
3^{-2}, and $(-5)^{-3}$.

Table 2	
1^0	?
2^0	?
3^0	?
4^0	?
5^0	?

2 **a.** To complete Table 2, use
a calculator to find the
value of the expression in
the first column.

b. What definition of x^0 do you think your
calculator uses? Check that your calculator also uses
this definition for negative values of x.

3 To see if your definitions for x^{-n} and x^0 work when $x = 0$,
use your calculator to evaluate 0^{-1}, 0^{-2}, and 0^0. What
happens? Why do you think this happens?

ZERO AND NEGATIVE EXPONENTS

Zero Exponent Rule

$a^0 = 1$ when $a \neq 0$

Negative Exponent Rule

$a^{-n} = \dfrac{1}{a^n}$ and $\dfrac{1}{a^{-n}} = a^n$ when $a \neq 0$

Objectives and Strands
See pages 56A and 56B.

Spiral Learning
See page 56B.

Materials List
➤ Scientific or graphics calculator
➤ Graphing software

Recommended Pacing
Section 2-6 is a two-day lesson.
Day 1
Pages 99–100: Exploration
through Sample 1, *Exercises 1–11*
Day 2
Pages 100–102: Exploration
through Look Back, *Exercises
12–43*

Extra Practice
See pages 616–617.

Warm-Up Exercises
Warm-Up Transparency 2-6

Support Materials
➤ Practice 14
➤ Enrichment 13 in the Activity
Bank
➤ Study Guide 2-6
➤ Problem Set 4
➤ Quiz 2-6
➤ Alternative Assessment 5

Answers to Exploration

1. a. 0.5; 0.25; 0.125; 0.0625;
0.03125

b. Check students'
calculations.

c. $x^{-n} = \dfrac{1}{x^n}$; $8^{-1} = 0.125 = \dfrac{1}{8}$;

$3^{-2} = 0.\overline{1} = \dfrac{1}{9}$;

$(-5)^{-3} = -0.008 = -\dfrac{1}{125}$

2. a. 1; 1; 1; 1; 1

b. $x^0 = 1$

3. A calculator will give an
error message when the
suggested values are en-
tered. Since x^{-n} is defined
as $\dfrac{1}{x^n}$, x^{-n} is not defined

when $x^n = 0$; $0^n = 0$ for all
positive numbers n. 0^0 is
not defined.

TEACHING

Exploration

The goal of the first Exploration is to have students use their calculators to arrive at an understanding of the meaning of a negative exponent and a zero exponent.

The second Exploration leads students to discover the meaning of the fractional exponents $\frac{1}{2}$ and $\frac{1}{3}$.

Additional Sample

S1 Simplify $4ax^{-3}y^{-2}c^0$. Write the answer with positive exponents.

$$4ax^{-3}y^{-2}c^0 = \frac{4a}{x^3y^2}$$

Mathematical Procedures

The two Explorations in this section illustrate the effective use of tables to analyze a mathematical situation. Organizing information in a table can often exhibit a pattern that may otherwise be difficult to discern.

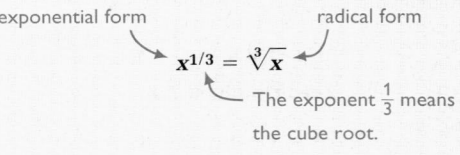

Sample 1

Simplify $6b^0a^{-4}$. Write the answer with positive exponents.

Sample Response

$$6b^0a^{-4} = 6 \cdot 1 \cdot a^{-4} \quad \longleftarrow \text{ Use the zero exponent rule.}$$

$$= 6\left(\frac{1}{a^4}\right) \quad \longleftarrow \text{ Use the negative exponent rule.}$$

$$= \frac{6}{a^4}$$

► Now you are ready for:
Exs. 1–11 on p. 102

EXPLORATION

(What) definition of $x^{1/2}$ and $x^{1/3}$ does your calculator use?

* **Materials: scientific or graphics calculators**
* **Work with another student.**

① Use a calculator to complete the table.

② **a.** Compare the numbers in the last two columns of your completed table. Make a conjecture about the meaning of $x^{1/2}$. Use your calculator to test your conjecture for several more values of x.

x	$\sqrt{x}$	$x^{1/2}$
1	?	?
2	?	?
3	?	?
4	?	?
5	?	?

b. Does your definition work for negative values of x? Why or why not?

③ Make a conjecture about the meaning of $x^{1/3}$. Use your calculator to test your conjecture for several positive values of x and several negative values of x. Do your results support your conjecture?

In the Exploration, you found that square roots and cube roots can be expressed using fractional exponents.

X : Lab

FRACTIONAL EXPONENTS

exponential form   radical form

$$x^{1/2} = \sqrt{x} \text{ when } x \geq 0$$

The exponent $\frac{1}{2}$ means the nonnegative square root.

$$x^{1/3} = \sqrt[3]{x}$$

The exponent $\frac{1}{3}$ means the cube root.

100   **Unit 2** Models of Variation and Growth

Answers to Exploration

1.

x	$\sqrt{x}$	$x^{1/2}$
1	1	1
2	1.414214	1.414214
3	1.732051	1.732051
4	2	2
5	2.236068	2.236068

2. a. The numbers in the last two columns in step 1 are the same.
Conjecture: $\sqrt{x} = x^{1/2}$.

b. No; only positive numbers have a real square root so if $x \leq 0$, $x^{1/2}$ is not a real number.

3. Conjecture: $\sqrt[3]{x} = x^{1/3}$; examples: $\sqrt[3]{1} = 1$; $\sqrt[3]{6} \approx 1.817$; $\sqrt[3]{27} = 3$; $\sqrt[3]{-1} = -1$; $\sqrt[3]{-14} \approx -2.41$; $\sqrt[3]{-64} = -4$. The results support the conjecture.

Simplify.

1. $81^{1/2}$ 2. $27^{1/3}$ 3. $(-8)^{1/3}$

4. Let $a = 9$ and $b = 16$. Find the value of $a \cdot b^{1/2}$ and of $(ab)^{1/2}$. How do the values compare?

The radical form of the expression $(2y)^{1/3}$ is $\sqrt[3]{2y}$. Rewrite each expression in the form indicated.

5. $(5x)^{1/2}$ in radical form   6. $4\sqrt[3]{n}$ in exponential form

Sample 2

You can use the formula below to estimate the speed v (in feet per second) that a roller coaster car must travel in order to stay on a vertical loop of track with radius r (in feet).

$$v = (32r)^{1/2}$$

About how fast must a roller coaster car travel on a vertical loop of track with radius 23 ft? Round your answer to the nearest foot per second.

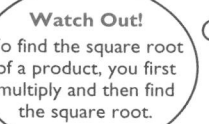

Watch Out!
To find the square root of a product, you first multiply and then find the square root.

Loop-and-screw roller coaster, Seibuen Park, Saitama Prefecture, Japan

Sample Response

Problem Solving Strategy: Use a formula.

$v = (32r)^{1/2}$

$= (32 \cdot 23)^{1/2}$ ⟵ Substitute 23 for r.

$= 736^{1/2}$

≈ 27.13 ⟵ Use the exponent key on your calculator.

The speed of the roller coaster car must be about 27 ft/s.

BY THE WAY...

The Moonsault Scramble coaster at the Fujikyu Highland Park, near Kawaguchi Lake, Japan, is 207 ft tall. When it was built, it was the tallest above-ground roller coaster in the world.

2-6 Using Powers   **101**

Look Back

You may wish to suggest that students illustrate their summaries with examples. ....●

APPLYING

Suggested Assignment

Day 1

Standard 1–11

Extended 1–11

Day 2

Standard 12–28, 34–43

Extended 12–32, 34–43

Integrating the Strands

Number Exs. 39–42

Algebra Exs. 1–36, 39–43

Geometry Exs. 28, 35, 36, 38

Logic and Language Exs. 1, 11, 37, 38

Error Analysis

It is common for students to make aithmetic or algebraic errors when working with negative and fractional exponents. A thorough review of the answers to Exs. 2–9 and 12–27 will help students to identify and correct any errors.

Reasoning

Ex. 11 requires students to expand the results of the Exploration on page 99 and of Ex. 10 to explain why $\frac{1}{a^{-n}} = a^n$.

▶ **Now you are ready for:**
Exs. 12–43 on pp. 102–104

Look Back ←

Summarize the meaning of each type of exponent: positive integer, negative integer, zero, one half, and one third.

2-6 Exercises and Problems

BY THE WAY...

The idea of zero arose separately in ancient India, Iraq, and Central and South America.

1. **Reading** For what value(s) of x does $x^0 \neq 1$?

Simplify. Write answers with positive exponents.

2. $-4s^0r^{-3}$

3. $\dfrac{45u^{-5}}{9}$

4. $(2 + x^0)(y^{-6})$

5. $(4m^{-2})(3n^{-4})$

6. $(b^0c^{-1})(d^4)$

7. $\dfrac{4}{v^{-2}}$

8. $\dfrac{4 + 7g^0}{h^{-3}}$

9. $\dfrac{15n^{-5}}{p^{-4}}$

10. To understand the zero and negative exponent rules, Le Ly looked at powers of 2. She noticed a pattern.

   a. Describe the pattern that Le Ly noticed.

   b. When Le Ly continues the pattern, what will she write for 2^0? for 2^{-1}? for 2^{-2}?

   c. Does Le Ly's method work for bases other than 2?

11. **Writing** Explain why $\dfrac{1}{a^{-n}} = a^n$ when a is not equal to zero.

$$\begin{aligned}
2^4 &= 16 \\
2^3 &= 8 \\
2^2 &= 4 \\
2^1 &= 2 \\
2^0 &= \\
2^{-1} &= \\
2^{-2} &=
\end{aligned}$$

Simplify.

12. $49^{1/2}$

13. $64^{1/2}$

14. $125^{1/3}$

15. $(-27)^{1/3}$

Rewrite each expression using fractional exponents.

16. $3\sqrt{a}$

17. $-2\sqrt[3]{x}$

18. $\sqrt[3]{3ab}$

19. $\sqrt{s} \cdot \sqrt[3]{t}$

20. $\sqrt{5x}$

21. $7\sqrt{8x}$

22. $-9\sqrt{p} \cdot \sqrt[3]{4q}$

23. $\sqrt{\dfrac{s}{2}}$

Rewrite each expression in radical form.

24. $5x^{1/2}$

25. $-6w^{1/3}$

26. $(3j)^{1/3}$

27. $\left(\dfrac{4}{r}\right)^{1/2}$

28. **a.** The formula $V = \frac{4}{3}\pi r^3$ gives the volume of a sphere of radius r. By solving the formula for r, show that $r = \left(\dfrac{3V}{4\pi}\right)^{1/3}$.

   b. Find the radius of a sphere with volume 200 cm³.

   c. Will the sphere in part (b) fit inside a cube with an edge that is 6 cm long?

Answers to Look Back

Positive integer exponents represent powers. Negative integer exponents represent reciprocals of powers. Any number to a zero exponent is 1 except for 0^0, which is undefined. An exponent of one-half represents the square root. An exponent of one-third represents the cube root.

Answers to Exercises and Problems

1. when $x = 0$

2. $\dfrac{-4}{r^3}$

3. $\dfrac{5}{u^5}$

4. $\dfrac{3}{y^6}$

5. $\dfrac{12}{m^2n^4}$

6. $\dfrac{d^4}{c}$

7. $4v^2$

8. $11h^3$

9. $\dfrac{15p^4}{n^5}$

10. **a.** Descriptions may vary. An example is given. Every time the exponent in a power of 2 is decreased by 1, the result is the previous answer divided by 2.

   b. $1, \dfrac{1}{2^1} = \dfrac{1}{2}, \dfrac{1}{2^2} = \dfrac{1}{4}$

   c. Yes.

11. $\dfrac{1}{a^{-n}} = \dfrac{1}{\frac{1}{a^n}} = \dfrac{1 \cdot a^n}{\frac{1}{a^n} \cdot a^n} = \dfrac{a^n}{1} = a^n$ when $a \neq 0$.

12. 7

13. 8

14. 5

15. –3

16. $3a^{1/2}$

17. $-2x^{1/3}$

18. $(3ab)^{1/3}$

19. $s^{1/2}t^{1/3}$

20. $(5x)^{1/2}$

21. $7(8x)^{1/2}$

22. $-9p^{1/2}(4q)^{1/3}$

23. $\left(\dfrac{s}{2}\right)^{1/2}$

24. $5\sqrt{x}$

25. $-6\sqrt[3]{w}$

26. $\sqrt[3]{3j}$

27. $\sqrt{\dfrac{4}{r}}$

For Exercises 29 and 30, use this information.

The period p (in seconds) of a pendulum is given by this formula:

$$p = 2\pi\left(\frac{l}{9.8}\right)^{1/2}$$

29. a. Find the period of a pendulum that is 1 m long.

b. Find the period of a pendulum that is 2 m long.

c. How do you think doubling the length of a pendulum affects the period? Check your answer for another pair of lengths.

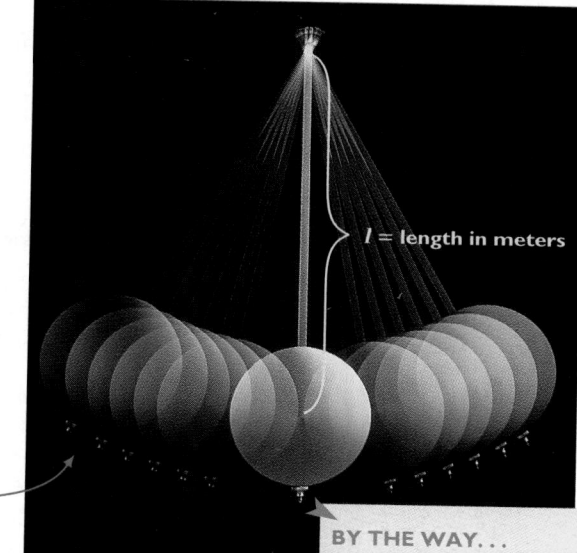

l = length in meters

> The *period* is the time it takes a pendulum to complete a swing.

BY THE WAY...

In 1851 Jean Foucault used a pendulum to prove that Earth rotates on its axis. Foucault's pendulum appeared to rotate because it stayed in the same place while Earth rotated.

30. Writing Do you think that changing the weight of a pendulum changes its period? Explain your answer. (*Hint:* How can you use the formula for p to decide?)

31. Open-ended Pendulums were replaced—first by springs and gears and then by quartz crystals—in clocks and watches. Why do you think that was?

32. Wind Power The wind speed s (in miles per hour) needed to generate W watts of electric power is given by this formula:

$$s = \left(\frac{W}{1.5 \times 10^{-2}}\right)^{1/3}$$

How fast would the wind have to blow in order to generate 180 watts of power? Round your answer to the nearest mile per hour.

33 TECHNOLOGY Use a graphics calculator or graphing software.

a. Graph each pair of functions on the same screen. Include all four quadrants in the viewing window.

$y = x^2$ and $y = x^{1/2}$ $\qquad$ $y = x^3$ and $y = x^{1/3}$

b. How are the graphs in each pair alike? How are they different?

c. How are the graphs of $y = x^{1/2}$ and $y = x^{1/3}$ alike? How are they different?

d. Are there any values of x for which $x^{1/2} > x^2$?

e. Are there any values of x for which $x^{1/3} > x^3$?

Answers to Exercises and Problems ····································

28. a. $V = \frac{4}{3}\pi r^3$

$\frac{3V}{4\pi} = r^3$

$\sqrt[3]{\frac{3V}{4\pi}} = r$

$\left(\frac{3V}{4\pi}\right)^{1/3} = r$

b. about 3.628 cm

c. No, since the diameter of the sphere would be

about 7.256 cm, so it would be too big to fit in the cube.

29. a. about 2.0 s

b. about 2.8 s

c. The period is increased by a factor of about 1.4 or about $\sqrt{2}$. Answers may vary. An example is given. The period is about 3.5 for a length of 3 and 4.9 for a length of

6. The period again increased by a factor of about $\sqrt{2}$.

30. No. Since the period depends only on the length of the pendulum (l is the only control variable), changing the weight will not change the period.

31–33. See answers in back of book.

103

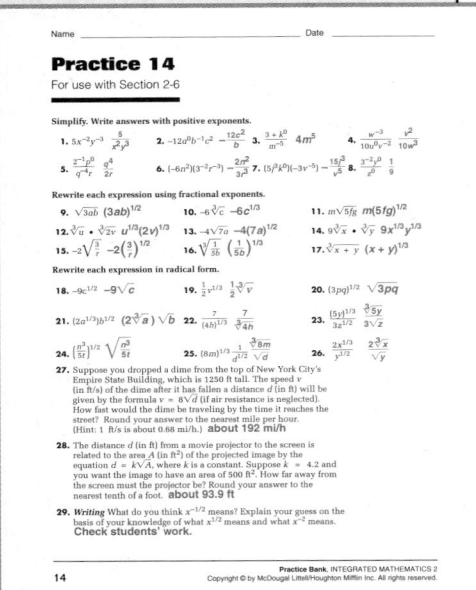
Ongoing ASSESSMENT

34. a. Find each value and arrange in order from least to greatest:

$$7^0 \qquad 7^3 \qquad (-7)^3 \qquad 7^{-3} \qquad (-7)^{-3} \qquad 7^{1/3} \qquad (-7)^{1/3}$$

   b. **Writing** Suppose your friend was absent when Section 2-6 was discussed. Explain to your friend why $a^n > a^{-n}$ when n is positive and $a > 1$.

   c. **Writing** Explain to your friend why $a^3 > a^{1/3}$ when $a > 1$.

Review PREVIEW

Write an equation that models each situation. Use k to represent the variation constant. *(Section 2-5)*

35. The area of a square room varies directly with the square of the length of the room.

36. The volume of a globe varies directly with the cube of its radius.

Tell whether each statement is an example of *inductive reasoning* or *deductive reasoning*. *(Section 1-6)*

37. Stephen King's new novel must be a horror story since all his previous best-selling novels have been horror stories.

38. If the measures of two angles of a triangle are 35° and 56°, then the measure of the third angle is 89°.

Simplify. *(Toolbox Skill 9)*

39. $18 \cdot 2^3$ **40.** $120 \cdot 4^2$ **41.** $5^4 \cdot 3^2$ **42.** $(2^4 \cdot 3^3)^2$

2 Working on the Unit Project

This exercise will help you to see how a drop in the water level of a lake affects the sizes of populations of animals living in the water.

43. In 1985, one cubic foot of water in Mono Lake held 1.9×10^3 brine shrimp. There were about 8.4×10^{10} cubic feet of water in the lake.

   a. In 1985 about how many brine shrimp were there in Mono Lake?

   b. One brine shrimp weighs about 2.7×10^{-3} oz. What was the approximate total weight of brine shrimp in Mono Lake in 1985?

   c. In 1985 the depth of Mono Lake was about 50 ft. Suppose the water level dropped 15 ft. About how much less water would be in the lake? Assume that the lake is a cylinder.

   d. About how many fewer shrimp can the lake hold at the water level in part (c)?

   e. About how many pounds do the brine shrimp in part (d) weigh?

This brine shrimp is about 8 times actual size.

Answers to Exercises and Problems

34. a. $7^0 = 1$; $7^3 = 343$; $(-7)^3 = -343$; $7^{-3} = 0.00291$; $(-7)^{-3} = -0.00291$; $7^{1/3} = 1.9129$; $(-7)^{1/3} = -1.9129$; From least to greatest: $(-7)^3, (-7)^{1/3}, (-7)^{-3}, 7^{-3}, 7^0, 7^{1/3}, 7^3$

   b. Answers may vary. An example is given. a^n is a constant raised to a power and a^{-n} is the inverse of that power.

Therefore, $a^n > a^{-n}$ whenever $a > 1$ and n is positive.

   c. a^3 is cubing the value of a and therefore increases it; $a^{1/3}$ is taking the cube root of a and therefore decreases it.

35. $A = kx^2$

36. $V = kr^3$

37. inductive

38. deductive

39. 144

40. 1920

41. 5625

42. 186,624

43. a. about 1.596×10^{14} brine shrimp in 1985

   b. About 4.3092×10^{11} oz was the total weight of shrimp in 1985.

   c. about 2.52×10^{10} fewer cubic feet of water

   d. about 4.788×10^{13} fewer shrimp

   e. about 8.07975×10^9 pounds

Focus
Explore situations
in which quantities
repeatedly double
or split in half.

Doubling and Halving

way **2** go!

EXPLORATION

(How) fast do numbers grow as they double?

• **Materials: newspapers, rulers**

• **Work with another student.**

Table 1	
Number of tears	**Area of each piece**
0	
1	
2	
3	
⋮	

Table 2	
Number of tears	**Number of pieces**
0	1
1	2
2	
3	
⋮	

① Read step 2. Predict how many times you will be able to tear the stack of newspaper pieces.

② **a.** Unfold a sheet of newspaper. Measure its area. Copy Table 1 and record the area in the first row.

b. Fold the sheet of newspaper in half. Tear along the fold so that you have two pieces. What is the area of each piece? Record the area in Table 1.

c. Stack the pieces of newspaper on top of each other. Fold the stack in half and tear along the fold. Copy Table 2 and record the number of pieces. Record the area of each piece in Table 1.

d. Repeat part (c) until you cannot tear the stack again. Extend Tables 1 and 2 as needed to record the number of pieces and the area of each piece.

③ Suppose you could tear the stack as many times as you predicted in step 1. How many pieces would you have?

④ Measure the height of your stack of pieces of newspaper. Estimate how tall the stack would be if you could make ten tears.

105

PLANNING

Objectives and Strands
See pages 56A and 56B.

Spiral Learning
See page 56B.

Materials List
➤ Newspaper
➤ Ruler
➤ Graph paper
➤ Graphics calculator
➤ 8.5 in. × 11 in. typing paper

Recommended Pacing
Section 2-7 is a two-day lesson.
Day 1
Pages 105–107: Exploration through Exponential Functions with Base 2, *Exercises 1–11*
Day 2
Pages 107–109: Halving through Look Back, *Exercises 12–33*

Extra Practice
See pages 616–617.

Warm-Up Exercises
Warm-Up Transparency 2-7

Support Materials
➤ Practice 15
➤ Enrichment 14 in the Activity Bank
➤ Study Guide 2-7
➤ Problem Set 4
➤ Diagram Masters 1, 2, 15 in the Explorations Lab Manual
➤ McDougal Littell Mathpack software: *Function Investigator*
➤ Using TI-81 and TI-82 Calculators: Using Tables to Solve Doubling and Halving Problems
➤ Quiz 2-7
➤ Test 6
➤ Alternative Assessment 6

Answers to Exploration

1. Answers may vary.

2. **a–d.** Answers may vary. Examples are given for an actual trial. The newspaper sheet in the example was 27.5 in. by 22.75 in. to begin. Six tears were made. To find the area of each piece after the first, dimensions were calculated, not measured.

3, 4. See answers in back of book.

Table 1			Table 2	
Number of tears	**Area of each piece**		**Number of tears**	**Number of pieces**
0	625.625		0	1
1	312.8125		1	2
2	156.40625		2	4
3	78.203125		3	8
4	39.1015625		4	16
5	19.55078125		5	32
6	9.775390625		6	64

The goal the Exploration is to have students discover how fast a number increases when it is repeatedly doubled. These observations lead to the more general concepts of exponential growth on pages 106 and 107.

Additional Sample

S1 Suppose Alfonso invests $2500 in a mutual fund at age 25. If the value of his investment doubles every seven years, what will be the value of the fund when Alfonso is 60 years old?

First find the number of doubling periods.

60 − 25 = 35

35 ÷ 7 = 5

There are 5 doubling periods.

Use an equation.

Let v = the value of the fund.

$v = 2500 \cdot 2^5$

$= 2500 \cdot 32$

$= 80,000$

The value of the fund when Alfonso is 60 years old will be $80,000.

The Daily Herald
Wednesday, October 18, 2000

Vol. 274, No. 49   28 pages   50 cents

Town Landfill Hits 50,000 Cubic Meters
Volume Doubling Every 3 Years

Doubling

Suppose it always takes the same amount of time for a quantity to double. This amount of time is called the **doubling period.**

The volume of the landfill in the newspaper headline has a doubling period of three years. The table shows the relationship between the *number of* doubling periods and the volume.

Number of 3-year doubling periods	Volume V (cubic meters)
0	$50,000 \times 2^0 = 50,000$
1	$50,000 \times 2 = 50,000 \times 2^1 = 100,000$
2	$100,000 \times 2 = 50,000 \times 2 \times 2 = 50,000 \times 2^2 = 200,000$
3	$200,000 \times 2 = 50,000 \times 2 \times 2 \times 2 = 50,000 \times 2^3 = 400,000$
4	$400,000 \times 2 = 50,000 \times 2 \times 2 \times 2 \times 2 = 50,000 \times 2^4 = 800,000$
⋮	⋮
n	(previous volume) $\times 2$ = (original volume) $\times$ (n factors of 2) = V

Sample 1

Suppose the volume of the landfill in the newspaper headline continues to double every three years. Find the volume 24 years from now.

Sample Response

First find the number of doubling periods.

total time → $\dfrac{24 \text{ years}}{3 \text{ years}} = 8$ ← number of doubling periods
doubling period →

Then use an equation.

$V = 50,000 \cdot 2^n$ ← The equation gives the volume V after n three-year doubling periods.

Watch Out!
Be sure to evaluate 2^8 *before* you multiply by 50,000.

$= 50,000 \cdot 2^8$ ← Substitute 8 for n.

$= 50,000 \cdot 256$

$= 12,800,000$

The volume of the landfill will be 12.8 million m³.

Unit 2 Models of Variation and Growth

1. a. What do you think the volume of the landfill was three years before the newspaper report?

   b. What value of n would you use to represent the time three years before the newspaper report? Find the value of V for this value of n.

   c. Find the value of V for $n = -2$. What does this quantity represent?

2. To graph the equation $V = 50{,}000 \cdot 2^n$, plot the points in the table on page 106 and the points you found in question 1.

   a. Is the graph *linear* or *nonlinear*? Does it show *growth* or *decay*?

   b. What does the vertical intercept represent?

   c. Does the graph ever touch the horizontal axis? Why or why not?

   d. What part of the graph do you think models the volume of the landfill? Explain.

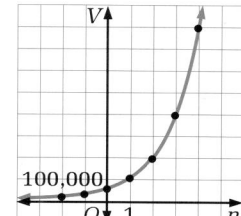

The equation $V = 50{,}000 \cdot 2^n$ from Sample 1 represents an **exponential function**. The general form is $y = ab^x$, where $a > 0$, $b > 0$, and $b \neq 1$.

EXPONENTIAL FUNCTIONS WITH BASE 2

x is the number of doubling periods.

$$y = a \cdot 2^x$$

a is the original amount when $x = 0$. The value of a cannot equal 0.

y is the amount after x doubling periods.

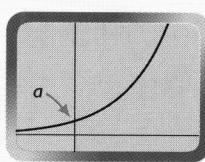

·····► Now you are ready for:
Exs. 1–11 on p. 110

Halving

Look at the data you recorded in Tables 1 and 2 in the Exploration. The doubling of the number of pieces of newspaper after each tear is an example of **exponential growth**. The decrease in the area of each piece is an example of **exponential decay**.

2-7 Doubling and Halving

107

Answers to Talk it Over

1. a. 25,000 m³

   b. $n = -1$; $V = 25{,}000$ m³

   c. 12,500 m³; the volume of the landfill 6 years before the newspaper report

2. a. nonlinear; growth

   b. present volume of the landfill

   c. No; if the graph were to intersect the horizontal axis, it would be at $V = 0$. Although at some point the actual volume of the landfill was zero, the value of the function $50{,}000(2^n)$ is never zero.

   d. Answer may vary. An example is given. The part of the graph that models the volume of the landfill is the portion for a few doubling periods before and after the year the report was written, that is, -3 or $-2 \leq n \leq 2$ or 3. Past doubling probably occurred only a few times. At some time in the future, the landfill will be completely filled up. Trash will be disposed of in some other manner.

Questions 3 and 4 allow students to explore exponential decay using data from the Exploration on page 105. Question 4 points out that in exponential decay, as in exponential growth, the dependent variable never assumes zero or negative values.

Assessment: Research

Students should investigate the half-life of several radioactive elements, such as carbon 14. They then should write an exponential model for each element.

Talk it Over

3. Use the data you recorded in Table 1 of the Exploration. Write an equation for the area A of one piece of your newspaper after n tears.

4. a. Suppose you could continue tearing the stack of newspaper pieces. Would the area of one piece ever be zero? Explain.

   b. Explain what your answer to part (a) means about the graph of the equation you wrote in question 3. Graph your equation in question 3.

An exponential function with base $\frac{1}{2}$ models a quantity that is halved again and again in equal time periods. The amount of time it takes for the quantity to divide in half is called the **half-life.**

EXPONENTIAL FUNCTIONS WITH BASE $\frac{1}{2}$

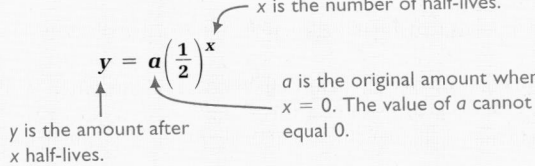

x is the number of half-lives.

$$y = a\left(\frac{1}{2}\right)^x$$

y is the amount after x half-lives.

a is the original amount when x = 0. The value of a cannot equal 0.

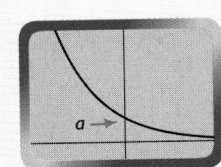

You can use the function $y = a\left(\frac{1}{2}\right)^x$ to model the decay of *radioactive* substances. As a substance gives off radiation, the amount of radioactive material decreases exponentially. Each radioactive substance has a specific half-life.

Radioactive iodine is used by doctors to diagnose and treat some thyroid problems.

Sample 2

One form of radioactive iodine has a half-life of about 8 days.

a. Write an equation that models the exponential decay of 500 g of this form of radioactive iodine.

b. How long will it be before only 50 g of the radioactive iodine is left?

Unit 2 Models of Variation and Growth

Answers to Talk it Over

3. The area of the original piece in the data in Table 1 was 625.625 in.^{2}. After n tears, the area is
$$A = 625.625\left(\frac{1}{2}\right)^n \text{ in.}^2.$$

4. a. No; the dimensions of each sheet would get smaller and smaller but would never reach zero.

b. The graph of the function never intersects the horizontal axis.

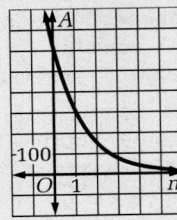

Sample Response

a. Let x = the number of 8-day half-lives.

Let y = the amount (in grams) of radioactive iodine.

$$y = a\left(\frac{1}{2}\right)^x \qquad \longleftarrow \text{ Use an exponential function with base } \frac{1}{2}.$$

$$y = 500\left(\frac{1}{2}\right)^x \qquad \longleftarrow \text{ The original amount is 500 g. Substitute 500 for } a.$$

The equation $y = 500\left(\frac{1}{2}\right)^x$ models the exponential decay of 500 g of this form of radioactive iodine.

b. Method ❶

Problem Solving Strategy: Use a table.

Use the equation from part (a) to make a table of values.

Number of half-lives	Amount of radioactive iodine (g)
0	500
1	250
2	125
3	62.5
4	31.25

50 occurs between the 3rd and 4th half-lives.

Since the half-life is 8 days, there will be 50 g of this form of radioactive iodine left after $8 \cdot 3 = 24$ days and before $8 \cdot 4 = 32$ days.

Method ❷

Problem Solving Strategy: Use a graph.

Use a graphics calculator. Trace the graph of the equation in part (a).

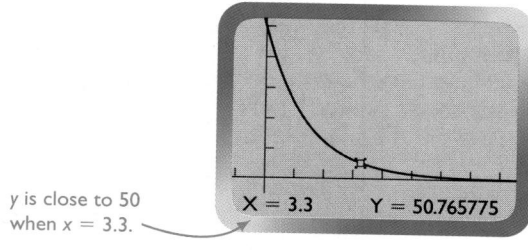

y is close to 50 when $x = 3.3$.

X = 3.3   Y = 50.765775

Since x is the number of 8-day half-lives, there will be 50 g of this form of radioactive iodine left after about $8(3.3) = 26.4$ days.

Look Back

Describe how to recognize a table that represents an exponential function with base 2. Describe how to recognize a graph that represents an exponential function with base $\frac{1}{2}$.

···▶ Now you are ready for:
Exs. 12–33 on pp. 110–112

Answers to Look Back

Descriptions may vary. An example is given. If the values in one column of the table increase by 1 and the values in the other column double, the table represents an exponential function with base 2. A graph of an exponential function with base $\frac{1}{2}$ is an example of nonlinear decay in quadrants I and II. It gets closer and closer to the horizontal axis but never reaches it. Each value of the dependent variable is equal to the product of the vertical intercept and $\frac{1}{2}$ raised to a power equal to the corresponding value of the control value.

Using Technology

The *Function Investigator* software can be used for Method 2 of Sample 2.

Additional Sample

S2 Suppose a radioactive substance has a half-life of about 30 days.

a. Write an equation that models the exponential decay of 10 g of this substance.

Let x = number of 30-day half-lives.

Let y = the number of grams of the radioactive substance.

$$y = a\left(\frac{1}{2}\right)^x$$

$$y = 10\left(\frac{1}{2}\right)^x$$

The equation $y = 10\left(\frac{1}{2}\right)^x$ models the exponential decay of 10 g of the radioactive substance.

b. How long will it be before less than 1 g of the radioactive substance is left?

Method 1: Use a table.

Number of half-lives	Amount of radioactive substance (g)
0	10
1	5
2	2.5
3	1.25
4	0.625

It will take between 3 and 4 half-lives or between 90 and 120 days before less than 1 g of the substance is left.

Method 2: Use a graphics calculator. Trace the graph of the equation $y = 10\left(\frac{1}{2}\right)^x$.

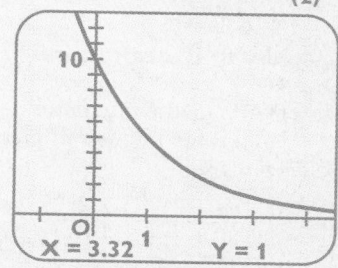

X = 3.32   Y = 1

Since x is the number of 30-day half-lives, there will be less than 1 g of the substance after about $30(3.32) = 99.6$ or 100 days.

109

Suggested Assignment

Day 1

Standard 1–10

Extended 1–11

Day 2

Standard 16–19, 21–33

Extended 12–14, 16–19, 21–33

Integrating the Strands

Algebra Exs. 1–28, 33

Functions Exs. 1–7, 9–21, 33

Geometry Exs. 29–32

Using Technology

Students can use the *Function Investigator* software to create graphs for the exercises for this section.

Career Note

During the past two or three decades, many people in the United States and in other countries have become increasingly concerned about the quality of their country's environment. Air quality, water quality, wetlands control, use of forests, waste disposal, and other environmental issues are often in the news. The need to manage the environment has created many new types of jobs, such as that of an environmental engineer in Ex. 3, who is concerned with recycling programs. An interesting activity would be to ask students about any environmental issues they may have read about and the types of job opportunities they think might be related to these issues.

2-7 Exercises and Problems

1. **a.** Use the data you recorded in Table 2 in the Exploration. Write an equation to model the data.

   b. Graph your equation from part (a).

2. Suppose the thickness of the sheet of newspaper you used in the Exploration is 2.2×10^{-3} in.

   a. Write an equation to model the height h of your stack of newspaper pieces after n tears.

   b. What would be the height of the stack if you could make 15 tears?

3. **Reading** The newspaper article shown on page 106 quotes an environmental engineer:

   Find the landfill's volume 24 years from now, if the doubling period is four years. Compare your answer to the answer in Sample 1.

   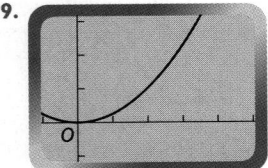

   "An aggressive recycling program could immediately increase the volume's doubling period to four years."

For Exercises 4–7, use the equation $y = 58 \cdot 2^x$. Find the value of y for each value of x.

4. $x = 0$ 5. $x = 5$ 6. $x = 10$ 7. $x = 20$

Tell if each graph represents an exponential function with base 2. Write *Yes* or *No*. Explain your answer.

8.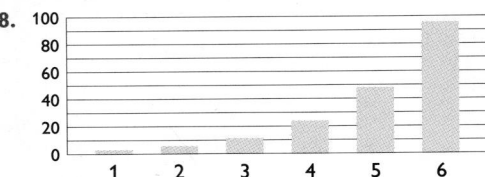

9.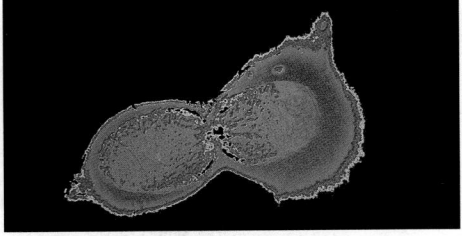

10. **Biology** A type of bacteria reproduces by dividing into two bacteria every 20 min. If you start with one bacterium, how many bacteria will there be after one hour? after two hours?

11. **Open-ended** Make up a situation that can be modeled by the equation $y = 100 \cdot 2^x$.

Number of tears	Area of each piece (in.²)
0	600
1	300
2	150
3	75
4	37.5
5	18.75

For Exercises 12 and 13, use the area data that Lydia and Al recorded when they did the Exploration using a sheet of newspaper with dimensions 20 in. × 30 in.

12. **a.** Describe the change in the area of one piece each time they tear the stack.

   b. Lydia modeled their data with the equation $A = 600\left(\frac{1}{2}\right)^n$. Explain how she might have arrived at this equation.

Answers to Exercises and Problems

1. **a.** Let n be the number of tears and p the number of pieces; $p = 2^n$.

   b.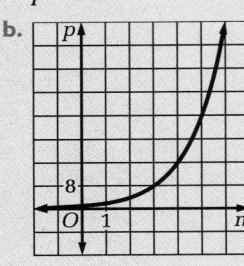

2. **a.** $h = (2.2 \times 10^{-3})(2^n)$

   b. about 72.1 in.

3. 3.2 million m³; This is one-fourth of the volume if the doubling period is three years.

4. 58

5. 1,856

6. 59,392

7. 60,817,408

8. Answers may vary. Yes; the value of the dependent variable roughly doubles when the value of the control variable is increased by 1.

9. No; the graph intersects the horizontal axis.

10. 8; 64

11. Answers may vary. An example is given. The population of a village was 100 in 1750. The population doubled every 25 years.

12. **a.** The area of one piece is halved.

   b. The area of the original piece was 600 in.². The areas are halved at regular intervals, so the area can be modeled by an exponential function with base $\frac{1}{2}$. The

13. a. Graph the equation $A = 600\left(\frac{1}{2}\right)^n$. Include points with negative

n-coordinates. Which points on the graph represent areas of Lydia's and Al's pieces of newspaper?

b. **Writing** Compare the graph of the equation $A = 600\left(\frac{1}{2}\right)^n$ to the graph

of the equation $V = 50{,}000 \cdot 2^n$ shown on page 107. How are they alike? How are they different?

For Exercises 14 and 15, use the information in Exercises 12 and 13. Suppose Lydia and Al are able to continue tearing their stack of newspaper pieces.

14. Use a table to find the number of tears after which the area of each piece is less than 1 in.²

15 TECHNOLOGY Use a graphics calculator to find the number of tears after which the area of each piece is less than 0.1 in.²

16. a. Graph the equation $y = 4\left(\frac{1}{2}\right)^x$.

b. Use your graph to estimate the value of x when $y = 3$.

17. One form of radium decays exponentially with a half-life of 1600 years.

a. Use an equation to model the exponential decay of 120 g of this form of radium.

b. How long will it take 120 g of the radium to decay to 5 g of radium?

18. **Sports** There are 64 teams in the first round of an NCAA basketball championship. In each round, every team in the round plays a game against one other team in the round. Only the winning teams advance to the next round.

a. Explain why the number of teams in each round can be modeled by an equation that represents exponential decay.

b. Write an exponential equation that you can use to find the number of teams in any round.

c. What does the exponent in your equation represent?

19. **Demographics** Brunei is a tiny, thinly populated country with a high standard of living. In 1999, the population of Brunei was 329,000. It was doubling approximately every 18 years. Suppose the population continues to grow at the same rate.

a. Write an equation that models the population growth.

b. In what year will the population exceed 5,000,000?

c. Do you think the population can continue to double every 18 years? Why or why not?

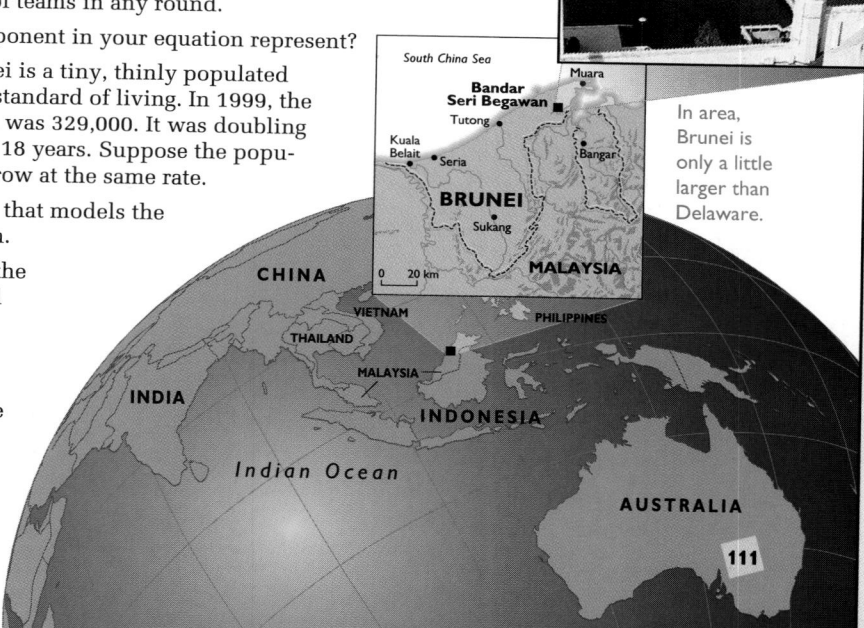

In area, Brunei is only a little larger than Delaware.

111

16. a.

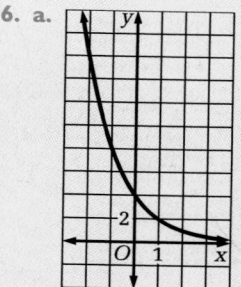

b. about 0.42

17. a. Let x be the number of 1600-year half-lives that have passed and y be the amount in grams of radium present; $y = 120\left(\frac{1}{2}\right)^x$.

b. about 7336 years

18. a. The number of teams is cut in half after each round.

b. Let x be the number of rounds and y be the number of teams in that round; $y = 64\left(\frac{1}{2}\right)^x$.

c. The exponent represents the number of rounds that have been played in the tournament.

19. See answers in back of book.

Answers to Exercises and Problems

appropriate equation is $A = 600\left(\frac{1}{2}\right)^n$.

13. a.

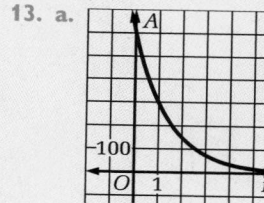

The points with integer coordinates between 0 and 5 (that is, (0, 600), (1, 300), (2, 150), (3, 75), (4, 37.5), (5, 18.75)).

b. Summaries may vary but should include these points: the graphs of $A = 600\left(\frac{1}{2}\right)^n$ and $V = 50{,}000(2^n)$ are both

nonlinear; both graphs are in quadrants I and II; both graphs cross the y-axis; both graphs approach the x-axis but do not cross it; one graph shows decay, the other shows growth.

14. 10 tears

15. 13 tears

Quick Quiz (2-4 through 2-7)

See page 114.

20. **Using Manipulatives** Begin with a sheet of typing paper with dimensions 8.5 in. × 11 in. Follow these steps:

Step 1 Fold the paper in half so that the short sides meet, and then tear the paper in half along the fold.

Step 2 Take one of the pieces and fold it in half so that the short sides meet, and then tear along the fold.

Step 3 Repeat step 2 until you can no longer fold and tear.

a. After how many tears is the area of the smallest piece of paper less than 1 in.^{2}?

b. What are the dimensions of the smallest piece of paper?

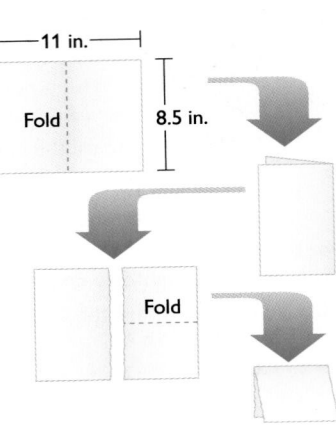

Ongoing **ASSESSMENT**

21. **Writing** Use Lydia's and Al's area data from Exercise 12 on page 110. Part (b) of Exercise 12 gives the equation $A = 600\left(\frac{1}{2}\right)^n$ as Lydia's model of the data. Al says they can model the data with the equation $A = 600 \cdot 2^{-n}$. Do you agree with him? Explain your reasoning.

Review **PREVIEW**

Simplify. Write answers with positive exponents. *(Section 2-6)*

22. $(6y^0)(6x^{-4})$

23. $\dfrac{7y^{-6}}{x^4}$

24. $(2n^3)^0$

Find the slope of each line. *(Section 2-2)*

25. $y = 3x - 5$

26. $y = 5$

27. $y = -\frac{1}{2}x + 4$

28. $x = -2$

What name best describes each shape? *(Toolbox Skill 27)*

29.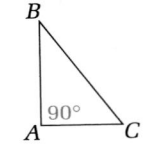

30.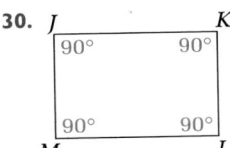

31.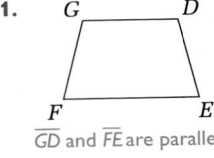
$\overline{GD}$ and $\overline{FE}$ are parallel.

32.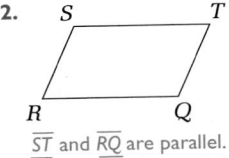
$\overline{ST}$ and $\overline{RQ}$ are parallel.
$\overline{RS}$ and $\overline{QT}$ are parallel.

  Working on the Unit Project

33. Between 1942 and 1992, the salinity of Mono Lake doubled. *Salinity* is the number of grams of salt per liter of water. In 1942 the salinity of Mono Lake was about 51.3 g/L.

Suppose the salinity doubles at regular intervals.

a. What would be the doubling period for the salinity?

b. After two more doubling periods, what would be the salinity?

Answers to Exercises and Problems

20. a. 7 tears
   b. $1\frac{1}{16}$ in. $\times \frac{11}{16}$ in.

21. Yes; the two equations are equivalent since $2^{-n} = \left(\frac{1}{2}\right)^n$.

22. $\dfrac{36}{x^4}$

23. $\dfrac{7}{x^4y^6}$

24. 1

25. 3

26. 0

27. $-\dfrac{1}{2}$

28. undefined

29. right triangle

30. rectangle

31. trapezoid

32. parallelogram

33. a. 50 years
    b. 410.4 g/L

Completing the Unit Project

Now you are ready to make a set of note cards for your Mono Lake guided tour.

Your note cards should include these things:

➤ a description of the major features of the Mono Lake ecosystem

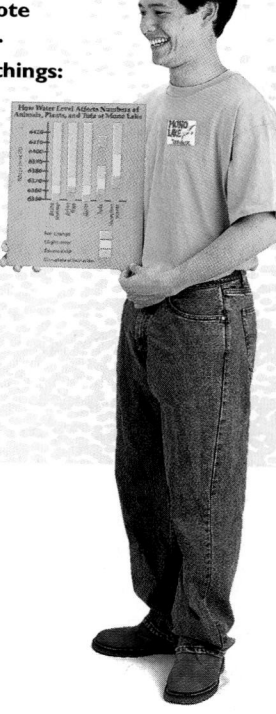

➤ historical information about changes in the ecosystem

➤ predictions about the future of the ecosystem

➤ interesting details to enliven your tour

➤ backup information for answering visitors' questions

Look Back

How did the use of mathematical models help you to better understand an ecosystem?

Assessment

A scoring rubric for the Unit Project can be found on pages 56 and 57 of this Teacher's Edition and also in the *Project Book*.

Alternative Projects

Project 1: Tropical Rain Forest

Research tropical rain forest ecosystems. Apply the models of variation and growth you learn about in this unit to write a report that includes:

➤ how rain forests affect the global climate

➤ how logging affects the world's rain forests

Project 2: Population Growth

Obtain population data for your state as far back as possible. Analyze the data. Determine whether or not there is a constant doubling period. Graph the data and use it to predict population changes for the next 20 years. If professional forecasts are available, compare them with your predictions. What factors account for any differences between the various professional forecasts and your predictions?

Quick Quiz (2-4 through 2-7)

1. What is the surface area of a sphere whose diameter is 20 cm? [2-4] about 1257 cm²

2. What is another way of saying that y varies directly with x^2? [2-5]
   y is proportional to x^2.

3. If $y = 2.5x^3$, find the value of x when $y = 160$. [2-5]
   y = 4

4. Simplify $\dfrac{16k^0 n^2 m^{-3}}{4m^{-2}}$. Write the answer with positive exponents. [2-6] $\dfrac{4n^2}{m}$

5. What is the value of $12^{1/2}$ to the nearest tenth? [2-6]
   3.5

6. A radioactive substance has a half-life of 500 years. How many years will it take for 10 grams of the substance to decay to 0.625 grams? [2-7] 2000 years

Answers to Unit 2 Review and Assessment

1. dependent variable: freshman enrollment; control variable: years

2. domain: 1993–2000; range: about 392,000–425,000

3. The graph is drawn in linear segments. It is decreasing from 1993 to 1995; increasing from 1995 to 1997; and decreasing from 1997 to 2000.

4. a. 3   b. 5
   c. $y = 3x + 5$ d. 3
   e. Let x represent the number of CD's ordered and y represent the total cost. Then $3x$ would be the cost for the CD's plus $5 handling charge to arrive at the equation $y = 3x + 5$.

For Questions 1–3, use the graph.   2-1

1. Name the dependent and control variables.

2. What is the domain of the function represented by the graph? What is the range?

3. Use the terms *linear* or *nonlinear* and *increasing*, *decreasing*, or *constant* to describe the graph.

4. A line contains two points with coordinates (8, 29) and (−1, 2).   2-2
   a. What is the slope of the line?
   b. What is the vertical intercept of the line?
   c. Write an equation of the line.
   d. Find the value of x when $y = 14$.
   e. **Writing** Explain why the equation you wrote can be used to model the mail-order charge when the shipping charge is $3 per CD plus a handling charge of $5.

Writing Is *direct variation* or *inverse variation* a good model for the data in each table? Explain how you made your decision.   2-2, 2-3

5.

x	y
4.4	4.96
4.6	5.04
4.8	5.12
5.0	5.20

6.

x	y
5.4	2.27
5.5	2.23
5.6	2.19
5.7	2.15

7. a. Rewrite the equation $xy = 144$ so that it can be entered on a graphics calculator.   2-3
   b. Find y when $x = 20$.

8. What is the volume of a sphere with radius 3 in.?   2-4

9. The ratio of the radii of two spheres is 3:5.
   a. What is the ratio of the surface areas of the two spheres?
   b. The surface area of the larger sphere is 100 ft². What is the surface area of the smaller sphere?

Use this information for Questions 10–12.   2-5

In flight, the weight of birds, insects, and aircraft is carried by the wings. The equation $w \approx (9 \times 10^{-5})s^2$ relates the wing loading w (g/cm²) and the minimum speed s (km/h) for level flight.

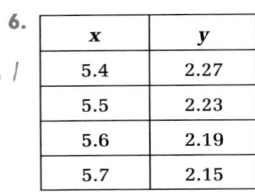

Wing loading is the weight supported by each square unit of wing surface.

10. What type of variation is modeled by the equation?

11. Estimate the minimum flying speed for an insect with $w = 0.02$ g/cm².

12. Estimate the wing loading for an aircraft with a minimum flying speed of 80 km/h.

---

5. Explanations may vary. An example is given. direct variation; Each of the quotients $\dfrac{y}{x}$ is approximately equal to 1.1.

6. Explanations may vary. An example is given: inverse variation. Each of the products xy is approximately equal to 12.26.

7. a. $y = \dfrac{144}{x}$
   b. 7.2

8. about 113.1 in.³

9. a. 9:25
   b. 36 ft²

10. direct variation with the square

11. about 15 km/h

12. about 0.576 g/cm²

13. $\dfrac{x^9}{y}$

14. g^2

15. $-\dfrac{20r}{t^3}$

16. $\dfrac{1}{64}$

17. 33.3 km/h

18. Descriptions may vary. An example is given. The graph of an exponential function with base 2 gets closer and closer to the horizontal axis but does not intersect it, yet it does intersect the vertical axis. As the value of the control variable increases, the value of the dependent value increases without bound.

Simplify. Write answers with positive exponents.

2-6

13. x^9y^{-1} **14.** $\dfrac{5^0}{g^{-2}}$ **15.** $(5r)(-4t^{-3})$ **16.** $(2^{-6})(3^0)$

17. Another way of writing the equation relating speed and wing loading from Questions 10–12 is $s = 105.4w^{1/2}$. Find the minimum speed required for level flight with a wing loading of 0.1 g/cm².

18. **Writing** Describe the important characteristics of the graph of an exponential function with base 2.

2-7

19. The graph models the decay of a form of radioactive bismuth. The half-life is five days.

a. What was the original amount of the radioactive substance?

b. Estimate the number of days after which less than $\dfrac{1}{10}$ of the original amount is left.

c. Write an exponential equation that models the decay of this form of radioactive bismuth.

d. Find the amount of radioactive bismuth left after one year.

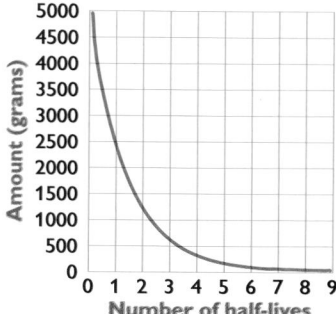

20. **Self-evaluation** What have you added to your understanding of direct variation as a result of your work in this unit?

21. **Group Activity** Work in a group of three to six students.

a. Sit in a circle. Choose someone to write each of these phrases on a separate sheet of paper.

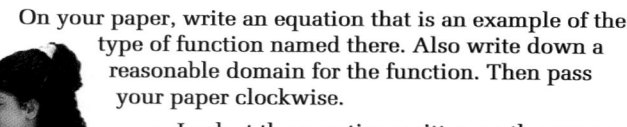

direct variation	inverse variation
varies with the square	varies with the cube
exponential growth (doubling)	exponential decay (half-life)

b. Each of you should choose a sheet of paper at random. Put aside the papers not chosen.

On your paper, write an equation that is an example of the type of function named there. Also write down a reasonable domain for the function. Then pass your paper clockwise.

c. Look at the equation written on the paper you receive. On the same piece of paper, sketch a graph of the equation over the domain stated on the paper. Again pass your paper clockwise.

d. Describe a situation that is modeled by the equation and the graph on the paper you receive. Be sure to include values for at least two points.

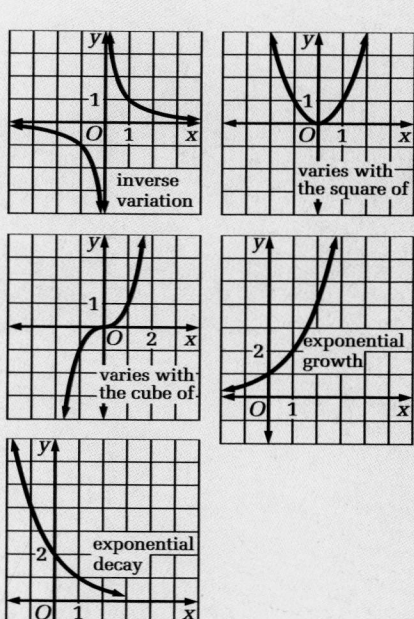

115

Answers to Unit 2 Review and Assessment

19. a. 5000 g

b. about 17 days

c. Let x be the number of 5-day half-lives that have passed and y be the amount (in grams) of the substance present; $y = 5000\left(\dfrac{1}{2}\right)^x$.

d. 5.29×10^{-19} g

20. Answers may vary.

21. a, b. direct variation: $y = kx$; inverse variation: $y = \dfrac{k}{x}$; varies with the square: $y = kx^2$; varies with the cube: $y = kx^3$; exponential growth (doubling): $y = k(2^x)$; exponential decay (half-life): $y = \left(\dfrac{1}{2}\right)^x$;

Domains may vary, but for inverse variation must exclude zero.

c. Graphs may vary. Examples are given.

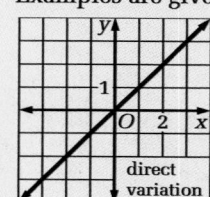

d. Descriptions may vary. Examples are given. direct variation: cost as a function of the number of items purchased; inverse variation: length as a function of width for a rectangle of fixed area; varies with the square: cost of a number of tiles as a function of the length of a side; varies with the cube: volume of a cube as a function of the length of a side; exponential growth: reproduction of one-celled organisms by splitting; exponential decay: radioactive decay

IDEAS AND (FORMULAS) $= x^2$

- The graphs of functions can be examples of linear growth, nonlinear growth, linear decay, nonlinear decay, or a constant. *(p. 61)*

- Graphs of functions can have different characteristics over different intervals. *(p. 61)*

- Functions, tables, graphs, equations, and inequalities can be used as mathematical models of situations. *(p. 67)*

- Linear functions can be written in slope-intercept form $y = mx + b$: *(p. 68)*

$$\underset{\text{variable}}{\text{dependent}} = \text{slope} \times \underset{\text{variable}}{\text{control}} + \underset{\text{intercept}}{\text{vertical}}$$

- The slope m of the line between (x_1, y_1) and (x_2, y_2) is: *(p. 68)*

$$m = \frac{y_2 - y_1}{x_2 - x_1}$$

- In a direct variation situation, two quantities have a constant ratio. An algebraic model for "y varies directly with x" is $y = kx$ when $k \neq 0$. *(p. 70)*

- In an inverse variation situation, two quantities have a constant product. An algebraic model for "y varies inversely with x" is $y = \frac{k}{x}$ when $k \neq 0$ and $x \neq 0$. *(pp. 76–77)*

- A model for "y varies directly with x^2" is $y = kx^2$ when $k \neq 0$. The model represents direct variation with the square. *(p. 92)*

- A model for "y varies directly with x^3" is $y = kx^3$ when $k \neq 0$. The model represents direct variation with the cube. *(p. 94)*

- The following rules apply to the exponent zero and negative exponents when $a \neq 0$. *(p. 99)*

$$a^0 = 1 \qquad a^{-n} = \frac{1}{a^n} \text{ and } \frac{1}{a^{-n}} = a^n$$

- Square roots and cube roots can be expressed using fractional exponents: $x^{1/2} = \sqrt{x}$ when $x \geq 0$, and $x^{1/3} = \sqrt[3]{x}$. *(p. 100)*

- Exponential functions with base 2, such as $y = a \cdot 2^x$ when $a \neq 0$, model the doubling of a quantity in equal time periods. *(p. 107)*

- Exponential functions with base $\frac{1}{2}$ model the halving of a quantity in equal time periods. *(p. 108)*

- Functions in the form $y = a\left(\frac{1}{2}\right)^x$ when $a \neq 0$ model the decay of radioactive substances. *(p. 108)*

Unit 2 Models of Variation and Growth

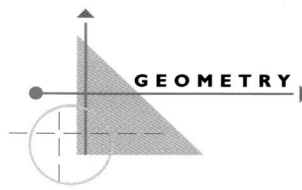

GEOMETRY

➤ Through any two points there is exactly one line. *(p. 68)*

➤ The graph of inverse variation is a hyperbola in Quadrants I and III or Quadrants II and IV. *(p. 77)*

➤ For a sphere with radius r: Surface Area (S.A.) $= 4\pi r^2$ *(p. 85)*

  Volume $(V) = \frac{4}{3}\pi r^3$ *(p. 85)*

➤ All spheres are similar space figures. *(p. 86)*

➤ The ratio of the surface areas of two spheres is the ratio of the squares of their radii. *(p. 86)*

  The ratio of the volumes of two spheres is the ratio of the cubes of their radii. *(p. 86)*

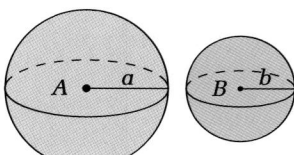

$$\frac{\text{S.A. of sphere } A}{\text{S.A. of sphere } B} = \frac{a^2}{b^2}$$

$$\frac{\text{volume of sphere } A}{\text{volume of sphere } B} = \frac{a^3}{b^3}$$

➤ The graph of direct variation with the square is a parabola. *(p. 92)*

➤ The graph of direct variation with the cube is a curve through the origin. *(p. 94)*

Key Terms

- **linear** (p. 60)
- **decay graph** (p. 61)
- **range** (p. 62)
- **slope-intercept form** (p. 68)
- **direct variation** (p. 70)
- **hyperbola** (p. 77)
- **diameter of a sphere** (p. 85)

- **doubling period** (p. 106)
- **exponential decay** (p. 107)

- **function** (p. 60)
- **constant graph** (p. 61)
- **mathematical model** (p. 67)
- **slope** (p. 68)
- **variation constant** (p. 70)
- **sphere** (p. 84)
- **direct variation with the square** (p. 92)

- **exponential function** (p. 107)
- **half-life** (p. 108)

- **growth graph** (p. 61)
- **domain** (p. 62)
- **linear function** (p. 68)
- **vertical intercept** (p. 68)
- **inverse variation** (p. 76)
- **radius of a sphere** (p. 85)
- **direct variation with the cube** (p. 94)

- **exponential growth** (p. 107)

Linear Systems and Matrices

OVERVIEW

➤ **Unit 3** covers methods of solving systems of linear equations: graphing, the substitution method, the addition-or-subtraction method, and using matrices. Systems of linear inequalities are included. A review of graphing equations and inequalities is provided in the **Student Resources Toolbox** on pages 649–654. The work on systems includes the number and type of solutions, and systems involving parallel and perpendicular lines.

➤ Matrices and basic operations on matrices are covered. Work with matrices is extended to solving a system of linear equations on a graphics calucaltor by using the inverse of a matrix.

➤ The theme of the Unit Project is nutrition. Students examine food and dietary needs for Calories from protein, fats, and carbohydrates.

➤ Connections to public transportation, movie salaries, jewelry making, sports stores, and codes are integrated into the teaching materials and exercises.

➤ Graphics calculators are used in Section 3-1 to graph systems of equations, in Section 3-3 to explore the relationships between the slopes of parallel and perpendicular lines, in Section 3-5 to multiply a matrix by a scalar, in Section 3-7 to multiply two matrices, and in Section 3-8 to find the inverse of a matrix and to solve a linear system using the matrix functions of a graphics calculator. Computer software, such as Plotter Plus (Macintosh version), can be used in Sections 3-5, 3-7, and 3-8 to explore operations with matrices.

➤ Problem-solving strategies used in Unit 3 include using graphs, technology, patterns, tables, diagrams, linear systems of equations, and matrices.

Unit Objectives

Section	Objectives	NCTM Standards
3-1	• Solve systems of linear equations by graphing.	1, 2, 4, 5, 8
	• Graph systems of linear inequalities.	
3-2	• Solve systems of equations by substitution.	1, 2, 4, 5
3-3	• Understand and use the relationships between the slopes of parallel and perpendicular lines.	1, 2, 4, 5, 8
3-4	• Solve systems of equations using addition-or-subtraction and choose a method for solving a system of equations.	1, 2, 4, 5
3-5	• Use matrices to represent data sets and use matrix operations.	1, 2, 4, 5, 12
3-6	• Use matrices to represent changes in the size or position of a polygon.	1, 2, 4, 5, 8, 12
3-7	• Recognize when matrices can be multiplied and find the product of two matrices.	1, 2, 4, 5, 12
3-8	• Use technology to find inverse matrices.	1, 2, 4, 5, 12
	• Use inverse matrices to solve systems of equations.	

Skills Bank To extend the curriculum and provide practice with skills, you may wish to assign the following topics from the **Skills Bank** ancillary: determinants and inverses of matrices (for use after Section 3-8) and Cramer's rule (for use after Section 3-8).

Section	Connections to Prior and Future Concepts
3-1	**Section 3-1** covers solving a system of equations by graphing. Students can review graphing a straight line in the Student Resources Toolbox. Graphing systems to find a solution was first introduced in Section 8-5 of Book 1. Work on this topic is continued in Unit 1 of Book 3.
3-2	**Section 3-2** covers solving systems of equations by using the substitution method. This skill was first introduced in Section 5-8 of Book 1. Applications are tied to geometric concepts, which can be reviewed in the Toolbox.
3-3	**Section 3-3** uses the slope-intercept form of a linear equation, first presented in Section 8-1 of Book 1, to determine the nature and number of solutions of a system of linear equations. The concept of slope, first presented in Section 7-1 of Book 1, is extended to parallel and perpendicular lines.
3-4	**Section 3-4** covers the addition-or-subtraction method of solving a system of linear equations. Systems of linear equations were introduced in Unit 8 of Book 1, and are used in Units 3, 4, and 9 of Book 2, and Unit 1 of Book 3.
3-5	**Section 3-5** covers representing data with matrices. All three books use this form of representation extensively. Scalar multiplication is introduced.
3-6	**Section 3-6** covers using matrices to represent geometric transformations. These transformations include dilations and translations, which were first covered in Sections 4-3 and 6-6 of Book 1. This topic is extended in Unit 9 of Book 3.
3-7	**Section 3-7** extends operations on matrices to include matrix multiplication. This skill is used again in Section 3-8 and Unit 5 of Book 2, and in Units 1 and 9 of Book 3, for applications in solving systems of equations and performing geometric transformations.
3-8	**Section 3-8** covers using a graphics calculator to obtain the inverse of a matrix, and using the inverse to solve a system of equations written in matrix form. Unit 1 of Book 3 extends this skill to 3×3 linear systems.

Integrating the Strands

Strands	Sections
Algebra	3-1, 3-2, 3-3, 3-4, 3-5, 3-6, 3-7, 3-8
Geometry	3-1, 3-2, 3-3, 3-4, 3-5, 3-6, 3-7
Statistics and Probability	3-4
Discrete Mathematics	3-1, 3-5, 3-6, 3-7, 3-8
Logic and Language	3-1, 3-2, 3-3, 3-4, 3-5, 3-6, 3-7, 3-8

Section Planning Guide

➤ Essential exercises and problems are indicated in boldface.
➤ Ongoing work on the Unit Project is indicated in color.
➤ Exercises and problems that require student research, group work, manipulatives, or graphing technology are indicated in the column headed "Other."

Section	Materials	Pacing	Standard Assignment	Extended Assignment	Other
3-1	graphics calculator	Day 1 Day 2	**1–8**, 10, **12**, **14** **15–18**, 19, **20–23**, 24–31, 32	**1–8**, 9–11, **12**, 13, **14** **15–18**, 19, **20–23**, 24–31, 32	
3-2		Day 1	**1–15**, 19–28, 29	**1–15**, 16–28, 29	19
3-3	graphics calculator, protractor	Day 1 Day 2	1, 2, **3–12** 16, **17–29**, 30–37, 38	1, 2, **3–12**, 13, 14 16, **17–29**, 30–37, 38	15 38
3-4		Day 1 Day 2	1, **2–9**, **13–15** **19–27**, **29–32**, 34–37, 38	1, **2–9**, 10–12, **13–15**, 16–18 **19–27**, 28, **29–32**, 34–37, 38	33
3-5	graphics calculator	Day 1 Day 2	**1–5**, 6–10 **14–18**, 19, **20**, 21, 24–34, 35	**1–5**, 6–13 **14–18**, 19, **20**, 21–34, 35	
3-6		Day 1	1, **2–16**, 19–25, 26	1, **2–16**, 17–25, 26	
3-7	graphics calculator	Day 1 Day 2	1, **2–5**, 6–9 **10–14**, 16–18, 19–26, 27	1, **2–5**, 6–9 **10–14**, 15, **16–18**, 19–26, 27	
3-8	graphics calculator	Day 1	**1, 2**, 17–25, 26	**1, 2**, 7, 8, 17–25, 26	3–6, 9–17
Review Test		**Day 1** **Day 2**	**Unit Review** **Unit Test**	**Unit Review** **Unit Test**	

Yearly Pacing	Unit 3 Total	Units 1–3 Total	Remaining	Total
	17 days (2 for Unit Project)	49 days	111 days	160 days

Support Materials

➤ See **Project Book** for notes on Unit 3 Project: Create a Daily Menu.
➤ "UPP" and "disk" refer to **Using Plotter Plus** booklet and **Plotter Plus** disk.
➤ "TI-81/82" refers to **Using TI-81 and TI-82 Calculators** booklet.
➤ Warm-up exercises for each section are available on **Warm-Up Transparencies**.
➤ "FI," "GI," and "MA" refer, respectively, to the McDougal Littell Mathpack software Activity Books for **Function Investigator, Geometry Inventor,** and **Matrix Analyzer.**

Section	Study Guide	Practice Bank	Problem Bank	Activity Bank	Explorations Lab Manual	Assessment Book	Visuals	Technology
3-1	3-1	Practice 17	Set 5	Enrich 15	Masters 1, 2	Quiz 3-1		UPP, p. 39
3-2	3-2	Practice 18	Set 5	Enrich 16	Master 2	Quiz 3-2		
3-3	3-3	Practice 19	Set 5	Enrich 17	Master 2	Quiz 3-3	Folder 3	FI Act. 10 and GI Act. 15
3-4	3-4	Practice 20	Set 5	Enrich 18		Quiz 3-4 Test 9		FI Act. 11 UPP, p. 40
3-5	3-5	Practice 21	Set 6	Enrich 19	Add. Expl. 5	Quiz 3-5		UPP (Mac), pp. 41–42 Matrix Calculator (disk)
3-6	3-6	Practice 22	Set 6	Enrich 20	Master 2	Quiz 3-6		TI-81/82, p. 38
3-7	3-7	Practice 23	Set 6	Enrich 21		Quiz 3-7		MA Act. 1 UPP (Mac), pp. 41–42 Matrix Calculator (disk)
3-8	3-8	Practice 24	Set 6	Enrich 22		Quiz 3-8 Test 10		TI-81/82, p. 39 UPP (Mac), pp. 41–42 Matrix Calculator (disk) UPP (IBM), pp. 41–42 Matrix Reducer (disk)
Unit 3	Unit Rev.	Practice 25	Unif. Prob. 3	Fam. Inv. 3		Tests 11, 12		

UNIT TESTS

Software Support

McDougal Littell Mathpack
Function Investigator
Geometry Inventor
Matrix Analyzer

Plotter Plus
Macintosh and MS-DOS
(worksheets included)

Outside Resources

Books/Periodicals

Cooper, Patricia. "Supply & Demand: An Application of Linear Equations." *Mathematics Teacher* (October 1991): pp. 554–559.

Glidden, Peter. "Graphs to Matrices." *Mathematics Teacher* (February 1990): pp. 127–134.

Activities/Manipulatives

Levine, Maita, Robert Plummer, and Raymond Rolwing. "Using TI-81 to Analyze Sports Data." *Mathematics Teacher* (November 1993): pp. 636–641.

Software

North Carolina School of Science and Math. *Matrices: New Topics for Secondary School Mathematics.* NCTM, 1993. IBM.

Videos

College Algebra: In Simplest Terms. Program No. 21: Systems of Linear Inequalities. COMAP Inc., 1991.

Landscape of Geometry. Program No. 8: Range of Change. Ontario Educational Communications Authority, 1983.

Video for Unit Project: *Our Human Body.* Episode 10: Nutrition. Agency for Instructional Technology, 1992.

Form A

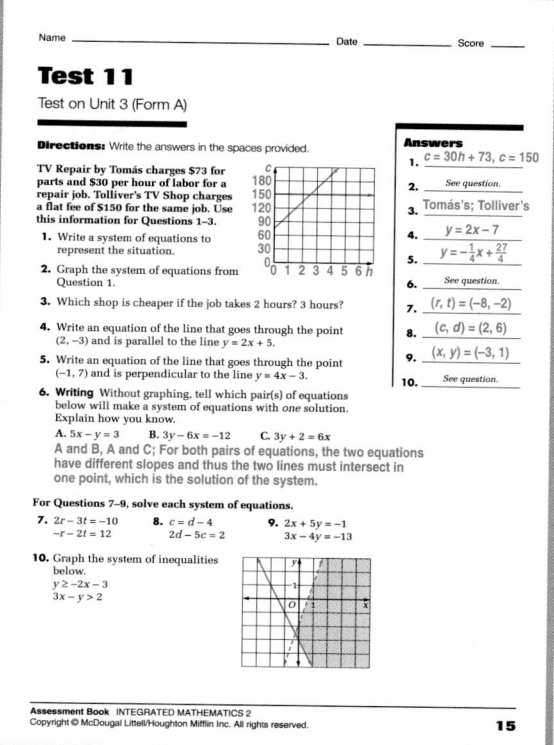

Test 11

Test on Unit 3 (Form A)

Directions: Write the answers in the spaces provided.

TV Repair by Tomás charges $73 for parts and $30 per hour of labor for a repair job. Tolliver's TV Shop charges a flat fee of $150 for the same job. Use this information for Questions 1–3.

1. Write a system of equations to represent the situation.
2. Graph the system of equations from Question 1.
3. Which shop is cheaper if the job takes 2 hours? 3 hours?
4. Write an equation of the line that goes through the point $(2, -3)$ and is parallel to the line $y = 2x + 5$.
5. Write an equation of the line that goes through the point $(-1, 7)$ and is perpendicular to the line $y = 4x - 3$.
6. **Writing** Without graphing, tell which pair(s) of equations below will make a system of equations with *one* solution. Explain how you know.
   A. $5x - y = 3$ B. $3y - 6x = -12$ C. $3y + 2 = 6x$
   A and B, A and C; For both pairs of equations, the two equations have different slopes and thus the two lines must intersect in one point, which is the solution of the system.

For Questions 7–9, solve each system of equations.
7. $2r - 3t = -10$ 8. $c = d - 4$ 9. $2x + 5y = -1$
   $-r - 2t = 12$ $2d - 5c = 2$ $3x - 4y = -13$
10. Graph the system of inequalities below.
    $y \geq -2x - 3$
    $3x - y > 2$

Answers
1. $c = 30h + 73$, $c = 150$
2. *See question.*
3. Tomás's; Tolliver's
4. $y = 2x - 7$
5. $y = -\frac{1}{4}x + \frac{27}{4}$
6. *See question.*
7. $(r, t) = (-8, -2)$
8. $(c, d) = (2, 6)$
9. $(x, y) = (-3, 1)$
10. *See question.*

16

Test 11 *(continued)*

Directions: Write the answers in the spaces provided.

Find the coordinates of each vertex of rhombus *ABCD* after each transformation. Write each answer as a matrix.

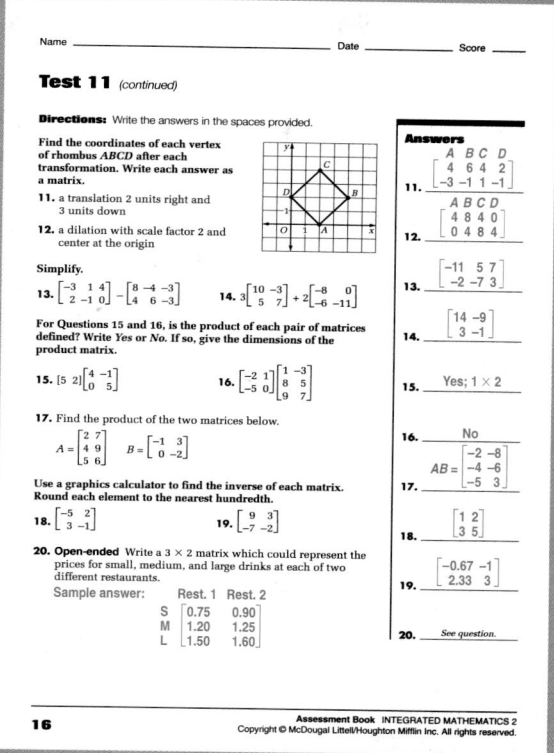

11. a translation 2 units right and 3 units down
12. a dilation with scale factor 2 and center at the origin

Simplify.

13. $\begin{bmatrix} -3 & 1 & 4 \\ 2 & -1 & 0 \end{bmatrix} - \begin{bmatrix} 8 & -4 & -3 \\ 4 & 6 & -3 \end{bmatrix}$ 14. $\begin{bmatrix} 10 & -3 \\ 5 & 7 \end{bmatrix} + 2\begin{bmatrix} -8 & 0 \\ -6 & -11 \end{bmatrix}$

For Questions 15 and 16, is the product of each pair of matrices defined? Write *Yes* or *No*. If so, give the dimensions of the product matrix.

15. $[5 \; 2]\begin{bmatrix} 4 & -1 \\ 0 & 5 \end{bmatrix}$ 16. $\begin{bmatrix} -2 & 1 \\ -5 & 0 \end{bmatrix}\begin{bmatrix} 1 & -3 \\ 8 & 5 \\ 9 & 7 \end{bmatrix}$

17. Find the product of the two matrices below.
    $A = \begin{bmatrix} 2 & 7 \\ 4 & 9 \\ 5 & 6 \end{bmatrix}$ $B = \begin{bmatrix} -1 & 3 \\ 0 & -2 \end{bmatrix}$

Use a graphics calculator to find the inverse of each matrix. Round each element to the nearest hundredth.

18. $\begin{bmatrix} 5 & 2 \\ 3 & -1 \end{bmatrix}$ 19. $\begin{bmatrix} 9 & 3 \\ -7 & -2 \end{bmatrix}$

20. **Open-ended** Write a 3 × 2 matrix which could represent the prices for small, medium, and large drinks at each of two different restaurants.

Sample answer:
	Rest. 1	Rest. 2
S	0.75	0.90
M	1.20	1.25
L	1.50	1.60

Answers
11. $\begin{matrix} A & B & C & D \\ \begin{bmatrix} 4 & 6 & 4 & 2 \\ -3 & -1 & 1 & -1 \end{bmatrix} \end{matrix}$
12. $\begin{matrix} A & B & C & D \\ \begin{bmatrix} 4 & 8 & 4 & 0 \\ 0 & 4 & 8 & 4 \end{bmatrix} \end{matrix}$
13. $\begin{bmatrix} -11 & 5 & 7 \\ -2 & -7 & 3 \end{bmatrix}$
14. $\begin{bmatrix} 14 & -9 \\ 3 & -1 \end{bmatrix}$
15. Yes; 1×2
16. No
17. $AB = \begin{bmatrix} -2 & -8 \\ -4 & -6 \\ -5 & 3 \end{bmatrix}$
18. $\begin{bmatrix} 1 & 2 \\ 3 & 5 \end{bmatrix}$
19. $\begin{bmatrix} -0.67 & -1 \\ 2.33 & 3 \end{bmatrix}$
20. *See question.*

Form B

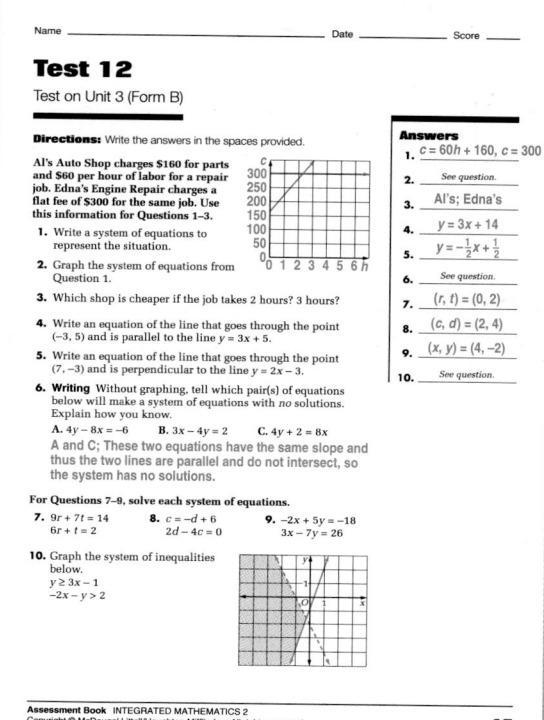

Test 12

Test on Unit 3 (Form B)

Directions: Write the answers in the spaces provided.

Al's Auto Shop charges $160 for parts and $60 per hour of labor for a repair job. Edna's Engine Repair charges a flat fee of $300 for the same job. Use this information for Questions 1–3.

1. Write a system of equations to represent the situation.
2. Graph the system of equations from Question 1.
3. Which shop is cheaper if the job takes 2 hours? 3 hours?
4. Write an equation of the line that goes through the point $(-3, 5)$ and is parallel to the line $y = 3x + 5$.
5. Write an equation of the line that goes through the point $(7, -3)$ and is perpendicular to the line $y = 2x - 3$.
6. **Writing** Without graphing, tell which pair(s) of equations below will make a system of equations with *no* solutions. Explain how you know.
   A. $4y - 8x = -6$ B. $3x - 4y = 2$ C. $4y + 2 = 8x$
   A and C; These two equations have the same slope and thus the two lines are parallel and do not intersect, so the system has no solutions.

For Questions 7–9, solve each system of equations.
7. $9r + 7t = 14$ 8. $c = -d + 6$ 9. $-2x + 5y = -18$
   $6r + t = 2$ $2d - 4c = 0$ $3x - 7y = 26$
10. Graph the system of inequalities below.
    $y \geq 3x - 1$
    $-2x - y > 2$

Answers
1. $c = 60h + 160$, $c = 300$
2. *See question.*
3. Al's; Edna's
4. $y = 3x + 14$
5. $y = -\frac{1}{2}x + \frac{1}{2}$
6. *See question.*
7. $(r, t) = (0, 2)$
8. $(c, d) = (2, 4)$
9. $(x, y) = (4, -2)$
10. *See question.*

18

Test 12 *(continued)*

Directions: Write the answers in the spaces provided.

Find the coordinates of each vertex of △*ABC* after each transformation. Write each answer as a matrix.

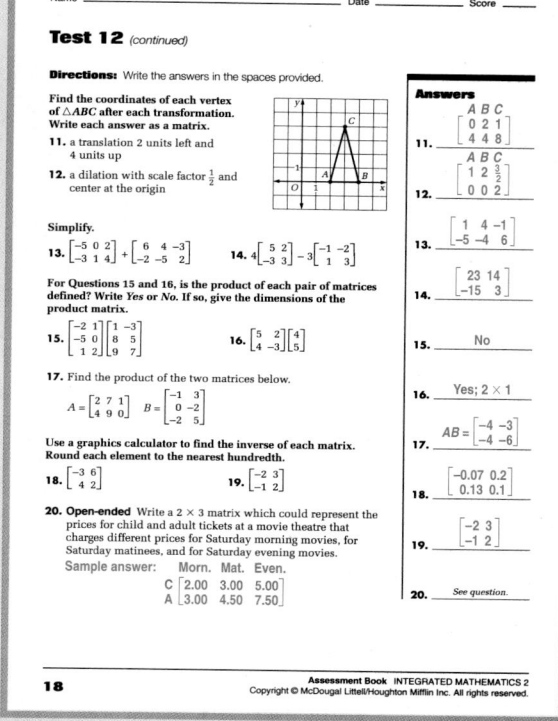

11. a translation 2 units left and 4 units up
12. a dilation with scale factor $\frac{1}{2}$ and center at the origin

Simplify.

13. $\begin{bmatrix} -5 & 0 & 2 \\ -3 & 1 & 4 \end{bmatrix} + \begin{bmatrix} 6 & 4 & -3 \\ -2 & -5 & 2 \end{bmatrix}$ 14. $\begin{bmatrix} 5 & 2 \\ -3 & 3 \end{bmatrix} - 3\begin{bmatrix} -1 & -2 \\ 1 & 3 \end{bmatrix}$

For Questions 15 and 16, is the product of each pair of matrices defined? Write *Yes* or *No*. If so, give the dimensions of the product matrix.

15. $\begin{bmatrix} -2 & 1 \\ -5 & 0 \\ 1 & 2 \end{bmatrix}\begin{bmatrix} 1 & -3 \\ 8 & 5 \\ 9 & 7 \end{bmatrix}$ 16. $\begin{bmatrix} 5 & 2 \\ 4 & -3 \end{bmatrix}\begin{bmatrix} 4 \\ 5 \end{bmatrix}$

17. Find the product of the two matrices below.
    $A = \begin{bmatrix} 2 & 7 & 1 \\ 4 & 9 & 0 \end{bmatrix}$ $B = \begin{bmatrix} -1 & 3 \\ 0 & -2 \\ -2 & 5 \end{bmatrix}$

Use a graphics calculator to find the inverse of each matrix. Round each element to the nearest hundredth.

18. $\begin{bmatrix} -3 & 6 \\ 1 & 2 \end{bmatrix}$ 19. $\begin{bmatrix} -2 & 3 \\ -1 & 2 \end{bmatrix}$

20. **Open-ended** Write a 2 × 3 matrix which could represent the prices for child and adult tickets at a movie theatre that charges different prices for Saturday morning movies, for Saturday matinees, and for Saturday evening movies.

Sample answer:
	Morn.	Mat.	Even.
C	2.00	3.00	5.00
A	3.00	4.50	7.50

Answers
11. $\begin{matrix} A & B & C \\ \begin{bmatrix} 0 & 2 & 1 \\ 4 & 4 & 8 \end{bmatrix} \end{matrix}$
12. $\begin{matrix} A & B & C \\ \begin{bmatrix} 1 & 2 & \frac{1}{2} \\ 0 & 0 & 2 \end{bmatrix} \end{matrix}$
13. $\begin{bmatrix} 1 & 4 & -1 \\ -5 & -4 & 6 \end{bmatrix}$
14. $\begin{bmatrix} 23 & 14 \\ -15 & 3 \end{bmatrix}$
15. No
16. Yes; 2×1
17. $AB = \begin{bmatrix} -4 & -3 \\ -4 & -6 \end{bmatrix}$
18. $\begin{bmatrix} -0.07 & 0.2 \\ 0.13 & 0.1 \end{bmatrix}$
19. $\begin{bmatrix} -2 & 3 \\ -1 & 2 \end{bmatrix}$
20. *See question.*

PROJECT GOALS

➤ Students create a day's menu for three people with different activity levels and different body weights.

➤ Students determine a person's daily Calorie needs as a function of body weight and activity level.

➤ Students analyze and adjust the nutritional value of the three menus.

PROJECT PLANNING

Materials List

➤ Cookbooks

➤ Restaurant menus

➤ Calorie chart

➤ Drawings or pictures from magazines or newspapers

Project Teams

As students plan three different daily menus, they should investigate the four food groups, foods from around the world, and menus of local restaurants. Mathematically, students should look at Calorie consumption as a function of an individual's activity level and body weight.

Have students work on the project in groups of three. One way for the individuals in the group to distribute the work is as follows:

1. Coordinator: collects local restaurant menus and a variety of cookbooks, coordinates the groups ideas about menus for the three people, and checks numerical facts about the body's ability to use Calories and the Calories in each menu.

2. Writer: writes a description of how each menu was developed and revised, of how linear systems were used to analyze the menus, and of the nutritional content.

3. Illustrator: illustrates the menus with pictures from magazines or newspapers.

unit 3

Linear Systems and Matrices

FOOD

Imagine cookouts without ketchup, corn on the cob, or potatoes. Dessert without chocolate or vanilla flavoring. Thanksgiving dinner without turkey, cranberry sauce, sweet potatoes, or pumpkin pie. That would be our fate if the people native to the Americas had not been cultivating wild plants and domesticating wild animals over thousands of years.

special diets

Nutritionists plan high-carbohydrate menus for athletes in training, school lunches for growing children, and special diets for people with health problems. They also show families how to create nutritious meals on a budget.

118

Suggested Rubric for Unit Project

4 Students have correctly determined a person's daily Calorie requirements as a function of body weight and activity level in preparing their three different daily menus. Their description of how each menu was developed is based upon the Food Guide Pyramid, the serving size table, and a Calorie chart. The description also includes an explanation of how linear systems were used to analyze the menus, and an analysis of the nutritional content of each menu. The finished project is well organized, correct in all details, and attractively presented.

3 Students have incorporated all of the major elements of the project in creating their daily menus. One of the menus does not supply a completely healthful balance of nutrients and Calories. The mathematics supporting the menus is satisfactory but is not correct in all details. The descriptions of how each menu was developed and refined are not complete. There are some misconceptions regarding the analysis of the nutritional content of each menu and how each menu fulfills the requirements of the Food Guide Pyramid and other nutritional guidelines.

Create a Daily Menu

Your project is to create a day's menu for three people with different activity levels and different body weights. Each person's meals must supply a healthful balance of nutrients and all the Calories needed for one day but without too many extra Calories. After you have completed the "Working on the Unit Project" exercises for Section 3-1, you will be able to determine a person's daily Calorie requirements as a function of body weight and activity level. Using this information, the Food Guide Pyramid, the serving size table on page 120, and a Calorie chart, your group will plan three menus. Then you will learn how to analyze and adjust the nutritional content of your menus.

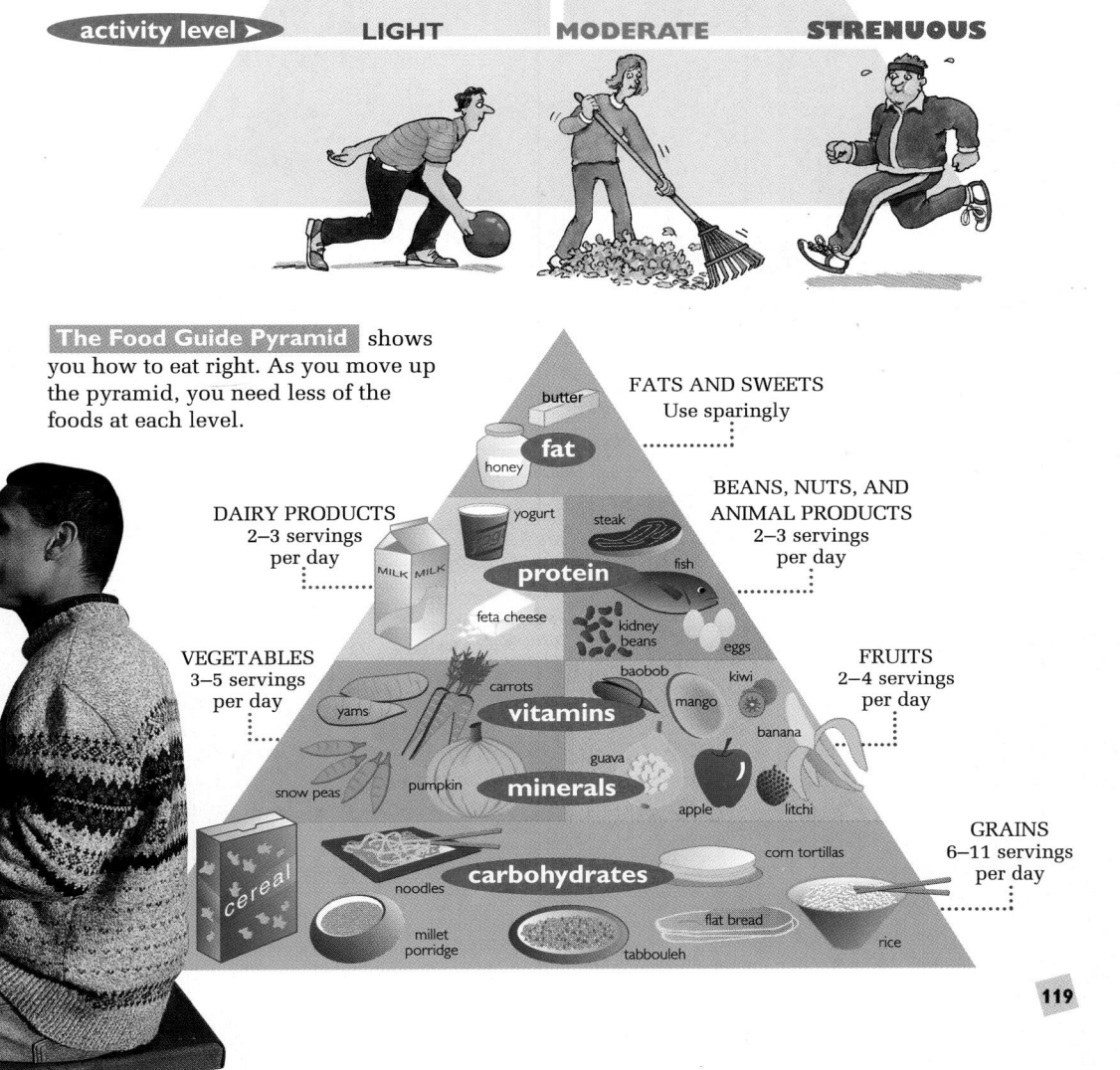

activity level ▶   **LIGHT**   **MODERATE**   **STRENUOUS**

The Food Guide Pyramid shows you how to eat right. As you move up the pyramid, you need less of the foods at each level.

FATS AND SWEETS
Use sparingly

butter
fat
honey

DAIRY PRODUCTS
2–3 servings
per day

yogurt
MILK MILK
feta cheese
protein

BEANS, NUTS, AND
ANIMAL PRODUCTS
2–3 servings
per day

steak
fish
kidney beans
eggs

VEGETABLES
3–5 servings
per day

carrots
yams
vitamins
snow peas
pumpkin
minerals

baobab
mango
kiwi
banana
guava
apple
litchi

FRUITS
2–4 servings
per day

cereal
noodles
carbohydrates
millet porridge
tabbouleh
flat bread
corn tortillas
rice

GRAINS
6–11 servings
per day

119

Support Materials

The *Project Book* contains information about the following topics for use with this Unit Project.

➤ Project Description
➤ Teaching Commentary
➤ Working on the Unit Project Exercises
➤ Completing the Unit Project
➤ Assessing the Unit Project
➤ Alternative Projects
➤ Outside Resources

ADDITIONAL BACKGROUND

Multicultural Note

In the evenings, Japanese workers in Tokyo often eat dinner or have a quick snack in the numerous, informal street stalls. Common foods sold at these stands include *oden*, a shellfish stew with Japanese radish and eggs; *ramen*, boiled Chinese noodles; *yakitori*, grilled chicken on skewers; and *nikumanju*, hot meat-filled buns. When it is cold outside, *yakiimo* venders stay busy serving baked sweet potatoes.

Ethiopian cuisine is noted for its delicious sauces, some delicate, others spicy, that are cooked with lentils or other vegetables, or with chicken, lamb or beef. *Doro wat*, one traditional dish, is made of simmered chicken, spices, herb butter, and garlic. It is often served with soft, spongy bread.

Many popular American dishes reflect West African influences. These include gumbo, black-eyed peas and rice, sweet potato pie with molasses, and banana pudding.

Calories and Fat as a Percent of Calories

Saturated fat is the chief culprit in heart disease and cholesterol is an accomplice. On the average, people would be healthier if they ate no more than 300 milligrams of cholesterol and 35 to 40 grams of total fat each day, of which 20 grams or less were in the form of saturated fat. •••••••••••••••••

ALTERNATIVE PROJECTS

Project 1, page 180

Using Matrices for Secret Codes

Prepare a classroom display on secret codes by doing some library research about the history of secret codes and the use of matrices in constructing them. Use methods introduced in the exercises in preparing the display.

Project 2, page 180

Create a Daily Menu for a Person with Special Nutritional Needs

Research the special nutritional needs of a young child, a senior citizen, or a person on a restricted diet due to a health problem such as heart disease or diabetes.

Getting Started

Serving sizes for each food group
Grains   1 slice of bread   1 ounce of dry cereal $\frac{1}{2}$ cup cooked cereal, rice, or pasta
Vegetables   1 cup raw leafy vegetables $\frac{1}{2}$ cup of others $\frac{3}{4}$ cup juice
Fruits   1 medium apple, etc. $\frac{1}{2}$ cup cooked $\frac{3}{4}$ cup juice
Dairy Products   1 cup milk or yogurt $1\frac{1}{2}$ oz cheese
Beans, Nuts, Meat   2–3 oz cooked lean fish, poultry, or meat $\frac{1}{2}$ cup cooked beans   1 egg   2 tbsp nut butter

For this project you should work in a group of three students. Here are some ideas to help you get started.

☞ Make a list of foods from the five food groups shown that are eaten in your communities and in other countries.

☞ Plan to learn more about foods around the world by looking at cookbooks and restaurant menus.

☞ Discuss how you will illustrate your group's menus.

☞ Make plans to obtain a Calorie chart.

☞ Plan to meet again after completing the "Working on the Unit Project" exercises for Section 3-1 to choose body weights and activity levels for which to plan your menus.

Can We Talk FOOD

 Working on the Unit Project

Your work in Unit 3 will help you create a daily menu.

Related Exercises:
Section 3-1, Exercise 32
Section 3-2, Exercise 29
Section 3-3, Exercise 38
Section 3-4, Exercise 38
Section 3-5, Exercise 35
Section 3-6, Exercise 26
Section 3-7, Exercise 27
Section 3-8, Exercise 26

Alternative Projects p. 180

➤ On a typical day, do you eat many different foods or only a few that you like? Which levels of the food pyramid do they come from?

➤ How can the way food is prepared affect the nutritional content of the food? Are there any foods that you like prepared in a variety of ways? Which ones?

➤ How do the sizes of the servings shown in the table above compare with those you eat?

➤ What activities do you participate in? Would you describe your overall activity level as light, moderate, or strenuous?

➤ In your family or community, what are some favorite foods? Are special foods served on holidays and birthdays? Are recipes passed down from generation to generation?

120   **Unit 3** Linear Systems and Matrices

Answers to Can We Talk?

➤ Answers may vary. An example is given. I eat many different foods on a typical day. Most of the foods I eat come from the carbohydrates and protein levels.

➤ Answers may vary. An example is given. What food is cooked in or how it is prepared can influence the nutritional content of the food. For example, chicken that is baked or broiled does not contain as much fat as fried chicken, and salad that is prepared or garnished with other vegetables such as carrots, spinach, cabbage, celery, and tomatoes provides a better variety of vegetables. Yes. I like ground beef prepared as hamburgers, in tacos, and as meatballs with spaghetti. I also like fruits plain, in gelatin, and as a fruit salad.

➤ Answers may vary. An example is given. I usually eat portions larger than those shown in the table.

➤ Answers may vary. An example is given. I play soccer and run cross country. My activity level is strenuous.

➤ Answers may vary. Examples are given. In my family, pizza, hamburgers, and fish are some favorite foods. Special foods are served on holidays and recipes are passed down from generation to generation.

Systems and Graphs

At the Crossroads

At the Crossroads

Focus
Solve systems of linear equations by graphing and graph systems of linear inequalities.

FitnessPLUS
Initiation Fee $50
Monthly Fee $60

Cost of membership		
	FitnessPLUS	Bodyworks
5 months	?	?
10 months	?	?

Talk it Over

1. Candra Reeves wants to join a health club. Use the rate sheets at the left to fill in this table.

2. Which health club membership will cost less if Candra joins for five months? for ten months?

You can write two equations to compare the costs of belonging to each health club.

Let c = the total cost of membership.   Let n = the number of months of membership.

	total cost	=	initiation fee	+	the monthly fee times n
FitnessPLUS:	c	=	50	+	$60n$
Bodyworks:	c	=	225	+	$35n$

Two or more equations that state relationships between the same variable quantities are called a **system of equations.** Since the two cost equations are linear, they are a **linear system.**

Talk it Over

3. Without graphing, identify the slope and the vertical intercept of the graph of each cost equation. Explain the meaning of each number in terms of the total cost of belonging to each health club.

4. Find the cost of a seven-month membership for each health club. What do you notice?

3-1 Systems and Graphs

121

PLANNING

Objectives and Strands
See pages 118A and 118B.

Spiral Learning
See page 118B.

Materials List
➤ Graph paper
➤ Graphics calculator

Recommended Pacing
Section 3-1 is a two-day lesson.
Day 1
Pages 121–124: Talk it Over 1 through Talk it Over 8, *Exercises 1–14*
Day 2
Pages 124–125: Systems of Inequalities through Look Back, *Exercises 15–32*

Toolbox References
➤ **Toolbox Skill 23:** Using $y = mx + b$
➤ **Toolbox Skill 25:** Graphing an Inequality in Two Variables

Extra Practice
See pages 618–619.

Warm-Up Exercises
Warm-Up Transparency 3-1

Support Materials
➤ Practice 17
➤ Enrichment 15 in the Activity Bank
➤ Study Guide 3-1
➤ Problem Set 5
➤ Diagram Masters 1, 2 in the Explorations Lab Manual
➤ McDougal Littell Mathpack software: *Function Investigator*
➤ Using Plotter Plus: Applications of Linear Inequalities
➤ Quiz 3-1
➤ Alternative Assessment 1

Answers to Talk it Over

1.
Cost of Membership

	FitnessPLUS	Bodyworks
5 months	350	400
10 months	650	575

2. FitnessPLUS costs less for 5 months; Bodyworks costs less for 10 months.

3. FitnessPLUS: slope = 60, y-intercept = 50; Bodyworks: slope = 35, y-intercept = 225. The y-intercepts represent the initiation fee to join, and the slope represents the monthly dues or the rate at which the total cost is increasing.

4. FitnessPLUS: $470; Bodyworks: $470. After seven months, the costs have averaged out. However, you will be paying $25 more each month forever at FitnessPLUS.

TEACHING

Talk it Over

Questions 1 and 2 motivate the development of a linear system of two equations. Questions 3 and 4 have students analyze the system of equations in terms of slope, vertical intercept, and total costs, and then at a particular point. Questions 5 and 6 direct students' thinking to the specific meaning of the solution point (7, 470) and to a more general analysis of the relationship between the two graphs.

Teaching Tip

Solving a system of equations by graphing, either by hand or by using a graphics calculator, is the first of three methods for solving systems discussed in this unit. The other two are the method of elimination by substitution (Section 3-2) and the method of elimination by addition or subtraction (Section 3-4).

Additional Sample

S1 Solve this system of equations by graphing.

$p + q = 9$

$q = \frac{1}{5}p - 3$

Method 1: Graph the equations of the system by hand.

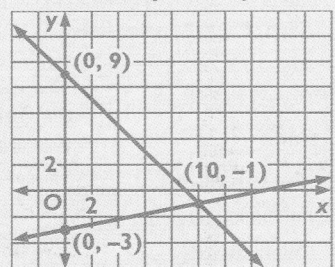

The solution is at about (10, –1).
Method 2: Use a graphics calculator. Using a graphics calculator with appropriate settings for the viewing window will show that the solution is at (10, –1).

A **solution of a system of equations** is an ordered pair whose coordinates make all the equations true. One method of solving a system of equations is *solving by graphing*.

> Graphing both equations on the same axes helps you "see" the solution.

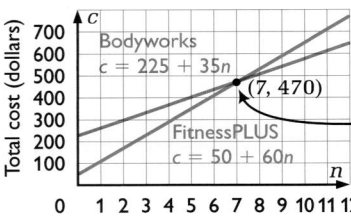

The coordinates of the intersection point make both equations true. The solution (n, c) is $(7, 470)$.

Talk it Over

5. Explain what each coordinate of the intersection point means in terms of the cost of a membership for each health club.

6. Which health club costs less to belong to for one year? How can you use the graph to answer this question?

Student Resources Toolbox
pp. 652–653   *Graphs, Equations, and Inequalities*

Sample 1

Solve this system of equations by graphing: $v + w = 3$

$w = \frac{2}{3}v - 5$

Sample Response

Method ①   Graph the equations of the system by hand.

Note: When either variable may be the control variable, let the letter that occurs earlier in the alphabet be the control variable.

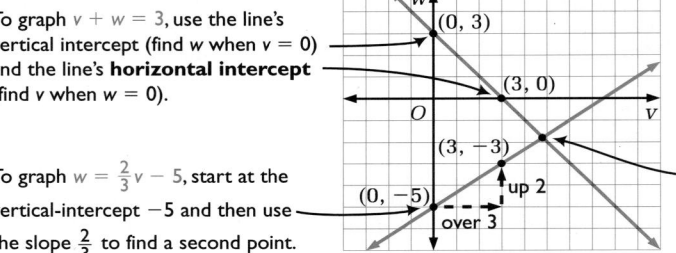

To graph $v + w = 3$, use the line's vertical intercept (find w when $v = 0$) and the line's **horizontal intercept** (find v when $w = 0$).

To graph $w = \frac{2}{3}v - 5$, start at the vertical-intercept -5 and then use the slope $\frac{2}{3}$ to find a second point.

Estimate the coordinates of the intersection point. The lines intersect at about $(4.8, -1.8)$.

The solution (v, w) is about $(4.8, -1.8)$.

122   **Unit 3** Linear Systems and Matrices

Answers to Talk it Over

5. The x-coordinate is the number of months. The y-coordinate is the cost.

6. Bodyworks; For every value of $n > 7$, the graph of the Bodyworks function is under the graph of the FitnessPLUS function, and therefore is less expensive since the y-axis represents the cost.

Method ② Use a graphics calculator.

Enter the equations in slope-intercept form. Use x for the control variable and y for the dependent variable.

Then use ZOOM and TRACE to find the coordinates of the intersection point to the nearest tenth.

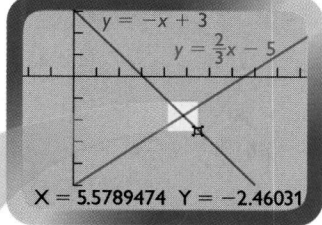

$y = -x + 3$
$y = \frac{2}{3}x - 5$

X = 5.5789474 Y = −2.46031

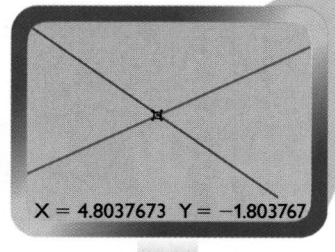

X = 4.8037673 Y = −1.803767

TECHNOLOGY NOTE

For information on using ZOOM, see the Technology Handbook, pp. 607–608.

The solution (v, w) is about $(4.8, -1.8)$. ← Be sure to use the original variable names when you write the solution.

Sample 2

Writing To use a locker at FitnessPLUS you can pay either $45 per year or $5.25 per month. How many months per year do you have to use a locker to make it worth paying the yearly rate? Explain, using this graph.

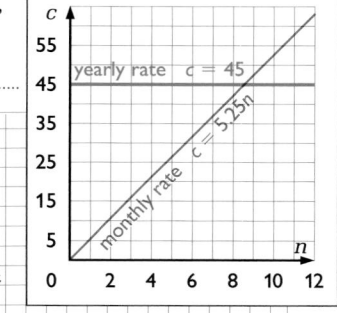

Sample Response

It is worth paying the yearly rate if you use a locker for 9 or more months per year. Here is how the graph shows this.

The graphs intersect between $n = 8$ and $n = 9$.

To the right of the intersection point the monthly-rate graph is above the yearly-rate graph.

This graph shows that after 8 months, the total cost (the c-value on the graph) is greater when you pay the monthly rate.

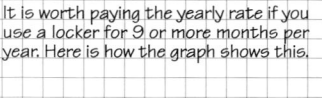

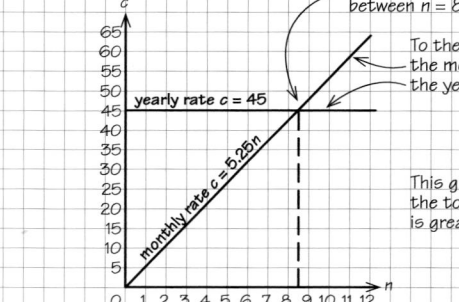

3-1 Systems and Graphs

123

Mathematical Procedures

Solving a system of equations by graphing by hand can only lead, in general, to approximate solutions. If the coordinates of the point of intersection of the two lines are not integers, then students have to estimate the coordinates. This often results in small discrepancies in answers among students.

Visual Thinking

Ask students to explain what happens when they use ZOOM. How does the image change on their screen? What happens when they use TRACE? How is this helpful? This activity involves the visual skills of *recognition* and *interpretation*.

Using Technology

Students can also use the *Function Investigator* software for Method 2 of Sample 1.

The use of a graphics calculator can yield an approximate solution to many decimal places and thus to a greater degree of precision than is required in most practical problems.

Additional Sample

S2 Season tickets for State University's 15 home basketball games has a package price of $120 or $12 per game if purchased individually. How many games does a fan have to attend to make it worth buying the season package? Draw a graph to support your answer. **It is worth buying the season package if a fan attends 11 or more games. The graph shows that after 10 games, the package rate is below the per-game rate.**

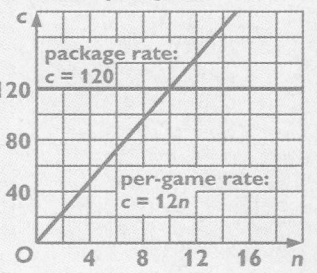

123

Talk it Over

Questions 9–11 introduce students to a system of inequalities. Students discover that such a system can have more than one point as a solution and that the solution points lie in a region of the coordinate plane.

Additional Sample

S3 Graph this system of inequalities.

$$y < 2x + 1$$
$$x + y \geq -3$$

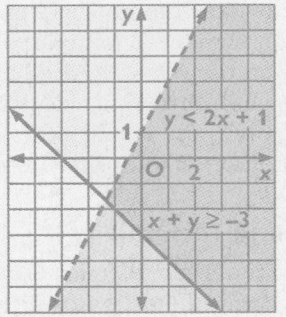

The points inside the region of overlap make both inequalities true.

······► **Now you are ready for:**
Exs. 1–14 on pp. 125–127

Talk it Over

7. Use the graph in Sample 2 to estimate the solution of this system of equations. ► $c = 5.25n$ $c = 45$

8. Do you need to know the exact solution of the system in order to answer the question asked in Sample 2? Explain.

Systems of Inequalities

Sonya is budgeting for her trip to Japan. She plans to spend no more than $50 (about 5000 yen) for lunch and dinner each day.

Talk it Over

9. Let l = dollars spent for lunch. Let d = dollars spent for dinner. ► $l + d \leq 50$ $l \geq 0$ $d \geq 0$

Explain why you can use this **system of inequalities** to describe the possible combinations of Sonya's daily lunch and dinner costs.

10. Which of the labeled points on the graph make the inequality $l + d \leq 50$ true? make $l \geq 0$ true? make $d \geq 0$ true?

11. Which of the labeled points make all three inequalities true? Describe the region of the coordinate plane that contains all points that are possible combinations of Sonya's daily lunch and dinner costs.

The graph of the points that make all the inequalities in a system true is called the **solution region** of the system of inequalities.

Student Resources Toolbox
p. 654 *Graphs, Equations, and Inequalities*

Sample 3

Graph this system of inequalities: $y \geq -x + 4$
   $2x - y > -2$

Unit 3 Linear Systems and Matrices

124

Answers to Talk it Over

7. From the graph, $n \approx 8.5$; $(n, c) \approx (8.5, 45)$.

8. No. Since you cannot rent a locker for a portion of a month, you only need to see between which two months the answers lies.

9. The maximum amount spent will be the cost of lunch and dinner and will be less than or equal to $50

(but no more than $50). The cost of the lunch and dinner is positive or zero for each.

10. (10, 40), (20, 10), (0, 30), (30, 0), (−10, −10), and (−20, 10), for $l + d \leq 50$; (10, 40), (0, 30), (20, 10), (30, 0), and (50, 30), for $l \geq 0$; (30, 0), (−20, 10), (20, 10), (0, 30), (10, 40), and (50, 30), for $d \geq 0$.

11. (10, 40), (0, 30), (30, 0), and (20, 10); The region is the triangle portion of the graph bounded by the equation $l + d = 50$, the l-axis, and the d-axis.

Sample Response

1 Graph the inequality $y \geq -x + 4$.

Graph $y = -x + 4$ as a *solid line*.

Test the point $(0, 0)$.
$$y > -x + 4$$
$$0 \overset{?}{>} -0 + 4$$
$$0 > 4 \text{ (false)}$$

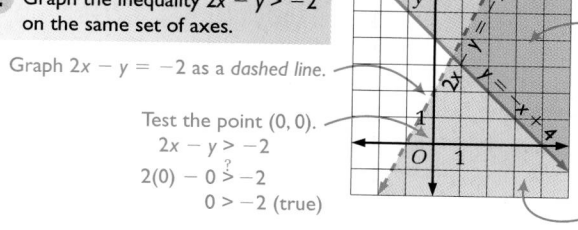

$(0, 0)$ is not a solution. Shade the region on the *opposite side* of the line from $(0, 0)$.

2 Graph the inequality $2x - y > -2$ on the same set of axes.

Graph $2x - y = -2$ as a *dashed line*.

Test the point $(0, 0)$.
$$2x - y > -2$$
$$2(0) - 0 \overset{?}{>} -2$$
$$0 > -2 \text{ (true)}$$

You may want to darken the region of overlap.

$(0, 0)$ is a solution. Shade the region on the *same side* of the line as $(0, 0)$.

3 Find the solution region for the system. The points inside the region of overlap make both inequalities true.

> Now you are ready for:
> Exs. 15–32 on pp. 127–128

Look Back

Describe how you can decide which side of the line to shade when you graph an inequality.

3-1 ## Exercises and Problems

1. **Reading** What is the solution of a system of equations? How is the solution related to the graphs of the equations?

Estimate the solution of each linear system.

2.
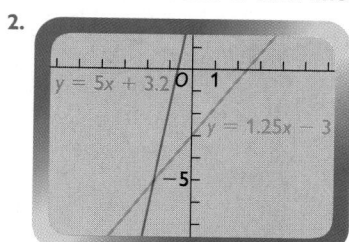
$y = 5x + 3.2$
$y = 1.25x - 3$

3.
$y = 2x + 8.5$
$y = -0.7x + 3$

Answers to Look Back

Test the point $(0, 0)$ to determine if it is a solution. If it is, shade the region on the same side as the point $(0, 0)$. If it is not a solution, shade the region opposite that containing the point $(0, 0)$.

Answers to Exercises and Problems

1. The solution of a system of equations is the ordered pair(s) for which both equations are true. The solution is the point of intersection of the graphs of the equations.

2. $(-1.6, -5)$

3. $(-2, 4.5)$

Reasoning

The use of the point $(0, 0)$ as a test point in the Sample 3 Response is a quick and simple way to determine which side of the line should be shaded. Students should understand that a solution point, when substituted into the original inequality, always makes the inequality a *true* statement. If the result of the substitution is a false statement, then the point is *not* a solution and the solutions must be on the other side of the line.

APPLYING

Suggested Assignment

Day 1

Standard 1–8, 10, 12, 14

Extended 1–14

Day 2

Standard 15–32

Extended 15–32

Integrating the Strands

Algebra Exs. 1–32

Geometry Exs. 1–24, 32

Discrete Mathematics Exs. 4, 9–11, 13, 32

Logic and Language Exs. 1, 9, 11, 24

Communication: Reading

Ex. 1 has students focus on the meaning and interpretation of the solution for a system of equations. Students need to recall that all the points on the graph of a linear equation are solutions of the equation. In other words, the graph of a linear equation is the graph of its solution set, which is a straight line. Thus, if two lines intersect, the point of intersection is a solution of both equations.

FotoRite
Frequent Buyers' Club
save over 10¢ per print
Club Membership Cost: $15.00
Member cost per print: $.25
Non-member cost per print: $.40

4. Use the information on the Frequent Buyers' Club card.

a. Write an equation for the total cost for a club member to have n prints made. Write an equation for the total cost for a non-member to have n prints made.

b. Graph the system of equations in part (a).

c. Use your graph to find the solution of the system of equations. Explain the meaning of the solution in this situation.

Solve each system of equations by graphing.

5. $y = x$
$y = 1.8x + 3$

6. $a - b = 1$
$b = -4a$

7. $2x + 5y = 5$
$y = \frac{2}{5}x + 5$

8. $n = 0.5p + 1$
$n = 0.2p + 2$

Public Transportation **For Exercises 9 and 10, use this information about public transportation fares in Boston.**

Bus and subway riders can either pay single-ride fares or buy monthly passes at the prices shown. A *combo pass* lets you ride both the bus and the subway.

$46

$20
(Single ride: $.60)

direction of motion

direction of motion

$27
(Single ride: $.85)

9. **Writing** Suppose you ride the bus every day and you sometimes ride the subway. How many times per month must you ride the subway to make it worth buying a combo pass? Explain, using this graph to support your answer.

combo pass $c = 46$

bus pass/subway rides $c = 20 + 0.85r$

Cost (dollars)

Number of rides

10. Yukiko is trying to decide whether to buy a combo pass or to buy a subway pass and then pay the single-ride fare when she rides the bus.

a. Write a system of equations that models Yukiko's choices.

b. Graph the system of equations that you wrote in part (a).

c. Suppose Yukiko usually rides the bus 20 times per month. Should she buy a combo pass? How does your graph support your answer?

126 **Unit 3** Linear Systems and Matrices

Answers to Exercises and Problems

4. a. $c = 15 + 0.25n$; $c = 0.4n$

b.

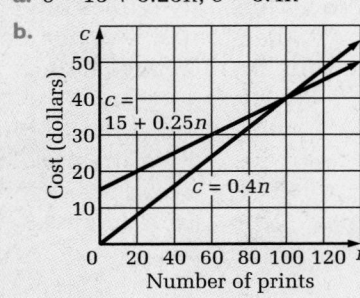

Cost (dollars)

$c = 15 + 0.25n$

$c = 0.4n$

Number of prints

c. (100, 40); When you make 100 copies, the total cost will be $40 whether you are a member or a non-member.

5–10. See answers in back of book.

11. a. Descriptions may vary. An example is given. A name brand soda on sale costs $1.49 for a two-liter bottle and $.99 for each 16-ounce bottle. The store brand soda costs $1.99 for a two-liter bottle and $.89 for each 16-ounce bottle. If you buy one two-liter bottle of soda, and several 16-ounce bottles, at what price can you get the same number of 16-ounce bottles of the name brand soda as the store brand soda?

b. The y-intercept in each equation is the price of one two-liter bottle. The slope is the cost per 16-ounce bottle of soda.

12. a. $\left(\frac{1}{2}, 3\right)$

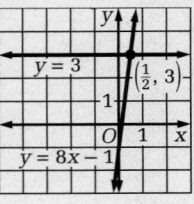

$y = 3$

$\left(\frac{1}{2}, 3\right)$

$y = 8x - 1$

11. a. **Open-ended** Describe a real-world situation that can be modeled by this linear system.

$$y = 0.99x + 1.49$$
$$y = 0.89x + 1.99$$

b. Without graphing, tell how the slope and vertical intercept of the graph of each equation in part (a) are related to the situation you described.

12. a. Solve this system of equations by graphing.

$$y = 3$$
$$y = 8x - 1$$

b. Solve the equation $3 = 8x - 1$ for x.

c. Describe what the system in part (a) has in common with the equation in part (b). Explain how to use the system to solve the equation.

d. Write a system of equations that you can use to solve $4x = x - 12$.

13. Candra Reeves is considering another health club.

a. Write a cost equation for Neighborhood Health Club.

b. Compare the equation you wrote for part (a) with the equations on page 121. Which of the equations has the graph with the greatest slope? the greatest vertical intercept?

c. Graph all three equations on the same axes.

d. Suppose Candra Reeves plans to join a health club for three months. Which plan is the cheapest? Suppose she plans to join for seven months. Which plan is the cheapest? Explain how the graph supports your answers.

14. a. Solve this system of equations by graphing.

$$y = x^2 + 4$$
$$y = 4$$

b. Is the system in part (a) a linear system? Explain why or why not.

Graph each system of inequalities.

15. $y \leq 3x - 3$
$y > -\frac{1}{2}x + 2$

16. $y < 3x$
$3y - 2x \geq 9$

17. $x < 2$
$y < x + 5$
$x + 2y > -2$

18. $y - 3x \geq 5$
$2y + 5x < 7$

19. a. Write an equation for each side of this trapezoid.

b. Write a system of inequalities that describes the shaded region.

c. Choose a point inside the shaded region and show that its coordinates make all your inequalities in part (b) true.

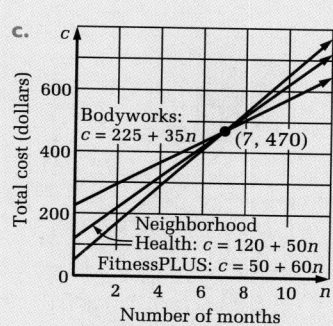

Graph each system of inequalities. Write the specific name of the shape of each solution region.

20. $2x + y \leq 4$
$y \geq -3$
$x \geq -1$

21. $y \geq -1$
$y \leq x + 1$
$3x + 2y \leq 16$
$y \leq 2$

22. $3 < x < 5$
$0 < y < 2$

23. $-4 \leq x \leq 2$
$-3 \leq y \leq 1$

3-1 Systems and Graphs

Communication: Writing

Ex. 11 gives students an opportunity to relate a system of equations to a real-world situation. Most responses will probably focus on purchases as students relate the given numbers to dollar amounts.

Multicultural Note

Subway systems are full of fascinating stories—from archaeologists unearthing ancient relics during construction to besieged citizens finding shelter within them during war. In Mexico City, tens of thousands of artifacts from the past six centuries were unearthed during construction of the subway system, including delicate leather jewelry and a 22-ton Aztec calendar stone. Many of these treasures are now displayed throughout the concourses: each subway stop highlights some aspect of Mexican history or daily life. During World War II, more than 200,000 people slept each night in bomb shelters established within the London Underground. British Prime Minister Winston Churchill and Allied Commander Dwight Eisenhower each had a war office in a subway station.

Communication: Discussion

A discussion of Ex. 12 will prepare students for the topic of the next section, solving systems by substitution.

Assessment: Standard

For Ex. 13, students should be able to discuss how the value of the slope and the value of the y-intercept affect the total cost.

Cooperative Learning

You may wish to have students work in groups of three or four to do Exs. 15–23. In doing so, students can compare graphs and share ideas about graphing systems of inequalities.

Answers to Exercises and Problems

b. $x = \frac{1}{2}$

c. When $y = 3$ is substituted into $y = 8x - 1$, you get $3 = 8x - 1$, and solving for x will yield the solution of the system. The point $\left(\frac{1}{2}, 3\right)$ is the point of intersection of the two equations.

d. $y = 4x$
$y = x - 12$

13. a. $c = 120 + 50n$

b. greatest slope: FitnessPLUS, where $c = 50 + 60n$; greatest intercept: Bodyworks, where $c = 225 + 35n$

c.

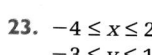
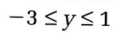

Bodyworks: $c = 225 + 35n$ (7, 470)

Neighborhood Health: $c = 120 + 50n$
FitnessPLUS: $c = 50 + 60n$

Total cost (dollars) vs. Number of months n

13d–23. See answers in back of book.

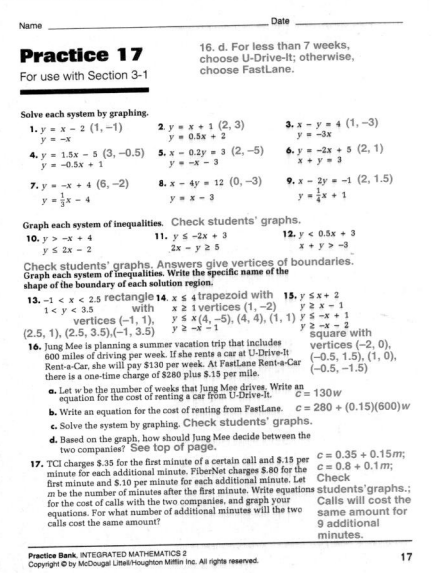
Answers to Exercises and Problems

24. Graph $y = -x + 8$ and $x - 2y = -22$ on the same set of axes. Find the point of intersection to solve the system.

25. $y = 100\left(\frac{1}{2}\right)^n$, where n = the number of 1600-year half-lives.

26. $(8x)^{1/2}$ 27. $-5t^{1/3}$

28. $(7m)^{1/3}$ 29. $m = 7.5$

30. $a = -12$ 31. $n = \frac{15}{7}$

32. **a.** $4c$ = Calories from c grams of carbohydrates; $9f$ = Calories from f grams of fat; Since you take 10% of your daily Calories from protein, the balance of 90%, or 0.9, comes from carbohydrates and fats. Then $4c + 9f = 0.9 \times$ daily Calories.

Answers for 32b–f may vary. Examples are given based upon a person weighing 120 lb.

b. light activity: $14 \times 120 = 1680$ Calories; strenuous: $16 \times 120 = 1920$ Calories

c. $4c + 9f = 1512$; $4c + 9f = 1728$

---

24. **Writing** Describe how to solve this system of equations by graphing: $y = -x + 8$ $x - 2y = -22$

Review **PREVIEW**

25. Radium-226 decays exponentially with a half-life of 1600 years. Use an equation to model the exponential decay of 100 g of radium-226. *(Section 2-7)*

Rewrite each expression using a fractional exponent. *(Section 2-6)*

26. $\sqrt{8x}$ 27. $-5\sqrt[3]{t}$ 28. $\sqrt[3]{7m}$

Solve. *(Toolbox Skill 13)*

29. $15 = \frac{8}{5}m + 3$ 30. $7(a + 10) = -14$ 31. $4(6 - 3n) = -6 + 2n$

Working on the Unit Project

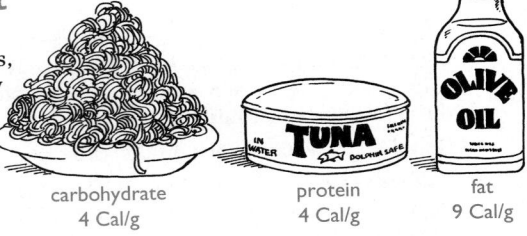

carbohydrate 4 Cal/g   protein 4 Cal/g   fat 9 Cal/g

32. **a.** Calories in food come from carbohydrates, protein, and fat. About 10% of your daily Calories should come from protein.

Let c = grams of carbohydrate.
Let f = grams of fat.

Explain why you can use the equation

$$4c + 9f = 0.9 \times \text{daily Calories}$$

to model the possible combinations of amounts of fats and carbohydrates that you should eat in one day.

b. Your daily Calorie needs depend on your weight and your activity level.

Daily Calorie needs = Activity rating × weight (lb)

Estimate your daily Calorie needs on two activity levels: light and strenuous.

c. Use the two numbers you found in part (b) to write two equations like the one shown in part (a).

d. Graph the two equations you wrote in part (c) on the same axes.

Activity Rating	Activity Level	
14	light	walking casually, bowling, doing auto repair
15	moderate	walking briskly, climbing stairs, doing yard work
16	strenuous	moving heavy objects, dancing, jogging

e. Suppose you want your daily intake of fats and carbohydrates to be no more than you need for strenuous activity and no less than you need for light activity. Shade the region of your graph that shows the combinations of amounts of fats and carbohydrates you can consider.

f. Dietitians recommend that your daily fat intake be less than 30% of your total daily Calories. Pick several points in the shaded region of your graph. Which of them show combinations of fats and carbohydrates that meet this goal?

g. Write down at least two ideas about a healthy diet from this exercise that you may want to remember when you create menus for your project.

---

d–e.

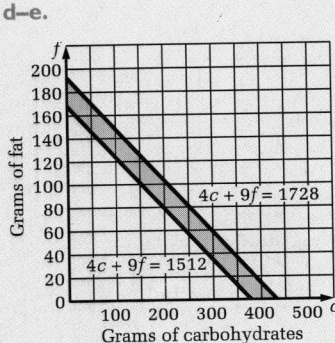

Grams of fat vs. Grams of carbohydrates; lines labeled $4c + 9f = 1728$ and $4c + 9f = 1512$

f. Only points in approximately the lower third of the shaded region will meet a goal of fat intake less than 30% of the total daily Calories. Actual points will vary according to the person's weight estimate.

g. Ideas may vary. Examples are given. Pick the majority of your diet from carbohydrates and proteins. Approximately 10% of your daily Calorie intake should come from protein.

Solving Systems by Substitution

Focus
Solve systems of equations by substitution.

"My point, exactly"

REACH THE BREAK-EVEN POINT IN YOUR LIGHT...

One electronic bulb lasts as long as twenty 100-watt incandescent bulbs.

*based on average use of 4 hours per day

COMPARE

Cost per bulb..........................$24 ....$.75
Cost of electricity per day....$.01............$.04*

Bakeerah brought this ad to school to discuss with her math class. The class wondered if using an electronic bulb really would save money as the ad claims. They wrote and graphed these two equations, where x is the number of days of use and y is the total cost.

Electronic bulb: $y = 24 + 0.01x$
Twenty 100-watt bulbs: $y = 15 + 0.04x$

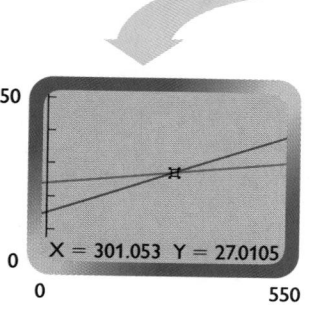

X = 301.053 Y = 27.0105

Talk it Over

1. Use the information in the ad to explain how the two cost equations represent the situation.

2. Use the graph of the system of equations. About how many days do you have to use one electronic bulb before it becomes cheaper than using twenty 100-watt bulbs? Explain.

3. Are the TRACE values shown on the calculator screen an exact solution of the system of cost equations? Explain.

3-2 Solving Systems by Substitution

129

PLANNING

Objectives and Strands
See pages 118A and 118B.

Spiral Learning
See page 118B.

Materials List
➤ Graph paper

Recommended Pacing
Section 3-2 is a one-day lesson.

Toolbox References
➤ **Toolbox Skill 26:** Finding Unknown Angle Measures
➤ **Toolbox Skill 28:** Using Formulas from Geometry

Extra Practice
See pages 618–619.

Warm-Up Exercises
Warm-Up Transparency 3-2

Support Materials
➤ Practice 18
➤ Enrichment 16 in the Activity Bank
➤ Study Guide 3-2
➤ Problem Set 5
➤ Diagram Master 2 in the Explorations Lab Manual
➤ Quiz 3-2

Answers to Talk it Over

1. The cost to use one electronic bulb is the initial cost ($24) plus $.01/day for electricity. The total cost is $c = 24 + 0.01x$, where x = number of days used. The cost to use the equivalent in 100-watt bulbs is the cost of twenty bulbs at $.75 each ($15) plus $.04/day for electricity.

The total cost is $c = 15 + 0.04x$, where x = number of days used.

2. about 301 days; At that point, the graphs of the two equations intersect and from there on the electronic bulb costs less in total cost.

3. No. It is a very close estimate, but although these two coordinates are on the graph of $y = 24 + 0.01x$, they are not *exactly* on the graph of $y = 15 + 0.04x$. The exact intersection point cannot be read all the time.

Talk it Over

Questions 1–3 analyze a system of cost equations using graphing methods. Students see in question 3 that the solution is not exact. This prepares them to understand that one of the principal advantages of algebraic methods is that they yield exact solutions. After completing questions 4 and 5, students obtain the exact solution to the system.

Additional Sample

S1 Solve this system of equations by substitution.

$x + 2y = 1$
$5x - 4y = -23$

Step 1. Solve the first equation for x.

$x + 2y = 1$
$\quad x = 1 - 2y$

Step 2. Substitute $1 - 2y$ for x in the second equation.

$5(1 - 2y) - 4y = -23$

Step 3. Solve the new equation for y.

$5 - 10y - 4y = -23$
$\quad -14y = -28$
$\quad\quad y = 2$

Step 4. Find the value for x when $y = 2$.

$x = 1 - 2y$
$\quad = 1 - 4$
$\quad = -3$

The solution (x, y) is $(-3, 2)$.

....

Problem Solving

Students can try different substitutions in Sample 1 to see that there is more than one way to solve the system. For example, both equations can be solved for x to yield $x = 2y - 11$ and $x = 4 - y$. Then $4 - y$ can be substituted for x in the other equation to yield $4 - y = 2y - 11$. Now this equation can be solved for y and this value can be used to solve for x.

You can use algebra to find the exact solution of the system of cost equations. At the intersection point of the graphs of the equations, *the y-values are the same.*

Replace y in one equation with the expression for y from the other equation.

$$\left. \begin{array}{l} y = 24 + 0.01x \\ y = 15 + 0.04x \end{array} \right\}$$

Use the *two* equations in x and y to write *one* equation that you can solve for x.

$$24 + 0.01x = 15 + 0.04x$$

This method of solving a system of equations is called *solving by substitution.*

Talk it Over

4. Solve the third equation shown above for x. Compare the answer to your answer for question 2 on page 129.

5. Substitute the value of x you found in question 4 into each cost equation. What value do you get for y?

Solve this system of equations by substitution: $x - 2y = -11$
$x + y = 4$

Sample Response

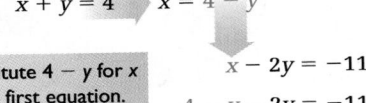

1 Solve the second equation for x.

$x + y = 4 \quad\Rightarrow\quad x = 4 - y$

2 Substitute $4 - y$ for x in the first equation.

$x - 2y = -11$
$4 - y - 2y = -11$

3 Solve the new equation for y.

$4 - 3y = -11$
$-3y = -15$

This is the y-value of the solution. ⟶ $y = 5$

4 To find the x-value, substitute 5 for y in either of the original equations.

$x + y = 4$
$x + 5 = 4$
$x = -1$

The solution (x, y) is $(-1, 5)$.

Talk it Over

6. Check that the solution found in Sample 1 makes both equations true.

7. Graph the equations $x - 2y = -11$ and $x + y = 4$ on one set of axes. Explain how to use your graph to check that the solution found in Sample 1 is reasonable.

130   **Unit 3** Linear Systems and Matrices

Answers to Talk it Over

4. $x = 300$ days, as compared to 301 days solving by graphing and using TRACE

5. $y = 27$

6. $x - 2y = -11$ gives
$-1 - 2(5) = -1 - 10 = -11$ ✓;
$x + y = 4$ gives $-1 + 5 = 4$ ✓.

7. Graphing both equations on one set of axes, you find the graphs intersect at $(-1, 5)$, so $(-1, 5)$ is the

solution of the system.

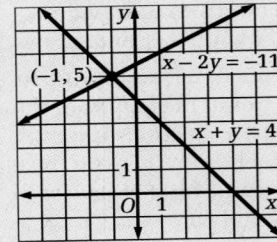

GLORY
12:30 3:00 5:30 8:00 10:30
ADULTS $7 CHILDREN $4

Movie theaters keep track of how many tickets they sell. For a 5:30 showing, this movie theater sold 272 tickets and took in $1694. How many of each type of ticket were sold?

Sample Response

Problem Solving Strategy: Use a system of equations.

You know two totals — the number of tickets sold and the amount of money taken in. Each total comes from sales of both adults' and children's tickets.

1 Write an expression for each total in terms of two variables. A table may help you organize the information.

	Number of tickets sold	Dollar amount taken in
Adult	a	$7a$
Child	c	$4c$
Total	$a + c$	$7a + 4c$

2 Use what you know about the totals to write a system of equations.

$a + c = 272$
$7a + 4c = 1694$

3 Solve the system by substitution.

$a + c = 272$ ▶ $c = 272 - a$ ◀── Solve one equation for c in terms of a.

$7a + 4c = 1694$ ◀── Substitute $272 - a$ for c in the other equation and solve for a.

$7a + 4(272 - a) = 1694$

$7a + 1088 - 4a = 1694$

$3a + 1088 = 1694$

$3a = 606$

$a = 202$

$a + c = 272$ ◀── To find c, substitute 202 for a in either of the original equations.

$202 + c = 272$

$c = 70$

The solution (a, c) of the system is (202, 70).
There were 202 adults' tickets and 70 children's tickets sold.

Look Back ◀

For each linear system, tell how you would begin solving by substitution. Which equation would you solve for what variable?

a. $3x - y = 5$
$4x + y = 9$

b. $3a - 5b = 10$
$a + 7b = 12$

c. $r + 2t = 5$
$2r + t = -2$

3-2 Solving Systems by Substitution

131

Answers to Look Back

Answers may vary. Examples are given. For system (a), solve $3x - y = 5$ for y to obtain $y = 3x - 5$ and substitute for y in the equation $4x + y = 9$. For system (b), solve the second equation for a to obtain $a = 12 - 7b$ and substitute in $3a - 5b = 10$. For system (c), solve the first equation for r to obtain $r = 5 - 2t$ and substitute in $2r + t = -2$.

Additional Sample

S2 A total of 1096 people attended the concert at the County Fair. Reserved seats cost $25 each and unreserved seats cost $20 each. If $26,170 was collected, how many of each type of ticket was sold?

Step 1. Write an expression for each total in terms of two variables. Let r = reserved seats. Let u = unreserved seats. Number of tickets sold:
$r + u = 1096$
Dollar amount collected:
$25r + 20u = 26,170$
Step 2. Write a system of equations.
$r + u = 1096$
$25r + 20u = 26,170$
Step 3. Solve the system by substitution.
$r = 1096 - u$
$25(1096 - u) + 20u = 26,170$
$27,400 - 25u + 20u = 26,170$
$-5u = -1230$
$u = 246$
To find r, substitute 246 for u in the equation
$r = 1096 - u$.
$r = 1096 - 246$
$r = 850$
The solution (r, u) of the system is (850, 246). There were 850 reserved seats and 246 unreserved seats sold.

Error Analysis

Sample 2 illustrates that solving a real-world problem first involves translating the conditions of the problems into equations (or inequalities). This is often a difficult step for many students and, consequently, they may write incorrect equations. The use of a table to organize the information given in a problem, as in Sample 2, is an excellent technique to help students with the translation process.

Look Back

This question helps students to synthesize their thinking on how to start solving a system by substitution. They see that the easiest variable to solve for in either equation is the variable whose coefficient is one.

Reasoning

Some students might wish to explore the thinking that supports the process of solving a system by substitution. In Ex. 2, for example, the equation $y = 4x$ has an infinite number of solutions. For any arbitrarily selected value of x, there is a corresponding value of y and the ordered pairs $(x, 4x)$ are the solutions. However, as soon as $4x$ is substituted for y in the equation $y = -x - 15$ to yield the equation $4x = -x - 15$, then the condition is imposed that whatever value of y satisfies the first equation must also satisfy the second equation. In other words, the value of y becomes a fixed value by the substitution—it must be the same value. This means that x can no longer be an arbitrary value but must be a single value, and it must be a solution of the equation $4x = -x - 15$. The solution of this equation is $x = -3$, which means that $y = -12$. Therefore, the unique solution of the system is $(-3, -12)$.

Students Acquiring English

Many students acquiring English are not likely to be familiar with *mutual funds.* Explain that a mutual fund is a type of investment. People buy shares in a mutual fund with the expectation that they will receive dividends (income on the investment) in addition to being able to sell their shares in the future for more than they paid for them.

3-2 Exercises and Problems

1. a. Estimate the solution of this system of equations by graphing:
$$y = x - 4$$
$$y = \tfrac{1}{3}x - 9$$

    b. Solve the system in part (a) using substitution.

Solve each system of equations by substitution.

2. $y = 4x$
   $y = -x - 15$

3. $b = a + 5$
   $b = 3a - 1$

4. $y = \tfrac{1}{2}x$
   $y = \tfrac{5}{2}x + 8$

5. $x - y = 1$
   $x + y = -1$

6. $c + 2d = 12$
   $c + d = 2$

7. $f - 3g = 9$
   $5f + g = -3$

8. Choose one of the systems of equations you solved in Exercises 2–7. Check your solution by solving the system by graphing.

9. Melissa and Bjorn started solving Exercise 5 two different ways.

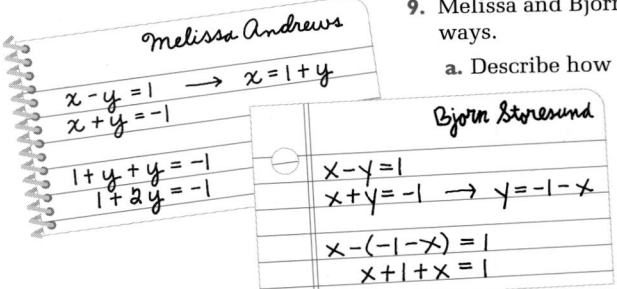

    a. Describe how their methods are different.

    b. Will they get the same results? Explain why or why not.

    c. **Writing** Which method do you think is easier for solving this system of equations? Do you think that the same method is best for all systems of equations? Explain why or why not.

10. a. Solve this system of equations by substitution:
$$F = 1.8C + 32$$
$$F = C$$

    b. You can use the first equation in part (a) to convert a temperature in degrees Celsius (C) to a temperature in degrees Fahrenheit (F). Explain what the solution of the system of equations represents.

Use a system of equations to answer each question.

11. Use the information shown on the refrigerator price tags. After how many years of use is the cost of the Cold-air the same as the cost of the Cool-spot?

12. Investment Theo and Mona Northrop have saved $5500. They want the amount they invest in a mutual fund to be three times the amount they leave in their savings account. How much money should the Northrops put in the mutual fund?

13. Tickets to the school play cost $2.50 for general admission or $2.00 for students. On opening night, 319 tickets were sold. The total receipts were $694. How many of each kind of ticket were sold?

Answers to Exercises and Problems

1. See answers in back of book.

2. $(-3, -12)$ **3.** $(3, 8)$

4. $(-4, -2)$ **5.** $(0, -1)$

6. $(-8, 10)$ **7.** $(0, -3)$

8. Choices of equation may vary. Graphs will confirm the solution of the exercise chosen.

9. a. Melissa solved for x in the first equation and substituted that value into the second equation to solve for y. Bjorn solved the second equation for y and substituted that value into the first equation to solve for x.

    b. Yes. After solving for the first variable and then substituting into the original equation to solve for the second variable, both will get the same result. They just did it in different orders.

    c. Answers may vary. An example is given. Melissa's method is easier for this system of equations. At different times, different methods are easier. It depends upon the equations as to which way is easiest.

Use a system of equations to find x and y in each situation.

14.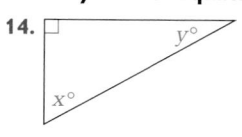

x is twice as big as y.

15.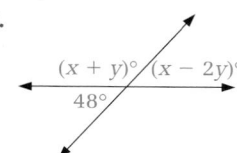

$(x + y)° / (x - 2y)°$
$48°$

Student Resources Toolbox
p. 655 *Formulas and Relationships*

16. **Reading** Here is another way to solve the problem in Sample 2.

   a. Explain how the entry for number of children's tickets sold is related to the solution on page 131.

   b. Explain how the equation
   $$7a + 4(272 - a) = 1694$$
   is related to the solution on page 131.

	Number of tickets sold	Dollar amount taken in
Adult	a	$7a$
Child	$272 - a$	$4(272 - a)$

\$ from adults + \$ from children = 1694

$$7a + 4(272 - a) = 1694$$

17. **Movie Salaries** In 1916, Mary Pickford's contract stated that her earnings that year would be half the profits of all her movies that year, plus \$340,000 in bonuses. Charlie Chaplin's contracted salary that year was \$670,000.

   a. Write an equation for Mary Pickford's earnings. Let s represent her earnings and p represent the profits of all her movies.

   b. Write an equation for Charlie Chaplin's salary. Let s represent his salary.

   c. What would the profits of Mary Pickford's movies have to be in order for her earnings to equal Charlie Chaplin's salary?

BY THE WAY...

Mary Pickford was a good businesswoman as well as a popular actress. "It took longer to make one of Mary's contracts than it did to make one of Mary's pictures," said her studio boss.

WHO'S PAID MOST?

Two of the highest paid actors in Hollywood are Sylvester Stallone and Jack Nicholson. For his work on *Rocky V*, Stallone was said to have received about \$27 million plus 35% of the film's gross earnings. This puts Sly in the same income bracket as Nicholson, who is believed to have made a cool \$60 million for his role as the Joker in *Batman*.

18. a. **Movie Salaries** Use the information in this article to write a system of equations that represents the earnings of Sylvester Stallone from *Rocky V* and the earnings of Jack Nicholson from *Batman*.

   b. Suppose both actors' earnings were the same. Use your system of equations from part (a) to find the gross earnings of *Rocky V*.

3-2 Solving Systems by Substitution

133

Answers to Exercises and Problems

10. a. $(-40, -40)$

   b. The solution represents the point at which the temperature in degrees Fahrenheit equals the temperature in degrees Celsius.

11. $7\frac{1}{2}$ years

12. \$4125

13. 112 general admission tickets; 207 student tickets

14. $(60, 30)$

15. $(104, 28)$

16. a. The number of tickets sold was $202 + 70 = 272$, so the number of children's tickets sold is the total number of tickets sold minus the adult tickets sold, or $272 - a$.

   b. This step represents the substitution of one equation into the other.

17. a. $s = \frac{1}{2}p + 340,000$

   b. $s = 670,000$

   c. \$660,000

18. a. Stallone: $e = 27,000,000 + 0.35g$; Nicholson: $e = 60,000,000$

   b. \$94,285,714.29

133

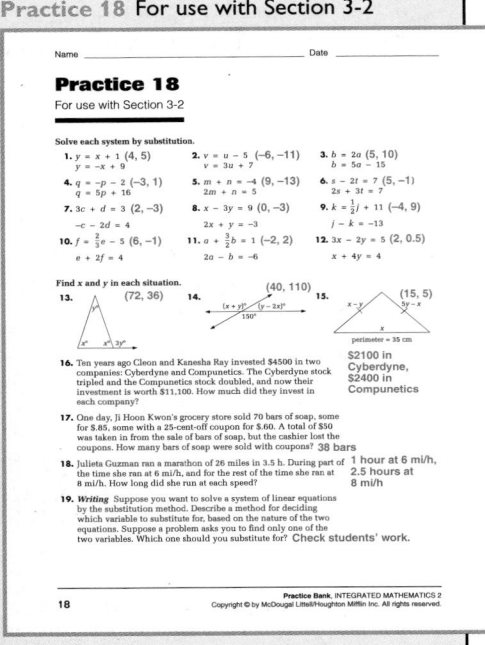
19. **Group Activity** Work with another student.

   a. Each of you should write a system of inequalities whose solution region is a right triangle. Then trade papers.

   b. Graph the system of inequalities that you were given. Find the coordinates of the vertices of the triangle.

   c. Find the area of the right triangle.

   d. Trade papers again and check each other's work.

Review **PREVIEW**

20. Graph this system of inequalities: $3x + 5y > -10$ *(Section 3-1)*
$$y \le 3$$

Expand each product. *(Toolbox Skill 11)*

21. $x(-3x + 4)$ 22. $(x - 9)(x + 6)$ 23. $-5x(x - 10)$ 24. $(2x - 7)(3x + 8)$

Without graphing, find the slope of each line. *(Toolbox Skill 15, Section 2-2)*

25. $y = \frac{1}{4}x + 6$ 26. $y = \frac{2}{3}$ 27. $-3x + y = 11.5$ 28. $x = -9$

 Working on the Unit Project

29. This graph is based on the information in Exercise 32 on page 128. These are the equations of the three lines.

   strenuous: $f = 0.53w$
   moderate: $f = 0.50w$
   light: $f = 0.47w$

   a. Explain what the graph shows.

   b. Suppose you solved this system of equations by substitution:
   $$f = 0.47w$$
   $$w = 120$$
   Tell what the solution means in this situation.

   c. Write a system of equations whose solution gives a recommended maximum daily fat intake for a moderately active 150 lb adult.

   d. Solve the system of equations you wrote in part (c). Explain the meaning of each coordinate of the solution.

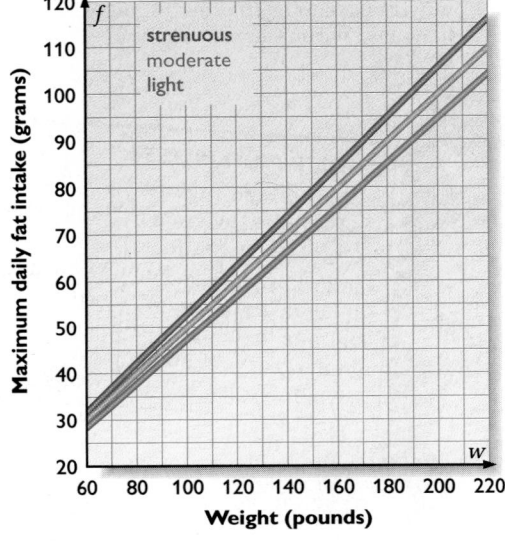

Unit 3 Linear Systems and Matrices

Answers to
Exercises and Problems

19. Systems may vary. An example is given.

   a. $x + y \le 4$, $x \ge 0$, $y \ge 0$

   b. vertices: $(0, 0)$, $(4, 0)$, $(0, 4)$

   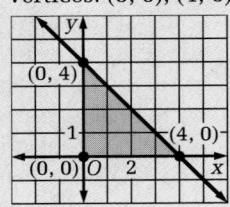

   c. area $= \frac{1}{2} \cdot 4 \cdot 4 = 8$

   d. Check students' work.

20.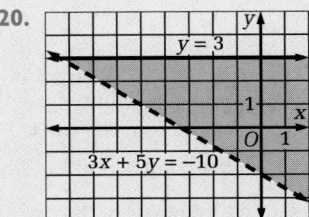

21. $-3x^2 + 4x$

22. $x^2 - 3x - 54$

23. $-5x^2 + 50x$

24. $6x^2 - 5x - 56$

25. $\frac{1}{4}$

26. 0

27. 3

28. undefined

29. a. The graph shows the maximum amount of fat one should eat daily (in grams) for a given weight of a person (in pounds) for three different levels of exercise activity (light, moderate, and strenuous).

   b. The solution $(120, 56.4)$ means that a person who exercises lightly and weighs 120 pounds should eat a maximum of 56.4 grams of fat daily.

   c. $f = 0.50w$
   $w = 150$

   d. $(150, 75)$; A person who weighs 150 pounds and who exercises moderately should take in a maximum of 75 grams of fat daily.

Focus
Understand and use the relationships between the slopes of parallel and perpendicular lines.

Slopes and Systems

Hit the Slopes

EXPLORATION

Can you predict whether two lines will intersect?

- Materials: graphics calculator or graph paper
- Work with another student.

① Use these equations.

$$y = 3x \qquad y = 3x + 3 \qquad y = 3x - 4$$

a. How are the equations alike? How are they different?

b. Graph the equations on the same set of axes.

c. Describe the graphs. How are they alike? How are they different?

② **a.** Write an equation of another line with the same slope as the line $y = 3x$.

b. Predict whether the line will intersect the graphs in step 1.

c. Test your prediction by graphing your equation on the same set of axes that you used in step 1.

③ **a.** Write an equation of a line that you think will intersect all the graphs in step 1.

b. Graph your equation on the same set of axes that you used in step 1. Check whether the graph intersects the other lines.

④ For each linear system, predict whether the lines will intersect if you graph the equations on the same set of axes.

a. $y = -2x + 1$ **b.** $y = -2x + 7$ **c.** $y = x - 5$
     $y = -4x - 4$ $x - y = 8$ $2x - 2y = 16$

⑤ Test your predictions in step 4 by graphing each system of equations. Discuss any unexpected results.

3-3 Slopes and Systems   **135**

Answers to Exploration

1. a. All equations have $y = 3x$ in common and a slope of 3. All equations have different constants or y-intercepts, namely 0, 3, and -4.

b. See graph at right.

c. All lines are parallel to each other and have the same slope but different y-intercepts.

b.
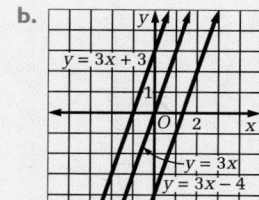

2. a. Equations may vary. An example is given. $y = 3x - 1$. Anything of the form $y = 3x + b$, where b is any number other than 0, 3, or -4 will work.

b. No.

c.
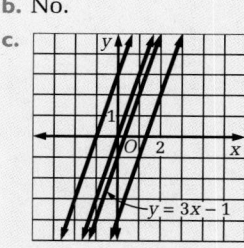

3–5. See answers in back of book.

TEACHING

Exploration

The goal of the Exploration is to have students discover that lines with equal slopes and different vertical intercepts are parallel. They also check to see that lines with different slopes do, in fact, intersect.

Teaching Tip

Under Types of Linear Systems, students should verify that the equations $b = a + 2$ and $-2a + 2b = 4$ for the *One line, Many solutions* graph are the same equation.

Additional Sample

S1 Use this system of equations.

$9x - 3y = 10$
$4y = 12x + 7$

a. Without graphing, describe the relationship between the graphs of the equations.

Write both equations in slope-intercept form.

$9x - 3y = 10$
$\quad -3y = -9x + 10$
$\quad\quad y = 3x - \dfrac{10}{3}$

$4y = 12x + 7$
$\quad y = 3x + \dfrac{7}{4}$

The equations have the same slope but different y-intercepts. The graphs of the equations are parallel lines.

b. Tell whether the system of equations has *no solution*, *one solution*, or *many solutions*. Identify the system as *consistent* or *inconsistent*.

The system has no solution and is inconsistent.

The graphs of two equations in a linear system can be related in one of three ways. You can use the relationship between the two graphs to tell how many solutions the system has.

TYPES OF LINEAR SYSTEMS

Two intersecting lines One solution	One line Many solutions	Parallel lines No solutions
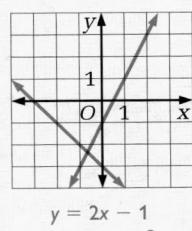	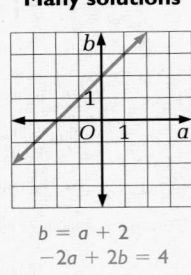	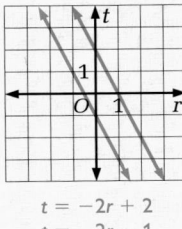
$y = 2x - 1$ $y = -x - 3$	$b = a + 2$ $-2a + 2b = 4$	$t = -2r + 2$ $t = -2r - 1$

A linear system that has one or more solutions is called a **consistent system**.

A linear system that has no solutions is called an **inconsistent system**.

Sample 1

Use this system of equations: $4x - y = 2$
$ 3y = 12x - 6$

a. Without graphing, describe the relationship between the graphs of the equations.

b. Tell whether the system of equations has *no solution*, *one solution*, or *many solutions*. Identify the system as *consistent* or *inconsistent*.

Sample Response

a. Write both equations in slope-intercept form.

$4x - y = 2$
$\quad -y = -4x + 2$
$\quad\quad y = 4x - 2$

$3y = 12x - 6$
$\quad \dfrac{3y}{3} = \dfrac{12x}{3} - \dfrac{6}{3}$
$\quad\quad y = 4x - 2$

same slope
same y-intercept

The graphs of the equations are one line.

b. The system of equations has many solutions, because the graphs are one line. The system is consistent.

→ **Now you are ready for:**
Exs. 1–15 on pp. 139–140

136   **Unit 3** Linear Systems and Matrices

How are the slopes of perpendicular lines related?

- **Materials:** graph paper, protractor
- **Work in a group of three students.**

(1) Each of you should copy one of these segments on graph paper. Put one endpoint at the edge of your paper.

Segment A   **Segment B**   **Segment C**

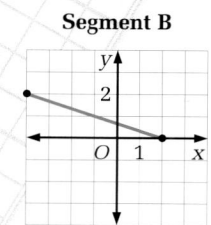

(2) Find the slope of your segment.

(3) Fold the graph paper so that the endpoints of your segment meet.

(4) Unfold the paper. Trace the fold line. Find its slope.

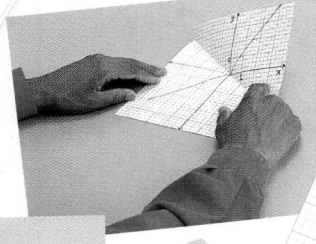
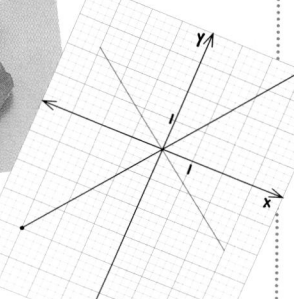

(5) Record your group's results from steps 2 and 4 in a table like this. Discuss any patterns that you see.

	Slope of segment	Slope of fold line
Segment A	?	?
Segment B	?	?
Segment C	?	?

(6) Look again at your graph paper. What do you think is the measure of the angle formed by each segment and its fold line? Use a protractor to check your guess.

(7) Use your group's results from steps 5 and 6 to make a conjecture about how the slopes of any two perpendicular lines are related.

3-3 Slopes and Systems

137

Reasoning

In the response to Sample 1, students see that the system of equations is really just the same equation, $y = 4x - 2$, written in two different ways. They should also understand that if the y-intercept of $y = 4x - 2$ is changed, for example, from 2 to 3, then the changed equation, $y = 4x - 3$, represents a line parallel to $y = 4x - 2$. If the slope of $y = 4x - 2$ is changed, for example, from 4 to 5, then the changed equation, $y = 5x - 2$, represents a line that intersects $y = 4x - 2$.

Exploration

Working in groups of three, students use graphs of line segments and paper-folding activities to collect data on the slopes of perpendicular segments. In step 7, they use their group's results to make a conjecture about how the slopes of perpendicular lines are related.

Using Technology

Activity 15 in the *Geometry Inventor Activity Book* is an exploration of the slopes of perpendicular and of parallel lines.

Answers to Exploration

1. Check students' work.

2. $\frac{4}{3}$; $-\frac{1}{3}$; -2

3. Check students' work.

4. $-\frac{3}{4}$; 3; $\frac{1}{2}$

5. See table at right.

6. 90°

7. The slopes of two perpendicular lines are negative reciprocals of each other.

5.

	Slope of segment	Slope of fold line
Segment A	$\frac{4}{3}$	$-\frac{3}{4}$
Segment B	$-\frac{1}{3}$	3
Segment C	-2	$\frac{1}{2}$

Talk it Over

Question 1 has students apply their conjectures from the Exploration on page 137 to other lines. Question 2 leads students to think about the relationship between the slopes of horizontal and vertical lines.

Communication: Writing

You may wish to anticipate Ex. 16 on page 140 by asking students to multiply the slopes of two perpendicular lines. They should write: $m\left(-\frac{1}{m}\right) = -1$.

This equation shows that the product of the slopes of two perpendicular lines is always -1.

Additional Sample

S2 Write an equation of the line p that goes through the point $(-3, 4)$ and is perpendicular to the line $y = -5x + 1$.

The slope of $y = -5x + 1$ is -5, so the slope of the perpendicular line p is $\frac{1}{5}$.

$y = mx + b$

$4 = \frac{1}{5}(-3) + b$

$4 = -\frac{3}{5} + b$

$\frac{23}{5} = b$

An equation of the perpendicular line p is $y = \frac{1}{5}x + \frac{23}{5}$.

Reasoning

Sample 2 is equivalent to the problem of writing an equation of a line given one point on the line and its slope. The same type of problem is presented again in Talk it Over question 4. The slope is known because the lines are parallel.

Look Back

After discussing this Look Back, ask students what they should do to the equations in any system if they want to know if the system is consistent or inconsistent. (Write the equations in slope-intercept form.)

Talk it Over

1. Use your conjecture from the Exploration. What do you think is the slope of a line perpendicular to the line $y = 5x - 4$? to the line $y = -\frac{3}{4}x + 7$?

2. What is the slope of a horizontal line? What is the slope of a vertical line? Does your conjecture from the Exploration apply to horizontal and vertical lines? Explain.

PARALLEL LINES AND PERPENDICULAR LINES

When the slope of a line is m, the slope of a parallel line is m.

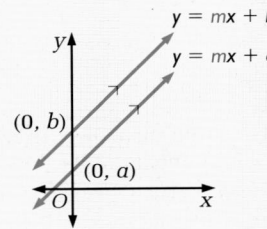

When the slope of a line is m, $(m \neq 0)$, the slope of a perpendicular line is $-\frac{1}{m}$.

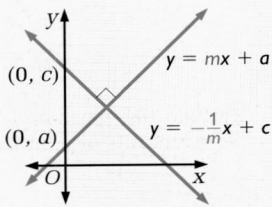

Sample 2

Write an equation of the line p that goes through the point $(-6, -1)$ and is perpendicular to the line $y = -2x - 3$.

Sample Response

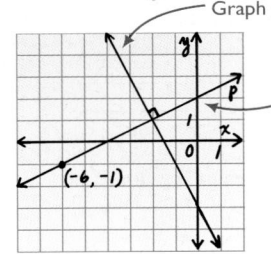

Drawing a picture may help you understand the problem.

Graph $y = -2x - 3$.

Sketch a line p through $(-6, -1)$ that is perpendicular to the line $y = -2x - 3$.

To write an equation of line p, you need to know the slope. The slope of $y = -2x - 3$ is -2, so the slope of the perpendicular line p is $-\left(\frac{1}{-2}\right)$ or $\frac{1}{2}$.

$y = mx + b$ ← Use slope-intercept form.

$-1 = \frac{1}{2}(-6) + b$ ← p goes through $(-6, -1)$ and has slope $\frac{1}{2}$.

$-1 = -3 + b$

$2 = b$

An equation of the perpendicular line p is $y = \frac{1}{2}x + 2$.

138 **Unit 3** Linear Systems and Matrices

Answers to Talk it Over

1. $-\frac{1}{5}; \frac{4}{3}$

2. 0; undefined; No, because the slope of a vertical line is undefined.

3. The slope in the sample graph appears to be $\frac{1}{2}$ $\left(\frac{\text{rise}}{\text{run}} = \frac{2}{4}\right)$ and the y-intercept 2, so $\frac{1}{2}$ and 2 are reasonable values for m and b.

4. The slope will be the same, -2; substitute -6 for x, -1 for y, and -2 for m in the equation $y = mx + b$, so $-1 = (-2)(-6) + b$ and $b = -13$. The equation is $y = -2x - 13$.

5. $x = 4$

Answers to Look Back

Equations are consistent if their slopes are different or if one equation is a multiple of the other. They are inconsistent if they have the same slope and different y-intercepts.

3. Explain how you can use the graph in Sample 2 to check that $\frac{1}{2}$ and 2 are reasonable values for m and b in the equation for the perpendicular line p.

4. Describe how to find an equation of the line that goes through the point $(-6, -1)$ and is *parallel* to the line $y = -2x - 3$.

5. Find an equation of the line that goes through the point $(4, 3)$ and is perpendicular to the line $y = 3$.

Look Back ◄

Suppose the equations of a linear system are in slope-intercept form. Describe how to tell if the system of equations is consistent or inconsistent.

⋯► Now you are ready for:
Exs. 16–38 on pp. 140–141

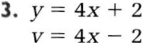

3-3 Exercises and Problems

1. Which linear system in step 4 of the Exploration on page 135 has equations whose graphs are parallel lines? Write equations of two more lines that are parallel to the lines in this system.

2. **Reading** Describe three ways in which the graphs of two linear equations can be related.

For each system of equations:

a. Without graphing, describe the relationship of the graphs of the equations.

b. Tell whether the system of equations has *no solution*, *one solution*, or *many solutions*. Identify the system as *consistent* or *inconsistent*.

3. $y = 4x + 2$
   $y = 4x - 2$

4. $p = 4n - 2$
   $5p = 20n - 10$

5. $3v + 2w = -6$
   $5v - 2w = -10$

6. $3y = 2x - 1$
   $12y = 8x - 4$

7. a. Find the slope of $\overline{AB}$, of $\overline{BC}$, of $\overline{CD}$, and of $\overline{AD}$.

   b. What type of polygon is $ABCD$? Explain how you know.

8. a. Graph these equations on the same set of axes.

   $y = x + 2$ $y = x - 3$ $y = 1$ $y = -3$

   b. What type of polygon do the lines form? Explain how you know.

   c. Find the area of the polygon.

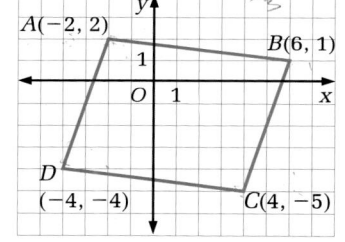

Without graphing, tell whether each line is parallel to, intersects, or is the same line as the line $2x - 5y = 10$.

9. $5y = 2x + 10$

10. $4x = 10y + 20$

11. $6x = 10 + 10y$

12. $x - 2.5y = 5$

Answers to Exercises and Problems

1. c; Equations may vary. Examples are given.
   $y = x + 2$ and $x - y = 3$

2. The graphs may be intersecting lines, in which case the system of equations has one solution. They may be the same line, in which case the system has many solutions. They may be parallel lines, in which case the system has no solution.

3. a. parallel lines
   b. no solutions, inconsistent

4. a. same line
   b. many solutions, consistent

5. a. intersecting lines
   b. one solution, consistent

6. a. same line
   b. many solutions, consistent

7, 8. See answers in back of book.

9. parallel

10. same line

11. intersects

12. same line

139

13. **Movie Salaries** At one time, Arnold Schwarzenegger's fee for a film was reported to be between $10 million and $13 million, plus 15% of the profits.

    a. Suppose his fee was $10 million, plus 15% of the profits. Use two variables to write an equation for this fee.

    b. Suppose his fee was $13 million, plus 15% of the profits. Use the same two variables to write an equation for this fee.

    c. Graph the equations from parts (a) and (b) on the same set of axes.

    d. Describe your graph. Is your system of equations *consistent* or *inconsistent*?

14. **Economics** To find a country's trade balance with Japan, you subtract the value of the products that the country *buys from* Japan from the value of the products that the country *sells to* Japan.

    a. Describe the slope of the graph for Russia from 1997 to 1998. Do the same for France. Explain what the slopes mean in terms of Japan's trade balance with each of the two countries.

    b. Repeat part (a) for Malaysia and Russia from 1995 to 1996.

15. **Research** In a newspaper, magazine, or another textbook, find a graph that contains two lines. Describe the information that the graph shows. Tell if the graph represents a system that is *consistent* or *inconsistent*.

16. a. Use the table that you made in step 5 of the Exploration on page 137. For each segment, find this product:

    slope of segment × slope of fold line

    b. Use your results in part (a) to make a conjecture about the product of the slopes of two perpendicular lines.

17. Find the slope of a line that is perpendicular to the line $-3x + y = \frac{1}{2}$.

18. Find the slope of a line that is parallel to the line $4x + 5y = -10$.

Write an equation of the line that fits each description.

19. a line through the point $(-3, 2)$ and parallel to the line $y = -4x + 1$

20. a line through the point $(4, 7)$ and parallel to the line $y = 2$

21. a line through the point $(-3, 2)$ and perpendicular to the *y*-axis

22. a line through the point $(-2, 6)$ and perpendicular to the line $y = -2x + 2$

23. a line through the point $(-4, 0)$ and parallel to the line $y = 3x - 9$

24. a line through the point $(0, 5)$ and perpendicular to the *x*-axis

25. **Writing** You know how to find an equation of these lines:

    ➤ a line through a given point and *perpendicular* to a given line
    ➤ a line through a given point and *parallel* to a given line

    How are the procedures alike? How are they different?

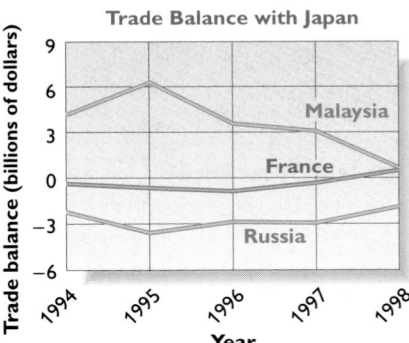

Trade Balance with Japan

Trade balance (billions of dollars) vs *Year* (1994, 1995, 1996, 1997, 1998), showing Malaysia, France, and Russia.

 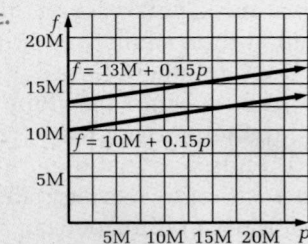

For Exercises 26 and 27, tell what type of polygon ABCD is. Explain how you know.

26. $A(-8, 3)$, $B(2, 5)$, $C(3, 0)$, $D(-2, -1)$

27. $A(-4.8, 3.6)$, $B(-0.8, 5.6)$, $C(2.8, -1.6)$, $D(-1.2, -3.6)$

28. Write an equation of the line that goes through $(-3, 2)$ and is parallel to the line that goes through $(6, -3)$ and $(3, 1)$.

29. Two lines rise from left to right and cross the x-axis at an angle of 45°. One line goes through the point $(-1, 0)$ and the other line goes through the point $(2, 1)$.

　　a. Find the slope of each line. (*Hint:* See Exercise 32 on page 73.)

　　b. Write an equation for each line.

　　c. Tell whether the system of equations you wrote in part (b) has *no solution, one solution,* or *many solutions.*

Ongoing **ASSESSMENT**

30. **Open-ended** Write equations of two parallel lines. Graph and label them l_1 and l_2. Write and graph an equation of a line that is perpendicular to l_1. Label it l_3. Tell whether l_3 is parallel or perpendicular to l_2.

Review **PREVIEW**

Solve each system of equations. *(Section 3-2)*

31. $a + b = 10$
$3a + 2b = 40$

32. $5x - y = 15$
$x - 4y = 22$

33. $2k + 3n = 10$
$10k - 3n = -4$

34. Tell whether you think the inequality $x < 2x$ is true for all values of x. If not, give a counterexample. *(Section 1-5)*

Solve. *(Toolbox Skill 13)*

35. $6(3y - 4) = 3$

36. $9 = -3(5 - 2x)$

37. $-8(-3 - 5n) = 0$

 Working on the Unit Project

38. **Research** Does your family have recipes that are passed down from generation to generation? Choose an old family recipe or the recipe for a favorite food. Find the fat, protein, carbohydrate, and Calorie content of each ingredient. You can find tables that give this information about foods in these sources:

➤ *The New Laurel's Kitchen* by Laurel Robertson, Carol Flinders, and Brian Ruppenthal (vegetarian only)

➤ *Nutrition Almanac* by Lavon J. Dunne

➤ *Nutritive Value of Foods,* Home and Garden Bulletin Number 72, United States Department of Agriculture

Gallina en Pepitoria
Puerto Rico (Chicken in Almond Sauce)
3½-pound chicken
½ cup (2 oz) blanched almonds
2-inch piece stick cinnamon
¼ cup olive oil
½ cup tomato,
2 cups chicke
2 eggs
2 tsp lime or lemon juice
4 whole cloves
1 clove garlic, chopped
1 medium onion, chopped
¼ tsp white pepper

3-3 Slopes and Systems

141

Using Technology

The *Function Investigator* software can be used to graph the equations for Ex. 13 on page 140.

Assessment: Open-ended

For Ex. 29, students should be able to explain why the two lines are parallel before they find the slope of each line.

Working on the Unit Project

You may wish to check with your school librarian to see if the publications listed in Ex. 38 are available for student use.

Practice 19 For use with Section 3-3

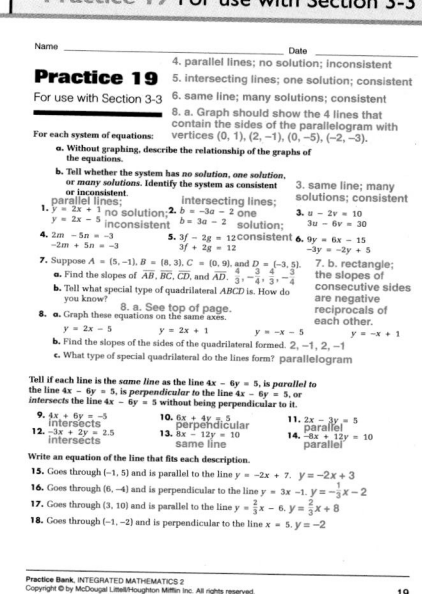

Answers to Exercises and Problems

a parallel line, you use the slope of the given line. If you are finding an equation of a perpendicular line, you use the negative reciprocal of the slope of the given line.

26. a trapezoid since only two sides are parallel

27. a rectangle since there are two pairs of parallel sides and two pairs of perpendicular sides

28. $y = -\frac{4}{3}x - 2$

29. a. $m = 1$

　　b. $y = x + 1$; $y = x - 1$

　　c. no solution

30. Answers may vary. An example is given. Let the equations be: l_1: $y = 3x$; l_2: $y = 3x - 2$; l_3: $y = -\frac{1}{3}x + 1$; l_3 is perpendicular to line l_2.

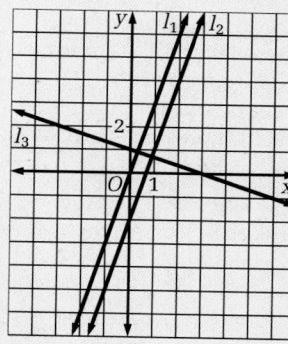

31. $(20, -10)$

32. $(2, -5)$

33. $\left(\frac{1}{2}, 3\right)$

34. No; if $x = -1$, then -1 is not less than -2.

35. $y = \frac{3}{2}$

36. $x = 4$

37. $n = -\frac{3}{5}$

38. Research may vary.

141

Objectives and Strands
See pages 118A and 118B.

Spiral Learning
See page 118B.

Recommended Pacing
Section 3-4 is a two-day lesson.

Day 1
Pages 142–145: Talk it Over 1 through Talk it Over 10, *Exercises 1–18*

Day 2
Pages 145–147: Sample 3 through Look Back, *Exercises 19–38*

Extra Practice
See pages 618–619.

Warm-Up Exercises
Warm-Up Transparency 3-4

Support Materials
➤ Practice 20
➤ Enrichment 18 in the Activity Bank
➤ Study Guide 3-4
➤ Problem Set 5
➤ McDougal Littell Mathpack software: *Function Investigator*
➤ Function Investigator with Matrix Analyzer Activity Book: Function Investigator Activity 11
➤ Using Plotter Plus: Looking at the Addition-or-Subtraction Method
➤ Quiz 3-4
➤ Test 9
➤ Alternative Assessment 3

Section 3-4

Solving Systems by Addition-or-Subtraction

Focus
Solve systems of equations using addition-or-subtraction and choose a method for solving a system of equations.

Disappearing Act

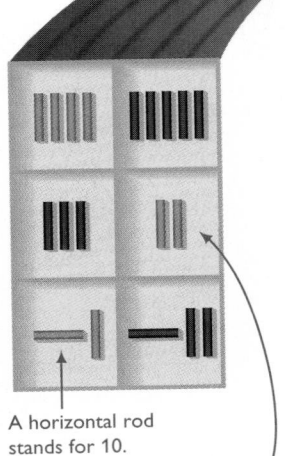

A horizontal rod stands for 10.

Two vertical rods stand for 2.

Talk it Over

People in ancient China used red and black counting rods arranged in a checkerboard pattern to solve linear systems. The diagram shows this linear system:

$$4x - 3y = 11$$
$$-5x + 2y = -12$$

1. What number does each group of counting rods represent?

2. How are the colors red and black used?

3. Compare the diagram to the modern way of writing the linear system. How are they alike? How are they different?

4. Explain why it is not easy to solve the linear system by substitution. (This system of equations is solved in Sample 3.)

The Chinese book *Nine Chapters on the Mathematical Art* (completed before the first century A.D.) contains the first known use of the *addition-or-subtraction method* for solving a linear system. This method involves combining the like terms of the two equations to make a new equation with just one variable.

Unit 3 Linear Systems and Matrices

142

Answers to Talk it Over

1. The first column of rods (red, black, red) represent the numbers 4, –3, 11. The second column (black, red, black) represent –5, 2, –12.

2. red: positive; black: negative

3. Each column of the diagram represents an equation with the variables in the same position. Each equation is written in vertical form rather than in horizontal form; the Chinese method does not explicitly use variables.

4. because the coefficients of none of the variables is 1

Here are two ways to begin solving a linear system:

Substitution Method

$x + y = -3$
$x - y = -1$

Solve the first equation for y. →
$y = -x - 3$

Substitute for y in the second equation. →
$x - (-x - 3) = -1$
$x + x + 3 = -1$
$2x = -4$

Addition-or-Subtraction Method

$x + y = -3$
$+ \quad x - y = -1$
$(x + y) + (x - y) = -3 + (-1)$
$2x = -4$

Add $x - y$ to the left side of the first equation and -1 to the right side.

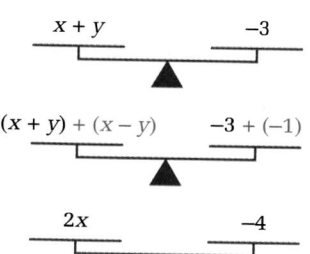

$x + y$ ⟷ -3

$(x + y) + (x - y)$ ⟷ $-3 + (-1)$

$2x$ ⟷ -4

:::: **Talk it Over**

5. Both methods shown above lead to the same equation. Find the solution of the system of equations.

6. Compare the number of steps needed in each method to reach the equation $2x = -4$. Which method do you think is easier to use for this system of equations? Why?

7. The balance scales show the addition-or-subtraction method. Why do the scales remain balanced?

Sample 1

Solve by the addition-or-subtraction method.

a. $3y = 2x + 2$
   $3y = x - 2$

b. $5a + 2b = 23$
   $7a - 2b = 13$

Sample Response

You can compare the coefficients of the like terms to decide which operation will *eliminate* one of the variables.

a. The coefficients of y are *the same*. *Subtract* to eliminate the y-terms.

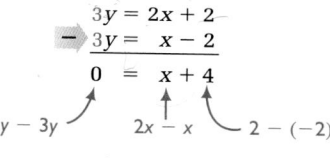

$3y = 2x + 2$
$- \quad 3y = x - 2$
$0 = x + 4$

$3y - 3y$ ↗ $2x - x$ ↑ $2 - (-2)$ ↘

$0 = x + 4$
$-4 = x$

$3y = -4 - 2$
$3y = -6$
$y = -2$

The solution (x, y) is $(-4, -2)$.

Solve the new equation.

Substitute in one of the original equations to find the other variable.

b. The coefficients of b are *opposites*. *Add* to eliminate the b-terms.

$5a + 2b = 23$
$+ \quad 7a - 2b = 13$
$12a + 0 = 36$

$5a + 7a$ ↗ $2b + (-2b)$ ↑ $23 + 13$ ↘

$12a = 36$
$a = 3$

$5(3) + 2b = 23$
$15 + 2b = 23$
$2b = 8$
$b = 4$

The solution (a, b) is $(3, 4)$.

3-4 Solving Systems by Addition-or-Subtraction

143

Answers to Talk it Over

5. $(-2, -1)$

6. The substitution method uses more steps than the addition-or-subtraction method. Answers may vary. An example is given. The addition-or-subtraction method is easier because it requires fewer steps.

7. In the first step, the scales remain balanced because equal amounts were added to each side. In the second step, the scales remain balanced because nothing was added or subtracted, just simplified.

Error Analysis

A common type of error made by some students using the addition-or-subtraction method is to not change the sign of each term of an equation when subtracting to eliminate one of the variables. When multiplication is also involved, as in Sample 2, errors can be made by not multiplying each term on both sides of an equation by the chosen multiplier. These types of errors may be eliminated by highlighting them in class discussions so as to make students more aware of them.

Additional Sample

S2 Solve this system of equations.

$x - 3y = 10$
$3x + y = 2$

To make the coefficients of the y-terms the same, multiply both sides of the second equation by 3.

$x - 3y = 10$
$3(3x + y) = 3 \cdot 2$

Solve the system by adding to eliminate the y-terms.

$$\begin{array}{r} x - 3y = 10 \\ + \ 9x + 3y = \ 6 \\ \hline 10x \quad\quad = 16 \\ x = 1.6 \end{array}$$

Substitute $x = 1.6$ in $x - 3y = 10$ to find y.

$1.6 - 3y = 10$
$-3y = 8.4$
$y = -2.8$

The solution (x, y) is $(1.6, -2.8)$.

Multiplying Before Using Addition-or-Subtraction

Sometimes the equations in a system of equations do not have any like terms with the same or opposite coefficients. You can change the coefficients by multiplying both sides of either equation by a constant.

Sample 2

The readouts on the stair machine and the treadmill tell Raquel how many Calories she burns. How many minutes should she spend on each machine if she exercises for 30 min and wants to burn 200 Cal?

Sample Response

Problem Solving Strategy: Use a system of equations.

Let x = the number of minutes on the stair machine.
Let y = the number of minutes on the treadmill.

Write two equations that relate x and y.

$x + y = 30$ ← Raquel exercises for 30 min.

$5.7x + 7.3y = 200$ ← Raquel wants to burn a total of 200 Cal.

To make the coefficients of the x-terms the same, multiply both sides of the first equation by 5.7.

$5.7(x + y) = 5.7(30)$ → $5.7x + 5.7y = 171$

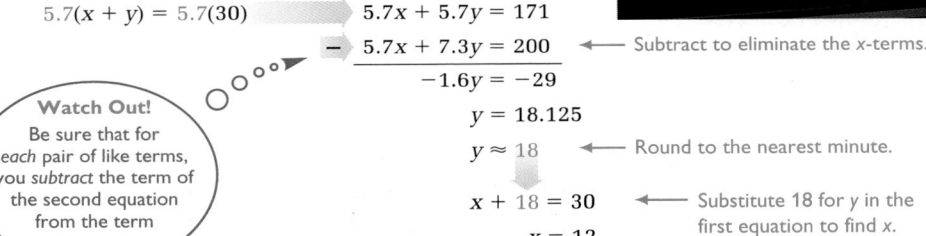

Watch Out!
Be sure that for *each* pair of like terms, you *subtract* the term of the second equation from the term above it.

$$-\ \begin{array}{r} 5.7x + 5.7y = 171 \\ 5.7x + 7.3y = 200 \\ \hline -1.6y = -29 \end{array}$$ ← Subtract to eliminate the x-terms.

$y = 18.125$

$y \approx 18$ ← Round to the nearest minute.

$x + 18 = 30$ ← Substitute 18 for y in the first equation to find x.

$x = 12$

Raquel should spend about 12 min on the stair machine and about 18 min on the treadmill.

8. In Sample 2, suppose you multiply both sides of the first equation by −5.7 instead of 5.7. How does this change the other steps of the solution?

9. Describe the steps you can take if you choose to eliminate y in solving the system of equations in Sample 2.

▶ Now you are ready for:
Exs. 1–18 on pp. 147–148

10. Describe the first step you would take to solve this system of equations.

$$5s + 2t = 11$$
$$-10s - 6t = -18$$

To solve the system of equations shown on page 142, you need to change the coefficients of both equations.

Sample 3

Solve this system of equations: $4x - 3y = 11$
$-5x + 2y = -12$

Sample Response

To make the coefficients of the x-terms opposites, multiply both sides of each equation by a constant.

$$5(4x - 3y) = 5(11) \qquad \longleftarrow \text{Multiply both sides by 5.}$$
$$4(-5x + 2y) = 4(-12) \qquad \longleftarrow \text{Multiply both sides by 4.}$$

$$\begin{array}{r} 20x - 15y = 55 \\ + \quad -20x + 8y = -48 \\ \hline -7y = 7 \\ y = -1 \end{array}$$

$\longleftarrow$ Add to eliminate the x-terms.

You can use the addition-or-subtraction method to find x also.

$$4x - 3y = 11$$
$$-5x + 2y = -12$$

$\longleftarrow$ Use the original equations.

$$2(4x - 3y) = 2(11) \qquad \longleftarrow \text{Multiply both sides by 2.}$$
$$3(-5x + 2y) = 3(-12) \qquad \longleftarrow \text{Multiply both sides by 3.}$$

$$\begin{array}{r} 8x - 6y = 22 \\ + \quad -15x + 6y = -36 \\ \hline -7x = -14 \\ x = 2 \end{array}$$

$\longleftarrow$ Add to eliminate the y-terms.

The solution (x, y) is $(2, -1)$.

BY THE WAY...

Chapter 8 of *Nine Chapters on the Mathematical Art* covers solving linear systems. It also introduces arithmetic of positive and negative numbers. The Chinese are believed to be the first people to use negative numbers.

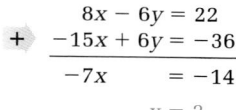

$y = -1$

$x = 2$

Questions 8 and 9 lead students through an analysis of different approaches that could have been used to solve the system in Sample 2. Students learn, therefore, that they have some flexibility in the steps that can be used to solve a system of equations. This flexibility of approach can be demonstrated by using question 10.

Additional Sample

S3 Solve this system of equations.
$$2x + 4y = 9$$
$$-3x - 5y = 2$$

To make the coefficients of the x-terms opposites, multiply both sides of each equation by a constant.
$$3(2x + 4y) = 3(9)$$
$$2(-3x - 5y) = 2(2)$$
Add to eliminate the x-terms.
$$\begin{array}{r} 6x + 12y = 27 \\ + -6x - 10y = 4 \\ \hline 2y = 31 \\ y = 15.5 \end{array}$$
Substitute 15.5 into the equation $2x + 4y = 9$ to find x.
$$2x + 4(15.5) = 9$$
$$2x + 62 = 9$$
$$2x = -53$$
$$x = -26.5$$
The solution (x, y) is $(-26.5, 15.5)$.

Answers to Talk it Over

8. The only difference is that you would add to eliminate the x-terms instead of subtracting. The result would be $1.6y = 29$ or $y = 18.125$.

9. If you want to eliminate y, multiply both sides of the first equation by 7.3 and subtract to eliminate the y-terms.

10. Multiply both sides of the first equation by 2.

You now know three methods for solving a system of equations. Here are some suggestions for choosing which method to use.

CHOOSING A METHOD TO SOLVE A LINEAR SYSTEM

You might solve by...	when...
graphing 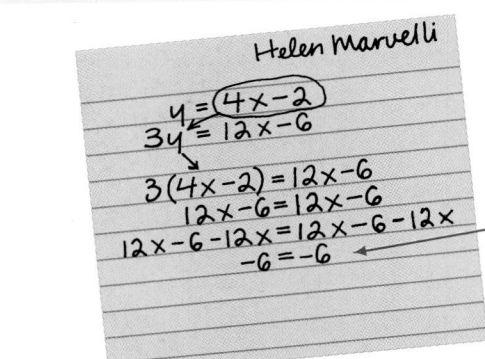	➤ an approximate solution is acceptable. ➤ you want to tell when one quantity is greater than or less than another quantity. ➤ the lines are easy to graph by hand, or a graphics calculator is available. ➤ you want to check that a solution found by another method is reasonable.
substitution $b = a + 5$ $b = 3a - 1$	➤ at least one equation is solved for one of the variables. ➤ at least one equation has a variable with coefficient 1.
addition-or-subtraction $+$ $\rightarrow$	➤ the like terms of the two equations are in the same order and on the same side of the equation. ➤ the coefficients of at least one pair of like terms in the two equations are the same or are opposites. ➤ no variable in either equation has a coefficient of 1.

Remember that not all systems have exactly one solution. What happens if you use algebra to solve a system that has no solution or many solutions? For this system, Helen chose solving by substitution.

You can see that this equation is true for all values of *x*.

You end up with a *true* statement without variables. This means that the system is consistent and has many solutions.

Talk it Over

11. For another system of equations, Daryl chose the addition-or-subtraction method. Compare the last line of her work with the last line of Helen's work above. How are they alike? How are they different? What do you think Daryl's result means?

146   **Unit 3** Linear Systems and Matrices

Tell which method you would use to solve each system of equations. Give a reason for your choice.

12. $c = 6d + 7$
$12d - 2c = -14$

13. $w = \frac{2}{3}v + 2$
$w = \frac{2}{3}v - 1$

14. $2x + y = 17$
$2x - 5y = 11$

15. Solve the system in question 12. Explain the result.

Look Back ◄

Samples 1, 2, and 3 show how to use addition-or-subtraction to solve four different systems of linear equations. Explain the differences in how you apply the method in each case.

·····► Now you are ready for:
Exs. 19–38 on pp. 148–150

3-4 Exercises and Problems

1. a. Reading Sample 1 shows how to use addition-or-subtraction to solve a system of equations. How do you decide whether to add or subtract?

b. To solve the system in Exercise 2, will you add or subtract? Why?

Solve each system of equations.

2. $-3a - 5b = -17$
$3a + 8b = 5$

3. $p - 6q = 14$
$2p + 6q = 10$

4. $-2c + 9d = 35$
$6c + 7d = 65$

5. $-5m + 3n = 12$
$5m - 8n = 23$

6. $7j - 3k = -14$
$2j + 3k = 32$

7. $y = 4x + 5$
$y = 2x - 7$

8. $2x + y = 5$
$3x - 2y = 4$

9. $4w - v = 15$
$-2w + 6v = -2$

10. Open-ended Write two different systems of equations that both have (2, 3) as a solution.

11. A problem in *Nine Chapters on the Mathematical Art* can be represented by this system of equations. Solve the system.
$9x - y = 11$
$6x - y = -16$

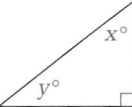

For Exercises 12–15, use a system of equations to solve each problem.

12. Fitness Liam burns 8.3 Cal/min when using a rowing machine, and 5.9 Cal/min when using an exercise bike. He plans to exercise for 45 min and wants to burn 300 Cal. How many minutes should he spend on each machine?

13. x is 15 more than four times y. Find the measure of each angle.

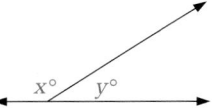

14. The difference between x and y is 12. Find the measure of each angle.

15. Each of two sides of a triangle is 8 in. longer than the third side. The perimeter is 43 in. How long is each side of the triangle?

3-4 Solving Systems by Addition-or-Subtraction **147**

Answers to Exercises and Problems

1. a. If like terms have the same coefficients, you subtract. If the like terms have opposite coefficients, you add.

b. add; the coefficients of a are opposites.

2. $\left(\frac{37}{3}, -4\right)$

3. $(8, -1)$

4. $(5, 5)$

5. $\left(-\frac{33}{5}, -7\right)$

6. $\left(2, \frac{28}{3}\right)$

7. $(-6, -19)$

8. $(2, 1)$

9. $(1, 4)$

10. $y = x + 1$ $x + y = 5$
$y = 2x - 1$ $2x - 3y = -5$

11. $(9, 70)$

12. about 14 min. on the rowing machine and 31 min. on the exercise bike

13. $x = 147°, y = 33°$

14. $x = 51°, y = 39°$

15. 9 in., 17 in., 17 in.

Suggested Assignment
Day 1
Standard 1–9, 13–15
Extended 1–18
Day 2
Standard 19–27, 29–32, 34–38
Extended 19–32, 34–38

Integrating the Strands
Algebra Exs. 1–38
Geometry Exs. 13–15
Statistics and Probability Exs. 35–37
Logic and Language Exs. 1, 10, 24–27

Assessment: Standard
For Exs. 2–9, students should describe verbally which method they would use to solve each system. If the choice is addition-or-subtraction, they should describe the steps they would use to solve the system.

Problem Solving
The open-ended problem in Ex. 10 involves a situation in which students have to use a given solution and work backward to construct two different systems of equations. Since two points determine a line, there are an infinite number of lines through a single point. Thus, there are also an infinite number of systems that have (2, 3) as a solution.

147

Career **For Exercises 16–18, use this information on jewelry making.**

Some jewelers make the gold that they use from pure gold and a combination of other metals. The *karat* of the gold depends on the percent of pure gold used.

Karat	24	22	18	14	10
% pure gold	100	91.7	75	58.3	41.7

Note: Weights of precious metals are given in *pennyweights* (abbreviated dwt), where 20 dwt = 1 ounce.

16. A jeweler has on hand some 14-karat gold and some 24-karat gold. The jeweler needs to know how much of each to use to make 8 dwt of 18-karat gold for a bracelet ordered by a customer.

    a. Let x = the amount of 14-karat gold needed (dwt).
       Let y = the amount of 24-karat gold needed (dwt).

       Explain the meaning of each equation in this system of equations. (*Hint:* Use the information in the table above.)

       $x + y = 8$
       $0.583x + 1y = 0.75(8)$

    b. Solve the system of equations in part (a). Give the values of x and y to the nearest tenth. Explain the meaning of the solution.

17. How much 10-karat gold and how much 22-karat gold should be combined to make 10 dwt of 14-karat gold?

18. How much 24-karat gold should be added to 50 dwt of 14-karat gold to make 18-karat gold? How much 18-karat gold will there be?

Solve each system of equations.

19. $3x - 2y = 2$
    $10x - 3y = -8$

20. $2r + 2t = -14$
    $-5r + 3t = -45$

21. $4a + 15b = 10$
    $3a + 10b = 5$

22. $3u + 2v = -6$
    $5u - 4v = 1$

23. The Broadcast Club at Curie High School plans to spend $200 on tapes and CDs for the school radio station. Cherub Records offers to sell them tapes for $6 and CDs for $12. At Flower's Music, tapes cost $8 and CDs cost $10.

    a. Use this graph. What do the variables t and c represent? Which line represents Cherub Records? Flower's Music?

    b. Use the graph to estimate the solution of the system of equations.

    c. Solve the system using addition-or-subtraction.

    d. For which values of t is it cheaper to buy at Cherub Records? For which values of t is it cheaper to buy at Flower's Music?

    e. **Writing** Do you think the system is easier to solve by *graphing* or by *addition-or-subtraction*? Explain your choice.

Answers to Exercises and Problems

16. a. $x + y = 8$ represents that the jeweler needs x dwt of 14-karat gold and y dwt of 24-karat gold for a total of 8 dwt of 18-karat gold. $0.583x$ is the amount of pure gold in x ounces of 14-karat gold, $1y$ is the amount of pure gold in y ounces of 24-karat gold, which when added together will give $0.75(8) = 6$ or the total amount of pure gold in the 18-karat gold piece.

    b. (4.8, 3.2); It takes 4.8 dwt of 14-karat gold and 3.2 dwt of 24-karat gold to make 8 dwt of 18-karat gold.

17. 6.7 dwt of 10-karat gold; 3.3 dwt of 22-karat gold

18. 33.4 dwt of 24-karat gold; 83.4 dwt of 18-karat gold

19. (−2, −4)   20. (3, −10)

21. (−5, 2)

22. $\left(-1, -\frac{3}{2}\right)$

23. a. t represents the number of tapes that are bought; c represents the number of CDs that are bought. The line labeled $6t + 12c = 200$ represents Cherub Records; the line labeled $8t + 10c = 200$ represents Flower's Music.

    b. (11, 11)

    c. $\left(11\frac{1}{9}, 11\frac{1}{9}\right)$

    d. For $0 \le t \le 11$, it is cheaper to buy at Flower's Music. For $12 \le t \le 33$, you get more for your money at Cherub Records.

    e. Answers may vary. An example is given. Graphing is visual and

148

Writing Tell what method you would use to solve each system of equations. Give a reason for your choice.

24. $y = 2x + 13$
$3x + y = 15$

25. $5k - 3n = -4$
$6k - 5n = 1$

26. $-4a + b = 10$
$4a + 2b = -1$

27. $y = \frac{1}{2}x + 6$
$y = -2x + 1$

28. Dan solved a system of equations using the addition-or-subtraction method.

   a. Explain his solution.

   b. Write each equation in the system in slope-intercept form. What do you know about the graphs of the equations? What type of system is this?

Solve each system of equations. If there is no solution, write *no solution*.

29. $3a - 2b = 24$
$6a - 4b = -6$

30. $y = 9x - 3$
$4x + 2y = 5$

31. $2x + 9y = 20$
$5x + 6y = 17$

32. $3r - 3s = 18$
$r = s + 6$

> Dan O'Brien
>
> $2x + 3y = 1$
> $4x + 6y = -2$
>
> $2(2x + 3y) = 2(1)$
>
> $4x + 6y = 2$
> $4x + 6y = -2$ (Subtract)
> $0 = 4$ ALWAYS FALSE!

....
Ongoing **ASSESSMENT**

33. **Group Activity** Work in a group of three students.

   Use this system of equations: $y = 3x + 14$
   $2y = -x + 7$

   a. Solve the system of equations by substitution, addition-or-subtraction, and graphing. Each of you should use a different method.

   b. With your group, decide which method you think is best for solving the system. Give a reason for your choice.

....
Review **PREVIEW**

34. Write an equation of the line that goes through the point $(-3, 2)$ and is parallel to the line $y = -2x + 2$. *(Section 3-3)*

Use the information in the table to find each probability. *(Toolbox Skill 6)*

35. Suppose a resident of Maine is picked at random. What is the probability that the person lives in a rural area?

36. Suppose a resident of a rural area in New England is picked at random. What is the probability that the person lives in Maine?

37. Suppose a resident of New England is picked at random. What is the probability that the person lives in a rural area?

State	Populations of the New England States (1990)	
	Total population (thousands)	Rural population (thousands)
Connecticut	3287	686
Maine	1228	680
Massachusetts	6016	947
New Hampshire	1109	544
Rhode Island	1003	140
Vermont	563	382

3-4 Solving Systems by Addition-or-Subtraction

Cooperative Learning

You may wish to expand the group activity presented in Ex. 33 to Exs. 24–27 and 29–32.

....
Assessment: Task

For Ex. 33, students should review and check each other's solution. You may wish to call upon a few groups to see if they selected different methods.

....
Using Technology

Function Investigator Activity 11 in the *Function Investigator with Matrix Analyzer Activity Book* can be used to extend the section by examining graphically what happens when you solve a system of linear equations by multiplying before using addition-or-subtraction.

Answers to Exercises and Problems

gives a better overall picture. The addition-or-subtraction method is more cumbersome.

24. substitution; One equation is already solved for y.

25. addition-or-subtraction; It is easier to multiply both equations by a number than to solve one or both of the equations for a variable.

26. addition-or-subtraction; This will eliminate the a-term.

27. graphing; Both equations are in slope-intercept form and the lines are perpendicular.

28. a. Dan doubled both sides of the first equation to yield like terms and then subtracted to give the false statement

$0 = 4$. Therefore, the lines are parallel.

   b. $y = -\frac{2}{3}x + \frac{1}{3}$
   $y = -\frac{2}{3}x - \frac{1}{3}$; The graphs are parallel lines; inconsistent system

29. no solution

30. $\left(\frac{1}{2}, \frac{3}{2}\right)$

31. $(1, 2)$

32. infinitely many solutions

33. a. $(-3, 5)$

   b. Answers may vary. An example is given. Substitution may be best since one equation is already solved for y.

34. $y = -2x - 4$

35. 0.55

36. 0.20

37. 0.26

149

Practice 20 For use with Section 3-4

3 Working on the Unit Project

38. For a backpacking trip, Selena wants to make a snack of raisins and peanuts so that the mix has half her daily allowances for protein and fat. Her daily allowances are 55 grams of protein and 73 grams of fat. How many cups of each food should she use? Round to the nearest half cup.

	protein (g)	fat (g)
raisins (1 cup)	4	1
peanuts (1 cup)	38	70

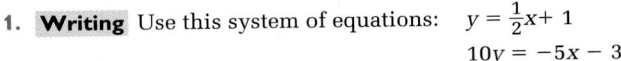

Unit 3 CHECKPOINT

1. **Writing** Use this system of equations:
   $$y = \tfrac{1}{2}x + 1$$
   $$10y = −5x − 3$$

   Does the system have *no solution, one solution,* or *many solutions*? Explain how you can tell without graphing the system.

2. The town of Reedsville pays $400 per ton to dispose of cardboard waste. If the town rents a cardboard compactor for $350, then they will pay only $80 per ton to dispose of cardboard waste. **3-1**

   a. Write a system of equations that models the town's costs for each cardboard waste disposal plan.

   b. Graph the system of equations in part (a).

   c. Which disposal plan is cheaper if the town has one ton of cardboard waste? if the town has two tons of cardboard waste? Explain how the graph supports your answers.

3. Graph this system of inequalities:
   $$y \le −2x + 1$$
   $$y > 1.5x − 3$$

Solve each system of equations by substitution. **3-2**

4. $y = 3x − 1$
   $y = −5x + 3$

5. $x + y = 461$
   $6x + 5y = 2530$

6. Write an equation of the line that goes through (2, 5) and is parallel to the line $y = −3x + 4$. **3-3**

7. Write an equation of the line that goes through (−2, 0) and is perpendicular to the line $y = −3x + 4$.

Solve each system of equations. **3-4**

8. $4y = 3x + 1$
   $−8y = −3x − 5$

9. $2y = 12x + 4$
   $−y = −6x − 2$

10. $3x − y = −1$
    $4x − y = 4$

11. Tell what method you would use to solve this system. Give a reason for your choice.
    $y = −5x$
    $2x + y = 9$

Unit 3 Linear Systems and Matrices

BY THE WAY...

Businesses are trying to turn trash into profit. Recycled cardboard is used to make a variety of products from pencils to building materials. The pencils shown are made from recycled cardboard and newspaper fiber.

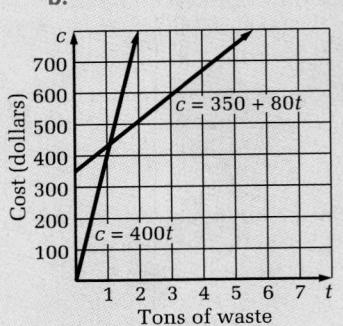

150

Answers to Exercises and Problems

38. about 2 cups of raisins; about $\tfrac{1}{2}$ cup of peanuts

Answers to Checkpoint

1. one solution; Putting the second equation in slope-intercept form, $m = −\dfrac{1}{2}$.

   Since the two slopes are different, the lines intersect and there is one solution.

2. a. Let c = costs and t = tons of waste. Then the system of equations is
   $c = 400t$
   $c = 350 + 80t$.

   b.

   [Graph: Cost (dollars) vs Tons of waste, with lines $c = 350 + 80t$, $c = 400t$]

   c. Direct disposal is cheaper for one ton of cardboard waste. Using a compactor is cheaper for two tons of cardboard waste. The point when the costs are equal is at slightly more than one ton of waste.

3-5

Matrix Operations

~On the Menu~

Real-world data that belong to more than one category are often displayed in a table or *matrix*.

PLANNING

Objectives and Strands
See pages 118A and 118B.

Spiral Learning
See page 118B.

Materials List
➤ Graphics calculator

Recommended Pacing
Section 3-5 is a two-day lesson.
Day 1
Pages 151–153: Opening paragraph through Talk it Over 7, *Exercises 1–13*
Day 2
Pages 154–155: Matrix Addition and Subtraction through Look Back, *Exercises 14–35*

Extra Practice
See pages 618–619.

Warm-Up Exercises
Warm-Up Transparency 3-5

Support Materials
➤ Practice 21
➤ Enrichment 19 in the Activity Bank
➤ Study Guide 3-5
➤ Problem Set 6
➤ Additional Exploration 5
➤ McDougal Littell Mathpack software: *Matrix Analyzer*
➤ Function Investigator with Matrix Analyzer Activity Book: *Matrix Analyzer Activity 1*
➤ Using Plotter Plus: *Matrix Calculations (Mac version)*
➤ Using Mac Plotter Plus Disk: *Matrix Calculator*
➤ Quiz 3-5
➤ Alternative Assessment 4

Bombay House
Luncheon Specials
Monday – Friday, 11:00 – 2:00

	Curry	Kurma
Chicken	$3.75	$4.25
Lamb	$4.00	$4.50
Shrimp	$5.25	$5.75

In mathematics a **matrix** is an arrangement of numbers, called **elements,** in rows and columns. (*Note:* The plural of *matrix* is *matrices.*)

The numbers in a matrix are written inside large square brackets ([ ]).

Write category labels outside the brackets.

The element 4.25 is in row 1, column 2.

$$P = \begin{array}{c} \text{chicken} \\ \text{lamb} \\ \text{shrimp} \end{array} \begin{bmatrix} 3.75 & 4.25 \\ 4.00 & 4.50 \\ 5.25 & 5.75 \end{bmatrix}$$

curry   kurma

3 rows

2 columns

You can name a matrix with a single capital letter.

The number of rows and the number of columns, *in that order,* are the **dimensions** of the matrix. The dimensions of this price matrix are 3 × 2, read "three by two."

Answers to Checkpoint

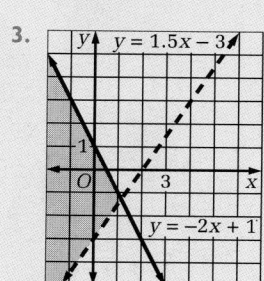

3.

4. $\left(\dfrac{1}{2}, \dfrac{1}{2}\right)$

5. (225, 236)

6. $y = -3x + 11$

7. $3y = x + 2$

8. (1, 1)

9. infinitely many solutions

10. (5, 16)

11. substitution, because one equation is already solved for y; The solution is (–3, 15).

Talk it Over

1. In which row and column is the price for an order of lamb curry?

BY THE WAY...

Curry dishes are cooked with curry powder, which is a combination of the spices cumin, tumeric, and coriander. Kurma dishes are cooked with yogurt, cream, almonds, and sweet spices.

Bombay House

$$P = \begin{array}{c} \\ \text{chicken} \\ \text{lamb} \\ \text{shrimp} \end{array} \begin{array}{cc} \text{curry} & \text{kurma} \\ \begin{bmatrix} 3.75 & 4.25 \\ 4.00 & 4.50 \\ 5.25 & 5.75 \end{bmatrix} \end{array}$$

2. What does the element in row 3, column 2 of the price matrix represent?

3. Suppose the owner of Bombay House wants to expand the menu to show prices for vegetable curry and vegetable kurma. What would be the dimensions of the new price matrix?

4. Use the original price matrix P. Suppose the owner wants to raise prices at Bombay House by 4%.

   a. Explain why the owner can multiply each price by 1.04 in order to find the new price.

   b. What will be the dimensions of the new price matrix?

To multiply the matrix P by the number 1.04, you multiply each element of P by 1.04.

Multiplying a matrix by a number is called *scalar multiplication*.

$$1.04P = 1.04 \begin{bmatrix} 3.75 & 4.25 \\ 4.00 & 4.50 \\ 5.25 & 5.75 \end{bmatrix} = \begin{bmatrix} 1.04(3.75) & 1.04(4.25) \\ 1.04(4.00) & 1.04(4.50) \\ 1.04(5.25) & 1.04(5.75) \end{bmatrix} = \begin{bmatrix} 3.90 & 4.42 \\ 4.16 & 4.68 \\ 5.46 & 5.98 \end{bmatrix}$$

Sample 1

	A	B	C	D	E
		rock/pop	jazz	classical	other
1					
2	CDs	1913	139	333	388
3	tapes	843	61	119	164

February Sales

Bill Chee uses spreadsheet software to keep track of sales data at his music store. In March, he hopes to increase sales in all categories by 7%.

a. Write the February sales data in a matrix.

b. Use scalar multiplication to find how many of each type of recording in each category the store needs to sell to meet the March sales goal.

Answers to Talk it Over

1. row 2, column 1

2. the price of shrimp kurma

3. 4×2

4. a. 1.04 is the same as 100% + 4% when you multiply by the price.

   b. 3×2

a. Give the matrix a name and include category labels.

February Sales

$$A = \begin{array}{l} \text{CDs} \\ \text{tapes} \end{array} \begin{bmatrix} \overset{\text{rock/pop}}{1913} & \overset{\text{jazz}}{139} & \overset{\text{classical}}{333} & \overset{\text{other}}{388} \\ 843 & 61 & 119 & 164 \end{bmatrix}$$

b. To increase each element of the February sales matrix by 7%, multiply the matrix A by 1.07.

Method ❶ Use arithmetic.

You can leave off the category labels while you do the calculations.

$$1.07A = 1.07 \begin{bmatrix} 1913 & 139 & 333 & 388 \\ 843 & 61 & 119 & 164 \end{bmatrix}$$

Multiply each element of A by 1.07.

$$= \begin{bmatrix} (1.07)1913 & (1.07)139 & (1.07)333 & (1.07)388 \\ (1.07)843 & (1.07)61 & (1.07)119 & (1.07)164 \end{bmatrix}$$

$$= \begin{bmatrix} 2046.91 & 148.73 & 356.31 & 415.16 \\ 902.01 & 65.27 & 127.33 & 175.48 \end{bmatrix}$$

Enter each result in the corresponding position of the product matrix.

Write the answer as a matrix with labels.

Method ❷ Use a graphics calculator.

Enter the February sales matrix in matrix A. Then find $1.07A$.

1.07[A]
```
[ 2046.91 148.7...
   902.01  65.2...
```

Recordings are sold in whole units. Round off each element to the nearest whole number.

March Sales Goals

$$\begin{array}{l} \text{CDs} \\ \text{tapes} \end{array} \begin{bmatrix} \overset{\text{rock/pop}}{2047} & \overset{\text{jazz}}{149} & \overset{\text{classical}}{356} & \overset{\text{other}}{415} \\ 902 & 65 & 127 & 175 \end{bmatrix}$$

TECHNOLOGY NOTE

To see all the elements of a matrix, you may need to use the arrow keys to scroll right and left. For more information on using the matrix functions of a graphics calculator, see the Technology Handbook, p. 609.

Talk it Over

5. How many jazz tapes does Bill Chee hope to sell in March?

6. In Sample 1, what are the dimensions of the February sales matrix A? What are the dimensions of the matrix $1.07A$?

7. Will the dimensions of a matrix M and a scalar multiple of M always be the same? Explain.

Now you are ready for:
Exs. 1–13 on pp. 155–157

3-5 Matrix Operations

Using Technology

Students can use the *Matrix Analyzer* software or a graphics calculator for Sample 1.

On the TI-81, TI-82, TI-83, or TI-83 Plus, enter a matrix by first pressing MATRX (on the TI-81, TI-82, or TI-83) or 2nd [MATRX] (on the TI-83 Plus) and selecting the EDIT menu. Choose the name you want for the matrix ([A], [B], and so on). On the first line of the screen, enter the dimensions of the matrix. Then enter the matrix elements one at a time. For example, the pair of numbers 1,1 indicates the matrix element for row 1, column 1; the pair 2,4 indicates the element for row 2, column 4. *Note:* for the TI-81, elements that are fractions must be entered in decimal form. On the TI-82, TI-83, and TI-83 Plus you can type the fraction, press ENTER, and the conversion to decimal form will be done for you.

For Method 2 of the Sample response, enter [A] to start the calculation. When you have entered [A], press 2nd [QUIT] to go to the home screen. On the TI-82 or TI-83, press 1.07 MATRX 1 ENTER to find 1.07[A]. On the TI-83 Plus, press 2nd [MATRX] 1 ENTER. On the TI-81, press 1.07 2nd [[A]] ENTER. In all cases, after you press ENTER, the calculator will display the answer.

Answers to Talk it Over

5. 65

6. 2×4; 2×4

7. Yes. You are multiplying each entry by a single number, or scalar, not another matrix.

Teaching Tip

You may wish to discuss with students why two matrices having different dimensions cannot be added or subtracted. (All of their elements are not in corresponding positions.) This discussion, complete with examples of what happens if you try to add or subtract matrices with different dimensions, should help solidify students' knowledge of when matrices can be added or subtracted.

Using Technology

Students can use the *Matrix Analyzer* software or a graphics calculator for Sample 2.

Additional Sample

S2 Each matrix below indicates the number of tickets sold for a student play in both the fall and spring for the Friday evening and Saturday evening performances. How many tickets were sold in each category for the two seasons. Write the answer as a matrix.

Fall Season:

$$\begin{array}{c} \\ \text{Fri.} \\ \text{Sat.} \end{array} \begin{array}{cc} \text{Student} & \text{Adult} \\ \left[\begin{array}{cc} 112 & 230 \\ 157 & 265 \end{array}\right] \end{array}$$

Spring Season:

$$\begin{array}{c} \\ \text{Fri.} \\ \text{Sat.} \end{array} \begin{array}{cc} \text{Student} & \text{Adult} \\ \left[\begin{array}{cc} 119 & 285 \\ 184 & 273 \end{array}\right] \end{array}$$

Add the two matrices.

$$\left[\begin{array}{cc} 112 & 230 \\ 157 & 265 \end{array}\right] + \left[\begin{array}{cc} 119 & 285 \\ 184 & 273 \end{array}\right] = \left[\begin{array}{cc} 231 & 515 \\ 341 & 538 \end{array}\right]$$

Two Seasons:

$$\begin{array}{c} \\ \text{Fri.} \\ \text{Sat.} \end{array} \begin{array}{cc} \text{Student} & \text{Adult} \\ \left[\begin{array}{cc} 231 & 515 \\ 341 & 538 \end{array}\right] \end{array}$$

Matrix Addition and Subtraction

When two matrices have the same dimensions, you can add or subtract the matrices by adding or subtracting the elements in corresponding positions.

Sample 2

These spreadsheets show the January and February sales at the music store in Sample 1. Find the total sales in each category for January and February combined. Write the answer as a matrix.

January Sales

	A	B rock/pop	C jazz	D classical	E other
1		rock/pop	jazz	classical	other
2	CDs	1837	131	319	393
3	tapes	839	63	127	158

February Sales

	A	B rock/pop	C jazz	D classical	E other
1		rock/pop	jazz	classical	other
2	CDs	1913	139	333	388
3	tapes	843	61	119	164

Sample Response

1 Write the January and February data in matrices.

January Sales

$$B = \begin{array}{c} \\ \text{CDs} \\ \text{tapes} \end{array} \begin{array}{cccc} \text{rock/pop} & \text{jazz} & \text{classical} & \text{other} \\ \left[\begin{array}{cccc} 1837 & 131 & 319 & 393 \\ 839 & 63 & 127 & 158 \end{array}\right] \end{array}$$

February Sales

$$A = \begin{array}{c} \\ \text{CDs} \\ \text{tapes} \end{array} \begin{array}{cccc} \text{rock/pop} & \text{jazz} & \text{classical} & \text{other} \\ \left[\begin{array}{cccc} 1913 & 139 & 333 & 388 \\ 843 & 61 & 119 & 164 \end{array}\right] \end{array}$$

2 To find the total sales in each category, add the matrices.

$$B + A = \left[\begin{array}{cccc} 1837 & 131 & 319 & 393 \\ 839 & 63 & 127 & 158 \end{array}\right] + \left[\begin{array}{cccc} 1913 & 139 & 333 & 388 \\ 843 & 61 & 119 & 164 \end{array}\right]$$

Add the elements in corresponding positions.

$$= \left[\begin{array}{cccc} (1837 + 1913) & (131 + 139) & (319 + 333) & (393 + 388) \\ (839 + 843) & (63 + 61) & (127 + 119) & (158 + 164) \end{array}\right]$$

$$= \left[\begin{array}{cccc} 3750 & 270 & 652 & 781 \\ 1682 & 124 & 246 & 322 \end{array}\right]$$

Enter each result in the corresponding position of the sum matrix.

3 Write the answer as a matrix with labels.

January/February Sales

$$\begin{array}{c} \\ \text{CDs} \\ \text{tapes} \end{array} \begin{array}{cccc} \text{rock/pop} & \text{jazz} & \text{classical} & \text{other} \\ \left[\begin{array}{cccc} 3750 & 270 & 652 & 781 \\ 1682 & 124 & 246 & 322 \end{array}\right] \end{array}$$

154 **Unit 3** Linear Systems and Matrices

Answers to Talk it Over

8. 652

9. a. how many more CDs and tapes were sold in February than in January

   b. Negative numbers mean the music store sold less in that category in February than in January.

8. How many classical CDs were sold in January/February?

9. You can subtract matrices by subtracting elements in corresponding positions. Use matrices B and A in Sample 2:

$$A - B = \begin{bmatrix} 1913 & 139 & 333 & 388 \\ 843 & 61 & 119 & 164 \end{bmatrix} - \begin{bmatrix} 1837 & 131 & 319 & 393 \\ 839 & 63 & 127 & 158 \end{bmatrix}$$

$$= \begin{bmatrix} 76 & 8 & 14 & -5 \\ 4 & -2 & -8 & 6 \end{bmatrix} \quad \longleftarrow 388 - 393 = -5$$

a. Explain the meaning of the matrix $A - B$ in terms of sales at Bill Chee's music store.

b. What do the negative numbers in the matrix $A - B$ mean?

MATRIX OPERATIONS

Scalar multiplication

➤ To multiply matrix A by a constant c, multiply each element of A by c.

Matrix addition or subtraction

➤ To add or subtract two matrices, add or subtract the elements that are in corresponding positions.

➤ Matrices can be added or subtracted only if they have the same dimensions.

> ······➤ Now you are ready for:
> Exs. 14–35 on pp. 157–158

Look Back ◄────

How is scalar multiplication like matrix addition or subtraction? How is it different?

> ············
> **3-5** **Exercises and Problems**

1. **Reading** How many elements does a matrix with dimensions 3×4 have?

What are the dimensions of each matrix?

2. $\begin{bmatrix} 4 & 7 \\ 8 & 2 \end{bmatrix}$

3. $\begin{bmatrix} 67 & 32 & 18 & 5 & 0 \\ 53 & 12 & 6 & 41 & 11 \\ 2 & 8 & 0 & 4 & 72 \end{bmatrix}$

4. $\begin{bmatrix} 6 \\ 17 \\ 3 \end{bmatrix}$

5. $\begin{bmatrix} 0 & 25 & 16 & 70 \end{bmatrix}$

3-5 Matrix Operations

155

Talk it Over

Question 9 introduces the procedure for subtracting matrices. Parts (a) and (b) of this question focus on what matrix $A - B$ means in terms of the data represented by each matrix. It is important that students recognize the real-world meaning of the numbers in matrix $A - B$. In this situation, positive numbers represent an increase in sales from January to February and negative numbers show a decrease.

Look Back

You might wish to have students make a list of their responses to these questions and suggest that they keep it in their journals for future reference. ········●

APPLYING

Suggested Assignment

Day 1
Standard 1–10
Extended 1–13

Day 2
Standard 14–21, 24–35
Extended 14–35

Integrating the Strands

Algebra Exs. 1–32, 35
Geometry Exs. 33, 34
Discrete Mathematics Exs. 1–24, 35
Logic and Language Exs. 1, 13, 22–24

Answers to Look Back ········

Answers to Exercises and Problems ·····

Answers may vary. An example is given. Scalar multiplication, addition, and subtraction all result in a matrix with the same dimensions as the original matrix. Scalar multiplication multiplies each element of one matrix by a constant. Matrix addition or subtraction combines two matrices of the same dimension into one.

1. 12 elements
2. 2×2
3. 3×5

4. 3×1
5. 1×4

Interdisciplinary Problems

Since matrices can be used in any situation involving discrete data, they have a broad application to many real-world situations. In this section, there are exercises relating to biology, business, baking, basketball, and social studies.

Reasoning

For Exs. 6–10, students see a matrix whose elements are different in meaning than those presented previously in this section. In this situation, the numbers 0 and 1 are being used in a non-numerical way as general symbols or elements to indicate the capture status of a particular duck. You may wish to ask students if it makes any sense to multiply this matrix by a scalar or to add or subtract it to another matrix. (No.)

Mathematical Procedures

The algebra of matrices defines a matrix as a rectangular array of elements in which the elements are usually considered to be real numbers. In general, the elements of a matrix must be mathematical entities for which addition and multiplication are uniquely defined. Thus, the elements are not necessarily numbers but could be, for example, polynomials or rational fractions with integral coefficients. In real life, the concept of a matrix has been adapted to represent any rectangular array of elements, where the elements can almost be anything, for example, the names of people or the colors of cars. Obviously, mathematical operations cannot be performed on such "matrices."

connection to **BIOLOGY**

This duck is being banded as part of a program to estimate the nesting duck population in Central Oregon.

For Exercises 6–10, use this information.

Biologists use *capture-recapture models* to estimate how many animals are in an area. The biologists repeatedly capture, tag, and release samples of the animals. They use a *capture-history matrix* to keep track of which animals are captured each time.

Suppose this capture-history matrix records the results of five samples of a duck population.

Each column represents a time when biologists captured a sample of ducks.

Each row of the matrix represents a duck.

Capture-History Matrix

$$
\begin{array}{c}
\text{duck } A \\
\text{duck } B \\
\text{duck } C
\end{array}
\begin{bmatrix}
1 & 0 & 0 & 1 & 0 \\
1 & 0 & 1 & 0 & 1 \\
0 & 1 & 0 & 0 & 1
\end{bmatrix}
$$

The element "0" means the duck was not captured.

The element "1" means the duck was captured.

6. What are the dimensions of the capture-history matrix?

7. What do the dimensions mean in this situation?

8. How many times was duck *A* captured?

9. Which duck was captured the greatest number of times?

10. What does the element in row 3, column 4 mean in this situation?

11. **Sales** A sports store is planning a 20% off sale on all basketball, cycling, and running clothes and shoes.

    a. Write the price data in a matrix.

    b. Explain why you can multiply each price by 0.80 to find each sale price.

    c. Use scalar multiplication to find the sale price of each item.

    d. What is the sale price of cycling shorts?

	Original Price (Dollars)		
	Basketball	Cycling	Running
Shirts	9.99	16.99	10.99
Shorts	16.99	9.99	9.99
Shoes	64.99	59.99	54.99

12. **Baking** Use this table from a box of biscuit mix.

	MIX	MILK	SUGAR	EGGS	SHORTENING
Biscuits	1⅓ cups	½ cup	none	none	none
Muffins	1⅓ cups	¾ cup	¼ cup	1	2 tablespoons
Coffee Cake	1⅓ cups	½ cup	¼ cup	1	none

    a. Write the ingredients table as a matrix.

    b. Multiply the ingredients matrix by 3.

    c. What does scalar multiplication by 3 mean in this situation?

Unit 3 Linear Systems and Matrices

Answers to Exercises and Problems

6. 3×5

7. Each row represents a particular duck, each labeled *A*, *B*, and *C*. The columns represent the five different times biologists captured a sample of ducks.

8. twice

9. duck *B*

10. On the fourth sample, duck *C* was not captured.

11. a. $\begin{bmatrix} 9.99 & 16.99 & 10.99 \\ 16.99 & 9.99 & 9.99 \\ 64.99 & 59.99 & 54.99 \end{bmatrix}$

    b. Each item will be 80% of the original price, so multiply each element by 0.80.

    c. $\begin{bmatrix} 7.99 & 13.59 & 8.79 \\ 13.59 & 7.99 & 7.99 \\ 51.99 & 47.99 & 43.99 \end{bmatrix}$

    d. $7.99

12. a. $\begin{bmatrix} 1\frac{1}{3} & \frac{1}{2} & 0 & 0 & 0 \\ 1\frac{1}{3} & \frac{3}{4} & \frac{1}{4} & 1 & 2 \\ 1\frac{1}{3} & \frac{1}{2} & \frac{1}{4} & 1 & 0 \end{bmatrix}$

    b. $\begin{bmatrix} 4 & 1\frac{1}{2} & 0 & 0 & 0 \\ 4 & 2\frac{1}{4} & \frac{3}{4} & 3 & 6 \\ 4 & 1\frac{1}{2} & \frac{3}{4} & 3 & 0 \end{bmatrix}$

13. **Open-ended** Describe a situation that can be represented by a matrix for which scalar multiplication does *not* give a sensible answer.

Simplify.

14. $\begin{bmatrix} -1 & 0 \\ 3 & -5 \end{bmatrix} + \begin{bmatrix} 4 & -6 \\ 1 & 0 \end{bmatrix}$

15. $\begin{bmatrix} 2.4 & -1.3 \\ 5.2 & 1.8 \\ -3.1 & 2.7 \end{bmatrix} - \begin{bmatrix} 1.3 & 6.2 \\ 7.1 & 0.5 \\ -2.1 & -4.0 \end{bmatrix}$

16. $5\begin{bmatrix} -3 \\ 4 \\ 0 \end{bmatrix} + \begin{bmatrix} 15 \\ -7 \\ -9 \end{bmatrix}$

17. $3\begin{bmatrix} 2 \\ 0 \\ 11 \end{bmatrix} + 2\begin{bmatrix} 4 \\ 13 \\ 9 \end{bmatrix}$

18. Is it possible to add the matrices $\begin{bmatrix} 12 & 14 & 2 & 5 \\ 76 & 42 & 9 & 1 \\ 18 & 7 & 58 & 3 \end{bmatrix}$ and $\begin{bmatrix} 56 & 11 \\ 5 & 3 \\ 0 & 3 \end{bmatrix}$?

Explain why or why not.

19. **Business** In March, Bill Chee sold 2082 rock/pop CDs, 143 jazz CDs, 327 classical CDs, 423 other CDs, 865 rock/pop tapes, 64 jazz tapes, 149 classical tapes, and 167 other tapes at his music store.

a. Organize the data in a matrix with dimensions 2×4.

b. Did Bill Chee reach his sales goal for March?
(See Sample 1 response on page 153.)

c. Use the music sales data in Sample 2 on page 154. What are the total sales at Bill Chee's music store for the first quarter of the year?

20. Use the matrices $B = \begin{bmatrix} 14 & 48 & 18 \\ 5 & 30 & 2 \end{bmatrix}$ and $D = \begin{bmatrix} 56 & 48 & 13 \\ 80 & 36 & 1 \end{bmatrix}$.

a. Find $B + D$ and $D + B$. Does the order in which you add two matrices matter? Explain why or why not.

b. Find $B - D$ and $D - B$. Does the order in which you subtract two matrices matter? Explain why or why not.

21. **Basketball** Use the two win-loss tables.

**Top Three Western Conference Teams
1998–1999 Basketball Season**

HOME GAMES		
	WINS	LOSSES
San Antonio	21	4
Utah	22	3
Portland	22	3

AWAY GAMES		
	WINS	LOSSES
San Antonio	16	9
Utah	15	10
Portland	13	12

a. Write the information in each table in a 3×2 matrix.

b. Add the matrices in part (a).

c. What does the sum of the matrices mean in this situation?

d. Subtract the matrices in part (a).

e. What does the difference of the matrices mean in this situation?

3-5 Matrix Operations

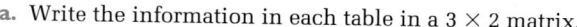

Answers to Exercises and Problems

c. ingredients for making a triple batch of biscuits, muffins, and coffee cake

13. Answers may vary. Examples are given. The capture-history matrix in Exs. 6–10 has no sensible scalar multiple. Also, in a set of test answers, multiplying by $\frac{1}{2}$ would give results on half of a test. This does not make sense.

14. $\begin{bmatrix} 3 & -6 \\ 4 & -5 \end{bmatrix}$

15. $\begin{bmatrix} 1.1 & -7.5 \\ -1.9 & 1.3 \\ -1.0 & 6.7 \end{bmatrix}$

16. $\begin{bmatrix} 0 \\ 13 \\ -9 \end{bmatrix}$

17. $\begin{bmatrix} 14 \\ 26 \\ 51 \end{bmatrix}$

18. No; they are different dimensions.

19. See answers in back at book.

20. a. $B + D = \begin{bmatrix} 70 & 96 & 31 \\ 85 & 66 & 3 \end{bmatrix}$;
$D + B = \begin{bmatrix} 70 & 96 & 31 \\ 85 & 66 & 3 \end{bmatrix}$;
No, order does not matter. Using the addition property of equality, $B + D = D + B$.

Assessment: Open-ended

Students should be prepared to support their situations with valid reasons as to why scalar multiplication does not give a sensible answer.

Research

For Ex. 19, students could research how a matrix and spreadsheet are similar. Ask students to explain how they would use either one to keep a cumulative record of Bill Chee's sales for an entire year.

Reasoning

In Ex. 20, students see that the addition of matrices is commutative but subtraction is not. Students should be able to reason that this is a consequence of (1) how these operations are defined for matrices and (2) the properties of real numbers.

Using Technology

Students can use the *Matrix Analyzer* software to do Exs. 11, 12, 14–17, and 19–21.

b. $B - D = \begin{bmatrix} -42 & 0 & 5 \\ -75 & -6 & 1 \end{bmatrix}$;
$D - B = \begin{bmatrix} 42 & 0 & -5 \\ 75 & 6 & -1 \end{bmatrix}$;
Yes, order matters. $D - B = -(B - D)$. Subtraction is not commutative.

21. a. $\begin{bmatrix} 21 & 4 \\ 22 & 3 \\ 22 & 3 \end{bmatrix}$; $\begin{bmatrix} 16 & 9 \\ 15 & 10 \\ 13 & 12 \end{bmatrix}$

b. $\begin{bmatrix} 37 & 13 \\ 37 & 13 \\ 35 & 15 \end{bmatrix}$

c. the total wins and total losses for the season for each team (home and away games)

d. $\begin{bmatrix} 5 & -5 \\ 7 & -7 \\ 9 & -9 \end{bmatrix}$

e. how many more games they won or lost at home than they did away (home court advantage)

For Exercises 22 and 23, use these matrices.

Women in the Labor Force (millions)					
All Women			**Women with Children**		
	married	other*		married	other*
1996	33.4	27.8	1996	17.8	6.9
1997	33.9	29.0	1997	18.2	7.5
1998	34.1	29.8	1998	18.1	7.5

* widowed, divorced, separated, or single

22. **Writing** Does adding the matrices give a meaningful result in this situation? Why or why not?

23. **Writing** Does subtracting the matrices give a meaningful result in this situation? Why or why not?

Ongoing **ASSESSMENT**

24. **Open-ended** Write a five-question quiz on this section. Include questions using scalar multiplication and addition or subtraction of matrices.

Review **PREVIEW**

Solve each system of equations. If there is no solution, write *no solution*. *(Section 3-4)*

25. $-4w + 6v = -1$
$4w - 9v = 13$

26. $2c + d = 15$
$4c + 2d = 39$

27. $8a - b = -3$
$7a + b = -2$

28. $3x - 5y = 22$
$5x - 4y = 28$

Simplify. Write answers with positive exponents. *(Section 2-6)*

29. $3^{-2}c^{-5}d^4$

30. $\dfrac{8^0 m^3}{n^{-4}}$

31. $(6a^{-3})(-3b^2)$

32. $\dfrac{27x^{-3}y^0}{3}$

Tell whether each diagram shows a *dilation*, a *rotation*, a *reflection*, or a *translation*. *(Toolbox Skills 33, 34, 35, 36)*

33.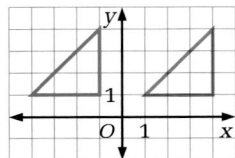

34.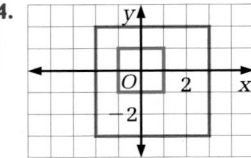

3 Working on the Unit Project

35. For one day's breakfast, lunch, and dinner, record the number of servings you eat from each of these food groups: grains, vegetables, fruits, milk products, and other protein foods (meats, beans, etc.). Organize the information in a 5 × 3 matrix. (See page 120 for suggested serving sizes.)

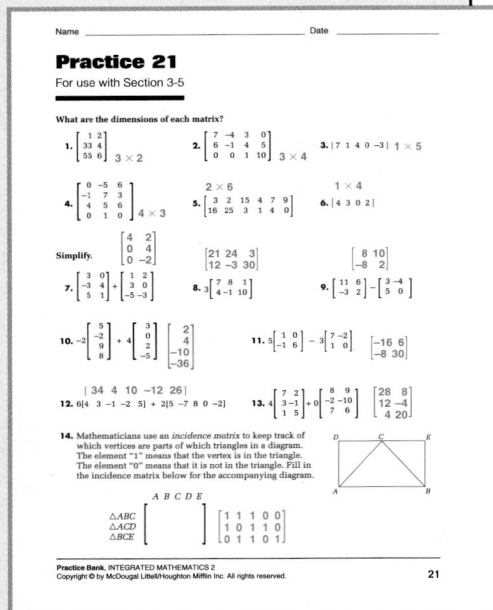

Practice 21 For use with Section 3-5

Practice 21
For use with Section 3-5

Answers to Exercises and Problems

22. No, adding the matrices would not be meaningful because some women would be counted twice. Women with children are already included in the first matrix.

23. Yes, subtracting the matrices will give the number of women in the work force for 1996, 1997, and 1998 without children. Since the women represented in the second matrix are also in the first, it makes sense to subtract the second matrix from the first.

24. Quizzes may vary.

25. $\left(-4, -\dfrac{23}{4}\right)$

26. no solution

27. $\left(-\dfrac{1}{3}, \dfrac{1}{3}\right)$

28. $(4, -2)$

29. $\dfrac{d^4}{9c^5}$

30. $m^3 n^4$

31. $\dfrac{-18b^2}{a^3}$

32. $\dfrac{9}{x^3}$

33. translation

34. dilation

35. Answers may vary. The result will be a 5 × 3 matrix. Columns will be breakfast, lunch, and dinner. Rows will be grains, vegetables, fruits, milk products, and other. Each element will record the number of servings eaten for that meal from that group.

16. Codes Use the coded message, the coding matrix, and the other matrices that you wrote for Exercise 15 on page 172.

Decoding your message involves using the inverse of your 3×3 coding matrix.

  a. TECHNOLOGY Use a graphics calculator to find the inverse of your coding matrix. (See Exercise 15 on page 178.)

  b. **Group Activity** Trade your coded message and the inverse matrix you found in part (a) with another student. Write the coded message you receive as three 3×1 matrices. Multiply each of the three 3×1 matrices by the inverse matrix you receive.

  c. Rewrite the product matrices in part (b) using letters. Use A for 1, B for 2, and so on. Compare the decoded message with your partner's original message.

BY THE WAY...

Jim Sanborn is a sculptor whose artwork carries encoded messages. In *The Code Room*, the message is encoded and written in the Cyrillic alphabet. The word *Medusa* is a key to unraveling part of the code.

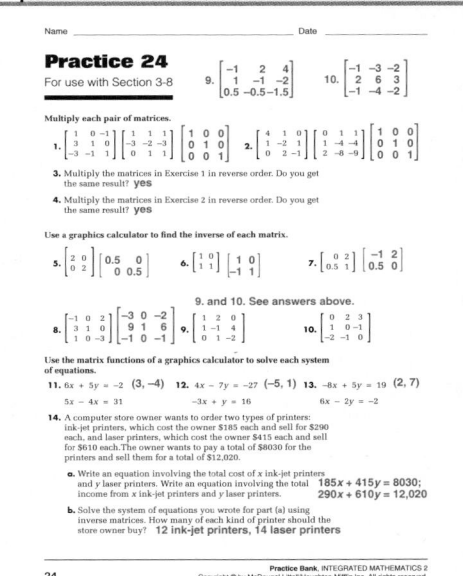

Ongoing **ASSESSMENT**

17. Group Activity Work in a group of four students.

  a. Each of you should solve this linear system using a different method: *graphing, substitution, addition-or-subtraction,* or *inverse matrices.* Compare your solutions and correct any mistakes.

$$2x + 5y = -1$$
$$x + 3y = -1$$

  b. Decide with your group which method you think is easiest to use for this system.

Review **PREVIEW**

Multiply each pair of matrices. *(Section 3-7)*

18. $\begin{bmatrix} 1 & -2 \\ 7 & -1 \end{bmatrix}\begin{bmatrix} 25 \\ 7 \end{bmatrix}$ **19.** $\begin{bmatrix} 2 & 15 & 1 \end{bmatrix}\begin{bmatrix} 9 & 14 \\ 3 & -8 \\ 0 & 4 \end{bmatrix}$ **20.** $\begin{bmatrix} 0 \\ 11 \end{bmatrix}\begin{bmatrix} -5 & 3 \end{bmatrix}$

21. Use deductive reasoning to reach a conclusion. *(Section 1-6)*

If you are in Port Moresby, then you are in Papua New Guinea.
If you are in Papua New Guinea, then you are south of the equator.

Evaluate $x^2 + 3x + 14$ for each value of x. *(Toolbox Skill 9)*

22. $x = 4$ **23.** $x = -3$ **24.** $x = 0$ **25.** $x = \frac{2}{3}$

Working on the Unit Project

26. Describe one way that you will use a linear system and one way that you will use matrices in revising and presenting your menus.

3-8 Using Technology and Matrices with Systems

179

Working on the Unit Project

Each group should discuss Ex. 26 before writing out a description that they can use when completing the Unit Project.

Quick Quiz (3-5 through 3-8)

See page 181.

Practice 24 For use with Section 3-8

Name _____ Date _____

Practice 24
For use with Section 3-8

9. $\begin{bmatrix} -1 & 2 & 4 \\ 1 & -1 & -2 \\ 0.5 & -0.5 & -1.5 \end{bmatrix}$ 10. $\begin{bmatrix} -1 & -3 & -2 \\ 2 & 6 & 3 \\ -1 & -4 & -2 \end{bmatrix}$

Multiply each pair of matrices.

1. $\begin{bmatrix} 1 & 0 & -1 \\ 3 & 1 & 0 \\ -3 & -1 & 1 \end{bmatrix}\begin{bmatrix} 1 & 1 & 1 \\ -3 & -2 & -3 \\ 0 & 1 & 1 \end{bmatrix}\begin{bmatrix} 1 & 0 & 0 \\ 0 & 1 & 0 \\ 0 & 0 & 1 \end{bmatrix}$ 2. $\begin{bmatrix} 4 & 1 & 0 \\ 1 & -2 & 1 \\ 2 & 3 & -1 \end{bmatrix}\begin{bmatrix} 0 & 1 & 1 \\ 1 & -4 & -4 \\ 2 & 8 & -9 \end{bmatrix}\begin{bmatrix} 1 & 0 & 0 \\ 0 & 1 & 0 \\ 0 & 0 & 1 \end{bmatrix}$

3. Multiply the matrices in Exercise 1 in reverse order. Do you get the same result? **yes**

4. Multiply the matrices in Exercise 2 in reverse order. Do you get the same result? **yes**

Use a graphics calculator to find the inverse of each matrix.

5. $\begin{bmatrix} 2 & 0 \\ 0 & 2 \end{bmatrix}\begin{bmatrix} 0.5 & 0 \\ 0 & 0.5 \end{bmatrix}$ 6. $\begin{bmatrix} 1 & 0 \\ 1 & 1 \end{bmatrix}\begin{bmatrix} 1 & 0 \\ -1 & 1 \end{bmatrix}$ 7. $\begin{bmatrix} 0 & 2 \\ 0.5 & 1 \end{bmatrix}\begin{bmatrix} -1 & 2 \\ 0.5 & 0 \end{bmatrix}$

9. and 10. See answers above.

8. $\begin{bmatrix} -1 & 0 & 2 \\ 3 & 1 & 0 \\ 1 & 0 & -3 \end{bmatrix}\begin{bmatrix} -3 & 0 & -2 \\ 9 & 1 & 6 \\ -1 & 0 & -1 \end{bmatrix}$ 9. $\begin{bmatrix} -1 & 0 & -2 \\ 1 & -1 & 4 \\ 0 & 1 & -2 \end{bmatrix}$ 10. $\begin{bmatrix} 0 & 2 & 3 \\ 1 & 0 & -1 \\ -2 & -1 & 0 \end{bmatrix}$

Use the matrix functions of a graphics calculator to solve each system of equations.

11. $6x + 5y = -2$ (3, −4) 12. $4x - 7y = -27$ (−5, 1) 13. $-8x + 5y = 19$ (2, 7)
$\quad 5x - 4x = 31$ $\quad -3x + y = 16$ $\quad 6x - 2y = -2$

14. A computer store owner wants to order two types of printers: ink-jet printers, which cost the owner $185 each and sell for $290 each, and laser printers, which cost the owner $415 each and sell for $610 each. The owner wants to pay a total of $8030 for the printers and sell them for a total of $12,020.

  a. Write an equation involving the total cost of x ink-jet printers and y laser printers. Write an equation involving the total income from x ink-jet printers and y laser printers. $185x + 415y = 8030;$ $290x + 610y = 12,020$

  b. Solve the system of equations you wrote for part (a) using inverse matrices. How many of each kind of printer should the store owner buy? **12 ink-jet printers, 14 laser printers**

24   **Practice Bank,** INTEGRATED MATHEMATICS 2
Copyright © by McDougal Littell/Houghton Mifflin Inc. All rights reserved.

Answers to Exercises and Problems

b. $\begin{bmatrix} 40 \\ 26 \\ 12 \end{bmatrix}\begin{bmatrix} 63 \\ 28 \\ 71 \end{bmatrix}\begin{bmatrix} 93 \\ 50 \\ 61 \end{bmatrix}$;

$A^{-1}\begin{bmatrix} 40 \\ 26 \\ 12 \end{bmatrix} = \begin{bmatrix} 9 \\ 1 \\ 13 \end{bmatrix}$;

$A^{-1}\begin{bmatrix} 63 \\ 28 \\ 71 \end{bmatrix} = \begin{bmatrix} 8 \\ 21 \\ 14 \end{bmatrix}$;

$A^{-1}\begin{bmatrix} 93 \\ 50 \\ 61 \end{bmatrix} = \begin{bmatrix} 7 \\ 18 \\ 25 \end{bmatrix}$

c. I AM HUNGRY; it works!

17. a. $(2, -1)$

  b. Answers may vary.

18. $\begin{bmatrix} 11 \\ 168 \end{bmatrix}$

19. $\begin{bmatrix} 63 & -88 \end{bmatrix}$

20. $\begin{bmatrix} 0 & 0 \\ -55 & 33 \end{bmatrix}$

21. If you are in Port Moresby, then you are south of the equator.

22. 42

23. 14

24. 14

25. $16\frac{4}{9}$

26. Descriptions may vary.

179

Completing the Unit Project

Now you are ready to complete your menus. Your finished project should include these things:

➤ three different daily menus for people with different body weights and activity levels

➤ a description of how each menu was developed and refined. You should also show how you used linear systems to analyze the menus.

➤ an analysis of the nutritional content of each menu and an explanation of how each fulfills the requirements of the Food Guide Pyramid and other nutritional guidelines explored in the "Working on the Unit Project" exercises throughout this unit

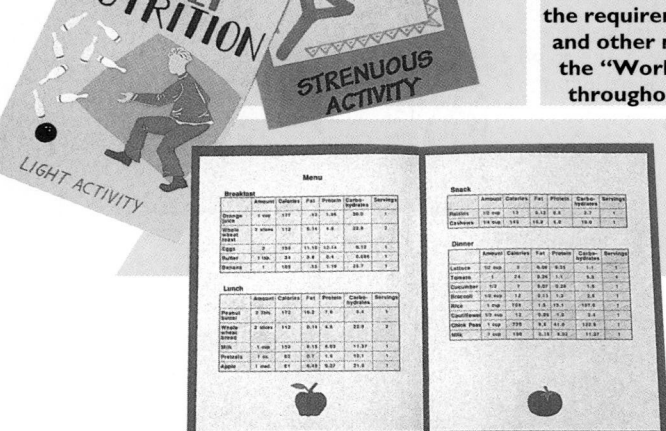

Look Back

How has learning about nutrition and exercise changed your ideas about what you should eat and how much you should exercise?

Alternative Projects

Project 1: Using Matrices for Secret Codes

Prepare a classroom display on secret codes. Do some library research to learn about the history of secret codes and about the contributions of mathematician Lester S. Hill, who was one of the first people to apply matrices to this field.

Also include in your display an example of the use of 2 × 2 matrices to code/decode a secret message using the methods introduced in Exercise 15 on page 172 and Exercise 16 on page 179 for 3 × 1 matrices. (Be sure to check that your coding matrix has an inverse.)

Project 2: Create a Daily Menu for a Person with Special Nutritional Needs

Research the special nutritional needs of a young child, a senior citizen, or a person on a restricted diet due to a health problem such as heart disease or diabetes. Carry out the project described on page 119 for someone in this category.

Answers to Unit 3 Review and Assessment ······················

1. **a.** $c = 93 + 42h$
   $c = 225$

b.

c. ABC Auto Repair is cheaper if repairs take 2 hours. Bob's Auto Shop is cheaper if the repairs take 4 hours. The graph shows a "break-even point" at slightly more than three hours.

1. ABC Auto Repair charges $93 for parts and $42 per hour of labor for a repair job. Bob's Auto Shop charges a flat fee of $225 for the same job.   **3-1**

   a. Write a system of equations to represent the situation.

   b. Graph the system of equations in part (a).

   c. Which estimate is cheaper if the job takes two hours? Four hours? Explain how the graph supports your answers.

2. Graph this system of inequalities: $y \le -2x + 1$
   $0.5x - y < 2$

3. **Investment** Lee Wong invested $3000, some in certificates of deposit (CDs) and some in a money market fund. The CDs paid 4% annual interest and the fund paid 2% annual interest. Her total annual income from interest was $101. How much money did she invest in CDs?   **3-2**

For Questions 4 and 5, use equations A–C.   **3-3**

   A. $2y - 8 = 8x$ **B.** $4x - y = 1$ **C.** $2y = 8x - 2$

4. Without graphing, tell which pair(s) of equations will make a system of equations with many solutions. Explain how you know.

5. Without graphing, tell which pair(s) of equations will make an inconsistent system of equations. Explain how you know.

6. Write an equation of the line that goes through the point (1, 8) and is perpendicular to the line $y = \frac{1}{3}x + 2$.

Solve each linear system. Use a different method for each system.   **3-4**

7. $y = 2x - 3$ 8. $3x + 2y = 7$ 9. $y = 13$
   $2y - 4x = -6$ $-4x - y = -11$ $8x - 3 = y$

10. **Open-ended** Write a 3 × 5 matrix that represents the amount that three students paid for their lunches each day one week.   **3-5**

11. Betty's Boutique is having a 20% off sale.

   a. Use scalar multiplication to write a matrix representing 20% of the pre-sale prices. Then use matrix subtraction to find the sale prices.

   b. Multiply the pre-sale prices matrix by 0.8. Compare your answer to your answer in part (a).

Pre-Sale Price ($)

	Juniors	Misses	Tall
turtlenecks	12	15	20
sweaters	35	40	50
jeans	40	40	50

Find the coordinates of the vertices of △*ABC* after each transformation. Write each answer as a matrix.   **3-6**

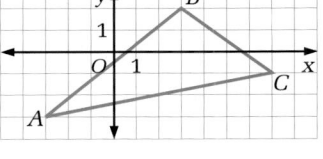

12. a dilation with scale factor $\frac{1}{3}$ and center at the origin

13. a translation 1 unit left and 2 units down

14. Find the product of these two matrices: $A = \begin{bmatrix} 6 & 1 \\ -1 & 5 \end{bmatrix}$ $B = \begin{bmatrix} 10 & -2 \\ 0 & 2 \\ -1 & 5 \end{bmatrix}$ **3-7**

Quick Quiz (3-5 through 3-8)

1. What are the dimensions of this matrix? [3-5]
   $$\begin{bmatrix} 2 & 7 & 6 & 1 & 5 \\ 3 & 9 & 0 & 8 & 4 \end{bmatrix}$$
   2 × 5

2. Simplify. [3-5]
   $$\begin{bmatrix} 0 & -1 \\ -1 & 2 \end{bmatrix} + \begin{bmatrix} 5 & -6 \\ -3 & 7 \end{bmatrix}$$
   $$\begin{bmatrix} 5 & -7 \\ -4 & 9 \end{bmatrix}$$

3. Describe the transformation represented by each matrix. [3-6]

   a. $\frac{3}{4}\begin{bmatrix} x \\ y \end{bmatrix}$ dilation

   b. $\begin{bmatrix} x \\ y \end{bmatrix} + \begin{bmatrix} 6 \\ -6 \end{bmatrix}$ translation

4. Multiply. [3-7]
   $$\begin{bmatrix} 2 & -1 \\ -2 & 2 \end{bmatrix}\begin{bmatrix} 4 & 0 & -3 \\ 5 & -2 & -6 \end{bmatrix}$$
   $$\begin{bmatrix} 3 & 2 & 0 \\ 2 & -4 & -6 \end{bmatrix}$$

5. Write the system as a matrix equation. [3-8]
   $4x + 3y = -9$
   $-5x + 7y = 11$
   $$\begin{bmatrix} 4 & 3 \\ -5 & 7 \end{bmatrix}\begin{bmatrix} x \\ y \end{bmatrix} = \begin{bmatrix} -9 \\ 11 \end{bmatrix}$$

Answers to Unit 3 Review and Assessment

2.
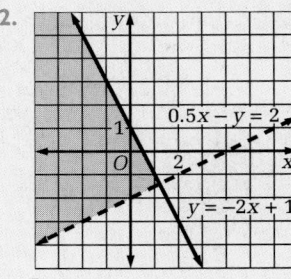

3. $2050

4. B and C because they are the same line (C is just twice B)

5. A and C or A and B will be inconsistent. A and C both have $8x - 2y$ in common but different constants c when written in the form $ax + by = c$. So A and C are parallel lines and the system is inconsistent. If you multiply equation B by two, you obtain an equivalent equation to that of C, so A and B are also inconsistent.

6. $y = -3x + 11$

7. infinitely many solutions

8. $(3, -1)$ 9. $(2, 13)$

10. Answers may vary. An example is given.
   $$\begin{bmatrix} 1.75 & 1.25 & 2.00 & 1.50 & 1.50 \\ 0 & 2.00 & 1.50 & 0 & 0 \\ 1.25 & 2.00 & 1.50 & 1.50 & 1.50 \end{bmatrix}$$

11. See answers in back of book.

12. $\begin{bmatrix} -1 & 1 & \frac{7}{3} \\ -1 & \frac{2}{3} & -\frac{1}{3} \end{bmatrix}$

13. $\begin{bmatrix} -4 & 2 & 6 \\ -5 & 0 & -3 \end{bmatrix}$

14. $BA = \begin{bmatrix} 62 & 0 \\ -2 & 10 \\ -11 & 24 \end{bmatrix}$

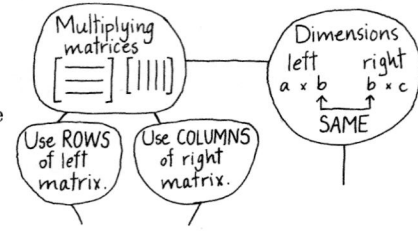

15. **Writing** Jennifer started this concept map for matrix multiplication. Complete her map or create a new one. Describe the ideas your map shows.

16 TECHNOLOGY Use the matrix functions of a graphics calculator to solve this linear system.

$$-x - y = -5$$
$$2x - 15y = 3$$

3-8

17. **Self-evaluation** What method (*graphing*, *substitution*, or *addition-or-subtraction*) would you prefer to use to solve this linear system? Why? Describe the difficulties you find with the methods you do not prefer.

$$y = 10x + 5$$
$$y = -2x - 3$$

18. **Group Activity** Work with another student.

a. Choose a point P. One student should write the equation of the line that goes through P and is parallel to $y = 2x$. The other student should write the equation of the line that goes through P and is perpendicular to $y = 2x$.

b. Write an equation of a line that intersects both lines from part (a) and does not go through P.

c. Graph the three equations that you wrote in parts (a) and (b). What are the coordinates of the vertices of the triangle formed by the lines? Write the answer as a matrix.

d. Each of you should write a transformation in matrix form. Use each other's matrix to transform the triangle in part (c). What are the new coordinates of the vertices?

IDEAS AND (FORMULAS)

ALGEBRA

➤ To solve a linear system by graphing, estimate the intersection point of the graphs of the equations. *(p. 122)*

➤ You can use the graphs of the equations of a linear system to compare the quantities represented by the equations. *(p. 123)*

➤ To solve a system of equations by substitution, solve one equation for one variable. Replace that variable in the other equation with the resulting expression. *(p. 130)*

➤ The graphs of the equations of a linear system can be intersecting lines, the same line, or parallel lines. You can use the relationship of the graphs to tell how many solutions the system has, and whether the system is consistent. *(p. 136)*

➤ You can use the slope-intercept form of the equations of a linear system to recognize several characteristics of the system without graphing the lines or solving the system. *(p. 136)*

➤ When the slope of a line is m, the slope of a parallel line is m and the slope of a perpendicular line is $-\frac{1}{m}$. *(p. 138)*

Answers to Unit 3
Review and Assessment

15.

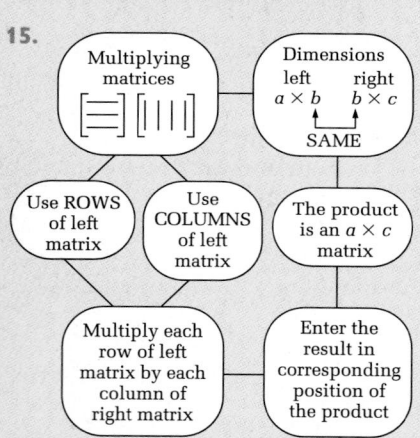

The map shows how to set up two matrices in order to multiply them. It also shows how to do the multiplication and the dimensions of the product.

16. about (4.59, 0.412)

17. Answers may vary. An example is given. Substitution would be the easiest since both equations are already in terms of y. It might be difficult to get exact answers by graphing since x and y are not whole numbers.

18. a. Choices of point may vary. An example is given. Point $P(2, 1)$; $y = 2x - 3$ for the parallel line; $y = -\frac{1}{2}x + 2$ for the perpendicular line

b. Equations may vary. An example is given.
$$y = \frac{1}{3}x + 2$$

$$\begin{bmatrix} 2 & 3 & 0 \\ 1 & 3 & 2 \end{bmatrix}$$

c.

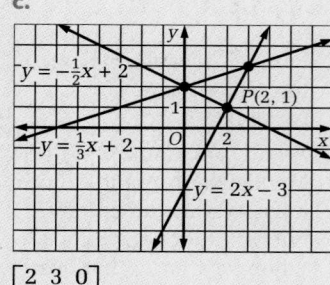

d. Transformations may vary. An example is given. 1 unit right, 3 units up:

$$\begin{bmatrix} 2 & 3 & 0 \\ 1 & 3 & 2 \end{bmatrix} + \begin{bmatrix} 1 & 1 & 1 \\ 3 & 3 & 3 \end{bmatrix} = \begin{bmatrix} 3 & 4 & 1 \\ 4 & 6 & 5 \end{bmatrix}$$

182

➤ To solve a linear system by addition-or-subtraction, combine the like terms of the equations to make a new equation with just one variable. You may need to multiply both sides of one or both equations by a constant. *(pp. 143–145)*

➤ You can use matrices to organize data that belong to more than one category. *(p. 151)*

➤ Scalar multiplication involves multiplying each element of a matrix by the same number. *(pp. 152–153, 155)*

➤ You add or subtract two matrices with the same dimensions by adding or subtracting the elements in corresponding positions. *(pp. 154–155)*

➤ To multiply a row of matrix L by a column of matrix R, add the products of the corresponding elements of the row and the column. *(pp. 165–166)*

➤ To find the matrix product LR, multiply each row of L by each column of R. Enter the result in the corresponding row-column position of the product matrix. *(pp. 166–168)*

➤ The matrix product LR is defined only if the number of columns of L equals the number of rows of R. *(pp. 168, 170)*

➤ The matrix product LR has the same number of rows as L and the same number of columns as R. *(pp. 168, 170)*

➤ Generally, matrix multiplication is not commutative. *(p. 170)*

➤ You can use a matrix equation to represent a linear system.

The solution of the equation $A\begin{bmatrix} x \\ y \end{bmatrix} = B$ is $A^{-1}B$. *(pp. 175–176)*

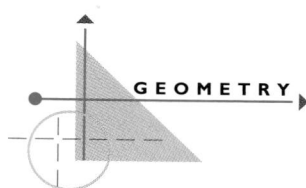

GEOMETRY ➤ You can use scalar multiplication to represent a dilation with center at the origin. *(pp. 159–160)*

➤ You can represent a translation with matrix addition. *(p. 161)*

.... **Key Terms**

- **system of equations** (p. 121)
- **horizontal intercept** (p. 122)
- **consistent system** (p. 136)
- **element of a matrix** (p. 151)
- **transformation** (p. 159)
- **center of dilation** (p. 159)
- **inverse matrices** (p. 174)

- **linear system** (p. 121)
- **system of inequalities** (p. 124)
- **inconsistent system** (p. 136)
- **dimensions of a matrix** (p. 151)
- **dilation** (p. 159)
- **scale factor** (p. 159)
- **A^{-1}** (p. 174)

- **solution of a system of equations** (p. 122)
- **solution region** (p. 124)
- **matrix** (p. 151)
- **scalar multiplication** (p. 155)
- **image** (p. 159)
- **translation** (p. 161)
- **matrix equation** (p. 175)

183

Quick Quiz (3-1 through 3-4)

1. Solve this system of equations by graphing. [3-1]

$x + y = 6$
$x - y = 0$

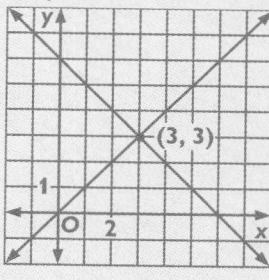

The solution is (3, 3).

2. Solve this system of equations by substitution. [3-2]

$y = -3x$
$y = 2x - 10$

The solution is (2, –6).

3. Identify the system as *consistent* or *inconsistent*. [3-3]

$y = \frac{2}{3}x + 3$

$y = \frac{3}{2}x - 3$

The system is consistent.

4. Solve this system by using addition-or-subtraction. [3-4]

$2x - 3y = 9$
$4x + 3y = 15$

The solution is $\left(4, -\frac{1}{3}\right)$.

OVERVIEW

➤ **Unit 4** discusses quadratic functions and equations, including graphing and translating graphs of quadratic functions. Quadratic equations are solved by taking the square root of both sides of the equation, by factoring, and by using the quadratic formula. Students examine the discriminant of the quadratic formula to determine the nature of the roots, which leads to a discussion of complex numbers and operations on them. Quadratic systems of equations are introduced.

➤ The theme of the Unit Project is designing a water fountain. Students study a variety of situations in which water is sprayed into an arc. The path of the water is modeled by an equation, and students take measurements to write equations from their own experiments.

➤ Connections to oceanography, games, wave lengths, cliff diving, fire fighting, acrobatics, basketball, baseball, and water slides are integrated into the teaching materials and exercises.

➤ Graphics calculators are used in Sections 4-1 and 4-6 to graph quadratic functions, in Section 4-2 to explore translations of parabolas, in Sections 4-3 and 4-4 to solve quadratic equations, and in Section 4-7 to solve quadratic systems. Computer software, such as Plotter Plus, can be used in Sections 4-1 and 4-2 to explore the properties of parabolas.

➤ Problem-solving strategies used in Unit 4 include using formulas, graphs, transformations, patterns, technology, manipulatives, and mathematical models.

Unit Objectives

Section	Objectives	NCTM Standards
4-1	• Understand how the coefficients of a quadratic function influence its graph: the direction it opens, its vertex, its line of symmetry, and its y-intercept.	1, 2, 3, 4, 5, 6, 8
4-2	• Explore translations of parabolas.	1, 2, 3, 4, 5, 6, 8
4-3	• Solve simple quadratic equations by graphing and undoing.	1, 2, 4, 5, 6, 8
4-4	• Solve quadratic equations by factoring.	1, 2, 5
4-5	• Use the quadratic formula to solve quadratic equations.	1, 2, 5
4-6	• Use the discriminant to find the number of real solutions of a quadratic equation.	1, 2, 3, 4, 5
	• Add, subtract, and multiply complex numbers.	
4-7	• Solve problems involving quadratic systems.	1, 2, 4, 5, 8

Skills Bank To extend the curriculum and provide practice with skills, you may wish to assign the following topics from the **Skills Bank** ancillary: completing the square (for use after Section 4-4) and division of complex numbers (for use after Section 4-6).

Section	Connections to Prior and Future Concepts
4-1	**Section 4-1** presents quadratic functions and their graphs. The coefficients of a quadratic function are examined to determine the characteristics of the related parabola. Parabolas were explored in Unit 10 of Book 1, and are used in Units 2, 4, and 9 of Book 2, and in Unit 2 of Book 3.
4-2	**Section 4-2** explores translations of a parabola. This topic was first introduced in Section 10-2 of Book 1. Standard form, from Section 10-7 of Book 1, is reviewed as a means of finding the coordinates of the vertex of a parabola. This skill is important in Unit 2 of Book 3 for solving optimization problems.
4-3	**Section 4-3** introduces solving a quadratic equation by taking the square root of both sides of the equation. Students can find extra practice on taking square roots in the Toolbox.
4-4	**Section 4-4** uses algebra tiles to illustrate factoring. Special quadratics, whose factors follow specific patterns, are introduced. Factors for quadratic expressions were explored in Unit 10 of Book 1 and will be used again in Unit 2 of Book 3. Factoring quadratic expressions leads to solving quadratic equations by factoring.
4-5	**Section 4-5** reviews the quadratic formula, first developed in Section 10-8 of Book 1. This skill is used in Unit 9 of Book 2 and Unit 2 of Book 3. Solving a quadratic equation by completing the square, an extension of Section 4-3 of Book 2, is found in the exercise set.
4-6	**Section 4-6** uses the discriminant of the quadratic formula to determine the number and nature of the solutions of a quadratic equation. This discussion leads to the development of the set of complex numbers. Students are introduced to operations on the complex numbers.
4-7	**Section 4-7** introduces solving a system of quadratic equations. Students find the point(s) of intersection of two parabolas by graphical and algebraic methods. The algebraic method is the substitution method, which is used in all three books for solving systems of linear equations.

Integrating the Strands

Strands	Sections
Number	4-5
Algebra	4-1, 4-2, 4-3, 4-4, 4-5, 4-6, 4-7
Functions	4-1, 4-2, 4-3, 4-4, 4-5, 4-6, 4-7
Geometry	4-2, 4-5, 4-7
Statistics and Probability	4-6
Discrete Mathematics	4-5
Logic and Language	4-1, 4-2, 4-3, 4-4, 4-5, 4-6, 4-7

Korrie
11).

Section Planning Guide

➤ Essential exercises and ...
➤ Ongoing work on the U...
➤ Exercises and problems ... up work, manipulatives, or graphing technology ar... "Other."

Section	Materials	Pacing	Standard Assignment	Extended Assignment	Other
4-1	graphing technology	Day 1	2, 3, **4–17**	1–3, **4–17**, 18–20	
		Day 2	**21–28**, 29–36, 37–40	**21–28**, 29–36, 37–40	38, 40
4-2	graphics calculator, tracing paper, tape measure, water hose	Day 1	**1–9**	**1–9**, 10	11
		Day 2	**13–18**, 21–28, 29	12, **13–18**, 19–28, 29	29
4-3	graphics calculator	Day 1	**2–24**, 25, 26, 31–38, 39	1, **2–24**, 25–38, 39	
4-4	algebra tiles, graphics calculator	Day 1	**4–15**, 18	1–3, **4–15**, 16, 18	17
		Day 2	**20–35**, 36, 38–44, 45	19, **20–35**, 36, 38–44, 45	37
4-5	graphics calculator	Day 1	**5–14**, **17–19**	1, 2, 4, **5–14**, 15, **17–19**	3, 16
		Day 2	**24–35**, 39, 44–51, 52	20–23, **24–35**, 36–51, 52	52
4-6	graphics calculator	Day 1	**3–15**	1, 2, **3–15**, 16–18	
		Day 2	**20–43**, 46–52, 53	19, **20–43**, 44, 46–52, 53	45
4-7	graphics calculator	Day 1	**2–18**, 22–29, 30	1, **2–18**, 19–29, 30	
Review		**Day 1**	Unit Review	Unit Review	
Test		**Day 2**	Unit Test	Unit Test	

Yearly Pacing	Unit 4 Total	Units 1–4 Total	Remaining	Total
	16 days (2 for Unit Project)	65 days	95 days	160 days

Support Materials

➤ See **Project Book** for notes on Unit 4 Project: Design a Fountain.
➤ "UPP" and "disk" refer to **Using Plotter Plus** booklet and **Plotter Plus** disk.
➤ "TI-81/82" refers to **Using TI-81 and TI-82 Calculators** booklet.
➤ Warm-up exercises for each section are available on **Warm-Up Transparencies.**
➤ "FI," "PC," "GI," "MA," and "Stats!" refer, respectively, to the McDougal Littell Mathpack software Activity Books for **Function Investigator, Probability Constructor, Geometry Inventor, Matrix Analyzer,** and **Stats!.**

Section	Study Guide	Practice Bank	Problem Bank	Activity Bank	Explorations Lab Manual	Assessment Book	Visuals	Technology
4-1	4-1	Practice 26	Set 7	Enrich 23		Quiz 4-1		TI-81/82, p. 40 Parabola Plotter (disk)
4-2	4-2	Practice 27	Set 7	Enrich 24	Master 2	Quiz 4-2		FI Acts. 12–15 Parabola Quiz (disk)
4-3	4-3	Practice 28	Set 7	Enrich 25		Quiz 4-3		
4-4	4-4	Practice 29	Set 7	Enrich 26	Masters 2–4	Quiz 4-4 Test 13	Folder 4	FI Act. 16
4-5	4-5	Practice 30	Set 8	Enrich 27		Quiz 4-5		TI-81/82, p. 41
4-6	4-6	Practice 31	Set 8	Enrich 28	Add. Expl. 6	Quiz 4-6		TI-81/82, p. 41
4-7	4-7	Practice 32	Set 8	Enrich 29		Quiz 4-7 Test 14		TI-81/82, p. 42 UPP, p. 43
Unit 4	Unit Review	Practice 33	Unifying Problem 4	Family Involve 4		Tests 15, 16		

UNIT TESTS

Spanish versions of these tests are on pages 130–133 of the **Assessment Book.**

Form A

Name _____ Date _____ Score _____

Test 15
Test on Unit 4 (Form A)

Directions: Write the answers in the spaces provided.

1. Open-ended Write a function whose graph is a translation of the graph of the function $y = x^2$ in two directions. Describe the translation.

Sample answer: $y = (x - 3)^2 + 2$; The graph of $y = (x - 3)^2 + 2$ is a translation of the graph of $y = x^2$ 3 units right and 2 units up.

For Questions 2 and 3, find the vertex and the y-intercept of the graph of each function.

2. $y = -4x^2 - 3$ **3.** $y = 2(x - 4)^2 + 5$

Solve.

4. $3x^2 - 6 = 6$ **5.** $3(x - 1)^2 + 24 = 72$
6. $5(x + 2)^2 - 16 = 64$ **7.** $3x^2 - 4x - 4 = 0$

Factor.

8. $x^2 - 3x + 2$ **9.** $4x^2 - 9$ **10.** $6x^2 + 7x - 3$

Solve using the quadratic formula. Round answers to the nearest hundredth.

11. $x^2 + 3x = 9$ **12.** $-3x^2 = 2x - 4$
13. $2(x - 1)^2 - 1 = 2$ **14.** $3x^2 - 5x - 7 = 0$

Match each function with its graph.

15. $y = 2(x - 3)^2$
16. $y = -2x^2 - 3$
17. $y = -2(x + 3)^2$
18. $y = 2x^2 + 3$

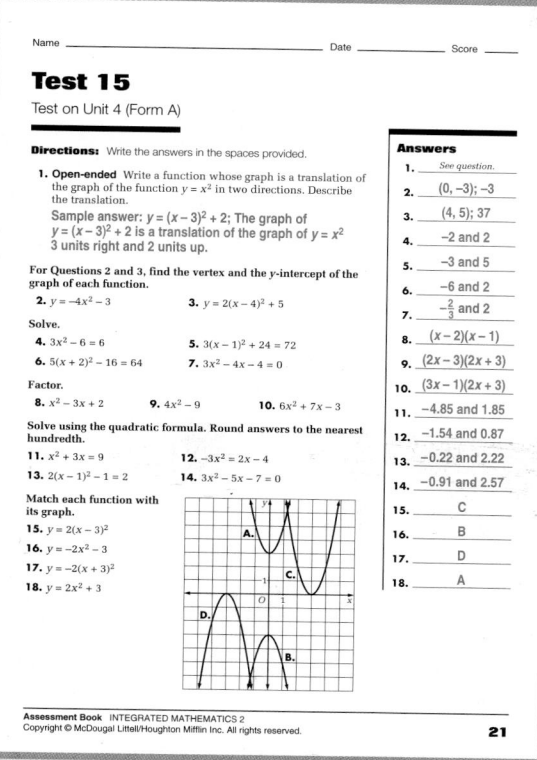

Answers
1. _See question._
2. $(0, -3)$; -3
3. $(4, 5)$; 37
4. -2 and 2
5. -3 and 5
6. -6 and 2
7. $-\frac{2}{3}$ and 2
8. $(x - 2)(x - 1)$
9. $(2x - 3)(2x + 3)$
10. $(3x - 1)(2x + 3)$
11. -4.85 and 1.85
12. -1.54 and 0.87
13. -0.22 and 2.22
14. -0.91 and 2.57
15. C
16. B
17. D
18. A

21

Name _____ Date _____ Score _____

Test 15 (continued)

Directions: Write the answers in the spaces provided.

Solve by graphing the related function.

19. $(x - 2)^2 = 0$ **20.** $-2(x + 1)^2 = -8$

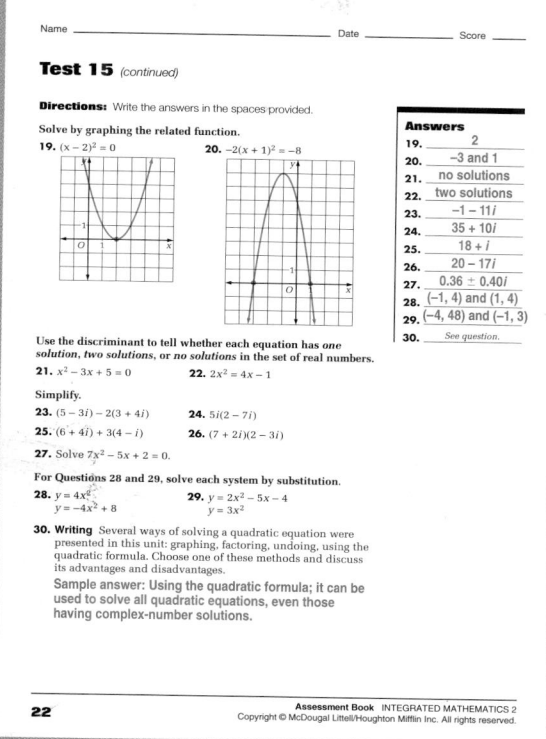

Use the discriminant to tell whether each equation has one solution, two solutions, or no solutions in the set of real numbers.

21. $x^2 - 3x + 5 = 0$ **22.** $2x^2 = 4x - 1$

Simplify.

23. $(5 - 3i) - 2(3 + 4i)$ **24.** $5i(2 - 7i)$
25. $(6 + 4i) + 3(4 - i)$ **26.** $(7 + 2i)(2 - 3i)$
27. Solve $7x^2 - 5x + 2 = 0$.

For Questions 28 and 29, solve each system by substitution.

28. $y = 4x^2$ **29.** $y = 2x^2 - 5x - 4$
$\quad y = -4x^2 + 8$ $\quad y = 3x^2$

30. Writing Several ways of solving a quadratic equation were presented in this unit: graphing, factoring, undoing, using the quadratic formula. Choose one of these methods and discuss its advantages and disadvantages.

Sample answer: Using the quadratic formula; it can be used to solve all quadratic equations, even those having complex-number solutions.

Answers
19. 2
20. -3 and 1
21. no solutions
22. two solutions
23. $-1 - 11i$
24. $35 + 10i$
25. $18 + i$
26. $20 - 17i$
27. $0.36 \pm 0.40i$
28. $(-1, 4)$ and $(1, 4)$
29. $(-4, 48)$ and $(-1, 3)$
30. _See question._

Form B

Name _____ Date _____ Score _____

Test 16
Test on Unit 4 (Form B)

Directions: Write the answers in the spaces provided.

1. Open-ended Write a function whose graph is a translation of the graph of the function $y = x^2$ in two directions. Describe the translation.

Sample answer: $y = (x - 3)^2 + 2$; The graph of $y = (x - 3)^2 + 2$ is a translation of the graph of $y = x^2$ 3 units right and 2 units up.

For Questions 2 and 3, find the vertex and the y-intercept of the graph of each function.

2. $y = 2x^2 + 3$ **3.** $y = -3(x + 2)^2 - 4$

Solve.

4. $-4x^2 + 8 = -56$ **5.** $2(x - 1)^2 + 24 = 32$
6. $3(x + 2)^2 - 16 = 11$ **7.** $3x^2 - 11x - 20 = 0$

Factor.

8. $x^2 + 3x - 10$ **9.** $9x^2 - 16$ **10.** $10x^2 - 13x - 3$

Solve using the quadratic formula. Round answers to the nearest hundredth.

11. $x^2 + 8x = 7$ **12.** $-3x^2 = 2x - 2$
13. $3(x - 1)^2 + 2 = 4$ **14.** $4x^2 - 7x - 3 = 0$

Match each function with its graph.

15. $y = 2(x + 4)^2 - 4$
16. $y = -2x^2 - 4$
17. $y = -2(x - 4)^2$
18. $y = 2x^2 + 4$

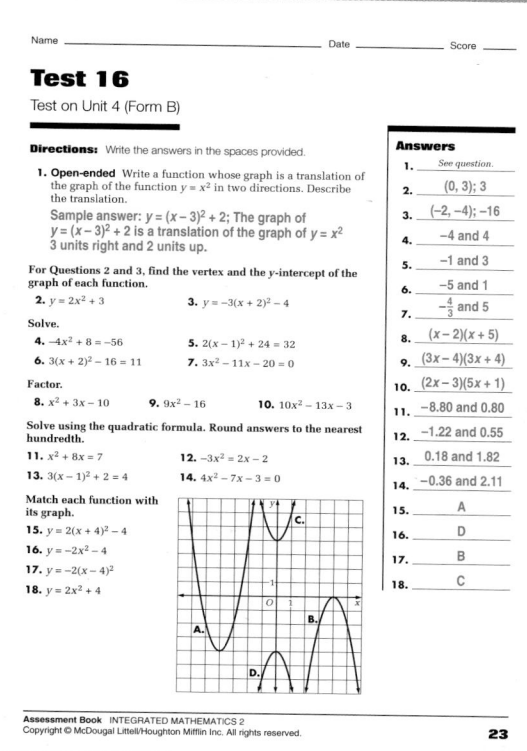

Answers
1. _See question._
2. $(0, 3)$; 3
3. $(-2, -4)$; -16
4. -4 and 4
5. -1 and 3
6. -5 and 1
7. $-\frac{4}{3}$ and 5
8. $(x - 2)(x + 5)$
9. $(3x - 4)(3x + 4)$
10. $(2x - 3)(5x + 1)$
11. -8.80 and 0.80
12. -1.22 and 0.55
13. 0.18 and 1.82
14. -0.36 and 2.11
15. A
16. D
17. B
18. C

23

Name _____ Date _____ Score _____

Test 16 (continued)

Directions: Write the answers in the spaces provided.

Solve by graphing the related function.

19. $(x - 3)^2 = 0$ **20.** $-(x - 4)^2 + 1 = 0$

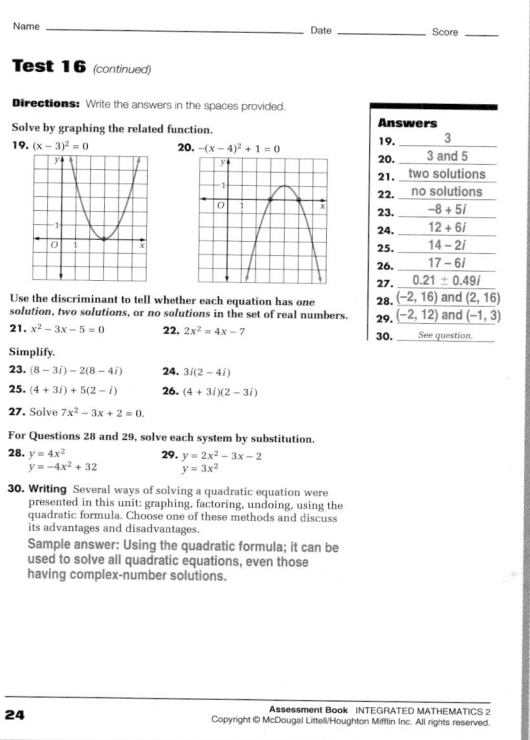

Use the discriminant to tell whether each equation has one solution, two solutions, or no solutions in the set of real numbers.

21. $x^2 - 3x - 5 = 0$ **22.** $2x^2 = 4x - 7$

Simplify.

23. $(8 - 3i) - 2(8 - 4i)$ **24.** $3i(2 - 4i)$
25. $(4 + 3i) + 5(2 - i)$ **26.** $(4 + 3i)(2 - 3i)$
27. Solve $7x^2 - 3x + 2 = 0$.

For Questions 28 and 29, solve each system by substitution.

28. $y = 4x^2$ **29.** $y = 2x^2 - 3x - 2$
$\quad y = -4x^2 + 32$ $\quad y = 3x^2$

30. Writing Several ways of solving a quadratic equation were presented in this unit: graphing, factoring, undoing, using the quadratic formula. Choose one of these methods and discuss its advantages and disadvantages.

Sample answer: Using the quadratic formula; it can be used to solve all quadratic equations, even those having complex-number solutions.

Answers
19. 3
20. 3 and 5
21. two solutions
22. no solutions
23. $-8 + 5i$
24. $12 + 6i$
25. $14 - 2i$
26. $17 - 6i$
27. $0.21 \pm 0.49i$
28. $(-2, 16)$ and $(2, 16)$
29. $(-2, 12)$ and $(-1, 3)$
30. _See question._

Software Support

McDougal Littell Mathpack
Function Investigator

Plotter Plus
Macintosh and MS-DOS
(worksheets included)

Outside Resources

Books/Periodicals

Owens, John F. "Families of Parabolas." *Mathematics Teacher* (September 1992): pp. 477–479.

Activities/Manipulatives

Howden, Hilde. *Algebra Tiles for the Overhead Projector.* Cuisinaire Co, 1985.

Laycock, Mary and Reuben Schadler. *Algebra in the Concrete.* Hayward, CA: Activities Resource Co., 1987.

Software

Goodson, B. *Artillery.* San Mateo, CA: CUF, 1981. (Apple Shareware Game to match project.)

Logal Company. *Physics Explorer Series: One Body.* Pleasantville, NY: Sunburst, 1994. Macintosh and Windows.

Videos

Futures with Jaime Escalante. Program No. 12: Sports Performance. PBS, 1990.

Videodisk: "Projectile Motion." *Science: Forces & Energy;* (Side A). Macmillan/McGraw-Hill, 1993.

➤ Students design a fountain with a least two interesting parabolic water arcs for a park in their community.

➤ Students make a poster to display the fountain design and separate graphs for each of the parabolic water arcs.

➤ Students work in a cooperative group and appreciate each other's contribution.

PROJECT PLANNING

Materials List

➤ Markers
➤ Poster board
➤ Graph paper
➤ Protractor

Project Teams

Have students work on the project in groups of four. One way for the individuals in the group to distribute the work is as follows:

1. Coordinator: collects and summarizes all possible ideas about size, location, and purpose of the fountain from the group.

2. Designer: plans a scale model of the fountain, including the heights and widths of all water arcs, water speed, and measure of the stream angle.

3. Writer: describes the size, location, and purpose of the fountain and explains all of the mathematical equations and measurements used to make the fountain functional.

4. Illustrator: assembles material from the designer and the writer, creates the poster, and includes all measurements and equations.

Have you ever seen water play leapfrog? In a fountain at Epcot Center, the water almost seems to be alive. It jumps and plays like a sprightly puppy.

The effect of air resistance on the flow of water has to be considered by people who design fountains. To produce water arcs of the desired height and width, **fountain designers** must determine how fast the water should flow and at what angle it should come out of the nozzle.

water arcs

STREAM BREAKS UP DUE TO AIR RESISTANCE

At first, a stream of water follows the same type of parabolic path as a ball thrown across a field.

At this point the path of the water changes sharply.

WATER ARC

PARABOLA

ANGLE OF NOZZLE

As a result, a stream of water does not travel as far as a ball that starts out along the same parabolic flight path.

184

Suggested Rubric for Unit Project

4 Students use the equation for the path of a parabolic water arc correctly in designing their water fountain. Their sketch of the fountain is accurate, clear, and includes the heights and widths of all water arcs. The graphs of the water arcs are drawn correctly and the equations of the arcs, stream angles, and water speeds are free of error. The poster is attractively presented and shows a fountain design that is supported by the mathematics of this unit.

3 Students' posters lack some of the details regarding heights and widths of the water arcs, the equations of the arcs, the measures of the stream angles, or the water speeds. The sketch of the fountain is somewhat rough and could be improved. There may be some minor errors in applying the mathematics needed to design the fountain.

Design a Fountain

Your project is to design a fountain for a park in your community. Include at least two intersecting water arcs in your fountain. Each water arc should meet these requirements: ····················▶

STARTING POINT
ground level

HEIGHT
between 30 ft and 60 ft

WATER SPEED
between 6 ft/s and 70 ft/s

ANGLE
between 15° and 75°

For this range of angles, a parabola is a reasonable model for a water arc. To determine the angle and water speed of each parabolic water arc, you will use an equation given in the "Working on the Unit Project" exercises for the unit.

Make a poster to display your fountain design. Include a sketch of your fountain as well as graphs of the paths of the water arcs.

Support Materials
The *Project Book* contains information about the following topics for use with this Unit Project.

➤ Project Description
➤ Teaching Commentary
➤ Working on the Unit Project Exercises
➤ Completing the Unit Project
➤ Assessing the Unit Project
➤ Alternative Projects
➤ Outside Resources

ADDITIONAL BACKGROUND

Multicultural Note

Buenos Aires, the capital of Argentina, is home to more than a third of the country's population. The city has the country's busiest port and is the primary industrial center.

The leaders of Paris have a long tradition of enhancing the beauty of their city. During the Renaissance, French kings hired artisans to construct Greek- and Roman-style palaces, squares, and boulevards. In the 1800s, Napoleon laid out elegant public gardens.

Brisbane, Australia is situated on the Brisbane River, nine miles from the Pacific Ocean. In 1824, Brisbane was established as a penal settlement. Free settlers were not allowed to live there until 1842. The city is known for its varied architectural styles.

Kyoto, Japan is on the island of Honshu. From A.D. 794 to 1868, Kyoto was the capital of Japan. Kyoto is home to many Shinto shrines and Buddhist temples containing exquisite works of art.

Madrid is the capital of Spain. The Muslim emir Muhammad I named the city Magerit and built a fortress where the Royal Palace now stands. Modern Madrid is graced with numerous palaces, fountains, and parks.

FOUNTAINS AROUND THE WORLD

Buenos Aires, Argentina

Brisbane, Australia

Kyoto, Japan

Portland, Oregon

Paris, France

185

Suggested Rubric for Unit Project

2 Students' posters are lacking in many essential details. The sketch of the fountain is careless and demonstrates superficial work. Students do not fully understand how to use the equation for the path of a parabolic water arc to design their fountain.

1 Students' posters show a sketch of a fountain, but most details are missing or are incorrect. The equation of the arcs are incorrect as are other data associated with them. The group should be encouraged to speak with the teacher as soon as possible to review their work and to make a new start on the project.

Hong Kong is situated just off the southern coast of China. In 1898, Hong Kong Island and the adjacent Kowloon Peninsula were leased to Great Britain for 99 years. Hong Kong is a leading center of international commerce and trade.

Heights of Water Arcs

Typical heights of water arcs are anywhere from a few feet to 100 ft. It is possible to have water arcs rising 250–400 ft in the air, but unlikely to find one rising 500 ft or more into the air. The speeds required to push water that far would atomize the water into a mist. This is the physical limitation on fountain size. A mile-high fountain crossing the Mississippi River would not be possible.

ALTERNATIVE PROJECTS

Project 1, page 236

Investigating Water Arcs by Experiments

Use a large coffee can or juice can with holes punched in the side at several different heights to conduct the experiment. Fill the can with water and mark points where the water arcs hit the surface. Describe the experiment, draw a graph of the water arcs, list the coordinates where the arcs intersect, and write equations for the arcs.

Project 2, page 236

Using Straight Lines to Draw a Parabola

Follow a procedure for drawing straight lines in a coordinate system to create a parabola. Analyze the parabola, discuss its line of symmetry, vertex, intercepts, and identify the transformation of $y = x^2$ that would produce its graph. If possible, write the parabola's equation.

Getting Started

For this project you should work in a group of four students. Here are some ideas to help you get started.

☞ In your group, decide where you will locate your fountain. What size would be appropriate for the location? Who will visit your fountain?

☞ An equation for the path of a parabolic water arc is stated and applied in the "Working on the Unit Project" exercises throughout the unit. Plan to meet later to discuss how to use this equation to design your fountain.

Moroccan Embassy, Spain

Hong Kong

Madrid, Spain

FOUNTAIN PLAN
Location:
Size:
Visitors:

Working on the Unit Project

Your work in Unit 4 will help you design your fountain.

Related Exercises:

Section 4-1, Exercises 37–40
Section 4-2, Exercise 29
Section 4-3, Exercise 39
Section 4-4, Exercise 45
Section 4-5, Exercise 52
Section 4-6, Exercise 53
Section 4-7, Exercise 30

Alternative Projects p. 236

Can We Talk

➤ To the ancient Greeks, water was one of the four basic elements along with earth, air, and fire. Today, water is known to be essential for life. How is water used by people and other living things?

➤ Some of the earliest fountains were built around 4000 B.C. in what is now Iran. These fountains may have been used to decorate gardens. What other uses for fountains do you know about?

➤ Where else besides fountains have you seen water arcs? Which of these water arcs are natural and which are made by people?

➤ A rainbow is a different kind of water arc. It is formed when tiny droplets of water in the air act like prisms, separating light into the various colors within it. When and where have you seen a rainbow? What legends or stories do you know in which a rainbow is important?

Unit 4 Quadratic Functions and Graphs

Answers to Can We Talk?

➤ Answers may vary. Examples are given. Different types of fish, as well as whales and other creatures live in the water. All plants need water to grow and some plants, such as algae, grow immersed in water. Animals drink water and need it to survive. Humans use water for drinking, bathing, cooking, and swimming, just to name a few uses.

➤ Answers may vary. Examples are given. Fountains are used for tourist attractions, as decorations inside and outside of buildings, as a place for fish to swim, to water flowers or other plants, or to move water from one location to another.

➤ Answers may vary. Examples are given. A squirt bottle, a garden hose, a boat used to extinguish fires on boats or other things in lakes or rivers,

a geyser, and a mineral spring. The squirt bottle, garden hose, and the boat are all made by people. The geyser and mineral spring are natural.

➤ Answers may vary. Examples are given. In the sky after it rains, spraying water from a garden hose in the sun, and at Niagara Falls on a sunny day. Leprechauns are said to have a pot of gold that can be found at the end of a rainbow.

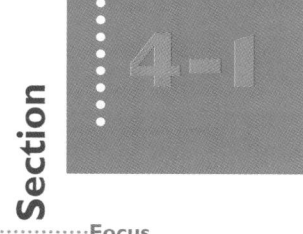

Graphing Quadratic Functions

Here's Looking at ∨

The water cannon is about 10 ft above the river.

On the north bank of the Chicago River, the Water Arc sprays recirculated water across the river toward a terrace along the south bank. The curve of water is big enough for boats to sail under.

The path of the water is an example of a **parabola,** a curve that can be modeled with a quadratic function. A **quadratic function** is a function that can be written in the **standard form**

$$y = ax^2 + bx + c, \text{ where } a \neq 0.$$

The path of the Water Arc can be modeled using the function

$$y = -0.006x^2 + 1.2x + 10.$$

Talk it Over

BY THE WAY...

The Water Arc sprays at a rate of 2100 gallons per minute with a water pressure of 375 pounds per square inch.

1. Use a graphics calculator or software to graph the function. The water cannon is about 10 ft above the river surface.

   a. What point on your graph represents the water cannon?

   b. What is the greatest height the water reaches?

   c. How far across the river does the water reach?

2. What happens to the graph if you change the coefficient of x^2 in the equation from -0.006 to 0.006? Describe the new graph.

4-1 Graphing Quadratic Functions

187

 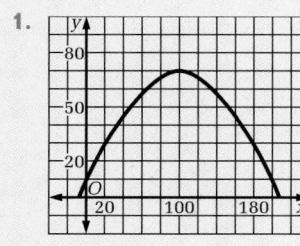

Using Technology

Graphing technology such as the *Function Investigator* software and graphics calculators can be used very effectively to graph quadratic equations. The discussion on page T34 of this Teacher's Edition provides information relevant to this topic as does the Technology Handbook on pages 611–617.

You can use tables to find a good graph screen for a parabolic graph. For example, consider the Water Arc function on page 187. Clear the Y= list and enter $Y_1 = -0.006X^2 + 1.2X + 10$. If you are using the TI-82 or TI-83, build a table that starts with X = 0 and uses an increment of 10. (See the TI-81/82/83 Manual section on tables.) As you scroll through the X values in the table, you see Y_1 values go from −16.4 (at X = −20) to a maximum of 70 (at X = 100) and then to −31.4 (at X = 230). Thus, for a good graph screen, you can use Xmin = −20, Xmax = 230 and Ymin = −50, Ymax = 90.

Teaching Tip

A quadratic function always contains a squared term, such as x^2. Because of the squared term, the graphs of quadratic functions are curves.

Talk it Over

Question 2 illustrates that changing the sign of the coefficient of x^2 in the equation for the path of the water arc influences the direction of the graph. The simple sign change from negative 0.006 to positive 0.006 reverses the direction of the parabola from opening down to opening up.

X Lab

ORIENTATIONS OF PARABOLAS

When a is negative, the graph of $y = ax^2 + bx + c$ is a parabola that opens down.

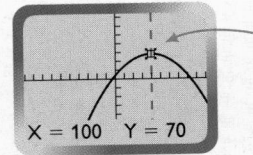

X = 100   Y = 70

The **vertex** is on the line of symmetry. Here it is a **maximum**.

$y = -0.006x^2 + 1.2x + 10$

When a is positive, the graph of $y = ax^2 + bx + c$ is a parabola that opens up.

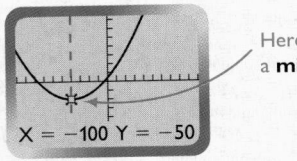

X = −100 Y = −50

Here the vertex is a **minimum**.

$y = 0.006x^2 + 1.2x + 10$

The formula for the line of symmetry is $x = -\dfrac{b}{2a}$.

Sample 1

Use the function $y = -3x^2 + 2x + 1$.

a. Tell whether the graph opens *up* or *down*.

b. Tell whether the vertex is a *maximum* or a *minimum*.

c. Find an equation for the line of symmetry.

d. Find the coordinates of the vertex.

Sample Response

The function $y = -3x^2 + 2x + 1$ is in the form $y = ax^2 + bx + c$.

a. The value of a is −3. It is negative, so the graph opens down.

b. Because the graph opens down, the vertex is a maximum.

c. $x = -\dfrac{b}{2a}$ ⟵ Write the formula for the line of symmetry.

$x = -\dfrac{2}{2(-3)}$ ⟵ Substitute 2 for b and −3 for a.

$x = \dfrac{1}{3}$

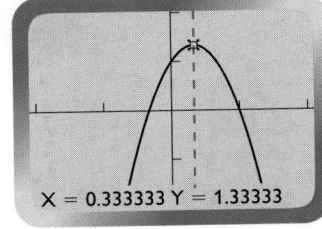

X = 0.333333 Y = 1.33333

d. The vertex lies on the line of symmetry, so $x = \dfrac{1}{3}$.

$y = -3x^2 + 2x + 1$ ⟵ Write the original function.

$y = -3\left(\dfrac{1}{3}\right)^2 + 2\left(\dfrac{1}{3}\right) + 1$ ⟵ Substitute $\dfrac{1}{3}$ for x.

$y = 1\dfrac{1}{3}$ ⟵ This is the y-value of the vertex.

The coordinates of the vertex are $\left(\dfrac{1}{3},\ 1\dfrac{1}{3}\right)$.

▶ Now you are ready for:
Exs. 1–20 on pp. 190–191

The vertex is one point that helps you sketch a parabola.

The intercepts, where the parabola crosses the *x*-axis and *y*-axis, also help you sketch a graph.

Here are graphs of the Water Arc.

One *x*-intercept is about −8.

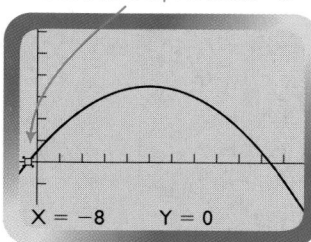

X = −8   Y = 0

The *y*-intercept is 10.

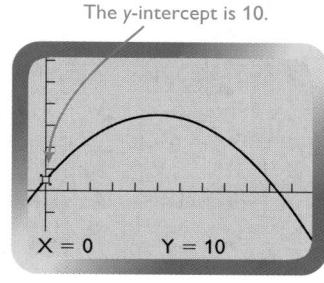

X = 0   Y = 10

The other *x*-intercept is about 208.

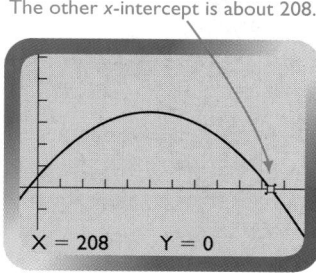

X = 208   Y = 0

You can find the **y-intercept** of an equation by substituting 0 for *x* in the equation. You can find **x-intercepts** by substituting 0 for *y*, but for now, you should estimate them from a graph.

Sample 2

Use the function $y = x^2 + 0.5x − 3.74$.

a. Find the *y*-intercept of the graph.

b. Use a graph to estimate the *x*-intercepts. Check one *x*-intercept by substitution.

Sample Response

a. $y = x^2 + 0.5x − 3.74$ ⟵ Write the function.

$= (0)^2 + 0.5(0) − 3.74$ ⟵ Substitute 0 for *x*.

$= −3.74$

The *y*-intercept is −3.74.

b. Make a table of values or use a graphics calculator.

The *x*-intercepts are −2.2 and 1.7.

Check Substitute 1.7 for *x* and 0 for *y*.

$y = x^2 + 0.5x − 3.74$

$0 \stackrel{?}{=} (1.7)^2 + 0.5(1.7) − 3.74$

$0 \stackrel{?}{=} 2.89 + 0.85 − 3.74$

$0 = 0$ ✔

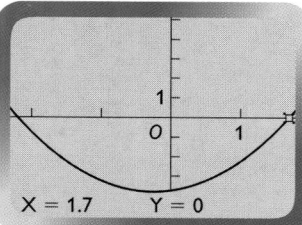

X = −2.2   Y = 0

X = 1.7   Y = 0

4-1 Graphing Quadratic Functions

....
Additional Sample

S1 Use the function
$y = 2x^2 + 3x − 1$.

a. Tell whether the graph opens up or down. **The graph opens up.**

b. Tell whether the vertex is a *maximum* or a *minimum*. **The vertex is a minimum.**

c. Find an equation for the line of symmetry. $x = −\frac{3}{4}$

d. Find the coordinates of the vertex. $\left(−\frac{3}{4}, −2\frac{1}{8}\right)$

....
Mathematical Procedures

The orientation of parabolas can be summarized by using inequalities. When $a < 0$, the parabola opens down and has a maximum point. When $a > 0$, the parabola opens up and has a minimum point.

....
Reasoning

By definition, the *y*-intercept of an equation is the *y*-coordinate of the point at which the graph of the equation crosses the *y*-axis. Since all points on the *y*-axis have 0 as their *x*-coordinate, the *y*-intercept of an equation can be found by substituting 0 for *x* in the equation. Using the standard form of a quadratic function, $y = ax^2 + bx + c$, if $x = 0$, then the *y*-intercept is simply the value of *c*.

....
Additional Sample

S2 Use the function
$y = x^2 + 0.6x − 7.75$.

a. Find the *y*-intercept of the graph. **The y-intercept is −7.75.**

b. Use a graph to estimate the *x*-intercepts. Check one *x*-intercept by substitution. **The x-intercepts are 2.5 and −3.1.**

Check. Substitute 2.5 for *x* in the original equation.

$y \stackrel{?}{=} (2.5)^2 + 0.6(2.5) − 7.75$

$y \stackrel{?}{=} 6.25 + 1.5 − 7.75$

$y = 0$ ✓

189

····▶ Now you are ready for:
Exs. 21–40 on pp. 191–192

Look Back

In order to frame a correct explanation, students need to recall the standard form of a quadratic function, $y = ax^2 + bx + c$; the influence of the coefficient a on the orientation of the function; the formula for the line of symmetry, $x = -\dfrac{b}{2a}$; and how to find the y-coordinate of the maximum or minimum value. ················•

APPLYING

Suggested Assignment

Day 1

Standard 2–17

Extended 1–20

Day 2

Standard 21–40

Extended 21–40

Integrating the Strands

Algebra Exs. 1–40

Functions Exs. 4–29, 34–40

Logic and Language Exs. 1, 20, 29

Communication: Discussion

Some of the Exercises and Problems on pages 190–192 can be completed in class verbally by having individual students discuss the answers. Exs. 1–10 and 24–28 fall into this category.

Interdisciplinary Problems

The paths of moving objects, such as the Water Arc and the gymnast in Exs. 2 and 3, can be represented by a parabola. Parabolas appear frequently in sports, science, and engineering. The cables on some suspension bridges assume the form of parabolas. Parabolic shapes are also commonly used as reflectors, such as in car headlights, electric heaters, or large broadcasting or receiving antennas.

Look Back ◀

Explain how you would find the maximum or minimum value of a quadratic function.

4-1 Exercises and Problems

1. **Reading** How are the graph of the Water Arc and the graph in Sample 1 alike? How are they different?

Estimate the vertex of the parabola that describes the movement of each gymnast.

2.

3.

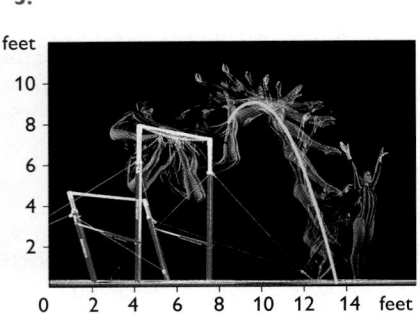

Match each function with its graph.

4. $y = 0.5x^2 + x$

5. $y = -0.5x^2 + x$

6. $y = -0.15x^2 + 3$

7. $y = 0.15x^2 - 3$

A.
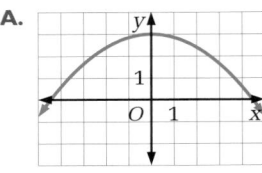

B.
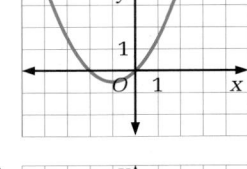

C.
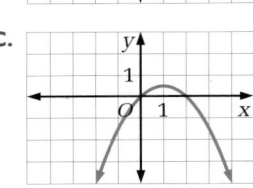

D.
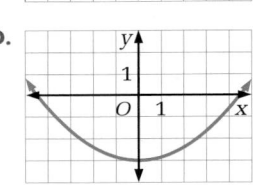

Without graphing, tell whether the graph of each function opens *up* or *down*.

8. $y = -5x^2 + 6$ 9. $y = x^2 - 3$ 10. $y = -0.7x^2 - 6x$

Find an equation for the line of symmetry for the graph of each function.

11. $y = -2x^2 + 6x$ 12. $y = x^2 + 3$ 13. $y = 3x^2 - 6x + 17$

190   **Unit 4** Quadratic Functions and Graphs

Answers to Look Back········

First find the equation of the line of symmetry for the function in the form $y = ax^2 + bx + c$. It will have the form $x = \dfrac{-b}{2a}$.

Since $\dfrac{-b}{2a}$ is the x-coordinate of the vertex, substitute $x = \dfrac{-b}{2a}$ in the original equation to find the y-coordinate of the vertex. If a is positive, the vertex is a minimum. If a is negative, the vertex is a maximum.

Answers to Exercises and Problems·······

1. Both functions have negative values for a so both have a maximum vertex and open downward. The water arc has a y-intercept of 10, while the graph in Sample 1 has a y-intercept of 1. The x-intercepts and vertices are also different.

2. (11, 8)

3. (9, 9)

4. B   5. C

6. A   7. D

8. down   9. up

10. down

11. $x = \dfrac{3}{2}$

12. $x = 0$ or y-axis

13. $x = 1$

14. (3, 4); maximum

15. (−2, −1); minimum

Find the coordinates of the vertex of the graph of each function.
Tell whether the vertex is a *maximum* or a *minimum*.

14. $y = -2x^2 + 12x - 14$ **15.** $y = x^2 + 4x + 3$ **16.** $y = -0.25x^2 - 0.5x + 2.5$

17. Choose one of the equations from Exercises 14–16 and graph it.
Label the vertex with its coordinates.

18. Use the function for the Chicago Water Arc on page 187.

   a. Find an equation for the line of symmetry for its graph.

   b. Find the vertex of its graph.

19. **Open-ended** Create three different quadratic functions that have the line
$x = 2$ as their line of symmetry. Sketch their graphs.

20. **Writing** How is the graph of $y = ax^2 + bx + c$ affected if a, b, or c is 0?
Draw sketches to support your conclusions.

Find the *y*-intercept of the graph of each function.

21. $y = 2x^2 + x - 3$ **22.** $y = -4x^2 - x + 3$ **23.** $y = \frac{1}{2}x^2 + 3x - 2$

**Use the graph to estimate the *x*-intercepts. Check one *x*-intercept
by substitution.**

24. $y = -\frac{1}{3}x^2 + \frac{2}{3}x + 1$ **25.** $y = \frac{1}{2}x^2 - 2x$

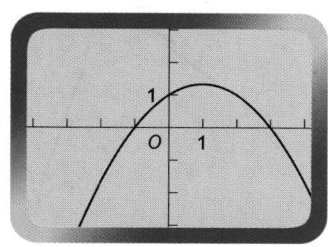   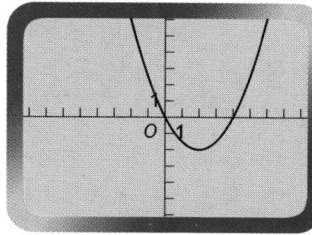

26. $y = -x^2 - 6x - 5$ **27.** $y = 0.2x^2 - 0.2x - 4$

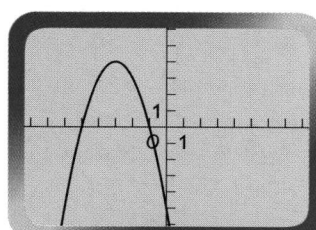   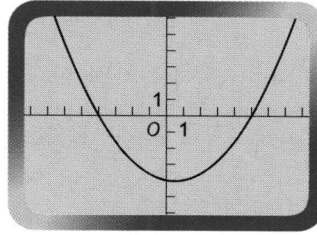

28. a. What do the graphs of the functions $y = -0.006x^2 + 1.2x + 10$ and
   $y = 0.006x^2 - 1.2x + 10$ have in common?

   b. What do the graphs of the functions $y = 0.006x^2 + 1.2x + 10$ and
   $y = -0.006x^2 - 1.2x + 10$ have in common?

   c. What point do all four graphs in parts (a) and (b) have in common?

4-1 Graphing Quadratic Functions   **191**

Answers to Exercises and Problems

16. (−1, 2.75); maximum

17. Choice of parabola may
vary. All parabolas are
given.
$y = -2x^2 + 12x - 14$

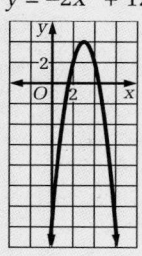

$y = x^2 + 4x + 3$

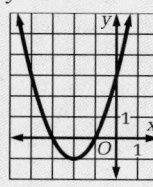

$y = -0.25x^2 - 0.5x + 2.5$

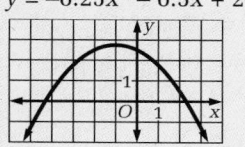

18. $x = 100$; (100, 70)

19. Answers may vary. Examples are given. (Any equation where b is −4 times
the value of a will work.)

$y = x^2 - 4x + 2$

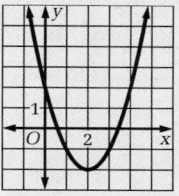

The concept of function was
introduced in the first section
of Unit 2 of this book. It reap-
pears in this unit on quadratic
functions and their graphs.
Functions are pervasive
throughout almost all of mathematics and are so fundamental
that they have great power as a
unifying or integrating concept.
The emphasis in this unit is on
the connection of functions and
algebra. Many of the exercises
on pages 190–192 explicitly
involve algebraic functions.

Integrating the Strands

The concept of function was
introduced in the first section
of Unit 2 of this book. It reap-
pears in this unit on quadratic
functions and their graphs.
Functions are pervasive
throughout almost all of mathematics and are so fundamental
that they have great power as a
unifying or integrating concept.
The emphasis in this unit is on
the connection of functions and
algebra. Many of the exercises
on pages 190–192 explicitly
involve algebraic functions.

Research

The text on page 187 points out
that a parabola is a curve that
can be modeled with a quadratic function. An important question that some students may
wish to research is the following: Are all parabolas graphs of
quadratic functions? (No.) You
might suggest that students
begin by reviewing the definition of a function given on
page 60 in Unit 2.

19. $y = -x^2 + 4x$ $y = \frac{1}{2}x^2 - 2x + 1$

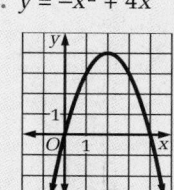   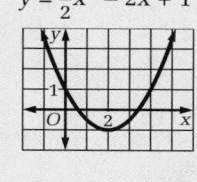

20. If $a = 0$, then $y = bx + c$, and the
graph is a line. If $b = 0$, then
$y = ax^2 + c$, and the graph is a
parabola with a line of symmetry
$x = 0$. If $c = 0$, then $y = ax^2 + bx$,
and the graph is a parabola that
passes through the origin and the
point $\left(\frac{-b}{a}, 0\right)$. Examples are
shown.

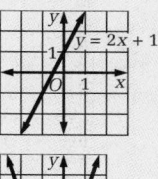   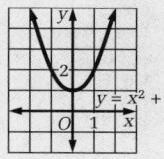

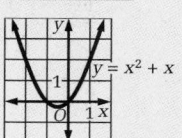

21. −3   **22.** 3   **23.** −2

24–28. See answers in back of book.

Practice 26 For use with Section 4-1

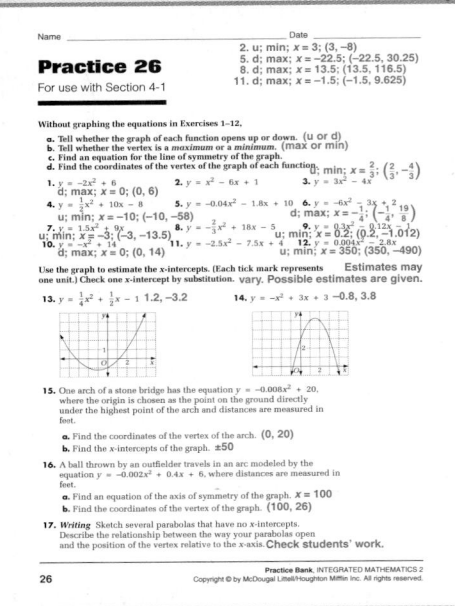

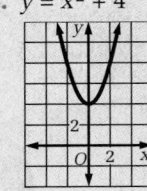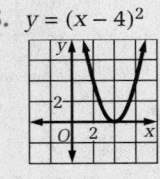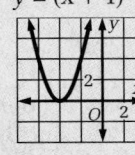

29. **Writing** Explain how to find the y-intercept of the graph of the function $y = ax^2 + bx + c$. Choose values for a, b, and c and use them in an example.

Review **PREVIEW**

Write each system as a matrix equation. *(Section 3-8)*

30. $3x + 2y = 5$
$4x - y = 3$

31. $4x - 2y = 8$
$-3x + 5y = -6$

32. $y = 3x - 4$
$y = -2x + 21$

33. What is the radius of a circle with an area of 50 cm²? *(Toolbox Skill 28)*

Graph each function. *(Toolbox Skill 20)*

34. $y = x^2 + 4$

35. $y = (x - 4)^2$

36. $y = (x + 4)^2$

Working on the Unit Project

Use this function for the path of a water arc whose speed, v, is measured in feet per second. Angle A is the angle of the nozzle.

$$y = \frac{-16}{v^2(\cos A)^2}x^2 + (\tan A)x$$

37. Suppose a water hose sprays water at an angle of 40° and at a speed of v ft/s. Write a function describing the water's path. (Your equation will involve v.)

38. Use a graphics calculator.

   a. Graph the equation you wrote in Exercise 37 for these values of v: 50 ft/s, 60 ft/s, and 70 ft/s.

   b. As v increases how does the maximum height of the water's path change?

   c. As v increases how does the distance that the water travels across the ground change?

   d. What do the x-intercepts of the graphs represent?

39. Suppose a second water hose sprays water at an angle A and at a speed of 65 ft/s. Write an equation describing the water's path. (Your equation will involve angle A.)

40. Use a graphics calculator.

   a. Graph the equation you wrote in Exercise 39 for these measures of angle A: 25°, 35°, 45°, and 55°.

   b. For which angle A is the maximum height of the water the greatest?

   c. For which angle A is the distance the water travels across the ground the greatest?

37. $y = \dfrac{-16}{v^2(\cos 40°)^2}x^2 + (\tan 40°)x$, or $y \approx \dfrac{-16}{0.77v^2}x^2 + 0.84x$

38. a.
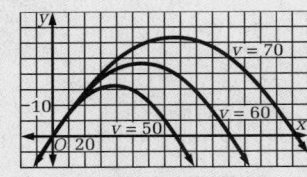

b. The maximum height increases.

c. The distance increases.

d. the location of the nozzle and the distances from the nozzle at which the water hits the ground

39. $y = \dfrac{-16}{65^2(\cos A)^2}x^2 + (\tan A)x$, or $y = \dfrac{-16}{4225(\cos A)^2}x^2 + (\tan A)x$

40. a.
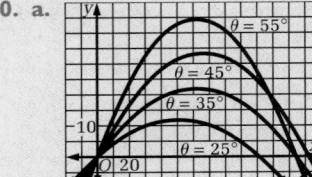

b. 55°   **c.** 45°

Translating Parabolas

Focus

Explore translations of parabolas.

SLIDE ─◐►VER

EXPLORATION

(How) *do changes in the equation affect the graph of a parabola?*

- **Materials: graphics calculators**
- **Work with another student.**

① Graph $y = x^2$, $y = 2x^2$, $y = 5x^2$, and $y = 12x^2$ on the same axes. What happens to the graph of $y = x^2$ when the coefficient of x^2 is greater than 1?

② Graph $y = x^2$, $y = \frac{1}{2}x^2$, $y = \frac{1}{4}x^2$, and $y = \frac{1}{10}x^2$ on the same axes. What happens to the graph of $y = x^2$ when the coefficient of x^2 is between 0 and 1?

③ How do you think the graphs in steps 1 and 2 will change when the coefficient of x^2 is negative? Check your answer by graphing some examples.

④ Graph $y = 5x^2$, $y = 5x^2 + 3$, and $y = 5x^2 - 3$ on the same axes. How does the graph of $y = 5x^2$ change when you add 3 to $5x^2$? when you subtract 3 from $5x^2$?

⑤ Predict what the graph of $y = 5x^2 - 7$ looks like. Check your answer by graphing.

⑥ Graph each function on the same axes as $y = 2x^2$. Describe how the graph of each function is different from the graph of $y = 2x^2$.

  a. $y = 2(x + 2)^2$ **b.** $y = 2(x - 3)^2$ **c.** $y = 2(x - 6)^2$

⑦ What relationship do you see between the equations in step 6, parts (a)–(c), and their graphs?

⑧ Use what you discovered in steps 4 and 6 to predict what the graph of $y = (x - 7)^2 + 4$ will look like. Sketch your prediction on a piece of paper. Then check your prediction by graphing.

⑨ Describe how the graph of $y = 2(x + 3)^2 - 1$ is different from the graph of $y = x^2$.

4-2 Translating Parabolas

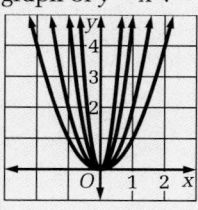
193

PLANNING sidebar

Objectives and Strands
See pages 184A and 184B.

Spiral Learning
See page 184B.

Materials List
➤ Graphics calculator
➤ Graph paper
➤ Tracing paper
➤ Tape measure
➤ Water hose

Recommended Pacing
Section 4-2 is a two-day lesson.
Day 1
Pages 193–194: Exploration through Talk it Over 6, *Exercises 1–11*
Day 2
Pages 195–196: Top of page 195 through Look Back, *Exercises 12–29*

Extra Practice
See pages 620–621.

Warm-Up Exercises
Warm-Up Transparency 4-2

Support Materials
➤ Practice 27
➤ Enrichment 24 in the Activity Bank
➤ Study Guide 4-2
➤ Problem Set 7
➤ Diagram Master 2 in the Explorations Lab Manual
➤ McDougal Littell Mathpack software: *Function Investigator*
➤ Function Investigator with Matrix Analyzer Activity Book: Function Investigator Activities 12–15
➤ Using IBM/Mac Plotter Plus Disk: Parabola Quiz
➤ Quiz 4-2
➤ Alternative Assessment 2

Answers to Exploration

1. The innermost parabola is the graph of $y = 12x^2$; the outermost parabola is the graph of $y = x^2$.

Descriptions may vary. An example is given. For coefficients of x^2 greater than 1, the parabola becomes steeper and narrower.

2. See answers in back of book.

3. Answers may vary. An example is given. When the coefficient of x^2 is negative, the parabola opens down. The graph of $y = -ax^2$ is the image of the graph of $y = ax^2$ under a reflection over the horizontal axis.

4–9. See answers in back of book.

Exploration

The goal of the Exploration is to have students investigate how changes in a quadratic equation affect the graph of a parabola. Students explore changes in the shape and position of the graph. Changes in shape are explored in steps 1 and 2. Step 3 considers reflections of the graphs used in steps 1 and 2. Steps 4–9 explore changes in position.

Using Technology

For the Exploration, optimal graph screens for the graphs are as follows:

Step 1: $-2 \le x \le 2$ and $-1 \le y \le 2$;

Step 2: $-10 \le x \le 10$ and $-5 \le y \le 10$;

Step 4: $-2 \le x \le 2$ and $-5 \le y \le 10$;

Step 6: $-5 \le x \le 8$ and $-5 \le y \le 10$.

Students can also use the *Function Investigator* software to graph the functions.

Teaching Tip

A translation changes a graph's position by moving the graph up or down, to the left or right, or some combination of an up-down movement with a left-right movement. The graph of $y = (x + 3)^2 + 2$ is a translation of $y = x^2$ three (3) units to the left and two (2) units up.

Additional Sample

S1 Tell how to translate the graph of $y = 0.3x^2$ in order to produce the graph of each function.

a. $y = 0.3x^2 + 4$
   Translate the graph of $y = 0.3x^2$ up 4 units.

b. $y = 0.3(x - 2)^2$
   Translate the graph of $y = 0.3x^2$ to the right 2 units.

c. $y = 0.3(x + 6)^2 - 5$
   Translate the graph of $y = 0.3x^2$ to the left 6 units and down 5 units.

The graph of $y = (x + 3)^2 + 2$ is a translation of the graph of $y = x^2$. A translation changes only a graph's position. It does not change a graph's size or shape or the direction in which a graph opens.

Talk it Over

Tell whether the graph of each function is a translation of $y = x^2$.

1. $y = x^2 + 6$ 2. $y = 3x^2$ 3. $y = (x - 1)^2$

4. Describe the information you can get about the graph of a parabola from its equation.

Sample 1

Tell how to translate the graph of $y = -0.5x^2$ in order to produce the graph of each function.

   a. $y = -0.5x^2 - 2$ **b.** $y = -0.5(x + 4)^2$ **c.** $y = -0.5(x - 1)^2 + 3$

Sample Response

a. $y = -0.5x^2 - 2$

Translate the graph of $y = -0.5x^2$ 2 units *down*.

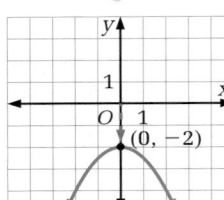

b. $y = -0.5(x + 4)^2$

Translate the graph of $y = -0.5x^2$ 4 units to the *left*.

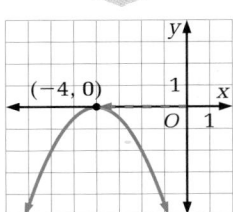

c. $y = -0.5(x - 1)^2 + 3$

Translate the graph of $y = -0.5x^2$ 1 unit to the *right* and 3 units *up*.

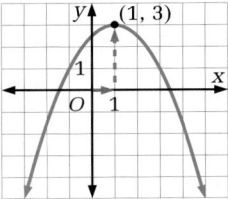

▶ Now you are ready for:
Exs. 1–11 on pp. 196–197

Talk it Over

5. What is the vertex of the graph of $y = 4x^2$? What is the vertex of the graph of $y = 4x^2 + 3$? Describe the change in the position of the vertex when 3 is added to $4x^2$.

6. For each parabola in Sample 1, describe the translation of the vertex.

194   **Unit 4** Quadratic Functions and Graphs

Answers to Talk it Over

1. Yes.

2. No.

3. Yes.

4. Answers may vary. An example is given. You can tell if the graph has the same shape or position as a parabola with a simpler equation. You can determine the coordinates of the vertex and tell whether the parabola opens up or down.

5. (0, 0); (0, 3); The vertex is translated 3 units up.

6. In equation (a), the vertex is translated down 2 units; in equation (b), the vertex is translated 4 units to the left; in equation (c), the vertex is translated 1 unit to the right and 3 units up.

Sometimes you want to write a quadratic function in *standard form* before you use it to get information about the graph.

Sample 2

Find the coordinates of the vertex of the graph of
$y = 3(x - 4)^2 + 1.$

Sample Response

Method ❶ Use a formula.

The formula for the line of symmetry, $x = -\frac{b}{2a}$, gives the x-coordinate of the vertex. You need to write the function in standard form to use the formula.

$$y = 3(x - 4)^2 + 1$$
$$= 3(x - 4)(x - 4) + 1 \quad \longleftarrow \quad \text{Rewrite } (x - 4)^2.$$
$$= 3(x^2 - 8x + 16) + 1 \quad \longleftarrow \quad \text{Use the distributive property: } (x - 4)x - (x - 4)4.$$
$$= 3x^2 - 24x + 48 + 1 \quad \longleftarrow \quad \text{Use the distributive property.}$$
$$= 3x^2 - 24x + 49 \quad \longleftarrow \quad \text{Combine like terms.}$$

The equation $y = 3x^2 - 24x + 49$ is in the form $y = ax^2 + bx + c$. Find the x-coordinate of the vertex.

$$x = -\frac{b}{2a} \quad \longleftarrow \quad \text{Use the formula for the line of symmetry.}$$
$$= -\frac{-24}{2(3)} \quad \longleftarrow \quad \text{Substitute } -24 \text{ for } b \text{ and } 3 \text{ for } a.$$
$$= 4$$

Use this value to find the y-coordinate of the vertex.

$$y = 3(x - 4)^2 + 1 \quad \longleftarrow \quad \text{Write the original function.}$$
$$= 3(4 - 4)^2 + 1 \quad \longleftarrow \quad \text{Substitute 4 for } x.$$
$$= 1$$

The coordinates of the vertex are (4, 1).

Method ❷ Use a translation.

The graph of $y = 3(x - 4)^2 + 1$ is a translation of the graph of $y = 3x^2$. Translate the vertex of $y = 3x^2$ to the right 4 units and up 1 unit to find the vertex of $y = 3(x - 4)^2 + 1$.

$$(0, 0) \quad \longleftarrow \quad \text{Write the vertex of the parabola } y = 3x^2.$$
$$(0 + 4, 0 + 1) \quad \longleftarrow \quad \text{The vertex is translated } \mathbf{4} \text{ units right and } \mathbf{1} \text{ unit up.}$$
$$(4, 1)$$

The coordinates of the vertex are (4, 1).

4-2 Translating Parabolas

195

195

For question 8, students can also tell that the two functions are equivalent by referring back to Method 1 of Sample 2. The expansion of $y = 3(x - 4)^2 + 1$ yields the equivalent equation $y = 3x^2 - 24x + 49$.

Using Technology

You can use the TI-81/82/83 to help write a function of the form $y = ax^2 + bx + c$ in the form $y = a(x + h)^2 + k$. Consider $y = 5x^2 + 7x + 1$. Graph the function on the standard graph screen. Locate the vertex by finding the minimum point. With the TI-82 or TI-83, you can do this quickly by using 3:minimum from the CALCULATE menu. With the TI-81, you will get similar coordinates for the minimum point by zooming and tracing. The results indicate that the vertex is at $(-0.7, -1.45)$. The vertex $(0, 0)$ of the "parent" function $y = 5x^2$ seems to have been translated 0.7 units to the left and 1.45 units down. You can verify algebraically that $y = 5x^2 + 7x + 1$ is equivalent to $y = 5(x + 0.7)^2 + (-1.45)$. Alternatively, graph both functions. The graphs coincide.

Look Back

The movements of the graph of the function $y = x^2$ can be summarized by using the single function $y = a(x + h)^2 + k$.

If $h > 0$, $y = x^2$ moves left h units.

If $h < 0$, $y = x^2$ moves right h units.

If $k > 0$, $y = x^2$ moves up k units.

If $k < 0$, $y = x^2$ moves down k units.

Using Technology

Function Investigator Activities 12–15 in the *Function Investigator with Matrix Analyzer Activity Book* can be used to further explore how changing the equation of a quadratic function changes its graph.

Talk it Over

7. In Method 1 of Sample 2, does it matter whether you distribute the 3 before you expand $(x - 4)^2$? Why or why not?

8. Graph $y = 3(x - 4)^2 + 1$ and $y = 3x^2 - 24x + 49$ on the same set of axes. What do the graphs tell you about the two functions?

Look Back

In the Exploration, you discovered that changes to the function $y = x^2$ can move its graph up, down, left, or right. Describe a way to remember the effect that each change in the function has on the graph.

▶ Now you are ready for:
Exs. 12–29 on pp. 197–198

4-2 Exercises and Problems

1. **Reading** Which of the parabolas in the Exploration are translations of the graph of $y = x^2$?

2. Without graphing, list the functions in order from the one with the narrowest graph to the one with the widest graph.

$y = \frac{2}{3}x^2 + 1$ $y = 12x^2 - 5$ $y = 0.01x^2$ $y = 5x^2 + 8$

3. Without graphing, list the functions in order beginning with the one whose graph has the vertex farthest to the left.

$y = \frac{2}{3}(x + 1)^2$ $y = 12(x - 5)^2$ $y = 0.01(x - 3)^2$ $y = 5(x + 8)^2$

For Exercises 4–7, tell how to translate the graph of $y = -3x^2$ in order to produce the graph of each function.

4. $y = -3(x + 7)^2$

5. $y = -3(x - 2)^2 + 3$

6. $y = -3(x - 1)^2 - 2$

7. $y = -3(x + 2)^2 + 5$

Each graph is a translation of $y = \frac{1}{3}x^2$. Write a function for each graph.

8.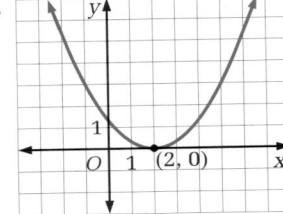

9.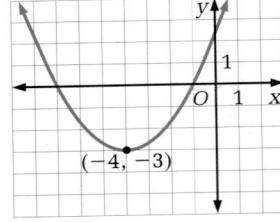

Answers to Talk it Over

7. Yes. Explanations may vary. An example is given. According to the order of operations, the power should be simplified first. Then the expression can be multiplied by 3. If you distribute the 3 first and then simplify the power, you actually multiply each term by 3^2 or 9.

8. The equations have the same graph; they are equivalent equations.

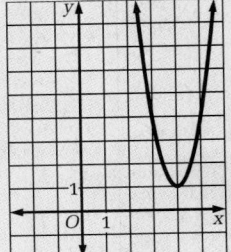

Answers to Look Back

Answers may vary. An example is given. The equation $y = (x + a)^2$ has a horizontal translation of a units left or right (left if a is positive); the equation $y = x^2 + b$ has a vertical translation of b units up or down (up if b is positive).

10. Make a concept map to describe the ways the graph of $y = 3x^2$ can be translated. Give examples of at least two functions for each type of translation. Use functions that show vertical translations, horizontal translations, or both vertical and horizontal translations.

11. a. **Using Manipulatives** Make a coordinate grid on graph paper. Place tracing paper on top of the graph paper.

   Graph $y = \frac{2}{5}x^2$ on your tracing paper.

   b. Move the tracing paper so that the parabola is translated up 6 units. What is the y-intercept? the line of symmetry? Rewrite the equation $y = \frac{2}{5}x^2$ to show the translation.

   c. Repeat part (b) but translate the original parabola 4 units to the left.

   d. Repeat part (b) but translate the original parabola 2 units down and 3 units to the right.

   e. Repeat part (b) but reflect the original parabola over the x-axis.

12. **Writing** Jack says that the y-intercept of the graph of $y = 3(x + 1)^2 - 8$ is -8. Lindsey rewrites the function in standard form and says the y-intercept of the graph is -5. Who do you think is right? Why?

For the graph of each function:

a. Find the coordinates of the vertex.

b. Find the y-intercept.

13. $y = (x + 6)^2$

14. $y = (x + 3)^2 - 4$

15. $y = (x - 5)^2 + 2$

16. $y = 2(x + 4)^2 - 18$

17. $y = 5(x - 1)^2 + 11$

18. $y = -4(x - 2)^2 + 9$

19. The equation for the area of a circle is written $A = \pi r^2$.

   a. When you rewrite $A = \pi r^2$ using x for the radius and y for the area, you get $y = \pi x^2$. Graph the function $y = \pi x^2$. (Use $\pi \approx 3.14$.)

   b. What is a reasonable domain for this function?

Answers to Exercises and Problems

1. the graph in step 8,
   $y = (x - 7)^2 + 4$

2. $y = 12x^2 - 5$, $y = 5x^2 + 8$,
   $y = \frac{2}{3}x^2 + 1$, $y = 0.01x^2$

3. $y = 5(x + 8)^2$, $y = \frac{2}{3}(x + 1)^2$,
   $y = 0.01(x - 3)^2$,
   $y = 12(x - 5)^2$

4. Move the graph 7 units to the left.

5. Move the graph 2 units to the right and 3 units up.

6. Move the graph 1 unit to the right and 2 units down.

7. Move the graph 2 units to the left and 5 units up.

8. $y = \frac{1}{3}(x - 2)^2$

9. $y = \frac{1}{3}(x + 4)^2 - 3$

10. See answers in back of book.

11. a. Check students' graphs.

   b. 6; $x = 0$; $y = \frac{2}{5}x^2 + 6$

c. 6.4; $x = -4$; $y = \frac{2}{5}(x + 4)^2$

d. 1.6; $x = 3$;
   $y = \frac{2}{5}(x - 3)^2 - 2$

e. 0; $x = 0$; $y = -\frac{2}{5}x^2$

12. Lindsey is right; when
   $x = 0$, $3(x + 1)^2 - 8 =$
   $3(0 + 1)^2 - 8 = 3 - 8 = -5$.
   Jack found the y-intercept
   of $y = 3x^2 - 8$.

13-19. See answers in back of book.

Suggested Assignment

Day 1

Standard 1–9

Extended 1–10

Day 2

Standard 13–18, 21–29

Extended 12–29

Integrating the Strands

Algebra Exs. 1–29

Functions Exs. 1–25, 29

Geometry Exs. 19, 20

Logic and Language Exs. 1, 10, 12

Communication: Reading

For Ex. 1, discuss also the effect that changing the value of a has on the graph of $y = ax^2$ (Exploration steps 1 and 2). For $a > 1$, increasing values of a make the shape of the parabola more narrow. For $a < 1$, decreasing values of a make the shape wider. If the sign of a changes (step 3), then the direction in which the graph of $y = ax^2$ opens is changed from up to down or down to up.

Communication: Discussion

The use of concept maps in Ex. 10 can stimulate a discussion among students as they compare their maps and examples. These activities would provide an excellent summary of the ideas associated with translating the graph of a parabola.

Assessment: Task

For Ex. 20, students should be able to analyze the quadratic equation function $y = \pi(x^2 - 4)$ and describe the coordinates of the vertex. What portion of the graph should be considered, remembering that this is the area as a function of the radius? Do both x-intercepts have physical meaning? Why? If the radius of the larger circle is double the radius of the smaller circle, what is the shaded region? Students should analyze the geometric sketch and correlate the findings on the graphics calculator with their analysis.

Working on the Unit Project

Students can work on Ex. 29 at home or at some other place where they have access to an outdoor faucet. Their experience with the graph of the path of the water will help them to design a fountain.

Practice 27 For use with Section 4-2

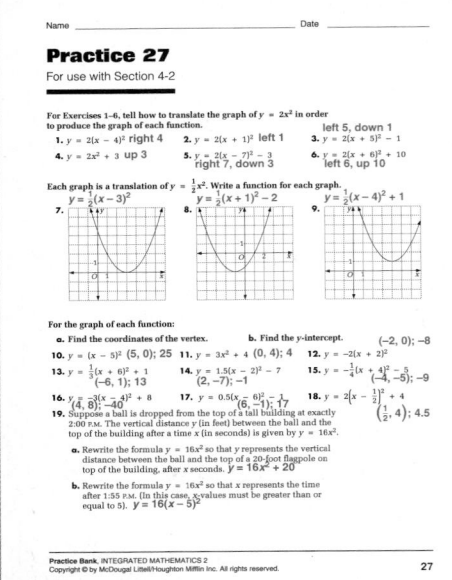

Answers to Exercises and Problems

20. a. 4π square units

b. πx^2

c. $y = \pi x^2 - 4\pi$; The graph shows $y = \pi x^2$ translated 4π units down.

d. all real numbers $x \geq 2$

e. 2 and −2; The positive x-intercept represents the value of x for which the area of the shaded region is 0, that is, when the two circles are the same. The negative x-intercept is not in the domain.

f. The graph of $y = \pi(x - 4)^2$, not the graph of $y = \pi(x^2 - 4)$, is the graph of $y = \pi x^2$ translated 4 units to the right. The graph of $y = \pi(x^2 - 4)$ is not the same as the graph of $y = \pi(x - 4)^2$ because you are squaring a different quantity in the two equations.

---

20. a. Use the formula $A = \pi r^2$ to find the area of the small circle.

b. Use the formula $A = \pi r^2$ to write an expression for the area of the large circle.

c. Use your answers to parts (a) and (b) to write an equation for the area of the shaded region. Then graph the equation and tell what translation of $y = \pi x^2$ produces the graph.

d. What is a reasonable domain for this function?

e. Estimate the x-intercepts of your graph. What do the x-intercepts represent?

f. Describe the error Yael made in describing the translation of the graph of $y = \pi x^2$ in part (c).

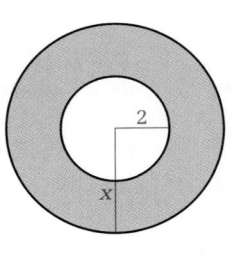

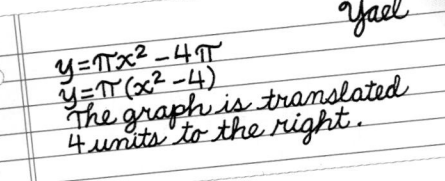

Yael
$y = \pi x^2 - 4\pi$
$y = \pi(x^2 - 4)$
The graph is translated 4 units to the right.

Ongoing ASSESSMENT

21. **Open-ended** Write three examples of quadratic functions whose graphs fit each description.

a. open down

b. have a narrower opening than $y = x^2$

c. have a wider opening than $y = x^2$

d. have a line of symmetry of $x = 3$

Review PREVIEW

For each function, find the coordinates of the vertex of the graph and tell if the vertex is a *maximum* or a *minimum*. (Section 4-1)

22. $y = \frac{1}{2}x^2 + 6x - 5$

23. $y = 5x^2 + 2x + 4$

24. $y = -2x^2 + 12x - 8$

25. Graph the equation $y = 3(2^n)$. Does your graph represent *exponential growth* or *exponential decay*? Explain. (Section 2-7)

Solve. (Toolbox Skill 16)

26. $x^2 = 169$

27. $x^2 = 784$

28. $x^2 = 64$

Working on the Unit Project

29. **Group Activity** Work with another student. You will need a tape measure and a water hose connected to a faucet outdoors.

a. One person should hold the hose's nozzle as close to the ground as possible at a 45° angle up from the ground.

b. The other person should turn on the water at full force and measure the distance d in feet between the nozzle and the point on the ground where the water lands.

c. Sketch a graph of the path of the water arc on a coordinate plane. Let the origin correspond to the nozzle of the hose. Label the x-intercepts with their coordinates.

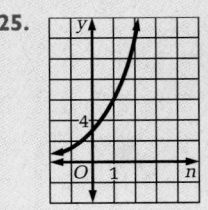

198   Unit 4 Quadratic Functions and Graphs

---

21. Answers may vary. Examples are given.

a. $y = -x^2$; $y = -3(x + 1)^2$; $y = -\frac{1}{2}x^2 + 3$

b. $y = 3x^2$; $y = 8(x - 1)^2$; $y = 20(x + 3)^2$

c. $y = \frac{1}{2}x^2$; $y = \frac{3}{8}(x - 2)^2$; $y = \frac{1}{9}x^2$

d. $y = (x - 3)^2$; $y = \frac{1}{2}(x - 3)^2 + 1$; $y = -(x - 3)^2 - 5$

22. $(-6, -23)$; minimum

23. $\left(-\frac{1}{5}, \frac{19}{5}\right)$; minimum

24. $(3, 10)$; maximum

25.

Since the equation $y = 3(2^n)$ is an exponential function with base 2, its graph represents exponential growth.

26. 13 and −13

27. 28 and −28

28. 8 and −8

29. a, b. Check students' work.

c. Answers may vary. An example is given.

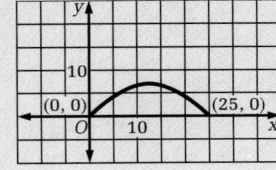

198

Solving Equations Using Square Roots

------Focus
Solve simple quadratic equations by graphing and undoing.

MAKING WAVES

BY THE WAY...

Oceanographers forecast wave patterns so that shipping companies can plan routes. Wave patterns can affect travel time, cargo safety, and passenger comfort.

Oceanographers have identified several kinds of waves. A wave in ocean water that is deeper than half the wavelength is called a *deep water wave*.

The speed of a deep water wave is independent of the depth of the ocean. The relationship between wave speed and wavelength can be modeled with a quadratic function.

$$2\pi C^2 = 9.8L$$

C = wave speed (meters per second)

L = wavelength (meters)

The *wavelength* is the distance from crest to crest.

crest

sea level

For deep water waves, the depth of the water is more than half the wavelength.

4-3 Solving Equations Using Square Roots

199

PLANNING

Objectives and Strands
See pages 184A and 184B.

Spiral Learning
See page 184B.

Materials List
➤ Graphics calculator

Recommended Pacing
Section 4-3 is a one-day lesson.

Toolbox References
➤ **Toolbox Skill 8:** Finding Geometric Probability

Extra Practice
See pages 620–621.

Warm-Up Exercises
Warm-Up Transparency 4-3

Support Materials
➤ Practice 28
➤ Enrichment 25 in the Activity Bank
➤ Study Guide 4-3
➤ Problem Set 7
➤ McDougal Littell Mathpack software: *Function Investigator*
➤ Quiz 4-3
➤ Alternative Assessment 3

TEACHING

Teaching Tip

The equation $2\pi C^2 = 9.8L$ that relates the speed of a deep water wave (C) to its wavelength (L) can be used to find either C or L if one of the two values is known. In Sample 1, L is given as 15 m. This value is substituted into the equation $2\pi C^2 = 9.8L$, which is then solved to find the value of C.

Additional Sample

S1 A deep water wave has a wave speed of 3.9 m/s. Find its wavelength.

$$2\pi C^2 = 9.8L$$
$$\frac{2\pi(3.9)^2}{9.8} = L$$
$$L \approx 9.75$$

The wavelength is approximately 9.75 m.

Talk it Over

Question 1 asks students to relate the possible mathematical answers to the real-world situation of a moving wave. A negative solution is not realistic.

Additional Sample

S2 Solve $2x^2 + 9 = 19$.

Method 1. Use algebra.

$$2x^2 + 9 = 19$$
$$2x^2 = 10$$
$$x^2 = 5$$
$$x = \pm\sqrt{5}$$
$$x \approx \pm 2.2$$

The solutions are about 2.2 and about −2.2.

Method 2. Use a graph. Rewrite the equation in the form $ax^2 + bx + c = 0$.

$$2x^2 + 9 = 19$$
$$2x^2 - 10 = 0$$

Graph $y = 2x^2 - 10$.

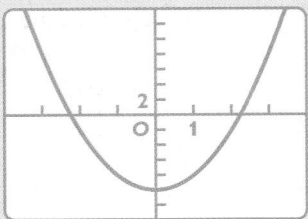

Sample 1

A deep water wave has a wavelength of 15 m. Find the wave speed. Use the information on page 199.

Sample Response

$$2\pi C^2 = 9.8L \qquad \longleftarrow \text{Use the equation.}$$
$$2\pi C^2 = (9.8)(15) \qquad \longleftarrow \text{Substitute 15 for } L.$$
$$2\pi C^2 = 147$$
$$\frac{2\pi C^2}{2\pi} = \frac{147}{2\pi} \qquad \longleftarrow \text{Divide both sides by } 2\pi.$$
$$C^2 = \frac{147}{2\pi}$$
$$C = \pm\sqrt{\frac{147}{2\pi}} \qquad \longleftarrow \text{Undo the squaring.}$$
$$C \approx 4.8 \qquad \longleftarrow \text{Find the positive square root.}$$

The wave speed is approximately 4.8 m/s.

Talk it Over

1. In Sample 1, why should you look only for the positive square root?

2. Are $2\pi C^2 = 9.8L$ and $L = \dfrac{2\pi C^2}{9.8}$ equivalent? Why or why not?

3. Is the relationship between L and C an example of direct variation with the square? Why or why not?

Sample 2

Solve $4x^2 - 7 = 21$.

Sample Response

Method ❶ Use algebra.

$$4x^2 - 7 = 21$$
$$4x^2 = 28 \qquad \longleftarrow \text{Add 7 to both sides.}$$
$$x^2 = 7 \qquad \longleftarrow \text{Divide both sides by 4.}$$
$$x = \pm\sqrt{7} \qquad \longleftarrow \text{Undo the squaring.}$$
$$x \approx \pm 2.6$$

The solutions are about 2.6 and about −2.6.

Unit 4 Quadratic Functions and Graphs

Answers to Talk it Over

1. The number represented by the variable is a speed. A negative value would not make sense.

2. Yes; the solution set of an equation is not changed when both sides of the equation are divided by the same nonzero number.

3. Yes; $\dfrac{2\pi}{9.8}$ is a constant coefficient for C^2.

Method ② Use a graph.

Rewrite the equation in the form $ax^2 + bx + c = 0$.

$$4x^2 - 7 = 21$$
$$4x^2 - 28 = 0 \qquad \longleftarrow \text{Subtract 21 from both sides.}$$

Graph the related function $y = 4x^2 - 28$. Use ZOOM and TRACE to estimate the x-intercepts to the nearest tenth. They are the solutions.

Watch Out!
Unless you know that the value you are looking for is positive, be sure to find both the positive and the negative square root.

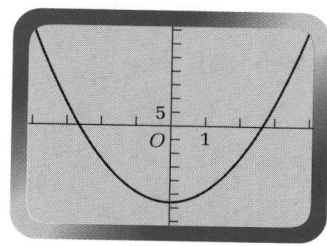

Zoom to estimate one x-intercept.

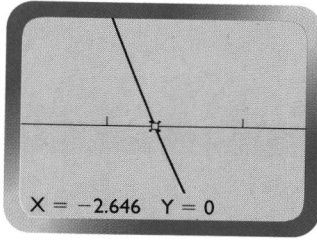

X = −2.646 Y = 0

Zoom to estimate the other x-intercept.

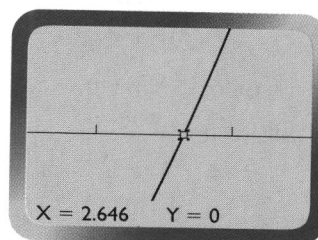

X = 2.646 Y = 0

The solutions are about 2.6 and about −2.6.

The equation $4x^2 - 7 = 21$ is a *quadratic equation*. A **quadratic equation** is one that can be written in the form $ax^2 + bx + c = 0$, where $a \neq 0$. This form is called **standard form**.

When $4x^2 - 7 = 21$ is written as $4x^2 - 28 = 0$, it is in the standard form $ax^2 + bx + c = 0$, where $b = 0$.

The x-intercepts of the graph of $y = ax^2 + bx + c$ are the solutions of the equation $0 = ax^2 + bx + c$.

Talk it Over

4. What is the relationship between the x-intercepts of the graph in Method 2 of Sample 2 and the solutions of the original equation?

5. How is the equation solving process in Sample 1 like the process in Method 1 of Sample 2? How is it different?

4-3 Solving Equations Using Square Roots

201

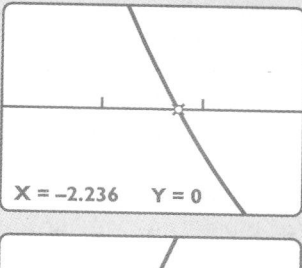
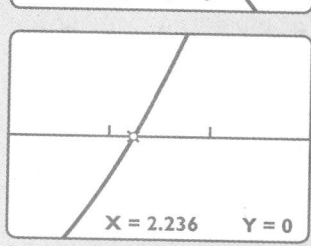

Quadratic Equations Involving Parentheses

Operations inside parentheses come first in the order of operations. When you solve quadratic equations by undoing, you reverse the order of operations and undo operations inside parentheses last.

Sample 3

Solve $(x - 3)^2 + 1 = 17$.

Sample Response

$(x - 3)^2 + 1 = 17$

$(x - 3)^2 = 16$ ←——— Subtract 1 from both sides.

$x - 3 = \pm 4$ ←——— Undo the squaring.

$x = \pm 4 + 3$ ←——— Add 3 to both sides.

$x = 4 + 3 \qquad or \qquad x = -4 + 3$

$= 7 \qquad\qquad\qquad\qquad = -1$

The solutions are 7 and -1.

Sample 4

Solve $2(x + 5)^2 - 4 = 18$.

Sample Response

$2(x + 5)^2 - 4 = 18$

$2(x + 5)^2 = 22$ ←——— Add 4 to both sides.

$(x + 5)^2 = 11$ ←——— Divide both sides by 2.

$x + 5 = \pm\sqrt{11}$ ←——— Undo the squaring.

$x + 5 \approx \pm 3.3$

$x \approx \pm 3.3 - 5$ ←——— Subtract 5 from both sides.

$x \approx 3.3 - 5 \qquad or \qquad x \approx -3.3 - 5$

$\approx -1.7 \qquad\qquad\qquad \approx -8.3$

The solutions are about -1.7 and about -8.3.

Talk it Over

6. How could you check the solutions in Sample 3?

7. How could you solve the equation in Sample 4 using a graph?

Unit 4 Quadratic Functions and Graphs

Answers to Talk it Over

6. Check by substituting both values for x in the original equation.

7. Check by graphing the related equation $y = 2(x + 5)^2 - 22$ and finding the x-intercepts.

Look Back ←

Describe how to solve a quadratic equation using a graph.
Describe how to solve a quadratic equation by undoing.

4-3 Exercises and Problems

1. **Reading** In Sample 3 on page 202, why should you add 3 to both sides as the last step rather than as the first step?

Use the graph of the related function to estimate the solutions of each equation.

2. $0 = 2x^2 - 3$

3. $0 = 0.5(x + 2)^2$

4. $0 = -(x - 3)^2 + 4$

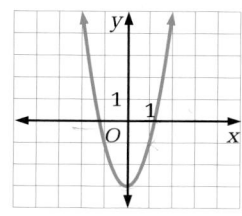

$y = 2x^2 - 3$

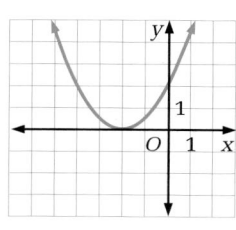

$y = 0.5(x + 2)^2$

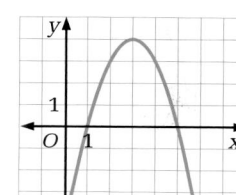

$y = -(x - 3)^2 + 4$

5. Use the graph and the equations in Exercise 4.

   a. Find the mean of the solutions.

   b. Use the graph to find an equation of the line of symmetry.

   c. Write the quadratic function in standard form.

   d. Use the formula $x = -\dfrac{b}{2a}$ to find the equation of the line of symmetry.

   e. Compare the results of parts (a), (b), and (d). What do you notice?

Find the value of x in each figure.

6.

Area = 1600 yd²

7.

x   362 yd

23 yd

8.

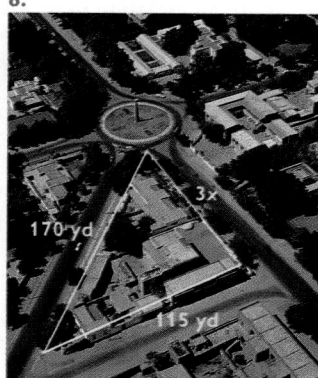

3x   170 yd

115 yd

4-3 Solving Equations Using Square Roots

Look Back

Students can frame their responses to the Look Back by using specific equations. For example, by using the equation $3(x + 4)^2 + 2 = 12$, specific statements can be made about how to solve it by using a graph or by undoing.

APPLYING

Suggested Assignment

Standard 2–26, 31–39

Extended 1–39

Integrating the Strands

Algebra Exs. 1–34, 36–39

Functions Exs. 1–34, 36–39

Logic and Language Exs. 1, 30, 31, 35

Answers to Look Back

To solve an equation such as $3(x + 4)^2 + 2 = 12$ using a graph, graph the related equation $y = 3(x + 4)^2 - 10$ and find the x-intercepts. To solve such an equation by undoing, reverse the order of operations. First, subtract 2 from both sides of the equation; next, divide both sides by 3; then undo the squaring; finally, subtract 4 from both sides.

Answers to Exercises and Problems

1. When you solve quadratic equations by undoing, you reverse the order of operations and undo operations inside parentheses last.

2. Estimates may vary. Examples are given. 1.2 and −1.2

3. −2

4. 1, 5

5. a. 3

   b. $x = 3$

   c. $y = -x^2 + 6x - 5$

   d. $x = -\dfrac{-6}{2} = 3$

   e. The equation of the line of symmetry found from the graph and the equation found from the formula are the same, $x = 3$; and the mean of the solutions is also 3.

6. $x = 40$

7. $x \approx 57.58$

8. $x \approx 41.73$

Exs. 26–28 involve a functional relationship between two variables, namely the desired probability and the length of the side of the square or the radius of the circle. If the probability is increased to 25%, for example, the square and circles would have to be made larger (to increase their areas). If the probability were decreased to say 10%, then the square and circles would have to be smaller. You might wish to consider these other possibilities with students to more fully develop their understanding of the functional relationship involved.

Career Note

Oceanographers are highly educated scientists employed by universities and some private industries, such as shipping companies, to study the physical nature of Earth's oceans. The study of oceans includes their biology, chemistry, geology, and physics. The study of waves and tides, the most familiar features of oceans, requires a strong knowledge of mathematics and physics.

In connection with Ex. 29 on page 205, some students may wish to pursue the study of *tsunamis*, or tidal waves, which may have wave lengths that are hundreds of miles long. A brief report to the class on the nature, characteristics, and devastation caused by tsunamis in the Pacific Ocean would be fascinating to most students.

Solve using mental math.

9. $x^2 = 1600$

10. $x^2 = 144$

11. $x^2 = 49$

12. Compare your answers to Exercises 6 and 9. How are they alike? How are they different?

For each equation, solve by graphing and solve using algebra.

13. $4x^2 - 2 = 10$

14. $(x + 5)^2 = 49$

15. $(x - 1)^2 - 15 = 0$

Solve.

16. $3x^2 + 5 = 32$

17. $(x + 3)^2 = 25$

18. $(x + 5)^2 - 8 = 8$

19. $2(x - 3)^2 = 60$

20. $-2x^2 + 6 = -18$

21. $3(x - 2)^2 = 48$

22. $(x - 2)^2 + 16 = 66$

23. $9(x + 23)^2 - 111 = 987$

24. $25(x - 15)^2 - 27 = 106$

25. Here are samples of two students' work for solving $(x + 2)^2 = 7$.

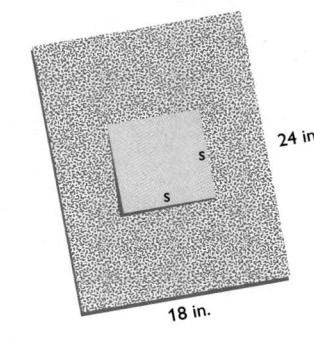

Charlie Bennett
$(x+2)^2 = 7$
$x+2 = \pm\sqrt{7}$
$x+2 \approx \pm 2.6$

$x \approx 2.6 - 2$
≈ 0.6
OR
$x \approx -2.6 - 2$
≈ -4.6

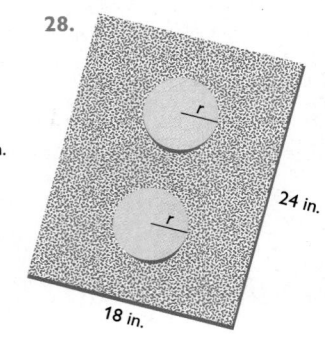

James Martin
$(x+2)^2 = 7$
$\pm(x+2) = \sqrt{7}$
$\pm(x+2) \approx 2.6$

$x + 2 \approx 2.6$
$x \approx 0.6$
OR
$-x - 2 \approx 2.6$
$-x \approx 4.6$
$x \approx -4.6$

a. Compare the methods. How are they alike? How are they different?

b. Do both methods give the same results?

c. Which method seems easier to you? Why?

Games Nadine is designing dart boards. If a dart lands on the board, she wants the probability of getting the dart in the unshaded region to be 15%. She assumes that a dart has an equal chance of landing anywhere on a dart board.

For each dart board:

a. **Write an equation in terms of the given variable for the probability P of getting a dart in the unshaded region.**

b. **Solve the equation in part (a) when $P = 15\%$.**

Student Resources Toolbox
p. 639 *Probability*

26.

24 in.

s

s

18 in.

27.

24 in.

r

18 in.

28.

r

r

24 in.

18 in.

Answers to Exercises and Problems

9. 40 and −40   10. 12 and −12

11. 7 and −7

12. The corresponding equations have one solution in common. The equation in Ex. 9 has two solutions, while the corresponding equation in Ex. 6 has only one, since the solution is a length and must be positive.

13. about 1.7, about −1.7; $\pm\sqrt{3}$

14. 2, −12

15. about 4.9, about −2.9; $1 \pm \sqrt{15}$

16. 3, −3

17. 2, −8

18. −1, −9

19. $3 \pm \sqrt{30}$; about 8.5, about −2.5

20. $\pm 2\sqrt{3}$; about 3.5, about −3.5

21. 6, −2

22. $2 \pm 5\sqrt{2}$; about 9.1, about −5.1

23. $-23 \pm \sqrt{122}$; about −12, about −34

24. $15 \pm \dfrac{\sqrt{133}}{5}$; about 17.3, about 12.7

25. a. Both methods use undoing to solve the equation. When you undo squaring, you need to account for the fact that every positive number

has two square roots. Charlie accounted for that fact by writing $\pm\sqrt{7}$; James wrote $\pm(x + 2)$.

b. Yes.

c. Answers may vary. An example is given. I feel Charlie's method is easier since James's method involves solving two more equations.

29. Science Use this information about deep water waves.

$$2\pi C^2 = 9.8L$$

$C =$ wave speed (meters per second)

$L =$ wavelength (meters)

a. A deep water wave has a wavelength of 25 m. Find the wave speed.

b. Convert the wave speed you found in part (a) to kilometers per hour.

30. a. Writing Explain how to solve $2x^2 + 3 = 8$ by using a graph.

b. **Writing** Explain how to solve $2x^2 + 3 = 8$ by using algebra.

Ongoing **ASSESSMENT**

31. Writing Lyle solved the equation $0 = 3(x - 2)^2 - 27$ and got the solutions -1 and 5. Based on his solutions to the first equation, he decided that the solutions to the equation $0 = 3(x - 5)^2 - 27$ must be 2 and 8. Do you agree with him? Explain your reasoning.

Review **PREVIEW**

Find the coordinates of the vertex of the graph of each function. *(Section 4-2)*

32. $y = 3x^2 - 1$

33. $y = -2(x + 15)^2$

34. $y = -7(x - 2)^2 + 11$

35. Determine whether the conclusion in the following statement is correct. If not, give a counterexample. *(Section 1-7)*

If Sara is sitting in her drama class, then she is in school. Sara is in school.
Conclusion: Sara is in drama class.

Find each product. *(Toolbox Skill 11)*

36. $(x + 3)(x - 5)$

37. $(y - 8)(2y - 4)$

38. $2(3z + 1)(6z - 9)$

 Working on the Unit Project

39. Use the Water Arc equation on page 192 and the data you gathered in Exercise 29 on page 198.

a. Substitute values you know for $m\angle A$, x, and y in the equation and then solve to find the water speed v.

b. Use the result of part (a) to help you write an equation for the water's path.

c. Use the equation you wrote in part (b) to find the maximum height of the water above the ground.

4-3 Solving Equations Using Square Roots

Practice 28 For use with Section 4-3

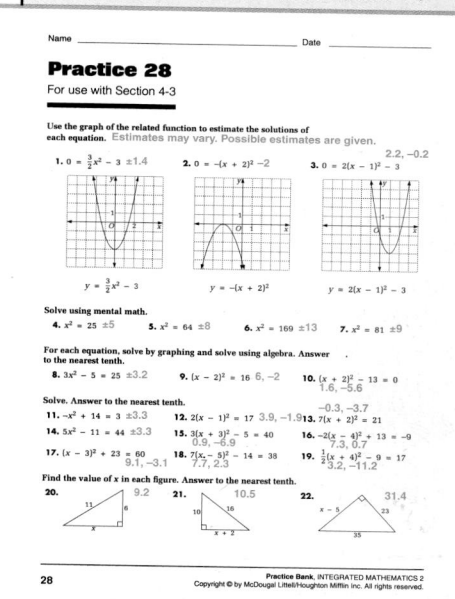

Assessment: Standard

Ex. 31 assesses students' knowledge of the effect of a translation on the graph of a specific quadratic function and thus on the solutions to the corresponding equation.

Working on the Unit Project

Students will need the water arc equation to design their fountains.

Answers to Exercises and Problems

26. a. $P = \dfrac{s^2}{432}$

b. $s \approx 8$ in.

27. a. $P = \dfrac{\pi r^2}{432}$

b. $r \approx 4.5$ in.

28. a. $P = \dfrac{2\pi r^2}{432} = \dfrac{\pi r^2}{216}$

b. $r \approx 3.2$ in.

29. a. about 6.2 m/s

b. about 22.32 km/h

30. a. Subtract 8 from both sides of the equation to get $2x^2 - 5 = 0$. Then graph the related equation $y = 2x^2 - 5$ and find the x-intercepts. They are the solutions of the original equation.

b. Begin undoing using the reverse order of operations. That is, first subtract 3 from both sides. Next, divide both sides of the equation by 2. Finally, undo the squaring to get $x = \pm\sqrt{\dfrac{5}{2}}$.

31. Lyle is correct. The solutions of the equation $0 = 3(x - 5)^2 - 27$ are the x-intercepts of the graph of $y = 3(x - 5)^2 - 27$. That graph is the graph of $y = 3(x - 2)^2 - 27$ translated 3 units to the right. By translating the x-intercepts of the graph of

$y = 3(x - 2)^2 - 27$, Lyle found the solutions to be $-1 + 3 = 2$ and $5 + 3 = 8$.

32. $(0, -1)$ **33.** $(-15, 0)$ **34.** $(2, 11)$

35. False. For example, Sarah might be in some other classroom, the cafeteria, or a hallway.

36. $x^2 - 2x - 15$

37. $2y^2 - 20y + 32$

38. $36z^2 - 42z - 18$

39. See answers in back of book.

Section 4-4

Solving Equations Using Factoring

factor*fiction*

Focus
Solve quadratic equations by factoring.

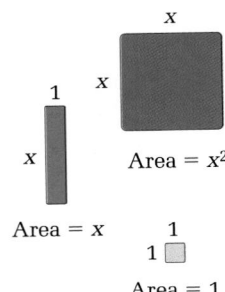

x

x

1

Area = x^2

x

Area = x

1

1

Area = 1

EXPLORATION

(How) can algebra tiles help you factor trinomials?

- **Materials:** algebra tiles (x^2-tiles, x-tiles, and 1-tiles)
- **Work in a group of three students.**

A **monomial** is a number, a variable, or the product of a number and one or more variables. A **trinomial** is a sum of three monomials. You can model a trinomial with a set of algebra tiles. The trinomial is an expression for the area covered by the tiles.

Suppose you can build a rectangle with the tiles. The expressions for the length and the width of the rectangle are the factors of the trinomial.

① **a.** Build a rectangle for $x^2 + 7x + 6$. The tiles should touch but not overlap.

b. Use the dimensions of the tiles to complete the variable expressions for the length and the width of the rectangle.

$$\text{Area} = x^2 + 7x + 6 = (x + \underline{?})(x + \underline{?})$$

② **a.** Build a rectangle for $2x^2 + 5x + 3$. Is building a rectangle more difficult when the coefficient of the x^2-term is greater than one?

b. Use the dimensions of the tiles to complete the variable expressions for the length and the width of the rectangle.

$$\text{Area} = 2x^2 + 5x + 3 = (2x + \underline{?})(x + \underline{?})$$

③ Discuss how modeling with algebra tiles can help you factor trinomials.

④ Try to build a rectangle for $3x^2 + 2x + 1$. What is your conclusion about factoring this trinomial?

Unit 4 Quadratic Functions and Graphs

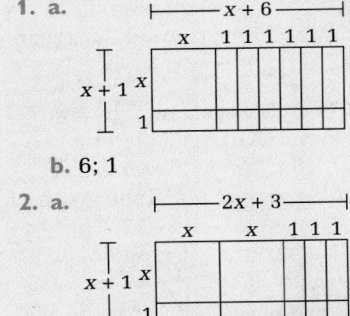

Factor $2x^2 + 5x + 3$.

Sample Response

Method ❶ Use algebra tiles.

Build a rectangle for $2x^2 + 5x + 3$ with tiles.

The length of the rectangle is $2x + 3$ and the width of the rectangle is $x + 1$.

$2x^2 + 5x + 3 = (2x + 3)(x + 1)$

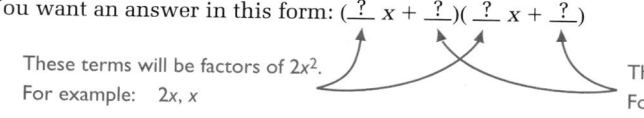

Method ❷ Use trial and error.

You want an answer in this form: $(\underline{?}\,x + \underline{?})(\underline{?}\,x + \underline{?})$

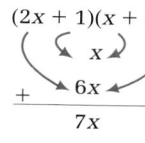 These terms will be factors of $2x^2$.
For example: $2x, x$

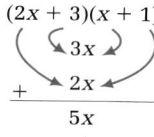 These terms will be factors of 3.
For example: $1, 3$
$-1, -3$

Try different combinations. Focus on getting the correct middle term.

$(2x + 1)(x + 3)$ $(2x + 3)(x + 1)$ $(2x - 1)(x - 3)$ $(2x - 3)(x - 1)$

x $3x$ $-x$ $-3x$

$+\;\;\;\; 6x$ $+\;\;\;\; 2x$ $+\;\;\;\; -6x$ $+\;\;\;\; -2x$

$\quad\;\; 7x$ $5x$ $-7x$ $-5x$

The second pair of factors gives the correct middle term.

$2x^2 + 5x + 3 = (2x + 3)(x + 1)$

Talk it Over

1. Suppose the trinomial in Sample 1 had been $2x^2 - 5x + 3$. Look at the list of possible factors in the Sample Response. Factor this new trinomial.

2. Suppose the trinomial in Sample 1 had been $2x^2 - 5x - 3$.
   a. What are the factors of the third term, -3?
   b. Factor the trinomial.

3. The first step in factoring any trinomial is to look for common factors in each term of the trinomial. Suppose the trinomial in Sample 1 had been $4x^2 + 10x + 6$.
   a. What is the greatest common factor of each term?
   b. Factor out this common factor: $4x^2 + 10x + 6 = \underline{?}\,(\underline{?})$
   c. Factor completely: $4x^2 + 10x + 6 = \underline{?}\,(\underline{?})(\underline{?})$

4. Which is the correct way to factor $12x^2 + 16x + 5$?
   a. $(6x + 1)(2x + 5)$ b. $(6x + 5)(2x + 1)$ c. $(4x + 5)(3x + 1)$

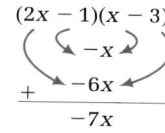 **Now you are ready for:**
Exs. 1–18 on pp. 210–211

4-4 Solving Equations Using Factoring

 **207**

Answers to Talk it Over

1. $(2x - 3)(x - 1)$
2. a. 1 and -3 or -1 and 3
   b. $(2x + 1)(x - 3)$
3. a. 2
   b. $2(2x^2 + 5x + 3)$
   c. $2(2x + 3)(x + 1)$
4. b

TEACHING

Exploration

Working in groups of three, students use algebra tiles to model trinomials and learn that the dimensions of a rectangle modeling a trinomial can be used as the factors of a trinomial. In step 4, students learn the important fact that not all trinomials can be factored.

Teaching Tip

An expression such as $2a + 4b + c$ is a trinomial because it has three unlike terms. In this section, *quadratic trinomials* are considered, that is, trinomials of the form $ax^2 + bx + c$.

Additional Sample

S1 Factor $3x^2 + 7x + 2$.

Method 1. Use algebra tiles.

$(3x^2 + 7x + 2) = (3x + 1)(x + 2)$

Method 2. Use trial and error.
$(\underline{?}\,x + \underline{?})(\underline{?}\,x + \underline{?})$
$(3x + 2)(x + 1) = 3x^2 + 5x + 2$
No.
$(3x + 1)(x + 2) = 3x^2 + 7x + 2$
Yes.

Talk it Over

Question 3 introduces a trinomial that has a common numerical factor in each term. Before attempting to factor this trinomial into a product of two binomials, the greatest common factor of each term is factored out. Then the remaining trinomial is factored, if possible. In this case, the factors are $2(2x + 3)(x + 1)$.

207

208

Reasoning

In order to use the special factoring patterns, students need to be able to recognize that a particular trinomial, such as $x^2 + 20x + 100$, has the same form as one of the special patterns. In this case, $x^2 + 20x + 100$ can be rewritten as $x^2 + 2 \cdot 10x + 10^2$, which matches the pattern $a^2 + 2ab + b^2$ ($b = 10$, $2b = 20$, and $a = x$). Therefore, $x^2 + 20x + 100 = (x + 10)^2$.

Additional Samples

S2 Factor $25x^2 - 81$.

$25x^2 - 81 = (5x + 9)(5x - 9)$

S3 Factor $16x^2 + 56x + 49$.

$16x^2 + 56x + 49 = (4x + 7)^2$

Error Analysis

Errors in factoring trinomials are made by most students as they search for the right combinations of terms in each pair of factors. Before students conclude, however, that they have indeed found the correct factors, they should always check the factors by multiplying them together to see if the product is the original trinomial. If it is not, then the factors are not the correct ones.

The results of Exercises 17 and 18 on page 211 lead you to these special factoring patterns.

SPECIAL FACTORING PATTERNS

To factor a *difference of two squares*:

$$a^2 - b^2 = (a + b)(a - b)$$

To factor a *perfect square trinomial*:

$$a^2 + 2ab + b^2 = (a + b)^2$$
$$a^2 - 2ab + b^2 = (a - b)^2$$

Examples

$x^2 - 100 = (x + 10)(x - 10)$

$x^2 + 20x + 100 = (x + 10)^2$

$x^2 - 20x + 100 = (x - 10)^2$

Sample 2

Factor $16x^2 - 9$.

Sample Response

Test whether the expression is a difference of two squares. Ask these questions:

Is the expression a difference?	Yes.
Is the first term a square?	Yes: $16x^2 = (4x)^2$
Is the second term a square?	Yes: $9 = 3^2$

$16x^2 - 9 = (4x)^2 - 3^2$

$\qquad = (4x + 3)(4x - 3)$ ⟵ —— Use the pattern: $a^2 - b^2 = (a + b)(a - b)$

Sample 3

Factor $9x^2 - 30x + 25$.

Sample Response

Test whether the trinomial is a perfect square trinomial. Ask these questions:

Is the first term a square?	Yes: $9x^2 = (3x)^2$
Is the last term a square?	Yes: $25 = 5^2$
Is the middle term twice the product of $3x$ and 5?	Yes: $30x = 2(3x)(5)$

$9x^2 - 30x + 25 = (3x)^2 - 2(3x)(5) + 5^2$

$\qquad = (3x - 5)^2$ ⟵ —— Use the pattern: $a^2 - 2ab + b^2 = (a - b)^2$

Unit 4 Quadratic Functions and Graphs

Solving Equations by Factoring

Some quadratic equations can be solved by factoring and then using the *zero-product property*.

Sample 4

Solve $4x^2 - x = 5$.

Sample Response

$$4x^2 - x = 5$$
$$4x^2 - x - 5 = 0 \quad \longleftarrow \quad \text{Rewrite the equation in standard form.}$$
$$(4x - 5)(x + 1) = 0 \quad \longleftarrow \quad \text{Factor the trinomial by trial and error.}$$

$$4x - 5 = 0 \quad \text{or} \quad x + 1 = 0 \quad \longleftarrow \quad \text{Use the } \textbf{zero-product property.} \text{ When a}$$
$$4x = 5 \qquad\qquad x = -1 \qquad\qquad \text{product of factors is equal to 0, one or}$$
$$x = 1.25 \qquad\qquad\qquad\qquad\qquad \text{more of the factors equals 0.}$$

The solutions are 1.25 and -1.

Sample 5

Solve $5n^2 - 15n - 20 = 0$.

Sample Response

$$5n^2 - 15n - 20 = 0$$
$$5(n^2 - 3n - 4) = 0 \quad \longleftarrow \quad \text{Factor out the greatest common factor.}$$
$$5(n - 4)(n + 1) = 0 \quad \longleftarrow \quad \text{Factor the remaining trinomial.}$$

$$n - 4 = 0 \quad \text{or} \quad n + 1 = 0 \quad \longleftarrow \quad \text{Use the zero-product property.}$$
$$n = 4 \qquad\qquad n = -1$$

The solutions are 4 and -1.

> **BY THE WAY...**
>
> Factoring was not used to solve quadratic equations until 1631.

Talk it Over

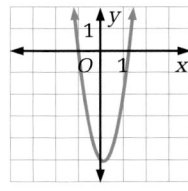

5. In Sample 4, describe how you can check whether 1.25 and -1 are solutions.

6. Use the graph shown at the left to estimate the x-intercepts of the graph of $y = 4x^2 - x - 5$.

7. How do the x-intercepts relate to the solutions of the equation $4x^2 - x - 5 = 0$ in Sample 4?

4-4 Solving Equations Using Factoring

Teaching Tip

The zero-product property can be stated mathematically as follows: If a and b are real numbers and if $a \cdot b = 0$, then $a = 0$ or $b = 0$. In mathematics, the word *or* is always used in the *inclusive* sense; in other words, to say that $a = 0$ or $b = 0$ means that both a and b can be 0.

Additional Samples

S4 Solve $7x^2 + 18x = -8$.
$$7x^2 + 18x = -8$$
$$7x^2 + 18x + 8 = 0$$
$$(7x + 4)(x + 2) = 0$$
$$7x + 4 = 0 \quad \text{or} \quad x + 2 = 0$$
$$7x = -4 \qquad\qquad x = -2$$
$$x = -\frac{4}{7}$$
The solutions are $-\frac{4}{7}$ and -2.

S5 Solve $2x^2 + 20x + 32 = 0$.
$$2x^2 + 20x + 32 = 0$$
$$2(x^2 + 10x + 16) = 0$$
$$2(x + 8)(x + 2) = 0$$
$$x + 8 = 0 \quad \text{or} \quad x + 2 = 0$$
$$x = -8 \qquad\qquad x = -2$$
The solutions are -8 and -2.

Talk it Over

Question 6 reinforces the fact that the x-intercepts of a quadratic equation are the solutions of the equation.

Answers to Talk it Over

5. Substitute -1 and 1.25 for x in the original equation.

6. about -1 and about 1.25

7. The x-intercepts of the graph of $y = 4x^2 - x - 5$ are the solutions of the equation $4x^2 - x - 5 = 0$.

Suggested Assignment

Day 1

Standard 4–15, 18

Extended 1–16, 18

Day 2

Standard 20–36, 38–45

Extended 19–36, 38–45

Integrating the Strands

Algebra Exs. 1–45

Functions Exs. 32–37, 45

Logic and Language Exs. 1, 16, 17, 19, 38

Communication: Writing

For Ex. 3, students should write out all 12 possible factors of the trinomial with their middle terms. As students gain experience in factoring, however, they will be able to eliminate incorrect factors mentally and thus save time by not writing them all down.

Assessment: Standard

For Exs. 4–15, students should write out what they think are the correct factors and then check their work by multiplying the factors to recreate the original trinomial.

Answers to Look Back

Answers may vary. An example is given. The terms of the trinomial in Sample 1 have no common factors. The first and third terms are not squares, so the trinomial is neither the difference of squares nor a perfect square trinomial. The trinomial must be factored by trial and error. The terms of the trinomial in Sample 2 have no common factors. However, the two terms are both perfect squares, so $16x^2 - 9$ is the difference of two squares. The terms of the trinomial in Sample 3 have no common factors. It is not a difference, but the first and third terms are perfect squares and the middle term is twice the product of the first and third terms. So $9x^2 - 30x + 25$ is a perfect square trinomial. The trinomial in Sample 4 does not meet any of the

GUIDELINES FOR FACTORING COMPLETELY

1. Factor out the greatest common factor first.
2. Look for a difference of two squares.
3. Look for a perfect square trinomial.
4. If a trinomial is not a perfect square, use trial and error to look for a pair of factors.

► **Now you are ready for:**
Exs. 19–45 on pp. 211–213

Look Back ◄

Describe how each sample in this section illustrates the guidelines above.

4-4 Exercises and Problems

1. **Reading** When you build a rectangle with algebra tiles to model a trinomial, how do you find the factors of the trinomial from the rectangle?

2. In the Exploration, was there more than one rectangle you could form to represent $2x^2 + 5x + 3$?

3. Use the trinomial $6m^2 - 5m - 4$ and the table at the right.

   a. Complete the first column.

   b. Complete the second column.

   c. Make a table that shows the possible factors of the trinomial and the possible middle terms. Which middle term is correct?

   d. Factor the trinomial.

Factors of $6m^2$	Factors of -4
?, m	1, ?
$3m$, ?	-1, ?
—	2, ?

Factor.

4. $x^2 + 2x - 15$ 5. $2x^2 - 7x + 3$ 6. $3m^2 + 2m - 21$

7. $7n^2 + 17n + 6$ 8. $5x^2 - 14x + 8$ 9. $12x^2 - 5x - 3$

10. $4x^2 + 32x + 15$ 11. $24z^2 - 14z - 5$ 12. $3x^2 - 18x - 48$

13. $6x^2 - 27x + 21$ 14. $18x^2 + 14x - 4$ 15. $12d^2 - 34d + 20$

16. **Open-ended**

   a. Write a trinomial that cannot be factored.

   b. Make a sketch or build a model of the trinomial to show that you cannot form a rectangle using algebra tiles.

Answers to Exercises and Problems

first three guidelines, so it is factored by trial and error. The trinomial in Sample 5 has a common factor which is factored out first. The remaining trinomial has first and third terms that are perfect squares, but the second term is not twice the product of the first and third terms, so the trinomial is factored by trial and error.

1. The factors of the trinomial are the length and width of the rectangle.

2. The only other rectangle was one in which the width is $2x + 3$ and the length $x + 1$. A trinomial can be factored completely in only one way, unless you consider the order of the factors. That is, $2x^2 + 5x + 3$ can only be

factored as $(2x + 3)(x + 1)$ or $(x + 1)(2x + 3)$.

3. a. $6m$; $2m$

   b. -4; 4; -2

   c. See answers in back of book.

   d. $(3m - 4)(2m + 1)$

4. $(x + 5)(x - 3)$

5. $(2x - 1)(x - 3)$

6. $(3m - 7)(m + 3)$

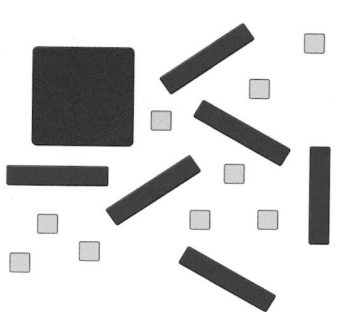

17. Using Manipulatives

a. Model $x^2 + 6x + 9$ using algebra tiles and arrange the tiles to form a rectangle.

b. Make a sketch of your arrangement. What special kind of rectangle is it?

c. Use the dimensions of your rectangle to complete:
$$x^2 + 6x + 9 = (\underline{\ ?\ })(\underline{\ ?\ }) = (\underline{\ ?\ })^2$$

d. The product $3 \cdot 3$ is 9. The product $(-3)(-3)$ is also 9. Use this result to factor the trinomial $x^2 - 6x + 9$.

e. **Writing** The type of trinomial factored in parts (c) and (d) is called a *perfect square trinomial*. Explain how you know when a trinomial is a perfect square trinomial.

18. For parts (a)–(d), find each product.

a. $(x + 1)(x - 1)$ b. $(x + 9)(x - 9)$ c. $(x + 8)(x - 8)$ d. $(x + 6)(x - 6)$

e. What patterns do you notice?

f. Use the patterns to find the product $(x + k)(x - k)$.

19. Writing Which of the special factoring patterns described on page 208 does the diagram model? Explain.

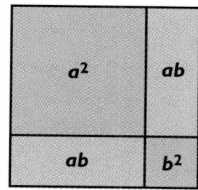

Factor.

20. $x^2 + 4x + 4$ **21.** $x^2 - 14x + 49$ **22.** $16n^2 - 8n + 1$

23. $x^2 - 16$ **24.** $9m^2 - 4$ **25.** $x^2 - 25y^2$

Solve.

26. $0 = 2x^2 - 3x - 5$ **27.** $0 = 9x^2 + 6x - 3$ **28.** $x^2 = 4x + 5$

29. $-1 = x^2 - 2x$ **30.** $2 = 10x^2 + 11x - 4$ **31.** $0 = 8x^2 - 8x - 6$

Match each function with its graph.

32. $y = (x + 1)(x - 2)$

33. $y = 2(x + 1)(x - 2)$

34. $y = -(x + 1)(x - 2)$

35. $y = 0.5(x + 1)(x - 2)$

A.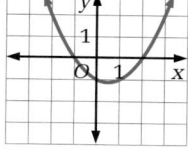

B.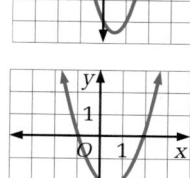

C.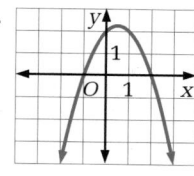

D.

4-4 Solving Equations Using Factoring   **211**

Answers to Exercises and Problems

7. $(7n + 3)(n + 2)$

8. $(5x - 4)(x - 2)$

9. $(3x + 1)(4x - 3)$

10. $(2x + 15)(2x + 1)$

11. $(4z + 1)(6z - 5)$

12. $3(x + 2)(x - 8)$

13. $3(x - 1)(2x - 7)$

14. $2(9x - 2)(x + 1)$

15. $2(6d - 5)(d - 2)$

16. a. Answers may vary. Example: $x^2 + 3x + 1$

b. Answers may vary. An example is given.

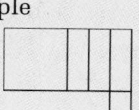

b.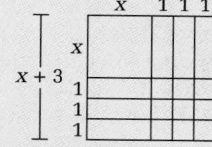

a square

17. a. Check students' work.

c. $(x + 3)(x + 3) = (x + 3)^2$

d. $(x - 3)(x - 3) = (x - 3)^2$

Cooperative Learning

Ex. 17 can be used as a group activity with students working in groups of three, as was done for the Exploration on page 206. The remaining factoring exercises on this page (Exs. 20–25) also can be included as part of the group work. In so doing, some students may be able to assist others who are experiencing difficulties with factoring.

17. e. Answers may vary. An example is given. A trinomial is a perfect square trinomial when the first and third terms are perfect squares and the second term is twice the product of the square roots of the first and third terms.

18. a. $x^2 - 1$ **b.** $x^2 - 81$

c. $x^2 - 64$ **d.** $x^2 - 36$

e. There are no middle terms.

f. $x^2 - k^2$

19. Answers may vary. The diagram models a perfect square trinomial; either $a^2 + 2ab + b^2 = (a + b)^2$ or $a^2 - 2ab + b^2 = (a - b)^2$.

20. $(x + 2)^2$ **21.** $(x - 7)^2$

22. $(4n - 1)(4n - 1)$

23. $(x + 4)(x - 4)$

24. $(3m + 2)(3m - 2)$

25. $(x - 5y)(x + 5y)$

26. $-1, \frac{5}{2}$ **27.** $-1, \frac{1}{3}$

28. $-1, 5$ **29.** 1

30. $\frac{2}{5}, -\frac{3}{2}$ **31.** $\frac{3}{2}, -\frac{1}{2}$

32. D   **33.** B

34. C   **35.** A

36. a. Factor $ax^2 + bx$.

   b. Solve the equation $0 = ax^2 + bx$ for x.

   c. What do the two solutions in part (b) represent for the graph of the function $y = ax^2 + bx$?

   d. Write an expression for the average of the solutions in part (b).

   e. How is your answer to part (d) related to the line of symmetry of the graph of $y = ax^2 + bx$?

   f. Explain why the line of symmetry of $y = ax^2 + bx + c$ is also $x = -\dfrac{b}{2a}$.

37 TECHNOLOGY Use a graphics calculator.

   a. Choose one of the equations in Exercises 26–31.

   b. On the same set of axes, graph the function related to the equation given in the exercise and the function for the factored form.

   c. What do you notice?

Ongoing **ASSESSMENT**

38. **Writing** A basketball player shoots at a basket that is 10 ft from the floor. The function in the photo gives the distance from the ball to the floor, in feet.

   a. Explain how the equation $10 = -16t^2 + 20t + 6$ or $0 = -16t^2 + 20t - 4$ can help you find when the ball is at basket level.

   b. Solve $0 = -16t^2 + 20t - 4$ by factoring. Which solution represents the time that the ball passes through the basket?

   c. Explain how the equation $0 = -16t^2 + 20t + 6$ can help you find when the ball hits the ground.

   d. Solve $0 = -16t^2 + 20t + 6$ by factoring. Which solution makes sense as the time the ball hits the ground?

$d = -16t^2 + 20t + 6$

Review **PREVIEW**

Solve. *(Section 4-3)*

39. $3x^2 - 13 = 14$ **40.** $(x - 5)^2 = 5$ **41.** $2(x + 2)^2 - 8 = 10$

For Exercises 42 and 43, assume that the time it takes to travel a distance of 150 mi varies inversely with the speed you are traveling. *(Section 2-3)*

42. Model the situation with an equation.

43. Find the time it would take to travel the 150 miles at 50 mi/h.

44. Use the proportion $\dfrac{x}{18} = \dfrac{5}{6}$. *(Toolbox Skill 17)*

   a. What are the cross products of the proportion?

   b. Solve the proportion.

212   **Unit 4** Quadratic Functions and Graphs

45. Near the town of Cairo, Illinois, the Mississippi River is 4500 ft across. Suppose an ambitious engineer wants to design a water gun that sprays water across the Mississippi at Cairo. The engineer would like the water arc to reach a maximum height of 1 mi (5280 ft) as shown.

Do parts (a)–(f) to find the necessary water speed v and angle A of the water gun.

a. Draw the water arc on a coordinate plane, using the location of the water gun for the origin. Label the coordinates of the arc's vertex and two endpoints.

b. Use the graph from part (a) to find the x-intercepts.

c. The equation of a parabola may be written in factored form as $y = a(x - p)(x - q)$, where p and q are the x-intercepts. For the equation of the water arc, you know p, q, and the coordinates of the vertex. Use this information to find a and to write the equation of the water arc in factored form.

d. Rewrite the equation you wrote in part (c) in the standard form $y = ax^2 + bx + c$.

e. Use the fact that $b = \tan A$ to find the angle A at which the water gun should be tilted.

f. Use the fact that $a = \dfrac{-16}{v^2(\cos A)^2}$ to find the water speed v needed to make the arc reach across the Mississippi. Does this speed seem reasonable to you?

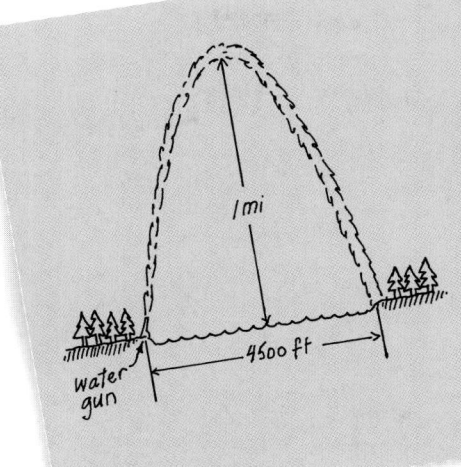

Unit 4   **CHECKPOINT**

1. Writing Can all quadratic equations be solved by factoring? Explain.

Find the coordinates of the vertex of the graph of each function. Tell whether the vertex is a *maximum* or a *minimum*.   4-1

2. $y = 3x^2 - 6x + 7$ **3.** $y = -x^2 + x$

Tell how to translate the graph of $y = 0.5x^2$ to produce the graph of each function.   4-2

4. $y = 0.5(x - 1)^2 + 5$ **5.** $y = 0.5(x + 2)^2$

Solve.   4-3, 4-4

6. $7x^2 - 22 = 34$ **7.** $3(x + 6)^2 = 33$

8. $2(x - 8)^2 - 25 = 25$ **9.** $3x^2 = 31x - 36$

10. $9x^2 + 5 = 30$ **11.** $5x^2 + 30x + 45 = 0$

4-4 Solving Equations Using Factoring   **213**

Practice 29 For use with Section 4-4

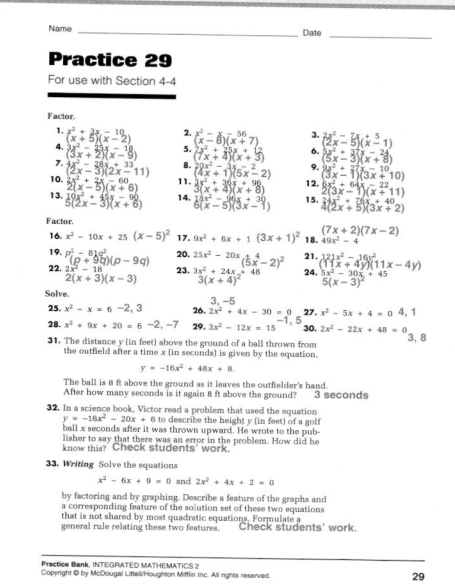

Answers to Checkpoint

1. No; there are some trinomials that cannot be factored. For example, $2x^2 + 3x + 5$ cannot be factored, so $2x^2 + 3x + 5 = 0$ cannot be solved by factoring.

2. $(1, 4)$; minimum

3. $\left(\dfrac{1}{2}, \dfrac{1}{4}\right)$; maximum

4. 1 unit to the right, 5 units up

5. 2 units to the left

6. $\pm 2\sqrt{2}$; about 2.8, about −2.8

7. $-6 \pm \sqrt{11}$; about −2.7, about −9.3

8. 13, 3

9. $9, \dfrac{4}{3}$

10. $\dfrac{5}{3}, -\dfrac{5}{3}$

11. −3

Answers to Exercises and Problems

45. a.

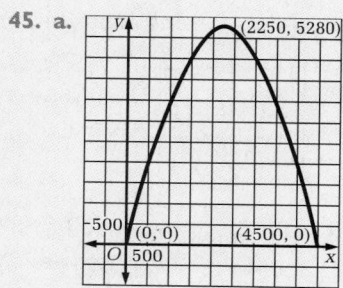

b. 0 and 4500

45. c–f. Estimates may vary. Examples are given.

c. about −0.001;
$y = -0.001x(x - 4500)$

d. $y = -0.001x^2 + 4.5x$

e. about 77°

f. The speed would need to be about 566 ft/s, or about 386 mi/h. Answers may vary. An example is given. This speed seems too fast to be a reasonable speed for the water gun; pumps described elsewhere in the unit had maximum speeds of 50 ft/s, 60 ft/s, and 70 ft/s.

Objectives and Strands
See pages 184A and 184B.

Spiral Learning
See page 184B.

Materials List
➤ Graphics calculator

Recommended Pacing
Section 4-5 is a two-day lesson.
Day 1
Pages 214–216: Talk it Over 1 through Talk it Over 8, *Exercises 1–19*
Day 2
Pages 216–217: Sample 2 through Look Back, *Exercises 20–52*

Extra Practice
See pages 620–621.

Warm-Up Exercises
Warm-Up Transparency 4-5

Support Materials
➤ Practice 30
➤ Enrichment 27 in the Activity Bank
➤ Study Guide 4-5
➤ Problem Set 8
➤ McDougal Littell Mathpack software: *Function Investigator*
➤ Using TI-81 and TI-82 Calculators: Approximating Solutions Using a Quadratic Formula Program
➤ Quiz 4-5

Section

4-5

---➤Focus
Use the quadratic formula to solve quadratic equations.

The Quadratic Formula

The Golden Solution

Mill-owners' Association Building, Ahmedabac, India. Designed by Charles Édouard Jeanneret, known as Le Corbusier.

Talk it Over

Golden rectangles are often used in art and architecture because their shape is considered pleasing to the eye. There is a special relationship between the sides of a golden rectangle.

This ratio is called the *golden ratio*. ➜

$$\frac{\text{length of short side}}{\text{length of long side}} = \frac{\text{length of long side}}{\text{length of short side} + \text{length of long side}}$$

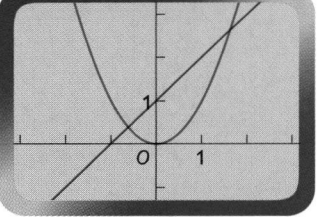

1. The rectangle in the photograph is a golden rectangle with sides of length 1 and x. Write a proportion to show the relationship between the sides.

2. Rewrite the proportion from question 1 using cross products. Can you use factoring to solve this equation? Explain.

3. Use a graphics calculator to graph $y = x^2$ and $y = x + 1$. What do the points of intersection represent?

4. Use TRACE to approximate the x-values for the points where the two graphs intersect. What does the positive x-value represent?

5. Another way to solve $x + 1 = x^2$ is to graph $y = x^2 - x - 1$. Use TRACE to approximate the x-intercepts of this graph.

6. Describe the relationship between the x-values you found in question 4 and the x-intercepts of the graph of $y = x^2 - x - 1$ that you found in question 5.

214   **Unit 4** Quadratic Functions and Graphs

Answers to Talk it Over

1. $\frac{1}{x} = \frac{x}{x+1}$

2. $x + 1 = x^2$; No. To solve the equation $x^2 - x - 1 = 0$ by factoring, you consider the factors of the first term and the third term. The only possible factoring is $(x + 1)(x - 1)$, which does not produce the correct middle term.

3. the numbers x for which $x + 1 = x^2$

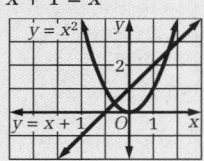

4. about -0.6 and about 1.6; The positive value is close to the golden ratio.

5. about -0.6 and about 1.6

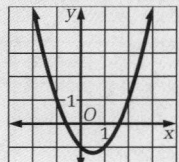

6. The x-coordinates of the points of intersection are the x-intercepts of $y = x^2 - x - 1$.

Using the Quadratic Formula

You can use a graph to find approximate solutions of the equation $x + 1 = x^2$. You can also use the quadratic formula.

QUADRATIC FORMULA

The solutions of the quadratic equation $0 = ax^2 + bx + c$, when $a \neq 0$ are given by this formula:

x-coordinate of the vertex, which is on the line of symmetry ⟶

distance from each x-intercept to the line of symmetry ⟵

$$x = -\frac{b}{2a} \pm \frac{\sqrt{b^2 - 4ac}}{2a}$$

"$\pm$" means there are two solutions.

The solutions are:

$$x = -\frac{b}{2a} + \frac{\sqrt{b^2 - 4ac}}{2a} \quad \text{and} \quad x = -\frac{b}{2a} - \frac{\sqrt{b^2 - 4ac}}{2a}$$

Sample 1

Solve $x + 1 = x^2$.

Sample Response

First, write the equation in standard form.

$$x + 1 = x^2$$

$$0 = x^2 - x - 1 \quad \longleftarrow \text{ This is in the form } 0 = ax^2 + bx + c.$$

Then use the quadratic formula.

$$x = -\frac{b}{2a} \pm \frac{\sqrt{b^2 - 4ac}}{2a} \quad \longleftarrow \text{ Write the quadratic formula.}$$

$$= -\frac{(-1)}{2(1)} \pm \frac{\sqrt{(-1)^2 - 4(1)(-1)}}{2(1)} \quad \longleftarrow \text{ Substitute 1 for } a, -1 \text{ for } b, \text{ and } -1 \text{ for } c.$$

$$= \frac{1}{2} \pm \frac{\sqrt{5}}{2}$$

$$\approx 0.5 \pm 1.12$$

$$x \approx 0.5 + 1.12 \quad or \quad x \approx 0.5 - 1.12$$

$$\approx 1.62 \qquad\qquad \approx -0.62$$

The solutions are about 1.6 and about −0.6.

> **BY THE WAY...**
>
> In A.D. **628**, the Hindu mathematician Brahmagupta found one of the solutions of a quadratic equation. His method was one which was used to develop the quadratic formula.

TEACHING

Talk it Over

Questions 1 and 2 use the special relationship between the sides of a golden rectangle to write a proportion whose cross products give rise to a quadratic equation ($x + 1 = x^2$) that cannot be solved by using factoring methods developed in the previous section.

Questions 3–6 show that graphing techniques can be used to find the solutions to the equation $x + 1 = x^2$ (or the equivalent equation $x^2 - x - 1 = 0$), which are approximately −0.6 and 1.6.

Although graphing techniques are useful, they can only yield approximate solutions. Other techniques are needed that yield exact solutions, such as the use of the quadratic formula.

Teaching Tip

Sample 1 uses the equation that results from Talk it Over question 2. The positive solution to this equation (1.62) is approximately equal to the golden ratio. This ratio also can be written as $\frac{1 + \sqrt{5}}{2}$.

Additional Sample

S1 Solve $x + 4 = x^2$.

$$0 = x^2 - x - 4$$

$$x = -\frac{(-1)}{2(1)} \pm \frac{\sqrt{(-1)^2 - 4(1)(-4)}}{2(1)}$$

$$x = \frac{1}{2} \pm \frac{\sqrt{17}}{2}$$

$$x \approx 0.5 \pm 2.06$$

$$x \approx 2.56 \text{ or } x \approx -1.56$$

Talk it Over

Questions 7 and 8 on page 216 help students to equate the numerical values in a quadratic equation to the values of a, b, and c in the quadratic formula. This is an essential step if the formula is to be applied correctly.

Additional Sample

S2 A baseball player throws a ball from center field to home plate in an attempt to get a runner out at the plate. The height in meters t seconds after the ball is thrown is given by the function $h = -0.45t^2 + 0.25t + 3.11$. How long will it take the ball to reach home plate?

When the ball reaches home plate, its height is 0 m. Substitute 0 for h.

$0 = -0.45t^2 + 0.25t + 3.11$

Use the quadratic formula to find the values of t when $h = 0$.

$$t = \frac{(-0.25)}{2(-0.45)} \pm$$

$$\frac{\sqrt{(0.25)^2 - 4(-0.45)(3.11)}}{2(-0.45)}$$

$t \approx 0.28 \pm \dfrac{\sqrt{5.65}}{-0.9}$

$t \approx 0.28 \pm (-2.64)$

$t \approx 0.28 + (-2.64)$ or

$t \approx 0.28 + 2.64$

$t \approx -2.36$ or $t \approx 2.92$

The ball will reach home plate in about 3 s.

Talk it Over

Question 9 makes students think about interpreting solutions to equations in a real-world context. Very often, equations have solutions that do not make sense in realistic situations. These solutions are then discarded and only those that are valid for the situation are retained.

Now you are ready for:
Exs. 1–19 on pp. 217–218

Talk it Over

7. Suppose an equation is given as $3x^2 = 2x - 5$. What values of a, b, and c would you use in the quadratic formula?

8. In the equation $2x^2 - 6 = 0$, what is the value of b? Explain.

Sample 2

A cliff diver in Acapulco, Mexico, jumps from about 17 m above the water. His height in meters from the water t seconds after he jumps is given by the function $h = -4.9t^2 + 1.5t + 17$. How long will it take for the diver to reach the water?

Sample Response

$0 = -4.9t^2 + 1.5t + 17$ ← The diver's height when he reaches the water is 0 m. Substitute 0 for h.

$t = -\dfrac{b}{2a} \pm \dfrac{\sqrt{b^2 - 4ac}}{2a}$ ← Use the quadratic formula to find the values for t when $h = 0$.

$= -\dfrac{(1.5)}{2(-4.9)} \pm \dfrac{\sqrt{(1.5)^2 - 4(-4.9)(17)}}{2(-4.9)}$ ← Substitute −4.9 for a, 1.5 for b, and 17 for c.

$\approx 0.15 \pm \dfrac{\sqrt{335.45}}{-9.8}$

$\approx 0.15 \pm -1.87$

$t \approx 0.15 + (-1.87)$ or $t \approx 0.15 - (-1.87)$

≈ -1.72 ≈ 2.02

The diver will reach the water in about 2 seconds.

Talk it Over

9. a. Give a mathematical reason why $t \approx -1.72$ is a valid solution for the equation in Sample 2.

   b. Give a reason why $t \approx -1.72$ is not a valid solution for the situation in Sample 2.

   c. Describe the difference between a valid mathematical solution and a valid solution for a situation.

10. Find the vertex of the parabola given by the function in Sample 2. What does the vertex represent in this situation?

Answers to Talk it Over

7. $a = 3$, $b = -2$, $c = 5$

8. There is no x-term so $b = 0$.

9. a. When −1.72 is substituted for t in the original equation, the resulting statement is true.

   b. Since t represents a time, its value must be nonnegative.

   c. A valid mathematical solution must make sense in real terms in order to be a valid solution for a situation.

10. about (0.15, 17.11); The vertex represents the maximum height the cliff diver reaches. The first coordinate indicates the time at which he reaches his maximum height above the water and the second coordinate indicates that height.

Answers to Look Back

Answers may vary. An example is given. You might use the quadratic formula when you want an exact answer, rather than the approximate answers you might get from a graph. You might use a graph when approximate answers are enough or when you also want the additional information you can get from a graph, such as the coordinates of the vertex, the line of symmetry, the shape of the graph, and so on. Aside from giving exact solutions, the quadratic formula can be used to find solutions quickly with a calculator. When a trinomial cannot be factored by any other method, you can use the quadratic formula to find the factors.

······▶ Now you are ready for:
: Exs. 20–52 on pp. 218–221

Look Back ◀——

When might you choose to use the quadratic formula to solve a quadratic equation? When might you choose to use graphing? What are some advantages of using the quadratic formula?

4-5 Exercises and Problems

1. **Reading** What are golden rectangles? Where are they used?

2. Gabrielle copied her graph of $y = x^2$ and $y = x + 1$ on a piece of graph paper and used one of the intersection points to make the rectangle shown.

   a. Find the ratio of the longer side of the rectangle to the shorter side. What does this tell you about this rectangle?

   b. Find the ratio of the shorter side of the rectangle to the longer side. How is this ratio related to the ratio you found in part (a)? How is this ratio related to the negative x-value you found in *Talk it Over* question 4?

3. **Research** Look around your home for objects that are in the shape of a golden rectangle. Measure the dimensions to see how close they are to the golden ratio.

Exercise 4 refers to the *Fibonacci sequence*. The sequence of numbers 1, 1, 2, 3, 5, 8, 13, 21, 34, . . . is known as the Fibonacci sequence.

4. a. What is the next number in the Fibonacci sequence? What rule do you use to get the next number in the sequence?

   b. Complete the table with the correct ratios of the Fibonacci numbers. What do you notice about the ratios?

larger number	2	3	5	8	13	21	34
smaller number	1	2	3	5	8	13	21
ratio of larger to smaller	2	1.5	?	?	?	?	?

BY THE WAY...

When you are standing, your height divided by the distance from the floor to your navel is about 1.618 . . . . the Golden Ratio!

Solve using the quadratic formula.

5. $0 = x^2 + 9x + 14$

6. $0 = x^2 + 7x + 12$

7. $0 = z^2 - 12z + 27$

8. $0 = 2n^2 + 9n + 4$

9. $0 = 3x^2 + 5x + 2$

10. $0 = 2x^2 + x - 3$

11. Solve one of the equations in Exercises 5–10 by factoring and show that the solutions match the results you got by using the quadratic formula.

Solve using cross products and the quadratic formula.

12. $\dfrac{3}{x} = \dfrac{x}{x+3}$

13. $\dfrac{5}{x} = \dfrac{x}{x+5}$

14. $\dfrac{8}{x} = \dfrac{x}{x+8}$

4-5 The Quadratic Formula

217

Answers to Exercises and Problems

1. Golden rectangles are rectangles in which the ratio of the longer side to the shorter side is about 1.618. Such rectangles are often used in art and architecture.

2. a. The ratio is about 1.62. The proportions of the rectangle are roughly those of a golden rectangle.

   b. about 0.62; This ratio is the inverse of the ratio in part (a). It is also the opposite of the negative x-value found in Question 4.

3. Answers may vary.

4. a. 55; Beginning with the third number, each number in the sequence is the sum of the two preceding numbers.

   b. 1.67; 1.6; 1.63; 1.62; 1.62 (Answers are rounded to the nearest hundredth.) The ratios get closer and closer to the golden ratio.

5. $-7, -2$

6. $-4, -3$

7. $9, 3$

8. $-4, -\dfrac{1}{2}$

9. $-1, -\dfrac{2}{3}$

10. $1, -\dfrac{3}{2}$

Answers continued on next page.

Answers continued on next page.

APPLYING

Suggested Assignment

Day 1

Standard 5–14, 17–19

Extended 1, 2, 4–15, 17–19

Day 2

Standard 24–35, 39, 44–52

Extended 20–52

Integrating the Strands

Number Ex. 4

Algebra Exs. 2, 5–47, 49–51

Functions Exs. 20–22, 36, 37, 39

Geometry Exs. 1, 3, 4

Discrete Mathematics Ex. 48

Logic and Language Exs. 1, 15, 23, 38, 40–44, 52

Multicultural Note

Leonardo Fibonacci (1175?–1240?) was an influential Italian mathematician who helped introduce the Hindu-Arabic numeral system to Western Europeans. Fibonacci learned the system during his early travels in the Middle East. In 1202, he published *Liber Abaci (Book of the Abacus)*, which discusses the numerals 0–9 and arithmetic methods to solve commercial problems. It also contains the famous Fibonacci sequence. The sequence can be found in the spiral growth of certain leaves and in many other natural patterns.

Integrating the Strands

The Fibonacci sequence discussed in Ex. 4 is an interesting pattern of numbers that has a surprising number of applications to real-world phenomena. Just as fascinating is the fact that the ratios shown in the table approach the golden ratio 1.62, which also shows up as the solution to a quadratic equation. Thus, 1.62 appears in a number of different mathematical contexts: the dimensions of a rectangle that is most pleasing to the human eye, a very important number sequence, and the solution to an algebraic equation.

217

15. **a.** **Reading** Look at the statement of the quadratic formula on page 215. Why do you think it says $a \neq 0$?

   b. Write an equation in the form $y = ax^2 + bx + c$, where $a = 0$. Describe the graph of this equation. What kind of equations produce this type of graph?

16. **a.** **Using Manipulatives** The tiles shown at the right can represent the equation $x^2 + 4x + 1 = 0$. Can you use factoring to solve this equation?

   b. How many more 1-tiles do you need to add to be able to form a square? Add this number to both sides of the equation in part (a). What is the new equation?

   c. Factor the left side of the equation in part (b). How does this expression relate to the square you made with tiles?

   d. Here is what Rodrigo did next. Describe his steps.

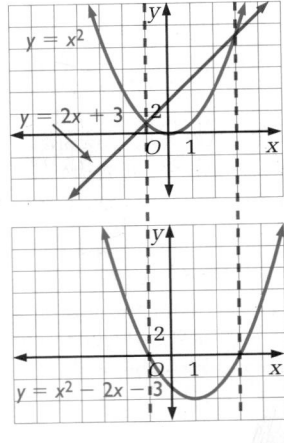

Rodrigo

$$(x+2)^2 = 3$$
$$\sqrt{(x+2)^2} = \pm\sqrt{3}$$
$$x+2 = \pm\sqrt{3}$$
$$x+2-2 = -2\pm\sqrt{3}$$
$$x = -2\pm\sqrt{3}$$

The solutions are:
$$x = -2 + \sqrt{3} \text{ and}$$
$$x = -2 - \sqrt{3}$$

The method used in Exercise 16 is called **completing the square.** Use this method to solve each equation.

17. $x^2 + 6x + 4 = 0$

18. $x^2 + 8x + 10 = 0$

19. $x^2 + 10x + 15 = 0$

Cliff Diving Use the cliff diver equation, $h = -4.9t^2 + 1.5t + 17$, to find the time elapsed for each height above the water. Give your answer to the nearest hundredth of a second.

20. $h = 10$ m   21. $h = 6$ m   22. $h = 3$ m

23. **a.** How do the x-coordinates for the points where the line and parabola intersect in the top graph compare to the x-intercepts in the bottom graph?

   b. How does the solution of the equation $0 = x^2 - 2x - 3$ compare with the solution of this system of equations:
   $$y = x^2$$
   $$y = 2x + 3$$

   c. **Writing** Use what you observed in parts (a) and (b) to describe two methods for solving the equation $x^2 = 2x + 3$.

Solve each equation by factoring, by graphing, or by using the quadratic formula. Use each method at least once. Explain how you decided which method to use.

24. $2x^2 + 3x + 7 = 9$

25. $6x^2 - 7x - 2 = 0$

26. $-2x^2 = x - 5$

27. $-3x + 1 = 4x^2$

28. $5x^2 - 4 = 3x$

29. $3(x + 1)^2 - 4 = 12$

Use the quadratic formula to find the solutions of each equation.

30. $x^2 - 5x - 8 = 0$

31. $x^2 - 7 = 0$

32. $2x^2 + x = 3$

33. $3x^2 = 9x - 5$

34. $2(x - 1)^2 + 5 = 6$

35. $3(x + 4)^2 - 22 = 14x + 28$

36. **Baseball** In his first time at bat in a game at Fenway Park, Cecil Fielder hits a baseball toward left center field. The distance in feet, d, and height, h, can be modeled by the equation $h = -0.002d^2 + 0.18d + 4$.

a. What is the highest point the ball reaches? How far from home plate is the ball when it reaches this height?

b. Which player is more likely to catch the ball, the shortstop or the center fielder?

37. **Baseball** In his second time at bat, the equation $h = -0.0015d^2 + 0.5d + 4$ can be used to model the path of the baseball hit by Cecil Fielder. The ball is hit toward the portion of the left field wall that is 347 ft from home plate.

a. The left field wall in Fenway Park is 37 ft high. Did Cecil Fielder hit the ball over the wall for a home run? Explain.

b. Along the third base line, the wall is 315 ft from home plate. Assume that the angle between the third base line and the wall is a right angle. Find the value of x in the diagram.

38. a. **Open-ended** Write a quadratic equation that has the solutions $x = -\frac{3}{8} \pm \frac{\sqrt{5}}{8}$.

b. Graph the equation you wrote in part (a). What is the line of symmetry?

c. Compare the equation for the line of symmetry with the solutions in part (a). Explain how you can find the line of symmetry of the graph from the solutions of the equation.

wall
center fielder ≈ 330 ft
347 ft
shortstop ≈ 130 ft
third base
first base
third base line
315 ft
$x°$
home plate

BY THE WAY...

Baseball parks are usually built so that the line from home plate to the pitcher's mound faces east-northeast. This is done so that the batter does not have to look into the sun while trying to hit the ball.

4-5 The Quadratic Formula

219

Problem Solving

Students need to apply their knowledge of parabolas and solving quadratic equations to answer the questions for Exs. 36 and 37. Also, a good approach for most students would be to employ the problem-solving strategy of *make a sketch*. By doing so, they can illustrate the physical aspects of a baseball field and the positions of the players involved, for example, the shortstop and center fielder in Ex. 36.

Interdisciplinary Problems

Problems that involve the motion or path of a projectile, such as a baseball in Exs. 36 and 37, the cliff diver in Sample 2, water from a firehouse (Ex. 39), or the cannonballs in Exs. 40–43, can be modeled using quadratic equations. The path followed by a projectile is called its *trajectory*, which is a parabola. Students who take a course in physics will study motion problems involving projectiles in detail.

Assessment: Open-ended

For Ex. 38, students should be given several sets of solutions and asked to find the quadratic equations having these solutions.

Using Technology

Students can use the *Function Investigator* software to graph the equation in Ex. 38.

Answers to Exercises and Problems

b. The solutions are the same.

c. You can solve $x^2 = 2x + 3$ by graphing $y = x^2$ and $y = 2x + 3$ on the same set of axes and finding the points of intersection, or you can graph $y = x^2 - 2x - 3$ and find the x-intercepts.

24–29. Choices and explanations may vary.

24. $-2, \frac{1}{2}$

25. about 1.4, about −0.24

26. about −1.9, about 1.4

27. $-1, \frac{1}{4}$

28. about 1.2, about −0.6

29. about −3.3, about 1.3

30. about −1.3, about 6.3

31. about −2.6, about 2.6

32. $1, -\frac{3}{2}$

33. about 2.3, about 0.7

34. about 1.7, about 0.3

35. about 0.2, about −3.5

36. a. 8.05 ft; 45 ft

b. the shortstop

37. a. No; the ball (if it was not caught) landed before reaching the wall.

b. about 25°

38. a. Answers may vary. An example is given. $16x^2 + 12x + 1 = 0$

b. $x = -\frac{3}{8}$

c. The equation of the line of symmetry can be found by finding the average of the solutions. Since the form of the solutions will always be $a + b$ and $a - b$, the average is $\frac{2a}{2}$ or a.

The Connection to Literature excerpt, and some of the language in the introduction to it (tall tales, excerpt) will be challenging for students acquiring English. Before students read the passage, discuss the meanings of these words: *reconnaissance, disposition, encampment,* and *seize.*

25 ft

?

39. Firefighting A firefighter aims a hose at a window 25 ft above the ground. The equation $y = -0.05x^2 + 2x + 5$ describes the path of the water.

a. An equation to find the distance between the firefighter and the building is $-0.05x^2 + 2x + 5 = \underline{\quad?\quad}$.

b. Rewrite the equation from part (a) so one side equals zero. Use the quadratic formula to solve the equation. How far from the building is the firefighter?

c. Suppose the firefighter wants the water to hit a window 20 ft above the ground, without changing the angle of the hose. Find two distances he can stand from the building.

connection to **LITERATURE**

Baron von Münchhausen was famous for telling tall tales. This is part of one of his stories, retold by a great-great-great-great-great-grandniece, Angelita von Münchhausen.

In this story, the Baron tells how he got information about enemy forces in a nearby town.

40. Were the two cannonballs the Baron rode fired at the same time?

41. Did the Baron switch cannonballs exactly halfway between his encampment and the town? If not, was he closer to his encampment or the town?

42. Did the Baron spend more time in the air by switching cannonballs than he would have if he stayed on the first cannonball?

43. Draw a sketch showing what the paths of the cannonballs might have looked like, and what the Baron's flight path was.

THE REAL MÜNCHHAUSEN

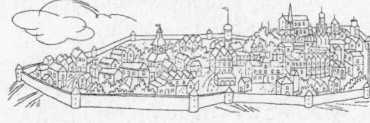

Since there was no convenient hill overlooking the town, ... it fell to my lot to provide the necessary reconnaissance. Directing my men to fire our largest cannon at my signal, I climbed a tree just in front of it and hanging by my hands gave the command, "FIRE!" ... Catching the ball between my legs as one would ride a horse, I let go the branch and soared off through the air. ... Below me I could see the astonished faces of my colleagues and the startled look on the faces of the people and soldiers within the town. Just as I flew over, another cannon was fired from within the town walls, and the ball headed straight toward me. I had already seen the disposition of the enemy's forces and would only have met disaster if I had continued to ride the ball until it arrived at its destination. So, as the enemy's ball neared me I quickly changed "horses" in midair and flew back to our own encampment. ... and as the ball passed through a clump of trees I was enabled to seize a branch and thus to descend safely to the ground.

Answers to Exercises and Problems

39. a. $-0.05x^2 + 2x + 5 = 25$

b. $-0.05x^2 + 2x - 20 = 0$; 20 is the only solution. 20 ft

c. 10 ft or 30 ft

40. No.

41. No; he was closer to the town.

42. Yes.

43.

Path of Cannon Balls

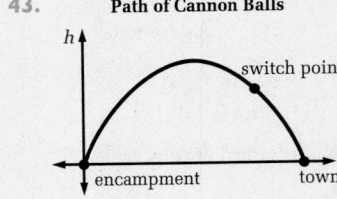

switch point

encampment   town

Baron's Flight Path

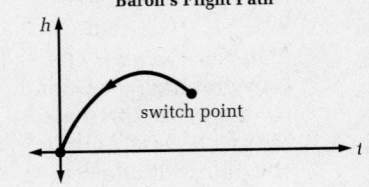

switch point

44. a. The height of a football in feet, t seconds after it has been kicked, is given by the equation $h = -16t^2 + 45t + 2.8$. Solve the equation using the quadratic formula. What do the two solutions represent in this situation?

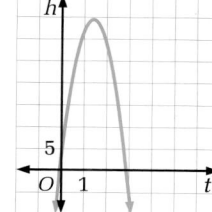

b. Writing How are the solutions of a quadratic equation represented on a graph?

Review **PREVIEW**

Factor each expression. *(Section 4-4)*

45. $x^2 - 5x + 6$ **46.** $2x^2 + 11x + 12$ **47.** $3x^2 - 5x - 8$

48. The president of the student council distributes copies of a survey to every fifth student who enters the cafeteria during the lunch hour. What type of sample is this? *(Section 1-3)*

Find each product. *(Toolbox Skill 11)*

49. $x(2x - 3)$ **50.** $(-5x + 2)(y - 1)$ **51.** $(4k + 9)(7k - 2)$

 Working on the Unit Project

52. Research Look in books, magazines, or encyclopedias for examples of interesting fountains. Think about whether you can use some of their features in the fountain you are designing.

Working on the Unit Project

The various project groups should share their resources for ideas on designing a fountain.

Practice 30 **For use with Section 4-5**

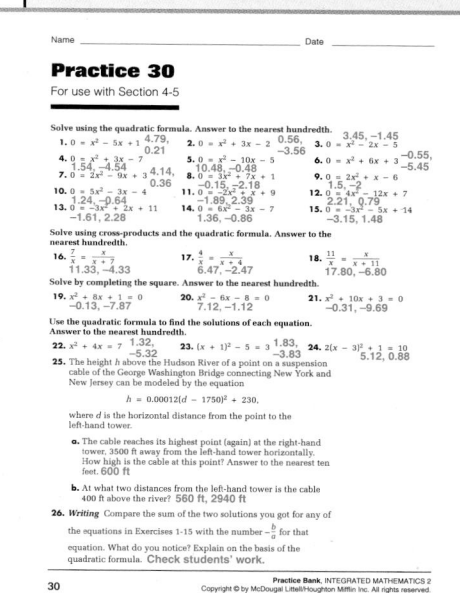

Answers to Exercises and Problems

44. a. about 2.9, about −0.06; The positive solution represents the time it takes the ball to reach the ground (known as the "hang time"). The negative solution has no meaning in this situation.

  b. The solutions are the x-intercepts.

45. $(x - 3)(x - 2)$

46. $(2x + 3)(x + 4)$

47. $(3x - 8)(x + 1)$

48. systematic

49. $2x^2 - 3x$

50. $-5xy + 5x + 2y - 2$

51. $28k^2 + 55k - 18$

52. Answers may vary.

Objectives and Strands
See pages 184A and 184B.

Spiral Learning
See page 184B.

Materials List
➤ Graphics calculator

Recommended Pacing
Section 4-6 is a two-day lesson.

Day 1

Pages 222–224: Exploration through Discriminants and Solutions, *Exercises 1–18*

Day 2

Pages 224–227: Complex Numbers through Look Back, *Exercises 19–53*

Extra Practice
See pages 620–621.

Warm-Up Exercises
Warm-Up Transparency 4-6

Support Materials
➤ Practice 31
➤ Enrichment 28 in the Activity Bank
➤ Study Guide 4-6
➤ Problem Set 8
➤ Additional Exploration 6
➤ McDougal Littell Mathpack software: *Function Investigator*
➤ Using TI-81 and TI-82 Calculators: Approximating Solutions Using a Quadratic Formula Program
➤ Quiz 4-6
➤ Alternative Assessment 5

Section 4-6

The Discriminant and Complex Numbers

The *i*'s Have It

Focus

Use the discriminant to find the number of real solutions of a quadratic equation. Add, subtract, and multiply complex numbers.

EXPLORATION

Can you predict the number of solutions of a quadratic equation?

- **Materials:** graphics calculators
- **Work with another student.**

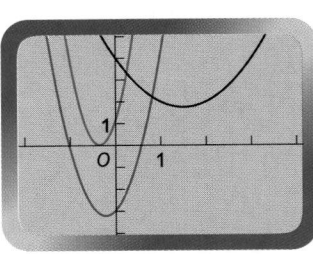

① Graph each quadratic function. Find the *x*-intercepts of each graph.

   a. $y = 5x^2 + 2x - 3$ **b.** $y = 9x^2 + 6x + 1$

   c. $y = x^2 - 3x + 4$ **d.** $y = -4x^2 + 4x - 1$

   e. $y = 2x^2 + x + 5$ **f.** $y = -3x^2 + 2x + 1$

② What differences do you notice among the six graphs in step 1? What similarities do you see?

③ How many *x*-intercepts can the graph of a quadratic function have? Is the number of *x*-intercepts the same for all quadratic functions?

④ Use the results of step 1 to tell whether each quadratic equation has one solution, two solutions, or no solutions in the set of real numbers.

   a. $0 = 5x^2 + 2x - 3$ **b.** $0 = 9x^2 + 6x + 1$

   c. $0 = x^2 - 3x + 4$ **d.** $0 = -4x^2 + 4x - 1$

   e. $0 = 2x^2 + x + 5$ **f.** $0 = -3x^2 + 2x + 1$

⑤ The **discriminant** $b^2 - 4ac$ is the part of the quadratic formula under the radical sign. Find the value of the discriminant for each quadratic equation in step 4. Tell whether each discriminant is positive, negative, or zero.

$$x = -\frac{b}{2a} \pm \frac{\sqrt{b^2 - 4ac}}{2a} \quad \longleftarrow \text{ discriminant}$$

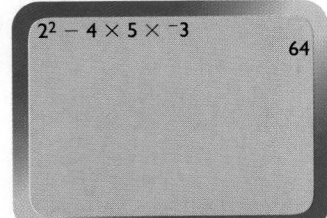

⑥ Compare the results of steps 4 and 5. Make a conjecture about the relationship between the discriminant and the real-number solutions of a quadratic equation.

Unit 4 Quadratic Functions and Graphs

Answers to Exploration

1. Check students' graphs. Estimates of *x*-intercepts may vary. Examples are given.

   a. 0.6, –1

   b. about –0.3

   c. none

   d. 0.5

   e. none

   f. 1, about –0.3

2. Answers may vary. An example is given. Some of the graphs open up, some open down. Some of the graphs have two *x*-intercepts, some have one, some have none. All the graphs are parabolas. All the graphs intercept the vertical axis.

3. 0, 1, or 2; No.

4. a. two solutions

   b. one solution

   c. no solutions

   d. one solution

   e. no solutions

   f. two solutions

5. a. 64; positive

   b. 0

   c. –7; negative

Using the Discriminant

Without graphing you can use the discriminant to find out whether or not a quadratic equation has real-number solutions.

Sample 1

istance above the ground

$y = -0.2x^2 + 3x + 3$

x = distance along the ground from the seesaw

As part of a Shanghai Circus act, one acrobat jumps onto a seesaw to propel another acrobat into the air.

The equation

$$y = -0.2x^2 + 3x + 3$$

describes the parabolic path of the flying acrobat's center of gravity. Does her center of gravity ever reach a height of 15 ft above the ground?

Sample Response

Step 1 Decide on a problem solving strategy.

The equation tells you how high off the ground the acrobat's center of gravity is at any point during her flight. Find out whether there are real-number solutions of the equation when $y = 15$.

Step 2 Use the given equation.

$y = -0.2x^2 + 3x + 3$

$15 = -0.2x^2 + 3x + 3$ ←——— Substitute 15 for y.

$0 = -0.2x^2 + 3x - 12$ ←——— Write the equation in standard form.

Step 3 Evaluate the discriminant.

$b^2 - 4ac = (3)^2 - 4(-0.2)(-12)$ ←——— Substitute **-0.2** for **a**, **3** for **b**, and **-12** for **c**.

$= 9 - 9.6$

$= -0.6$

Step 4 Interpret the result.

The discriminant is negative. You cannot find the square root of a negative number in the set of real numbers, so the equation has no real-number solutions. This means that at no time during her flight is the acrobat's center of gravity 15 ft above the ground.

4-6 The Discriminant and Complex Numbers

Answers to Exploration

d. 0

e. −39; negative

f. 16; positive

6. Answers may vary. Examples are given. For parts (a) and (f), the discriminant is positive and the equation has two real-number solutions. For parts (b) and (d), the dis-

criminant is zero and the equation has one real-number solution. For parts (c) and (e), the discriminant is negative and the equation has no real-number solutions. Conjecture: If the discriminant for a quadratic equation is positive, the equation has two real-number solutions. If the

discriminant is zero, the equation has one real-number solution. If the discriminant is negative, the equation has no real-number solutions.

DISCRIMINANTS AND SOLUTIONS

Here are the possible types of solutions for an equation in the form $0 = ax^2 + bx + c$, where a, b, and c are real numbers and $a \neq 0$.

When $b^2 - 4ac > 0$, there are two different real-number solutions.

The graph of $y = ax^2 + bx + c$ has two *x*-intercepts.

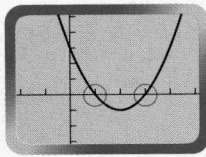

When $b^2 - 4ac = 0$, there is one real-number solution.

The graph of $y = ax^2 + bx + c$ has one *x*-intercept.

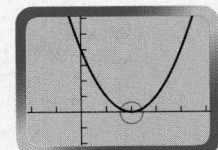

When $b^2 - 4ac < 0$, there are no real-number solutions.

The graph of $y = ax^2 + bx + c$ has no *x*-intercept.

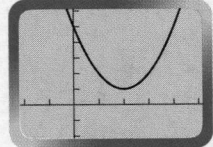

······▶ Now you are ready for:
Exs. 1–18 on pp. 227–228

Complex Numbers

A quadratic equation with a negative discriminant does not have any real-number solutions. However, such an equation does have solutions in another set of numbers, the *complex numbers*. Physics and engineering are two fields that use complex numbers.

To understand complex numbers, you have to understand the *imaginary unit*.

Calvin and Hobbes   by Bill Watterson

Unit 4 Quadratic Functions and Graphs

The **imaginary unit** i is defined as follows:

$$i = \sqrt{-1} \quad \text{and} \quad i^2 = -1$$

The square root of a negative number is defined as follows:

$$\sqrt{-a} = i\sqrt{a} \text{ when } a > 0$$

Sample 2

Simplify.

a. $\sqrt{-81}$

b. $\sqrt{-33}$

Sample Response

a. $\sqrt{-81} = i\sqrt{81} = 9i$

b. $\sqrt{-33} = i\sqrt{33} \approx 5.7i$

COMPLEX NUMBERS

A **complex number** is a number of the form $a + bi$, where a and b are real numbers and i is the imaginary unit $\sqrt{-1}$.

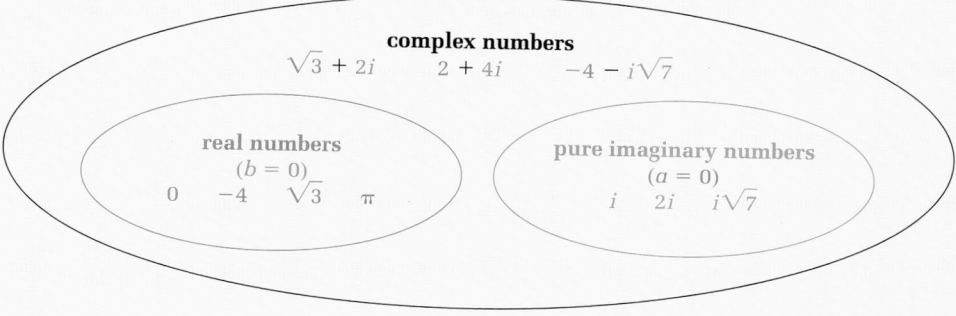

complex numbers
$\sqrt{3} + 2i \qquad 2 + 4i \qquad -4 - i\sqrt{7}$

real numbers
$(b = 0)$
$0 \quad -4 \quad \sqrt{3} \quad \pi$

pure imaginary numbers
$(a = 0)$
$i \quad 2i \quad i\sqrt{7}$

Operations with Complex Numbers

You can use what you know about adding like terms and multiplying binomials to do operations with complex numbers.

S3 Simplify.

a. $(11i)(-9i)$

$$(11i)(-9i) = -99i^2$$
$$= -99(-1)$$
$$= 99$$

b. $(3 - 4i) + (7 + 2i)$

$$(3 - 4i) + (7 + 2i)$$
$$= 3 - 4i + 7 + 2i$$
$$= (3 + 7) + (-4 + 2)i$$
$$= 10 - 2i$$

c. $(6 + 3i)(4 - 9i)$

$$(6 + 3i)(4 - 9i)$$
$$= (6 + 3i)4 + (6 + 3i)(-9i)$$
$$= 24 + 12i - 54i - 27i^2$$
$$= 24 - 42i - 27(-1)$$
$$= 24 - 42i + 27$$
$$= 51 - 42i$$

S4 Solve $0 = 9x^2 - 3x + 11$.

$$x = -\frac{(-3)}{2(9)} \pm \frac{\sqrt{(-3)^2 - 4(9)(11)}}{2(9)}$$
$$= \frac{3}{18} \pm \frac{\sqrt{9 - 396}}{18}$$
$$= \frac{1}{6} \pm \frac{\sqrt{-387}}{18}$$
$$= \frac{1}{6} \pm \frac{i\sqrt{387}}{18}$$
$$\approx 0.17 \pm 1.093i$$
$$x \approx 0.17 + 1.093i \text{ or }$$
$$x \approx 0.17 - 1.093i$$

The complex solutions are 0.17 + 1.093i and 0.17 − 1.093i.

Mathematical Procedures

Students need to understand that operations with complex numbers, in particular operations with numbers expressed in terms of i, are carried out in exactly the same way as operations involving variables, such as x, y, or z.

Using Technology

Students can use the *Function Investigator* software to graph the functions in Exs. 6–14 on page 227.

Sample 3

Simplify.

a. $(9i)(3i)$ **b.** $(2 + 6i) - (1 - 3i)$ **c.** $(5 + 7i)(4 + 8i)$

Sample Response

a. $(9i)(3i) = 27i^2$

$$= 27(-1) \quad \longleftarrow \text{Substitute} -1 \text{ for } i^2.$$
$$= -27$$

> **Watch Out!**
> Be careful distributing. Remember that $-(1 - 3i) = -1 + 3i$.

b. $(2 + 6i) - (1 - 3i) = 2 + 6i - 1 + 3i$ Group real parts

$$= (2 - 1) + (6 + 3)i \quad \longleftarrow \text{ and group imaginary parts.}$$
$$= 1 + 9i$$

c. $(5 + 7i)(4 + 8i) = (5 + 7i)4 + (5 + 7i)8i$

$$= 20 + 28i + 40i + 56i^2$$
$$= 20 + 68i + 56(-1)$$
$$= 20 + 68i - 56$$
$$= -36 + 68i$$

Sample 4

Solve $0 = 3x^2 + 2x + 5$.

Sample Response

Use the quadratic formula.

$$x = -\frac{b}{2a} \pm \frac{\sqrt{b^2 - 4ac}}{2a}$$

$$= -\frac{2}{2(3)} \pm \frac{\sqrt{2^2 - 4(3)(5)}}{2(3)} \quad \longleftarrow \text{Substitute 3 for } a, \text{ 2 for } b, \text{ and 5 for } c.$$

$$= -\frac{2}{6} \pm \frac{\sqrt{-56}}{6}$$

$$= -\frac{1}{3} \pm \frac{i\sqrt{56}}{6}$$

$$\approx -0.33 \pm 1.247i$$

$$x \approx -0.33 + 1.247i \quad \text{or} \quad x \approx -0.33 - 1.247i$$

The solutions are about $-0.3 + 1.2i$ and about $-0.3 - 1.2i$.

Answers to Talk it Over

1. none

2. infinitely many; Every point on the graph represents an ordered pair of real numbers that is a solution of the equation.

Answers to Look Back

Determine whether the discriminant is positive, zero, or negative. If it is positive, the equation has two different real-number solutions. If it is zero, the equation has one real-number solution. If it is negative, it has no real-number solutions.

Talk it Over

For questions 1 and 2, use the results of Sample 4.

1. Suppose you graph the function $y = 3x^2 + 2x + 5$ on a coordinate plane. How many x-intercepts will it have?

2. The equation $0 = 3x^2 + 2x + 5$ does not have any real-number solutions. Does $y = 3x^2 + 2x + 5$ have any real-number solutions? Why or why not?

Look Back

How can you use the discriminant to tell how many real-number solutions a quadratic equation has?

▶ Now you are ready for:
Exs. 19–53 on pp. 228–229

4-6 Exercises and Problems

1. **Reading** What is meant by the "discriminant" in the quadratic formula?

2. **Open-ended** Why do you think $b^2 - 4ac$ is called the discriminant?

Use the graph of the related function to tell whether the discriminant for each equation is *positive, negative,* or *zero*.

3. $0 = 1.5(x + 3)^2$

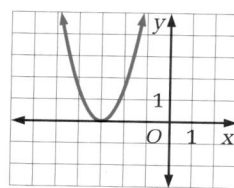

$y = 1.5(x + 3)^2$

4. $0 = 0.25(x - 2)^2 - 3$

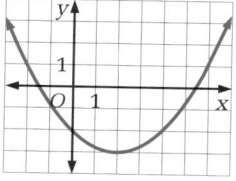

$y = 0.25(x - 2)^2 - 3$

5. $0 = -x^2 - 1$

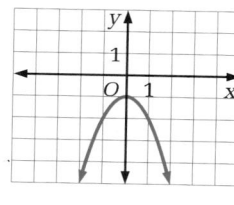

$y = -x^2 - 1$

For Exercises 6–14:

a. Use the discriminant to tell whether each equation has *one solution, two solutions,* or *no solutions* in the set of real numbers.

b. Solve each equation that has at least one real-number solution.

c. Graph the related quadratic function for each equation that has no real-number solutions.

6. $x^2 + 2x - 8 = 0$

7. $x^2 - 6x + 9 = 0$

8. $x^2 + 2x + 7 = 0$

9. $2x^2 + 5x + 3 = 0$

10. $3x^2 + x + 2 = 0$

11. $x^2 - 0.25x + 0.125 = 0$

12. $9x^2 + 16x = 12$

13. $-2x^2 + x = 5$

14. $4x^2 - 4x = -1$

4-6 The Discriminant and Complex Numbers   **227**

Answers to Exercises and Problems

1. The discriminant is the part of the quadratic formula under the radical sign.

2. Answers may vary. An example is given. The discriminant "discriminates," or makes a clear distinction among equations with one real-number solution, two real-number solutions, or no real-number solutions.

3. zero
4. positive
5. negative
6. a. two solutions
   b, c. 2, –4
7. a. one solution
   b, c. 3
8. a, b. no solutions

c.

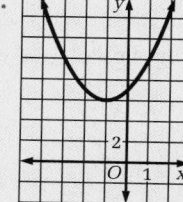

9. a. two solutions
   b, c. –1, –1.5
10. a, b. no solutions

10. c.

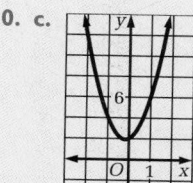

11. a, b. no solutions

c.

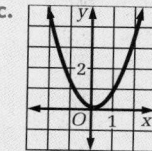

12. a. two solutions
   b, c. about –2.35, about 0.57
13. a, b. no solutions

c.

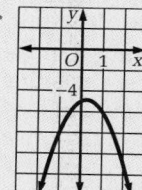

14. a. one solution   b, c. 0.5

227

15. Use the equation $x^2 + kx + 9 = 0$. Tell what values of k satisfy each condition.

   a. The equation has only one real-number solution.

   b. The equation has two real-number solutions.

   c. The equation has no real-number solutions.

Acrobatics Use the equation $y = -0.2x^2 + 3x + 3$ from the Shanghai Circus situation in Sample 1.

16. How high is the acrobat's center of gravity when she is at the halfway point between the edge of the seesaw and the tower of acrobats?

17. When the acrobat's center of gravity is 5 ft above the ground, how far along the ground from her starting point is she?

18. Suppose the equation for the acrobat's center of gravity is $y = -0.2x^2 + 4x + 3$. Will she reach a height of 15 ft?

19. **Writing** Explain how you can use the discriminant to tell whether the solutions of a quadratic equation are real or complex.

Simplify.

20. $\sqrt{-100}$
21. $\sqrt{-0.25}$
22. $\sqrt{-17}$
23. $\sqrt{-83}$

24. $(5i)(7i)$
25. $(4i)(-3i)(0.5i)$
26. $9i(1 - 8i)$
27. $-7i(12 + 3i)$

28. $(8 - 14i) + (10 - 5i)$
29. $(-4 + 2i) - (9 - 9i)$
30. $(3 + 4i) - (-7 + 11.5i)$

31. $(5 + 4i)(6 - 12i)$
32. $(-2 + 8i)(1 + 0.2i)$
33. $(4 - 10i)(4 + 10i)$

34. Describe the pattern shown at the right.

$i^1 = i$	$i^5 = i$	$i^9 = i$
$i^2 = -1$	$i^6 = -1$	$i^{10} = -1$
$i^3 = -i$	$i^7 = -i$	$i^{11} = -i$
$i^4 = 1$	$i^8 = 1$	$i^{12} = 1$

Use the result of Exercise 34 to complete each ? .

35. $i^{16} = $?
36. $i^{99} = $?
37. $i^{401} = $?

Solve.

38. $x^2 - 3x + 5 = 0$
39. $25x^2 - 16x + 2 = 0$
40. $-3x^2 + x - 5 = 0$

41. $4x^2 + 40x + 100 = 0$
42. $-2x^2 + 7x - 12 = 0$
43. $6x^2 + 6x + 2 = 0$

44. **a.** Average the solutions of each equation in Exercises 38–40.

   b. Graph the related quadratic function for each equation that has complex solutions.

   c. What characteristic of each graph that you drew in part (b) is related to your corresponding answer in part (a)?

Ongoing ASSESSMENT

45. Group Activity Work with another student.

a. Write a quadratic equation in standard form.

b. Use algebra to decide whether your equation has real-number solutions or complex solutions and find the solutions.

c. Exchange equations. (Do not exchange your solutions yet.)

d. Graph the related quadratic function for the equation you received in part (c).

e. Compare your answers for parts (b) and (d). How are they related?

Review PREVIEW

Tell which method you would use to solve each equation. Then solve.
(Section 4-5)

46. $-(x + 5)^2 + 8 = 3$ **47.** $4x^2 + 12x + 9 = 0$ **48.** $-2x + 7 = 6x^2$

49. A survey of Asa Hirata's students showed that 4 out of 150 students own motorcycles. Estimate the number of students in the total school population of 1200 who own motorcycles. *(Section 1-1)*

Solve each system of equations. *(Sections 3-2, 3-4)*

50. $x + y = 3$ **51.** $-x + 5y = 8$ **52.** $2x + 3y = -4$
$\quad\ \ y = -2x$ $\quad\ \ 2x - 10y = -16$ $\quad\ \ 4x - y = 6$

Working on the Unit Project

53. Michael is designing a fountain with one water arc. His fountain nozzle will spray water at 55 ft/s, and he wants the water arc to reach at least 30 ft into the air. At what angle A should he tilt the nozzle? Do parts (a) and (b) to find out. Use this function from page 192:

$$y = \frac{-16}{v^2(\cos A)^2} x^2 + (\tan A)x$$

a. Write an equation involving A that describes all the possible water arcs.

b. Substitute these values for $m \angle A$ into your equation from part (a):

$$m \angle A = 20°, 40°, 60°, 80°$$

Use the discriminant to decide whether each value of $m \angle A$ will produce a water arc that reaches 30 ft high.

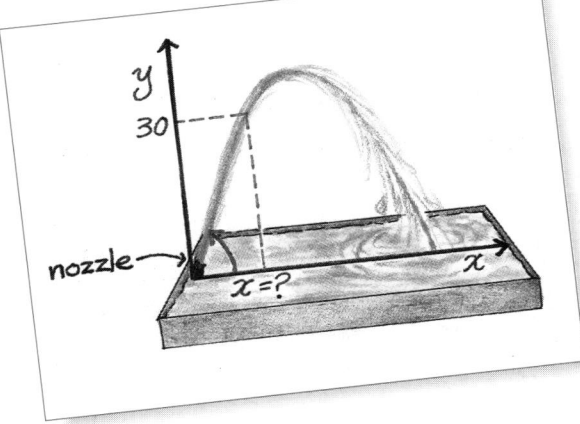
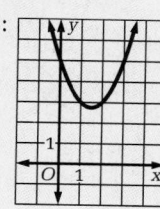
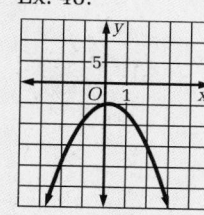

4-6 The Discriminant and Complex Numbers   **229**

Answers to Exercises and Problems

44. a. Ex. 38: about 1.5;
Ex. 39: about 0.35;
Ex. 40: about 0.2

b. Ex. 38:

Ex. 40:

c. the line of symmetry

45. a–e. Answers may vary.
Check students' work.

If the equation written for part (a) has real-number solutions, the graph in part (d) will have one or two x-intercepts. If the equation has complex solutions, the graph in part (d) will have no x-intercepts.

46, 47. Solution methods may vary. Examples are given.

Practice 31 For use with Section 4-6

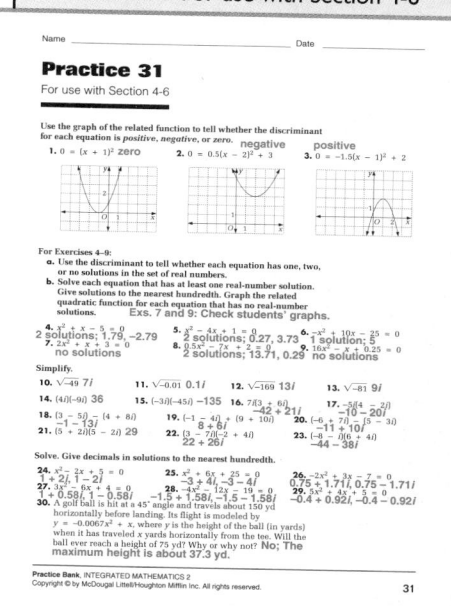

46. undoing; about -2.8, about -7.2

47. factoring; -1.5

48. the quadratic formula; about 0.9, about -1.3

49. 32 students

50. $(-3, 6)$

51. infinitely many solutions

52. $(1, -2)$

53. a. $y = \dfrac{-0.005}{(\cos A)^2} x^2 + (\tan A)x$

b. 20°: $-0.006x^2 + 0.36x - 30 = 0$; No.
40°: $-0.009x^2 + 0.84x - 30 = 0$; No.
60°: $-0.02x^2 + 1.73x - 30 = 0$; Yes.
80°: $-0.17x^2 + 5.67x - 30 = 0$; Yes.

PLANNING

Objectives and Strands
See pages 184A and 184B.

Spiral Learning
See page 184B.

Materials List
➤ Graphics calculator

Recommended Pacing
Section 4-7 is a one-day lesson.

Extra Practice
See pages 620–621.

Warm-Up Exercises
Warm-Up Transparency 4-7

Support Materials
➤ Practice 32
➤ Enrichment 29 in the Activity Bank
➤ Study Guide 4-7
➤ Problem Set 8
➤ McDougal Littell Mathpack software: *Function Investigator*
➤ Using TI-81 and TI-82 Calculators: Finding Intersections of Parabolas
➤ Using Plotter Plus: Estimating Solutions of Quadratic Systems
➤ Quiz 4-7
➤ Test 14

Section 4-7 Quadratic Systems

Focus
Solve problems involving quadratic systems.

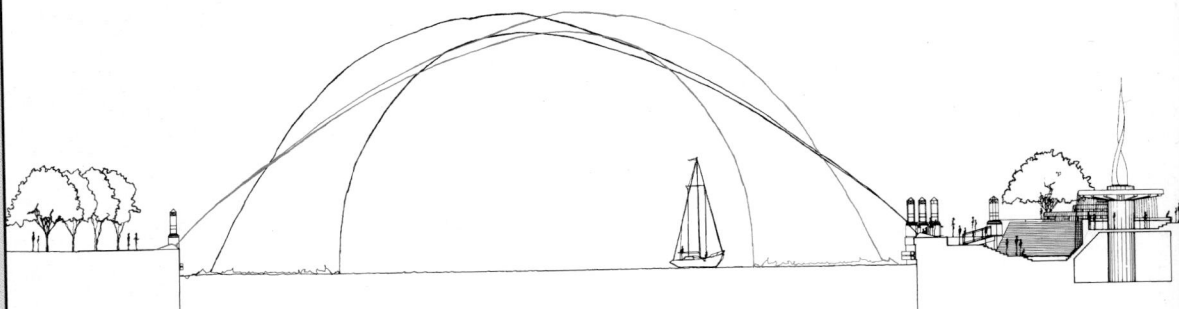

The Water Arc crosses the Chicago River from the north bank toward the south bank. If the designers decided to add a similar arc going in the other direction, where would the water arcs intersect? Assume the river is 220 ft wide.

Sample 1

These equations represent the paths of the two water arcs.

$$y = -0.006x^2 + 1.2x + 10$$
$$y = -0.006x^2 + 1.44x - 16.4$$

Find the point of intersection of the two graphs.

Sample Response

Substitute $-0.006x^2 + 1.44x - 16.4$ for y in the first equation.

$-0.006x^2 + 1.44x - 16.4 = -0.006x^2 + 1.2x + 10$

$1.44x - 16.4 = 1.2x + 10$ ⟵ Add $0.006x^2$ to both sides.

$0.24x = 26.4$

$x = \dfrac{26.4}{0.24}$

$x = 110$

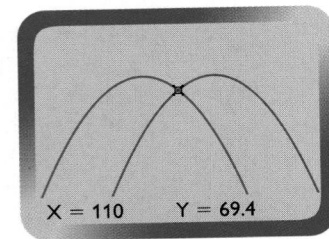

X = 110   Y = 69.4

To find where the arcs intersect, use substitution.

$y = -0.006x^2 + 1.2x + 10$ ← Use one of the original equations.

$= -0.006(110)^2 + 1.2(110) + 10$ ← Substitute 110 for x.

$= -72.6 + 132 + 10$

$= 69.4$

The point of intersection is (110, 69.4).

The water arcs intersect 110 ft from the north bank and 69.4 ft above the river.

> **Talk it Over**
>
> 1. Does it make sense that the water arcs intersect 110 ft from the north bank? Explain.
> 2. Explain why it does not matter which of the two original equations you use to find y after you know x.
> 3. Substitute x into the other equation to check that you get the same value for y.
> 4. Check the solution of the system of quadratic equations using a graphics calculator or software.

Two or more quadratic functions with the same variables are called a **quadratic system**. A system of two quadratic functions can be graphed as two parabolas. The points where the parabolas intersect are the real-number solutions of the system.

There will be zero, one, or two real-number solutions, depending on whether the parabolas intersect in zero, one, or two points.

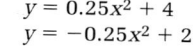
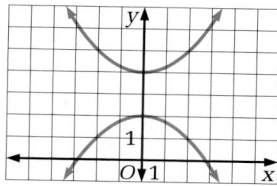

The parabolas do not intersect.

The system has zero real-number solutions.

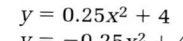
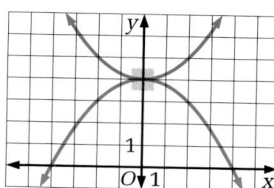

The parabolas intersect in one point.

The system has one real-number solution.

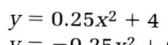
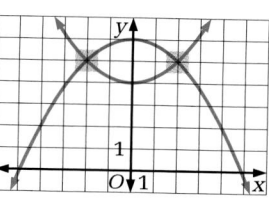

The parabolas intersect in two points.

The system has two real-number solutions.

You can use algebra to find the solutions of a quadratic system.

Answers to Talk it Over

1. Yes; the arcs intersect over the middle of the river and 110 ft is halfway across.

2. Since x is the first coordinate of the point of intersection, you will get the same value for y from either equation.

3. $-0.006(110)^2 + 1.44(110) - 16.4 = -72.6 + 158.4 - 16.4 = 69.4$ ✓

4. The solution should be about (110, 69.4).

Teaching Tip

Sample 1 uses the method of substitution to find the point of intersection of two parabolas. The method is applied in the same way it would be to find the point of intersection of two straight lines.

Visual Thinking

Encourage students to create a sketch of the situation described showing both arcs. Ask them to use their sketches to explain where the arcs would intersect. The activity involves the visual skills of *generalization* and *communication*.

Additional Sample

S1 These equations represent the paths of two moving objects traveling in opposite directions. Find the point of intersection of the two graphs.

$y = -0.05x^2 + 2.1x + 5$

$y = -0.05x^2 + 2.5x - 12.3$

Substitute $-0.05x^2 + 2.5x - 12.3$ for y in the first equation.

$-0.05x^2 + 2.5x - 12.3 = -0.05x^2 + 2.1x + 5$

$2.5x - 12.3 = 2.1x + 5$

$0.4x = 17.3$

$x = \frac{17.3}{0.4}$

$x = 43.25$

$y = -0.05x^2 + 2.1x + 5$

$= -0.05(43.25)^2 + 2.1(43.25) + 5$

$= -93.53 + 90.83 + 5$

$= 2.3$

The point of intersection is (43.25, 2.3).

Talk it Over

Questions 2 and 3 have students verify that the method of substitution works equally well if either of the two equations is used to find y when x is known.

Using Technology

Students can use the *Function Investigator* software to graph quadratic systems.

Sample 2

Solve the system: $y = x^2 - 5x + 4$

$y = -2x^2 + 7x - 1$

Sample Response

Step 1 Substitute $-2x^2 + 7x - 1$ for y in the first equation.

$-2x^2 + 7x - 1 = x^2 - 5x + 4$

$0 = 3x^2 - 12x + 5$ ◄—— Rewrite the equation in standard form.

$x = -\dfrac{-12}{2(3)} \pm \dfrac{\sqrt{(-12)^2 - 4(3)(5)}}{2(3)}$ ◄—— Substitute **3** for a, **–12** for b, and **5** for c in the quadratic formula.

$x \approx 2 \pm 1.53$

$x \approx 2 + 1.53$ *or* $x \approx 2 - 1.53$

≈ 3.53 ≈ 0.47

Step 2 Substitute each x-value into one of the original two equations to find the corresponding y-value.

➤ Substitute 3.53 for x.

$y = x^2 - 5x + 4$

$\approx (3.53)^2 - 5(3.53) + 4$

≈ -1.19

One solution is about $(3.53, -1.19)$.

➤ Substitute 0.47 for x.

$y = x^2 - 5x + 4$

$\approx (0.47)^2 - 5(0.47) + 4$

≈ 1.87

The other solution is about (0.47, 1.87).

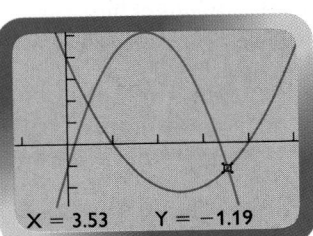

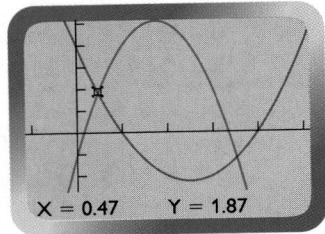

Sometimes when you try to solve a system, you get an equation that is never true. In that case, there is no solution of the system.

Sample 3

Solve the system: $y = -0.1x^2 - 2$

$y = -0.1x^2 + 3$

Unit 4 Quadratic Functions and Graphs

Sample Response

$$-0.1x^2 + 3 = -0.1x^2 - 2 \qquad \leftarrow \text{Substitute } -0.1x^2 + 3 \text{ for } y \text{ in the first equation.}$$
$$3 = -2 \qquad \leftarrow \text{Add } 0.1x^2 \text{ to both sides.}$$

This equation is never true.
There is no solution of the system.

If you graph these equations, you see that the parabolas never intersect. One parabola is always five units above the other.

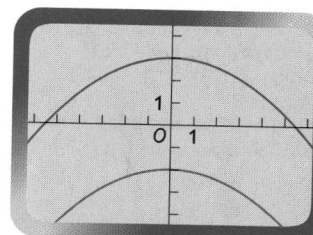

Look Back

How is solving quadratic systems similar to solving linear systems? How is it different?

Exercises and Problems

1. **Reading** Two parabolas are graphed on the same coordinate axes. How many points might the two parabolas have in common?

Solve each system by substitution.

2. $y = 3x^2$
$y = 3x^2 - 12x + 12$

3. $y = -x^2 + 5$
$y = -0.5x^2 + 3$

4. $m = n^2 - 3n$
$m = -2n^2 - 3n$

5. $y = 2x^2 - 4x + 2$
$y = -2x^2 - 4x - 2$

6. Choose two of the systems from Exercises 2–5 and graph them to check your solutions.

Estimate the solutions of each system of quadratic equations shown.

7. $y = x^2 - 12$
$y = -x^2 + 6$

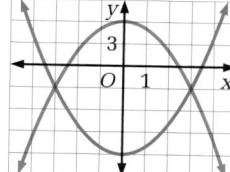

8. $y = x^2$
$y = -x^2 + 4x$

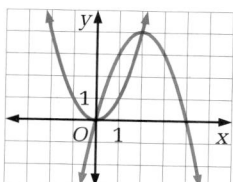

9. $y = \frac{1}{3}x^2$
$y = -\frac{1}{3}x^2 + 4x - 6$

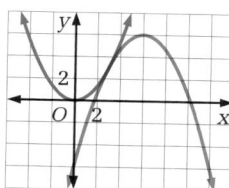

4-7 Quadratic Systems

233

Look Back

Quadratic and linear systems can both be solved algebraically by using the method of substitution or by using graphs. The methods are the same in both cases. A linear system, however, unlike a quadratic system, cannot have two solutions because two lines can intersect in only one point.

APPLYING

Suggested Assignment
Standard 2–18, 22–30
Extended 1–30

Integrating the Strands
Algebra Exs. 1–26
Functions Exs. 2–22, 30
Geometry Exs. 27–29
Logic and Language Exs. 1, 22

Using Technology

With the TI-82 and TI-83, you can find approximate solutions of quadratic systems by using 5:intersect from the CALCULATE menu. With the TI-81, TI-82, or TI-83, you can find approximate solutions by zooming and tracing. Usually this is easy to do, but it may be difficult if the graphs are tangent or have two points of intersection that are very close. In such cases, the curves appear to merge. (The system in Ex. 9 is an example.) One way around the difficulty (which is more visual than mathematical) is to graph the difference of the two functions. The x-intercepts of the graph of the difference function are the x-coordinates of the points of intersection of the original functions. You can graph all three functions on the same screen. After you have found the x-intercept for the difference function, use the ▼ or ▲ key to find the approximate y-coordinate of the points of intersection of the original graphs.

Answers to Look Back

Summaries may vary. An example is given. To solve either a quadratic system or a linear system, you can use graphing or algebra to find the solution(s) of both systems. A quadratic system may have one or two real-number solutions or it may have none. A linear system has either one solution, no solutions, or infinitely many solutions. The solutions of a linear system are real numbers.

Answers to Exercises and Problems

1. two, one, or none
2. (1, 3)
3. (2, 1), (−2, 1)
4. (0, 0)
5. no real solutions
6. Check students' graphs.
7. (−3, −3), (3, −3)
8. (0, 0), (2, 4)
9. (3, 3)

Draw a sketch of each situation.

10. two parabolas that intersect in 2 points

11. two parabolas that intersect in 1 point

12. two parabolas that do not intersect

Solve each system by graphing.

13. $y = x^2 - 2x + 3$
    $y = 0.5x^2 + 3x + 1$

14. $y = 0.7x^2 - 2x$
    $y = 0.7x^2 + 1.5x - 4$

15. $y = x^2 - 4x$
    $y = 0.2x^2 + 6x$

16. $y = -5x^2 + 5x + 2$
    $y = x^2 + 4x - 1$

Write variable expressions for the coordinates of the solutions of each system of equations.

17. $y = ax^2 + b$
    $y = cx^2 + d$

18. $y = ax^2 + bx$
    $y = cx^2 + dx$

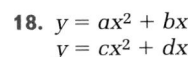 connection to **PHYSICS**

The Waimea Wave water slide near Salt Lake City, Utah, sends riders into the air for a part of their trip. The path depends on the rider's speed at liftoff, which is influenced by the friction between the rider and the waterslide.

Fred Langford, the designer of the slide, had to calculate the parabolic path of a typical rider in order to design protective walls and insure that landings would not be too rough.

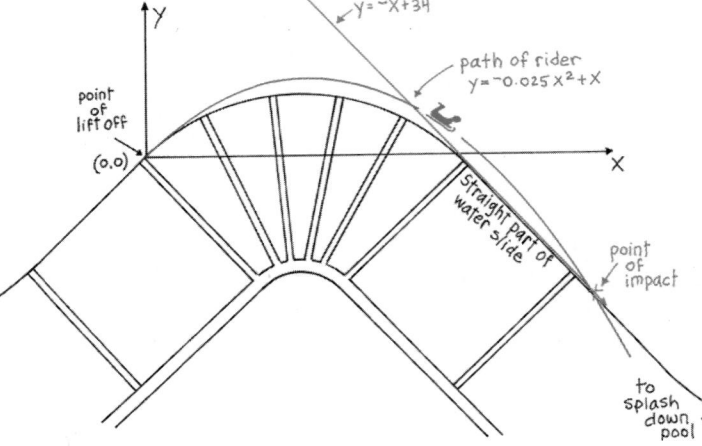

Suppose the point of liftoff is at (0, 0). An equation for the path of a rider through the air is $y = -0.025x^2 + x$. An equation for the straight part of the water slide where the rider lands is $y = -x + 34$. (All distances are measured in feet.)

19. **a.** Find the solutions of the system of two equations.

    b. Which of the solutions represents the point of impact where the rider lands?

    c. What are the coordinates of the highest point along the rider's path through the air?

20. If there is more friction, the path of a rider through the air might be represented by the equation $y = -0.028x^2 + x$. How do the two paths compare? Find the coordinates of the new point of impact.

21. Which ride would you prefer, the one with more or less friction?

 234

Answers to Exercises and Problems

10–12. Sketches may vary. Examples are given.

10.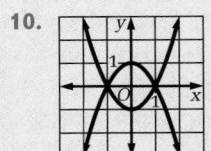

11.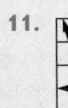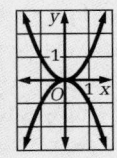

12.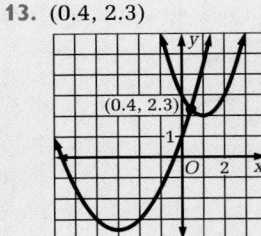

13–16. Estimates may vary. Examples are given.

13. (0.4, 2.3)

(0.4, 2.3)

14. (1.1, −1.4)

(1.1, −1.4)

15–21. See answers in back of book.

Ongoing ASSESSMENT

22. **Open-ended** Write a system of two quadratic equations that has solutions at $(2, 4)$ and $(-2, 4)$.

Review PREVIEW

Use the discriminant to tell whether each equation has *one solution*, *two solutions*, or *no solutions* in the set of real numbers. *(Section 4-6)*

23. $x^2 - 5x + 4 = 0$ **24.** $2x^2 + 3x - 5 = 0$ **25.** $-6x^2 - 7x = 3$

26. Solve this system of linear equations. *(Section 3-4)*

$$x + 2y = 14$$
$$-x - y = -2$$

Sketch an example of each figure. Then find each area. *(Toolbox Skill 28)*

27. a rectangle with base = 7 in., height = 6 in.

28. a parallelogram with base = 4.5 m, height = 3 m

29. a trapezoid with base$_1$ = 3 cm, base$_2$ = 5 cm, height = 4 cm

 Working on the Unit Project

30. Latricia designed a fountain with two intersecting water arcs. The fountain, shown below, is in a circular pool 100 ft in diameter, and the vertices of the two arcs lie directly above the pool's center.

  a. Write an equation for the wide arc. (*Hint:* Substitute values into the factored form $y = a(x - p)(x - q)$ as you did in Exercise 45 of Section 4-4.)

  b. Latricia designed the narrow arc to have half the width and twice the height of the wide arc. Write an equation for the narrow arc.

  c. Find the points where the arcs intersect.

  d. For what values of x is the narrow arc above the wide arc?

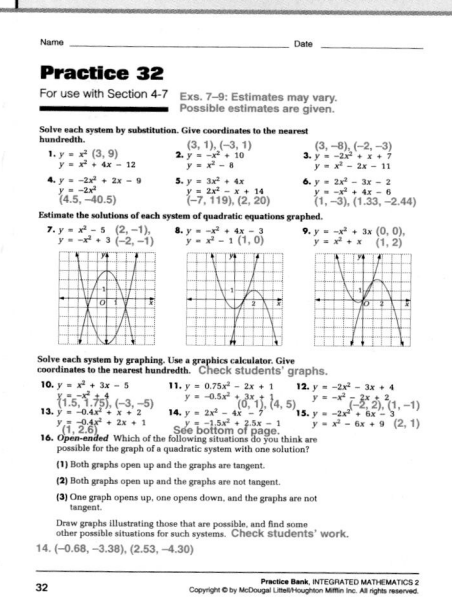

4-7 Quadratic Systems

235

Assessment: Open-ended

In Ex. 22, students need to reason backward from a solution to a system of equations having that solution. They should reverse the process after the equations are written to check their work.

Quick Quiz (4-5 through 4-7)

See page 237.

Practice 32 For use with Section 4-7

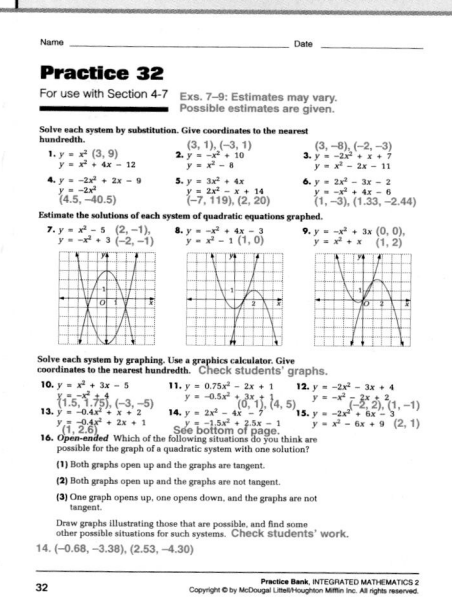

Answers to Exercises and Problems

22. Answers may vary.
Example: $y = x^2$,
$y = -x^2 + 8$

23. two solutions

24. two solutions

25. no solutions

26. $(-10, 12)$

27. Area = 42 in.^{2}

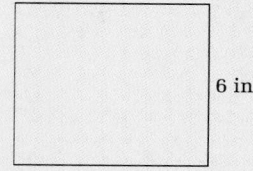

6 in.

7 in.

28. Area = 13.5 m^2

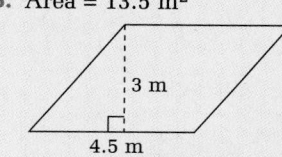

3 m

4.5 m

29. Area = 16 cm^2

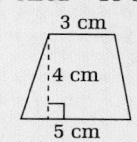

3 cm

4 cm

5 cm

30. a. $y = -\dfrac{1}{36}(x - 20)(x - 80)$

  b. $y = -\dfrac{2}{9}(x - 35)(x - 65)$

  c. about $(38.7, 21.4)$, about $(61.3, 21.4)$

  d. $38.7 < x < 61.3$

Assessment

A scoring rubric for the Unit Project can be found on pages 184 and 185 of this Teacher's Edition and also in the *Project Book*.

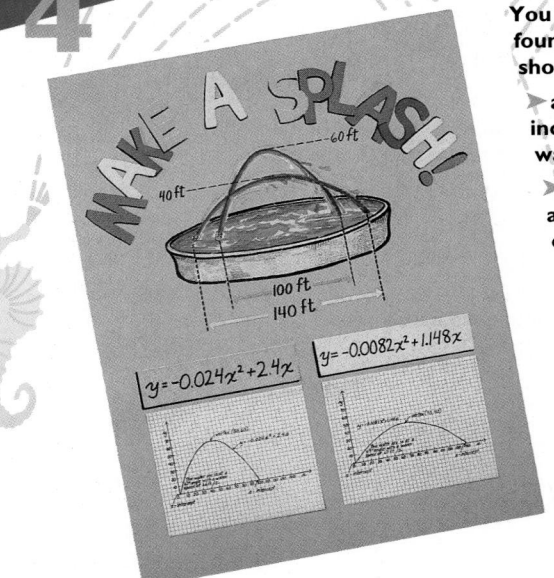

Unit Project 4

Completing the Unit Project

You are now ready to present your fountain design. Your completed poster should include the following:

➤ a detailed sketch of your fountain, including the heights and widths of all water arcs

➤ separate graphs of each of the water arcs. On each graph, write the equation of the arc, the measure of the stream angle, and the water speed. Label the coordinates of the vertex and the *x*-intercepts.

Look Back ◄

Explain how your knowledge of quadratic functions and graphs helped you design your fountain.

Alternative Projects

Project 1: Investigating Water Arcs by Experiment

Punch holes at several different heights in the side of a large can. Place the can on a large sheet of plastic in a sink or shallow tub. Fill the can with water and mark the points where the arcs hit the surface.

Describe the relationship between the height of a hole and how far the water travels. Choose an origin and graph the paths of the water arcs. Write the equations of all the arcs and find the coordinates of the points where pairs of arcs intersect.

Project 2: Using Straight Lines to Draw a Parabola

Follow this procedure to create a parabola with straight lines:

Draw a set of axes on graph paper. Label the axes from 1 to 20. With a ruler, draw lines connecting (0, 20) with (1, 0), (0, 19) with (2, 0), (0, 18) with (3, 0), and so on in this pattern until every labeled point on the vertical axis is connected to a labeled point on the horizontal axis.

Use what you have learned about parabolas in this unit to analyze the parabola formed by straight lines. Discuss the parabola's line of symmetry, vertex, and intercepts, as well as what transformations of $y = x^2$ will produce its graph. If possible, write an equation for the parabola.

Find the vertex and y-intercept of the graph of each function.

4-1

1. $y = 0.5x^2$ **2.** $y = 0.5x^2 + 4$ **3.** $y = 0.5x^2 + 6x + 10$

4. **Open-ended** Write a quadratic equation whose graph opens down and whose line of symmetry is $x = -3$.

Find the vertex of the graph of each function. Tell whether the graph opens *up* or *down*.

4-2

5. $y = -3(x - 3)^2 - 16$ **6.** $y - 1 = -(x - 1)^2$

7. a. **Open-ended** Write an equation for a parabola whose vertex is $(3, 4)$ and opens down.

    b. **Open-ended** Write an equation for a parabola whose vertex is $(3, 4)$, that opens down, and that is wider than the parabola in part (a).

    c. **Writing** Is the parabola in part (b) a translation of the parabola in part (a)? Explain.

Match each function with its graph.

8. $y = -0.25(x + 3)^2$

9. $y = -0.25x^2 - 3$

10. $y = -0.25(x - 3)^2$

11. $y = 0.25x^2 - 3$

A.

B.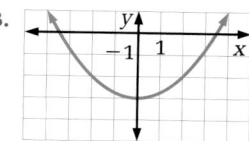

C.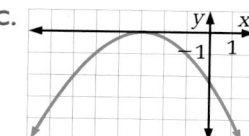

D.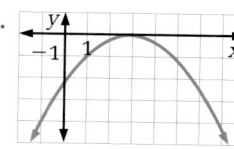

Solve by graphing.

4-3

12. $-(x - 4)^2 = 0$ **13.** $2x^2 - 3 = 1$ **14.** $0.2(x + 1)^2 = 4$

Solve by undoing.

15. $5x^2 - 10 = 20$ **16.** $2(x + 5)^2 - 228 = 222$ **17.** $3(x - 2)^2 - 11 = 10$

Factor.

4-4

18. $2x^2 - 3x - 20$ **19.** $4n^2 - 81$ **20.** $16x^2 - 24x + 9$

21. Solve $9x^2 - 15x + 6 = 0$ by factoring.

Solve using the quadratic formula.

4-5

22. $3x^2 + 9x + 10 = 6$ **23.** $-2x^2 = 3x - 5$ **24.** $3(x - 2)^2 = 8$

Use the discriminant to tell whether each equation has *one solution*, *two solutions*, or *no solutions* in the set of real numbers.

4-6

25. $x^2 - 6x = -9$ **26.** $5x^2 + 3 = -9x$ **27.** $4(x + 0.5)^2 - 20 = -21$

Simplify.

28. $4i(3 - 6i)$ **29.** $(8 - 4i) - 6(2 + 9i)$ **30.** $(5 + 7i)(7 - 3i)$

Unit 4 Review and Assessment   **237**

Unit Support Materials

➤ Unit 4 Cumulative Practice 33

➤ Unit 4 Study Guide Review

➤ Unifying Problem 4 in the Problem Bank

➤ Unit Tests 15 and 16

➤ Spanish versions of the Unit Tests are in the Assessment Book.

➤ Teacher's Resources for Transfer Students

Quick Quiz (4-5 through 4-7)

1. Solve using the quadratic formula. $5x^2 + 3x - 4 = 0$ [4-5] $x \approx 0.64$ or $x \approx -1.24$

2. Are the solutions of the equation $10x^2 + 9x + 11 = 0$ real or complex? [4-6] complex

3. Simplify $\sqrt{-19}$. [4-6] $i\sqrt{19}$

4. Simplify $(3 - 4i)(7 + 2i)$. [4-6] $29 - 22i$

5. Solve the system.
$y = 3x^2 + 4x - 5$
$y = -2x^2 - x - 3$
The solutions are about $(0.31, -3.49)$ and about $(-1.31, -5.11)$.

13. about 1.4, about -1.4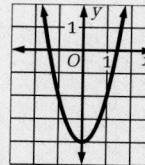

14. about 3.5, about -5.5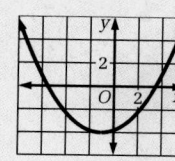

15. about 2.4, about -2.4

16. $10, -20$

17. about 4.6, about -0.6

18. $(2x + 5)(x - 4)$

19. $(2n - 9)(2n + 9)$

20. $(4x - 3)^2$

21. $\frac{2}{3}, 1$

22. about -0.5, about -2.5

23. $1, -2.5$

24. about 0.4, about 3.6

25. one solution   **26.** two solutions

27. no solutions   **28.** $24 + 12i$

29. $-4 - 58i$ **30.** $56 + 34i$

Answers to Unit 4 Review and Assessment

1. $(0, 0); 0$

2. $(0, 4); 4$

3. $(-6, -8); 10$

4. Answers may vary.
Example: $y = -x^2 - 6x - 9$

5. $(3, -16)$; down

6. $(1, 1)$; down

7. a, b. Answers may vary. Examples are given.

a. $y = -x^2 + 6x - 5$
[or $y = -(x - 3)^2 + 4$]

b. $y = -\frac{1}{2}x^2 + 3x - \frac{1}{2}$
[or $y = -\frac{1}{2}(x - 3)^2 + 4$]

c. No; parabolas that are translations of each other have the same shape.

8. C   **9.** A

10. D   **11.** B

12. 4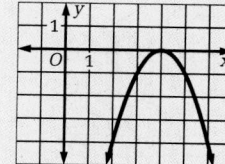

Find all real and complex solutions.

31. $5 - 6x = -6x^2$

32. $0.25x^2 + 3x = -1$

33. $4x^2 + x + 3 = 0$

4-7

Solve each system by substitution.

34. $y = x^2 - 6x + 12$
   $y = x^2 + 3$

35. $y = 3x^2 - 5x + 1$
   $y = 2x^2 + x + 1$

Solve each system by graphing.

36. $y = -2x^2$
   $y = 2x^2 - 3$

37. $y = -0.2x^2 - x + 3$
   $y = 0.25x^2$

38. **Self-evaluation** Make a list of the different methods for solving quadratic equations. Which do you think are easier to use? Why?

39. **Group Activity** Work in a group of three students. For each equation in parts (a)–(d), one student should try to solve by factoring, one student should solve by using the quadratic formula, and one student should solve by graphing. Each student should use each method at least once.

   a. Solve $3x^2 - 2x - 8 = 0$.

   b. Find the x-intercepts of $y = 8x^2 - 14x + 3$.

   c. Find the x-intercepts of $y = 2x^2 - 15x + 4$.

   d. A pitcher throws a warm-up pitch in a softball game. The path of the ball is modeled by the equation $h = -16t^2 + 12t + 4$ where h represents the height of the ball after t seconds. How long will it take for the ball to hit the catcher's mitt at ground level?

   e. For each equation in parts (a)–(d), discuss which solution method you think works best. Give a reason why. Can you decide which method to use by looking at the equation?

IDEAS AND (FORMULAS) $= X^2$

ALGEBRA $) X^2$

➤ The standard form of the equation for a parabola is $y = ax^2 + bx + c, a \neq 0$. *(p. 187)*

➤ When a is negative, the parabola opens down and has a maximum. When a is positive, the parabola opens up and has a minimum. *(p. 188)*

➤ The formula for the line of symmetry of a parabola is $x = -\dfrac{b}{2a}$. *(p. 188)*

➤ You can solve a quadratic equation by undoing the squaring. *(p. 200)*

Unit 4 Quadratic Functions and Graphs

Answers to Unit 4 Review and Assessment ···

31. about $0.5 + 0.76i$, about $0.5 - 0.76i$

32. about -0.3, about -11.7

33. about $-0.1 + 0.9i$, about $-0.1 - 0.9i$

34. $(1.5, 5.25)$

35. $(0, 1)$, $(6, 79)$

36. about $(-0.9, -1.5)$, about $(0.9, -1.5)$

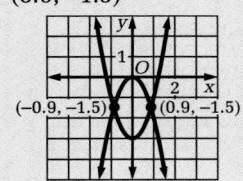

37. about $(-3.9, 3.8)$, about $(1.7, 0.7)$

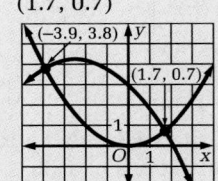

38. Quadratic equations can be solved by graphing, undoing, factoring, and the quadratic formula. Choices may vary.

39. a. $2, -\dfrac{4}{3}$

   b. 1.5 and 0.25

   c. about 7.2 and about 0.3

   d. 1 s

➤ You can solve a quadratic equation by graphing the related function and finding the x-intercepts of the graph. *(p. 201)*

➤ You can factor the difference of two squares. *(p. 208)*

$$a^2 - b^2 = (a + b)(a - b)$$

➤ You can factor a perfect square trinomial. *(p. 208)*

$$a^2 + 2ab + b^2 = (a + b)^2 \qquad a^2 - 2ab + b^2 = (a - b)^2$$

➤ You can use the quadratic formula $x = -\dfrac{b}{2a} \pm \dfrac{\sqrt{b^2 - 4ac}}{2a}$
to solve an equation of the form $0 = ax^2 + bx + c$, when $a \neq 0$. *(p. 215)*

➤ The discriminant of a quadratic equation of the form $0 = ax^2 + bx + c$ is $b^2 - 4ac$, when $a \neq 0$. If the discriminant is *positive*, the equation has two real-number solutions. If the discriminant is *zero*, the equation has one real-number solution. If the discriminant is *negative*, the equation has no real-number solutions but has two complex solutions. *(pp. 222, 224)*

➤ Complex numbers can be added, subtracted, and multiplied like binomials. *(p. 226)*

➤ You can solve a system of quadratic equations by substitution. *(p. 230)*

➤ You can solve a system of quadratic equations by graphing them and finding their point(s) of intersection, if any. *(p. 231)*

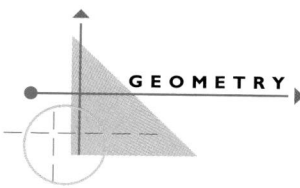
GEOMETRY

➤ The graphs of parabolas in the form $y = a(x + b)^2 + c$ follow these patterns.

As a gets closer to 0, the parabola gets wider. *(p. 193)*

When b is positive, the graph of $y = ax^2$ is translated b units to the left. When b is negative, the graph is translated b units to the right. *(p. 194)*

When c is positive, the graph $y = ax^2$ is translated c units up. When c is negative, the graph is translated c units down. *(p. 194)*

Key Terms

- **parabola** (p. 187)
- **vertex** (p. 188)
- **y-intercept** (p. 189)
- **monomial** (p. 206)
- **quadratic formula** (p. 215)
- **complex number** (p. 225)
- **quadratic system** (p. 231)

- **quadratic function** (p. 187)
- **maximum** (p. 188)
- **x-intercept** (p. 189)
- **trinomial** (p. 206)
- **discriminant** (p. 222)
- **real number** (p. 225)

- **standard form** (pp. 187, 201)
- **minimum** (p. 188)
- **quadratic equation** (p. 201)
- **zero-product property** (p. 209)
- **imaginary unit** (p. 225)
- **pure imaginary number** (p. 225)

Unit 4 Review and Assessment

Quick Quiz (4-1 through 4-4)

1. Without graphing, tell whether the graph of $y = 2x^2 - 7$ opens *up* or *down*. [4-1] up

2. Find the y-intercept of the graph of $y = -4x^2 + 5x - 9$. [4-1] –9

3. Find the coordinates for the vertex of $y = -2(x - 1)^2 + 3$. [4-2] (1, 3)

4. Solve the equation $(x + 5)^2 = 36$. [4-3] $x = 1$ or $x = -11$

5. Factor $2x^2 - 6x - 20$. [4-4] $2(x + 2)(x - 5)$

6. Solve $3x^2 + 4x - 4 = 0$. [4-4] $x = \frac{2}{3}$ or $x = -2$

Answers to Unit 4 Review and Assessment

e. Answers may vary. Examples are given. The equations in parts (a), (b), and (d) are easily factored. Graphing each equation by hand involves estimating x-intercepts; using the TRACE feature on a graphics calculator yields answers quite easily. The equation in part (c) is best solved using the quadratic formula or graphing with a graphics calculator.

OVERVIEW

Internet Resources
Visit our Web site www.mcdougallittell.com for additional resources when teaching this unit.

➤ **Unit 5** covers coordinate geometry and quadrilaterals. Students develop classification skills and learn coordinate geometry formulas. Matrices are used to represent transformations. Standard position is introduced and properties are explored.

➤ The distance formula and midpoint formula are introduced. Coordinates are used to represent vertices of figures placed on the coordinate plane and properties of polygons involving length and midpoints are explored.

➤ The Unit Project is based on creating a board game. Students analyze given game boards for design and relationships to the coordinate system. Diagonals of quadrilaterals are examined in relation to designing the board. One activity includes examining tangrams.

➤ Connections to biology, geography, swimming, literature, and stamps and coins are some of the topics included in the teaching materials and the exercises.

➤ Graphing software can be used in Section 5-4 to explore coordinates and transformations and in Section 5-6 to explore proportions of the diagonals of a trapezoid.

➤ Problem-solving strategies used in Unit 5 include using diagrams and properties of geometric figures, deductive reasoning, formulas, patterns, coordinates, and transformations.

Unit Objectives

Section	Objectives	NCTM Standards
5-1	• Describe characteristics of quadrilaterals and develop classification skills.	1, 2, 3, 4, 7
5-2	• Use formulas for the distance and slope between two points to show relationships in quadrilaterals.	1, 2, 4, 5, 8
5-3	• Use a formula to find the midpoint of a segment.	1, 2, 4, 5, 8
5-4	• Transform geometric figures and learn how transformations affect their properties.	1, 2, 4, 5, 8
5-5	• Represent figures on a coordinate plane using as few variables for coordinates as possible.	1, 2, 4, 5, 8
5-6	• Use coordinate geometry and deductive reasoning to verify some properties of polygons.	1, 2, 3, 4, 5, 8

Skills Bank To extend the curriculum and provide practice with skills, you may wish to assign the following topic from the **Skills Bank** ancillary: poiny symmetry and reflections over $y = x$ (for use after Section 5-4).

Section	Connections to Prior and Future Concepts
5-1	**Section 5-1** reviews characteristics of quadrilaterals. Students develop classification skills by examining diagrams and statements about quadrilaterals. These relationships are used throughout all three books.
5-2	**Section 5-2** introduces the distance formula and reviews finding the slope when given two points on a line. Slope was first introduced in Section 7-2 of Book 1, and is used in Units 7 and 8 of Book 1, Unit 4 of Book 2, and Units 2 and 3 of Book 3. The distance formula is extended to three dimensions in Section 10-5 of Book 2 and is used in Unit 3 of Book 3.
5-3	**Section 5-3** introduces the midpoint formula. This formula is used in Section 5-6 of Book 2 and Unit 3 of Book 3. The problem-solving strategy, *Use a Formula*, is used to find the coordinates of an endpoint of a line segment when the midpoint and the other endpoint are known.
5-4	**Section 5-4** reviews transformations of geometric figures on the coordinate plane. These transformations were first introduced in Sections 4-3, 4-4, and 6-6 of Book 1. Transformations are examined for their effect on segment length and change in slope of the segments. Transformations are extended to the graphs of functions in Unit 9 of Book 3.
5-5	**Section 5-5** examines methods of placing geometric figures on the coordinate plane. The goal is to use as few variables as possible to represent the coordinates of the vertices of the figure. This skill is useful in coordinate proofs, covered in Unit 3 of Book 3.
5-6	**Section 5-6** introduces using coordinate geometry and deductive reasoning to verify some properties about polygons. These properties involve lengths of sides and diagonals, and the line segment joining the midpoints of two sides of a triangle. The midpoint formula was first introduced in Section 5-3 of Book 2. Deductive reasoning was first introduced in Section 9-1 of Book 1, and is used in Units 1 and 7 of Book 2 and Unit 3 of Book 3.

Integrating the Strands

Strands	Sections
Algebra	5-1, 5-2, 5-3, 5-4, 5-5
Functions	5-2
Measurement	5-1
Geometry	5-1, 5-2, 5-3, 5-4, 5-5, 5-6
Statistics and Probability	5-2, 5-6
Logic and Language	5-1, 5-2, 5-3, 5-4, 5-5, 5-6

Coordinate Geometry and Quadrilaterals

Section Planning Guide

➤ Essential exercises and problems are indicated in boldface.
➤ Ongoing work on the Unit Project is indicated in color.
➤ Exercises and problems that require student research, group work, manipulatives, or graphing technology are indicated in the column headed "Other."

Section	Materials	Pacing	Standard Assignment	Extended Assignment	Other
5-1	scissors	Day 1	**1, 3–12**	1, 2, **3–12**, 13–17	
		Day 2	18–28, **29–35**, 37–43, 44–46	18–28, **29–35**, 37–43, 44–46	36
5-2	dice	Day 1	1, **2–4**, 5, **6–14**	1, **2–4**, 5, **6–14**, 15, 16	
		Day 2	**17–29**, 31–38, 39–42	**17–29**, 31–38, 39–42	30, 39
5-3		Day 1	**2–13, 15**, 18–23, 25–34, 35, 36	1, **2–13**, 14, **15**, 16–23, 25–34, 35, 36	24
5-4		Day 1	**1, 2, 6–14**, 15	1, 2, 3–5, **6–14**, 15	
		Day 2	**16–21**, 22, **23–30**, 37–41, 42–44	**16–21**, 22, **23–30**, 31–35, 37–41, 42–44	36
5-5		Day 1	1, **9–21**, 22–33, 34–40	1–8, **9–21**, 22–33, 34–40	
5-6	scissors, protractor, graphing software	Day 1	**1–5**	**1–5**	
		Day 2	**8–10**, 11, 13–15, 17–23, 24, 25	6, **8–10**, 11, 13–15, 17–23, 24, 25	7, 12, 16
Review		**Day 1**	**Unit Review**	**Unit Review**	
Test		**Day 2**	**Unit Test**	**Unit Test**	

Yearly Pacing	Unit 5 Total	Units 1–5 Total	Remaining	Total
	14 days (2 for Unit Project)	79 days	81 days	160 days

Support Materials

➤ See **Project Book** for notes on Unit 5 Project: Create a Board Game.
➤ "UPP" and "disk" refer to **Using Plotter Plus** booklet and **Plotter Plus** disk.
➤ "TI-81/82" refers to **Using TI-81 and TI-82 Calculators** booklet.
➤ Warm-up exercises for each section are available on **Warm-Up Transparencies.**
➤ "FI," "PC," "GI," "MA," and "Stats!" refer, respectively, to the McDougal Littell Mathpack software Activity Books for **Function Investigator, Probability Constructor, Geometry Inventor, Matrix Analyzer,** and **Stats!.**

Section	Study Guide	Practice Bank	Problem Bank	Activity Bank	Explorations Lab Manual	Assessment Book	Visuals	Technology
5-1	5-1	Practice 34	Set 9	Enrich 30	Master 16	Quiz 5-1		
5-2	5-2	Practice 35	Set 9	Enrich 31	Master 2	Quiz 5-2		
5-3	5-3	Practice 36	Set 9	Enrich 32		Quiz 5-3 Test 17		
5-4	5-4	Practice 37	Set 10	Enrich 33	Masters 2, 17	Quiz 5-4	Folder 5	GI Acts. 16–24 TI-81/82, p. 38
5-5	5-5	Practice 38	Set 10	Enrich 34		Quiz 5-5		
5-6	5-6	Practice 39	Set 10	Enrich 35	Master 2	Quiz 5-6 Test 18		GI Acts. 7 and 8
Unit 5	Unit Review	Practice 40	Unifying Problem 5	Family Involve 5		Tests 19–21		

UNIT TESTS

Name _____ Date _____ Score _____

Test 19

Test on Unit 5 (Form A)

Directions: Write the answers in the spaces provided.

The vertices of quadrilateral *ABCD* are *A*(–2, –5), *B*(8, –5), *C*(6, –1), and *D*(0, –1).

1. Find the slope of each side of *ABCD*.
   AB: 0, *BC*: –2, *CD*: 0, *AD*: 2
2. Find the length of each side of *ABCD*.
   AB = 10, *BC* = $2\sqrt{5}$, *CD* = 6, *AD* = $2\sqrt{5}$
3. What type of quadrilateral is *ABCD*? Explain your reasoning.
   An isosceles trapezoid; the figure has two parallel sides of unequal length with the other two sides being of the same length.

For Questions 4–6, use the points *A*(5, 5) and *B*(–4, 2).

4. Find the distance between *A* and *B*.
5. Find the coordinates of the midpoint of $\overline{AB}$.
6. Suppose *B* is the midpoint of $\overline{AC}$. Find the coordinates of *C*.

For Questions 7 and 8, tell whether each statement is *True* or *False.*

7. All rectangles are squares.
8. If a quadrilateral is a kite, then it is a rhombus.
9. Plot the points *A*(0, –4), *B*(4, –3), and *C*(–3, –3).
10. Which point is farthest from the origin? closest to the origin?
11. **Open-ended** Find a fourth point, *D*, so that a parallelogram is formed using the vertices *A*, *B*, *C*, and *D* in any order. Plot your point and draw the parallelogram on the coordinate grid for Question 9.
    Three answers are possible: D_1(1, –2), D_2(7, –4), or D_3(–7, –4). Check students' graphs.

Answers
1. See question.
2. See question.
3. See question.
4. $3\sqrt{10} \approx 9.5$
5. $\left(\frac{1}{2}, \frac{7}{2}\right)$
6. (–13, –1)
7. False
8. False
9. See question.
10. *B*; *A*
11. See question.

27

Name _____ Date _____ Score _____

Test 19 *(continued)*

Directions: Write the answers in the spaces provided.

For Questions 12 and 13, find the coordinates of the image described.

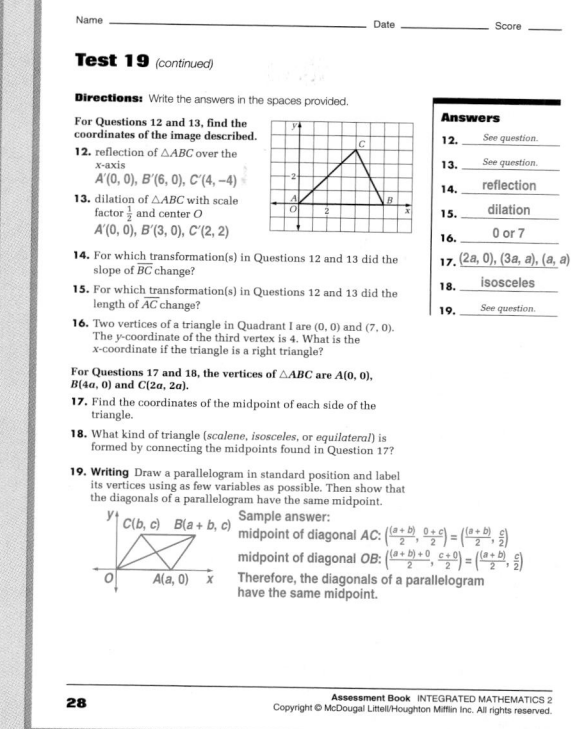

12. reflection of △*ABC* over the *x*-axis
    A′(0, 0), *B*′(6, 0), *C*′(4, –4)
13. dilation of △*ABC* with scale factor $\frac{1}{2}$ and center *O*
    A′(0, 0), *B*′(3, 0), *C*′(2, 2)
14. For which transformation(s) in Questions 12 and 13 did the slope of $\overline{BC}$ change?
15. For which transformation(s) in Questions 12 and 13 did the length of $\overline{AC}$ change?
16. Two vertices of a triangle in Quadrant I are (0, 0) and (7, 0). The *y*-coordinate of the third vertex is 4. What is the *x*-coordinate if the triangle is a right triangle?

For Questions 17 and 18, the vertices of △*ABC* are *A*(0, 0), *B*(4*a*, 0) and *C*(2*a*, 2*a*).

17. Find the coordinates of the midpoint of each side of the triangle.
18. What kind of triangle (*scalene, isosceles,* or *equilateral*) is formed by connecting the midpoints found in Question 17?
19. **Writing** Draw a parallelogram in standard position and label its vertices using as few variables as possible. Then show that the diagonals of a parallelogram have the same midpoint.

Sample answer:
midpoint of diagonal *AC*: $\left(\frac{(a+b)}{2}, \frac{0+c}{2}\right) = \left(\frac{(a+b)}{2}, \frac{c}{2}\right)$
midpoint of diagonal *OB*: $\left(\frac{(a+b)+0}{2}, \frac{c+0}{2}\right) = \left(\frac{(a+b)}{2}, \frac{c}{2}\right)$
Therefore, the diagonals of a parallelogram have the same midpoint.

Answers
12. See question.
13. See question.
14. reflection
15. dilation
16. 0 or 7
17. (2*a*, 0), (3*a*, *a*), (*a*, *a*)
18. isosceles
19. See question.

28

Form B

Name _____ Date _____ Score _____

Test 20

Test on Unit 5 (Form B)

Directions: Write the answers in the spaces provided.

The vertices of quadrilateral *ABCD* are *A*(–6, –2), *B*(0, –2), *C*(4, 2), and *D*(2, 6).

1. Find the slope of each side of *ABCD*.
   AB: 0, *BC*: 1, *CD*: –2, *AD*: 1
2. Find the length of each side of *ABCD*.
   AB = 6, *BC* = $4\sqrt{2}$, *CD* = $2\sqrt{5}$, *AD* = $8\sqrt{2}$
3. What type of quadrilateral is *ABCD*? Explain your reasoning.
   A trapezoid; the figure has two parallel sides but none of the sides are of equal length.

For Questions 4–6, use the points *A*(–5, –1) and *B*(–2, 0).

4. Find the distance between *A* and *B*.
5. Find the coordinates of the midpoint of $\overline{AB}$.
6. Suppose *B* is the midpoint of $\overline{AC}$. Find the coordinates of *C*.

For Questions 7 and 8, tell whether each statement is *True* or *False.*

7. Every square is a rhombus.
8. If a quadrilateral is a parallelogram, then it is a rhombus.
9. Plot the points *A*(0, –5), *B*(4, –3), and *C*(–3, –3).
10. Which point is farthest from the point (1, 1)? closest to the origin?
11. **Open-ended** Find a fourth point, *D*, so that a parallelogram is formed using the vertices *A*, *B*, *C*, and *D* in any order. Plot your point and draw the parallelogram on the coordinate grid for Question 9.
    Three answers are possible: (1, –1), (7, –5), or (–7, –5). Check students' graphs.

Answers
1. See question.
2. See question.
3. See question.
4. $\sqrt{10} \approx 3.2$
5. $\left(-\frac{7}{2}, -\frac{1}{2}\right)$
6. (1, 1)
7. True
8. False
9. See question.
10. *A*; *C*
11. See question.

29

Name _____ Date _____ Score _____

Test 20 *(continued)*

Directions: Write the answers in the spaces provided.

For Questions 12 and 13, find the coordinates of the image described.

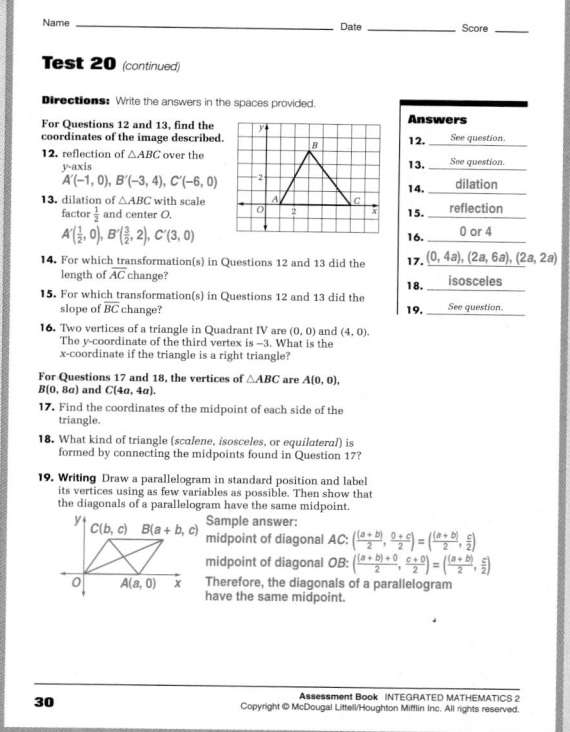

12. reflection of △*ABC* over the *y*-axis
    A′(–1, 0), *B*′(–3, 4), *C*′(–6, 0)
13. dilation of △*ABC* with scale factor $\frac{1}{2}$ and center *O*.
    A′$\left(\frac{1}{2}, 0\right)$, *B*′$\left(\frac{3}{2}, 2\right)$, *C*′(3, 0)
14. For which transformation(s) in Questions 12 and 13 did the length of $\overline{AC}$ change?
15. For which transformation(s) in Questions 12 and 13 did the slope of $\overline{BC}$ change?
16. Two vertices of a triangle in Quadrant IV are (0, 0) and (4, 0). The *y*-coordinate of the third vertex is –3. What is the *x*-coordinate if the triangle is a right triangle?

For Questions 17 and 18, the vertices of △*ABC* are *A*(0, 0), *B*(0, 8*a*) and *C*(4*a*, 4*a*).

17. Find the coordinates of the midpoint of each side of the triangle.
18. What kind of triangle (*scalene, isosceles,* or *equilateral*) is formed by connecting the midpoints found in Question 17?
19. **Writing** Draw a parallelogram in standard position and label its vertices using as few variables as possible. Then show that the diagonals of a parallelogram have the same midpoint.

Sample answer:
midpoint of diagonal *AC*: $\left(\frac{(a+b)}{2}, \frac{0+c}{2}\right) = \left(\frac{(a+b)}{2}, \frac{c}{2}\right)$
midpoint of diagonal *OB*: $\left(\frac{(a+b)+0}{2}, \frac{c+0}{2}\right) = \left(\frac{(a+b)}{2}, \frac{c}{2}\right)$
Therefore, the diagonals of a parallelogram have the same midpoint.

Answers
12. See question.
13. See question.
14. dilation
15. reflection
16. 0 or 4
17. (0, 4*a*), (2*a*, 6*a*), (2*a*, 2*a*)
18. isosceles
19. See question.

30

Software Support

McDougal Littell Mathpack

Geometry Inventor
Matrix Analyzer

Outside Resources

Books/Periodicals

Maletsky, Evan. *Teaching with Student Math Notes, Volume 2.* NCTM, 1993: p. 27, Fair Games and p. 46, Midpoint Madness.

McClintock, Ruth. "Pixy Stix Segments and Midpoint Connections." *Mathematics Teacher* (November 1993): pp. 668–675.

Software

Cabri Geometry II. Houghton Mifflin-Texas Instruments, 1994. Macintosh (geometric constructions with coordinate geometry capabilities).

Schwartz, Judah L. and Michal Yerushalmy. *Geometric Super Supposer.* Pleasantville, NY: Sunburst, 1994. Macintosh and IBM.

Videos

Mathematical Eye. Program No. 9: Symmetry. Journal Films, 1988.

College Algebra: In Simplest Terms. Program No. 6: Probability. COMAP Inc., 1991.

Landscape of Geometry. Program No. 8: Range of Change. Ontario Educational Communications Authority, 1983. (Animation explains translations, rotations, and reflections.)

Futures with Jaime Escalante. Program No. 5: Cartography. PBS, 1990.

240D

PROJECT GOALS

➤ Students create a board game for at least four players that incorporates a coordinate grid.

➤ Before creating a game, students research some board games and discuss their features.

➤ Students incorporate in the board or in the rules at least three math topics from this unit. ....•

PROJECT PLANNING

Materials List

➤ Poster board

➤ Markers

➤ Dice or cards

➤ Tokens or game pieces

➤ Variety of board games

Project Teams

Have students work on the project in groups of four. One way for the individuals in the group to distribute the work is as follows:

1. Researcher: selects board and computer games to analyze, summarizes all ideas from the group about the object of each game, its rules, playing pieces, and strategies.

2. Designer: plans the layout of the game board, creates the playing pieces, and determines how the players will decide the order of taking turns.

3. Writer: writes a complete and concise set of rules for the players to follow and to determine the winner.

4. Game Master: explains the object of the game, the strategies involved, and how the math topics from this unit are used in the game.

Coordinate Geometry and Quadrilaterals

GAMES

It's only a game, or is it? Many of today's games originally had a serious purpose. Some, like tug of war and hopscotch, were rituals for controlling the weather and other powerful natural forces. Others, such as chess, darts, and shuttlecock, were used to train young people in mental and physical skills.

computers

LEVEL 2

SCORE 002289
LINES 011

HIGH SCORE 005047

As a teenager in Moscow in the early 1970s, **Aleksei Pajitnov** played puzzle games to keep busy when he broke his leg. His interest in games continued while he studied applied mathematics and then worked as a programmer at a computer institute. In 1985, in his spare time, Aleksei Pajitnov invented the popular computer game shown above.

START

ALQUERQUE, or el-quirkat (Middle East) Ancestor of checkers. ②

SNAKES AND LADDERS (India) ③ Slide up the ladders toward the 100th square or down the snakes' tails toward square 1.

TANGRAM (China) Use seven basic pieces to make designs. ④

CAT'S CRADLE (Inuit people of the Arctic) Make complex patterns from looped string. ① 240

Suggested Rubric for Unit Project

4 Students' board games apply three or more mathematical topics from this unit in a mathematically sound way. The game board incorporates a coordinate grid, game pieces for at least four players, and dice, cards, or both for determining moves and the order of play. The written instructions are clear and complete. The instructions are easy to follow and the game is fun to play.

3 Students' board games incorporate the appropriate mathematical topics from the unit correctly and have the correct number of game pieces. Dice or cards are used for moves and the order of play. The major difficulty is with the written instructions, which are not entirely clear or complete.

2 Students' board games have some major flaws in applying the mathematical topics from the unit. The procedures for determining the moves and the order of play is not always clear. The instructions are somewhat confusing and incomplete.

Create a Board Game

Your project is to create a board game for four or more players.

Your group should design and build the board and four or more game pieces, and make up rules for your game. Be sure to tell the number of players, how to choose the order of the players, how moves are determined, and how to win the game.

Like the boards for Alquerque, Go, and Snakes and Ladders, your board should have a coordinate grid.

In the board or the rules you should apply at least three mathematical topics from this unit:

➤ properties of quadrilaterals
➤ the distance formula
➤ the midpoint formula
➤ slopes of perpendicular and parallel lines
➤ transformations
➤ coordinate geometry

◄ Go being played in Kyoto, Japan.

GO
(Japan)
Similar to chess.
5

AWITHLAKNANNAI
(Zuni people of New Mexico)
The first player to capture the other player's pieces is the winner.
8

FINISH

PATOLLI
(Aztec people of Mexico)
Similar to backgammon.
6

WARI
(Africa)
Starting with 2 empty cups and 4 pieces in each of 12 cups, try to capture the other player's pieces.
7

241

Suggested Rubric for Unit Project

1 Students' board games essentially do not work. The mathematical topics are applied incorrectly, moves and order of play do not make sense, and the written instructions are incomplete and can- not be followed by the players. The group should be encouraged to speak with the teacher as soon as possible to review their work and to make a new start on the project.

Support Materials

The *Project Book* contains information about the following topics for use with this Unit Project.

➤ Project Description
➤ Teaching Commentary
➤ Working on the Unit Project Exercises
➤ Completing the Unit Project
➤ Assessing the Unit Project
➤ Alternative Projects
➤ Outside Resources

Students Acquiring English

Creating a board game is a valuable project for students acquiring English. These students can add a unique perspective by describing games from their native countries, and by using words and phrases from their languages that could be incorporated into the games. Before students begin, help them choose the math topics that they wish to apply to the project.

ADDITIONAL BACKGROUND

Multicultural Note

The board game *snakes and ladders* is based on a game from India called *moksha-patamu*. The game symbolizes the struggles in life between good and evil. The most ancient hopscotch game pattern known is inscribed into the floor of the Forum, a central public gathering place in ancient Rome. Roman soldiers taught the game to children who lived in what is now Great Britain, France, and Germany. Alquerque is a battle game from Egypt and the Middle East that dates to at least 1400 B.C. It is a predecessor of checkers. To win the game, a player must get five stones in a row.

241

Time Limits and Chess

Time limits are important in many board games. Tournament chess is played with a time limit of two hours per player, during which each player must make 40 moves. In a 1931 tournament, City College of New York was playing Columbia University when the CCNY team captain realized that one of his players had not yet arrived. A phone call to the player's home woke him up and he raced by bus and subway to the tournament site. The player arrived with 40 seconds remaining of his allotted two hours to make 40 moves. His opponent used a standard opening found in many chess books. Since the player was able to anticipate all threats, he traded down pieces to a draw position. His opponent offered to call the game a draw at move 38 when the player had 3 seconds left on his clock. The player had made 38 moves in 37 seconds and turned a certain loss into a draw. ....●

ALTERNATIVE PROJECTS

Project 1, page 287

Design Your Own House

Design a house that could be located in your neighborhood. Use properties of quadrilaterals, the distance and midpoint formulas, and coordinate geometry to draw a floor plan. Combine the floor plan and siting plan in a visual display.

Project 2, page 287

Treasure Hunt

Design a treasure hunt. Draw a treasure map on a grid and write clues that use the properties of quadrilaterals, the midpoint and distance formulas, and coordinate geometry.

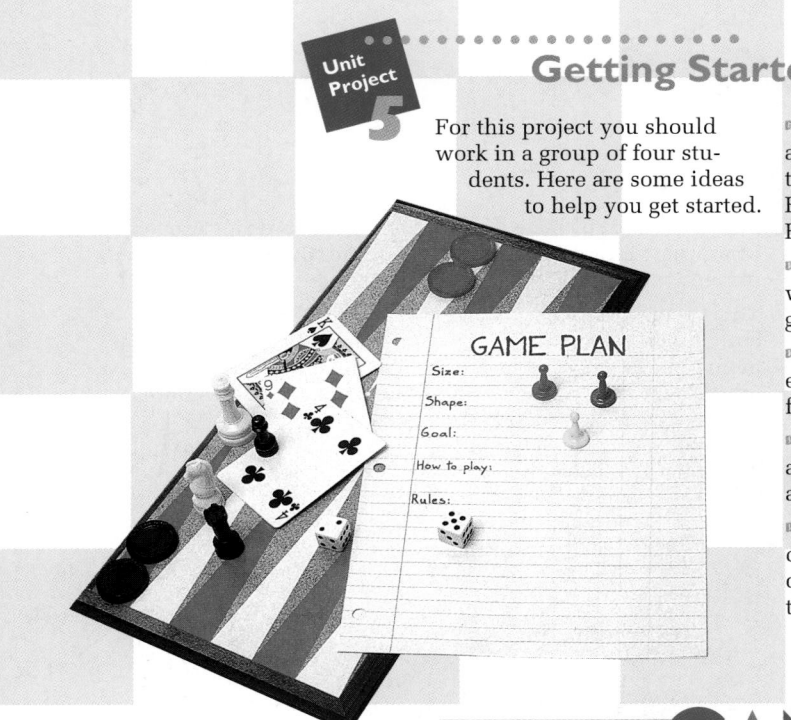

Unit Project 5

Getting Started

For this project you should work in a group of four students. Here are some ideas to help you get started.

☞ Bring in some board games and discuss their features with the members of your group. How are the games alike? How are they different?

☞ Decide what materials you will use to build the board and game pieces.

☞ Discuss ways in which players can decide who will go first, second, and so on.

☞ Your group may wish to talk about the balance between skill and chance in your game.

☞ Plan to meet later to discuss how to include three of this unit's mathematical topics in your game.

Can We Talk

> Have you played any of the games pictured here, or any similar games? What do you like best about these or any other board games you have played?

> Are there any board games that are played by several generations of your family or in your community? If so, why do you think these games are still popular?

> Which of the board games and computer games that you have played use a coordinate grid? How is the grid used in each game?

> In what ways are board and computer games alike? How are they different?

> In which board and computer games that you have played is winning mainly a matter of luck? In which is ability the most important factor? In which are luck and ability about equally important? How do you know?

> What kinds of skills or information do you think you learn from board and computer games? Which skills or information do you think will be helpful in school? at work?

Working on the Unit Project

Your work in Unit 5 will help you create your board game.

Related Exercises:
Section 5-1, Exercises 44–46
Section 5-2, Exercises 39–42
Section 5-3, Exercises 35, 36
Section 5-4, Exercises 42–44
Section 5-5, Exercises 34–40
Section 5-6, Exercises 24, 25

Alternative Projects   p. 287

Unit 5 Coordinate Geometry and Quadrilaterals

Answers to Can We Talk?

> Answers may vary. An example is given. Yes. I like most card games and games that involve using a die or dice such as backgammon.

> Answers may vary. An example is given. Yes. Checkers and chess. Because each game is different every time you play it.

> Answers may vary. Examples are given. Chess or checkers. The grid is used to indicate where pieces can move.

> Answers may vary. Examples are given. They both can be played with more than one person, and they can be played using a grid. Board games cannot be played with one person but computer games can.

> Answers may vary. An example is given. In the board and computer games that I have played, ability is the most important factor. Luck is involved somewhat in backgammon or other games where dice are used.

> Answers may vary. Examples are given. Hand-eye coordination, making a plan, taking turns, and logical reasoning. Making a plan, taking turns, and logical reasoning will be most helpful in school and at work.

Focus
Describe characteristics of
quadrilaterals and develop
classification skills.

Quadrilaterals

THE **QUAD** CLASSIFIED **SQUAD**

EXPLORATION

How can quadrilaterals be classified?

- **Work in a group of four students.**

1. Your group will be investigating quadrilaterals. Each of
you should make a copy of the table shown to record your
results.

2. Look at the twelve numbered quadrilaterals. Which shapes
have *two pairs of parallel sides*? Write the numbers of the
shapes that fit this description in the appropriate column
of the table.

Read "congruent."

Continued on next page.

5-1 Quadrilaterals

243

PLANNING

Objectives and Strands
See pages 240A and 240B.

Spiral Learning
See page 240B.

Materials List
➤ Scissors

Recommended Pacing
Section 5-1 is a two-day lesson.
Day 1
Pages 243–244: Exploration,
Exercises 1–17
Day 2
Pages 244–246: A Quadrilateral
Chart through Look Back,
Exercises 18–46

Extra Practice
See pages 622–623.

Warm-Up Exercises
Warm-Up Transparency 5-1

Support Materials
➤ Practice 34
➤ Enrichment 30 in the Activity
  Bank
➤ Study Guide 5-1
➤ Problem Set 9
➤ Diagram Master 16 in the
  Explorations Lab Manual
➤ Quiz 5-1
➤ Alternative Assessment 1

Answers to Exploration

1. Check students' work.

2, 3.

2 pairs of ∥ sides	4 ≅ sides	4 rt. angles	4 ≅ sides and 4 rt. angles	2 pairs of consecutive ≅ sides	4 sides
2, 3, 4, 5, 6, 11	2, 3, 6	3, 4, 6	3, 6	2, 3, 6, 7, 10	1, 2, 3, 4, 5, 6, 7, 8, 9, 10, 11, 12

Exploration

The goal of the Exploration is to introduce students to the idea that some quadrilaterals are special cases of others by looking at a set of shapes and determining which of them have certain properties. In so doing, the Exploration sets the stage for the development of the quadrilateral chart on page 245.

Teaching Tip

You may wish to reproduce the table students need for the Exploration and provide copies for each group. Then students can use all of their time working on steps 2–8. Also, before students start step 2, make sure they understand the meaning of the markings on the sides of the figures.

Reasoning

After students decide whether each statement in step 8 of the Exploration is true or false, you might wish to relate these statements to the study of converses in Unit 1 on page 46. Students can rewrite parts (a), (c), and (d) as if-then statements and then examine the converse of each one to see if it is true or false.

Communication: Reading

In order to check that students can read and understand the quadrilateral chart, ask them to identify the three most general families that are in the quadrilateral family. (trapezoid, parallelogram, and kite)

Notice that the definition of a trapezoid does not specify *at least one* or *exactly one* pair of parallel sides. As students explore quadrilaterals further, they will be better able to understand why mathematicians use a definition that specifies *at least one* pair of parallel sides. The quadrilateral hierarchy will be revisited and extended in *Integrated Mathematics 3*.

③ Repeat step 2 for each of these characteristics.

Remember: Congruent sides are equal in measure.

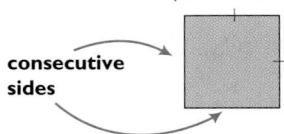

consecutive sides

- four congruent sides
- four right angles
- four congruent sides and four right angles
- two pairs of consecutive, congruent sides
- four sides

④ Which shapes are in all six columns? Which are in the fewest columns?

⑤ Place each of the words *square*, *quadrilateral*, *rectangle*, and *parallelogram* at the top of the column it best describes. Be sure that the members of your group agree. Use the glossary at the back of this book if necessary.

⑥ Read the definitions below. Place each of the words *kite* and *rhombus* at the top of the column it best describes. Be sure that the members of your group agree.

A **kite** is a quadrilateral with two pairs of consecutive sides that are equal in measure. These pairs do not have a side in common.

These sides are congruent.

These sides are congruent.

A **rhombus** is a quadrilateral with four sides of equal measure.

---

⑦ Are there columns of quadrilaterals that are completely included in the parallelogram column? If so, which columns?

⑧ With your group, decide whether each statement is *True* or *False*.

  a. Every rectangle is a parallelogram.

  b. If a quadrilateral is a square, then it is a rectangle.

  c. All rhombuses are squares.

  d. Every rhombus is a parallelogram.

▶ Now you are ready for:
Exs. 1–17 on pp. 246–247

A Quadrilateral Chart

It is easier to see the relationships among quadrilaterals using a chart. Each quadrilateral belongs to the family of quadrilaterals linked to it above and has its characteristics.

Answers to Exploration

4. Shapes 3 and 6 are in all six columns. Shapes 1, 9, and 12 are each in only one column.

5, 6.

parallelogram	rhombus	rectangle	square	kite	quadrilateral
2 pairs of ‖ sides	4 ≅ sides	4 rt. angles	4 ≅ sides and 4 rt. angles	2 pairs of consecutive ≅ sides	4 sides
2, 3, 4, 5, 6, 11	2, 3, 6	3, 4, 6	3, 6	2, 3, 6, 7, 10	1, 2, 3, 4, 5, 6, 7, 8, 9, 10, 11, 12

7. Yes; rhombus, rectangle, square.

8. **a.** True. **b.** True. **c.** False. **d.** True.

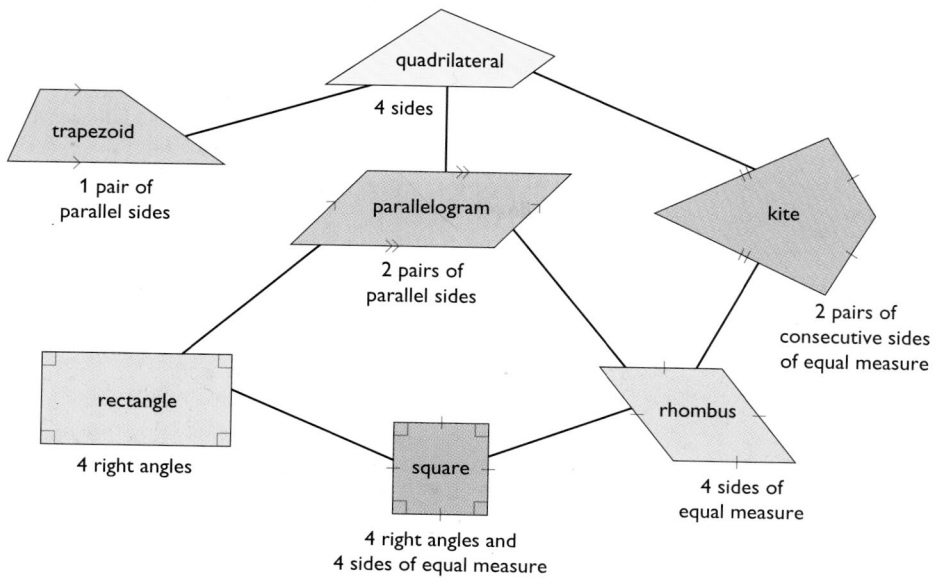

Sample

Complete each sentence so that it is a true statement. Be as specific as possible. Use the quadrilateral chart to explain your choice.

a. All rectangles are also _?_.

b. Every rhombus is also a _?_ and a _?_.

Sample Response

a. All rectangles are **parallelograms**. In the chart parallelograms and quadrilaterals are linked to rectangles from above. Parallelograms are more specific.

b. Every rhombus is also a **kite** and a **parallelogram**. In the chart kites, parallelograms, and quadrilaterals are linked to rhombuses from above. Kites and parallelograms are more specific.

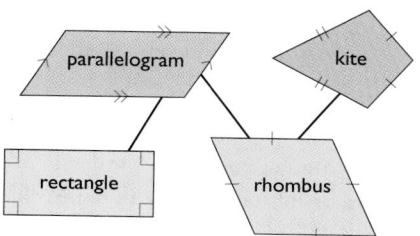

Talk it Over

1. After looking at the quadrilateral chart, Tyler decided that all parallelograms are rectangles. Explain the error he made in using the chart.

2. Do you think that all squares are parallelograms? Why or why not?

5-1 Quadrilaterals

Look Back

The characteristic that all quadrilaterals have in common is having 4 sides, which is the *most general* characteristic. Other characteristics add more specificity to a quadrilateral and, in so doing, help to define different types of quadrilaterals.

APPLYING

Suggested Assignment

Day 1

Standard 1, 3–12

Extended 1–17

Day 2

Standard 18–35, 37–46

Extended 18–35, 37–46

Integrating the Strands

Algebra Exs. 37–43

Measurement Ex. 35

Geometry Exs. 1–12, 29–36, 43–46

Logic and Language Exs. 13–34

Communication: Reading

In Exs. 3–8, the words *all, every, some,* and *if-then* are used. Some students may need help in relating or differentiating the meanings of these words. *Every* has the same meaning as *all. Some* does not mean *all* or *every* but means *at least one.* Thus, Ex. 5 can be translated to this sentence: There is at least one parallelogram that is a rectangle. In Ex. 7, the *if-then* sentence can be reworded as an equivalent sentence using *all* or *every;* for example: All parallelograms are rectangles.

······▶ Now you are ready for:
Exs. 18–46 on pp. 248–250

Look Back ◀

What characteristic do all the figures in the quadrilateral chart have in common? Which quadrilaterals are special cases of a parallelogram? Which are special cases of a kite?

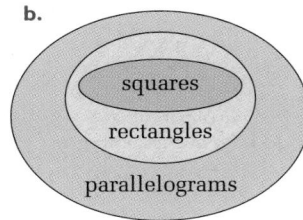

5-1 Exercises and Problems

1. Based on the results of the Exploration, choose the letter of the Venn diagram that shows the correct relationship between squares, rectangles, and parallelograms.

a.
b.
c.

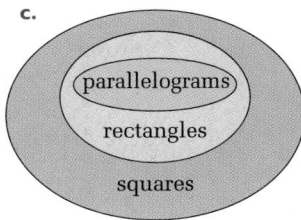

2. **Reading** Use the glossary at the back of this book to find the definitions of *square*, *rectangle*, and *parallelogram*. For each column in your table from the Exploration, tell whether the quadrilaterals in the column fit the definition.

For Exercises 3–7, tell whether each statement is *True* or *False*.

3. All squares are rectangles.

4. Every rectangle is a square.

5. Some parallelograms are rectangles.

6. All parallelograms are quadrilaterals.

7. If a quadrilateral is a parallelogram, then it is a rectangle.

8. **a.** Draw a Venn diagram to show the relationship between kites, rhombuses, and squares.

   b. Write three sentences to show relationships between pairs of shapes in your diagram. For each sentence, use a different pair of shapes and a different one of the words *all*, *every*, and *if-then*.

Use the definition of a kite to determine whether each of these quadrilaterals is a kite. Explain your reasoning.

9.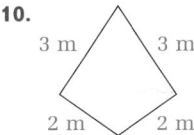

10.
11.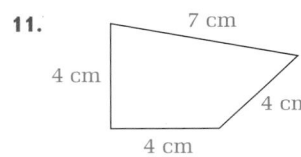

12. What characteristic(s) do rhombuses have that not all kites have?

Answers to Look Back ·······:

4 sides; rhombus, rectangle, square; rhombus, square

Answers to Exercises and Problems ·····················

1. b

2. Check students' work. The definition should describe the shapes.

3. True.

4. False.

5. True.

6. True.

7. False.

8. **a.**

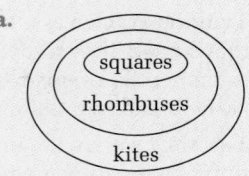

b. All squares are rhombuses. Every rhombus is a kite. If a quadrilateral is a square, then the quadrilateral is a kite.

In Thornton Wilder's play, *Our Town*, Rebecca Gibb tells her older brother, George, about a letter received by her friend.

REBECCA: I never told you about that letter Jane Crofut got from her minister when she was sick. He wrote Jane a letter and on the envelope the address was like this: It said: Jane Crofut; The Crofut Farm; Grover's Corners; Sutton County; New Hampshire; United States of America.

GEORGE: What's funny about that?

REBECCA: But listen, it's not finished: the United States of America; Continent of North America; Western Hemisphere; the Earth; the Solar System; the Universe; … —that's what it said on the envelope.

GEORGE: What do you know!

REBECCA: And the postman brought it just the same.

13. According to the letter, if you live in Grover's Corners then you live in New Hampshire. Write three other true statements using the address on Jane Crofut's letter.

14. Complete the diagram at the right to describe the items included in the address.

15. How would someone address a letter to you using the style on Jane Crofut's letter?

16. a. Address a letter to someone who lives in the city of Puebla using the style on Jane Crofut's letter.

b. Write at least two true statements using the Puebla address.

17. a. Address a letter to someone in the country of Morocco using the style on Jane Crofut's letter.

b. Write at least two true statements using the Morocco address.

5-1 Quadrilaterals

---

connection to **BIOLOGY**

A system of classifying living things by phylum, class, order, family, genus, and species was developed by Carolus Linnaeus in 1758. This chart shows a portion of one of the eleven phyla, the Chordates. Mammals are one of seven classes of Chordates.

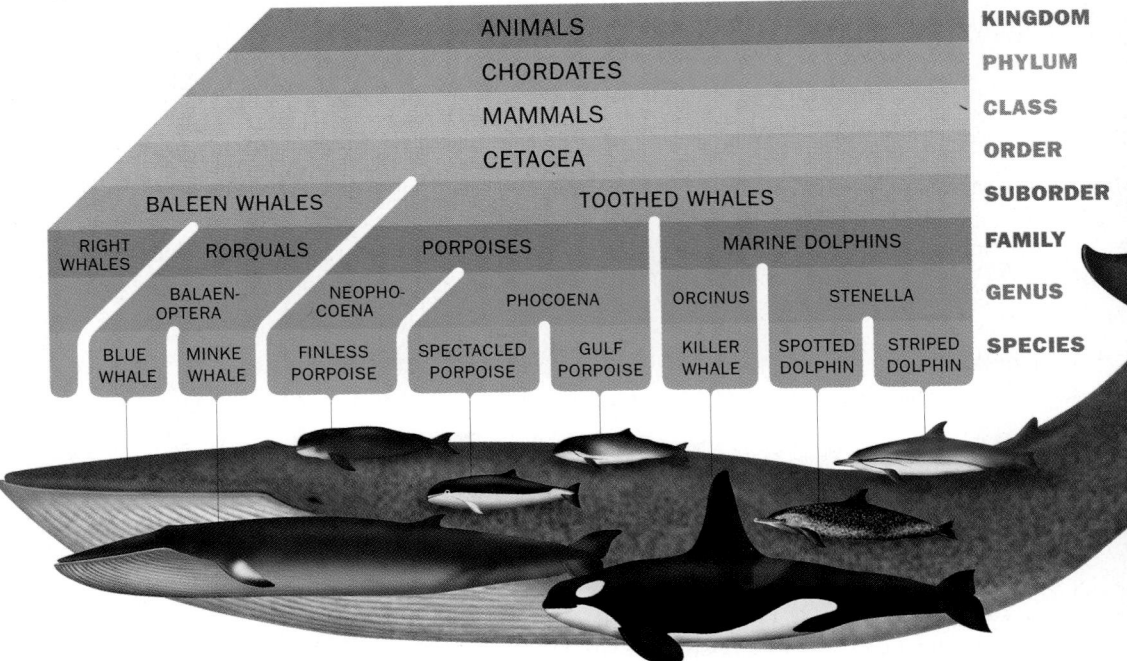

Use the chart for Exercises 18–28.

18. Which species are part of the Porpoise family?

19. Name all the groups that a spotted dolphin belongs to.

20. How is a killer whale like a minke whale?

21. In *Moby Dick*, the author uses the word *Cetacea* to refer to the whale. Why do you think he chose this word?

22. According to the chart, how are members of the Rorqual family different from members of the Porpoise family?

For Exercises 23–28, tell whether each statement is *True* or *False*.

23. All Baleen whales are Mammals.

24. If an animal is a killer whale, then it is a Marine dolphin.

25. Every blue whale is a member of the Right whale family.

26. If an animal is a spectacled porpoise, then it is a member of the Toothed whales suborder.

27. Every striped dolphin is a member of the *Orcinus* genus.

28. All blue whales are minke whales.

> **BY THE WAY...**
>
> Blue whales, the largest animals on Earth, have *baleen* plates instead of teeth. The plates are made out of the same type of material as human fingernails. In a single day, a blue whale is likely to eat up to eight TONS of krill!

248   **Unit 5** Coordinate Geometry and Quadrilaterals

Complete each sentence so that it is a true statement. Be as specific as possible. Use the quadrilateral chart to explain your choice.

29. Every kite is also a __?__ .

30. All __?__ are also rhombuses.

31. Every square is also a __?__ and a __?__ .

32. All parallelograms are also __?__ .

33. If a quadrilateral is a rectangle, then it is also a __?__ .

34. When Carly looked in the glossary of a friend's math book, she found this definition.

When Silas looked in another math book, he found this definition.

> *trapezoid:* A quadrilateral with at least one pair of parallel sides.

> **trapezoid:** A quadrilateral with exactly one pair of parallel sides.

a. How are the definitions different?

b. Which of these quadrilaterals are trapezoids if you use the definition Carly found? if you use the definition Silas found?

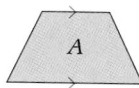 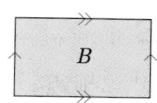 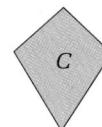 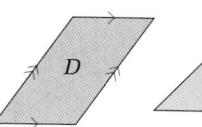 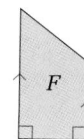

c. Which definition would you be using if you drew the quadrilateral chart with a link between trapezoid and parallelogram? Explain.

35. a. Use the formula $A = \frac{1}{2}h(b_1 + b_2)$ to find the area of trapezoid *ABCD*.

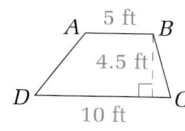

b. Use the formula $A = \frac{1}{2}h(b_1 + b_2)$ to find the area of parallelogram *JKLM*. Do you get the same area if you use $A = bh$?

c. For which types of quadrilaterals can you use the formula $A = \frac{1}{2}h(b_1 + b_2)$ to find the area?

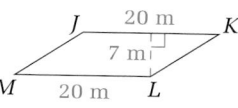

Ongoing **ASSESSMENT**

36. Group Activity Work with at least one other student.

a. Draw and cut out large copies of the quadrilaterals shown. Use paper folding to find the lines of symmetry, if any, for each shape. Draw the lines of symmetry on a copy of the quadrilateral chart.
  • kite   • rhombus   • square   • rectangle   • parallelogram

b. Which figure has no line of symmetry?

c. How do the lines of symmetry for a rhombus compare with the lines of symmetry for a kite?

d. Find the lines of symmetry for a square. How many are there? How are they related to the lines of symmetry for other quadrilaterals?

e. Which figure in the quadrilateral chart has the most lines of symmetry?

 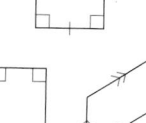 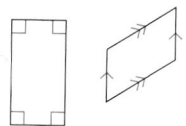

Assessment: Standard

For Ex. 35, students should be able to explain why $\frac{1}{2}(b_1 + b_2)$ is equal to *bh* for a parallelogram, rectangle, square, and rhombus. (Since $b_1 = b_2$, then $b_1 + b_2 = 2b$ and $\frac{1}{2}h(b_1 + b_2) = \frac{1}{2}h(2b) = bh$.)

Research

The prefix *quad-* comes from the Latin *quadri-* (meaning four) and is used in the formation of compound words such as quadrilateral, quadrant, and quadruple. Second-degree equations in algebra, however, such as those in Exs. 37–39, are called quadratic equations, which may lead some students to wonder why they are not fourth-degree equations. The answer to this seemingly misuse of the prefix *quad-* can be found in thinking about the area of a square (a quadrilateral) whose sides have length *x*. The area, of course, is $A = x^2$. It is this historical connection to the area of a square that gave rise to the term *quadratic* (and also to the expression to *square a number*, meaning to multiply a number by itself or to raise it to the second power). Research by students of the early history of mathematics will bring out the historical meaning of the term *quadratic*.

Answers to Exercises and Problems

36. a.

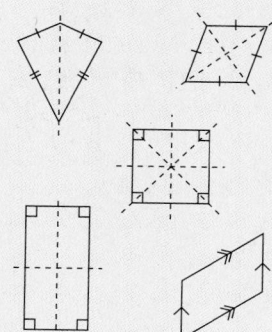

b. parallelogram

c. The lines of symmetry for a kite and a rhombus are along a diagonal.

d. four; The lines of symmetry of a square are the diagonals and the two lines connecting the centers of opposite sides. Since every square is a rectangle and a rhombus, a square has the lines of symmetry of both figures.

e. square

Solve each system. *(Section 4-7)*

37. $y = -0.5x^2 + 2$
$y = 0.8x^2 - 4$

38. $y = 0.25x^2 + 2$
$y = -x^2 + 1$

39. $y = x^2 - 3x + 2$
$y = x^2 + 3x + 2$

**For Exercises 40–42, write the equation of the line that is perpendicular to
each line and goes through the given point.** *(Section 3-3)*

40. $y = -\frac{1}{2}x + 6$; $(1, -2)$

41. $y = 5$; $(-2, 5)$

42. $x = -3$; $(-3, 4)$

43. Use the Pythagorean theorem to find the length of the hypotenuse of
a right triangle with legs of 7 cm and 24 cm. *(Toolbox Skill 31)*

Working on the Unit Project

As you complete Exercises 44–46, think about how you might use
quadrilaterals and their properties in the game you design.

The game of *Alquerque* starts with the pieces arranged on the game board
as shown.

1 A player moves to any
adjacent empty space.

2 If the space behind
your opponent's piece
is empty, your piece
may jump over your
opponent's piece
and into the space.
You then remove
your opponent's
piece.

3 Players are allowed to
move in any direction
and to make multiple
jumps in one turn.

4 The first player to
capture all the
opponent's pieces
wins.

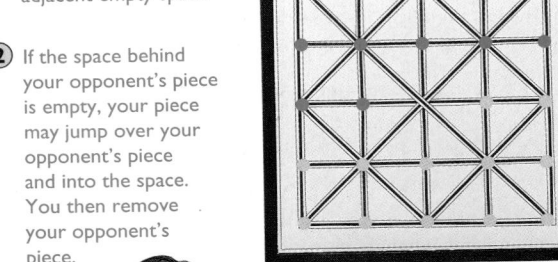

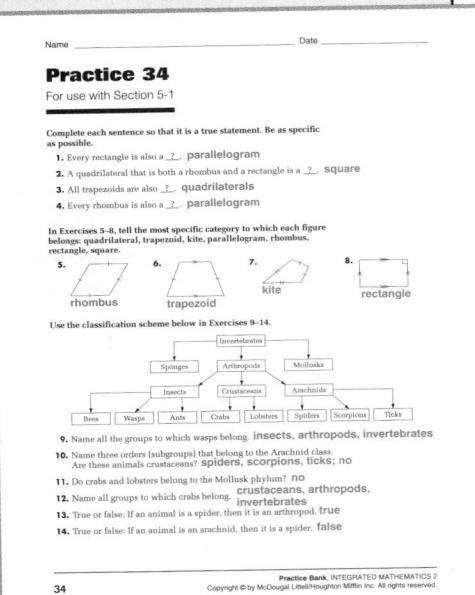

Use the Alquerque board.

44. Do any of the lines form a rhombus
that is not a square? If so, draw the
rhombus on a copy of the board. If
not, explain why not.

45. Some of the lines form a trapezoid.
Find one and draw the trapezoid on
a copy of the board.

46. Describe the game board to someone who cannot see it.

*Pakistan: An Alquerque game
in progress.*

Unit 5 Coordinate Geometry and Quadrilaterals

Answers to Exercises and Problems

37. about $(-2.148, -0.308)$; about
$(2.148, -0.308)$

38. no solution

39. $(0, 2)$

40. $y = 2x - 4$

41. $x = -2$

42. $y = 4$

43. 25 cm

44. No; every angle of each rhombus
is formed by a pair of perpendicular lines.

45. Examples are shown.

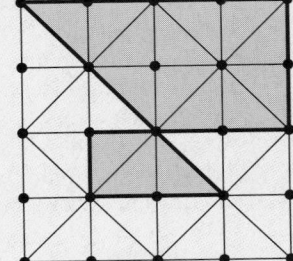

46. Summaries may vary. Use
graph paper to draw a
square. Draw the lines connecting the centers of the
opposite sides to form four
smaller squares. Draw the
lines connecting the cen-
ters of the opposite sides of
the four smaller squares.
Finally, draw the diagonals
of the larger square and the
remaining diagonals of
each of the four smaller
squares.

The Distance Formula and Quadrilaterals

Focus
Use formulas for the distance and slope between two points to show relationships in quadrilaterals.

MORE THAN MEETS THE EYE

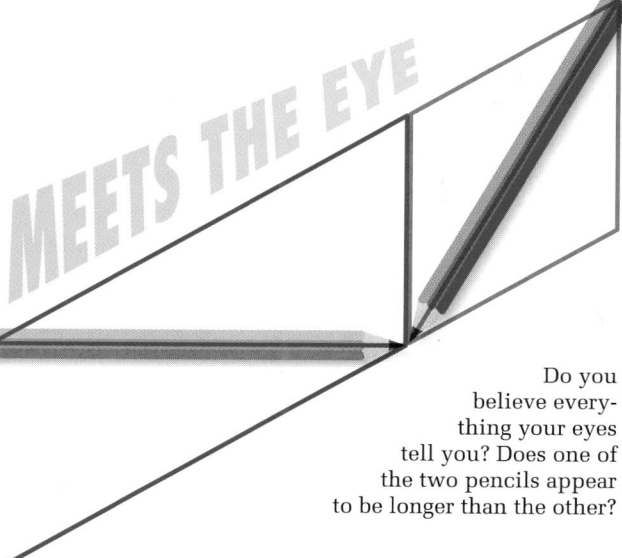

Do you believe every-thing your eyes tell you? Does one of the two pencils appear to be longer than the other?

EXPLORATION

Are the two pencils the same length?

- **Materials: graph paper**
- **Work with another student.**

① The diagram represents the optical illusion above. Copy the diagram on graph paper.

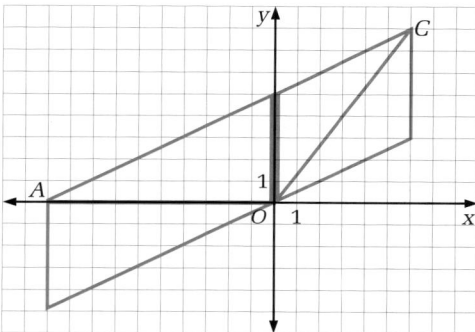

② Find the length of $\overline{AO}$. Describe your method.

③ Discuss with your partner whether you can use the same method to find the length of $\overline{OC}$.

④ Draw a segment straight down from point C to the x-axis. Discuss how you can use the Pythagorean theorem to find OC. Find OC.

⑤ Compare AO and OC. Is the result what you expected?

5-2 The Distance Formula and Quadrilaterals

251

Answers to Exploration

1. Check students' work.

2. 10; Methods may vary. An example is given. Count the number of units along the x-axis.

3. No.

4. Call the point where the line you have drawn meets the x-axis X. $\triangle OCX$ is a right triangle with hypotenuse $\overline{OC}$. Use the Pythagorean theorem:
$OC^2 = OX^2 + CX^2 = 6^2 + 8^2 = 100; OC = 10.$

5. $AO = OC$; Answers may vary. Some may have expected OC to be less than AO.

The Exploration demonstrates that appearances can be misleading, and motivates the need for the use of mathematics to actually find the lengths of the two segments so they can be compared.

Using Technology

The coordinate geometry feature of the *Geometry Inventor* software can be used for the Exploration.

Integrating the Strands

This section begins the study of coordinate geometry, which is perhaps the most important and powerful integration of the major strands of algebra and geometry. By means of the concept of the coordinate grid, geometric concepts can be expressed in algebraic terms, using variables and equations.

Teaching Tip

Students are used to thinking of the Pythagorean theorem in terms of the squares of the *lengths* of the legs and hypotenuse of a right triangle. You may need to connect the terms *distance, change in x,* and *change in y* to the term *length* of a segment. The changes in x and y could be positive or negative, depending upon how the coordinates are subtracted. Of course, the positive change only is the same as the lengths of the segments.

Talk it Over

Questions 1–3 help students to understand the distance formula and how it can be applied to the situation in the Exploration.

Additional Sample

S1 Find the distance between the points (2, 1) and (7, 9).

$$\text{distance} = \sqrt{(7-2)^2 + (9-1)^2}$$
$$= \sqrt{25 + 64}$$
$$= \sqrt{89}$$
$$\approx 9.4$$

The distance between the points is about 9.4 units.

When you know the coordinates of two points, you can find the distance between the points. You can draw a right triangle and use the Pythagorean theorem.

second point $P_2(x_2, y_2)$

distance

change in y

first point

$P_1(x_1, y_1)$ **change in x**

$$(\text{distance})^2 = (\text{change in } x)^2 + (\text{change in } y)^2$$
$$\text{distance} = \sqrt{(\text{change in } x)^2 + (\text{change in } y)^2}$$

Distance is positive. Use the positive square root.

To get a general formula, you can write the change in x and the change in y as the differences of the coordinates of the two points.

THE DISTANCE FORMULA

This is the distance d between the points $P_1(x_1, y_1)$ and $P_2(x_2, y_2)$:

$$\text{distance} = \sqrt{(\text{change in } x)^2 + (\text{change in } y)^2}$$
$$d = \sqrt{(x_2 - x_1)^2 + (y_2 - y_1)^2}$$

Talk it Over

1. Suppose you use the distance formula to find OC in the Exploration. What are the values of x_1, x_2, y_1, and y_2?

2. When you use the distance formula, does it matter if the change in x or the change in y is negative? Explain.

3. Explain why the distance formula can also be written as
$$\text{distance} = \sqrt{(x_1 - x_2)^2 + (y_1 - y_2)^2}.$$

Sample 1

Find the distance between the points (−4, 6) and (0, 3).

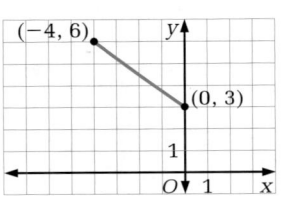

Unit 5 Coordinate Geometry and Quadrilaterals

Answers to Talk it Over ·····:

1. Answers may vary. Let $O = P_1$ and $C = P_2$. Then $x_1 = 0$, $x_2 = 6$, $y_1 = 0$, and $y_2 = 8$.

2. No; both changes are squared.

3. Since $x_2 - x_1 = -(x_1 - x_2)$, $(x_2 - x_1)^2 = [-(x_1 - x_2)]^2 = (x_1 - x_2)^2$. Similarly, $(y_2 - y_1)^2 = (y_1 - y_2)^2$.

Sample Response

$$\text{distance} = \sqrt{(x_2 - x_1)^2 + (y_2 - y_1)^2}$$ ← Use the distance formula.

$$= \sqrt{(0 - (-4))^2 + (3 - 6)^2}$$ ← Substitute $(-4, 6)$ for (x_1, y_1) and $(0, 3)$ for (x_2, y_2).

$$= \sqrt{4^2 + (-3)^2}$$

$$= \sqrt{16 + 9}$$

$$= \sqrt{25}$$

$$= 5$$

The distance between the two points is 5 units.

TECHNOLOGY NOTE

To use the distance formula on a calculator, you may need to use the parentheses keys to get the correct result.

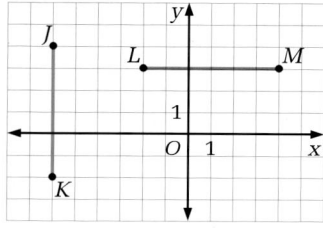

Talk it Over

4. Suppose two points lie on a horizontal line. What is the change in y?

5. What is an easy way to find the distance between two points that lie on a vertical line?

Use the diagram.

6. Find JK.

7. Find LM.

▶ Now you are ready for:
Exs. 1–16 on pp. 255–256

Exploring Quadrilaterals on the Coordinate Plane

The definitions of some types of quadrilaterals involve parallel sides or sides of equal measure. The distance formula and the relationship between the slopes of parallel lines can help you identify a specific type of quadrilateral. Remember that two different lines with the same slope are parallel.

Examples of Parallel Lines

same positive slope   same negative slope   slope = 0   undefined slope

5-2 The Distance Formula and Quadrilaterals

253

Talk it Over

Questions 4–7 consider the two special cases of horizontal and vertical segments. For those situations, the length of each segment can be determined by simply finding the *positive* change in x or y. The distance formula does not have to be used.

Communication: Discussion

A brief discussion of slope would be appropriate. Ask students to describe the slopes of the parallel lines shown. For example, lines with the same positive slope always slope upward to the right. Also, in preparation for Sample 2, the ratio for calculating the slope of a line should be reviewed:
$$\text{slope} = \frac{\text{rise}}{\text{run}}, \text{ or } \frac{\text{change in } y}{\text{change in } x}.$$

Using Technology

Repetitive calculations for figures in the coordinate plane usually can be done by means of simple programs that students can write and execute on the TI-82 or TI-83. Constructing such programs gives an easy introduction to programming. For example, the following program allows you to input the coordinates of two points, (A, B) and (C, D), and find the distance between them.

: Disp "1ST X COORD"
: Input A
: Disp "1ST Y COORD"
: Input B
: Disp "2ND X COORD"
: Input C
: Disp "2ND Y COORD"
: Input D
: Disp "DIST IS",$\sqrt{((C - A)^2 + (D - B)^2)}$

You may need to show students how to name a new program. Program names may have no more than eight characters. Both *Disp* and *Input* are found by pressing PRGM and going to the I/O (input/output) menu.

Answers to Talk it Over

4. 0

5. Subtract the y-coordinates.

6. 6

7. 6

S2 Ann and Phil Graham wanted the design of their new patio to be made up of colored bricks laid out in the shape of parallelograms. They made a pattern for the design on graph paper. Are the opposite sides of their figure parallel? Is the figure a parallelogram?

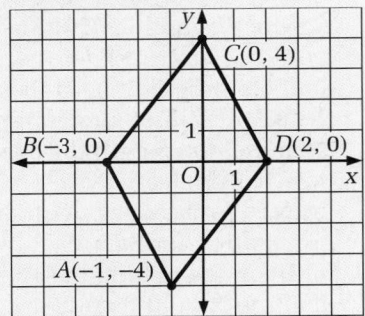

slope of $\overline{BA} = \dfrac{0-(-4)}{-3-(-1)} = \dfrac{4}{-2} = -2;$

slope of $\overline{CD} = \dfrac{4-0}{0-2} = \dfrac{4}{-2} = -2;$

$\overline{AB}$ is parallel to $\overline{CD}$.

slope of $\overline{BC} = \dfrac{4-0}{0-(-3)} = \dfrac{4}{3};$

slope of $\overline{AD} = \dfrac{0-(-4)}{2-(-1)} = \dfrac{4}{3};$

$\overline{BC}$ is parallel to $\overline{AD}$.
The figure is a parallelogram.

Talk it Over

Question 8 provides students with an opportunity to calculate slopes and distances using the distance formula.

Multicultural Note

In 1966, Dr. Maulana Karenga developed the African-American celebration called Kwanzaa, which is celebrated between December 26 and January 1. He envisioned it as fostering cultural and personal goals, political awareness, and connections to Africa. Intrinsic to Kwanzaa are these seven principles: Umoja (unity), Kujichagulia (self-determination), Ujima (collective work and responsibility), Ujamaa (cooperative economics), Nia (purpose), Kuumba (creativity, and Imani (faith).

Sample 2

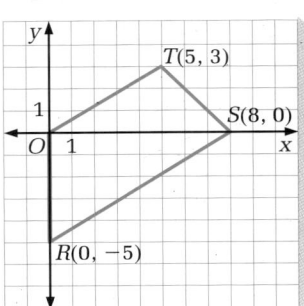

Writing Phelton and Odessa want to include a special design on each family member's Kwanzaa outfit. Phelton made a pattern for the design on graph paper.

For the design to fit together properly, the shape needs to be a trapezoid.

Phelton thinks that sides $\overline{OT}$ and $\overline{RS}$ are parallel, but Odessa does not. Who do you think is correct? Why?

Sample Response

I think Odessa is right. The slopes of the two sides are not equal, so $\overline{OT}$ is not parallel to $\overline{RS}$.

slope of $\overline{OT} = \dfrac{3-0}{5-0} = \dfrac{3}{5} = 0.6$

slope of $\overline{RS} = \dfrac{0-(-5)}{8-0} = \dfrac{5}{8} = 0.625$

The other pair of opposite sides is not parallel either. Therefore ORST is not a trapezoid.

BY THE WAY...

Kwanzaa is a holiday that celebrates African American heritage and achievements. For the festival, women wear traditional African dresses called *lappas* and men wear *dashikis*.

Perpendicular lines can also help you identify quadrilaterals. Remember that when the slope of a line is m, the slope of a perpendicular line is $-\dfrac{1}{m}$.

Talk it Over

8. Show that a quadrilateral with vertices $A(-3, 4)$, $B(3, 1)$, $C(6, -5)$, and $D(0, -2)$ is a rhombus.

9. How can you verify that a quadrilateral is a rectangle?

Look Back

How can you remember the distance formula? If you forget it, how can you find the distance between two points?

Now you are ready for:
Exs. 17–42 on pp. 256–258

Unit 5 Coordinate Geometry and Quadrilaterals

Answers to Talk it Over

8. Answers may vary. An example is given. $AB = \sqrt{(-3-3)^2 + (4-1)^2} = \sqrt{36+9} = \sqrt{45} = 3\sqrt{5};$

$BC = \sqrt{(3-6)^2 + (1-(-5))^2} = \sqrt{9+36} = \sqrt{45} = 3\sqrt{5};$

$CD = \sqrt{(6-0)^2 + (-5-(-2))^2} = \sqrt{36+9} = \sqrt{45} = 3\sqrt{5};$

$DA = \sqrt{(0-(-3))^2 + (-2-4)^2} = \sqrt{9+36} = \sqrt{45} = 3\sqrt{5};$

Since the four sides are equal in measure, $ABCD$ is a rhombus.

9. Answers may vary. An example is given. Show that each pair of consecutive sides is perpendicular.

5-2 Exercises and Problems

1. **Open-ended** The picture of the two pencils at the beginning of the section is called an *optical illusion.* Describe another optical illusion you have seen. Why do you suppose your eyes play tricks on you?

For Exercises 2–4, study each optical illusion to answer the question.

2. Are the columns parallel?

3. Which of the two lines continues to the single line?

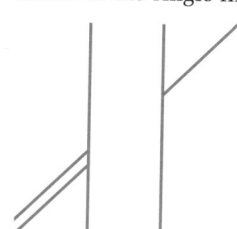

4. Are the diagonal lines parallel?

5. **Reading** How is the distance formula related to the Pythagorean theorem?

Find the distance between each pair of points.

6. (5, 8) and (10, 4)

7. (−6, 2) and (1, −4)

8. (2, 8) and (−7, 8)

Find each distance.

9. *LM*

10. *GJ*

11. *JL*

12. *GH*

13. *JK*

14. *GM*

Aviation The length of runway needed for a plane to land safely depends on the plane's weight, the airport's elevation, and the temperature.

15. **a.** The plan for an airport runway system is shown. Estimate the length of each runway: *AB*, *CD*, *EF*, *GH*, and *CJ*.

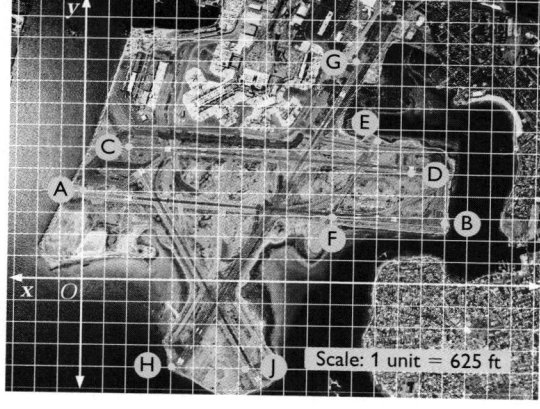

Scale: 1 unit = 625 ft

b. Suppose a jet needs about 7500 ft to land. Which runways can it land on?

c. Repeat part (b) for a small plane that needs about 2150 ft to land.

d. Repeat part (b) for a space shuttle that needs an average of about 9925 ft to land.

▶ **BY THE WAY...**

Planes need more room to take off and land in hot weather and at high elevations. It is not uncommon for a plane in Arizona to unload cargo so that it will have enough runway space to take off.

5-2 The Distance Formula and Quadrilaterals **255**

APPLYING

Suggested Assignment

Day 1

Standard 1–14

Extended 1–16

Day 2

Standard 17–29, 31–42

Extended 17–29, 31–42

Integrating the Strands

Algebra Exs. 5–8, 17–29, 33–35

Functions Exs. 33–35

Geometry Exs. 2–32. 39, 41

Statistics and Probability Exs. 36–38, 41

Logic and Language Exs. 1, 26, 31, 32, 39–42

Research

Students interested in aviation might wish to research the question of why planes need more room to take off and land in hot weather and at high elevations.

Answers to Look Back

Summaries may vary. An example is given. Remember that the distance is the positive square root of [(change in x)^2 + (change in y)^2]. If you forget the formula, draw a right triangle and use the Pythagorean theorem.

Answers to Exercises and Problems

1. Answers may vary. An example is given. One commonly seen optical illusion is a pair of parallel line segments the same length in which one segment has regular arrowheads at the endpoints and the other has outward-pointing arrowheads. The segment with the outward-pointing arrowheads appears longer.

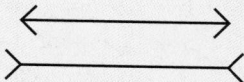

2. Yes.

3. the lower line

4. Yes.

5. The distance formula is derived by drawing a right triangle and using the lengths of horizontal and

vertical lines, whose lengths can be found by subtracting x-coordinates and y-coordinates of points, respectively. These distances are then used in the Pythagorean theorem to find the length of the hypotenuse.

6. $\sqrt{41} \approx 6.40$

7. $\sqrt{85} \approx 9.22$

8. 9

9. 3

10. 4

11. 5

12. $\sqrt{40} \approx 6.3$

13. $\sqrt{29} \approx 5.4$

14. $5\sqrt{2} \approx 7.07$

15. **a.** $AB \approx 10{,}000$ ft
$CD \approx 7800$ ft
$EF \approx 2500$ ft
$GH \approx 10{,}000$ ft
$CJ \approx 7100$ ft

b. *AB*, *CD*, *GH*

c. all of them

d. *AB* and *GH*

Application

In competitive swimming, the differences between the times of the swimmers finishing in first, second, and third places are usually only hundredths or thousandths of a second. This makes the calculation and use of a swimmer's advantage time extremely important. By applying the distance formula in Ex. 16, the advantage time for each swimmer can be found. Since the actual time a swimmer takes to finish a race is a little more than the recorded time, the swimmer's advantage is added to the recorded time to find the actual time.

Problem Solving

Exs. 17–19 provide problem-solving experiences with particular figures and prepare students for solving similar but more general problems in Sections 5-5 and 5-6.

Mathematical Procedures

For Exs. 17–29, algebraic procedures that involve the distance formula and the ratio for finding the slope of a line are used to answer questions and solve problems that involve properties of geometric figures. This connection of algebra and geometry provides students with some powerful problem-solving techniques and expands significantly the strategies now available to solve problems.

---

16. In competitive swimming, when the starter fires a shot, the timers start their watches and the swimmers dive into the water. The time it takes for the sound of the shot to travel to the swimmers and timers can give some swimmers an advantage. To make the contest fair, a correction is made to each swimmer's finishing time.

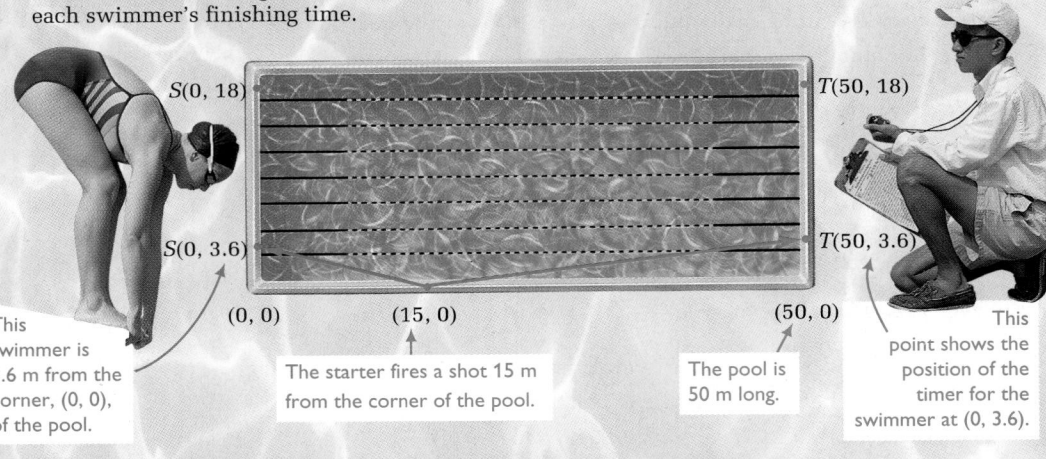

S(0, 18)   *T*(50, 18)

S(0, 3.6)   *T*(50, 3.6)

(0, 0)   (15, 0)   (50, 0)

This swimmer is 3.6 m from the corner, (0, 0), of the pool.

The starter fires a shot 15 m from the corner of the pool.

The pool is 50 m long.

This point shows the position of the timer for the swimmer at (0, 3.6).

For parts (a)–(e), use the diagram above. Assume that sound travels at 346 m/s. Round your answers to the nearest thousandth of a second.

a. Calculate the distance from the starter to the swimmer at *S*(0, 3.6). Find the time it takes for sound to travel from the starter to the swimmer.

b. Calculate the distance from the starter to the timer at *T*(50, 3.6). Find the time it takes for sound to travel from the starter to the timer.

c. The positive difference between the two times you found in parts (a) and (b) is the swimmer's advantage. What is this swimmer's advantage?

d. What is the advantage for the swimmer at (0, 18)?

e. **Writing** Explain how you think the judges of a swimming competition should use the advantages in order to determine the winner.

BY THE WAY…

At some swimming competitions, horns are placed under each person's starting point so that the signal reaches every swimmer at the same time. Individual electronic timers begin when the horns sound and stop when a swimmer touches a sensor at the end of the pool.

For Exercises 17–19, use the distance formula and slope to show that the quadrilateral is the type specified.

17. Show that *TUVW* is a parallelogram.

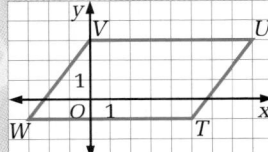

18. Show that *EFGH* is a kite.

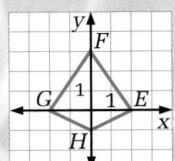

19. Show that *JKLM* is a square.

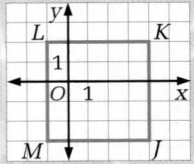

256   **Unit 5** Coordinate Geometry and Quadrilaterals

Answers to Exercises and Problems

16. a. about 15.43 m; about 0.045 s

   b. about 35.18 m; about 0.102 s

   c. about 0.057 s

   d. 0.046 s

   e. The advantage of a given swimmer should be added to that swimmer's time.

17. slope of $\overline{VU}$ = slope of $\overline{WT}$ = 0; slope of $\overline{VW}$ = slope of $\overline{UT}$ = $\frac{4}{3}$;

$\overline{VU} \parallel \overline{WT}$ and $\overline{VW} \parallel \overline{UT}$ so *TUVW* is a parallelogram.

18. $GH = HE = \sqrt{5}$ and $GF = FE = \sqrt{13}$ so *EFGH* is a kite.

19. $LM = LK = KJ = JM = 5$; $\overline{LK}$ and $\overline{MJ}$ have 0 slope and $\overline{LM}$ and $\overline{KJ}$ have undefined slope, so $\overline{LK} \perp \overline{LM}$, $\overline{LK} \perp \overline{KJ}$, $\overline{MJ} \perp \overline{LM}$, and $\overline{MJ} \perp \overline{KJ}$. *JKLM* has four congruent

sides and four right angles, so *JKLM* is a square.

20. Opposite sides are parallel.

21. Two pairs of consecutive sides are congruent.

22. One pair of sides is parallel.

23. All sides are congruent and consecutive sides are perpendicular.

24. a. −1; 1; 0; 1

b. Since $\overline{SK}$ and $\overline{PG}$ have the same slope, $\overline{SK} \parallel \overline{PG}$ and *GSKP* is a trapezoid.

25. a. Rectangles may vary.

   b. most likely result: The diagonals are congruent.

   c. The results should be the same. The diagonals of a rectangle are congruent.

Suppose you have a quadrilateral. What do you have to know about its sides to show that it is the special quadrilateral described?

20. a parallelogram   **21.** a kite

22. a trapezoid   **23.** a square

24. Use quadrilateral *GSKP*.

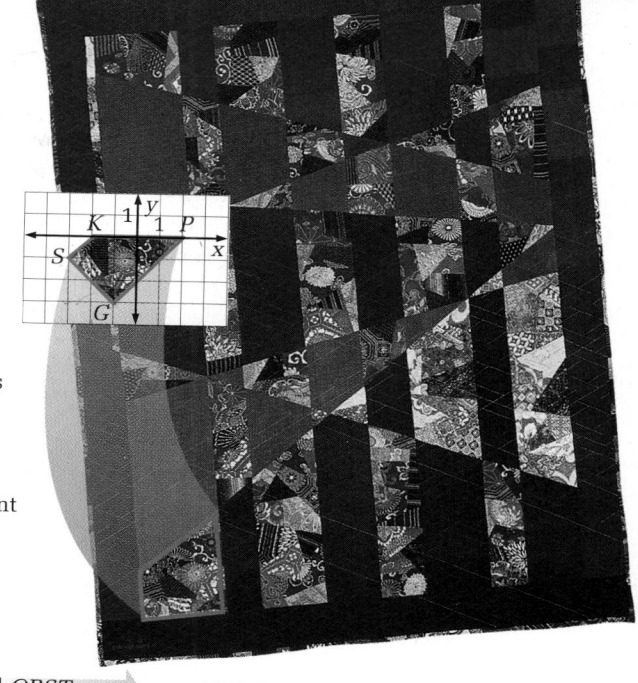

  a. Find the slope of $\overline{GS}$, $\overline{SK}$, $\overline{KP}$, and $\overline{PG}$.

  b. Show that *GSKP* is a trapezoid.

25. a. **Open-ended** Draw a rectangle on a coordinate plane. Give the coordinates of its vertices.

  b. Find the length of each diagonal of your rectangle.

  c. Repeat steps (a) and (b) using a different rectangle.

  d. Make a conjecture about the diagonals of any rectangle.

  e. In part (d), did you use *inductive reasoning* or *deductive reasoning*?

26. **Writing** Jennika thinks that quadrilateral *QRST* is a kite. Do you agree or disagree? Explain your reasoning.

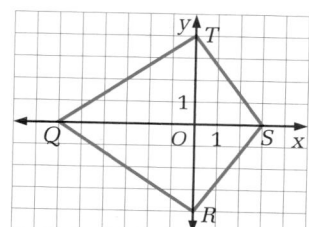

27. Alan claims that quadrilateral *JKLM* is a rhombus. Its vertices are *J*(0, 0), *K*(7, 2), *L*(11, 8), and *M*(4, 6).

  a. Draw *JKLM* on graph paper and measure each side as best you can. Do your measurements indicate that *JKLM* is a rhombus?

  b. Use the distance formula to find the exact length of each of the sides. Do you think that *JKLM* is a rhombus? Why or why not?

  c. Show that *JKLM* is a parallelogram.

  d. **Writing** Look back at parts (a) and (b). Why do you suppose mathematicians prefer to verify information using formulas instead of measurements or drawings?

28. Use quadrilateral *OQRS*.

  a. Show that *OQRS* is a parallelogram.

  b. Show that the opposite sides of *OQRS* are equal in measure.

29. A quadrilateral has vertices *A*(0, 0), *B*(8, 0), *C*(7, 5), and *D*(3, 5).

  a. What type of quadrilateral is *ABCD*?

  b. Find the length of each side to the nearest tenth of a unit.

  c. Use the formula $A = \frac{1}{2}h(b_1 + b_2)$ to find the area of *ABCD*.

  d. Find the perimeter of *ABCD*.

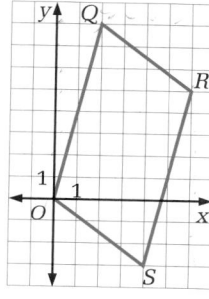

5-2 The Distance Formula and Quadrilaterals

Answers to Exercises and Problems

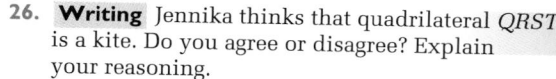

  d. The diagonals of a rectangle are congruent.

  e. inductive reasoning

26. agree; $QT = QR = 2\sqrt{13}$ and $RS = TS = 5$; Two pairs of consecutive sides are congruent, so *QRST* is a kite.

27. a. Measurements and answers may vary. The four sides of the figure are very close in length.

  b. $JM = KL = \sqrt{52} \approx 7.2$; $JK = ML = \sqrt{53} \approx 7.3$; *JKLM* is not a rhombus because all four sides are not congruent.

  c. slope of $\overline{JM}$ = slope of $\overline{KL} = \frac{3}{2}$; slope of $\overline{JK}$ = slope of $\overline{ML} = \frac{2}{7}$; $\overline{JM} \parallel \overline{KL}$ and $\overline{JK} \parallel \overline{ML}$, so *JKLM* is a parallelogram.

  d. Answers may vary. An example is given. Drawings may be deceptive; segments that appear to be congruent may not be and may be so close that even measuring will not establish the truth. For example, in a drawing, two segments that are 32.8 mm and 32.7 mm long will certainly appear to be congruent

and could not be measured accurately with a ruler.

28. a. slope of $\overline{OQ}$ = slope of $\overline{SR} = 4$; slope of $\overline{OS}$ = slope of $\overline{QR} = -\frac{3}{4}$; $\overline{OQ} \parallel \overline{SR}$ and $\overline{OS} \parallel \overline{QR}$, so *OQRS* is a parallelogram.

  b. $OS = QR = 5$ and $OQ = SR = 2\sqrt{17} \approx 8.2$

29. a. trapezoid

  b. $AB = 8$; $BC = 5.1$; $CD = 4$; $AD = 5.8$

  c. 30 square units

  d. about 22.9

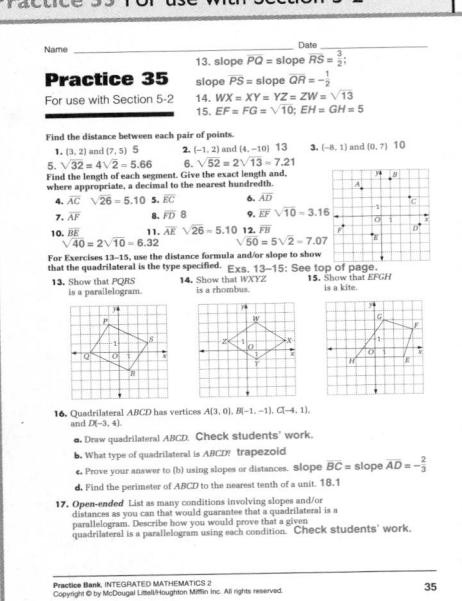
30. Group Activity Work with another student.

a. Each of you should draw a figure on a coordinate plane that looks like a trapezoid, a parallelogram, a kite, or a rhombus. Try to make your figure an optical illusion. Make it appear to be something it is not.

b. Label your figure with the coordinates of its vertices.

c. Trade the figures with each other. Use the distance formula and the slope formula to decide whether the figure you have received is what it appears to be.

Review **PREVIEW**

Tell whether each statement is *True* or *False*. *(Section 5-1)*

31. All kites are parallelograms.

32. Every square is a kite.

For each function, describe how *y* changes when *x* is halved. *(Section 2-5)*

33. $y = 4x^2$

34. $y = \dfrac{-3}{x}$

35. $y = \dfrac{2}{5}x^3$

For Exercises 36–38, find the mean of the data points. *(Toolbox Skill 4)*

36. Winter temperatures (°F):
32, −5, 10, −3, 15, 28

37. Ice skating scores:
5.7, 5.9, 5.8, 5.4, 5.7

38. Test scores:
85, 75, 92, 83, 60, 98, 87

Working on the Unit Project

Exercises 39–42 use the *distance-formula game*.

In the distance-formula game, two dice are used to determine a point (*x, y*) in the coordinate plane. To start, roll the dice to determine the *target point*.

Have each player roll the dice in turn. Record the coordinates rolled. The player whose point is closest to the target point wins the round. The game ends when one player has won three rounds.

39. a. Group Activity Play the game with another student.

b. List the materials you need to play this game. Describe when and how players use the distance formula.

c. Writing Are the directions for the game clear? How could they be made better?

d. Writing How can you make the directions for your game easy to read and understand?

40. List all the possible target points.

41. How many ways can the distance from a player's point be less than 2 units from the target point (4, 3)?

42. Can two players tie in a round of the game? If so, how could you break the tie?

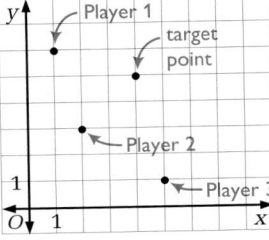

One die represents the *y*-coordinate…

…and the other represents the *x*-coordinate.

Answers to Exercises and Problems

30. a–c. Answers may vary. Check students' work.

31. False; if all four sides of a kite are not congruent, the kite is not a parallelogram.

32. True.

33. *y* is divided by 4.

34. *y* is doubled.

35. *y* is divided by 8.

36. about 12.8°F

37. 5.7

38. about 82.9

39. See answers in back of book.

40. (1, 1), (1, 2), (1, 3), (1, 4), (1, 5), (1, 6), (2, 1), (2, 2), (2, 3), (2, 4), (2, 5), (2, 6), (3, 1), (3, 2), (3, 3), (3, 4), (3, 5), (3, 6), (4, 1), (4, 2), (4, 3), (4, 4), (4, 5), (4, 6), (5, 1), (5, 2), (5, 3), (5, 4), (5, 5), (5, 6), (6, 1), (6, 2), (6, 3), (6, 4), (6, 5), (6, 6)

41. 9

42. Yes. Answers may vary. An example is given. Those two players should roll again to determine a winner.

Section 5-3

Midpoints

Focus
Use a formula to find the midpoint of a segment.

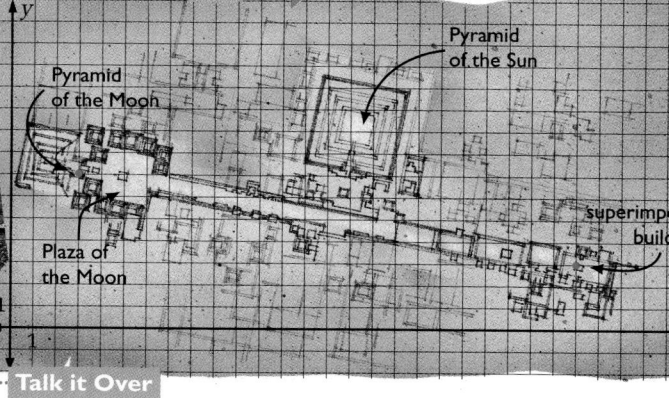

Meet Me Halfway

Talk it Over

1. At Teotihuácan, a Mesoamerican ceremonial center in Mexico, the halfway point along the street connecting the Pyramid of the Moon and the superimposed buildings is directly in front of the Pyramid of the Sun. Estimate the coordinates of the halfway point.

2. What *x*-coordinate is halfway between 3 and 25? Explain.

3. What *y*-coordinate is halfway between 7 and 3? Explain.

4. Based on your answers to questions 2 and 3, find more precise coordinates of the halfway point.

The point halfway between the endpoints of a segment is called the **midpoint.** You can find the coordinates of the midpoint of a segment by finding the mean of the *x*-coordinates and the mean of the *y*-coordinates.

THE MIDPOINT FORMULA

The midpoint of a segment with endpoints (x_1, y_1) and (x_2, y_2) has coordinates

$$\left(\frac{x_1 + x_2}{2}, \frac{y_1 + y_2}{2}\right).$$

the mean of the *x*'s   the mean of the *y*'s

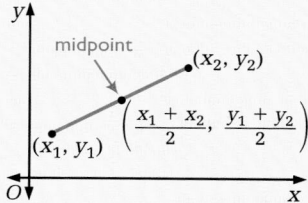

5-3 Midpoints **259**

PLANNING

Objectives and Strands
See pages 240A and 240B.

Spiral Learning
See page 240B.

Recommended Pacing
Section 5-3 is a one-day lesson.

Extra Practice
See pages 622–623.

Warm-Up Exercises
Warm-Up Transparency 5-3

Support Materials
➤ Practice 36
➤ Enrichment 32 in the Activity Bank
➤ Study Guide 5-3
➤ Problem Set 9
➤ Quiz 5-3
➤ Test 17

Answers to Talk it Over

1. about (15, 5)

2. 14; The average of 3 and 25 is 14.

3. 5; The average of 7 and 3 is 5.

4. (14, 5)

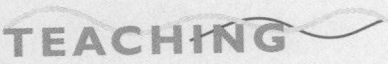

TEACHING

Talk it Over

Questions 1–4 prepare students for the symbolic statement of the midpoint formula by first using the numerical coordinates of two points.

Teaching Tip

Some students may need to be reminded that the *mean* of two numbers is the average of the numbers.

Additional Samples

S1 Find the coordinates of the midpoint of the segment whose endpoints are (−8, 10) and (12, 6).

$\frac{-8 + 12}{2} = 2$ and $\frac{10 + 6}{2} = 8$

The coordinates of the midpoint are (2, 8).

S2 M is the midpoint of $\overline{RT}$. Find the coordinates of T.

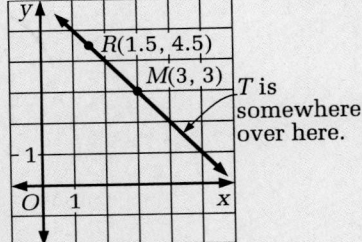

Find the x-coordinate of T.

$\frac{1.5 + x_2}{2} = 3$

$1.5 + x_2 = 6$

$x_2 = 4.5$

Find the y-coordinate of T.

$\frac{4.5 + y_2}{2} = 3$

$4.5 + y_2 = 6$

$y_2 = 1.5$

The coordinates of T are (4.5, 1.5).

Sample 1

Find the coordinates of the midpoint of the segment whose endpoints are (9, −14) and (3, 4).

Sample Response

Let (x_1, y_1) be $(9, -14)$ and let (x_2, y_2) be $(3, 4)$.

The x-coordinate of the midpoint is $\frac{x_1 + x_2}{2} = \frac{9 + 3}{2} = 6$.

The y-coordinate of the midpoint is $\frac{y_1 + y_2}{2} = \frac{-14 + 4}{2} = -5$.

The coordinates of the midpoint are (6, −5).

Sample 2

M is the midpoint of $\overline{AB}$. Find the coordinates of B.

B is somewhere over here.

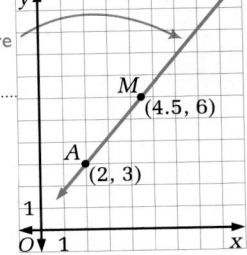

Sample Response

Use a formula.

Let the coordinates of B be (x_2, y_2).

Find the x-coordinate of B.

$\frac{2 + x_2}{2} = 4.5$ ← Substitute 2 for x_1 in $\frac{x_1 + x_2}{2} = 4.5$.

$2 + x_2 = 9$ ← Multiply both sides by 2.

$x_2 = 7$

Find the y-coordinate of B.

$\frac{3 + y_2}{2} = 6$ ← Substitute 3 for y_1 in $\frac{y_1 + y_2}{2} = 6$.

$3 + y_2 = 12$ ← Multiply both sides by 2.

$y_2 = 9$

The coordinates of B are (7, 9).

Look Back

State the distance formula and the midpoint formula in words. How is each formula used?

Answers to Look Back

distance formula: Given two points, (x_1, y_1) and (x_2, y_2), add the square of the difference between the x-coordinates to the square of the difference between the y-coordinates and take the positive square root of the sum; midpoint formula: Given two points, (x_1, y_1) and (x_2, y_2), find the mean of the x-coordinates and the mean of the y-coordinates. The distance formula is used to find the distance between two points, given their coordinates. The midpoint formula is used to find the coordinates of the midpoint of a line segment, given the coordinates of its endpoints.

Exercises and Problems

1. Reading Compare the method you used in *Talk it Over* questions 2 and 3 on page 259 to using the midpoint formula. How are they alike? How are they different?

For each graph, find the midpoint of $\overline{AB}$.

2.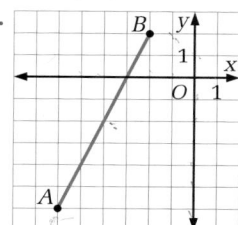

3.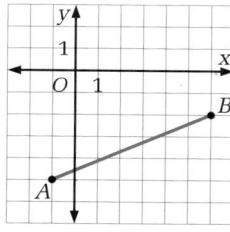

4.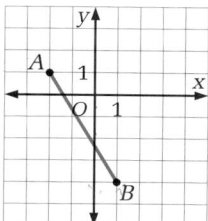

Find the coordinates of the midpoint of each segment whose endpoints are given.

5. $(0, 6)$ and $(-2, 4)$

6. $(-3, 8)$ and $(5, -2)$

7. $(-6, 7)$ and $(1, 3)$

8. $\left(\frac{1}{2}, -\frac{3}{4}\right)$ and $(-4, 2)$

9. $(4.5, 0.15)$ and $(-1.2, 3.8)$

10. $\left(\frac{3}{8}, -\frac{2}{3}\right)$ and $\left(\frac{1}{4}, -\frac{5}{6}\right)$

For Exercises 11–13, M is the midpoint of $\overline{CD}$. Find the coordinates of D.

11. $C(4, -2)$; $M(4, 4)$

12. $C(1, -3)$; $M(-5, 1)$

13. $C(-2, -8)$; $M(2, -3)$

14. Nayati and Blaire each used a formula to show that *M* is the midpoint of $\overline{FG}$. Here is each person's method.

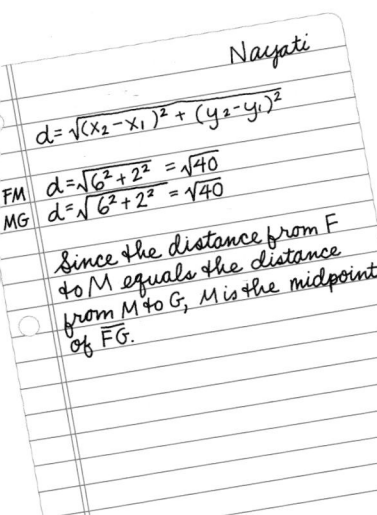

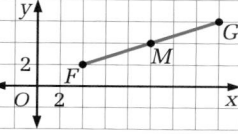

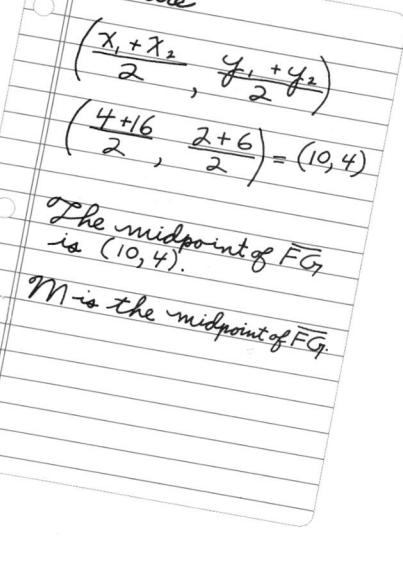

a. Explain Nayati's method. Did he show that *M* is the midpoint of $\overline{FG}$?

b. Explain Blaire's method. Did she show that *M* is the midpoint of $\overline{FG}$?

c. Which method do you prefer? Why?

APPLYING

Suggested Assignment
Standard 2–13, 15, 18–23, 25–36
Extended 1–23, 25–36

Integrating the Strands
Algebra Exs. 1–36
Geometry Exs. 2–4, 11–24, 31–36
Logic and Language Exs. 1, 16, 21, 22

Reasoning
In Ex. 14, Nayati used correct reasoning to show that *M* is the midpoint of $\overline{FG}$ by using the distance formula. Blaire's method applied the midpoint formula directly. Students may express preferences for either method.

Answers to Exercises and Problems

1. Answers may vary. An example is given. In *Talk it Over* questions 2 and 3, the x-coordinate and y-coordinate are found separately by finding the means of the coordinates of the endpoints. In the midpoint formula, the same method is used, but coordinates are found at the same time.

2. $(-4, -2)$

3. $\left(2\frac{1}{2}, -3\frac{1}{2}\right)$

4. $\left(-\frac{1}{2}, -1\frac{1}{2}\right)$

5. $(-1, 5)$

6. $(1, 3)$

7. $\left(-2\frac{1}{2}, 5\right)$

8. $\left(-1\frac{3}{4}, \frac{5}{8}\right)$

9. $(1.65, 1.975)$

10. $\left(\frac{5}{16}, -\frac{3}{4}\right)$

11. $D(4, 10)$

12. $D(-11, 5)$

13. $D(6, 2)$

14. a. Nayati showed that the distance from *E* to *M* is the same as the distance from *G* to *M*. Then, since $FM + GM = FG$, $GM = \frac{1}{2}FG$ and $FM = \frac{1}{2}FG$. So Nayati showed that *M* is halfway between *F* and *G* and *M* is the midpoint of $\overline{FG}$.

b. Blaire used the midpoint formula. Yes.

c. Answers may vary. An example is given. I prefer Blaire's method, using the midpoint formula, because it is easier.

261

Ex. 22 on page 263 involves students in thinking about the concept of a *continuous* sequence of points or a *discrete* sequence of points. These two different ideas can, in fact, be used to categorize mathematics into two main overarching strands: a strand that involves the concept of continuity as studied in calculus, and a strand that involves distinct, separate phenomena, studied in discrete mathematics.

Continuous mathematics underlies most of algebra and calculus, which use real or complex numbers as a domain for their functions. Discrete mathematics involves functions defined on finite sets of numbers. Discrete mathematics is becoming more important today because of its many applications in business and in computer science, where computational methods play such a central role. Approaches to solving real-world problems that involve concepts from both continuous and discrete mathematics often complement each other and shed light on a problem in different ways.

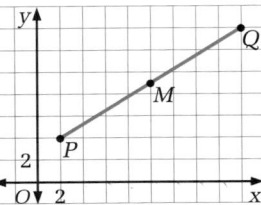

15. Show that $\overline{PQ}$ is twice as long as $\overline{PM}$.

16. **Writing** Explain how finding the midpoint of a segment is like finding the mean of the endpoints.

17. The midpoint formula uses means to divide a segment into two equal parts. Describe a method to divide a segment into three equal parts.

---

connection to HISTORY

The *Midway Islands* have that name because ships used the islands as a halfway stopping point between North America and Asia.

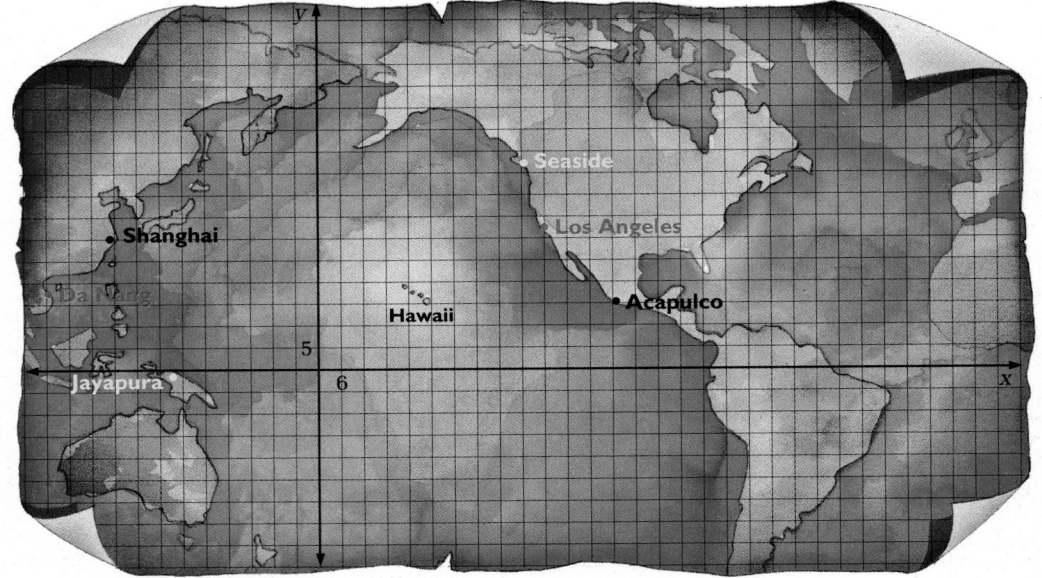

For Exercises 18–20, use the coordinate grid to find the midpoint between each pair of cities.

18. Los Angeles, California, and Da Nang, Vietnam

19. Acapulco, Mexico, and Shanghai, China

20. Seaside, Oregon, and Jayapura, New Guinea

For Exercise 21, use your answers to Exercises 18–20.

21. **a.** Find the mean of the *x*-coordinates and the mean of the *y*-coordinates of the three midpoints.

   b. Use your answer to part (a) to estimate the coordinates of the Midway Islands.

   c. **Writing** On this map, the coordinates of the Midway Islands are (3, 28). Do you think the Midway Islands are "midway" between North American and Asian cities? Explain your reasoning.

262   **Unit 5** Coordinate Geometry and Quadrilaterals

Answers to
Exercises and Problems

15. $PQ = \sqrt{(18 - 2)^2 + (14 - 4)^2} = \sqrt{256 + 100} = 2\sqrt{89}$;
$PM = \sqrt{(10 - 2)^2 + (9 - 4)^2} = \sqrt{64 + 25} = \sqrt{89}$

16. To find the mean of the two numbers, you add them together and divide by 2. To find the midpoint of a segment, you add the *x*-coordinates and divide by 2 and add the *y*-coordinates and divide by 2. You have found the mean of each coordinate.

17. Divide the horizontal distance between the endpoints of the segment by 3. Move that distance from each endpoint along the horizontal. Then move vertically to intersect the segment at the two points that divide the segment into thirds. The coordinates of the points are

$\left(\dfrac{2x_1 + x_2}{3}, \dfrac{2y_1 + y_2}{3}\right)$ and $\left(\dfrac{x_1 + 2x_2}{3}, \dfrac{y_1 + 2y_2}{3}\right)$.

18. $(-6, 25)$

19. $\left(12, 22\frac{1}{2}\right)$

20. $\left(7\frac{1}{2}, 22\frac{1}{2}\right)$

21. **a.** mean of *x*-coordinates: $4\frac{1}{2}$; mean of *y*-coordinates: $23\frac{1}{3}$

   b. about $\left(4\frac{1}{2}, 23\frac{1}{3}\right)$

   c. Answers may vary. An example is given. The Midway Islands appear to be midway between the east coast of Asia and the west coast of North America because the coordinates for the average midway point between 3 North American west coast cities and 3 Asian east coast cities is very close to the coordinates, (3, 28), for the Midway Islands.

22. **a.** Each midpoint divides the previous segment in half.

   b. $\dfrac{1}{16}, \dfrac{1}{32}$

   c. discrete

   d. No; the only logical end would be 0 and there is no number *n* for which $\dfrac{1}{n} = 0$.

22. Leann found the midpoint of $\overline{AB}$. Then she found the midpoints of $\overline{AC}$ and $\overline{AD}$. Her results are shown.

a. Describe the pattern.

b. What are the next two numbers in the sequence $\frac{1}{2}, \frac{1}{4}, \frac{1}{8}, \dots$?

c. Is the sequence of midpoints *continuous* or *discrete*?

d. Will the sequence ever end? Explain.

e. In the fifth century B.C., the Greek mathematician Zeno presented a version of this puzzle that is described below. How does his reasoning relate to Leann's sequence?

f. Do you agree with Zeno's reasoning? Why or why not?

$$
\begin{array}{ccccc}
A & E & D & C & B \\
\bullet & \bullet & \bullet & \bullet & \bullet \\
0 & \frac{1}{8} & \frac{1}{4} & \frac{1}{2} & 1
\end{array}
$$

A PERSON IS WALKING FROM POINT A TO POINT B.

POINT A   POINT B

The person must first walk half of the distance.

Then the person must walk half of the remaining distance.

Then half of the remaining distance.

There will always be half of the remaining distance to walk, so the person will never reach point B.

23. a. Show that *LMNO* is a rhombus.

b. Are the diagonals $\overline{LN}$ and $\overline{MO}$ perpendicular to each other? Verify your answer.

c. What is the midpoint of $\overline{LN}$? What is the midpoint of $\overline{MO}$? How do they compare?

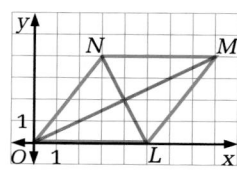

***Ongoing* ASSESSMENT**

24. Group Activity Work with another student.

a. *P*, *Q*, and *R* are the midpoints of the three sides of $\triangle ABC$. Find the coordinates of *P*, *Q*, and *R*.

b. Show that these lines are parallel: $\overline{QP}$ and $\overline{AB}$, $\overline{RQ}$ and $\overline{BC}$, $\overline{RP}$ and $\overline{AC}$.

c. Find the perimeter of $\triangle PQR$. How does it compare to the perimeter of $\triangle ABC$?

d. How do you think the areas of $\triangle PQR$ and $\triangle ABC$ compare?

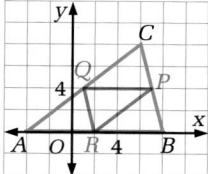

5-3 Midpoints

263

Answers to Exercises and Problems

e. If the person begins walking at point *A* in the drawing, the numbers in the sequence represent the portions of the distance that remain to be covered.

f. Answers may vary. An example is given. In reality, the distance remaining would become insignificant.

23. a. $OL = NM = 5$; $ON = \sqrt{(3-0)^2 + (4-0)^2} = \sqrt{9+16} = 5$; $LM = \sqrt{(8-5)^2 + (4-0)^2} = \sqrt{9+16} = 5$; Since all four sides of *OLMN* are congruent, *OLMN* is a rhombus.

b. Yes. slope of $\overline{OM} = \frac{4-0}{8-0} = \frac{1}{2}$; slope of $\overline{LN} = $

$\frac{4-0}{3-5} = -2$; Since the slopes of $\overline{OM}$ and $\overline{LN}$ are negative reciprocals of each other, $\overline{OM} \perp \overline{LN}$.

c. (4, 2); (4, 2); The segments have the same midpoint.

Answers continued on next page.

263

Find the distance between each pair of points. *(Section 5-2)*

25. (5, 10) and (8, 4) **26.** (−7, 6) and (1, −2) **27.** (−1, −9) and (4, 3)

Solve. *(Section 4-3)*

28. $3x^2 + 8 = 56$ **29.** $(x − 5)^2 + 6 = 66$ **30.** $−5(x + 2)^2 + 16 = −59$

Tell if the image is a *translation, rotation, dilation,* or *reflection* of the original figure and name the coordinates of the image. *(Toolbox Skills 33–36)*

31. 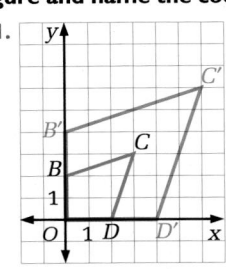 **32.** 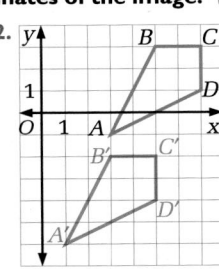 **33.** 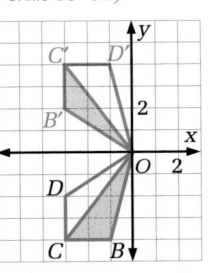 **34.**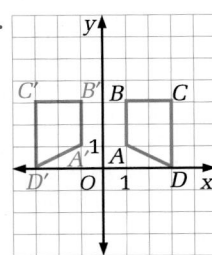

 Working on the Unit Project

People in China developed the puzzle game *tangram* in about 1800. To complete a tangram puzzle, a person must use all seven pieces to form a design. None of the pieces, known as *tans*, may overlap.

35. Make a sketch that shows how to arrange the tans to form one of designs A through I.

36. a. **Writing** Describe how to use midpoints to create a set of tangram pieces from a square.

 b. **Writing** Describe how you could use the midpoint formula in the design or play of your game.

Example

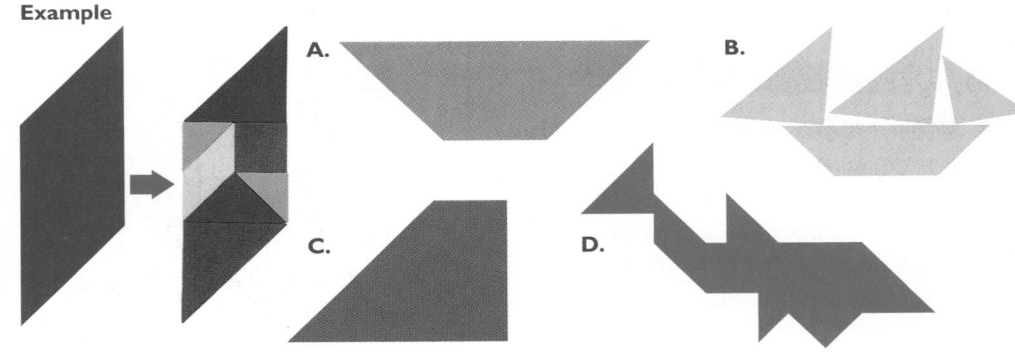

A. **B.** **C.** **D.**

264 **Unit 5** Coordinate Geometry and Quadrilaterals

Answers to
Exercises and Problems

24. a. $P(7, 4)$; $Q(1, 4)$; $R(2, 0)$

 b. slope of $\overline{QP}$ = slope of $\overline{AB}$ = 0 so $\overline{QP} \parallel \overline{AB}$; slope of $\overline{RQ}$ = slope of $\overline{BC}$ = −4 so $\overline{RQ} \parallel \overline{BC}$; slope of $\overline{RP}$ = slope of $\overline{AC}$ = $\frac{4}{5}$ so $\overline{RP} \parallel \overline{AC}$.

 c. perimeter of $\triangle PQR$ = 6 + $\sqrt{41}$ + $\sqrt{17}$ ≈ 16.5; perimeter of $\triangle ABC$ = 12 + 2$\sqrt{41}$ + 2$\sqrt{17}$ ≈ 33; perimeter of $\triangle PQR = \frac{1}{2} \cdot$ perimeter of $\triangle ABC$

 d. area of $\triangle PQR = \frac{1}{4} \cdot$ area of $\triangle ABC$

25. $3\sqrt{5} \approx 6.71$

26. $8\sqrt{2} \approx 11.31$

27. 13

28. 4, −4

29. $5 \pm 2\sqrt{15}$; about 12.75, about −2.75

30. $x = −2 \pm \sqrt{15}$; about 1.87, about −5.87

31. dilation; $O'(0, 0)$; $B'(0, 4)$; $C'(6, 6)$; $D'(4, 0)$

32. translation; $A'(1, −6)$; $B'(3, −2)$; $C'(5, −2)$; $D'(5, −4)$

33. rotation; $O'(0, 0)$; $B'(−3, 2)$; $C'(−3, 4)$; $D'(−1, 4)$

34. reflection; $A'(−1, 1)$; $B'(−1, 3)$; $C'(−3, 3)$; $D'(−3, 0)$

35. Sketches may vary. An example is given using design B.

36. a. Descriptions may vary. An example is given. Draw a square on graph paper. Label the vertices A, B, C, and D. Draw $\overline{BD}$. Locate E, the midpoint of $\overline{BD}$. Draw $\overline{AE}$. Find the midpoint of $\overline{DE}$ and label it F. Find the midpoint of $\overline{DC}$ and label it G. Draw $\overline{FG}$. Find the midpoint of $\overline{BC}$ and label it H. Draw $\overline{GH}$. Find the midpoint of $\overline{GH}$ and label it J. Draw $\overline{EJ}$. Find the midpoint of $\overline{EB}$ and label it K. Draw $\overline{JK}$.

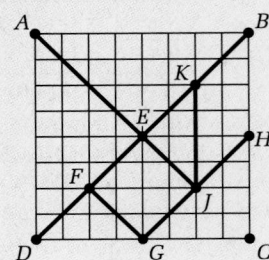

b. Answers may vary. An example is given. I might have special cards that direct players where to move. One direction might be something like, "Move to the midpoint between these two locations: (5, 7) and (4, 9)."

264

1. **Writing** What properties do you need to show before you can say that a quadrilateral is a parallelogram? a rectangle? a rhombus? a square? What algebra skills do you use?

2. Quadrilateral *ABCD* has these vertices:

   A(1, 2), *B*(12, 4), *C*(15, −1), and *D*(4, −3)

   a. Find the slope of each side of quadrilateral *ABCD*.

   b. What type of quadrilateral is *ABCD*? Why can you make this conclusion?

3. Quadrilateral *WXYZ* has these vertices:

   W(−4, −1), *X*(−3, 4), *Y*(2, 3), and *Z*(1, −2)

   a. Find the slope of each side of quadrilateral *WXYZ*.

   b. Find the length of each side of quadrilateral *WXYZ*.

   c. Based on your answers to parts (a) and (b), what type of quadrilateral is *WXYZ*?

5-1

5-2

BY THE WAY...

There are at least 1600 designs that can be made using tangram pieces. Some of these designs are found on dishes, boxes, and tables made in nineteenth century China.

For each pair of points A and B:

a. Find the distance between the points.

b. Find the coordinates of the midpoint of $\overline{AB}$.

5-3

4. *A*(5, −2) and *B*(−7, 0)
5. *A*(3, 0) and *B*(−4, 12)
6. *A*(−8, −5) and *B*(12, −6)
7. *A*(3, −1) and *B*(6, −5)

For Exercises 8–11, M is the midpoint of $\overline{CD}$. Find the coordinates of D.

8. *C*(4, 3); *M*(−2, 0)
9. *C*(−6, 3); *M*(−1, 2)
10. *C*(−1, 5); *M*(3, −2)
11. *C*(3, −2); $M\left(\frac{1}{2}, 3\right)$

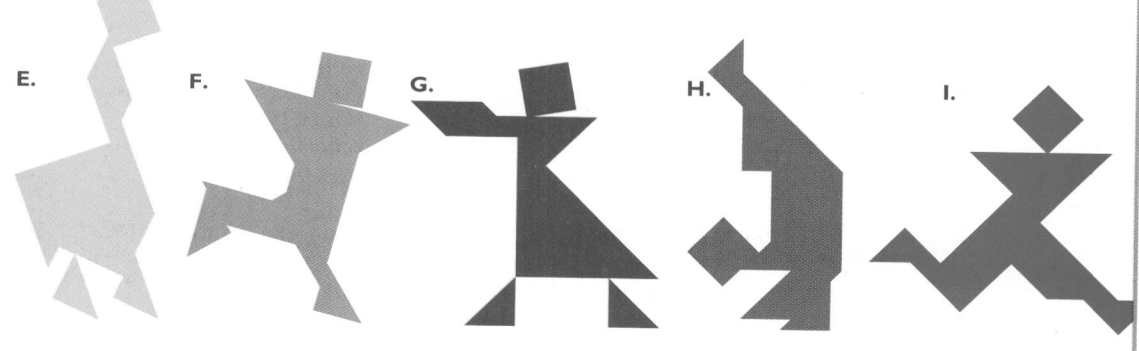

E. **F.** **G.** **H.** **I.**

5-3 Midpoints

265

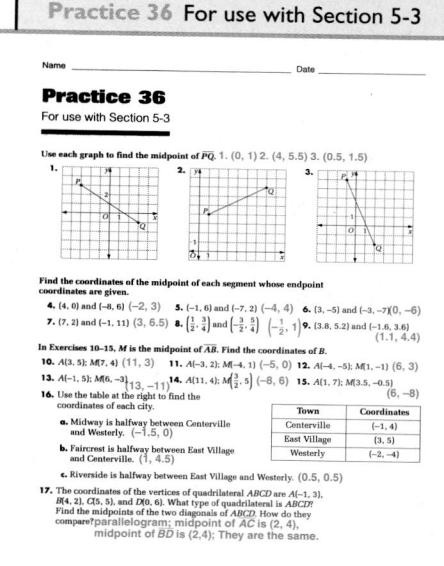

Answers to Checkpoint

1. two pairs of parallel sides; four right angles; four congruent sides; four congruent sides and four right angles; You would find the slope of a segment to determine if sides are parallel or if they meet at right angles. You would use the distance formula to show that the lengths of the sides are equal in measure.

2. **a.** slope of $\overline{AB}$ = slope of $\overline{DC} = \frac{2}{11}$; slope of $\overline{AD}$ = slope of $\overline{BC} = -\frac{5}{3}$

   b. *ABCD* is a parallelogram since it has two pairs of parallel sides. *ABCD* is not a rectangle since the slopes of adjacent sides are not negative reciprocals. It is not a rhombus since it does not have four congruent sides.

3. **a.** slope of $\overline{WX}$ = slope of $\overline{ZY}$ = 5; slope of $\overline{XY}$ = slope of $\overline{WZ} = -\frac{1}{5}$

   b. *WX* = *XY* = *YZ* = *WZ* = $\sqrt{26}$

   c. *WXYZ* is a square, since it is both a rectangle and a rhombus.

4. **a.** $2\sqrt{37} \approx 12.17$
   b. (−1, −1)
5. **a.** $\sqrt{193} \approx 13.89$
   b. (−0.5, 6)
6. **a.** $\sqrt{401} \approx 20.02$
   b. (2, −5.5)
7. **a.** 5
   b. (4.5, −3)
8. (−8, −3)
9. (4, 1)
10. (7, −9)
11. (−2, 8)

PLANNING

Objectives and Strands
See pages 240A and 240B.

Spiral Learning
See page 240B.

Materials List
➤ Graph paper

Recommended Pacing
Section 5-4 is a two-day lesson.

Day 1
Pages 266–267: Exploration through Talk it Over 1, *Exercises 1–15*

Day 2
Pages 268–270: Sample 1 through Look Back, *Exercises 16–44*

Toolbox References
➤ **Toolbox Skill 12:** Simplifying Expressions with Radicals

Extra Practice
See pages 622–623.

Warm-Up Exercises
Warm-Up Transparency 5-4

Support Materials
➤ Practice 37
➤ Enrichment 33 in the Activity Bank
➤ Study Guide 5-4
➤ Problem Set 10
➤ Diagram Masters 2, 17 in the Explorations Lab Manual
Overhead Visual 5
➤ McDougal Littell Mathpack software: *Geometry Inventor* and *Matrix Analyzer*
➤ Geometry Inventor Activity Book: Activities 16–24
➤ Using TI-81 and TI-82 Calculators: Transformations Using Matrices and Draw Feature
➤ Quiz 5-4
➤ Alternative Assessment 3

Coordinates and Transformations

Focus
Transform geometric figures and learn how transformations affect their properties.

EXPLORATION

(How) are the coordinates of an image different after a transformation?

- **Work with another student.**

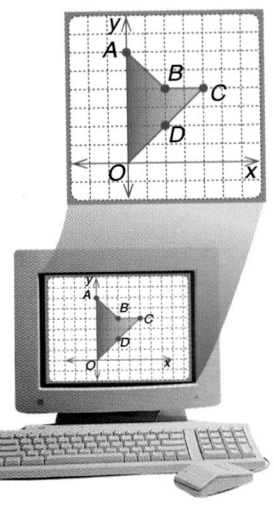

1. Danielle is designing a kaleidoscope pattern on her computer. She draws the figure shown. What are the coordinates of points *A*, *B*, *C*, and *D*? Copy the table and record the coordinates in the row labeled *original*.

Transformations	Coordinates of Points			
original	A(?, ?)	B(?, ?)	C(?, ?)	D(?, ?)
x-axis reflection	A'(?, ?)	B'(?, ?)	C'(?, ?)	D'(?, ?)
y-axis reflection	?	?	?	?
180° rotation	?	?	?	?
270° counterclockwise	?	?	?	?
90° counterclockwise	?	?	?	?
horizontal translation	?	?	?	?
vertical translation	?	?	?	?
horz/vert translation	?	?	?	?

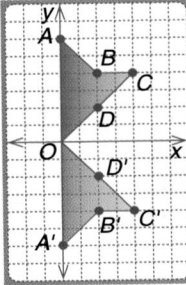

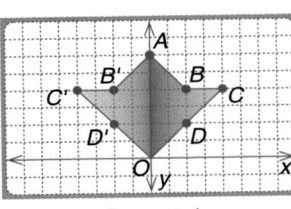

flip vertical

2. Danielle used the *flip vertical* and *flip horizontal* features on her computer. Which type of flip is a **reflection** over the x-axis? over the y-axis?

flip horizontal

3. Record the coordinates of each image in your table. How do the coordinates of each image compare to the original coordinates? Discuss any patterns you see.

Unit 5 Coordinate Geometry and Quadrilaterals

Answers to Exploration

See answers in back of book.

④ Danielle used the *rotate* feature on the computer to create the images below. Which image is a **rotation** of 180°? of 270° counterclockwise? of 90° counterclockwise? Repeat step 3 for the rotated images.

Image 1

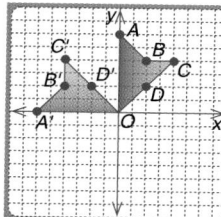

Image 2

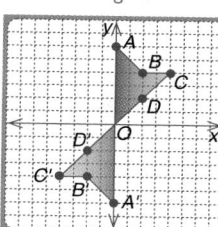

Image 3

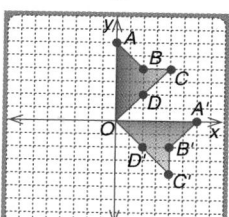

⑤ Images 4, 5, and 6 show the results of a horizontal translation, a vertical translation, and a combined horizontal and vertical translation. Repeat step 3 for the translated images.

Image 4

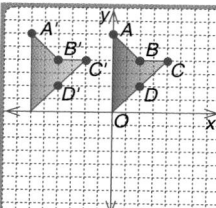

Image 5

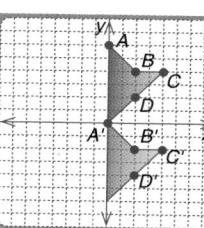

Image 6

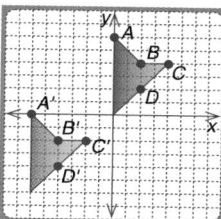

⑥ For each type of transformation, write a general rule to show how the coordinates change.

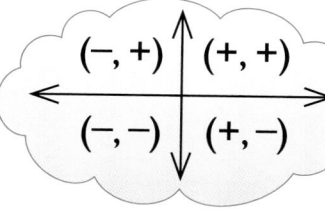

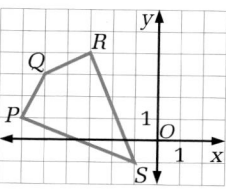

⤑ Now you are ready for:
Exs. 1–15 on pp. 270–271

Talk it Over

1. To find the coordinates of a reflected image, Sergio first determines which quadrant the reflection is in. Then he thinks about the sign of each coordinate in that quadrant. Use Sergio's method to find the reflection of kite *PQRS* over the *y*-axis.

5-4 Coordinates and Transformations

Answers to Talk it Over

1. $P'(6, 1)$, $Q'(5, 3)$, $R'(3, 4)$, $S'(1, -1)$

TEACHING

Exploration

The goal of the Exploration is to discover general rules for the transformations presented in steps 2–5. The results of each transformation should be entered into the table established in step 1. The rule for each transformation can be determined by observing how the coordinates of the original points change.

Talk it Over

The reflection of *PQRS* over the *y*-axis changes each (x, y) coordinate to a $(-x, y)$ coordinate. Since the *x*-coordinates of the points are all negative, their image points are given by $-x$, which are all positive numbers.

Using Technology

In Sample 2 on page 268, matrix multiplication is used to transform a quadrilateral. Students can use the *Matrix Analyzer* software or a graphics calculator to do matrix multiplication. Suppose you want to find

$$\begin{bmatrix} 1 & 0 \\ 0 & -1 \end{bmatrix} \begin{bmatrix} 3 & -2 & -3 & 5 \\ 5 & -4 & -1 & 2 \end{bmatrix}$$ on the TI-82, TI-83, and TI-83 Plus.

Press MATRX (on the TI-82 or TI-83) or 2nd [MATRX] (on the TI-83 Plus). Select EDIT, and then press 1 to enter the first matrix as matrix [A]. Press 2 ENTER 2 ENTER to enter the dimensions of the matrix. Then enter the elements of the matrix one at a time, row by row. When you are done, press MATRX (on the TI-82 or TI-83) or 2nd [MATRX] (on the TI-83 Plus) and follow the same procedure to enter matrix [B]. To find [A][B], press 2nd [QUIT] to return to the home screen. Press MATRX 1 MATRX 2 (on the TI-82 or TI-83) or 2nd [MATRX]1 2nd [MATRX]2 (on the TI-83 Plus) to display [A][B]. Then press ENTER to multiply the matrices and display the product.

Using Technology

Students can use the *Geometry Inventor* software to transform a geometric figure.

Additional Samples

S1 Find the coordinates of the image described.

a. Reflect △*ABC* over the *y*-axis. **See graph below.**
$A(2, 0) \rightarrow A'(-2, 0)$
$B(6, 1) \rightarrow B'(-6, 1)$
$C(1, 3) \rightarrow C'(-1, 3)$

b. Translate △*ABC* 2 units left and 3 units up. **See graph below.**
$A(2, 0) \rightarrow A'(0, 3)$
$B(6, 1) \rightarrow B'(4, 4)$
$C(1, 3) \rightarrow C'(-1, 6)$

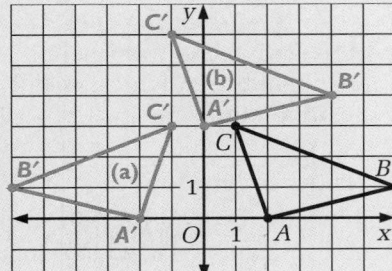

S2 Use matrix multiplication to transform *KLMN*. Then sketch *KLMN* and its image. Describe the transformation.

$$\begin{array}{cccc} K & L & M & N \end{array}$$
$$\begin{bmatrix} 1 & 0 \\ 0 & -1 \end{bmatrix} \begin{bmatrix} 1 & 2 & 6 & 6 \\ 1 & 4 & 5 & 1 \end{bmatrix}$$
$$\begin{array}{cccc} K & L & M & N \end{array}$$
$$\begin{bmatrix} 1 & 0 \\ 0 & -1 \end{bmatrix} \begin{bmatrix} 1 & 2 & 6 & 6 \\ 1 & 4 & 5 & 1 \end{bmatrix} =$$
$$\begin{bmatrix} 1 & 2 & 6 & 6 \\ -1 & -4 & -5 & -1 \end{bmatrix}$$

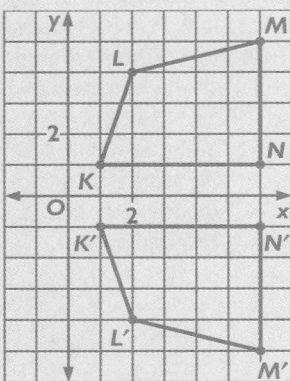

The coordinates of the vertices of *K' L' M' N'* are *K'*(1, −1), *L'*(2, −4), *M'*(6, −5), and *N'*(6, −1). The image is a reflection over the *x*-axis.

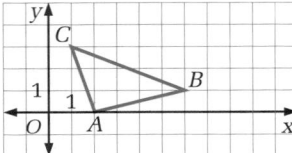

Find the coordinates of the image described.

a. Reflect △*ABC* over the *x*-axis.

b. Translate △*ABC* 3 units right and 2 units down.

Sample Response

a. The image is on the opposite side of the *x*-axis, so each *y*-coordinate is the opposite of the original. Each *x*-coordinate stays the same. The rule is $P(x, y) \rightarrow P'(x, -y)$.

$A(2, 0) \rightarrow A'(2, 0)$
$B(6, 1) \rightarrow B'(6, -1)$
$C(1, 3) \rightarrow C'(1, -3)$

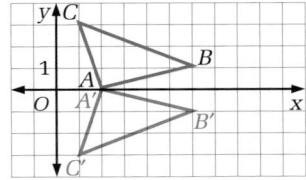

b. Add 3 to each *x*-coordinate and subtract 2 from each *y*-coordinate. The rule is $P(x, y) \rightarrow P'(x + 3, y - 2)$.

$A(2, 0) \rightarrow A'(5, -2)$
$B(6, 1) \rightarrow B'(9, -1)$
$C(1, 3) \rightarrow C'(4, 1)$

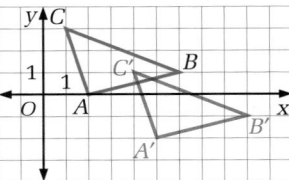

The coordinates of quadrilateral *ABCD* are listed below in a matrix. Use matrix multiplication to transform *ABCD*. Then sketch *ABCD* and its image. Describe the transformation.

$$\begin{array}{cccc} A & B & C & D \end{array}$$
$$\begin{bmatrix} 1 & 0 \\ 0 & -1 \end{bmatrix} \begin{bmatrix} 3 & -2 & -3 & 5 \\ 5 & 4 & 1 & 1 \end{bmatrix}$$
← the *x*-coordinates of *ABCD*
← the *y*-coordinates of *ABCD*

Sample Response

$$\begin{bmatrix} 1 & 0 \\ 0 & -1 \end{bmatrix} \begin{bmatrix} 3 & -2 & -3 & 5 \\ 5 & 4 & 1 & 1 \end{bmatrix} = \begin{bmatrix} 1(3) + 0(5) & 1(-2) + 0(4) & 1(-3) + 0(1) & 1(5) + 0(1) \\ 0(3) + (-1)(5) & 0(-2) + (-1)(4) & 0(-3) + (-1)(1) & 0(5) + (-1)(1) \end{bmatrix}$$

$$= \begin{bmatrix} 3 & -2 & -3 & 5 \\ -5 & -4 & -1 & -1 \end{bmatrix}$$

The coordinates of the vertices of the image of *ABCD* are $A'(3, -5)$, $B'(-2, -4)$, $C'(-3, -1)$, and $D'(5, -1)$. The image is a reflection over the *x*-axis.

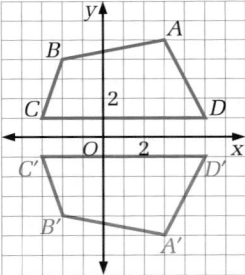

Unit 5 Coordinate Geometry and Quadrilaterals

Effects of Transformations

When a geometric figure is transformed, some properties stay the same and some change. The formulas for slope and distance can help you decide which properties stay the same.

Talk it Over

Use the graphs in Sample 1.

2. Find the length of $\overline{AB}$ and of $\overline{A'B'}$ in each image. Does the length of $\overline{AB}$ change when the triangle is reflected? when it is translated?

3. Does $\overline{A'B'}$ have the same slope as $\overline{AB}$ when the triangle is reflected? when it is translated?

4. Suppose you rotated $\triangle ABC$ 90° clockwise around the origin. Would $\overline{AB}$ and $\overline{A'B'}$ be the same length? Would they have the same slope? Explain.

5. Do the results you found in questions 2–4 about $\overline{AB}$ also apply to $\overline{BC}$? Why or why not?

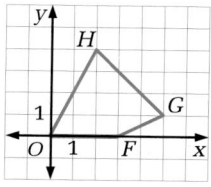

Sample 3

a. Find the coordinates of the image of *OFGH* after a dilation with center at the origin and scale factor 3.

b. Find the length of $\overline{HG}$ and of $\overline{H'G'}$. How do they compare?

c. Find the slope of $\overline{HG}$ and of $\overline{H'G'}$. How do they compare?

Sample Response

a. Multiply each coordinate of the original figure by the scale factor of 3 to get the coordinates of the image.

$O(0, 0) \rightarrow O'(0, 0)$

$F(3, 0) \rightarrow F'(9, 0)$

$G(5, 1) \rightarrow G'(15, 3)$

$H(2, 4) \rightarrow H'(6, 12)$

b. Use the formula $d = \sqrt{(x_2 - x_1)^2 + (y_2 - y_1)^2}$.

$HG = \sqrt{(5 - 2)^2 + (1 - 4)^2} = \sqrt{18} = \sqrt{9 \cdot 2} = 3\sqrt{2}$

$H'G' = \sqrt{(15 - 6)^2 + (3 - 12)^2} = \sqrt{162} = \sqrt{81 \cdot 2} = 9\sqrt{2}$

The length of $\overline{H'G'}$ is three times the length of $\overline{HG}$.

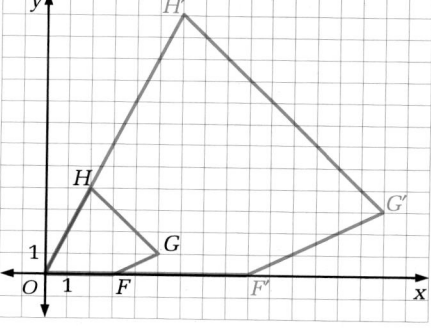

Student Resources Toolbox
p. 642 *Algebraic Expressions*

Continued on next page.

5-4 Coordinates and Transformations

269

Answers to Talk it Over

2. $AB = \sqrt{17}$; $A'B' = \sqrt{17}$; No; No.

3. No; Yes.

4. Yes. No; the slope of $\overline{AB}$ is positive and the slope of $\overline{A'B'}$ is negative.

5. Yes; $\overline{BC}$ is another side in the same triangle. Therefore, it will be affected in the same manner as other sides of the triangle by a transformation.

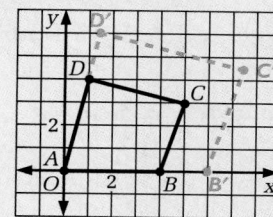

Additional Sample (continued)

c. Find the slope of $\overline{BC}$ and of $\overline{B'C'}$. How do they compare?

The slope of $\overline{BC} = \dfrac{3-0}{5-4} = \dfrac{3}{1}$.

The slope of $\overline{B'C'} = \dfrac{4.5-0}{7.5-6} = \dfrac{4.5}{1.5} = 3$.

The slopes are the same.

Look Back

It may not be obvious to students that a reflection changes the slope of a segment as is shown by Talk it Over question 3. However, it should be clear to all students that rotations (except for multiples of 180°) change the slope of a segment.

APPLYING

Suggested Assignment

Day 1

Standard 1, 2, 6–15

Extended 1–15

Day 2

Standard 16–30, 37–44

Extended 16–35, 37–44

Integrating the Strands

Algebra Exs. 31–35, 37–40

Geometry Exs. 1–39, 41–44

Logic and Language Exs. 6–8, 44

Communication: Discussion

Exs. 1–15 can be discussed verbally by the whole class. For Exs. 9–14, students may want to refer to the table they completed for the Exploration on page 266. In particular, the pattern column would be helpful for these exercises.

---

c. The slope of $\overline{HG} = \dfrac{4-1}{2-5} = \dfrac{3}{-3} = -1.$ ⬅ Use $H(2, 4)$ and $G(5, 1)$ and the formula $m = \dfrac{y_2 - y_1}{x_2 - x_1}$.

The slope of $\overline{H'G'} = \dfrac{12-3}{6-15} = \dfrac{9}{-9} = -1.$ ⬅ Use $H'(6, 12)$ and $G'(15, 3)$.

The slopes are the same.

⋯▶ **Now you are ready for:**
Exs. 16–44 on pp. 272–273

Look Back ◄

Which of the four transformations change the slope of a segment? Which changes the length of a segment?

5-4 Exercises and Problems

Name the transformation that was used to create each design.

Original Figure

1.

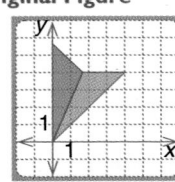

2.

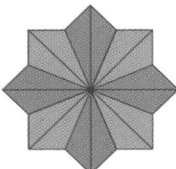

Stamps or coins with errors can be collectors' items. Describe the transformation(s) that may have occurred to cause these errors.

3.

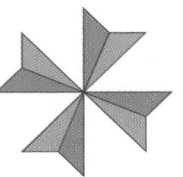

4.

5.

For Exercises 6–8:

a. Tell what kind of transformation is shown.

b. Write a rule to describe what must be done to the coordinates of the original figure to get the coordinates of the image.

6.

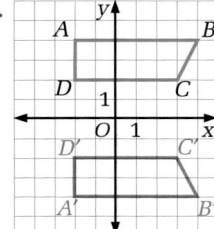

7.

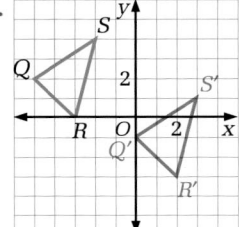

8.

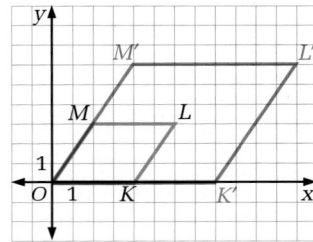

Answers to Look Back

reflections and rotations; dilations

Answers to Exercises and Problems

1. rotation of 90°, 180°, 270°

2. combinations of rotations in Ex. 1 and reflection

3. vertical translation

4. 180° rotation

5. 180° rotation

6. **a.** reflection over the x-axis

   b. To get the coordinates of the image of *ABCD*, keep the same x-coordinate as the original, but take the opposite of the original y-coordinate.
   $(x, y) \rightarrow (x, -y)$

7. **a.** a translation 5 units to the right, 3 units down

   b. To get the coordinates of the image of $\triangle QRS$, add 5 to the original x-coordinate and subtract 3 from the original y-coordinate.
   $(x, y) \rightarrow (x + 5, y - 3)$

For Exercises 9–14, use quadrilateral QRST. Tell what type of transformation is described. Then copy QRST and sketch its image.

9. The figure is shifted 2 units right and 5 units down.

10. Each point on the image has the opposite *x*-coordinate and the opposite *y*-coordinate of the corresponding point on the original.

11. The coordinates of the image are three times the corresponding coordinates of the original.

12. Each point on the image has the same *x*-coordinate as the original point, but the opposite *y*-coordinate.

13. Each *x*-coordinate of the image is 4 more than the corresponding *x*-coordinate of the original. The *y*-coordinates are the same in both figures.

14. Each coordinate of the image is two thirds of the corresponding original coordinate.

connection to **EARTH SCIENCE**

15. Geologists believe that all of the world's continents were once connected into one super-continent that is called *Pangaea*. These computer images show the possible path of the continents when the Atlantic Ocean formed.

   a. What types of transformations describe the movement of the continents?

   b. **Open-ended** Describe where you think the continent that you live on will be 100 million years from now.

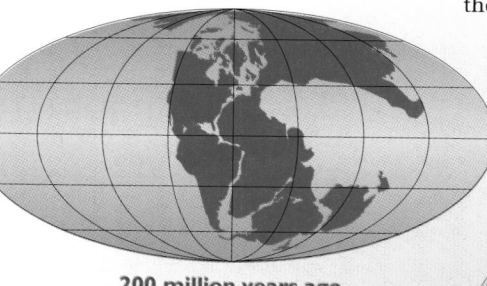

200 million years ago

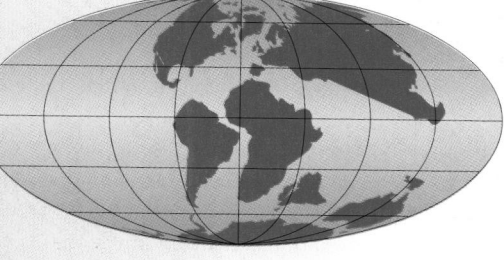

100 million years ago

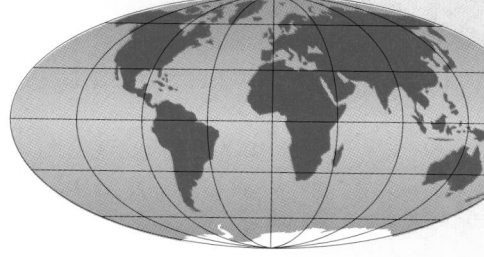

Present

5-4 Coordinates and Transformations

271

Answers to Exercises and Problems

8. **a.** dilation with a scale factor 2

   b. To get the coordinates of the image of *JKLM*, double the value of each *x*-coordinate and each *y*-coordinate.
   $(x, y) \rightarrow (2x, 2y)$

9. translation 2 units to the right, 5 units down

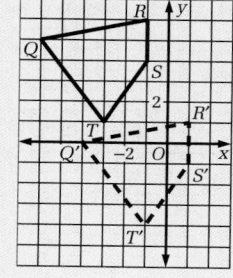

10. rotation 180°

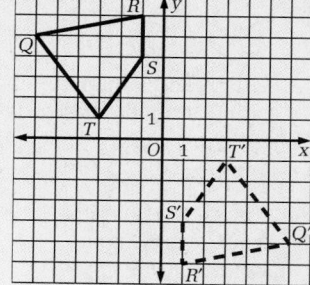

11, 12. See answers in back of book.

13. translation 4 units to the right

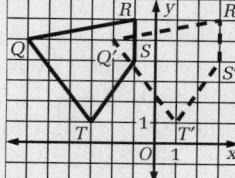

14. dilation with center at the origin and scale factor $\frac{2}{3}$

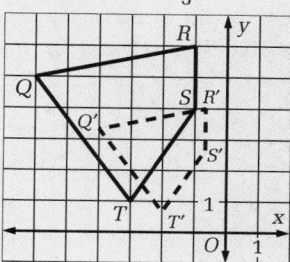

15. **a.** translation

   b. Answers may vary. An example is given. North America seems to be drifting westward. So it is likely that our continent will be even farther from Europe than it is now.

271

Reasoning

For Exs. 16–21, students should try to form a mental image of a point (or a figure) in a coordinate plane and then picture what happens to the point using the given rule. This reasoning process will lead them to the correct transformation in the second column.

Mathematical Procedures

In Exs. 23–29, students use inductive reasoning to make conjectures about transformations. The examination of specific examples to make conjectures is a well-established and often productive procedure for discovering new mathematical facts. Deductive reasoning must then be applied to the general situation in order to establish a conjecture as a fact.

Using Technology

A graphics calculator can be used to find the coordinates of the vertices of the image figure for a counterclockwise rotation through θ degrees. Be sure that the mode setting is *degrees* and not radians. Use the matrix product

$$\begin{bmatrix} \cos\theta & -\sin\theta \\ \sin\theta & \cos\theta \end{bmatrix} \begin{bmatrix} x_1 & x_2 & \cdots & x_n \\ y_1 & y_2 & \cdots & y_n \end{bmatrix}$$

where the second matrix is the matrix for the vertices of the figure whose image you want to find. For the TI-82 or TI-83, you can enter the *expressions* for the elements. The calculator will enter the values of the expressions as you go. For example, for a counterclockwise rotation of 30°, you would enter cos 30 on the TI-82 or cos (30) on the TI-83 for the element in row 1 column 1. The calculator will display .86603 for that element. This method produces values that are accurate to several decimal places. Once you have entered both matrices, find their product in the usual way.

For Exercises 16–21, match each rule with the transformation it describes.

16. $(x, y) \rightarrow (x, y - 5)$
17. $(x, y) \rightarrow (y, -x)$
18. $(x, y) \rightarrow (x, -y)$
19. $(x, y) \rightarrow (-x, -y)$
20. $(x, y) \rightarrow (5x, 5y)$
21. $(x, y) \rightarrow (-y, x)$

A. dilation with scale factor 5
B. 90° counterclockwise rotation
C. 180° rotation
D. 270° counterclockwise rotation
E. translation 5 units down
F. reflection over the x-axis

22. **Reading** What properties of a geometric figure may change when a figure is transformed? What formulas can help you decide?

Animators can use many different transformations to animate an image. For each transformation, sketch the image of △ABC and label the coordinates of the vertices. (Save your sketches for Exercises 28 and 29.)

23. reflection over the y-axis
24. translation 2 units left and 5 units up
25. dilation with scale factor 4 and center at O
26. translation 3 units down
27. 90° clockwise rotation around O

For Exercises 28 and 29, use your sketches from Exercises 23–27.

28. a. Find the length of $\overline{BC}$.
    b. Find the length of $\overline{B'C'}$ for each transformation.
    c. For which transformations did the length of the segment stay the same? For which transformations did the length change?
    d. Are the results in part (c) true in general? Why or why not?

29. a. Find the slope of $\overline{BC}$.
    b. Find the slope of $\overline{B'C'}$ for each transformation.
    c. For which transformations did the slope stay the same? For which transformations did the slope change?
    d. Are the results in part (c) true in general? Why or why not?

30. Which transformations create an image that is *congruent* to the original image? that is *similar* to the original image?

Use matrix multiplication to transform each figure. Then sketch each figure and its image. Describe each transformation.

31. quadrilateral *ABCD*

$$\begin{bmatrix} -1 & 0 \\ 0 & 1 \end{bmatrix} \begin{matrix} A & B & C & D \\ \end{matrix} \begin{bmatrix} 1 & 2 & 5 & 5 \\ -1 & 2 & 1 & -5 \end{bmatrix}$$

32. triangle *EFG*

$$\begin{bmatrix} 0 & 1 \\ -1 & 0 \end{bmatrix} \begin{matrix} E & F & G \\ \end{matrix} \begin{bmatrix} -4 & -3 & 1 \\ 2 & 5 & 3 \end{bmatrix}$$

33. quadrilateral *JKLM*

$$\begin{bmatrix} -1 & 0 \\ 0 & -1 \end{bmatrix} \begin{matrix} J & K & L & M \\ \end{matrix} \begin{bmatrix} 0 & 1 & 3 & 4 \\ 2 & 4 & 3 & 0 \end{bmatrix}$$

Unit 5 Coordinate Geometry and Quadrilaterals

Answers to Exercises and Problems ·····················

16. E
17. D
18. F
19. C
20. A
21. B

22. length and slope; the distance and slope formulas

23–29. See answers in back of book.

30. Rotations, reflections, and translations create congruent images; dilations create images similar to the original figure.

31. $A'(-1, -1)$, $B'(-2, 2)$, $C'(-5, 1)$, $D'(-5, -5)$; reflection over the y-axis

32. $E'(2, 4)$, $F'(5, 3)$, $G'(3, -1)$; 90° clockwise rotation

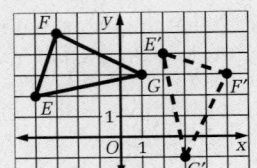

For Exercises 34 and 35:

a. Describe each transformation in words.

b. Give a rule, $(x, y) \rightarrow (\underline{\ ?\ }, \underline{\ ?\ })$, for each transformation.

34. $P \qquad P'$

$$\begin{bmatrix} x \\ y \end{bmatrix} \rightarrow 2\begin{bmatrix} x \\ y \end{bmatrix}$$

35. $P \qquad\qquad P'$

$$\begin{bmatrix} x \\ y \end{bmatrix} \rightarrow \begin{bmatrix} x \\ y \end{bmatrix} + \begin{bmatrix} 3 \\ -2 \end{bmatrix}$$

Ongoing **ASSESSMENT**

36. **Group Activity** Work with another student.

a. Each of you should give each other the coordinates of the vertices of a quadrilateral and a rule to describe the coordinates of an image.

b. Exchange papers and write the coordinates of the image using each other's rule. Then sketch the original figure and its image.

c. Calculate the lengths of the sides and the slopes of the sides in the original figure and in the image.

d. Did any properties change? If so, which ones?

Review **PREVIEW**

Find the coordinates of the midpoint of each segment whose endpoints are given. *(Section 5-3)*

37. $(0, 0)$ and $(100, -100)$ 38. $(3, 7)$ and $(5, -1)$ 39. $(-4, 6)$ and $(1, -2)$

40. Use the equation $y = \dfrac{3}{x^2}$. *(Section 2-5)*

a. Find the value of y when $x = 7$.

b. Find the value of x when $y = \dfrac{1}{12}$.

41. Find the length of each side of trapezoid $ABCD$ with vertices $A(0, 1)$, $B(2, 5)$, $C(6, 5)$, and $D(10, 1)$. *(Section 5-2)*

 Working on the Unit Project

Open-ended For Exercises 42 and 43, describe how you could use each transformation. Give examples.

a. translation   b. reflection   c. rotation

42. designing the pattern on your game board

43. directing players' moves in your game

44. **Writing** How could you use transformations to make your game board look the same to all the players?

Practice 37 For use with Section 5-4

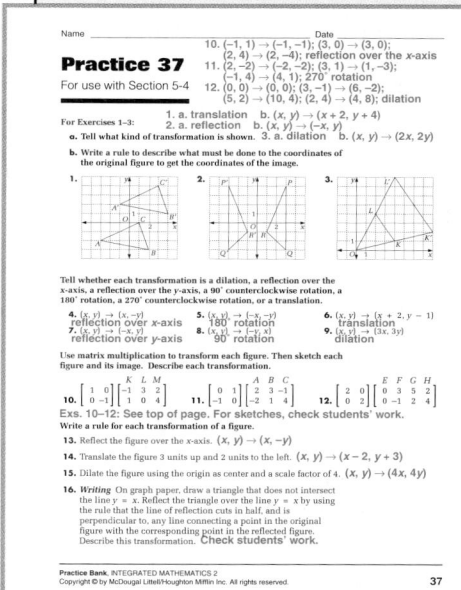

Answers to Exercises and Problems

33. $J'(0, -2)$, $K'(-1, -4)$, $L'(-3, -3)$, $M'(-4, 0)$; 180° rotation

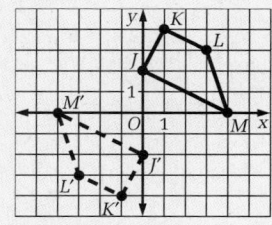

34. a. dilation with a scale factor 2

b. $(x, y) \rightarrow (2x, 2y)$

35. a. translation 3 units to the right, 2 units down

b. $(x, y) \rightarrow (x + 3, y - 2)$

36. a–c. Check students' work.

d. Dilations cause distance to change; reflections and rotations other than rotations that are multiples of 180° cause slope to change.

37. $(50, -50)$ 38. $(4, 3)$

39. $(-1.5, 2)$

40. a. $\dfrac{3}{49}$ or about 0.061

b. 6, -6

41. $AB = \sqrt{20} \approx 4.5$, $BC = 4$, $CD = \sqrt{32} \approx 5.7$, $AD = 10$

42–44. Answers may vary. Examples are given.

42. a. Draw a polygon. Use translations to create a tessellation.

b. Draw a square and the segments connecting the midpoints of opposite sides. Draw a pattern on one of the smaller squares and reflect it, respectively, over each of the four segments produced.

c. Proceed as in part (b), but rotate the design about the intersection of the segments drawn.

43, 44. See answers in back of book.

273

Objectives and Strands
See pages 240A and 240B.

Spiral Learning
See page 240B.

Recommended Pacing
Section 5-5 is a one-day lesson.

Extra Practice
See pages 622–623.

Warm-Up Exercises
Warm-Up Transparency 5-5

Support Materials
➤ Practice 38
➤ Enrichment 34 in the Activity Bank
➤ Study Guide 5-5
➤ Problem Set 10
➤ Quiz 5-5
➤ Alternative Assessment 4

Section 5-5

Coordinates for Triangles and Quadrilaterals

Focus
Represent figures on a coordinate plane using as few variables for coordinates as possible.

Príme POsítíOn

Many cars have two odometers.

One shows how many total miles the car has been driven.

34302.6
0000

reset button

The trip odometer may be reset to zero to show the distance traveled from a starting point.

Talk it Over

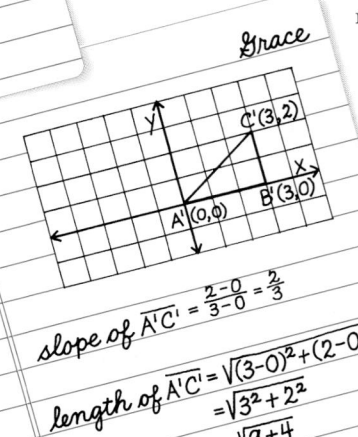

1. Suppose you traveled from Cleveland, Ohio, to Gary, Indiana, and back. Your odometer read 34,302.6 at the beginning of the trip and 34,879.2 at the end. How many miles did you travel?

2. Suppose you set the car's trip odometer to zero at the beginning of a trip from Cleveland to Gary. How will this setting make it easier to find how far you traveled?

3. In a homework problem Luiz and Grace found the slope and the length of the hypotenuse of $\triangle ABC$. Luiz used the given coordinates. Grace first translated the triangle 2 units right and 1 unit up.

   a. Whose calculations look simpler? Why?

   b. Did Grace's translation of the triangle affect its size or shape?

Luiz

slope of $\overline{AC} = \dfrac{1-(-1)}{1-(-2)} = \dfrac{1+1}{1+2} = \dfrac{2}{3}$

length of $\overline{AC} = \sqrt{[1-(-2)]^2 + [1-(-1)]^2}$
$= \sqrt{(1+2)^2 + (1+1)^2}$
$= \sqrt{3^2 + 2^2}$
$= \sqrt{9+4}$
$= \sqrt{13}$

Grace

slope of $\overline{A'C'} = \dfrac{2-0}{3-0} = \dfrac{2}{3}$

length of $\overline{A'C'} = \sqrt{(3-0)^2 + (2-0)^2}$
$= \sqrt{3^2 + 2^2}$
$= \sqrt{9+4}$
$= \sqrt{13}$

274

Answers to Talk it Over

1. 576.6 mi

2. You will be able to read the miles traveled directly from the trip odometer.

3. a. Grace's; The arithmetic is simpler because more zeroes are involved.

   b. No.

Triangles and Quadrilaterals in Standard Position

Any triangle or quadrilateral can be placed with a vertex at $(0, 0)$ and a side along the x-axis. This placement is called **standard position**. Calculations of slope and length are often easier when figures are in standard position.

FIGURES IN STANDARD POSITION

Triangle

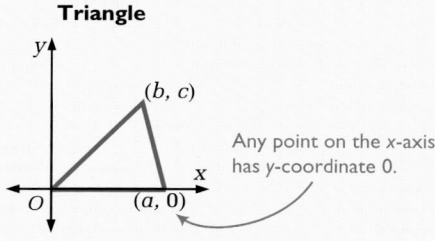

Any point on the x-axis has y-coordinate 0.

Use three variables to name the coordinates.

Quadrilateral

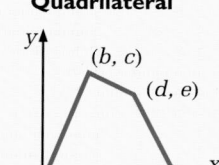

Use five variables to name the coordinates.

Coordinates for Special Quadrilaterals

In trapezoid $OPQR$ the sides $\overline{OP}$ and $\overline{RQ}$ are parallel. You can use the coordinates of the vertices of a quadrilateral in standard position to show that the y-coordinates of R and Q are the same. The slopes of the parallel sides, $\overline{OP}$ and $\overline{RQ}$, are equal.

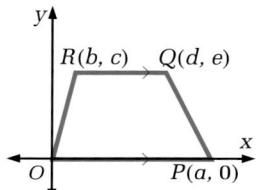

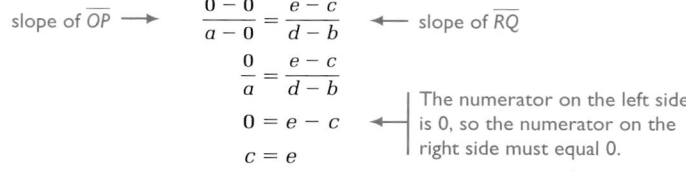

slope of $\overline{OP}$ → $\dfrac{0 - 0}{a - 0} = \dfrac{e - c}{d - b}$ ← slope of $\overline{RQ}$

$\dfrac{0}{a} = \dfrac{e - c}{d - b}$

$0 = e - c$ ← The numerator on the left side is 0, so the numerator on the right side must equal 0.

$c = e$

Since $c = e$, you can replace e with c. The coordinates of Q are (d, c).

276

Communication: Discussion

In the Special Quadrilaterals in Standard Position box, it is important that students understand why the coordinates of one vertex of the parallelogram are $(a + b, c)$. A brief discussion of the rationale for $a + b$ would be helpful for some students.

Talk it Over

Questions 4 and 5 help students relate the coordinates of specific points to the values given by the letters a, b, c, d, and e on the figures in standard position.

Additional Sample

$\triangle OBC$ is a right triangle. Name the missing coordinate without introducing a new variable.

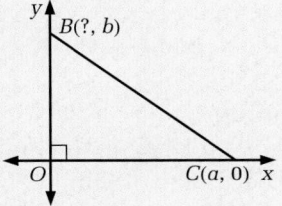

Since B is on the y-axis, its x-coordinate is zero. Vertex B can be labeled $(0, b)$.

Look Back

Students will experience the usefulness of the placement of geometric figures in standard position when they have to calculate distances or slopes and when they have to show or prove that various geometric figures have certain properties.

You have just seen that the coordinates of a trapezoid can be named using just four variables. The coordinates of other special quadrilaterals can also be named using fewer than five variables. You will show this in Exercises 22 and 23.

SPECIAL QUADRILATERALS IN STANDARD POSITION

Trapezoid

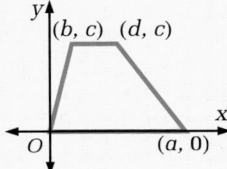

Parallelogram

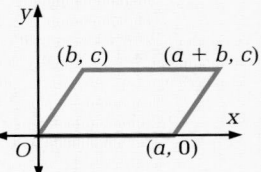

Rectangle

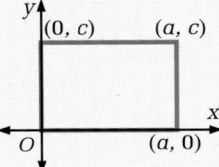

Talk it Over

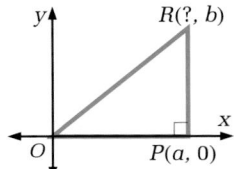

For questions 4 and 5, refer to the diagrams for quadrilaterals in standard position.

4. For parallelogram $OQRS$, what are the values of a, b, and c?

5. The vertices of quadrilateral $OJKL$ are $O(0, 0)$, $J(9, 0)$, $K(6, 10)$, and $L(2, 5)$. Find the values of a, b, c, d, and e.

6. Draw a square with one vertex at the origin and one side along the x-axis. Label the coordinates using variables. How many different variables do you need for the coordinates?

Sample

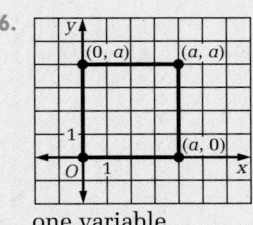

$\triangle OPR$ is a right triangle. Name the missing coordinate without introducing a new variable.

Sample Response

Since there is a right angle at P, $\overline{PR}$ is a vertical line.

R is directly above P and has the same x-coordinate as P.

The missing coordinate is a and vertex R can be labeled (a, b).

Look Back

How can placing a geometric figure with one vertex at the origin and one side along the x-axis be helpful?

Answers to Talk it Over

4. $a = 4$, $b = 2$, $c = 3$

5. $a = 9$, $b = 2$, $c = 5$, $d = 6$, $e = 10$

6.

one variable

Answers to Look Back

It allows you to use zeroes for at least three of the coordinates, thus simplifying the arithmetic.

Exercises and Problems

1. **Reading** When a triangle is placed in standard position, what are the coordinates of the two vertices that are on the *x*-axis?

For Exercises 2–6, use the map and time zone chart.

2. Which country is in the same time zone as one region of the United States? How can you tell?

3. a. Lorina lives in Seattle, Washington. At 10 A.M. she calls Kenya. What time is it in Kenya?

   b. Arman lives in Dayton, Ohio. At 10 A.M. he calls Kenya. What time is it in Kenya?

   c. Were Lorina and Arman calling Kenya at the same time? Explain your reasoning.

4. Create a table that describes the time zones in the United States if all your calls originate in Tahiti.

5. What is the time difference from Costa Rica to India?

6. How does a caller's "origin" influence how he or she calculates time zone differences?

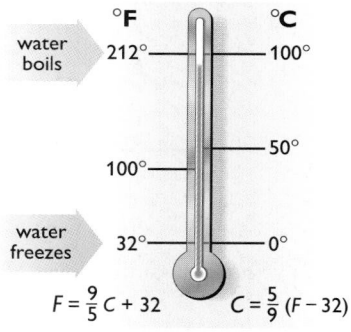

	PACIFIC	MOUNTAIN	CENTRAL	EASTERN	USA TIME
					COUNTRY
COSTA RICA	+2	+1	+0	−1	
KENYA	+11	+10	+9	+8	
TAHITI	−2	−3	−4	−5	
INDIA	$+13\frac{1}{2}$	$+12\frac{1}{2}$	$+11\frac{1}{2}$	$+10\frac{1}{2}$	

°F water boils 212° — 100° **°C**
— 50°
100° —
water freezes 32° — 0°

$$F = \frac{9}{5}C + 32 \qquad C = \frac{5}{9}(F - 32)$$

7. **Writing** In 1742, Anders Celsius developed a new temperature scale to make calculations easier.

   a. Explain why calculations are easier on a Celsius scale.

   b. How is the scale Anders Celsius developed like a figure placed in standard position?

8. a. **Literature** The title of Ray Bradbury's book *Fahrenheit 451* is based on the Fahrenheit scale. Find the Celsius temperature when the Fahrenheit scale reads 451°.

   b. What would the book's title have been if Bradbury had used the Celsius scale to name his book?

Name each missing coordinate without introducing a new variable.

9. isosceles right triangle

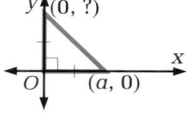

y (0, ?) x O (a, 0)

10. right triangle

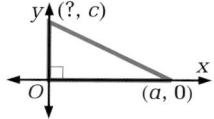

y (?, c) x O (a, 0)

11. triangle

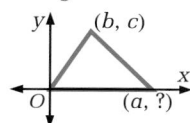

y (b, c) x O (a, ?)

12. rectangle

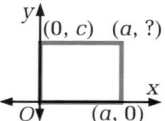

y (0, c) (a, ?) x O (a, 0)

13. trapezoid

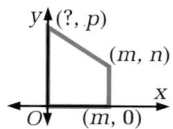

y (?, p) (m, n) x O (m, 0)

14. parallelogram

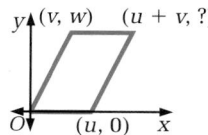

y (v, w) (u + v, ?) x O (u, 0)

5-5 Coordinates for Triangles and Quadrilaterals **277**

APPLYING

Suggested Assignment
Standard 1, 9–40
Extended 1–40

Integrating the Strands
Algebra Exs. 29–33
Geometry Exs. 1, 9–28, 34–39
Logic and Language Exs. 1–8, 24–26, 40

Communication: Reading
Ex. 1 checks students' understanding of the key idea of a triangle being in standard position. You may wish to follow up this question by asking students if the type of triangle would influence its standard position.

Teaching Tip
Exs. 2–7 illustrate the use of the idea of an origin or starting point to make certain calculations easier. This idea is then applied to the placement of geometric figures in order to achieve the same result of making calculations easier.

Interdisciplinary Problems
Authors sometimes entitle their books after events in the physical world. In Ex. 8, for example, it is interesting to note that 451°F is the burning point of paper. A recent book by Murray Gell-Mann, winner of the Nobel Prize in Physics, is called *The Quark and the Jaguar* (copyright 1994). Quarks are fundamental particles of matter that constitute the neutrons and protons of atomic nuclei. Jaguars are large and ferocious wild cats, and like everything else in the universe, they are made up of quarks.

Answers to Exercises and Problems

1. (0, 0) and (*a*, 0)

2. Costa Rica; The time difference between Costa Rica and the Central time zone of the United States is +0 on the chart.

3. a. 9 P.M.   b. 6 P.M.

   c. No; when Lorina was calling Kenya at 10 A.M. in Seattle, it was 1:00 P.M. in Dayton.

4. See answers in back of book.

5. $11\frac{1}{2}$ hours

6. If a call originates in a time zone that is east of the time zone called, the caller must subtract hours from his or her time; if a call originates in a time zone that is west of the time zone called, the caller must add hours to his or her time.

7. a. The freezing point is 0°C and the boiling point is 100°C.

   b. The scale begins at zero.

8. a. about 233°C

   b. Celsius 233

9. *a*   10. 0

11. 0   12. *c*

13. 0   14. *w*

For Exercises 15–17:

a. Describe the transformation needed for each polygon to be in the first quadrant with one vertex at (0, 0).

b. Give the coordinates of the vertices for the image of each polygon.

15.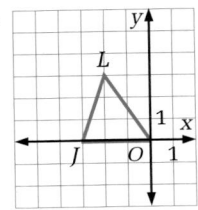

16.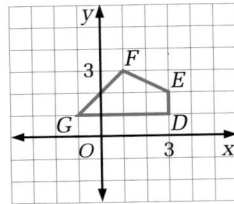

17.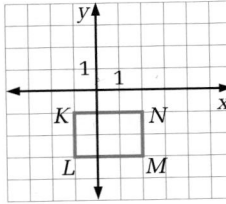

18. Quadrilateral *PQRS* has vertices *P*(0, 0), *Q*(7, 0), *R*(8, 4), and *S*(1, 4).

  a. Use slopes to show that *PQRS* is a parallelogram.

  b. Use the diagram for a parallelogram in standard position. Find the values of *a*, *b*, and *c*.

When polygons are symmetric, you can represent them using fewer variables by placing the axes along lines of symmetry. For Exercises 19–21, name the missing coordinates without introducing a new variable.

19. rectangle

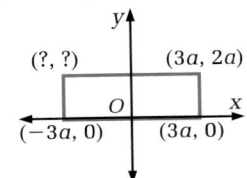

20. rectangle

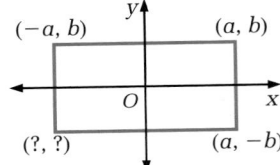

21. isosceles triangle

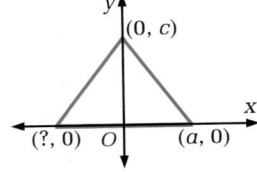

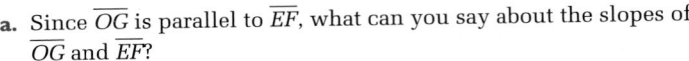

22. Quadrilateral *OEFG* is a parallelogram.

  a. Since $\overline{OG}$ is parallel to $\overline{EF}$, what can you say about the slopes of $\overline{OG}$ and $\overline{EF}$?

  b. **Writing** Since *OEFG* is a quadrilateral in standard position, the coordinates of its vertices can be written *O*(0, 0), *E*(a, 0), *F*(d, e), and *G*(b, c). Use the slope of $\overline{OE}$ and of $\overline{GF}$ to show that *e* = *c*.

  c. Use the slope of $\overline{OG}$ and of $\overline{EF}$ to show that *d* = *a* + *b*.

  d. How many different variables do you need to represent the coordinates of the vertices of a parallelogram in standard position?

23. Quadrilateral *OJKL* is a rectangle.

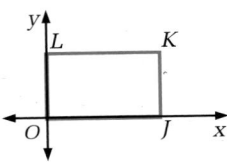

  a. What is the *x*-coordinate of *L*?

  b. **Writing** Since *OJKL* is also a parallelogram, the coordinates of its vertices can be written *O*(0, 0), *J*(a, 0), *K*(a + b, c), and *L*(b, c). Tell why the *x*-coordinate of point *K* can be written as *a* instead of the general *a* + *b*.

  c. How many different variables do you need to represent the coordinates of the vertices of a rectangle in standard position?

278

Unit 5 Coordinate Geometry and Quadrilaterals

Answers to Exercises and Problems

15. a. There are two possible answers: translate the triangle three units to the right or reflect the triangle over the *y*-axis.

  b. translation: *J*′(0, 0), *O*′(3, 0), *L*′(1, 3); reflection: *J*′(3, 0), *O*′(0, 0), *L*′(2, 3)

16. a. Translate the polygon one unit right and one unit down.

  b. *G*′(0, 0), *D*′(4, 0), *E*′(4, 1), *F*′(2, 2)

17. a. Translate the polygon one unit right and three units up.

  b. *L*′(0, 0), *M*′(3, 0), *N*′(3, 2), *K*′(0, 2)

18. a. slope of $\overline{PS} = \frac{4-0}{1-0} = 4$ and slope of $\overline{QR} = \frac{4-0}{8-7} = 4$; slope of $\overline{PQ} = \frac{0-0}{7-0} = 0$ and slope of

$SR = \frac{4-4}{8-1} = 0$; Since the slopes of the opposite sides are equal, $\overline{PS} \parallel \overline{QR}$ and $\overline{PQ} \parallel \overline{SR}$; thus, *PQRS* is a parallelogram.

  b. *a* = 7, *b* = 1, and *c* = 4

19. (−3a, 2a)

20. (−a, −b)

21. −a

22. See answers in back of book.

23. a. 0

  b. Since *L* is on the vertical axis, *b* = 0. Then *a* + *b* = *a* and the *x*-coordinate of *K* can be written as *a*.

  c. two

24. a. $\sqrt{a^2 + e^2}$; $\sqrt{a^2 + e^2}$

  b. $\sqrt{a^2 + b^2}$; $\sqrt{a^2 + b^2}$

24. a. Find the length of $\overline{LM}$ and the length of $\overline{MJ}$.

b. Find the length of $\overline{LK}$ and the length of $\overline{KJ}$.

c. Is *JKLM* a kite? Why or why not?

d. Which of the three variables used to name the coordinates represents a negative number?

25. Suppose that *JKLM* is a rhombus.

a. What is the relationship between $\overline{LK}$ and $\overline{LM}$?

b. Show that $e^2 = b^2$.

c. **Writing** Explain why $e = -b$.

d. Suppose rhombus *JKLM* has the x-axis and y-axis as lines of symmetry and two vertices at $J(4, 0)$ and $K(0, 3)$. Find the coordinates of the other two vertices.

26. Writing Copy the portion of the quadrilateral chart on page 245 that includes these figures: quadrilateral, trapezoid, parallelogram, rectangle, square. Label the coordinates of the vertices for each figure in standard position. Use as few variables as possible. Describe any patterns you see.

For each transformation, find the coordinates of the vertices of the image of △ABC. *(Section 5-4)*

27. reflection over the y-axis

28. translation 1 unit left and 1 unit down

Simplify. *(Section 4-6)*

29. $\sqrt{-25}$

30. $\sqrt{-30}$

31. $6i(1 - 4i)$

32. $(7 - 2i) + (5 - 3i)$

33. Rita made a conjecture that $\frac{1}{x} < x$. Do you think the conjecture is *True* or *False*? Explain. If false, give a counterexample. *(Section 1-5)*

 Working on the Unit Project

In the game of Alquerque, the point at the center of the grid is left empty when the pieces are put in place before play begins.

For Exercises 34–39, the point in the center of the board is the origin. What are the coordinates of the vertices of each figure?

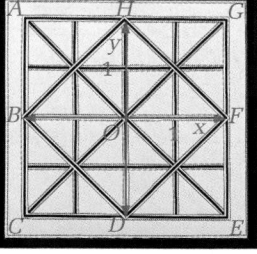

34. square *BDFH*

35. △*CEA*

36. trapezoid *CEOB*

37. △*OGA*

38. square *OFGH*

39. △*COA*

40. Open-ended How could you choose the origin on your game board in order to make it easier to locate points on the board?

5-5 Coordinates for Triangles and Quadrilaterals

279

Practice 38 For use with Section 5-5

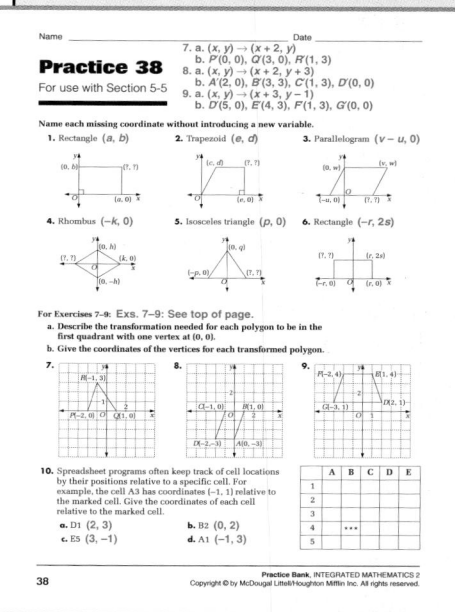

Answers to Exercises and Problems

c. Yes; it has two pairs of congruent adjacent sides.

d. *e*

25. a. $LK = LM$

b. *JKLM* is a rhombus so $KL = LM$; $\sqrt{a^2 + e^2} = \sqrt{a^2 + b^2}$. By squaring both sides, $a^2 + e^2 = a^2 + b^2$ and $e^2 = b^2$.

c. Since $e^2 = b^2$, when you undo the square, $e = \pm b$. If $e = b$, then K and M would be the same point and you would not have a rhombus. Therefore, $e = -b$.

d. $L(-4, 0)$; $M(0, -3)$

26. See answers in back of book.

27. $A'(-1, -2)$, $B'(-3, 1)$, $C'(-2, 2)$

28. $A'(0, -3)$, $B'(2, 0)$, $C'(1, 1)$

29. $5i$

30. $i\sqrt{30}$

31. $24 + 6i$

32. $12 - 5i$

33. False; for example, when $x = \frac{1}{2}$, $\frac{1}{\frac{1}{2}} = 2$ which is greater than $\frac{1}{2}$.

34. $B(-2, 0)$, $D(0, -2)$, $F(2, 0)$, $H(0, 2)$

35. $C(-2, -2)$, $E(2, -2)$, $A(-2, 2)$

36. $C(-2, -2)$, $E(2, -2)$, $O(0, 0)$, $B(-2, 0)$

37. $O(0, 0)$, $G(2, 2)$, $A(-2, 2)$

38. $O(0, 0)$, $F(2, 0)$, $G(2, 2)$, $H(0, 2)$

39. $C(-2, -2)$, $O(0, 0)$, $A(-2, 2)$

40. Answers may vary. An example is given. If you use a square game board divided into geometric figures, position the origin so that it lies at the intersection of as many lines of symmetry as possible.

Section 5-6

Exploring Properties

Focus
Use coordinate geometry and deductive reasoning to verify some properties of polygons.

AMAZING DIAGONALS

EXPLORATION

How are the diagonals in special quadrilaterals related?

- **Materials:** scissors, rulers, protractors
- **Work in a group of four students.**

Always start with a rectangular piece of paper.

① Each of you should make a different one of these quadrilaterals using paper folding and cutting.

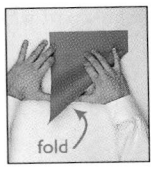
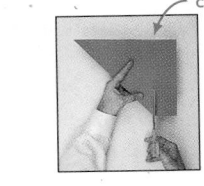

square

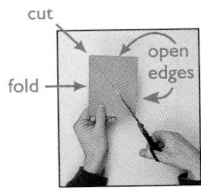

rhombus

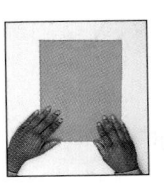

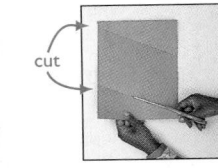
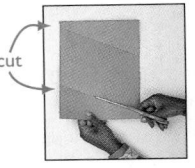

parallelogram

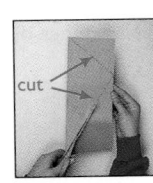
kite

280

Unit 5 Coordinate Geometry and Quadrilaterals

Answers to Exploration

1. Check students' work.

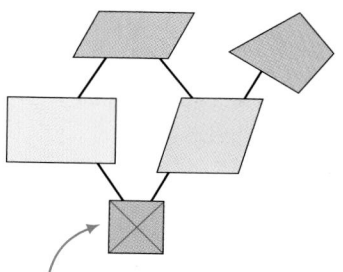

Diagonals have the same midpoint.
Diagonals are perpendicular.
Diagonals are equal in measure.

② The **diagonal** of a polygon is a segment joining two non-consecutive vertices. Show that the square has each of these properties. Use a ruler and a protractor if necessary.

  a. The diagonals have the same midpoint.

  b. The diagonals are perpendicular to each other.

  c. The diagonals are equal in measure.

③ Decide whether each of the other quadrilaterals you made in step 1 has any or all of the properties listed in step 2. The person who made the square should explore the properties of a rectangle.

④ Organize your results from step 3 in a quadrilateral chart like the one at the left.

Verifying Properties with Coordinates

In the Exploration, you used inductive reasoning to support your findings. You can also use coordinates and deductive reasoning to prove conjectures.

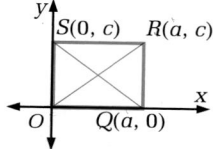

Sample 1

Use the coordinates of a rectangle in standard position to show that the diagonals of every rectangle have each property.

a. The diagonals are equal in measure.

b. The diagonals have the same midpoint.

Sample Response

a. Use the distance formula. Find the length of each diagonal and compare.

$$OR = \sqrt{(a - 0)^2 + (c - 0)^2} = \sqrt{a^2 + c^2}$$
$$SQ = \sqrt{(a - 0)^2 + (0 - c)^2} = \sqrt{a^2 + c^2}$$

These are equal, so the diagonals are equal in measure.

b. Use the midpoint formula. Find the midpoints and compare.

The midpoint of $\overline{OR}$ is $\left(\dfrac{0 + a}{2}, \dfrac{0 + c}{2}\right) = \left(\dfrac{a}{2}, \dfrac{c}{2}\right)$.

The midpoint of $\overline{SQ}$ is $\left(\dfrac{0 + a}{2}, \dfrac{c + 0}{2}\right) = \left(\dfrac{a}{2}, \dfrac{c}{2}\right)$.

The midpoints of the two diagonals are the same. The diagonals *bisect* each other.

▶ Now you are ready for:
Exs. 1–5 on p. 284

Answers to Exploration

2. A square has all three properties listed.

3. rhombus: a and b; parallelogram: a; kite: b; rectangle: a and c

4.

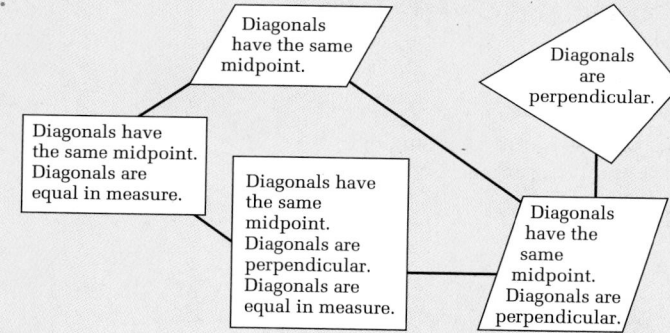

Shared Properties

Coordinate geometry can be used to show that the diagonals of special quadrilaterals have the properties you have been exploring. Here is a summary of those properties.

DIAGONALS OF SPECIAL QUADRILATERALS

In a *parallelogram*, the diagonals have the same midpoint.

In a *kite*, the diagonals are perpendicular to each other.

In a *rectangle*, the diagonals are equal in measure.

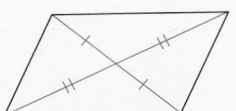
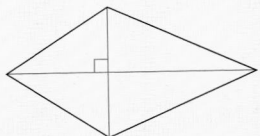
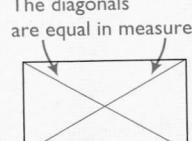

The diagonals are equal in measure.

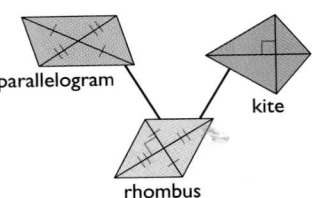

parallelogram

kite

rhombus

Every special quadrilateral shares the properties of the family of quadrilaterals to which it belongs. For example, a rhombus is a kite and a parallelogram. As you saw in the Exploration, its diagonals are perpendicular and have the same midpoint.

Here is another property of special quadrilaterals that is explored in Exercise 4.

OPPOSITE SIDES OF A PARALLELOGRAM

In a *parallelogram*, opposite sides are equal in measure.

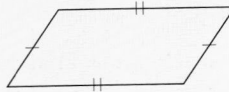

> **Talk it Over**
>
> **Use the quadrilateral chart that you made in the Exploration. Name all special quadrilaterals that have each property.**
>
> 1. The diagonals have the same midpoint.
> 2. The diagonals are perpendicular to each other.
> 3. The diagonals are equal in measure.
> 4. Opposite sides are equal in measure.

Unit 5 Coordinate Geometry and Quadrilaterals

B

W

Z

O

C

Properties of Triangles

This sculpture was created by Joan Brossa in 1984. It is one of a series of sculptures around Barcelona, Spain.

Sample 2

Imagine $\triangle OBC$ in the photo. $\overline{WZ}$ connects the midpoints of $\overline{OB}$ and $\overline{CB}$. Show that $\overline{WZ}$ is parallel to $\overline{OC}$ and that it is half as long.

Sample Response

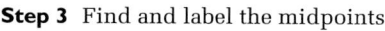

Step 1 Place the triangle in standard position.

Step 2 Use convenient coordinates. Finding midpoints involves dividing by 2, so use variable coordinates that are multiples of 2.

Step 3 Find and label the midpoints.

Step 4 Find each slope.

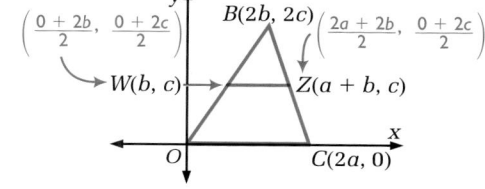

$\left(\frac{0 + 2b}{2}, \frac{0 + 2c}{2}\right)$ B(2b, 2c) $\left(\frac{2a + 2b}{2}, \frac{0 + 2c}{2}\right)$

W(b, c)   Z(a + b, c)

O   C(2a, 0)

The slope of $\overline{WZ}$ is $\dfrac{c - c}{a + b - b} = \dfrac{0}{a} = 0$.

The slope of $\overline{OC}$ is $\dfrac{0 - 0}{2a - 0} = \dfrac{0}{2a} = 0$.

The slopes are equal, so the segments are parallel.

Step 5 Find the length of each segment. Assume that $a > 0$.

$WZ = \sqrt{(a + b - b)^2 + (c - c)^2} = \sqrt{a^2 + 0^2} = a$

$OC = \sqrt{(2a - 0)^2 + (0 - 0)^2} = \sqrt{4a^2 + 0^2} = 2a$

$WZ = \frac{1}{2}OC$

A PROPERTY OF TRIANGLES

In a triangle, a segment that connects the midpoints of two sides is parallel to the third side and half as long.

$$MN = \frac{1}{2}PR$$

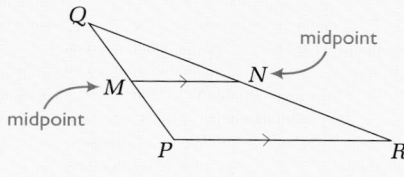

Q

midpoint

M   N

midpoint

P   R

Talk it Over

5. How many segments like $\overline{MN}$ are there for a triangle? Does each segment have the property described above?

5-6 Exploring Properties

Answers to Talk it Over

5. three segments; Yes.

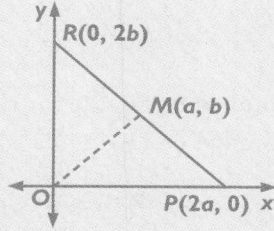

····▶ **Now you are ready for:**
Exs. 6–25 on pp. 284–286

Look Back ◄

How can you show that two segments are equal in measure? that they are parallel? that they are perpendicular?

5-6 Exercises and Problems

1. Parallelogram $OUVW$ has vertices $O(0, 0)$, $U(10, 0)$, $V(12, 5)$ and $W(2, 5)$. Show that the diagonals $\overline{OV}$ and $\overline{UW}$ have the same midpoint.

2. Use the coordinates in the diagram to show that the two diagonals of any parallelogram have the same midpoint.

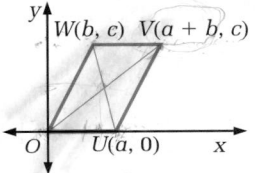

3. Suppose you are trying to convince a friend that the two diagonals of *every* parallelogram have the same midpoint. Which would be more convincing, your computations from Exercise 1 or Exercise 2? Why?

4. Another property of parallelograms is that opposite sides are equal in measure.

   a. Show that this is true for the parallelogram in Exercise 1.

   b. Show that this is true for all parallelograms using the coordinates in Exercise 2.

5. Use the coordinates of $OQRS$ in the diagram to show that a square has each property.

   a. $\overline{OR}$ and $\overline{QS}$ have the same midpoint.

   b. $\overline{OR}$ is perpendicular to $\overline{QS}$.

   c. $\overline{OR}$ is equal in measure to $\overline{QS}$.

6. **Reading** Did you use *inductive* or *deductive* reasoning in the Exploration on page 280? in Sample 1 on page 281? in Sample 2 on page 283?

7 TECHNOLOGY Use graphing software.

   a. Draw a trapezoid $ABCD$ so that no two sides are the same length and $\overline{AB}$ is parallel to $\overline{DC}$. Draw the diagonals and label the point where they intersect E.

   b. Measure to find the ratios AE to EC and BE to ED. Record your results.

   c. Repeat parts (a) and (b) for five more trapezoids. Describe any patterns you see in your results.

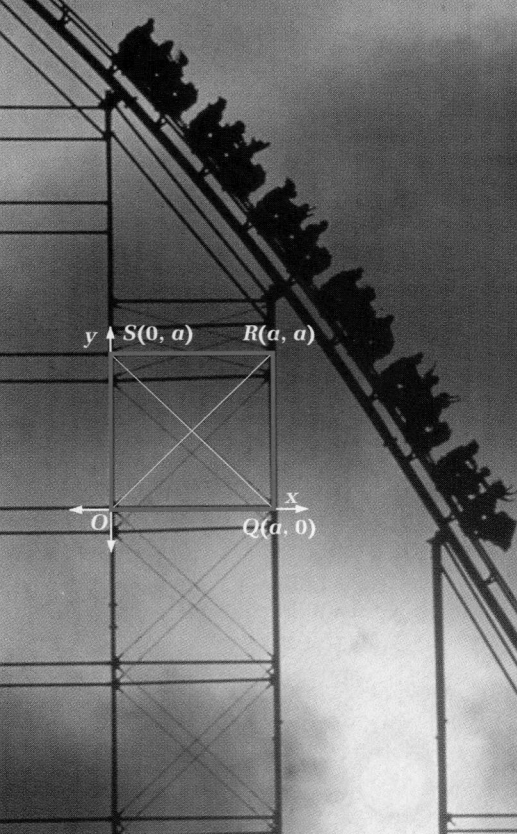

---

8. In trapezoid *OFGH*, *M* and *N* are the midpoints of $\overline{OH}$ and $\overline{FG}$. Use the coordinates in the diagram.

   a. Find the coordinates of *M* and *N*.

   b. Show that $\overline{MN}$ is parallel to $\overline{OF}$.

   c. Show that $MN = \frac{1}{2}(OF + GH)$.

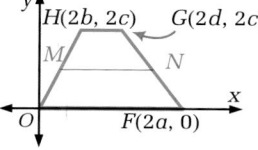

9. The midpoints of the sides of rectangle *LMNO* are *P*, *Q*, *R*, and *S*.

   a. Find the coordinates of *P*, *Q*, *R*, and *S*.

   b. What type of special quadrilateral is *PQRS*?

   c. Use the coordinates you found in part (a) to verify the conjecture you made in part (b).

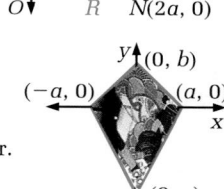

10. A kite can be represented as shown. Use the diagram to explain why the diagonals of a kite must be perpendicular to each other.

For Exercises 11–14, use the following two statements.

(1) If a parallelogram is a rectangle, then it has diagonals that are equal in measure.

(2) If a parallelogram has diagonals that are equal in measure, then it is a rectangle.

11. What is the relationship between the two statements?

12. **Using Manipulatives** Cut two equal strips of paper. Make them intersect so that a parallelogram is formed by joining their endpoints. What is special about this parallelogram?

13. Use the diagram to show that statement (2) is true. (*Hint:* Use the distance formula to find *OL* and *KM*, then set them equal. Then show that *OKLM* must be a rectangle.)

14. **Career** Carpenters use geometry to create the frames for buildings, decks, and other projects. Read below about the method carpenters use and decide which statement is being applied.

To make a frame, a carpenter cuts the opposite sides of the frame equal in length.

The sides of the frame form a parallelogram but not necessarily a rectangle.

The carpenter "squares up" the parallelogram by adjusting the angle until the two diagonals are equal in measure.

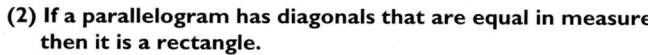

Using Technology

Activity 7 in the *Geometry Inventor Activity Book* can be used with Ex. 8.

Communication: Writing

In Ex. 8, $\overline{MN}$ is the *median* of the trapezoid and $\overline{HG}$ and $\overline{OF}$ are its *bases.* Using this language, ask students to write a statement that describes the results of their work. (The median of a trapezoid is parallel to its bases and has a length equal to half the sum of the lengths of the bases.) Students also can write the result of Ex. 8 without using the terms *median* and *base.* If you wish, have students write down the results of Ex. 9 as well.

Cooperative Learning

Students may find Ex. 13 to be somewhat complicated. You may wish to have students work this exercise in groups.

9. a. *P*(*a*, 2*c*); *Q*(2*a*, *c*); *R*(*a*, 0); *S*(0, *c*)

   b. rhombus

   c. $PQ = \sqrt{(2a - a)^2 + (c - 2c)^2} = \sqrt{a^2 + c^2}$; $QR = \sqrt{(2a - a)^2 + (c - 0)^2} = \sqrt{a^2 + c^2}$; $SR = \sqrt{(a - 0)^2 + (0 - c)^2} = \sqrt{a^2 + c^2}$; $PS = \sqrt{(a - 0)^2 + (2c - c)^2} = \sqrt{a^2 + c^2}$; all four sides are equal in measure, so *PQRS* is a rhombus.

10. The diagonals lie on the *x*-axis and the *y*-axis, which are perpendicular.

11. The statements are converses.

12. The parallelogram is a rectangle.

13. See answers in back of book.

14. Statement 2

Answers to Exercises and Problems

5. a. midpoint of $\overline{OR} = \left(\frac{a + 0}{2}, \frac{a + 0}{2}\right) = \left(\frac{a}{2}, \frac{a}{2}\right)$; midpoint of $\overline{QS} = \left(\frac{0 + a}{2}, \frac{a + 0}{2}\right) = \left(\frac{a}{2}, \frac{a}{2}\right)$

   b. slope of $\overline{OR} = \frac{a - 0}{a - 0} = 1$; slope of $\overline{QS} = \frac{a - 0}{0 - a} = \frac{a}{-a} = -1$; Since the slope of $\overline{OR}$ is the negative reciprocal of the slope of $\overline{QS}$, $\overline{OR} \perp \overline{QS}$.

   c. $OR = a\sqrt{2}$ and $QS = a\sqrt{2}$, so the diagonals have the same length.

6. inductive; deductive; deductive

7. a. Check students' work.

   b. The ratios should be equal or almost equal.

   c. $\frac{BE}{ED} = \frac{AE}{EC}$

8. a. *M*(*b*, *c*); *N*(*a* + *d*, *c*)

   b. slope of $\overline{MN} = \frac{c - c}{a + d - b} = \frac{0}{a + d - b} = 0$; slope of $\overline{OF} = \frac{0 - 0}{2a - 0} = 0$; slope of $\overline{MN} =$ slope of $\overline{OF}$ so $\overline{MN} \parallel \overline{OF}$.

   c. $\overline{MN}$, $\overline{OF}$, and $\overline{GH}$ are horizontal so $MN = a + d - b$; $OF + GH = 2a + 2d - 2b = 2(a + d - b)$; $MN = \frac{1}{2}(OF + GH)$.

15. **Writing** Write a quiz that covers all the properties of quadrilaterals and triangles that are covered in Section 5-6.

Ongoing ASSESSMENT

16. **Group Activity** Work in a group of four students.

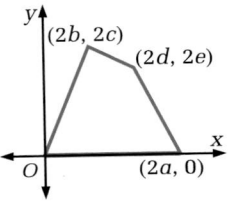

a. Each of you should draw a different quadrilateral on a coordinate grid. Find the midpoints of each side.

b. Join the midpoints to make another quadrilateral. Look for a pattern in your results. Make a conjecture about the type of quadrilateral you get.

c. Use the diagram at the right to verify your conjecture from part (b).

Review PREVIEW

Name the missing coordinates without introducing a new variable. *(Section 5-5)*

17. rectangle

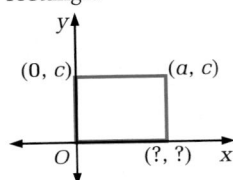

18. right triangle

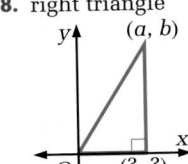

19. parallelogram

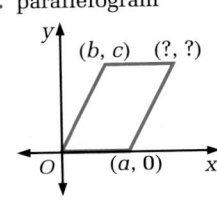

What can you conclude from each statement? *(Section 1-6)*

20. Carlos is taller than Gus and Gus is taller than Ben.

21. If Julie enters the race, then she will win. If she wins, then she will get a prize.

Use this information for Exercises 22 and 23. *(Toolbox Skill 7)*

Kim entered her name in a contest to win a free book at a bookstore. In all, 80 people entered their names. The winner's name will be chosen at random.

22. Find the probability that Kim will win a free book.

23. Find the probability that Kim will not win a free book.

Working on the Unit Project

24. A possible game board pattern is shown. Use what you know about the diagonals of quadrilaterals and coordinate geometry to copy this pattern on a coordinate grid.

25. **Open-ended** How could you use what you know about the diagonals of quadrilaterals in designing your game board? in directing players' moves?

286   **Unit 5** Coordinate Geometry and Quadrilaterals

Answers to Exercises and Problems

15. Check students' work.

16. See answers in back of book.

17. $(a, 0)$

18. $(a, 0)$

19. $(a + b, c)$

20. Carlos is taller than Ben.

21. If Julie enters the race, then she will get a prize.

22. $\frac{1}{80}$

23. $\frac{79}{80}$

24.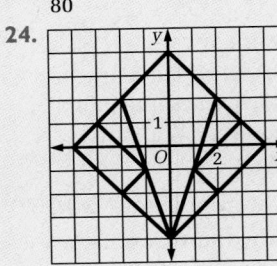

25. The design of the paths for the game pieces to move around the board could be along diagonals. At each corner, a player can move horizontally, vertically, and along a diagonal.

Completing the Unit Project

Now you are ready to finish making your game.
Your finished game should include these things:

➤ **a game board that incorporates a coordinate grid**

➤ **enough game pieces for at least four players**

➤ **dice, cards, or both for determining the moves and the order of play**

➤ **clear, complete written instructions for playing the game**

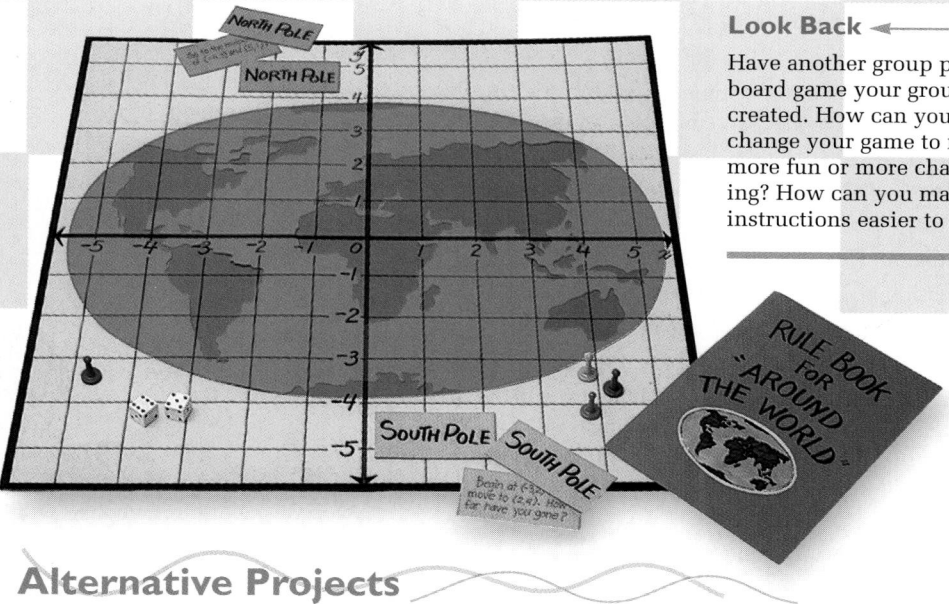

Look Back

Have another group play the board game your group has created. How can you change your game to make it more fun or more challenging? How can you make the instructions easier to follow?

Assessment

A scoring rubric for the Unit Project can be found on pages 240 and 241 of this Teacher's Edition and also in the *Project Book*.

Alternative Projects

Project 1: Design Your Own House

Design a house for a lot in your neighborhood. Make a siting plan by locating the center of the house and the outer walls. Use properties of quadrilaterals, the distance and midpoint formulas, and coordinate geometry to draw a floor plan. Combine your floor plan and siting plan in a visual display that demonstrates how you created the plans.

Project 2: Treasure Hunt

Design a treasure hunt. Draw a map on a coordinate grid and write clues that use the properties of quadrilaterals, the midpoint and distance formulas, and a coordinate grid.

Quick Quiz (5-4 through 5-6)

1. Name the type of transformation described by the rule $(x, y) \rightarrow (x + 3, y - 2)$. [5-4] translation

2. What type of transformation causes length to change? [5-4] dilation

3. Name the missing coordinates without introducing a new variable. [5-5] (a, b)

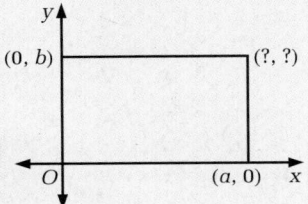

4. How would you show that two lines are parallel? [5-5]
   Show that they have the same slope.

5. Classify each statement as *True* or *False*. [5-6]

   a. The diagonals of a parallelogram are equal in measure. False.

   b. The diagonals of a square are perpendicular to each other. True.

   c. The diagonals of a parallelogram have the same midpoint. True.

6. The diagonal of a rhombus has slope $\frac{a}{b}$. What is the slope of its other diagonal? [5-6] $-\frac{b}{a}$

For Exercises 1–4, tell whether each statement is *True* or *False*. If the statement is false, give a counterexample.   5-1

1. All rhombuses are parallelograms.

2. If a quadrilateral is a rhombus, then it is a kite.

3. Every square is a rhombus.

4. All squares are parallelograms.

5. Make a concept map to show how these shapes are related: *square, rectangle, quadrilateral, trapezoid, rhombus, kite, parallelogram*

6. a. Plot the points $A(0, 6)$, $B(2, 5)$, and $C(-3, 4)$.   5-2

   b. Which point is closest to the origin?

   c. Which point is farthest from the origin?

7. Explain how you can use the Pythagorean theorem to help you remember the distance formula.

For Exercises 8 and 9, use the two figures at the right.

8. Show that *FGHJ* is a kite.

9. Show that *MNOP* is a parallelogram.

10. The endpoints of $\overline{KL}$ are $K(8, 3)$ and $L(-2, -5)$.   5-3

    a. Find the coordinates of M, the midpoint of $\overline{KL}$.

    b. Suppose L is the midpoint of $\overline{KN}$. Find the coordinates of N.

11. **Open-ended** Create a real-life problem for which you use the distance formula to find the solution. Show how to solve it.

For each transformation in Exercises 12–14, sketch the image of △ABC and label the coordinates of the vertices.   5-4

12. reflection over the *y*-axis

13. translation 1 unit up and 8 units left

14. dilation with scale factor 3 and center at O

15. In Exercises 12–14, for which transformations did the slope of $\overline{AC}$ change? For which transformations did the length of $\overline{AC}$ *not* change?

16. **Open-ended** Pick any four points in the coordinate plane and draw quadrilateral *PQRS* connecting them. For parts (a) and (b), tell what type of transformation is described and sketch the original and its image.

    a. The image has opposite *x*-coordinates, but the same *y*-coordinates.

    b. The image has opposite *x*-coordinates and opposite *y*-coordinates.

17. **Writing** For figures drawn in the first quadrant, does a reflection over the *x*-axis give you the same image as a 90° clockwise rotation? Explain why or why not.

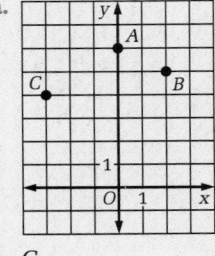

Answers to Unit 5 Review and Assessment

1. True.   2. True.   3. True.   4. True.

6. a.

5.

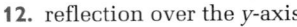

- quadrilaterals
- trapezoids
- kites
- parallelograms
- rectangles
- rhombuses
- squares

b. *C*

c. *A*

18. Find the missing coordinate of a parallelogram with vertices (0, 0), (8, 0), (?, 7), and (2, 7). 5-5

19. A triangle has vertices (0, 0), (6, 0), and (?, 7).

   a. What could the missing coordinate be if the triangle is a right triangle?

   b. What could the missing coordinate be if the triangle is isosceles?

20. Quadrilateral *HIJK* has coordinates $H(-4, -12)$, $I(6, -12)$, $J(5, -8)$, and $K(-5, -8)$.

   a. Sketch the quadrilateral.

   b. Sketch the image of the quadrilateral in standard position.

   c. What kind of quadrilateral is *HIJK*?

21. Plot the points $O(0, 0)$, $Q(4a, 0)$, and $R(2a, 2c)$. Show that $\triangle OQR$ is an isosceles triangle. 5-6

22. **Self-evaluation** You have seen properties of geometric figures demonstrated with inductive reasoning using numbers for coordinates and with deductive reasoning using variables for coordinates. Which method do you find easier? Which reasoning do you think is better? Why?

23. **Group Activity** Work in a group of four students. Each member of your group should choose one of these shape names: *rectangle*, *kite*, *rhombus*, or *parallelogram*.

For each of the properties listed in (a)–(g), discuss with your group members these two questions:

➤ Do *any* quadrilaterals with your shape's name have the given property?

➤ Does *every* quadrilateral with your shape's name have the given property?

   a. two pairs of parallel sides

   b. two pairs of opposite sides that are equal in measure

   c. two pairs of consecutive sides that are equal in measure

   d. diagonals that are equal in measure

   e. diagonals that have the same midpoint

   f. diagonals that are perpendicular

   g. sides that are perpendicular

Unit 5 Review and Assessment   289

---

since *MNOP* has two pairs of parallel sides, *MNOP* is a parallelogram.

10. a. (3, −1) **b.** (−12, −13)

11. Answers may vary. An example is given. Suppose the coordinates (1980, 1020) and (1990, 980) represent two points on a fitted line that describes your school's enrollment from 1980 to the present. You can use the midpoint formula to estimate your school's enrollment in 1985:
$$\left(\frac{1980 + 1990}{2}, \frac{1020 + 980}{2}\right) =$$
(1985, 1000); your school's enrollment was about 1000 in 1985.

12.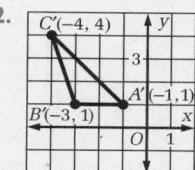

13.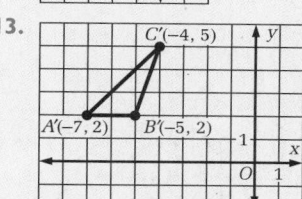

14.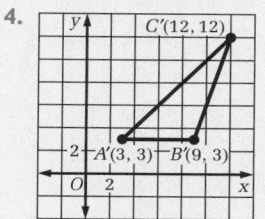

15. Ex. 12; Exs. 12 and 13

16. Check students' sketches.

   a. The image is a reflection over the *y*-axis.

   b. The image is a 180° rotation.

17. No; a reflection over the *x*-axis maps (x, y) to $(x, -y)$. A 90° clockwise rotation maps (x, y) to $(y, -x)$.

18. 10

19. a. 6 or 0 **b.** 3

20. a.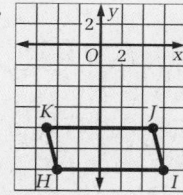

   b.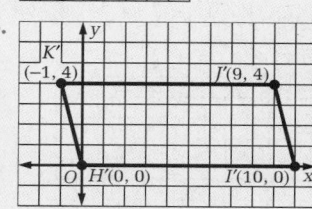

   c. parallelogram

Answers continued on next page.

Answers to Unit 5 Review and Assessment

7. The Pythagorean theorem tells how to find the square of the distance between the two endpoints of a hypotenuse of a right triangle: (distance)^2 = (change in x)^2 + (change in y)^2. Taking the same square root of both sides gives the distance formula: distance = $\sqrt{(\text{change in }x)^2 + (\text{change in }y)^2}$.

8. $FG = \sqrt{(-3 - 0)^2 + (0 - 2)^2}$ $= \sqrt{13}$; $HG =$ $\sqrt{(-3 - 0)^2 + (0 - (-2))^2} =$ $\sqrt{13}$; $FJ =$ $\sqrt{(2 - 0)^2 + (0 - 2)^2} = \sqrt{8}$; $HJ =$ $\sqrt{(2 - 0)^2 + (0 - (-2))^2} =$ $\sqrt{8}$; Since *FGHJ* has two pairs of adjacent congruent sides, *FGHJ* is a kite.

9. slope of $\overline{MN} = \frac{3 - 5}{-1 - (-5)} =$ $-\frac{1}{2}$; slope of $\overline{PO} = \frac{2 - 0}{-4 - 0} =$ $-\frac{1}{2}$; slope of $\overline{MP} =$ $\frac{5 - 2}{-5 - (-4)} = -3$; slope of $\overline{NO} = \frac{3 - 0}{-1 - 0} = -3$; slope of $\overline{MN}$ = slope of $\overline{PO}$ so $\overline{MN} \parallel \overline{PO}$; slope of $\overline{MP} =$ slope of $\overline{NO}$ so $\overline{MP} \parallel \overline{NO}$;

289

IDEAS AND (FORMULAS) = X^2

ALGEBRA $)X^2$

$(\times$

➤ **Measurement** To find the distance between two points, find the change in the x-coordinates and the change in the y-coordinates. *(p. 252)*

$$\text{distance} = \sqrt{(\text{change in } x)^2 + (\text{change in } y)^2}$$

➤ **Measurement** The distance d between the points (x_1, y_1) and (x_2, y_2) is given by the formula $d = \sqrt{(x_2 - x_1)^2 + (y_2 - y_1)^2}$. *(p. 252)*

➤ You can use the distance formula and what you know about the slopes of parallel and perpendicular lines to show that a figure is a certain kind of quadrilateral. *(pp. 253–254)*

➤ To find the midpoint of a segment, find the mean of the x-coordinates and the mean of the y-coordinates. *(p. 259)*

➤ You can use a formula to find the midpoint of a segment: If the endpoints of a segment have coordinates (x_1, y_1) and (x_2, y_2), then the midpoint has coordinates $\left(\dfrac{x_1 + x_2}{2}, \dfrac{y_1 + y_2}{2}\right)$. *(p. 259)*

➤ The distance and slope formulas may be used to show properties of geometric figures. *(p. 281)*

LOGICAL REASONING
if - then

➤ Special types of quadrilaterals may be organized in a chart. Each quadrilateral is a special case of the quadrilateral(s) it is connected to from above. *(pp. 244–245)*

➤ You can use the quadrilateral chart to make statements of the form: *All* ? *are* ? or *Every* ? *is a* ? or *If a quadrilateral is a* ?, *then it is a* ?. *(p. 245)*

➤ A property may be investigated using inductive reasoning by demonstrating the property in many specific cases or with variable coordinates in a general case using deductive reasoning. *(p. 281)*

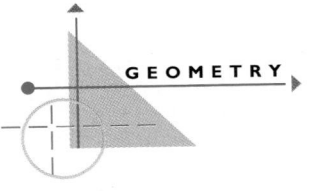

GEOMETRY

➤ Dilations affect length, but not slope. Rotations and reflections affect slope, but not length. Translations do not affect slope or length. *(pp. 269–270)*

➤ **Problem Solving** Placing a figure in standard position on a coordinate plane may make calculations easier. *(p. 275)*

➤ The vertices of a special quadrilateral can be named using four variables or less. *(p. 276)*

290

Unit 5 Coordinate Geometry and Quadrilaterals

Answers to Unit 5 Review and Assessment

21. $OR = \sqrt{(2a - 0)^2 + (2c - 0)^2} = 2\sqrt{a^2 + c^2}$;

$QR = \sqrt{(2a - 4a)^2 + (2c - 0)^2} = 2\sqrt{a^2 + c^2}$

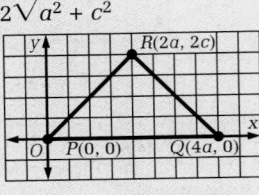

22. Answers may vary. Which reasoning is "better" depends on what you are attempting to do. If you are demonstrating properties, inductive reasoning is sufficient. If you want to prove that a property is always true, the deductive method is better.

23. a. all rectangles, rhombuses, parallelograms; some kites

b. all rectangles, rhombuses, parallelograms

c. all kites, rhombuses; some rectangles, parallelograms

d. all rectangles; some kites, rhombuses, parallelograms

e. all rectangles, rhombuses, parallelograms; some kites

f. all kites, rhombuses; some rectangles, parallelograms

g. all rectangles; some kites, rhombuses, parallelograms

➤ Coordinate geometry may be used to show that *all* geometric figures of a particular type have certain properties. (*p. 282*)

➤ Quadrilaterals "inherit" properties of the family to which they belong. (*p. 282*)

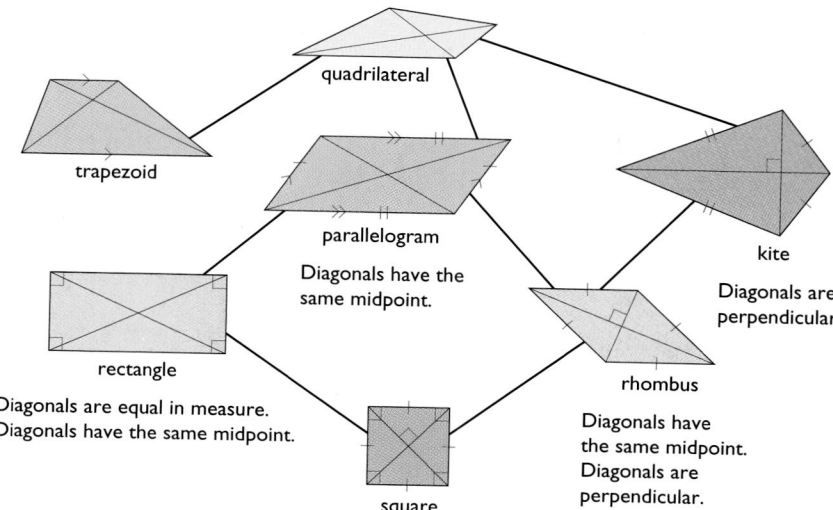

quadrilateral

trapezoid

parallelogram
Diagonals have the
same midpoint.

kite
Diagonals are
perpendicular.

rectangle
Diagonals are equal in measure.
Diagonals have the same midpoint.

rhombus
Diagonals have
the same midpoint.
Diagonals are
perpendicular.

square
Diagonals are equal in measure.
Diagonals have the same midpoint.
Diagonals are perpendicular.

➤ The diagonals of a parallelogram have the same midpoint. The diagonals of a kite are perpendicular to each other. The length of the diagonals of a rectangle are equal in measure. Opposite sides of a parallelogram are equal in measure. (*p. 282*)

➤ In every triangle, a segment that connects the midpoints of two sides is parallel to and half the length of the third side. (*p. 283*)

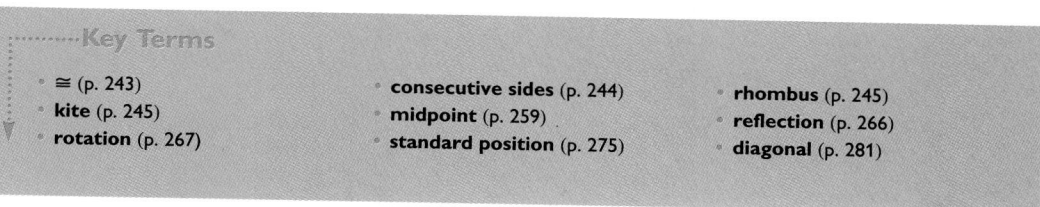

Key Terms

- ≅ (p. 243)
- **kite** (p. 245)
- **rotation** (p. 267)
- **consecutive sides** (p. 244)
- **midpoint** (p. 259)
- **standard position** (p. 275)
- **rhombus** (p. 245)
- **reflection** (p. 266)
- **diagonal** (p. 281)

1. Decide whether each statement is *True* or *False*. [5-1]

   a. If a quadrilateral is a parallelogram, then it is a rhombus. False.

   b. Every square is a rhombus. True.

2. Find the distance, d, between points $A(5, 2)$ and $B(-3, -4)$. [5-2] $d = 10$

3. How would you use the slope formula to show that a parallelogram is a rectangle? [5-2] Find the slopes of consecutive sides and check to see if their product is –1.

4. Find the midpoint of $\overline{CD}$. $C(7, -3)$; $D(-4, 9)$ [5-3] (1.5, 3)

5. If M is the midpoint of $\overline{XY}$, then $2 \times XM = $ _?_. [5-3] XY

OVERVIEW

➤ **Unit 6** presents techniques for solving probability problems. Students investigate the counting principle, permutations, and combinations as means of counting events. Probability is applied to mutually exclusive events, dependent and independent events, and complementary events, as well as to binomial experiments. Students can review basic topics of probability in the **Student Resources Toolbox** on pages 637–639.

➤ Pascal's triangle is introduced and connected to combinations and to expanding powers of binomials.

➤ Developing an interest profile based on birthdays and interest in school subjects is the theme of the Unit Project. Students write and conduct a survey, then find the probabilities of events relating to the survey.

➤ Connections to acting, business travel, basketball lotteries, biology, music, and literature are integrated into the teaching materials and exercises.

➤ Graphics calculators are used in Section 6-2 to find factorials and permutations, in Section 6-5 to find combinations, and in Section 6-8 to generate random test results.

➤ Problem-solving strategies used in Unit 6 include using diagrams, tables, systematic lists, patterns, formulas, counting techniques, Pascal's triangle, and the binomial theorem.

Unit Objectives

Section	Objectives	NCTM Standards
6-1	• Use diagrams and tables to count possibilities.	1, 2, 4, 5, 10
6-2	• Use the multiplication counting principle to find a number of possible arrangements of items.	1, 2, 4, 5, 10
6-3	• Find the probability of an event and of mutually exclusive events. • Relate probability to odds.	1, 2, 4, 5, 10, 11
6-4	• Find the probability of independent and dependent events.	1, 2, 4, 5, 10, 11
6-5	• Find the number of ways to select some items from a group.	1, 2, 4, 5, 10, 11
6-6	• Find patterns in Pascal's triangle. • Recognize the elements of Pascal's triangle as combinations.	1, 2, 4, 5, 10, 11
6-7	• Find probabilities for experiments that have two outcomes for each trial and where the probability of each outcome is one half.	1, 2, 4, 5, 10, 11
6-8	• Find probabilities for binomial experiments where the probability of each outcome is not one half.	1, 2, 4, 5, 10, 11
6-9	• Find powers of binomials.	1, 2, 4, 5, 10, 11

Skills Bank To extend the curriculum and provide practice with skills, you may wish to assign the following topics from the **Skills Bank** ancillary: permutations with repeated elements (for use after Section 6-2) and compound probability (for use after Section 6-5).

Topic Spiraling

Section	Connections to Prior and Future Concepts
6-1	**Section 6-1** introduces counting techniques with tree diagrams, tables, and systematic lists. Skills with counting techniques are essential when students determine possible outcomes for an event. These techniques are used in Unit 7 of Book 3.
6-2	**Section 6-2** develops the counting principle to determine the number of possible arrangements or outcomes. Permutations are introduced as an arrangement of items in a particular order. Counting techniques are needed in Unit 7 of Book 3.
6-3	**Section 6-3** investigates and then defines mutually exclusive events. Students apply counting techniques to probability problems. Complementary events and odds are introduced. These skills are used in Unit 7 of Book 3.
6-4	**Section 6-4** introduces compound events, the difference between independent and dependent events, and the effect they have on a probability situation. Skills with independent events are used in Unit 7 of Book 3.
6-5	**Section 6-5** explores the concept of combinations. The relationship between combinations and permutations is covered. These concepts are used in Unit 7 of Book 3.
6-6	**Section 6-6** relates the patterns found in Pascal's triangle to combinations. Pascal's triangle is applied to counting problems.
6-7	**Section 6-7** introduces binomial experiments in which the outcomes are equally likely. Topics from Sections 6-3 and 6-4 are tied in with binomial experiments to determine the probabilities connected with these experiments. The probability of an event is limited to $\frac{1}{2}$ in this section. The concept of a binomial experiment is extended in Section 6-8 of Book 2 and in Unit 7 of Book 3.
6-8	**Section 6-8** extends binomial experiments to include experiments in which the outcomes are not equally likely.
6-9	**Section 6-9** introduces the binomial theorem. The coefficients of a binomial expansion are related to the entries of Pascal's triangle and to combinations. These topics were introduced in Section 6-6 of Book 2.

Integrating the Strands

Strands	Sections
Number	6-5, 6-6, 6-9
Algebra	6-1, 6-2, 6-3, 6-4, 6-6, 6-8, 6-9
Functions	6-6
Geometry	6-1, 6-5, 6-6, 6-7, 6-8, 6-9
Statistics and Probability	6-1, 6-2, 6-3, 6-4, 6-5, 6-6, 6-7, 6-8, 6-9
Logic and Language	6-1, 6-2, 6-3, 6-4, 6-5, 6-6, 6-7, 6-8, 6-9

Section Planning Guide

➤ Essential exercises and problems are indicated in boldface.
➤ Ongoing work on the Unit Project is indicated in color.
➤ Exercises and problems that require student research, group work, manipulatives, or graphing technology are indicated in the column headed "Other."

Section	Materials	Pacing	Standard Assignment	Extended Assignment	Other
6-1		Day 1	**1–12**, 15–30, 31, 32	**1–12**, 13–30, 31, 32	
6-2	four index cards per group	Day 1	**1–10**, 13, 14, 16	**1–10**, 11–16	12c
		Day 2	**17–28**, 31–39, 40–44	**17–28**, 29, 31–39, 40–44	30
6-3	removable notes, spinner, paper clip	Day 1	1, 2, **3–13**, 15–19	1, 2, **3–13**, 15–21	14
		Day 2	**22–29**, 30–32, 40–46, 47–52	**22–29**, 30–32, 34–46, 47–52	33
6-4	spinner, paper clip	Day 1	**1–5**, 6–8	**1–5**, 6–8, 10–13	9
		Day 2	**15–19**, 20–29, 30, 31	14, **15–19**, 20–29, 30, 31	
6-5		Day 1	**1–14, 16–18**, 19, 20, 25–30, 31, 32	**1–14**, 15, **16–18**, 19–23, 25–30, 31, 32	24
6-6		Day 1	1, 3, **5–19**, 23–28, 29, 30	1, 3, **5–19**, 20–28, 29, 30	2, 4
6-7	four coins per group	Day 1	**3–5, 7, 8**, 11–21, 22, 23	1, 2, **3–5, 7, 8**, 9–21, 22, 23	6
6-8	calculator or telephone book	Day 1	**2–7**, 8–13, 18–23, 24, 25	1, **2–7**, 8–13, 15–23, 24, 25	14, 24
6-9		Day 1	**1–8**	**1–8**	
		Day 2	**9–20**, 23, 25–31, 32	**9–20**, 21–31, 32	
Review		Days 1, 2	**Unit Review**	**Unit Review**	
Test		Day 3	**Unit Test**	**Unit Test**	

Yearly Pacing	Unit 6 Total	Units 1–6 Total	Remaining	Total
	18 days (2 for Unit Project)	97 days	63 days	160 days

Support Materials

➤ See **Project Book** for notes on Unit 6 Project: Develop an Interest Profile.
➤ "UPP" and "disk" refer to **Using Plotter Plus** booklet and **Plotter Plus** disk.
➤ "TI-81/82" refers to **Using TI-81 and TI-82 Calculators** booklet.
➤ Warm-up exercises for each section are available on **Warm-Up Transparencies.**
➤ "PC" refers to the McDougal Littell Mathpack software Activity Book for **Probability Constructor.**

Section	Study Guide	Practice Bank	Problem Bank	Activity Bank	Explorations Lab Manual	Assessment Book	Visuals	Technology
6-1	6-1	Practice 41	Set 11	Enrich 36		Quiz 6-1		PC Acts. 17–19
6-2	6-2	Practice 42	Set 11	Enrich 37	Add. Expl. 7	Quiz 6-2		
6-3	6-3	Practice 43	Set 11	Enrich 38		Quiz 6-3	Folder 1	PC Act. 20
6-4	6-4	Practice 44	Set 11	Enrich 39		Quiz 6-4 Test 22		
6-5	6-5	Practice 45	Set 12	Enrich 40		Quiz 6-5		
6-6	6-6	Practice 46	Set 12	Enrich 41	Add. Expl. 8 Master 6	Quiz 6-6		TI-81/82, pp. 43–44
6-7	6-7	Practice 47	Set 12	Enrich 42	Masters 1, 6, 18	Quiz 6-7 Test 23		
6-8	6-8	Practice 48	Set 13	Enrich 43		Quiz 6-8		
6-9	6-9	Practice 49	Set 13	Enrich 44	Master 6	Quiz 6-9 Test 24		
Unit 6	Unit Review	Practice 50	Unifying Problem 6	Family Involve 6		Tests 25, 26		

UNIT TESTS

Spanish versions of these tests are on pages 138–141 of the **Assessment Book**.

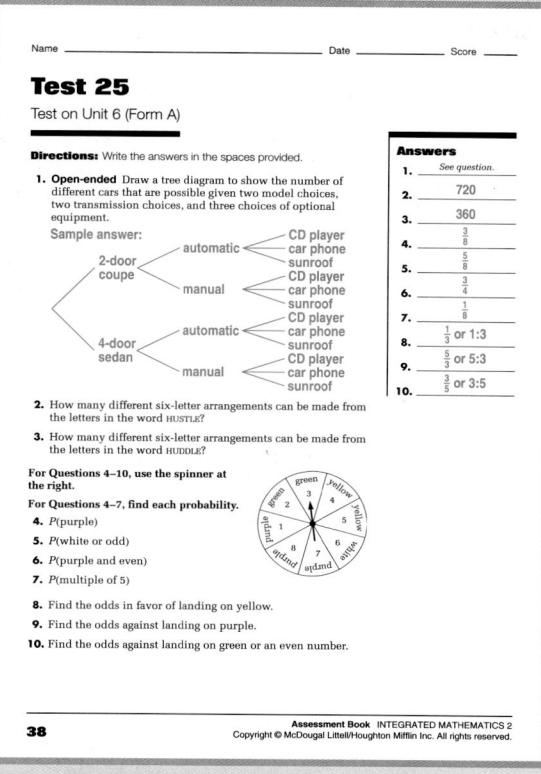

Name _____ Date _____ Score _____

Test 25
Test on Unit 6 (Form A)

Directions: Write the answers in the spaces provided.

1. **Open-ended** Draw a tree diagram to show the number of different cars that are possible given two model choices, two transmission choices, and three choices of optional equipment.

Sample answer:

2. How many different six-letter arrangements can be made from the letters in the word HUSTLE?

3. How many different six-letter arrangements can be made from the letters in the word HUDDLE?

For Questions 4–10, use the spinner at the right.

For Questions 4–7, find each probability.

4. $P(\text{purple})$

5. $P(\text{white or odd})$

6. $P(\text{purple and even})$

7. $P(\text{multiple of 5})$

8. Find the odds in favor of landing on yellow.

9. Find the odds against landing on purple.

10. Find the odds against landing on green or an even number.

Answers

1. _See question._
2. 720
3. 360
4. $\frac{3}{8}$
5. $\frac{5}{8}$
6. $\frac{3}{4}$
7. $\frac{1}{8}$
8. $\frac{1}{3}$ or 1:3
9. $\frac{5}{3}$ or 5:3
10. $\frac{3}{5}$ or 3:5

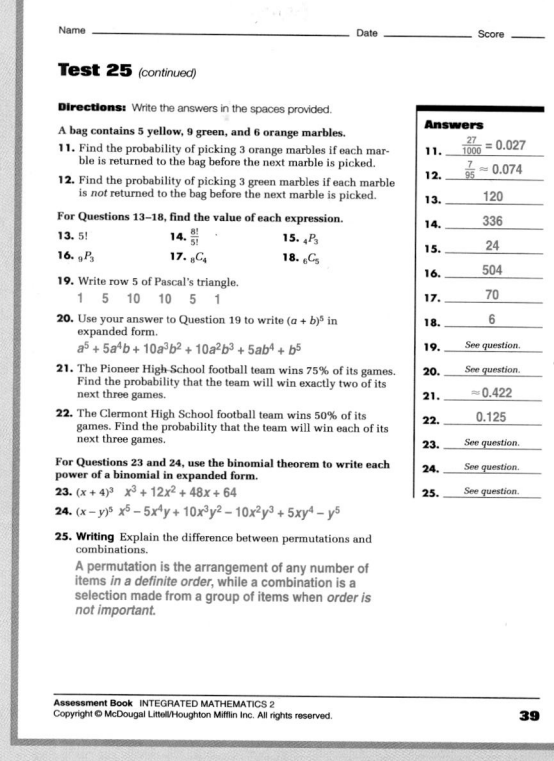

Name _____ Date _____ Score _____

Test 25 (continued)

Directions: Write the answers in the spaces provided.

A bag contains 5 yellow, 9 green, and 6 orange marbles.

11. Find the probability of picking 3 orange marbles if each marble is returned to the bag before the next marble is picked.

12. Find the probability of picking 3 green marbles if each marble is *not* returned to the bag before the next marble is picked.

For Questions 13–18, find the value of each expression.

13. 5!   14. $\frac{8!}{5!}$ 15. $_4P_3$

16. $_9P_3$ 17. $_8C_4$ 18. $_6C_5$

19. Write row 5 of Pascal's triangle.

1   5   10   10   5   1

20. Use your answer to Question 19 to write $(a + b)^5$ in expanded form.

$a^5 + 5a^4b + 10a^3b^2 + 10a^2b^3 + 5ab^4 + b^5$

21. The Pioneer High School football team wins 75% of its games. Find the probability that the team will win exactly two of its next three games.

22. The Clermont High School football team wins 50% of its games. Find the probability that the team will win each of its next three games.

For Questions 23 and 24, use the binomial theorem to write each power of a binomial in expanded form.

23. $(x + 4)^3$ $x^3 + 12x^2 + 48x + 64$

24. $(x - y)^5$ $x^5 - 5x^4y + 10x^3y^2 - 10x^2y^3 + 5xy^4 - y^5$

25. **Writing** Explain the difference between permutations and combinations.

A permutation is the arrangement of any number of items *in a definite order*, while a combination is a selection made from a group of items when *order is not important.*

Answers

11. $\frac{27}{1000} = 0.027$
12. $\frac{7}{95} \approx 0.074$
13. 120
14. 336
15. 24
16. 504
17. 70
18. 6
19. _See question._
20. _See question._
21. ≈ 0.422
22. 0.125
23. _See question._
24. _See question._
25. _See question._

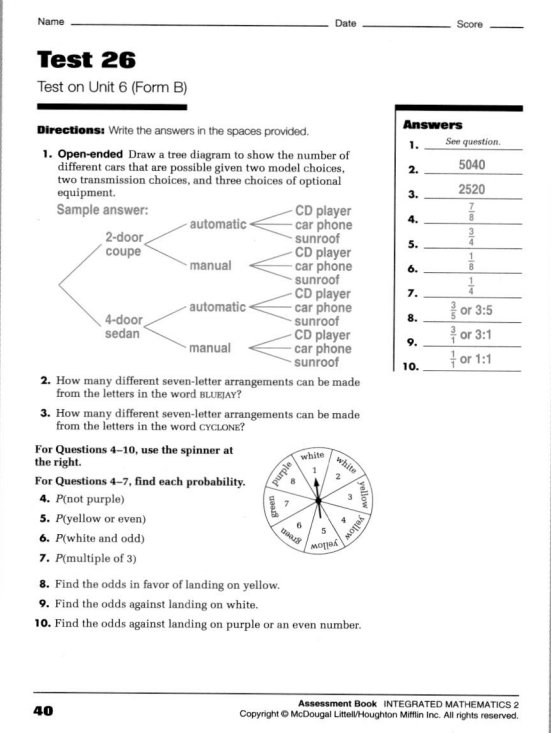

Name _____ Date _____ Score _____

Test 26
Test on Unit 6 (Form B)

Directions: Write the answers in the spaces provided.

1. **Open-ended** Draw a tree diagram to show the number of different cars that are possible given two model choices, two transmission choices, and three choices of optional equipment.

Sample answer:

2. How many different seven-letter arrangements can be made from the letters in the word BLUEJAY?

3. How many different seven-letter arrangements can be made from the letters in the word CYCLONE?

For Questions 4–10, use the spinner at the right.

For Questions 4–7, find each probability.

4. $P(\text{not purple})$

5. $P(\text{yellow or even})$

6. $P(\text{white and odd})$

7. $P(\text{multiple of 3})$

8. Find the odds in favor of landing on yellow.

9. Find the odds against landing on white.

10. Find the odds against landing on purple or an even number.

Answers

1. _See question._
2. 5040
3. 2520
4. $\frac{7}{8}$
5. $\frac{3}{4}$
6. $\frac{1}{8}$
7. $\frac{1}{4}$
8. $\frac{3}{5}$ or 3:5
9. $\frac{3}{1}$ or 3:1
10. $\frac{1}{1}$ or 1:1

Name _____ Date _____ Score _____

Test 26 (continued)

Directions: Write the answers in the spaces provided.

A bag contains 8 yellow, 5 green, and 7 orange marbles.

11. Find the probability of picking 3 yellow marbles if each marble is returned to the bag before the next marble is picked.

12. Find the probability of picking 3 yellow marbles if each marble is *not* returned to the bag before the next marble is picked.

For Questions 13–18, find the value of each expression.

13. 4!   14. $\frac{9!}{5!}$ 15. $_5P_3$

16. $_7P_4$ 17. $_9C_4$ 18. $_8C_5$

19. Write row 6 of Pascal's triangle.

1   6   15   20   15   6   1

20. Use your answer to Question 19 to write $(x + y)^6$ in expanded form.

$x^6 + 6x^5y + 15x^4y^2 + 20x^3y^3 + 15x^2y^4 + 6xy^5 + y^6$

21. The Pioneer High School football team wins 70% of its games. Find the probability that the team will win exactly one of its next three games.

22. The Clermont High School football team wins 50% of its games. Find the probability that the team will win at least two of its next three games.

For Questions 23 and 24, use the binomial theorem to write each power of a binomial in expanded form.

23. $(x + 2)^5$ $x^5 + 10x^4 + 40x^3 + 80x^2 + 80x + 32$

24. $(x - y)^3$ $x^3 - 3x^2y + 3xy^2 - y^3$

25. **Writing** Explain the difference between probability and odds.

The probability of an event is the ratio of the number of favorable outcomes for that event to the total number of possible outcomes, while the odds in favor of an event are the ratio of the number of favorable outcomes for that event to the number of unfavorable outcomes for the event.

Answers

11. $\frac{8}{125} = 0.064$
12. $\frac{14}{285} \approx 0.049$
13. 24
14. 3024
15. 60
16. 840
17. 126
18. 56
19. _See question._
20. _See question._
21. 0.189
22. 0.5
23. _See question._
24. _See question._
25. _See question._

Software Support

McDougal Littell Mathpack
Probability Constructor

Outside Resources

Books/Periodicals

Ericksen, Donna B., Martha L. Frank, and Ryan Kelley. "WITPO: What is the Probability of?" *Mathematics Teacher* (April 1991): pp. 258–264.

Shutte, Albert. *Teaching Statistics and Probability.* 1981 Yearbook. NCTM, 1981.

Activities/Manipulatives

Duncan, David and Bonnie Litwiller. "Combinatorics Connections: Playoff Series and Pascal's Triangle." *Mathematics Teacher* (October 1992): pp. 532–535.

Software

Bretl, C. Donna and Lois Edwards. *A Chance Look.* Pleasantville, NY: Sunburst, 1991. Apple.

Casino Master Gold. Centron Software, 1994. Macintosh

Videos

College Algebra: In Simplest Terms. Program No. 5: Probability. COMAP Inc., 1991.

Video for Unit Project: *Mathematical Eye.* Program No. 6: Probability. Journal Films, 1988. (Explores factors that affect probability. Shows how graphing can help uncover what is affecting probability.)

Counting Strategies, Probability, Binomials

PROFILES

➤ Students develop two interest profiles that represent a sample of students in their school.

➤ A survey is developed and distributed to determine students' birthdays and to rate their interest level for five school subjects.

➤ Students present the profiles in a visual display and describe them in a written report. ....●

PROJECT PLANNING

Materials List

➤ Graph paper

➤ Drawings or photos for visual display

Project Teams

Have students work on the project in groups of four. One way for the individuals in the group to distribute the work is as follows:

1. Coordinator: coordinates and summarizes the discussion about which subjects to include in the survey, the sampling methods, sample size, how to use the related exercises in the unit, the written report, and the visual display.

2. Surveyor: conducts the survey in a manner selected by the group and tallies the data.

3. Writer: gives a written description of the profiles and an analysis of the questionnaire including all computed probabilities and a summary of the data.

4. Illustrator: uses drawings or photos to create a visual display showing the interest profile for the two groups of students.

Can you easily bend your thumb back to touch your wrist? Can you do a back bend? If you can, you are among the small percentage of people who are called *double-jointed* because some of their joints are unusually flexible.

flexibility

A recent study revealed a positive correlation between being double-jointed and being a musician. Although rare in the general population, double-jointedness occurs in about 63% of the flutists in the survey and almost 50% of the players of stringed instruments.

music

On the other hand, whether the apparently high incidence of musical talent among scientists and mathematicians represents a positive correlation is still an open question.

science

Science & Music
Is there a correlation?

H_2O

Jamel Lamonté Oeser-Sweat
Age: 17
Science project: medicine
(loofa sponges as source of bacterial infections)
Musical talent: drums

292

Suggested Rubric for Unit Project ·······························

4 Students' interest profiles are complete in that they include all the things listed on page 358 (Completing the Unit Project). The visual display is attractive and includes the probabilities based on the survey results. The group's survey, analysis of the survey, data display, written descrip-

tions of the profiles, and probabilities are accurate, clear, and mathematically correct. The procedures or methods used to develop the profiles are supported by the mathematics of this unit.

3 Students' interest profiles have been developed using the correct survey techniques and

an accurate calculation of the probabilities. The written report contains the survey, a data display of the survey results, and an analysis of the survey. The report is adequate but could have been organized better and written more clearly. The visual display is acceptable but could have been improved with more work.

Unit Project 6

Develop an Interest Profile

An *interest profile* is a summary of the interests of an individual or the interests common to a group of people.

Your project is to develop two interest profiles that represent a sample of the students in your school. You will make separate profiles for students with birthdays from January 1 through June 30 and from July 1 through December 31.

You will develop and distribute a survey asking students to state their birthday and to rate five school subjects on their level of interest alone.

You will present your profiles in a visual display that includes probabilities based on your survey results. You will describe your profiles in a written report that also contains your survey, a data display of the survey results, and an analysis of your survey.

4 Winners of a Science Talent Search

Jennifer Yu-Fe Lin
Age: 17
Science project: biology
(factors controlling cell growth)
Musical talent: classical piano

careers

What do you want to do when you finish school? **Interest inventory tests** are designed to help people select a career. When you fill out an interest inventory, you are comparing your interests with the interest profiles for various career fields.

Rajen Arun Sheth
Age: 17
Science project: engineering
(effect of intelligent vehicle/highway systems on vehicle efficiency)
Musical talent: violin

Jessica Hammer
Age: 17
Science project: psycholinguistics
(how nonverbal cues affect language learning)
Musical talent: jazz music

293

Suggested Rubric for Unit Project

2 Students' finished projects are somewhat incomplete by not including all of the things listed on page 358 (Completing the Unit Project). There are some problems with the survey questions. The visual display is not clear, and the written report is not only lacking in data but is also somewhat disorganized.

1 Students have essentially not completed the project. The interest profiles are not supported by the results of the survey. The procedures or methods employed are mathematically incorrect. The group should be encouraged to speak with the teacher as soon as possible to review their work and to make a new start on the project.

Support Materials

The *Project Book* contains information about the following topics for use with this Unit Project.

➤ Project Description
➤ Teaching Commentary
➤ Working on the Unit Project Exercises
➤ Completing the Unit Project
➤ Assessing the Unit Project
➤ Alternative Projects
➤ Outside Resources

ADDITIONAL BACKGROUND

Multicultural Note

Musicians and composers listen to music of other cultures for inspiration. Here are some notable examples: Antonín Dvořák was a Czech composer who gained inspiration from Czech and Slavonic folk music. In 1893, he composed the famous Symphony in E Minor (*From the New World*), which has melodies similar to those of African-American and Native American music. Miles Davis was an American composer and trumpeter whose highly acclaimed album *Sketches of Spain* (1959–1960) features jazz impressions of Spanish compositions. Carlos Chávez was a Mexican composer and conductor whose *Sinfonia India* (1935) displays Mexican and Indian influences. Stephane Grappelli, a classically trained jazz violinist from France, performed in the 1930s with such jazz luminaries as Josephine Baker and Louis Armstrong, as well as with the great American composer-pianist George Gershwin. Fela Kuti, a Nigerian composer and band leader of Afro-beat music, studied classical theory at London's Trinity College of Music early in his career.

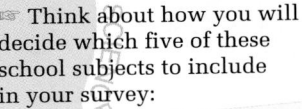

MATICS SOCIAL STUDIES LANGUAGE ARTS

BUSINESS

Getting Started

For this project you should work in a group of four students. Here are some ideas to help you get started.

☞ Think about how you will decide which five of these school subjects to include in your survey:

> mathematics, social studies, language arts, science, art, music, physical education, industrial technology, languages, business

☞ In your group, discuss various kinds of sampling methods. Decide which method to use for your survey.

☞ Review the related exercises in the unit. Decide how you will use the answers with your profiles and in your report.

☞ Think about how to create an appropriate data display for your survey results.

☞ Begin to collect drawings and photos for use in your visual display.

Working on the Unit Project

Your work in Unit 6 will help you create your interest profiles.

Related Exercises:

Section 6-1, Exercises 31, 32
Section 6-2, Exercises 40–44
Section 6-3, Exercises 47–52
Section 6-4, Exercises 30, 31
Section 6-5, Exercises 31, 32
Section 6-6, Exercises 29, 30
Section 6-7, Exercises 22, 23
Section 6-8, Exercises 24, 25
Section 6-9, Exercise 32

Alternative Projects p. 358

294

Can We Talk PROFILES

➤ Do you think the positive correlation between being double-jointed and being a musician reflects a cause-effect relationship between the two characteristics? Why or why not?

➤ Where have you seen other profiles of people?

➤ What are some factors other than interests that affect the choice of a career?

➤ Do you think interest inventory tests can predict whether a person will be successful in a particular career? Why or why not?

Unit 6 Counting Strategies, Probability, Binomials

Answers to Can We Talk?

➤ Answers may vary. An example is given. No. Because not every double-jointed person is a musician and not every musician is double-jointed.

➤ Answers may vary. Examples are given. In magazines, newspapers, pamphlets, and on television.

➤ Answers may vary. Examples are given. Ability, determination, level of education required, career location, and knowledge about career choices.

➤ Answers may vary. An example is given. No. There are many factors necessary to being successful, such as hard work and dedication. An interest inventory measures interest, not desire, work habits, or other factors.

Exploring Counting Problems

Focus
Use diagrams and tables to count possibilities.

Let Me **COUNT** the Ways

Talk it Over

1. a. Suppose you are packing for a trip and can take only one small bag of clothes. How do you decide what to pack?

   b. Suppose you decide to take three shirts, a pair of jeans, and a pair of shorts, all of which are color-coordinated. How can you make a complete list of all the possible outfits without counting any outfit more than once?

2. Suppose you are having posters for a play printed in two colors. Your color choices are black, blue, red, green, and purple. How can you make a complete list of all the possible pairs of colors without counting any pair more than once?

3. How are the situations in questions 1(b) and 2 alike? How are they different?

You can organize information in a systematic way so that you list all possibilities without listing anything more than once.

6-1 Exploring Counting Problems

295

PLANNING

Objectives and Strands
See pages 292A and 292B.

Spiral Learning
See page 292B.

Recommended Pacing
Section 6-1 is a one-day lesson.

Extra Practice
See pages 623–624.

Warm-Up Exercises
Warm-Up Transparency 6-1

Support Materials
➤ Practice 41
➤ Enrichment 36 in the Activity Bank
➤ Study Guide 6-1
➤ Problem Set 11
➤ McDougal Littell Mathpack software: *Probability Constructor*
➤ Probability Constructor Activity Book: Activities 17–19
➤ Quiz 6-1
➤ Alternative Assessment 1

Answers to Talk it Over

1–3. Answers may vary. Examples are given.

1. a. Items to consider include the purpose of the trip, the weather, any special occasions to be attended, and so on.

   b. Draw a tree diagram with one column of branches for the shirts and one for the shorts or the jeans.

2. Draw a tree diagram with one column of branches for the first color and one for the second.

3. Both involve choosing a combination of items from a list of several items. There are more possible choices in question 2. Also, in question 2, the choices from the second category depend on the choice for the first.

Talk it Over

Questions 1 and 2 ask students to consider two situations for which there is a need to organize information in a list. Both situations prepare students to think about ways in which information can be presented to show all the distinct possibilities involved.

Additional Sample

S1 A furniture store sells a reclining chair that is available in 4 different styles, 3 different colors, and 2 different sizes. How many different chairs are there to choose from?

Make a tree diagram with a column of branches for each style, color, and size. Label style and color with a different letter. The sizes can be labeled 1 and 2.

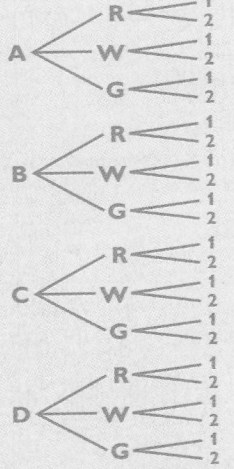

There are 24 different chairs to choose from.

Reasoning

Some students might reason their way to answer Talk it Over question 5 as follows: For each main dish, there are two side dish choices. Therefore, for 3 main dishes, there are 3×2 or 6 possibilities for side dishes. For each of these 6 possibilities, there are 2 drink choices. Therefore, there are 6×2 or 12 outcomes altogether.

MENU

MAIN DISHES $2.75
Tacos, Burritos, Enchiladas

SIDE DISHES $.50
Rice, Pinto Beans

DRINKS $.75
Lemonade, Spring Water

COMPLETE MEAL $3.50
Includes a main dish, a side dish, and a drink.

Sample 1

Suppose you go to a snack bar that has the menu shown and buy a "complete meal." How many different meals are there to choose from?

Sample Response

Problem Solving Strategy: Use a diagram.

Make a **tree diagram** with a column of branches for each category. To keep it simple, label each branch in each category with a single letter. Use a different letter for each item.

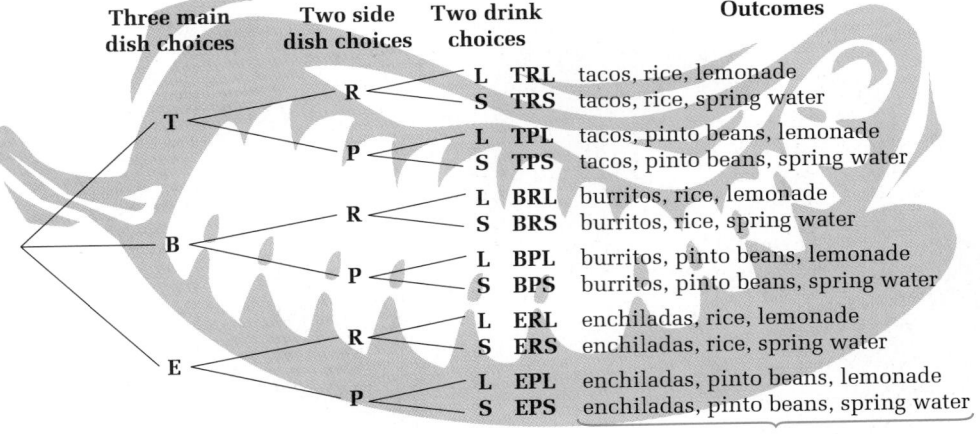

Three main dish choices	Two side dish choices	Two drink choices		Outcomes
		L	TRL	tacos, rice, lemonade
		S	TRS	tacos, rice, spring water
		L	TPL	tacos, pinto beans, lemonade
		S	TPS	tacos, pinto beans, spring water
		L	BRL	burritos, rice, lemonade
		S	BRS	burritos, rice, spring water
		L	BPL	burritos, pinto beans, lemonade
		S	BPS	burritos, pinto beans, spring water
		L	ERL	enchiladas, rice, lemonade
		S	ERS	enchiladas, rice, spring water
		L	EPL	enchiladas, pinto beans, lemonade
		S	EPS	enchiladas, pinto beans, spring water

Each of the 12 different possibilities is an **outcome**.

There are 12 different meals to choose from.

Talk it Over

Use the situation in Sample 1.

4. Make another tree diagram in which you select the drink first, the side dish second, and the main dish third. How do the results compare with those in the Sample?

5. Describe another way to find the total number of meals (outcomes) without drawing a tree diagram.

6. An **event** is a set of outcomes. How many outcomes are there for each event?

   a. having a meal with tacos

   b. having a meal with rice

Unit 6 Counting Strategies, Probability, Binomials

Answers to Talk it Over

4.

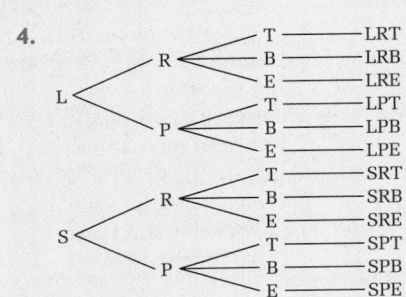

The meals are the same; the parts of the meal are listed in a different order.

5. Answers may vary. An example is given. You could make a chart with three columns, one for each choice. List one main dish in the first column, first row and one side dish in the second column, first row. Then list one drink choice in the third column, first row. Then with the same entries in the first

Outcomes from Rolling Dice

Many games use *dice*. Dice are cubes that have a different number of dots from 1 to 6 on each face. A single cube is called a *die*.

Sample 2

Suppose you are playing a board game that involves rolling two dice and counting the number of dots showing on the top of each die. One die is red, the other is white. How many different outcomes are there?

Sample Response

Problem Solving Strategy: Make a table.

1 List the outcomes for the red die.

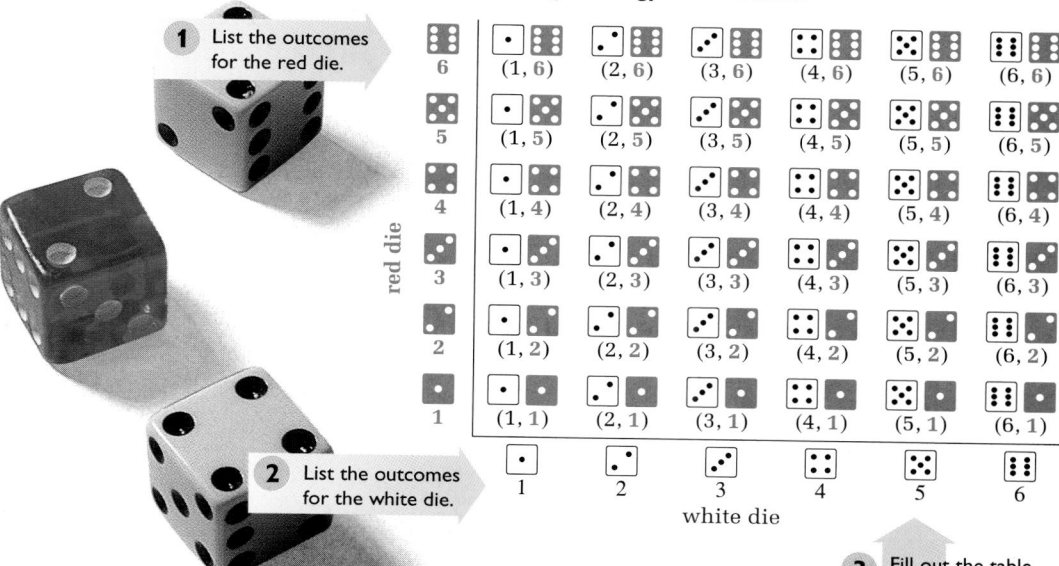

2 List the outcomes for the white die.

3 Fill out the table with the possible outcomes for both dice.

There are 36 different outcomes.

Talk it Over

7. Do you know a quicker way to find the number of outcomes in Sample 2? If so, describe your method.

Use the table in Sample 2. Find the number of possible outcomes for each event.

8. a sum of 8   9. a product over 25   10. an even sum

Answers to Talk it Over

two columns of the second row, list the next drink choice in the third column, second row. Proceed until all possible choices are listed. There will be twelve rows in the table.

6. a. 4 choices
   b. 6 choices

7. Answers may vary. An example is given. Without making a table, you may be able to think of the outcomes as ordered pairs with six different first coordinates and six different second coordinates.

8. 5 outcomes

9. 3 outcomes

10. 18 outcomes

Multicultural Note

Dice most likely originated in Asia. It is known that Asian women and girls played a dice game similar to jacks. References to dice are found also in ancient Greek and Roman documents, and dice have been recovered from ancient Egyptian tombs. Cultures throughout the world have used dice for both religious purposes and for games of chance. The design of the modern die comes mostly from India, where at least 2000 years ago cubical dice marked with "birds-eye" spots were used.

Additional Sample

S2 Suppose you are playing a board game that involves rolling three tetrahedrons (4 sides) and recording the numbers on the bottom of each one. There is a red, a green, and a white tetrahedron, each with the numbers 1, 2, 3, and 4 on them. How many different outcomes are there?

Make a table. For each row, keep the numbers on the first two tetrahedrons constant, and vary the third number from 1 to 4.

(1,1,1) (1,1,2) (1,1,3) (1,1,4)
(1,2,1) (1,2,2) (1,2,3) (1,2,4)
(1,3,1) (1,3,2) (1,3,3) (1,3,4)
(1,4,1) (1,4,2) (1,4,3) (1,4,4)
(2,1,1) (2,1,2) (2,1,3) (2,1,4)
(2,2,1) (2,2,2) (2,2,3) (2,2,4)
(2,3,1) (2,3,2) (2,3,3) (2,3,4)
(2,4,1) (2,4,2) (2,4,3) (2,4,4)
(3,1,1) (3,1,2) (3,1,3) (3,1,4)
(3,2,1) (3,2,2) (3,2,3) (3,2,4)
(3,3,1) (3,3,2) (3,3,3) (3,3,4)
(3,4,1) (3,4,2) (3,4,3) (3,4,4)
(4,1,1) (4,1,2) (4,1,3) (4,1,4)
(4,2,1) (4,2,2) (4,2,3) (4,2,4)
(4,3,1) (4,3,2) (4,3,3) (4,3,4)
(4,4,1) (4,4,2) (4,4,3) (4,4,4)

There are 64 different outcomes.

Using Technology

Activities 17–19 in the *Probability Constructor Activity Book* explore the use of tree diagrams to represent all possible outcomes for rolling one or two dice and for tossing two coins.

Additional Sample

S3 Val is building a new house. Her builder asks her to consider additional options for the house that include air conditioning, a security system, a fireplace, and a central vacuum system. Val plans to add at least one of the options to the house. How many combinations are possible?

Make a systematic list. List each possible event and the number of outcomes for each event.

(1) **Val wants all 4 of the options.**
  - air conditioning, security system, fireplace, central vacuum system

Number of outcomes: 1

(2) **Val wants 3 of the options.**
  - air conditioning, security system, fireplace
  - air conditioning, security system, central vacuum system
  - air conditioning, fireplace, central vacuum system
  - security system, fireplace, central vacuum system

Number of outcomes: 4

(3) **Val wants 2 of the options.**
  - air conditioning, security system
  - air conditioning, fireplace
  - air conditioning, central vacuum system
  - security system, fireplace
  - security system, central vacuum system
  - fireplace, central vacuum system

Number of outcomes: 6

(4) **Val wants 1 of the options.**
  - air conditioning
  - security system
  - fireplace
  - central vacuum system

Number of outcomes: 4

Fifteen different option combinations are possible.

Leaving Out Choices

You do not always have to choose something from every category when you make a selection.

Sample 3

Suppose you are thinking about buying any one, two, or three of the following accessories for a camera: lens, flash, tripod. You will not buy more than one of each type of accessory. How many accessory combinations are possible?

Sample Response

Problem Solving Strategy: Make a systematic list.

You may buy three accessories, two accessories, or one accessory.

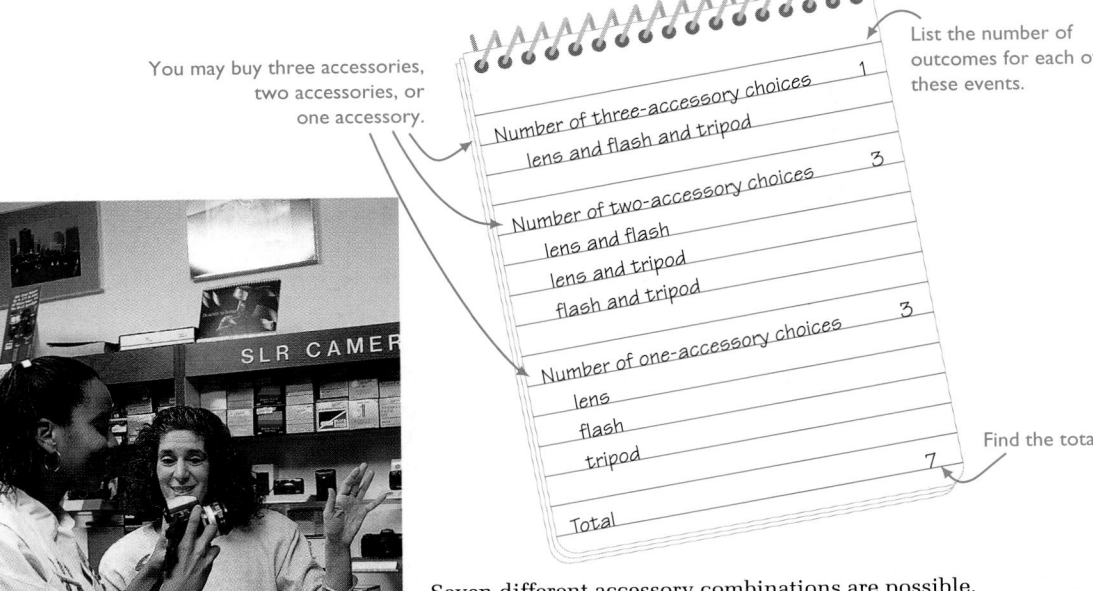

List the number of outcomes for each of these events.

Number of three-accessory choices 1
  lens and flash and tripod

Number of two-accessory choices 3
  lens and flash
  lens and tripod
  flash and tripod

Number of one-accessory choices 3
  lens
  flash
  tripod

Find the total.

Total 7

Seven different accessory combinations are possible.

Talk it Over

11. How is the situation in Sample 3 different from the situation in Sample 1?

12. Suppose a camera bag is added to the choices in Sample 3. How many different accessory combinations will be possible?

Answers to Talk it Over

11. In Sample 1, exactly one item is chosen from each category. In Sample 3, you do not have to choose an item from each category.

12. 15 accessory combinations

Answers to Look Back

Summaries may vary. Information can be organized in a tree diagram, a table, or a systematic list. All three methods make it possible to keep track of all possible choices and to list outcomes. A tree diagram may take up a lot of space if there are more than a few choices in each category or more than a few categories. In the beginning, it may not be clear how big either a table or tree diagram will be. If a choice does not have to be made from each category, a standard tree diagram or table would have to be altered.

Look Back ←

What are some methods for organizing information to include all possible choices? What are some advantages and disadvantages of each?

6-1 Exercises and Problems

Reading Use the table in Sample 2 on page 297. How many outcomes are there for each event when you roll one red die and one white die?

1. rolling exactly one 6

2. rolling exactly one even number

3. rolling two odd numbers

For Exercises 4 and 5, find all the possible outcomes for each situation.

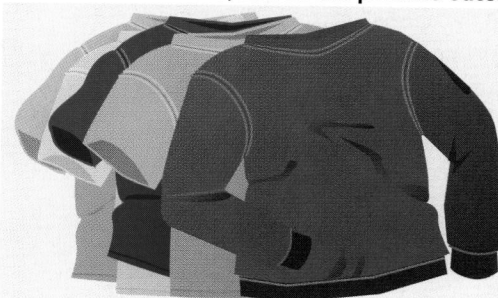

4. Raúl is ordering a shirt. The catalog offers his size in the five colors and two sleeve lengths shown.

T-Shirt: long and short sleeve
Colors: spruce, yellow, white, oatmeal, or purple

Sizes: S, M, L, XL

5. Evetta is buying a telephone. She plans to choose one option, but not both.

Color	white, gray, black
Style	corded, cordless
Options	built-in answering machine, speakerphone

6. **Open-ended** Write a problem that you could solve using this tree diagram. Then solve your problem.

7. Deb drops a nickel, a dime, and a quarter. None lands on its edge. How many possible ways can the coins show heads or tails?

8. Charlotte is playing a board game that involves rolling a pair of dice. The number of spaces that she moves depends on the sum of the dots on the top faces. How many different sums are there?

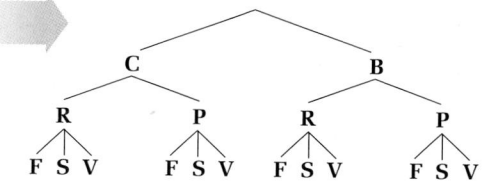

9. Tobias is playing a board game that involves rolling a pair of dice. The red die shows how many spaces he will move, and the white die shows the category of the question he must answer. How many different outcomes are there?

10. **Writing** Compare Exercises 8 and 9. How are they alike? How are they different?

6-1 Exploring Counting Problems **299**

Answers to Exercises and Problems

1. 10 outcomes

2. 18 outcomes

3. 9 outcomes

4. short, spruce; short, yellow; short, white; short, oatmeal; short, purple; long, spruce; long, yellow; long, white; long, oatmeal; long, purple

5. white corded with built-in answering machine, white corded with speakerphone, white cordless with built-in answering machine, white cordless with speakerphone, gray corded with built-in answering machine, gray corded with speakerphone, gray cordless with built-in answering machine, gray cordless with speakerphone, black corded with built-in answering machine, black corded with speakerphone, black cordless with built-in answering machine, black cordless with speakerphone

6–10. See answers in back of book.

Problem Solving

Three problem-solving strategies have now been introduced to solve counting problems: making a tree diagram, a table, or a systematic list.

Look Back

Student volunteers can provide answers to these questions. A thorough discussion of the advantages and disadvantages of each method will help students to choose the most desirable method to use in problem-solving situations. ···········•

APPLYING

Suggested Assignment
Standard 1–12, 15–32
Extended 1–32

Integrating the Strands
Algebra Exs. 23–30
Geometry Exs. 16–19, 21, 22
Statistics and Probability Exs. 1–20, 31, 32
Logic and Language Exs. 6, 10, 13, 20

Problem Solving

In Ex. 6, students need to write a problem that can be solved by using the given tree diagram. When they try to solve their problems, some students may discover that the tree diagram does not work. They then have to go back and make adjustments to their original problems. The thinking involved in doing Ex. 6 will help students to develop their problem-solving skills.

Using Technology

The *Probability Constructor* software can be used to create probability tree diagrams that represent all possible outcomes for an event.

299

Teaching Tip

If two or more students use different methods to work Exs. 7–9 and 11–15, ask them to explain why they used the method they did. This will help all students to compare and contrast methods and to see which ones work best for different problem situations.

Students Acquiring English

In Ex. 15, you may need to clarify these expressions for students acquiring English: *narrowed your search* and *optional features.* Discuss these terms using an automobile advertisement from a newspaper or magazine.

Research

For Ex. 15, you might wish to have some students research information about the cost of a car, the number of different options for the model they want, and the total number of possible combinations of options. Research can be conducted at a local automobile dealership. The results can be shared with the class.

Assessment: Standard

For Ex. 15, students should be able to justify each part using an organized list or a tree diagram.

Answers to
Exercises and Problems

11. 16 ways   **12.** 15 choices

13. a. four videos: drama, first comedy, second comedy, musical
three videos: drama, first comedy, second comedy; drama, first comedy, musical; drama, second comedy, musical; first comedy, second comedy, musical
two videos: drama, first comedy; drama, second comedy; drama, musical; first comedy, second comedy; first comedy, musical; second comedy, musical
one video: drama; first comedy; second comedy; musical

300

---

11. Manuel Arias has four men and four women in his ballet. In how many ways can he assign dance partners that include one man and one woman?

12. A yogurt shop offers raisins, granola, coconut, and walnuts as toppings. A customer may choose one or more toppings. How many choices are there?

13. Amanda rented four videos for the weekend: one drama, two comedies, and one musical. She may watch one, two, three, or all four videos.

  a. Make a diagram to show all of Amanda's choices.

  b. **Writing** Write a story explaining why Amanda might not have watched all four videos and how she decided which videos to watch.

14. Five actresses try out for a play.

  a. In how many ways can the five actresses be cast for these five roles: detective, business executive, salesperson, house cleaner, journalist?

  b. In how many ways can the five actresses be cast if the part of the salesperson is cut?

  c. What if two parts are cut, the salesperson and the journalist?

  d. Describe any patterns you see in your answers to parts (a)–(c).

15. **Consumerism** Suppose you have narrowed your search for a car to five car models, two colors, and the four optional features shown. You are considering all five models and both colors. How many different cars are there to choose from in each case?

  a. You do not want any of the optional features.

  b. You want all four optional features.

  c. You can afford only one of the optional features.

  d. You can afford any two of the optional features.

  e. You can afford any number of the optional features, but you are not sure you want them all.

BY THE WAY...

Henry Ford commented about the color choices for the Model T Ford in these words, "Any color — so long as it's black."

Unit 6 Counting Strategies, Probability, Binomials

---

b. Answers may vary. An example is given. On Friday evening, Amanda had no time, so she did not watch any videos. On Saturday, it was gloomy and raining, so Amanda watched both comedies after she finished her chores. On Sunday, Amanda had to finish a book report on the book on which the drama was based, so she watched the drama to refresh her memory.

14. a. 120 ways
  b. 120 ways
  c. 60 ways
  d. In part (a), the total is $5 \cdot 4 \cdot 3 \cdot 2 \cdot 1$; in part (b), the total is $5 \cdot 4 \cdot 3 \cdot 2$; in part (c), the total is $5 \cdot 4 \cdot 3$.

15. a. 10 cars
  b. 10 cars
  c. 40 cars
  d. 60 cars

  e. If you choose any number of the optional features from 0 to 4, the total number of choices is 160.

16. 10 segments
17. 10 triangles
18. 5 quadrilaterals
19. 20 rays
20. Answers may vary.
21. False.
22. True.

300

Use the coordinate plane.

16. How many segments can be drawn between any two of the five points?

17. How many triangles can be drawn connecting any three of the five points?

18. How many quadrilaterals can be drawn connecting any four of the five points?

19. How many rays can be drawn between any two of the five points?

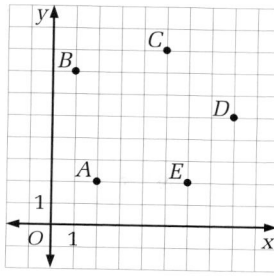

Ongoing **ASSESSMENT**

20. **Writing** Write and solve a counting problem that you consider challenging. Explain your method for solving it.

Review **PREVIEW**

Tell whether each statement is *True* or *False*. *(Section 5-6)*

21. The diagonals of a parallelogram are perpendicular and have the same midpoint.

22. The diagonals of a square are equal in measure, have the same midpoint, and are perpendicular.

Simplify. Write each answer with positive exponents. *(Section 2-6)*

23. $(10a^5)(5b^{-2})$

24. $25x^4y^{-3}$

25. $(18m^0)(2n^{-6})$

26. One form of radioactive iodine has a half-life of about 8 days. Make a table to find how long it will be before 600 g of this iodine decays to only 100 g. *(Section 2-7)*

Evaluate each expression for the given values. *(Toolbox Skill 9)*

27. $x(x-1)(x-2)$; $x = 3$

28. $ab(b-7)$; $a = -6$, $b = 2$

29. $\frac{4z}{z-1}$; $z = -3$

30. $\frac{m(m-1)}{m-p}$; $m = -1$, $p = 7$

 Working on the Unit Project

31. List all the different groups of five subjects that you can select from the list on page 294 that include music and art.

32. One part of your survey should consist of questions like this:

> Which subject do you prefer in each pair? Circle one.
>
> **2. a.** Music   **b.** Art

When students have completed this part of the survey, they should have compared each of the five selected subjects with every one of the others. How many questions like this will you need to include in your survey? How did you determine your answer?

6-1 Exploring Counting Problems

301

Answers to Exercises and Problems

23. $\frac{50a^5}{b^2}$

24. $\frac{25x^4}{y^3}$

25. $\frac{36}{n^6}$

26.

Number of half-lives	Amount present (g)
0	600
1	300
2	150
3	75

Since the half-life is 8 days, there will be 100 g left after 16 days and before 24 days.

27. 6

28. 60

29. 3

30. −0.25

31. There are 56 groups of five subjects that include music and art.

32. 20; Each of the five subjects must be compared to each of the four remaining subjects. So for each subject, there are four possibilities, for a total of $5 \cdot 4 = 20$ questions.

PLANNING

Objectives and Strands
See pages 292A and 292B.

Spiral Learning
See page 292B.

Materials List
➤ Four index cards per group

Recommended Pacing
Section 6-2 is a two-day lesson.

Day 1

Pages 302–304: Exploration through paragraph at top of page 304, *Exercises 1–16*

Day 2

Pages 304–306: Permutations through Look Back, *Exercises 17–44*

Extra Practice
See pages 623–624.

Warm-Up Exercises
Warm-Up Transparency 6-2

Support Materials
➤ Practice 42
➤ Enrichment 37 in the Activity Bank
➤ Study Guide 6-1
➤ Problem Set 11
➤ Additional Exploration 7
➤ Quiz 6-2
➤ Alternative Assessment 2

Section 6-2

Counting and Permutations

REARRANGED GRANDER ERA

Focus
Use the multiplication counting principle to find a number of possible arrangements of items.

EXPLORATION

Can you find all possible arrangements of a group of letters?

• **Materials: four index cards**

• **Work with another student.**

① Print one letter of the word HEAR on each of the index cards. Find all possible four-letter arrangements. The arrangements do not have to form real words. Record your strategies and the arrangements you find.

② Compare your list of letter arrangements with the list from another group. Compare strategies. Was your list complete? If not, how might you improve your strategy?

③ Make a tree diagram to show all possible four-letter arrangements.

④ In your tree diagram, how many choices are there for the first letter of an arrangement? How many choices for the second letter? for the third? for the fourth? Make a conjecture about how your answers relate to the total number of arrangements.

⑤ Suppose a fifth letter is added, making the word HEART. Discuss with your partner how you can modify your tree diagram to find all the five-letter arrangements. How many arrangements are there now?

⑥ Suppose one more letter is added, making the word HEARTS. How many arrangements are there?

Unit 6 Counting Strategies, Probability, Binomials

302

Answers to Exploration

1. Strategies may vary. An example is given. Use a table or tree diagram.
HEAR, HERA, HAER, HARE, HREA, HRAE, EHAR, EHRA, EAHR, EARH, ERHA, ERAH, AHER, AHRE, AEHR, AERH, ARHE, AREH, RHEA, RHAE, REHA, REAH, RAHE, RAEH

2. Answers may vary. An example is given. If there are the same number of letter arrangements beginning with each of the four letters, it is reasonable to assume that the list was complete; some may have been overlooked.

3.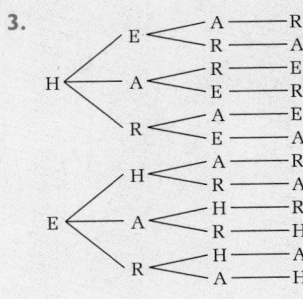

In the Exploration, you may have noticed that the number of possible letter arrangements was the product of the number of choices you had at each stage of the tree diagram.

MULTIPLICATION COUNTING PRINCIPLE

The number of possible outcomes for an event is found by multiplying the number of choices at each stage of the event.

Sample 1

How many different four-letter arrangements can be made from the letters in the word GRATES? Assume that a letter cannot be used more than once.

Sample Response

Use the multiplication counting principle.

> There are 6 choices for the first letter.

> There are 4 choices left for the third letter.

$$6 \cdot 5 \cdot 4 \cdot 3 = 360$$

> There are 5 choices left for the second letter.

> There are 3 choices left for the fourth letter.

There are 360 different four-letter arrangements that can be made.

Talk it Over

1. a. How many different two-letter arrangements can be made from the letters in the word GRATES? Assume that a letter cannot be used more than once.

   b. List one or more of these two-letter arrangements that form an English word. Can you form words from another language besides English with two letters in the word GRATES? If so, what words?

2. a. How many different three-letter arrangements can be made from the letters in the word GRATES? Assume that a letter cannot be used more than once.

   b. List one or more of these three-letter arrangements that form an English word. Can you form words from another language besides English with three letters in the word GRATES? If so, what words?

6-2 Counting and Permutations

303

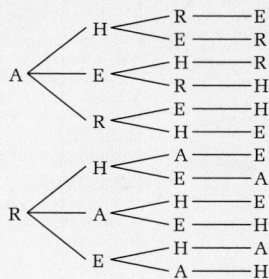

Teaching Tip

The multiplication counting principle can be explained by using an example involving pigeons. If you have six pigeons and six pigeonholes, the pigeons can be placed in the holes as follows. For the first hole, any one of the 6 pigeons can be placed in it. There are now 5 pigeons left, so any one of these 5 can be placed in the second hole. Thus, there are 6 · 5 or 30 ways to fill the first two pigeonholes. The third hole can be filled in 4 ways, the fourth hole in 3 ways, the fifth hole in 2 ways, and the sixth hole in 1 way. Therefore, there are 6! possible ways to place the pigeons in their holes.

Communication: Reading

The development of the formula for finding the number of permutations of n items arranged r at a time builds upon the activities of the Exploration and Sample 1. In the expression for finding $_6P_4$ as $\frac{6!}{(6-4)!}$, have students read the equation from right to left as well as from left to right. Some students may find it easier to accept the middle portion containing the facts 2 · 1 in both the numerator and denominator by using a right-to-left approach.

Reasoning

It is always useful to have a formula in mathematics to do a calculation, and students should remember the formula $_nP_r = \frac{n!}{(n-r)!}$. However, if they can recall the reasoning process that led to the formula, answers to permutation problems can be found without using the formula. For example, $_{10}P_3 = 10 \cdot 9 \cdot 8 = 720$ by reasoning, and $_{10}P_3 = \frac{10!}{(10-4)!} = 720$ by formula.

The symbol **!** is called **factorial** and is used in mathematics in a specific way.

You read the symbol 6! as "six factorial." Here is what it means:

$$6! = 6 \cdot 5 \cdot 4 \cdot 3 \cdot 2 \cdot 1$$

Start with the positive integer. → Multiply by each next-smaller integer.

By definition, 0! = 1.

▶ Now you are ready for:
Exs. 1–16 on pp. 306–308

Permutations

The arrangement of any number of items in a definite order is called a **permutation**. The symbol for the number of different arrangements when n items are arranged r at a time is $_nP_r$.

In the Exploration with HEARTS, 6 letters are arranged 6 at a time. You can use the multiplication counting principle to find the number of possible arrangements.

$$_6P_6 = 6 \cdot 5 \cdot 4 \cdot 3 \cdot 2 \cdot 1 = 720$$

6 items ⌐ ⌐ arranged 6 at a time

In Sample 1, 6 letters are arranged 4 at a time.

$$_6P_4 = \underline{6} \cdot \underline{5} \cdot \underline{4} \cdot \underline{3}$$

└── the number of factors

You can also write this using factorials.

$$_6P_4 = 6 \cdot 5 \cdot 4 \cdot 3 = \frac{6 \cdot 5 \cdot 4 \cdot 3 \cdot 2 \cdot 1}{2 \cdot 1} = \frac{6!}{2!} = \frac{6!}{(6-4)!}$$

This is the difference between the total number of items and the number of items being arranged.

PERMUTATIONS OF n ITEMS ARRANGED r AT A TIME

The number of permutations of n items arranged r at a time ($r < n$) is given by this formula.

$$_nP_r = \underbrace{n(n-1)(n-2) \cdots}_{r \text{ factors}} = \frac{n!}{(n-r)!}$$

Example

$$_{10}P_3 = 10 \cdot 9 \cdot 8 = \frac{10!}{(10-3)!} = 720$$

Talk it Over

3. What does the symbol $_8P_5$ mean?

TECHNOLOGY NOTE

See whether your calculator has a factorial key or menu item. Find $(8 - 5)!$. See whether your calculator has a permutation key or menu item. Find $_8P_5$. ←

Talk it Over

3. What does the symbol $_8P_5$ mean?

4. How do you simplify $(8 - 5)!$?

5. Explain how to find the number of permutations of 8 items arranged 5 at a time.

6. Find the number of three-letter arrangements of the letters in the word ITCH using the multiplication counting principle. Then find the number of three-letter arrangements using the formula $_nP_r = \dfrac{n!}{(n - r)!}$. Compare the methods.

Sample 2

Ching's crossword puzzle clue is "anagram of the word FREE." He knows that an anagram of a word is found by rearranging the letters of the word. (SLIP is an anagram of LIPS.) How many arrangements are there of the letters in the word FREE?

Sample Response

Problem Solving Strategy: Make a systematic list.

Ching notices that FREE looks the same if he interchanges the E's. If he uses the formula $_4P_4$, he will find the number of possible arrangements of the letters of FREE, but some arrangements will be the same. Ching decides to make a systematic list to count the different arrangements.

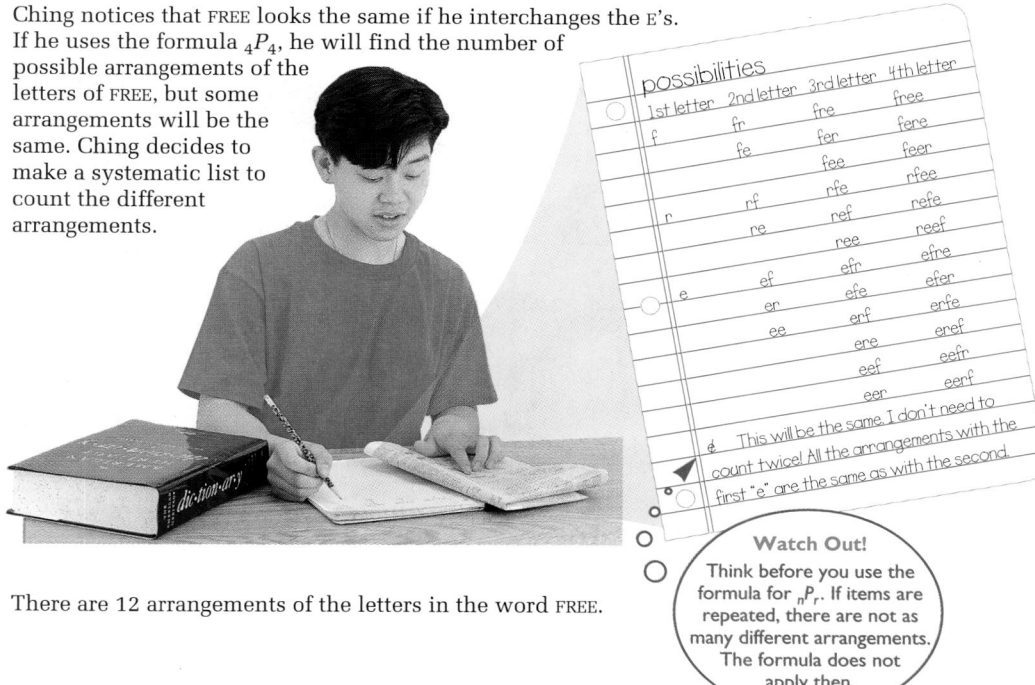

possibilities

1st letter	2nd letter	3rd letter	4th letter
f	fr	fre	free
	fe	fer	fere
		fee	feer
r	rf	rfe	rfee
	re	ref	refe
		ree	reef
e	ef	efr	efre
	er	efe	efer
	ee	erf	erfe
		ere	eref
		eef	eefr
		eer	eerf

¢ This will be the same. I don't need to count twice! All the arrangements with the first "e" are the same as with the second.

There are 12 arrangements of the letters in the word FREE.

Watch Out!
Think before you use the formula for $_nP_r$. If items are repeated, there are not as many different arrangements. The formula does not apply then.

6-2 Counting and Permutations

305

Talk it Over

Questions 3–5 check students' understanding of permutation and factorial notation and how to find the number of permutations of n items arranged r at a time. In question 6, students see that the methods are equivalent since they produce the same result.

Using Technology

The TI-81, TI-82, and TI-83 all have factorial as a menu item. They also have $_nP_r$. On the TI-81, press MATH 5 to access factorial. You can find 6!, for example, by typing 6 MATH 5 ENTER. On the TI-82 or TI-83, factorial is accessed by pressing the MATH key and choosing ! from the PRB menu. Thus, to find 6!, you would press 6 MATH ◄ 4 ENTER. On the TI-81, TI-82, and TI-83, you access $_nP_r$ by pressing MATH and selecting item 2 from the PRB menu. Thus, to find $_8P_5$, press 8 MATH ◄ 2, followed by 5 ENTER. The calculator will immediately display the result, 6720.

Additional Sample

S2 How many arrangements would Lena find for the letters in the word TOOT?
Make a systematic list.
TOOT TOTO TTOO
OTTO OTOT OOTT
Lena would find 6 arrangements.

305

Answers to Talk it Over

3. the number of arrangements when 8 items are arranged 5 at a time

4. $(8 - 5)! = 3! = 6$

5. $_8P_5 = \dfrac{8!}{(8 - 5)!} = \dfrac{8!}{3!} = 8 \cdot 7 \cdot 6 \cdot 5 \cdot 4 = 6720$

6. There are four choices for the first letter, three for the second, and two for the third. By the multiplication counting principle, the number of arrangements is $4 \cdot 3 \cdot 2 = 24$. Using the permutations formula,
$_4P_3 = \dfrac{4!}{(4 - 3)!} = \dfrac{4!}{1!} = 4 \cdot 3 \cdot 2 \cdot 1 = 24$. Both methods produce the same result.

Problem Solving

Making a systematic list is helpful when the list is not too long, such as in Sample 2. However, if Ching had to make a list to find the number of arrangements for the letters in the word APPLE (there are 60), it would take a long time and the list might not be complete. Another method for finding the arrangements when some items are repeated is to use the formula $\frac{n!}{(r_1! \cdot r_2! \cdot r_3! \cdot \ldots)}$, where n is the total number of items and each r represents the number of times each item repeats. For example, the word APPLE has five letters: A occurs once, P occurs twice, L occurs once, and E occurs once. Using the formula gives $\frac{5!}{(1! \cdot 2! \cdot 1! \cdot 1!)} = \frac{120}{2} = 60$. You might want to consider some other words in which letters are repeated, for example, *bookmark*, *football*, and *Mississippi*.

APPLYING

Suggested Assignment

Day 1

Standard 1–10, 13, 14, 16

Extended 1–16

Day 2

Standard 17–28, 31–44

Extended 17–29, 31–44

Integrating the Strands

Algebra Exs. 33–35

Statistics and Probability Exs. 1–32, 36–44

Logic and Language Exs. 6, 11, 13–16, 30, 31

Interdisciplinary Problems

Counting problems and permutations can arise in many areas of life. Exs. 2–6, 12–15, 29, and 40–44 involve business, sports, graphic design, license plates, language arts, games, and surveys.

Now you are ready for:
Exs. 17–44 on pp. 308–309

Look Back

For what situations can you use the multiplication counting principle? How are permutations a special case of the multiplication counting principle?

6-2 Exercises and Problems

1. **Reading** How do you read 9! ? What product does it represent?

2. **Business Travel** A company in New York City keeps travel profiles for its employees. A profile includes the preferred airport of departure, the seating class, and the seating preference.

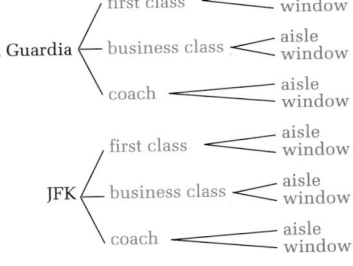

a. How many different travel profiles does the tree diagram represent?

b. How could you use the multiplication counting principle instead of this tree diagram to find the number of different travel profiles possible?

3. There are eight people hiking together. They walk single file on a narrow section of the trail. How many ways can they be lined up on the trail?

4. **Art** Robin is designing a poster for an exhibit of Egyptian art. She wants the border to be a repeated pattern of the four hieroglyphs shown. How many different ways can she arrange the four hieroglyphs in a row?

mouth　folded cloth　owl　hand

BY THE WAY...

Egyptian hieroglyphs are pictures, but each one generally represents a letter or a sound. A hieroglyph means what it pictures when it has a *determinative stroke*.

5. a. Suppose you add an "O" to the letters represented by the hieroglyphs. How many different five-letter arrangements can you make?

b. Suppose you add an "O" and an "E" to the letters represented by the hieroglyphs. How many different six-letter arrangements can you make?

c. If possible, list one or more words in English or another language that can be formed by the letters in part (a). Do the same for part (b).

Unit 6 Counting Strategies, Probability, Binomials

Answers to Look Back

The multiplication counting principle is used to count outcomes of a sequence of choices from a number of possibilities. In permutations, the order of the choices is significant and there is one less item to choose from at each stage.

Answers to Exercises and Problems

1. 9 factorial; $9 \cdot 8 \cdot 7 \cdot 6 \cdot 5 \cdot 4 \cdot 3 \cdot 2 \cdot 1 = 362{,}880$

2. a. 12 profiles

b. Since there are 2 choices for the preferred airport, 3 for the seating class, and 2 for the seating preference, the number of different travel profiles is $2 \cdot 3 \cdot 2 = 12$.

3. 40,320 ways

4. 24 ways

5. a. 120 arrangements

b. 720 arrangements

c. Answers may vary. Examples are given. molds; models, seldom

6. a. 362,880 ways

b. Yes, if the pitcher is always introduced last, there are only 8

6. a. In how many different ways can the nine starting players on a baseball team be introduced?

b. **Writing** Does the number change if the pitcher is always last? Explain.

Find each value.

7. 2! **8.** 0! **9.** 7! **10.** 1!

11. **Writing** Would you prefer to *make an organized list, make a tree diagram,* or *use the multiplication counting principle* to find the number of possible four-letter arrangements of the letters in the word HEARTS? Explain your preference.

12. License Plates In California standard license plates have this form.

any digit from 1 to 9 any three letters except "O" any three digits from 0 to 9

a. How many different license plates can be created under this system, without letters or digits repeated? with letters or digits repeated?

b. Why do you think some possible plates are not printed?

c. **Research** Can you have personalized plates in your state? If so, what restrictions are there on them?

---

connection to **LANGUAGE ARTS**

13. a. Use the sentence MY SHOELACE IS UNTIED. How many arrangements of all the words are possible?

b. Assume you can use a period or a question mark as punctuation. Which arrangements make meaningful sentences?

14. a. How many five-word arrangements can you make using these words: SAID, HERE, WAIT, MIMI, NELSON?

b. Use only commas, a period, and quotation marks as punctuation. Write at least five meaningful sentences using all the words in part (a).

15. a. **Open-ended** Write a three-word sentence that has an adjective, a noun, and a verb. How many arrangements of all the words are possible?

b. Which arrangements make meaningful sentences?

c. Add two words to your sentence in part (a). One word should be an adverb and the other an adjective. How many arrangements of all the words are now possible?

d. Write as many meaningful sentences as you can using all the words in part (c).

Communication: Writing

Ex. 11 gives students an opportunity to think about and compare the three ways of finding arrangements. As they explain their preferences, students can gain deeper insight into each method and thus be better prepared to apply the methods to solve problems.

Assessment: Standard

For Ex. 11, students should be able to show that each method produces equivalent results and then state their preference.

14. b. Twelve meaningful sentences are given.
Mimi Nelson said, "Wait here."
"Wait here," Mimi Nelson said.
Nelson said, "Wait here, Mimi."
Mimi said, "Wait here, Nelson."
"Wait here, Mimi," Nelson said.
"Wait here, Nelson," Mimi said.
"Wait here, Nelson," said Mimi.
"Wait here, Mimi," said Nelson.
"Nelson," said Mimi, "Wait here."
"Mimi," said Nelson, "Wait here."
"Nelson," Mimi said, "Wait here."
"Mimi," Nelson said, "Wait here."

15. Answers may vary. Examples are given.

a. Newborn babies cry. 6 arrangements

b. Answers may vary according to the sentence. For the given example, a second meaningful sentence is "Cry, newborn babies!"

c. Hungry newborn babies cry frequently. 120 arrangements

d. Answers may vary according to the sentence. For the given example, the given sentence, "Frequently hungry newborn babies cry," and "Hungry newborn babies frequently cry" are two other meaningful sentences.

---

positions to be considered. Then there are 40,320 different ways of introducing the team.

7. 2

8. 1

9. 5040

10. 1

11. Answers may vary. An example is given. I prefer using the multiplication

counting principle because it is easier than making a tree diagram or an organized list where some arrangements may be overlooked.

12. a. 62,596,800; 140,625,000

b. Answers may vary. An example is given. Some letters and digits might be easily confused (zero

and Q, for example). Also, some letters may form phrases considered offensive.

c. Answers may vary.

13. a. 24 arrangements

b. "My shoelace is untied." "Is my shoelace untied?" "Untied, is my shoelace."

14. a. 120 arrangements

16. **a.** Find how many different five-letter arrangements can be made from the letters in the word MOUSE.

    b. Find how many different five-letter arrangements can be made from the letters in the word MOOSE.

    c. **Writing** Compare the results of parts (a) and (b). How are they different?

Find each value.

17. $\dfrac{8!}{3!}$ **18.** $\dfrac{7!}{(7-3)!}$ **19.** $_{10}P_4$ **20.** $_{12}P_3$

How many different permutations are there of all the letters in each word?

21. MAINE

French settlers may have named this state after the French province *Mayne* or used their word for *mainland*.

22. WYOMING

This state got its name from the Native American term *mecheweaming*, which is a term for "at the big flats."

23. IOWA

This state name comes from *ayuxwa*, which is a Native American tribal name. It means "one who puts to sleep."

For Exercises 24–27, find each number of permutations.

24. 8 books, arranged 2 at a time

25. 4 desserts, arranged in a row on a display

26. 7 bushes, arranged 5 in a row along the side of a house

27. a list of 6 students' last names, when no names are repeated

28. There are eight people in a race. First, second, and third places will be awarded. How many different ways could the awards be won?

29. **Games** Ji Sun is playing a word game and has the tiles C, T, A, and C.

    a. List the three-letter permutations.   **b.** List the two-letter permutations.

    c. Using the multiplication counting principle, check that you found all the permutations in parts (a) and (b).

    d. How could Ji Sun build on the tiles shown to form another word?

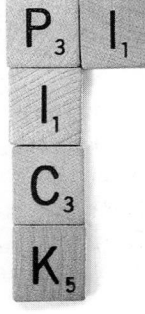

30. **Group Activity** Work with another student.

    a. Agree with your partner on the choice of three colors. One of you writes the colors down in a row and hides them with your hand.

    b. One partner guesses the colors in order, and the other tells how many of the guesses are correct. Keep guessing until the correct order is found.

    c. Discuss strategies for finding the correct order with the fewest guesses.

    d. Repeat the procedure with four colors. Discuss the mathematical reasons why this may take more guesses than using three colors.

Answers to Exercises and Problems

16. a. 120 arrangements

    b. 60 arrangements

    c. For five-letter arrangements of a five-letter word, when no letters are repeated, there are twice as many arrangements as when one letter repeats.

17. 6720   **18.** 210

19. 5040   **20.** 1320

21. 120   **22.** 5040

23. 24   **24.** 56

25. 24   **26.** 2520

27. 720   **28.** 336

29. a. cta, cat, act, atc, tca, tac, cct, cca, ctc, cac, tcc, acc

    b. ct, ca, cc, tc, ta, ac, at

    c. According to the multiplication counting principle, there are 24 three-letter permutations and 12 two-letter permutations. But since two letters are the same,

there are only 12 distinct three-letter permutations, and there are only 7 distinct two-letter combinations.

    d. Answers may vary. An example is given. Ji Sun could make the word "PICA" by placing the C and A tiles to the right of the P and I tiles.

30. a, b. Answers may vary.

    c. It may help to begin with a systematic list of the possible orders and mark off guesses to cover all possibilities and avoid repeating incorrect guesses.

    d. There are four times as many possible arrangements.

Ongoing ASSESSMENT

31. **Open-ended** Write two words with six letters each. One word should not have any letters repeated. The other should have a single letter repeated. Find how many permutations there are of all the letters in each word. Are the numbers of permutations the same? Why or why not?

Review PREVIEW

32. Lani, Eve, Derek, and Peter are four models posing for a photograph. One model is standing on each of four steps. List all the possible ways the models can be arranged on the four steps. *(Section 6-1)*

Factor. *(Section 4-4)*

33. $2x^2 - x - 6$

34. $9x^2 - 25$

35. $25x^2 + 20x + 4$

Use a number anywhere on the scale to estimate the probability of each event. *(Toolbox Skill 6)*

36. The sun will not rise next week.

37. You will eat cereal some day next week.

38. You will find a penny on the ground this month.

39. It will snow in your city or town next month.

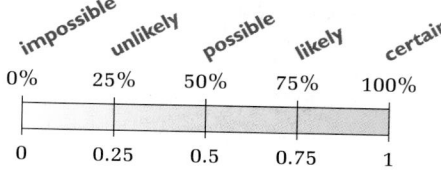

Working on the Unit Project

40. Look back at your answer to Exercise 32 in Section 6-1. In how many different ways can you arrange the questions on the part of your survey in which students compare the five selected subjects with one another?

41. Your survey should consist of one question asking students whether their birthday is in the first or second half of the year, along with the questions mentioned in Exercise 40.

   a. How many questions will your survey have in all?

   b. In how many different ways can you arrange the questions on your survey if the birthday question is the first question?

42. Write your survey. Put the birthday question first.

43. Look at these possible student answers for your survey:

   Student 1: 1. a, 2. a, 3. b …

   Student 2: 1. a, 2. b, 3. a …

   How many possible answer lists are there?

44. Distribute your survey.

> **INTEREST SURVEY**
> 1. In which half of the year is your birthday? Circle one.
>   a. January 1—June 30
>   b. July 1—December 31
> Which subject do you prefer in each pair? Circle one.
> 2. a. Music   b. Art
> 3. a. Music   b. Science

Answers to Exercises and Problems

31. If there are no letters repeated, there are 720 permutations. If one letter is repeated, there are 360 permutations since half of these 720 permutations will be the same.

32. Lani, Evetta, Derek, Peter;
Lani, Evetta, Peter, Derek;
Lani, Derek, Evetta, Peter;
Lani, Derek, Peter, Evetta;
Lani, Peter, Derek, Evetta;

Lani, Peter, Evetta, Derek;
Evetta, Lani, Derek, Peter;
Evetta, Lani, Peter, Derek;
Evetta, Derek, Lani, Peter;
Evetta, Derek, Peter, Lani;
Evetta, Peter, Derek, Lani;
Evetta, Peter, Lani, Derek;
Derek, Evetta, Lani, Peter;
Derek, Evetta, Peter, Lani;
Derek, Lani, Evetta, Peter;
Derek, Lani, Peter, Evetta;
Derek, Peter, Evetta, Lani;

Derek, Peter, Lani, Evetta;
Peter, Derek, Evetta, Lani;
Peter, Derek, Lani, Evetta;
Peter, Evetta, Derek, Lani;
Peter, Evetta, Lani, Derek;
Peter, Lani, Derek, Evetta;
Peter, Lani, Evetta, Derek

33. $(2x + 3)(x - 2)$

34. $(3x - 5)(3x + 5)$

35. $(5x + 2)^2$

Working on the Unit Project

As students work in their project groups of four, they can share the task of writing the survey questions for Ex. 42. For Ex. 44, one individual in each group can be responsible for distributing the survey.

Practice 42 For use with Section 6-2

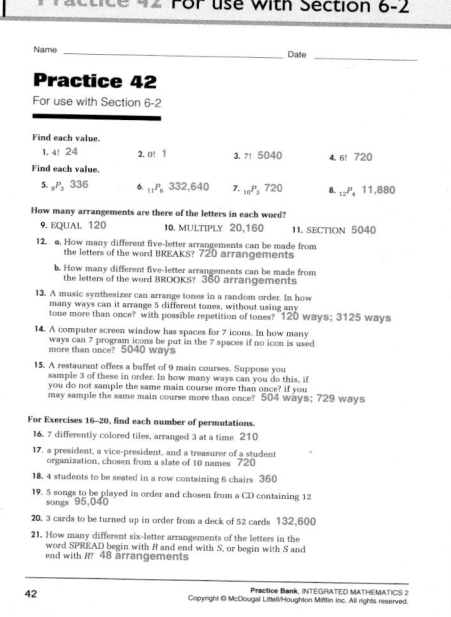

36–39. Answers may vary. Examples are given.

36. 0%; The sun rises every day.

37. 100%; I usually have cereal for breakfast.

38. 10%; Most of the ground is snow-covered now.

39. 50%; In New England, it is possible to have snow in December.

40. $20! \approx 2.4 \times 10^{18}$ ways

41. a. 21 questions

   b. $20! \approx 2.4 \times 10^{18}$ ways

42. Check students' surveys.

43. $2^{21} = 2{,}097{,}152$ lists

44. Check distributions of surveys.

Materials List
➤ Removable notes
➤ Spinner
➤ Paper clip

Recommended Pacing
Section 6-3 is a two-day lesson.

Day 1

Pages 310–312: Opening paragraph through Sample 2, *Exercises 1–21*

Day 2

Pages 313–315: Counting Techniques and Probability through Look Back, *Exercises 22–52*

Toolbox References
➤ **Toolbox Skill 7:** Finding Theoretical Probability
➤ **Toolbox Skill 8:** Finding Geometric Probability

Extra Practice
See pages 623–624.

Warm-Up Exercises
Warm-Up Transparency 6-3

Support Materials
➤ Practice 43
➤ Enrichment 38 in the Activity Bank
➤ Study Guide 6-3
➤ Problem Set 11
○ Overhead Visual 1
➤ McDougal Littell Mathpack software: *Probability Constructor*
➤ Probability Constructor Activity Book: Activity 20
➤ Quiz 6-3
➤ Alternative Assessment 3

Section 6-3 Probability and Odds

Focus
Find the probability of an event and of mutually exclusive events. Relate probability to odds.

Chances Are

Playing cards have been used in many countries around the world for hundreds of years. The French introduced the four *suits* in the 1500s.

A standard deck of playing cards consists of 52 cards, with 13 cards in each of four suits: clubs, spades, diamonds, and hearts. *Face cards* are jacks, queens, and kings.

	A ACE	2 TWO	3 THREE	4 FOUR	5 FIVE	6 SIX	7 SEVEN	8 EIGHT	9 NINE	10 TEN	JACK	QUEEN	KING
Clubs													
Spades													
Diamonds													
Hearts													

Talk it Over

How many of each kind of card are in a standard deck?

1. a 2
2. a red card
3. a red 2
4. a face card

Jeannine picked one card from a standard deck and Chris picked one card from another standard deck. They tried to guess each other's card.

5. Jeannine gave this clue: "My card is a 2 and it is red." What are the possible cards that Jeannine could have?

6. Chris gave this clue: "My card is a 2 or it is red." How is his clue different from Jeannine's? Will it be easier or harder to guess his card? Why?

7. Can you pick one card that is an ace and a jack from a standard deck? Why or why not?

Unit 6 Counting Strategies, Probability, Binomials

Answers to Talk it Over

1. 4
2. 26
3. 2
4. 12
5. 2 of diamonds, 2 of hearts

6. Jeannine's clue indicates her card is both a 2 and red; Chris's indicates his is one or the other. His will be harder to guess because his clue describes many more cards. Also, it is not clear if he means his card is not both.

7. No; each card has only one label.

Sample 1

In a card game, you are dealing the first card from a well-mixed standard deck. Find the probability of each event.

a. dealing an ace or a jack   b. dealing a face card or a spade

Sample Response

Student Resources Toolbox
p. 638 *Probability*

There are 52 possible outcomes.

a. There are 8 favorable outcomes: 4 aces and 4 jacks.

> Read as "the probability of an ace or a jack."

$P(\text{ace or jack}) = \frac{8}{52} \approx 0.15$

> You can also write this as 15%.

b. There are 22 favorable outcomes:
12 face cards and 10 other spades.

Clubs

Spades

Diamonds

> You count the jack, queen, and king of spades only once each.

Hearts

$P(\text{face card or spade}) = \frac{22}{52} \approx 0.42$

In Sample 1(a) you cannot deal one card that is both an ace and a jack. These two events cannot happen at the same time. That makes the events **mutually exclusive**. Notice this relationship:

$$P(\text{ace or jack}) = \frac{4}{52} + \frac{4}{52} = \frac{8}{52}$$

$P(\text{ace})$ ⤴   ⤴ $P(\text{jack})$

PROBABILITY OF MUTUALLY EXCLUSIVE EVENTS

When two events are mutually exclusive, you can add to find the probability that either one occurs.

For mutually exclusive events A and B:

$$P(A \text{ or } B) = P(A) + P(B)$$

6-3 Probability and Odds

311

TEACHING

Talk it Over

Questions 1–4 check students' understanding of a standard deck of playing cards. Questions 5–7 involve the selection of cards from a deck and have students explore events related by *and* and *or* in anticipation of a discussion of mutually exclusive events.

Additional Sample

S1 Suppose you select a number cube from a bag without looking. In the bag are three red cubes numbered 1, 2, and 3, six blue cubes numbered 1 through 6, and one green cube with a 1 on it. Find the probability of each event.

a. selecting a red or a green cube **There are 10 possible outcomes. There are 4 favorable outcomes: 3 red cubes and 1 green cube.**
$P(\text{red or green}) = \frac{4}{10} = \frac{2}{5}$ **or 0.4 or 40%**

b. selecting a cube that is blue or has a 1 on it. **There are 10 possible outcomes. There are 8 favorable outcomes: 6 cubes are blue, the green cube is numbered 1, and a red cube has the number 1 on it. (The blue cube with a 1 on it is not counted a second time.)**
$P(\text{blue or 1}) = \frac{8}{10} = \frac{4}{5}$ **or 0.8 or 80%**

Students Acquiring English

You may need to clarify the phrase *mutually exclusive* for students acquiring English. Use actual playing cards to demonstrate the concept.

311

Question 9 prepares students for understanding the concept of complementary events.

Teaching Tip

Remind students that the probability of an event that is certain to occur is 1. The probability of an impossible event occurring is 0. Thus, probabilities are fractions between 0 and 1.

Additional Sample

S2 Suppose you again select number cubes from a bag without looking. In the bag are three red cubes numbered 1, 2, and 3, six blue cubes numbered 1 through 6, and one green cube with a 1 on it. Find P(not a 2).

There are 10 possible outcomes.
Method 1: Count or list the favorable outcomes (not a 2).
red–1, red–3, blue–1, blue–3, blue–4, blue–5, blue–6, green–1
There are 8 favorable outcomes.
P(not a 2) $= \frac{8}{10} = 0.8$
Method 2: Count or list the unfavorable outcomes (a 2).
red–2, blue–2
There are 2 unfavorable outcomes.
P(not a 2) $= 1 - P$(a 2) $=$
$1 - \frac{2}{10} = \frac{10}{10} - \frac{2}{10} = \frac{8}{10} = 0.8$

Using Technology

Activity 20 in the *Probability Constructor Activity Book* can be used to explore the probability of events that are mutually exclusive or complementary.

---

8. Are the events dealing a face card and dealing a spade mutually exclusive? Why or why not?

9. Suppose you are choosing a card from a standard deck.

   a. How many outcomes are there for the event "heart"? for the event "not a heart"?

   b. Are the events "heart" and "not a heart" mutually exclusive? Why or why not?

   c. Find P(heart or not a heart).

Complementary Events

Two events are **complementary events** if they are mutually exclusive and together they include all the possibilities. The events "heart" and "not a heart" are complementary events.

The sum of the probabilities of complementary events is 1.

$$P(\text{event}) = 1 - P(\text{not the event})$$

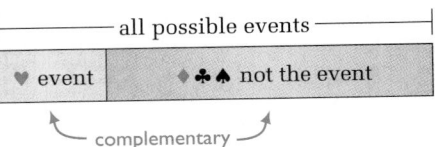

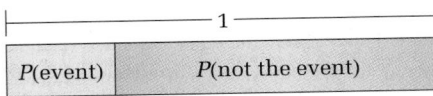

Sample 2

Find P(not a face card) when a card is randomly chosen from a standard deck.

Sample Response

There are 52 possible outcomes.

Method ❶ Count the favorable outcomes (not a face card).
There are 40 cards that are not face cards: 10 clubs, 10 spades, 10 diamonds, and 10 hearts.

Aces are not considered face cards.

P(not a face card) $= \frac{40}{52} \approx 0.77$

Method ❷ Count the unfavorable outcomes (a face card).
There are 12 cards that are face cards: 3 clubs, 3 spades, 3 diamonds, and 3 hearts.

P(not a face card) $= 1 - P$(face card) $= 1 - \frac{12}{52} = \frac{52}{52} - \frac{12}{52} = \frac{40}{52} \approx 0.77$

▶ Now you are ready for:
Exs. 1–21 on pp. 315–316

Unit 6 Counting Strategies, Probability, Binomials

312

Answers to Talk it Over

8. No; there are three cards that are both spades and face cards.

9. a. 13; 39

   b. Yes; a card cannot be a heart and not a heart at the same time.

   c. 1

Counting Techniques and Probability

You can sometimes use the multiplication counting principle and permutations to find the number of possible outcomes when you are finding the probability of an event.

Sample 3

Find the probability that no two people in a group of five people have the same birthday (month and day).

Sample Response

Assume that there are 365 birthdays in a year to choose from.

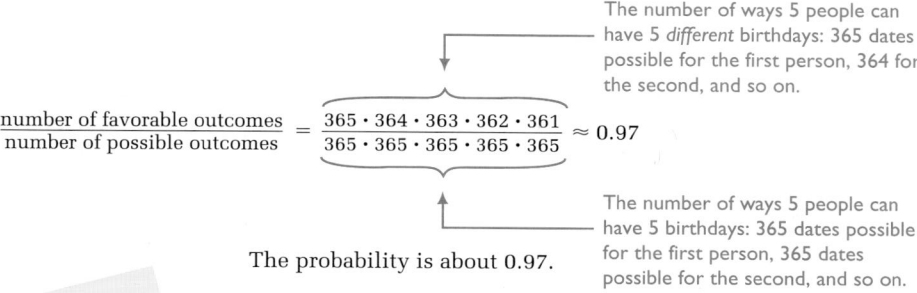

The number of ways 5 people can have 5 *different* birthdays: 365 dates possible for the first person, 364 for the second, and so on.

$$\frac{\text{number of favorable outcomes}}{\text{number of possible outcomes}} = \frac{365 \cdot 364 \cdot 363 \cdot 362 \cdot 361}{365 \cdot 365 \cdot 365 \cdot 365 \cdot 365} \approx 0.97$$

The number of ways 5 people can have 5 birthdays: 365 dates possible for the first person, 365 dates possible for the second, and so on.

The probability is about 0.97.

Talk it Over

10. The complement of "no two people" is "at least two people." Use this fact and the result of Sample 3 to find the probability that at least two people in a group of five people have the same birthday.

11. Explain how to find the probability that at least two people in a group of six people have the same birthday.

12. a. How likely do you think it is that at least two people in your class have the same birthday?

    b. Write the month and date of your birthday, not the year, on a removable note. At the front of the classroom make a histogram (by month) with the notes for the entire class. Are at least two birthdays the same?

April 1st

June 26th

September 8th

possible outcomes	
favorable outcomes	unfavorable outcomes

Odds

Odds are another way of stating the likelihood of an event. Suppose the *odds against* winning a contest are 5:2 (read "five to two"). This means that for every 5 chances of losing, there are 2 chances of winning.

LIKELIHOOD OF AN EVENT

Suppose each outcome of an event is equally likely.

Probability of the event = $\dfrac{\text{number of favorable outcomes}}{\text{number of possible outcomes}}$

Odds in favor of the event = $\dfrac{\text{number of favorable outcomes}}{\text{number of unfavorable outcomes}}$

Odds against the event = $\dfrac{\text{number of unfavorable outcomes}}{\text{number of favorable outcomes}}$

Example Suppose 2 out of 7 outcomes are **favorable**.

probability = $\frac{2}{7} \approx 0.29$

odds in favor = $\frac{2}{5}$, or 2:5

odds against = $\frac{5}{2}$, or 5:2

In this book, assume that each outcome is equally likely when you toss a coin, roll a die, or spin a spinner with equal sections.

Sample 4

In some ice skating competitions, the order in which the competitors perform is determined by a random drawing. Suppose a competition involves five skaters with different names.

a. Find the probability that the skaters will perform in alphabetical order.

b. Find the odds in favor of the skaters performing in alphabetical order.

Sample Response

There is only 1 way to arrange 5 skaters in alphabetical order.

a. P(5 skaters perform in alphabetical order) = $\frac{1}{120} \approx 0.01$

The number of arrangements of 5 different skaters is 5!.

b. Odds in favor of performing in alphabetical order = $\frac{1}{119}$, or 1:119.

favorable

unfavorable = possible − favorable = 5! − 1

Answers to Talk it Over

13. 119:1
14. about 99%
15. 6:19; 19:6

Answers to Look Back

The two ratios are reciprocal. If the odds in favor of an event are $\frac{m}{n}$, then the probability of the event is $\frac{m}{m + n}$.

13. For the situation in Sample 4, what are the odds against the five skaters performing in alphabetical order?

14. For the situation in Sample 4, what is the probability that the five skaters will not perform in alphabetical order?

15. Suppose that the probability of an event is 24%. What are the odds in favor of that event? against that event?

Look Back

What is the relationship between the odds in favor of an event and the odds against an event? How can you find the probability of an event if you know the odds in favor of the event?

Now you are ready for:
Exs. 22–52 on pp. 316–318

6-3 Exercises and Problems

1. a. **Reading** What two events in Sample 1 are mutually exclusive?

   b. **Open-ended** Give another example of mutually exclusive events.

2. **Reading** Are complementary events always mutually exclusive?

Suppose you roll a die. Find each probability.

3. $P(6)$

4. $P(\text{prime})$

5. $P(\text{a factor of 6})$

6. $P(6 \text{ or prime})$

7. $P(6 \text{ or a factor of 6})$

8. $P(\text{not a factor of 6})$

9. Which of the events in Exercises 3–5 are mutually exclusive?

10. Which of the events in Exercises 3–8 are complementary?

11. Suppose $P(\text{rain tomorrow}) = 75\%$. Find $P(\text{no rain tomorrow})$.

12. Suppose the probability of not getting the flu if you get a flu shot is 85%. What is the probability of getting the flu if you get a flu shot?

13. A store selects one student at random from the 2000 students at Plainfield High School to win a graphics calculator. The school has 40 students on its mathematics team. What is the probability that no one on the team will win the calculator?

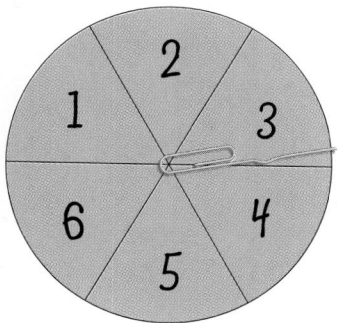

14. a. **Writing** Write and solve a probability problem about this spinner that involves complementary events.

   b. **Using Manipulatives** Make a spinner like the one shown. You can unfold a paper clip to use for a pointer and hold it in place with a pencil. Do an experiment to find the experimental probability for the problem you wrote in part (a).

   c. Compare the probabilities you found in parts (a) and (b). Were they exactly the same? Should they be exactly the same? Why or why not?

Answers to Exercises and Problems

1. a. dealing an ace and dealing a jack

   b. Answers may vary. An example is given. dealing a red card and dealing a spade

2. Yes.

3. about 17%

4. 50%

5. about 67%

6. about 67%

7. about 67%

8. about 33%

9. rolling a 6 and rolling a prime

10. rolling a factor of 6 and rolling a number not a factor of six; rolling 6 or a factor of 6 and rolling a number not a factor of 6

11. 25%

12. 15%

13. 98%

Answers continued on next page.

Talk it Over

Questions 14 and 15 lead students to analyze the situation in Sample 4 in terms of both odds and probability.

Look Back

In answering these questions, students can consolidate their understanding of the concepts of odds and probability. A written summary can be used for a journal entry.

APPLYING

Suggested Assignment

Day 1

Standard 1–13, 15–19

Extended 1–13, 15–21

Day 2

Standard 22–32, 40–52

Extended 22–32, 34–52

Integrating the Strands

Algebra Exs. 42–45

Statistics and Probability Exs. 1–41, 46–52

Logic and Language Exs. 1, 2, 14, 33, 40, 52

Communication: Reading

Exs. 1 and 2 require students to reach conclusions about mutually exclusive events based on what they have read.

Using Manipulatives

You may wish to roll die to illustrate Exs. 3–8.

Communication: Writing

Ex. 14, parts (a) and (c) require students to create and solve a probability problem and then organize and express their thoughts about the different results from the theoretical and experimental probabilities.

Using Technology

The *Probability Constructor* software can be used to simulate the experiment in Ex. 14.

Research

An interesting research project for students would be to find the probability of a large meteor striking Earth. Two important factors to consider are meteor strikes by size and according to time periods. For example, students can research a specific questions such as: What is the probability of a very large meteor striking Earth during the next one thousand years. This question can then be modified by changing the time periods.

Assessment: Standard

For Exs. 15–21, include as part of the assessment the odds for and against each event. Have students relate in writing how to find each of the other two facts when only one of the following is given: odds for an event, odds against an event, probability of an event occurring.

	Area in square kilometers
Earth	510,066,000
Land	148,429,000
Water	361,637,000
Asia	44,485,900
Africa	30,269,680
North America	24,235,280
South America	17,820,770
Antarctica	13,209,000
Europe	10,530,750
Australia	7,682,300
Pacific Ocean	166,241,000
Atlantic Ocean	86,557,000
Indian Ocean	73,427,000
Arctic Ocean	9,485,000

Student Resources Toolbox
p. 639 *Probability*

connection to SCIENCE

Suppose that a meteor that strikes Earth is equally likely to land anywhere on Earth. Find the probability of each event.

15. The meteor lands in an ocean.

16. The meteor does not land in an ocean.

17. The meteor lands in Africa.

18. The meteor does not land in Africa.

19. The meteor lands in South America or North America.

Use the information below for Exercises 20 and 21.

Gwen plans to call Lisa's house on Saturday at a random time between 8:00 A.M. and 12:00 P.M. Gwen does not know that Lisa does not get up until 10:30 A.M. on Saturdays.

20. a. What is the probability that Gwen will call before Lisa gets up?

b. What is the probability that Gwen will call after Lisa gets up?

21. a. Suppose that Lisa's parents leave at 9:15 A.M. on Saturdays to take her brother to play soccer. What is the probability that Gwen will call before Lisa's family leaves?

b. What is the probability that Gwen will call before Lisa's family leaves or after Lisa gets up?

c. What is the probability that Gwen will call after Lisa's family leaves but before Lisa gets up?

22. CD Players Suppose there are 10 songs on a CD. You program the CD player to play the songs at random without any repeats.

a. In how many different orders can 10 songs be played?

b. What is the probability that the songs will be played in the order in which they are arranged on the CD?

23. Ja-Wen, Phelton, Ryan, and Deanna stand in a row to rehearse a song. They are equally likely to stand in any order.

a. What is the probability that they stand in alphabetical order from left to right?

b. What are the odds in favor of them standing in alphabetical order from left to right?

c. No two are the same age. When they stand in alphabetical order from left to right, they are not in order by age. What is the probability that they stand in alphabetical order or in order by age (youngest to oldest) from left to right?

316

Answers to Exercises and Problems

14. Answers may vary. Examples are given.

a. Find $P(\text{odd})$ and $P(\text{even})$; (50%; 50%).

b. Spin the spinner 50 times. Record the number of times the spinner lands on an odd number and the number of times it lands on an even number. (Results may vary.)

c. They are not necessarily the same, but if the number of trials is high enough, they should be similar. In the actual experiment, there are physical factors that affect the outcome. For example, the spinner might be slightly bent or the surface slightly uneven.

15. about 66%

16. about 34%

17. about 6%

18. about 94%

19. about 8%

20. a. 62.5%

b. 37.5%

21. a. 31.25%

b. 68.75%

c. 31.25%

22. a. 3,628,800

b. $\frac{1}{3,628,000}$ or about 0.000028%

23. a. $\frac{1}{24}$ or about 4.17%

b. 1:23

c. $\frac{1}{12}$ or about 8.3%

Camp counselors are packing lunches for a hiking trip. Suppose that each item in the menu below is equally likely to be selected and that a meal includes an item from each category.

For Exercises 24–27, find the probability of each event.

24. packing a lunch that includes a turkey sandwich

25. packing a lunch that does not include a turkey sandwich

26. packing a lunch that includes a turkey sandwich, an apple, and milk

27. packing a lunch that includes a turkey sandwich or a lunch that includes an apple

Sandwiches	Fruit	Drink
turkey	banana	milk
tuna	apple	apple juice
vegetarian	orange	lemonade
ham and cheese		

28. Find the odds in favor of the event in Exercise 25.

29. Find the odds against the event in Exercise 26.

connection to **HEALTH**

The data in the diagram are percentages of blood types in the United States. Each blood type can be divided into two categories, positive and negative. This is called the *Rh factor*.

Suppose you choose Person X at random from the population of the United States.

30. **a.** What are the odds in favor of Person X having AB blood?

   b. What are the odds against Person X having AB blood?

31. The odds in favor of Person X having AB negative (AB⁻) blood, which is the least common blood type, are 7 to 993.

   a. What are the odds against Person X having AB⁻ blood?

   b. What is the probability that Person X has AB⁻ blood? AB⁺ blood?

Type O 46.1% Type A 38.8% Type B 11.1% Type AB 3.9%

32. Someone with type O blood is called a *universal donor* because type O blood can be donated to anyone, as long as the Rh factors match.

   a. What are the odds in favor of Person X being a universal donor?

   b. What are the odds against Person X being a universal donor?

   c. Suppose 200 donors are signed up to give blood at a blood drive. How many of them might you expect to be universal donors?

33. **Research** Find out what the term *universal recipient* means. Find the odds in favor of Person X being a universal recipient.

Application

Exs. 30–33 present a real-world application of the concepts of odds and probability to blood types in the United States. An understanding of the probabilities of various blood types existing in a population is critical information for medical professionals.

Career Note

Students would probably be amazed at the large number of occupations associated with the field of health. Doctors and nurses are obvious examples to everyone. But there are also health professionals in other areas that do not deal directly with patients. To help students gain some perspective on careers in health, you might wish to spend a few minutes of class time to develop a list of occupations. The list can be organized into two parts: those people who work directly with patients, such as a physical therapist, and those people who do not, such as a sales representative for a pharmaceutical company.

Answers to Exercises and Problems

24. 25%

25. 75%

26. about 2.8%

27. 50%

28. 3:1

29. 35:1

30. **a.** $\frac{39}{961}$

   b. $\frac{961}{39}$

31. **a.** 993:7

   b. 0.7%; 3.2%

32. **a.** 461 to 539 or about 46 to 54

   b. 539 to 461 or about 54 to 46

   c. about 92 donors

33. A person with blood type AB+ is a universal recipient; the odds in favor of Person X being a universal recipient are 4 to 121.

For each number of people:

a. Find the probability that no two birthdays match.

b. Find the probability that at least two birthdays match.

34. 6   **35.** 7   **36.** 8

37. How are the events in parts (a) and (b) of Exercises 34–36 related?

38. How can you find the probability that at least two people in any size group have the same birthday? Describe your method in words or in symbols.

39. How large a group you do need before the probability of having at least two people with the same birthday is 50%?

Ongoing **ASSESSMENT**

40. **Open-ended** A car wash decides to give a free wash to any customer who comes in on his or her birthday. In July and August, the car wash had 10,000 customers and gave 1000 free washes. Do you think this information helps the owner of the car wash predict the number of free washes that will be given during the rest of the year? Why or why not?

Review **PREVIEW**

41. How many different three-letter arrangements can be made from the letters in the word PRICES? How many five-letter arrangements? *(Section 6-2)*

Simplify. *(Section 4-6)*

42. $\sqrt{-81}$ **43.** $(6i)(-2i)(5i)$ **44.** $(6 - 2i)(4 + 5i)$ **45.** $(1 + 8i) - (4 - 7i)$

46. Rama is dressing a mannequin for a window display. She has a pair of blue slacks, a pair of green slacks, a yellow sweater, and a black sweater to work with. Make a table to show all the ways Rama could dress the mannequin in pants and a sweater. *(Section 6-1)*

Working on the Unit Project

47. Alphabetize the subject areas included in your survey and number them.

For Exercises 48–51, use your survey results.

a. Find the probability of each event.

b. Find the odds in favor of each event.

48. A person with a birthday in the second half of the year prefers subject 3 to subject 1.

49. A person with a birthday in the first half of the year prefers subject 3 to subject 1.

50. A person with a birthday in the second half of the year prefers subject 2 to subject 4.

51. A person with a birthday in the first half of the year prefers subject 2 to subject 4.

52. **Writing** Are the events in Exercises 48 and 49 mutually exclusive? How do you know?

Practice 43 For use with Section 6-3

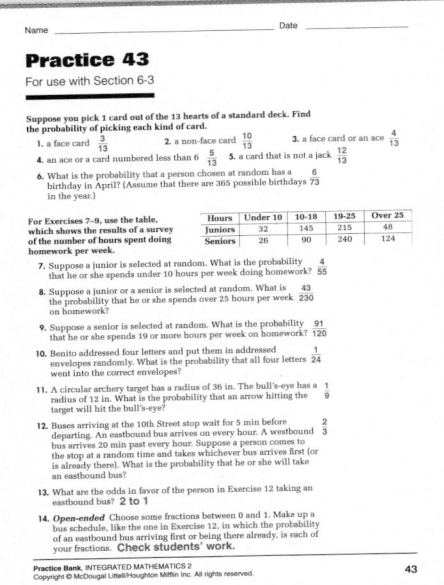

Answers to Exercises and Problems

34. a. about 96%   **b.** about 4%

35. a. about 94%   **b.** about 6%

36. a. about 93%   **b.** about 7%

37. The events are complementary.

38. Summaries may vary. Let n be the size of the group. The probability that at least two people in a group of n people have the same birthday is
$$\frac{365^n - (365)(364) \ldots (365 - (n-1))}{365^n}.$$

39. 23 people

40. Answers may vary. Some items to consider are: In areas with heavy snowfall in the winter where the roads are heavily salted, car washes may increase significantly, but a person who might not think to use a car wash on his or her birthday might still take advantage of the free wash. Then using the ratio of free washes to customers might not help. The owner might consider that he or she gave away about 500 washes per month, and, assuming births are evenly distributed over the year, might assume that number might be fairly constant with a slight increase in the winter months.

41. 120; 720   **42.** $9i$

43. $60i$ **44.** $34 + 22i$

45. $-3 + 15i$

46.

slacks color	yellow sweater	black sweater
blue	blue slacks, yellow sweater	blue slacks, black sweater
green	green slacks, yellow sweater	green slacks, black sweater

47–51. Answers may vary. Check students' work.

52. No. Students with a birthday in either half of the year may prefer subject 3 to subject 1.

Focus
Find the probability of independent and dependent events.

Compound Events

Before and After

Table tennis balls were used to represent each team's entries. The balls were placed in a clear cylinder, thoroughly mixed, and then drawn by vacuum to the top. The ball that came to the top first determined which team got the first choice.

After the first three balls were drawn, a team's win-loss record determined the order, with the team having the worst record getting the next choice.

BY THE WAY...

Orlando won the lottery in both 1992 and 1993. This prompted the NBA Board of Governors to modify the lottery system.

Every spring, the National Basketball Association (NBA) holds a lottery to find the order in which professional teams can choose new members from college players. The lottery system that was in place from 1990 to 1993 is described at the left.

The 11 teams that did not qualify for the professional playoffs participated each year.

1992		1993	
Team standings in reverse order	Entries	Team standings in reverse order	Entries
Minnesota	11	Dallas	11
Orlando	10	Minnesota	10
Dallas	9	Washington	9
Denver	8	Sacramento	8
Washington	7	Philadelphia	7
Sacramento	6	Milwaukee	6
Milwaukee	5	Golden State	5
Charlotte	4	Denver	4
Philadelphia	3	Miami	3
Atlanta	2	Detroit	2
Houston	1	Orlando	1

Each team got from 1 to 11 entries in the lottery. The team with the worst record got the most entries.

Talk it Over

1. How would you find the probability that a particular team wins the lottery (gets the first choice)?

2. What was the probability that the Orlando team would win the lottery in 1992? in 1993?

6-4 Compound Events

PLANNING

Objectives and Strands
See pages 292A and 292B.

Spiral Learning
See page 292B.

Materials List
➤ Spinner
➤ Paper clip

Recommended Pacing
Section 6-4 is a two-day lesson.

Day 1
Pages 319–321: Opening paragraph through Sample 2, *Exercises 1–13*

Day 2
Pages 322–323: Dependent Events through Look Back, *Exercises 14–31*

Extra Practice
See pages 623–624.

Warm-Up Exercises
Warm-Up Transparency 6-4

Support Materials
➤ Practice 44
➤ Enrichment 39 in the Activity Bank
➤ Study Guide 6-4
➤ Problem Set 11
➤ McDougal Littell Mathpack software: *Probability Constructor*
➤ Quiz 6-4
➤ Test 22
➤ Alternative Assessment 4

Answers to Talk it Over

1. Divide the number of entries the team has by the total number of entries.

2. about 0.152; about 0.015

Talk it Over

Questions 1 and 2 require that students use their understanding of how to find a probability to arrive at the answers. This leads to determining the probabilities of independent and dependent events.

Teaching Tip

Stress that independent events have nothing to do with each other.

Talk it Over

Questions 3–6 check students' understanding of the difference between independent and dependent events. Explanations could involve the notion that events having nothing to do with each other cannot, therefore, affect one another and thus are independent.

Additional Sample

S1 Suppose you roll a die and spin a spinner. Find the probability of getting "3" on the die and "3" on the spinner, or P(3 and 3).

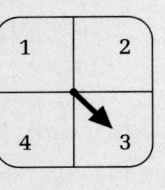

Make a table of outcomes.

SPINNER

DIE	1	2	3	4
1	1,1	1,2	1,3	1,4
2	2,1	2,2	2,3	2,4
3	3,1	3,2	3,3	3,4
4	4,1	4,2	4,3	4,4
5	5,1	5,2	5,3	5,4
6	6,1	6,2	6,3	6,4

The sample space represented by the table contains 24 possible outcomes.
P(3 and 3) = $\frac{1}{24} \approx 0.04$

Communication: Reading

The term *sample space* is defined at the bottom of this page. You might wish to have students read aloud the set of possible outcomes for Sample 1.

Compound Events

When you look at the 1992 and 1993 basketball lotteries together, you are looking at a *compound event*. A **compound event** is an event made of two or more events that can happen either at the same time or one after the other. The events can be either *independent events* or *dependent events*.

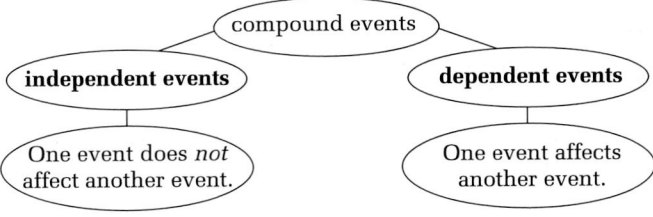

Talk it Over

Tell whether each pair of events is *independent* or *dependent*. Explain.

3. earning grades on your tests and earning your final semester grade

4. selecting a red apple and then a green apple from a bag of 6 red and 4 green apples, if no apples are returned to the bag

5. selecting a red apple and then a green apple from a bag of 6 red and 4 green apples, if the first apple is returned to the bag before the next selection

6. tossing a coin and rolling a die

Sample 1

Suppose you toss a coin and roll a die. Find the probability of getting heads on the coin and "5" on the die, or P(H and 5).

Sample Response

Problem Solving Strategy: Make a table.

Only one outcome has heads and a "5."

		Outcomes for rolling a die					
		1	2	3	4	5	6
Outcomes for tossing a coin	H	H, 1	H, 2	H, 3	H, 4	H, 5	H, 6
	T	T, 1	T, 2	T, 3	T, 4	T, 5	T, 6

The table contains twelve possible outcomes. A set of all possible outcomes, with no repeats, is called a **sample space**.

$$P(\text{H and 5}) = \frac{1}{12} \approx 0.08$$

Answers to Talk it Over

3. dependent

4. dependent

5. independent

6. independent

The diagram shows how you can use the probability of each event in Sample 1 to find the probability of both. Notice that the probability of heads on the coin and "5" on the die can be found by multiplying the probabilities.

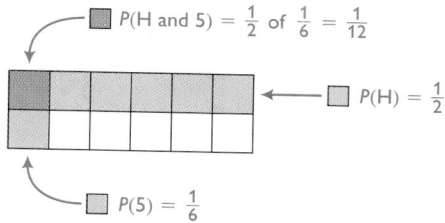

$$P(\text{H and 5}) = \tfrac{1}{2} \text{ of } \tfrac{1}{6} = \tfrac{1}{12}$$
$$P(\text{H}) = \tfrac{1}{2}$$
$$P(5) = \tfrac{1}{6}$$

$$P(\text{H and 5}) = P(\text{H}) \cdot P(5) = \tfrac{1}{2} \cdot \tfrac{1}{6} = \tfrac{1}{12} \approx 0.08$$

PROBABILITY OF INDEPENDENT EVENTS

When two events are independent, you can multiply to find the probability that both occur.

For independent events A and B:

$$P(A \text{ and } B) = P(A) \cdot P(B)$$

Sample 2

Use the information about the basketball lottery on page 319. What was the probability that the Orlando team would win *both* the 1992 and 1993 lotteries?

Sample Response

First decide if the events are independent or dependent. →

Winning the lottery in 1992 had no effect on the lottery in 1993, so the events are independent. Multiply to find the probability that both events occur.

$$P(\text{Orlando would win the 1992 lottery}) = \tfrac{10}{66}$$

$$P(\text{Orlando would win the 1993 lottery}) = \tfrac{1}{66}$$

Add all entries. There are 66 altogether.

$$P(\text{Orlando would win in 1992 } and \text{ 1993}) = \tfrac{10}{66} \cdot \tfrac{1}{66} = \tfrac{10}{4356} \approx 0.002$$

The probability that the Orlando team would win *both* the 1992 and 1993 lotteries was about 0.002.

► Now you are ready for:
Exs. 1–13 on pp. 323–325

6-4 Compound Events

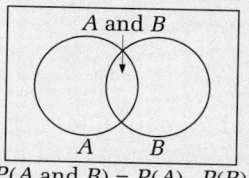

Dependent Events

With dependent events, the outcome of the first event affects the outcome of the second event. You need to consider this when you figure probabilities.

Sample 3

There are five discs in a CD player. The player has a "random" button that selects songs at random and does not repeat until all songs are played. What is the probability that the first song is selected from disc 3 and the second song is selected from disc 5?

Sample Response

The selection of the first song does affect the possibilities for the second song, so the events are dependent.

1 Find the probability that the first song is selected from disc 3.

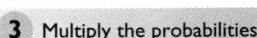

$P(\text{disc 3 song}) = \frac{13}{50}$ ← 13 songs on disc 3
← 50 songs altogether

2 Find the probability that the second song is selected from disc 5.

Because songs *cannot* repeat, there is *one less song* possible for the second song.

$P(\text{disc 5 song after disc 3 song}) = \frac{10}{49}$ ← 10 songs on disc 5
← 49 songs left

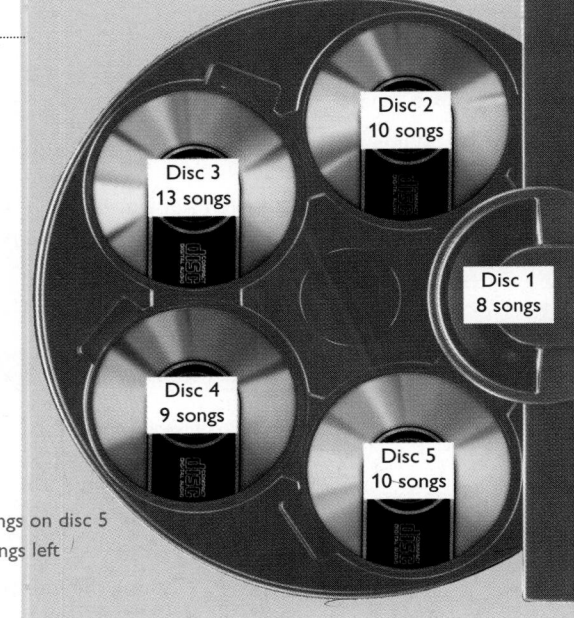

Disc 2
10 songs

Disc 3
13 songs

Disc 1
8 songs

Disc 4
9 songs

Disc 5
10 songs

3 Multiply the probabilities.

$P(\text{disc 3 song, then disc 5 song}) = P(\text{disc 3 song}) \cdot P(\text{disc 5 song after disc 3 song})$

$$= \frac{13}{50} \cdot \frac{10}{49}$$

$$= \frac{13}{245}$$

$$\approx 0.053$$

The probability that the first song is selected from disc 3 and the second song is selected from disc 5 is about 0.05.

Answers to Talk it Over

7. In Sample 3, the list of possible choices changes after the first choice. In Sample 2, the list does not change. In Sample 3, since songs do not repeat, the song chosen first is no longer a possible choice. There are only 49 possible choices remaining.

8. a. independent; The choice of the first song has no effect on the choice of the second.

b. 0.052

X Lab

PROBABILITY OF DEPENDENT EVENTS

For dependent events A and B:

$$P(A \text{ and } B) = P(A) \cdot P(B \text{ after } A)$$

Talk it Over

7. Explain why the denominators change for each successive event in Sample 3 but not in Sample 2.
8. Suppose songs in Sample 3 can repeat.
   a. Tell whether the choice of a first song and the choice of a second song are *independent* or *dependent* events. Explain.
   b. Find the probability that the first song is selected from disc 3 and the second song is selected from disc 5.

Now you are ready for:
Exs. 14–31 on pp. 325–327

Look Back

What is meant by independent events? How are they different from dependent events? How is the probability that two dependent events will happen different from the probability that two independent events will happen?

6-4 Exercises and Problems

Suppose you roll one red and one blue eight-sided game piece and that each piece is numbered from 1 to 8. Find each probability.

1. P(red 8 and blue 8)
2. P(red 1 and blue 6)
3. P(even red and blue 4)

For Exercises 4 and 5, imagine that you are using the spinner shown.

4. In two spins what is the probability of landing on a "3" then on a "2"?
5. a. Copy and complete this table for the sum of any two spins.

+	1	2	3	3
1	2	3	4	4
2	?	?	?	?
3	?	?	?	?
3	?	?	?	?

   b. List the sample space for the sum of any two spins.
   c. Which sum is most likely? What is its probability?
   d. What is the probability that the sum is 6?
   e. Which is greater, the probability of an odd sum or an even sum? Explain.

Mathematical Procedures

For dependent events A and B, the probability of event A is determined by using the entire sample space, that is, all possible outcomes. Event B is an event in a subset of the original sample space. This subset is arrived at by placing a *condition* on the original sample space. The probability associated with an event in the subset of a sample space is called a *conditional* probability.

Look Back

A class discussion of these questions should not only help to sharpen students' understanding of the concepts of this section, but should also help to clear up any misunderstandings.

APPLYING

Suggested Assignment

Day 1

Standard 1–8

Extended 1–8, 10–13

Day 2

Standard 15–31

Extended 14–31

Integrating the Strands

Algebra Exs. 26–28

Statistics and Probability Exs. 1–25, 29–31

Logic and Language Exs. 9, 24, 30, 31

Answers to Look Back

Events are independent if one event does not affect the other event. Events are dependent if one event does affect the other. If two events are independent, the probability that both will occur is the product of the probabilities that each will occur. If the events are dependent, the probability is the product of the probability that the first will occur and the probability that the second will occur after the first has occurred.

Answers to Exercises and Problems

1. about 0.016
2. about 0.016
3. about 0.063
4. 0.125
5. a.

+	1	2	3	3
1	2	3	4	4
2	3	4	5	5
3	4	5	6	6
3	4	5	6	6

   b. 2, 3, 4, 5, 6
   c. 4; 0.3125
   d. 0.25
   e. The probability of an even sum is greater. P(even sum) = 0.625; P(odd sum) = 0.375

connection to **SCIENCE**

Career Geneticists study how traits are passed from parents to their offspring through *genes*. Genes come in pairs, one from each parent. Sometimes one gene in a pair is considered *dominant* and the other gene is considered *recessive*. It takes two recessive genes to produce a recessive trait, but only one dominant gene to produce a dominant trait.

6. Use the table at the right. Suppose a rabbit with two dominant black-fur genes (BB) mates with a rabbit that has two recessive brown-fur genes (bb). What is the probability that their offspring will have brown fur? black fur?

7. Suppose a rabbit with two dominant black-fur genes (BB) mates with a rabbit that has one dominant and one recessive fur gene (Bb).

   a. Make a table to model this situation.

   b. What is the probability that their offspring will have brown fur? black fur?

8. Repeat Exercise 7 for a rabbit with two recessive brown-fur genes (bb) and a rabbit with one dominant and one recessive fur gene (Bb).

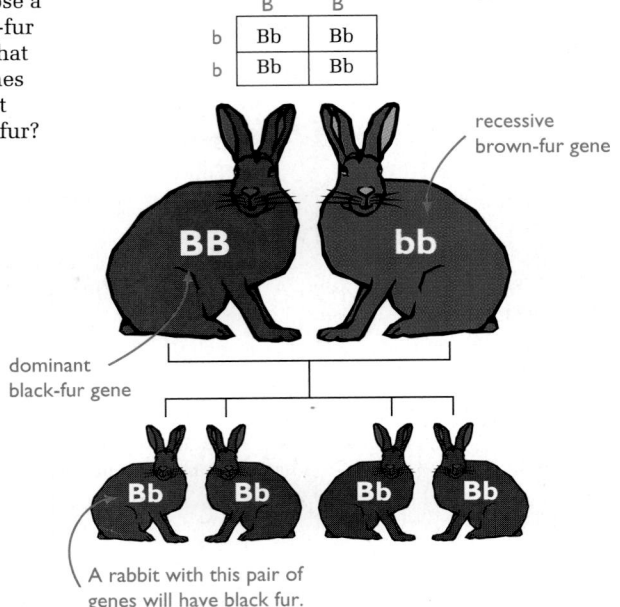

	B	B
b	Bb	Bb
b	Bb	Bb

recessive brown-fur gene

BB   **bb**

dominant black-fur gene

Bb   **Bb**   **Bb**   **Bb**

A rabbit with this pair of genes will have black fur.

Spinner *M*   Spinner *N*

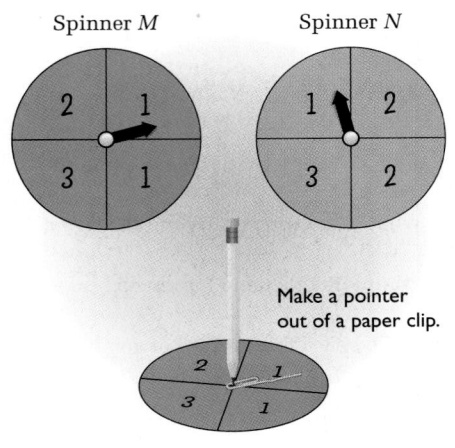

Make a pointer out of a paper clip.

9. **Group Activity** Work with another student.

   a. **Using Manipulatives** Make two spinners that match the ones shown.

   b. Predict the most likely sum when spinning both spinners once.

   c. Copy and complete the table for 50 trials. Each of you should spin a different spinner.

Sum	2	3	4	5	6
Tally	?	?	?	?	?

   d. **Writing** Were you surprised by the results? Why or why not?

Unit 6 Counting Strategies, Probability, Binomials

Answers to Exercises and Problems

6. P(brown fur) = 0; P(black fur) = 1

7. a.

	B	B
B	BB	BB
b	Bb	Bb

   b. P(brown fur) = 0, P(black fur) = 1

8. a.

	B	b
b	Bb	bb
b	Bb	bb

b. P(brown fur) = 0.5; P(black fur) = 0.5

9. a. Check students' work.

   b. The most likely sum is 3 or 4, each with probability 0.3125.

   c. The table shows expected results based on actual probabilities. Experimental results may vary.

Sum	2	3	4	5	6
Tally	about 6	about 16	about 16	about 9	about 3

d. Answers may vary. Actual results may vary from expected results.

10. 25%; 0.5%

11. about 17%; about 1.5%

12. 0.14%

Basketball **For Exercises 10–12, use the table.**

The lottery system was revised in 1993 so that each team is now assigned combinations of four numbers from 1 to 14 (such as 1, 7, 9, and 12). The team with the worst record is assigned 250 number combinations. The four balls that come to the top first determine which team gets the first choice.

10. Under this system, what is the probability that the first draft pick will go to the team with the worst record? to the team in the lottery with the best record?

11. Under the system described on page 319, what was the probability that the first draft pick would go to the team with the worst record? to the team in the lottery with the best record?

12. Use the standings for 1992 and 1993 from the table on page 319. If the revised system were in place in 1992 and 1993, what would have been Orlando's chances of winning *both* the 1992 and 1993 lotteries?

13. **Basketball** Marisela's free-throw percentage is 0.700.

   a. Which part of the area diagram below best represents the probability of her making two free throws in a row?

   b. Which part of the tree diagram below best represents the probability of her making two free throws in a row?

   c. What do the other parts of the two diagrams represent?

   d. Find the probability that Marisela makes two free throws in a row.

TEAM STANDINGS IN REVERSE ORDER	Entries
Team 1	250
Team 2	200
Team 3	157
Team 4	120
Team 5	89
Team 6	64
Team 7	44
Team 8	29
Team 9	18
Team 10	11
Team 11	7
Team 12	6
Team 13	5
TOTAL	1000

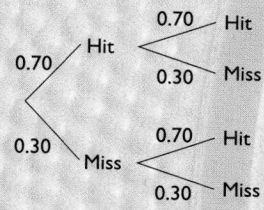

14. **Reading** Give examples from pages 319–322 of a pair of independent events and a pair of dependent events.

15. A bag contains three red marbles and seven blue marbles.

   a. Find the probability of picking two red marbles, if the first marble is returned to the bag before the second is picked.

   b. Find the probability of picking two red marbles, if the first marble is *not* returned to the bag before the second is picked.

Answers to Exercises and Problems

13. a. A

   b. Hit–Hit

   c. B and Miss–Hit branches: miss first, make second; C and Hit–Miss branches: make first, miss second; D and Miss–Miss branches: miss both

   d. 49%

14. Answers may vary. Examples are given. Independent events: choosing one team's draft picks by lottery for two consecutive years; getting heads on a coin toss and rolling a 5 on a die; Dependent events: selecting two songs from a CD by random selection if songs cannot repeat; choosing the draft picks of the team that got second pick after choosing the draft picks of the team that got first pick

15. a. 0.09

   b. about 0.067

Use this situation for Exercises 16–19.

Suppose you are playing a card game with a standard deck of playing cards and are dealt four cards, one after another, from the top of the deck.

16. Are these four events *independent* or *dependent*?

Find each probability.

17. P(four aces)

18. P(four hearts)

19. P(four face cards)

20. Jury Selection In the Massachusetts jury selection process, about one of every three people called for jury duty actually appears on the given date. These people can then be assigned to one of 10 panels of prospective jurors. Assume that all panels are the same size.

  a. What is the probability that a person called for jury duty appears?

  b. What is the probability that a person called for jury duty appears and is then assigned to Panel 2?

21. Lotteries A state lottery begins with choosing a ball from 30 table tennis balls that are numbered 1 through 30 in a bin. The first ball is put on display and a second ball is then chosen. Find the probability that the 6 is chosen and then the 21 is chosen. Round to the nearest thousandth.

22. Ali flipped a coin to determine the five answers on a true-false quiz. What is the probability that her five answers match all five correct answers?

23. Sharla and her two brothers pick cards at random every weekend to decide who has to clean each room of the house. Suppose it is Sharla's turn to pick her two rooms first. What is the probability that Sharla will have to clean both bathrooms?

Ongoing ASSESSMENT

24. Open-ended Describe a situation about finding a probability that involves independent events. Change the situation slightly to describe a situation about finding a probability that involves dependent events. Find each probability.

Review PREVIEW

25. A bag contains two green marbles, four white marbles, and four red marbles. One marble is selected at random. *(Section 6-3)*

  a. Find the probability of selecting a white marble.

  b. Find the odds in favor of selecting a white marble.

Solve each equation for the variable shown in red. *(Toolbox Skill 15)*

26. $I = prt$

27. $3x - y = 40$

28. $mx + ny = p$

29. a. What does the symbol $_9P_2$ mean? *(Section 6-2)*

  b. Find the number of permutations of the letters in the word MARVELOUS arranged two at a time.

Answers to Exercises and Problems

16. dependent

17. about 0.000004

18. about 0.003

19. about 0.002

20. a. about 0.333

  b. about 0.033

21. 0.001

22. about 0.031

23. about 0.067

24. Answers may vary. An example is given. Independent: A jar contains 10 green marbles, 5 yellow marbles, and 15 blue marbles. You close your eyes and take out a marble. You replace the first marble, close your eyes and take out a second marble. What is the probability that both marbles are yellow? (The probability is about 0.028.) Dependent: Repeat the above, but do not replace the first marble. (The probability is about 0.023.)

25. a. 0.4

  b. 2:3

26. $P = \dfrac{I}{rt}$

27. $x = \dfrac{y + 40}{3}$

28. $y = \dfrac{p - mx}{n}$

29. a. the number of arrangements when 9 are arranged 2 at a time

  b. 72

30–31. Answers may vary.

Working on the Unit Project

Use your survey results and the list from Exercise 47 in Section 6-3.

a. Find the probability of each compound event.

b. Tell whether the events in each pair are *independent* or *dependent*.

c. **Writing** Explain how you arrived at your answer to part (b).

30. A person with a birthday in the first half of the year prefers subject 4 to both subject 2 and subject 5.

31. A person with a birthday in the second half of the year prefers subject 4 to both subject 2 and subject 5.

Working on the Unit Project
Remind students to keep a record of their answers to Exs. 30 and 31. They will need to refer to the probabilities when developing their interest profiles.

Quick Quiz (6-1 through 6-4)
See page 360.

Unit 6 — CHECKPOINT 1

1. Writing Carl is playing a board game and wants to land on the "Free" space and then on the "Lucky Draw" space. He needs to roll two dice and get a total of 6, followed by a roll that gives a total of 9. Explain how to find the probability that he will roll the totals he needs.

2. John has a new bank card to use at automatic teller machines. For his security code he uses the four digits on the keypad that correspond to the letters in his name.   **6-1**

  a. List the letter arrangements John can use.

  b. Do you think it is a good idea for John to use an arrangement of the letters in his name for a security code? Why or why not?

3. How many seven-letter arrangements can be made from the letters in GRAVITY if you use each letter once?   **6-2**

4. How many permutations are there of 12 birds arranged 3 at a time on a telephone line?

For Exercises 5–7, each letter of the word ALGEBRA is put on one of seven cards. The cards are shuffled and one is chosen at random.   **6-3**

  5. Find P(vowel). Find P(consonant).

  6. Are the two events in Exercise 5 mutually exclusive? Are they complementary? Why or why not?

  7. What are the odds against choosing a vowel?

  8. Suppose a red die and a blue die are tossed. Find P(red 6 and blue 1).   **6-4**

  9. Suppose you are playing a card game with a standard deck of playing cards and are dealt two cards from the top of the deck. Find P(two 3s).

6-4 Compound Events

327

Practice 44 For use with Section 6-4

Name _____   Date _____

Practice 44
For use with Section 6-4

For Exercises 1–4, a card is drawn from a standard 52-card deck. Then a die is rolled. Find the probability of each compound event.

1. A heart is drawn and a 6 is rolled. $\frac{1}{24}$

2. A seven is drawn and an even number is rolled. $\frac{1}{26}$

3. A face card is drawn and a number less than 6 is rolled. $\frac{5}{26}$

4. An ace or a king is drawn and a 2 is rolled. $\frac{1}{39}$

5. A drawer contains 4 green socks and 5 blue socks. One sock is drawn at random. Then another sock is drawn at random.

   a. Suppose the first sock is returned to the drawer before the second is drawn. Find the probability that both are blue. $\frac{25}{81}$

   b. Suppose the first sock is not returned to the drawer before the second is drawn. Find the probability that both socks are blue. $\frac{5}{18}$

6. Suppose two cards are dealt, one after another, from a standard deck. The first card is not returned to the deck before the second is drawn. Find the probability of each event.

   a. The first card is an ace and the second card is a king. $\frac{4}{663}$

   b. The first card is a heart and the second card is not a heart. $\frac{13}{68}$

7. Does either of the experiments in Exercise 6 consist of two independent events? If so, which one(s)? no

8. Find the probabilities in Exercises 6(a) and 6(b) assuming the first card is returned to the deck before the second card is drawn. $\frac{1}{169}, \frac{3}{16}$

9. Wenona's batting average is .410. This is the probability of her getting a hit in her next official at-bat. (Ignore changes to her average caused by her next few at-bats.)

   a. What is the probability that Wenona will get hits in her next two official at-bats? .168

   b. What is the probability that Wenona will get hits in her next two official at-bats and not get a hit in the at-bat after those? .099

10. **Writing** Suppose you have a large number of white marbles, an equal number of black marbles, and three bags. A friend is going to choose one of the bags and then draw a marble at random from that bag. How can you distribute the marbles to maximize the probability of drawing a black marble? What will this probability be, approximately? (Hint: You can make it more than $\frac{2}{3}$.) Check students' work.

44

Answers to Checkpoint

1. First, determine how many sums are possible when two dice are rolled. Next, determine the probability of getting a total of 6 and the probability of getting a total of 9. Finally, multiply the two probabilities.

2. a. JOHN, JONH, JHON, JHNO, JNOH, JNHO, OJHN, OJNH, OHJN, OHNJ, ONJH, ONHJ, HOJN, HONJ, HJON, HJNO, HNJO, HNOJ, NOJH, NOHJ, NJOH, NJHO, NHJO, NHOJ

b. Answers may vary. An example is given. No; it may not be a good idea, since his four-letter name is an obvious choice and there are only 24 permutations. With three chances to guess the code, a thief would have a 12.5% chance of doing so.

3. 5040   **4.** 1320

5. P(vowel) ≈ 0.429; P(consonant) ≈ 0.571

6. The events are mutually exclusive since none of the letters is both a vowel and a consonant. The events are complementary since they are mutually exclusive and together they include all the possibilities.

7. 4 : 3

8. about 0.028

9. about 0.005

Objectives and Strands
See pages 292A and 292B.

Spiral Learning
See page 292B.

Recommended Pacing
Section 6-5 is a one-day lesson.

Extra Practice
See pages 623–624.

Warm-Up Exercises
Warm-Up Transparency 6-5

Support Materials
➤ Practice 45
➤ Enrichment 40 in the Activity Bank
➤ Study Guide 6-5
➤ Problem Set 12
➤ Quiz 6-5
➤ Alternative Assessment 5

Section **6-5**

Combinations

Choices, Choices

Focus
Find the number of ways to select some items from a group.

Julian likes five of the yogurt flavors at O'Leary's Frozen Yogurt Shop: vanilla, coffee, strawberry, peach, and mocha chip. Here is a partial list of the ways that Julian can order a cone with three scoops from these five flavors. Each scoop is a different flavor.

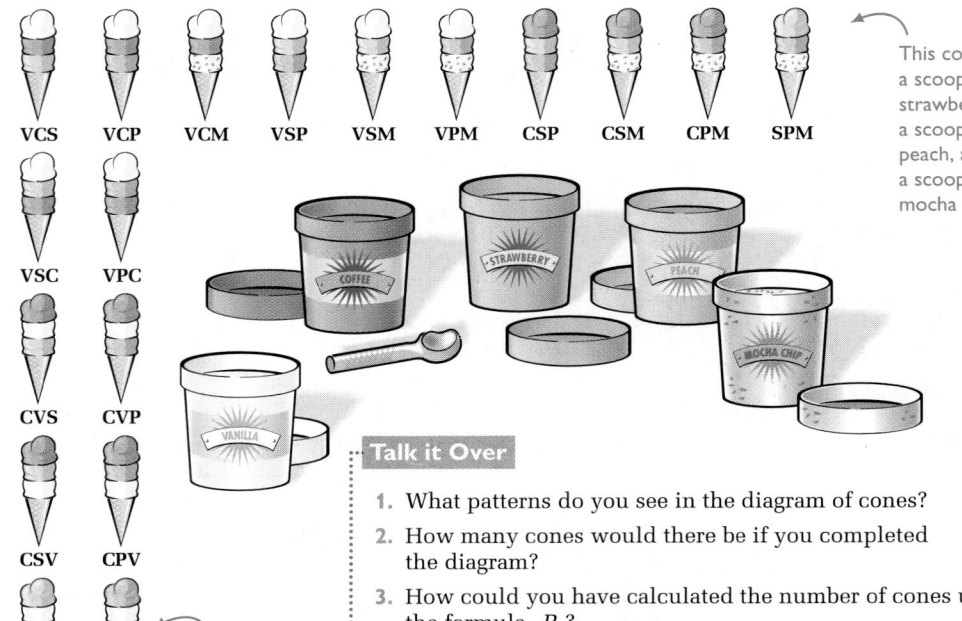

VCS   VCP   VCM   VSP   VSM   VPM   CSP   CSM   CPM   SPM

VSC   VPC

CVS   CVP

CSV   CPV

SVC   PVC

SCV   PCV

This cone has a scoop of strawberry, a scoop of peach, and a scoop of mocha chip.

This cone has a scoop of peach, a scoop of vanilla, and a scoop of coffee.

Talk it Over

1. What patterns do you see in the diagram of cones?

2. How many cones would there be if you completed the diagram?

3. How could you have calculated the number of cones using the formula $_5P_3$?

4. How many cones would there be *in each column* if you completed the diagram? How can you represent this number using permutation notation?

5. Suppose Julian orders a dish of yogurt instead of a cone, so that the order of the scoops does not matter. How many dishes of yogurt are there with a different group of three flavors from Julian's five flavors?

6. What fraction of the possible three-scoop cones from Julian's five flavors is the number of possible three-scoop dishes?

328

Unit 6 Counting Strategies, Probability, Binomials

Answers to Talk it Over

1. Answers may vary. An example is given. The cones in the first column show all the ways the first three flavors can be arranged. The second column shows the ways the first two and the fourth can be combined, and so on.

2. 60 cones

3. $_5P_3 = \dfrac{5!}{(5-3)!} = \dfrac{5!}{2!} = \dfrac{120}{2} = 60$

4. 6; $_3P_3$

5. 10 dishes

6. $\dfrac{1}{6}$

Order matters when you make a cone. Six different cones can have these flavors.

All dishes that have one peach, one strawberry, and one coffee scoop would be considered the same.

A selection made from a group of items when order is not important is called a **combination**. The symbol for the number of different combinations when n items are selected r at a time is $_nC_r$.

In the situation on page 328, there are 60 permutations of 5 flavors arranged 3 at a time. However, there are only 10 combinations of 5 flavors selected 3 at a time. There is a connection between the number of permutations and the number of combinations.

$$10 = \frac{60}{6} = \frac{_5P_3}{3!} = {}_5C_3$$

Since order does not matter, you have to divide by the number of arrangements of 3 flavors, 3!.

COMBINATIONS OF n ITEMS SELECTED r AT A TIME

The number of combinations of n items selected r at a time ($r < n$) is given by this formula.

$$_nC_r = \frac{_nP_r}{r!} = \frac{n!}{(n-r)!\,r!}$$

Example

$$_9C_5 = \frac{_9P_5}{5!} = \frac{9!}{(9-5)!5!} = 126$$

Sample

How many different groups of 3 actresses can be chosen to play the witches in *Macbeth* from these 6 actresses who audition: Val, Carla, Susan, Pat, Mimi, and Rose?

Sample Response

Order does not matter in this situation. You have to find the number of combinations of 6 items selected 3 at a time.

Method ❶

Problem Solving Strategy: Make a systematic list.

Represent each actress with one letter.

VCS	VSP	VPM	VMR	CSP	CPM	CMR	SPM	SMR	PMR
VCP	VSM	VPR		CSM	CPR		SPR		
VCM	VSR			CSR					
VCR									

20 different groups of 3 actresses can be chosen from 6 actresses.

Continued on next page.

6-5 Combinations

329

TEACHING

Talk it Over

Questions 1–6 lead students to consider the difference in counting when the order of the selected items does not matter. In so doing, these questions prepare students for a more formal presentation of the relationship between permutations and combinations.

Teaching Tip

In order to reinforce the difference between a permutation and a combination, ask students how many permutations and combinations there are of the letters A, B, and C. (6 and 1, respectively)

Reasoning

Students should understand that dividing by $r!$ in the combination formula, $_nC_r = \frac{_nP_r}{r!}$, eliminates the duplication of selected items when order does not matter.

Additional Sample

How many different groupings of 3 pieces of furniture can be chosen for a living room from these 5 possibilities: high back chair, low back chair, rocking chair, ottoman, and swivel rocking chair?

Method 1: Make a systematic table. Represent each piece of furniture with one letter.

HLR	HLO	HLS
HRO	HRS	
HOS		
LRO	LRS	
LOS		
ROS		

There are 10 different groupings of 3 pieces of furniture that can be chosen from 5 pieces of furniture.

Method 2: Use a formula.

$$_5C_3 = \frac{5!}{(5-3)!3!} = \frac{5!}{2!3!} = \frac{5 \cdot 4}{2} = 10$$

There are 10 different groupings of 3 pieces of furniture that can be chosen from 5 pieces of furniture.

Method ❷

Problem Solving Strategy: Use a formula.

$$_6C_3 = \frac{6!}{(6-3)!\,3!} = \frac{6!}{3!\,3!} = \frac{6 \cdot 5 \cdot 4 \cdot 3 \cdot 2 \cdot 1}{3 \cdot 2 \cdot 1 \cdot 3 \cdot 2 \cdot 1} = 20$$

20 different groups of 3 actresses can be chosen from 6 actresses.

Talk it Over

Celia is choosing two photographs to decorate a bulletin board for a play. She has six good photographs to choose from.

7. How many different pairs of photographs can Celia choose out of six photographs?

8. How many ways can Celia arrange two photographs side by side when she has six to choose from?

9. Is question 7 asking for a number of *permutations* or a number of *combinations*? What about question 8?

Look Back

How are combinations and permutations different? If you know the number of permutations of a group of items, how can you find the number of combinations of those items?

6-5 Exercises and Problems

Reading Tell the meaning of each expression.

1. $_7P_4$ 2. $_7C_4$ 3. $_8P_5$ 4. $_8C_5$

5. Which is smaller, $_8P_5$ or $_8C_5$? How many times smaller? Why?

Find the value of each expression.

6. $_4P_3$ 7. $_3C_3$ 8. $_3C_0$ 9. $_6C_2$

10. $_6C_4$ 11. $_9C_3$ 12. $_9C_6$ 13. $_8P_4$

TECHNOLOGY NOTE

Some calculators have keys or menu items for combinations.

14. Describe any patterns you notice in the number of combinations in Exercises 7–12.

15. **Politics** The Springfield school board has seven members.

a. The board must have three officers: a chairperson, an assistant chairperson, and a secretary. How many different sets of these officers can be formed from this board?

b. How many three-person committees can be formed from this board?

c. Is part (a) asking for a number of *permutations* or a number of *combinations*? What about part (b)?

d. How are your answers to parts (a) and (b) related?

Unit 6 Counting Strategies, Probability, Binomials

Answers to Talk it Over

7. 15 pairs

8. 30 ways

9. combinations; permutations

Answers to Look Back

A permutation is a selection made from a group of items where order is important. A combination is a selection made from a group of items where order is not important. Given the number of permutations of a group of items, determine how many permutations there are for each combination and divide to find the number of combinations.

For Exercises 16–18, tell whether each situation is asking for a number of *permutations* or a number of *combinations*. Then answer each question.

Rubén Eugenio has room for three plants on a windowsill.

16. In how many different ways can three plants be arranged on his windowsill?

17. Suppose Rubén has six plants. How many groups of three plants can he put on his windowsill?

18. Suppose Rubén has nine plants. How many ways can three of these plants be arranged on his windowsill?

19. Security To open a combination lock, you dial a sequence of three numbers called the lock's *combination.* You turn the dial right for the first number, left for the second, and right again for the third.

   a. How many *combinations* are possible for a lock like the one shown?

   b. **Writing** Do you think a lock's combination is like a combination in mathematics? Why or why not?

20. Cheerleading Suppose fifteen people qualify for a college cheerleading squad, six women and nine men.

   a. How many six-member squads can be selected?

   b. Suppose that exactly two members of the six-member squad must be male. How many six-member squads can be selected?

   c. Find the probability of the event in part (b).

21. a. Copy and complete the table.

Numbers of Segments Connecting Points						
Number of points	3	4	5	6	...	n
Ways to connect points	△	▱	⋰⋱	⋰⋱	...	—
Number of segments	3	6	?	?	...	?

   b. How are the numbers of segments that can be drawn connecting any two of the points like combinations of items?

22. Music The ten band directors at a summer band camp are planning to give a performance. One of the pieces they want to play calls for a French horn, a tuba, a trombone, and a trumpet. Each of the band directors can play all four instruments. How many different quartets can they have?

6-5 Combinations

331

Answers to Exercises and Problems

1. the number of permutations of 7 items arranged 4 at a time

2. the number of combinations of 7 items selected 4 at a time

3. the number of permutations of 8 items arranged 5 at a time

4. the number of combinations of 8 items selected 5 at a time

5. $_8C_5$; 120 times; For every combination of 5 items, there are 120 arrangements of the 5 items.

6. 24

7. 1

8. 1

9. 15

10. 15

11. 84

12. 84

13. 1680

14. $_nC_n = {}_nC_0 = 1; {}_nC_r = {}_nC_{n-r}$

15. **a.** 210 sets

   b. 35 committees

c. permutations; combinations

d. The number of committees, 35, is the number of sets of officers, 210, divided by the number of permutations of 3 people, 6.

16. permutations; 6 ways

17. combinations; 20 sets

Answers continued on next page.

331

23. Business Suppose Carmeta Jackson owns a pizzeria and offers the options shown.

   a. How many ways can a customer order two toppings? three toppings?

   b. If a customer can order from zero to seven toppings, how many different groups of toppings can be ordered?

   c. How many different pizzas can a customer order at her pizzeria?

   d. **Writing** Write a radio advertisement for her pizzeria that includes your answer to part (c).

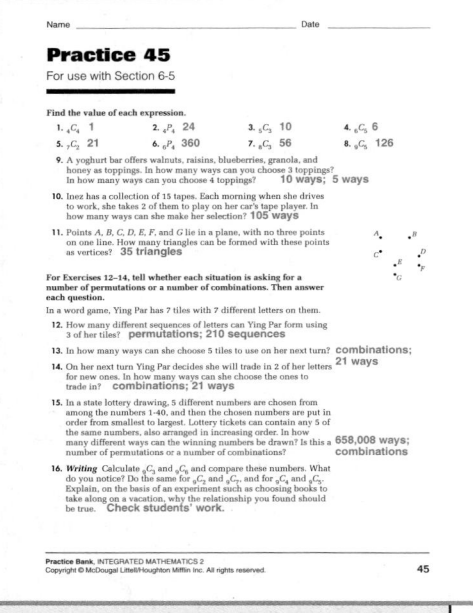
Answers to
Exercises and Problems ....

18. permutations; 504 ways

19. **a.** 59,280 combinations

   b. Answers may vary. An example is given. It might be more appropriate to call the lock a permutation lock, since the order of the numbers is significant.

20. **a.** 5005

   b. 540

   c. about 0.11

21. **a.**

Number of points	5	6	n
Ways to connect points			—
Number of segments	10	15	$_nC_2$

   b. The number of segments is the same as the combination of the number of points taken 2 at a time.

22. 5040 quartets

Ongoing ASSESSMENT

24. Group Activity Work with another student.

   a. You should each write one problem that can be solved using permutations and a related problem that can be solved using combinations.

   b. Solve the problems together.

   c. Discuss whether the problems are clearly of one type or the other. Work together to revise them if necessary.

Review PREVIEW

25. The athletic director at Piedmont High School picks names from a hat to decide who gets the door prizes at the awards banquet. Suppose the hat contains 15 names on green paper and 35 names on yellow paper. Find the probability of picking 2 names on green paper, if the first name is not returned to the bag before the second is picked. *(Section 6-4)*

Find the area of each figure. *(Toolbox Skill 28)*

26. a trapezoid with base$_1$ = 15 ft, base$_2$ = 5 ft, and height = 9 ft

27. a parallelogram with base = 90 mm and height = 48 mm

Predict the next number or term in each pattern. *(Section 1-5)*

28. 1, 3, 6, 10, 15, ___?   **29.** 5, 15, 45, 135, ___?   **30.** 2x, 4x, 16x, 256x, ___?

Working on the Unit Project

31. Suppose your survey included all the subjects listed on page 294. How many interest questions like those described in Exercise 32 on page 301 would appear on your survey?

32. Suppose you want to extend your survey to include all basic courses in each subject area. If there are 23 basic courses, how many interest questions would appear on your survey?

332   **Unit 6** Counting Strategies, Probability, Binomials

23. **a.** 21 ways; 35 ways

   b. 128 groups

   c. 768 pizzas

   d. Answers may vary. An example is given. We make pizza *your* way. At our pizzeria, you can choose from 768 different pizzas.

24. **a–c.** Answers may vary.

25. about 0.086

26. 90 ft^2

27. 4320 mm^2

28. 21

29. 405

30. 65,536x

31. 45 questions

32. 253 questions

Pascal's Triangle

Shortcuts

Focus
Find patterns in Pascal's triangle. Recognize the elements of Pascal's triangle as combinations.

This triangular pattern was pictured in a Chinese book entitled *Precious Mirror of the Four Elements* in A.D. 1303. The author, Chu Shih-Chieh, referred to it as "The Old Method." Evidence suggests that it originated with Liu Ju-Hsieh around A.D. 1100.

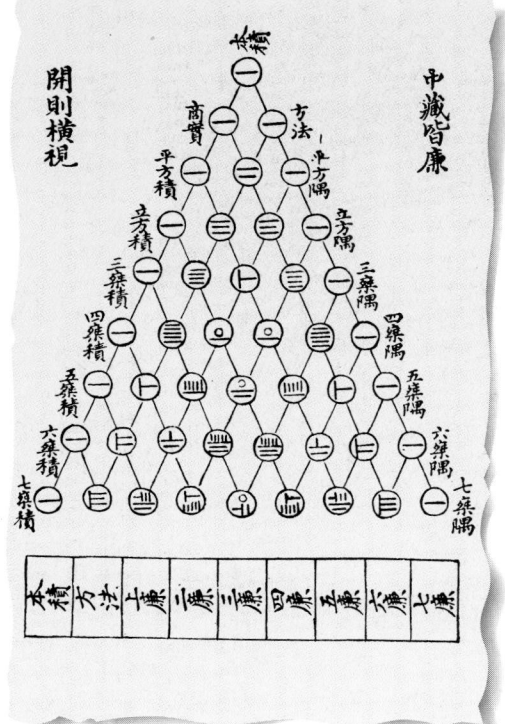

BY THE WAY...

The Chinese pattern has a modern form named after Blaise Pascal (1623–1662), a French mathematician and essay writer. He explored many of its properties, particularly those related to the study of probability.

Talk it Over

1. Ignoring the Chinese characters, what symmetry do you see in the triangle?

2. How do the symbols in the first four rows seem to relate to each other?

3. What do you think the symbol ⊢ means?

4. What do you think the symbol ○ means?

6-6 Pascal's Triangle

333

PLANNING

Objectives and Strands
See pages 292A and 292B.

Spiral Learning
See page 292B.

Recommended Pacing
Section 6-6 is a one-day lesson.

Extra Practice
See pages 623–624.

Warm-Up Exercises
Warm-Up Transparency 6-6

Support Materials
➤ Practice 46
➤ Enrichment 41 in the Activity Bank
➤ Study Guide 6-6
➤ Problem Set 12
➤ Additional Exploration 8
➤ Diagram Master 6 in the Explorations Lab Manual
➤ Using TI-81 and TI-82 Calculators: Permutations, Combinations, and Pascal's Triangle
➤ Quiz 6-6
➤ Alternative Assessment 6

Answers to Talk it Over

1. A line drawn through the center of the top circle and perpendicular to the opposite side of the triangle is an axis of symmetry.

2. Summaries may vary. An example is given. The first and last symbols in each row are the same. The other symbols appear to be made by adding the number of marks on the two circles above a given symbol.

3. 6

4. 10

Multicultural Note

The binomial combinations referred to by Chu Shih-Chieh as "The Old Method" were first calculated in 1100 by Liu Ju-Hsieh in *Piling-Up Powers and Unlocking Coefficients*. Other mathematical "firsts" of the Chinese include the decimal system, traced to the fourteenth century B.C. but apparently in use long before that; negative numbers, used as early as the second century B.C.; and the use of algebraic equations to describe geometrical shapes, developed in the third century A.D.

Talk it Over

Questions 1–4 familiarize students with the ancient Chinese triangular pattern that is now called Pascal's triangle. Students look for patterns and identify the meaning of two symbols. In so doing, they should be able to recognize that the triangular pattern is an arrangement of numbers.

Exploration

Working in pairs, students are led to discover some of the patterns in Pascal's triangle, particularly those related to combinations. Step 6 is an open-ended question. You might wish to call upon each pair of students to identify any other patterns they see and start a list of them.

Integrating the Strands

Pascal's triangle is a geometric arrangement of numbers that exhibits some remarkable properties that are developed in this section and used throughout the remainder of the unit. Implicit in the triangle is an integration of the strands of number, algebra, geometry, and statistics and probability.

* **Work with another student.**

① Each of you should copy the portion of **Pascal's triangle** shown below. Notice that the first row is row 0 and the first diagonal is diagonal 0.

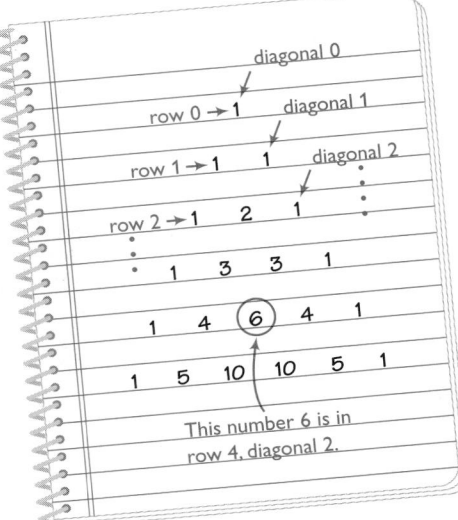

② To locate a number in Pascal's triangle, you specify its row number and diagonal number. Each of you should pick a number in the triangle. Tell your partner its location. Make sure you agree on what number is in that location.

③ There is a rule for creating each row from the numbers in the row above it. With your partner, figure out the rule and use it to create row 6.

④ For each row, find the sum of the numbers. What pattern do you see in the sums? Predict the sum of the numbers in row 7.

⑤ **a.** Use a formula to calculate these combinations:

$$_4C_0 \qquad _4C_1 \qquad _4C_2 \qquad _4C_3 \qquad _4C_4$$

b. In what row and diagonal of Pascal's triangle do you see each of the results from part (a)?

c. Predict where to find $_3C_2$ in Pascal's triangle. Test your prediction.

⑥ Discuss any other number patterns you see in Pascal's triangle. Write down at least one.

Unit 6 Counting Strategies, Probability, Binomials

334

Answers to Exploration

1. Check students' work.

2. Answers may vary. An example is given. The number 5 is in row 5, diagonal 1, and row 5, diagonal 4.

3. The first number in each row is 1. The last number in each row is also 1. To find the number that goes in any other position, add

the two numbers above that position; row 6: 1 6 15 20 15 6 1

4. row 0: 1; row 1: 2; row 2: 4; row 3: 8; row 4: 16; row 5: 32; The sum of the numbers in the nth row is 2^n. The sum of the numbers in row 7 is $2^7 = 128$.

5. **a.** 1, 4, 6, 4, 1

   b. row 4; diagonals 0 to 4

   c. row 3, diagonal 2

6. Answers may vary. An example is given. Pascal's triangle demonstrates that $_nC_r = {}_nC_{n-r}$.

Denise finds four different paperback books that she wants to buy but has enough money for only three books. Use Pascal's triangle to find the number of ways she can select three of the four books.

Sample Response

The notation $_4C_3$ represents the number of combinations of three different books that Denise can select from four different books. Locate the number in row 4, diagonal 3, to find the number of combinations.

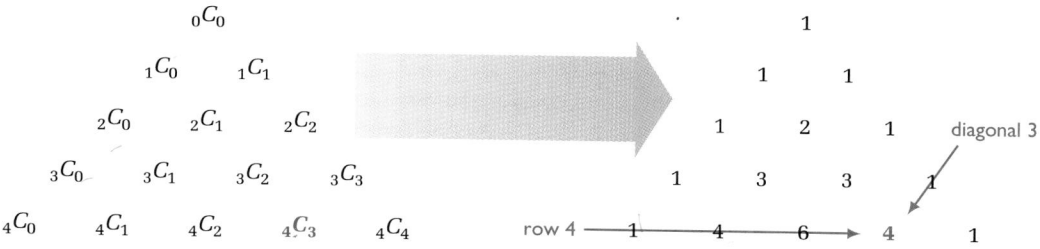

There are four ways Denise can select three of the four books.

SOME PROPERTIES OF PASCAL'S TRIANGLE

Each number (except the 1's) is the sum of the two numbers just above it.

The number in row n, diagonal r, is $_nC_r$.

The sum of the numbers in row n is 2^n.

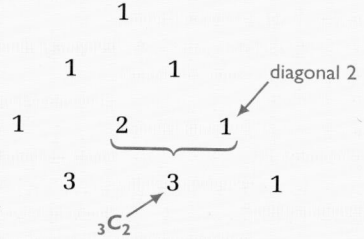

Talk it Over

5. How could you use a formula to find the answer to the Sample?

6. For the situation in the Sample, how could you use a formula to find the total number of ways to select no books, one book, two books, or three books?

6-6 Pascal's Triangle

Answers to Talk it Over

5. $_4C_3 = \dfrac{4!}{3!1!} = \dfrac{24}{6} = 4$

6. $_4C_0 + {}_4C_1 + {}_4C_2 + {}_4C_3 =$
$\dfrac{4!}{0!4!} + \dfrac{4!}{1!3!} + \dfrac{4!}{2!2!} + \dfrac{4!}{3!1!} =$
$1 + 4 + 6 + 4 = 15$

Additional Sample

Use Pascal's triangle to find the number of ways that two items can be selected from five items. The notation $_5C_2$ represents the number of combinations of two different items selected from five items. Use Pascal's triangle to locate the number in row 5 on diagonal 2.

There are 10 different ways to select two of five items.

Using Technology

You can use the TABLE feature of the TI-82 or TI-83 to display the numbers for a row of Pascal's triangle. For example, to display the number for row 3, press [Y=] and enter the equation Y1= 3 nCr X. Then, on the TI-82, press [2nd][TblSet] and for TABLE SETUP use TblMin=0, ΔTbl=1. On the TI-83, press [2nd][TblSet] and for TABLE SETUP use TblStart=0, ΔTbl=1. Finally, press [2nd][TABLE]. The Y1-column displays, in order, the numbers for row 3 of Pascal's triangle. To display the numbers for row 7, use Y1= 7 nCr X for the equation in the Y= list. Use the up and down arrow keys to scroll through the full set of numbers in the Y1-column. (The calculator displays 0's for table entries that do not correspond to numbers for Pascal's triangle. Simply ignore them.)

Teaching Tip

Have students develop Pascal's triangle for seven or eight rows using the pattern shown on this page. For each row, they can then verify that the sum of its numbers is 2^n.

335

Look Back

Ask students to write down their responses to this activity. Then ask a few volunteers to explain their responses. Students should be able to state clearly their understanding of patterns in Pascal's triangle.

APPLYING

Suggested Assignment

Standard 1, 3, 5–19, 23–30

Extended 1, 3, 5–30

Integrating the Strands

Number Exs. 1–3, 5–18, 22, 23, 29, 30

Algebra Exs. 25–27

Functions Exs. 25–27

Geometry Ex. 2

Statistics and Probability Exs. 1–24, 28–30

Logic and Language Exs. 1–4, 21–23

Communication: Reading

Ex. 1 requires students to read, analyze, and respond to questions about Pascal's triangle.

Cooperative Learning

Ex. 2 will require some class time for students to complete. Ex. 3 can be done individually and then discussed with the group partner.

Look Back ←

Choose a row and a number in that row to illustrate each of the properties of Pascal's triangle listed on page 335.

6-6 Exercises and Problems

1. **a.** **Reading** What number is in row 3, diagonal 3, of Pascal's triangle?

   b. Describe how you could locate the number in Pascal's triangle that is the same as $_{15}C_5$.

   c. Without adding, find the sum of the numbers in row 10.

2. **Group Activity** Work with another student.

   a. Copy the Pascal's triangle shown and complete through row 9.

   b. For each row from rows 2–8, choose one number that is surrounded by six others. Find the product of the six numbers surrounding that number.

   c. Make a conjecture about the product of the six numbers surrounding any number.

$$1$$
$$1 \quad 1$$
$$1 \quad 2 \quad 1$$
$$1 \quad 3 \quad 3 \quad 1$$

3. Use the triangle you made for Exercise 2(a).

   a. Find the sum of the first five numbers in diagonal 1. Find that number on the next diagonal.

   b. Repeat part (a), using the first six numbers in diagonal 3.

   c. Make a conjecture about how to find the sum of the first n numbers of any diagonal without adding.

4. **Research** Find out what Pascal's law is. Also find all you can about a unit called a *pascal*.

Find each value using Pascal's triangle.

5. $_5C_2$ 6. $_4C_4$ 7. $_6C_5$ 8. $_6C_2$

9. $_7C_1$ 10. $_7C_6$ 11. $_5C_5$ 12. $_6C_3$

13. Use Pascal's triangle to find all the values of n and r for which $_nC_r = 6$.

For Exercises 14–18, suppose you have just a penny, a nickel, and a dime in your pocket. In how many ways can you choose each of the following?

14. no coins   15. exactly one coin   16. exactly two coins   17. three coins

18. **a.** Which row of Pascal's triangle gives you the answers to Exercises 14–17?

   b. How can you use the row you indicated in part (a) to find the total number of ways to choose no coins, one coin, two coins, or three coins?

   c. **Reading** How could you use a formula to answer part (b)?

19. Nita has six different pens in her book bag. Without looking she grabs three pens at random from the bag. How many three-pen combinations are possible?

Answers to Look Back

Answers may vary. An example is given. Consider row 5. The second number is 5, which is 1 + 4. The third is 10, which is 4 + 6. The fourth is 10, which is 6 + 4. The fifth is 5, which is 4 + 1. The number in row 5, diagonal 3 is 10, which is equal to $_5C_3$. The sum of the numbers in row 5 is 1 + 5 + 10 + 10 + 5 + 1 = 32 = 2^5.

Answers to Exercises and Problems

1. **a.** one

   b. Given the first sixteen rows of Pascal's triangle, find the number in row 15, diagonal 5. Remember that the first row and diagonal are row 0 and diagonal 0.

   c. 1024

2. See answers in back of book.

3. **a.** 15   **b.** 126

   c. Find the nth number on the next diagonal. (Move one row down and one place to the right from the last number in the sum.)

4. Pascal's Law states that whenever the pressure in a confined liquid is increased or diminished at any point, this change in pressure is transmitted equally throughout the entire liquid. Pascal's Law has many practical applications, including the hydraulic brakes on a car. A *pascal* (symbol *Pa*) is a unit of pressure equal to one newton per square meter.

5. 10   6. 1

7. 6   8. 15

9. 7   10. 7

20. Career Artists who do printmaking sometimes choose a variety of color combinations for the same design. Suppose the artist who made the prints shown chose from among eight colors. How many different three-color mixtures were possible?

21. Writing Which method did you use to answer Exercise 20? Explain why you chose that method.

22. Suppose you toss four coins. Use Pascal's triangle to find each number.

  a. number of outcomes that have exactly three heads

  b. number of outcomes that have at least three heads

  c. Compare the situations in parts (a) and (b). How are they alike? How are they different?

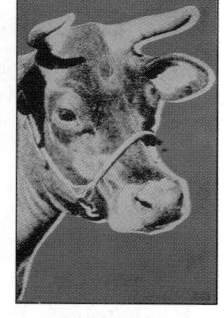

These cows by Andy Warhol were printed on wallpaper.

Ongoing **ASSESSMENT**

23. Open-ended Choose a row of Pascal's triangle. Describe a situation involving combinations where the solution is a number in that row.

Review **PREVIEW**

24. Use a formula to find the number of possible ways to assign a pair of roommates from a group of 120 women in a college dormitory. *(Section 6-5)*

Without graphing, identify the slope and the vertical intercept of the graph of each function. Then graph each function and tell if it is an *increasing function,* **a** *decreasing function,* **or a** *constant function.* *(Section 2-2)*

25. $y = 4x$ **26.** $y = -2x + 3$ **27.** $y = -3$

28. Make a tree diagram that shows all the possible outcomes when you toss three pennies. *(Section 6-1)*

 Working on the Unit Project

29. Look back at Exercises 31 and 32 in Section 6-5. Explain how you can use Pascal's triangle to find the answers.

30. a. How could you use your survey results to find out which subject(s) students born in each half of the year find most interesting?

  b. Use the method you described in part (a) to identify the subject(s) students born in each half of the year find the most interesting.

6-6 Pascal's Triangle   **337**

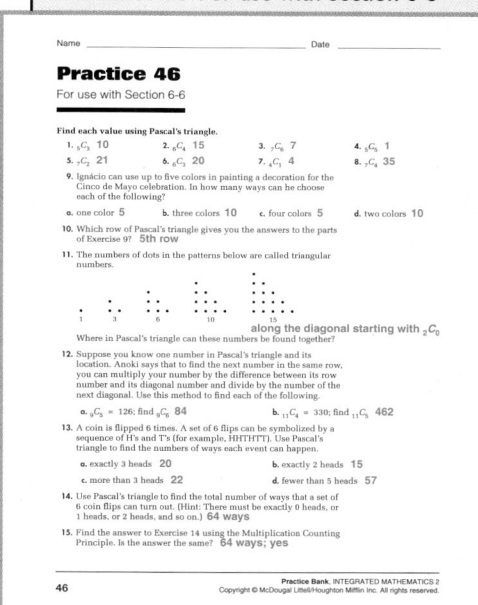

Answers to Exercises and Problems

11. 1

12. 20

13. $n = 4, r = 2; n = 6, r = 1;$ $n = 6, r = 5$

14. 1 way   **15.** 3 ways

16. 3 ways   **17.** 1 way

18. a. row 3

  b. Add the numbers in the row.

  c. $2^n = 2^3 = 8$

19. 20 combinations

20. 56 mixtures

21. Answers may vary. If a written-out triangle including the eighth row is not available, it is easier to use the formula. If such a triangle is available, using it rather than the formula could help avoid arithmetic errors. You might also want to use both as a check.

22. a. 4 outcomes

  b. 5 outcomes

  c. Answers may vary. An example is given. The 5 outcomes included in part (b) include the 4 from part (a) along with the outcome HHHH.

23–29. See answers in back of book.

30. a. Answers may vary. An example is given. Rank each student's responses in order from least interesting to most interesting and weight the answers. For example, if 10 subjects are ranked, give a subject 1 point for a first place (least interesting) and 10 points for a last place (most interesting). Then find the highest weighted average.

  b. Answers may vary. Check students' work.

337

PLANNING

Objectives and Strands
See pages 292A and 292B.

Spiral Learning
See page 292B.

Materials List
Four coins per group
Graph paper

Recommended Pacing
Section 6-7 is a one-day lesson.

Extra Practice
See pages 623–624.

Warm-Up Exercises
Warm-Up Transparency 6-7

Support Materials
➤ Practice 47
➤ Enrichment 42 in the Activity Bank
➤ Study Guide 6-7
➤ Problem Set 12
➤ Diagram Masters 1, 6, 18 in the Explorations Lab Manual
➤ McDougal Littell Mathpack software: *Probability Constructor*
➤ Quiz 6-7
➤ Test 23
➤ Alternative Assessment 7

Section 6-7

Binomial Experiments with $P = \frac{1}{2}$

IT'S A TOSSUP

Focus
Find probabilities for experiments that have two outcomes for each trial and where the probability of each outcome is one half.

EXPLORATION

What are you likely to get when you toss four coins?

- **Materials: four coins**
- **Work with another student.**

① Copy the table.

Number of heads	0	1	2	3	4	Total tosses
First person's results	?	?	?	?	?	20
Second person's results	?	?	?	?	?	20
Total so far	?	?	?	?	?	40
Another team's results	?	?	?	?	?	40
Total for the two teams	?	?	?	?	?	80
Experimental probability	?	?	?	?	?	—

② One person tosses a group of four coins twenty times. The other person tallies in the table whether there are 0, 1, 2, 3, or 4 heads each time.

③ Change roles and repeat step 2.

④ Total the results of steps 2 and 3.

⑤ Combine results with another team and then calculate the experimental probability of each event to the nearest hundredth. For example:

$$P(0 \text{ heads}) = \frac{\text{total number of times no heads were tossed}}{80}$$

This is the total number of tosses for the two teams.

⑥ Make a graph of the probabilities you found. Label the axes as shown.

⑦ Discuss and summarize your findings.

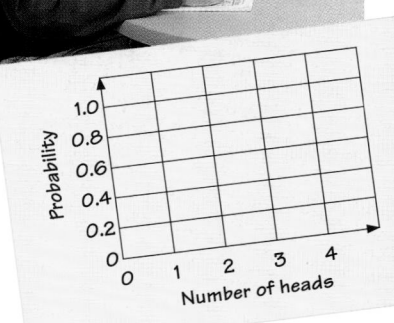

Answers to Exploration

1–7. Actual results may vary. The theoretical probabilities are: 0 heads: 0.0625; 1 head: 0.25; 2 heads: 0.375; 3 heads: 0.25; 4 heads: 0.0625. The graph for these possibilities is shown.

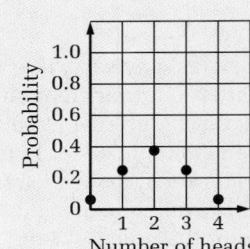

Binomial Experiments

Each time you tossed four coins in the Exploration, you performed a *binomial experiment*, which has the following characteristics.

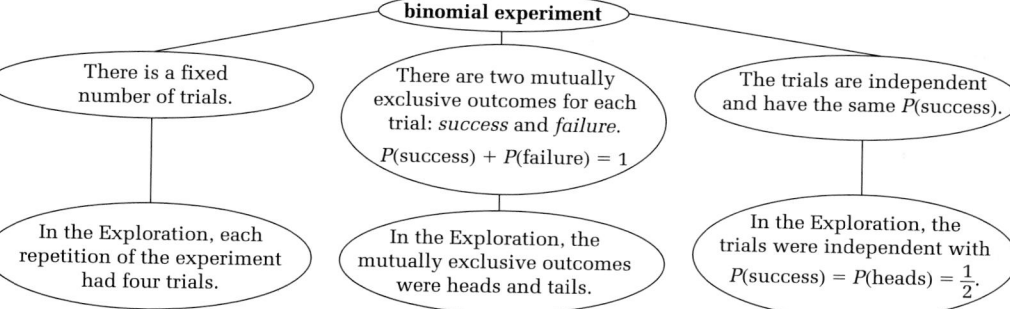

By repeating the binomial experiment many times you were able to find and graph the experimental probability of getting exactly 0, 1, 2, 3, or 4 heads when you toss four coins.

Sample

Find the theoretical probability of getting exactly two heads when four coins are tossed.

Sample Response

Method ❶ **Problem Solving Strategy:** Draw a diagram.

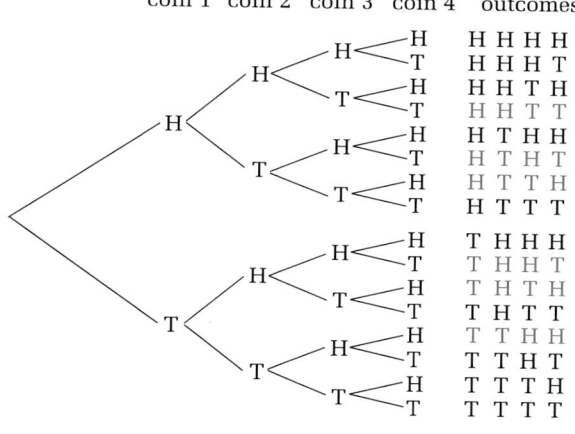

There are 6 favorable outcomes for the event "exactly 2 heads" out of 16 possible outcomes.

$$P(\text{exactly 2 heads out of 4}) = \frac{\text{number of favorable outcomes}}{\text{number of possible outcomes}} = \frac{6}{16} = \frac{3}{8} = 0.375$$

6-7 Binomial Experiments with $P = \frac{1}{2}$

Exploration

The goal of the Exploration is to have students carry out a typical binomial experiment and get an intuitive sense of the results. To save class time, you could provide students with a copy of the table.

Using Technology

The *Probability Constructor* software can be used to simulate the experiment in the Exploration.

Teaching Tip

Consider using a large piece of graph paper or a transparency for displaying the combined results of step 5 of the Exploration. Students should see a general pattern that is bell-shaped and somewhat symmetric. The graph has this shape because more outcomes are a mix of heads and tails rather than just heads or just tails.

Reasoning

In the discussion of a binomial experiment, students learn that in such an experiment for each trial, there are two *mutually exclusive* outcomes, and the trials are *independent*. There is a danger of students confusing *mutually exclusive* events with *independent* events. They are not the same, and the distinction can be made by using the tree diagram in the Sample Response. When the coins are tossed, there are two mutually exclusive outcomes for each coin, namely heads (H) or tails (T). However, an outcome such as HHHH, or any of the 15 others, have events in common which are not mutually exclusive but which are independent; that is, the outcome of each coin has no effect on the outcomes of the other coins. The probability of HHHH is $\left(\frac{1}{2}\right)^4 = \frac{1}{16}$.

Additional Sample

Find the theoretical probability of getting exactly three tails when four coins are tossed.

Method 1: Draw a diagram.
Students can use the diagram and the outcomes identified in the Sample Response to answer this question.
There are four favorable outcomes for the event "exactly 3 tails": HTTT, THTT, TTHT, TTTH.
There are 16 possible outcomes.
P(exactly 3 tails out of 4) $= \frac{4}{16} = \frac{1}{4}$
$= 0.25$

Method 2: Use Pascal's triangle.
The number of favorable outcomes is $_4C_3$. You can find this number in row 4, diagonal 3, of Pascal's triangle. It is 4.
The number of possible outcomes is the sum of the numbers in row 4 of Pascal's triangle:
$1 + 4 + 6 + 4 + 1 = 16$.
P(exactly 3 tails out of 4) $= \frac{4}{16} = \frac{1}{4}$
$= 0.25$

Mathematical Procedures

The Sample compares the experimental probability of the Exploration with the theoretical probability as developed by using a tree diagram or by using the rows and diagonals of Pascal's triangle. Students may use either method for their own problem-solving activities. In Method 2, remind students that they can also use powers of 2 to find the sum of the numbers in any row of Pascal's triangle.

Look Back

Ask all students to write a few sentences to answer this question and then randomly select a few students to present their answers to the class.

Method 2 Use Pascal's triangle.

The number of favorable outcomes is the number of ways you can toss four coins and get two heads, or $_4C_2$. You find this number in row 4, diagonal 2, of Pascal's triangle.

$$
\begin{array}{ccccc}
& & _0C_0 & & \\
& _1C_0 & & _1C_1 & \\
_2C_0 & & _2C_1 & & _2C_2 \\
_3C_0 & _3C_1 & & _3C_2 & _3C_3 \\
_4C_0 & _4C_1 & _4C_2 & _4C_3 & _4C_4 \\
\end{array}
\qquad
\begin{array}{ccccc}
& & 1 & & \\
& 1 & & 1 & \\
1 & & 2 & & 1 \\
1 & 3 & & 3 & 1 \\
1 & 4 & 6 & 4 & 1 \\
\end{array}
$$

The number of possible outcomes is the sum of the number of ways four coins can land. This is the sum of the numbers in row 4 of Pascal's triangle.

$\underbrace{1 + 4 + 6 + 4 + 1}_{\text{sum of numbers in row 4}} = 16$ or $\underset{\text{sum of numbers in row } n = 2^n}{2^4 = 16}$

$P(\text{exactly 2 heads out of 4}) = \dfrac{\text{number of favorable outcomes}}{\text{number of possible outcomes}} = \dfrac{6}{16} = \dfrac{3}{8} = 0.375$

Talk it Over

1. a. Which of the methods in the Sample do you prefer? Why?

   b. How could you use a formula to find the number of favorable outcomes?

2. Find P(exactly 1 head) when four coins are tossed.

3. Find P(exactly 2 heads) when five coins are tossed.

4. The graph shows the theoretical probability of getting exactly 0, 1, 2, 3, 4, 5, or 6 heads when you toss six coins. Use the graph to estimate the probability of getting four heads when you toss six coins.

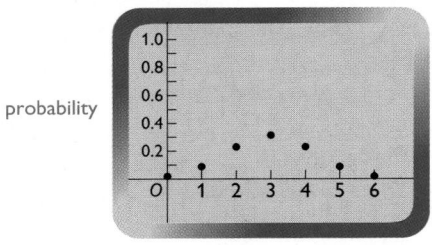

Look Back

How do binomial experiments relate to Pascal's triangle?

Answers to Talk it Over

1. a. Answers may vary. I prefer Pascal's triangle, since it involves less work than making a diagram and it is not necessary to know what the actual outcomes are.

   b. $_4C_2 = \dfrac{4!}{2!2!} = \dfrac{24}{2 \cdot 2} = 6$

2. 0.25

3. 0.3125

4. about 0.23

Answers to Look Back

In a binomial experiment, the number of favorable outcomes for r successes in n tries is given by the number in row n and diagonal r of Pascal's triangle ($_nC_r$).

Exercises and Problems

1. **Reading** Explain why the experiment in the Sample on page 339 is a binomial experiment.

2. a. **Reading** Use the tree diagram in the Sample on page 339 to complete this table.

Ways of Getting Heads When Tossing Four Coins						
Number of heads	0	1	2	3	4	Total
Number of outcomes	?	?	?	?	?	?
Probability	?	?	?	?	?	?

b. Make a graph of the probability of each number of heads in part (a).

c. **Writing** Compare the graph you made in part (b) with the graph you made in step 6 of the Exploration on page 338. How are they alike? How are they different?

Find the probability of the event shown when each group of coins is tossed.

3.

4.

5.

For Exercises 6–8, assume that the birth of a boy and the birth of a girl are equally likely.

6. A three-child family might include 0, 1, 2, or 3 girls.

   a. Why is this a binomial situation?

   b. **Using Manipulatives** Do a simulation. Let heads represent girls and tails represent boys. Toss a group of 3 coins 25 times and tally in a table whether there are 0, 1, 2, or 3 girls in the family.

   c. **Group Activity** Combine results with another student. Then calculate the experimental probability of each event to the nearest hundredth.

   d. Find the theoretical probability of each event.

   e. On the same axes, graph the experimental and theoretical probability of each event. Compare the graphs.

7. Find the probability of a six-child family including exactly three girls.

8. a. Predict whether the probability that a four-child family will include exactly two girls is *50%*, *greater than 50%*, or *less than 50%*. Explain your reasoning.

   b. Find the probability that a four-child family will include exactly two girls.

6-7 Binomial Experiments with $P = \frac{1}{2}$

341

---

1. There is a fixed number of trials. The two outcomes are mutually exclusive and $P(\text{heads}) + P(\text{tails}) = 1$. The trials are independent and $P(\text{heads}) = P(\text{tails}) = \frac{1}{2}$.

2. a.

Number of heads	0	1	2	3	4	Total
Number of outcomes	1	4	6	4	1	16
Probability	0.0625	0.25	0.375	0.25	0.0625	1

b.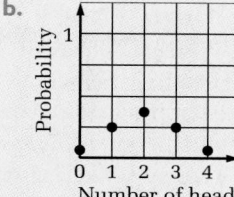

Probability / Number of heads

Suggested Assignment
Standard 3–5, 7, 8, 11–23
Extended 1–5, 7–23

Integrating the Strands
Geometry Exs. 19, 20
Statistics and Probability
Exs. 1–18, 21–23
Logic and Language Exs. 1, 2, 10–12, 17

Using Technology
The *Probability Constructor* software can be used to simulate the coin tossing in Ex. 6.

2. c. Answers may vary. It is possible that the graphs are exactly alike, very similar, or not similar at all, except in the x-coordinates of the points and the fact that the y-coordinates are all less than 1.

3. 0.375

4. 0.125

5. 0.3125

6. a. There is a fixed number of trials, 3. There are two mutually exclusive outcomes for each trial: *boy* and *girl*. Finally, the trials are independent and $P(\text{boy}) = P(\text{girl}) = \frac{1}{2}$.

   b. Check students' work.

   c. Results may vary.

   d. 0 girls: 0.125; 1 girls: 0.375; 2 girls: 0.375; 3 girls: 0.125

   e. Answers may vary. It is possible that the graphs are exactly alike, very similar, or not similar at all, except in the x-coordinates of the points and the fact that the y-coordinates are all less than 1. The graph of the theoretical probability is given.

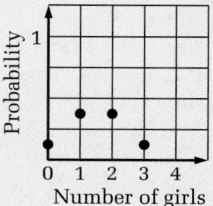

Probability / Number of girls

7. 0.3125

Answers continued on next page.

Interdisciplinary Problems

Students know that mathematics is a useful tool for solving real-world problems. In the Connection to Literature and in Exs. 9 and 10, students see that other individuals, such as authors of plays, also use mathematics, but to entertain rather than to solve problems. Clearly, author Tom Stoppard knows about probability and the fact that the product of 2 and any odd or even number is always even (Ex. 10).

Rosencrantz and Guildenstern Are Dead by Tom Stoppard is a twentieth century play about two characters from Shakespeare's *Hamlet*. It begins with the title characters on stage. They both have large leather money bags, but Guildenstern's (GUIL) is almost empty and Rosencrantz's (ROS) is almost full.

GUIL *takes a coin out of his bag, spins it, letting it fall.*

ROS: Heads. *He picks it up and puts it in his bag. The process is repeated.*

Heads. *Again.*

Heads. *Again.*

Heads. *Again.*

Heads.

GUIL . . . *flips over two more coins.* . . . ROS *announces each of them as "heads."*

ROS: Eighty-five in a row—beaten the record!

GUIL . . .: And if you'd lost? If they'd come down against you, eighty-five times, one after another, just like that?

ROS . . .: Eighty-five in a row? *Tails?*

GUIL: Yes! What would you think?

ROS (*doubtfully*): Well . . . . Well, I'd have a good look at your coins for a start! . . .

GUIL: It must be indicative of something, besides the redistribution of wealth. . . . each individual coin spun individually (*he spins one*) is as likely to come down heads as tails and therefore should cause no surprise each individual time it does. . . . The equanimity of your average tosser of coins depends upon a law, or rather a tendency, or let us say a probability, or at any rate a mathematically calculable chance, which ensures that he will not upset himself by losing too much or upset his opponent by winning too often.

9. a. In all, 92 coins came down heads 92 times. Based on the experimental results of Rosencrantz and Guildenstern's coin tossing, what is the experimental probability that a tossed coin comes down heads?

   b. What is the theoretical probability that 92 tosses all come down heads?

10. Later in the play Guildenstern makes another wager, "Bet me then. . . . Year of your birth. Double it. Even numbers I win, odd numbers I lose." What is the probability that he will win? Explain.

Unit 6 Counting Strategies, Probability, Binomials

Answers to Exercises and Problems

8. a. Answers may vary. An example is given. less than 50%; The probability is the same as that of getting exactly two heads when four coins are tossed. Since the probability that any one of the children is a girl is 50%, it may seem to some students that the probability that half of the children are girls is 50%. That is not true.

   b. 0.375

9. a. 1

   b. $(0.5)^{92} \approx 2.02 \times 10^{-28}$

10. 1; Doubling any whole number produces an even number.

11. a. There is a fixed number of trials, 5. There are two mutually exclusive outcomes for each trial: *true* and *false*. The trials are independent and $P(\text{true}) = P(\text{false}) = \frac{1}{2}$.

   b. 32   **c.** 1

   d. 0.03125

   e. Answers may vary. An example is given. Find the answer to part (b) by adding the numbers in row 5 of Pascal's triangle or by finding 2^5. Find the answer to part (c) by finding the number in row 5, diagonal 5 of Pascal's triangle.

12. a. 3

   b. 10 ways

   c. Answers may vary. An example is given. Calculate $_5C_3$ or find the element in row 5, diagonal 3 of Pascal's triangle.

   d. 0.5

342

11. Suppose you select the five answers on a true-false quiz at random.

   a. Why is this a binomial situation?

   b. How many different ways could you answer the five questions?

   c. How many ways could you answer the five questions correctly?

   d. What is the probability of getting all the answers correct?

   e. **Writing** Which method did you use to answer part (b)? part (c)? Tell why you chose each method.

12. Suppose a score of at least 60% is needed to pass a true-false quiz with five questions.

   a. At least how many correct answers are needed to pass?

   b. How many ways can you get at least enough correct answers to pass?

   c. Describe the method you used to get your answer in part (b).

   d. Find the probability of getting at least a 60% on a true-false quiz with five questions by answering randomly.

13. Graph the probabilities associated with getting 0, 1, 2, 3, 4, or 5 questions correct on a true-false quiz with five questions.

14. Marcus makes half of the free-throw shots he attempts in basketball. He shoots four free-throw shots. What is the probability that he will make all four shots?

15. Half of the 70 teachers at Grant High School are married. You need to find 5 chaperones for a dance. If you ask 10 teachers at random to chaperone, what is the probability that you will ask exactly 5 married teachers?

16. Phyllis Hayashibara has a part-time job. There is a 50% chance that she will have to work on any given evening. She has already worked Friday and Saturday evenings. What is the probability that she will have to work on Sunday evening? Explain your answer.

Ongoing ASSESSMENT

17. **Writing** Samantha says that the probability of getting exactly *two* heads when five coins are tossed is the same as the probability of getting exactly *three* heads when five coins are tossed. Do you agree? Why or why not?

Quiz: *Voting Rights*

Mark whether each statement is *True* or *False*.

T F 1. In 1878 Susan B. Anthony succeeded in bringing the 19th Amendment, which guaranteed voting rights to women in the United States, before a senate committee.

T F 2. Carrie Chapman Catt was instrumental in getting the 19th Amendment ratified in 1920.

T F 3. The 15th Amendment guaranteed African Americans the right to vote. The 24th Amendment eliminated poll taxes as an obstacle to voting.

T F 4. In 1893, New Zealand gave women full voting rights.

T F 5. In 1971, United States citizens 18 years of age and over were guaranteed the right to vote.

Answers to Exercises and Problems

13.

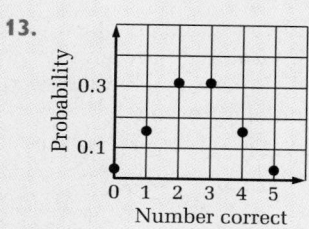

14. 0.0625

15. about 0.246

16. 50%; Since the probability that she will work on any given evening is 50%, whether she works on Sunday is independent of whether she worked on Friday or Saturday.

17. Yes. Reasoning may vary. An example is given. When five coins are tossed, the probability of getting two heads is the same as that of getting three tails. But the probability of getting three tails is the same as that of getting three heads. Alternatively, note that $_5C_2 = {}_5C_3$ and that the number is row 5, diagonal 2 of Pascal's triangle is the same as the one in row 5, diagonal 3.

Review **PREVIEW**

18. Use Pascal's triangle to find the number of possible ways two students could tie in a six-person race. *(Section 6-6)*

Find the coordinates of each image described. *(Section 5-4)*

19. translation of *QRST* 2 units left and 2 units down

20. dilation of *QRST* with scale factor 2 and center at the origin

21. Suppose you roll a die. *(Section 6-3)*

   a. Find *P*(5).

   b. Find *P*(prime).

   c. Are the events in parts (a) and (b) mutually exclusive? Why or why not?

Working on the Unit Project

22. Suppose it is equally likely that a person chosen at random has a birthday in the first or second half of the year.

   a. What is the theoretical probability that a person chosen at random has a birthday in the first half of the year? in the second half of the year?

   b. Find the probability that exactly two of six people chosen at random have a birthday in the second half of the year.

23. Based on your survey results, what is the experimental probability that a person chosen at random has a birthday in the first half of the year? in the second half of the year?

Unit 6   **CHECKPOINT 2**

1. **Writing** Describe how you can use Pascal's triangle to find the number of combinations of five things selected four at a time.

2. a. How many different groups of five trophies can you select from nine trophies?   6-5

   b. How many different ways can you arrange five trophies in a row?

3. What are the numbers in row 3 of Pascal's triangle? Show how you can find the numbers.   6-6

4. Use combination notation to describe the number of ways two items can be chosen from four items. Then use Pascal's triangle to find the number of combinations.

5. Find *P*(exactly 3 heads) when three coins are tossed.   6-7

6. Find *P*(exactly 4 heads) when five coins are tossed.

Unit 6 Counting Strategies, Probability, Binomials

Answers to Exercises and Problems

18. 15 ways

19. *Q*′(−1, 0); *R*′(1, 0); *S*′(1, −4); *T*′(−3, −3)

20. *Q*′(2, 4); *R*′(6, 4); *S*′(6, −4); *T*′(−2, −2)

21. a. about 0.167

   b. 0.5

   c. No; the events can happen at the same time since five is a prime number.

22. a. 0.5; 0.5

   b. about 0.234

23. Answers may vary.

Answers to Checkpoint

1. Find the number in row 5, diagonal 4. (5)

2. a. 126 groups

   b. 120 ways

3. 1 3 3 1; Answers may vary. An example is given. The first and fourth numbers are 1. To find the second number, add the first and second numbers of row 2. To find the third number, add the second and third numbers of row 2.

4. $_4C_2$; 6

5. 0.125

6. 0.15625

Section 6-8

Binomial Experiments with $P \neq \dfrac{1}{2}$

Focus
Find probabilities for binomial experiments where the probability of each outcome is not one half.

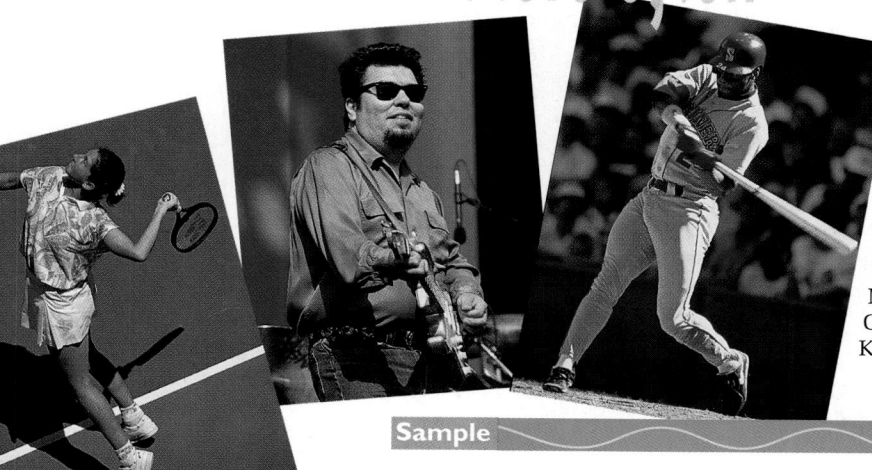

More Often Than Not

The probability of being left-handed is about 10%. These are some notable left-handed people: Monica Seles, Cesar Rosas, and Ken Griffey, Jr.

Sample

Find the probability that exactly two out of three students chosen at random are left-handed.

Sample Response

This is a binomial experiment. There are two outcomes, left-handed and right-handed, and each trial is independent.

Method ❶ Use Pascal's triangle.

Step 1

Find the probability of each outcome that has exactly two left-handed students.

$P(L) \cdot P(L) \cdot P(R) = (0.1)(0.1)(0.9)$
$= 0.009$

You can multiply the probabilities because the events are independent.

Step 2

The number of ways to select two out of three students is found in row 3, diagonal 2.

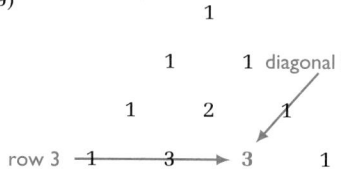

```
              1

          1       1  diagonal 2

      1       2       1

row 3 —1———— 3 ——→ 3       1
```

Step 3

Multiply. The probability of choosing exactly two left-handed students is

$3(0.009) = 0.027.$

6-8 Binomial Experiments with $P \neq \dfrac{1}{2}$ 345

PLANNING

Objectives and Strands
See pages 292A and 292B.

Spiral Learning
See page 292B.

Materials List
➤ Calculator or telephone book

Recommended Pacing
Section 6-8 is a one-day lesson.

Extra Practice
See pages 623–624.

Warm-Up Exercises
💡 Warm-Up Transparency 6-8

Support Materials
➤ Practice 48
➤ Enrichment 43 in the Activity Bank
➤ Study Guide 6-8
➤ Problem Set 13
➤ McDougal Littell Mathpack software: *Probability Constructor*
➤ Quiz 6-8
➤ Alternative Assessment 8

Additional Sample

In a certain school, it is known that about 20% of the students walk to school. Find the probability that exactly three out of four students chosen at random walk to school.

This is a binomial experiment. There are two outcomes, either a student walks to school or rides to school, and each trial is independent.

Method 1: Use Pascal's triangle.
Step 1. Find the probability of each outcome that has exactly three out of four students walking to school.
P(walks) · P(walks) · P(walks) · P(rides) = (0.2)(0.2)(0.2)(0.8) = 0.0064
Step 2. The number of ways to select three out of four students is in row 4, diagonal 3. This number is 4.
Step 3. Multiply. The probability of choosing exactly 3 out of 4 students who walk is 4(0.0064) = 0.0256.

Method 2: Use a diagram.
Step 1. Draw a tree diagram. Use W for walks and R for rides. See diagram at bottom of page.
Step 2. Find the probability of each outcome with exactly three out of four students walking.
P(WWWR) = 0.0064
P(WWRW) = 0.0064
P(WRWW) = 0.0064
P(RWWW) = 0.0064
Step 3. The probability of choosing exactly 3 students out of 4 who walk is the sum of the individual probabilities because the events are mutually exclusive.
0.0064 + 0.0064 + 0.0064 + 0.0064 = 0.0256

Method ❷ Problem Solving Strategy: Draw a diagram.

Step 1 Draw a tree diagram.

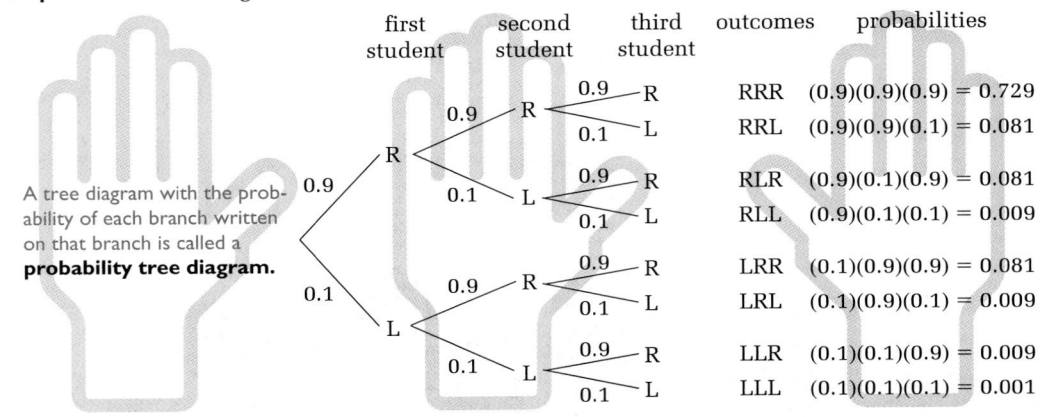

A tree diagram with the probability of each branch written on that branch is called a **probability tree diagram.**

	first student	second student	third student	outcomes	probabilities
			0.9 R	RRR	(0.9)(0.9)(0.9) = 0.729
	0.9 R	0.9 R	0.1 L	RRL	(0.9)(0.9)(0.1) = 0.081
R 0.9		0.1 L	0.9 R	RLR	(0.9)(0.1)(0.9) = 0.081
			0.1 L	RLL	(0.9)(0.1)(0.1) = 0.009
	0.9 R		0.9 R	LRR	(0.1)(0.9)(0.9) = 0.081
L 0.1		0.1 L	0.1 L	LRL	(0.1)(0.9)(0.1) = 0.009
			0.9 R	LLR	(0.1)(0.1)(0.9) = 0.009
	0.1 L		0.1 L	LLL	(0.1)(0.1)(0.1) = 0.001

Step 2 Find the probability of each outcome with exactly two left-handed students.

P(RLL) = 0.009   P(LRL) = 0.009   P(LLR) = 0.009

Step 3 The probability of choosing exactly two left-handed students is:

0.009 + 0.009 + 0.009 = 0.027 ← You can add the probabilities because the outcomes are mutually exclusive.

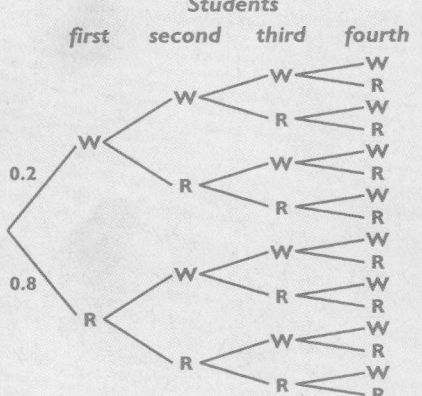

Combinations with at least one left-handed student:
RRL   RLL   LLL
RLR   LRL
LRR   LLR
3(0.081) + 3(0.009) + 0.001
0.271

"at least one" and "none" are complements.
P(at least one) = 1 − P(none)
= 1 − P(RRR)
= 1 − 0.729
= 0.271

When the outcomes are *not equally likely,* as in the Sample, you cannot divide favorable outcomes by total outcomes to find a probability.

$$\frac{\text{favorable}}{\text{total}} = \frac{3}{8} = 0.375 \neq 0.027$$

Talk it Over

Use the Sample.

1. Why are the outcomes not equally likely?

2. Show how to use the formula $_3C_2$ to find the number of ways to select exactly two students from three students.

3. Suppose your friend thinks that you can just multiply (0.1)(0.1)(0.9) to find the probability that exactly two out of three students chosen at random are left-handed. How can you show your friend that he or she is mistaken?

4. Two students used information from the tree diagram in the Sample to find the probability that *at least* one out of three students chosen at random is left-handed. Their work is shown at the left. Which method do you prefer? Why?

5. Find the probability that at least two out of three students chosen at random are left-handed.

Unit 6 Counting Strategies, Probability, Binomials

	Students			Outcomes	Probabilities
first	second	third	fourth		
				WWWW	(0.2)(0.2)(0.2)(0.2) = 0.0016
	W	W		WWWR	(0.2)(0.2)(0.2)(0.8) = 0.0064
		R		WWRW	(0.2)(0.2)(0.8)(0.2) = 0.0064
0.2	W			WWRR	(0.2)(0.2)(0.8)(0.8) = 0.0256
		W		WRWW	(0.2)(0.8)(0.2)(0.2) = 0.0064
	R	R		WRWR	(0.2)(0.8)(0.2)(0.8) = 0.0256
				WRRW	(0.2)(0.8)(0.8)(0.2) = 0.0256
				WRRR	(0.2)(0.8)(0.8)(0.8) = 0.1024
		W		RWWW	(0.8)(0.2)(0.2)(0.2) = 0.0064
0.8	W			RWWR	(0.8)(0.2)(0.2)(0.8) = 0.0256
		R		RWRW	(0.8)(0.2)(0.8)(0.2) = 0.0256
	R			RWRR	(0.8)(0.2)(0.8)(0.8) = 0.1024
		W		RRWW	(0.8)(0.8)(0.2)(0.2) = 0.0256
	R			RRWR	(0.8)(0.8)(0.2)(0.8) = 0.1024
		R		RRRW	(0.8)(0.8)(0.8)(0.2) = 0.1024
				RRRR	(0.8)(0.8)(0.8)(0.8) = 0.4096

Answers to Talk it Over

1. The probability of being left-handed is 0.1 and the probability of being right-handed is 0.9.

2. $_3C_2 = \dfrac{3!}{(3-2)!2!} = \dfrac{3 \cdot 2 \cdot 1}{1 \cdot 2 \cdot 1} = 3$

3. Answers may vary. An example is given. The number of left-handed students may be 0, 1, 2, or 3. Using the reasoning described, the probabilities would be 0 students: 0.729; 1 student: 0.081; 2 students: 0.009; 3 students: 0.001. The sum of those probabilities is only 0.82.

4–9. See answers in back of book.

Experiments with more than two outcomes can be binomial experiments if you consider one outcome to be "favorable" and the remaining outcomes to be "unfavorable."

For example, suppose you roll a die and consider a "1" to be a favorable outcome. Then 2, 3, 4, 5, and 6 are the unfavorable outcomes.

Talk it Over

6. Suppose you roll a die. What is the probability of the favorable outcome, rolling a "1"?

7. What is the probability of not rolling a "1"?

8. Suppose you roll a die three times and consider a "1" to be a favorable outcome. Draw a probability tree diagram for this situation.

9. Use your diagram from question 8. Are the outcomes equally likely? Why or why not?

Look Back

How are binomial experiments with $P \neq \frac{1}{2}$ like binomial experiments with $P = \frac{1}{2}$? How are they different?

6-8 Exercises and Problems

1. **Reading** Why is the answer to the Sample not $\frac{3}{8}$?

For Exercises 2–5, use the special coin described below.

A special coin has been created for a magic trick. The probability of its landing on heads is 0.25 and on tails is 0.75.

2. Draw a probability tree diagram for three tosses of the coin.

3. Find the probability of tossing three consecutive heads.

4. Find the probability of tossing exactly two heads in three tosses.

5. Find the probability of tossing at least two heads in three tosses.

6. Cassandra generally wins three games out of five when she plays table tennis with Alec. What is the probability of her winning at least two of the next five games?

7. Suppose you want to find the probability of rolling at least one "1" on three rolls of a die.

   a. Tell how this problem meets the criteria for a binomial experiment.

   b. Solve the problem. Show your work.

Answers to Look Back

Being binomial experiments, both have a fixed number of trials with two mutually exclusive outcomes. Trials are independent. However, in the experiments with $P \neq \frac{1}{2}$, the outcomes do not have the same probability. Therefore, you cannot find a probability by dividing favorable outcomes by total outcomes.

Answers to Exercises and Problems

1. because $P(R) \neq P(L)$

2.

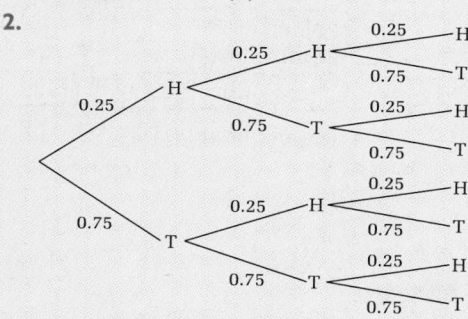

Answers continued on next page.

Answers to
Exercises and Problems

3. about 0.016

4. about 0.141

5. 0.15625

6. 0.91296

7. a. There are a limited number of trials. The two possible outcomes ("1" and "not 1") are mutually exclusive and $P(1) + P(\text{not } 1) = 1$. The trials are independent.

   b. Solution method may vary. An example is given. Use the tree diagram shown in the answer for Talk it Over question 8. Since "rolling at least one 1" and "rolling no 1's" are complementary, find $P(\text{no 1's})$. The only favorable outcome is NNN with probability $\left(\frac{5}{6}\right)^3 \approx$ 0.579. Then $P(\text{at least one 1}) \approx$ 0.421.

---

8. **Writing** Compare the two situations represented by the tables below. How are they alike? How are they different?

Ways of Getting Left-handed Students When Selecting Three Students					
Number of "lefties"	0	1	2	3	Total
Number of outcomes	1	3	3	1	8
Probability	0.729	0.243	0.027	0.001	1

Ways of Getting Heads When Tossing Three Coins					
Number of heads	0	1	2	3	Total
Number of outcomes	1	3	3	1	8
Probability	0.125	0.375	0.375	0.125	1

Health The graph shows the range of success rates for some vaccines. All the rates apply to people who have received the minimum number of doses (usually three). All the vaccines protect people through at least the age of ten.

Suppose four children under the age of ten have each had the minimum number of doses of all the vaccines. Find the range of probabilities for each situation.

9. All four children are exposed to measles. All four children get the disease.

10. All four children are exposed to polio. None of the children gets the disease.

11. All four children are exposed to mumps. Only one child gets the disease.

12. All four children are exposed to pertussis. At least three children get the disease.

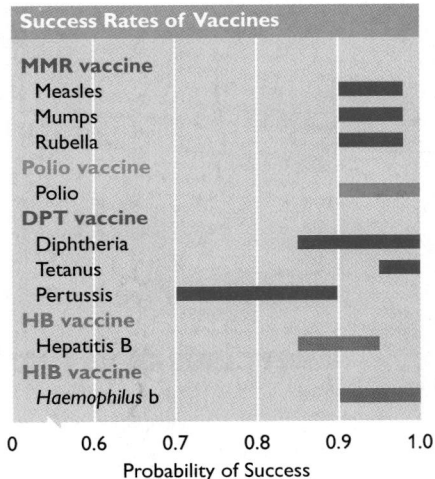

13. Each of the five questions on a multiple-choice test has four choices.

   a. What is the probability of guessing correctly on any single question?

   b. What is the probability of guessing incorrectly on any single question?

   c. Copy and complete the table.

Ways of Getting Correct Answers						
Number correct	0	1	2	3	4	5
Number of outcomes	?	?	?	?	?	?
Probability	?	?	?	?	?	?

   d. Use your completed table to find the probability of getting at least three out of five questions correct just by guessing.

Unit 6 Counting Strategies, Probability, Binomials

---

8. Both are binomial experiments. In the first table, $P \neq \frac{1}{2}$. In the second table, $P = \frac{1}{2}$.

9. 0.00000016 to 0.0001

10. 0.6561 to 1

11. 0.075 to 0.2916

12. 0.0037 to 0.0837

13. a. 0.25

   b. 0.75

c.

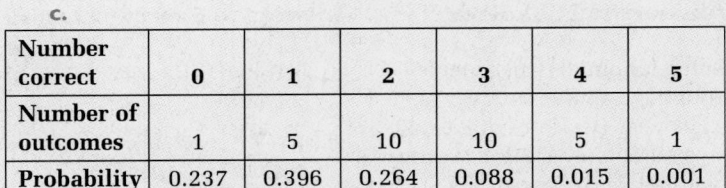

Number correct	0	1	2	3	4	5
Number of outcomes	1	5	10	10	5	1
Probability	0.237	0.396	0.264	0.088	0.015	0.001

   d. about 0.104

14 TECHNOLOGY Mike receives an "A" on tests 90% of the time. You will use a calculator to generate random test results for Mike. You should count any number from 0 to 0.9 as an "A."

Alternative Approach Generate random numbers from a telephone book (see page 19).

a. Why does it make sense to count numbers from 0 to 0.9 as "A's"?

b. Generate a group of five random numbers between 0 and 1. Tally in a table whether Mike gets 0, 1, 2, 3, 4, or 5 "A's."

c. Repeat part (b) for a total of 25 trials.

d. Find the experimental probability of each event in your table.

e. Find the theoretical probability of each event in your table.

For Exercises 15–17, use the matrices below.

Colleges must have an idea of how many students will drop out each year in order to decide how many students they can accept. Matrix A contains the drop-out rates by class for each of three colleges. Matrix B contains enrollment figures at the three colleges.

Matrix A

	A	B	C	D	E
1		fresh.	soph.	jr.	sr.
2	College 1	0.22	0.15	0.12	0.08
3	College 2	0.07	0.03	0.02	0.01
4	College 3	0.35	0.22	0.13	0.07
5					
6					

Matrix B

	A	B	C	D
1		Coll. 1	Coll. 2	Coll. 3
2	fresh.	416	2215	500
3	soph.	324	2060	324
4	jr.	275	1994	252
5	sr.	241	1950	218
6				

15. Find out how many students at each college will drop out. Describe your method.

16. What is the probability that exactly five out of six sophomores chosen at random from College 1 will stay for another year?

17. What is the probability that exactly four out of six freshmen chosen at random from College 3 will stay for another year?

Ongoing **ASSESSMENT**

18. a. **Open-ended** Write and solve a multiple-choice quiz for this section of the unit. Your quiz should have four questions, and there should be five choices for each question.

b. Find the probability of getting exactly two questions correct just by guessing on your quiz.

Using Technology

The random-number feature of the *Probability Constructor* software can be used to do the experiment in Ex. 14.

Assessment: Standard

Ex. 18 offers a good opportunity for students to demonstrate their understanding of this section. Students can be assessed not only on how well they do on their own quizzes, but also on how complete their quizzes are.

Answers to Exercises and Problems

14. a. A random number generator will theoretically generate numbers from 0 to 0.9 90% of the time and numbers between 0.9 and 1, including 1, 10% of the time.

b–d. Results may vary.

e. $P(0 \text{ A's}) = 0.00001$;
$P(1 \text{ A}) = 0.00045$;
$P(2 \text{ A's}) = 0.0081$;

$P(3 \text{ A's}) = 0.0729$;
$P(4 \text{ A's}) = 0.32805$;
$P(5 \text{ A's}) = 0.59049$

15. College 1: 192 students
College 2: 276 students
College 3: 294 students
For each college, multiply the dropout rate for each of the 4 classes by the number in each class. Then add the four numbers.

16. about 0.399

17. about 0.328

18. a. Answers may vary. Check students' work.

b. 0.1536

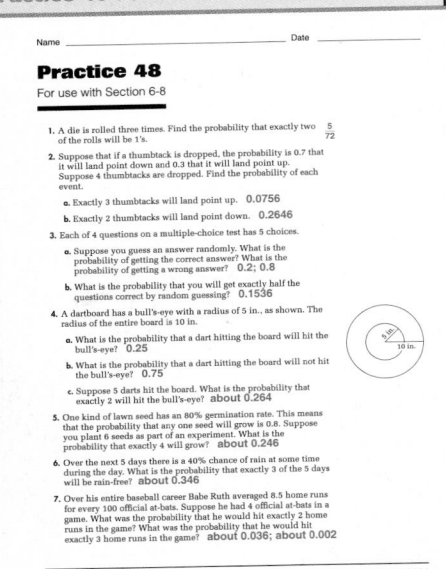
19. Find the probability of getting exactly three heads when five coins are tossed. *(Section 6-7)*

Estimate the solutions of each system of quadratic equations shown. *(Section 4-7)*

20. $y = 0.5x^2$
    $y = 2x^2 + 3x - 3$

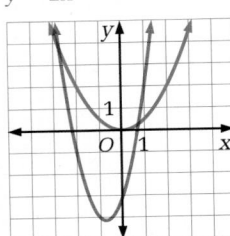

21. $y = x^2 + 0.75$
    $y = -x^2 + 1.25$

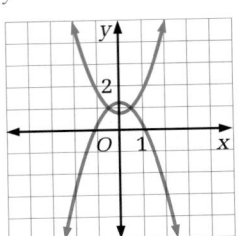

Write and simplify an expression for the volume of each box. *(Toolbox Skills 10, 28)*

22.

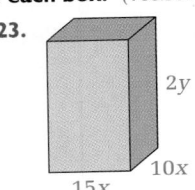

$3a$
$3a$
$6a$

23.

$2y$
$10x$
$15x$

Working on the Unit Project

24. a. **Research** Find out the number of births in each month over the past few years in your city, town, or county, or at a large hospital in your community.
    b. What is the probability that a person chosen at random from the sample you chose in part (a) has a birthday in the first half of the year? in the second half of the year?
    c. Look back at your answer to Exercise 23 in Section 6-7. Are the probabilities you found in your survey close to the probabilities based on the data you got in part (a)? If not, why do you think there is a significant difference?

25. Use your survey results.
    a. Find the probability that exactly two out of six people chosen at random have a birthday in the second half of the year.
    b. How does your answer to part (a) compare to your answer to part (b) of Exercise 22 in Section 6-7?

Answers to Exercises and Problems

19. 0.3125

20–21. Answers may vary. Examples are given.

20. (–2.7, 3.6) and (0.7, 0.3)

21. (–0.5, 1) and (0.5, 1)

22. $V = 3a \cdot 3a \cdot 6a = 54a^3$

23. $V = 15x \cdot 10x \cdot 2y = 300x^2y$

24. a–c. Answers may vary.

25. a, b. Answers may vary.

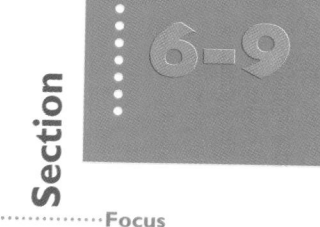

Focus
Find powers of binomials.

The Binomial Theorem

EXPAND Your Horizons

An expression that can be written as the sum of two monomials, such as $a + b$, is a **binomial**. Here are some powers of binomials:

$$(a + b)^2, (a + b)^3, \text{ and } (a + b)^4$$

You can write these powers in *factored form* or *expanded form*.

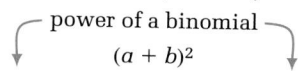

power of a binomial
$(a + b)^2$

factored form   **expanded form**

written as a product → $(a + b)(a + b) = a^2 + 2ab + b^2$ ← written as a sum

You can use models to show these two forms.

Talk it Over

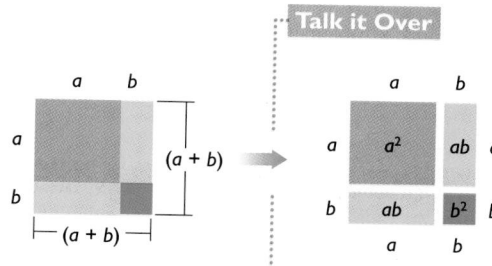

1. Use the area model of $(a + b)^2$. Explain how it shows that the factored form and expanded form are equal.

2. Explain how to use the distributive property to rewrite the product $(a + b)(a + b)$ in expanded form.

Use the volume models below.

3. Explain how you know that each of the three gold prisms in the diagram has a volume of a^2b cubic units.

4. Explain how you know that each of the three green prisms in the diagram has a volume of ab^2 cubic units.

5. Explain how to use the distributive property to rewrite $(a + b)(a + b)(a + b)$ in expanded form.

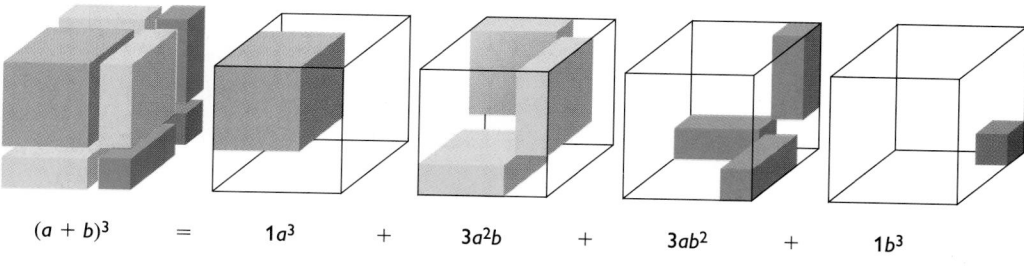

$(a + b)^3 \quad = \quad 1a^3 \quad + \quad 3a^2b \quad + \quad 3ab^2 \quad + \quad 1b^3$

6-9 The Binomial Theorem

PLANNING

Objectives and Strands
See pages 292A and 292B.

Spiral Learning
See page 292B.

Recommended Pacing
Section 6-9 is a two-day lesson.

Day 1
Pages 351–353: Opening paragraph through Talk it Over 11, *Exercises 1–8*

Day 2
Pages 353–354: The Binomial Theorem through Look Back, *Exercises 9–32*

Extra Practice
See pages 623–624.

Warm-Up Exercises
Warm-Up Transparency 6-9

Support Materials
➤ Practice 49
➤ Enrichment 44 in the Activity Bank
➤ Study Guide 6-9
➤ Problem Set 13
➤ Diagram Master 6 in the Explorations Lab Manual
➤ Quiz 6-9
➤ Test 24

Answers to Talk it Over

1. Both models have length $a + b$ and width $a + b$. The area of the figure on the left is $(a + b)^2$. The total area of the figures on the right is $a^2 + 2ab + b^2$.

2. $(a + b)(a + b) = (a + b)(a) + (a + b)(b) = a(a) + b(a) + a(b) + b(b) = a^2 + 2ab + b^2$

3. Each gold prism has a square base with side length equal to a, and a height equal to b, so the volume is $a \cdot a \cdot b = a^2b$.

4. Each green prism has a square base with side length equal to b, and a height equal to a, so the volume is $b \cdot b \cdot a = b^2a$.

5. Answers may vary. Example: $(a + b)(a + b)(a + b) = (a + b)[(a + b)(a + b)] = (a + b)(a^2 + 2ab + b^2) = a(a^2 + 2ab + b^2) + b(a^2 + 2ab + b^2) = a(a^2) + a(2ab) + a(b^2) + b(a^2) + b(2ab) + b(b^2) = a^3 + 2a^2b + ab^2 + a^2b + 2ab^2 + b^3 = a^3 + 3a^2b + 3ab^2 + b^3$

TEACHING

Talk it Over

Questions 1, 3, and 4 ask students to review and extend the area model for multiplying binomials to a three-dimensional model representing the cube of a binomial. Questions 2 and 5 review the use of the distributive property to rewrite products in expanded form. Questions 6–9 lead students to discover the relationship between the coefficient in the expanded form of $(a + b)^n$ and the number in the nth row of Pascal's triangle.

Additional Sample

S1 Write $(a + b)^4$ in expanded form.

Use Pascal's triangle to determine the coefficients in the expanded form.
Step 1. Since the power is 4, look at row 4. The numbers are: 1, 4, 6, 4, 1. These numbers will be the coefficients for the five terms.
Step 2. Write the powers of a in decreasing order starting with a^4 and the powers of b in increasing order from b^0. The order is a^4b^0, a^3b^1, a^2b^2, a^1b^3, a^0b^4.
Step 3. Write the coefficients from step 1 with each corresponding set of variables from step 2.
$1a^4b^0 + 4a^3b^1 + 6a^2b^2 + 4a^1b^3 + 1a^0b^4$
Step 4. Simplify. Variables with exponents of 0 can be omitted, and it is not necessary to write an exponent or coefficient of 1.
$a^4 + 4a^3b + 6a^2b^2 + 4ab^3 + b^4$

Look at the patterns in the following expanded forms of the powers of the binomial $a + b$. Coefficients and exponents of 1 are shown to help you see the patterns.

$$(a + b)^0 = 1$$
$$(a + b)^1 = 1a^1 + 1b^1$$
$$(a + b)^2 = 1a^2 + 2a^1b^1 + 1b^2$$
$$(a + b)^3 = 1a^3 + 3a^2b^1 + 3a^1b^2 + 1b^3$$

Talk it Over

6. What pattern do you see in the coefficients?

7. What pattern do you see in the exponents of the a variables? of the b variables?

8. Since $b^0 = 1$ and $a^0 = 1$, you could write
$$(a + b)^2 = 1a^2b^0 + 2a^1b^1 + 1a^0b^2$$
Do the exponents follow the pattern you saw in question 7?

9. Rewrite the expanded form of $(a + b)^3$ using zeros as exponents where appropriate.

The coefficients you use in the expanded form of $(a + b)^n$ are found in the nth row of Pascal's triangle.

Sample 1

Write $(a + b)^5$ in expanded form.

```
                1
              1   1
            1   2   1
          1   3   3   1
        1   4   6   4   1
      1   5  10  10   5   1
```

Sample Response

Use Pascal's triangle to find the coefficients in the expanded form.

Step 1 Because the power is 5, look at the fifth row of Pascal's triangle. Write the six numbers, leaving space for the variables.

$$1 \quad + 5 \quad + 10 \quad + 10 \quad + 5 \quad + 1$$

Step 2 Write powers of a next to each coefficient, starting with a^5 and decreasing from there.

$$1a^5 \quad + 5a^4 \quad + 10a^3 \quad + 10a^2 \quad + 5a^1 \quad + 1a^0$$

Step 3 Write powers of b next to each power of a, starting with b^0 and increasing from there.

$$1a^5b^0 + 5a^4b^1 + 10a^3b^2 + 10a^2b^3 + 5a^1b^4 + 1a^0b^5$$

Step 4 Simplify. Coefficients and exponents of 1 are usually not written. Also, variables with an exponent of 0 can be omitted because they equal 1.

$$a^5 + 5a^4b + 10a^3b^2 + 10a^2b^3 + 5ab^4 + b^5$$

Answers to Talk it Over

6. The coefficients of $(a + b)^n$ are the numbers in row n of Pascal's triangle.

7. The exponents of the a variables in $(a + b)^n$ are decreasing consecutive integers from n to 0. The exponents of the b variables in $(a + b)^n$ are increasing consecutive integers from 0 to n.

8. Yes.

9. $1a^3b^0 + 3a^2b^1 + 3a^1b^2 + 1a^0b^3$

Now you are ready for:
Exs. 1–8 on pp. 354–355

Talk it Over

10. **a.** How many terms are there in the expanded form of $(a + b)^6$?

    b. Write $(a + b)^6$ in expanded form.

11. How many terms are there in the expanded form of $(a + b)^n$?

The Binomial Theorem

You can rewrite the expanded form in Sample 1 using the $_nC_r$ notation instead of numbers from Pascal's triangle.

$$(_5C_0)a^5b^0 + (_5C_1)a^4b^1 + (_5C_2)a^3b^2 + (_5C_3)a^2b^3 + (_5C_4)a^1b^4 + (_5C_5)a^0b^5$$

This pattern can be generalized.

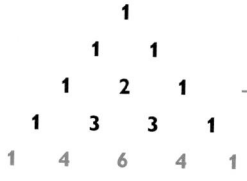

THE BINOMIAL THEOREM

If n is a positive integer, then this is the expanded form of $(a + b)^n$:

$$(_nC_0)a^nb^0 + (_nC_1)a^{n-1}b^1 + (_nC_2)a^{n-2}b^2 + \cdots$$

$$\cdots + (_nC_{n-2})a^2b^{n-2} + (_nC_{n-1})a^1b^{n-1} + (_nC_n)a^0b^n$$

The coefficients of the form $(_nC_r)$ are numbers in the nth row of Pascal's triangle.

Sample 2

Write $(x + 3)^4$ in expanded form.

Sample Response

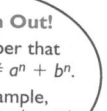

```
        1
      1   1
    1   2   1
  1   3   3   1
1   4   6   4   1
```

Use the binomial theorem with $n = 4$.

For coefficients, use the fourth row of Pascal's triangle.

$$(a + b)^4 = 1a^4b^0 + 4a^3b^1 + 6a^2b^2 + 4a^1b^3 + 1a^0b^4$$

Substitute x for a and 3 for b. Simplify.

$$(x + 3)^4 = 1x^4(3)^0 + 4x^3(3)^1 + 6x^2(3)^2 + 4x^1(3)^3 + 1x^0(3)^4$$

$$= 1x^4(1) + 4x^3(3) + 6x^2(9) + 4x^1(27) + 1x^0(81)$$

$$= x^4 + 12x^3 + 54x^2 + 108x + 81$$

Watch Out!
Remember that
$(a + b)^n \neq a^n + b^n$.
For example,
$(x + 3)^4 \neq x^4 + 3^4$.

Answers to Talk it Over

10. **a.** 7 terms

    b. $a^6 + 6a^5b + 15a^4b^2 + 20a^3b^3 + 15a^2b^4 + 6ab^5 + b^6$

11. $n + 1$

Talk it Over

Questions 10 and 11 require that students recognize and generalize that there is always one more term in a binomial expansion than the degree of expansion.

Communication: Reading

You may wish to ask for a volunteer to read the binomial theorem using the $_nC_r$ notation to the class. Ask also why this theorem is called the binomial theorem. (because it involves the expansion of a binomial $(a + b)$ to an integral power n)

Additional Sample

S2 Write $(2 + y)^3$ in expanded form. Use the binomial theorem with $n = 3$. Use row 3 of Pascal's triangle for the coefficients.

$(a + b)^3 = 1a^3b^0 + 3a^2b^1 + 3a^1b^2 + 1a^0b^3$

Substitute 2 for a and y for b. Simplify.

$(2 + y)^3 = (2)^3y^0 + 3(2)^2y^1 + 3(2)^1y^2 + 1(2)^0y^3$
$= 8 + 12y + 6y^2 + y^3$

S3 Write $(z - 4)^3$ in expanded form. **Think of $(z - 4)$ as $(z + (-4))$. Substitute z for a and (-4) for b in the expanded form of $(a + b)^3$. Then simplify.**

$$(z - 4)^3 = 1z^3(-4)^0 + 3z^2(-4)^1 + 3z^1(-4)^2 + 1z^0(-4)^3$$
$$= z^3 - 12z^2 + 48z - 64$$

Talk it Over

Questions 12–14 focus students' attention on the effect of a negative factor in each term in the expansion of a binomial. Students need to observe that the even and odd powers of a negative factor cause the signs to alternate.

Look Back

Ask students to write a response to this question. Then have students check with a partner to refine their descriptions. A few sample responses can be read to the class. •

APPLYING

Suggested Assignment

Day 1

Standard 1–8

Extended 1–8

Day 2

Standard 9–20, 23, 25–32

Extended 9–32

Integrating the Strands

Number Exs. 2, 21, 22

Algebra Exs. 1–25

Geometry Exs. 1, 3, 23, 24, 27

Statistics and Probability Exs. 1–22, 25, 32

Logic and Language Exs. 21, 22, 25, 28–32

Sample 3

Write $(p - q)^5$ in expanded form.

Sample Response

Use the binomial theorem with $n = 5$.

For coefficients, use the fifth row of Pascal's triangle.

$$(a + b)^5 = 1a^5b^0 + 5a^4b^1 + 10a^3b^2 + 10a^2b^3 + 5a^1b^4 + 1a^0b^5$$

Think of $(p - q)$ as $(p + (-q))$. Substitute p for a and $-q$ for b.

$$(p - q)^5 = 1p^5(-q)^0 + 5p^4(-q)^1 + 10p^3(-q)^2 + 10p^2(-q)^3 + 5p^1(-q)^4 + 1p^0(-q)^5$$
$$= 1p^5(q^0) + 5p^4(-q^1) + 10p^3(q^2) + 10p^2(-q^3) + 5p^1(q^4) + 1p^0(-q^5)$$
$$= 1p^5q^0 + (-5p^4q^1) + 10p^3q^2 + (-10p^2q^3) + 5p^1q^4 + (-1p^0q^5)$$
$$= p^5 - 5p^4q + 10p^3q^2 - 10p^2q^3 + 5pq^4 - q^5$$

Watch Out!
Be careful about signs when you simplify the powers of $-q$.

Talk it Over

12. Explain why the coefficients in the final expanded form of Sample 2 are not found in a row of Pascal's triangle.

13. Explain why $10p^3(-q)^2$ simplifies to $10p^3(q^2)$ in Sample 3.

14. Why do the signs alternate $+$ and $-$ in the final expanded form of Sample 3?

Look Back

How do you use the patterns in Pascal's triangle and decreasing and increasing powers to write any power of a binomial?

▶ Now you are ready for:
Exs. 9–32 on pp. 355–357

6-9 Exercises and Problems

1. Use the area model to write $(x + 3)^2$ in expanded form.

2. Use the distributive property to write $(x + 7)^2$ in expanded form.

3. **a.** Use the volume model to write $(m + 2)^3$ in expanded form.

   b. Describe the volumes of the eight blocks in the model.

4. **Reading** Where in Pascal's triangle are the coefficients of the terms in the expanded form of $(a + b)^7$?

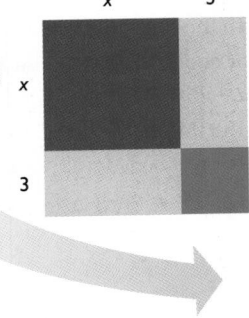
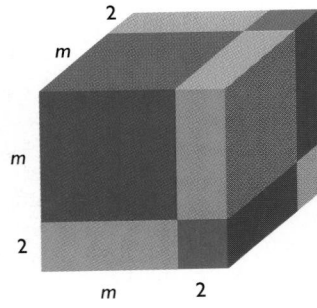

Unit 6 Counting Strategies, Probability, Binomials

Answers to Talk it Over

12. The second term of the binomial is a constant, not a variable, so the coefficients of Pascal's triangle are multiplied by the constant raised to the correct power.

13. Even powers of negative numbers are always positive.

14. because even and odd powers of negative numbers alternate signs

Answers to Look Back

To expand $(a + b)^n$, use the nth row of Pascal's triangle for coefficients. Write powers of a next to each coefficient, starting with a^n and decreasing to 0 by intervals of 1. Write powers of b next to each power of a, starting with b^0 and increasing to n by intervals of 1. Finally, rewrite the resulting expression omitting coefficients and exponents of 1 and variables with exponent 0.

Use Pascal's triangle and patterns of exponents to write each power of a binomial in expanded form.

5. $(c + d)^3$
6. $(p + q)^4$
7. $(x + y)^5$
8. Write the expanded form of $(a + b)^6$ using ${}_nC_r$ notation instead of numbers from Pascal's triangle for the coefficients.

Use the binomial theorem to write each power of a binomial in expanded form.

9. $(x + 2)^3$
10. $(z + 2)^5$
11. $(y - 2)^4$
12. $(c + 3)^4$
13. $(x + 3)^3$
14. $(x - 3)^3$
15. $(a + 1)^{10}$
16. $(m - 1)^9$

Will numbers from a row of Pascal's triangle appear in the expanded form of each binomial? Explain why or why not.

17. $(p + q)^6$
18. $(p + 2)^3$
19. $(p + 2q)^3$
20. Write $(x - 2y)^3$ in expanded form.
21. a. Describe the number pattern for powers of 11 shown below.

			+100000
		+10000	+50000
	+1000	+4000	+10000
+100	+300	+600	+1000
+20	+30	+40	+50
+1	+1	+1	+1
$11^2 = 121$	$11^3 = 1331$	$11^4 = 14641$	$11^5 = 161051$

b. Write the expanded form of $(10 + 1)^6$ using the binomial theorem. Stack the terms to make the next sum in the number pattern. Check your answer by finding 11^6 with a calculator.

c. Explain how the number pattern is related to the expanded form of $(10 + 1)^n$.

22. a. Describe the number pattern for powers of 9 shown below.

			+100000
		+10000	−50000
	+1000	−4000	+10000
+100	−300	+600	−1000
−20	+30	−40	+50
+1	−1	+1	−1
$9^2 = 81$	$9^3 = 729$	$9^4 = 6561$	$9^5 = 59049$

b. Write the expanded form of $(10 - 1)^6$ using the binomial theorem. Stack the terms to make the next sum in the number pattern. Check your answer by finding 9^6 with a calculator.

c. Explain how the number pattern is related to the expanded form of $(10 - 1)^n$. Why do the signs in this pattern alternate + and −?

Assessment: Standard

When students are expanding a binomial, as in Exs. 5–16, it might be beneficial for them to turn their papers sideways so that they have ample room to write each part of the term, especially when the second term in the binomial is negative. Check that students have written the proper coefficients from Pascal's triangle into their calculations. Suggest that they write these coefficients above their calculations. To assess students' ability to use this technique, have them write a step-by-step method to expand a binomial.

Integrating the Strands

Exs. 21 and 22 reveal how mathematical concepts are often interrelated. In these two exercises, concepts from the strands of number, algebra, statistics and probability, and logic and language are involved.

Answers to Exercises and Problems

1. $x^2 + 6x + 9$
2. $x^2 + 14x + 49$
3. a. $m^3 + 6m^2 + 12m + 8$
   b. There is one block with volume m^3 and one with volume 8. There are three blocks with volume $2m^2$ and three with volume $4m$.
4. row 7
5. $c^3 + 3c^2d + 3cd^2 + d^3$
6. $p^4 + 4p^3q + 6p^2q^2 + 4pq^3 + q^4$
7. $x^5 + 5x^4y + 10x^3y^2 + 10x^2y^3 + 5xy^4 + y^5$
8. ${}_6C_0a^6 + {}_6C_1a^5b + {}_6C_2a^4b^2 + {}_6C_3a^3b^3 + {}_6C_4a^2b^4 + {}_6C_5\,ab^5 + {}_6C_6b^6$
9. $x^3 + 6x^2 + 12x + 8$
10. $z^5 + 10z^4 + 40z^3 + 80z^2 + 80z + 32$
11. $y^4 - 8y^3 + 24y^2 - 32y + 16$
12. $c^4 + 12c^3 + 54c^2 + 108c + 81$
13. $x^3 + 9x^2 + 27x + 27$
14. $x^3 - 9x^2 + 27x - 27$
15. $a^{10} + 10a^9 + 45a^8 + 120a^7 + 210a^6 + 252a^5 + 210a^4 + 120a^3 + 45a^2 + 10a + 1$
16. $m^9 - 9m^8 + 36m^7 - 84m^6 + 126m^5 - 126m^4 + 84m^3 - 36m^2 + 9m - 1$
17. Yes; each term of the expansion has the form ${}_6C_rp^{(6-r)}q^r$.
18. No; each term of the expansion has the form ${}_6C_rp^{(6-r)}2^r$. When these terms are simplified, the coefficient of each term except the first is multiplied by a power of 2.
19. No; each term of the expansion has the form ${}_3C_rp^{(3-r)}(2q)^r$. When these terms are simplified, the coefficient of each term except the first is multiplied by a power of 2.
20. $x^3 - 6x^2y + 12xy^2 - 8y^3$
21. a. The boldface digits in the addends of each sum are rows 2–5 of Pascal's triangle.
    b. $10^6 + 6 \cdot 10^5 + 15 \cdot 10^4 + 20 \cdot 10^3 + 15 \cdot 10^2 + 6 \cdot 10 + 1$

       1000000
       + 600000
       + 150000
       + 20000
       + 1500
       + 60
       + 1
       $11^6 = 1771561$
    c. The number pattern is derived by expanding $(10 + 1)^n$. The expanded form of $(10 + 1)^n$ has terms that are the numbers of row n of Pascal's triangle times powers of ten.
22. See answers in back of book.

356

Using Manipulatives

Ex. 23 can be modeled using sugar cubes, small wooden cubes, or plastic cubes. The large cube can be assembled from the small cubes and then painted with diluted food coloring, a marker pen, or with small colored stickers. Students can be encouraged to make their own model at home, or a model could be available in the classroom.

Research

Some students may find it interesting to research how to make a model of a hypercube. The research should include a description of some of the mathematical properties of a hypercube and why it is important in mathematics.

23. A cube with sides of length $(n + 2)$ is dipped in a bucket of paint and then cut into unit cubes. In this exercise you will find how many of these unit cubes have 0, 1, 2, and 3 faces painted.

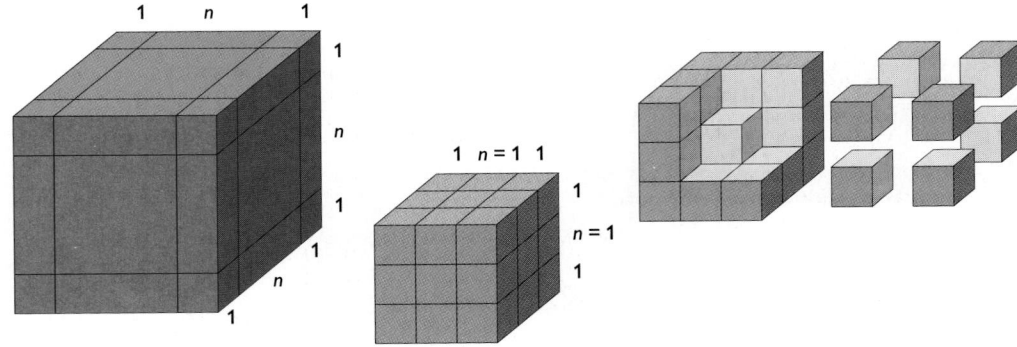

a. Complete the table for values of n from 0 to 3.

n	$n + 2$	Total number of unit cubes	Unit cubes painted on 0 faces	Unit cubes painted on 1 face	Unit cubes painted on 2 faces	Unit cubes painted on 3 faces
0	2	8	0	0	0	8
1	3	27	1	6	?	?
2	4	?	?	?	?	?
3	?	?	?	?	?	?
n	$n + 2$	$(n + 2)^3$	?	?	?	?

b. Complete the table for row n.

c. Explain how the expanded form of $(n + 2)^3$ is related to the entries in row n.

24. You saw that $(a + b)^2$ can be modeled as a *square* made of 4 rectangles, 1 with area a^2, 2 with area ab, and 1 with area b^2.

You also saw that $(a + b)^3$ can be modeled as a *cube* made of 8 prisms, 1 with volume a^3, 3 with volume a^2b, 3 with volume ab^2, and 1 with volume b^3.

A *hypercube* is a four-dimensional cube. Consider a hypercube of length $(a + b)$ on each side.

a. Write a power of a binomial that expresses the "hyper-volume" of the hypercube.

b. If you "explode" the hypercube in the same way that the square and cube were exploded in this section, how many pieces do you expect?

c. How many different "hyper-volumes" will there be among the pieces? What are they?

d. How many pieces do you expect will have each "hyper-volume"? Show how your answer is related to the expanded form of $(a + b)^4$.

Unit 6 Counting Strategies, Probability, Binomials

Answers to Exercises and Problems

23. a, b.

n	$n + 2$	Total number of unit cubes	Unit cubes painted on 0 faces	Unit cubes painted on 1 face	Unit cubes painted on 2 faces	Unit cubes painted on 3 faces
0	2	8	0	0	0	8
1	3	27	1	6	12	8
2	4	64	8	24	24	8
3	5	125	27	54	36	8
n	$n + 2$	$(n + 2)^3$	n^3	$6n^2$	$12n$	8

c. The entries in row n, columns 4–7, are the terms of the expanded form $(n + 2)^3$.

24. a. $(a + b)^4$

b. 16 pieces

c. five "hyper-volumes"; $a^4, a^3b, a^2b^2, ab^3, b^4$

25. a. If you toss 4 coins, how many different ways can you get exactly 4 heads? exactly 3 heads and 1 tail? exactly 2 heads and 2 tails? exactly 1 head and 3 tails? exactly 4 tails?

b. Write an expanded form of $(h + t)^4$.

c. **Writing** How does your expression in part (b) relate to the situation of the possible outcomes when tossing 4 coins? Describe the significance of the coefficients and exponents of each term of the expanded form.

Review **PREVIEW**

26. Terry misses the school bus 5% of the time. What is the probability that he will miss the bus exactly three out of five days this week? *(Section 6-8)*

27. Show that $ABCD$ is a rhombus. *(Section 5-2)*

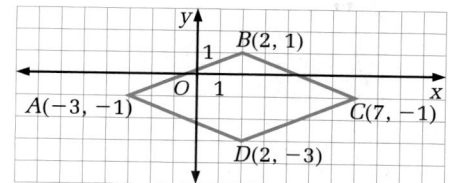

Tell whether each statement about animals is *True* or *False*. *(Section 1-6)*

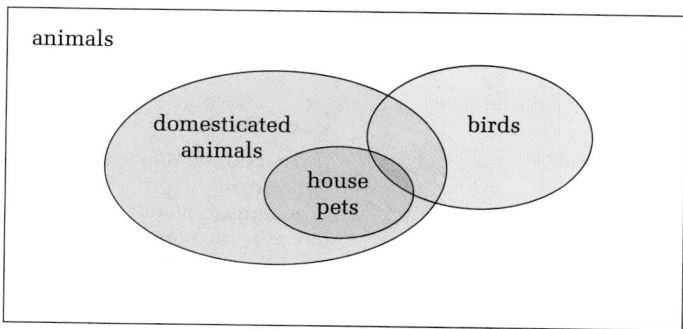

28. If an animal is a house pet, then it is domesticated.

29. Every bird is a domesticated animal.

30. Some domesticated animals are birds.

31. All animals that are not domesticated are not house pets.

 ## Working on the Unit Project

32. **Writing** Use your survey results. Describe any positive or negative correlations between having a birthday in the first or second half of the year and interest in the school subjects included in your survey. If you found no strong correlations, provide a possible explanation.

6-9 The Binomial Theorem

357

Practice 49 For use with Section 6-9

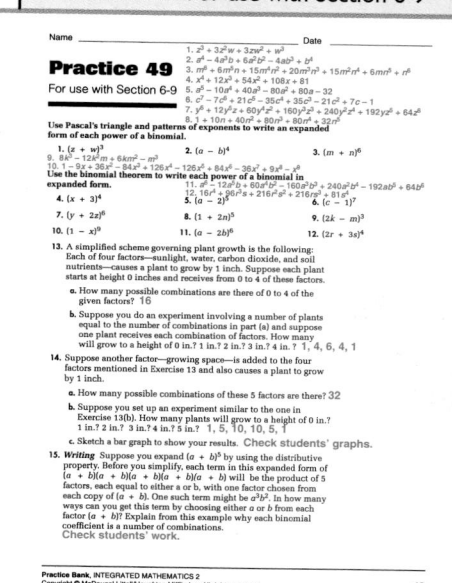

Answers to Exercises and Problems

d. a^4: 1 piece; a^3b: 4 pieces; a^2b^2: 6 pieces; ab^3: 4 pieces; b^4: 1 piece; The number of pieces with each "hyper-volume" is the coefficient of the appropriate term in the expanded form of $(a + b)^4$.

25. a. 1; 4; 6; 4; 1

b. $h^4 + 4h^3t + 6h^2t^2 + 4ht^3 + t^4$

c. The coefficients are, in order, the number of different ways of getting exactly 4, 3, 2, 1, or 0 heads. The term $_nC_r h^{(n-r)}t^r$ indicates that there are $_nC_r$ ways of getting exactly $n - r$ heads and r tails.

26. about 0.001

27. slope of $\overline{AB} = \frac{1 + 1}{2 + 3} = \frac{2}{5}$ and

slope of $\overline{CD} = \frac{-1 + 3}{7 - 2} = \frac{2}{5}$;

slope of $\overline{AD} = \frac{-3 + 1}{2 + 3} = -\frac{2}{5}$

and slope of $\overline{BC} = \frac{-1 - 1}{7 - 2} = -\frac{2}{5}$; $AB =$

$\sqrt{(2 + 3)^2 + (1 + 1)^2} = \sqrt{29}$;

$BC = \sqrt{(7 - 2)^2 + (-1 - 1)^2}$

$= \sqrt{29}$; $CD =$

$\sqrt{(7 - 2)^2 + (-1 + 3)^2} =$

$\sqrt{29}$; $AD = \sqrt{(2 + 3)^2 + (-3 + 1)^2}$

$= \sqrt{29}$; Since $ABCD$ has two pairs of parallel sides and all four sides have the same measure, $ABCD$ is a rhombus.

28. True.

29. False.

30. True.

31. True.

32. Answers may vary.

Assessment

A scoring rubric for the Unit Project can be found on pages 292 and 293 of this Teacher's Edition and also in the *Project Book*.

Unit Project 6

Completing the Unit Project

Develop your interest profiles. Your finished project should include these things:

➤ a copy of your group's survey

➤ the analysis of your survey based on your answers to "Working on the Unit Project" exercises

➤ a data display of the survey results

➤ the probabilities you computed in the "Working on the Unit Project" exercises, and any others you feel are appropriate

➤ a written description of your profiles

➤ a visual display showing an interest profile for students with birthdays in the first half of the year and an interest profile for students with birthdays in the second half of the year

JAN-JUNE
Visual Arts 58%
Music 29%
Social Studies 41%
Science 41%
Physical Education 29%

JULY-DEC
Visual Arts 59%
Music 58%
Social Studies 26%
Physical Education 11%
Science 42%

Look Back

If you had the opportunity to improve the procedures or methods you used to develop your profiles, what changes would you make?

Alternative Projects

Project 1: Mendel's Theory of Heredity

Research the principles of heredity developed by Gregor Mendel. Prepare a poster describing the principles. Include a Punnett square and explain how to use it to predict the inheritance of genetic traits.

Project 2: Odds of Winning a Lottery

If your state or a neighboring one runs a lottery, contact the lottery commission to find out the odds of winning, how the odds are computed, and when and how the odds may change. At the same time, interview some people who regularly buy lottery tickets, some who never buy them, and some who only occasionally buy them. Ask them the same questions. Use the information you collected to write an article with the title, "State Lotteries: Fact vs. Fiction."

358   **Unit 6** Completing the Unit Project

Answers to Unit 6
Review and Assessment

1.
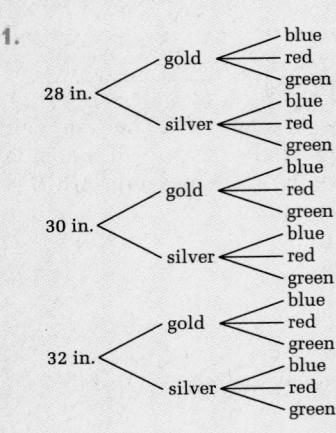

28 in.
- gold — blue, red, green
- silver — blue, red, green

30 in.
- gold — blue, red, green
- silver — blue, red, green

32 in.
- gold — blue, red, green
- silver — blue, red, green

2. 6,084,000 plates

3. 2,948,400 plates

4. $_{15}P_{10} = 10{,}897{,}286{,}400$

5. about 0.333

6. about 0.833

7. about 0.667

8. 1 : 2

9. 3 : 1

10. about 0.037

11. about 0.018

12. 495

13. $_5P_3 = 60$; $_5C_3 = 10$; $_5C_3 = \dfrac{_5P_3}{_3P_3}$

14. 1, 4, 6, 4, 1; $_4C_0$, $_4C_1$, $_4C_2$, $_4C_3$, $_4C_4$

15. The number in row n, diagonal r of Pascal's triangle is equal to the number of combinations of n items selected r at a time.

16. 0.3125

1. Make a tree diagram to show the possible necklaces from these choices: 28 in., 30 in., or 32 in. long; gold or silver finish; with all blue stones, all red stones, or all green stones. — 6-1

One format for making license plates is to use two letters followed by four digits. For Questions 2 and 3, how many different license plates are possible for each situation? — 6-2

2. Zero cannot be the first digit and repeats are allowed.

3. Zero cannot be the first digit and repeats are not allowed.

4. There are spaces for 10 bicycles in the rack next to the library. One afternoon 15 people who rode bicycles were there at the same time. Write a mathematical expression for determining the number of ways the bicycles could be arranged in the rack.

For Questions 5–9, use the spinner. — 6-3

5. Find P(landing on red).

6. Find P(landing on blue or on an odd).

7. Find P(not landing on green).

8. Find the odds in favor of landing on blue.

9. Find the odds against landing on a 1.

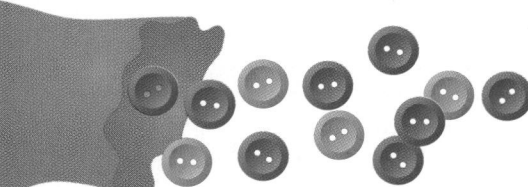

A bag contains twelve buttons as shown. — 6-4

10. Find the probability of picking three red buttons if each button is returned to the bag before the next button is picked.

11. Find the probability of picking three red buttons if each button is *not* returned to the bag before the next button is picked.

12. Four is the minimal number of colors you need to shade a map so that no region is the same color as one next to it. Colored pencils are sold in boxes of twelve different colors. How many ways can you select four colors to shade a map so that no region is the same color as one next to it? — 6-5

13. Find $_5P_3$ and $_5C_3$. Compare the two values.

14. Write the fourth row of Pascal's triangle in the following ways. — 6-6

   a. Use numerical values.

   b. Use combination notation.

15. **Writing** Describe the relationship between Pascal's triangle and combinations.

16. **Baseball** Mathias successfully steals half of the stolen bases he attempts to steal. What is the probability that he will successfully steal exactly two of the next five bases he attempts to steal? — 6-7

Unit Support Materials

➤ Unit 6 Cumulative Practice 50

➤ Unit 6 Study Guide Review

➤ Unifying Problem 6 in the Problem Bank

➤ Unit Tests 25 and 26

➤ Spanish versions of the Unit Tests are in the Assessment Book.

➤ Teacher's Resources for Transfer Students

Quick Quiz (6-8 through 6-9)

A special coin created for a magic trick has a 60% probability of landing on heads.

1. Draw a probability tree diagram for three tosses of the coin. [6-8] **See diagram below.**

2. Find the probability of tossing exactly two heads in three tosses. [6-8] P(exactly 2 heads out of 3 tosses) = 0.144 + 0.144 + 0.144 = 0.432

3. Find the probability of tossing at least two heads in three tosses. [6-8] P(at least 2 heads out of 3 tosses) = 0.432 + 0.216 = 0.648

4. Use the binomial theorem to write $(x - 1)^5$ in expanded form. [6-9] $x^5 - 5x^4 + 10x^3 - 10x^2 + 5x - 1$

5. What is the fourth term in the expanded form of $(y + 2)^6$? [6-9] fourth term: $20(y^3)(2^3) = 160y^3$

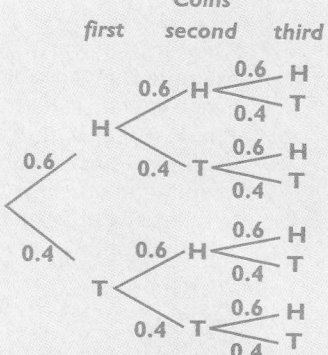

	Coins			Outcomes	Probabilities
	first	second	third		
				HHH	$(0.6)(0.6)(0.6) = 0.216$
				HHT	$(0.6)(0.6)(0.4) = 0.144$
				HTH	$(0.6)(0.4)(0.6) = 0.144$
				HTT	$(0.6)(0.4)(0.4) = 0.096$
				THH	$(0.4)(0.6)(0.6) = 0.144$
				THT	$(0.4)(0.6)(0.4) = 0.096$
				TTH	$(0.4)(0.4)(0.6) = 0.096$
				TTT	$(0.4)(0.4)(0.4) = 0.064$

1. Sherrine is playing a board game and it is her turn to roll a pair of dice. She does not want to land on the *Lose a Turn* space, but she will if she rolls a total of 8. Explain how to find the probability that she will not lose a turn. [6-1]

Answers may vary. Students might use complementary events after determining the number of outcomes when rolling two dice. Determine the number of outcomes for rolling a total of 8 and subtract the probability of that event from 1. Example:
P(not rolling 8) =
1 − P(rolling 8) =
$1 - \frac{5}{36} = \frac{31}{36} \approx 0.86$

2. How many permutations are there of 8 necklaces arranged 4 at a time in a jewelry display case? [6-2]

$_8P_4 = \frac{8!}{(8-4)!} = \frac{8!}{4!} = 8 \cdot 7 \cdot 6 \cdot 5 = 1680$

For Exs. 3–5, the suit of all hearts is removed from a standard deck of playing cards. The remaining cards are shuffled, one is drawn at random for Exs. 3 and 4, and two are drawn at random for Ex. 5.

3. Find P(diamond) and P(a card from a black suit). [6-3] There are 52 cards in a standard deck, 13 cards in each suit, and 39 cards in this reduced deck.

$P(\text{diamond}) = \frac{13}{39} = \frac{1}{3}$ or about 0.33

$P(\text{a card from a black suit}) = \frac{26}{39} = \frac{2}{3}$ or about 0.67

4. What are the odds against choosing a card from a black suit? [6-3] Odd against a card from a black suit =

$\frac{\text{unfavorable outcomes}}{\text{favorable outcomes}} = \frac{13}{26} = \frac{1}{2}$ or 1 to 2

5. Find P(two Jacks). [6-4]
P(two Jacks) = P(first Jack) ·
P(second Jack) $= \frac{3}{39} \cdot \frac{2}{38} = \frac{6}{1482}$ or about 0.004

17. **Open-ended** Find an example of an event with two equal outcomes in everyday life and write a probability problem about it.

Aidan sees a movie on Friday nights 60% of the time. 6-8

18. Find P(Aidan sees a movie on exactly three of the next four Fridays).

19. Find P(Aidan sees a movie on at least three of the next four Fridays).

Write each power of a binomial in expanded form. 6-9

20. $(x + 2)^4$ **21.** $(x - 3)^5$ **22.** $(x + y)^3$ **23.** $(r - s)^3$

24. **Self-evaluation** How are counting methods used in probability? Which of the counting methods from this unit (tree diagram, organized list/table, combinations, permutations) makes the most sense to you? Why?

25. **Group Activity** Work in a group of three students. Read and discuss the following problem.

Stan Musial had a lifetime batting average of 0.331, which means he got a hit about one third of the times that he had an official at bat. What is the probability that he would not get exactly two hits in five consecutive at bats?

a. One student should draw a diagram of the problem. A second student should show how to use Pascal's triangle to solve the problem. The third student should draw and use a spinner to solve the problem experimentally.

b. Were all three results the same? Why or why not? Which method seemed to work best?

IDEAS AND (FORMULAS) $= X^2$

➤ **Problem Solving** Tree diagrams, tables, and organized lists are used to count small numbers of outcomes. *(pp. 296–298)*

➤ The multiplication counting principle is used to find the total number of outcomes of a series of selections. *(p. 303)*

➤ The number of arrangements (permutations) of *n* distinct objects is *n*!. *(p. 304)*

➤ The number of permutations of *n* different objects arranged *r* at a time (*r* < *n*) is given by this formula. When items are repeated, this formula does not necessarily apply. *(p. 304)* $_nP_r = \frac{n!}{(n-r)!}$

➤ The number of combinations of *n* items selected *r* at a time (*r* < *n*) is given by this formula. With combinations, order does not matter. *(p. 329)* $_nC_r = \frac{n!}{(n-r)!r!}$

➤ **Problem Solving** You can use Pascal's triangle to find combinations. The number in row *n*, diagonal *r*, is $_nC_r$. The sum of the numbers in row *n* is 2^n. *(p. 335)*

diagonal 0

row 0 ⟶ 1

1 1

1 2 1

1 3 3 1

1 4 6 4 1

1 5 10 10 5 1

360 **Unit 6** Counting Strategies, Probability, Binomials

Answers to Unit 6 Review and Assessment ·····························

17. Answers may vary. An example is given. For the event "a baby is born," P(boy) = P(girl). If twelve babies are born at a local hospital on one day, what is the probability that at least half of them are boys?

18. 0.3456

19. 0.4752

20. $x^4 + 8x^3 + 24x^2 + 32x + 16$

21. $x^5 - 15x^4 + 90x^3 - 270x^2 + 405x - 243$

22. $x^3 + 3x^2y + 3xy^2 + y^3$

23. $r^3 - 3r^2s + 3rs^2 - s^3$

24. Summaries may vary. Counting methods are used to determine the number of favorable or unfavorable outcomes and the total number of outcomes. Tree diagrams and organized lists or tables may make the most sense when you want to know not only how many outcomes are possible but also what they are. When the numbers involved are large, especially if you do not need to know what the outcomes are, combinations and permutations may make more sense.

STATISTICS & PROBABILITY

➤ To find the probability of mutually exclusive events A and B, add: $P(A \text{ or } B) = P(A) + P(B)$. (p. 311)

➤ The sum of the probabilities of complementary events is 1: $P(\text{event}) + P(\text{not the event}) = 1$. (p. 312)

➤ These ratios apply to equally likely outcomes. (p. 314)

$$\text{Probability of an event} = \frac{\text{number of favorable outcomes}}{\text{number of possible outcomes}}$$

$$\text{Odds in favor of an event} = \frac{\text{number of favorable outcomes}}{\text{number of unfavorable outcomes}}$$

$$\text{Odds against an event} = \frac{\text{number of unfavorable outcomes}}{\text{number of favorable outcomes}}$$

➤ To find the probability of independent events A and B, multiply the probabilities of the individual events: $P(A \text{ and } B) = P(A) \cdot P(B)$. (p. 321)

➤ To find the probability of dependent events A and B, multiply the probability of A by the probability of B after A: $P(A \text{ and } B) = P(A) \cdot P(B \text{ after } A)$. (p. 323)

➤ You can use Pascal's triangle or a probability tree diagram to find the probability of binomial events whether the two outcomes are equally likely or not. (pp. 339–340, 345–346)

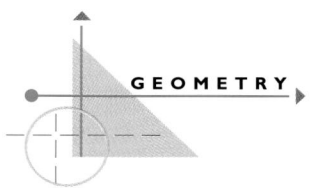

GEOMETRY

➤ You can use area models to represent the probability of a compound event. (pp. 321, 325)

➤ You can use an area model to represent $(a + b)^2$ and a volume model to represent $(a + b)^3$. (p. 351)

ALGEBRA

➤ The binomial theorem is used to expand expressions of the form $(a + b)^n$, where n is a positive integer. The coefficients of the form $_nC_r$ are numbers in the nth row of Pascal's triangle. (p. 353)

$$(_nC_0)a^n b^0 + (_nC_1)a^{n-1}b^1 + (_nC_2)a^{n-2}b^2 + \cdots$$
$$\cdots + (_nC_{n-2})a^2 b^{n-2} + (_nC_{n-1})a^1 b^{n-1} + (_nC_n)a^0 b^n$$

Key Terms

- **tree diagram** (p. 296)
- **outcome** (p. 296)
- **event** (p. 296)
- **factorial, !** (p. 304)
- **permutation** (p. 304)
- **mutually exclusive events** (p. 311)
- **complementary events** (p. 312)
- **odds in favor, odds against** (p. 314)
- **compound events** (p. 320)
- **independent events** (p. 320)
- **dependent events** (p. 320)
- **sample space** (p. 320)
- **combination** (p. 329)
- **Pascal's triangle** (p. 334)
- **binomial experiment** (p. 339)
- **probability tree diagram** (p. 346)
- **binomial** (p. 351)
- **factored form** (p. 351)
- **expanded form** (p. 351)
- **binomial theorem** (p. 353)

Unit 6 Review and Assessment

361

361

Answers to Unit 6 Review and Assessment

25. **a.** Diagrams may vary. An example is given. The tree diagram would show 32 possible outcomes of the type HHNHN, which symbolizes hit, hit, no hit, hit, no hit. The probability of Musial *not* getting 2 hits in 5 consecutive at bats is the complement of his getting exactly 2 hits. In the probability tree diagram, there are 10 outcomes in which Musial would get exactly 2 hits. Each of these outcomes has a probability of $(0.331)^2(0.669)^3 \approx 0.033$. Thus, the probability of his getting exactly 2 hits is about $10(0.033) = 0.330$, and the probability of his not getting exactly 2 hits is about $1 - 0.330 = 0.670$. To use Pascal's triangle, go to row 5, diagonal 2 to find the number of ways of getting exactly 2 hits in 5 consecutive at bats. Then use the reasoning described for the tree diagram to determine the probability of his not getting exactly 2 hits. To make a spinner, divide a circle into 3 parts, one labeled "hit" and two labeled "no hit." For each trial, spin the spinner five times and record results.

b. The calculated results should be the same. The experimental probability may or may not be close. The greater the number of trials, the closer it may be.

361

OVERVIEW

> **Unit 7** introduces many of the elements necessary to write a proof. Conjunctions, disjunctions, and biconditionals are introduced as types of statements. Students learn to make implications, write good definitions, and distinguish between valid arguments and invalid arguments.

> Two-column proofs, paragraph proofs, and flow proofs are introduced as ways of proving statements. Definitions, postulates, and theorems are presented as ways to justify statements in a proof.

> Students are supplied with a variety of statements to prove, including aspects from everyday life, theorems about angles, and theorems about parallel lines.

> Writing a mystery story is the theme of the Unit Project. Students research logic as it applies to creating a story line and writing clues for the reader to follow.

> Connections to museums, electronic circuits, jewelry, literature, flight schedules, and the Declaration of Independence are integrated into the teaching materials and exercises.

> Problem-solving strategies in Unit 7 include using tables, graphs, Venn diagrams, deductive reasoning, rules of logic, and proofs.

Internet Resources
Visit our Web site www.mcdougallittell.com for additional resources when teaching this unit.

Unit Objectives

Section	Objectives	NCTM Standards
7-1	• Learn the meaning of the words *and*, *or*, and *not*. • Graph algebraic sentences that use these words.	1, 2, 3, 4, 5, 12
7-2	• Translate among various forms of implications.	1, 2, 3, 4, 5, 12
7-3	• Distinguish valid arguments from invalid arguments.	1, 2, 3, 4, 5, 12
7-4	• Recognize and write biconditionals. • Use biconditionals to make valid arguments and to recognize and write good definitions.	1, 2, 3, 4, 5, 12
7-5	• Become familiar with key elements of proof and formats for two-column, paragraph, and flow proofs.	1, 2, 3, 4, 5, 12, 14
7-6	• Use postulates of algebra to write proofs.	1, 2, 3, 4, 5, 12, 14
7-7	• Recognize the value of definitions and postulates in proofs. • Write proofs about angles.	1, 2, 3, 4, 5, 12, 14
7-8	• Write proofs for properties of parallel lines.	1, 2, 3, 4, 5, 12, 14

Skills Bank To extend the curriculum and provide practice with skills, you may wish to assign the following topics from the **Skills Bank** ancillary: DeMorgan's laws (for use after Section 7-1), related conditional statements (for use after Section 7-4), coordinate proof (for use after Section 7-5), and mathematical systems (for use after Section 7-6).

Section	Connections to Prior and Future Concepts
7-1	**Section 7-1** uses the words *and*, *or*, and *not* to form conjunctions, disjunctions, and negations of logical statements. Students demonstrate the meaning of these statements through the use of Venn diagrams and graphing inequalities on number lines. Graphing inequalities was introduced in Section 3-3 of Book 1.
7-2	**Section 7-2** introduces the symbolism used in logical implications. The truth values of an implication and its converse are examined. Converses were introduced in Section 9-3 of Book 1, and are used in Units 1, 7, and 8 of Book 2, and in Unit 3 of Book 3.
7-3	**Section 7-3** introduces rules of logic—the direct argument, the indirect argument, the chain rule, and the "or" rule. Students use these rules to distinguish a valid argument from one that is not valid. These skills are used in the remainder of Unit 7 of Book 2 and in Unit 3 of Book 3.
7-4	**Section 7-4** introduces biconditionals as a way to make valid arguments. Conditions about identifying a good definition are stressed. Definitions are a vital part of the proofs found in Units 7 and 8 of Book 2 and Unit 3 of Book 3.
7-5	**Section 7-5** introduces the key elements of a proof: the "given," the "prove," the "statements," and the "justifications." The forms of proof developed include the two-column proof, paragraph proof, and flow proof. Skill with proofs is further developed in the remainder of Unit 7, in Unit 8 of Book 2, and in Unit 3 of Book 3.
7-6	**Section 7-6** introduces the concept of a postulate. Students explore using postulates from algebra to write proofs. This work with algebraic postulates is extended to geometric postulates in Sections 7-7 and 7-8 of Book 2.
7-7	**Section 7-7** develops proofs about angles using definitions and postulates. Using a previously proved theorem is introduced as a justification in a proof. Proofs are further developed in Section 7-8 of Book 2 and in Unit 3 of Book 3.
7-8	**Section 7-8** develops proofs about parallel lines and the angles they form. These proofs build upon concepts concerning angles that were developed in Section 7-7 of Book 2. Geometric proofs are continued in Unit 8 of Book 2 and Unit 3 of Book 3.

Integrating the Strands

Strands	Sections
Number	7-4, 7-5, 7-6
Algebra	7-1, 7-2, 7-3, 7-4, 7-5, 7-6, 7-7, 7-8
Geometry	7-1, 7-2, 7-3, 7-4, 7-5, 7-6, 7-7, 7-8
Statistics and Probability	7-1, 7-3, 7-4
Discrete Mathematics	7-1, 7-2, 7-3, 7-4, 7-5, 7-6
Logic and Language	7-1, 7-2, 7-3, 7-4, 7-5, 7-6, 7-7, 7-8

Section Planning Guide

➤ Essential exercises and problems are indicated in boldface.
➤ Ongoing work on the Unit Project is indicated in color.
➤ Exercises and problems that require student research, group work, manipulatives, or graphing technology are indicated in the column headed "Other."

Section	Materials	Pacing	Standard Assignment	Extended Assignment	Other
7-1		Day 1	**2–8**, 12, **13–20**	1, **2–8**, 9–12, **13–20**	
		Day 2	**21–40**, 41–47, 48	**21–40**, 41–47, 48	
7-2		Day 1	**1–13**, 14–19, 25–31, 32, 33	**1–13**, 14–31, 32, 33	
7-3		Day 1	**1–11**, 15–20, 22–28, 29	**1–11**, 12–20, 22–28, 29	21
7-4		Day 1	**1–15**	**1–15**	
		Day 2	**16–23**, 24–28, **29–31**, 35–42, 43	**16–23**, 24–28, **29–31**, 32–42, 43	43
7-5		Day 1	1, **2–5**	1, **2–5**	6
		Day 2	**7–10**, 11, 14–23, 24	**7–10**, 11–23, 24	
7-6	scissors	Day 1	**1–10**, **12–14**, **18**, 19–23, 24	**1–10**, 11, **12–14**, 15, 16, **18**, 19–23, 24	17, 24
7-7		Day 1	**1–15**, 19–23, 24	**1–15**, 17, 19–23, 24	16, 18
7-8	protractor, four straws, four straight pins, scissors	Day 1	**1–10**	**1–10**	11
		Day 2	**12–19**, 21–26, 27	**12–19**, 20–26, 27	
Review		**Day 1**	Unit Review	Unit Review	
Test		**Day 2**	Unit Test	Unit Test	

Yearly Pacing	Unit 7 Total	Units 1–7 Total	Remaining	Total
	16 days (2 for Unit Project)	113 days	47 days	160 days

Support Materials

➤ See **Project Book** for notes on Unit 7 Project: Write a Mystery Story.
➤ "UPP" and "disk" refer to **Using Plotter Plus** booklet and **Plotter Plus** disk.
➤ "TI-81/82" refers to **Using TI-81 and TI-82 Calculators** booklet.
➤ Warm-up exercises for each section are available on **Warm-Up Transparencies.**
➤ "FI," "PC," "GI," "MA," and "Stats!" refer, respectively, to the McDougal Littell Mathpack software Activity Books for **Function Investigator, Probability Constructor, Geometry Inventor, Matrix Analyzer,** and **Stats!**.

Section	Study Guide	Practice Bank	Problem Bank	Activity Bank	Explorations Lab Manual	Assessment Book	Visuals	Technology
7-1	7-1	Practice 51	Set 14	Enrich 45	Add. Expl. 9 Master 2	Quiz 7-1		TI-81/82, p. 45
7-2	7-2	Practice 52	Set 14	Enrich 46	Master 2	Quiz 7-2		
7-3	7-3	Practice 53	Set 14	Enrich 47		Quiz 7-3 Test 27		
7-4	7-4	Practice 54	Set 15	Enrich 48		Quiz 7-4		
7-5	7-5	Practice 55	Set 15	Enrich 49		Quiz 7-5		
7-6	7-6	Practice 56	Set 15	Enrich 50		Quiz 7-6 Test 28		
7-7	7-7	Practice 57	Set 16	Enrich 51		Quiz 7-7	Folder 6	GI Acts. 1 and 10
7-8	7-8	Practice 58	Set 16	Enrich 52	Add. Expl. 10	Quiz 7-8 Test 29		
Unit 7	Unit Review	Practice 59	Unifying Problem 7	Family Involve 7		Tests 30, 31		

UNIT TESTS

Spanish versions of these tests are on pages 142–145 of the **Assessment Book**.

Form A

Name _____ Date _____ Score _____

Test 30
Test on Unit 7 (Form A)

Directions: Write the answers in the spaces provided.

For Questions 1–4, determine whether each statement is *True* or *False*.

1. If two angles are supplements of the same angle, then they are equal in measure.

2. The converse of a true implication is always true.

3. A conjunction is true when at least one of the two statements is true.

4. True biconditionals make good definitions.

For Questions 5 and 6, decide if the argument is *valid* or *invalid*. If the argument is valid, tell which rule of logic is used. If the argument is invalid, tell why.

5. Juan will pass biology or Juan will fail biology.
   Juan did not fail biology.
   Therefore, Juan passed biology.
   valid; *or* rule

6. If a quadrilateral is a rectangle, then it is a parallelogram.
   Quadrilateral *ABCD* is a parallelogram.
   Therefore, quadrilateral *ABCD* is a rectangle.
   invalid; converse error (*ABCD* could be a rhombus.)

7. **Open-ended** Write a valid argument using the chain rule.
   Sample answer: If a figure is a square, then it is a rectangle. If a figure is a rectangle, then it is a parallelogram. Therefore, if a figure is a square, then it is a parallelogram.

8. Write the pair of conditionals below as a biconditional using "if and only if."
   If $6x^2 = 24$, then $x = 2$.
   If $x = 2$, then $6x^2 = 24$. $6x^2 = 24$ if and only if $x = 2$.

9. Is the biconditional you wrote in Question 8 *True* or *False*? If it is false, rewrite it so it is true.
   False; $6x^2 = 24$ if and only if $x = \pm2$.

10. Replace ? to complete a valid implication.
   If $\angle G$ and $\angle H$ are supplementary and $m\angle H = 73°$, then ? .

Answers	
1.	True
2.	False
3.	False
4.	True
5.	See question.
6.	See question.
7.	See question.
8.	See question.
9.	See question.
10.	$m\angle G = 107°$

Name _____ Date _____ Score _____

Test 30 (continued)

Directions: Write the answers in the spaces provided.

11. **Writing** Explain the format and the parts of a good flow proof.
   Sample answer: A good flow proof reads from left to right, beginning with the given information and ending with the statement to be proved, with each statement connected to the next statement by a numbered arrow (the arrows are numbered consecutively). Justifications for the statements, numbered to correspond to the arrows, complete the flow proof.

12. Write a paragraph proof of this statement: If $12 - 7x = 40$, then $x = -4$.
   Given: $12 - 7x = 40$ *Prove:* $x = -4$
   You can use the subtraction property of equality to subtract 12 from both sides of $12 - 7x = 40$. Therefore, $-7x = 28$. Then you can use the division property of equality to divide both sides by -7. Therefore, $x = -4$.

13. Complete the two-column proof.
   Given: Lines q and r are parallel.
   Transversal t intersects lines q and r.
   Prove: $m\angle 2 = m\angle 8$

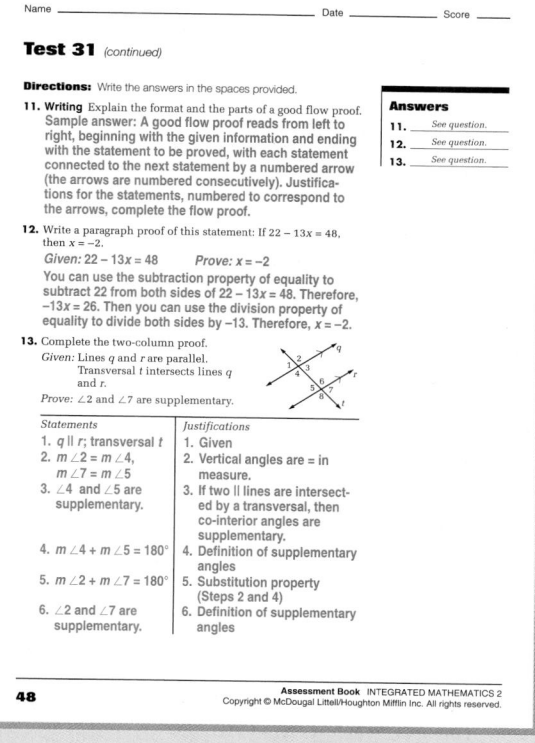

Statements	Justifications
1. $q \parallel r$; transversal t	1. Given
2. $m\angle 2 = m\angle 6$	2. If 2 ∥ lines are intersected by a transversal, then corresponding angles are = in measure.
3. $m\angle 6 = m\angle 8$	3. Vertical angles are = in measure.
4. $m\angle 2 = m\angle 8$	4. Substitution property (Steps 2 and 3)

Answers	
11.	See question.
12.	See question.
13.	See question.

Form B

Name _____ Date _____ Score _____

Test 31
Test on Unit 7 (Form B)

Directions: Write the answers in the spaces provided.

For Questions 1–4, determine whether each statement is *True* or *False*.

1. If two angles are supplements of the same angle, then the two angles are right angles.

2. The converse of a true implication is never true.

3. Vertical angles are equal in measure.

4. A disjunction is true when at least one of the two statements is true.

For Questions 5 and 6, decide if the argument is *valid* or *invalid*. If the argument is valid, tell which rule of logic is used. If the argument is invalid, tell why.

5. If a figure is a quadrilateral, then it is a polygon.
   I have drawn a figure that is a polygon.
   Therefore, the figure I drew is a quadrilateral.
   invalid; converse error (The figure could have been a triangle.)

6. When going to town, Mei Li walks or she rides her bicycle.
   When Mei Li went to town this morning, she did not walk.
   Therefore, Mei Li rode her bicycle to town this morning.
   valid; *or* rule

7. **Open-ended** Write a valid argument using the *or* rule.
   Sample answer: The light is red or the light is green. The light is not red. Therefore, the light is green.

8. Write the pair of conditionals below as a biconditional using "if and only if."
   If $7x^2 = 112$, then $x = 4$.
   If $x = 4$, then $7x^2 = 112$. $7x^2 = 112$ if and only if $x = 4$.

9. Is the biconditional you wrote in Question 8 *True* or *False*? If it is false, rewrite it so it is true.
   False; $7x^2 = 112$ if and only if $x = \pm4$.

10. Replace ? to complete a valid implication.
   If $\angle R$ and $\angle S$ are complementary and $m\angle R = 25°$, then ? .

Answers	
1.	False
2.	False
3.	True
4.	True
5.	See question.
6.	See question.
7.	See question.
8.	See question.
9.	See question.
10.	$m\angle S = 65°$

Name _____ Date _____ Score _____

Test 31 (continued)

Directions: Write the answers in the spaces provided.

11. **Writing** Explain the format and the parts of a good flow proof.
   Sample answer: A good flow proof reads from left to right, beginning with the given information and ending with the statement to be proved, with each statement connected to the next statement by a numbered arrow (the arrows are numbered consecutively). Justifications for the statements, numbered to correspond to the arrows, complete the flow proof.

12. Write a paragraph proof of this statement: If $22 - 13x = 48$, then $x = -2$.
   Given: $22 - 13x = 48$ *Prove:* $x = -2$
   You can use the subtraction property of equality to subtract 22 from both sides of $22 - 13x = 48$. Therefore, $-13x = 26$. Then you can use the division property of equality to divide both sides by -13. Therefore, $x = -2$.

13. Complete the two-column proof.
   Given: Lines q and r are parallel.
   Transversal t intersects lines q and r.
   Prove: $\angle 2$ and $\angle 7$ are supplementary.

Statements	Justifications
1. $q \parallel r$; transversal t	1. Given
2. $m\angle 2 = m\angle 4$, $m\angle 7 = m\angle 5$	2. Vertical angles are = in measure.
3. $\angle 4$ and $\angle 5$ are supplementary.	3. If two ∥ lines are intersected by a transversal, then co-interior angles are supplementary.
4. $m\angle 4 + m\angle 5 = 180°$	4. Definition of supplementary angles
5. $m\angle 2 + m\angle 7 = 180°$	5. Substitution property (Steps 2 and 4)
6. $\angle 2$ and $\angle 7$ are supplementary.	6. Definition of supplementary angles

Answers	
11.	See question.
12.	See question.
13.	See question.

Software Support

McDougal Littell Mathpack
Geometry Inventor

Outside Resources

Books/Periodicals

Barber, Jacqueline. *Crime Lab Chemistry*. GCMG. Lawrence Hall of Science, 1987.

Carcis, Frances and Lewis J. McNeece. "Case of Video Viewing, Reading and Writing in Mathematics Class—Solving the Mystery." *Mathematics Teacher* (November 1993): pp. 682–685.

Holden, Linda. *Thinker Tasks Critical Thinking Activities Book 1: Attributes and Logic*. Creative Publications, 1986.

Activities/Manipulatives

Marolda, Maria. *Exploring Attributes*. Dale Seymour Publications, 1990.

Software

Clough, Scott and Donna Stanger. *High Wire Logic*. Sunburst, 1985. Apple and IBM.

Grim, Perl, and Robinett. Teacher's Guide: Perl, Teri. *Gertrude's Puzzles*. Learning Company, 1982. Apple.

Videos

Landscape of Geometry. Program No. 3: Lines That Cross. Ontario Educational Communications Authority, 1983.

Landscape of Geometry. Program No. 4: Lines That Don't Cross. Ontario Educational Communications Authority, 1983.

PROJECT GOALS

➤ Students create an outline of a mystery story that contains valid logic arguments leading to the solution of the mystery.

➤ Students write a mystery story with a plot that involves a travel itinerary and at least two geometry theorems from this unit.

➤ Students read mysteries written by their classmates and give a written report based on specific criteria.

➤ Students work together in a cooperative group and all contribute to the project's success.

PROJECT PLANNING

Materials List

➤ Plane, train or bus schedules (optional)

Project Teams

Have students work on the project in groups of four. One way for the individuals in the group to distribute the work is as follows:

1. Editor: coordinates and collects the brainstorming ideas for the mystery story, checks that all aspects of the mystery are covered, and helps the writer revise the outline and story as needed.

2. Writer: writes and revises the story outline and the final draft of the story.

3. Mathematician: contributes to and checks on the correct use of at least two logical reasoning arguments and at least two geometry theorems from this unit.

4. Evaluator: writes the evaluation of another group's mystery story based on the specific criteria listed on page 363.

unit **7**

Logic and Proof

How good a detective are you? What clues can you find in this picture that could help you determine **WHODUNIT?** For instance, what day and time did the crime likely take place? Can you tell whether the writer was left-handed or right-handed? What do you think the message on the paper means? Does it look as if anything was removed from the desk?

whoDUNit?

Mystery stories have been popular in many countries for centuries. Among the mystery writers whose books have served as the basis for TV programs or movies are British author Agatha Christie and French author Maurice Leblanc. In their stories the mystery is solved by the police or by detectives like Jane Marple and Arsène Lupin.

362

Suggested Rubric for Unit Project

4 Students' mystery stories have been constructed from an outline that contains at least two valid logical arguments leading to the solution of the mystery. The stories have a plot that involves a travel itinerary and they apply two or more geometry postulates and theorems from this unit. Readers of the stories want to continue reading them to solve the mystery. The stories are well written and the mystery is challenging to solve.

3 Students' mystery stories are interesting but the clues to the mystery do not fit together clearly enough to point to the solution. Logical arguments and at least two geometry postulates and theorems are used; however, a reader would have difficulty determining a clear-cut solution to the mystery.

2 Students' mystery stories are only partially complete. Important clues are missing and it is not possible to solve the mystery. Readers tend to be confused by the story and do not want to continue reading it.

Write a Mystery Story

Your project is to write a mystery story. To structure your story, you will need an outline that contains all the clues you give the reader. Your outline should show how the clues fit together to point to the solution of your mystery. As you outline your story, use two of the techniques of logical argument presented in the unit.

Also include in your story a travel itinerary and applications of at least two of the postulates and theorems about angles and parallel lines that you study in the unit.

When all the groups have completed their stories, have the members of another group read your group's story. Ask them to evaluate it according to the following criteria.

❓ Does the reader want to continue reading in order to solve the mystery?

❓ Does the reader have enough clues to solve the mystery?

❓ Does solving the mystery challenge, surprise, or inform the reader?

In real life not all mysteries are solved by amateur, police, or private detectives. Specialists in many fields use logic and reasoning to solve mysteries.

archaeology

Archaeologists dig for evidence of the existence of a mythic empire like the Toltec empire in central Mexico.

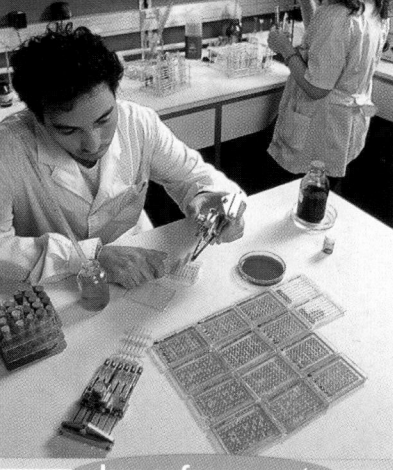

law enforcement

Forensic, or legal, scientists analyze the DNA in samples of blood or hair to determine if they came from a suspect in the case.

art history

Art historians are able to date paintings by determining the elements contained in the paint.

Support Materials

The *Project Book* contains information about the following topics for use with this Unit Project.

➤ Project Description
➤ Teaching Commentary
➤ Working on the Unit Project Exercises
➤ Completing the Unit Project
➤ Assessing the Unit Project
➤ Alternative Projects
➤ Outside Resources

ADDITIONAL BACKGROUND

Multicultural Note

Paco Ignacio Taibo II, who now lives in Mexico, was born in Gijón, Spain in 1949. Besides writing novels, Taibo has been a freelance journalist, the president of the International Association of Crime Writers, and a professor at the Universidad Autónoma de México in Mexico City. Some of his popular novels have been adapted to film and TV and translated into other languages. *An Easy Thing and Some Clouds* feature the cynical half-Basque, half-Irish Hector Belascoarán Shayne, a detective who has "a degree in engineering from the National University, and one eye less than most people." In 1987, Taibo received the Premio Hammett award for *La vida misma*, recognizing it as the best crime fiction novel in Spanish.

Suggested Rubric for Unit Project

1 Students' mystery stories are incomplete. The plot is inadequate. Valid logical arguments and geometry postulates and theorems from this unit are only vaguely incorporated into the story. Readers do not want to continue reading the story soon after starting it. The group should be encouraged to speak with the teacher as soon as possible to review their work and to make a new start on the project.

Forensic Medicine

Forensic scientists are physicians trained in pathology who are concerned with criminal law. They often work like detectives and follow medical clues to solve crimes. New tests involving DNA (deoxyribo nucleic acid) profiling can be used to identify which person a trace of blood, skin, or hair belongs to. DNA is the hereditary material in genes that plays a vital role in cell development. Since it is unique for each person, DNA profiling can identify the individual who has that DNA precisely. ·············●

ALTERNATIVE PROJECTS

Project 1, page 423

Testing the Validity of Arguments in the News Media

Collect and analyze examples of implications in ads, editorials, or news stories found in current newspapers or magazines. Identify arguments based on the implications, write some of your own if none exist, and discuss the validity of the arguments and your reasoning.

Project 2, page 423

Analyzing a Mystery Story

Read or watch a mystery story. List the clues, identify the important premises and conditionals, and write an outline in the form of a series of valid arguments.

Getting Started

For this project you should work in a group of four students. Here are some ideas to help you get started.

☞ Decide where your story will take place and list the characters. The setting for your story could be a place you know, a place you read about, or even a place you make up.

☞ Think of a mystery that you can write about. You might write about a missing object, a person who disappears, an unexplained sound, or an object that turns up in an unexpected place.

☞ Discuss possible clues to the solution of your mystery.

☞ Plan to meet later to discuss how you can: use logical arguments to develop an outline for your story; use a travel itinerary as a plot element; and apply theorems and postulates about angles or parallel lines.

Settings
- ~~school~~
- museum
- ~~boat~~
- ~~train~~
- apartment building
- ~~hospital~~
- woods

Working on the Unit Project

Your work in Unit 7 will help you write your mystery story.

Related Exercises:
Section 7-1, Exercise 48
Section 7-2, Exercises 32, 33
Section 7-3, Exercise 29
Section 7-4, Exercise 43
Section 7-5, Exercise 24
Section 7-6, Exercise 24
Section 7-7, Exercise 24
Section 7-8, Exercise 27

Alternative Projects p. 423

Can We Talk   Mysteries

➤ Why do you think mystery stories have been popular for so long in different cultures?

➤ Science is full of unsolved mysteries, such as why the dinosaurs became extinct. What other unsolved scientific mysteries have you heard about? What solutions have some scientists proposed?

➤ Which medium do you think is best for presenting a mystery story—books, movies, TV, or live theater? Why do you think so?

➤ What skills do you think private detectives, medical detectives, archaeologists, forensic scientists, and art historians have in common?

Answers to Can We Talk?

➤ Answers may vary. An example is given. Because they are challenging to the mind and are fun to try to solve. I think people in many cultures enjoy mental challenges.

➤ Answers may vary. Examples are given. The Mayan ruins, Stonehenge, who the first humans were and where they lived, how does the human brain work, and when an earthquake will occur. Some scientists have proposed theories about why the Mayan cities were abandoned and what the architecture and design of their buildings means, that the first humans were from Africa, and that the human brain works through a series of electrical impulses that come from and are sent to all parts of the body. Most of these are theories and we may never know if they are true or false. Scientists still are not able to predict when an earthquake will occur.

➤ Answers may vary. An example is given. I think books are the best medium because you can describe details that can be overlooked or missed using the three other visual mediums.

➤ Answers may vary. Examples are given. The are all curious, like to solve puzzles or mysteries, have an interest in history, can put clues together to solve problems, and are good problem solvers.

364

Using And, Or, Not

ConJunction

Focus

Learn the meaning of the words *and*, *or*, and *not*. Graph algebraic sentences that use these words.

Bridget was researching part-time jobs for herself and some friends. She made a table of all the information she found. This type of organized listing is sometimes called a **database**.

Business	Job	Location	Hours/week	Hourly pay ($)
Cow Bar	ice cream server	South Mall	10	6.00
Bond's	filing clerk	South Mall	12	6.00
Food Stuff	stock clerk	South Mall	15	6.50
Lunch Bag	ice cream server	North Mall	20	6.25
Shop-All	stock clerk	North Mall	10	6.75
Great Lawns	yard worker	neighborhood	10	9.50
Pooch's	dog walker	neighborhood	15	5.50

Many people use databases in their work. Usually the information is stored in a computer.

You can search a database using the words *and*, *or*, and *not*.

7-1 *Using And, Or, Not*

365

PLANNING

Objectives and Strands
See pages 362A and 362B.

Spiral Learning
See page 362B.

Materials List
➤ Graph paper

Recommended Pacing
Section 7-1 is a two-day lesson.

Day 1

Pages 365–367: Opening paragraph through Talk it Over 4, *Exercises 1–20*

Day 2

Page 368: Logic with Graphs through Look Back, *Exercises 21–48*

Extra Practice
See pages 625–626.

Warm-Up Exercises
Warm-Up Transparency 7-1

Support Materials
➤ Practice 51
➤ Enrichment 45 in the Activity Bank
➤ Study Guide 7-1
➤ Problem Set 14
➤ Additional Exploration 9
➤ Diagram Master 2 in the Explorations Lab Manual
➤ Using TI-81 and TI-82 Calculators: Guess My Number
➤ Quiz 7-1
➤ Alternative Assessment 1

TEACHING

Teaching Tip

In the introduction on page 365, students are introduced to a small database as a vehicle for thinking about the logical connectors *and*, *or*, and *not*. Some students may be familiar with doing key word searches in a library or with using other databases. Ask students if they have had any experiences using databases and, if so, to share them with the class.

Additional Sample

S1 Use Bridget's database on page 365.

a. Suppose Kayla is looking for a job that is for 20 hours per week *and* that pays over $6.25 per hour. Which jobs should Kayla consider? **There is no such job. The job for 20 hours per week pays only $6.25 per hour.**

b. Suppose Lucas wants a job that is for 25 hours per week *or* that pays over $8.00 per hour. Which jobs should Lucas consider? **He should consider the job at Great Lawns.**

c. Suppose Jason is willing to take any job that is not more than 10 hours per week. Which jobs should Jason consider? **He should consider jobs at Cow Bar, Shop-All, and Great Lawns.**

Talk it Over

Questions 1 and 2 provide students with more experiences using the database. These questions and Sample 1 should lead students to understand that the word *and* means that *both* conditions must be met. When *or* is used, then *either* condition or *both* conditions must be met. The word *and*, therefore, is a more restrictive term than *or*. Any search of a database using *and* will generally result in fewer items of data being selected than if *or* were used.

BY THE WAY...

About 80% of high school students have an after-school job sometime during their high school career. On any given day about one third of high school students are scheduled to work.

Sample 1

Use Bridget's database.

a. Kayla is looking for a job that is for 15 or more hours per week *and* that pays over $6.00 per hour. Which jobs should Kayla consider?

b. Lucas wants a job that is for 15 or more hours per week *or* that pays over $6.00 per hour. Which jobs should Lucas consider?

c. Jason is willing to take any job but has no transportation to the North Mall. Which jobs should Jason consider?

Sample Response

Here are the conditions involved in parts (a)–(c).

15 or more hours per week ▓   pay over $6.00 ▓   not at North Mall ▓

Business	Job	Location	Hours/week	Hourly pay ($)
Cow Bar	ice cream server	South Mall	10	6.00
Bond's	filing clerk	South Mall	12	6.00
Food Stuff	stock clerk	South Mall	15	6.50
Lunch Bag	ice cream server	North Mall	20	6.25
Shop-All	stock clerk	North Mall	10	6.75
Great Lawns	yard worker	neighborhood	10	9.50
Pooch's	dog walker	neighborhood	15	5.50

a. Kayla wants a job that meets both conditions ▓ *and* ▓. She should consider a job as a stock clerk at Food Stuff or as an ice cream server at Lunch Bag.

b. Lucas wants a job that meets condition ▓ *or* ▓ or both. He should consider the jobs at Food Stuff, Lunch Bag, Shop-All, Great Lawns, and Pooch's.

c. Jason wants a job that meets condition ▓. He should consider the jobs at Cow Bar, Bond's, Food Stuff, Great Lawns, and Pooch's.

Talk it Over

Use the database above. Recommend which job(s) each person should consider. Explain your reasoning.

1. Jean is willing to work as a stock clerk or to work at the North Mall.

2. Shenida wants a job that pays over $6.50 per hour and is for 20 or more hours per week.

Unit 7 Logic and Proof

Answers to Talk it Over

1. stock clerk at Food Stuff or Shop-All, ice cream server at Lunch Bag; Jean wants a job as a shop clerk *or* to work at North Mall *or* both.

2. none; The only job that is for 20 or more hours per week pays less than $6.50 per hour.

Venn Diagrams for Logic

Statements involving *and*, *or*, and *not* have special names as described below.

Two statements connected by *and* form a **conjunction**. It is true when both statements are true.

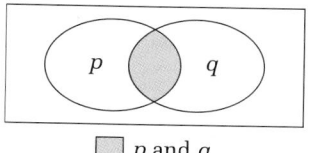

☐ *p* and *q*

Two statements connected by *or* form a **disjunction**. It is true when at least one statement is true.

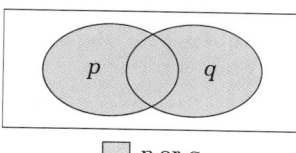

☐ *p* or *q*

A statement involving *not* is called a **negation**.

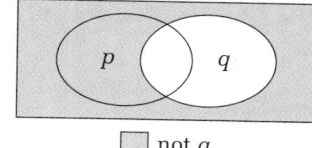

☐ not *q*

Reasoning with Or

In everyday language, *or* can mean two different things.

In the first situation *or* means at the library or on the field, *not both*. This is called an *exclusive or*.

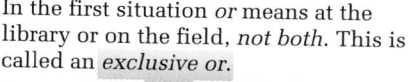

"At 4:00, I'll be at the library...

not both

...or on the playing field."

In the second situation *or* can mean being at the library, listening to music, or doing both. This is called an *inclusive or*.

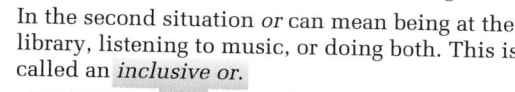

"At 4:00, I'll be at the library or listening to music."

Logical statements in mathematics and in this book use the *inclusive or*.

Talk it Over

Tell whether the *inclusive or* or the *exclusive or* is being used.

3. To meet graduation requirements Joe needs to take a writing course or a literature course next semester. He chooses to take creative writing and American literature.

4. Wakenda can afford to buy Bena either a classical music tape or a reggae tape for her birthday. Wakenda buys a reggae tape.

······► Now you are ready for:
Exs. 1–20 on pp. 369–371

7-1 Using And, Or, Not

Answers to Talk it Over ······

3. inclusive *or*
4. exclusive *or*

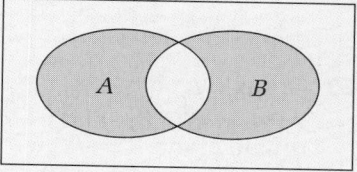

S2 Use a mathematical statement and a number line to show the ages of people who do *not* pay the regular admission price at the art museum. Let *b* represent the ages of people who do not pay the regular admission price. $b \leq 5$ or $b \geq 65$

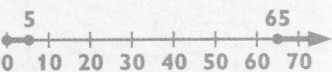

S3 Graph the conjunction $y \geq 2x$ and $x > -3$ on a coordinate plane. Tell which points are on the graph.

Step 1. Graph the line $y = 2x$ as a solid line and shade above the line where y is greater than $2x$.

Step 2. Graph the line $x = -3$ as a dashed line and shade to the right where x is greater than -3.

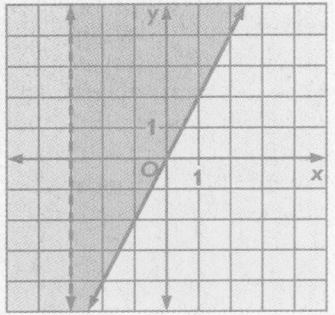

The two conditions are joined by *and*, so the graph is all the points that satisfy *both* conditions. These are the points that have been shaded twice.

Error Analysis

Students may make errors in drawing lines as solid or dashed when working with inequalities such as those in Sample 3. Stress that if the inequality is greater than or equal to ($\geq$) or less than or equal to ($\leq$), the *equal to* part means the points on the line are included in the graph and thus the line is *solid*. For other inequalities ($<$ or $>$), the points are not included in the graph and the line is dashed to represent this situation.

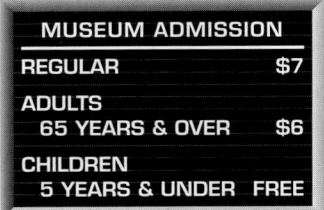

MUSEUM ADMISSION	
REGULAR	$7
ADULTS	
65 YEARS & OVER	$6
CHILDREN	
5 YEARS & UNDER	FREE

Logic with Graphs

Some mathematical statements involving a conjunction or a disjunction can be graphed on a number line or a coordinate plane.

Sample 2

Use a mathematical statement and a number line to show the ages of people who pay the regular admission price at the art museum.

Sample Response

People who are over 5 *and* under 65 pay the regular admission price. Let *a* represent the ages of people who pay the regular admission price. Then $a > 5$ and $a < 65$.

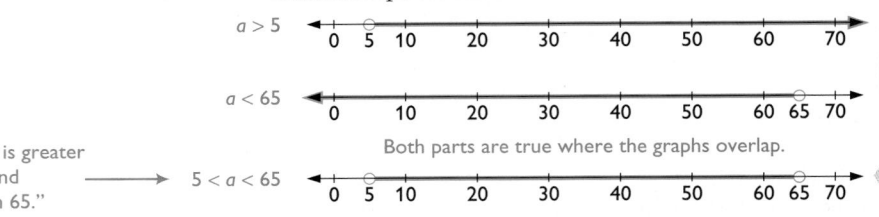

Read "*a* is greater than 5 and less than 65." $\rightarrow$ $5 < a < 65$

Both parts are true where the graphs overlap.

Sample 3

Graph the disjunction $y \geq x$ or $x < 3$ on a coordinate plane. Tell which points are on the graph.

Sample Response

1 Graph the line $y = x$ and shade above where y is greater than x.

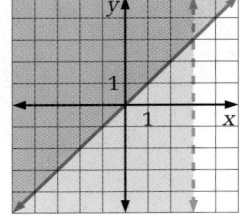

2 Graph the line $x = 3$ and shade to the left where x is less than 3.

The two conditions are joined by *or*, so the graph is all the points that satisfy one condition , the other condition , or both conditions . These are all the points that have been shaded.

Look Back

What is a conjunction? When is it true? What is a disjunction? When is it true? What is a negation?

⤑ Now you are ready for:
Exs. 21–48 on pp. 371–372

368   **Unit 7** Logic and Proof

Answers to Look Back

A conjunction is two statements connected by *and*. It is true when both statements are true. A disjunction is two statements connected by *or.* It is true when at least one of the statements is true. A negation is a statement involving *not.*

Exercises and Problems

1. **Reading** What does the shaded portion of each Venn diagram on page 367 mean?

For Exercises 2–4, use this part of a database for the Museum of Fine Arts in Boston.

Detail from woven and embroidered Peruvian cloak, A.D. 50–100

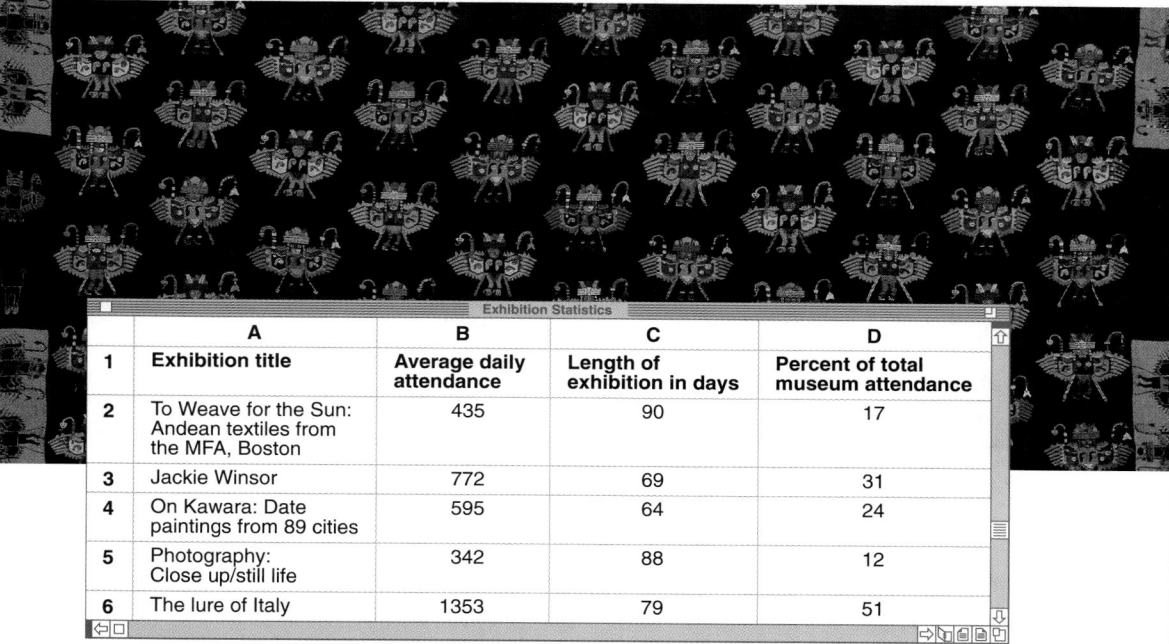

	A	B	C	D
	Exhibition title	Average daily attendance	Length of exhibition in days	Percent of total museum attendance
1				
2	To Weave for the Sun: Andean textiles from the MFA, Boston	435	90	17
3	Jackie Winsor	772	69	31
4	On Kawara: Date paintings from 89 cities	595	64	24
5	Photography: Close up/still life	342	88	12
6	The lure of Italy	1353	79	51

Exhibition Statistics

2. Which exhibition(s) lasted more than 75 days and had an average daily attendance greater than 500?

3. For which exhibition(s) was the average daily attendance over 600 or the percent of total museum attendance greater than 20?

4. **Writing** Describe two ways to search the database to find exhibitions that lasted more than 80 days and did not have a percent of total attendance less than 15.

For Exercises 5–8, use the Venn diagram showing seniors ( ) taking creative writing ( ). Match each letter W–Z with the student it represents.

5. Joan is a senior and is taking creative writing.

6. Sheila is a junior and is not taking creative writing.

7. Linh is a junior and is taking creative writing.

8. Lee is a senior and is not taking creative writing.

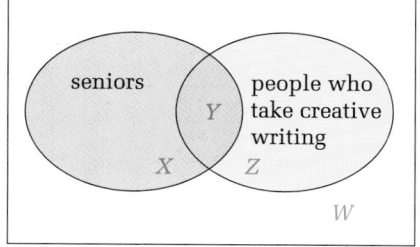

seniors | Y | people who take creative writing

X Z

W

7-1 *Using And, Or, Not*

APPLYING

Suggested Assignment

Day 1
Standard 2–8, 12–20
Extended 1–20

Day 2
Standard 21–48
Extended 21–48

Integrating the Strands
Algebra Exs. 21–30, 34–40, 42
Geometry Exs. 12, 31–40
Statistics and Probability Exs. 43–46
Discrete Mathematics Exs. 1–41, 47, 48
Logic and Language Exs. 1–41, 47, 48

Communication: Discussion
Exs. 1–8 can be done verbally in class to review the use of conjunctions, disjunctions, and negations to search a database and to interpret the meaning of a Venn diagram.

Answers to Exercises and Problems

1. the conditions under which the statement is true

2. the lure of Italy

3. Jackie Winsor, The lure of Italy, On Kawara

4. Answers may vary. Examples are given. Search for exhibitions that lasted more than 80 days. From those exhibitions, choose the ones whose percent of total attendance was not less than 15. Another way is to search for exhibitions whose percent of total museum attendance was greater than or equal to 15, and then choose only those exhibits that also lasted for more than 80 days.

5. *Y*
6. *W*
7. *Z*
8. *X*

connection to SCIENCE

To make electrical current flow, a *circuit*, or continuous path for the current, is needed. These diagrams show the two main ways circuits can be connected.

Parallel Circuit

Series Circuit

9. Use the parallel circuit.

   a. Will one light bulb stay lit if the other bulb is removed from its base?

   b. Liz says that when one bulb or the other bulb is lit, current is flowing. She knows that current is flowing when both bulbs are lit. Is the *or* that Liz is using *inclusive* or *exclusive*?

10. Use the series circuit.

    a. Will one light bulb stay lit if the other bulb is removed from its base?

    b. Write a statement that describes the conditions for both bulbs to remain lit. Tell whether your statement is a *conjunction* or *disjunction*.

11. A red light bulb, a green bulb, and a yellow bulb are connected in a series circuit. Describe which bulbs must be in their bases for all the bulbs to be lit. Tell whether your statement is a *conjunction* or *disjunction*.

12. a. Use triangles *A–G*. Copy the table. Show where each triangle should be placed. Triangle *G* has been done for you.

	Acute	Right	Obtuse
Scalene	?	G	?
Isosceles	?	?	?
Equilateral	?		

   b. List the triangles that are isosceles and obtuse.

   c. List the triangles that are isosceles or obtuse.

Answers to Exercises and Problems

9. a. Yes.

   b. inclusive *or*

10. a. No.

    b. Both light bulbs will remain lit only if when one light bulb is in its base, the other light bulb is also in its base; conjunction.

11. The red light bulb, the green light bulb, and the yellow light bulb must all be in their bases for all the light bulbs to remain lit; conjunction.

12. See answers in back of book.

13. I'm outside.

14. The footprints are Caitlin's or Kyra's.

15. If the inclusive *or* is being used, the conclusion is not justified because it is possible to eat pizza while at a ball game. The conclusion would be justified only if the exclusive *or* were being used.

16. This conclusion is not justified because the voice could have been either Rose's or Talia's.

17. Yes.   18. No.

What conclusion can you reach from each set of conditions?

13. I am in the house or outside. I am not in the house.

14. The footprints are those of Caroline, Caitlin, or Kyra. The footprints are not Caroline's.

For Exercises 15 and 16, each conclusion is not justified. Explain why.

15. We are at the ball game or we are eating pizza. We are eating pizza. Conclusion: We are not at the ball game.

16. The person leaving a message on my recorder is Lily, Rose, or Talia. It is not Lily's voice. Conclusion: It is Talia's voice.

**Thomas is at a food store. He says, "I will buy peanuts or I will buy raisins."
For each situation, tell whether his statement was accurate.**

17. He buys peanuts only.

18. He buys cashews only.

19. He buys a mixture of peanuts and raisins.

20. Suppose Thomas had said, "I will buy peanuts and raisins." He bought only peanuts. Was his statement accurate?

For Exercises 21–23, match each conjunction or disjunction with the letter of its graph.

21. $x > -20$ and $x \le 10$

22. $x < -20$ or $x \ge 10$

23. $x > -20$ or $x \ge 10$

A. 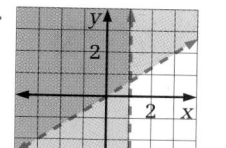 B. 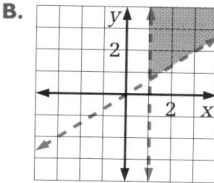 C.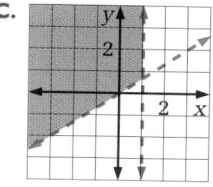

Graph each conjunction or disjunction on a number line.

24. $x \le 7$ or $x \ge 10$

25. $x > 7$ and $x < 10$

26. $x > 7$ and $x > 10$

27. $x < 7$ or $x > 10$

28. $x \le 7$ and $x < 10$

29. $x > 7$ or $x < 10$

30. Which of Exercises 24–29 can be written $7 < x < 10$?

Open-ended Write a conjunction or disjunction whose graph fits each description.

31. a segment

32. no points

33. the entire number line

Match each conjunction or disjunction with the letter of its graph.

34. $y > \frac{2}{3}x$ and $x < 1$

35. $y > \frac{2}{3}x$ and $x > 1$

36. $y > \frac{2}{3}x$ or $x < 1$

A. B. C.

Graph each conjunction or disjunction on a coordinate plane. Tell which points are on the graph.

37. $y \ge 2x$ and $y > 5$

38. $y > x + 4$ or $y \le x - 3$

39. $y < 2x$ or $y < 5$

40. $y > -x$ and $y < -x - 1$

7-1 Using And, Or, Not

371

Answers to Exercises and Problems

19. Yes.

20. No.

21. C

22. B

23. A

24.

25.

26.

27.

28.

29.

30. Ex. 25

31–33. Answers may vary. Examples are given.

31. $5 \le x \le 9$

32. $x < 3$ and $x > 7$

33. $x > 5$ or $x < 7$

34. C

35. B

36. A

37.

38.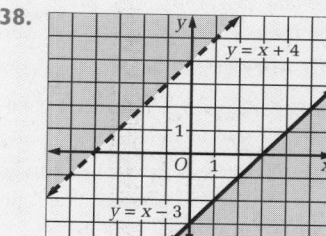

39.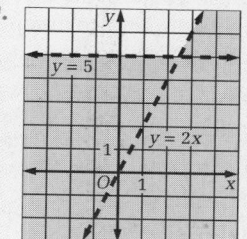

40.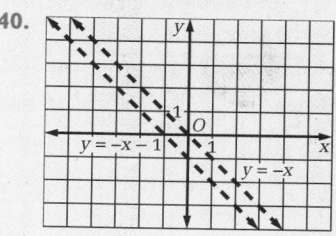

371

Working on the Unit Project

For Ex. 48, students can assemble in their project groups to discuss the clues in part (a) and to complete part (b). They should make a database like the one shown in the textbook.

Practice 51 For use with Section 7-1

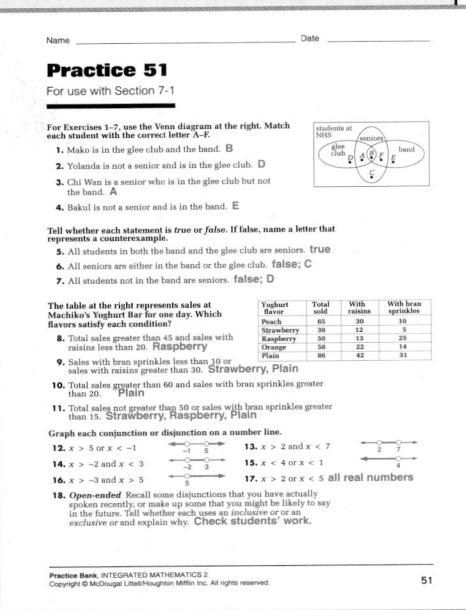

Answers to
Exercises and Problems

41. Answers may vary. Examples are given.

Conjunction: Use the data from Sample 2. Let y represent the ages of people who must pay an admission fee and are older than 30. The figure shows the graph of $y > 5$ and $y > 30$.

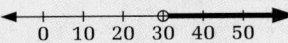

Disjunction: Again use the data from Sample 2. Let x represent the ages of people who pay $6 or $7. The figure shows the graph of $x > 5$ or $x \geq 65$.

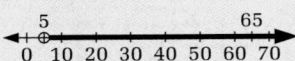

42. $x^3 + 9x^2 + 27x + 27$

43. 100%   **44.** 40%

45. 40%   **46.** 60%

---

41. **Open-ended** Represent two situations involving inequalities as in Sample 2. Make one situation a conjunction and one a disjunction. Label each one and draw its graph on a number line.

42. Write $(x + 3)^3$ in expanded form. *(Section 6-9)*

Use the Museum of Fine Arts database from Exercises 2–4. Suppose you choose an exhibition at random. Find each probability. *(Section 6-3)*

43. P(exhibit lasts more than 60 days)

44. P(exhibit lasts less than 70 days)

45. P(the average daily attendance is greater than 500 and the percent of total attendance is greater than 30)

46. P(the average daily attendance is greater than 500 or the percent of total attendance is greater than 30)

47. Draw a Venn diagram that shows the relationships among quadrilaterals, parallelograms, and rectangles. *(Section 5-1)*

7 Working on the Unit Project

You can use a database to store information about the characters in your story.

48. a. Use the clues about Characters A, B, and C to complete this database. Write *Yes* or *No* in each box.

Clue 1	Each character is on only one team.
Clue 2	Each character is from only one country.
Clue 3	Character A has never been to Thailand.
Clue 4	Character B is allergic to the chlorine used in swimming pools.
Clue 5	The character who plays volleyball is from Ireland.
Clue 6	Character C plays basketball.

	A	B	C
Basketball	?	?	?
Volleyball	?	?	?
Swimming	?	?	?
Ireland	?	?	?
Thailand	?	?	?
Costa Rica	?	?	?

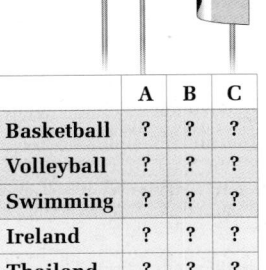

b. Tell which team each character plays on and which country each character comes from.

47.

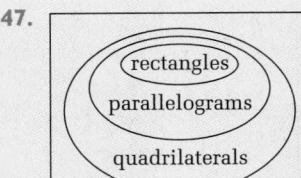

48. a.

	A	B	C
Basketball	No.	No.	Yes.
Volleyball	No.	Yes.	No.
Swimming	Yes.	No.	No.
Ireland	No.	Yes.	No.
Thailand	No.	No.	Yes.
Costa Rica	Yes.	No.	No.

b. Character A swims and is from Costa Rica, Character B plays volleyball and is from Ireland, and Character C plays basketball and is from Thailand.

Implications

Focus
Translate among various forms of implications.

Mind Your P's and Q's

Biologists use classifications to organize information.

All prairie dogs are rodents.

There are several other ways to say the same thing. Examples are given below. The Venn diagram represents them all.

rodents

prairie dogs

➤ **If** an animal is a prairie dog, **then** it is a rodent.

➤ **Every** prairie dog is a rodent.

➤ The fact that an animal is a prairie dog **implies** that it is a rodent.

➤ An animal is a prairie dog **only if** it is a rodent.

You can represent these statements with symbols.

Read "p implies q" or "if p, then q."

$$p \rightarrow q$$

Let p represent the "if" part or **hypothesis** "an animal is a prairie dog."

Let q represent the "then" part or **conclusion** "an animal is a rodent."

Statements that can be written in the form $p \rightarrow q$ are called **implications** or **conditionals**.

7-2 Implications

BY THE WAY...

Prairie dogs are not dogs, and guinea pigs are not pigs. They are both rodents, which are characterized by large front teeth used to gnaw. Mice, beavers, chinchillas, and porcupines are rodents, too.

PLANNING

Objectives and Strands
See pages 362A and 362B.

Spiral Learning
See page 362B.

Materials List
➤ Graph paper

Recommended Pacing
Section 7-2 is a one-day lesson.

Extra Practice
See pages 625–626.

Warm-Up Exercises
Warm-Up Transparency 7-2

Support Materials
➤ Practice 52
➤ Enrichment 46 in the Activity Bank
➤ Study Guide 7-2
➤ Problem Set 14
➤ Diagram Master 2 in the Explorations Lab Manual
➤ Quiz 7-2
➤ Alternative Assessment 2

TEACHING

Additional Sample

Use the implication "All kites have perpendicular diagonals."

a. Rewrite the implication in four different ways.
If a figure is a kite, then it has perpendicular diagonals.
Every kite has perpendicular diagonals.
The fact that a figure is a kite implies that it has perpendicular diagonals.
A figure is a kite only if it has perpendicular diagonals.

b. Tell whether the implication is *True* or *False.* If it is true, draw a Venn diagram for the implication. If it is false, give a counterexample. **True.**

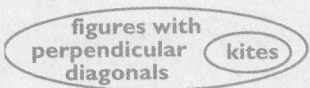

c. Suppose $p \to q$ represents the implication. What do p and q represent in this case?
p means "a figure is a kite."
q means "a figure has perpendicular diagonals."

d. Write the converse of the implication. Tell whether it is *True* or *False.* If it is false, give a counterexample. **The converse is "If a figure has perpendicular diagonals, then it is a kite." The converse is false. Counterexample: The quadrilateral shown has perpendicular diagonals but is not a kite.**

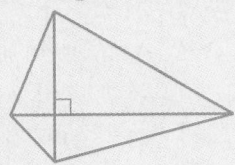

Use the implication "All rectangles have congruent diagonals."

a. Rewrite the implication in four different ways.

b. Tell whether the implication is *True* or *False.* If it is true, draw a Venn diagram for the implication. If it is false, give a counterexample.

c. Suppose $p \to q$ represents the implication. What do p and q represent in this case?

d. Write the *converse* of the implication. Tell whether it is *True* or *False.* If it is false, give a counterexample.

Sample Response

hypothesis ┐   ┌ conclusion

a. If a figure is a rectangle, then it has congruent diagonals.

Every rectangle has congruent diagonals.

The fact that a figure is a rectangle implies that it has congruent diagonals.

A figure is a rectangle only if it has congruent diagonals.

figures with congruent diagonals
rectangles

b. True. (See page 281.)

c. *p* means "a figure is a rectangle." *q* means "a figure has congruent diagonals."

d. The converse is "If a figure has congruent diagonals, then it is a rectangle." The converse is false. Here is a counterexample.

This trapezoid has congruent diagonals, but it is not a rectangle.

NORTH AMERICA

Canada

United States

Mexico

Talk it Over

1. Use the implication "I am in Canada only if I am in North America." Write the implication in if-then form. Then represent the implication with a Venn diagram.

2. Use this implication, "$x + 5 = 9$ implies that $x = 4$."
   a. Tell whether the implication is *True* or *False.*
   b. Write the converse of the implication.
   c. Tell whether the converse is *True* or *False.* If it is false, give a counterexample.

Unit 7 Logic and Proof

Answers to Talk it Over

1. If I am in Canada, then I am in North America.

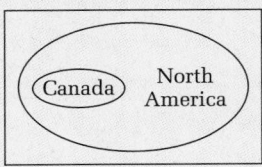
Canada — North America

2. **a.** True.
   b. If $x = 4$, then $x + 5 = 9$.
   c. True.

3. If an animal is a chinchilla, then it is a rodent.

4.
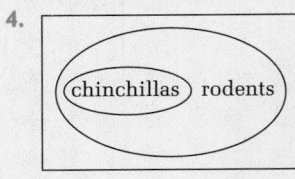
chinchillas — rodents

5. No.   6. Yes.

Answers to Look Back

See answers in back of book.

Cautions with If-then

Here is another way you can write the implication in the Sample.

If a figure is a rectangle , then it has congruent diagonals.

A figure has congruent diagonals if it is a rectangle .

This new type of translation is not the converse. This sentence is still symbolized $p \rightarrow q$, since the "if" part is still the same.

Remember, "*p only if q*" says the same thing as "If p, then q."

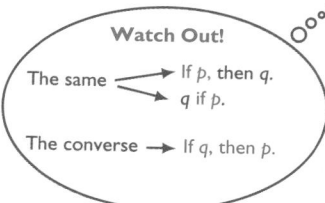

Watch Out!

The same → If p, then q.
             q if p.

The converse → If q, then p.

Talk it Over

3. Write "An animal is a chinchilla only if it is a rodent" in if-then form.

4. Draw a Venn diagram for the implication.

5. Is it possible to be in the *chinchilla* loop of your diagram without being in the *rodent* loop?

6. Is it possible to be in the *rodent* loop of your diagram without being in the *chinchilla* loop?

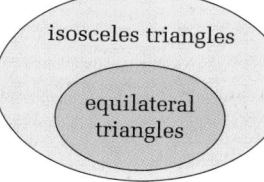

isosceles triangles

equilateral triangles

Look Back

Write at least four equivalent implications for this Venn diagram. Write the converse of one of your statements. Tell whether the converse is *True* or *False*.

7-2 Exercises and Problems

1. **Reading** Which part of an implication is the hypothesis?

2. What are four translations of $p \rightarrow q$?

3. Use symbols to write the converse of $p \rightarrow q$.

For Exercises 4–7:

a. Suppose $p \rightarrow q$ represents each implication. What do p and q represent in each case?

b. Rewrite each implication in an equivalent form using the key word(s) indicated.

c. Draw a Venn diagram for each implication.

4. If a figure is a rhombus, then its diagonals are perpendicular. (*all*)

5. A figure is a square only if it is a rhombus. (*implies*)

6. Whenever it is Saturday, it is a day of the weekend. (*every*)

7. If a figure is a cylinder, then the formula for its volume is $V = Bh$. (*only if*)

7-2 Implications

375

Answers to Exercises and Problems

1. the "if" part

2. Forms may vary. Seven translations are given. All p are q. If p, then q. Every p is q. p is a subset of q. p only if q. p implies q. q if p.

3. $q \rightarrow p$

4. a. p: a figure is a rhombus; q: a figure has perpendicular diagonals.

b. All rhombuses have perpendicular diagonals.

c.
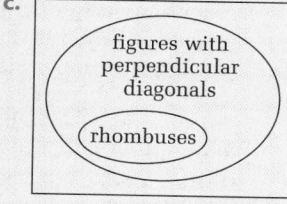
figures with perpendicular diagonals
rhombuses

5. a. p: a figure is a square; q: a figure is a rhombus.

b. The fact that a figure is a square implies that it is a rhombus.

c.
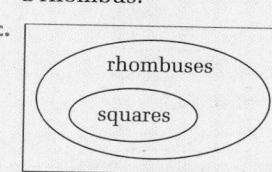
rhombuses
squares

6, 7. See answers at back of book.

Interdisciplinary Problems

Exs. 14–22 and 24 illustrate how implications can be applied to situations involving the chemistry of metals, a social situation involving jewelry worn by women in northern Algeria, and a game of tick-tack-toe. Of course, since an implication can be stated in abstract form as *if p, then q, p* and *q* can be any statements involving any real-world situation. Thus, there is no limit to the use of implications in interdisciplinary situations.

Answers to
Exercises and Problems

8. a. If the probability of an event is zero, then the event is impossible. True.

   b. If an event is impossible, then the probability of the event is zero. True.

9. a. If a figure is a rectangle, then it is a parallelogram. True.

   b. If a figure is a parallelogram, then it is a rectangle. False; a rhombus is also a parallelogram.

10. a. If a state is in New England, then it is east of the Mississippi River. True.

    b. If a state is east of the Mississippi River, then it is in New England. False; Virginia is east of the Mississippi, but it is not in New England.

11. a. If today is Valentine's Day, then this month is February. True.

    b. If this month is February, then today is Valentine's Day. False; it could be February 1 instead of February 14.

12. a. If a number ends in zero, then it is divisible by 2. True.

    b. If a number is divisible by 2, then the number ends in zero. False; 24 is divisible by 2, but it does not end in zero.

13. a. If Cleo is a golden retriever, then Cleo is a dog. True.

    b. If Cleo is a dog, then Cleo is a golden retriever. False; Cleo could be an Irish setter.

14. Yes.   15. Yes.

16. No.   17. Yes.

18. No.   19. Yes.

For Exercises 8–13:

a. **Rewrite each implication in if-then form. Tell whether each implication is *True* or *False*. If it is false, give a counterexample.**

b. **Write the converse of each implication. Tell whether each converse is *True* or *False*. If it is false, give a counterexample.**

8. Whenever the probability of an event is zero, the event is impossible.

9. Rectangles are parallelograms.

10. The New England states are east of the Mississippi River.

11. This month is February if today is Valentine's Day.

12. A number ending in 0 implies that it is divisible by 2.

13. Cleo is a golden retriever only if Cleo is a dog.

connection to CHEMISTRY

Many of the elements that make up the substances in the universe are classified as metals. One category of metals is *transition metals*. Examples of transition metals include copper, silver, nickel, and gold.

PERIODIC TABLE

☐ Alkali metals
☐ Alkaline earth metals
☐ Transition metals
☐ Lanthanide series
☐ Actinide series
☐ Other metals
☐ Nonmetals
☐ Noble gases

For Exercises 14–17, tell whether each implication is represented by the Venn diagram. Write *Yes* or *No*.

14. A transition metal is one type of metal.

15. All transition metals are metals.

16. If an element is a metal, then it is a transition metal.

17. An element is a transition metal only if it is a metal.

18. Does the fact that tin is a metal imply that it is a transition metal?

19. Does the fact that copper is a transition metal imply that it is a metal?

376   **Unit 7** Logic and Proof

---

20. If a woman's tabzimt is part of her dowry, then she wears the tabzimt around her neck. If a woman's tabzimt was given to her by her husband on the birth of their first son, then she wears the tabzimt on her forehead.

21. She had the tabzimt in her dowry before she was married and had a son.

22. True.

23. a. Yes.

    b. If a segment is a diameter of a circle, then it is a chord of the circle.

    c. If a segment is a chord of a circle, then it is a diameter of the circle. No; the converse is false. A chord is a diameter only if it passes through the center of the circle.

24.
X_1	O_2	X_7
X_9	O_4	O_8
O_6	X_5	X_3

b. Answers may vary. An example is given. Each move involves blocking the opponent. The implication is "if an opponent has two marks in a row, column, or diagonal, then you will put your mark in a free space in that row, column, or diagonal.

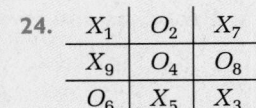

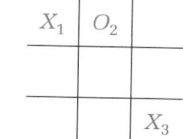

The piece of jewelry shown is a *tabzimt*. It is worn by Kabyle women of northern Algeria. A woman wears it at her neck if it is in her dowry when she marries. She wears it on her forehead if it is given by her husband on the birth of their first son.

20. Write each of the two conditionals in the above paragraph in if-then form.

21. Suppose a married Kabyle woman with a son wears a tabzimt at her neck. Explain why she may be wearing it there.

22. Is this statement *True* or *False*? If the materials in the tabzimt shown include silver, coral, and enamel, then the tabzimt has a transition metal in it. (See Exercises 14–19.)

23. A *chord* is a segment whose endpoints are on a circle.

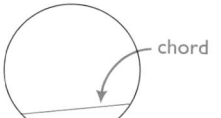

    a. Is a diameter of a circle a chord?

    b. Write an implication about chords and diameters.

    c. **Writing** Write the converse of your implication. Is it true? Explain.

24. **Games** In the game *tick-tack-toe*, players take turns putting Xs and Os in a 3-by-3 grid. Three of the same symbol in a row wins. The game at the right is in progress. The numbers below the letters tell the order in which they were played. Player X went first.

X_1	O_2	
	X_3	

    a. Assume that each player blocks a win whenever the other player has two in a row. Show how this game will finish.

    b. **Writing** Explain how each move is an example of an implication.

Ongoing ASSESSMENT

25. **Writing** Rewrite one statement from each of the previous six units as an implication. Use as many different forms of implications as you can.

Review PREVIEW

26. Graph the conjunction $y < 4$ and $y < \frac{3}{2}x$ on a coordinate plane. *(Section 7-1)*

The Venn diagram shows how students responded to a survey on three specific activities done during lunch time. Tell whether each statement about the students in the survey is *True* or *False*. *(Section 1-6)*

27. If a student eats lunch, then the student does not do homework.

28. All students who eat lunch do homework.

29. Some students visit with friends and do homework.

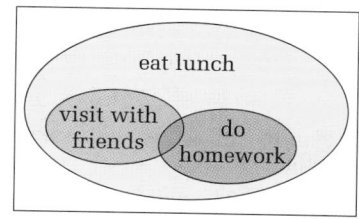

Using Technology

With the TI-82 and TI-83, it is sometimes possible to use tables to test implications. It is especially easy to do this if you use the ideas in the Technology Note on page 370 to get 0's and 1's in the Y_1- and Y_2-columns. For example, consider $(x > 2) \rightarrow (x > -1)$. Clear the Y= list and enter $Y_1 = X > 2$ and $Y_2 = X > -1$. On the TI-82, press [2nd] [TblSet] and set TblMin=−10, ΔTbl=1. On the TI-83, press [2nd] [TblSet] and set TblStart=−10, ΔTbl=1. Then press [2nd] [TABLE]. Press [▼] to look at the table entries for greater and greater values of x. In no case do you find a 1 in the Y_1-column paired with a 0 in the Y_2-column. Since 1 means true and 0 means false, there are no values observed where the hypothesis is true and the conclusion false. This supports the idea that $(x > 2) \rightarrow (x > -1)$ is true. (It does not *prove* the implication true, because the table cannot show all values of x.)

If you try the same idea with $(x^2 > 4) \rightarrow (x > 2)$, you see that for $x = -3$ you have $Y_1 = 1$ and $Y_2 = 0$. This is enough to show that the implication is not true for all values of x. The value −3 for x is a counterexample.

Students Acquiring English

Some English learners may not be familiar with the game of tick-tack-toe in Ex. 24. Have volunteers explain how the game is played. Encourage students to use the following phrases in their explanation: *in a row, blocks a win*.

Answers to Exercises and Problems

25. Answers may vary. Examples are given. Unit 1: If each member of a population has an equally likely chance of being selected for a sample, then the sample is a random sample. Unit 2: All graphs of inverse variations are hyperbolas. Unit 3: Every consistent system of linear equations has at least one solution. Unit 4: The equation $ax^2 + bx + c = 0$ has one solution only if the discriminant is zero. Unit 5: The set of squares is a subset of the set of rhombuses. Unit 6: The fact that two events are mutually exclusive implies that the probability that either occurs is the sum of the probabilities that each will occur.

26.

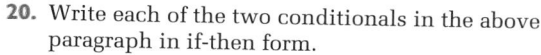

27. False.

28. False.

29. True.

Practice 52 For use with Section 7-2

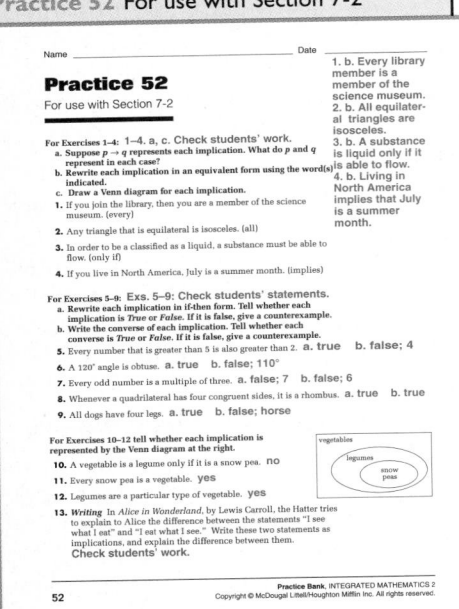

30. Murphy's Market charges these prices for the brands of peanut butter it sells. *(Section 3-5)*

	12 oz	**18 oz**	**40 oz**
Jem	$1.69	$2.29	$3.89
MJ's	$1.75	$2.49	$4.19
Susan's Best	$2.19	$2.79	$4.99

   a. Write the prices in the table as a 3×3 matrix.

   b. Use scalar multiplication to write a matrix representing a 7% increase in peanut butter prices.

31. **Writing** Use the Venn diagram to write three true statements, one each using *and*, *or*, and *not*. *(Section 7-1)*

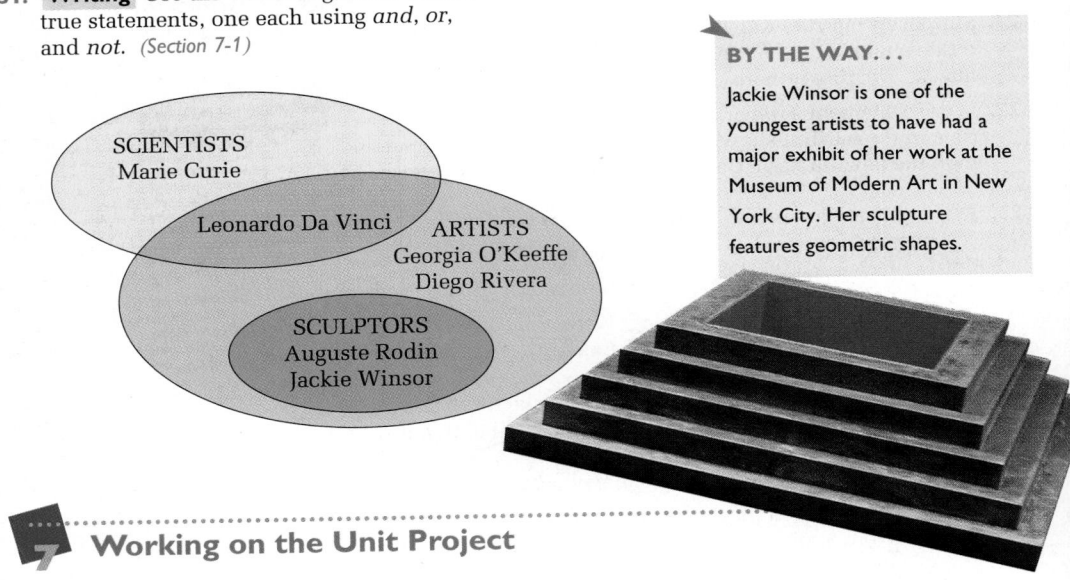

BY THE WAY...

Jackie Winsor is one of the youngest artists to have had a major exhibit of her work at the Museum of Modern Art in New York City. Her sculpture features geometric shapes.

Working on the Unit Project

For Exercises 32 and 33, use this excerpt from Michael Crichton's book *The Andromeda Strain*. The characters are trying to solve a mystery about an infection.

"The child was normal," Hall said. "It could cry, and disrupt its acid-base balance. That would prevent the Andromeda Strain from getting into its bloodstream....Sooner or later it would stop....Then it would be vulnerable to Andromeda....When the child stopped crying, either the organism was no longer there—or else the organism—"

"Changed," Stone said. "Mutated."

"Yes. Mutated to a noninfectious form. And perhaps it is still mutating. Now it is no longer directly harmful to man,..."

32. Identify at least two implications in the excerpt and write each in if-then form.

33. **Writing** The child stopped crying. Do you think it was harmed by the Andromeda organism?

378   **Unit 7** Logic and Proof

Answers to Exercises and Problems

30.
$$\begin{bmatrix} 1.69 & 2.29 & 3.89 \\ 1.75 & 2.49 & 4.19 \\ 2.19 & 2.79 & 4.99 \end{bmatrix}$$

$$\begin{bmatrix} 1.81 & 2.45 & 4.16 \\ 1.87 & 2.66 & 4.48 \\ 2.34 & 2.99 & 5.34 \end{bmatrix}$$

31. Answers may vary. Examples are given. Leonardo Da Vinci was an artist and a scientist. Rodin was a sculptor or Marie Curie was a scientist. Diego Rivera was not a scientist.

32. Answers may vary. Examples are given. If the child was normal, then it could cry. If the child could cry, then it would disrupt its acid-base balance. If the child disrupted its acid-base balance, then the child would prevent the Andromeda Strain from getting into the child's bloodstream. If the child stopped crying, then it became vulnerable to the Andromeda Strain.

33. Answers may vary. Examples are given. No; the organism probably mutated to a noninfectious form which is no longer directly harmful to man.

Focus

Distinguish valid arguments from invalid arguments.

PREMISES,
Premises

EXPLORATION

(Who) is going to the party?

- **Work in a group of four students.**

Clue 1 If Don is going, then Eve is going.

How often have you heard friends say, "I'll go if you'll go"? You will use these clues to determine who is going to the party:

Clue 2 Ben is not going to the party.

Clue 3 If Al is going, then Ben is going.

Clue 4 If Carla is going, then Don is going.

In your group, discuss which clues can lead you to an answer to each of these questions. Then agree on an answer.

1. Is Ben going to the party?
2. Is Al going to the party?
3. Is Carla going to the party?
4. Is Don going to the party?
5. Is Eve going to the party?
6. List the students who are going to the party. Compare your list with another group's list. If there are any differences, try to convince the others that your reasoning is valid.

Clue 5 Al or Carla is going to the party.

Answers to Exploration

1. No.
2. No.
3. Yes.
4. Yes.
5. Yes.
6. Carla, Don, Eve

PLANNING

Objectives and Strands
See pages 362A and 362B.

Spiral Learning
See page 362B.

Recommended Pacing
Section 7-3 is a one-day lesson.

Extra Practice
See pages 625–626.

Warm-Up Exercises
Warm-Up Transparency 7-3

Support Materials
➤ Practice 53
➤ Enrichment 47 in the Activity Bank
➤ Study Guide 7-3
➤ Problem Set 14
➤ Quiz 7-3
➤ Test 27
➤ Alternative Assessment 3

Exploration

Working in groups of four, students explore informally a series of clues and questions that may lead them intuitively to some of the rules of logic presented on this page.

Teaching Tip

For each rule of logic, ask students to identify each premise and conclusion. Also, see if students can relate any of the four rules to their answers for the Exploration questions.

Visual Thinking

Assign students to work in teams to consider real-life examples for each of the Venn diagrams shown in the Rules of Logic table. Ask each team to present its examples to the class. This activity involves the visual skills of *interpretation* and *communication.*

Reasoning

There is a subtle distinction between the truth of a statement and the validity of an argument. A statement is true if it is an established fact of the real-world or if it is assumed to be true (as the postulates of geometry are assumed to be true). An argument is valid if its conclusion is a logical consequence of its premises. The actual truth of the premises is irrelevant to judging whether an argument is valid or not. For example, if it is assumed that all Americans are North Americans, and if Carmen is an American, then the conclusion that Carmen is a North American is a *valid consequence* of our assumptions. However, it is not necessarily a true conclusion because Carmen could be from South America.

In the Exploration you may have used patterns of reasoning called *rules of logic.* Each rule of logic shown below involves two given statements called **premises** and produces a statement called a **conclusion.**

When both premises are true, the conclusion *must* be true. Such reasoning produces a **valid argument.**

RULES OF LOGIC

X shows what is true.

Direct Argument

If p is true, then q is true.
p is true.

Therefore, q is true.

$p \rightarrow q$
p

$\therefore q$ ←Read "Therefore q."

Indirect Argument

If p is true, then q is true.
q is not true.

Therefore, p is not true.

$p \rightarrow q$
not q

$\therefore$ not p

Chain Rule

If p is true, then q is true.
If q is true, then r is true.

Therefore, if p is true, then r is true.

$p \rightarrow q$
$q \rightarrow r$

$\therefore p \rightarrow r$

***Or* Rule**

p is true or q is true.
p is not true.

Therefore, q is true.

p or q
not p

$\therefore q$

Talk it Over

Tell which rule of logic is used in these valid arguments.

1. John is in his room or John is in the kitchen. John is not in the kitchen. Therefore, John is in his room.

2. If I take the Number 10 bus, then I can get to the mall. If I can get to the mall, then I can go to the movies. Therefore, if I take the Number 10 bus, then I can go to the movies.

3. If Manuela has eaten guacamole, then she has tasted avocado. Manuela has eaten guacamole. Therefore, she has tasted avocado.

Unit 7 Logic and Proof

Answers to Talk it Over

1. *or* rule
2. chain rule
3. direct argument

Sample 1

What conclusion can you reach when both premises are true?

a. Premise 1: If an animal is an insect, then it has exactly six legs.
   Premise 2: A spider does not have exactly six legs.

b. Premise 1: If a polygon is a square, then it is a rectangle.
   Premise 2: If a polygon is a rectangle, then it is a parallelogram.

Sample Response

Translate each premise into its symbolic form.

a. *insect* → *six legs* | These are the premises | $p \rightarrow q$
   not *six legs* | of an indirect argument. | not q
                                                          | $\therefore$ not p

Conclusion: A spider is not an insect.

b. *square* → *rectangle* | These are the premises | $p \rightarrow q$
   rectangle → *parallelogram* | of a chain rule argument. | $q \rightarrow r$
                                                          | $\therefore p \rightarrow r$

Conclusion: Therefore, if a polygon is a square,
it is a parallelogram.

Invalid Arguments

Arguments that do not use rules of logic are considered errors,
or **invalid arguments**.

Sample 2

Decide if each argument is *valid* or *invalid*. Explain your reasoning.

a. All multiples of 20 are multiples of five.
   Sam's locker number is a multiple of five.
   Therefore, Sam's locker number is a multiple of 20.

b. Every member of a youth hostel club (YHC) likes to travel.
   Indira is not a member of a youth hostel club.
   Therefore, Indira does not like to travel.

Continued on next page.

7-3 Valid and Invalid Arguments

381

S1 What conclusion can you
reach when both premises
are true?

a. Premise 1: If a plant is a
   flower, then its color is
   white.
   Premise 2: A rose is a
   flower.
   Translate each premise
   into its symbolic form.
   flower → white $p \rightarrow q$
   flower p
                      $\overline{\therefore q}$
   These are the premises of
   a direct argument.
   Conclusion: Therefore, a
   rose is white.

b. Premise 1: Figure *ABCD*
   is a trapezoid or figure
   ABCD is a
   parallelogram.
   Premise 2: Figure *ABCD*
   is not a trapezoid.
   trapezoid or
   parallelogram p or q
                  not p
                  $\overline{\therefore q}$
   These are the premises of
   an *or rule* argument.
   Conclusion: Therefore,
   figure *ABCD* is a
   parallelogram.

S2 Decide if each argument is
valid or *invalid*. Explain
your reasoning.

a. All parallelograms are
   quadrilaterals. Figure
   RSTP is a quadrilateral.
   Therefore, figure *RSTP*
   is a parallelogram. This
   argument is invalid. It
   assumes that the converse
   of every statement is true.

b. If a figure is a square,
   then it is a polygon. Figure *ABC* is not a square.
   Therefore, figure *ABC* is
   not a polygon. The argument is invalid. It is possible that figure *ABC* is a triangle, which is a polygon.

381

382

Reasoning

The converse of the statement *if p, then q* is *if q, then p*. The inverse of the statement *if p, then q* is *if not p, then not q*. Sample 2 shows that neither the converse nor the inverse of a statement is logically equivalent to the original statement. The only statement logically equivalent to *if p, then q* is *if not q, then not p*, which is called the *contrapositive*; it has been presented on page 380 as the indirect argument rule of logic. The term *contrapositive* is introduced in *Integrated Mathematics 3*.

Talk it Over

Question 4 looks somewhat like the chain rule argument, but it is not. It has the form $p \rightarrow q$ and $p \rightarrow r$, $\therefore q \rightarrow r$, which is not a valid argument. Question 5 is a valid indirect argument. The use of symbols $(p \rightarrow q)$ makes the structure of these arguments very clear.

Error Analysis

Students tend to make errors in reasoning logically because they think about the *content* of the statements and do not focus on the *form* of the argument. The rules of logic are valid arguments because of their form and not because of any meaning attached to the symbols p and q.

Sample Response

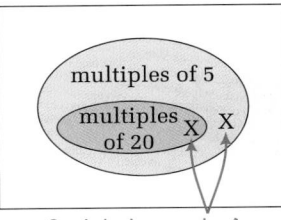

Sam's locker number?

Write the premises as if-then statements. Then use symbols and Venn diagrams to examine the argument.

a. If a number is a multiple of 20, then it is a multiple of 5. $p \rightarrow q$
   Sam's locker number is a multiple of 5. q

   Therefore, Sam's locker number is a multiple of 20. $\therefore p$

This argument is invalid. It does not use a rule of logic and assumes that the converse of every statement is true. This is called a *converse error*. An example of a multiple of 5 that is not a multiple of 20 is 10.

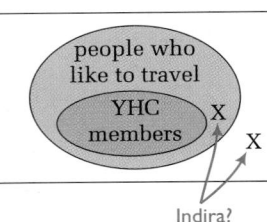

Indira?

b. If a person is a member of YHC, then the person likes to travel. $p \rightarrow q$
   Indira is not a member of YHC.   not p

   Therefore, Indira does not like to travel. $\therefore$ not q

This argument is invalid. It does not use a rule of logic and is called an *inverse error*. The diagram shows that it is possible that Indira likes to travel.

Talk it Over

Do you think each argument is valid? Why or why not?

4. If we visit Hong Kong, then we will eat well.
   If we visit Hong Kong, then we will see Victoria Harbor.
   Therefore, if we eat well, then we will see Victoria Harbor.

5. If $x = 5$, then $2x + 3 = 13$.
   $2x + 3 \neq 13$.
   Therefore, $x \neq 5$.

Look Back

Look again at the rules of logic on page 380. In each argument, tell whether each statement is a premise or a conclusion.

7-3 Exercises and Problems

1. **Reading** What does "$\therefore q$" mean?

For Exercises 2–5, what conclusion can you reach when both premises are true?

2. If an animal has a backbone, it is a vertebrate. A horse has a backbone.

3. If a triangle is isosceles, then it has at least two angles equal in measure.
   $\triangle ABC$ does not have at least two angles equal in measure.

4. If $2x + 3 = 21$, then $2x = 18$.
   If $2x = 18$, then $x = 9$.

5. If $P(A) = 0$, then A is an impossible event.
   A is not an impossible event.

Answers to Talk it Over

4. No; it has the form $p \rightarrow q$ and $p \rightarrow r$, $\therefore q \rightarrow r$, which is not a valid argument.

5. Yes; it is an indirect argument.

Answers to Look Back

The first two statements in each argument are the premises. The statements following the word *Therefore* are the conclusions in the arguments.

6. For each of steps 2–5 in the Exploration, you used rules of logic to find out which students were going to the party. For each student, name the rule of logic you used.

connection to HISTORY

For Exercises 7 and 8, what conclusion can you reach when both premises are true? For each exercise, the first premise is from an amendment to the Constitution.

7. "The right of citizens . . ., who are 18 years of age or older, to vote shall not be denied . . . ." Kerry is a citizen and is 19 years old.

8. "No person shall be elected to the office of the President more than twice . . . . ." Ronald Reagan was elected President twice.

Decide if each argument is *valid* or *invalid*. Explain your reasoning.

9. $q \to r$
   not r
   ————
   $\therefore$ not q

10. s or t
    not s
    ————
    $\therefore$ not t

11. $v \to w$
    w
    ————
    $\therefore v$

connection to LITERATURE

In *A Case of Identity*, a Sherlock Holmes mystery story, James Windibank has tried unsuccessfully to disguise himself as Hosmer Angel. Sherlock Holmes explains how he uncovered the deception.

> ...Then the fact that the two men were never together, but that the one always appeared when the other was away, was suggestive. So were the tinted spectacles and the curious voice, which both hinted at a disguise, as did the bushy whiskers. My suspicions were all confirmed by his peculiar action in typewriting his signature, which of course inferred that his handwriting was so familiar to her [Angel's stepdaughter] that she would recognize even the smallest sample of it....these isolated facts, together with many minor ones, all pointed in the same direction.

For Exercises 12 and 13, decide if each argument is *valid* or *invalid*. Explain your reasoning.

12. If a person wears tinted glasses, then he may be wearing a disguise. James Windibank wears tinted glasses. Conclusion: James Windibank may be wearing a disguise.

13. If James and Hosmer appear together, they are different people. James and Hosmer did not appear together. Conclusion: James and Hosmer are not different people.

14. Write a valid argument based on Sherlock Holmes's remarks.

APPLYING

....
Suggested Assignment
Standard 1–11, 15–20, 22–29
Extended 1–20, 22–29
....
Integrating the Strands
Algebra Exs. 4, 24
Geometry Exs. 3, 15, 18, 23
Statistics and Probability
Exs. 5, 26–28
Discrete Mathematics
Exs. 1–25, 29
Logic and Language Exs. 1–25, 29
....
Interdisciplinary Problems
The exercises in this section illustrate the interdisciplinary nature of logic using examples from algebra, probability, geometry, history, literature, sports, geology, advertising, and everyday life. This selection of topics reinforces the fact that the logical arguments discussed on page 380 are independent of the statements substituted for *p* and *q* and depend entirely on the form or structure of the argument.

Answers to Exercises and Problems

1. therefore q

2. A horse is a vertebrate.

3. $\triangle ABC$ is not isosceles.

4. If $2x + 3 = 21$, then $x = 9$.

5. $P(A) \neq 0$.

6. Ben is not going. (given) Al is not going by indirect argument. ($p \to q$; not q; $\therefore$ not p) Carla is going by the *or* rule. (p or q, not p; $\therefore q$) Don is going by direct argument. ($p \to q$; p; $\therefore q$)

Eve is going by the chain rule. ($p \to q$; $q \to r$; $\therefore p \to r$)

7. Kerry has the right to vote.

8. Ronald Reagan cannot be elected to the presidency of the U.S. again.

9. valid; indirect argument

10. invalid; It has the form p or q; not p; $\therefore$ not q, which is not a valid argument.

11. invalid; It has the form $p \to q$; q; $\therefore p$, which is not a valid argument.

12. valid; direct argument

13. invalid; It has the form $p \to q$; not p; $\therefore$ not q, which is not a valid argument.

14. Answers may vary. Examples are given. If two people do not appear together, then they could be the same person. Angel and Windibank never appeared together. Therefore, they could be the same person. If you talk in a curious voice, wear tinted spectacles, and wear bushy whiskers, then you could be wearing a disguise. If you type your signature, then you might not want anyone to recognize it. Windibank typed his signature. Therefore, he did not want anyone (his stepdaughter) to recognize it.

Answers to
Exercises and Problems

15. invalid; $p \to q$; q; $\therefore p$ is not a rule of logic.

16. invalid; $p \to q$; not p; $\therefore q$ is not a rule of logic.

17. valid; *or* rule

18. valid; chain rule

19. valid; indirect argument

20. invalid; converse error

21. Answers may vary. An example is given for an airlines advertisement. If I purchase tickets to fly to Europe before February 11, then I will pay the low fare price. I buy my tickets on February 9. Therefore I pay the low fare price; $(p \to q; p; \therefore q)$; direct argument

22. Answers may vary. An example is given. If you buy Sparkle Flakes, your laundry will be soft and fluffy. If your laundry is soft and fluffy, you and your family will be happy and comfortable. Therefore, if you buy Sparkle Flakes, you and your family will be happy and comfortable. $(p \to q; q \to r; \therefore p \to r)$; chain rule

23. a. If an angle is obtuse, then it measures between 90° and

---

Decide if each argument is *valid* or *invalid*. Explain your reasoning.

15. If a polygon is a rhombus, then it is a parallelogram. *PQRS* is a parallelogram. Therefore, *PQRS* is a rhombus.

16. If today is Monday, then I go to school. Today is not Monday. Therefore, I do not go to school.

17. Jim Burks or Lonnie Foy dropped the pass. Lonnie Foy did not drop the pass. Therefore, Jim Burks dropped the pass.

18. All pyramids are polyhedrons. All polyhedrons have polygonal faces. Therefore, all pyramids have polygonal faces.

19. If Amy hits a home run, then she is credited with an RBI. Amy is not credited with an RBI. Therefore, Amy did not hit a home run.

20. **Geology** If minerals are hematite, then they leave rust-colored streaks. Therefore, these minerals are hematite.

21. **Research** Find three examples of valid or invalid arguments in advertisements, comics, or newspaper articles. Explain the error in reasoning or the rule of logic used.

Ongoing ASSESSMENT

22. **Open-ended** Write an advertisement that uses a valid argument to convince someone to buy Sparkle Flakes. Identify the rule of logic it uses.

Review PREVIEW

For Exercises 23–25: *(Section 7-2)*

a. **Rewrite each implication in if-then form. Tell whether each implication is *True* or *False*. If it is false, give a counterexample.**

b. **Write the converse of each implication. Tell whether the converse of each implication is *True* or *False*. If it is false, give a counterexample.**

23. An angle is obtuse only if the measure of the angle is between 90° and 180°.

24. The fact that $x = 5$ implies that $x < 8$.

25. You are in a state bordering the Pacific Ocean if you are in California.

Find the probability of each event. *(Section 6-7)*

26. getting no heads when two coins are tossed

27. getting exactly three heads when three coins are tossed

28. getting exactly three heads when four coins are tossed

180°. True.

b. If an angle measures between 90° and 180°, then it is an obtuse angle. True.

24. a. If $x = 5$, then $x < 8$. True.

b. If $x < 8$, then $x = 5$. False; for example, x might be $3\frac{1}{2}$.

25. a. If you are in California, then you are in a state bordering the Pacific

Ocean. True.

b. If you are in a state bordering the Pacific Ocean, then you are in California. False; you might be in Oregon, for example.

26. 25%   27. 12.5%

28. 25%

29. Argument 1: If cadmium sulfide yellow and chromium oxide green pigments were used in the painting, the painting was painted

after 1863. Cadmium sulfide yellow and chromium oxide green pigments were used in the painting. Therefore, the painting was painted after 1863.

Argument 2: If Francisco de Zurbarán painted the painting, it was painted before the end of 1664. The painting was not painted before the end of 1664. Therefore, the painting was not painted by Francisco de Zurbarán.

You may want to create a series of valid arguments as a framework for your mystery story. You can use the arguments to write clues.

29. A painting credited to Francisco de Zurbarán (1598–1664) contained the pigments cadmium sulfide yellow and chromium oxide green. Tests showed that graphite filled the cracks of the painting like dust. The graphite had been applied all at once.

Use any of these clues to write an argument to convince someone that the painting is a fake.

Clue 1 Dust accumulates over centuries.

Clue 2 Graphite can look like dust but is actually different from it.

Clue 3 Cadmium sulfide yellow and chromium oxide green pigments were invented after 1863.

Working on the Unit Project
Ex. 29 will help students to understand the need to identify the valid arguments they want to use in their mystery story before trying to write the story. Students can do Ex. 29 as a group activity.

Quick Quiz (7-1 through 7-3)
See page 426.

Unit 7 CHECKPOINT

1. **Writing** Suppose you want to convince a friend to apply to become an astronaut. Write a valid argument using three implications and the chain rule.

Graph each conjunction or disjunction on a coordinate plane. Tell which points are on each graph.   7-1

2. $x < 5$ and $y \geq 2$ 3. $y < x$ or $y \geq x$

4. Use a mathematical statement and a number line to show the ages of people who pay the adult admission price at the movies.

     Adults: $6.50   Children 13 and under: $3.00   Seniors 55 or over: $4.00

For Exercises 5–7, rewrite each implication in if-then form.   7-2

5. Corey is a high school student only if he is a teenager.

6. Every multiple of 4 is also a multiple of 2.

7. All matrices with 4 columns and 3 rows have the dimensions 3×4.

8. What conclusion can you reach when both premises are true? If Jana scores 85 or less, she lowers her average. Jana did not lower her average.   7-3

9. Decide if this argument is *valid* or *invalid*. Explain your reasoning.

If a figure is a parallelogram, then it has two pairs of parallel sides. A square is a parallelogram. Therefore, a square has two pairs of parallel sides.

7-3 Valid and Invalid Arguments   **385**

Practice 53 For use with Section 7-3

Practice 53
For use with Section 7-3

Name _____ Date _____

For Exercises 1–8, what conclusion can you reach when both premises are true?

1. If a quadrilateral is a rhombus, then its diagonals are perpendicular. Quadrilateral *ABCD* is a rhombus.

2. If the density of an object is greater than the density of water, then the object will sink in water. A pine log floats on water.

3. If Uranium 238 decays radioactively, then it emits alpha particles. If Uranium 238 emits alpha particles, then it eventually turns into lead.

4. If you order two large pizzas, you get a small pizza free. Ernesto ordered two large pizzas.

5. Every warm-blooded animal is either a bird or a mammal. A platypus is warm-blooded and not a bird.

6. If an integer *n* is evenly divisible by 6, then *n* is evenly divisible by 3. The integer 5014 is not evenly divisible by 3.

7. If a substance is a mineral, then it is a solid. Quartz is a mineral.

8. Ishana went to the school play on either Friday or Saturday night. She did not go to the school play on Saturday night.

Decide if each argument is *valid* or *invalid*. Explain your reasoning.

9. $p \to q$
$r \to q$
$\therefore p \to r$

10. *p* or *q*
not *p*
$\therefore q$

11. $u \to v$
not *u*
$\therefore$ not *v*

Decide if each argument is *valid* or *invalid*. Explain your reasoning.

12. Every person in X Block math class has at least a B average in math. Aretha is not in X Block math class. Therefore, Aretha does not have at least a B average in math.

13. In order to be the winning pitcher in a baseball game, you must pitch at least 5 innings. Hee Sun pitched 5 innings. Therefore, she was the winning pitcher.

14. Every rectangle is a parallelogram. Quadrilateral *ABCD* is a rectangle. Therefore, quadrilateral *ABCD* is a parallelogram.

1. The diags. of quad. *ABCD* are perpendicular.
2. The density of a pine log is not greater than the density of water.
3. If Uranium 238 decays radioactively, then it eventually turns into lead.
4. Ernesto got a small pizza free.
5. A platypus is a mammal.
6. 5014 is not evenly divisible by 6.
7. Quartz is a solid.
8. Ishana went to the school play Friday night.
9. invalid; If a no. is div. by 18, then div. by 6; if a no. is div. by 12, then div. by 6; but not true that if div. by 18, then div. by 12.
10. valid, Or rule
11. invalid; If a figure is a triangle then it is a polygon. A square is not a triangle; but it is a polygon.
12. invalid, same kind of argument as in Ex. 11
13. invalid; The argument is similar to "If a number is prime, then it is >1; 4 > 1; so 4 is prime." This starts with two true statements but the conclusion is false.
14. valid; direct argument

Answers to Checkpoint

1. Answers may vary. An example is given. If you apply to the program, then you will get accepted. If you get accepted, you will be trained to fly on the space shuttle. If you fly on the space shuttle, you may get to walk in space. Therefore, if you apply to the program, you may get to walk in space.

2. [graph showing $y = 2$ and $x = 5$]

3. [graph showing $y = x$]

4. $13 < x < 55$; [number line marked 13 and 55, scale 0 10 20 30 40 50 60 70]

5. If Corey is a high school student, then he is a teenager.

6. If a number is a multiple of 4, then it is also a multiple of 2.

7. If a matrix has 4 columns and 3 rows, then the dimensions of the matrix are 3×4.

8. Jana scored higher than 85.

9. valid; direct argument

Objectives and Strands
See pages 362A and 362B.

Spiral Learning
See page 362B.

Recommended Pacing
Section 7-4 is a two-day lesson.

Day 1

Pages 386–387: Talk it Over 1 through Talk it Over 5, *Exercises 1–15*

Day 2

Pages 388–389: Good Definitions through Look Back, *Exercises 16–43*

Extra Practice
See pages 625–626.

Warm-Up Exercises
Warm-Up Transparency 7-4

Support Materials
➤ Practice 54
➤ Enrichment 48 in the Activity Bank
➤ Study Guide 7-4
➤ Problem Set 15
➤ Quiz 7-4

Section **7-4**

Bicondititionals and Good Definitions

Focus
Recognize and write biconditionals. Use biconditionals to make valid arguments and to recognize and write good definitions.

Two *ifs* are better than one

I'll have a hoagie.

Could I have a grinder?

One hero, please.

How about a sub?

May I have an Italian sandwich?

Talk it Over

1. What communication problem does the photo suggest?
2. Describe the sandwich they are all ordering.

Biconditionals

For people to communicate, they must agree on the meanings of words.

If a sandwich is a hoagie , then it is a grinder .

and

If a sandwich is a grinder , then it is a hoagie .

When a conditional and its converse are true, the conjunction of the two conditionals is a true statement called a **biconditional.**

You can also write a biconditional using the phrase "if and only if."

A sandwich is a hoagie *if and only if* it is a grinder.

A biconditional is true when both of its conditionals are true.

Unit 7 Logic and Proof

386

Answers to Talk it Over

1. All the talking heads are using different names for the same thing.
2. The sandwich usually consists of sandwich meats with lettuce, tomato, and dressing, and may also have onions, peppers, and other vegetables.

You can use Venn diagrams to show the relationship between a hoagie and a grinder.

If a sandwich is a hoagie, then it is a grinder.

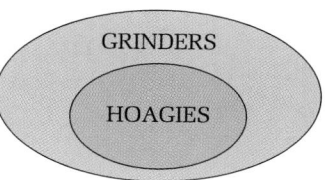

hoagie → grinder

If a sandwich is a grinder, then it is a hoagie.

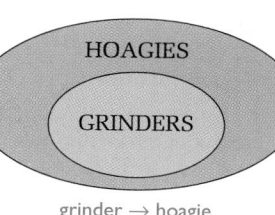

grinder → hoagie

A sandwich is a hoagie if and only if it is a grinder.

GRINDERS
HOAGIES

hoagie ↔ grinder

You can represent "if and only if" symbolically by a double arrow.

$q \rightarrow p$ and $p \rightarrow q$
p is true if q is true and
p is true only if q is true.

$$p \leftrightarrow q$$

p is true if and only if q is true.

Sample 1

Write the pair of conditionals as a biconditional using "if and only if."

If an angle has a measure of 90°, then it is a right angle.

If an angle is a right angle, then it has a measure of 90°.

Sample Response

An angle has a measure of 90° if and only if it is a right angle.

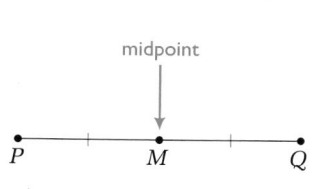

midpoint

P M Q

> Now you are ready for:
> Exs. 1–15 on pp. 389–390

Talk it Over

3. For each statement in parts (a) and (b), identify the hypothesis and conclusion.

   a. A point on a segment is the same distance from each endpoint if it is the midpoint of the segment.

   b. A point on a segment is the same distance from each endpoint only if it is the midpoint of the segment.

4. Write the pair of conditionals in question 3 as a biconditional using "if and only if."

5. a. Write the two implications represented by this biconditional: A quadrilateral is a rectangle if and only if the quadrilateral is a parallelogram.

   b. Is the biconditional in part (a) *True* or *False*?

7-4 Biconditionals and Good Definitions

387

TEACHING

Talk it Over

Questions 1 and 2 lead students to think about the fact that clear communication by people depends on a common understanding of the meanings of words.

Communication: Reading

Students need to remember when they read the term *conditional* that this is just another name for an implication. Since a biconditional is the *conjunction* (two statements connected by *and*) of a statement and its converse, students may need to be reminded that a conjunction is true when *both* statements are true. Therefore, in order to write a biconditional, the converse of a conditional must be true.

Additional Sample

S1 Write the pair of conditionals as a biconditional using "if and only if."
If a triangle is equilateral, then it is equiangular.
If a triangle is equiangular, then it is equilateral.
A triangle is equilateral if and only if it is equiangular.

Talk it Over

Question 3 illustrates that the definition of midpoint can be written as a biconditional and, and in so doing, prepares students for understanding the requirements of a good definition.

Answers to Talk it Over

3. a. hypothesis: A point is the midpoint of a segment. conclusion: The point is the same distance from each endpoint of the segment.

   b. hypothesis: A point on a segment is the same distance from each endpoint. conclusion: The point is the midpoint of the segment.

4. A point on a segment is the midpoint of the segment if and only if the point is the same distance from each endpoint.

5. a. If a quadrilateral is a rectangle, then it is a parallelogram. If a quadrilateral is a parallelogram, then it is a rectangle.

   b. False; it is not true that if a quadrilateral is a parallelogram, then it is a rectangle.

387

Good Definitions

You can use biconditionals to write definitions. A good definition is built from a true conditional with a true converse. For example, consider this definition of a rectangle:

> A *rectangle* is a parallelogram with four right angles.

This definition asserts two true conditionals:

> If a figure is a rectangle, then it is a parallelogram with four right angles.

> If a figure is a parallelogram with four right angles, then it is a rectangle.

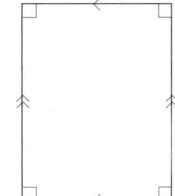

Sample 2

Rewrite this definition using "if and only if":

> A *square* is a rectangle with congruent sides.

Sample Response

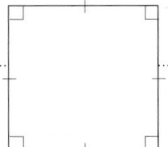

A figure is a *square* if and only if it is a rectangle with congruent sides.

Sample 3

Writing Tell what is wrong with each attempted definition and give a good definition.

a. An angle is *acute* if the measure of the angle is 85°.

b. The number *b* is a *square root* of *a* if and only if $b = \sqrt{a}$.

Sample Response

a. *Peter Wong*

The statement is true but it is not a biconditional.

Here is a good definition: An angle is acute if and only if the measure of the angle is between 0° and 90°.

b. *Karen Miller*

The biconditional is not true because one of its conditionals is not true.

For example, the square roots of 4 are 2 and -2, but the symbol √ means the positive square root. √4 = 2

Here is a good definition: the number b is a square root of a if and only if $b^2 = a$.

Unit 7 Logic and Proof

6. What is wrong with this definition?
   A polygon is a *rhombus* if it is a square.

7. Give a good definition of a rhombus.

This is a Hmong textile from Laos. Do you think it is a square?

Biconditionals and Valid Arguments

You can make valid arguments using biconditionals just as you do with implications.

A figure is a square if and only if it is a rectangle with four congruent sides. $p \leftrightarrow q$

QRST is a rectangle with four congruent sides. q

Therefore, *QRST* is a square. $\therefore p$

This is a special case of direct argument. If either p or q is true, the other is true.

You can also use biconditionals in indirect arguments.

$x = 12$ if and only if $3x = 36$ $p \leftrightarrow q$

$x \neq 12$ not p

Therefore, $3x \neq 36$. $\therefore$ not q

This is a special case of indirect argument. If either p or q is false, the other is false.

▶ Now you are ready for:
Exs. 16–43 on pp. 390–393

Look Back ◄

Describe several different ways of representing biconditionals.

7-4 Exercises and Problems

1. **Reading** What does "p if and only if q" mean?

Write each pair of conditionals as a biconditional using "if and only if."

2. If it is my birthday, then I was born on this date.
   If I was born on this date, then it is my birthday.

3. If $5x = 20$, then $x = 4$.
   If $x = 4$, then $5x = 20$.

4. A polygon is a quadrilateral if it has four sides.
   A polygon has four sides if it is a quadrilateral.

Look Back

You may wish to extend the different ways of representing biconditionals by introducing the symbol *iff* as a shorthand way of writing if and only if.

APPLYING

Suggested Assignment

Day 1

Standard 1–15

Extended 1–15

Day 2

Standard 16–31, 35–43

Extended 16–43

Integrating the Strands

Number Exs. 20, 38–40

Algebra Exs. 3, 5, 31, 37, 40, 42

Geometry Exs. 4, 6, 7, 10, 11, 17, 19, 21–27, 29, 30

Statistics and Probability Exs. 16, 18

Discrete Mathematics Exs. 1–37, 41, 42

Logic and Language Exs. 1–37, 41–43

Communication: Discussion

Exs. 1–12 can be done by having students provide verbal instead of written answers. Many of these exercises provide a good review and reinforcement of ideas about quadrilaterals and their properties.

Answers to Talk it Over

6. The statement is true, but it is not biconditional.

7. Wording may vary. An example is given. A figure is a rhombus if and only if it has four congruent sides.

Answers to Look Back

For implication $p \rightarrow q$ and $q \rightarrow p$, the related biconditional can be represented as $p \rightarrow q$ and $q \rightarrow p$, p if and only if q, or $p \leftrightarrow q$.

Answers to Exercises and Problems

1. Answers may vary. Examples are given. If p, then q and if q, then p; $p \rightarrow q$ and $q \rightarrow p$; or $p \leftrightarrow q$.

2–4. Biconditionals may be written $p \leftrightarrow q$ or $q \leftrightarrow p$. One order is given.

2. It is my birthday if and only if I was born on this date.

3. $5x = 20$ if and only if $x = 4$.

4. A polygon is a quadrilateral if and only if it has four sides.

Integrating the Strands

Many of the exercises on pages 389–391 integrate the strands of logic and geometry. In particular, the use of implications, biconditionals, and valid arguments impose a structure on geometric statements that makes the study of geometry more organized and systematic. This can help students to sort out, learn, and remember a large number of geometric facts regarding properties of various figures.

Answers to
Exercises and Problems

5. a. Yes. **b.** Yes.
c. $\frac{x}{2} = 7$ if and only if $x = 14$.

6. a. No. **b.** Yes.
c. not possible

7. a. Yes. **b.** No.
c. not possible

8. False; the conditional "If I can afford a snack that costs $.40, then I have $1" is not true.

9. False; both conditionals are not true.

10. False; the conditional "If all sides of a quadrilateral are congruent, then the quadrilateral is a square" is not true.

11. True; the two conditionals "If a figure is a parallelogram with four right angles, then it is a rectangle" and "If a figure is a rectangle, then it is a parallelogram with four right angles" are both true.

12. False; the conditional "If an instrument is a stringed instrument, then it is a violin" is not true.

13.
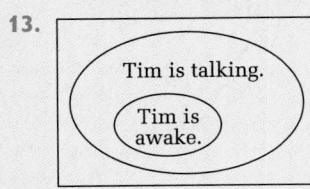

BY THE WAY...

Ostriches are the largest living birds. They may be nearly 8 ft high and weigh 300 lb. Ostriches cannot fly but can run as fast as 40 mi/h.

Represent each statement by a Venn diagram.

13. If Tim is awake, then he is talking. (Label one circle "Tim is awake" and the other "Tim is talking.")

14. A basketball is a sphere only if it is inflated.

15. If Sandy is tired, then she yawns; and if Sandy yawns, then she is tired.

Rewrite each definition using "if and only if."

16. In a set of data, the *mean* is the sum of the items divided by the number of items.

17. A *scalene* triangle has three sides that are not equal in measure.

18. The *probability* of an event E is the ratio of the number of outcomes favoring E to the total number of equally likely outcomes.

For Exercises 5–7:

a. Are the implications converses of each other?

b. Is each implication true?

c. If you answered *yes* to parts (a) and (b), rewrite the pair of implications as a biconditional.

5. If $\frac{x}{2} = 7$, then $x = 14$.
If $x = 14$, then $\frac{x}{2} = 7$.

6. A quadrilateral is a square only if it is a rectangle.
If a quadrilateral is a square, then it is a rectangle.

7. A space figure is a cube if it has six faces.
A space figure has six faces if it is a cube.

Tell whether each biconditional is *True* or *False*. Explain your reasoning.

8. I can afford a snack that costs $.40 if and only if I have $1.

9. An animal is a bird if and only if it flies.

10. A quadrilateral is a square if and only if all of its sides are equal in measure.

11. A figure is a rectangle if and only if it is a parallelogram with four right angles.

12. An instrument is a stringed instrument if and only if it is a violin.

14.
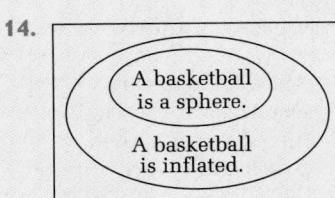

15.

Sandy is tired.
Sandy yawns.

16–18. Definitions may be written *p if and only if q* or *q if and only if p*. One order is given.

16. In a set of data, a number is the mean if and only if the number is the sum of the items divided by the number of items in the data set.

17. A triangle is *scalene* if and only if it has three sides that are not equal in measure.

18. A number is the *probability* of an event if and only if it is the ratio of the number of outcomes favoring E divided by the total number of equally likely outcomes.

19. No; the conditional "If an angle is obtuse, then the measure of the angle is 150°" is not true.

20. Yes; the conditionals "If b is a square root of a, then $b = \pm\sqrt{a}$" and "If $b = \pm\sqrt{a}$, then b is a square root of a" are both true.

390   **Unit 7** Logic and Proof

Writing For Exercises 19–22, tell whether each statement is a good definition. Explain your reasoning.

19. An angle is *obtuse* if and only if the measure of the angle is 150°.

20. The number b is a *square root* of a if and only if $b = \pm\sqrt{a}$.

21. Two lines are *perpendicular* if and only if they intersect to form a right angle.

22. *Perpendicular* lines intersect to form at least two congruent angles.

23. Here is a good definition of a square:
    "A *square* is a rectangle with four congruent sides."
    Write the two implications that make up this definition.

Writing For Exercises 24–26, decide whether each statement can be rewritten using "if and only if" to make a good definition. If so, rewrite it. If not, explain why not.

24. A figure with four sides equal in measure is a *parallelogram*.

25. A *parallelogram* is a polygon with two pairs of opposite sides parallel.

26. A *parallelogram* is a quadrilateral with at least one pair of parallel sides.

27. Write a good definition of *parallelogram*.

28. People in different parts of the country call the same kind of drink "soda," "pop," "soda pop," "tonic," or "soft drink." What do you call this drink? Write a good definition for the word you use.

Decide whether each argument is *valid* or *invalid*.

29. A figure is a rhombus if and only if it is a quadrilateral with four congruent sides.

    Quadrilateral *PQRS* is not a rhombus.

    Therefore, *PQRS* does not have four congruent sides.

30. A quadrilateral is a kite if and only if it has two pairs of consecutive sides equal in measure. These pairs do not have a side in common.

    DEFG is a quadrilateral with two pairs of consecutive sides equal in measure. These pairs do not have a side in common.

    Therefore, *DEFG* is a kite.

31. $x = 4$ if and only if $\frac{x}{4} = 1$

    $x \neq 4$

    $\therefore \frac{x}{4} \neq 1$

Reasoning

Exs. 19–28 pertain to good definitions. A major concern when introducing geometric concepts is a careful attention to definitions. Thus, the material in this section provides students with excellent opportunities to reason about definitions and prepares them for their continuing study of geometry in this book and in subsequent mathematics courses.

Assessment: Performance Task

After completing Exs. 23–27, students should be able to list the different types of quadrilaterals discussed previously. For each quadrilateral, they should be able to write a definition using *if and only if* form. Definitions may differ and students should compare definitions to see if they are good ones.

Answers to Exercises and Problems

21. Yes; the conditionals "If two lines are perpendicular, they intersect to form a right angle" and "If two lines intersect to form a right angle, then the lines are perpendicular" are both true.

22. No; the conditional "If two lines intersect to form at least two congruent angles, then the lines are perpendicular" is not true.

23. If a figure is a square, then it is a rectangle with four congruent sides. If a figure is a rectangle with four congruent sides, then the figure is a square.

24. No; the conditional "If a figure is a parallelogram, then it has four congruent sides" is not true. In a parallelogram, adjacent sides are not always congruent.

25. No; the conditional "If a figure is a polygon with two pairs of opposite sides parallel, then it is a parallelogram" is not true. For example, a regular hexagon is not a parallelogram.

26. No; the conditional "If a figure is a quadrilateral with at least one pair of parallel sides, then it is a parallelogram" is not true.

27. Wording may vary. An example is given. A parallelogram is a quadrilateral with two pairs of parallel sides.

28. Answers may vary. An example is given. A drink is a soft drink if and only if it is a nonalcoholic carbonated beverage.

29. valid

30. valid

31. valid

connection to BIOLOGY

The yew and rhododendron are common plants.

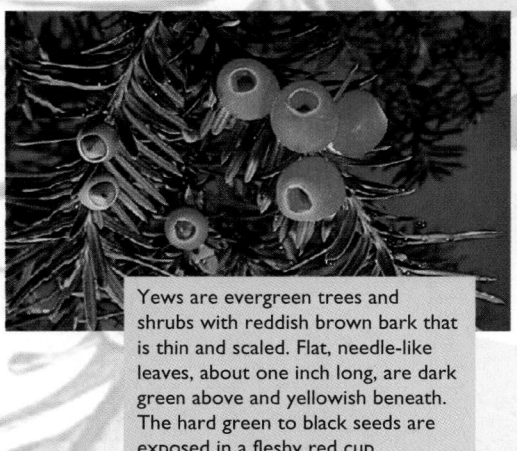

Yews are evergreen trees and shrubs with reddish brown bark that is thin and scaled. Flat, needle-like leaves, about one inch long, are dark green above and yellowish beneath. The hard green to black seeds are exposed in a fleshy red cup.

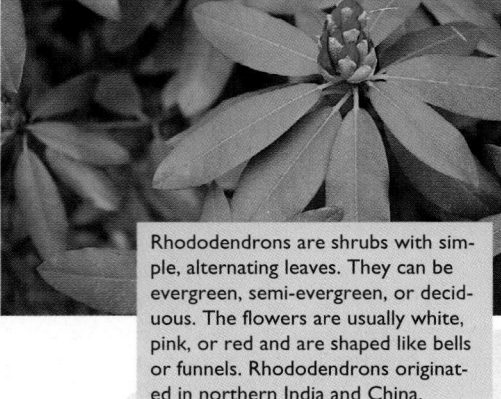

Rhododendrons are shrubs with simple, alternating leaves. They can be evergreen, semi-evergreen, or deciduous. The flowers are usually white, pink, or red and are shaped like bells or funnels. Rhododendrons originated in northern India and China.

32. a. What is wrong with this definition of a yew?
A *yew* is a tree or shrub with reddish brown bark and needle-like leaves.

 b. Write a better definition of a yew.

 c. Is your definition a good definition? Why or why not?

33. Which plant do you think would be easier to identify if you have never seen it before? Explain.

34. Tell whether the following argument is *valid* or *invalid*. Explain.

If a plant is a rhododendron, then it is a shrub with simple, alternating leaves.

All rhododendrons originated in northern India and China.

Therefore, if a plant is a shrub with simple, alternate leaves, then it originated in northern India and China.

Ongoing ASSESSMENT

35. Open-ended Write good definitions for three mathematical terms. Make a convincing case that all three of your definitions are good.

Review PREVIEW

Decide if each argument is *valid* or *invalid*. *(Section 7-3)*

36. If today is Tuesday, then I am going to the dentist. I am not going to the dentist today. Therefore, today is not Tuesday.

37. *x* is greater than 3. 3 is greater than *y*. Therefore, *y* is greater than *x*.

Answers to Exercises and Problems

32–34. Answers may vary. Examples are given.

32. a. This description probably fits many other trees and shrubs that are not yews.

 b. A yew is an evergreen tree or shrub with reddish brown bark that is thin and scaled, with flat needle-like leaves about one inch long that grow in opposite pairs along alternate twigs, and with hard, green to black seeds that are exposed in a fleshy red cup.

 c. Answers may vary. The description in part (b) is detailed and specific enough to allow an observer to distinguish a yew from other plants.

33. The definition given in the box for yews is more specific than the one for rhododendrons, so a yew might be easier to recognize based on that definition.

Simplify. *(Toolbox Skill 12)*

38. $\sqrt{36}$

39. $\sqrt{50}$

40. $3\sqrt{7} \cdot 4\sqrt{14}$

What can you conclude from each statement? *(Section 7-3)*

41. Fran is taller than Danielle and Abby is shorter than Danielle.

42. $x = -4 + 10$ and $-4 + 10 = 6$

 Working on the Unit Project

43. **Research** Read one or more of these mysteries to get ideas for characters, plot elements, settings, or clues for your story. As you read, you may want to take notes on ideas to help your story.

Suggested Bibliography

➤ *The Adventures of Sherlock Holmes* by Arthur Conan Doyle

➤ *Coyote Waits* by Tony Hillerman

➤ "Euclid's Crop Circles; Off the Beat" by Ivars Peterson *Science News,* February 1, 1992

➤ "It ain't over till it's over. . . cold fusion" by Jerry E. Bishop *Popular Science,* August 1993

➤ *Miss Marple: The Complete Short Stories* by Agatha Christie

➤ *Pigeon Blood* by Alexander Gary

➤ *The Vandermark Mummy* by Cynthia Voigt

➤ *Too Close to the Edge* by Susan Dunlap

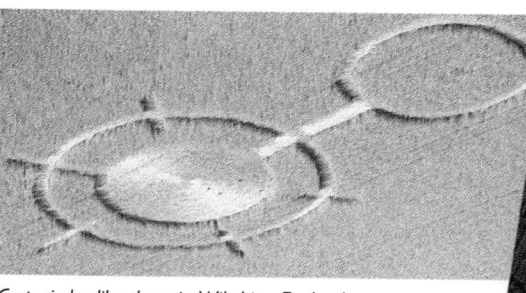

Crop circles like these in Wiltshire, England, intrigue scientists and investigators.

Practice 54 For use with Section 7-4

Name _____ Date _____

Practice 54

For use with Section 7-4

Write each pair of conditionals as a biconditional using "if and only if."

1. If two sides of a triangle are congruent, then two angles of the triangle are congruent.
If two angles of a triangle are congruent, then two sides of the triangle are congruent.

2. If today is Monday, then yesterday was Sunday.
If yesterday was Sunday, then today is Monday.

3. If an integer is odd, then the square of the integer is odd.
If the square of an integer is odd, then the integer is odd.

For each of Exercises 4 and 5:
a. Are the implications converses of each other?
b. Is each implication true?
c. If you answered yes to parts (a) and (b), rewrite the pair of implications as a biconditional.

4. If you are at least 18 years of age, then you have the right to vote.
If you have the right to vote, then you are at least 18 years of age.

5. If you are in California, then you are in a western state.
You are in California only if you are in a western state. **no; yes**

Tell whether each biconditional is *True* or *False*. Explain your reasoning.

6. $x^2 = 9$ if and only if $x = 3$. **false; x could be −3.**

7. A triangle is equilateral if and only if it has three congruent sides.

8. You can see the sun in the sky if and only if it is daytime.

Tell whether each definition is a good definition. Explain your reasoning.

9. The mean of a set of numbers is between the smallest and largest numbers in the set. **no; 2 is between 1 and 5 but is not their mean.**

10. An integer is a multiple of 5 if and only if it is a whole number exactly divisible by 5. **no; omits numbers like −15**

11. *Open-ended* Bessie defined the Mona Lisa as "the most beautiful painting in the world." Why isn't this a good definition? State some other definitions that are not good for the same reason.

1. Two sides of a triangle are cong. if and only if two angles of the triangle are congruent.

2. Today is Monday if and only if yesterday was Sunday.

3. An integer is odd if and only if its square is odd.

4. yes; yes; You have the right to vote if and only if you are at least 18 years of age.

7. true; Each conditional is true.
8. false; It could be cloudy.

Check students' work.

Answers to Exercises and Problems

34. invalid; It has the form $p \to q$, $p \to r$, $\therefore q \to r$, which is not a valid argument.

35. Answers may vary. Examples are given. A relationship is a *function* if and only if there is only one value of the dependent variable for each value of the control variable. An angle is *acute* if and only if its measure is between 0° and 90°. A segment is a *diagonal* of a polygon if and only if it joins two non-consecutive vertices of the polygon.

36. valid

37. invalid

38. 6

39. 7.07 to the nearest hundredth

40. $84\sqrt{2}$

41. Frank is taller than Abby.

42. $x = 6$

43. Research may vary.

Objectives and Strands
See pages 362A and 362B.

Spiral Learning
See page 362B.

Recommended Pacing
Section 7-5 is a two-day lesson.

Day 1
Pages 394–396: Opening paragraph through Talk it Over 5, *Exercises 1–6*

Day 2
Pages 396–397: Forms for Proofs through Look Back, *Exercises 7–24*

Extra Practice
See pages 625–626.

Warm-Up Exercises
Warm-Up Transparency 7-5

Support Materials
➤ Practice 55
➤ Enrichment 49 in the Activity Bank
➤ Study Guide 7-5
➤ Problem Set 15
➤ Quiz 7-5
➤ Alternative Assessment 4

Section 7-5

Introduction to Proof

Focus

Become familiar with key elements of proof and formats for two-column, paragraph, and flow proofs.

GO with the flow

Suppose you are a ticket agent for Euclid Airlines. Your specialty is planning routes, or itineraries, between the most populous cities of the world. The map shows the available flights and flight numbers.

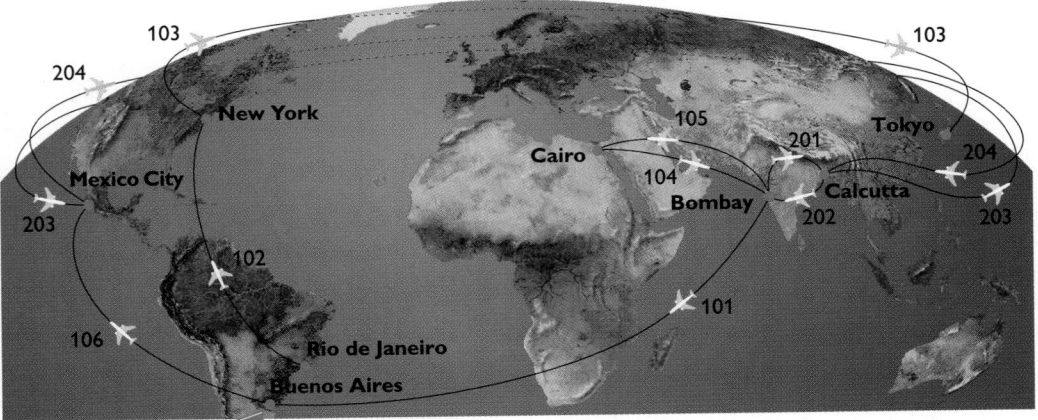

Here is a sample itinerary for a trip from Bombay to Mexico City.

City	Flight
Bombay	Departure point
Buenos Aires	Flight 101: Bombay → Buenos Aires
Mexico City	Flight 106: Buenos Aires → Mexico City

Read as "to."

Talk it Over

1. a. What is the first flight taken?
   b. How do you know that it goes *from* Bombay?

2. Use the map to plan a different itinerary to make the trip from Bombay to Mexico City. Write it in the same form as above.

3. Write an itinerary for a trip from Mexico City to Bombay.

394   **Unit 7** Logic and Proof

Proofs and Itineraries

The itinerary on page 394 shows that it is possible to fly from Bombay to Mexico City on Euclid Airlines. A logical demonstration such as this itinerary is called a *proof*.

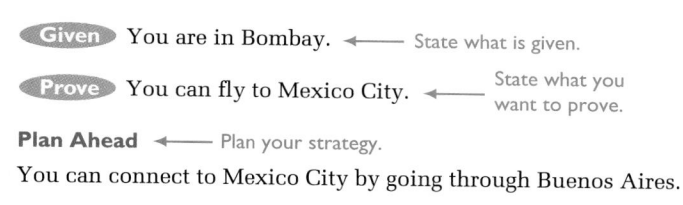

Write a proof of this statement: You can fly from Bombay to Mexico City.

Sample Response

Given You are in Bombay. ←— State what is given.

Prove You can fly to Mexico City. ←— State what you want to prove.

Plan Ahead ←— Plan your strategy.

You can connect to Mexico City by going through Buenos Aires.

Show Your Reasoning

Justify each statement.

Statements	**Justifications**
1. You are in Bombay.	1. Given
2. You can fly to Buenos Aires.	2. Flight 101: Bombay → Buenos Aires
3. You can fly to Mexico City.	3. Flight 106: Buenos Aires → Mexico City

Notice these similarities between itineraries and proofs.

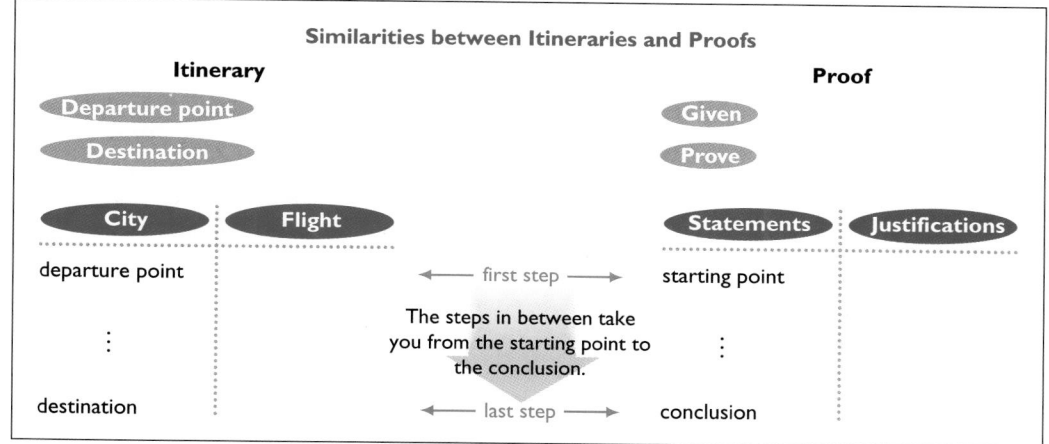

Similarities between Itineraries and Proofs

7-5 Introduction to Proof

395

Talk it Over

Questions 1–3 use the idea of a travel itinerary to introduce students to the concept of proof.

Students Acquiring English

Before English learners begin this section, make sure that they understand the following terms: *routes, itineraries, departure point,* and *destination.* Point out how the key words *from* and *to* relate to a trip's departure point and destination.

Additional Sample

S1 Write a proof to prove this statement: You can fly from Bombay to Mexico City and not go through Buenos Aires.

Given: You are in Bombay.
Prove: You can fly to Mexico City and not go through Buenos Aires.
Plan Ahead. You can connect to Mexico City by going through Calcutta.
Statements:
1. You are in Bombay.
2. You can fly to Calcutta.
3. You can fly to Mexico City.
Justifications:
1. Given
2. Flight 201: Bombay → Calcutta
3. Flight 203: Calcutta → Mexico City

Teaching Tip

Justifications in a proof can also be called Reasons. They are *facts* that support the statements.

Mathematical Procedures

Writing proofs is a fundamental procedure in the use of deductive reasoning. Students need to understand that a proof is a logical demonstration that links together a series of steps from a starting point to a conclusion.

395

Question 5 can be used to help students understand that a proof is really just a solution to a problem. Thus, just as there is often more than one way to solve a problem, there is often more than one way to prove a statement.

Communication: Writing

Students should be able to write proofs using any of the three forms discussed on this page. As they gain experience in writing proofs, the paragraph form should evolve as the desired form because it is the one most often used in more advanced mathematics courses.

Students Acquiring English

Allow English learners to write proofs in two-column or flow form if the paragraph form is too challenging.

Talk it Over

When students finish writing their three proofs for questions 6–8, they should see that the form of the proofs is secondary to the proof itself.

Teaching Tip

Since a proof is a logical demonstration, as stated on page 395, students should intuitively expect the rules of logic to play a role in writing proofs. These rules are usually not stated explicitly when proofs are written, but they are demonstrated here to show how they apply.

> Now you are ready for:
> Exs. 1–6 on pp. 397–398

Talk it Over

4. Write a proof of this statement: You can fly from Buenos Aires to Calcutta. Use the map on page 394.

5. Can there be more than one itinerary for a trip? Do you think there can be more than one proof of a statement? Explain.

Forms of Proofs

There are many forms of proofs. The form you just used is called a **two-column proof** because of the layout of the chart.

Another form is a **paragraph proof.** Here is a paragraph proof of the Bombay-Mexico City itinerary:

Notice that the statements of the proof are written in sentences to form a paragraph.

> It is possible to fly from Bombay to Mexico City. From Bombay you can fly to Buenos Aires because Flight 101 goes from Bombay to Buenos Aires. From Buenos Aires you can fly to Mexico City because Flight 106 goes from Buenos Aires to Mexico City.

Justifications are written where needed.

Another form of proof is a **flow proof.** It is a diagram using arrows to show how to get from one statement to the next.

Statements

Circled numbers refer to the justifications for the statements of the proof.

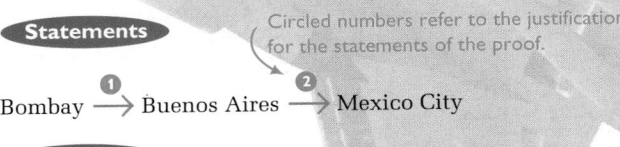

Bombay ──①── Buenos Aires ──②── Mexico City

Justifications

❶ Flight 101

❷ Flight 106

Justifications are given in a numbered list.

Talk it Over

Write a proof in each form to show that Euclid Airlines can take you from Rio de Janeiro to Tokyo.

6. two-column form   7. paragraph form   8. flow form

Unit 7 Logic and Proof

396

Answers to Talk it Over

4. *Given:* Buenos Aires
   Prove: Buenos Aires to Calcutta

Statements	Justifications
1. Buenos Aires	1. Given
2. Mexico City	2. Flight 106: Buenos Aires → Mexico City
3. Calcutta	3. Flight 204: Mexico City → Calcutta

5. Yes; Yes. There are often many ways to prove a statement just as there can be many ways to solve a problem.

6. *Given:* Rio de Janeiro
   Prove: Tokyo

Statements	Justifications
1. Rio de Janeiro	1. Given
2. New York City	2. Flight 102: Rio de Janeiro → New York City
3. Tokyo	3. Flight 103: New York City → Tokyo

7. It is possible to fly from Rio de Janeiro to Tokyo. You can take Flight 102 from Rio de Janeiro to New York City. Then you can take Flight 103 from New York City to Tokyo.

8. See answers in back of book.

Rules of Logic and Proofs

You can think of the statements of a proof as using rules of logic in a different format.

Sample 2

Tell which rule of logic is used to go from statement 1 to statement 2 on page 395. Then tell which rule of logic is used to go from statement 1 to statement 2 to statement 3.

Sample Response

Rewrite the statements as premises and a conclusion.

Itinerary	Logic
If you are in Bombay, then you can fly to Buenos Aires.	$p \to q$
You are in Bombay.	p
Therefore, you can fly to Buenos Aires.	$\therefore q$

Direct argument is used to go from statement 1 to statement 2.

	Logic
If you are in Bombay, then you can fly to Buenos Aires.	$p \to q$
If you are in Buenos Aires, then you can fly to Mexico City.	$q \to r$
Therefore, if you are in Bombay, then you can fly to Mexico City.	$\therefore p \to r$

The chain rule is used to go from statement 1 to statement 2 to statement 3.

Look Back

How are the three forms of proof in this section alike? How are they different?

Now you are ready for:
Exs. 7–24 on pp. 398–400

7-5 Exercises and Problems

1. **Reading** List some of the similarities between itineraries and proofs.

2. Fill in the missing parts of this nonsense proof.

   Given You are here.

   Prove You can go someplace.

   Statements
   1. You are here.
   2. You can go __?__.
   3. You can go wherever.
   4. You can go someplace.

   Justifications
   1. Given
   2. Here → There
   3. There → __?__
   4. __?__ → __?__

7-5 Introduction to Proof

397

Additional Sample

S2 For the proof you wrote for Talk it Over question 4 on page 396, would you use the same or different rules of logic than those used in Sample 2? Why?

The same rules would be used as in Sample 2 because each itinerary involves traveling from one city to another, and then continuing on from that city to a third city. Direct argument is used for the first leg of the trip. The chain rule applies to the whole trip.

Look Back

These two questions will help students to summarize their understanding of what a proof is and the forms in which it can be written.

APPLYING

Suggested Assignment

Day 1
Standard 1–5
Extended 1–5

Day 2
Standard 7–11, 14–24
Extended 7–24

Integrating the Strands

Number Ex. 13
Algebra Exs. 21–23
Geometry Exs. 18–20
Discrete Mathematics Exs. 1–20, 24
Logic and Language Exs. 1–20, 24

Answers to Look Back

Each type of proof begins with given information and uses rules of logic to demonstrate that the desired conclusion is justified. All three forms use the same information and logic; however, they present the information in different forms.

Answers to Exercises and Problems

1. Answers may vary. Examples are given. The "departure point" in an itinerary is like the "given" in a proof. The last statement in a proof corresponds to the last city in an itinerary. The order of steps matters. Steps may not be skipped.

2. *Given:* You are here.
   Prove: You can go someplace.

Statements	Justifications
1. You are here.	1. Given
2. You can go there.	2. Here → There
3. You can go wherever.	3. There → Wherever
4. You can go someplace.	4. Wherever → Someplace

397

Students Acquiring English

Ex. 11 is an excellent vocabulary-building activity for students who are acquiring English. Students might be encouraged to make cut-out alphabet cards and use them to complete parts (a) and (b) as well as Ex. 12.

Problem Solving

Ex. 13 can be used to relate the ideas of a solution to a problem and a proof of a statement. A solution to a problem is, in fact, a logical demonstration of a statement. The statement of the problem in Ex. 13 is the description of the pattern.

Answers to
Exercises and Problems

3.

City	Flight
Calcutta	Departure point
Bombay	Flight 202: Calcutta → Bombay
Buenos Aires	Flight 101: Bombay → Buenos Aires

4. *Given:* Calcutta
Prove: Calcutta to Buenos Aires

Statements	Justifications
1. Calcutta	1. Given
2. Bombay	2. Flight 202: Calcutta → Bombay
3. Buenos Aires	3. Flight 101: Bombay → Buenos Aires

5. It is impossible to go from Tokyo to New York City because Euclid Airlines does not have any flights out of Tokyo.

6. Starting points, destinations, and forms of itineraries may vary. Examples are given.

   a. Cairo to Mexico City

   b. *Given:* Cairo
   Prove: Mexico City

Statements	Justifications
1. Cairo	1. Given
2. Bombay	2. Flight 104: Cairo → Bombay
3. Calcutta	3. Flight 201: Bombay → Calcutta
4. Mexico City	4. Flight 203: Calcutta → Mexico City

7. direct argument

For Exercises 3–5, use the map on page 394.

3. Write an itinerary showing that it is possible to fly on Euclid Airlines from Calcutta to Buenos Aires.

4. Rewrite the itinerary you wrote in Exercise 3 as a two-column proof.

5. Explain why it is impossible to fly on Euclid Airlines from Tokyo to New York City.

6. **Group Activity** Work with another student.

   a. Each of you should plan your own itinerary on Euclid Airlines. Do not show them to each other. On a separate piece of paper, write your starting point and destination.

   b. Trade papers. Try to find itineraries for each other's trips. Discuss your results.

For Exercises 7–9, use this proof.

Given You are in Cairo.

Prove You can fly to Calcutta.

Statements	Justifications
1. You are in Cairo.	1. Given
2. You can fly to Bombay.	2. Flight 104: Cairo → Bombay
3. You can fly to Calcutta.	3. Flight 201: Bombay → Calcutta

7. Tell which rule of logic is used to go from statement 1 to statement 2.

8. Tell which rule of logic is used to go from statement 1 to statement 2 to statement 3.

9. Rewrite the proof as a flow proof.

10. **Writing** Write a paragraph proof showing that you can fly on Euclid Airlines from Mexico City to Cairo.

11. **Games** Here is an example of a word game.
Change WARM to COLD. Rule: Form a real word at each step by changing just one letter at a time.
Solution: WARM → WORM → WORD → CORD → COLD

   a. Use the rules to change the word CAT into the word DOG.

   b. Use the rules to change the word TRY into the word WIN.

   c. **Writing** How is this puzzle like planning an itinerary?

12. **Open-ended** Create your own word puzzle like those in Exercise 11. Use five-letter words and at least four steps.

13. a. Rewrite each power as a number: 7^0, 7^1, 7^2, 7^3, 7^4, 7^5, 7^6, 7^7, 7^8, 7^9

   b. Describe any pattern you find in the unit's digit in part (a).

   c. Write a paragraph proof to prove that the pattern you described in part (b) holds for all powers of 7.

   d. **Writing** What is the unit's digit in 7^{100}? Explain.

W A R M
W O R M
W O R D
C O R D
C O L D

---

8. chain rule

9. **Statements**
Cairo →① Bombay →② Calcutta

   Justifications
① Flight 104
② Flight 201

10. It is possible to fly from Mexico City to Cairo. From Mexico City you can fly to Calcutta because Flight 204 goes from Mexico City to Calcutta. From Calcutta you can fly to Bombay because Flight 202 goes from Calcutta to Bombay. From Bombay you can fly to Cairo because Flight 105 goes from Bombay to Cairo.

11. Answers may vary. Example are given.

   a. cat → cot → cog → dog
   b. try → toy → ton → tin → win

   c. You begin at a given point of departure (the original word) and change one letter at a time (as you would take one flight at a time) to reach the desired destination (the final word).

12. Answers may vary. Example: paint → rails: paint → pains → rains → rails

13. See answers in back of book.

14. a. The drawing at the right shows five squares. Use logical reasoning to find the lengths of the sides of squares *A*, *B*, and *C*.

b. How is the way you solved this puzzle like writing proofs?

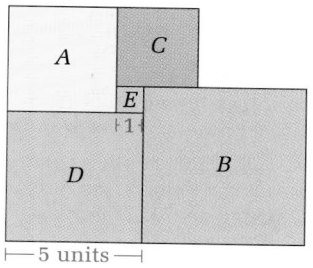

├── 5 units ──┤

connection to GEOLOGY

The Mesozoic Era is divided into three periods. The periods can be used to describe the age of fossils and rocks.

Period	Beginning of period (millions of years ago)
Cretaceous	138
Jurassic	205
Triassic	240

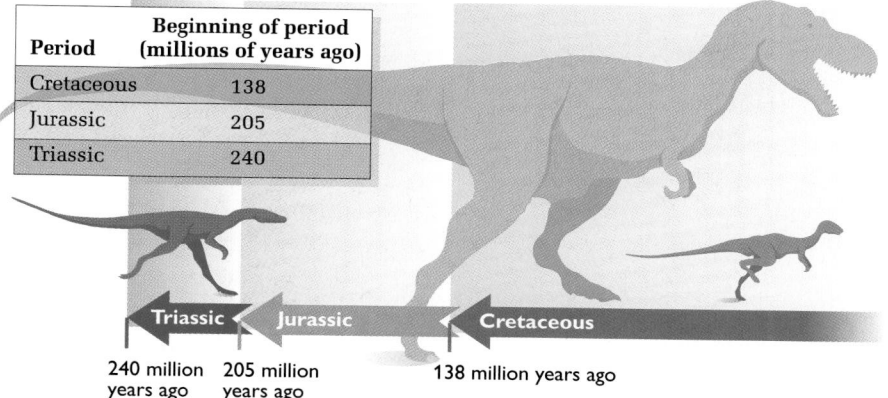

Triassic — Jurassic — Cretaceous

240 million years ago   205 million years ago   138 million years ago

15. Write a paragraph proof that a rock formed in the Cretaceous period did not exist in the Triassic period.

16. Tell which rule of logic you used in your proof.

Ongoing ASSESSMENT

17. Open-ended Plan your own itinerary on Euclid airlines. Write your itinerary in two different forms of proof. See page 394 for flights.

Review PREVIEW

For Exercises 18 and 19, tell whether each definition is a good definition, then write the two conditionals it uses. If it is not a good definition, tell why not. *(Section 7-4)*

18. A quadrilateral is a rhombus if and only if it has four congruent sides.

19. A quadrilateral is a rhombus if and only if it is a square.

20. Solve this system of equations by substitution. $x + y = 7$ *(Section 3-2)*
$$2x + 3y = 28$$

Solve each equation. *(Toolbox Skill 13)*

21. $n - 3 = 40$ **22.** $60 = 15x$ **23.** $24 = -3(a - 10)$

7-5 Introduction to Proof

399

Answers to Exercises and Problems

14. a. Let *a*, *b*, *c*, *d*, and *e* be the lengths of the sides of squares *A*, *B*, *C*, *D*, and *E*. Since $d = 5$, $e = 1$, and $a = d - e$, then $a = 4$. Since $b = d + e$, then $b = 6$. Since $c = a - e$, then $c = 3$.

b. Summaries may vary. An example is given. I began with given information and used logical reasoning to reach a desired destination.

15. If a rock was formed in the Cretaceous period, it was not formed more than 138 million years ago. If a rock was not formed more than 138 million years ago, it was not formed in the Triassic period. Therefore, a rock formed in the Cretaceous period did not exist in the Triassic period.

16. chain rule

17. See answers in back of book.

18. Yes. If a quadrilateral is a rhombus, then it has four congruent sides. If a quadrilateral has four congruent sides, then it is a rhombus.

19. No. If a quadrilateral is a rhombus, then the quadrilateral is a square. If a quadrilateral is a square, then the quadrilateral is a rhombus. If a quadrilateral is a rhombus, it is not necessarily a square.

20. $(-7, 14)$ **21.** $n = 43$

22. $x = 4$ **23.** $a = 2$

399

Working on the Unit Project

Project group members should work Ex. 24 individually. They can then meet as a group to share their itineraries and proofs.

As you complete this exercise, you will learn about one way to include a travel itinerary in your mystery story.

24. Zoe wants to add an early twentieth century European flavor to her mystery story. She researches the routes of the Orient-Express and creates this itinerary.

ORIENT EXPRESS

O-E 301: Paris → Vienna

O-E 302: Paris → Milan

O-E 410: Venice → Rome

O-E 412: Venice → Belgrade

O-E 701: Bucharest → Istanbul

O-E 503: Innsbruck → Munich

O-E 602: Milan → Venice

O-E 111: Vienna → Innsbruck

O-E 812: Belgrade → Istanbul

O-E 900: Munich → Vienna

a. Zoe could have her heroine take the Orient-Express from Paris directly to Istanbul but decides to make things more interesting by having a stop in Italy. Write a smaller itinerary that allows the heroine to go from Paris to Istanbul via Milan, Venice, or Rome.

b. Write a paragraph proof of the itinerary you wrote in part (a).

BY THE WAY...

The Orient-Express originated in 1883 to provide train service from Paris to Constantinople (now Istanbul). It actually was many connected train systems and included several destinations.

400   **Unit 7** Logic and Proof

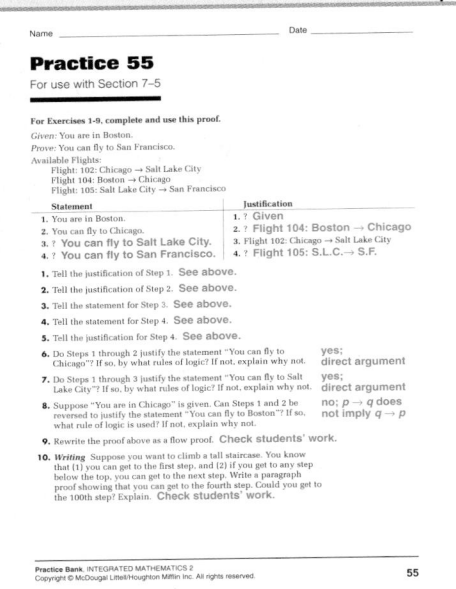

Name _____ Date _____

Practice 55
For use with Section 7–5

For Exercises 1-9, complete and use this proof.

Given: You are in Boston.
Prove: You can fly to San Francisco.
Available Flights:
  Flight: 102: Chicago → Salt Lake City
  Flight 104: Boston → Chicago
  Flight: 105: Salt Lake City → San Francisco

Statement	Justification
1. You are in Boston.	**1.** ? Given
2. You can fly to Chicago.	**2.** ? Flight 104: Boston → Chicago
3. ? You can fly to Salt Lake City.	**3.** ? Flight 102: Chicago → Salt Lake City
4. ? You can fly to San Francisco.	**4.** ? Flight 105: S.L.C.→ S.F.

1. Tell the justification of Step 1. **See above.**

2. Tell the justification of Step 2. **See above.**

3. Tell the statement for Step 3. **See above.**

4. Tell the statement for Step 4. **See above.**

5. Tell the justification for Step 4. **See above.**

6. Do Steps 1 through 2 justify the statement "You can fly to Chicago"? If so, by what rules of logic? If not, explain why not. **yes; direct argument**

7. Do Steps 1 through 3 justify the statement "You can fly to Salt Lake City"? If so, by what rules of logic? If not, explain why not. **yes; direct argument**

8. Suppose "You are in Chicago" is given. Can Steps 1 and 2 be reversed to justify the statement "You can fly to Boston"? If so, what rule of logic is used? If not, explain why not. **no; $p \rightarrow q$ does not imply $q \rightarrow p$**

9. Rewrite the proof above as a flow proof. **Check students' work.**

10. *Writing* Suppose you want to climb a tall staircase. You know that (1) you can get to the first step, and (2) if you get to any step below the top, you can get to the next step. Write a paragraph proof showing that you can get to the fourth step. Could you get to the 100th step? Explain. **Check students' work.**

Answers to Exercises and Problems

24. a.

City	Train
1. Paris	Departure point
2. Milan	O-E 302: Paris → Milan
3. Venice	O-E 602: Milan → Venice
4. Belgrade	O-E 412: Venice → Belgrade
5. Istanbul	O-E 812: Belgrade → Istanbul

b. Zoe's heroine can travel from Paris to Istanbul by taking the following trains on the Orient-Express. She can leave Paris on train 302 to Milan, where she can board train 602 to Venice. From Venice, she can catch train 412 to Belgrade, where she will have to make a final train change to train 812 from Belgrade to Istanbul.

Focus
Use postulates of algebra
to write proofs.

Postulates and Proofs in Algebra

Created Equal

At the beginning of the Declaration of Independence, the colonists explained why they wanted to break their ties with Great Britain.

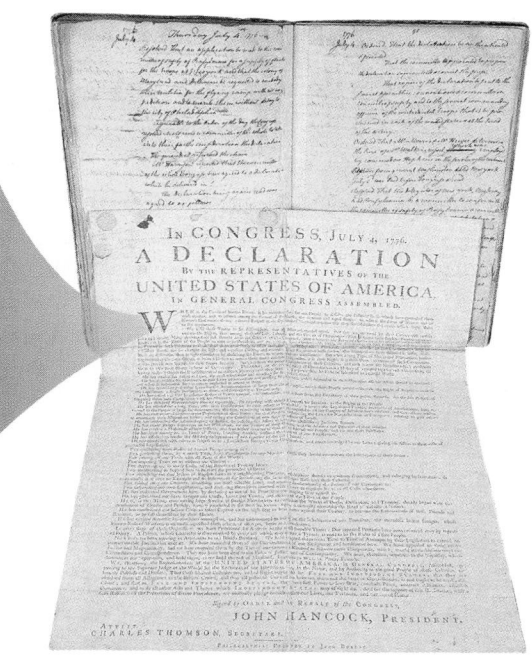

When in the course of human events, it becomes necessary for one people to dissolve the political bands which have connected them with another, ... they should declare the causes which impel them to the separation. We hold these truths to be self-evident, that all men are created equal, ...

Talk it Over

1. What did the colonists mean by the phrase "We hold these truths to be self-evident . . ."?

2. The colonists "declare the causes" for separation from Great Britain. What part of a mathematical proof is this similar to?

3. At the end of the Declaration, the colonists say "We, therefore ... declare, That these United Colonies are, and of Right ought to be Free and Independent States. . . ." What part of a proof in mathematics is this similar to?

7-6 Postulates and Proofs in Algebra

401

PLANNING

Objectives and Strands
See pages 362A and 362B.

Spiral Learning
See page 362B.

Materials List
Scissors

Recommended Pacing
Section 7-6 is a one-day lesson.

Extra Practice
See pages 625–626.

Warm-Up Exercises
Warm-Up Transparency 7-6

Support Materials
➤ Practice 56
➤ Enrichment 50 in the Activity Bank
➤ Study Guide 7-6
➤ Problem Set 15
➤ Quiz 7-6
➤ Test 28
➤ Alternative Assessment 5

Answers to Talk it Over

1. The colonists meant that these truths do not require a proof or explanation.

2. the statements

3. the conclusion

Questions 1–3 ask students how parts of the Declaration of Independence compare to the parts of a proof. In so doing, students learn that a proof can be written by starting with statements that are *assumed* to be true, that is, they do not require any prior justification.

Teaching Tip

Students should be familiar with many of the postulates of algebra from previous courses in mathematics. The use of the implication symbol in stating the postulates, however, may be new to them. Ask a few students to rephrase these postulates using the if-then form of an implication. Students will need to remember the names of the postulates to write algebraic proofs.

Additional Sample

S1 Prove that if $2x - 6 = -14$, then $x = -4$.

a. Write a flow proof.
Given: $2x - 6 = -14$
Prove: $x = -4$
Statements: $2x - 6 = -14$
$\overset{(1)}{\to} 2x = -8 \overset{(2)}{\to} x = -4$
Justifications:
(1) Addition property of equality
(2) Division property of equality

b. Write a paragraph proof.
Given: $2x - 6 = -14$
Prove: $x = -4$
You can use the addition property of equality to add 6 to both sides of $2x - 6 = -14$.
Therefore, $2x = -8$.
Then you can use the division property of equality to divide both sides by 2.
Therefore, $x = -4$.

In any logical argument, some statements must be assumed to be true to begin. These assumptions are called **postulates**.

SOME POSTULATES OF ALGEBRA

1. **Addition Property of Equality**	If the same number is added to equal numbers, the sums are equal.	$a = b \to a + c = b + c$
2. **Subtraction Property of Equality**	If the same number is subtracted from equal numbers, the differences are equal.	$a = b \to a - c = b - c$
3. **Multiplication Property of Equality**	If equal numbers are multiplied by the same number, the products are equal.	$a = b \to ac = bc$
4. **Division Property of Equality**	If equal numbers are divided by the same nonzero number, the quotients are equal.	$a = b$ and $c \neq 0 \to \frac{a}{c} = \frac{b}{c}$
5. **Reflexive Property of Equality**	A number is equal to itself.	$a = a$
6. **Substitution Property**	If values are equal, one value may be substituted for the other.	$a = b \to a$ may be substituted for b.
7. **Distributive Property**	An expression of the form $a(b + c)$ is equivalent to $ab + ac$.	$a(b + c) = ab + ac$

When you solve an equation in algebra, you are writing the steps of a proof. Here is how you solve $3x + 8 = 29$:

$3x + 8 = 29$ ⟵ Given
$3x = 21$ ⟵ Subtraction property of equality
$x = 7$ ⟵ Division property of equality

Sample 1

Prove that if $3x + 8 = 29$, then $x = 7$.

a. Write a flow proof.   **b.** Write a paragraph proof.

Sample Response

a. ⟨Given⟩ $3x + 8 = 29$ ⟨Prove⟩ $x = 7$

Plan Ahead
Get $3x$ alone on one side of the equation. Divide to find x.

Show Your Reasoning

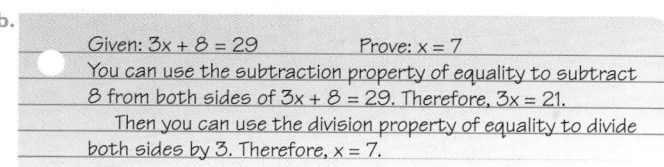

Statements

$$3x + 8 = 29 \xrightarrow{\text{①}} 3x = 21 \xrightarrow{\text{②}} x = 7$$

Justifications

① Subtraction property of equality

② Division property of equality

b.

> Given: $3x + 8 = 29$ Prove: $x = 7$
> You can use the subtraction property of equality to subtract
> 8 from both sides of $3x + 8 = 29$. Therefore, $3x = 21$.
>   Then you can use the division property of equality to divide
> both sides by 3. Therefore, $x = 7$.

Definitions can also be reasons in proofs. The following definition is used in Sample 2. A **square root** of a number is one of two equal factors of the number.

$$a^2 = n \leftrightarrow a = \pm\sqrt{n}$$

Sample 2

One fourth of the area of a square field is 16 square units. Prove that if $\frac{s^2}{4} = 16$, then $s = 8$.

Sample Response

Given $\frac{s^2}{4} = 16$ **Prove** $s = 8$

Plan Ahead

Get s alone on one side of the equation. Use the definition of a square root. Remember that the length of a field is positive.

Show Your Reasoning

Statements

$$\frac{s^2}{4} = 16 \xrightarrow{\text{①}} s^2 = 64 \xrightarrow{\text{②}} s = \pm 8 \left.\begin{array}{l} \\ s \text{ is positive.}\end{array}\right\} \xrightarrow{\text{③}} s = 8$$

Two premises must be true. Brace them together.

Justifications

① Multiplication property of equality

② Definition of square root

③ *Or* rule ($s = 8$ or $s = -8$. Since $s \neq -8$, $s = 8$ must be true.)

Look Back

Different students can provide the numerical examples of the postulates verbally. This is an excellent way of reviewing the meaning of each postulate.

Suggested Assignment

Standard 1–10, 12–14, 18–24

Extended 1–16, 18–24

Integrating the Strands

Number Ex. 15

Algebra Exs. 1–4, 7–10, 12–14, 16–19

Geometry Exs. 22, 23

Discrete Mathematics Exs. 1–24

Logic and Language Exs. 1–24

Communication: Reading

Have students read aloud Exs. 1–8 and provide their answers verbally. Other students listening to the answers can indicate their agreement or provide their own answers if they disagree.

Look Back

Give a numerical example of each of the postulates of algebra on page 402.

7-6 Exercises and Problems

Reading Identify which postulate or definition is used in each implication.

1. If $3x + 2 = 8$, then $3x = 6$.

2. If $3x = 6$, then $x = 2$.

3. If $x^2 = 9$, then $x = 3$ or $x = -3$.

4. If $5x = 15$, then $5x + 3 = 18$.

connection to HISTORY

The Woman's Rights Convention held in Seneca Falls, New York, in 1848 issued the first formal appeal for the right of women to vote. About 300 people approved a "Declaration of Sentiments."

5. The Declaration begins, "We hold these truths to be self-evident: that all men and women are created equal. . . ." How is this statement like a postulate?

6. The Declaration later states, ". . . let facts be submitted to a candid world." A listing of supporting reasons is similar to what part of a proof in mathematics?

Engraving of the convention

BY THE WAY...

Frederick Douglass, famous reformer and author, wrote, "If there is no struggle, there is no progress."

7. Copy and complete the two-column proof.

Given $x^2 + 8 = 24$
$\quad x > 0$

Prove $x = 4$

Statements	Justifications
1. $x^2 + 8 = 24$	1. ?
2. $x^2 = 16$	2. ?
3. ?	3. Definition of square root
4. $x > 0$	4. ?
5. ?	5. ?

Answers to Look Back

Addition Property of Equality:
$a = 5 \to a + 2 = 5 + 2$ or $a + 2 = 7$

Subtraction Property of Equality:
$a = 5 \to a - 2 = 5 - 2$ or $a - 2 = 3$

Multiplication Property of Equality:
$a = 5 \to a \cdot 2 = 5 \cdot 2$ or $2a = 10$

Division Property of Equality:
$a = 10 \to \dfrac{a}{2} = \dfrac{10}{2}$ or $\dfrac{a}{2} = 5$

Reflexive Property of Equality: $4 = 4$

Substitution Property: Since $4 = \dfrac{8}{2}$,
$4 + \dfrac{5}{2} = \dfrac{8}{2} + \dfrac{5}{2}$ or $\dfrac{13}{2}$

Distributive Property: $4(3 + 5) =$
$4 \cdot 3 + 4 \cdot 5 = 12 + 20 = 32$

Answers to Exercises and Problems

1. Subtraction property of equality

2. Division property of equality

3. Definition of square root

4. Addition property of equality

5. The colonists meant that these truths, like a postulate, do not require a proof or explanation.

6. Justifications

7. Given: $x^2 + 8 = 24$
$\quad\quad x > 0$
Prove: $x = 4$

Statements	Justifications
1. $x^2 + 8 = 24$	1. Given
2. $x^2 = 16$	2. Subtraction property of equality
3. $x = 4$ or $x = -4$	3. Definition of square root
4. $x > 0$	4. Given
5. $x = 4$	5. *Or* rule

8. Copy and complete the flow proof.

Given $2x - 15 = 25$

Prove $x = 20$

Statements

① ②
$2x - 15 = 25 \longrightarrow 2x = 40 \longrightarrow x = 20$

Justifications

① ?
② ?

9. a. Solve the equation $4x^2 + 6 = 330$ when $x > 0$. Show your steps in a two-column proof.

  b. Show your steps in a flow proof.

  c. Show your steps in a paragraph proof.

10. Solve the equation $\frac{x}{3} + 1 = 13$. Show your steps in a proof.

11. Writing Cam used equals signs instead of arrows between steps. What do you think is wrong with this?

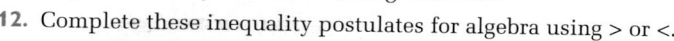

Cam Horton

If $3x + 8 = 29$, then $x = 7$.

Plan ahead. Get x alone.

Show your reasoning.
$3x + 8 = 29 = 3x = 21 = x = 7$

12. Complete these inequality postulates for algebra using > or <.

  a. If $a < b$, then $a + c$ _?_ $b + c$.

  b. If $a < b$, then $a - c$ _?_ $b - c$.

  c. If $a < b$ and $c > 0$, then ac _?_ bc.

  d. If $a < b$ and $c < 0$, then ac _?_ bc.

13. a. Writing Why do you think there are two inequality postulates involving multiplication in Exercise 12? Give examples to explain your reasoning.

  b. Write two postulates involving inequalities and division.

14. In solving quadratic equations you have used this postulate: If $ab = 0$, then $a = 0$ or $b = 0$.

  a. Write the postulate in words.

  b. How is this postulate different from the others you have studied?

  c. If $ab = 0$, can both a and b equal zero?

3-by-3 square

15. There are surprising numerical relationships on calendars.

  a. Use any month. Take any nine numbers that form a 3-by-3 square. What do you notice about their average?

  b. Let the number in the center of any 3-by-3 square be n. Prove that the average of the nine numbers equals the center number.

7-6 Postulates and Proofs in Algebra

405

Answers to Exercises and Problems

8. Justifications
❶ Addition property of equality
❷ Division property of equality

9. See answers in back of book.

10. *Given:* $\frac{x}{3} + 1 = 13$

Prove: $x = 36$

Statements	Justifications
1. $\frac{x}{3} + 1 = 13$	1. Given
2. $\frac{x}{3} = 12$	2. Subtraction property of equality
3. $x = 36$	3. Multiplication property of equality

11. When equal signs are used, untrue statements result. For example, it is not true that $29 = 3x$.

12. a. <
  b. <
  c. <
  d. >

Reasoning

Students need to understand that once they identify a postulate, as in Ex. 14, then they can use this postulate as a justification in proofs.

Problem Solving

Ex. 15 can be used to have students work on a different but related problem: Choose eight numbers on the calendar that form the outside of a 3-by-3 square. Find and prove another relationship involving these numbers. (The sum of the numbers is eight times the number inside the square.)

13. a. Answers may vary. An example is given. There are two inequality postulates because when you multiply an inequality by a positive number the inequality sign stays the same, but when you multiply an inequality by a negative number, the inequality sign is reversed. For example, for the inequality $2 < 5$, when both sides are multiplied by 3, then $6 < 15$. But when both sides are multiplied by -3, then $-6 > -15$.

  b. If $a < b$ and $c > 0$, then $\frac{a}{c} < \frac{b}{c}$.

  If $a < b$ and $c < 0$, then $\frac{a}{c} > \frac{b}{c}$.

14. a. If the product of two numbers is zero, then at least one of the numbers is zero.

  b. Answers may vary. The other postulates lead to just one conclusion. This postulate has two possible conclusions.

  c. Yes.

15. a. The average of the numbers is the number in the center of the 3-by-3 square.

  b. Let $n =$ the number in the center of the 3-by-3 square. Then the other numbers are $n - 8$, $n - 7$, $n - 6$, $n - 1$, $n + 1$, $n + 6$, $n + 7$, $n + 8$. The average of the numbers is the sum divided by how many numbers there are. So the average is $\frac{9n}{9} = n$, which is the middle number.

405

16. Camille proposed this postulate for squaring with inequalities:

If $a < b$, then $a^2 < b^2$.

   a. Give an example that shows when this is a true statement.

   b. Give a counterexample.

   c. **Writing** Did Camille write a postulate? Explain.

17. **Group Activity** Work in a group of four students.

   a. Use a large copy of the postulates on page 402. Cut it up to make 21 cards, each showing a postulate in words or symbols or its name. Turn the "cards" face down and mix them.

   b. Pick a card. Name the postulate and give it in words and symbols. You get one point for each correct answer. Let one person who does not play be the checker.

   c. Return the card to the table and scramble again. Play several rounds, so each person gets a chance to be the checker. High score wins.

18. a. **Writing** Explain why any even number can be represented by $2n$ and why any odd number can be represented by either $2n + 1$ or $2n - 1$.

   b. Complete this paragraph proof that the product of two consecutive numbers is an even number.

> I am given two consecutive numbers. Then one must be even and the other one odd.
>
> Let $2n$ be the even number and $2n + 1$ or $2n - 1$ be the odd number.
>
> Then the product is $2n(2n + 1)$ or $2n(2n - 1)$.
>
> The product has a factor of _?_, so the product must be an _?_ number.

Ongoing **ASSESSMENT**

19. **Open-ended** Write and solve your own equation. Present the solution as a flow proof or as a two-column proof.

20. Name and describe three forms of proof. *(Section 7-5)*

21. Arturo does a survey of attitudes about his school's sports program. He distributes the survey to every student he sees and asks that it be completed. Describe the problems in this method of surveying. *(Section 1-4)*

Tell if each definition is a good definition. If it is not, rewrite it so that it is a good definition. *(Section 7-4)*

22. A figure is a parallelogram if and only if the figure has two pairs of parallel sides.

23. A figure is a kite if it is a quadrilateral.

---

7 **Working on the Unit Project**

24. **Research** Edgar Allan Poe may be best known for his horror stories, including "The Pit and the Pendulum," and for his poetry, including "The Raven." He is also highly regarded as a literary theorist and as a short story writer.

Edgar Allan Poe set out guidelines for the use of ratiocination in what was to become the modern detective story. Find out what he meant by *ratiocination* and how he used it in mystery stories such as "The Murders in the Rue Morgue."

Unit 7   **CHECKPOINT**

1. **Writing** Explain why you need to plan ahead when writing a proof.

For Exercises 2 and 3, refer to this statement: **7-4**
A quadrilateral is a rectangle with parallel sides.

2. Write the statement as a biconditional.

3. Is the biconditional true? Explain.

4. Is the reasoning *valid* or *invalid*? Explain.
$16 + x = 12 \leftrightarrow x = -4$
$16 + x \neq 12$
Therefore, $x \neq -4$

For Exercises 5 and 6, replace each ? with the correct   **7-5**
word or phrase.

5. A ? is a diagram using arrows to show how to get from one statement to the next.

6. The destination of an itinerary is similar to the ? of a proof.

7. Prove that if $7x - 3 = 25$, then $x = 4$. Write a   **7-6**
two-column proof.

7-6 Postulates and Proofs in Algebra   **407**

Practice 56 For use with Section 7-6

Name _____ Date _____

Practice 56
For use with Section 7-6

1. add. prop. of = (add 7) or subt. prop. of = (subt. –7)
2. div. prop. of = (div. by 5) or mult. prop of = (mult. by $\frac{1}{5}$)
3. subt. prop. of = (subt. 3) or add. prop. of = (add –3)
4. mult. prop of = (mult. by 4) or div. prop of = (div. by $\frac{1}{4}$)

Identify which postulate is used in each implication.
1. If $5x - 7 = 33$, then $5x = 40$.
2. If $5x = 40$, then $x = 8$.
3. If $\frac{x}{4} + 3 = 15$, then $\frac{x}{4} = 12$.
4. If $\frac{x}{4} = 12$, then $x = 48$.

5. Copy and complete the two-column proof.
  Given: $3(x + 2) = 45$
  Prove: $x = 13$

Statement	Justification
1. $3(x + 2) = 45$	**1.** ? Given
2. $x + 2 = ?$ 15	**2.** ? Div. prop. of = (or mult. prop. of =)
3. $x = ?$ 13	**3.** ? Subt. prop. of = (or add. prop. of =)

6. Copy and complete the two-column proof.
  Given: $5x^2 = 180$, and $x < 0$
  Prove: $x = -6$

Statement	Justification
1. $5x^2 = 180$	**1.** ? Given
2. $x^2 = ?$ 36	**2.** ? Div. prop. of = (or mult. prop. of =)
3. $x = ?$ ±6	**3.** ? Definition of square root
4. ? x is not 6	**4.** ? Given
5. ? $x = -6$	**5.** ? Or rule

7. Misako proposed this postulate for square roots:
  If $a > 0$, then $\sqrt{a} \leq a$.
  a. Give a value of a for which this is a true statement. $a = 25$ ($\sqrt{25} \leq 25$)
  b. Give a counterexample. $a = \frac{1}{4}$ ($\sqrt{\frac{1}{4}} \leq \frac{1}{4}$ is **false.**)
  c. Is Misako's statement a postulate? no

8. Prove that the product of two consecutive even numbers is 1 less than the square of the odd number between them, or
$(2n)(2n + 2) = (2n + 1)^2 - 1$.
$2n(2n + 2) = 4n^2 + 4n = (4n^2 + 4n + 1) - 1 = (2n + 1)^2 - 1$

56   **Practice Bank,** INTEGRATED MATHEMATICS 2
Copyright © McDougal Littell/Houghton Mifflin Inc. All rights reserved.

Answers to Exercises and Problems

24. Answers may vary. An example is given. Ratiocination means to reason methodically and logically. In "The Murders in the Rue Morgue," Poe's character, detective Auguste Dupin, is able to demonstrate, by logic, that the murderer was an orangutan. Dupin was able to come to this conclusion by examining the evidence found at the scene of the crime. The evidence was the brutality of the murders; a loud screech that no witness could attribute to any human language; the fact that no one saw anyone escape, so the murderer must have gone out through a window; and the fact that the hair clutched in one of the victim's hands was not human.

Answers to Checkpoint

1. Answers may vary. An example is given. I need to plan ahead before I write a proof so that I can get from the premises to the conclusion in a straightforward, logical fashion.

2. A figure is a quadrilateral if and only if it is a rectangle with parallel sides.

3. No; any four-sided figure is a quadrilateral, not just rectangles.

4. valid; It is an indirect argument.

5. flow proof

6. conclusion

7. See answers in back of book.

Proofs for Angles

Focus
Recognize the value of definitions and postulates in proofs. Write proofs about angles.

Lawyers need to prove things in the courtroom. They cannot just say, "It is clear the defendant is guilty!"

The same is true in mathematics. When you make a conjecture, it needs to be proved.

Talk it Over

1. Write a good definition of **complementary angles** and a good definition of **supplementary angles.**

2. a. Think of two angles of the same measure. Find the *supplement* of each. What is true about the supplements?

   b. Make a conjecture about the supplements of angles equal in measure. Can you test your conjecture for all angles? Would a proof about angle supplements apply to all angle supplements?

In this book, you write $m \angle A = 30°$ to show that the measure of $\angle A$ is 30°. You write $m \angle A = m \angle B$ to show that the two angles are equal in measure. You write $\angle A \cong \angle B$ to show that $\angle A$ is congruent to $\angle B$.

Important statements you can prove are called **theorems.** To prove a statement, you can use rules of logic, postulates, definitions, given information, and proven theorems as justifications.

Watch Out!
Postulates are assumed to be true. Theorems must be proven true.

Unit 7 Logic and Proof

Answers to Talk it Over

1. Two angles are complementary if and only if the sum of their measures equals 90°. Two angles are supplementary if and only if the sum of their measures equals 180°.

2. a. The two supplements also have the same measure.

   b. If two angles are equal in measure, then their supplements are also equal in measure. No; an infinite number of cases cannot be tested. Yes.

3. **Statements**
   $\angle 1$ is supplementary to $\angle 2$. ❶→ $m \angle 1 + m \angle 2 = 180°$ ❷
   $\angle 3$ is supplementary to $\angle 2$. ❶→ $m \angle 3 + m \angle 2 = 180°$
   $m \angle 1 + m \angle 2 = m \angle 3 + m \angle 2$ ❸→ $m \angle 1 = m \angle 3$

   Justifications

   ❶ Definition of supplementary angles

   ❷ Substitution property

   ❸ Subtraction property of equality

Prove that supplements of the same angle are equal in measure.

Sample Response

If two angles are supplements of the same angle, then they are equal in measure.

← It helps to rewrite the statement in if-then form.

Given ∠1 is supplementary to ∠2.
∠3 is supplementary to ∠2.

← Make and label a diagram to represent the situation.

Prove m ∠1 = m ∠3 ← State what is given and what you need to prove.

Watch Out!
You cannot assume that angle measures are equal because they look equal in a diagram. If it is not given information, you have to prove it!

Plan Ahead

The sum of the measures of each pair of supplementary angles is 180°. Set the sums equal to each other. Subtract the common angle's measure.

Show Your Reasoning

Statements

1. ∠1 is supplementary to ∠2.
2. $m \angle 1 + m \angle 2 = 180°$
3. ∠3 is supplementary to ∠2.
4. $m \angle 3 + m \angle 2 = 180°$
5. $m \angle 1 + m \angle 2 = m \angle 3 + m \angle 2$
6. $m \angle 1 = m \angle 3$

Justifications

1. Given
2. Definition of supplementary ∡ ← Read "angles."
3. Given
4. Definition of supplementary ∡
5. Substitution property (Steps 2 and 4)
6. Subtraction property of equality

When you use more than one step, identify the steps.

Talk it Over

3. Rewrite the proof in flow form.

4. Prove in paragraph form that *complements* of the same angle are equal in measure.

SUPPLEMENTS AND COMPLEMENTS OF ANGLES

Theorem 7.1 If two angles are supplements of the same angle, then they are equal in measure.

Theorem 7.2 If two angles are complements of the same angle, then they are equal in measure.

Answers to Talk it Over

4. *Given:* ∠1 is complementary to ∠2; ∠3 is complementary to ∠2.
   Prove: m ∠1 = m ∠3

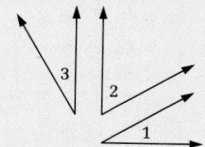

If two angles are complementary, then their sum is equal to 90°. Therefore, m ∠1 + m ∠2 = 90° and m ∠2 + m ∠3 = 90°.

Since the sums both equal 90°, you can say m ∠1 + m ∠2 = m ∠2 + m ∠3 by the substitution property. Then you can use the subtraction property of equality to subtract m ∠2 from both sides of the equation. Therefore, m ∠1 = m ∠3.

Two angles formed by intersecting lines and facing in opposite directions are **vertical angles.** To prove theorems about vertical angles, you need two more postulates.

∠**1** and ∠**3** are vertical angles.
∠**2** and ∠**4** are vertical angles.

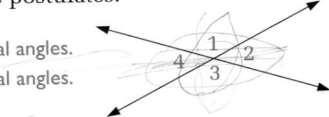

STRAIGHT ANGLE POSTULATE

Postulate 8   If the sides of an angle form a straight line, then the angle is a straight angle with measure 180°.

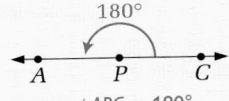

$m \angle APC = 180°$

The bottom edge of this fan forms a straight angle with measure 180°. The sum of the measures of the smaller angles is 180°.

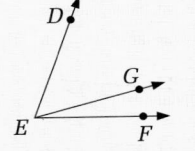

Watch Out!

The parts must not overlap!
$m \angle SPW \neq m \angle SPU + m \angle TPW$

WHOLE AND PARTS POSTULATE

Postulate 9   For any segment or angle, the measure of the whole is equal to the sum of the measures of its non-overlapping parts.

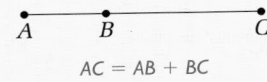

$AC = AB + BC$

$m \angle DEF = m \angle DEG + m \angle GEF$

Sample 2

Prove that vertical angles are equal in measure.

Sample Response

Given ∠1 and ∠2 are vertical angles.

Prove m ∠1 = m ∠2

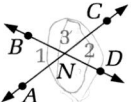

Plan Ahead

Use the straight angle postulate to show that m ∠1 + m ∠3 = m ∠2 + m ∠3. Then use the subtraction property of equality.

Show Your Reasoning

Statements

Lines *AC* and *BD* intersect at *N* **❶** m ∠ANC = 180° **❷**
to form vertical angles 1 and 2. → m ∠BND = 180° ⟶ m ∠ANC = m ∠BND

❸
m ∠ANC = m ∠1 + m ∠3   **❹**
m ∠BND = m ∠2 + m ∠3

❺
m ∠1 + m ∠3 = m ∠2 + m ∠3 ⟶ m ∠1 = m ∠2

Justifications

❶ If the sides of an angle form a straight line, then the angle is a straight angle with measure 180°.

❷ Substitution property

❸ For any angle, the measure of the whole is equal to the sum of the measures of its non-overlapping parts.

❹ Substitution property

❺ Subtraction property of equality

VERTICAL ANGLES THEOREM

Theorem 7.3 Vertical angles are equal in measure.

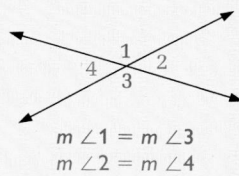

m ∠1 = m ∠3
m ∠2 = m ∠4

Additional Sample

S2 Angles *A* and *B* are vertical angles. The measure of angle *A* is 78°. What is the measure of angle *B*?
m ∠A = m ∠B = 78°

Communication: Writing

You might wish to have students write a two-column proof for Sample 2. If so, they can use the proof in Sample 1 on page 409 as a model.

Look Back

The answer to this question is given at the bottom of page 408. It is important for students to understand that justifications in proofs are either definitions, given information, or proven theorems.

APPLYING

Suggested Assignment

Standard 1–15, 19–24

Extended 1–15, 17, 19–24

Integrating the Strands

Algebra Exs. 19, 20–22

Geometry Exs. 1–15, 18, 23

Logic and Language Exs. 1–19, 24

Problem Solving

In Ex. 9, it seems clear from the diagram that the area of the new figure is twice that of the original square and that it is a square. Remind students, however, that they cannot use what appears to be true in a diagram as a justification for their reasoning. The proof of part (a) is fairly simple. For part (b), however, students need to write a proof showing that the new figure has four congruent sides and four right angles. A paragraph proof would be a good format for students to use to explain their reasoning.

Look Back

What kinds of statements can be used as justifications in proofs?

Reading Identify each type of statement as one or more of the following: a *definition*, a *postulate*, or a *theorem*.

1. a statement that is a biconditional

2. a statement that you assume is true, but do not prove

3. a statement that you may use as a justification in a proof

4. a statement that you can prove

In Exercises 5–7, state a conclusion that can be made in one step from the given information. Give a reason.

5. *Given:* $\angle Q$ is supplementary to $\angle R$.

6. *Given:* $\angle R$ and $\angle T$ are vertical angles.

7. *Given:* $\angle G$ is supplementary to $\angle H$. $\angle G$ is supplementary to $\angle J$.

8. Copy and complete the proof.

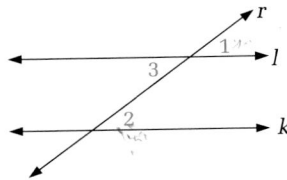

Given Line r intersects lines l and k.
$m \angle 1 = m \angle 2$

Prove $m \angle 3 = m \angle 2$

Statements	**Justifications**
1. l and r are intersecting lines.	1. Given
2. $\angle 1$ and $\angle 3$ are vertical angles.	2. _?_
3. _?_	3. Vertical $\angle$s are = in measure.
4. $m \angle 1 = m \angle 2$	4. _?_
5. _?_	5. Substitution property (Steps 3 and 4)

9. Laurie wants to double the area of a square. She first doubles each side. This gives her a square four times as large. Then she cuts each of the four squares in half.

   a. Is the area of the new figure twice the area of the original square?

   b. **Writing** How do you know for sure that the sides of the new figure are equal in measure? Explain your reasoning.

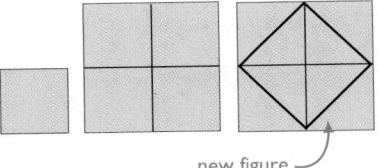

new figure

BY THE WAY...

The words *theorem* and *theater* both come from the same Greek root *to see*. At a theater you see a performance. In a theorem you see that a statement is true.

Answers to Look Back

Given information, postulates, definitions, and theorems may be used as justifications in proofs.

Answers to Exercises and Problems

1. definition

2. postulate

3. definition, postulate, theorem

4. theorem

5. $m \angle Q + m \angle R = 180°$; definition of supplementary angles

6. $m \angle R = m \angle T$; Vertical angles are equal in measure.

7. $m \angle H = m \angle J$; If two angles are supplements of the same angle, then they are equal in measure.

8. *Given:* Line r intersects lines l and k.
   $m \angle 1 = m \angle 2$
   Prove: $m \angle 3 = m \angle 2$

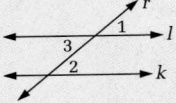

Statements	**Justifications**
1. l and r are intersecting lines.	1. Given
2. $\angle 1$ and $\angle 3$ are vertical angles.	2. Definition of vertical $\angle$s
3. $m \angle 1 = m \angle 3$	3. Vertical $\angle$s are = in measure.
4. $m \angle 1 = m \angle 2$	4. Given
5. $m \angle 3 = m \angle 2$	5. Substitution property (Steps 3 and 4)

10. Copy and complete the proof.

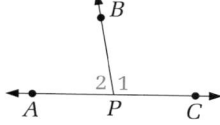

Given $\overrightarrow{PA}$ and $\overrightarrow{PC}$ form a straight angle.
$m \angle 1 = 100°$

Prove $m \angle 2 = 80°$

Statements

$\overrightarrow{PA}$ and $\overrightarrow{PC}$ form a straight angle. **①**→ $m \angle APC = 180°$

② $m \angle APC = m \angle 1 + m \angle 2$ **③**

$m \angle 1 + m \angle \underline{\ ?\ } = 180°$ **④**

$m \angle 1 = 100°$

$100° + m \angle 2 = 180°$ **⑤**→ $\underline{\ ?\ }$

Justifications

① $\underline{\ ?\ }$
② $\underline{\ ?\ }$
③ $\underline{\ ?\ }$
④ $\underline{\ ?\ }$
⑤ $\underline{\ ?\ }$

11. Write a flow proof: If $\angle 1$ and $\angle 2$ are complementary and $m \angle 1 = 75°$, then $m \angle 2 = 15°$.

12. Write a paragraph proof: If $\angle 1$ and $\angle 2$ form a straight angle and $m \angle 1 = 25°$, then $m \angle 2 = 155°$.

13. Law Do you think the statement "A person is innocent until proven guilty" is closer to a definition, a postulate, or a theorem?

14. What is the converse of Postulate 8? Is it true?

15. Write a proof of the following:

Given $\angle ABC$ is a straight angle.
$m \angle ABF = m \angle FBE$
$m \angle EBD = m \angle DBC$

Prove $\angle FBD$ is a right angle.

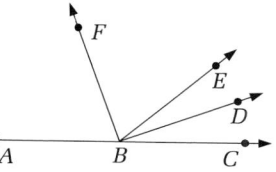

the salchow jump

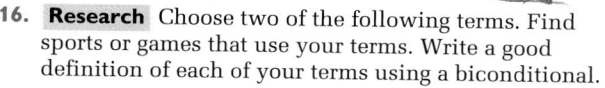

connection to **SPORTS**

Mathematics and the law have their own vocabularies and rules. So do many sports and games. All players must understand the terms and play by the same rules.

16. Research Choose two of the following terms. Find sports or games that use your terms. Write a good definition of each of your terms using a biconditional.

foul	starboard	netball	goal
salchow	stroke	out	checkmate

17. Open-ended Choose a game or a sport you know. Make up a situation where the players might have a dispute. Use the rules and definitions for your game or sport to decide on a ruling.

BY THE WAY...

Ulrich Salchow won the first men's figure skating event in the Olympics in 1908. He also won ten World and nine European Championships, representing Sweden.

7-7 Proofs for Angles

413

Answers to Exercises and Problems

9. a. Yes.
b. The sides of the new figure are all diagonals of congruent squares. These diagonals are all congruent.

10, 11. See answers in back of book.

12. *Given:* $\angle 1$ and $\angle 2$ form a straight angle.
$m \angle 1 = 25°$
Prove: $m \angle 2 = 155°$
If $\angle 1$ and $\angle 2$ form a straight angle, then $m \angle 1 + m \angle 2 = 180°$. If $m \angle 1 = 25°$, then $25° + m \angle 2 = 180°$ by the substitution property. Therefore, by the subtraction property of equality, $m \angle 2 = 155°$.

13. postulate

14. If an angle is a straight angle with measure of 180 degrees, then the sides of the angle form a straight line. Yes.

15. See answers in back of book.

413

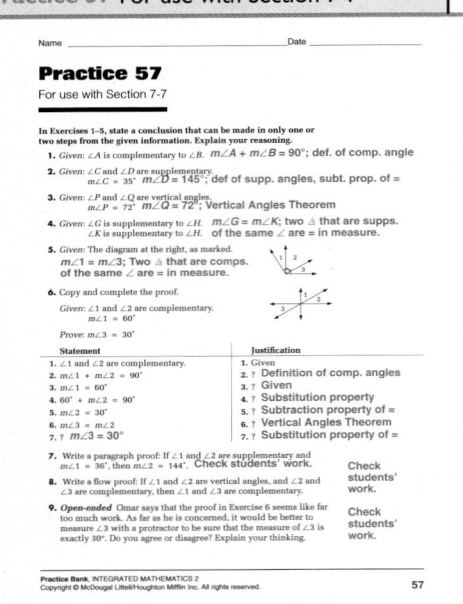
Ongoing ASSESSMENT

18. **Group Activity** Work with another student. Your goal is to prove that if ∠1 and ∠2 are supplementary angles and ∠1 and ∠3 are vertical angles, then ∠2 and ∠3 are supplementary angles.

   a. Plan your proof together. What form of proof will you use? You may want to draw a diagram.

   b. One of you should write the first statement and the other should write the justification. Then switch. Take turns writing the statements and justifications.

Review PREVIEW

19. Write a proof of the following: If $2(x + 7) = 3x$, then $x = 14$. *(Section 7-6)*

Tell whether each system of equations has *no solution, one solution,* or *many solutions.* *(Section 3-3)*

20. $y = 3x + 2$
    $y = -2x - 5$

21. $y = x - 1$
    $7y = 7x - 7$

22. $y = 2x - 2$
    $y = 2x + 2$

23. Name three kinds of quadrilaterals that are parallelograms. *(Section 5-1)*

Working on the Unit Project

24. Doctors, scientists, and engineers are sometimes called on to solve medical mysteries. When thousands of American Legionnaires met for a convention in Philadelphia in 1976, more than 200 came down with an unexplained illness. The symptoms were high fever, chest pains, and difficulty breathing.

Doctors found that blood samples showed a high level of a particular enzyme. Other samples revealed a bacterial infection. Six months after the convention, these clues led to finding the bacterium that causes Legionnaires' disease.

To solve your mystery story, readers need all the clues. List the clues that you plan to use in the order you will reveal them.

DISEASE DETECTIVES AT WORK

ATLANTA, GEORGIA—Officials at the U.S. Centers for Disease Control recently announced that their researchers have pieced together clues to discover the organism that caused Legionnaires' disease in Philadelphia. Physicians, biologists, chemists, bacteriologists, a microbiologists examin samples collected investigators. They final found that a previous unknown bacillus, new named *Legionell pneumophilia,* caused th disease.

414   **Unit 7** Logic and Proof

Answers to Exercises and Problems

18. See answers in back of book.

19. *Given:* $2(x + 7) = 3x$
    Prove: $x = 14$

Statements	Justifications
1. $2(x + 7) = 3x$	1. Given
2. $2x + 14 = 3x$	2. Distributive property
3. $14 = x$	3. Subtraction property of equality

20. one solution

21. many solutions

22. no solutions

23. rhombus, rectangle, square

24. Answers may vary.

Focus
Write proofs for properties
of parallel lines.

Proofs about Parallel Lines

Know all the Angles

EXPLORATION

(How) are angles and parallel lines related?

- **Materials: ruler or straight edge, protractor, lined notebook paper, blank paper**
- **Work in a group of four students.**

① Use lined notebook paper. Use a ruler to darken two parallel lines. Draw a dark line intersecting both parallel lines, but not perpendicular to them.

② Place a blank sheet of paper over your drawing. Trace one acute angle and label it *a*. Find all other angles of equal measure. Put a small *a* inside each angle with that measure.

③ Trace an obtuse angle and label it *o*. Find all other angles of equal measure. Put a small *o* inside each angle with that measure.

④ **a.** How many different angles did you find?

b. How are the acute and obtuse angles related to one another?

c. Describe any patterns you see in the results.

⑤ Can you find a pair of parallel lines and a transversal for which your observations do not hold?

⑥ Suppose all your classmates agree on relationships among the angles. What sort of reasoning are you using? Does this prove the relationships?

7-8 Proofs about Parallel Lines

415

Answers to Exploration

1–3. Check students' work.

4. **a.** There are three other acute angles with the same measure as *a*, and there are three other obtuse angles with the same measure as *o*.

b. The sum of their measures is 180°.

c. Answers may vary. Examples are given.

When two parallel lines are intersected by a transversal that is not perpendicular to them, there are two pairs of acute angles, all equal in measure, and there are two pairs of obtuse angles, all equal in measure. Each acute angle is supplementary to an obtuse angle.

5. Answers may vary.

6. Inductive reasoning is being used. It does not prove the relationship.

PLANNING

Objectives and Strands
See pages 362A and 362B.

Spiral Learning
See page 362B.

Materials List
➤ Ruler or straight edge
➤ Protractor
➤ Lined paper
➤ Blank paper
➤ Four straws
➤ Four straight pins
➤ Scissors

Recommended Pacing
Section 7-8 is a two-day lesson.
Day 1
Pages 415–417: Exploration through Talk it Over 6, *Exercises 1–11*
Day 2
Pages 417–419: Parallel Lines in Proofs through Look Back, *Exercises 12–27*

Extra Practice
See pages 625–626.

Warm-Up Exercises
Warm-Up Transparency 7-8

Support Materials
➤ Practice 58
➤ Enrichment 52 in the Activity Bank
➤ Study Guide 7-8
➤ Problem Set 16
➤ Additional Exploration 10
➤ McDougal Littell Mathpack software: *Geometry Inventor*
➤ Geometry Inventor Activity Book: Activities 1 and 10
➤ Quiz 7-8
➤ Test 29
➤ Alternative Assessment 7

Exploration

The goal of the Exploration is to have students discover that when two parallel lines are intersected by a third line not perpendicular to them, then pairs of congruent and supplementary angles are formed.

Using Technology

The *Geometry Inventor* software can be used to do the Exploration.

Transversals and Special Angle Pairs

It is helpful in talking about intersecting lines to agree on some terms.

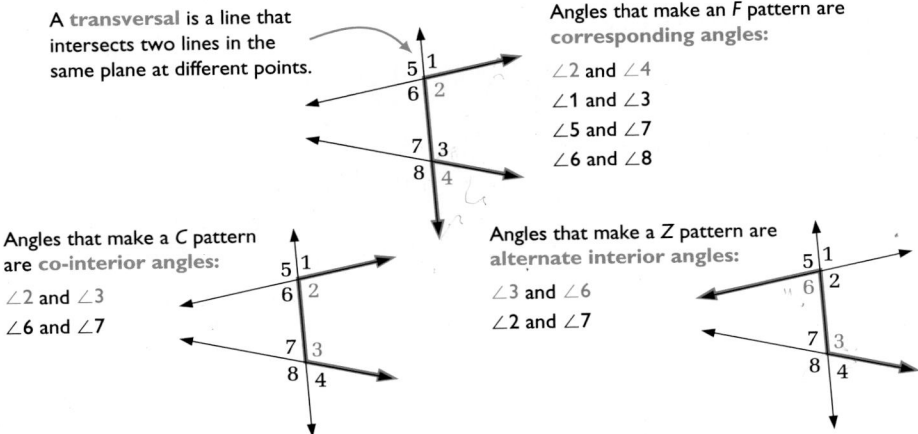

A **transversal** is a line that intersects two lines in the same plane at different points.

Angles that make an *F* pattern are **corresponding angles:**

∠2 and ∠4
∠1 and ∠3
∠5 and ∠7
∠6 and ∠8

Angles that make a *C* pattern are **co-interior angles:**

∠2 and ∠3
∠6 and ∠7

Angles that make a *Z* pattern are **alternate interior angles:**

∠3 and ∠6
∠2 and ∠7

Talk it Over

Use the diagram.

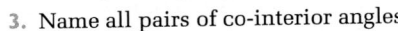

1. Name all pairs of alternate interior angles.

2. Name all pairs of corresponding angles.

3. Name all pairs of co-interior angles.

When lines are parallel, a transversal creates special angle pairs. As the Exploration suggests, some pairs are equal in measure and others are supplementary. If you assume Postulate 10, then you can prove that other relationships must be true.

A POSTULATE ABOUT PARALLEL LINES

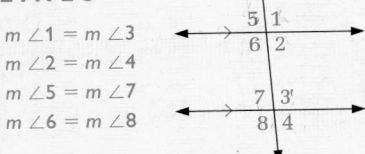

Postulate 10 If two parallel lines are intersected by a transversal, then corresponding angles are equal in measure.

$m \angle 1 = m \angle 3$
$m \angle 2 = m \angle 4$
$m \angle 5 = m \angle 7$
$m \angle 6 = m \angle 8$

Answers to Talk it Over

1. ∠3 and ∠5, ∠4 and ∠6

2. ∠1 and ∠5, ∠4 and ∠8, ∠2 and ∠6, ∠3 and ∠7

3. ∠4 and ∠5, ∠3 and ∠6

Here are statements of other patterns you may have observed in the Exploration.

THEOREMS ABOUT PARALLEL LINES

Theorem 7.4 If two parallel lines are intersected by a transversal, then alternate interior angles are equal in measure.

$m \angle 2 = m \angle 7$

$m \angle 3 = m \angle 6$

Theorem 7.5 If two parallel lines are intersected by a transversal, then co-interior angles are supplementary.

$m \angle 2 + m \angle 3 = 180°$

$m \angle 6 + m \angle 7 = 180°$

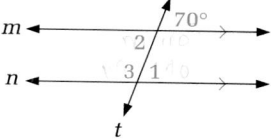

Talk it Over

4. In the diagram at the right, how do you know that $m \angle 1 = 70°$?

5. $\angle 1$ and $\angle 2$ are alternate interior angles. What are their measures? How do you know?

6. $\angle 2$ and $\angle 3$ are co-interior angles. What are their measures? How do you know?

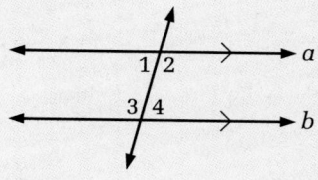

> ▶ Now you are ready for:
> Exs. 1–11 on pp. 419–420

Parallel Lines in Proofs

The symbol ∥ is read either as "parallel" (two ∥ lines) or as "is parallel to" ($m \parallel n$).

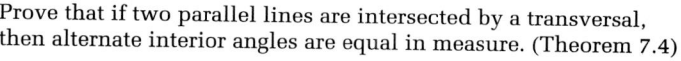
Sample 1

Prove that if two parallel lines are intersected by a transversal, then alternate interior angles are equal in measure. (Theorem 7.4)

Sample Response

Given Lines m and n are parallel.
Transversal t intersects lines m and n.

Prove $m \angle 1 = m \angle 2$

Plan Ahead

Think about which angle pairs are equal in measure. Show that $\angle 1$ and $\angle 2$ are both equal in measure to $\angle 3$. Then $\angle 1$ and $\angle 2$ are equal in measure.

Continued on next page.

7-8 Proofs about Parallel Lines

417

Answers to Talk it Over

4. Corresponding angles are equal in measure. The angle measuring 70° and $\angle 1$ are corresponding angles. Therefore, $m \angle 1 = 70°$.

5. Because $m \angle 1 = 70°$ (from question 4) and alternate interior angles are equal in measure, $m \angle 2 = m \angle 1 = 70°$.

6. $m \angle 2 = 70°$ (from question 5). Since co-interior angles are supplementary, $m \angle 2 + m \angle 3 = 180°$. By the substitution property, $70° + m \angle 3 = 180°$. Using the subtraction property of equality, $m \angle 3 = 110°$.

417

S2 Figure *RSTP* is a quadrilateral. Find the measure of each angle if $m \angle R = 110°$.

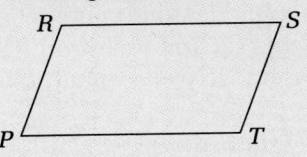

$m \angle S = 70°$
$m \angle T = 110°$
$m \angle P = 70°$

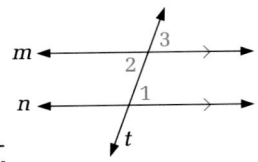

Show Your Reasoning

 **Statements**

$m \parallel n \xrightarrow{①} \left. \begin{array}{l} m \angle 1 = m \angle 3 \\ m \angle 2 = m \angle 3 \end{array} \right\} \xrightarrow{③} m \angle 1 = m \angle 2$

Justifications

① If two $\parallel$ lines are intersected by a transversal, then corresponding $\angle$s are $=$ in measure.

② Vertical $\angle$s are $=$ in measure.

③ Substitution property

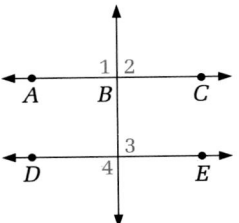

There are some things you can assume from a diagram and some you cannot. In this diagram you *can* assume:

All points shown are in the same plane.

Points *A*, *B*, and *C*, are on the same line.

$\angle 3$ and $\angle 4$ are vertical angles.

Here you *cannot* assume:

$\overleftrightarrow{AC}$ is parallel to $\overleftrightarrow{DE}$.

$m \angle 1 = m \angle 2$

$AB = BC$

Sample 2

Prove that if a quadrilateral is a parallelogram, then consecutive angles are supplementary.

Sample Response

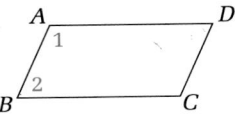

Given parallelogram *ABCD*

Prove $\angle 1$ is supplementary to $\angle 2$.

Plan Ahead

Find parallel lines intersected by a transversal for which $\angle 1$ and $\angle 2$ are co-interior angles. Then $\angle 1$ is supplementary to $\angle 2$.

Show Your Reasoning

Statements	**Justifications**
1. *ABCD* is a parallelogram.	1. Given
2. $\overline{AD}$ is parallel to $\overline{BC}$.	2. Definition of a parallelogram
3. $\angle 1$ is supplementary to $\angle 2$.	3. If two $\parallel$ lines are intersected by a transversal, then co-interior $\angle$s are supplementary.

Answers to Talk it Over

7. *Given:* parallelogram *ABCD*

   Prove: $m \angle 1 = m \angle 3$

   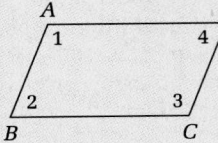

   Plan: $\angle 1$ and $\angle 3$ are both supplementary to $\angle 2$ by Theorem 7.6. Thus, $m \angle 1 = m \angle 3$ by Theorem 7.1.

PARALLELOGRAM ANGLE THEOREMS

Theorem 7.6 If a quadrilateral is a parallelogram,
then consecutive angles are supplementary.

$m \angle 1 + m \angle 2 = 180°$ $\quad$ $m \angle 2 + m \angle 3 = 180°$

$m \angle 3 + m \angle 4 = 180°$ $\quad$ $m \angle 4 + m \angle 1 = 180°$

Theorem 7.7 If a quadrilateral is a parallelogram,
then opposite angles are equal in measure.

$m \angle 1 = m \angle 3$ $\quad\quad\quad$ $m \angle 2 = m \angle 4$

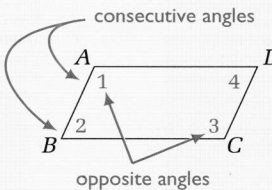

consecutive angles

opposite angles

Talk it Over

7. Write a plan to prove that if a quadrilateral is a parallelogram, then opposite angles are equal in measure.

Look Back ◄

What postulate was assumed in this lesson? What theorems
could be deduced from this postulate and previous theorems
and definitions?

······► **Now you are ready for:**
Exs. 12–27 on pp. 420–422

7-8 **Exercises and Problems**

For Exercises 1–6, use the diagram.

1. Name four pairs of corresponding angles.

2. Name two pairs of alternate interior angles.

3. Name two pairs of co-interior angles.

4. Name at least ten pairs of supplementary angles.

5. What might be a good name for the pair of angles numbered 1 and 4?

6. Suppose $m\angle 3 = 100°$. Find the measure of each angle.

   a. $\angle 1$ $\qquad$ **b.** $\angle 2$ $\qquad$ **c.** $\angle 4$ $\qquad$ **d.** $\angle 5$

   e. $\angle 6$ $\qquad$ **f.** $\angle 7$ $\qquad$ **g.** $\angle 8$

7. *ABCD* is a trapezoid.

   a. What type of angles are $\angle 1$ and $\angle 2$?

   b. What can you conclude about
   their measures?

   c. What is your justification?

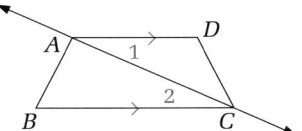

7-8 Proofs about Parallel Lines

419

Using Technology

Activity 1 in the *Geometry
Inventor Activity Book*
reinforces the postulates and
theorems about parallel lines.

Talk it Over

Question 7 asks students to
plan a proof of Theorem 7.7.
The plan involves a straightforward application of
Theorem 7.6.

Look Back

Students can list the postulate
and theorems by number or
you may wish to have them
write out the statements of
each one.

APPLYING

Suggested Assignment

Day 1

Standard 1–10

Extended 1–10

Day 2

Standard 12–19, 21–27

Extended 12–27

Integrating the Strands

Algebra Exs. 23–25

Geometry Exs. 1–22

Logic and Language Exs. 5,
7–22, 26, 27

Answers to Look Back ···········

Postulate assumed: If two parallel lines are intersected by a
transversal, then corresponding angles are equal in measure. Theorems deduced: If
two parallel lines are intersected by a transversal, then alternate interior angles are equal
in measure. If two parallel

lines are intersected by a
transversal, then co-interior
angles are supplementary. If a
quadrilateral is a parallelogram, then consecutive angles
are supplementary. If a quadrilateral is a parallelogram, then
opposite angles are equal in
measure.

Answers to Exercises and Problems ···········

1. $\angle 1$ and $\angle 3$, $\angle 2$ and $\angle 4$,
   $\angle 5$ and $\angle 7$, $\angle 6$ and $\angle 8$

2. $\angle 2$ and $\angle 7$, $\angle 3$ and $\angle 6$

3. $\angle 2$ and $\angle 3$, $\angle 6$ and $\angle 7$

4. Answers may vary.
   Examples are given.
   $\angle 1$ and $\angle 2$, $\angle 3$ and $\angle 4$,
   $\angle 5$ and $\angle 6$, $\angle 7$ and $\angle 8$,
   $\angle 1$ and $\angle 5$, $\angle 2$ and $\angle 6$,
   $\angle 3$ and $\angle 7$, $\angle 4$ and $\angle 8$,
   $\angle 2$ and $\angle 3$, $\angle 6$ and $\angle 7$,
   $\angle 1$ and $\angle 4$, $\angle 5$ and $\angle 8$

5. co-exterior angles

6. **a.** 100° $\qquad$ **b.** 80°

   c. 80° $\qquad$ **d.** 80°

   e. 100° $\qquad$ **f.** 80°

   g. 100°

7. **a.** alternate interior angles

   b. Their measures are equal.

   c. If two parallel lines are intersected by a transversal, then
   alternate interior angles are
   equal in measure.

connection to **GEOGRAPHY**

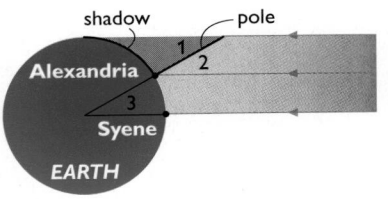

shadow pole

rays of sun

Alexandria

Syene

EARTH

(Not drawn to scale.)

Eratosthenes lived in northeast Africa in the 3rd century B.C. Exercises 8–10 show how he calculated the circumference of Earth using geometry. (Because the sun is so far from Earth, its rays can be considered parallel.)

He saw that on June 21 at noon, the sun cast no shadow in Syene. The sun *did* cast a shadow in Alexandria, north of Syene. Using the shadow cast by a pole, Eratosthenes found that the measure of ∠1 was 7.2°.

8. How are ∠1 and ∠2 related? ∠2 and ∠3?

9. What is the measure of ∠3?

10. a. Eratosthenes estimated the distance between Alexandria and Syene to be 5000 stadia. (One *stadium* is about 607 ft.) Use this proportion to estimate the circumference of Earth: $\dfrac{m\angle 3}{360°} = \dfrac{5000 \text{ stadia}}{\text{Earth circumference}}$

    b. What is the estimate in feet?

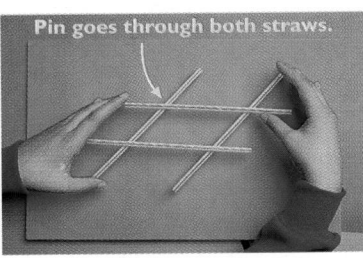

Pin goes through both straws.

11. **Using Manipulatives** You will need four straws, four straight pins, scissors, and blank paper.

    a. Hold two straws parallel, a few inches apart. Lay a straw across them and pin the intersections. Lay a fourth straw parallel to the third. Pin the intersections.

    b. **Writing** Gently shift the parallelogram so that the angles change size. Describe how consecutive pairs of angles are affected. Describe how opposite pairs of angles are affected.

12. Write a paragraph proof of Theorem 7.4: If two parallel lines are intersected by a transversal, then alternate interior angles are equal in measure.

13. Write a two-column proof of Theorem 7.5: If two parallel lines are intersected by a transversal, then co-interior angles are supplementary.

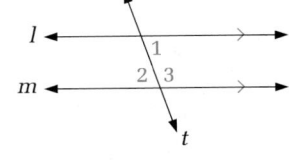

14. a. Given: Lines *q* and *r* are parallel.
       Prove: $m\angle 1 = m\angle 3$

    b. Write the conclusion of part (a) as a theorem using words.

15. *PQRS* is a parallelogram. What is the relationship between each pair of angles?
    a. ∠*P* and ∠*Q*   b. ∠*P* and ∠*R*

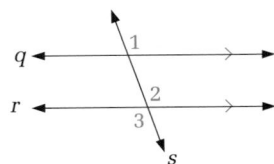

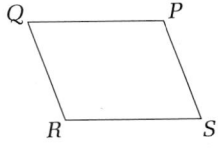

16. In parallelogram *ABCD*, $m\angle A = x°$.

    a. Write an expression for the measure of each of the other angles.

    b. Write an expression for the sum of the measures of the angles.

    c. Use your answer in part (b) to make a conjecture about the sum of the angles of a parallelogram.

420   **Unit 7** Logic and Proof

---

14. a. *Given:* Lines *q* and *r* are parallel and are intersected by line *s*.
       Prove: $m\angle 1 = m\angle 3$

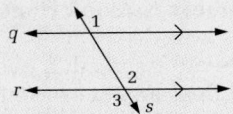

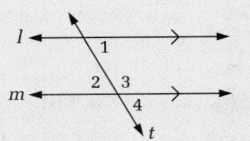

Since $l \parallel m$ and ∠1 and ∠4 are corresponding angles, $m\angle 1 = m\angle 4$. $m\angle 4$ is also equal to $m\angle 2$ because ∠4 and ∠2 are vertical angles. Therefore, by the substitution property, $m\angle 1 = m\angle 2$.

13. See answers in back of book.

Statements	Justifications
1. $q \parallel r$	1. Given
2. $m\angle 1 = m\angle 2$	2. If two ∥ lines are intersected by a transversal, then corresponding ⦞ are = in measure.
3. ∠2 and ∠3 are vertical ⦞.	3. Definition of vertical ⦞
4. $m\angle 2 = m\angle 3$	4. Vertical ⦞ are = in measure.
5. $m\angle 1 = m\angle 3$	5. Substitution property (Steps 2 and 4)

17. Copy and complete this proof.

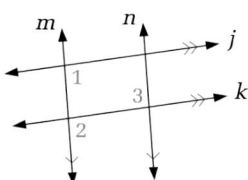

> **Given** Lines j and k are parallel.
> Lines m and n are parallel.

> **Prove** $m \angle 1 = m \angle 3$

Statements

$j \parallel k \xrightarrow{①} m \angle 1 = m \angle 2$

$m \parallel n \xrightarrow{②} m \angle 2 = \underline{?}$

$\Big\}$ $\xrightarrow{③}$ $m \angle 1 = \underline{?}$

Justifications

① $\underline{?}$

② If $\parallel$ lines are intersected by a transversal, then alternate interior $\angle$s are $=$ in measure.

③ Substitution property

18. Suppose a parallelogram has one right angle.

a. What can you conclude about the angles consecutive to this angle? Why?

b. What can you conclude about the angle opposite this angle? Why?

c. What special parallelogram is this?

d. **Writing** Decide whether this is a good definition: A parallelogram is a rectangle if and only if it has at least one right angle. Explain why or why not.

19. In parallelogram $QRST$, $m \angle Q = 123°$. Find the measures of the other angles.

Q $123°$ *T*
R *S*

connection to HEALTH

20. Physicians and physical therapists use a tool called a *goniometer* to measure range of motion.

a. The goniometer indicates that the range of motion of the knee shown is $30°$. The arms of the goniometer make a $150°$ angle. What do you think "range of motion" measures?

b. Find the center of the goniometer. Compare the angle formed by the lines through the center with the angle formed by the inside edges of the tool. Write a proof of why these angles must be equal in measure.

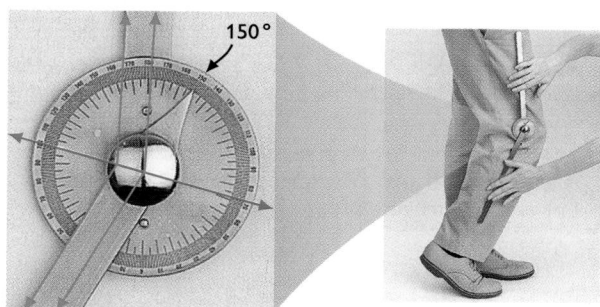

150°

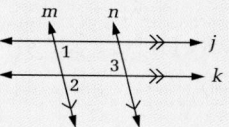

7-8 Proofs about Parallel Lines

421

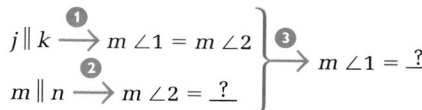

Working on the Unit Project

Each student in a project group should work on Ex. 27 individually. Then they can discuss the situation and compare sketches.

Quick Quiz (7-7 through 7-8)

See page 424.

Ongoing ASSESSMENT
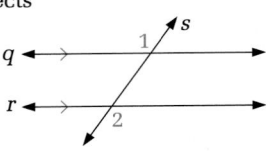

21. a. **Open-ended** Lines q and r are parallel. Transversal s intersects lines q and r. Create a reasonable name for a pair of angles positioned like $\angle 1$ and $\angle 2$.

    b. How do you think the measures of $\angle 1$ and $\angle 2$ are related?

    c. Prove your conjecture using two different forms of proof (paragraph, flow, or two-column).

Review PREVIEW
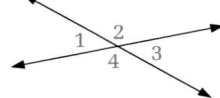

22. The measure of $\angle 1$ is 40°. What are the measures of $\angle 2$, $\angle 3$, and $\angle 4$? *(Section 7-7)*

Solve. *(Section 4-3)*

23. $2x^2 + 7 = 17$

24. $(x - 2)^2 + 5 = 21$

25. $4(x - 3)^2 - 1 = 15$

26. Write the converse of this statement: "If an animal has feathers, then it is a bird." *(Section 1-6)*

7 Working on the Unit Project

27. In the following situation, Carl claims he did not see Rowena waiting for him at 8:00. Suppose you are Carl. Explain why you did not see her. Make a sketch to support your argument.

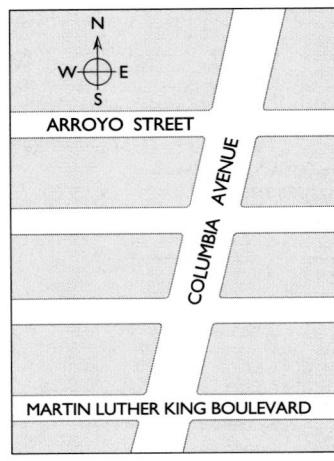

Rowena calls Carl. She says, "On the evening of the reunion, I will wait for you on the southeast corner of Columbia Avenue and Arroyo Street. I will stand on the north side of the block. If you are not there by 8:00, I'll take a taxi."

"OK," Carl answers, "I will be there on time if my car is running."

At 7:00 P.M. on the evening of the reunion, Carl is still fixing his car. He works under the hood for so long that he gets a stiff neck. He can not turn his head more than 70° in either direction.

At last the car starts! Carl drives northeast on Columbia Avenue. As he checks the time, he crosses Martin Luther King Boulevard.

At 8:00 P.M. Carl drives across the intersection of Columbia Avenue and Arroyo Street. He turns his head but does not see Rowena. He drives on to the reunion alone.

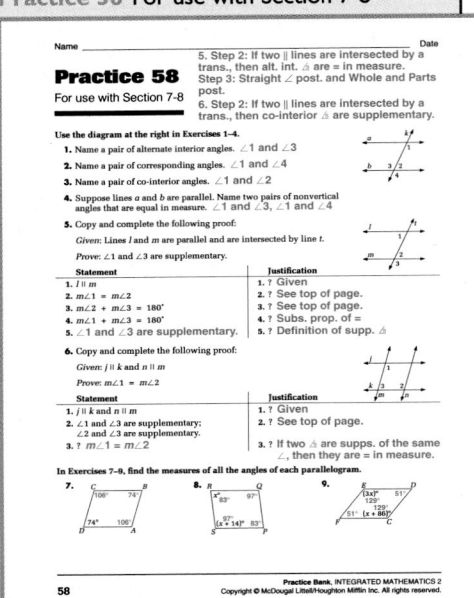

Answers to Exercises and Problems

21. a. Answers may vary. Example: alternate exterior angles

    b. They are equal.

    c. Given: Lines q and r are parallel.
    Prove: $m\angle 1 = m\angle 2$

    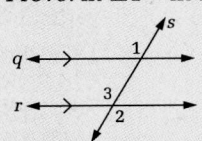

Statements	Justifications
1. $q \parallel r$	1. Given
2. $m\angle 1 = m\angle 3$	2. If two ∥ lines are intersected by a transversal, then corresponding ⦞ are = in measure.
3. ∠2 and ∠3 are vertical ⦞.	3. Definition of vertical ⦞
4. $m\angle 2 = m\angle 3$	4. Vertical ⦞ are = in measure.
5. $m\angle 1 = m\angle 2$	5. Substitution property (Steps 2 and 4)

22. $m\angle 2 = 140°$; $m\angle 3 = 40°$; $m\angle 4 = 140°$

23. $\sqrt{5}, -\sqrt{5}$

24. $-2, 6$

25. $1, 5$

26. If an animal is a bird, then it has feathers.

27. Carl does not see Rowena because he cannot turn his head more than 70°. She is on the south side of the intersection along Arroyo Street rather than on Columbia Avenue, where he is driving. He cannot turn his head enough to spot her.

Completing the Unit Project

Complete your mystery story. Your finished project should include these things:

➤ an outline that contains valid logical arguments leading to the solution of your mystery. Include at least two types of logical argument.

➤ an interesting mystery story with a plot that involves a travel itinerary and applications of at least two of the geometry postulates and theorems from this unit

➤ a written report of readers' reactions to your story

Look Back

How could you revise your story to make it more interesting? to make the mystery more challenging to solve?

Assessment

A scoring rubric for the Unit Project can be found on pages 362 and 363 of this Teacher's Edition and also in the *Project Book*.

Alternative Projects

Project 1: Testing the Validity of Arguments in the News Media

Collect examples of implications in advertisements, newspaper or magazine editorials, and news stories presenting various points of view on a controversial issue. Analyze the implications in the advertisements, editorials, and news stories. Identify arguments based on these implications. (If there are none, write some of your own.) Determine whether or not the arguments are valid. Discuss your reasoning.

Project 2: Analyzing a Mystery Story

Read a mystery story or watch a mystery movie or TV program. List the clues that are given to the reader or viewer. Identify the important premises and implications in the story. Write an outline of the story in the form of a series of valid arguments.

Unit Support Materials

- Unit 7 Cumulative Practice 59
- Unit 7 Study Guide Review
- Unifying Problem 7 in the Problem Bank
- Unit Tests 30 and 31
- Spanish versions of the Unit Tests are in the Assessment Book.
- Teacher's Resources for Transfer Students

Quick Quiz (7-7 through 7-8)

1. Angles C and D are supplements of angle E and $m\angle E = 37°$. What are the measures of angles C and D? [7-7] **$m\angle C = m\angle D = 143°$**

2. What is the difference between a postulate and a theorem? [7-7] **A postulate is assumed to be true. A theorem is proved to be true.**

3. Name all pairs of corresponding angles. [7-8]

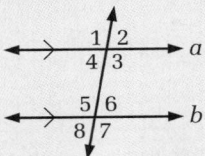

$\angle 2$ and $\angle 6$, $\angle 3$ and $\angle 7$.
$\angle 1$ and $\angle 5$, $\angle 4$ and $\angle 8$

4. Use the figure in Ex. 3 above to find the measure of each angle if $m\angle 1 = 100°$. [7-8]
$m\angle 2 = 80°$, $m\angle 3 = 100°$,
$m\angle 4 = 80°$, $m\angle 5 = 100°$,
$m\angle 6 = 80°$, $m\angle 7 = 100°$,
$m\angle 8 = 80°$

Answers to Unit 7 Review and Assessment

1. baseball, lacrosse ball

2. baseball, lacrosse ball, tennis ball, basketball, soccer ball, volleyball

3. $6.4 < x < 24$

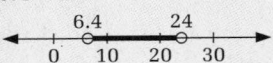

4. Ex. 1; Ex. 2   5. True.

6. If a ball has a mass over 100 g , then it has a leather cover. False; the lacrosse ball is 143 g and has a solid rubber cover.

7.

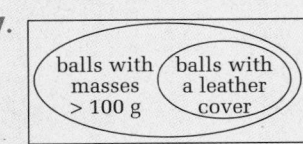

Tanya is working on a science project on the construction of balls used in different sports. She made this database.   7-1

Ball	Diam. (cm)	Mass (g)	Interior Construction	Exterior Construction
baseball	7.3	145	rubber or cork wrapped with yarn	leather cover
basketball	24.0	596	inflated rubber	leather or rubber cover
lacrosse	6.4	143	solid rubber	solid rubber cover
soccer	22.0	425	inflated shell	leather cover
tennis	6.5	57	hollow	cloth cover
volleyball	21.0	270	inflated rubber	leather or rubber cover

For Questions 1 and 2, find every ball that makes each statement true.

1. The ball has a diameter less than 10 cm and a mass greater than 140 g.

2. The ball has a diameter less than 10 cm or a mass greater than 140 g.

3. Use a mathematical statement and a graph to describe the range of diameters that are greater than that of a lacrosse ball and less than that of a basketball.

4. For Exercises 1 and 2, which statement is an example of a conjunction? a disjunction?

5. Is this statement *True* or *False* for the balls in the database?   7-2
Each ball with a leather cover has a mass over 100 g.

6. Write the converse of the statement in Question 5 and decide if it is *True* or *False*. If it is false, give a counterexample.

7. Draw a Venn diagram for the statement in Question 5.

For Questions 8 and 9, decide if the argument is *valid* or *invalid*.   7-3
If the argument is valid, tell which rule of logic was used. If the argument is invalid, tell why.

8. If a triangle is equilateral, then it is equiangular.
Triangle QRS is not equiangular.
Therefore, triangle QRS is not equilateral.

9. I will be home this afternoon or I will be at work. I will be at work. Therefore, I will not be home this afternoon.

10. **Open-ended** Write a valid argument using the chain rule.

11. Write the two implications in this biconditional using symbols and using words: $x^2 = 36 \leftrightarrow x = 6$ 7-4

12. Is the biconditional in Question 11 *True* or *False*? If it is false, rewrite it so it is true.

13. **Writing** Tell how you know that a biconditional is true.

---

8. valid; indirect argument

9. invalid; assumes exclusive *or*

10. Answers may vary. An example is given. Premise: If I go to school, then I will take the history exam. If I take the history exam, then I will pass it. Conclusion: If I go to school, then I will pass the history exam.

11. $x^2 = 36 \rightarrow x = 6$; $x = 6 \rightarrow x^2 = 36$; If the square of a number is 36, then the number is 6; if a number is 6, then its square is 36.

12. False; $x^2 = 36 \leftrightarrow x = 6$ or $x = -6$.

13. A biconditional is true when both of its conditionals are true.

14. a. It is possible to fly from Cairo to Mexico City. From Cairo you can fly to Bombay because Flight 104 goes from Cairo to Bombay. From Bombay you can fly to Calcutta because Flight 201 goes from Bombay to Calcutta. From Calcutta you can fly to Mexico City because Flight 203 goes from Calcutta to Mexico City.

14. Use the flight schedule to prove this statement: **7-5**
You can fly from Cairo to Mexico City.

  a. Write a paragraph proof.

  b. Write a two-column proof.

  c. Tell which rule of logic is used in the two-column proof in part (b).

15. Prove this statement:
If $3a^2 - 5 = 43$ and a is positive, then $a = 4$.   **7-6**

  a. Write a flow proof.

  b. Write a two-column proof.

16. Prove that if vertical angles are supplementary, then they are right angles.   **7-7**

  Given $\angle 1$ and $\angle 2$ are vertical angles.
$\angle 1$ is supplementary to $\angle 2$.

  Prove $\angle 1$ and $\angle 2$ are right angles.

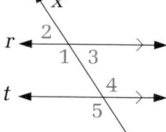

17. **Writing** Explain what postulates, definitions, and theorems are.

18. Write a two-column proof.   **7-8**

  Given Lines j and k are parallel.
Lines l and n are parallel.

  Prove $m \angle 1 = m \angle 3$

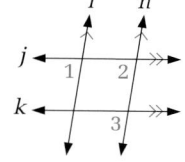

19. Lines r and t are parallel and intersected by line x.
$m \angle 1 = 122°$. Find the measure of each of the other angles.
Give reasons for your answers.

  a. $\angle 2$ **b.** $\angle 3$

  c. $\angle 4$ **d.** $\angle 5$

20. **Self-evaluation** Which method of proof do you prefer: the two-column proof, the flow proof, or the paragraph proof? Why? What features make your preferred form easier for you?

21. **Group Activity** Work in a group of three students. Each student should prove the statements in parts (a)–(c), one student by two-column proof, one student by flow proof, and one student by paragraph proof. Each student should use each method once.

  a. If $9x - 10 = -1$, then $x = 1$.

  b. If $\angle V$ and $\angle W$ are supplementary and $m \angle V = 75°$, then $m \angle W = 105°$.

  c. If lines l and k are parallel and intersected by line n, then $m \angle 1 = m \angle 3$.

  d. For each statement, discuss which method seems easiest to follow. Is there a way to decide which method to use before you start?

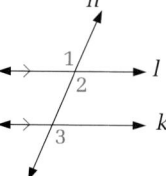

Unit 7 Review and Assessment   **425**

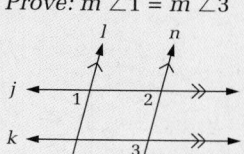

EUCLID AIRLINES

FLIGHT 102: RIO DE JANEIRO → NEW YORK CITY
FLIGHT 104: CAIRO → BOMBAY
FLIGHT 106: BUENOS AIRES → MEXICO CITY
FLIGHT 201: BOMBAY → CALCUTTA
FLIGHT 202: CALCUTTA → BOMBAY
FLIGHT 203: CALCUTTA → MEXICO CITY

---

15. b. *Given:* $3a^2 - 5 = 43$
$a > 0$
Prove: $a = 4$

Statements	Justifications
1. $3a^2 - 5 = 43$	1. Given
2. $3a^2 = 48$	2. Addition property of equality
3. $a^2 = 16$	3. Division property of equality
4. $a = 4$ or $a = -4$	4. Definition of square root
5. $a > 0$	5. Given
6. $a = 4$	6. *Or* rule (Steps 4 and 5)

16–17. See answers in back of book.

18. *Given:* Lines j and k are parallel.
Lines l and n are parallel.
Prove: $m \angle 1 = m \angle 3$

Statements	Justifications
1. $l \parallel n$	1. Given
2. $m \angle 1 = m \angle 2$	2. If two $\parallel$ lines are intersected by a transversal, then corresponding $\angle s$ are = in measure.
3. $j \parallel k$	3. Given
4. $m \angle 2 = m \angle 3$	4. If two $\parallel$ lines are intersected by a transversal, then corresponding $\angle s$ are = in measure.
5. $m \angle 1 = m \angle 3$	5. Substitution property (Steps 2 and 4)

19. 58°; $\angle 2$ and $\angle 1$ form a straight line and so are supplementary angles.
58°; $\angle 3$ and $\angle 1$ form a straight line and so are supplementary angles.
122°; $\angle 4$ and $\angle 1$ are alternate interior angles.
122°; $\angle 5$ and $\angle 1$ are corresponding angles.

20. Answers may vary. An example is given. I prefer the two-column proof because I can easily see the logic and development of the proof. I do not like the flow proof because I think it is harder to follow, especially if it is written horizontally and does not fit on one line. I also find the paragraph proof hard to follow.

21. See answers in back of book.

Answers to Unit 7 Review and Assessment ⋯⋯⋯⋯⋯⋯⋯⋯⋯⋯⋯⋯⋯⋯⋯⋯

b.

Statements	Justifications
1. Cairo	1. Given
2. Bombay	2. Flight 104: Cairo → Bombay
3. Calcutta	3. Flight 201: Bombay → Calcutta
4. Mexico City	4. Flight 203: Calcutta → Mexico City

c. chain rule

15. a. *Given:* $3a^2 - 5 = 43$
$a > 0$
Prove: $a = 4$

Statements

$3a^2 - 5 = 43 \overset{❶}{\rightarrow} 3a^2 = 48 \overset{❷}{\rightarrow} a^2 = 16 \overset{❸}{\rightarrow}$

$\left.\begin{array}{l} a = 4 \text{ or } a = -4 \\ a > 0 \end{array}\right\} \overset{❹}{\rightarrow} a = 4$

Justifications

❶ Addition property of equality

❷ Division property of equality

❸ Definition of square root

❹ *Or* rule

425

Quick Quiz (7-1 through 7-3)

1. Graph the conjunction $x < 4$ and $x \geq -2$ on a number line. [7-1]

   ```
   ←——+——+——+——+——+——+——+——+——→
     -3  -2  -1   0   1   2   3   4
   ```

2. What conclusion can you reach from each set of conditions? [7-1]
   I am in school or at home.
   I am not at home.
   I am in school.

3. Rewrite this implication in if-then form. [7-2]
   All squares have four sides equal in length.
   If a figure is a square, then it has four sides equal in length.

4. Write the converse of if t, then u. [7-2] **If u, then t.**

5. Is the following a *valid* or *invalid* argument? [7-3]
   If a is true, then b is true.
   a is not true.
   $\therefore b$ is not true.
   invalid

6. Name this rule of logic. [7-3]
   If p is true, then q is true.
   q is not true.
   $\therefore p$ is not true.
   indirect argument

Postulates of Algebra

➤ Addition Property of Equality: If the same number is added to equal numbers, the sums are equal. *(p. 402)*
$$a = b \rightarrow a + c = b + c$$

➤ Subtraction Property of Equality: If the same number is subtracted from equal numbers, the differences are equal. *(p. 402)*
$$a = b \rightarrow a - c = b - c$$

➤ Multiplication Property of Equality: If equal numbers are multiplied by the same number, the products are equal. *(p. 402)*
$$a = b \rightarrow ac = bc$$

➤ Division Property of Equality: If equal numbers are divided by the same nonzero number, the quotients are equal. *(p. 402)*
$$a = b \text{ and } c \neq 0 \rightarrow \frac{a}{c} = \frac{b}{c}$$

➤ Reflexive Property: A number is equal to itself. *(p. 402)*
$$a = a$$

➤ Substitution Property: If values are equal, one value may be substituted for the other. *(p. 402)*
$$a = b \rightarrow a \text{ may be substituted for } b.$$

➤ Distributive Property: An expression of the form $a(b + c)$ is equivalent to $ab + ac$. *(p. 402)*
$$a(b + c) = ab + ac$$

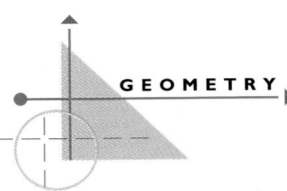

Postulates and Theorems of Geometry

➤ If two angles are supplements of the same angle, then they are equal in measure. *(p. 409)*

➤ If two angles are complements of the same angle, then they are equal in measure. *(p. 409)*

➤ If the sides of an angle form a straight line, then the angle is a straight angle with measure 180°. *(p. 410)*

➤ For any segment or angle, the measure of the whole is equal to the sum of the measures of its non-overlapping parts. *(p. 410)*

➤ Vertical angles are equal in measure. *(p. 411)*

➤ If two parallel lines are intersected by a transversal, then:
  • corresponding angles are equal in measure. *(p. 416)*
  • alternate interior angles are equal in measure. *(p. 417)*
  • co-interior angles are supplementary. *(p. 417)*

➤ If a quadrilateral is a parallelogram, then:
  • consecutive angles are supplementary. *(p. 419)*
  • opposite angles are equal in measure. *(p. 419)*

LOGICAL REASONING
p ↔ q
if - then

➤ A database stores information and may be searched using *and*, *or*, and *not*. *(p. 365)*

➤ A conjunction is true when both statements are true. A disjunction is true when at least one statement is true. *(p. 367)*

➤ Implications can be represented by Venn diagrams. *(p. 367)*

➤ There are several ways to state an implication: *(p. 373)*

If *p*, then *q*.   Every *p* is a *q*.   *p → q*
p implies *q*.   All *p* are *q*.   *p* only if *q*.
q if *p*. *(p. 375)*

➤ Direct Argument: If *p* is true, then *q* is true.
            p is true.
            Therefore, *q* is true. *(p. 380)*

➤ Indirect Argument: If *p* is true, then *q* is true.
                q is not true.
                Therefore, *p* is not true. *(p. 380)*

➤ Chain Rule: If *p* is true, then *q* is true.
            If *q* is true, then *r* is true.
            Therefore, if *p* is true, then *r* is true. *(p. 380)*

➤ *Or* Rule: *p* is true or *q* is true.
            p is not true.
            Therefore, *q* is true. *(p. 380)*

➤ Arguments that do not use rules of logic are invalid. *(p. 381)*

➤ The converse of a true implication is not necessarily true. *(p. 382)*

➤ A biconditional is true when both of its conditionals are true. *(p. 386)*

➤ Good definitions are made of true biconditionals. *(p. 388)*

➤ Proofs may be presented in two-column form, paragraph form, or flow form. *(p. 396)*

➤ The steps of a proof use rules of logic. *(p. 397)*

Quick Quiz (7-4 through 7-6)

1. Is the following statement *True* or *False*? [7-4] If a number *n* contains a factor of 2, then *n* is an even number. True.

2. Write the converse of the statement in Ex. 1 above. [7-4] If *n* is an even number, then *n* contains a factor of 2.

3. Is this statement *True* or *False*? [7-4] A number *n* contains a factor of 2 if and only if *n* is even. True.

4. Name the three different formats for writing a proof. [7-5] two-column, paragraph, flow

5. Prove that if $-4x + 5 = -15$, then $x = 5$. Use the paragraph format. [7-6] If $-4x + 5 = -15$, use the subtraction property of equality to subtract 5 from both sides of the equation: $-4x = -20$. Now, use the division property of equality to divide both sides of $-4x = -20$ by -4. Therefore, $x = 5$.

.... **Key Terms** ....

- **database** (p. 365)
- **negation** (p. 367)
- **implication** (p. 373)
- **valid argument** (p. 380)
- **indirect argument** (p. 380)
- **invalid argument** (p. 381)
- **paragraph proof** (p. 396)
- **square root** (p. 403)
- **m ∠A** (p. 408)
- **transversal** (p. 416)
- **co-interior angles** (p. 416)

- **conjunction** (p. 367)
- **hypothesis** (p. 373)
- **conditional** (p. 373)
- **∴** (p. 380)
- **chain rule** (p. 380)
- **biconditional** (p. 386)
- **flow proof** (p. 396)
- **complementary angles** (p. 408)
- **theorem** (p. 408)
- **corresponding angles** (p. 416)
- **‖** (p. 417)

- **disjunction** (p. 367)
- **conclusion** (pp. 373, 380)
- **premise** (p. 380)
- **direct argument** (p. 380)
- **or rule** (p. 380)
- **two-column proof** (pp. 395–396)
- **postulate** (p. 402)
- **supplementary angles** (p. 408)
- **vertical angles** (p. 410)
- **alternate interior angles** (p. 416)

OVERVIEW

➤ In **Unit 8,** theorems about parallel lines lead to the development of the triangle sum theorem. Students explore theorems about exterior angles, angle bisectors, perpendicular bisectors, and the geometric mean.

➤ Theorems and postulates concerning similar triangles and congruent triangles are developed. Relationships in right triangles are examined, and the study of special right triangles develops into a discussion of trigonometric ratios.

➤ The Unit Project is based on inventing a tool and completing a patent application for it. Properties of triangles are used to examine tools that were used for measurement in ancient civilizations, and those currently in use.

➤ Connections to art, billiards, architecture, Earth's atmosphere, and poetry are some of the topics included in the teaching materials and the exercises.

➤ Graphics calculators are used in Section 8-8 to find the values of trigonometric ratios.

➤ Problem-solving strategies used in Unit 8 include using deductive reasoning, proportions, patterns, diagrams, manipulatives, proofs, and trigonometric ratios.

Internet Resources
Visit our Web site www.mcdougallittell.com for additional resources when teaching this unit.

Unit Objectives

Section	Objectives	NCTM Standards
8-1	• Apply converses of parallel line theorems in proofs.	1, 2, 3, 4, 5, 7
8-2	• Prove the triangle sum theorem and apply it to numerical problems and proofs of other theorems.	1, 2, 3, 4, 5, 7
8-3	• Apply the properties of similar triangles. • Prove that triangles are similar.	1, 2, 3, 4, 5, 7
8-4	• Use two angles and a side in proofs about congruent triangles.	1, 2, 3, 4, 5, 7
8-5	• Use two sides and an angle or three sides in proofs about congruent triangles.	1, 2, 3, 4, 5, 7
8-6	• Apply properties of isosceles triangles, equilateral triangles, and perpendicular bisectors.	1, 2, 3, 4, 5, 7
8-7	• Identify similar right triangles and apply right triangle theorems. • Find geometric means.	1, 2, 3, 4, 5, 7
8-8	• Discover properties of 45°-45°-90° and 30°-60°-90° triangles. • Review the trigonometric ratios: sine, cosine, and tangent.	1, 2, 3, 4, 5, 7, 9

Skills Bank To extend the curriculum and provide practice with skills, you may wish to assign the following topics from the **Skills Bank** ancillary: angles of polygon (for use after Section 8-2), quadrilateral theorems (for use after Section 8-2), properties of proportions (for use after Section 8-3), triangle similarity theorems (for use after Section 8-3), proportional lengths (for use after Section 8-3), indirect proof (for use after Section 8-3), hypotenuse-leg (for use after Section 8-5), triangle inequalities (for use after Section 8-6), converse of the Pythagorean theorem (for use after Section 8-7), and constructions (for use after Section 8-8).

Section	Connections to Prior and Future Concepts
8-1	**Section 8-1** continues the study of parallel lines begun in Section 7-8 of Book 2. Students prove the converses of the theorems from that section. The concept of a transversal is extended to a transversal that is perpendicular to parallel lines.
8-2	**Section 8-2** introduces the unique parallel postulate, which is used to prove that the sum of the measures of the angles of a triangle is 180°. This relationship of the angles of a triangle was explored in Section 2-5 of Book 1.
8-3	**Section 8-3** covers concepts of congruent triangles and similar triangles. Similar triangles were first explored in Section 6-5 of Book 1. Students use AA similarity to prove that two triangles are similar. Students explore overlapping triangles to determine corresponding sides and angles.
8-4	**Section 8-4** introduces using ASA and AAS to prove that two triangles are congruent. Overlapping triangles are covered and using corresponding parts of congruent triangles is introduced as a justification in a proof. The concept of corresponding parts is used in the remainder of Unit 8 of Book 2.
8-5	**Section 8-5** introduces SSS and SAS as ways to prove that two triangles are congruent. Angle bisectors and segment bisectors are introduced. The concept of segment bisectors is extended to perpendicular bisectors in Section 8-6 of Book 2 and is used again in Unit 3 of Book 3.
8-6	**Section 8-6** explores theorems about isosceles and equilateral triangles. The distance formula, introduced in Section 5-2 of Book 2, is used in coordinate proof. The perpendicular bisector theorem builds on concepts from Section 5-5 of Book 2. Other properties of perpendicular bisectors are explored in Unit 3 of Book 3.
8-7	**Section 8-7** extends the concept of similarity to right triangles. The Pythagorean theorem, first used in Section 9-1 of Book 1, is reviewed and the geometric mean is introduced.
8-8	**Section 8-8** continues the study of right triangles to include the special relationships of 45°-45°-90° and 30°-60°-90° triangles. Measurements in right triangles lead to the trigonometric ratios of sine, cosine, and tangent. Sine and cosine ratios were introduced in Section 6-7 of Book 1 and the tangent ratio was introduced in Section 7-1 of Book 1. Trigonometric functions are explored more thoroughly in Units 8 and 10 of Book 3.

Integrating the Strands

Strands	Sections
Number	8-2, 8-7
Algebra	8-1, 8-2, 8-3, 8-4, 8-5, 8-6, 8-7, 8-8
Measurement	8-4, 8-6
Geometry	8-1, 8-2, 8-3, 8-4, 8-5, 8-6, 8-7, 8-8
Trigonometry	8-8
Statistics and Probability	8-5, 8-7
Discrete Mathematics	8-3
Logic and Language	8-1, 8-2, 8-3, 8-4, 8-5, 8-6, 8-7, 8-8

Section Planning Guide

➤ Essential exercises and problems are indicated in boldface.
➤ Ongoing work on the Unit Project is indicated in color.
➤ Exercises and problems that require student research, group work, manipulatives, or graphing technology are indicated in the column headed "Other."

Section	Materials	Pacing	Standard Assignment	Extended Assignment	Other
8-1	T-square, triangle, drawing software	Day 1	1, **2–14**	1, **2–14**	
		Day 2	**15, 19–22**, 23–27, 28	**15**, 16, 17, **19–22**, 23–27, 28	18
8-2	geometric drawing software, protractor, scissors	Day 1	2–7, 8–11, **13–17**	1, **2–7**, 8–12, **13–17**, 18, 20–22, 24, 25	19, 23
		Day 2	**26–34**, 36–43, 44	**26–34**, 36–43, 44	35, 44
8-3	mirror, straw, tape, string, weight, protractor	Day 1	**1–12**	**1–12**	19, 27
		Day 2	**13–15, 20, 21**, 22–26, 27	**13–15**, 16–18, **20, 21**, 22–26, 27	
8-4	geometric drawing software, protractor, straw, string, small wooden pole or stick, small piece of wood, nail	Day 1	**1–7**, 9	**1–7**, 9	8
		Day 2	**10–16**, 18–20, 21, 22	**10–16**, 18–20, 21, 22	17, 21
8-5	compass, straightedge	Day 1	**1–12**, 15–18, 19	**1–12**, 15–18, 19	13, 14
8-6	scissors, straightedge, compass	Day 1	**1–8, 10–16, 18–20**	**1–8, 10–16**, 17, **18–20**	9
		Day 2	**21–26**, 27–31, 32	**21–26**, 27–31, 32	
8-7	scissors	Day 1	**1–8**	**1–8**, 9	
		Day 2	**10–18, 21–25**, 27–29, 30	**10–18**, 20, **21–25**, 27–29, 30	19, 26
8-8	calculator	Day 1	**1–13**, 14	**1–13**, 14–18	
		Day 2	**19–31**, 32–37, 38	**19–31**, 32–37, 38	
Review		**Day 1**	**Unit Review**	**Unit Review**	
Test		**Day 2**	**Unit Test**	**Unit Test**	

Yearly Pacing	Unit 8 Total	Units 1–8 Total	Remaining	Total
	19 days (2 for Unit Project)	132 days	28 days	160 days

Support Materials

➤ See **Project Book** for notes on Unit 8 Project: Patent Your Idea.
➤ "UPP" and "disk" refer to **Using Plotter Plus** booklet and **Plotter Plus** disk.
➤ "TI-81/82" refers to **Using TI-81 and TI-82 Calculators** booklet.
➤ Warm-up exercises for each section are available on **Warm-Up Transparencies**.
➤ "GI" refers to the McDougal Littell Mathpack software Activity Book for **Geometry Inventor**.

Section	Study Guide	Practice Bank	Problem Bank	Activity Bank	Explorations Lab Manual	Assessment Book	Visuals	Technology
8-1	8-1	Practice 60	Set 17	Enrich 53		Quiz 8-1		
8-2	8-2	Practice 61	Set 17	Enrich 54	Master 19	Quiz 8-2	Folder 7	GI Acts. 3, 11, and 32
8-3	8-3	Practice 62	Set 17	Enrich 55	Add. Expl. 11	Quiz 8-3 Test 32	Folder 8	GI Act. 4
8-4	8-4	Practice 63	Set 18	Enrich 56	Master 2	Quiz 8-4		
8-5	8-5	Practice 64	Set 18	Enrich 57	Master 2	Quiz 8-5		
8-6	8-6	Practice 65	Set 18	Enrich 58	Master 2	Quiz 8-6 Test 33		GI Act. 29
8-7	8-7	Practice 66	Set 19	Enrich 59		Quiz 8-7		GI Act. 5
8-8	8-8	Practice 67	Set 19	Enrich 60		Quiz 8-8 Test 34		
Unit 8	Unit Review	Practice 68	Unifying Problem 8	Family Involve 8		Tests 35, 36		

Spanish versions of these tests are on pages 146–149 of the **Assessment Book**.

Form A

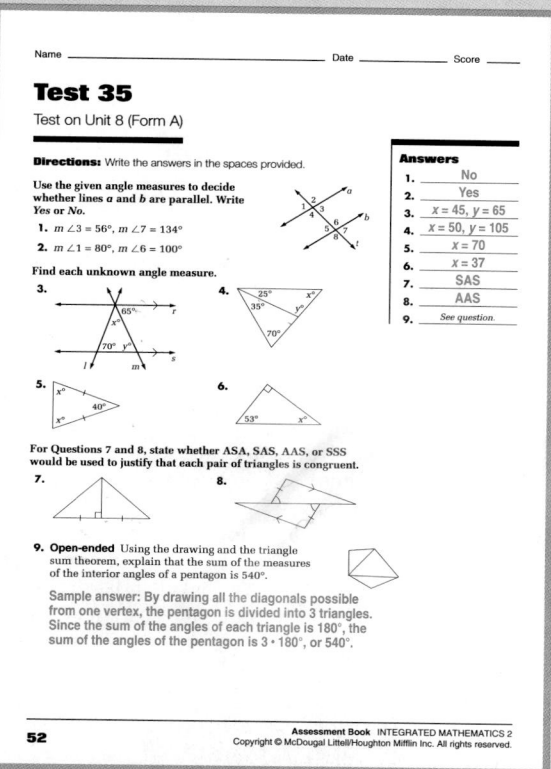

Name _____ Date _____ Score _____

Test 35
Test on Unit 8 (Form A)

Directions: Write the answers in the spaces provided.

Use the given angle measures to decide whether lines a and b are parallel. Write *Yes* or *No*.

1. $m\angle 3 = 56°$, $m\angle 7 = 134°$
2. $m\angle 1 = 80°$, $m\angle 6 = 100°$

Find each unknown angle measure.

3.
4.
5.
6.

For Questions 7 and 8, state whether ASA, SAS, AAS, or SSS would be used to justify that each pair of triangles is congruent.

7.
8.

9. **Open-ended** Using the drawing and the triangle sum theorem, explain that the sum of the measures of the interior angles of a pentagon is 540°.

Sample answer: By drawing all the diagonals possible from one vertex, the pentagon is divided into 3 triangles. Since the sum of the angles of each triangle is 180°, the sum of the angles of the pentagon is 3 · 180°, or 540°.

Answers
1. No
2. Yes
3. $x = 45$, $y = 65$
4. $x = 50$, $y = 105$
5. $x = 70$
6. $x = 37$
7. SAS
8. AAS
9. See question.

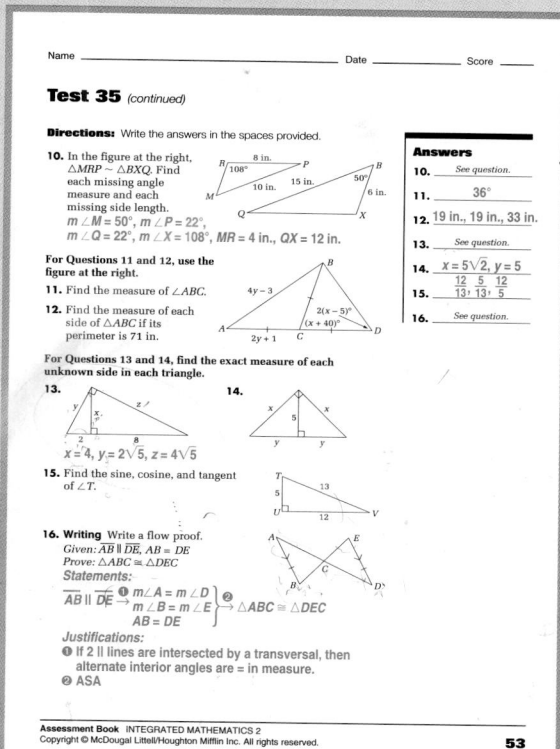

Name _____ Date _____ Score _____

Test 35 (continued)

Directions: Write the answers in the spaces provided.

10. In the figure at the right, $\triangle MRP \sim \triangle BXQ$. Find each missing angle measure and each missing side length.
$m\angle M = 50°$, $m\angle P = 22°$,
$m\angle Q = 22°$, $m\angle X = 108°$, $MR = 4$ in., $QX = 12$ in.

For Questions 11 and 12, use the figure at the right.

11. Find the measure of $\angle ABC$.
12. Find the measure of each side of $\triangle ABC$ if its perimeter is 71 in.

For Questions 13 and 14, find the exact measure of each unknown side in each triangle.

13.
$x = 4$, $y = 2\sqrt{5}$, $z = 4\sqrt{5}$

14.

15. Find the sine, cosine, and tangent of $\angle T$.

16. **Writing** Write a flow proof.
Given: $\overline{AB} \parallel \overline{DE}$, $AB = DE$
Prove: $\triangle ABC \cong \triangle DEC$
Statements:
$$\overline{AB} \parallel \overline{DE} \xrightarrow{\ ①\ } \left. \begin{array}{l} m\angle A = m\angle D \\ m\angle B = m\angle E \\ AB = DE \end{array} \right\} \xrightarrow{\ ②\ } \triangle ABC \cong \triangle DEC$$
Justifications:
① If 2 ∥ lines are intersected by a transversal, then alternate interior angles are = in measure.
② ASA

Answers
10. See question.
11. 36°
12. 19 in., 19 in., 33 in.
13. See question.
14. $x = 5\sqrt{2}$, $y = 5$
15. $\frac{12}{13}, \frac{5}{13}, \frac{12}{5}$
16. See question.

Form B

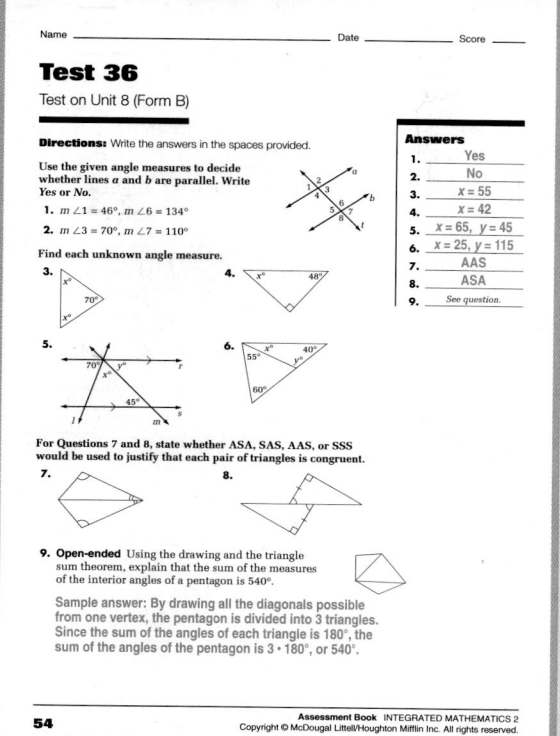

Name _____ Date _____ Score _____

Test 36
Test on Unit 8 (Form B)

Directions: Write the answers in the spaces provided.

Use the given angle measures to decide whether lines a and b are parallel. Write *Yes* or *No*.

1. $m\angle 1 = 46°$, $m\angle 6 = 134°$
2. $m\angle 3 = 70°$, $m\angle 7 = 110°$

Find each unknown angle measure.

3.
4.
5.
6.

For Questions 7 and 8, state whether ASA, SAS, AAS, or SSS would be used to justify that each pair of triangles is congruent.

7.
8.

9. **Open-ended** Using the drawing and the triangle sum theorem, explain that the sum of the measures of the interior angles of a pentagon is 540°.

Sample answer: By drawing all the diagonals possible from one vertex, the pentagon is divided into 3 triangles. Since the sum of the angles of each triangle is 180°, the sum of the angles of the pentagon is 3 · 180°, or 540°.

Answers
1. Yes
2. No
3. $x = 55$
4. $x = 42$
5. $x = 65$, $y = 45$
6. $x = 25$, $y = 115$
7. AAS
8. ASA
9. See question.

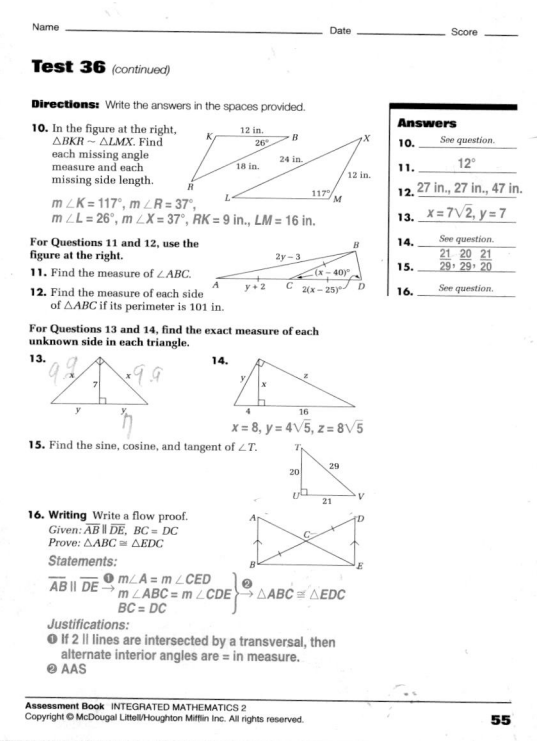

Name _____ Date _____ Score _____

Test 36 (continued)

Directions: Write the answers in the spaces provided.

10. In the figure at the right, $\triangle BKR \sim \triangle LMX$. Find each missing angle measure and each missing side length.
$m\angle K = 117°$, $m\angle R = 37°$,
$m\angle L = 26°$, $m\angle X = 37°$, $RK = 9$ in., $LM = 16$ in.

For Questions 11 and 12, use the figure at the right.

11. Find the measure of $\angle ABC$.
12. Find the measure of each side of $\triangle ABC$ if its perimeter is 101 in.

For Questions 13 and 14, find the exact measure of each unknown side in each triangle.

13.

14.
$x = 8$, $y = 4\sqrt{5}$, $z = 8\sqrt{5}$

15. Find the sine, cosine, and tangent of $\angle T$.

16. **Writing** Write a flow proof.
Given: $\overline{AB} \parallel \overline{DE}$, $BC = DC$
Prove: $\triangle ABC \cong \triangle EDC$
Statements:
$$\overline{AB} \parallel \overline{DE} \xrightarrow{\ ①\ } \left. \begin{array}{l} m\angle A = m\angle CED \\ m\angle ABC = m\angle CDE \\ BC = DC \end{array} \right\} \xrightarrow{\ ②\ } \triangle ABC \cong \triangle EDC$$
Justifications:
① If 2 ∥ lines are intersected by a transversal, then alternate interior angles are = in measure.
② AAS

Answers
10. See question.
11. 12°
12. 27 in., 27 in., 47 in.
13. $x = 7\sqrt{2}$, $y = 7$
14. See question.
15. $\frac{21}{29}, \frac{20}{29}, \frac{21}{20}$
16. See question.

Software Support

McDougal Littell Mathpack
Geometry Inventor

Outside Resources

Books/Periodicals

Macrina, George and Steve Okolica. "Integrating Transformation Geometry into Traditional High School Geometry." *Mathematics Teacher* (December 1992): pp. 716–719.

Activities/Manipulatives

Serra, Michael. *Patty Paper Geometry.* (Investigation Set 8). Key Curriculum Press, 1994.

Software

Cabri Geometry II. Houghton Mifflin-Texas Instruments, 1994. Macintosh (geometric constructions with coordinate geometry capabilities).

Jackiw, Nick. *Geometer's Sketchpad.* Berkeley, CA: Key Curriculum Press, 1994. Macintosh and IBM.

Videos

Project Mathematics. Program No. 3: Similarity. California Institute of Technology, 1993.

PROJECT GOALS

➤ Students invent a tool using at least two geometric ideas from this unit for the construction or operation of the tool.

➤ Students complete a patent application which contains sketches, diagrams, a written description of the tool, how it is made, and how to use it.

➤ Students give a presentation to classmates to convince them that their tool is worthy of a patent.

➤ Students work together in a cooperative group and all contribute to the project's success.

PROJECT PLANNING

Materials List

➤ Poster board or drawing paper
➤ Drawing tools
➤ Markers, pencils

Project Teams

Have students work on the project in groups of four. One way for the individuals in the group to distribute the work is as follows:

1. Coordinator: coordinates group activities, checks numerical facts for accuracy, and checks that the new tool involves an application of at least two geometric ideas from this unit.

2. Researcher: gathers books or articles containing information about patents and checks to ensure that their tool is new, useful, and that it works.

3. Designer: gives a clear and complete description for the creation and use of the tool, using both words and pictures.

4. Patent Applicant: gives a presentation to the class about the tool, how it is made, how it is used, and why it is important.

One day over fifty years ago, a Swiss mountain climber walked through some prickly bushes. As he struggled to remove the tiny thorns that stuck to his pants and socks, the idea for that sticky fastening tape today used on everything from athletic shoes to picture hangers popped into his head.

Inventions come about in many ways. Below are a few stories of how some everyday things began.

hooks — loops

To protect their inventions from being copied, many inventors apply for a patent. A **patent** gives an inventor the exclusive right to make and sell a product for a period of time. To receive a patent, an inventor must prove to the patent office that an invention works and that it is both new and useful.

Levi Strauss invented blue jeans for the miners of California.
1873

This roller skate curiously resembles the popular in-line skates of today.
1823

First century A.D.
Sneakers originated when the Mayans of Central America coated the soles of their feet with the sap of rubber trees.

1870
Brown paper bags are the result of machinery invented by Margaret Knight, who, starting at the age of 12, created over 27 inventions.

Margaret E. Knight Bag Machine Fig. 3

428

Suggested Rubric for Unit Project

4 Students are successful in inventing a tool. In the construction or operation of the tool, they have used geometric ideas correctly. The patent application is well written and includes easy to understand sketches and diagrams. The presentation to the class is effective and the patent is awarded.

3 Students are successful in inventing a tool. Their use of geometric ideas is appropriate. The patent application could be improved. It does not give as complete a description of the tool as it could. The explanation of how the tool works is not entirely clear.

2 Students invent a tool, but it is not clear how its construction or operation is based upon geometric ideas. The patent application is lacking in essential elements. Explanations are incomplete and sketches and diagrams are somewhat inaccurate.

Patent Your Idea

Your project is to invent a tool and write a patent application for it. The tool you design may combine and/or modify features of the tools you read about as you complete the "Working on the Unit Project" exercises.

Use at least two of these ideas in the construction or operation of your tool:

➤ properties of parallel lines

➤ the triangle sum theorem

➤ properties of similar triangles

➤ minimum conditions for congruent triangles

➤ right triangle trigonometry

In your patent application you should:

➤ Describe your invention clearly and completely.

➤ Explain how to make your invention.

➤ Explain how to use your invention.

➤ Include sketches and diagrams.

When all the groups have completed their patent application, have each group make a presention to the class. The class should decide whether to award a patent to each group.

The U.S. FIRST tournament makes heros out of inventors. In this technological superbowl the competing teams consist of working engineers paired with students from high schools across the nation. The 1994 games were won by the "orange cannon" robot designed by the team from Walnut High School in Cincinnati.

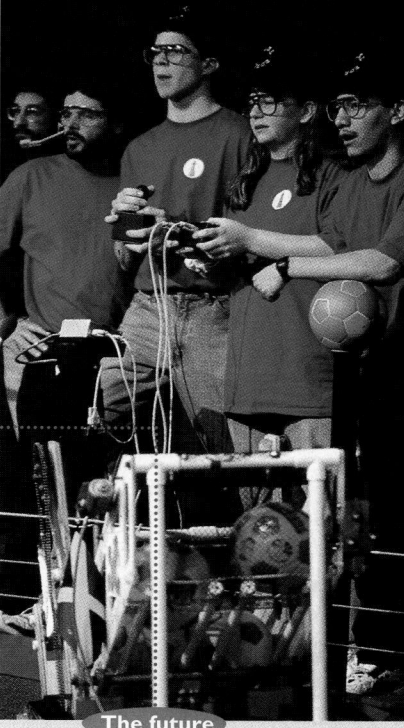

The future

Dedicated inventors working on two continents worked at perfecting the light bulb before Thomas Edison patented it.

1880

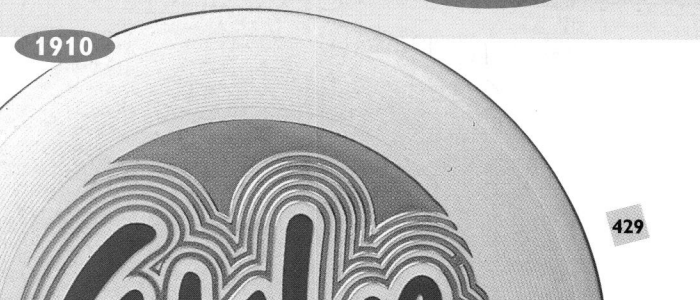

1910

The flying plastic disks so popular today originated when students at Yale University began tossing around pie tins.

429

Suggested Rubric for Unit Project

1 Students are not successful in inventing a tool, or if they have one, it does not work. Geometric ideas are lacking in the construction of the tool. The patent application is inad-equate. The group should be encouraged to speak with the teacher as soon as possible to review their work and to make a new start on the project.

Support Materials

The **Project Book** contains information about the following topics for use with this Unit Project.

➤ Project Description

➤ Teaching Commentary

➤ Working on the Unit Project Exercises

➤ Completing the Unit Project

➤ Assessing the Unit Project

➤ Alternative Projects

➤ Outside Resources

Students Acquiring English

Since the process of inventing a tool and applying for a patent draws upon kinesthetic and visual modalities as well as language skills, it offers excellent opportunities for students acquiring English to demonstrate mathematical and creative skills. Offer students the opportunity to incorporate words from their native language in the description of their new tools.

ADDITIONAL BACKGROUND

Multicultural Note

The Mayan civilization of southeastern Mexico and northern Central America has been in existence for more than 2,800 years. At various times, the Mayan Empire encompassed the Yucatan Peninsula in present-day Mexico, all of Guatemala and Belize, and parts of El Salvador and Honduras. Mayan culture reached its high point between A.D. 300 and 900, when many of the terraced pyramids were constructed. In that age, the Maya developed accurate solar and lunar calendars, gained considerable knowledge in astronomy, and developed an efficient mathematical system. They also developed a hieroglyphic writing system, which they used to keep scientific records.

U.S. Patent Office

By U.S. law, a patent may be granted for a term of 20 years and is restricted mainly to patents for inventions. Applications are usually considered in the order in which they are received. Patents are not granted for printed matter, for methods of doing business, or for devices for which claims contrary to physical laws are made. For example, applications for a perpetual motion machine have been made periodically, but no patent will be issued because the concept of perpetual motion violates known laws of physics.

The German naturalist, Alexander von Humboldt (1769–1859), is credited with saying that an invention goes through three stages: (1) doubt of its existence, (2) denial of its importance, and (3) credit for its discovery going to someone else. ....●

ALTERNATIVE PROJECTS

Project 1, page 497

Build the Tool You Design

Design and build a working model of a tool. Use the same guidelines presented in the Unit Project.

Project 2, page 497

A Pantograph

Build a pantograph, explain why it works, who would use the tool, and use it to enlarge or reduce a drawing.

Project 3, page 497

CAD Software

Use available CAD (computer-assisted design) software to design a tool. Apply the same guidelines presented in the Unit Project.

Getting Started

For this project you should work in a group of four students. Here are some ideas to help you get started.

☞ You may wish to obtain a book or article about patents in order to review some existing patents.

☞ In your group discuss how you will use words and pictures in your patent application to help make your explanations clear and complete. You may wish to look over some car repair manuals or assembly instructions to get ideas that you could apply in your patent application.

☞ Plan to meet later to discuss the features of the tool and which ideas from geometry will be applied in building or using it.

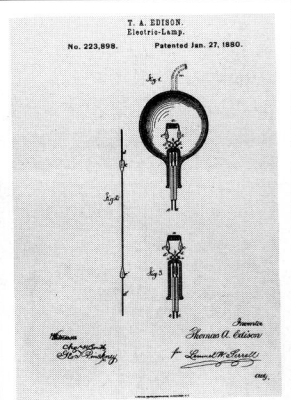

These pages are from the patent issued to Thomas A. Edison for the "electric lamp" on January 27, 1880.

 **Working on the Unit Project**

Your work in Unit 8 will help you design a tool and apply for a patent.

Related Exercises:

Section 8-1, Exercise 28
Section 8-2, Exercise 44
Section 8-3, Exercise 27
Section 8-4, Exercises 21, 22
Section 8-5, Exercise 19
Section 8-6, Exercise 32
Section 8-7, Exercise 30
Section 8-8, Exercise 38

Alternative Projects p. 497

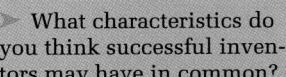 **Can We Talk**

➤ What characteristics do you think successful inventors may have in common?

➤ Some inventions remain "trade secrets." Do you think it is better to keep an invention secret or to patent it? Why?

➤ New products are being invented all the time. What new inventions have you heard or read about lately?

➤ Fewer than one out of a hundred patented inventions ever reach the market. What factors do you think may be responsible for this?

➤ The U.S. FIRST tournament is a competition modeled on a sporting event. It was created as a way of increasing respect for science and scientists. What other ways can you think of to accomplish the same goal?

Unit 8 Similar and Congruent Triangles

Answers to Can We Talk? ···

➤ Answers may vary. Examples are given. They have a desire to solve problems, are curious, have a strong determination, and enjoy helping people.

➤ Answers may vary. An example is given. I think it is better to patent an invention because then others can benefit from your knowledge, ingenuity, and hard work.

➤ Answers may vary. Examples are given. A cellular telephone that fits in your pocket, a camcorder the size of a person's hand, laser technology being used for medicine, cordless screwdrivers, and a refrigerator that uses thermal or heat energy to keep the things inside it cool.

➤ Answers may vary. An example is given. It takes more than an idea to bring a new product to the market. Most of the work involved comes after someone has built or thought of an invention and gotten a patent for it.

➤ Answers may vary. Examples are given. Visit places where scientists work, have scientists come to your school to talk about what they do, participate in a Science Fair in your school or town, or investigate ways that science is involved in the things that interest you.

Converses and Parallel Lines

T for Two

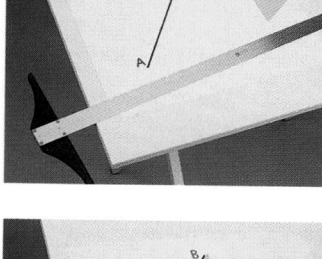

T-squares and triangles are drafting tools used to draw lines and
angles. The methods for using the tools are based on relationships from geometry.

With a T-square and a triangle, you can draw a line *CD* parallel
to another line *AB*.

1 Draw line *AB*.

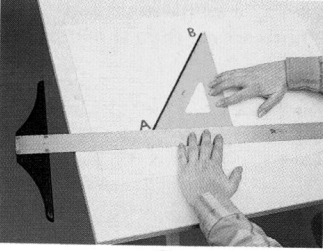

2 Position the tools so that
the hypotenuse of the triangle lines up with line *AB*.

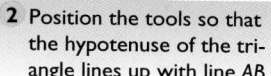

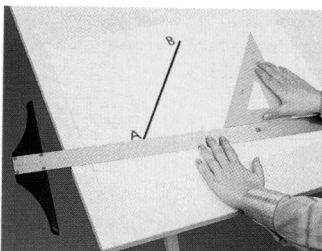

3 Slide the triangle along
the T-square.

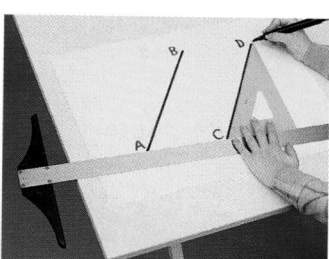

4 Draw line *CD* parallel
to line *AB*.

The method assumes that when corresponding angles are equal
in measure, the lines will be parallel. This assumption is true
and is stated as a postulate.

A POSTULATE ABOUT PARALLEL LINES

Postulate 11 If two lines are intersected by a transversal and
corresponding angles are equal in measure, then
the lines are parallel.

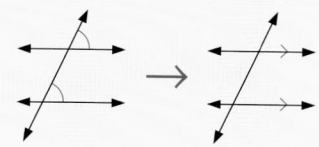

PLANNING

Objectives and Strands
See pages 428A and 428B.

Spiral Learning
See page 428B.

Materials List
➤ T-square
➤ Triangle
➤ Drawing software

Recommended Pacing
Section 8-1 is a two-day lesson.

Day 1

Pages 431–433: Opening paragraph through Theorems About
Parallel Lines, *Exercises 1–14*

Day 2

Pages 433–435: Middle of page
433 through Look Back, *Exercises
15–28*

Extra Practice
See pages 627–628.

Warm-Up Exercises
💡 Warm-Up Transparency 8-1

Support Materials
➤ Practice 60
➤ Enrichment 53 in the Activity
Bank
➤ Study Guide 8-1
➤ Problem Set 17
➤ McDougal Littell Mathpack
software: *Geometry Inventor*
➤ Quiz 8-1

TEACHING

Postulates 10 and 11 are converses of one another and can be stated as a biconditional: Two lines intersected by a transversal are parallel if and only if their corresponding angles are equal in measure. It may help some students to remember Postulates 10 and 11 by using the biconditional form.

Additional Sample

S1 Tell whether each pair of lines is parallel or not and why.

a.

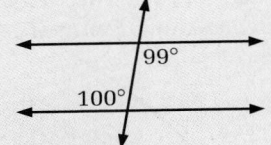

The lines are not parallel because the alternate interior angles are not equal in measure.

b.

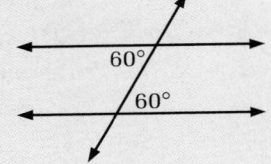

The lines are parallel because the alternate interior angles are equal in measure.

Talk it Over

1. In steps 1–4 on page 431, line *CD* is drawn parallel to line *AB*. Where are the corresponding angles that are equal in measure?

2. **a.** State the converse of Postulate 11.

   b. Look back at page 416 of Unit 7. Does your converse match Postulate 10?

3. **a.** State the converse of Theorem 7.4: If two parallel lines are intersected by a transversal, then alternate interior angles are equal in measure.

   b. State the converse of Theorem 7.5: If two parallel lines are intersected by a transversal, then co-interior angles are supplementary.

Watch Out!
The converse of a postulate or theorem is not necessarily true, but it is worthwhile to investigate converses. You may discover another theorem.

You can use Postulate 11 to investigate whether the converses you stated above are true.

Sample 1

Prove that if two lines are intersected by a transversal and alternate interior angles are equal in measure, then the lines are parallel.

Sample Response

Given Transversal *t* intersects lines *k* and *l*.
$m \angle 1 = m \angle 2$

State what is given and what you need to prove about your diagram.

Prove $k \parallel l$

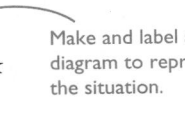

Make and label a diagram to represent the situation.

Plan Ahead

The lines are parallel if a pair of corresponding angles are equal in measure. Show that corresponding angles 1 and 3 are equal in measure.

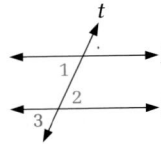

Show Your Reasoning

Method ❶ Write a two-column proof.

Statements	**Justifications**
1. $m \angle 1 = m \angle 2$	1. Given
2. $m \angle 2 = m \angle 3$	2. Vertical ∡ are = in measure.
3. $m \angle 1 = m \angle 3$	3. Substitution property (Steps 1 and 2)
4. $k \parallel l$	4. If two lines are intersected by a transversal and corresponding ∡ are = in measure, then the lines are ∥.

Answers to Talk it Over

1. $\angle BAC$ and the angle adjacent to $\angle DCA$

2. **a.** If two parallel lines are intersected by a transversal, then corresponding angles are equal in measure.

   b. Yes.

3. **a.** If two lines are intersected by a transversal and alternate interior angles are equal in measure, then the lines are parallel.

   b. If two lines are intersected by a transversal and co-interior angles are supplementary, then the lines are parallel.

**Method ② ** Write a paragraph proof.

> Alternate interior angles ∠1 and ∠2 are equal in measure
> (given). Since ∠2 and ∠3 are vertical angles, they are also
> equal in measure. Substitute m ∠3 for m ∠2 in the statement
> m ∠1 = m ∠2, and ∠1 must be equal in measure to ∠3. Since
> the corresponding angles ∠1 and ∠3 are equal in measure,
> the lines intersected by the transversal are parallel, so k ∥ l.

Sample 1 proves the first theorem below. You will prove the
second theorem in Exercise 12.

THEOREMS ABOUT PARALLEL LINES

Theorem 8.1 If two lines are intersected by a transversal and
alternate interior angles are equal in measure,
then the lines are parallel.

Theorem 8.2 If two lines are intersected by a transversal and
co-interior angles are supplementary, then the
lines are parallel.

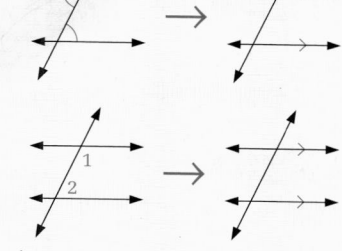

m ∠1 + m ∠2 = 180°

·····▸ **Now you are ready for:**
Exs. 1–14 on pp. 435–437

Drafters may also use perpendicular lines to draw parallel lines.
The triangle tool is a right triangle.

1 Place a leg of the
right triangle along
the T-square.

2 Draw line *EF* along the
other leg.

3 Slide the right triangle
along the T-square.

4 Draw line *GH*. Then line *GH*
is parallel to line *EF*.

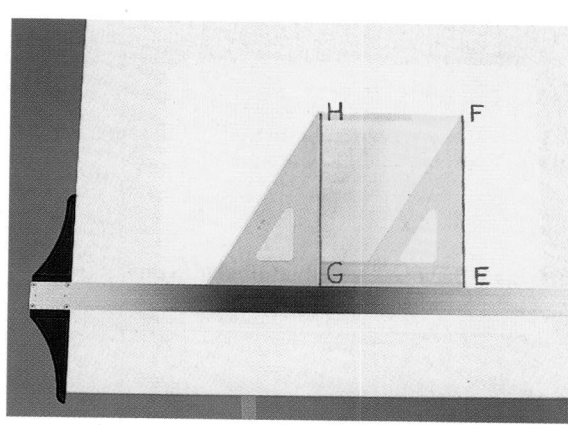

8-1 Converses and Parallel Lines

Communication: Discussion

The Talk it Over questions and
the Watch Out! on page 432
can serve as a springboard to a
discussion about the truth or
falsity of converses. You may
want to have students state theorems and postulates that are
true but whose converses are
false.

Error Analysis

In order to apply Theorems 8.1
and 8.2 correctly, students
need to be able to identify the
alternate interior angles or the
co-interior angles. If this is a
problem for some students,
refer them back to Unit 7,
page 416, where transversals
and special angle pairs are
introduced.

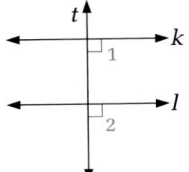
Additional Sample

S2 Line *t* is perpendicular to lines *p* and *q*. What is the degree measure of angles 1–8?

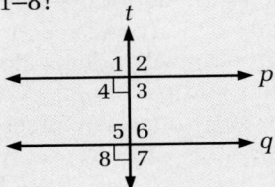

Each of the right angles has a degree measure of 90°.

Reasoning

Some students may be confused by the statement of Theorem 8.4 as the converse of Theorem 8.3 because of its wording. Students should try to write the converse of Theorem 8.3 without looking at their books. Then they will have to think through the meaning of the converse and will be led to the way it is expressed in the book.

Look Back

Students should write down their answers and include them in their notebooks or journals for future reference. ⋯⋯⋯●

Write a flow proof to prove that if two lines are perpendicular to the same transversal, then they are parallel.

Sample Response

Given Transversal *t* intersects lines *k* and *l*.
$k \perp t, l \perp t$

Prove $k \parallel l$ ⟵ Read "is perpendicular to."

Plan Ahead

The lines are parallel if a pair of corresponding angles are equal in measure. Show that angles 1 and 2 are equal in measure.

Show Your Reasoning

Statements

$$k \perp t \xrightarrow{①} m \angle 1 = 90° \,\Big|②$$
$$l \perp t \xrightarrow{①} m \angle 2 = 90° \,\Big\} \xrightarrow{} m \angle 1 = m \angle 2 \xrightarrow{③} k \parallel l$$

Justifications

① Definition of perpendicular lines
② Substitution property
③ If two lines are intersected by a transversal and corresponding ∠s are = in measure, then the lines are ∥.

The statement proved in Sample 2 is stated as Theorem 8.3. Theorem 8.4 is related and will be proved in Exercise 15.

$X_{(} \angle ab$

PERPENDICULAR AND PARALLEL LINES

Theorem 8.3 If two lines are perpendicular to the same transversal, then they are parallel.

Theorem 8.4 If a transversal is perpendicular to one of two parallel lines, then it is perpendicular to the other one also.

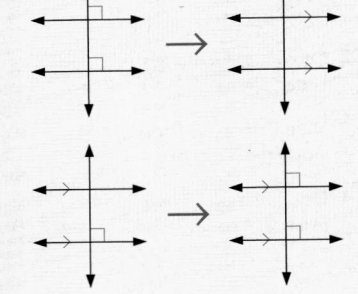

Answers to Look Back ⋯⋯⋯

The lines are parallel if corresponding angles are equal in measure, alternate interior angles are equal in measure, co-interior angles are supplementary, or if the transversal forms right angles with both lines.

▸ Now you are ready for:
Exs. 15–28 on pp. 437–438

Look Back ◂

Two lines are intersected by a transversal. Describe the angle relationships that can be used to decide whether the two lines are parallel.

8-1 Exercises and Problems

1. **Reading** How were corresponding angles used in Sample 1 to prove Theorem 8.1 about alternate interior angles?

For each figure, state a postulate or theorem that could be used to prove that lines *l* and *m* are parallel.

2.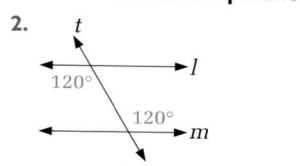
120°
120°

3.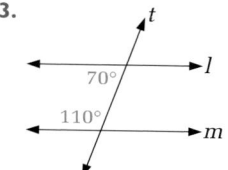
70°
110°

4.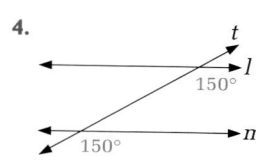
150°
150°

5.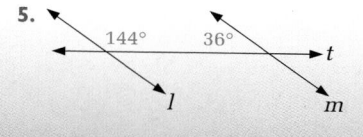
144°   36°

6.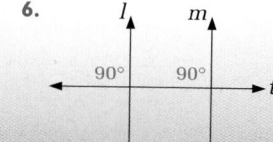
90°   90°

7.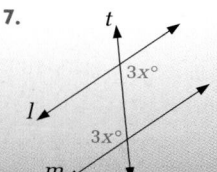
$3x°$
$3x°$

In the Arctic, the prevailing winds blow the snow to form parallel ridges called sastrugi. For centuries the Inuits have used this natural phenomenon to give them direction as they traveled along the frozen Arctic plain.

8-1 Converses and Parallel Lines

435

APPLYING

Suggested Assignment

Day 1

Standard 1–14

Extended 1–14

Day 2

Standard 15, 19–28

Extended 15–17, 19–28

Integrating the Strands

Algebra Ex. 27

Geometry Exs. 1–26, 28

Logic and Language Exs. 1–28

Multicultural Note

The traditional means of Inuit transportation are the kayak, the umiak, and the dog sled. The kayak is a light, canoe-like hunting boat designed for one rider. Its wooden frame is completely covered with sealskin except for a round opening at its center. Kayaks built in the fashion that is traditional in Greenland, northern Canada, and Alaska become watertight when the sealskin is laced tightly around the rider's waist. The umiak is a large, open boat (about 30 ft long and 8 ft wide) used to transport entire families and their belongings. It is usually made of a wooden frame covered with walrus skins. The dog sled is an open sled drawn by a team of native dogs. It is designed for travel over icy and snow-covered land. Today motorboats and snowmobiles are also important modes of travel for native Arctic peoples.

Answers to Exercises and Problems

1. We are given that a pair of alternate interior angles are equal in measure. By introducing a third angle, vertical to ∠2 and thus equal in measure to it, we showed that this angle was equal in measure to its corresponding angle and so the lines are parallel.

2. Theorem 8.1; If two lines are intersected by a transversal and alternate interior ∠s are = in measure, then the lines are ∥.

3. Theorem 8.2; If two lines are intersected by a transversal and co-interior ∠s are supplementary, then the lines are ∥.

4. Parallel Lines Postulate; If two lines are intersected by a transversal and corresponding ∠s are = in measure, then the lines are ∥.

5. Theorem 8.2; If two lines are intersected by a transversal and co-interior ∠s are supplementary, then the lines are ∥.

6. Theorem 8.3; If two lines are ⊥ to the same transversal, then they are parallel *or* Parallel Lines Postulate; If two lines are intersected by a transversal and corresponding ∠s are = in measure, then the lines are ∥.

7. Theorem 8.1; If two lines are intersected by a transversal and alternate interior ∠s are = in measure, then the lines are ∥.

435

436

For each of Exercises 8–11, use the given angle measures to decide whether lines *v* and *w* are parallel. Write *Yes* or *No.*

8. $m \angle 1 = 24°$, $m \angle 2 = 156°$

9. $m \angle 1 = 35°$, $m \angle 2 = 35°$

10. $m \angle 1 = 3x°$, $m \angle 2 = (180 - 3x)°$

11. $m \angle 1 = y°$, $m \angle 2 = (90 - y)°$

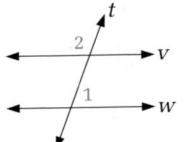

12. Copy and complete this proof of Theorem 8.2: If two lines are intersected by a transversal and co-interior angles are supplementary, then the lines are parallel.

> **Given** Transversal $\overleftrightarrow{EG}$ intersects line a at E and line b at F. $\angle 1$ and $\angle 2$ are supplementary.

> **Prove** $a \parallel b$

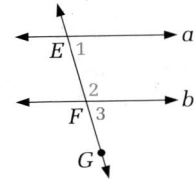

Statements	**Justifications**
1. $\angle 1$ and $\angle 2$ are supplementary.	1. Given
2. $m \angle 1 + m \angle 2 = 180°$	2. _?_
3. $m \angle EFG = 180°$	3. If the sides of an angle form a straight line, then the angle is a straight angle with measure 180°.
4. $m \angle EFG = m \angle 2 + m \angle \underline{?}$	4. For any angle, the measure of the whole is equal to the sum of the measures of its non-overlapping parts.
5. $m \angle 2 + m \angle 3 = 180°$	5. _?_ (Steps 3 and 4)
6. $m \angle 1 + m \angle 2 = m \angle 2 + m \angle 3$	6. _?_ (Steps _?_ and _?_)
7. $m \angle 1 = m \angle 3$	7. _?_
8. $a \parallel b$	8. _?_

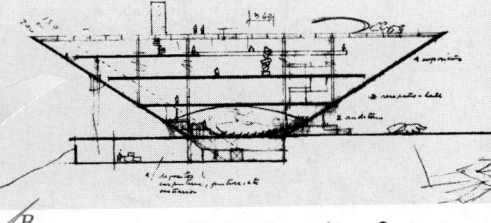

13. Copy and complete the flow proof.

> **Given** $\overrightarrow{MQ} \parallel \overline{SR}$
> $m \angle 1 = m \angle 2$

> **Prove** $m \angle 3 = m \angle 4$

Statements

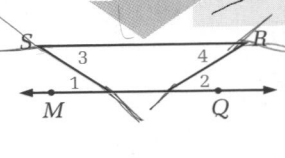

$\overrightarrow{MQ} \parallel \overline{SR}$ **①** $\begin{cases} m \angle 3 = m \angle \underline{?} \\ m \angle 4 = m \angle \underline{?} \\ m \angle 1 = m \angle 2 \end{cases}$ **②** $\rightarrow$ $m \angle \underline{?} = m \angle \underline{?}$

Justifications

① _?_

② _?_

In the mid-1950s, Brazilian architect Oscar Niemeyer drew this cross section for a proposed Modern Art Museum in Caracas, Venezuela.

436   **Unit 8** Similar and Congruent Triangles

---

14. Prove that lines parallel to the same line are parallel to each other.

> **Given** Transversal t intersects lines a, b, and c.
> $a \parallel b$, $c \parallel b$

> **Prove** $a \parallel c$

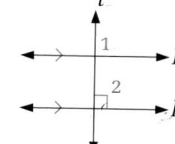

15. a. Copy and complete this proof of Theorem 8.4: If a transversal is perpendicular to one of two parallel lines, then it is perpendicular to the other one also.

> **Given** Transversal t intersects lines k and l.
> $k \parallel l$, $t \perp l$

> **Prove** $t \perp k$

Statements	**Justifications**
1. $k \parallel l$	1. __?__
2. $m \angle 1 = m \angle 2$	2. __?__
3. $t \perp l$	3. __?__
4. $m \angle 2 = 90°$	4. __?__
5. $m \angle 1 = 90°$	5. Substitution property (Steps __?__ and __?__)
6. $t \perp k$	6. __?__

b. Rewrite the two-column proof in part (a) as a paragraph proof.

---

connection to **INDUSTRIAL TECHNOLOGY**

A drafting student places a T-square parallel to the bottom edge of a rectangular sheet of paper.

16. The student then draws a line by placing a leg of a right triangle against the T-square and drawing along the other leg. How does the student know that the line drawn will be parallel to the left and right edges of the paper?

17. Suppose the student places the hypotenuse of the triangle along the T-square and draws a line along one leg. Will the line drawn be parallel to the left and right edges of the paper? Explain why or why not.

18. TECHNOLOGY Use drawing software to draw two parallel lines. Explain how you know that they are parallel.

8-1 Converses and Parallel Lines

437

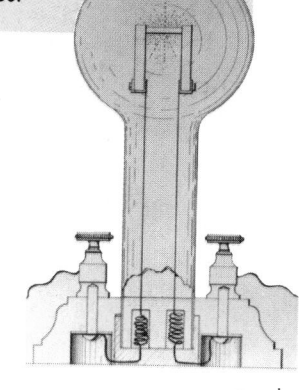

Answers to Exercises and Problems

Justifications
1. Given
2. If two $\parallel$ lines are intersected by a transversal, then corresponding $\angle$s are = in measure.
3. Substitution property (Step 2)
4. If two lines are intersected by a transversal and corresponding $\angle$s are = in measure, then the lines are $\parallel$.

15, 16. See answers in back of book.

17. No. If you extend the lines representing the edges of the paper and draw the line along the leg, the line drawn along the leg will intersect both edges of the paper. This is because the angle formed by the T-square and the triangle cannot be 90° since the right angle is opposite the edge of the T-square. Since the line intersects both edges of the paper, it is not $\parallel$ to them.

18. The lines are parallel because they are spaced exactly the same distance apart.

Practice 60 For use with Section 8-1

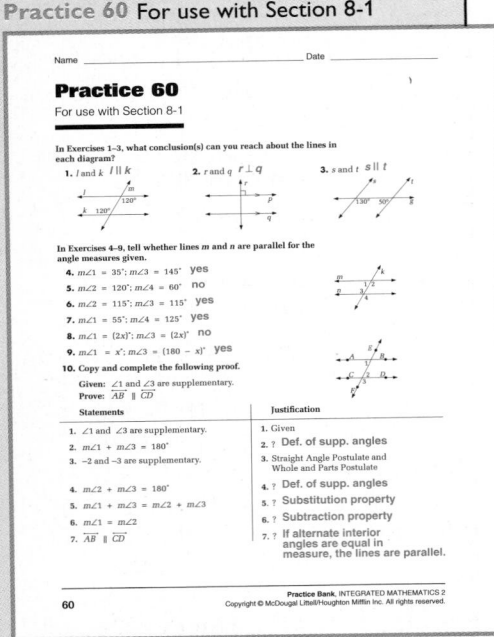

19. **Given** $\overline{GH} \perp \overline{HJ}$
    $m \angle KJH = 90°$
    Prove $\overline{GH} \parallel \overline{KJ}$

20. **Given** $\overleftrightarrow{LM} \parallel \overleftrightarrow{PQ}$
    $m \angle MRS = 90°$
    Prove $\overleftrightarrow{PQ} \perp \overleftrightarrow{RS}$

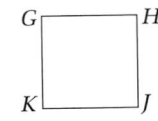  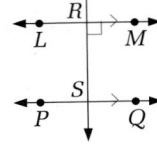

21. Prove that a quadrilateral with four right angles is a parallelogram.

22. **Writing** In Section 7-8, Exercise 18 stated that every parallelogram with at least one right angle is a rectangle. Is it accurate to say that every quadrilateral with at least one right angle is a rectangle? Explain.

Ongoing ASSESSMENT

23. **Open-ended** Write a statement for an angle relationship that you think produces parallel lines but has not been discussed in this section. Prove your statement using a flow proof.

Review PREVIEW

24. In a parallelogram *ABCD*, $m \angle D = 75°$. Find the measures of the other angles. *(Section 7-8)*

For Exercises 25 and 26, tell whether each implication is *True* or *False*. If it is false, give a counterexample. *(Sections 5-1, 7-2)*

25. If a figure has four sides, then it is a parallelogram.

26. All squares are kites.

27. Solve $5x + 2x + 40 = 180$. *(Toolbox Skill 13)*

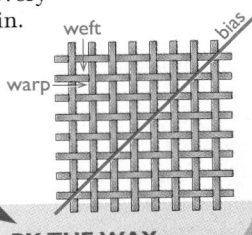

BY THE WAY...

Woven fabric will not stretch very much if it is pulled along a weft thread or along a warp thread. Fabric that is pulled along the bias, however, will stretch.

Mademoiselle Madeleine Vionnet, a dressmaker in Paris, introduced the bias cut. The dress shown was designed by Vionnet in 1926.

Working on the Unit Project

As you complete Exercise 28, think about how you can include properties of parallel and perpendicular lines in the tool you design.

28. A *parallel ruler* is an instrument used by navigators to draw parallel lines on navigation charts. It consists of two rulers joined by two clips. The clips rotate at the points where they are attached. This allows the two rulers to move apart while still remaining parallel.

   a. What properties of parallel lines could the tool-maker use when fastening the clips to the rulers? Can the tool-maker check only one property to verify that the rulers are parallel, or should all the properties be checked?

   b. The rulers are parallel in any position. What conjecture can you make about the clips in any position?

   c. What would you need to know to prove your conjecture from part (b)?

438   **Unit 8** Similar and Congruent Triangles

Answers to Exercises and Problems

19. *Given:* $\overline{GH} \perp \overline{HJ}$; $m \angle KJH = 90°$
    Prove: $\overline{GH} \parallel \overline{KJ}$
    Statements
    1. $\overline{GH} \perp \overline{HJ}$; $m \angle KJH = 90°$
    2. $\overline{KJ} \perp \overline{HJ}$
    3. $\overline{GH} \parallel \overline{KJ}$
    Justifications
    1. Given
    2. Definition of $\perp$ lines
    3. If two lines are $\perp$ to the same transversal, then they are $\parallel$.

20. *Given:* $\overleftrightarrow{LM} \parallel \overleftrightarrow{PQ}$;
    $m \angle MRS = 90°$
    Prove: $\overleftrightarrow{PQ} \perp \overleftrightarrow{RS}$
    Statements
    1. $\overleftrightarrow{LM} \parallel \overleftrightarrow{PQ}$
    2. $\angle MRS$ and $\angle QSR$ are supplementary.
    3. $m \angle MRS + m \angle QSR = 180°$
    4. $m \angle MRS = 90°$
    5. $90° + m \angle QSR = 180°$
    6. $m \angle QSR = 90°$
    7. $\overleftrightarrow{PQ} \perp \overleftrightarrow{RS}$
    Justifications
    1. Given
    2. If two $\parallel$ lines are intersected by a transversal, then co-interior $\angle$s are supplementary.
    3. Definition of supplementary
    4. Given
    5. Substitution property (Steps 3 and 4)
    6. Subtraction property of equality
    7. Definition of perpendicular

21–28. See answers in back of book.

Focus
Prove the triangle sum theorem and apply it to numerical problems and proofs of other theorems.

On the Level

The airplane instrument shown is called an *artificial horizon*, or *attitude indicator*. The instrument shows the position of the plane with respect to the horizon. There is only one position at which the plane is flying level and the plane's wings are parallel to the horizon.

horizon line

planes's wings

The photo shows that the left wing of the plane is up (the plane is "banking" to the right).

> **Talk it Over**
>
> 1. a. On a piece of paper, draw any line and any point not on the line.
>
>   b. Do you think there is a line through your point that is parallel to the line you drew?
>
>   c. Do you think there is more than one parallel line through your point?

THE UNIQUE PARALLEL POSTULATE

Postulate 12 Through a point not on a given line, there is one and only one line parallel to the given line.

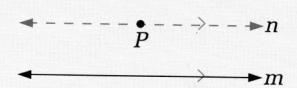

Folding Method

Tearing Method

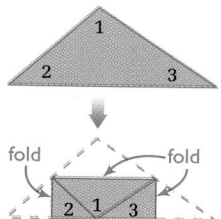

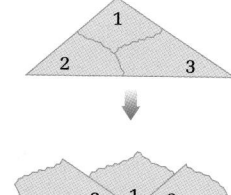

In an earlier course, you probably explored the relationship between angles in triangles by folding or tearing paper triangles.

Inductive reasoning led you to the conjecture that the sum of the measures of the angles of a triangle is 180°. The unique parallel postulate will help you prove this by deductive reasoning.

8-2 The Triangle Sum Theorem

439

Answers to Talk it Over

1. a. Check students' work.
   b. Yes.
   c. No.

Talk it Over

In question 1(c), students can try to draw more than one parallel line through their point; they will see that this is impossible and therefore accept Postulate 12 as a true statement.

Mathematical Procedures

Students are introduced to the notion of a *helping line* in Sample 1. This is probably their first experience involving the introduction of a new line to write a proof. This procedure is sometimes necessary in geometry, and since *when* and *how* to add such a line is often not obvious, proofs requiring a new line can be rather challenging.

Additional Sample

S1 a. Triangle *ABC* is an equilateral triangle. What is the measure of each angle? **60°**

b. Triangle *RST* is an isosceles right triangle. What is the measure of each angle if $m \angle R =$ 90°? *m∠ R = 90°, m∠ S = 45°, m∠ T = 45°*

Research

Postulate 12 is the most famous postulate in the history of geometry. It has played a pivotal role in the development of both Euclidean and non-Euclidean geometries. A brief research report on the history of this postulate by a few students should prove to be very interesting.

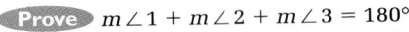
Prove that the sum of the measures of the angles of a triangle is 180°.

Sample Response

Given △*ABC*

Prove $m \angle 1 + m \angle 2 + m \angle 3 = 180°$

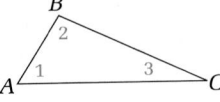

Plan Ahead

Draw a helping line through *B* parallel to $\overline{AC}$. Then use alternate interior angles and the whole and parts postulate to show that the sum of the measures of the angles of a triangle equals the sum of the measures of the parts of a straight angle.

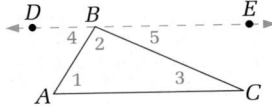

Show Your Reasoning

Statements	Justifications
1. *ABC* is a triangle.	1. Given
2. Draw helping line $\overleftrightarrow{DE}$ through *B* so that $\overleftrightarrow{DE} \parallel \overline{AC}$.	2. Through a point not on a given line, there is one and only one line parallel to the given line.
3. $m \angle DBE = 180°$	3. If the sides of an angle form a straight line, then the angle is a straight angle with measure 180°.
4. $m \angle DBE = m \angle 4 + m \angle 2 + m \angle 5$	4. For any angle, the measure of the whole is equal to the sum of the measures of its non-overlapping parts.
5. $m \angle 4 + m \angle 2 + m \angle 5 = 180°$	5. Substitution property (Steps 3 and 4)
6. $m \angle 1 = m \angle 4; m \angle 3 = m \angle 5$	6. If two ∥ lines are intersected by a transversal, then alternate interior ∠s are = in measure.
7. $m \angle 1 + m \angle 2 + m \angle 3 = 180°$	7. Substitution property (Steps 5 and 6)

THE TRIANGLE SUM THEOREM

Theorem 8.5 The sum of the measures of the angles of a triangle is 180°.

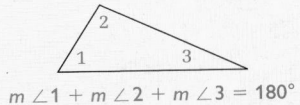

$m \angle 1 + m \angle 2 + m \angle 3 = 180°$

Sample 2

Write a paragraph proof to prove that the sum of the measures of the angles of a quadrilateral is 360°.

Sample Response

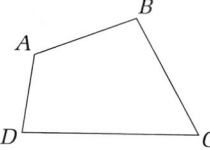

Given *ABCD* is a quadrilateral.

Prove $m \angle A + m \angle B + m \angle C + m \angle D = 360°$

Plan Ahead

Draw a diagonal helping line to divide the quadrilateral into two triangles. Then use the triangle sum theorem.

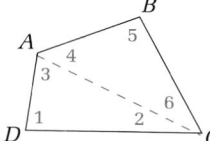

Show Your Reasoning

Draw the diagonal $\overline{AC}$ to form $\triangle ABC$ and $\triangle CDA$. The angles of the quadrilateral *ABCD* are made up of the angles of the two triangles. The sum of the angle measures of each triangle is 180°. The sum of the measures of the angles of the quadrilateral is 180° + 180°, which equals 360°.

The statement proved in Sample 2 can be used to prove other theorems about quadrilaterals. You will prove Theorem 8.7 in Exercise 17.

X.Lab

QUADRILATERAL THEOREMS

Theorem 8.6 The sum of the measures of the angles of a quadrilateral is 360°.

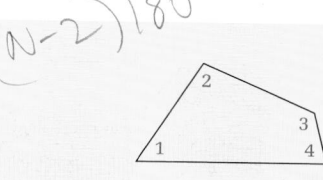

$$m \angle 1 + m \angle 2 + m \angle 3 + m \angle 4 = 360°$$

Theorem 8.7 If both pairs of opposite angles of a quadrilateral are equal in measure, then the quadrilateral is a parallelogram.

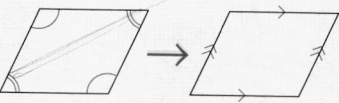

Additional Sample

S2 Use the reasoning of Sample 2 to find the sum of the measures of the angles of a pentagon. **540°**

Teaching Tip

Students should recognize the converse of Theorem 8.7 as a statement they proved about parallelograms on page 419 of Unit 7 (Talk it Over question 7).

Using Technology

Activity 11 in the *Geometry Inventor Activity Book* extends the section by leading students to discover a general formula for the sum of the interior angles of any polygon.

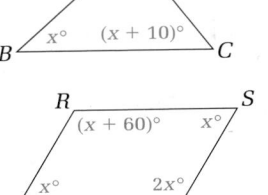

Talk it Over

2. **a.** Write an equation that represents the sum of the measures of the angles of △ABC.

   b. Solve the equation for x.

   c. Find the measures of the angles.

3. **a.** Write an equation for the sum of the measures of the angles of quadrilateral RSTU.

   b. Find the measures of the angles.

   c. Explain why RSTU is a parallelogram.

▶ **Now you are ready for:**
Exs. 1–25 on pp. 443–446

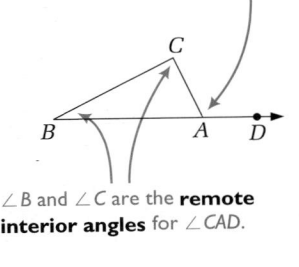

∠CAD is an exterior angle.

∠B and ∠C are the **remote interior angles** for ∠CAD.

EXPLORATION

(How) do the interior angles of a triangle relate to an exterior angle?

- **Materials: geometric drawing software or protractors**
- **Work with another student.**

① Draw any △ABC. Extend $\overline{BA}$ through a point D to form an exterior angle of △ABC.

② Measure ∠CAD, ∠B, and ∠C for your triangle. Complete the first row of the table.

	m ∠CAD	**m ∠B**	**m ∠C**	**m ∠B + m ∠C**
△ 1	?	?	?	?
△ 2	?	?	?	?
△ 3	?	?	?	?
△ 4	?	?	?	?
△ 5	?	?	?	?

③ Repeat steps 1 and 2 for four other triangles. Use a variety of types of triangles and choose different locations for the exterior angle.

④ Look at the completed table. Describe any patterns you see.

442

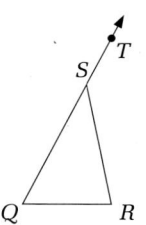

4. In the Exploration, why do you think $\angle B$ and $\angle C$ are called *remote* interior angles?

5. Which angles in the figure at the left are the remote interior angles for exterior $\angle RST$?

6. Suppose you extend $\overline{RS}$ through S to a point V. What are the remote interior angles for $\angle QSV$?

7. Do you think an exterior angle of a triangle can be acute? Why or why not?

In the Exploration, you may have seen the relationship described in Theorem 8.8. You will prove this theorem in Exercise 34.

EXTERIOR ANGLE THEOREM

Theorem 8.8 An exterior angle of a triangle is equal in measure to the sum of the measures of its two remote interior angles.

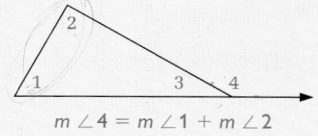

$$m \angle 4 = m \angle 1 + m \angle 2$$

Look Back

> Now you are ready for:
> Exs. 26–44 on pp. 447–448

Summarize the ideas developed in this section about angle measures.

8-2 Exercises and Problems

1. Reading How was the unique parallel postulate used in the proof of the triangle sum theorem in Sample 1?

For Exercises 2–7, find each unknown angle measure.

2.
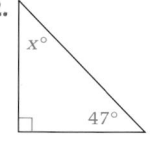

3.
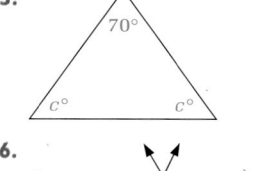

4.
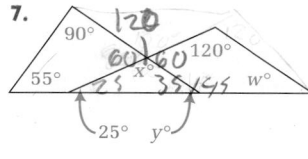

5.
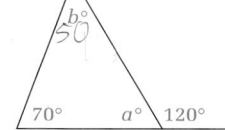

6.
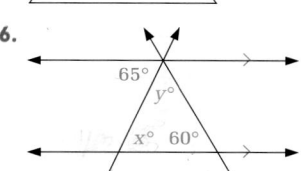

7.

8-2 The Triangle Sum Theorem

443

Students Acquiring English

Students who are unfamiliar with the word *remote* will not be able to answer Talk it Over question 4. Check students' understanding by asking them to describe a remote control for a television set.

Reasoning

The proof of Theorem 8.8 is asked for in Ex. 34. You may wish at this time, however, to have students sketch out a proof, which would go as follows:

$m \angle 1 + m \angle 2 + m \angle 3 = 180°$

$m \angle 3 + m \angle 4 = 180°$

$\therefore m \angle 1 + m \angle 2 + m \angle 3 = m \angle 3 + m \angle 4$

$\therefore m \angle 1 + m \angle 2 = m \angle 4.$

Using Technology

Activity 3 in the *Geometry Inventor Activity Book* reinforces the triangle sum and exterior angle theorems.

APPLYING

Suggested Assignment

Day 1

Standard 2–11, 13–17

Extended 1–18, 20–22, 24, 25

Day 2

Standard 26–34, 36–44

Extended 26–34, 36–44

Integrating the Strands

Number Exs. 10, 11

Algebra Exs. 2–7, 11, 13–16, 30–33, 41

Geometry Exs. 1–40, 43

Logic and Language Exs. 1, 11, 12, 21, 22, 35, 36, 42–44

Answers to Look Back

The sum of the measures of the angles of a triangle is 180°. The sum of the measures of the angles of a quadrilateral is 360°. If both pairs of opposite angles of a quadrilateral are equal in measure, then the quadrilateral is a parallelogram. Any exterior angle of a triangle is equal in measure to the sum of the measures of the two remote interior angles.

Answers to Exercises and Problems

1. A line was drawn through C parallel to $\overline{AB}$. The Parallel Postulate guarantees that there is such a line and there is only one such line.

2. $x° = 43°$

3. $c° = 55°$

4. $x° = 34°$, $(x + 10)° = 44°$, $3x° = 102°$

5. $a° = 60°$, $b° = 50°$

6. $x° = 65°$, $y° = 55°$

7. $w° = 35°$, $x° = 120°$, $y° = 35°$

Surveying The highest point on Earth is the summit of Mount Everest on the border of Nepal and China. In 1852, a government survey of India established the height of this mountain as 29,002 ft. Surveyors used a series of six triangles and averaged the results to find the distance between the peak and some inaccessible point directly below the summit. Calculations in the 1950s resulted in the official height accepted now, 29,028 ft.

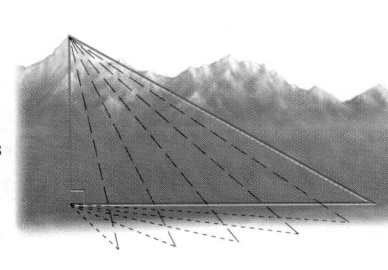

The tool used to measure angles from the plain to the summit is called a *theodolite*.

8. Suppose the angle measured at B for one triangle is 5°. What is the measure of $\angle A$?

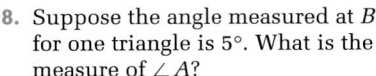

(Not drawn to scale.)

9. Suppose in another triangle that $m \angle ADN = 176°$. What is the measure of $\angle A$?

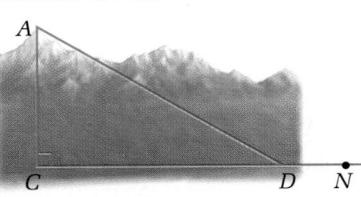

10. Which group of angle measures does not form a triangle? Explain your reasoning.

Group 1	Group 2	Group 3
35°, 72°, 83°	35°, 72°, 73°	27°, 38°, 115°

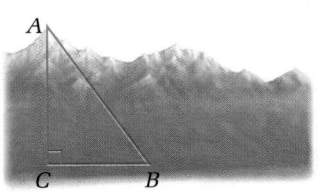

Brandon Reed

1:2:6

$x°$ = measure of smallest angle
$2x°$ = measure of middle angle
$6x°$ = measure of largest angle

$x + 2x + 6x = 180$
$9x = 180$
$x = 20$

So the measures are 20°, 40°, and 120°.

11. **a.** How did Brandon use the triangle sum theorem in his solution to the following question?

   "The measures of the angles of a triangle are in a ratio of 1:2:6. What are the measures of the three angles?"

   b. Use Brandon's method to find the measures of the three angles of a triangle where the angles are in a ratio of 1:3:5.

   c. Repeat part (b) for the angle measure ratio of 2:4:9.

   d. The measures of the angles of $\triangle CDE$ are in the ratio of 1:1:2. Is $\triangle CDE$ an *acute*, an *obtuse*, or a *right* triangle?

12. **Writing** Robin says that a triangle can have only one right angle. Do you agree or disagree with her? Explain your reasoning.

For Exercises 13–16:

a. Find the measure of each angle of quadrilateral *ABCD*.

b. Identify each quadrilateral. Be as specific as you can.

13. $m \angle A = x°$
    $m \angle B = x°$
    $m \angle C = x°$
    $m \angle D = x°$

14. $m \angle A = x°$
    $m \angle B = 2x°$
    $m \angle C = x°$
    $m \angle D = 2x°$

15. $m \angle A = 2x°$
    $m \angle B = 4x°$
    $m \angle C = 3x°$
    $m \angle D = 3x°$

16. $m \angle A = x°$
    $m \angle B = 2x°$
    $m \angle C = 4x°$
    $m \angle D = 3x°$

Unit 8 Similar and Congruent Triangles

17. Copy and complete this proof of Theorem 8.7: If both pairs of opposite angles of a quadrilateral are equal in measure, then the quadrilateral is a parallelogram.

Given *JKLM* is a quadrilateral.
$m\angle J = m\angle L$, $m\angle K = m\angle M$

Prove *JKLM* is a parallelogram.

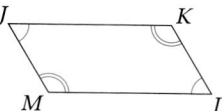

Statements

1. *JKLM* is a quadrilateral.
2. $m\angle J + m\angle K + m\angle L + m\angle M = 360°$
3. $m\angle J = m\angle L$, $m\angle K = m\angle M$
4. $m\angle J + m\angle M + m\angle J + m\angle M = 360°$
5. $2(m\angle J + m\angle M) = 360°$
6. $m\angle J + m\angle M = 180°$
7. $\angle J$ and $\angle M$ are supplementary angles.
8. $\overline{JK} \parallel \overline{ML}$
9. $m\angle J + m\angle K = 180°$
10. $\angle J$ and $\angle K$ are supplementary angles.
11. $\overline{JM} \parallel \overline{KL}$
12. *JKLM* is a parallelogram.

Justifications

1. ?
2. ?
3. ?
4. ?
5. ?
6. ?
7. ?
8. ?
9. Substitution property (Steps ? and ?)
10. ?
11. ?
12. ?

For Exercises 18 and 19, use this information.

A *tessellation* is a pattern formed when polygons cover a plane without gaps or overlaps.

18. a. Quadrilateral *ABCD* has been tessellated to cover a plane. What is the sum of the measures of the angles of *ABCD*?

b. What is the sum of the measures of the angles at any vertex not on the boundary of the tessellation?

c. Writing Describe any tessellations you see in the quilt at the right.

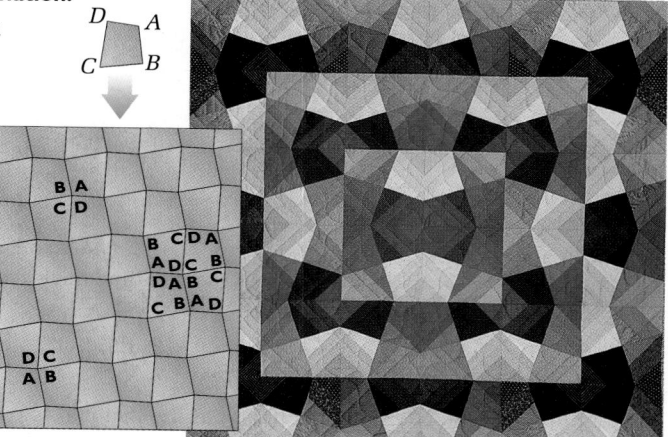

Thinking of Winter by Carol Gersen

8-2 The Triangle Sum Theorem

445

Research

Exs. 18 and 19 introduce students to the concept of tessellation. After doing these exercises, some students may wish to research how tessellations are used in art. Students should find many interesting examples in Islamic art and in the works of M. C. Escher.

Using Technology

Activity 32 in the *Geometry Inventor Activity Book* extends the ideas in Exs. 18 and 19.

Answers to Exercises and Problems

17. *Given: JKLM is a quadrilateral. $m\angle J = m\angle L$, $m\angle K = m\angle M$*
Prove: JKLM is a parallelogram.

Statements

1. *JKLM* is a quadrilateral.
2. $m\angle J + m\angle K + m\angle L + m\angle M = 360°$
3. $m\angle J = m\angle L$, $m\angle K = m\angle M$
4. $m\angle J + m\angle M + m\angle J + m\angle M = 360°$
5. $2(m\angle J + m\angle M) = 360°$
6. $m\angle J + m\angle M = 180°$
7. $\angle J$ and $\angle M$ are supplementary angles.
8. $\overline{JK} \parallel \overline{ML}$
9. $m\angle J + m\angle K = 180°$
10. $\angle J$ and $\angle K$ are supplementary angles.
11. $\overline{JM} \parallel \overline{KL}$
12. *JKLM* is a parallelogram.

Justifications

1. Given
2. The sum of the measures of the ∠s of a quadrilateral is 360°.
3. Given
4. Substitution property (Steps 2 and 3)
5. Distributive property
6. Division property of equality
7. Definition of supplementary angles
8. If two lines are intersected by a transversal and co-interior ∠s are supplementary, then the lines are ∥.
9. Substitution property (Steps 3 and 6)
10. Definition of supplementary angles
11. If two lines are intersected by a transversal and co-interior ∠s are supplementary, then the lines are ∥.
12. Definition of parallelogram

18. a. 360°

b. 360°

c. Answers may vary.

445

446

---

19. a. **Using Manipulatives** Draw any quadrilateral and make a tessellation with it. Make a sketch of the tessellation or cut out several copies of your quadrilateral and arrange them to model the tessellation.

b. What is the sum of the measures of the angles in your tessellation at any vertex not on the boundary?

c. Explain why the following statement is true. "Any quadrilateral will tessellate a plane."

20. Use the figure at the right to prove the triangle sum theorem.

21. a. Write the following statement in if-then form.

"The acute angles of a right triangle are complementary."

b. Prove the statement from part (a).

22. **Writing** Suppose you are tutoring a student. Describe how helping lines are used in the proofs of some theorems in this section.

---

connection to LITERATURE

Alfonsina Storni (1892–1938) was an Argentinian poet and teacher. Her emotional poetry is known for its symbolism, but she wrote about everyday life in everyday language.

23. a. **Group Activity** Work in a group of four students. Translate this poem from Spanish into English.

> ## CUADRADOS Y ÁNGULOS
>
> Casas enfiladas, casas enfiladas,
> Casas enfiladas.
> Cuadrados, cuadrados, cuadrados.
> Casas enfiladas.
> Las gentes ya tienen el alma cuadrada,
> Ideas en fila
> Y ángulo en la espalda.
> Yo misma he vertido ayer una lágrima,
> Dios mio, cuadrada.
> —Alfonsina Storni, 1918

b. How does Alfonsina Storni use squares and angles to express her feelings about the world she lived in?

24. **Writing** What feelings do the simple geometric shapes in the painting give you about New York?

25. **Writing** Think of a situation in your life that makes you think of angles, triangles, or quadrilaterals. Write a short paragraph about it.

This oil painting by Chilean artist Nemesio Antúnez is entitled New York, New York 10008 (1967).

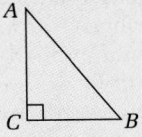

Name the remote interior angles for each exterior angle.

26. $\angle DAC$

27. $\angle EAB$

28. $\angle FBA$

29. $\angle GCA$

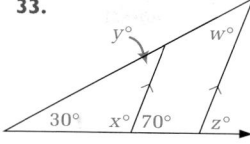

For Exercises 30–33, find each unknown angle measure.

30.

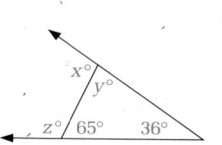

31.

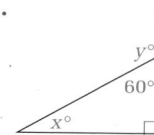

32.

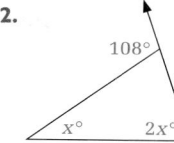

33.

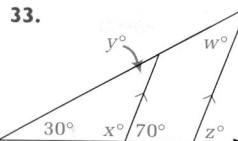

34. Copy and complete this proof of Theorem 8.8: An exterior angle of a triangle is equal in measure to the sum of its two remote interior angles.

Given $\triangle ABC$ with exterior $\angle 4$

Prove $m\angle 4 = m\angle 1 + m\angle 2$

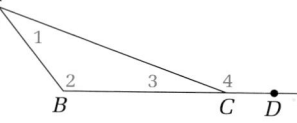

Statements

① $m\angle BCD = 180°$

② $m\angle BCD = m\angle 3 + m\angle 4$

③ $m\angle 3 + m\angle 4 = 180°$

④ $m\angle 1 + m\angle 2 + m\angle 3 = 180°$

⑤

⑥ $m\angle 3 + m\angle 4 = m\angle 1 + m\angle 2 + m\angle 3$

$m\angle 4 = m\angle 1 + m\angle 2$

Justifications

① ?

② ?

③ ?

④ ?

⑤ ?

⑥ ?

35. a. **Using Manipulatives** Draw a large $\triangle ABC$. Place your pencil at A as shown in step 1. Slide the pencil along $\overline{AB}$ until the eraser is at B and then rotate it around B as shown in step 2. Now slide it to C and rotate it around C (step 3). Finally slide it back to A and rotate it around A (step 4).

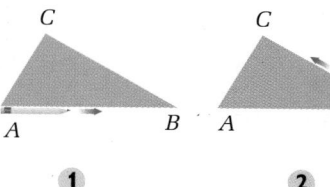 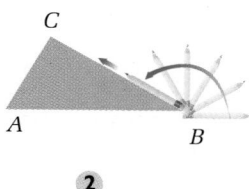 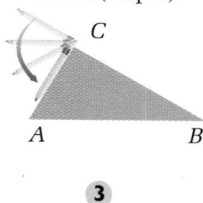 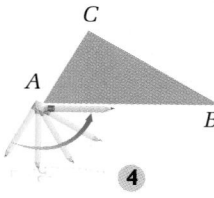

① ② ③ ④

b. What is the total number of degrees you have rotated your pencil?

c. What conclusion about the exterior angles of a triangle is suggested above?

d. **Writing** Do you think that the same conclusion is true for quadrilaterals? pentagons? hexagons? 12-gons? n-gons? Explain.

8-2 The Triangle Sum Theorem

447

23. a. SQUARES AND ANGLES

   Houses in a row, houses in a
      row,
   Houses in a row.
   Squares, squares, squares.
   Houses in a row.
   People all have square souls,
   Ideas in a row.
   Their backs in an angle.
   I myself shed a tear yesterday,
   And, my God, it was square!

b. Answers may vary. An example is given. The use of squares and angles expresses the writer's feelings about the sameness and hardness of the world.

24. Answers may vary.

25. Answers may vary. An example is given. A house has many places where angles, triangles, and quadrilaterals exist. The top of a roof or any corner of a room are examples of angles. The bottom of a corner cabinet or an open staircase are examples of triangles. A door or wall are examples of quadrilaterals.

26. $\angle 2$ and $\angle 3$ **27.** $\angle 2$ and $\angle 3$

28. $\angle 1$ and $\angle 2$ **29.** $\angle 1$ and $\angle 3$

30. $x° = 101°$, $y° = 79°$, $z° = 115°$

31. $x° = 30°$, $y° = 120°$

32. $x° = 36°$, $2x° = 72°$

33. $x° = 110°$, $y° = 40°$, $z° = 70°$, $w° = 40°$

34. See answers in back of book.

35. a. Drawings may vary.

b. 360°

c. The sum of the measures of the exterior angles of a triangle is 360°.

d. The sum of the measures of the exterior angles of all quadrilaterals is 360°; the same is true for pentagons, hexagons, 12-gons, and n-gons. The sum of the exterior angles of an n-gon is $180n - 180(n - 2)$ which equals 360°. (the sum of the number of straight angles less the measure of the sum of the interior angles)

Answers to Exercises and Problems

22. Answers may vary. An example is given. When proving certain theorems in geometry, it is often useful to introduce additional lines or line segments not included in the given figure. These lines are called helping lines. In the case of the Triangle Sum Theorem, we use the Parallel Postulate to draw a line parallel to one side of a triangle through the opposite vertex and then use the theorems about parallel lines and transversals to show that the measures of the angles of the triangle add up to a straight angle. In the case of the Quadrilateral Sum Theorem, we use the fact that there is one and only one line between two points to draw a diagonal helping line and divide the quadrilateral into two triangles. We obtain our result from the Triangle Sum Theorem.

447

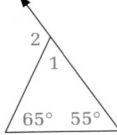

36. Writing Describe two ways to find the measure of $\angle 2$.

Review **PREVIEW**

For each of Exercises 37–40, use the given angle measures to decide whether lines l and m are parallel. Write Yes or No. *(Section 8-1)*

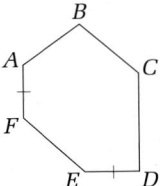

37. $m\angle 1 = 56°$, $m\angle 2 = 124°$ **38.** $m\angle 1 = 49°$, $m\angle 2 = 121°$

39. $m\angle 1 = 110°$, $m\angle 2 = 110°$ **40.** $m\angle 1 = 90°$, $m\angle 2 = 90°$

41. Solve this system of equations: $5x + y = 30$ *(Section 3-4)*
$$3x - 4y = 41$$

42. Explain how to solve the proportion $\frac{8}{5} = \frac{12}{x}$. *(Toolbox Skill 17)*

43. What do the markings in the diagram indicate? *(Toolbox Skill 27)*

Working on the Unit Project

44. Research Read about how some everyday or unusual tools were created, how they work, and how they were patented. See how words and diagrams work together to explain an invention. Here are some books that contain information:

➤ *Blacks in Science: Ancient and Modern* by Ivan Van Sertima, ed.

➤ *Black Pioneers of Science & Invention* by Louis Haber

➤ *Extraordinary Origins of Everyday Things* by Charles Panati

➤ *Mothers of Invention* by Ethlie A. Vare and Greg Ptacek

➤ *Panati's Browser's Book of Beginnings* by Charles Panati

➤ *The Real McCoy: African-American Invention & Innovation, 1619–1930* by Portia James

➤ *Steven Caney's Invention Book* by Steven Caney

➤ *The Way Things Work* by David Macaulay

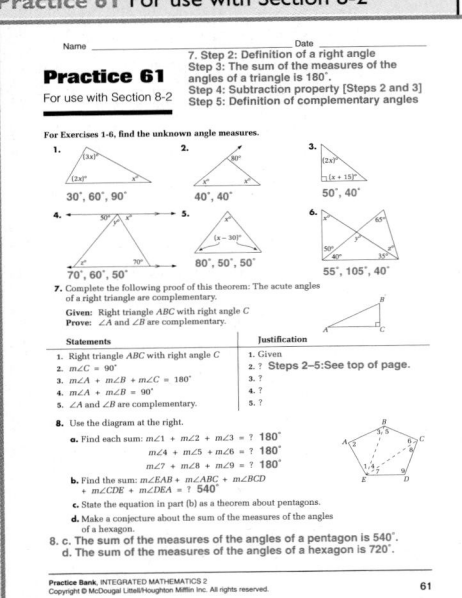

Answers to Exercises and Problems

36. Methods may vary. Examples are given.
(1) Use Theorem 8-8: An exterior angle of a triangle is equal in measure to the sum of the measures of its two remote interior angles.
(2) Use the Triangle Sum Theorem to find the measure of $\angle 1$ and then the Linear Pairs Postulate to find the measure of $\angle 2$.

37. No.

38. No.

39. Yes.

40. Yes.

41. $x = 7$, $y = -5$

42. Multiply $8 \cdot x$ and $5 \cdot 12$ to get the equation $8x = 60$. Divide both sides by 8 to obtain $x = 7.5$

43. $AF = DE$

44. Books chosen and information gathered may vary.

Similar Triangles

--- Focus

Apply the properties of similar triangles. Prove that triangles are similar.

SCALE THE HEIGHTS

The John Hancock Center in Chicago is the fifth tallest sky-scraper in the United States. The interesting patterns of *congruent* and *similar* triangles on the sides of the building offer excellent strength and support.

Talk it Over

1. Two triangles are **congruent** if and only if their vertices can be matched up so that the *corresponding parts* (angles and sides) of the triangles are equal in measure.

    a. What angle of △ABC is equal in measure to ∠D?

    b. What side of △DEC is equal in measure to $\overline{AC}$?

    c. Explain why △ABC ≅ △DEC.

    d. Vertices are named in the order that they correspond. Complete: △BCA ≅ ___?___.

    A 38° 100 ft 38° D
    175 ft 110° C   C 110° 175 ft
    115 ft
    B 32° 32° E

2. Two triangles are **similar** if and only if their vertices can be matched up so that corresponding angles are equal in measure and corresponding sides are *in proportion* (that is, the ratios of their measures are all equal).

    a. Are the angles of △DEC and △FGH equal in measure?

    b. Find the ratios $\frac{DE}{FG}$, $\frac{EC}{GH}$, and $\frac{DC}{FH}$. What do you notice?

    c. Explain why △DEC ~ △FGH.

    Read "is similar to." →

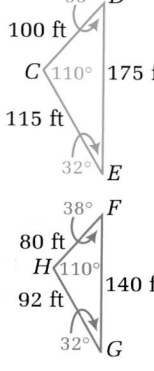

38° D
100 ft
C 110° 175 ft
115 ft
32° E

38° F
80 ft
H 110° 140 ft
92 ft
32° G

Answers to Talk it Over

1. a. ∠A

   b. $\overline{DC}$

   c. m∠B = m∠E; m∠C = m∠C; m∠A = m∠D; AB = DE; AC = DC; BC = EC; Since three pairs of sides are equal in measure and three pairs of angles are equal in measure, △ABC ≅ △DEC by definition.

   d. △ECD

2. a. Yes.

   b. $\frac{DC}{FH} = \frac{5}{4}$; $\frac{EC}{GH} = \frac{5}{4}$; $\frac{DE}{FG} = \frac{5}{4}$; They are all equal.

   c. m∠D = m∠F; m∠E = m∠G; m∠C = m∠H; $\frac{DC}{FH} = \frac{EC}{GH} = \frac{DE}{FG}$; Since three pairs of angles are equal in measure and three pairs of sides are in proportion, △DEC ~ △FGH by definition.

PLANNING

Objectives and Strands
See pages 428A and 428B.

Spiral Learning
See page 428B.

Materials List
➤ Mirror
➤ Straw
➤ Tape
➤ String
➤ Weight
➤ Protractor

Recommended Pacing
Section 8-3 is a two-day lesson.

Day 1
Pages 449–450: Opening paragraph through Sample 1, *Exercises 1–12*

Day 2
Pages 450–452: Overlapping Triangles through Look Back, *Exercises 13–27*

Extra Practice
See pages 627–628.

Warm-Up Exercises
Warm-Up Transparency 8-3

Support Materials
➤ Practice 62
➤ Enrichment 55 in the Activity Bank
➤ Study Guide 8-3
➤ Problem Set 17
➤ Additional Exploration 11
Overhead Visual 8
➤ McDougal Littell Mathpack software: *Geometry Inventor*
➤ Geometry Inventor Activity Book: Activity 4
➤ Quiz 8-3
➤ Test 32
➤ Alternative Assessment 2

The definitions of congruent and similar triangles are given in questions 1 and 2, respectively. Students can see that congruent triangles have the same size and shape, but that similar triangles only have the same shape. In question 2(b), it is important for students to understand that it is the ratios of *corresponding* sides that are equal in measure. Corresponding sides are those that are opposite equal angles.

Reasoning

You may wish to ask students why it is necessary to show only two pairs of angles equal in measure to conclude that triangles are similar rather than showing all three pairs. (If two pairs of angles are equal in measure, the third pair has to be equal by the triangle sum theorem.)

Additional Sample

S1 For each pair of triangles, tell whether the triangles are similar. Write *Yes* or *No*. Explain.

a.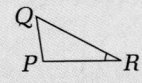

No. Only one pair of angles is equal in measure: $m \angle T = m \angle R$.

b.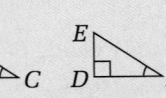

Yes. △ABC ~ △DEF. Two pairs of angles are equal in measure: $m \angle A = m \angle D$ and $m \angle C = m \angle F$.

c.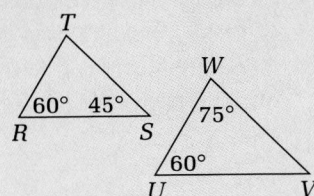

Yes; △RST ~ △UVW. By the triangle sum theorem, $m \angle T = 75°$ and $m \angle V = 45°$. Two pairs of angles are equal in measure: $m \angle R = m \angle U$ and $m \angle T = m \angle W$. (Also, $m \angle S = m \angle V$.)

450

Two triangles are similar by definition when *all* corresponding angles are equal in measure and *all* corresponding sides are in proportion. To prove that two triangles are similar, however, you only need to show that *two* pairs of angles are equal in measure.

Postulate 13 If two angles of one triangle are equal in measure to two angles of another triangle, then the two triangles are similar. (AA Similarity)

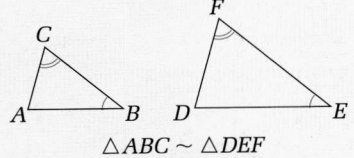

$$\triangle ABC \sim \triangle DEF$$

Sample 1

For each pair of triangles, tell whether the triangles are similar. Write *Yes* or *No*. Explain.

a.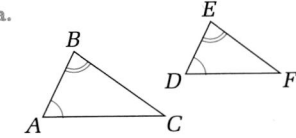

b.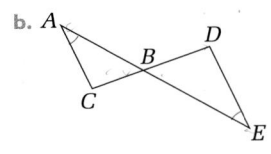

c.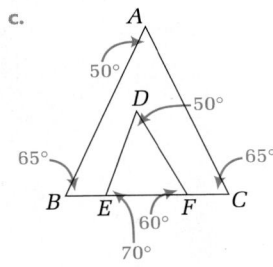

Sample Response

a. Yes, △ABC ~ △DEF. Two pairs of angles are equal in measure: $m \angle A = m \angle D$, $m \angle B = m \angle E$.

b. Yes, △ABC ~ △EBD. Two pairs of angles are equal in measure: $m \angle A = m \angle E$, $m \angle ABC = m \angle EBD$ (vertical angles).

c. No. Only one pair of angles is equal in measure: $m \angle A = m \angle D$.

> **Watch Out!**
> When you name pairs of congruent or similar triangles, be sure to list the corresponding vertices in the same order.

▶ Now you are ready for:
Exs. 1–12 on p. 453

Overlapping Triangles

Sometimes triangles in a diagram overlap. You may find it useful to separate the triangles. Label them to help you refer to the correct segments and angles.

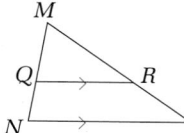

△**MQR** and △**MNP** are similar. Name the pairs of corresponding parts.

Sample Response

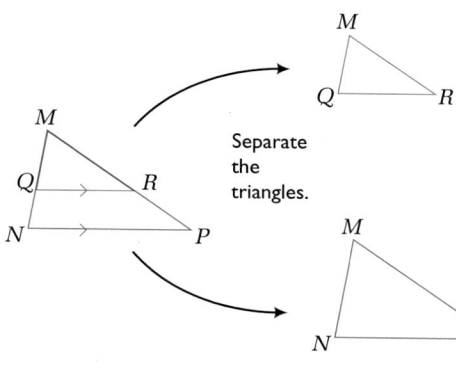

Separate the triangles.

Corresponding parts	
Angles	Sides
∠M, ∠M	$\overline{MQ}$, $\overline{MN}$
∠MQR, ∠MNP	$\overline{QR}$, $\overline{NP}$
∠MRQ, ∠MPN	$\overline{MR}$, $\overline{MP}$

Sample 3

Prove that a line drawn from a point on one side of a triangle parallel to another side forms a triangle similar to the original triangle.

Sample Response

 △ABC
$\overline{DE} \parallel \overline{BC}$

 △ADE ~ △ABC

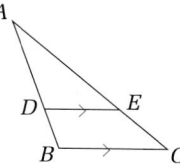

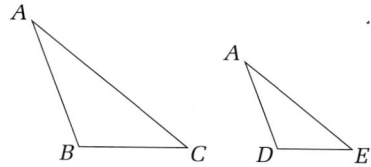

Plan Ahead

Separate and label the two triangles. Use parallel lines to show that two pairs of corresponding angles are equal in measure.

Show Your Reasoning

Statements

1. $\overline{DE} \parallel \overline{BC}$

2. m ∠ ADE = m ∠ ABC
   m ∠ AED = m ∠ ACB

3. △ADE ~ △ABC

Justifications

1. Given

2. If two ∥ lines are intersected by a transversal, then corresponding ∡ are = in measure.

3. AA Similarity

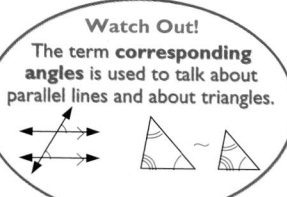

Watch Out!
The term **corresponding angles** is used to talk about parallel lines and about triangles.

8-3 Similar Triangles

451

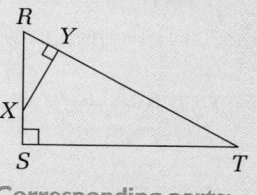
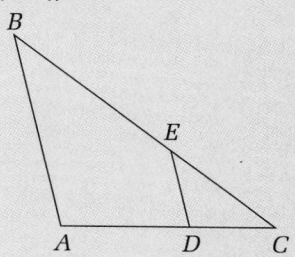

Teaching Tip

If students have difficulty setting up the proportion in Sample 4, point out that the ratio of AD to AB is that of the smaller side to the longer side. Therefore, the other ratio in the proportion must also be smaller side to longer side.

Additional Sample

S4 Find the measure of $\overline{ED}$.

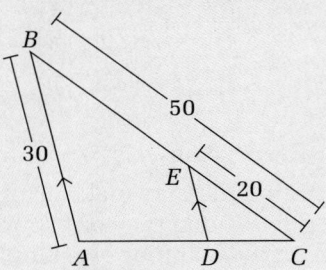

Since $\overline{AB} \parallel \overline{DE}$,
$\triangle ABC \sim \triangle DEC$.
$$\frac{ED}{AB} = \frac{EC}{BC}$$
$$\frac{ED}{30} = \frac{20}{50}$$
$$50(ED) = 600$$
$$ED = 12$$
The measure of $\overline{ED}$ is
12 units.

In Sample 3, a parallel line was drawn to form similar triangles. The parallel line drawn in a triangle may be parallel to any of the three sides. In each case, similar triangles are formed.

X·Lab

OVERLAPPING SIMILAR TRIANGLES

Theorem 8.9 If a line is drawn from a point on one side of a triangle parallel to another side, then it forms a triangle similar to the original triangle.

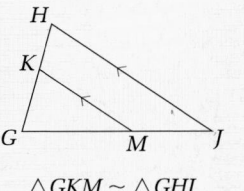

$$\triangle GKM \sim \triangle GHJ$$

Sample 4

Find the measure of $\overline{AD}$.

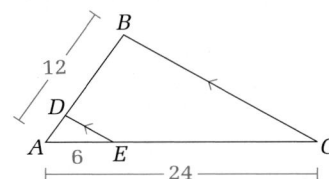

Sample Response

Use a proportion.
Since $\overline{DE} \parallel \overline{BC}$, $\triangle ADE \sim \triangle ABC$.

$$\frac{AD}{AB} = \frac{AE}{AC} \quad \longleftarrow \text{Corresponding sides of similar triangles are in proportion.}$$

$$\frac{AD}{12} = \frac{6}{24} \quad \longleftarrow \text{Substitute the measures you know.}$$

$$24(AD) = 72 \quad \longleftarrow \text{Use cross products.}$$

$$AD = 3 \quad \longleftarrow \text{Divide both sides by 24.}$$

The measure of $\overline{AD}$ is 3 units.

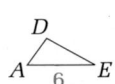

······► Now you are ready for:
Exs. 13–27 on pp. 453–456

Look Back

What should you look for to prove that two triangles are similar?

Unit 8 Similar and Congruent Triangles

Answers to Look Back ········

Find two angles of one triangle that are equal in measure to two angles of the other triangle.

Exercises and Problems

Reading Use the similar triangles △ABC and △DEF.

1. Name the corresponding angles.
2. Name the corresponding sides.
3. If m ∠A = 35° and m ∠E = 70°, what are the measures of the remaining angles?

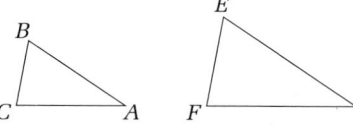

Explain why the triangles are similar.

4.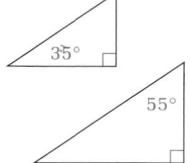
5.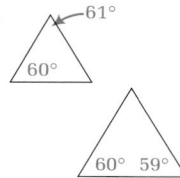
6.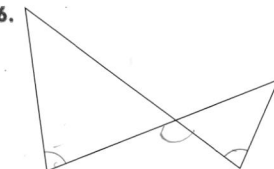

For Exercises 7 and 8, name the pairs of similar triangles.

7.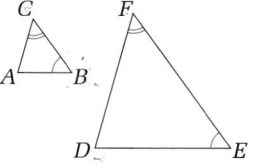
8.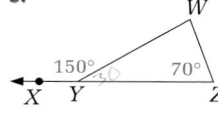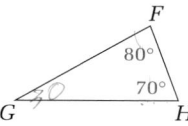

9. Write a paragraph proof.

> **Given** $\overline{AB} \parallel \overline{DE}$

> **Prove** $\triangle ABC \sim \triangle EDC$

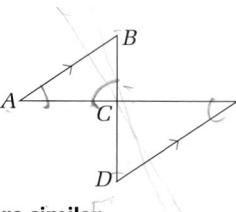

△MQR and △XYZ are similar.
Complete and solve each proportion.

10. $\frac{8}{16} = \frac{?}{a}$
11. $\frac{8}{16} = \frac{?}{b}$

Complete each equation.

12.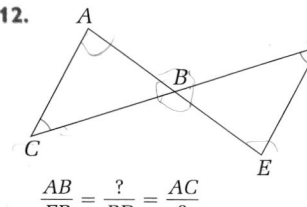
$$\frac{AB}{EB} = \frac{?}{BD} = \frac{AC}{?}$$

13.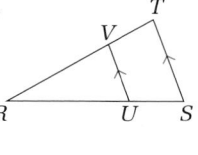
$$\frac{RV}{?} = \frac{RU}{RS} = \frac{?}{TS}$$

8-3 Similar Triangles

453

Suggested Assignment

Day 1
Standard 1–12
Extended 1–12

Day 2
Standard 13–15, 20–27
Extended 13–18, 20–27

Integrating the Strands
Algebra Exs. 10, 11, 25, 26
Geometry Exs. 1–23, 26, 27
Discrete Mathematics Exs. 24, 25
Logic and Language Exs. 1–4, 16–18, 22, 27

Communication: Reading
Exs. 1 and 2 check to see that students understand the basic ideas of corresponding angles and corresponding sides of similar triangles. Ex. 3 makes use of the fact that corresponding angles of similar triangles have equal measures.

Answers to Exercises and Problems

1. ∠A and ∠D; ∠B and ∠E; ∠C and ∠F
2. $\overline{AB}$ and $\overline{DE}$; $\overline{AC}$ and $\overline{DF}$; $\overline{BC}$ and $\overline{EF}$
3. ∠B = 70°, ∠C = 75°, ∠D = 35°, ∠B = 70°, ∠F = 75°
4. Two angles of each triangle are 35° and 55° (and one angle is 90°, the right angle).
5. Angles of both triangles are 59°, 60°, and 61°.
6. One pair of angles is shown to be equal, and a second pair of angles can be shown to be equal because they are vertical angles.
7. △ABC, △DEF
8. △WYZ, △FGH
9. Given: $\overline{AB} \parallel \overline{DE}$
   Prove: △ABC ~ △EDC
   Since $\overline{AB} \parallel \overline{DE}$, m ∠A = m ∠E and m ∠B = m ∠D because if two parallel lines are intersected by a transversal, then alternate interior angles are equal in measure. Then △ABC ~ △EDC by the AA Similarity Postulate.
10. $\frac{8}{16} = \frac{9}{a}$; a = 18
11. $\frac{8}{16} = \frac{12}{b}$; b = 24
12. $\frac{AB}{EB} = \frac{BC}{BD} = \frac{AC}{ED}$
13. $\frac{RV}{RT} = \frac{RU}{RS} = \frac{VU}{TS}$

453

14. **a.** Why is $\triangle FGH \sim \triangle JKH$?

    b. Find the values of x and y.

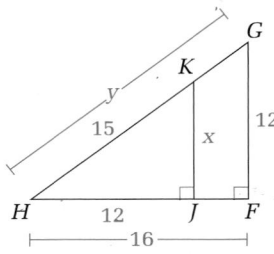

15. Prove that if a line is drawn from a point on one side of a triangle parallel to another side, then it divides the sides proportionally.

 **Given** $\overline{BC} \parallel \overline{DE}$

 **Prove** $\dfrac{AB}{BD} = \dfrac{AC}{CE}$

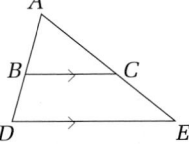

Plan Ahead

Show that $\triangle ABC$ and $\triangle ADE$ are similar and that the corresponding sides are in proportion. Then use $AD = AB + BD$ and $AE = AC + CE$.

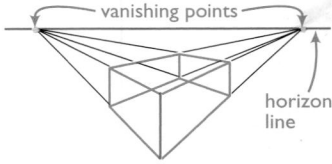

connection to ART

Artists may use *perspective* to represent three-dimensional objects on a two-dimensional surface. In many early Renaissance paintings the lines on tiled floors seem to meet at a single point, the *vanishing point*, at the "back" of the painting. Artists used vanishing points to pull a viewer into the painting.

16. The actual lines on the plaza floor shown would be parallel, but in the painting they also seem to meet at a single point. Where do the lines all seem to meet?

17. The horizontal lines in the floor are called *transversals*. What would you need to know about the transversals to prove that $\triangle ABC \sim \triangle DEC$?

18. **Writing** Explain how the figure below was drawn starting with the vertical blue line and using two vanishing points.

Unit 8 Similar and Congruent Triangles

19. **Using Manipulatives** Work with another student. You can use a mirror to measure the height of a tree indirectly. When you see an image in a mirror, the angles of incidence and reflection are equal in measure ($m \angle 1 = m \angle 2$).

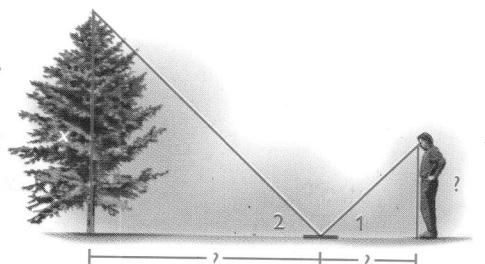

You will need a mirror and a tape measure. Place the mirror on the ground between the tree and yourself. Move away from the mirror until you see the top of the tree in the mirror. Use similar triangles to find the height of the tree (x).

20. If the ratio of the measures of the corresponding sides of two similar triangles is 1:1, what is the special relationship between the triangles?

21. a. Find the missing angle measures in each of the triangles.

b. Suppose you choose one of the six triangles at random. What is the probability that the triangle is similar to △I? Explain.

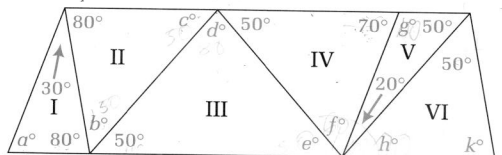

Ongoing **ASSESSMENT**

22. **Writing** Explain how each statement follows from the AA Similarity Postulate.

a. If an acute angle of one right triangle is equal in measure to an acute angle of another right triangle, then the triangles are similar.

b. If two triangles are similar to the same triangle, then they are similar to each other.

Review **PREVIEW**

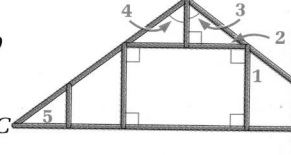

23. In △CDE the measure of ∠D is 37°. Find the measure of each numbered angle.
(Section 8-2)

For Exercises 24 and 25, tell whether each product is defined. If so, find the product matrix. *(Section 3-7)*

24. $\begin{bmatrix} 4 & 7 & 11 & 1.3 \end{bmatrix} \begin{bmatrix} 1 & 52 \\ 9.7 & 4 \end{bmatrix}$ **25.** $\begin{bmatrix} 1 & 2 & 3 \\ 2 & 5 & 6 \end{bmatrix} \begin{bmatrix} 1 \\ 2 \\ 3 \end{bmatrix}$

26. M is the midpoint of $\overline{AB}$. The coordinates of A and M are $A(-3, 7)$ and $M(0, 3)$.

a. Find the coordinates of B. *(Section 5-3)*

b. Find AB. *(Section 5-2)*

8-3 Similar Triangles

455

Application

Ex. 19 gives students an opportunity to perform a real-world activity involving similar triangles.

Assessment: Standard

For Ex. 19, students should explain which distances they will have to measure in order to find the height of the tree. They should also explain, from the sketch, which are the corresponding parts. In Ex. 21, students should justify each step in finding the missing angles.

Multicultural Note

The Arabic word for restoration and balancing, *al-jabru*, is the root of the English word *algebra*. During the 800s, Arab mathematicians made many contributions to algebra's development. They introduced the modern use of fractions, used positive and negative numbers, and expanded the use of zero. Between 813 and 833, al-Khwarizmi, a teacher in the mathematical school in Baghdad, collected and improved upon the advances of previous Hindu and Arab scholars. He also brought Chinese knowledge of algebra and geometry to the West. The Persian astronomer and poet Omar Khayyam (1050–1123) wrote a book on algebra in which he demonstrates how to express roots of cubic equations by line segments formed by intersecting conic sections.

Answers to Exercises and Problems

19. Check students' work.

20. They are congruent.

21. a. I: $a° = 70°$;
II: $b° = 50°$, $c° = 50°$;
III: $d° = 80°$, $e° = 50°$;
IV: $f° = 60°$;
V: $g° = 110°$;
VI: $h° = 50°$, $k° = 80°$

b. $\frac{1}{6}$ since △ I is similar only to itself and not to any of the other five triangles.

22. a. Since one acute angle of one triangle is equal in measure to an acute angle of the other, and the right angles are equal in measure, the triangles are similar by the AA Similarity Postulate.

b. If two triangles are similar to the same triangle, then they each have corresponding angles equal in measure to the angles of that triangle. By substitution and applying the AA Similarity Postulate, they are similar to each other.

23. $m \angle 1 = 53°$, $m \angle 2 = 37°$, $m \angle 3 = 53°$, $m \angle 4 = 53°$, $m \angle 5 = 37°$

24. Product is not defined.

25. $\begin{bmatrix} 1 & 2 & 3 \\ 2 & 5 & 6 \end{bmatrix} \begin{bmatrix} 1 \\ 2 \\ 3 \end{bmatrix} = \begin{bmatrix} 14 \\ 30 \end{bmatrix}$

26. a. $(3, -1)$

b. 10 units

455

Working on the Unit Project

For Ex. 27, students should pair up with another member of their project group. In order to expedite the making of a simple astrolabe by each group, you may wish to make available in class the objects needed in part (a). Students should keep a record of their work on this exercise for use in completing the Unit Project.

As you complete Exercise 27, think about how you can use the properties of similar triangles in the tool you design.

27. **Group Activity** Work with another student.

An astrolabe is a medieval instrument that was used to determine latitude by measuring the altitude of the sun and other stars. Although astrolabes were used in a variety of cultures, they were most widely used in the Islamic world.

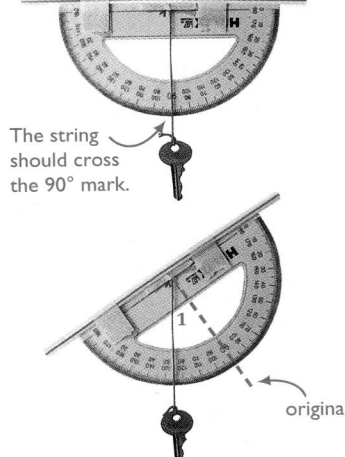

The string should cross the 90° mark.

original position

a. **Using Manipulatives** Make a simple astrolabe. You will need a protractor, a straw, a small weight or stone, and a piece of string about as long as the straw.

➤ Tie the weight to one end of the string. Tape the other end of the string to the center of the base of the protractor.

➤ Tape the straw to the base of the protractor.

b. Use your astrolabe to find your latitude.

➤ At night, look at the North Star through the straw.

➤ Have your partner note where the string crosses the protractor.

➤ Find the measure of the angle that the new position of the string makes with the original position of the string (∠1 at the left and in the diagram below).

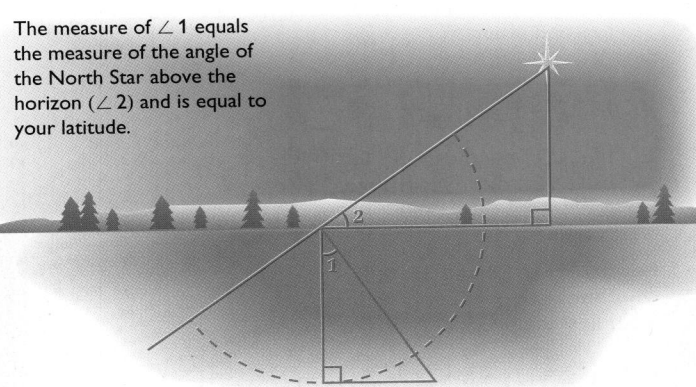

The measure of ∠1 equals the measure of the angle of the North Star above the horizon (∠2) and is equal to your latitude.

c. Each degree of latitude is equal to 111.2 km along Earth's surface. How far are you from the equator? (The equator has 0° latitude.)

d. Are the two triangles in the diagram similar? Explain.

Unit 8 Similar and Congruent Triangles

Answers to Exercises and Problems

27. a–c. Check students' work.

d. Yes; $m\angle 1 = m\angle 2$ and the two right angles are equal in measure. The triangles are similar by the AA Similarity Postulate.

1. **Writing** Write at least three things you have learned in this unit about angles and triangles.

2. **Given** $m \angle 1 = 80°$
$m \angle 2 = 100°$

   Prove $k \parallel l$

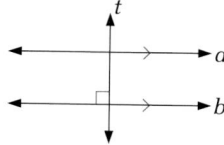

8-1

3. Explain how you know that $t \perp a$.

4. Find the value of x in each diagram.

8-2

a.
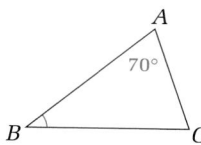
75°
55° $x°$

b.
145°
$x°$ 75°
78°

c.
35°
$x°$ 100°

5. Is there enough information given to prove that the triangles below are similar? Why or why not?

8-3

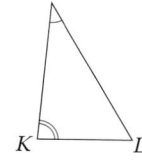

A
70°
B   C

71° D
E   F

6. a. Name the similar triangles.
   b. Name the corresponding angles.
   c. Name the corresponding sides.
   d. Write a proportion that shows how the measures of the sides are related.

G
H   I

J
K   L

7. Find the value of x.

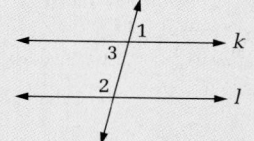
8
x
3   4

8-3 Similar Triangles

457

Quick Quiz (8-1 through 8-3)
See page 500.

Practice 62 For use with Section 8-3

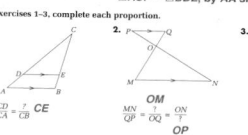

Name _____ Date _____

Practice 62
For use with Section 8-3

8. $CF \perp AB$; $DE \perp AB$; $m\angle 1 = m\angle 2$ (given). $CF \parallel DE$, since both are $\perp AB$. Thus, $m\angle 2 = m\angle 3$, since they are corr. $\angle$s. By substitution, $m\angle 1 = m\angle 3$. By def. of $\perp$ lines, $\angle CFA$ and $\angle DEB$ are rt. $\angle$s and $=$ in measure. $\triangle ACF \sim \triangle BDE$, by **AA** similarity.

For Exercises 1–3, complete each proportion.

1.
$\frac{CD}{CA} = \frac{?}{CB}$ **CE**

2.
$\frac{MN}{QP} = \frac{?}{OQ} = \frac{ON}{?}$
OM
OP

3.
$\frac{VW}{?} = \frac{VX}{ZX} = \frac{WX}{?}$
ZY
YX

For Exercises 4–7, use the diagram at the right. Use the given lengths of sides to find the missing side length.

4. $XH = 5$; $XF = 6$; $XK = 7.5$; $XG = ?$ **9**
5. $FG = 12$; $HK = 9$; $XH = 18$; $XF = ?$ **24**
6. $XK = 15$; $XG = 21$; $HK = 20$; $FG = ?$ **28**
7. $XG = 36$; $XH = 42$; $XK = 28$; $XF = ?$ **54**

8. Write a paragraph proof.
Given: $CF \perp AB$; $DE \perp AB$; $m\angle 1 = m\angle 2$
Prove: $\triangle ACF \sim \triangle BDE$

9. Suppose you stand near a tree so that the tip of your shadow (PH in the drawing) exactly coincides with the tip of the tree's shadow PT.
$\triangle PRQ \sim \triangle PTS$
a. Name a pair of similar triangles in the drawing.
b. Suppose you are 5 ft tall, your shadow is 6 ft long, and the shadow of the tree is 30 ft long. How tall is the tree? **25 ft**

10. **Writing** Are two isosceles triangles always similar? Are two equilateral triangles always similar? Give reasons for your answers to both questions. **no; yes; Check students' reasons.**

Justifications
1. Given
2. Addition property of equality
3. Definition of vertical angles
4. Vertical $\angle$s are $=$ in measure.
5. Substitution property (Steps 2 and 4)
6. Definition of supplementary angles
7. If two lines are intersected by a transversal and co-interior $\angle$s are supplementary, then the lines are $\parallel$.

3. If a transversal is perpendicular to one of two parallel lines, then it is perpendicular to the other. (Theorem 8.4)

4. a. $x° = 50°$
   b. $x° = 62°$
   c. $x° = 65°$

5. There is not enough information given to prove that the triangles are similar or that they are not similar. $m \angle A \neq m \angle D$, so $\triangle ABC \nsim \triangle DEF$, but it is possible that $\angle C = 71°$ and $\angle F = 70°$. Then $\triangle ABC \sim \triangle FED$ would be true.

6. a. $\triangle GHI$ and $\triangle JLK$
   b. $\angle G$ and $\angle J$; $\angle H$ and $\angle L$; $\angle I$ and $\angle K$
   c. $\overline{GH}$ and $\overline{JL}$; $\overline{GI}$ and $\overline{JK}$; $\overline{HI}$ and $\overline{LK}$
   d. $\frac{GI}{JK} = \frac{GH}{JL} = \frac{HI}{LK}$

7. $x = 6$

Answers to Checkpoint

1. Answers may vary. Examples are given. The sum of the measures of the angles of a triangle is 180°. Any exterior angle of a triangle is equal in measure to the sum of the measures of its two remote interior angles. If two angles of one triangle are equal in measure to two angles of another triangle, then the two triangles are similar.

2. Format and approach of proof may vary. An example is given.
Given: $m \angle 1 = 80°$;
$m \angle 2 = 100°$
Prove: $k \parallel l$

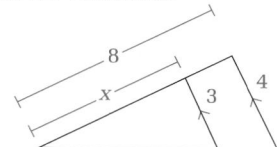
1
3   k
2
l

Statements
1. $m \angle 1 = 80°$;
$m \angle 2 = 100°$
2. $m \angle 1 + m \angle 2 = 180°$
3. $\angle 1$ and $\angle 3$ are vertical angles.
4. $m \angle 1 = m \angle 3$
5. $m \angle 2 + m \angle 3 = 180°$
6. $\angle 2$ and $\angle 3$ are supplementary.
7. $k \parallel l$

457

PLANNING

Objectives and Strands
See pages 428A and 428B.

Spiral Learning
See page 428B.

Materials List
- Geometric drawing software or
- Graph paper
- Ruler
- Protractor
- Straw
- String
- Small wooden pole or stick
- Small piece of wood
- Nail

Recommended Pacing
Section 8-4 is a two-day lesson.

Day 1
Pages 458–461: Exploration through Sample 2, *Exercises 1–9*

Day 2
Pages 461–462: Corresponding Parts of Congruent Triangles through Look Back, *Exercises 10–22*

Extra Practice
See pages 627–628.

Warm-Up Exercises
- Warm-Up Transparency 8-4

Support Materials
- Practice 63
- Enrichment 56 in the Activity Bank
- Study Guide 8-4
- Problem Set 18
- Diagram Master 2 in the Explorations Lab Manual
- McDougal Littell Mathpack software: *Geometry Inventor*
- Quiz 8-4

Section 8-4

Congruent Triangles: ASA and AAS

AS Alike AAS can be

Focus
Use two angles and a side in proofs about congruent triangles.

EXPLORATION

(How) *can you show that two triangles are congruent?*

- Materials: geometric drawing software or graph paper, rulers, and protractors
- **Work with another student.**

① Draw any △*ABC*. Measure the angles and sides of your triangle.

EXAMPLE

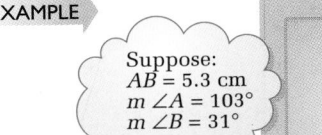
Suppose:
$AB = 5.3$ cm
$m \angle A = 103°$
$m \angle B = 31°$

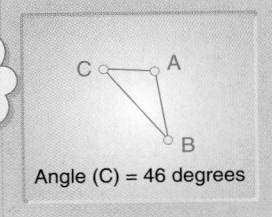
Angle (C) = 46 degrees

② Use the measures you found in step 1 for AB, $\angle A$, and $\angle B$ to draw △*EFG*.

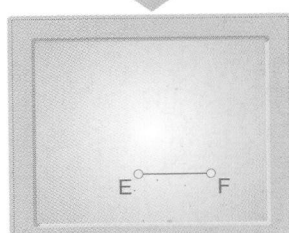
Draw $EF = AB = 5.3$ cm.

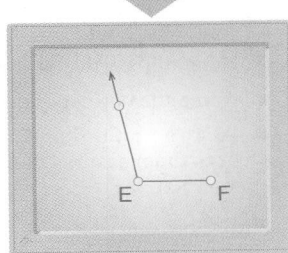
Draw $m \angle E = m \angle A = 103°$.

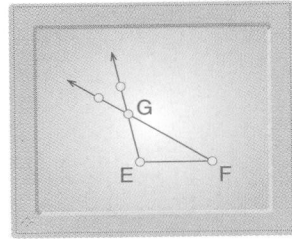
Draw $m \angle F = m \angle B = 31°$.

③ Measure the remaining angle and sides of △*EFG*.

④ Are △*ABC* and △*EFG* congruent? Do you think you could draw △*EFG* as instructed in step 2 so that △*ABC* and △*EFG* are not congruent? Explain why or why not.

Unit 8 Similar and Congruent Triangles

458

Answers to Exploration

1–3. Check students' work. Corresponding parts of △*EFG* and △*ABC* should have the same measure.

4. <u>Yes</u>; No. Once $\angle E$, $\angle F$, and $\overline{EF}$ were drawn, the position of the third vertex, G, was determined. There were no other locations for G that would result in a triangle, so every triangle produced using this method will be congruent to △*ABC*.

⑤ Use the measures you found in step 1 for AB, $\angle A$, and $\angle C$ to draw $\triangle QRS$.

Draw $QR = AB = 5.3$ cm.

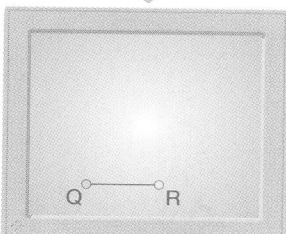

Draw $m \angle Q = m \angle A = 103°$.

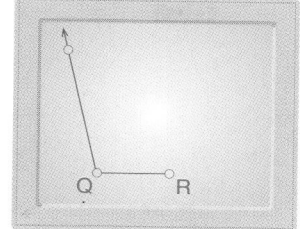

Draw $m \angle S = m \angle C = 46°$.

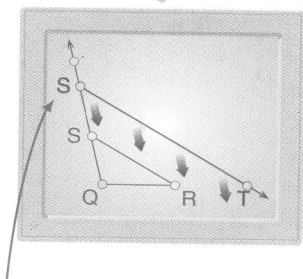

⑥ Measure the remaining sides and angle of $\triangle QRS$.

⑦ Are $\triangle ABC$ and $\triangle QRS$ congruent? Do you think you could draw $\triangle QRS$ as instructed in step 5 so that $\triangle ABC$ and $\triangle QRS$ are not congruent? Explain why or why not.

Draw $\vec{ST}$ so that $m \angle QST = 46°$. Adjust the position of $\vec{ST}$ until it passes through R.

To show that two triangles are congruent, it is not necessary to show that *all* pairs of angles are equal in measure and *all* pairs of sides are equal in measure.

THEOREMS ABOUT CONGRUENT TRIANGLES

The sides between the marked angles are called *included sides.*

Theorem 8.10 If two angles and the included side of one triangle are equal in measure to the corresponding angles and side of another triangle, then the triangles are congruent. (ASA, angle-side-angle)

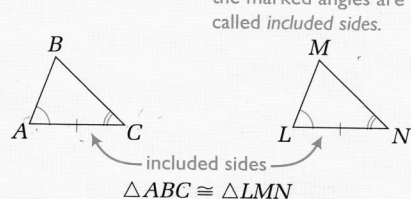

included sides

$\triangle ABC \cong \triangle LMN$

Theorem 8.11 If two angles and a non-included side of one triangle are equal in measure to the corresponding angles and side of another triangle, then the triangles are congruent. (AAS, angle-angle-side)

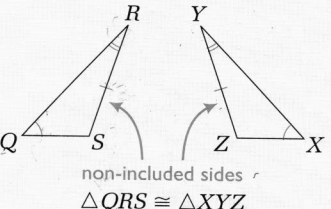

non-included sides

$\triangle QRS \cong \triangle XYZ$

8-4 Congruent Triangles: ASA and AAS

459

Answers to Exploration ·······································

5, 6. Check students' work. Corresponding parts of $\triangle QRS$ and $\triangle ABC$ should have the same measure.

7. Yes; <u>No</u>. Once $\angle Q$, $\angle S$, and $\overline{QR}$ were drawn, the position of the third vertex, S, was determined. There were no other locations for S that would result in a triangle, so every triangle produced using this method will be congruent to $\triangle ABC$.

Additional Sample

S1 Are triangles *ABC* and *DEF* congruent? Why?

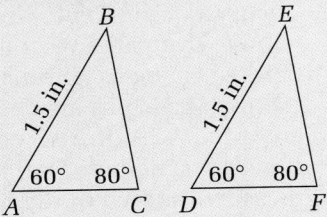

Yes; by **AAS** Theorem 8.11.

Reasoning

The key idea in planning the proof of Theorem 8.11, given in Sample 1, is to realize that if the two triangles are similar, then the ratio of the two corresponding sides must be equal to 1 because the sides are equal in length. This fact implies that the ratios of the other two pairs of corresponding sides must also equal 1, which, in turn, implies that these corresponding sides are also equal in length.

Talk it Over

Question 3 relates the proof of Theorem 8.11 to a possible proof of Theorem 8.10. Students should readily see that the location of the corresponding sides as included sides does not change the proof given for Theorem 8.11. The plan of this proof can be used to prove Theorem 8.10.

Use a two-column proof to prove Theorem 8.11.

Sample Response

> **Given** $m \angle Q = m \angle X$
> $m \angle R = m \angle Y$
> $RS = YZ$
>
> **Prove** $\triangle QRS \cong \triangle XYZ$

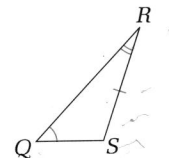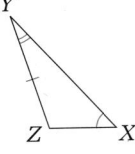

Plan Ahead

Prove that the triangles are similar. Show that the pairs of corresponding sides from the two triangles have a ratio of 1, so they are equal in measure.

Show Your Reasoning

Statements	Justifications
1. $m \angle Q = m \angle X$, $m \angle R = m \angle Y$	1. Given
2. $\triangle QRS \sim \triangle XYZ$	2. AA Similarity Postulate
3. $m \angle S = m \angle Z$	3. Definition of $\sim$ △ *Read "similar triangles."*
4. $\dfrac{RS}{YZ} = \dfrac{SQ}{ZX} = \dfrac{QR}{XY}$	4. Definition of $\sim$ △
5. $RS = YZ$	5. Given
6. $\dfrac{RS}{YZ} = 1$	6. Division property of equality
7. $1 = \dfrac{SQ}{ZX}$, $1 = \dfrac{QR}{XY}$	7. Substitution property (Steps 4 and 6)
8. $SQ = ZX$, $QR = XY$	8. Multiplication property of equality
9. $\triangle QRS \cong \triangle XYZ$	9. Definition of $\cong$ △ (Steps 1, 3, 5, and 8) *Read "congruent triangles."*

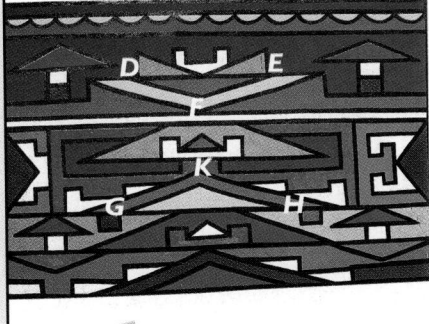

Talk it Over

1. In any $\triangle ABC$, what side is included between $\angle B$ and $\angle C$?
2. What do ASA and AAS stand for?
3. How would a proof of Theorem 8.10 compare with the proof of Theorem 8.11?
4. Suppose Nadine wants to prove that $\triangle DEF \cong \triangle GHK$. What information does she need to know to use AAS in her proof?

The photo shows a portion of a wall painted by two Ndebele women of the Transvaal region of South Africa.

Unit 8 Similar and Congruent Triangles

460

Answers to Talk it Over

1. $\overline{BC}$

2. ASA: angle-side-angle; AAS: angle-angle-side

3. The plan of the proof would be exactly the same. The proofs would differ only in that the sides used in Steps 5 and 6 would be the sides included between the congruent angles. If Theorem 8.11 were already proven, you would only need to show that the two triangles are similar and so the third pair of angles are equal in measure. Then you would have two angles and a non-included side all congruent, and you could use Theorem 8.11.

4. Nadine would need to know that two pairs of angles are congruent and that a pair of non-included sides are congruent.

For each pair of triangles, tell whether there is enough information to prove that the triangles are congruent. Write *Yes* or *No*. Explain.

a.
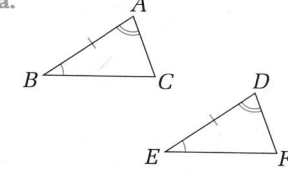

b.
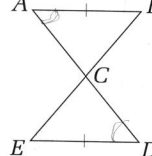

c.
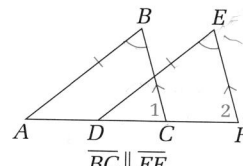

$\overline{BC} \parallel \overline{EF}$

Sample Response

a. Yes, $\triangle ABC \cong \triangle DEF$ by ASA. Two pairs of angles and the included sides are equal in measure: $m \angle B = m \angle E$, $m \angle A = m \angle D$, $AB = DE$.

b. No. Only one pair of angles and one pair of sides are known to be equal in measure: $m \angle ACB = m \angle DCE$ (vertical angles), $AB = DE$.

c. Yes, $\triangle ABC \cong \triangle DEF$ by AAS. Two pairs of angles and the corresponding non-included sides are equal in measure: $m \angle B = m \angle E$, $m \angle 1 = m \angle 2$ (corresponding angles formed by parallel lines and a transversal), $AB = DE$.

▶ Now you are ready for:
Exs. 1–9 on pp. 462–463

Corresponding Parts of Congruent Triangles

You can prove relationships between the corresponding parts of two triangles once you have proved that the triangles are congruent. Use the statement *Corresponding parts of congruent triangles are equal in measure.*

Some people abbreviate this statement as CPCTE.

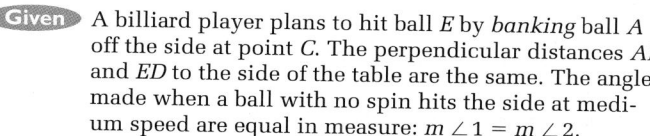

Sample 3

Given A billiard player plans to hit ball *E* by *banking* ball *A* off the side at point *C*. The perpendicular distances *AB* and *ED* to the side of the table are the same. The angles made when a ball with no spin hits the side at medium speed are equal in measure: $m \angle 1 = m \angle 2$.

Prove *C* is the midpoint of $\overline{BD}$.

Continued on next page.

8-4 Congruent Triangles: ASA and AAS

461

S2 For each pair of triangles, tell whether there is enough information to prove that the triangles are congruent. Write *Yes* or *No*. Explain.

a.
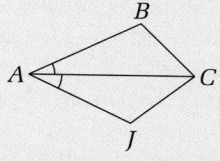

No. Only one pair of angles and a pair of sides are equal in measure.

b.
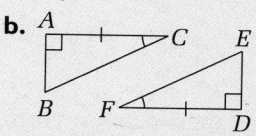

Yes. $\triangle ABC \cong \triangle DEF$ by ASA.

c.
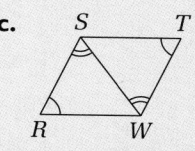

Yes. $\triangle RSW \cong \triangle TWS$ by AAS.

S3 Given: $\overline{AD} \cong \overline{AE}$
$\qquad m \angle B = m \angle C$
Prove: $CE = BD$

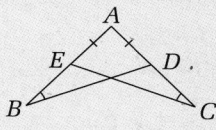

Plan: Show that $\triangle ABD \cong \triangle ACE$. Then corresponding parts of these triangles will be equal in measure.
$m \angle A = m \angle A$
$m \angle B = m \angle C$
$\overline{AD} \cong \overline{AE}$
$\therefore \triangle ABD \cong \triangle ACE$ by AAS.
$CE = BD$ because corresponding parts of congruent triangles are equal in measure.

461

Sample Response

Given $m \angle 1 = m \angle 2$
$AB = ED$
$\overline{AB} \perp \overline{BD}$ and $\overline{ED} \perp \overline{BD}$

Prove C is the midpoint of $\overline{BD}$.

Plan Ahead

Show that $\triangle ABC \cong \triangle EDC$. Then corresponding sides $\overline{BC}$ and $\overline{DC}$ will be equal in measure.

Show Your Reasoning

Statements

$\overline{AB} \perp \overline{BD}$
$\overline{ED} \perp \overline{BD}$ **①** $\rightarrow$ $m \angle ABC = 90°$
$m \angle EDC = 90°$ **②** $\rightarrow$ $m \angle ABC = m \angle EDC$
$m \angle 1 = m \angle 2$
$AB = ED$ **③**

$\rightarrow$ $\triangle ABC \cong \triangle EDC$ **④** $\rightarrow$ $BC = DC$ **⑤** $\rightarrow$ C is the midpoint of $\overline{BD}$.

Justifications

① Definition of perpendicular lines

② Substitution property

③ AAS

④ Corres. parts of $\cong \triangle$ are $=$ in measure.

⑤ Definition of midpoint

BY THE WAY...

The U.S. patent in 1869 for the new material celluloid resulted from the game of billiards. A billiards ball manufacturer had offered $10,000 for an inexpensive substitute for ivory.

Look Back

Explain why it may be necessary to first prove that two triangles are congruent in order to prove that certain sides or certain angles are equal in measure.

> Now you are ready for:
> Exs. 10–22 on pp. 464–465

Now you are ready for: Exs. 10–22 on pp. 464–465

8-4 **Exercises and Problems**

1. **Reading** Sketch a triangle XYZ. Copy and complete the table.

Sides	Included Angle
$\overline{XY}$ and $\overline{YZ}$	?
$\overline{YZ}$ and $\overline{ZX}$	?
$\overline{ZX}$ and $\overline{XY}$	?

Answers to Look Back

The logic involved with CPCTE (corresponding parts of congruent triangles are equal in measure) requires the use of congruent triangles.

Answers to Exercises and Problems

1.

Sides	Included Angle
$\overline{XY}$ and $\overline{YZ}$	$\angle Y$
$\overline{YZ}$ and $\overline{ZX}$	$\angle Z$
$\overline{ZX}$ and $\overline{XY}$	$\angle X$

2.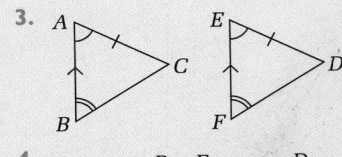

3.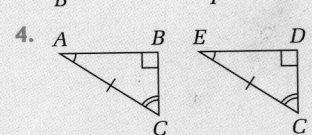

4.

5. b

6. $x° = 40°$, $y° = 20°$

7. Given: $m \angle TUW = m \angle VUW$; $\overline{UW} \perp \overline{TV}$
Prove: $\triangle TUW \cong \triangle VUW$

Statements

1. $m \angle TUW = m \angle VUW$
2. $\overline{UW} = \overline{UW}$
3. $\overline{UW} \perp \overline{TV}$
4. $m \angle UWT = 90°$
$m \angle UWV = 90°$
5. $m \angle UWT = m \angle UWV$
6. $\triangle TUW \cong \triangle VUW$

In each of Exercises 2–4, the triangles are congruent. Trace the triangles so that they are side by side with corresponding vertices in the same position. Mark the parts that are equal in measure. An example is done for you.

Example

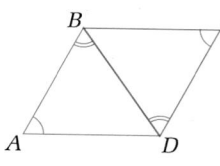 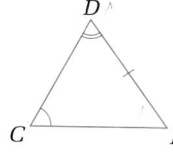

2.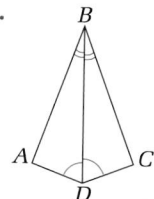

3.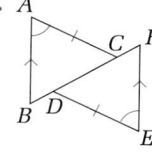

4. Given: $\overline{BD} \perp \overline{AB}$
$\overline{BD} \perp \overline{DE}$
C is the midpoint of $\overline{AE}$.

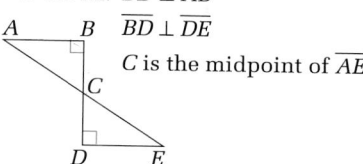

5. Use the triangles in the Exploration on pages 458–459. Choose the letter of the statement that correctly shows the relationship between the triangles.

a. $\triangle ABC \cong \triangle RQS$ **b.** $\triangle ABC \cong \triangle QRS$ **c.** $\triangle ABC \cong \triangle SRQ$

6. Find the value of x and the value of y.

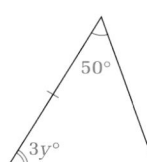

7. **Given** $m \angle TUW = m \angle VUW$
$\overline{UW} \perp \overline{TV}$

Prove $\triangle TUW \cong \triangle VUW$

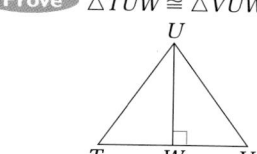

8. **Group Activity** Work with another student.

a. Plot the points $J(1, 9)$, $K(3, 3)$, and $L(6, 4)$ on a coordinate plane. Connect them. Find the slopes of $\overline{JK}$ and $\overline{LK}$. What is the measure of $\angle K$?

b. Plot the points $M(-2, -5)$, $N(-8, -3)$, and $P(-9, -6)$ on the same coordinate plane. Connect the points. Find the slopes of $\overline{MN}$ and $\overline{PN}$. What is the measure of $\angle N$?

c. Use the distance formula to show that $JL = MP$.

d. If $m \angle J = m \angle M$, what is the relationship between $\triangle JKL$ and $\triangle MNP$? Explain.

9. **Writing** Explain why two right triangles are congruent if the hypotenuse and an acute angle of one right triangle are equal in measure to the hypotenuse and an acute angle of the other right triangle.

8-4 Congruent Triangles: ASA and AAS

Answers to Exercises and Problems

Justifications
1. Given
2. Reflexive property of equality
3. Given
4. Definition of $\perp$ lines
5. Substitution property (Step 4)
6. ASA

8. a, b.

a. slope of $\overline{JK} = -3$; slope of $\overline{LK} = \frac{1}{3}$; $m \angle K = 90°$

b. slope of $\overline{MN} = -\frac{1}{3}$; slope of $\overline{PN} = 3$; $m \angle N = 90°$

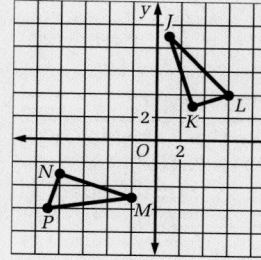

c. $JL = \sqrt{(9-4)^2 + (1-6)^2} = \sqrt{25 + 25} = 5\sqrt{2}$;
$MP = \sqrt{(-9+2)^2 + (-6+5)^2} = \sqrt{49 + 1} = 5\sqrt{2}$

d. $\triangle JKL \cong \triangle MNP$ by AAS.

9. Since the right angles are also equal in measure, the triangles are congruent by AAS.

For Exercises 10–12, suppose you had to prove each relationship given. What pair of triangles would you first need to prove congruent?

a. $m \angle 1 = m \angle 2$

b. $AB = CD$

10.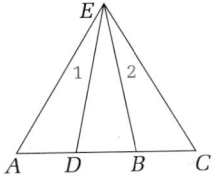

11.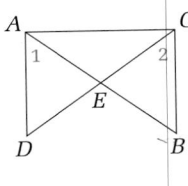

12.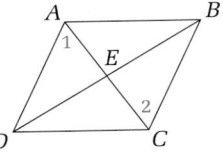

13. **Given**  $\overline{AC} \perp \overline{CB}$
$\overline{DB} \perp \overline{BC}$
$m \angle 1 = m \angle 2$

Prove $AC = DB$

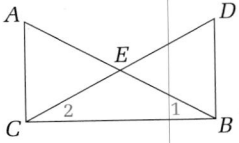

Find the value of x. If there is not enough information given, write *not enough information*.

14.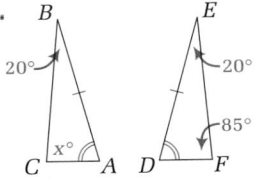

15.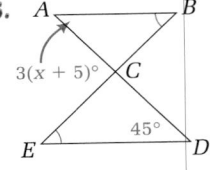

16.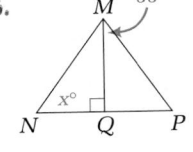

Ongoing **ASSESSMENT**

17. **Group Activity** Work with another student. You will need straws, string, a ruler, and a protractor.

a. Each of you should cut straws into pieces. Cut lengths of 4 in., 5 in., and 7 in. Now thread string through your straw pieces and connect them tightly to form a triangle.

b. Use the protractor to measure the angles of both triangles.

c. What relationship exists between your two triangles? Explain.

d. Compare your triangles to other groups' triangles. Does the relationship still hold?

e. The theorems in this section indicate that when you know that two pairs of corresponding angles and a pair of corresponding sides are equal in measure, then you can say that the triangles are congruent. What other group of three pairs of corresponding parts did you use in steps (a)–(d) to also guarantee congruent triangles?

464

Unit 8 Similar and Congruent Triangles

Answers to Exercises and Problems

10. a. $\triangle ADE \cong \triangle CBE$

b. $\triangle ABE \cong \triangle CDE$

11. a. $\triangle DEA \cong \triangle BEC$

b. $\triangle DAC \cong \triangle BCA$

12. a. $\triangle AED \cong \triangle CEB$ or
$\triangle ACD \cong \triangle CAB$

b. $\triangle ABE \cong \triangle CDE$ or
$\triangle ABC \cong \triangle CDA$

13. *Given:* $\overline{AC} \perp \overline{CB}; \overline{DB} \perp \overline{BC};$
$m \angle 1 = m \angle 2$
Prove: $AC = DB$
Statements
1. $\overline{AC} \perp \overline{CB}; \overline{DB} \perp \overline{BC}$
2. $m \angle ACB = 90°$
   $m \angle DBC = 90°$
3. $m \angle ACB = m \angle DBC$
4. $m \angle 1 = m \angle 2$
5. $BC = BC$
6. $\triangle ABC \cong \triangle DCB$
7. $AC = DB$

Justifications
1. Given
2. Definition of $\perp$ lines
3. Substitution property (Step 2)
4. Given
5. Reflexive property of equality
6. ASA
7. CPCTE

14. $x° = 85°$

15. $x° = 10°$

16. not enough information

17. a. Check students' work.

b. The angles are about 34°, 44° and 102°.

c. They are congruent since three pairs of sides and three pairs of angles have the same measure.

d. Yes.

464

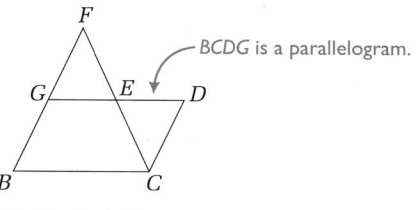

BCDG is a parallelogram.

Review **PREVIEW**

18. Identify the similar triangles. Identify the postulates or theorems that support your answer. *(Section 8-3)*

19. The measure of one exterior angle of a triangle is 35°. What type of triangle is it? *(Section 8-2)*

20. What is the justification for the statement $PR = PQ + QR$? *(Section 7-7)*

Working on the Unit Project

As you complete Exercises 21 and 22, think about how you can include the properties of congruent triangles in the tool you design.

A common problem for many land surveyors is how to measure distances considered "inaccessible" because they cannot be measured directly, like the distance across a canyon. In Exercise 21, you will explore a tool used to find such distances.

21. a. Using Manipulatives Find a wooden pole a little taller than yourself. Nail a stick of wood about the size of a ruler to the pole at a height less than or equal to your eye level. This stick should be movable, but should not hang freely. Follow the directions at the right.

b. What can you say about the two triangles formed? Explain.

c. What can you say about the bases of the two triangles? Measure to confirm your answer.

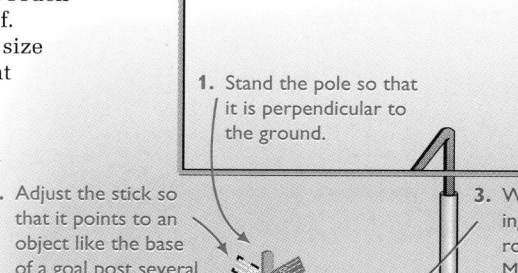

1. Stand the pole so that it is perpendicular to the ground.

2. Adjust the stick so that it points to an object like the base of a goal post several feet away from where you are standing.

3. Without readjusting the stick, rotate the pole. Mark a point *A*, where the stick is now pointing.

22. How can a surveyor use a similar tool to find the distance across a canyon?

465

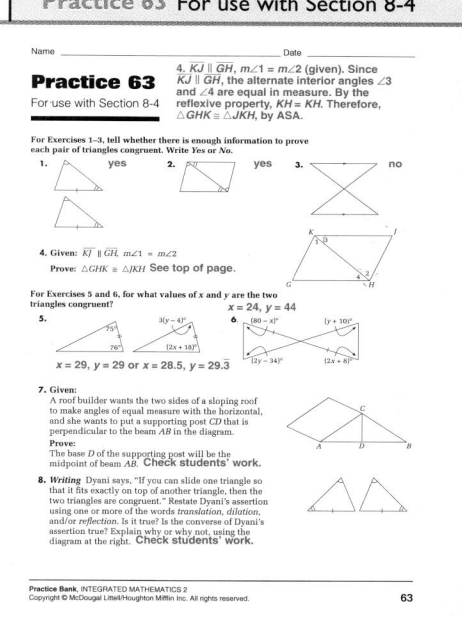

Practice 63 For use with Section 8-4

Answers to Exercises and Problems

e. Three pairs of corresponding sides were used.

18. △GEF ~ △DEC by the AA Similarity Postulate (vertical angles at *E*, and ∠EGF and ∠EDC being alternate interior angles). △GEF ~ △BCF by the Overlapping Similar Triangles Theorem (*GE* ∥ *BC* because GDBC is a parallelogram); △BCF ~ △DEC by the AA Similar-

ity Postulate (opposite angles *B* and *D* in the parallelogram and ∠BCF and ∠DEC being alternate interior angles).

19. obtuse

20. Whole and Parts Postulate: For any segment, the measure of the whole is equal to the sum of the measures of its non-overlapping parts.

21. a. Check students' work.

b. They are congruent. The two right angles are congruent to each other. The triangles have the wooden pole as a common side, and the angles formed by the pole and the stick are congruent as well. So by ASA, the triangles are congruent.

c. The bases are equal in measure by CPCTE.

22. The surveyor can sight a point on the opposite side of the canyon, then rotate the pole without adjusting the angle of the piece of wood and sight a point whose distance from the base of the pole can be measured directly.

465

Section 8-5

Congruent Triangles: SAS and SSS

Focus
Use two sides and an angle or three sides in proofs about congruent triangles.

Choosing SIDES

Structures that are made from triangles are stable. The angles in the structure cannot change without breaking the sides. A structure that is a quadrilateral, on the other hand, can be distorted. The angles can change while the measures of the sides stay the same.

One way to build two congruent triangles is to make them with sides of equal measures (SSS Postulate). You can also make two congruent triangles by making two pairs of sides and the angles between them equal in measure (SAS Postulate).

POSTULATES ABOUT CONGRUENT TRIANGLES

Postulate 14 If two sides and the included angle of one triangle are equal in measure to the corresponding sides and angle of another triangle, then the triangles are congruent. (SAS, side-angle-side)

The angles between the marked sides are called *included angles*.

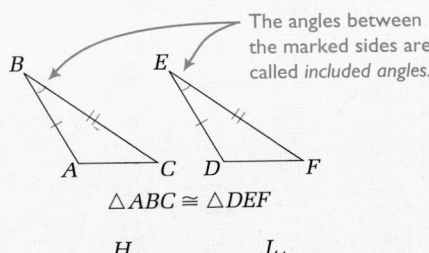

$\triangle ABC \cong \triangle DEF$

Postulate 15 If three sides of one triangle are equal in measure to the corresponding sides of another triangle, then the triangles are congruent. (SSS, side-side-side)

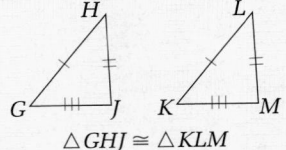

$\triangle GHJ \cong \triangle KLM$

For each pair of triangles, tell whether there is enough information to prove that the triangles are congruent. Write *Yes* or *No.*
Explain.

a.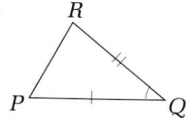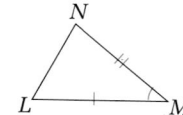

b. 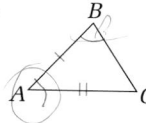 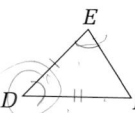 SSA

Sample Response

a. Yes, $\triangle PQR \cong \triangle LMN$ by SAS: $RQ = NM$, $m \angle Q = m \angle M$, $PQ = LM$.

b. No. The congruent angles are not included angles. You would need to know
that the third pair of sides is also congruent, or that a second pair of angles
is congruent, to prove that $\triangle ABC \cong \triangle DEF$.

Sample 2

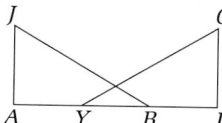

Given $JA = CI$ **Prove** $\triangle JAR \cong \triangle CIY$
$AY = IR$
$JR = CY$

Sample Response

Plan Ahead

Separate the triangles and mark the diagram
using the given information. Show that $AR = IY$
and then use SSS.

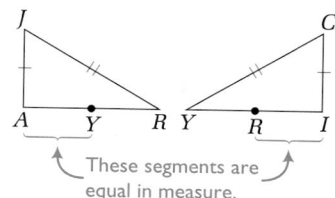

These segments are
equal in measure.

Show Your Reasoning

> $JA = CI$, $JR = CY$ (given). The remaining sides of $\triangle JAR$ and
> $\triangle CIY$ are $\overline{AR}$ and $\overline{IY}$. You know that $AY = IR$. Add YR to
> both sides. This gives $AY + YR = IR + RY$ (add. prop. of =).
> $AY + YR = AR$ and $IR + RY = IY$ (measure of whole equals
> sum of measures of non-overlapping parts). By
> substitution, $AR = IY$. Now $\triangle JAR \cong \triangle CIY$ by SSS.

8-5 Congruent Triangles: SAS and SSS

467

 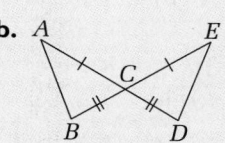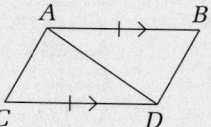
467

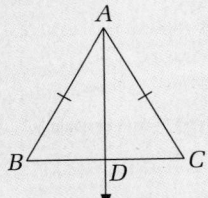
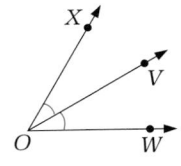

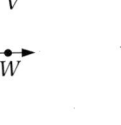

Bisectors

In the diagram at the left, $\overrightarrow{OV}$ bisects $\angle WOX$. An **angle bisector** is a ray that begins at the vertex of an angle and divides the angle into two angles of equal measure.

Sample 3

Given $\overrightarrow{AD}$ bisects $\angle BAC$.
$AB = AC$

Prove $BD = CD$

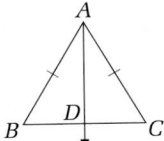

Sample Response

Plan Ahead

Show that $\triangle BAD \cong \triangle CAD$ by SAS. Then the corresponding parts $\overline{BD}$ and $\overline{CD}$ will be equal in measure.

Show Your Reasoning

Statements	Justifications
1. $AB = AC$	1. Given
2. $\overrightarrow{AD}$ bisects $\angle BAC$.	2. Given
3. $m \angle BAD = m \angle CAD$	3. Definition of angle bisector
4. $AD = AD$	4. Reflexive property of equality
5. $\triangle BAD \cong \triangle CAD$	5. SAS (Steps 1, 3, and 4)
6. $BD = CD$	6. Corres. parts of $\cong$ $\triangle$ are $=$ in measure.

Watch Out!
An angle bisector does not *always* bisect a side of a triangle. $\triangle ABC$ is a special case.

In Sample 3, $\overrightarrow{AD}$ bisects $\overline{BC}$. A **segment bisector** is a ray, line, or segment that divides a segment into two parts of equal measure. The bisector passes through the midpoint of the segment it bisects.

Unit 8 Similar and Congruent Triangles

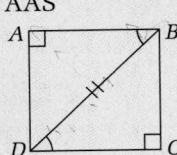
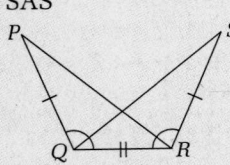
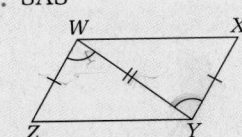

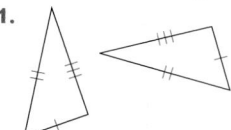

Look Back ◄

What information would you need in order to decide whether these two triangles are congruent? (There is more than one answer.)

 8-5 **Exercises and Problems**

For each pair of triangles, tell whether there is enough information to prove that the triangles are congruent. Write *Yes* or *No*. Explain.

1. 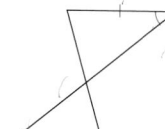 **2.** 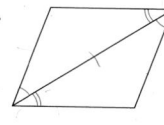 **3.** 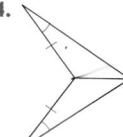 **4.**

Copy each figure and mark any parts that are equal in measure. Identify the postulate or theorem you would use to prove that each pair of triangles is congruent.

5. $\overline{AD} \perp \overline{AB}, \overline{BC} \perp \overline{CD}$
$m \angle ABD = m \angle CDB$

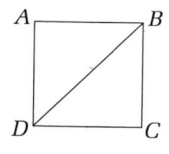

$\triangle ABD \cong \triangle CDB$

6. $m \angle PQR = m \angle SRQ$
$PQ = SR$

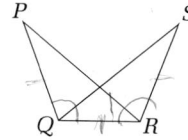

$\triangle PQR \cong \triangle SRQ$

7. $\overline{WZ} \parallel \overline{YX}$
$WZ = YX$

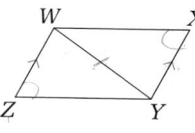

$\triangle WZY \cong \triangle YXW$

8. a. Plot the points $G(2, 2)$, $H(7, 2)$, and $J(3, 5)$ on a coordinate plane. Connect the points to form $\triangle GHJ$.

b. Plot the points $K(2, -1)$, $L(7, -1)$, and $M(3, -4)$ on a coordinate plane. Connect the points to form $\triangle KLM$.

c. Use the distance formula to prove that $\triangle GHJ \cong \triangle KLM$.

9. If you are given only the measures $AC = 3.5$ ft, $m \angle A = 42°$, and $m \angle B = 23°$, you can draw a triangle that will automatically be congruent to the triangle in the diagram. If you are given only the three angle measures, you cannot.

Make an organized list of all the sets of three measures that provide enough information to draw a triangle that will automatically be congruent to $\triangle ABC$.

This building at Futuroscope, a science-based theme park in France, resembles a quartz crystal.

8-5 Congruent Triangles: SAS and SSS

469

---

9. Using ASA
AC, $m \angle C$, $m \angle A$
AB, $m \angle A$, $m \angle B$
BC, $m \angle B$, $m \angle C$

Using SSS
AB, BC, AC

Using SAS
AC, AB, $m \angle A$
AB, BC, $m \angle B$
BC, AC, $m \angle C$

Using AAS
$m \angle A$, $m \angle B$, AC
$m \angle A$, $m \angle B$, BC
$m \angle B$, $m \angle C$, AB
$m \angle B$, $m \angle C$, AC
$m \angle A$, $m \angle C$, AB
$m \angle A$, $m \angle C$, BC

Answers to Exercises and Problems ································

8. a.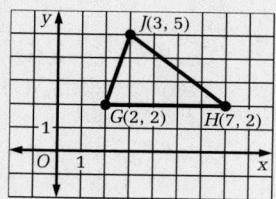

b.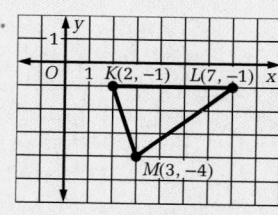

c. $GH = KL = 5$; $HJ = \sqrt{(5-2)^2 + (3-7)^2} = \sqrt{9 + 16} = \sqrt{25} = 5$;

$LM = \sqrt{(7-3)^2 + (-1+4)^2} = \sqrt{16 + 9} = \sqrt{25} = 5$; therefore, $HJ = LM$. $GJ = \sqrt{(5-2)^2 + (3-2)^2} = \sqrt{9 + 1} = \sqrt{10}$; $KM = \sqrt{(3-2)^2 + (-4+1)^2} = \sqrt{1 + 9} = \sqrt{10}$; therefore, $GJ = KM$. Then by SSS, $\triangle GHJ \cong \triangle KLM$.

10. **Reading** How are segment bisectors and angle bisectors alike? How are they different?

11. $\overrightarrow{BD}$ bisects $\angle ABC$. Find x.

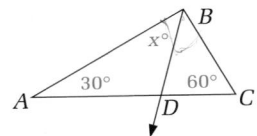

12. **Given** $\overline{PR}$ and $\overline{NS}$ bisect each other.

    Prove $\triangle NPQ \cong \triangle SRQ$

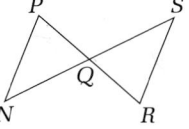

---

connection to **INDUSTRIAL TECHNOLOGY**

Drafters can duplicate line segments, angles, and geometric shapes using only a compass and a *straightedge* (a device for drawing straight lines that does not have marks for measuring).

13. **Using Manipulatives** Follow these steps to duplicate a triangle using only a compass and a straightedge.

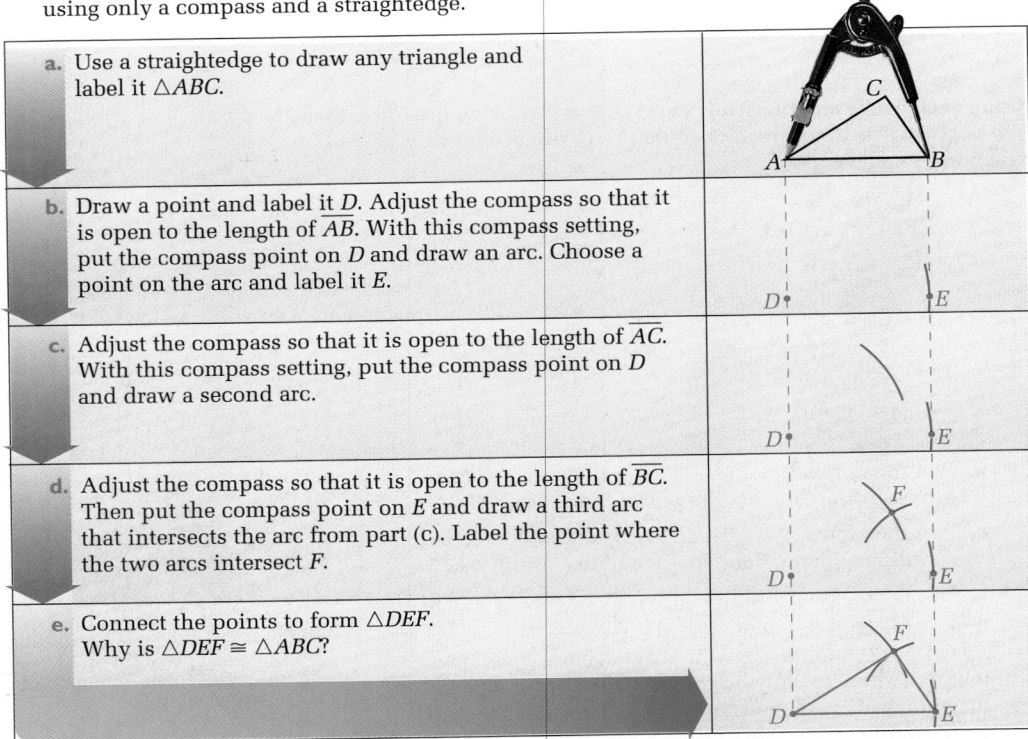

a. Use a straightedge to draw any triangle and label it $\triangle ABC$.

b. Draw a point and label it D. Adjust the compass so that it is open to the length of $\overline{AB}$. With this compass setting, put the compass point on D and draw an arc. Choose a point on the arc and label it E.

c. Adjust the compass so that it is open to the length of $\overline{AC}$. With this compass setting, put the compass point on D and draw a second arc.

d. Adjust the compass so that it is open to the length of $\overline{BC}$. Then put the compass point on E and draw a third arc that intersects the arc from part (c). Label the point where the two arcs intersect F.

e. Connect the points to form $\triangle DEF$. Why is $\triangle DEF \cong \triangle ABC$?

14. a. **Research** Find out if it is possible to bisect an angle using only a compass and straightedge. If so, describe how to do it.

    b. **Research** Find out if it is possible to *trisect* an angle using only a compass and straightedge. If so, describe how to do it.

 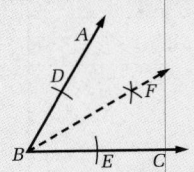
470

15. Writing Identify the theorem or postulate about congruent triangles that can be used to justify each statement. Explain your choice.

a. If the legs of one right triangle are equal in measure to the corresponding legs of another right triangle, then the triangles are congruent.

b. If any side and an acute angle of one right triangle are equal in measure to the corresponding side and acute angle of another right triangle, then the triangles are congruent.

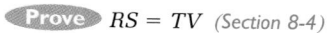 *Review* **PREVIEW**

16. ⟨Given⟩ $\overline{RS} \parallel \overline{VT}$
$RW = TW$

⟨Prove⟩ $RS = TV$ (Section 8-4)

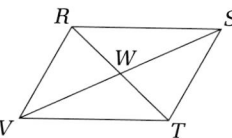

17. Joshua remembers that the last four digits of his friend's phone number are 3, 4, 6, and 8. Unfortunately he doesn't remember the order of the numbers. How many permutations of the four numbers are there? *(Section 6-2)*

18. Draw a Venn diagram for the implication "If a triangle is equilateral, then it is isosceles." *(Section 7-2)*

 Working on the Unit Project

As you complete Exercise 19, think about how you can use the properties of congruent triangles in the tool you design.

19. Ruth Levinson is surveying a piece of property. She needs to measure the distance between A and B across a pond. She drives in a stake at any point X. Then she uses her steel tape to measure $\overline{AX}$ and $\overline{BX}$. After more measuring, she drives in stakes at points Y and Z.

a. How long do you think she makes $\overline{XY}$? How long do you think she makes $\overline{XZ}$?

b. Ruth was very careful to make sure that point Y lies on $\overleftrightarrow{AX}$ and point Z lies on $\overleftrightarrow{BX}$. She knew this would guarantee that $m \angle YXZ = m \angle AXB$. Explain her reasoning.

c. Ruth measures $\overline{YZ}$. She finds that $YZ = 53$ ft. What is AB? How do you know?

Surveyors may use a *steel tape* when finding distances across lakes, canyons, and other geographical features whose dimensions cannot be measured directly. The flexible steel tape is rolled up on a reel. The tape can be reeled in like a line on a fishing rod.

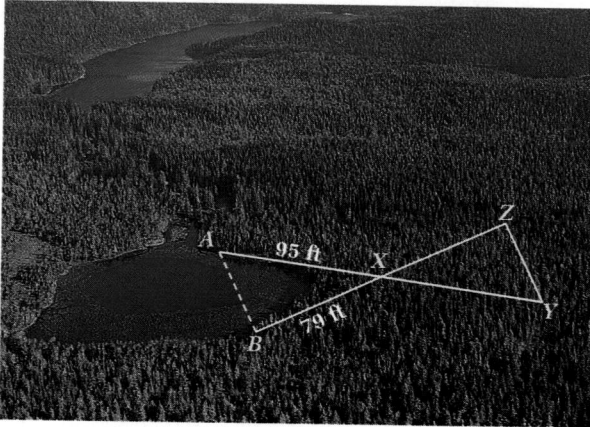

8-5 Congruent Triangles: SAS and SSS

471

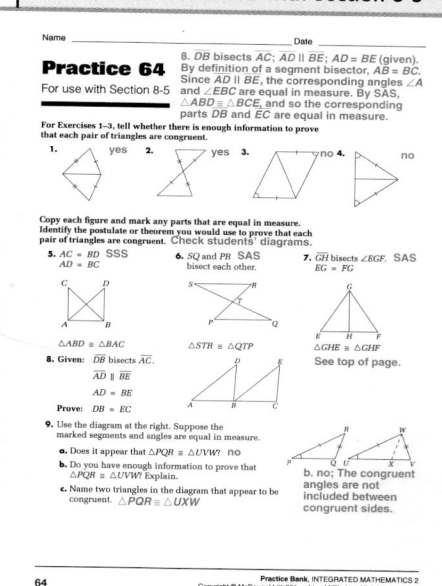

Assessment: Standard

Students should write a flow proof for proving parts (a) and (b) of Ex. 15. Also, students should be able to construct a triangle congruent to $\triangle ABC$ using SAS.

Working on the Unit Project

Students can work on Ex. 19 individually and then meet in their project groups to compare answers.

Answers to Exercises and Problems

16. *Given:* $\overline{RS} \parallel \overline{VT}$; $RW = TW$
Prove: $RS = TV$

Statements
1. $\overline{RS} \parallel \overline{VT}$
2. $m \angle RSV = m \angle SVT$
   $m \angle SRT = m \angle VTR$
3. $RW = TW$
4. $\triangle RSW \cong \triangle TVW$
5. $RS = TV$

Justifications
1. Given
2. If two ∥ lines are intersected by a transversal, then alternate interior ∠s are = in measure.
3. Given
4. AAS
5. CPCTE

17. 24

18.

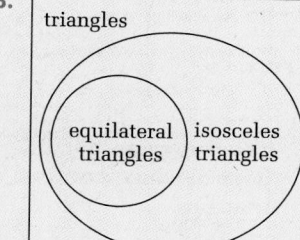

triangles

equilateral triangles / isosceles triangles

19. a. 95 ft; 79 ft

b. $\angle YXZ$ and $\angle AXB$ would be vertical angles and therefore equal in measure.

c. 53 ft; $\triangle AXB \cong \triangle YXZ$ by SAS and $AB = YZ$ by CPCTE.

PLANNING

Objectives and Strands

See pages 428A and 428B.

Spiral Learning

See page 428B.

Materials List

➤ Graph Paper

➤ Scissors

➤ Straightedge

➤ Compass

Recommended Pacing

Section 8-6 is a two-day lesson.

Day 1

Pages 472–474: Opening paragraph through Talk it Over 8, *Exercises 1–20*

Day 2

Page 475: Perpendicular Bisectors through Look Back, *Exercises 21–32*

Toolbox References

Toolbox Skill 12: Simplifying Expressions with Radicals

Extra Practice

See pages 627–628.

Warm-Up Exercises

💡 Warm-Up Transparency 8-6

Support Materials

➤ Practice 65

➤ Enrichment 58 in the Activity Bank

➤ Study Guide 8-6

➤ Problem Set 18

➤ Diagram Master 2 in the Explorations Lab Manual

➤ McDougal Littell Mathpack software: *Geometry Inventor*

➤ Geometry Inventor Activity Book: Activity 29

➤ Quiz 8-6

➤ Test 33

➤ Alternative Assessment 4

Congruence and Isosceles Triangles

UPON REFLECTION

Focus

Apply properties of isosceles triangles, equilateral triangles, and perpendicular bisectors.

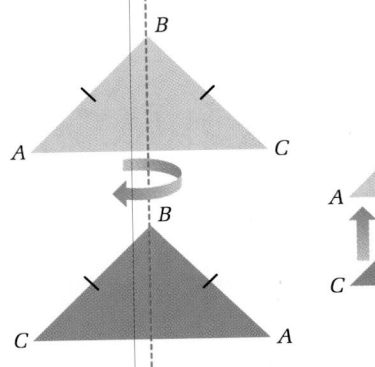
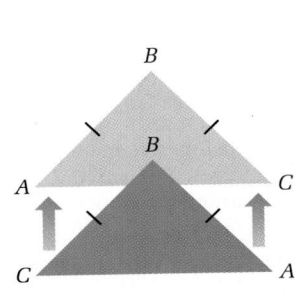
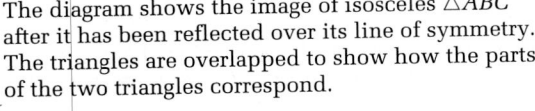

BY THE WAY...

The internal spaces in a vulture's metacarpal bone approximate isosceles triangles. This bone structure in the wing is lightweight but very strong. The structure resembles the bridge structure on page 466.

The diagram shows the image of isosceles △ABC after it has been reflected over its line of symmetry. The triangles are overlapped to show how the parts of the two triangles correspond.

Talk it Over

For question 1–5, use the figures above. For questions 1–3, tell which part of the image corresponds to each given part of the original triangle.

1. $\overline{AB}$ 2. ∠B 3. $\overline{CB}$

4. What postulate or theorem can you use to prove that △ABC ≅ △CBA?

5. Why must ∠A and ∠C be equal in measure?

6. What can you say about ∠X and ∠Z in isosceles △XYZ?

Theorem 8.12 summarizes the results of the questions you just answered. You will prove this theorem in Exercise 14 and its converse, Theorem 8.13, in Exercise 15.

Unit 8 Similar and Congruent Triangles

Answers to Talk it Over

1. $\overline{CB}$

2. ∠B

3. $\overline{AB}$

4. SAS

5. They are corresponding parts of congruent triangles.

6. They are equal in measure.

ISOSCELES TRIANGLE THEOREMS

Theorem 8.12 If two sides of a triangle are equal in measure, then the angles opposite those sides are equal in measure.

In an isosceles triangle, the sides of equal measure are called **legs** and the third side is called the **base**.

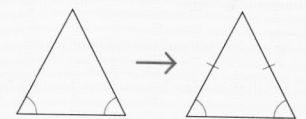

Theorem 8.13 If two angles of a triangle are equal in measure, then the sides opposite those angles are equal in measure.

The isosceles triangle theorems can help you find measures of sides and angles.

Sample 1

In a △GRE, GR = ER. The measure of ∠R is ten more than three times the measure of one of the other angles. Find the measures of all three angles.

Sample Response

Draw and label a diagram.

$GR = RE$, so △GRE is isosceles.

Let $x°$ = the measure of $\angle G$. Then $x°$ = the measure of $\angle E$, since $\angle G$ and $\angle E$ are angles opposite sides of equal measure.

Also, $(3x + 10)°$ = the measure of $\angle R$.

$m\angle G + m\angle E + m\angle R = 180°$ ← Use the triangle sum theorem.

$x + x + 3x + 10 = 180$

$5x + 10 = 180$

$5x = 170$

$x = 34$

Substitute 34 for x to find the measure of $\angle R$.

$3x + 10 = 3(34) + 10 = 102 + 10 = 112$

Then, $m\angle G = 34°$, $m\angle E = 34°$, and $m\angle R = 112°$.

This building is in the city of Sandakan in Malaysia.

TEACHING

Talk it Over

Questions 1–3 make use of the fact that a reflection of a triangle over a line does not alter the lengths of the segments or the measures of the angles that form the original triangle. Thus, in question 4, SAS can be used to conclude that △ABC ≅ △CBA, which implies that $m\angle A = m\angle C$.

Reasoning

Students should be able to state Theorems 8.12 and 8.13 as a biconditional. (Two sides of a triangle are equal in measure if and only if the angles opposite those sides are equal in measure.)

Additional Sample

S1 In △MNP, MN = NP. The measure of ∠N is 8 less than twice the measure of one of the other angles. Find the measures of all three angles.

Make a diagram.

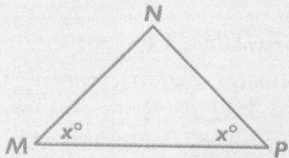

Let $x° = m\angle M$.
Then $x° = m\angle P$ by the isosceles triangle theorem. Use the triangle sum theorem.

$x + x + 2x - 8 = 180$

$4x = 188$

$x = 47$

$2x - 8 = 2(47) - 8 = 86$

Then, $m\angle M = 47°$,
$m\angle P = 47°$, and $m\angle N = 86°$.

473

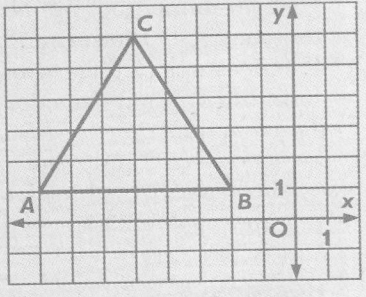
On a coordinate plane, plot the points $W(1, 5)$, $Q(5, 5)$, and $R(3, 1)$. Show that $m\angle W = m\angle Q$.

Sample Response

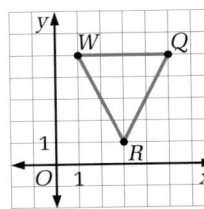

Use the distance formula $d = \sqrt{(x_2 - x_1)^2 + (y_2 - y_1)^2}$.

$WR = \sqrt{(3 - 1)^2 + (1 - 5)^2}$ $\qquad$ $QR = \sqrt{(3 - 5)^2 + (1 - 5)^2}$

$= \sqrt{(2)^2 + (-4)^2}$ $\qquad\qquad$ $= \sqrt{(-2)^2 + (-4)^2}$

$= \sqrt{4 + 16}$ $\qquad\qquad\qquad$ $= \sqrt{4 + 16}$

$= \sqrt{20}$ $\qquad\qquad\qquad\quad$ $= \sqrt{20}$

Since $WR = QR$, you can conclude that $m\angle W = m\angle Q$, because in a triangle that has two sides of equal measure, the angles opposite those sides are equal in measure.

Equilateral Triangles

Equilateral triangles have three sides of equal measure. They are a special type of isosceles triangle. You will investigate the following theorems about equilateral triangles in Exercise 17.

EQUILATERAL TRIANGLE THEOREMS

Theorem 8.14 If a triangle is equilateral, then it is also equiangular, with three 60° angles.

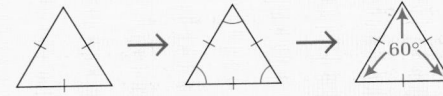

Theorem 8.15 If a triangle is equiangular, then it is also equilateral.

The angles of **equiangular** figures are all equal in measure.

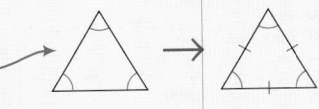

▶ Now you are ready for:
Exs. 1–20 on pp. 476–477

Talk it Over

7. What is the measure of $\angle ABD$? Explain.

8. What is the perimeter of an equiangular triangle with one side of measure 8 cm?

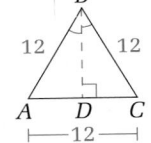

Perpendicular Bisectors

The **perpendicular bisector** of a segment is a line (or ray or segment) that bisects the segment and is perpendicular to it.

The diagrams below show how you can construct a perpendicular bisector using a straightedge and a compass.

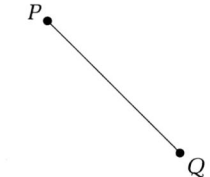

1 Draw $\overline{PQ}$.
Use P and Q as centers to draw two arcs with the same radius.

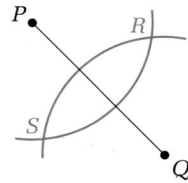

2 The two arcs intersect in two points when the radius used is greater than $\frac{1}{2}PQ$.

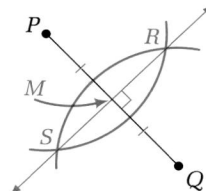

3 Draw $\overleftrightarrow{RS}$.
$\overleftrightarrow{RS}$ is the perpendicular bisector of $\overline{PQ}$.

The construction works because of the following theorem. You will prove Theorem 8.16 in Exercise 21.

PERPENDICULAR BISECTOR THEOREM

Theorem 8.16 If a point is the same distance from both endpoints of a segment, then it lies on the perpendicular bisector of the segment.

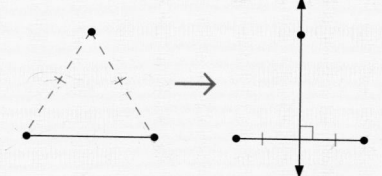

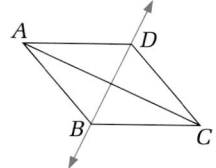

Talk it Over

9. *ABCD* is a rhombus. Explain why $\overleftrightarrow{BD}$ is the perpendicular bisector of $\overline{AC}$.

10. Name at least four pairs of angles that are equal in measure in the diagram of the rhombus at the left.

Look Back

What do you know is true about the triangle shown?

What else can be proven?

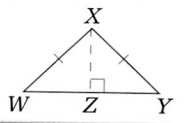

> ▶ Now you are ready for:
> Exs. 21–32 on pp. 478–480

8-6 Congruence and Isosceles Triangles

475

Communication: Drawing

Students are shown how to construct a perpendicular bisector of a segment. You may wish to have students perform this construction using their own compass and straightedge.

Look Back

The Look Back questions provide an opportunity for students to review may properties of isosceles triangles.

475

For each figure, identify the isosceles triangle(s) and identify the pair(s) of angles that are equal in measure.

1. 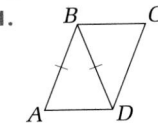   2. 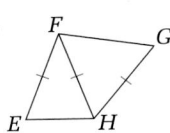   3. 4.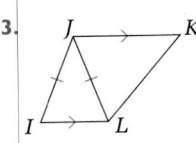

Find the value of x in each figure.

5. 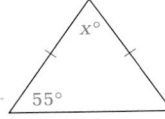   6. 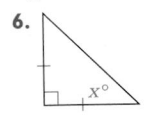   7. 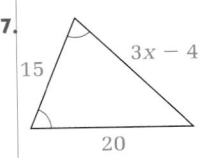   8.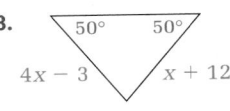

9. a. **Using Manipulatives** Cut a large isosceles triangle out of a piece of paper and fold it so the sides that are equal in measure match up.

   b. **Reading** What can you call the fold line?

   c. Use the results of part (a) and (b). Draw as many conclusions as possible about the angles, sides, and their measures in the isosceles triangle.

Use the diagram at the right for Exercises 10 and 11.

10. Identify two pairs of angles that are equal in measure.

11. Suppose $m \angle A = 2(x - 5)°$ and $m \angle ACB = (x + 50)°$. Find the measure of each angle of each triangle.

12. In △DEF, $m \angle E = m \angle F$. Write an expression for the perimeter of the triangle if $DE = 2x + 3$ and $EF = 4x - 2$.

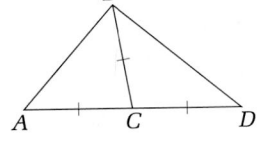

13. A *golden triangle* has two angles of equal measure that are each twice as large as the third angle. Find the measure of the angles of a golden triangle.

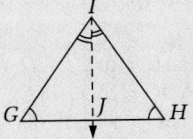

> **BY THE WAY...**
>
> In a golden triangle, the ratio of the lengths of a leg and the base is the golden ratio.
>
> $$\frac{\text{leg}}{\text{base}} \approx 1.618$$

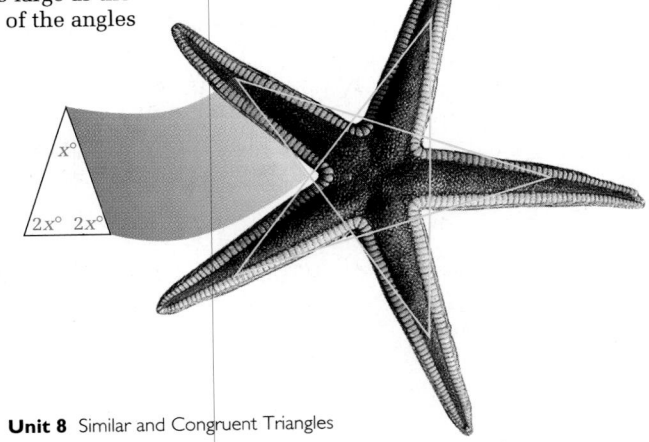

4. △GIJ ≅ △HIJ

5. $m \angle G = m \angle H$

Justifications
1. Given
2. Definition of angle bisector
3. Reflexive property of equality
4. SAS
5. CPCTE

15. *Given: $m \angle G = m \angle H$*
    Prove: GI = HI

Statements
1. $m \angle G = m \angle H$
2. Draw the angle bisector $\vec{IJ}$ as a helping line. Then $m \angle GIJ = m \angle HIJ$.
3. $IJ = IJ$
4. △GIJ ≅ △HIJ
5. $GI = HI$

Justifications
1. Given
2. Definition of angle bisector
3. Reflexive property of equality
4. AAS
5. CPCTE

16. Two sides of a triangle are equal in measure if and only if the angles opposite those sides are equal in measure. The biconditional is true because both conditionals are true.

14. Copy and complete this proof of Theorem 8.12.

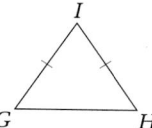

> **Given** $GI = HI$
>
> **Prove** $m \angle G = m \angle H$

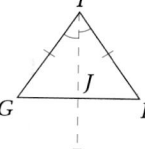

Statements	Justifications
1. $GI = HI$	1. Given
2. Draw the angle bisector $\overrightarrow{IJ}$ as a helping line. Then, $m \angle GIJ = m \angle HIJ$.	2. Definition of angle bisector
3. $IJ = IJ$	3. Reflexive property of equality
4. $\triangle GIJ \cong \triangle HIJ$	4. _?_
5. $m \angle G = m \angle H$	5. _?_

15. Write a two-column proof of Theorem 8.13, the converse of Theorem 8.12.

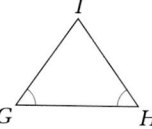

> **Given** $m \angle G = m \angle H$
>
> **Prove** $GI = HI$

16. Write Theorems 8.12 and 8.13 together as a biconditional. Why is it possible to restate these theorems in this way?

17. a. Use Theorem 8.12 to prove that if a triangle is equilateral, then all three angles are equal in measure.

  b. **Writing** Based on the result of part (a), explain how you could prove that the measure of every angle in an equilateral triangle is 60°.

  c. How would a proof of Theorem 8.15 be different from the proof of Theorem 8.14 in parts (a) and (b)?

18. a. On a coordinate plane, plot the points $P(4, 2)$, $E(3, 7)$, and $R(8, 6)$. Draw $\triangle PER$.

  b. Find PE, ER, and PR. What type of triangle is $\triangle PER$?

  c. Find the midpoint of $\overline{PR}$. Label this point S.

  d. Find the slopes of $\overline{ES}$ and $\overline{PR}$. What is the relationship between these segments?

19. a. On a coordinate plane, plot the points $A(-2, 0)$, $B(0, \sqrt{12})$, and $C(2, 0)$. Draw $\triangle ABC$.

  b. Show that $\triangle ABC$ is equiangular.

> **Student Resources Toolbox**
> p. 642 *Algebraic Expressions*

20. **Given** $LM = LO$
  $m \angle 1 = m \angle 3$

  Prove $MN = ON$

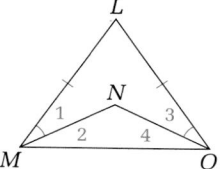

8-6 Congruence and Isosceles Triangles

477

---

18. a, c.

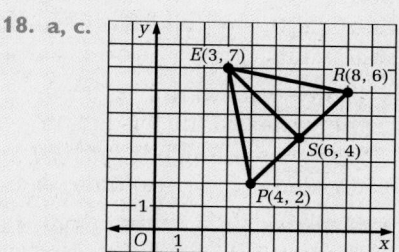

  a. See graph.

  b. $PE = \sqrt{26}$; $ER = \sqrt{26}$; $PR = 4\sqrt{2}$; $\triangle PER$ is an isosceles triangle.

  c. $\left(\frac{8 + 4}{2}, \frac{6 + 2}{2} \right) = (6, 4)$; See graph for location.

  d. slope of $\overline{ES} = \frac{7 - 4}{3 - 6} = -1$; slope of $\overline{PR} = \frac{6 - 2}{8 - 4} = 1$; Since the slopes are negative reciprocals, $\overline{ES} \perp \overline{PR}$.

19. See answers in back of book.

20. *Given:* $LM = LO$; $m \angle 1 = m \angle 3$
  Prove: $MN = ON$

  Statements
  1. $LM = LO$
  2. $m \angle LMO = m \angle LOM$
  3. $m \angle LMO = m \angle 1 + m \angle 2$
    $m \angle LOM = m \angle 3 + m \angle 4$
  4. $m \angle 1 + m \angle 2 = m \angle 3 + m \angle 4$
  5. $m \angle 1 = m \angle 3$
  6. $m \angle 2 = m \angle 4$
  7. $MN = ON$

  Justifications
  1. Given
  2. If two sides of a triangle are = in measure, then the ⚹ opposite those sides are = in measure.
  3. For any angle, the measure of the whole is equal to the sum of the measures of its non-overlapping parts.
  4. Substitution property (Steps 2 and 3)
  5. Given
  6. Subtraction property of equality
  7. If two ⚹ of a triangle are = in measure, then the sides opposite those ⚹ are = in measure.

Answers to Exercises and Problems

17. a. *Given:* $\triangle ABC$ is equilateral.
  Prove: $m \angle A = m \angle B = m \angle C$

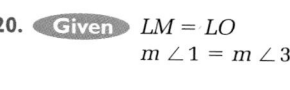

  Statements
  1. $\triangle ABC$ is equilateral.
  2. $AB = BC$
    $AB = AC$
  3. $m \angle A = m \angle C$
    $m \angle B = m \angle C$
  4. $m \angle A = m \angle B = m \angle C$

  Justifications
  1. Given
  2. Definition of an equilateral triangle
  3. If two sides of a triangle are = in measure, then the ⚹ opposite those sides are = in measure.
  4. Substitution property (Step 3)

  b. Since the three angles are equal in measure, let x represent the measure of each angle. Then $x + x + x = 180°$ or $3x = 180°$ and $x = 60°$.

  c. Essentially, the above proof would be completed in reverse except you would use the theorem that states if two ⚹ of a triangle are = in measure, then the sides opposite those ⚹ are = in measure.

477

21. Copy and complete this two-column proof of Theorem 8.16.

   Given $RP = RQ$

   Prove R lies on the perpendicular bisector of $\overline{PQ}$.

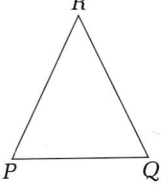

Plan Ahead

Draw $\overleftrightarrow{RM}$ through M, the midpoint of $\overline{PQ}$. Then use congruent triangles to prove that angles 1 and 2 are equal in measure. Show that these angles are right angles. Then $\overleftrightarrow{RM}$ is perpendicular to $\overline{PQ}$.

Show Your Reasoning

Statements	**Justifications**
1. $RP = RQ$	1. ___?___
2. Draw a line from R passing through the midpoint M of $\overline{PQ}$ so that $PM = QM$.	2. Definition of midpoint
3. $\overleftrightarrow{RM}$ bisects $\overline{PQ}$.	3. ___?___
4. $RM = RM$	4. Reflexive property of equality
5. $\triangle PRM \cong \triangle QRM$	5. ___?___ (Steps 1, 2, and 4)
6. $m \angle 1 = m \angle 2$	6. ___?___
7. $m \angle 1 + m \angle 2 = m \angle PMQ$	7. For any angle, the measure of the whole is equal to the sum of the measures of its non-overlapping parts.
8. $m \angle PMQ = 180°$	8. If the sides of an angle form a straight line, then the angle is a straight angle with measure 180°.
9. $m \angle 1 + m \angle 2 = 180°$	9. Substitution property (Steps ___?___ and ___?___)
10. $m \angle 1 + m \angle 1 = 180°$	10. Substitution property (Steps ___?___ and ___?___)
11. $2(m \angle 1) = 180°$	11. Distributive property
12. $m \angle 1 = 90°$	12. ___?___
13. $\overleftrightarrow{RM} \perp \overline{PQ}$	13. ___?___
14. $\overleftrightarrow{RM}$ is the perpendicular bisector of $\overline{PQ}$, so R lies on the perpendicular bisector of $\overline{PQ}$.	14. Definition of perpendicular bisector (Steps ___?___ and ___?___)

22. **Writing** The proof in Exercise 21 has many steps. Explain what happened in steps 6–13.

23. **a.** On a coordinate plane, plot the points $H(-2, -1)$, $J(4, -1)$, $K(1, 3)$, and $L(1, -4)$. Draw $HKJL$, $\overleftrightarrow{KL}$, and $\overline{HJ}$.
   b. Explain how you know that $\overleftrightarrow{KL}$ is the perpendicular bisector of $\overline{HJ}$.

An arrangement of Mayan buildings at Uaxactun, Guatemala, may have been used for solar observations and keeping the solar calendar. An observer at one structure looking east across an open plaza would see three buildings. The center building is due east of the observer. The outside buildings are due south and due north of the center building and equidistant from it.

The sun rose approximately above the northernmost building on the first day of summer.

The sun passed directly over the central building on both equinox days.

The sun rose over the southernmost building on the first day of winter.

(Perspective altered for illustrative purposes.)

24. What information in the paragraph above tells you that $DA = DB$? What information tells you that $\angle ADC$ and $\angle BDC$ are right angles?

25. How can you prove that $\triangle ADC \cong \triangle BDC$?

26. Explain how you would know that $\overrightarrow{CD}$ is the perpendicular bisector of $\overline{AB}$?

Ongoing **ASSESSMENT**

27. **Open-ended** Draw any large triangle on a piece of paper. Construct the perpendicular bisector of each side using a straightedge and compass as shown on page 475. What do you notice about the three bisectors?

Review **PREVIEW**

28. Tell whether there is enough information to prove that $\triangle ABC \cong \triangle XYZ$. Write *Yes* or *No*. Explain. *(Section 8-5)*

29. Factor $x^2 + 5x - 84$. *(Section 4-4)*

30. Solve the proportion $\frac{3}{8} = \frac{9}{x}$. *(Toolbox Skill 17)*

31. Find the area of $\triangle DEF$. *(Toolbox Skill 28)*

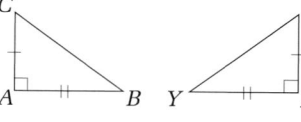

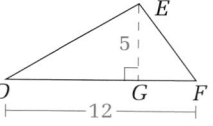

8-6 Congruence and Isosceles Triangles

479

Answers to Exercises and Problems

23. a.

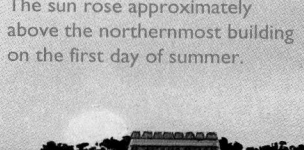

b. Using the distance formula, $HK = JK = 5$ and $HL = JL = 3\sqrt{2}$. Thus K is the same distance from H as from J, and L is the same distance from H as from J. By Theorem 8.16, both K and L lie on the $\perp$ bisector of $\overline{HJ}$, so $\overleftrightarrow{KL}$ is the $\perp$ bisector of $\overline{HJ}$.

24. The outside buildings are equidistant from the center building. The center building is due east of the observer, and the outer buildings are due north and due south of the center building.

25. Since $\angle ADC$ and $\angle BDC$ are right angles, $DA = DB$, and $DC = DC$, you know $\triangle ADC \cong \triangle BDC$ by SAS.

26. $\overrightarrow{CD}$ is perpendicular to $\overline{AB}$ because $\angle ADC$ and $\angle BDC$ are right angles. $\overrightarrow{CD}$ is a bisector of $\overline{AB}$ because $DA = DB$. So $\overrightarrow{CD}$ is the perpendicular bisector of $\overline{AB}$.

27. The lines intersect at the same point.

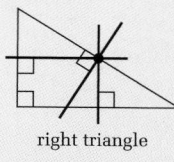 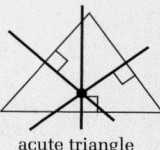

right triangle   acute triangle

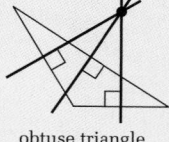

obtuse triangle

28. Yes; SAS.

29. $(x - 7)(x + 12)$

30. $x = 24$

31. 30 square units

Practice 65 For use with Section 8-6

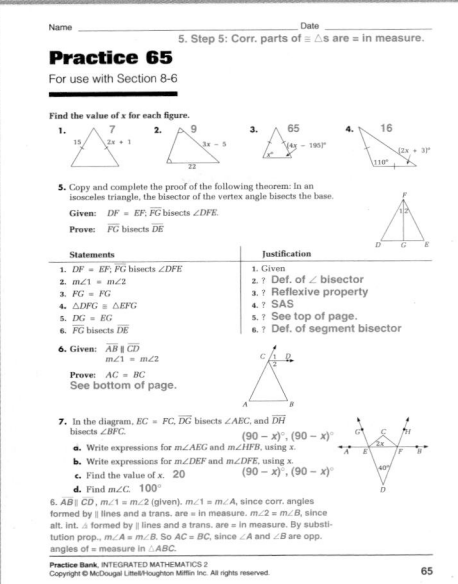

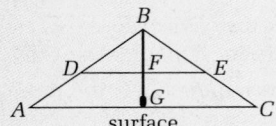

Working on the Unit Project

As you complete Exercise 32, think about how you can use the properties of isosceles triangles in the tool you design.

The ancient Egyptians used a tool called a *plumb level*. It was used to determine if a surface was level.

A *plumb level* consists of an A-frame and a weighted string that hangs from the vertex, B.

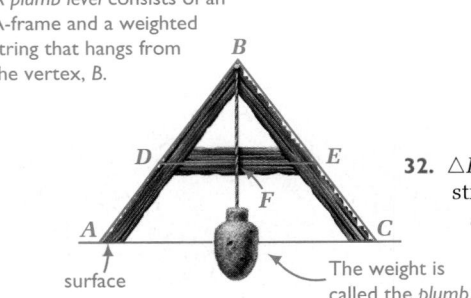

surface
The weight is called the *plumb*.

This temple for Queen Hatshepsut of Egypt was built at Dayr al-Bahri around 1460 B.C.

32. $\triangle DBE$ is isosceles with $DB = EB$, and $AB = CB$. The string is perpendicular to $\overline{DE}$ when the plumb level stands on a level surface—one that is not tilted. The Egyptians knew that if the surface was level, then the string would bisect $\overline{DE}$.

Prove that $\overline{DE} \parallel \overline{AC}$ when $\overleftrightarrow{BF}$ bisects $\overline{DE}$.

Unit 8   CHECKPOINT 2

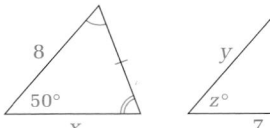

Exercise 2

1. **Writing** Describe how you might decide which method to use to show that two triangles are congruent.

2. Find the values of x, y, and z. Explain your reasoning.   8-4

For Exercises 3 and 4, identify the congruent triangles. How do you know they are congruent?   8-5

3. 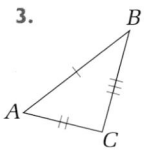   4.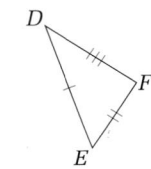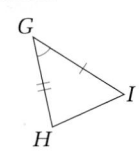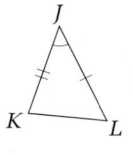

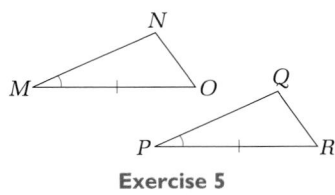

Exercise 5

5. Suppose you want to say that $\triangle MNO \cong \triangle PQR$. What additional information do you need?

6. On a coordinate plane, plot the points $S(1, 1)$, $T(3, -4)$, and $U(5, 1)$. What can you say about $\triangle STU$?   8-6

7. In $\triangle ABC$, $AB = CB$. The measure of $\angle B$ is four less than twice the measure of $\angle C$. Find the measures of all three angles.

480   **Unit 8** Similar and Congruent Triangles

Answers to Exercises and Problems

32. *Given:* $\triangle DBE$ is isosceles; $DB = EB$; $AB = CB$; $\overrightarrow{BF} \perp \overline{DE}$; $\overleftrightarrow{BF}$ bisects $\overline{DE}$.
Prove: $\overline{DE} \parallel \overline{AC}$

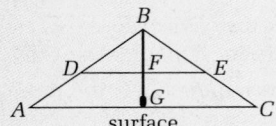

surface

Statements
1. $\triangle DBE$ is isosceles.
2. $DB = EB$
3. $BF = BF$
4. $m \angle BDF = m \angle BEF$
5. $\overleftrightarrow{BF} \perp \overline{DE}$
6. $m \angle BFD = 90°$; $m \angle BFE = 90°$
7. $m \angle BFD = m \angle BFE$
8. $\triangle BFD \cong \triangle BFE$
9. $m \angle DBF = m \angle EBF$
10. $BG = BG$
11. $AB = CB$
12. $\triangle ABG \cong \triangle CBG$
13. $AG = CG$
14. $\overleftrightarrow{BF}$ is the perpendicular bisector of $\overline{AC}$.
15. $\overline{DE} \parallel \overline{AC}$.

Justifications
1. Given
2. Given
3. Reflexive property of equality
4. If two sides of a triangle are = in measure, then the ∡ opposite those sides are = in measure.
5. Given
6. Definition of perpendicular lines
7. Substitution (Step 6)
8. AAS
9. CPCTE
10. Reflexive property of equality
11. Given
12. SAS
13. CPCTE
14. If a point is the same distance from both endpoints of a segment, then it lies on the perpendicular bisector of the segment.
15. If two lines are ⊥ to the same transversal, then they are ∥.

Answers to Checkpoint

See answers in back of book.

480

Similarity in Right Triangles

Two rights rights make a right

Focus

Identify similar right triangles and apply right triangle theorems. Find geometric means.

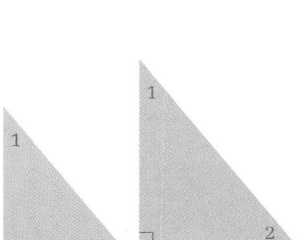

EXPLORATION

(How) can you make three similar triangles from one right triangle?

- **Materials: paper, rulers, scissors**
- **Work with another student.**

(1) Draw and cut out two congruent right triangles.

(2) On each triangle, label the corresponding acute angles "1" and "2." Mark the right angles.

(3) An **altitude** of a triangle is a segment from a vertex perpendicular to the line containing the opposite side.

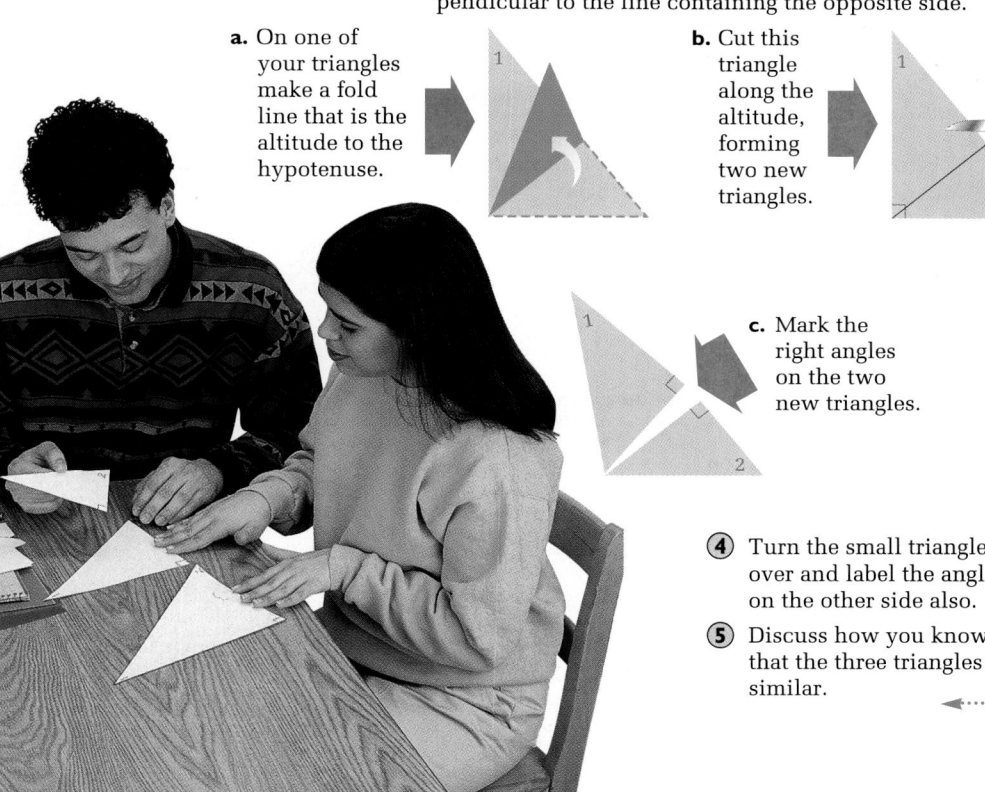

a. On one of your triangles make a fold line that is the altitude to the hypotenuse.

b. Cut this triangle along the altitude, forming two new triangles.

c. Mark the right angles on the two new triangles.

(4) Turn the small triangles over and label the angles on the other side also.

(5) Discuss how you know that the three triangles are similar.

481

PLANNING

Objectives and Strands
See pages 428A and 428B.

Spiral Learning
See page 428B.

Materials List
➤ Ruler
➤ Scissors

Recommended Pacing
Section 8-7 is a two-day lesson.
Day 1
Pages 481–482: Exploration through Talk it Over 2, *Exercises 1–9*
Day 2
Pages 483–484: The Geometric Mean through Look Back, *Exercises 10–30*

Extra Practice
See pages 627–628.

Warm-Up Exercises
Warm-Up Transparency 8-7

Support Materials
➤ Practice 66
➤ Enrichment 59 in the Activity Bank
➤ Study Guide 8-7
➤ Problem Set 19
➤ McDougal Littell Mathpack software: *Geometry Inventor*
➤ Geometry Inventor Activity Book: Activity 5
➤ Quiz 8-7

Answers to Exploration

1–4. Check students' work.

5. Each triangle has a right angle and at least one other angle marked either ∠1 or ∠2. So by the AA Similarity Postulate, they are all similar to one another.

Exploration

The goal of this Exploration is to have students discover Theorem 8.17 on page 482; that is, if the altitude is drawn to the hypotenuse of a right triangle, then the two triangles formed are similar to the original triangle and to each other. This conclusion is reached in step 5 by applying the AA similarity postulate.

Reasoning

Refer students to the definition of altitude in step 3 of the Exploration. Ask them two questions: Does a triangle have to be a right triangle to have an altitude? (No.) How many altitudes does a triangle have? (3)

Additional Sample

S1 In △ABC, $\overline{BD}$ is an altitude to hypotenuse $\overline{AC}$. Identify the similar triangles.

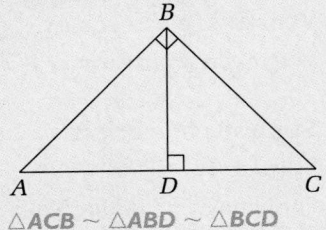

△ACB ~ △ABD ~ △BCD

Talk it Over

To answer question 1, students need to identify the corresponding sides of triangles RSQ and RSP. It might help them to think in terms of the two short legs of each triangle, the two longer legs, and the hypotenuse of each triangle as being the corresponding parts.

In the Exploration you may have observed this relationship.

SIMILAR RIGHT TRIANGLES THEOREM

Theorem 8.17 If the altitude is drawn to the hypotenuse of a right triangle, then the two triangles formed are similar to the original triangle and to each other.

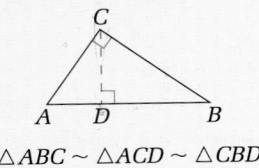

△ABC ~ △ACD ~ △CBD

Similar right triangles may be used to prove one of the most famous theorems in mathematics, the Pythagorean theorem. A proof is shown in Exercise 5.

THE PYTHAGOREAN THEOREM

Theorem 8.18 In any right triangle, the square of the length of the hypotenuse is equal to the sum of the squares of the lengths of the legs.

$$c^2 = a^2 + b^2$$

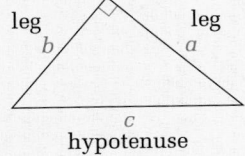

Sample 1

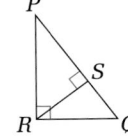

In △PQR, $\overline{RS}$ is the altitude to hypotenuse $\overline{PQ}$. Identify the similar triangles.

Sample Response

Sketch the large triangle and the two smaller triangles formed by the altitude to the hypotenuse. Mark the angles that are equal in measure.

Use the angle marks to write the corresponding vertices in the same order for each triangle: △PQR ~ △PRS ~ △RQS.

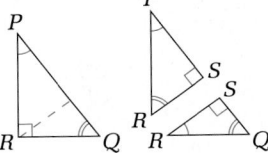

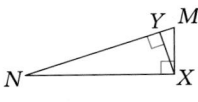

► Now you are ready for:
Exs. 1–9 on pp. 485–486

Talk it Over

1. Use the figure in Sample 1 to complete these statements.

   a. $\dfrac{QS}{RS} = \dfrac{?}{PS}$

   b. $\dfrac{QS}{QR} = \dfrac{?}{QP}$

2. In △MNX at the left, $\overline{XY}$ is an altitude to hypotenuse $\overline{MN}$. Identify the similar triangles.

Unit 8 Similar and Congruent Triangles

Answers to Talk it Over

1. a. RS
   b. QR
2. △MXN ~ △MYX ~ △XYN

The Geometric Mean

When you complete the proportion in *Talk it Over* question 1(a) on page 482, notice that RS appears in two places. The length RS is the *geometric mean* between the lengths QS and PS.

If a, x, and b are positive numbers and

$$\frac{a}{x} = \frac{x}{b},$$

then x is called the **geometric mean** between a and b. The geometric mean is always positive.

Sample 2

Find the geometric mean between 2 and 32.

Sample Response

Let x = the geometric mean between 2 and 32.
Write a proportion and solve it.

$\frac{2}{x} = \frac{x}{32}$ ◄——— Use the proportion $\frac{a}{x} = \frac{x}{b}$.

$64 = x^2$ ◄——— Use cross products.

$\sqrt{64} = x$ ◄——— The geometric mean is always positive. Find the positive square root.

$8 = x$

The geometric mean between 2 and 32 is 8.

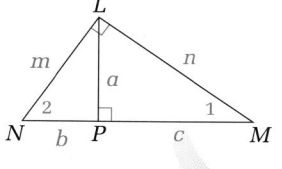

Talk it Over

Use the diagram below to complete each proportion.

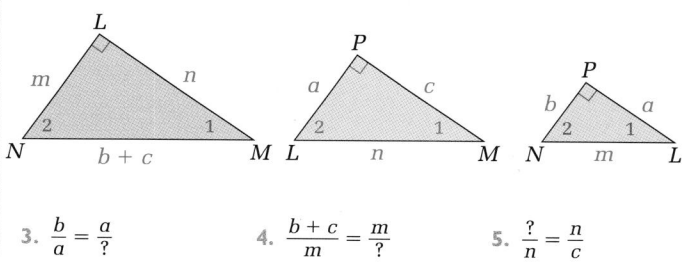

3. $\dfrac{b}{a} = \dfrac{a}{?}$ **4.** $\dfrac{b+c}{m} = \dfrac{m}{?}$ **5.** $\dfrac{?}{n} = \dfrac{n}{c}$

The results of *Talk it Over* question 3 can be generalized to Theorem 8.19, proved in Exercise 20. Questions 4 and 5 can be generalized to a theorem stated in Exercise 26.

8-7 Similarity in Right Triangles

Answers to Talk it Over

3. c

4. b

5. $b + c$

Communication: Discussion

A discussion of Theorem 8.19 should make it clear that the altitude involved is the one from the vertex of the right angle to the hypotenuse and not either of the other two altitudes of the triangle.

Additional Sample

S3 Find the lengths of m, n, and p.

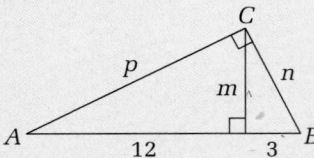

First find m.

$$\frac{3}{m} = \frac{m}{12}$$
$$m^2 = 36$$
$$m = 6$$

Use the Pythagorean theorem to find n and p.

$$3^2 + m^2 = n^2$$
$$3^2 + 6^2 = n^2$$
$$9 + 36 = n^2$$
$$45 = n^2$$
$$6.7 \approx n$$
$$12^2 + m^2 = p^2$$
$$12^2 + 6^2 = p^2$$
$$144 + 36 = p^2$$
$$180 = p^2$$
$$13.4 \approx p$$

The lengths of m, n, and p are 6, about 6.7, and about 13.4, respectively.

Look Back

Students may have to refer back to Talk it Over questions 3–5 on page 483 to give the two results asked for here.

GEOMETRIC MEAN THEOREM

Theorem 8.19 If the altitude is drawn to the hypotenuse of a right triangle, then the measure of the altitude is the geometric mean between the measures of the parts of the hypotenuse.

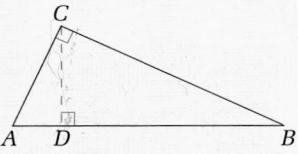

$$\frac{AD}{CD} = \frac{CD}{BD}$$

Sample 3

Find the lengths x, y, and z.

Sample Response

1 First find x. Write and solve a proportion involving x.

$$\frac{6}{x} = \frac{x}{10}$$ ← x is the geometric mean between the measures of the parts of the hypotenuse.

$$x^2 = 60$$ ← Use cross products.

$$x = \sqrt{60}$$ ← The geometric mean is always positive.

2 Use the value of x and the Pythagorean theorem to find y.

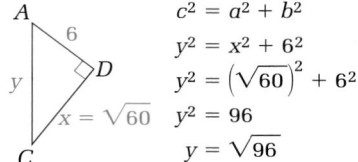

$$c^2 = a^2 + b^2$$
$$y^2 = x^2 + 6^2$$
$$y^2 = \left(\sqrt{60}\right)^2 + 6^2$$
$$y^2 = 96$$
$$y = \sqrt{96}$$

3 Use the value of x and the Pythagorean theorem to find z.

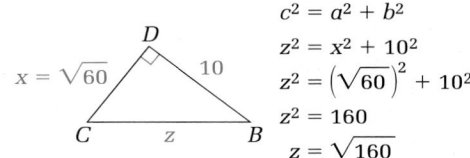

$$c^2 = a^2 + b^2$$
$$z^2 = x^2 + 10^2$$
$$z^2 = \left(\sqrt{60}\right)^2 + 10^2$$
$$z^2 = 160$$
$$z = \sqrt{160}$$

The lengths x, y, and z are $\sqrt{60}$, $\sqrt{96}$, and $\sqrt{160}$, or about 7.7, about 9.8, and about 12.6.

⋯⋯► Now you are ready for:
Exs. 10–30 on pp. 486–488

Look Back ◄

Altitude $\overline{ST}$ is drawn to the hypotenuse of right $\triangle QRS$. State two true relationships.

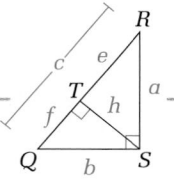

Answers to Look Back

$$\frac{f}{h} = \frac{h}{e}, \frac{c}{b} = \frac{b}{f}, \text{ and } \frac{c}{a} = \frac{a}{e}$$

Answers to Exercises and Problems

1.

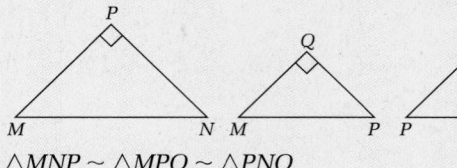

$$\triangle MNP \sim \triangle MPQ \sim \triangle PNQ$$

2.

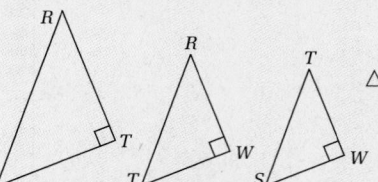

$$\triangle STR \sim \triangle TWR \sim \triangle SWT$$

For Exercises 1 and 2, draw and identify the similar triangles.

1.

2.

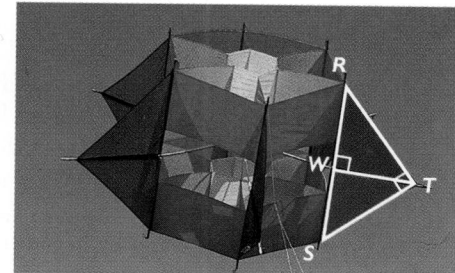

3. Reading What can you do to more easily identify angles that are equal in measure when similar triangles overlap?

4. In right $\triangle EFG$, $\overline{GH}$ is the altitude to the hypotenuse $\overline{EF}$. The measure of $\angle E$ is 65°. Draw $\triangle EFG$ and label the measures of all the angles.

5. Copy and complete this proof of the Pythagorean theorem.

Given $\triangle ABC$ with right $\angle C$.
$\overline{CD}$ is the altitude to the hypotenuse.

Prove $c^2 = a^2 + b^2$

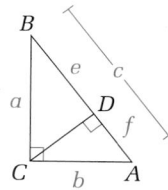

Statements

1. In $\triangle ABC$, $\angle C$ is a right angle. $\overline{CD}$ is the altitude to the hypotenuse.

2. $\triangle ABC \sim \triangle CBD$; $\triangle ABC \sim \triangle ACD$

3. $\dfrac{c}{a} = \dfrac{a}{e}$; $\dfrac{c}{?} = \dfrac{b}{f}$

4. $ce = \underline{?}$; $cf = \underline{?}$
5. $ce + cf = \underline{?} + \underline{?}$
6. $c(e + f) = \underline{?} + \underline{?}$
7. $e + f = c$
8. $c(\underline{?}) = a^2 + b^2$

9. $\underline{?} = a^2 + b^2$

Justifications

1. $\underline{?}$

2. If the altitude is drawn to the hypotenuse of a right triangle, then the two triangles formed are similar to the original triangle and to each other.

3. Definition of similar triangles: corresponding sides are in proportion.

4. $\underline{?}$
5. $\underline{?}$
6. $\underline{?}$
7. $\underline{?}$
8. $\underline{?}$ (Steps 6 and 7)

9. $\underline{?}$

Notice which sides correspond in the three right triangles.

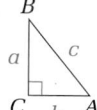 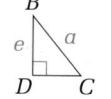 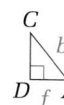

Suggested Assignment

Day 1
Standard 1–8
Extended 1–9

Day 2
Standard 10–18, 21–25, 27–30
Extended 10–18, 20–25, 27–30

Integrating the Strands
Number Ex. 9
Algebra Exs. 6–18
Geometry Exs. 1–9, 13–26
Statistics and Probability Ex. 28
Logic and Language Exs. 3, 26, 30

Students Acquiring English
Have students acquiring English work with partners to complete the proof of the Pythagorean theorem in Ex. 5.

Research
Ex. 5 presents a proof of the Pythagorean theorem that is based upon the use of similar triangles. As a research project, you may wish to have students find out how many different proofs of the Pythagorean theorem exist. Also, it would be a worthwhile activity for students to present a few of these alternative proofs to the class.

Answers to Exercises and Problems

3. Sketch both triangles separately. Mark all angles that are equal in measure.

4. Measures of sides may vary.

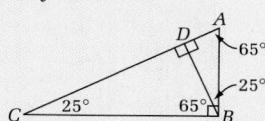

5. *Given:* $\triangle ABC$ with right $\angle C$; $\overline{CD}$ is the altitude to the hypotenuse.
Prove: $a^2 + b^2 = c^2$

Statements
1. $\triangle ABC$ with right $\angle C$; $\overline{CD}$ is the altitude to the hypotenuse.
2. $\triangle ABC \sim \triangle CBD$ $\triangle ABC \sim \triangle ACD$
3. $\dfrac{c}{a} = \dfrac{a}{e}$; $\dfrac{c}{b} = \dfrac{b}{f}$

4. $ce = a^2$; $cf = b^2$
5. $ce + cf = a^2 + b^2$
6. $c(e + f) = a^2 + b^2$
7. $e + f = c$
8. $c(c) = a^2 + b^2$
9. $c^2 = a^2 + b^2$

Justifications
1. Given
2. If the altitude is drawn to the hypotenuse of a right triangle, then the two triangles formed are similar to the original triangle and to each other.
3. Definition of similar triangles; corresponding sides are in proportion.
4. Multiplication property of equality
5. Addition property of equality
6. Distributive property
7. For any segment, the measure of the whole is equal to the sum of the measures of its non-overlapping parts.
8. Substitution property (Steps 6 and 7)
9. Definition of exponents

485

Find the measure of each unknown side.

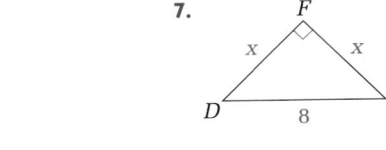

6.

7.

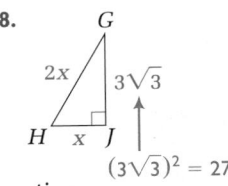

8.

$(3\sqrt{3})^2 = 27$

9. A *Pythagorean triple* is a group of three integers that satisfy the equation $c^2 = a^2 + b^2$ and that can be the lengths of the sides of a right triangle.

   a. Show that 5, 12, 13 is a Pythagorean triple.

   b. **Open-ended** Name two other Pythagorean triples.

   c. Show that multiplying the integers in a Pythagorean triple by a constant produces another Pythagorean triple.

   d. Suppose the integers of a Pythagorean triple are the lengths of the sides of a right triangle. If you multiply the integers in the triple by 2 and form a new triangle, how will the triangles be related to each other?

Solve each proportion.

10. $\frac{4}{x} = \frac{5}{10}$

11. $\frac{3}{x} = \frac{x}{12}$

12. $\frac{5 + x}{x} = \frac{4}{3}$

Find the geometric mean between each pair of numbers.

13. 6 and 24

14. 27 and 3

15. 4 and 16

16. 45 and 5

17. 12 is the geometric mean between 3 and what other number?

18. 10 is the geometric mean between 25 and what other number?

Architecture Andrea Palladio (1508–1580), an Italian Renaissance architect, proposed a method for determining a pleasing height for a room. Palladio suggested that in rooms with flat ceilings, the height should be equal to the width. In square rooms with vaulted ceilings, the height should be one third greater than the width.

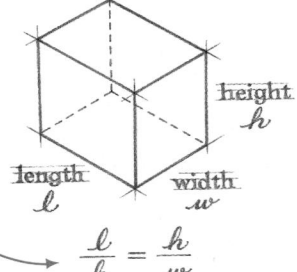

For many other rooms, Palladio suggested that the height should be equal to the geometric mean between the room's length and width.

$\frac{\ell}{h} = \frac{h}{w}$

The basilica, or public building, in Vicenza, Italy, was designed by Palladio.

19. **Group Activity** Work with at least one other student.

   a. Is your classroom floor a square? Does the room have a flat ceiling? Which of Palladio's suggestions applies to your classroom?

   b. Measure the actual length and width of the room.

   c. Calculate the proper height for the room, based on Palladio's suggestions.

   d. Measure the actual height of your classroom. Is the room's proper height the same as the actual height?

486

Unit 8 Similar and Congruent Triangles

Answers to Exercises and Problems

6. $6\sqrt{2} \approx 8.5$

7. $4\sqrt{2} \approx 5.7$

8. $HJ = 3; HG = 6$

9. a. $5^2 + 12^2 = 25 + 144 = 169 = 13^2$

   b. Answers may vary. Examples are given. 3, 4, 5 and 8, 15, 17

   c. If you multiply the numbers by a constant,

d, then $(ad)^2 + (bd)^2 \stackrel{?}{=} (cd)^2$. So $(ad)^2 + (bd)^2 = a^2d^2 + b^2d^2 = (a^2 + b^2)d^2 = c^2d^2$ ✓

   d. The triangles will be similar with a ratio of 2.

10. $x = 8$

11. $x = 6$ or -6

12. $x = 15$

13. 12

14. 9

15. 8

16. 15

17. 48

18. 4

19. a–d. Answers will vary depending upon actual classrooms.

20. *Given:* $\triangle ABC$ with right $\angle C; \overline{CD}$ is the altitude to the hypotenuse.

   Prove: $\frac{AD}{CD} = \frac{CD}{BD}$

486

20. Copy and complete this proof of Theorem 8.19.

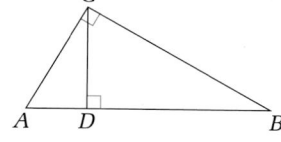

Given $\triangle ABC$ with right $\angle C$.
$\overline{CD}$ is the altitude to the hypotenuse.

Prove $\dfrac{AD}{CD} = \dfrac{CD}{BD}$

Statements

$\left.\begin{array}{l}\triangle ABC \text{ with right } \angle C.\\ \overline{CD} \text{ is the altitude to the hypotenuse.}\end{array}\right\}$ ①

① ⟶ $\triangle ADC \sim \triangle CDB$ ② $\dfrac{AD}{CD} = \dfrac{CD}{BD}$

Justifications

① $\underline{\text{?}}$

② $\underline{\text{?}}$

For Exercises 21–24, find the value of each variable.

21.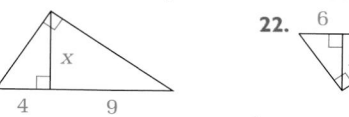

22.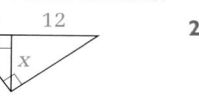

23.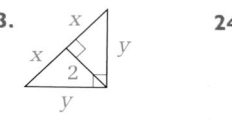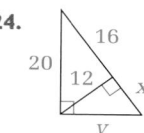

24.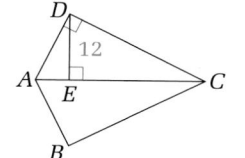

25. In kite $ABCD$, $\angle ADC$ is a right angle.
Find the length of diagonal $\overline{AC}$.

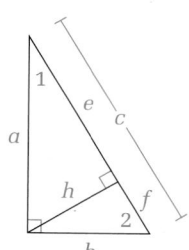

$AE = x$
$CE = x + 18$

.... **Ongoing ASSESSMENT**

26. **Group Activity** Work with another student.

a. Cut out two congruent right triangles.

b. As in the Exploration on page 481, label the corresponding acute angles "1" and "2." Mark the right angles.

c. Label the measures of the sides of the triangles. Label the hypotenuse c, the longer leg a, and the shorter leg b.

d. On one of the triangles make a fold line that is the altitude to the hypotenuse. Cut the triangle along the altitude.

e. On the two new triangles, label the side that was the fold line h.

f. Label the remaining sides of the two triangles e or f, as appropriate.

g. **Writing** Use your similar triangles to explain how the proportions $\dfrac{c}{a} = \dfrac{a}{e}$ and $\dfrac{c}{b} = \dfrac{b}{f}$ lead to this second geometric mean theorem:

If an altitude is drawn to the hypotenuse of a right triangle, then the measure of each leg is the geometric mean between the measure of the hypotenuse and the measure of the part of the hypotenuse that meets that leg.

8-7 Similarity in Right Triangles

Using Manipulatives

Ex. 26 allows students to use manipulatives in a group activity to discover a second geometric-mean theorem. By working with a partner, students can exchange ideas about how their triangles lead to this new theorem.

Answers to Exercises and Problems

Statements

$\left.\begin{array}{l}\triangle ABC \text{ with right } \angle C;\\ CD \text{ is the altitude to the hypotenuse.}\end{array}\right\}$ ① $\triangle ADC \sim \triangle CDB$ ②

$\dfrac{AD}{CD} = \dfrac{CD}{BD}$

Justifications

① If the altitude is drawn to the hypotenuse of a right triangle, then the two triangles formed are similar to the original triangle and to each other.

② Corresponding parts of similar triangles are in proportion.

21. $x = 6$

22. $x = 6\sqrt{2} \approx 8.5$

23. $x = 2$, $y = 2\sqrt{2} \approx 2.8$

24. $x = 9$, $y = 15$

25. $AC = 30$

26. **a–f.** Check students' triangles.

g. Using the Similar Right Triangles Theorem, you can show the three

triangles formed are similar. Then since corresponding parts of similar triangles are in proportion, you can show $\dfrac{c}{a} = \dfrac{a}{e}$ and $\dfrac{c}{b} = \dfrac{b}{f}$. This shows the measure of each leg is the geometric mean between the measure of the hypotenuse and the measure of the part of the hypotenuse that meets that leg.

Working on the Unit Project

You may wish to make a framing square available in class so students can handle it when doing Ex. 30.

27. **Given** $\triangle ABD$ is an equilateral triangle.
    $\overline{BC} \perp \overline{AD}$

    a. What is the measure of $\overline{AC}$? *(Section 8-6)*

    b. What is the measure of $\angle ABD$? What is the measure of $\angle ABC$?

    c. What is the measure of $\overline{BC}$?

28. How many different four-letter arrangements can be made from the letters in the word WISH? Assume that a letter cannot be used more than once. *(Section 6-2)*

29. Draw and label a right $\triangle JKL$ so that
    $\tan K = \dfrac{\text{measure of leg opposite } \angle K}{\text{measure of leg adjacent to } \angle K} = \dfrac{5}{12}.$ *(Toolbox Skill 29)*

Working on the Unit Project

As you complete Exercise 30, think about how you can use the properties of similar right triangles in the tool you design.

30. A carpenter uses a tool called a *framing square* to measure and draw right angles. A square consists of two rulers that form an "L."

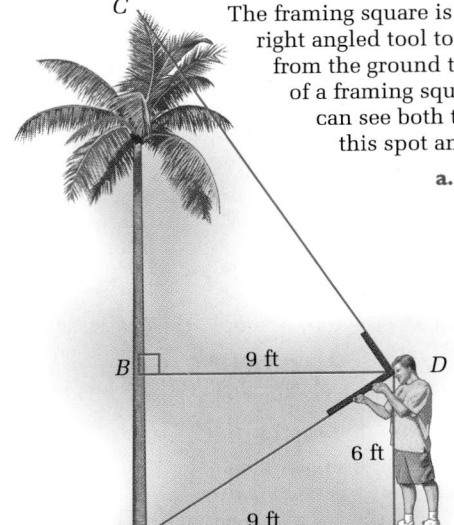

The framing square is in the shape of a right angle. Troy uses this right angled tool to estimate the height of a tree. The distance from the ground to Troy's eyes is 6 ft. He holds the corner of a framing square near his eye and moves back until he can see both the top and the bottom of the tree. Troy marks this spot and measures its distance from the tree.

a. Which triangles are congruent? Which triangles are similar?

b. Write a proportion and figure out the height of the tree.

c. Why is it important that the angle held near Troy's eye is a right angle?

488   **Unit 8** Similar and Congruent Triangles

Answers to Exercises and Problems

27. a. $AC = 5$

    b. $m \angle ABD = 60°$; $m \angle ABC = 30°$

    c. $BC = 5\sqrt{3} \approx 8.7$

28. 24

29. (Either $\angle L$ or $\angle J$ can be the right angle.)

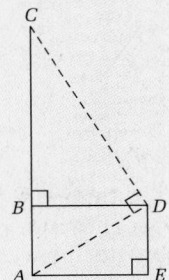

30. Label the diagram as shown.

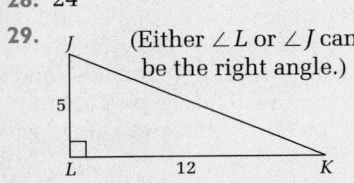

a. $\triangle ABD \cong \triangle DEA$;
   $\triangle ADC \sim \triangle ABD$;
   $\triangle ABD \sim \triangle DEC$;
   $\triangle DBC \sim \triangle DEA$

b. Let x be the height of the tree. Then $\dfrac{x-6}{9} = \dfrac{9}{6}$. The tree is about 19 ft 6 in. high.

c. If the angle is a right angle, Troy knows the length of the altitude to the hypotenuse that it determines. He can use the Geometric Mean Theorem to find the length of the hypotenuse, that is, the height of the tree.

Special Right Triangles and Trigonometry

PLANNING

Objectives and Strands
See pages 428A and 428B.

Spiral Learning
See page 428B.

Materials List
➤ Calculator

Recommended Pacing
Section 8-8 is a two-day lesson.
Day 1
Pages 489–490: Talk it Over 1 through Talk it Over 6, *Exercises 1–18*
Day 2
Pages 491–492: Trigonometry through Look Back, *Exercises 19–38*

Extra Practice
See pages 627–628.

Warm-Up Exercises
Warm-Up Transparency 8-8

Support Materials
➤ Practice 67
➤ Enrichment 60 in the Activity Bank
➤ Study Guide 8-8
➤ Problem Set 19
➤ Quiz 8-8
➤ Test 34
➤ Alternative Assessment 5

Focus
Discover properties of 45°-45°-90° and 30°-60°-90° triangles. Review the trigonometric ratios: sine, cosine, and tangent.

THE **RIGHT RATIO**

Talk it Over

Refer to △ABC below.

1. △*ABC* is an *isosceles right triangle*. It is a right triangle with legs of equal measure. What can you say about $m \angle A$ and $m \angle B$?

2. Why do you think that an isosceles right triangle is also called a *45°-45°-90° triangle*?

3. Use the Pythagorean theorem to find the length of $\overline{AB}$. Leave your answer in radical form.

4. This tapestry was woven in Turkey in the 19th Century. Suppose the weaver had used an isosceles right triangle whose legs were both 8 cm long. Find the length of the hypotenuse of that triangle.

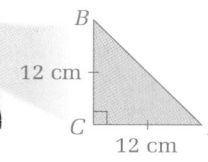

You can use the patterns below to find the lengths of the sides of some special right triangles. You will verify the relationships in 45°-45°-90° triangles and 30°-60°-90° triangles in Exercise 32.

RIGHT TRIANGLE RELATIONSHIPS

In a 45°-45°-90° triangle, the measure of the hypotenuse is $\sqrt{2}$ times the measure of a leg.

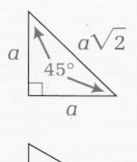

In a 30°-60°-90° triangle, the measure of the hypotenuse is twice the measure of the shorter leg. The measure of the longer leg is $\sqrt{3}$ times the measure of the shorter leg.

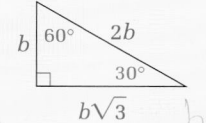

8-8 Special Right Triangles and Trigonometry

Answers to Talk it Over

1. $m \angle A = m \angle B = 45°$

2. because the angles of an isosceles right triangle always have measures of 45°, 45° and 90°

3. $12\sqrt{2}$ cm

4. $8\sqrt{2} \approx 11.3$ cm

Talk it Over

Questions 1–4 lead students to discover the properties of an isosceles right triangle and to the generalization that the measure of the hypotenuse is always $\sqrt{2}$ times the measure of the legs.

Reasoning

You might wish to explore with students the reasoning necessary to arrive at the relationship between the measures of the sides of a 30°-60°-90° triangle. Start with $\triangle ABC$ and then build on $\triangle AB'C$ as shown.

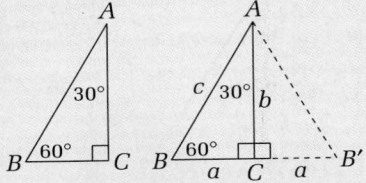

Ask students to supply justifications for each step, using postulates or theorems they have already learned.

1. $\triangle AB'C \cong \triangle ABC$

2. $m \angle B' = 60°$

3. $\triangle BAB'$ is equiangular.

4. $\triangle BAB'$ is equilateral.

5. $c = 2a$

6. $a^2 + b^2 = c^2$

7. $a^2 + b^2 = 4a^2$

8. $b^2 = 3a^2$

9. $b = a\sqrt{3}$

Additional Sample

S1 Find the exact measure of each unknown side in each triangle.

a.
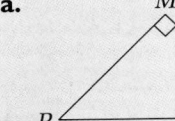

$MN = MP = 9$

b.

$ST = 10\sqrt{2}$
$RT = 10$

490

Find the exact measure of each unknown side in each triangle.

a.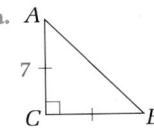

b.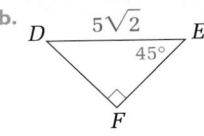

Sample Response

Use the relationships for an isosceles right, or 45°-45°-90°, triangle on page 489.

a. Substitute 7 for a in the diagram.

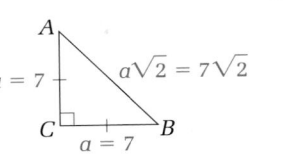

$AB = 7\sqrt{2}$
$CB = 7$

b. Substitute $5\sqrt{2}$ for $a\sqrt{2}$. Then solve for a.

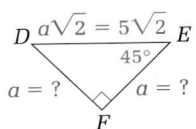

$a\sqrt{2} = 5\sqrt{2}$

$a = \dfrac{5\sqrt{2}}{\sqrt{2}}$

$a = 5$

$DF = 5$
$FE = 5$

Find the approximate measure of each unknown side in each triangle.

a.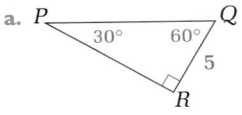

b.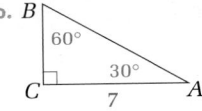

Sample Response

Use the relationships for a 30°-60°-90° triangle on page 489.

a. Substitute 5 for b in the diagram.

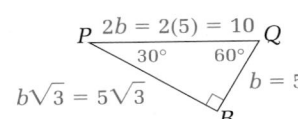

$PQ = 10$
$PR = 5\sqrt{3} \approx 8.7$

b. Substitute 7 for $b\sqrt{3}$. Then solve for b.

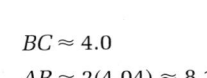

$b\sqrt{3} = 7$

$b = \dfrac{7}{\sqrt{3}}$

$b \approx 4.04$

$BC \approx 4.0$
$AB \approx 2(4.04) \approx 8.1$

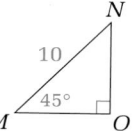

Talk it Over

5. Is △MNO isosceles? Explain.

6. Find *MO* and *NO* to the nearest tenth.

Trigonometry

The word *trigonometry* comes from the Greek language. It means *triangle measurement*. The Egyptians used trigonometry over 3800 years ago in constructing pyramids.

Each of the trigonometric ratios, **sine**, **cosine**, and **tangent**, compares the measures of two sides of a right triangle.

TRIGONOMETRIC RATIOS

$$\sin A = \frac{\text{measure of leg opposite } \angle A}{\text{measure of hypotenuse}} = \frac{BC}{AB}$$

$$\cos A = \frac{\text{measure of leg adjacent to } \angle A}{\text{measure of hypotenuse}} = \frac{AC}{AB}$$

$$\tan A = \frac{\text{measure of leg opposite } \angle A}{\text{measure of leg adjacent to } \angle A} = \frac{BC}{AC}$$

The symbols for the sine, cosine, and tangent are sin, cos, and tan.

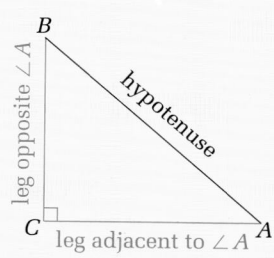

You can use the relationships between the sides of special right triangles to find the sine, cosine, and tangent of the acute angles in each triangle. The ratios are given in the table below.

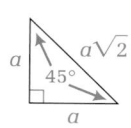
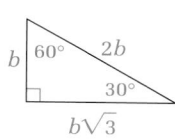

Watch Out!
The value of a trigonometric ratio depends only on the measure of the angle. No matter how large a 30°-60°-90° triangle is, $\cos 60° = \frac{1}{2}$.

Trigonometric Ratios for Special Right Triangles

		30° angle	45° angle	60° angle
sine =	$\frac{\text{opposite}}{\text{hypotenuse}}$	$\frac{b}{2b} = \frac{1}{2}$	$\frac{a}{a\sqrt{2}} = \frac{1}{\sqrt{2}}$	$\frac{b\sqrt{3}}{2b} = \frac{\sqrt{3}}{2}$
cosine =	$\frac{\text{adjacent}}{\text{hypotenuse}}$	$\frac{b\sqrt{3}}{2b} = \frac{\sqrt{3}}{2}$	$\frac{a}{a\sqrt{2}} = \frac{1}{\sqrt{2}}$	$\frac{b}{2b} = \frac{1}{2}$
tangent =	$\frac{\text{opposite}}{\text{adjacent}}$	$\frac{b}{b\sqrt{3}} = \frac{1}{\sqrt{3}}$	$\frac{a}{a} = 1$	$\frac{b\sqrt{3}}{b} = \sqrt{3}$

8-8 Special Right Triangles and Trigonometry

491

Answers to Talk it Over

5. Yes; the sum of the angle measures is 180°, so $m\angle N = 45°$. If two angles of a triangle are equal in measure, then the sides opposite those angles are equal in measure. △MNO has two sides equal in measure, so it is isosceles by definition.

6. $MO = NO \approx 7.1$

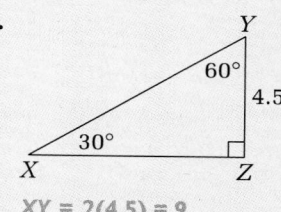
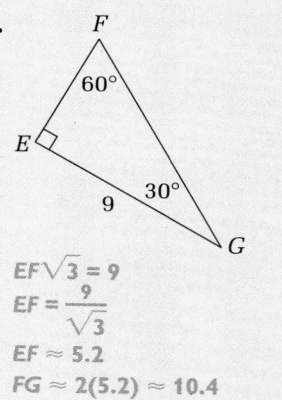
491

Additional Sample

S3 Find the value of the variable in each figure.

a.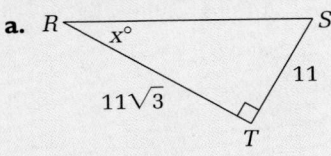

$$\tan x° = \frac{11}{11\sqrt{3}} = \frac{1}{\sqrt{3}}$$

$$\tan 30° = \frac{1}{\sqrt{3}}$$

$$x = 30$$

b.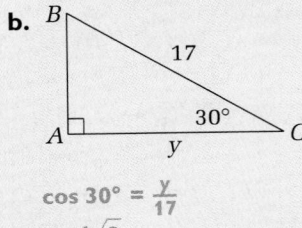

$$\cos 30° = \frac{y}{17}$$

$$\frac{\sqrt{3}}{2} = \frac{y}{17}$$

$$\frac{17\sqrt{3}}{2} = y$$

$$y \approx 14.7$$

c.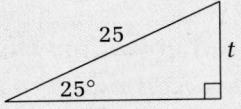

$$\sin 25° = \frac{t}{25}$$

Use a calculator or table to find sin 25°.

$$\sin 25° = 0.4226$$

$$0.4226 \approx \frac{t}{25}$$

$$t \approx 25(0.4226)$$

$$t \approx 10.6$$

Look Back

Students will most likely have different ways to remember these facts. If they can visualize the two triangles used to arrive at the values given in the chart on page 491, they will probably not have any difficulty reconstructing these values. •

Find the value of the variable in each figure.

a.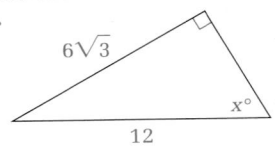

b.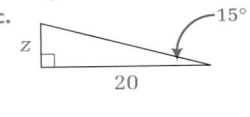

c. (figure with 15°, z, 20)

Sample Response

Decide which side measure(s) you know and which you want to know: opposite, adjacent, or hypotenuse. Use the trigonometric ratio that involves those sides.

a. Method ❶ Use the special triangle ratios. This is a 30°-60°-90° triangle.

$$\cos 30° = \frac{\text{adjacent}}{\text{hypotenuse}}$$

$$\frac{\sqrt{3}}{2} = \frac{23}{y}$$

$$y\sqrt{3} = 46 \quad \longleftarrow \text{ Use cross products.}$$

$$y = \frac{46}{\sqrt{3}} \approx 26.6$$

Method ❷ Use a calculator to find the trigonometric ratios.

$$\cos 30° = \frac{\text{adjacent}}{\text{hypotenuse}}$$

$$0.8660 \approx \frac{23}{y}$$

$$y \approx \frac{23}{0.8660}$$

$$y \approx 26.6$$

b. You know some side measures, but not the angle measure.

$$\sin x° = \frac{\text{opposite}}{\text{hypotenuse}} = \frac{6\sqrt{3}}{12} = \frac{\sqrt{3}}{2} \quad \text{Work backward.}$$

The measure of an angle with a sine of $\frac{\sqrt{3}}{2}$ is 60°. The value of x is 60.

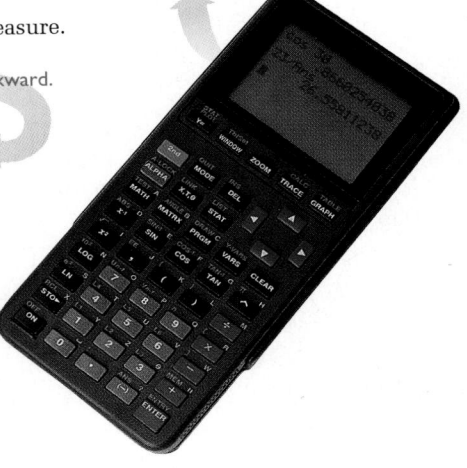

c. A triangle with a 15° angle is not one of the special right triangles.

$$\tan 15° = \frac{\text{opposite}}{\text{adjacent}}$$

$$0.2679 \approx \frac{z}{20} \quad \longleftarrow \text{ Use the } \boxed{\text{TAN}} \text{ key.}$$

$$z \approx 5.4$$

▸ Now you are ready for:
Exs. 19–38 on pp. 495–496

Look Back

Describe a way to remember the sine, cosine, and tangent of the acute angles of a 45°-45°-90° triangle. Describe a way to remember the sine, cosine, and tangent of each acute angle of a 30°-60°-90° triangle.

Unit 8 Similar and Congruent Triangles

Answers to Look Back

Summaries may vary. Examples are given. Sketch a 45°-45°-90° triangle. Label the measures of the legs x and the hypotenuse $x\sqrt{2}$. Then

$$\sin 45° = \cos 45° = \frac{x}{x\sqrt{2}} = \frac{1}{\sqrt{2}}$$

and tan 45° = 1. Similarly, sketch a 30°-60°-90° triangle and label the measures of the shorter and longer legs b and $b\sqrt{3}$ and the hypotenuse $2b$.

Then $\sin 30° = \cos 60° = \frac{b}{2b} = \frac{1}{2}$,

$$\sin 60° = \cos 30° = \frac{b\sqrt{3}}{2b} = \frac{\sqrt{3}}{2},$$

$$\tan 30° = \frac{b}{b\sqrt{3}} = \frac{1}{\sqrt{3}}, \text{ and}$$

$$\tan 60° = \frac{b\sqrt{3}}{b} = \frac{\sqrt{3}}{1}.$$

Exercises and Problems

Find the exact measure of each unknown side in each triangle.

1.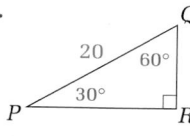

2.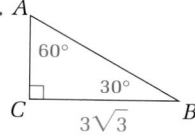

3.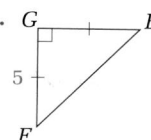

4.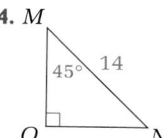

Find each measure to the nearest tenth.

5. the height of the parasailer above the ground

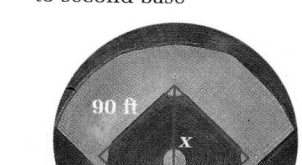

6. the length of a support in the skylight

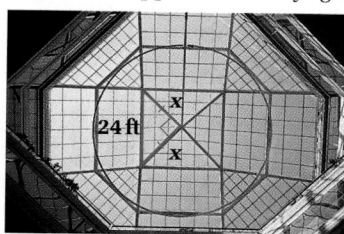

7. the distance from home plate to second base

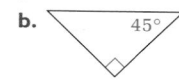

8. the length of the gangplank from the dock to the pier

9. Choose the letter of the triangle that must be an isosceles right triangle.

a. **b.** **c.**

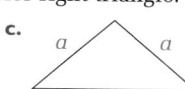

Find the measures of as many segments as possible in each figure.

10.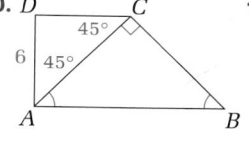

11.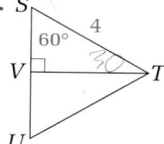

12.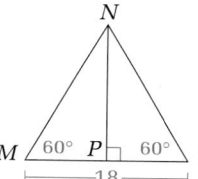

13.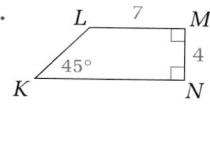

14. **Writing** Justify your answer to one of Exercises 10–13.

Suggested Assignment
Day 1
Standard 1–14
Extended 1–18
Day 2
Standard 19–38
Extended 19–38

Integrating the Strands
Algebra Exs. 23–28, 32
Geometry Exs. 1–18, 23–38
Trigonometry Exs. 19–31, 38
Logic and Language Exs. 14, 32

Error Analysis
Students get accustomed to seeing right triangles in the positions shown on this page, where the legs are parallel to the edges of the page. In seeing such triangles, they usually can apply the definitions of the trigonometric ratios correctly. The triangle shown in Ex. 9(b) is oriented differently, however, and some students tend to make errors in writing the ratios. You can help students by drawing many different right triangles on the board in many different positions and asking them to name the sine, cosine, and tangent of their angles.

Answers to Exercises and Problems

1. $QR = 10$; $PR = 10\sqrt{3}$

2. $AC = 3$; $AB = 6$

3. $EG = 5$; $EF = 5\sqrt{2}$

4. $MO = NO = 7\sqrt{2}$

5. 173.2 ft

6. 17.0 ft

7. 127.3 ft

8. 30.0 ft

9. b

10. $DC = 6$; $AC = BC = 6\sqrt{2}$; $AB = 12$

11. $SV = 2$; $VT = 2\sqrt{3}$

12. $MN = NO = 18$; $NP = 9\sqrt{3}$; $PO = PM = 9$

13. $KL = 4\sqrt{2}$; $KN = 11$

Research

Students may wish to research the various layers of Earth's atmosphere and the conditions present in each. Other students may wish to find out more about the Hubble Space Telescope.

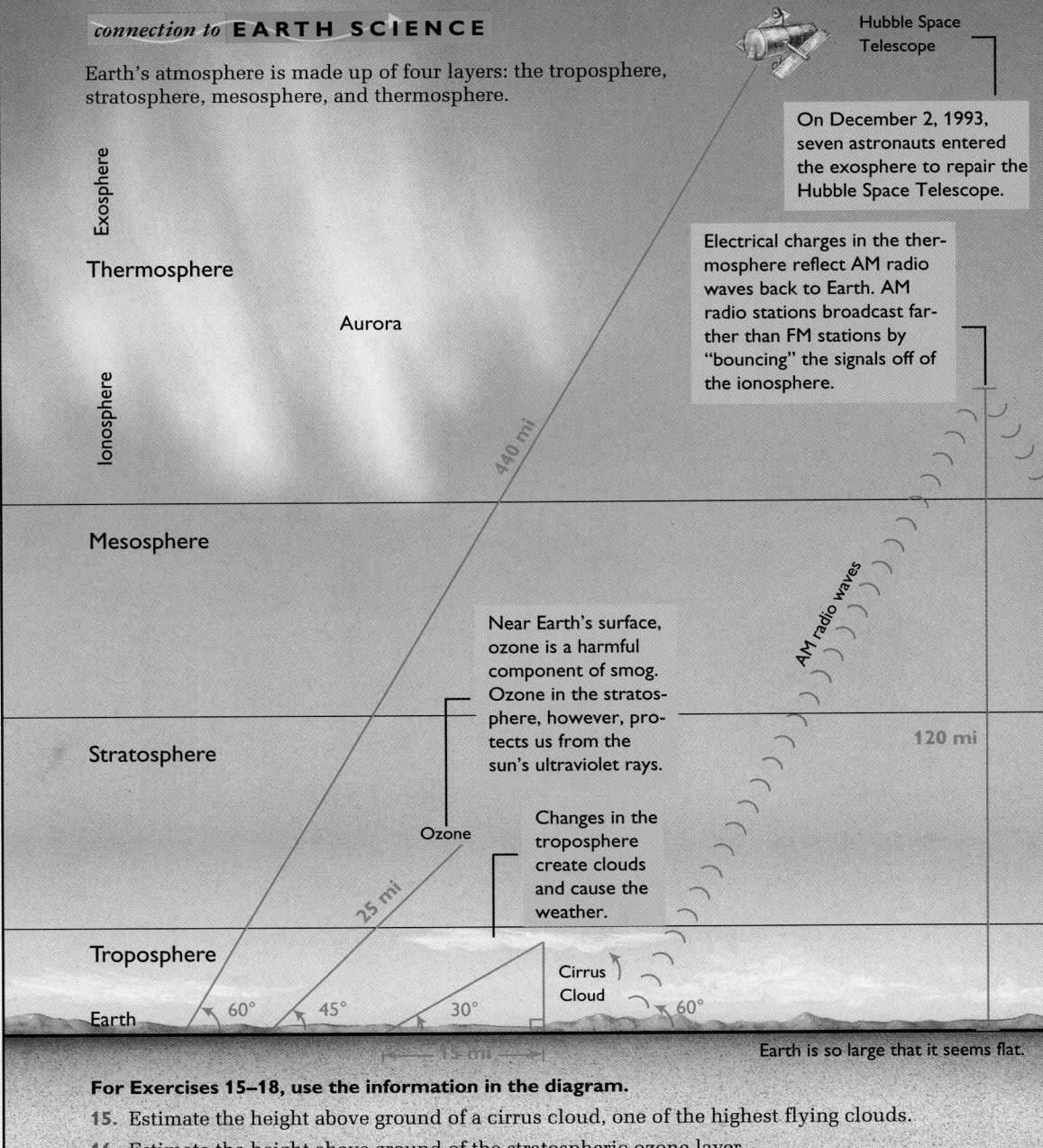

connection to **EARTH SCIENCE**

Earth's atmosphere is made up of four layers: the troposphere, stratosphere, mesosphere, and thermosphere.

Hubble Space Telescope

On December 2, 1993, seven astronauts entered the exosphere to repair the Hubble Space Telescope.

Electrical charges in the thermosphere reflect AM radio waves back to Earth. AM radio stations broadcast farther than FM stations by "bouncing" the signals off of the ionosphere.

Exosphere

Thermosphere

Aurora

Ionosphere

440 mi

Mesosphere

AM radio waves

Near Earth's surface, ozone is a harmful component of smog. Ozone in the stratosphere, however, protects us from the sun's ultraviolet rays.

Stratosphere

120 mi

Ozone

Changes in the troposphere create clouds and cause the weather.

25 mi

Troposphere

Cirrus Cloud

Earth   60°   45°   30°   60°

15 mi

Earth is so large that it seems flat.

For Exercises 15–18, use the information in the diagram.

15. Estimate the height above ground of a cirrus cloud, one of the highest flying clouds.

16. Estimate the height above ground of the stratospheric ozone layer.

17. About how far does the radio wave travel before it is reflected?

18. How high above Earth did the astronauts go to reach the Hubble?

(Not drawn to scale.)

494   **Unit 8** Similar and Congruent Triangles

Answers to Exercises and Problems

14. Answers may vary. An example is given for Ex. 10. By the converse of the Isosceles Triangle Theorem, $DC = DA$. $\triangle DAC$ is a 45°-45°-90° triangle, so $AC = (DA)(\sqrt{2})$. Again by the converse of the Isosceles Triangle Theorem, $BC = AC$. $\triangle ABC$ is also a 45°-45°-90° triangle, so $AB = (AC)(\sqrt{2})$.

15. about 8.7 mi

16. about 17.7 mi

17. about 138.6 mi

18. about 381.1 mi

19. $x° = 60°$

20. $y° = 45°$

21. $z° = 45°$

22. $w° = 30°$

23. $x = 6\sqrt{2} \approx 8.5$

24. $c = \dfrac{6.4}{\sqrt{3}} \approx 3.7$

25. $w° = 45°$

26. $r° = 60°$

27. $z \approx 12.9$

28. $y \approx 5.8$

29. $\sin \angle MNO = \dfrac{4}{5} = 0.8$;

$\cos \angle MNO = \dfrac{3}{5} = 0.6$;

$\tan \angle MNO = \dfrac{4}{3} \approx 1.33$

30. $\sin \angle BAC = \sin \angle BCA = \dfrac{1}{\sqrt{2}}$; $\cos \angle BAC =$

$\cos \angle BCA = \dfrac{1}{\sqrt{2}}$;

$\tan \angle BAC = \tan \angle BCA = 1$

31. a. $\sin 60° = \cos 30° = \dfrac{\sqrt{3}}{2}$

b. $\sin 30° = \cos 60° = \dfrac{1}{2}$

c. $\tan 60° = \sqrt{3}$; $\tan 30° = \dfrac{1}{\sqrt{3}}$

494

Reading Find the value of each variable.

19. $\cos x° = \dfrac{1}{2}$　　　**20.** $\sin y° = \dfrac{1}{\sqrt{2}}$　　**21.** $\tan z° = 1$　　　**22.** $\sin w° = \dfrac{1}{2}$

Find the value of the variable in each figure.

23.
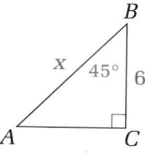

24.
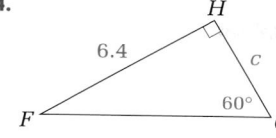

25.
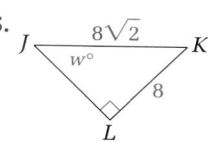

26.
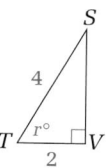

27.
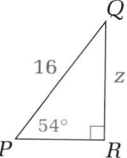

28.
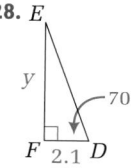

29. Find the sine, cosine, and tangent of $\angle MNO$.

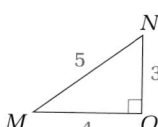

30. Find the sine, cosine, and tangent of the acute angles in $\triangle ABC$.

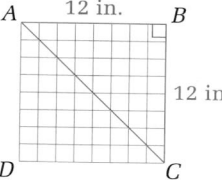

31. For parts (a)–(c), find each value.

　a. $\sin 60°$ and $\cos 30°$　　　**b.** $\sin 30°$ and $\cos 60°$　　　**c.** $\tan 60°$ and $\tan 30°$

　d. Find a pattern in your answers to parts (a)–(c). Make a conjecture. Support your conclusion.

Ongoing **ASSESSMENT**

32. **Writing** Use the figures at the right.

　a. Explain why $\triangle ABC \sim \triangle DEF$. Are all 45°-45°-90° triangles similar?

　b. Use the Pythagorean theorem to find AB.

　c. What is the ratio of corresponding sides in $\triangle ABC$ and $\triangle DEF$?

　d. Explain why $DE = a\sqrt{2}$.

　e. $\triangle GHJ$ is an equilateral triangle with altitude $\overline{GK}$. What kind of special triangle is $\triangle GHK$?

　f. Suppose $HK = 1$ unit. Find HJ and HG. Show your reasoning.

　g. Use the Pythagorean theorem to find GK.

　h. Suppose that $\triangle LMN \sim \triangle GHK$ and $MN = b$ units. Use similar triangles to find LN and LM. Show your reasoning.

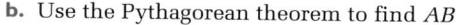
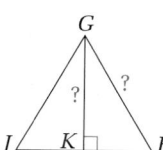
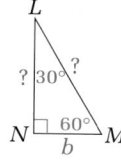

8-8 Special Right Triangles and Trigonometry

Assessment: Standard

Ex. 32 provides an excellent summary of the concepts presented in this section. In parts (b) and (g), students use the Pythagorean theorem to find AB and GK, respectively. They should also find these lengths by using trigonometric ratios.

Answers to Exercises and Problems

　d. If $\angle A$ and $\angle B$ are complementary, then $\sin A = \cos B$ and $\tan A = \dfrac{1}{\tan B}$. In $\triangle ABC$ with right $\angle C$, let $x° = m\angle A$ and $(90 - x)° = m\angle B$. Then $\sin x° = \sin A = \dfrac{BC}{AB}$, $\cos (90 - x)° = \cos B = \dfrac{BC}{AB}$, $\tan x° = \dfrac{BC}{AC}$,

$\tan (90 - x)° = \dfrac{AC}{BC} = \dfrac{\frac{1}{BC}}{\frac{1}{AC}} = \dfrac{1}{\tan x°}$.

32. a. $\triangle ABC \sim \triangle DEF$ because all pairs of corresponding angles have the same measure. Yes, all 45°-45°-90° triangles are similar.

　b. $AB = \sqrt{1^2 + 1^2} = \sqrt{2}$

　c. $\dfrac{1}{a}$ or $1: a$

　d. $DE = \sqrt{a^2 + a^2} = \sqrt{2a^2} = a\sqrt{2}$, or by ratios $\dfrac{1}{a} = \dfrac{\sqrt{2}}{?}$ and $? = a\sqrt{2}$

　e. $\triangle GHK$ is a 30°-60°-90° triangle.

　f. If $HK = 1$, then $HJ = 2$ and $HG = 2$. The perpendicular bisector of an equilateral triangle bisects the base so base

$HJ = 2(KH)$ and in an equilateral triangle, all sides have the same measure.

　g. $(GH)^2 = (GK)^2 + (KH)^2$; $2^2 = (GK)^2 + 1^2$; $4 = (GK)^2 + 1$; $3 = (GK)^2$; $GK = \sqrt{3}$

　h. If $MN = b$, then the ratio of similar triangles is $\dfrac{b}{1}$ or b. Therefore, $LN = b\sqrt{3}$ and $LM = 2b$.

495

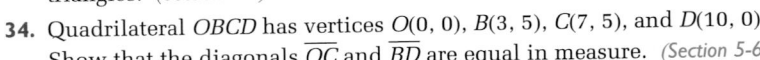

33. In $\triangle EHR$, $\overline{HJ}$ is the altitude to hypotenuse $\overline{ER}$. Identify the similar triangles. *(Section 8-7)*

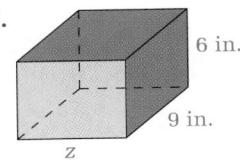

34. Quadrilateral $OBCD$ has vertices $O(0, 0)$, $B(3, 5)$, $C(7, 5)$, and $D(10, 0)$. Show that the diagonals $\overline{OC}$ and $\overline{BD}$ are equal in measure. *(Section 5-6)*

Find the value of the variable in each figure. *(Toolbox Skills 15 and 28)*

35.

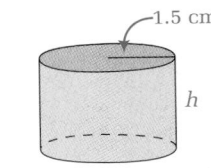

—1.5 cm

h

Volume ≈ 14.84 cm³

36.

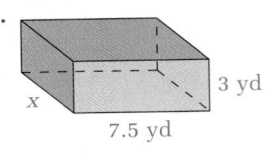

x

3 yd

7.5 yd

Volume = 126 yd³

37.

6 in.

9 in.

z

Surface Area = 348 in.²

Working on the Unit Project

As you complete Exercise 38, think about how you can use the properties of right triangles in the tool you design.

38. A *sextant* is a device that is normally used by navigators to help find a ship's position at sea. The instrument has two mirrors that allow a navigator to see the sun and horizon at the same time and to find the measure of the angle between them. This angle is always an angle of a right triangle.

the angle that the sextant measures

This sextant from about 1810 was used by a ship's captain.

Billie is out in a rowboat practicing using her sextant. When she sights the top and base of the lighthouse, the sextant gives Billie a reading of 30°. Suppose the lighthouse is 50 ft tall. About how far is Billie from the base? Round your answer to the nearest foot.

30°

(Not drawn to scale)

Unit 8 Similar and Congruent Triangles

496

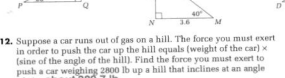
Answers to Exercises and Problems

33. $\triangle EHR \sim \triangle HJR \sim \triangle EJH$

34. $OC = \sqrt{7^2 + 5^2} =$
$\sqrt{49 + 25} = \sqrt{74}$; $BD =$
$\sqrt{(10 - 3)^2 + (0 - 5)^2} =$
$\sqrt{7^2 + (-5)^2} = \sqrt{49 + 25} =$
$\sqrt{74}$

35. $h \approx 2.10$ cm

36. $x = 5.6$ yd

37. $z = 8$ in.

38. about 87 ft

Completing the Unit Project

Complete your patent application. Your finished project should include these things:

➤ a clear, complete description—in words and pictures—of a new tool that applies at least two of the ideas from geometry in this unit

➤ an explanation of how the tool works

➤ an explanation of what the tool is used for

Look Back ◄

How can you increase your chances of receiving a patent for the tool you design?

Assessment

A scoring rubric for the Unit Project can be found on pages 428 and 429 of this Teacher's Edition and also in the **Project Book**.

Alternative Projects

Project 1: Build the Tool You Design

Design a tool according to the guidelines presented on page 429. Then build a working model of the tool.

Project 2: A Pantograph

A pantograph is a drawing tool used by mapmakers and artists to make an enlarged or reduced copy of an existing drawing. Find out how a pantograph is made. Explain how it works. Build your own pantograph and use it to enlarge or reduce a drawing.

Project 3: CAD Software

Many engineers use CAD (computer-aided design) software instead of hand-held drafting tools. If CAD software is available, use it to design a tool.

Unit Support Materials

➤ Unit 8 Cumulative Practice 68
➤ Unit 8 Study Guide Review
➤ Unifying Problem 8 in the Problem Bank
➤ Unit Tests 35 and 36
➤ Spanish versions of the Unit Tests are in the Assessment Book.
➤ Teacher's Resources for Transfer Students

Quick Quiz (8-7 through 8-8)

1. Name all similar triangles in this figure. [8-7]

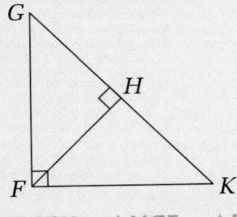

△FGK ~ △HGF ~ △HFK

2. Find the geometric mean between 4 and 36. [8-7]   **12**

3. In a 30°-60°-90° triangle, the side opposite the 30° angle is 7.5 units long. How long is the hypotenuse of the triangle? [8-8]
15 units

4. What is the tangent of 45°? [8-8]   **1**

5. Find the value of the variable. [8-8]

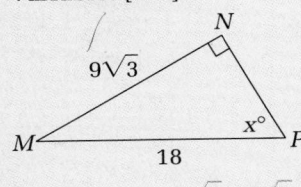

$\sin x° = \dfrac{MN}{MP} = \dfrac{9\sqrt{3}}{18} = \dfrac{\sqrt{3}}{2}$

$x = 60$

---

1. **Given** $\overrightarrow{AB} \parallel \overrightarrow{FC}$
∠B and ∠F are right angles.

Prove $\overrightarrow{FE} \parallel \overrightarrow{CD}$

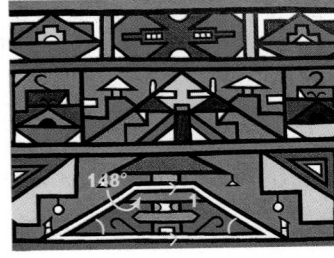

8-1

2. Find the measure of ∠1.

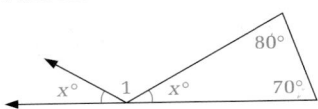

4. Find the measure of ∠1.

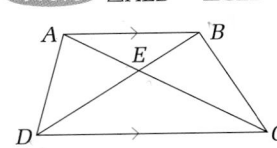

5. **Given** $\overline{AB} \parallel \overline{DC}$

Prove △AEB ~ △CED

6. Find the values of x and y.   8-3

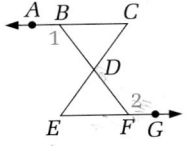

7. **Given** m∠1 = m∠2
BD = DF

Prove D is the midpoint of $\overline{CE}$.

8-4

8. **Open-ended** Name two everyday items that use triangles to give them rigidity.

9. **Given** B is the midpoint of $\overline{AE}$, $\overline{FC}$, and $\overline{GD}$.

Prove △ABG ≅ △EBD

8-5

10. **Writing** Do you agree or disagree with the statement, "The base angles of every isosceles triangle are acute angles"? Explain.

8-6

3. Is the quadrilateral a parallelogram? Why or why not?   8-2

The photos at left and above show two walls. The designs on the left wall were painted by an Ndebele woman in South Africa. The stone mosaic wall at the right is at Mitla, Oaxaca, Mexico.

498   Unit 8 Similar and Congruent Triangles

Answers to Unit 8
Review and Assessment

1. *Given:* $\overline{AB} \parallel \overline{FC}$; ∠B and ∠F are right angles.
Prove: $\overrightarrow{FE} \parallel \overrightarrow{CD}$

Statements
1. $\overline{AB} \parallel \overline{FC}$
2. m∠B = m∠FCD
3. ∠B is a right angle.
4. m∠B = 90°
5. m∠FCD = 90°
6. ∠FCD is a right angle.
7. $\overline{FC} \perp \overline{CD}$
8. ∠F is a right angle.

9. $\overrightarrow{FC} \perp \overrightarrow{FE}$
10. $\overrightarrow{FE} \parallel \overrightarrow{CD}$

Justifications
1. Given
2. If two ∥ lines are intersected by a transversal, then corresponding ∡ are = in measure.
3. Given
4. Definition of a right angle
5. Substitution property (Steps 2 and 4)

6. Definition of a right angle
7. Definition of perpendicular lines
8. Given
9. Definition of perpendicular lines
10. If two lines are ⊥ to the same transversal, then they are ∥.

2. 148°

3. Yes. If both pairs of opposite angles of a quadrilateral are = in measure, the

quadrilateral is a parallelogram.

4. m∠1 = 120°

5. *Given:* $\overline{AB} \parallel \overline{DC}$
Prove: △AEB ~ △CED

Statements
1. $\overline{AB} \parallel \overline{CD}$
2. m∠BAE = m∠DCE
3. m∠AEB = m∠CED
4. △AEB ~ △CED

Justifications
1. Given

498

11. Find the measures of the three angles in △QRS.

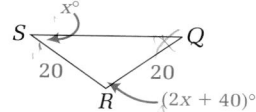

12. a. On a coordinate plane, plot the points $J(2, 2)$, $K(-3, 1)$, and $L(-1, 4)$. Draw △JKL.

  b. Show that △JKL is isosceles.

13. Explain how you know that $\overleftrightarrow{BD}$ is the perpendicular bisector of $\overline{AC}$.

14. Find the geometric mean between 100 and 4.

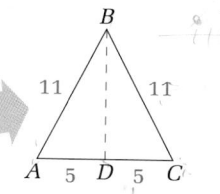

8-7

15. The logo shown is used by a shipbuilder. The artist drew the logo so that $\angle HKJ$ is a right angle. The measure of $\overline{HL}$ is 20 mm, and the measure of $\overline{LJ}$ is 16 mm.

  a. Identify the similar triangles.

  b. What is the measure of $\overline{KL}$?

  c. What is the measure of $\overline{HK}$?

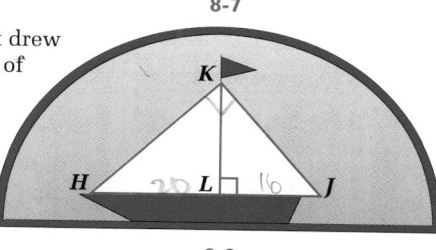

8-8

For Exercises 16 and 17:

a. Find the exact measure of each unknown side in each triangle.

b. Find the sine, cosine, and tangent of $\angle A$ in each triangle.

16.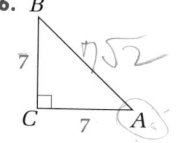

17.

Find the approximate value of x in each figure.

18.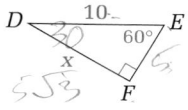

19.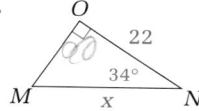

20. **Self-evaluation** What is some information you look for in diagrams involving lines intersected by a transversal or involving triangles? What are some questions you can ask yourself to help you think through a proof or problem?

21. **Group Activity** Work in a group of three students.

  a. Each student should write "given(s)" and a "prove" statement for a proof about parallel lines, similar triangles, congruent triangles, isosceles triangles, or right triangles.

  b. Trade your problem with another person in your group. Do the proof. Continue to trade until you have attempted each person's proof.

  c. Could all the proofs be completed given what you know? Why or why not?

Unit 8 Review and Assessment

499

Answers to Unit 8 Review and Assessment ·······

2. If two ‖ lines are intersected by a transversal, then alternate interior ∡ are = in measure.

3. Vertical ∡ are = in measure.

4. AA Similarity

6. $x = 20$, $y = 25$

7. Given: $m \angle 1 = m \angle 2$; $BD = DF$
Prove: D is the midpoint of $\overline{CE}$.

Statements
1. $m \angle 1 = m \angle 2$
2. $\overline{AC} \parallel \overline{EG}$
3. $m \angle BCD = m \angle FED$
4. $\angle BDC$ and $\angle FDE$ are vertical angles.
5. $m \angle BDC = m \angle FDE$
6. $BD = DF$
7. $\triangle BDC \cong \triangle FDE$
8. $ED = CD$
9. D is the midpoint of $\overline{CE}$.

Justifications
1. Given
2. If two lines are intersected by a transversal and alternate interior ∡ are = in measure, then the lines are ‖.
3. If two ‖ lines are intersected by a transversal, then alternate interior ∡ are = in measure.

4. Definition of vertical angles
5. Vertical ∡ are = in measure.
6. Given
7. AAS
8. CPCTE
9. Definition of midpoint

8. Answers may vary. Examples are given. bridges, roofs, swing sets, tripods, braces under a folding table, geodesic domes, trusses in houses, stepladders

9. *Given:* B is the midpoint of $\overline{AE}$, $\overline{FC}$, and $\overline{GD}$.
Prove: △ABG ≅ △EBD
Statements
1. B is the midpoint of $\overline{AE}$, $\overline{FC}$, and $\overline{GD}$.
2. $AB = BE$; $GB = BD$
3. $\angle ABG$ and $\angle EBD$ are vertical angles.
4. $m \angle ABG = m \angle EBD$
5. △ABG ≅ △EBD
Justifications
1. Given
2. Definition of midpoint
3. Definition of vertical angles
4. Vertical ∡ are = in measure.
5. SAS

10. agree; A triangle can have at most one right or obtuse angle since the sum of the measures of the angles is 180°. Therefore, two angles of a triangle must be acute, and in an isosceles triangle, these are the base angles since they are equal in measure.

11. 35°, 35°, 110°

12. a.

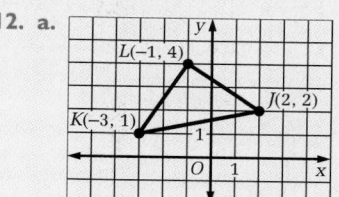

b. $JL = \sqrt{(2 - (-1))^2 + (2 - 4)^2} = \sqrt{9 + 4} = \sqrt{13}$; $KL = \sqrt{(-3 - (-1))^2 + (1 - 4)^2} = \sqrt{4 + 9} = \sqrt{13}$. Since sides JL and KL are equal in measure, △JKL is isosceles.

13. Since point B is the same distance from points A and C, and D is the midpoint of $\overline{AC}$, $\overleftrightarrow{BD}$ is the perpendicular bisector of $\overline{AC}$ by Theorem 8.16.

14. 20

15. a. △HKJ ~ △HLK ~ △KLJ

  b. $8\sqrt{5} \approx 17.9$mm

  c. about 26.8mm

Answers continued on next page.

499

Quick Quiz (8-1 through 8-3)

1. Is this statement *True* or *False*? If two lines are intersected by a transversal and corresponding angles are equal in measure, then the lines are parallel. [8-1]
True.

2. Name the pair of angles as *corresponding, alternate interior,* or *co-interior.* [8-1]

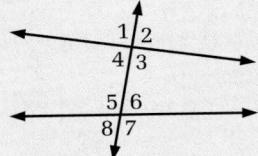

a. $\angle 4$ and $\angle 6$ alternate interior

b. $\angle 1$ and $\angle 5$ corresponding

c. $\angle 3$ and $\angle 6$ co-interior

3. A right triangle has one acute angle of 47°. What is the measure of the other acute angle? [8-2] 43°

4. Find the measure of $\angle B$. [8-2] $m \angle B = 50°$

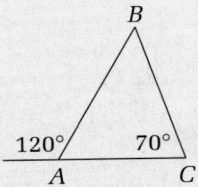

5. Name the similar triangles. [8-3] $\triangle ABD \sim \triangle ECD$

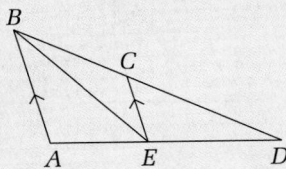

IDEAS AND (FORMULAS) = X²

ALGEBRA

➤ The proportion $\frac{a}{x} = \frac{x}{b}$ can be written and solved to find the positive value x that is the geometric mean between two positive numbers a and b. *(p. 483)*

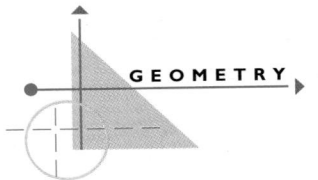

GEOMETRY

➤ Suppose two lines are intersected by a transversal. Then the lines are parallel under any of these conditions:
  • if corresponding angles are equal in measure *(p. 431)*
  • if alternate interior angles are equal in measure *(p. 433)*
  • if co-interior angles are supplementary *(p. 433)*

➤ If two lines are perpendicular to the same transversal, then they are parallel. *(p. 434)*

➤ If a transversal is perpendicular to one of two parallel lines, then it is perpendicular to the other one also. *(p. 434)*

➤ Through a point not on a given line, there is one and only one line parallel to the given line. (Unique Parallel Postulate) *(p. 439)*

➤ **Problem Solving** Drawing *helping lines* in a diagram can help you do a proof. *(p. 440)*

➤ **Measurement** The sum of the measures of the angles of a triangle is 180°. (Triangle Sum Theorem) *(p. 440)*

➤ **Measurement** The sum of the measures of the angles of a quadrilateral is 360°. *(p. 441)*

➤ If both pairs of opposite angles of a quadrilateral are equal in measure, then the quadrilateral is a parallelogram. *(p. 441)*

➤ **Measurement** An exterior angle of a triangle is equal in measure to the sum of the measures of its two remote interior angles. *(p. 443)*

➤ If two angles of one triangle are equal in measure to two angles of another triangle, then the two triangles are similar. (AA Similarity) *(p. 450)*

➤ If a line is drawn from a point on one side of a triangle parallel to another side, then it forms a triangle similar to the original triangle. *(p. 452)*

➤ Two triangles can be proven congruent when any of the following sets of corresponding parts are equal in measure:
  • two angles and the included side (ASA) *(p. 459)*
  • two angles and a non-included side (AAS) *(p. 459)*
  • two sides and the included angle (SAS) *(p. 466)*
  • three sides (SSS) *(p. 466)*

500

Unit 8 Similar and Congruent Triangles

Answers to Unit 8 Review and Assessment

16. $AB = 7\sqrt{2}$; $\sin A = \cos A = \frac{1}{\sqrt{2}}$; $\tan A = 1$

17. $BC = 4$; $AC = 4\sqrt{3}$; $\sin A = \frac{1}{2}$; $\cos A = \frac{\sqrt{3}}{2}$; $\tan A = \frac{1}{\sqrt{3}}$

18. $x = 5\sqrt{3} \approx 8.7$

19. $x \approx 26.5$

20. Answers may vary. An example is given. Look for parallel lines, alternate interior angles, corresponding angles, vertical angles, or exterior angles to find further information about parallel and perpendicular lines and congruent triangles to identify congruent parts. Can I find SSS, SAS, ASA, or AAS in a triangle so that I can prove two triangles are congruent? Are any triangles isosceles or equilateral? Ask yourself what parts you need to know to prove your conclusion and then look to see how you can prove that part or fact.

21. a–c. Answers may vary. Check students' work.

➤ You can prove that segments and angles are equal in measure if you can show that they are corresponding parts of congruent triangles. (CPCTE) *(p. 461)*

➤ If two sides of a triangle are equal in measure, then the angles opposite those sides are equal in measure. *(p. 473)*

➤ If two angles of a triangle are equal in measure, then the sides opposite those angles are equal in measure. *(p. 473)*

➤ A triangle is equilateral if and only if it is equiangular. An equiangular triangle has three 60° angles. *(p. 474)*

➤ If a point is the same distance from both endpoints of a segment, then it lies on the perpendicular bisector of the segment. *(p. 475)*

➤ In any right triangle, the square of the length of the hypotenuse is equal to the sum of the squares of the lengths of the legs. *(p. 482)*

➤ If the altitude is drawn to the hypotenuse of a right triangle:
  • then the two triangles formed are similar to the original triangle and to each other. *(p. 482)*
  • then the measure of the altitude is the geometric mean between the measures of the parts of the hypotenuse. *(p. 484)*

➤ **Measurement** The diagrams below show the relationships between the side measures in 45°-45°-90° triangles and 30°-60°-90° triangles. *(p. 489)*

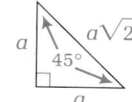 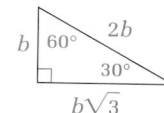

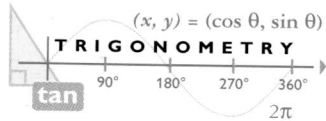

➤ The trigonometric ratios for 30°, 45°, and 60° angles can be found by using the relationships between the measures of the sides of 30°-60°-90° and 45°-45°-90° triangles. *(p. 491)*

➤ The sine, cosine, and tangent ratios can be used to find the measure of an unknown side of a triangle. *(pp. 491–492)*

Quick Quiz (8-4 through 8-6)

1. Triangle *ACB* is congruent to triangle *DEF*. Name the corresponding sides. [8-4]

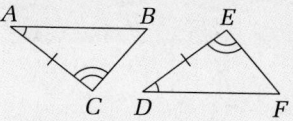

$\overline{AC}$ and $\overline{DE}$
$\overline{CB}$ and $\overline{EF}$
$\overline{AB}$ and $\overline{DF}$

2. Is there enough information to prove that the triangles are congruent? Write *Yes* or *No*. [8-5] No.

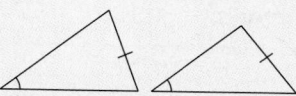

3. Find the measure of angles *R* and *T* in isosceles triangle *RST*. [8-6]

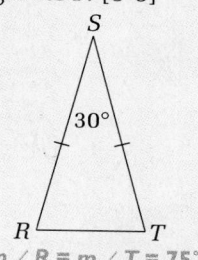

$m \angle R = m \angle T = 75°$

4. If △*MNP* and △*WXY* are both isosceles triangles, are they necessarily congruent triangles? Write *Yes* or *No*. [8-6] No.

501

Polynomial and Rational Functions

OVERVIEW

➤ **Unit 9** covers polynomial and rational functions. Students review rules of exponents. The graphs of polynomial functions are analyzed. Factoring is used in this analysis, as well as in solving polynomial equations. Polynomial equations are also solved by graphing and by applying the quadratic formula.

➤ Rational equations are used to model problems. Students solve rational equations that can be reduced to linear or quadratic forms. Parametric equations are used to solve problems.

➤ The Unit Project is based on power output as a function of wind speed. The goal of this project is for students to design their own wind machine by studying other wind machines and how wind speed affects power output.

➤ Connections to employment, finances, chemistry, volleyball, aviation, ornithology, and stocking a fish pond are some of the topics included in the teaching materials and the exercises.

➤ Graphics calculators are used in Section 9-4 to graph cubic and higher degree functions, and in Section 9-6 to graph parametric equations to solve problems. Computer software, such as Plotter Plus, can also be used in Section 9-4 to graph cubic functions.

➤ Problem-solving strategies used in Unit 9 include using diagrams, equations, manipulatives, tables, formulas, technology, breaking the problem into parts, graphs, and parametric equations.

Unit Objectives

Section	Objectives	NCTM Standards
9-1	• Model real-world situations with equations. • Classify expressions.	1, 2, 4, 5
9-2	• Use rules of exponents to simplify expressions.	1, 2, 4, 5, 6, 14
9-3	• Solve rational equations that simplify to linear or quadratic equations.	1, 2, 4, 5, 6
9-4	• Analyze graphs of polynomial functions written in factored form.	1, 2, 4, 5, 6, 8
9-5	• Solve cubic equations by various methods.	1, 2, 4, 5, 6, 8
9-6	• Graph parametric equations to solve problems.	1, 2, 4, 5, 6, 8

Skills Bank To extend the curriculum and provide practice with skills, you may wish to assign the following topics from the **Skills Bank** ancillary: factoring higher order polynomials (for use after Section 9-2), operations with polynomials (for use after Section 9-2), and operations with rational expressions (for use after Section 9-3).

Section	Connections to Prior and Future Concepts
9-1	**Section 9-1** introduces polynomial functions and rational functions. Students identify polynomial functions, determine the degree of a polynomial, and write a polynomial in standard form. Both functions are used to model problem situations. These skills are used in Unit 2 of Book 3.
9-2	**Section 9-2** reviews the rules of exponents, which were first explored in Section 10-4 of Book 1. These rules are extended to cover negative, zero, and fractional exponents, and to include the power of a power, power of a product, and power of a quotient rules. These rules are used in Unit 5 of Book 3. Factoring a polynomial is introduced. Factoring is used in the remainder of Unit 9, and in Unit 2 of Book 3.
9-3	**Section 9-3** introduces solving rational equations that simplify to either a linear equation or a quadratic equation. Students have encountered solving linear and quadratic equations in Units 2, 5, and 10 of Book 1, and in Unit 4 of Book 2. Work with rational functions is continued in Unit 2 of Book 3.
9-4	**Section 9-4** explores the characteristics of polynomial functions. Students examine a graph to determine where the zeros of a polynomial function are located and how many zeros exist. These skills are used in Unit 2 of Book 3.
9-5	**Section 9-5** explores solving a cubic equation. Work from Section 9-4 is extended to solving a cubic equation by factoring and by using the quadratic formula. The quadratic formula was first introduced in Section 10-8 of Book 1.
9-6	**Section 9-6** introduces the concept of parametric equations. Students explore using parameters to model situations. The skill of modeling with parametric equations is continued in Unit 8 of Book 3.

Integrating the Strands

Strands	Sections
Number	9-1, 9-2, 9-5
Algebra	9-1, 9-2, 9-3, 9-4, 9-5, 9-6
Functions	9-2, 9-3, 9-4, 9-5, 9-6
Measurement	9-1
Geometry	9-1, 9-2, 9-3, 9-4, 9-5, 9-6
Trigonometry	9-1, 9-6
Statistics and Probability	9-5
Discrete Mathematics	9-3, 9-4, 9-6
Logic and Language	9-1, 9-2, 9-3, 9-4, 9-5, 9-6

Planning the Unit

9 Polynomial and Rational Functions

Section Planning Guide

➤ Essential exercises and problems are indicated in boldface.
➤ Ongoing work on the Unit Project is indicated in color.
➤ Exercises and problems that require student research, group work, manipulatives, or graphing technology are indicated in the column headed "Other."

Section	Materials	Pacing	Standard Assignment	Extended Assignment	Other
9-1	5½ in. × 11 in. paper, scissors, tape	Day 1 Day 2	**2–8, 12–15** **17–25**, 26, 27, 29–36, 37, 38	1, **2–8**, 9, 10, **12–15** **17–25**, 26–36, 37, 38	11, 16 38
9-2		Day 1 Day 2	**1–19**, 21–29 **32–46**, 47–54, 55	**1–19**, 20, **21–29**, 30, 31 **32–46**, 47–54, 55	
9-3		Day 1 Day 2	**1–10** **11–16**, **18–22**, 25–34, 35–38	**1–10** **11–16**, 17, **18–22**, 23–34, 35–38	35–37
9-4	graphing technology	Day 1 Day 2	**2–16** **17–22**, **26**, 30–42, 43, 44	1, **2–16** **17–22**, **26**, 30–42, 43, 44	23–25, 27–29
9-5	graphics calculator	Day 1	**1–14**, 20–27, 28	**1–14**, 15–17, 19–27, 28	18, 19d
9-6	graphics calculator	Day 1 Day 2	**1–3, 5–8** **9–14**, 17–26, 27	**1–3**, 4, **5–8** **9–14**, 16–26, 27	15
Review Test		**Day 1** **Day 2**	**Unit Review** **Unit Test**	**Unit Review** **Unit Test**	

Yearly Pacing	Unit 9 Total 15 days (2 for Unit Project)	Units 1–9 Total 147 days	Remaining 13 days	Total 160 days

Support Materials

➤ See **Project Book** for notes on Unit 9 Project: Air Your Opinion.
➤ "UPP" and "disk" refer to **Using Plotter Plus** booklet and **Plotter Plus** disk.
➤ "TI-81/82" refers to **Using TI-81 and TI-82 Calculators** booklet.
➤ Warm-up exercises for each section are available on **Warm-Up Transparencies.**
➤ "FI," "PC," "GI," "MA," and "Stats!" refer, respectively, to the McDougal Littell Mathpack software Activity Books for **Function Investigator, Probability Constructor, Geometry Inventor, Matrix Analyzer,** and **Stats!.**

Section	Study Guide	Practice Bank	Problem Bank	Activity Bank	Explorations Lab Manual	Assessment Book	Visuals	Technology
9-1	9-1	Practice 69	Set 20	Enrich 61		Quiz 9-1		
9-2	9-2	Practice 70	Set 20	Enrich 62		Quiz 9-2		
9-3	9-3	Practice 71	Set 20	Enrich 63	Master 2	Quiz 9-3 Test 37		
9-4	9-4	Practice 72	Set 21	Enrich 64	Masters 2, 20	Quiz 9-4	Folder 9	FI Act. 18 TI-81/82, pp. 46–47 UPP, p. 44 UPP (disk): Function Plotter
9-5	9-5	Practice 73	Set 21	Enrich 65	Add. Expl. 12	Quiz 9-5	Folder 9	UPP, p. 45
9-6	9-6	Practice 74	Set 21	Enrich 66	Master 21	Quiz 9-6 Test 38		TI-81/82, pp. 48–49
Unit 9	Unit Review	Practice 75	Unifying Problem 9	Family Involve 9		Tests 39, 40		

UNIT TESTS

Spanish versions of these tests are on pages 150–153 of the **Assessment Book.**

Name _____ Date _____ Score _____

Test 39

Test on Unit 9 (Form A)

Directions: Write the answers in the spaces provided.

Tell whether each expression is a polynomial. Write *Yes* or *No*.

1. $2x^3 - x + 4$ **2.** $4x^{1/2} + 5x - 3$

3. $\frac{x+4}{x-7} - \frac{5}{x}$ **4.** $\frac{1}{6}x^2 - 3x - \frac{3}{4}$

Simplify. Write each answer without negative exponents.

5. $(s^3t^{-2})^{-1}$ **6.** $\frac{a^{-2}h^4}{a^{-3}h^2}$

7. $(2x^0)(5v^{-3})(5x)^{-2}$ **8.** $\frac{(w^0 2^{-2})^{-3}}{(w^{-1})^2}$

Factor completely.

9. $72r^5s^2 - 42r^3s^5$ **10.** $3w^4 - 12w^3 - 15w^2$

11. $36x^3z^4 - 24x^5z^2$ **12.** $4x^5 + 6x^4 - 18x^3$

Solve.

13. $\frac{1}{x^2} = \frac{1}{x+3}$ **14.** $\frac{a}{a-2} + \frac{1}{a} = 1$

15. $\frac{1}{x-2} = x + 6$ **16.** $\frac{20}{w^2-1} - \frac{10}{w-1} = -6$

For Questions 17–20, list the zeros of each cubic function. Tell which, if any, are double or triple zeros.

17. $y = (x-3)(x+2)^2$ **18.** $y = (x-2)^3$

19. $y = x(x+1)(x-5)$ **20.** $y = 3x^2(x-8)$

21. Open-ended Write a cubic function which has a graph that intersects the *x*-axis in exactly one point.
    Sample answer: $y = (x-5)^3$

Answers
1. Yes
2. No
3. No
4. Yes
5. $\frac{t^2}{s^3}$
6. $\frac{a}{h^2}$
7. $\frac{2}{w^2z^5}$ $\frac{5v^3x^2}{}$
8. w^2z^6
9. $6r^3s^2(12r^2 - 7s^3)$
10. $3w^2(w+1)(w-5)$
11. $12x^3z^2(3z^2 - 2x^2)$
12. $2x^3(2x-3)(x+3)$
13. $\frac{4}{2}$
14. $\frac{2}{3}$
15. $\frac{-2 \pm \sqrt{17}}{2}$
16. $\frac{3}{}$
17. -2 (double), 3
18. 2 (triple)
19. $-1, 0, 5$
20. 0 (double), 8
21. *See question.*

Name _____ Date _____ Score _____

Test 39 *(continued)*

Directions: Write the answers in the spaces provided.

Match each function with its graph.

22. $y = (x-3)^3$ **23.** $y = x^3 + 6x^2 + 9x$

24. $y = (x+2)(x-5)(x+4)$ **25.** $y = -(x-4)(x+1)^2$

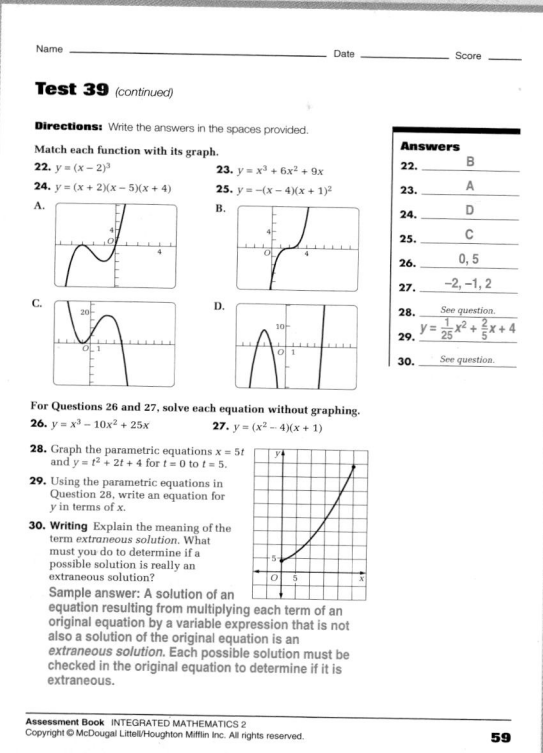

For Questions 26 and 27, solve each equation without graphing.

26. $y = x^3 - 10x^2 + 25x$ **27.** $y = (x^2 - 4)(x+1)$

28. Graph the parametric equations $x = 5t$ and $y = t^2 + 2t + 4$ for $t = 0$ to $t = 5$.

29. Using the parametric equations in Question 28, write an equation for *y* in terms of *x*.

30. Writing Explain the meaning of the term *extraneous solution*. What must you do to determine if a possible solution is really an extraneous solution?
Sample answer: A solution of an equation resulting from multiplying each term of an original equation by a variable expression that is not also a solution of the original equation is an *extraneous solution*. Each possible solution must be checked in the original equation to determine if it is extraneous.

Answers
22. B
23. A
24. D
25. C
26. 0, 5
27. $-2, -1, 2$
28. *See question.*
29. $y = \frac{1}{25}x^2 + \frac{2}{5}x + 4$
30. *See question.*

Name _____ Date _____ Score _____

Test 40

Test on Unit 9 (Form B)

Directions: Write the answers in the spaces provided.

Tell whether each expression is a polynomial. Write *Yes* or *No*.

1. $2x^{1/3} - 5x - 19$ **2.** $\frac{x+1}{x-4} - \frac{6}{x}$

3. $4x^3 - 3x + 7$ **4.** $\frac{1}{8}x^2 - \sqrt[3]{x} + 2$

Simplify. Write each answer without negative exponents.

5. $(x^4r^{-3})^{-2}$ **6.** $\frac{a^{-2}h^{-1}}{a^{-5}h^{-3}}$

7. $(7x^3)(4c^{-2})(7c)^{-2}$ **8.** $\frac{(w^{-1}z^{-3})^{-4}}{(w^0)^3}$

Factor completely.

9. $65a^3b^4 + 39a^2b^3$ **10.** $12v^5 - 20v^4 + 16v^3$

11. $81k^5n^2 + 45k^3n^4$ **12.** $12r^4 - 6r^3 - 90r^2$

Solve.

13. $\frac{1}{x^2-16} = \frac{1}{x-4}$ **14.** $\frac{2a}{a-4} + \frac{2}{a} = 1$

15. $\frac{-4}{x-3} = x + 2$ **16.** $\frac{6}{a^2-1} = \frac{3}{a-1} - \frac{3}{a+1}$

For Questions 17–20, list the zeros of each cubic function. Tell which, if any, are double or triple zeros.

17. $y = (x-2)^2(x+2)$ **18.** $y = (x+7)^3$

19. $y = x(x+4)(x-3)$ **20.** $y = 4x(x-1)^2$

21. Open-ended Write a cubic function which has a graph that intersects the *x*-axis in exactly two points.
    Sample answer: $y = (x-3)^2(x+5)$

Answers
1. No
2. No
3. Yes
4. No
5. $\frac{t^6}{x^8}$
6. a^3h^2
7. $\frac{4x^3}{7c^4}$
8. w^4z^{12}
9. $13a^2b^3(5ab + 3)$
10. $4v^3(3v^2 - 5v + 4)$
11. $9k^3n^2(9k^2 + 5n^2)$
12. $6r^2(2r + 5)(r - 3)$
13. -3
14. $-3 \pm \sqrt{17}$
15. $-1, 2$
16. 3
17. $-2, 2$ (double)
18. -7 (triple)
19. $-4, 0, 3$
20. 0, 1 (double)
21. *See question.*

Name _____ Date _____ Score _____

Test 40 *(continued)*

Directions: Write the answers in the spaces provided.

Match each function with its graph.

22. $y = (x-3)^3$ **23.** $y = x^3 + 4x^2 + 4x$

24. $y = (x+1)(x-4)(x+2)$ **25.** $y = (x-3)(x+4)^2$

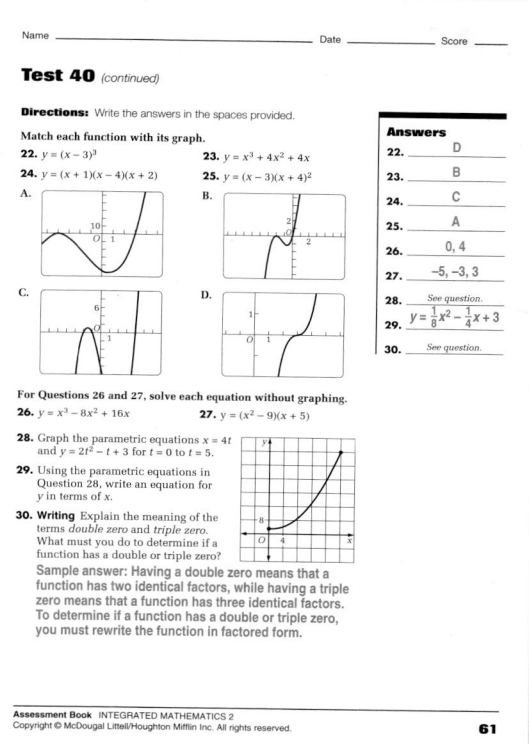

For Questions 26 and 27, solve each equation without graphing.

26. $y = x^3 - 8x^2 + 16x$ **27.** $y = (x^2 - 9)(x + 5)$

28. Graph the parametric equations $x = 4t$ and $y = 2t^2 - t + 3$ for $t = 0$ to $t = 5$.

29. Using the parametric equations in Question 28, write an equation for *y* in terms of *x*.

30. Writing Explain the meaning of the terms *double zero* and *triple zero*. What must you do to determine if a function has a double or triple zero?
Sample answer: Having a double zero means that a function has two identical factors, while having a triple zero means that a function has three identical factors. To determine if a function has a double or triple zero, you must rewrite the function in factored form.

Answers
22. D
23. B
24. C
25. A
26. 0, 4
27. $-5, -3, 3$
28. *See question.*
29. $y = \frac{1}{8}x^2 - \frac{1}{4}x + 3$
30. *See question.*

Software Support

McDougal Littell Mathpack
Function Investigator

Plotter Plus
Macintosh and MS-DOS
(worksheets included)

Outside Resources

Books/Periodicals

Fishman, Joseph. "Analyzing Energy and Resource Problems: An Interdisciplinary Approach with Mathematical Modeling." *Mathematics Teacher* (November 1993): pp. 628–633.

Activities/Manipulatives

Carlson, Ronald J. and Mary Jean Winter. *Algebra Experiment II.* Addison Wesley, 1993.

Software

Dugdale, Sharon and David Kibbey. Teacher's Guide: Edwards, Lois and Lisa Paul. *Graphing Equations and Green Globs.* Pleasantville, NY: Sunburst, 1985. Apple and IBM.

Videos

Project Mathematics. Program No. 4: Polynomials. California Institute of Technology, 1993.

Video for Unit Project: *Futures with Jaime Escalante.* Program No. 3: Advanced Energy. PBS, 1990.

Organizations

U.S. Dept. of Energy, Office of Science, Education, & Technology. Washington, DC 20585 Phone: (202) 586-8675

Polynomial and Rational Functions

ENERgy

PROJECT GOALS

➤ Students debate the pros and cons of using wind power to generate electricity.

➤ Students compile a list of advantages and disadvantages of converting to wind power.

➤ Students learn about the conditions that influence the amount of power produced by a wind machine and how to determine the power needs for a typical household.

PROJECT PLANNING

Project Teams

This project requires students to air their opinions by conducting a debate of the pros and cons of using wind power to generate electricity in your area.

Have students work on the project in groups of four. One way for the individuals in the group to distribute the work is as follows:

1. **Wind Power Researcher:** collects information about instruments used to measure the wind, the accuracy of measurements needed, a possible location for a wind turbine in your area, the effects on the environment, and the cost of installing a wind turbine.

2. **Electricity Researcher:** compiles a list of electrical appliances used each day by a typical household in your area, the amount of electricity used, and the approximate cost of purchasing it.

3. **Debater-Pro:** writes and presents the advantages of using wind power to generate electricity.

4. **Debater-Con:** writes and presents the disadvantages of using wind power to generate electricity.

Have you ever played hockey inside a mountain? At the 1994 Winter Olympics in Norway, hockey players went underground to take advantage of the insulating properties of a blanket of earth. An Olympic hockey stadium built deep inside a mountain uses 40% less energy than similar above-ground rinks.

underground

solar power

A thousand years ago, the Anasazi people of the American southwest built their houses out of **heat-absorbing stones**. These stones captured the warmth of the sun during the day and released it into their houses at night.

This kind of passive solar heating is still used today. An inside wall made of heat-absorbing material soaks up the sun's rays that stream in through large glass windows.

502

Suggested Rubric for Unit Project

4 Students have collected all the data they need to compile a list of the advantages and disadvantages of converting to wind power. They know how to determine the power needs of a typical household in your area and the conditions influencing the amount of power that can be produced by a wind machine. Their debate includes all five points listed on page 549 (Completing the Unit Project) and is very persuasive.

3 Students can debate the pros and cons of using wind power to generate electricity in your area. They most often can support the points they are trying to make in the debate with facts, but not always. Their point of view about wind power is persuasive.

2 Students have some difficulty supporting the points they are trying to make. Significant facts are lacking. They are not sure of how to determine the power needs of a typical household in your area. Their point of view is not persuasive.

Air Your Opinion

Your project is to debate the pros and cons of using wind power to generate electricity. As you complete the "Working on the Unit Project" exercises, you will learn how to determine the power needs of a typical household in your area

and what conditions influence the amount of power that can be produced by a wind machine in your area. You can use your findings to compile a list of the advantages and disadvantages of converting to wind power.

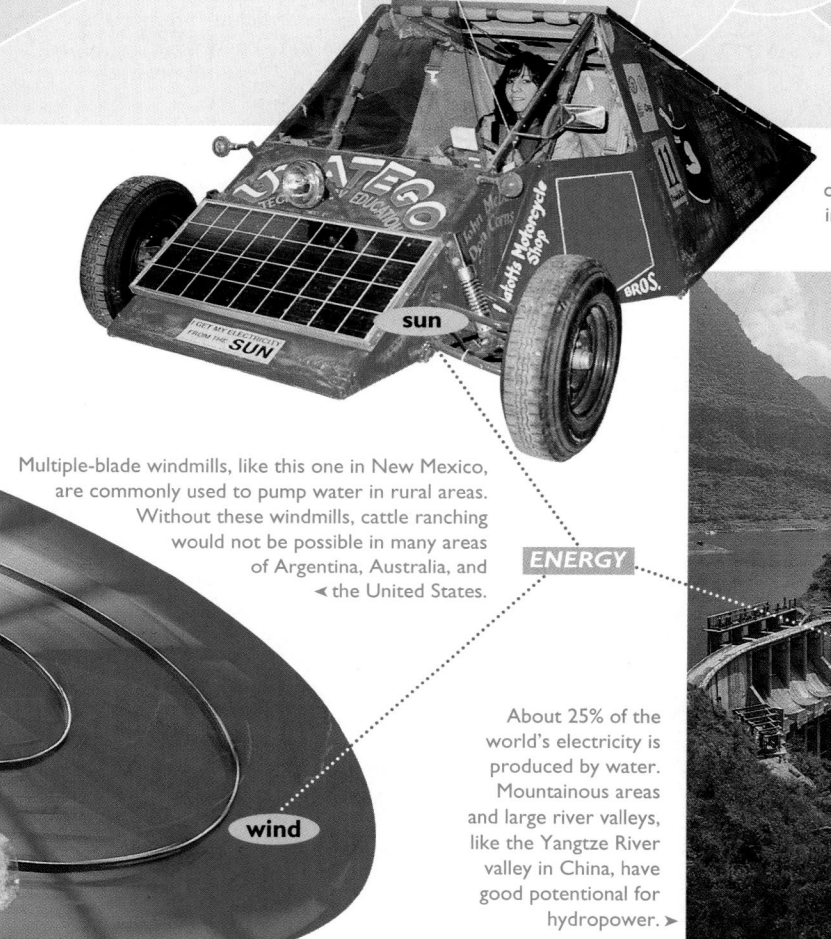

◄ Electric cars get their power from batteries and solar panels instead of gasoline. Many major car companies are developing electric cars in an effort to lower pollution.

sun

Multiple-blade windmills, like this one in New Mexico, are commonly used to pump water in rural areas. Without these windmills, cattle ranching would not be possible in many areas of Argentina, Australia, and ◄ the United States.

ENERGY

wind

About 25% of the world's electricity is produced by water. Mountainous areas and large river valleys, like the Yangtze River valley in China, have good potentional for hydropower. ►

water

503

Support Materials

The *Project Book* contains information about the following topics for use with this Unit Project.

➤ Project Description
➤ Teaching Commentary
➤ Working on the Unit Project Exercises
➤ Completing the Unit Project
➤ Assessing the Unit Project
➤ Alternative Projects
➤ Outside Resources

Students Acquiring English

This project gives students acquiring English practice in analyzing real-world data. You may wish to pair students with English proficient partners. Draw upon first-hand knowledge of those students whose native countries utilize wind power. Encourage them to explain orally or with a sketch how wind power works.

ADDITIONAL BACKGROUND

Multicultural Note

In ancient times, the Anasazi lived in the high desert where the states of Utah, New Mexico, Arizona, and Colorado now converge. Anasazi culture reached its height between A.D. 1050 and 1300. During that time, the Anasazi people built multistoried adobe structures, some of which were cut into rock walls of steep canyons. By the time Spanish *conquistadors* arrived in the Southwest, the cliff dwellings had been unoccupied for perhaps 200 years. Researchers still are not certain why the Anasazi abandoned these settlements and moved to other locations in the region. Today, visitors can view the remains of Anasazi cliff dwellings in Colorado's Mesa Verde National Park. The largest dwelling in Mesa Verde, the Cliff Palace, contains more than 200 rooms.

Suggested Rubric for Unit Project

1 Students are not prepared to give their opinion. They have not collected the information needed to make a list of the pros and cons of using wind power. They have not developed a point of view that

can be supported with facts. The group should be encouraged to speak with the teacher as soon as possible to review their work and to make a new start on the project.

World Wind Patterns

World wind patterns are known as doldrums, trade winds, westerlies, monsoons, roaring forties, and horse latitudes. The doldrums flow north and south away from the equator. Trade winds flow toward the equator. Westerlies flow toward mid-latitudes. Monsoons are seasonal reversals of wind direction. Wind patterns are displaced northward and southward on a seasonal basis and are affected by the rotation of Earth.

ALTERNATIVE PROJECTS

Project 1, page 549

Other Alternative Energy Sources

Write a research report about hydropower, solar power, geothermal power, and other alternative sources of energy. Include how and where they are used in other parts of the world.

Project 2, page 549

Using Parametric Equations

Students try the experiment in "Working on the Unit Project," which is Ex. 27 in Section 9-6. They use facial tissue in place of a feather and write parametric equations for this altered experiment. These equations are compared to those of Ex. 27.

Getting Started

For this project you should work in a group of four students. Here are some ideas to help you get started.

☞ In your group, make a list of the electrical appliances used each day by a typical household in your area.

☞ Discuss ways to estimate the amount of wind available at a possible location for a wind turbine.

☞ Discuss whether you think wind speed measurements made at the nearest airport give an accurate picture of the wind at your location.

☞ Suppose you had an instrument to measure wind speed directly. Consider how many measurements you would need to compile an accurate wind profile at a location.

List of appliances used each day:
lights
TV   stereo
VCR   hair dryer
heat   oven
        air conditioning

Working on the Unit Project

Your work in Unit 9 will help you prepare for the debate.

Related Exercises:

Section 9-1, Exercises 37, 38
Section 9-2, Exercise 55
Section 9-3, Exercises 35–38
Section 9-4, Exercises 43, 44
Section 9-5, Exercise 28
Section 9-6, Exercise 27

Alternative Projects p. 549

Can We Talk ENERGY

Wind, sun, and water are sometimes called "alternative" energy sources. Today, most of the energy produced in the United States comes from the burning of fuels like oil, coal, and natural gas.

➤ Can you think of some important ways in which alternative energy sources are different from such fuels? What are some advantages and disadvantages of both types of energy sources?

➤ What do you think are the advantages of an electric car over a gasoline-powered car? What are some possible disadvantages?

➤ How do you think climate and geography influence the ability to use alternative sources of energy?

➤ Do you think your town or city would be a good location for a wind turbine? a dam? a solar house? Why or why not?

➤ Do you know of any place in your area that uses wind, sun, or water to generate power? If so, what is the power used for?

Unit 9 Polynomial and Rational Functions

➤ Answers may vary. An example is given. When you use alternative energy sources, you are not burning them or depleting them. There is an unlimited supply of alternative energy sources, while the fuel supply is limited. Fuels can be used when needed while alternative energy sources may not be able to offer the energy when you need it (it may not be a windy or sunny day, or there may be a drought).

➤ Answers may vary. An example is given. An electric car does not emit any fumes or pollutants. An electric car does not go as far between recharges as a gasoline-powered car goes on a tank of gas, and it takes longer to recharge an electric car than it does to refill a tank with gasoline.

➤ Answers may vary. An example is given. If you live in a

cold climate, like Alaska, where the sun will not shine for part of the year, you would not be able to use solar power for energy. If you live in an area where the wind does not blow often, you would not be able to use the wind for energy.

➤ Answers may vary. An example is given. I think our town would be a good location for a solar house because the

sun shines almost every day, and we could use that energy for heat. I do not think our town would be a good location for a wind turbine or a dam because the wind is not very strong and the water does not flow quickly.

➤ Answers may vary. An example is given. A building downtown uses solar panels to trap energy from the sun for heating and cooling.

Focus
Model real-world situations with equations. Classify expressions.

Polynomial and Rational Models

On the Right Track

Heat makes metal expand. On hot days the rails of a railroad track get longer. If the ends of the rail cannot move, the middle of the rail may be pushed out of line. Some railroads have *expansion breaks* between sections of rail. On hot days the rails can expand into the breaks.

Sample 1

Suppose on a hot day, a 78 ft section of rail expands $\frac{1}{4}$ in. The middle of the rail curves out d inches. Write an equation to model the situation.

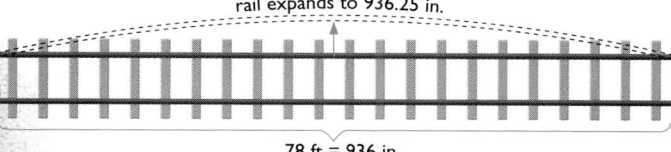

rail expands to 936.25 in.

78 ft = 936 in.

Sample Response

Let d = the distance (inches) that the middle of the rail curves out. Approximate the curve with two equal segments and form a right triangle. Use the Pythagorean theorem: $468^2 + d^2 = 468.125^2$

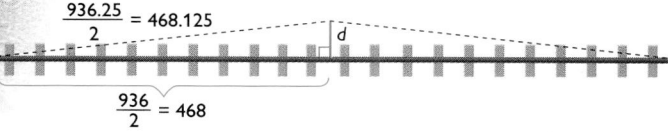

$\frac{936.25}{2} = 468.125$

d

$\frac{936}{2} = 468$

Talk it Over

1. Explain how to solve the equation $468^2 + d^2 = 468.125^2$.

2. Is it useful to use two line segments to model the expanded rail? Why or why not?

9-1 Polynomial and Rational Models

505

Answers to Talk it Over

1. First simplify 468^2 and 468.125^2, then subtract 468^2 from both sides of the equation. Undo the squaring on each side to find the positive square root.

2. It is useful because it simplifies the situation so that it can be easily modeled by using the Pythagorean theorem. The answer will only be an approximation, however, because a buckled railroad track is actually curved.

PLANNING

Objectives and Strands
See pages 502A and 502B.

Spiral Learning
See page 502B.

Materials List
➤ $5\frac{1}{2}$ in. × 11 in. paper
➤ Scissors
➤ Tape
➤ Ruler

Recommended Pacing
Section 9-1 is a two-day lesson.
Day 1
Pages 505–507: Opening paragraph through Talk it Over 5, *Exercises 1–16*
Day 2
Page 508: Rational Equations through Look Back, *Exercises 17–38*

Extra Practice
See pages 628–629.

Warm-Up Exercises
Warm-Up Transparency 9-1

Support Materials
➤ Practice 69
➤ Enrichment 61 in the Activity Bank
➤ Study Guide 9-1
➤ Problem Set 20
➤ Quiz 9-1
➤ Alternative Assessment 1

TEACHING

Additional Sample

S1 A 50 ft steam pipe that is held fast at either end expands when steam is passed through it. Suppose the pipe expands $\frac{1}{2}$ inch and its middle curves out d inches. Write an equation to model the situation.

Let d = the distance in inches that the middle of the steam pipe curves out. Approximate the curve with two equal segments and form a right triangle.

50 ft = 600 in.

The pipe expands to 600.5 in.;

600.5 ÷ 2 = 300.25.

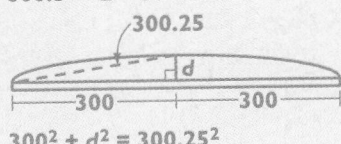

$300^2 + d^2 = 300.25^2$

Kia wants to save $3500 for a trip to Africa after graduation. At the beginning of tenth grade, she puts $1000 into a savings account. She plans to save $1000 every year until she graduates. She wonders what yearly interest rate she must get to reach her goal. Model the situation with an equation.

Sample Response

Think about what happens to a deposit of $1000 in one year.

    deposit + interest
        $1000 + 1000r$ ◀—— Let r = yearly interest rate.
        $1000(1 + r)$ ◀—— Use the distributive property.
        $1000g$ ◀—— Let $g = 1 + r$. The variable g is a *growth factor*.

Use the growth factor g to find Kia's balance after graduation.

Kia starts tenth grade and deposits $1000.

$1000

Kia ends tenth grade and deposits another $1000.

$1000g$ + $1000 ◀—— This is her balance as she starts eleventh grade.

Kia ends eleventh grade and deposits another $1000.

$1000g \cdot g$ + $1000g$ + $1000 ◀—— This is her balance as she starts twelfth grade.

Kia ends twelfth grade and graduates.

$1000g \cdot g \cdot g$ + $1000g \cdot g$ + $1000g$

$1000g^3$ + $1000g^2$ + $1000g$ ◀—— This is how much she has in her account for her trip.

The interest rate must be large enough so that Kia's balance is $3500.

$1000g^3 + 1000g^2 + 1000g = 3500$ ◀—— This equation models the situation.

BY THE WAY...

Africa has the world's longest river, the Nile (4145 mi), the world's largest desert, the Sahara (3.5 million mi²), and the world's longest freshwater lake, Tanganyika (420 mi). The climate varies widely. Within miles of each other there are ski slopes and deserts.

Talk it Over

Question 2 brings out the important idea that the Pythagorean theorem provides a useful approximation to the solution of the problem in Sample 1. The straight line segments approximate the actual curvature of the expanded rail, and because the expansion is rather small ($\frac{1}{4}$ in.), the approximation provides a useful solution.

Additional Sample

S2 Suppose in Sample 2 that Kia wants to save $4000 for her trip to Africa and instead of $1000, she saves $1200 every year until she graduates. Model the situation with an equation, using the variable g as a growth factor.

$1200g^3 + 1200g^2 + 1200g = 4000$

506   **Unit 9** Polynomial and Rational Functions

Polynomial Equations

The expression $1000g^3 + 1000g^2 + 1000g$ is an example of a *polynomial*. A **polynomial** is an expression that can be written as a monomial or sum of monomials with whole number exponents.

Each term is the product of a coefficient and a variable with a whole number exponent.

$$\overbrace{575x^3} - 12x^2 + 10x + 3$$

3 is the same as $3x^0$, since $x^0 = 1$.

The **degree** of a polynomial is the largest exponent. This polynomial has degree 3.

The exponent of this variable is 1, because $x^1 = x$.

Polynomials	Not polynomials
$1000g^3 + 1000g^2 + 1000g$	$1000g^{-3} + 1000g^{-2} + 1000g^{-1}$
πr^2	$\pi r^{1/2}$
$\frac{1}{3}b - b^2 + b^3$	$3\left(\frac{1}{b}\right) - b^2 + b^3$
$y + 1$	$\frac{y}{y+1}$
$4x^2 + 3xy$	$\frac{4x^2}{y} + \frac{3x}{y}$

A **polynomial equation** is an equation that can be written with a polynomial as one side and 0 as the other side.

Polynomials are usually written in **standard form.** Reading from left to right, the exponents go from largest to smallest.

$$\underset{4 \qquad 2 \qquad 1 \qquad 0}{2x^4 - 15x^2 + 4x + 50}$$

This polynomial is written in standard form.

➤ Now you are ready for:
Exs. 1–16 on pp. 509–510

Talk it Over

3. Explain why each expression in the second column of the table is not a polynomial.

4. Is $2(x + 3)$ a polynomial? Explain why or why not.

5. The expression $\sqrt{2}x^3 - \pi x^4 + 30$ is a polynomial.

   a. What is the degree of the polynomial?

   b. How would the polynomial be written in standard form?

   c. What is the exponent of x for the last term? ($30x^? = 30$)

Reasoning

A polynomial is defined as an expression that can be written as a monomial or *sum* of monomials with whole number exponents. Students should be able to explain why the polynomial $2x^4 - 15x^2 + 4x + 50$, used to demonstrate standard form, has a subtraction sign in it. (because $-15x^2$ can be rewritten as $+(-15x^2)$)

Talk it Over

Questions 3–5 provide opportunities for students to check their understanding of polynomials and the concepts associated with them.

Answers to Talk it Over

3. None of the five expressions is a polynomial because each contains a term that is not a monomial. None of the following can be written with a whole-number exponent: $1000g^{-3}$, $1000g^{-2}$, $1000g^{-1}$, $\pi r^{1/2}$, $3\left(\frac{1}{b}\right)$, $\frac{y}{y+1}$, $\frac{4x^2}{y}$, $\frac{3x}{y}$.

4. Yes; $2(x + 3)$ is a polynomial because it can be written as a monomial or a sum of monomials with exponents that are whole numbers: $2(x + 3) = 2x + 6$.

5. a. 4

   b. $-\pi x^4 + \sqrt{2}x^3 + 30$

   c. zero

507

508

When writing rational expressions or rational equations, it is sometimes stated, but always understood, that the domain for the variable excludes those values that make the denominator equal to zero.

Additional Sample

S3 Lucy is mixing a salad dressing for a large social function. It is suppose to be 50% salad oil. So far she has mixed 2.5 cups of vinegar, 0.5 cup of water, and 2.5 cups of salad oil. Lucy wonders how much more salad oil to add. Write an equation to model the situation.

Step 1. **Find out the percentage of salad oil that is already in the dressing.**

$$\frac{\text{cups of salad oil}}{\text{cups of salad dressing}} = \frac{2.5}{5.5} = 0.45$$

Step 2. **Find out how much salad oil Lucy needs to add to increase the percentage to 50%.**

Let x = **number of cups of salad oil Lucy adds.**

Then $2.5 + x$ = **the number of cups of salad oil in the dressing and** $5.5 + x$ = **the cups of dressing.**

Step 3. **Write an equation to model the situation.**

$$\frac{2.5 + x}{5.5 + x} = 0.50$$

Look Back

The Look Back questions raise the issue of whether polynomial equations are rational equations. Students should explain their reasoning by considering the relationship between integers and rational numbers.

Rational Equations

A rational number can be written as the quotient of two integers. 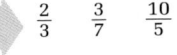 $\dfrac{2}{3}$ $\dfrac{3}{7}$ $\dfrac{10}{5}$

A **rational expression** is an expression that can be written as the quotient of two polynomials. 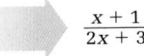 $\dfrac{x+1}{2x+3}$

A **rational equation** is an equation with only rational expressions on both sides. 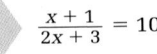 $\dfrac{x+1}{2x+3} = 10$

Sample 3

Ken is mixing fruit punch. It is supposed to be 30% orange juice. So far Ken has mixed two pints of cranberry juice, one pint of orange juice, and one pint of ginger ale. Ken wonders how much orange juice to add. Write an equation to model the situation.

Sample Response

Step 1 Find out the percent of orange juice that is already in the punch.

$$\frac{\text{pints of orange juice}}{\text{pints of fruit punch}} = \frac{1}{4} = 0.25 \longleftarrow \begin{array}{l}\text{Ken has 4 pt of punch.}\\ \text{The punch is 25\% orange juice.}\end{array}$$

Step 2 Choose a variable to represent the amount of orange juice Ken adds.

Let x = the number of pints of orange juice Ken adds.

Then $1 + x$ = the number of pints of orange juice in the punch and $4 + x$ = the number of pints of punch.

Step 3 Write an equation to model the situation.

The punch will be 30% orange juice when $\dfrac{\text{pints of orange juice}}{\text{pints of fruit punch}} = 0.30$.

$$\frac{1 + x}{4 + x} = 0.30 \longleftarrow \begin{array}{l}\text{This equation models}\\ \text{the situation.}\end{array}$$

⸺► **Now you are ready for:**
Exs. 17–38 on pp. 511–512

Look Back ◄

In Sample 2, Kia's savings were modeled by the polynomial equation $1000g^3 + 1000g^2 + 1000g = 3500$. Is this also a rational equation?

Answers to Look Back

Yes.

9-1 Exercises and Problems

1. **Reading** In Sample 2, what expression models Kia's savings account balance as she starts twelfth grade?

Write an equation to model the relationship among the measures in each figure.

2.

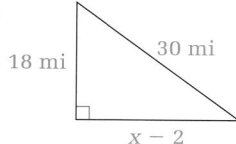

18 mi · 30 mi · $x - 2$

3.

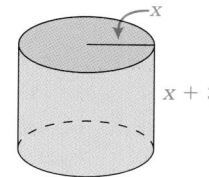

x · $x + 3$

Volume = 200π cm^3

4.

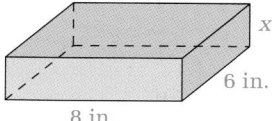

x · 6 in. · 8 in.

Surface Area = 152 in.^{2}

5.

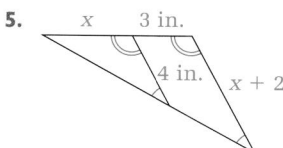

x · 3 in. · 4 in. · $x + 2$

6. Can all of your equations from Exercises 2–5 be written as polynomial equations? Explain.

7. Suppose there are no expansion breaks in a 500 m long straight railroad track. On a hot day, the rails expand 15 cm. The middle of one rail curves out d centimeters. Draw a sketch and write an equation to model the situation.

8. Maria is in tenth grade and wants to buy a $3000 used car after graduation. She plans to put $900 into a savings account every summer. She wonders what yearly interest rate she must get to have $3000 at the end of the summer after graduation. Model the situation with an equation.

9. The front of this Indonesian chest has dimensions in the golden ratio. The length of the chest is about 1.6 times the height. The width of the chest is equal to the height.

   a. An artist wants to create a replica of the chest with a volume of about 4500 in^3. The artist wonders what the height should be. Write an equation to model the situation. Let x = the height of the replica.

   b. Is your equation from part (a) a polynomial equation? Explain why or why not.

x · x · 1.6x

9-1 Polynomial and Rational Models · **509**

APPLYING

Suggested Assignment

Day 1

Standard 2–8, 12–15

Extended 1–10, 12–15

Day 2

Standard 17–27, 29–38

Extended 17–38

Integrating the Strands

Number Exs. 26, 37, 38

Algebra Exs. 1–29, 31–37

Measurement Exs. 2–5, 9, 16, 26, 30

Geometry Exs. 2–5, 9, 16, 27, 30

Trigonometry Ex. 30

Logic and Language Exs. 1, 29

Communication: Reading

In Ex. 1, students use critical thinking skills as they read and identify an appropriate expression to model a situation.

Application

Polynomials are used extensively in the solution of real-world problems. The three Sample problems in this section illustrate the use of polynomials in their solutions. Exs. 7–11, 16, and 26 are additional real-world situations that can be modeled using polynomial equations.

Answers to Exercises and Problems

1. $1000g^2 + 1000g + 1000$

2. $(x - 2)^2 + 18^2 = 30^2$

3. $\pi x^2(x + 3) = 200\pi$ or $x^2(x + 3) = 200$

4. $12x + 16x + 96 = 152$ or $28x + 96 = 152$

5. $\dfrac{x}{x + 3} = \dfrac{4}{x + 2}$

6. Yes. You can rewrite the equation in Ex.5 as a polynomial equation by using cross products.

7. $\dfrac{50,015}{2} = 25,007.5$

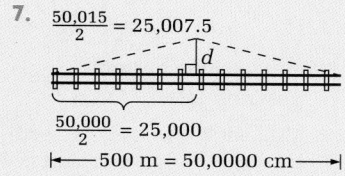

d

$\dfrac{50,000}{2} = 25,000$

500 m = 50,0000 cm

$25,000^2 + d^2 = 25,007.5^2$

8. $900g^2 + 900g + 900 = 3000$

9. a. $(x)(x)(1.6x) = 4500$

   b. Yes; $(x)(x)(1.6x) = 1.6x^3$, which is a polynomial.

Employment For Exercises 10 and 11, assume that employees earn time and a half for any time worked over 40 hours in one week. *Time and a half* means that a worker earns 1.5 times his or her regular hourly wage.

10. Linda Bowen worked 50 hours in one week. Her income before deductions was $325 for that week. Write an equation to model the situation. Let $p =$ her regular hourly wage.

11. a. **Research** Find out what the federal minimum wage is in the United States.

    b. Find the hourly wage of an employee who works 50 hours in one week and earns $300 before deductions.

    c. Suppose someone earning minimum wage wants to earn $300 a week before deductions. Write an equation to model the situation. Let $h =$ the number of hours of overtime worked.

For Exercises 12–15, use the polynomial $6x^9 + x^5 - 5x^2 + 2x - 15$.

12. What is the degree of the polynomial?

13. What is the coefficient of the third term from the left?

14. What is the exponent of the fourth term from the left?

15. Is the polynomial written in standard form? If not, rewrite it in standard form.

16. **Using Manipulatives** Use a $5\frac{1}{2}$ in. by 11 in. piece of paper, scissors, tape, and a ruler. Follow steps (a)–(c) to make a miniature pizza box.

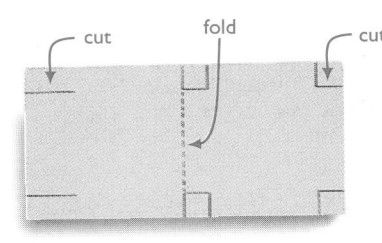

a. Fold the paper in half. Cut four identical squares out of the corners of one of the halves as shown.

b. Make two cuts on the uncut side as shown. Each cut should be twice as long as the squares from step (a).

c. Fold along the dotted lines as shown.

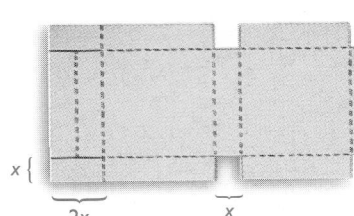  

d. Measure the dimensions of your box. Find its volume.

e. The employees at the Pizza Shop make their boxes out of 20 in. by 40 in. pieces of cardboard. Write an equation to model the volume of a Pizza Shop box. Let $x =$ the length of the sides of the square cutouts and let $V =$ the volume of the box.

510   **Unit 9** Polynomial and Rational Functions

Answers to Exercises and Problems

10. $40p + 10(1.5p) = 325$

11. a. $5.15 per hour

    b. $5.45

    c. $40(5.15) + 1.5(5.15)(h) = 300$

12. 9

13. −5

14. 1

15. Yes.

16. a–c. Check students' work.

    d. Answers may vary. The volume is given by the formula $(5.5 - 2x)^2(x)$.

    e. $(20 - 2x)^2(x) = V$

17. Yes; each term can be written with exponents that are whole numbers.

18. No; $\frac{3}{x}$ and $\frac{4}{x-2}$ are rational expressions but not polynomials.

19. Yes; each term can be written with exponents that are whole numbers.

20. Yes; each term can be written with exponents that are whole numbers.

21. No; $3x^{1/2}$ cannot be written as a polynomial.

22. No; x^{-2} and $-10x^{-1}$ can be written as the rational expressions $\frac{1}{x^2}$ and $\frac{-10}{x}$, but they are not polynomials.

Tell whether each expression is a polynomial. Write *Yes* or *No*.
Give a reason for your answer.

17. $3x^2 - 4x - 31$

18. $\frac{3}{x} + \frac{4}{x-2}$

19. $4x - 1$

20. $\frac{5}{3}r^3 - 3r - 2r^2 - 1$

21. $3x^{1/2} + 4x^3 + x^5$

22. $x^{-2} - 10x^{-1} + 2$

23. a. Is the equation $4x - 1 = 16$ linear?

   b. Are all linear equations also polynomial equations? Explain.

24. a. Is the equation $3x^2 - 4x - 31 = 0$ quadratic?

   b. Are all quadratic equations also polynomial equations? Explain.

25. Use cross products to solve the equation $\frac{1+x}{4+x} = 0.30$ from Sample 3.

26. Chemistry Laura Nyquist is a chemistry student. She mixes 5 mL acetic acid with 120 mL water to make a solution that should be 5% acid. Then she realizes she needs to add more acetic acid.

   a. Explain how Laura knows she needs to add more acetic acid.

   b. Laura wonders how much more acetic acid to add. Write an equation to model the situation.

   c. Is your equation in part (b) a rational equation?

27. Write an equation to model the relationship between the measures in the diagram.

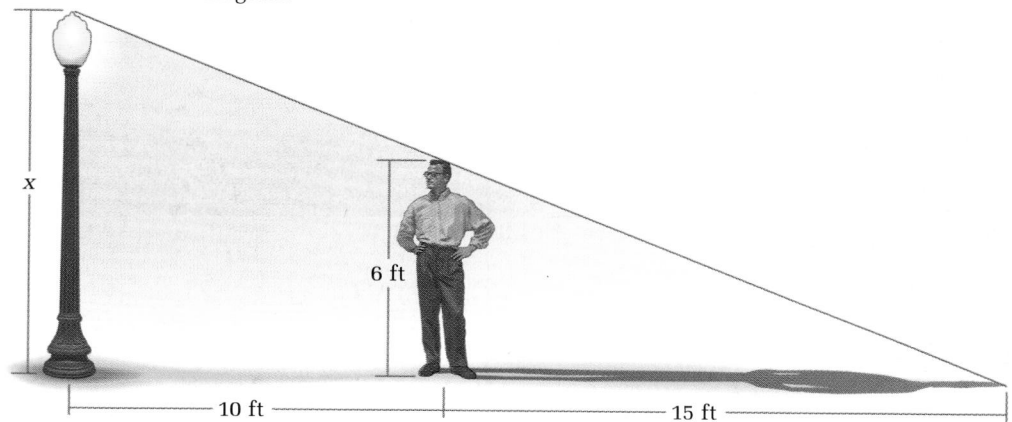

28. Open-ended Write two rational equations.

29. a. Writing Tell what you think the graph at the right means.

   b. Let n represent the number of oranges available. Let p represent the price of an orange. Can this situation be modeled with a polynomial equation? Explain.

Price and Supply

9-1 Polynomial and Rational Models

511

Answers to Exercises and Problems

23. a. Yes.

   b. Yes; all linear equations can be written in the form $ax + by + c = 0$, which is a polynomial equation for all values of a, b, and c.

24. a. Yes.

   b. Yes; all quadratic equations can be written in the form $ax^2 + bx + c = 0$, which is a polynomial equation for all values of a, b, and c.

25. $\frac{2}{7}$ or about 0.29

26. a. Since $\frac{\text{mL acetic acid}}{\text{mL solution}} = \frac{5}{125} = 0.04$, Laura knows

that her solution is only 4% acid.

   b. $\frac{5+x}{125+x} = 0.05$

   c. Yes.

27. Equations may vary. Example: $\frac{x}{6} = \frac{10+15}{15}$

28. Answers may vary. Examples: $2x^2 = 32$; $\frac{8x}{x+2} = 4$

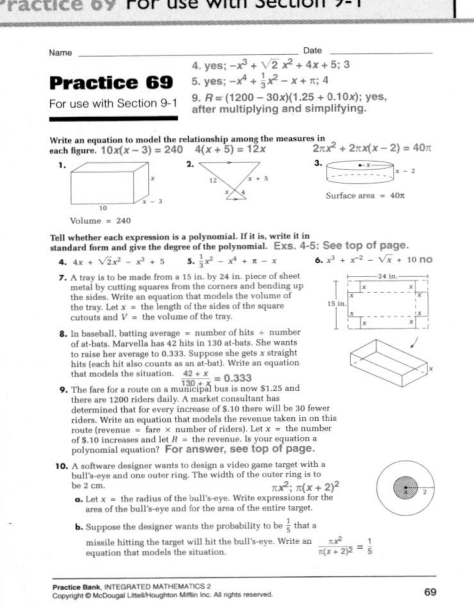

Review PREVIEW

30. **a.** Find the measures of as many segments as possible in $\triangle MNO$. *(Section 8-8)*

   b. Find the sine, cosine, and tangent of $\angle PNO$.

Simplify. *(Section 4-6)*

31. $3i - 6 - i^2 - 7i + 4$ **32.** $(2i)(5i)$ **33.** $(2 - i)(2 + i)$

34. Rewrite n^{-4} with a positive exponent. *(Section 2-6)*

35. Rewrite $\sqrt{x}$ with a fractional exponent. *(Section 2-6)*

36. What is the value of 2^0? of 99^0? of a^0? *(Section 2-6)*

Working on the Unit Project

The table shows the rate of electricity use for some common electrical appliances. It also shows the number of hours each appliance is typically used in one day. To find the amount of electricity used by each appliance in one day, you multiply the rate by the time.

rate of electricity use × average time of daily use = amount of electricity used in a day

   kilowatts (kW)   ×   hours (h)   =   kilowatt-hours (kW × h)

37. Use the table to estimate the total amount of electricity used in one day by a typical household in your area.

For appliances not in the table, read the power rating, in watts, on the appliance. Convert the rate to kilowatts by dividing by 1000. Then multiply by the estimated number of hours of daily use.

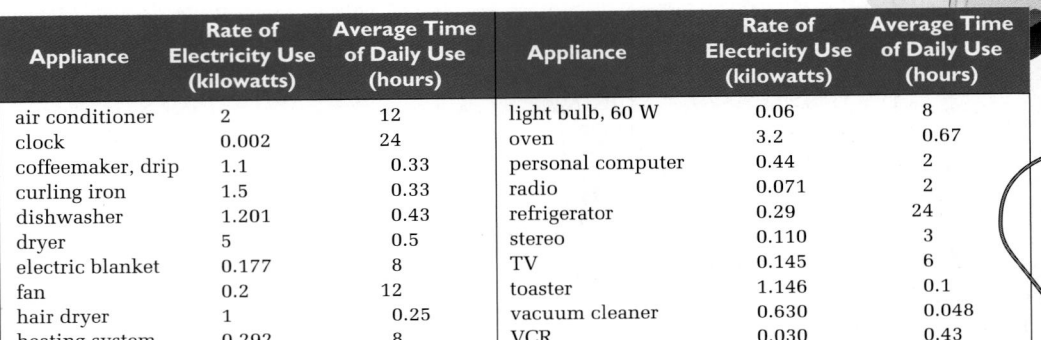

Appliance	Rate of Electricity Use (kilowatts)	Average Time of Daily Use (hours)	Appliance	Rate of Electricity Use (kilowatts)	Average Time of Daily Use (hours)
air conditioner	2	12	light bulb, 60 W	0.06	8
clock	0.002	24	oven	3.2	0.67
coffeemaker, drip	1.1	0.33	personal computer	0.44	2
curling iron	1.5	0.33	radio	0.071	2
dishwasher	1.201	0.43	refrigerator	0.29	24
dryer	5	0.5	stereo	0.110	3
electric blanket	0.177	8	TV	0.145	6
fan	0.2	12	toaster	1.146	0.1
hair dryer	1	0.25	vacuum cleaner	0.630	0.048
heating system	0.292	8	VCR	0.030	0.43
iron	1.1	0.17	water heater	4.5	3

38. **Research** Contact the company that supplies electricity in your area.

   a. Find out how much an average household in your area pays for electricity each month. How much is this per day? (Use 30 days for a month.)

   b. Find out the company's rate structure. Use it to estimate the daily cost of electricity for your group's typical household.

512   **Unit 9** Polynomial and Rational Functions

Answers to Exercises and Problems

30. **a.** $MN = 2\sqrt{2}$; $NO = 4$;
      $MP = 2$; $PO = 2\sqrt{3}$;
      $MO = 2 + 2\sqrt{3}$

   b. $\sin PNO = \dfrac{\sqrt{3}}{2} \approx 0.8660$;
      $\cos PNO = 0.5$;
      $\tan PNO = \sqrt{3} \approx 1.732$

31. $-4i - 1$

32. -10

33. 5

34. $\dfrac{1}{n^4}$

35. $x^{1/2}$

36. 1; 1; 1

37. Answers may vary. Check students' work.

38. Answers may vary. Check students' work.

Section 9-2

Power and Quotient Rules

Focus
Use rules of exponents to simplify expressions

Earth   Mars

Talk it Over

1. Complete. Describe any patterns you see.

   a. $x^3 \cdot x^2 = (x \cdot x \cdot x)(x \cdot x) = x^?$

   b. $x^4 \cdot x^2 = (x \cdot x \cdot x \cdot x)(x \cdot x) = x^?$

2. Write the product $x^{12} \cdot x^6$ as a power of x.

3. Complete. Describe any patterns you see.

   a. $\dfrac{a^5}{a^3} = \dfrac{\not{a} \cdot \not{a} \cdot \not{a} \cdot a \cdot a}{\not{a} \cdot \not{a} \cdot \not{a}} = a^?$

   b. $\dfrac{a^3}{a^5} = \dfrac{\not{a} \cdot \not{a} \cdot \not{a}}{\not{a} \cdot \not{a} \cdot \not{a} \cdot a \cdot a} = \dfrac{1}{a^?} = a^?$

   c. $\dfrac{a^5}{a^5} = \dfrac{\not{a} \cdot \not{a} \cdot \not{a} \cdot \not{a} \cdot \not{a}}{\not{a} \cdot \not{a} \cdot \not{a} \cdot \not{a} \cdot \not{a}} = 1 = a^?$

4. Write the quotient $\dfrac{x^7}{x^3}$ as a power of x.

The product of powers and quotient of powers rules describe the patterns you saw in questions 1–4.

RULES OF EXPONENTS

For all positive, negative, zero, or fractional exponents: **Examples**

Product of Powers Rule $a^m \cdot a^n = a^{m+n}$ $a^8 \cdot a^2 = a^{8+2} = a^{10}$

Quotient of Powers Rule $\dfrac{a^m}{a^n} = a^{m-n}, a \neq 0$ $\dfrac{a^8}{a^2} = a^{8-2} = a^6$

Answers to Talk it Over

1. a. 5

   b. 6; The exponent of the product is the sum of the exponents of the factors.

2. x^{18}

3. a. 2

   b. 2; −2

   c. 0; The exponent of the quotient is the difference of the exponents of the numerator and denominator.

4. x^4

PLANNING

Objectives and Strands
See pages 502A and 502B.

Spiral Learning
See page 502B.

Recommended Pacing
Section 9-2 is a two-day lesson.
Day 1
Pages 513–515: Talk it Over 1 through Talk it Over 8, *Exercises 1–31*
Day 2
Pages 515–517: More Rules of Exponents through Look Back, *Exercises 32–55*

Extra Practice
See pages 628–629.

Warm-Up Exercises
Warm-Up Transparency 9-2

Support Materials
➤ Practice 70
➤ Enrichment 62 in the Activity Bank
➤ Study Guide 9-2
➤ Problem Set 20
➤ Quiz 9-2
➤ Alternative Assessment 2

Talk it Over

Questions 1–4 lead students to see the patterns that are expressed in general form by the product of powers and quotient of powers rules.

Teaching Tip

In the quotient rule, if $m > n$, the exponent $m - n$ is positive; if $m < n$, then the exponent is negative. An expression containing a negative exponent should be rewritten using a positive exponent.

Additional Sample

S1 Simplify. Write each answer without negative exponents.

a. $x^{-4} \cdot x^6$
$x^{-4} \cdot x^6 = x^{-4+6} = x^2$

b. $(3x^2)(-5x^{-2})$
$(3x^2)(-5x^{-2}) =$
$(3)(-5)x^{2+(-2)} = -15x^0 = -15$

c. $\dfrac{w^3 t^4}{t^7}$ $\dfrac{w^3 t^4}{t^7} = w^3 t^{-3} = \dfrac{w^3}{t^3}$

Mathematical Procedures

Students learned in Unit 4 that to factor an algebraic expression, it was first necessary to find the greatest common factor of all the terms. The GCFs in Unit 4 involved numbers only. The product of powers rule now extends the use of the GCF to include variables.

Simplify. Write each answer without negative exponents.

a. $h^2 \cdot h^{-3} \cdot h$ b. $(-2x^{-5})(4x^8)$ c. $\dfrac{m^2 n^6}{n^9}$

Sample Response

a. $h^2 \cdot h^{-3} \cdot h = h^2 \cdot h^{-3} \cdot h^1$ ⟵ Rewrite h as h^1.

   $= h^{2+(-3)+1}$ ⟵ Use the product of powers rule.

   $= h^0$

   $= 1$ ⟵ Use the zero exponent rule.

b. $(-2x^{-5})(4x^8) = (-2 \cdot 4)(x^{-5} \cdot x^8)$ ⟵ Group numbers and group powers with the same base.

   $= (-2 \cdot 4)x^{-5+8}$ ⟵ Use the product of powers rule.

   $= -8x^3$

c. $\dfrac{m^2 n^6}{n^9} = m^2 \cdot \dfrac{n^6}{n^9}$ ⟵ Think of each variable separately.

   $= m^2 \cdot n^{6-9}$ ⟵ Use the quotient of powers rule.

   $= m^2 \cdot n^{-3}$

   $= m^2 \cdot \dfrac{1}{n^3}$ ⟵ Rewrite using a positive exponent.

   $= \dfrac{m^2}{n^3}$

Watch Out!
The bases m and n are not the same, so $\dfrac{m^2}{n^3}$ cannot be simplified.

Factoring Polynomials

Drew hits a volleyball up from a point near the ground. The height h of the ball t seconds after being hit can be modeled by the polynomial equation $h = 32t - 16t^2$. You can write this equation in factored form:

$h = 32t - 16t^2$

$h = (2 \cdot 16)t - 16t^2$ ⟵ Notice that 16 is a common factor of 32 and 16.

$h = 16(2t - t^2)$ ⟵ Notice that t is a common factor of both terms in parentheses.

$h = 16t(2 - t)$ ⟵ The greatest common factor of $32t - 16t^2$ is $16t$.

To factor a polynomial completely, you first need to find the greatest common factor (GCF) of all the terms.

Factor $6x^5 - 8x^7 + 10x^2$ completely.

Sample Response

$6x^5 - 8x^7 + 10x^2 = 6(x^2 \cdot x^3) - 8(x^2 \cdot x^5) + 10x^2$ ← Use the product of powers rule to find the GCF of the variable parts.

$= 2x^2(3x^3) - 2x^2(4x^5) + 2x^2(5)$ ← The GCF of the coefficients is 2. The GCF of the variable parts is x^2.

$= 2x^2(3x^3 - 4x^5 + 5)$

Talk it Over

Complete.

5. $12x^5 = 4x^2 \cdot \underline{?}$ 6. $16x^3y^5 = 4x^2y^3 \cdot \underline{?}$ 7. $20x^2 = 4x^2 \cdot \underline{?}$

8. Brian tried to factor the polynomial $3x^4 - 6x^3 - 45x^2$. He wrote $3x^2(x^2 - 2x - 15)$ as an answer. Has he factored the polynomial completely? If not, what else should he do?

▶ Now you are ready for:
Exs. 1–31 on pp. 517–518

More Rules of Exponents

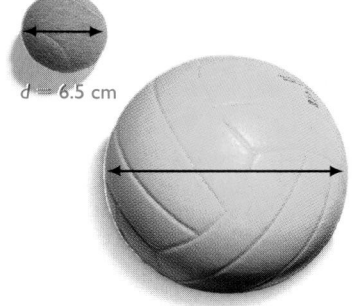

$d = 6.5$ cm

$d = 21$ cm

The ratio of the volumes of two spheres is equal to the ratio of the cubes of their diameters.

$$\frac{\text{volume of volleyball}}{\text{volume of tennis ball}} = \frac{(\text{diameter of volleyball})^3}{(\text{diameter of tennis ball})^3} = \frac{(21)^3}{(6.5)^3}$$

Talk it Over

9. Complete. Describe any patterns you see.

a. $\left(\dfrac{21}{6.5}\right)^3 = \left(\dfrac{21}{6.5}\right)\left(\dfrac{21}{6.5}\right)\left(\dfrac{21}{6.5}\right) = \dfrac{21^?}{6.5^?}$

b. $\left(\dfrac{2}{x}\right)^2 = \left(\dfrac{2}{x}\right) \cdot \left(\dfrac{2}{x}\right) = \dfrac{2^?}{x^?}$

10. Write $\left(\dfrac{a}{b}\right)^4$ as the quotient of a power of a and a power of b.

11. Complete. Describe any patterns you see.

a. $(3^2)^3 = 3^? \cdot 3^? \cdot 3^? = 3^?$ b. $(2^5)^2 = 2^? \cdot 2^? = 2^?$

12. Write $(a^2)^7$ as a power of a.

13. Complete. Describe any patterns you see.

a. $(3 \cdot 5)^2 = (3 \cdot 5)(3 \cdot 5) = (3 \cdot 3)(5 \cdot 5) = 3^? \cdot 5^?$

b. $(2x)^4 = (2x)(2x)(2x)(2x) = 2^? \cdot x^? = \underline{?}$

14. Write $(ab)^3$ as the product of a power of a and a power of b.

Watch Out!
$2x^4 = 2 \cdot x \cdot x \cdot x \cdot x$.
This is not the same as $(2x)^4$.

Answers to Talk it Over

5. $3x^3$

6. $4xy^2$

7. 5

8. No; he should factor $x^2 - 2x - 15$ as the product of two binomials, $x - 5$ and $x + 3$.

9. a. 3; 3

   b. 2; 2; The exponents of the numerator and denominator of the quotient on the right are both the same as the exponent of the quotient on the left.

10. $\dfrac{a^4}{b^4}$

11. a. 2; 2; 2; 6

   b. 5; 5; 10; The exponent on the right is the product of the exponents on the left.

12. a^{14}

13. a. 2; 2

   b. 4; 4; $16x^4$; The exponent of each factor on the right is the same as the exponent of the product on the left.

14. a^3b^3

Additional Sample

S2 Factor $9x^4 + 6x^3 + 3x^2$ completely.
$9x^4 + 6x^3 + 3x^2 =$
$3x^2(3x^2) + 3x^2(2x) + 3x^2(1) =$
$3x^2(3x^2 + 2x + 1)$

Talk it Over

Question 8 has students think about what it means to factor a polynomial completely. Students must also check to see whether the polynomial inside the parentheses can be factored. You can relate this question to the Sample 2 Response where the polynomial inside the parentheses cannot be factored further.

Questions 9–14 continue the use of patterns to provide a basis for establishing the three new rules of exponents given on page 516. These rules involve the *power* of a power, product, and quotient, respectively.

Visual Thinking

Ask students to create diagrams and mathematical models that demonstrate the ratios of the volume of spheres. Examples could include ping pong balls, tennis balls, different size marbles, or two planets. This activity involves the visual skills of *interpretation* and *self-expression*.

RULES OF EXPONENTS

For all positive, negative, zero, or fractional exponents:

Examples

Power of a Power Rule $\qquad (a^m)^n = a^{mn}$ $\qquad\qquad (a^2)^3 = a^{2 \cdot 3} = a^6$

Power of a Product Rule $\qquad (ab)^n = a^n b^n$ $\qquad\qquad (ab)^2 = a^2 \cdot b^2 = a^2 b^2$

Power of a Quotient Rule $\qquad \left(\dfrac{a}{b}\right)^n = \dfrac{a^n}{b^n},\ b \neq 0$ $\qquad \left(\dfrac{a}{b}\right)^3 = \dfrac{a^3}{b^3}$

Sample 3

Simplify. Write answers without negative exponents.

a. $(-2x^6)^4$ \qquad\qquad b. $(4b^{-5})^{-3}$ \qquad\qquad c. $\left(\dfrac{3y}{-2z}\right)^2$

Sample Response

a. $(-2x^6)^4 = (-2)^4 \cdot (x^6)^4$ ⟵ $-2x^6$ is the product of -2 and x^6. Use the power of a product rule.

$\qquad = 16 \cdot (x^6)^4$

$\qquad = 16 \cdot x^{(6 \cdot 4)}$ ⟵ $(x^6)^4$ is the fourth power of x^6. Use the power of a power rule.

$\qquad = 16x^{24}$

b. $(4b^{-5})^{-3} = 4^{-3} \cdot (b^{-5})^{-3}$ ⟵ $4b^{-5}$ is the product of 4 and b^{-5}. Use the power of a product rule.

$\qquad = \dfrac{1}{4^3} \cdot b^{(-5)(-3)}$ ⟵ Rewrite 4^{-3} with a positive exponent. Use the power of a power rule.

$\qquad = \dfrac{b^{15}}{64}$

c. $\left(\dfrac{3y}{-2z}\right)^2 = \dfrac{(3y)^2}{(-2z)^2}$ ⟵ Use the power of a quotient rule.

$\qquad = \dfrac{3^2 \cdot y^2}{(-2)^2 \cdot z^2}$ ⟵ Use the power of a product rule.

$\qquad = \dfrac{9y^2}{4z^2}$

Talk it Over

15. You know that $\sqrt{3} \cdot \sqrt{3} = 3$. Use the product of powers rule to show that $3^{1/2} \cdot 3^{1/2} = 3$.

16. Use the power of a power rule to show that $(x^{1/3})^3 = x$. How does this support the definition of $x^{1/3}$ as the cube root of x?

516 \qquad\qquad **Unit 9** Polynomial and Rational Functions

---

Teaching Tip

Students can remember these three rules of exponents as a group by seeing that they all involve expressions within parentheses being raised to a power. The power of each expression is the number of times the expression is multiplied by itself, as was apparent in Talk it Over questions 9–14.

Additional Sample

S3 Simplify. Write answers without negative exponents.

a. $(-4x^3)^2$
$(-4x^3)^2 = (-4)^2(x^3)^2 = 16x^6$

b. $(3x^{-2})^3$
$(3x^{-2})^3 = (3)^3(x^{-2})^3 = 27x^{-6} = \dfrac{27}{x^6}$

c. $\left(\dfrac{2x^3}{x^2}\right)^2$
$\left(\dfrac{2x^3}{x^2}\right)^2 = \dfrac{(2x^3)^2}{(x^2)^2} = \dfrac{4x^6}{x^4} = 4x^2$

Talk it Over

Questions 15 and 16 help strengthen students' understanding of the connection between fractional exponents and roots.

Answers to Talk it Over

15. $3^{1/2} \cdot 3^{1/2} = 3^{(1/2 + 1/2)} = 3^1 = 3$

16. $(x^{1/3})^3 = x^{(1/3)(3)} = x^1 = x$; The cube root of x is the number whose cube is x. Since $(x^{1/3})^3 = x$, $x^{1/3}$ is the cube root of x.

Answers to Look Back

Summaries may vary. Examples are given. Product of Powers Rule: The exponent of the product of two powers with the same base is the sum of the exponents of the powers; $2^2 \cdot 2^4 = 2^6$. Quotient of Powers Rule: The exponent of the quotient of two powers with the same base is the difference of the exponents of the powers if the base is not zero; $\dfrac{2^7}{2^4} = 2^{7-4} = 2^3$. Power of a Power Rule: The exponent of a power raised to a power is the product of the exponents; $(2^{1/2})^4 = 2^{(1/2)(4)} = 2^2$. Power of a Product Rule: If a product is raised to a power, the exponent of each factor of the product is the same as the power; $(2 \cdot 3)^2 = 2^2 \cdot 3^2$. Power of a Quotient Rule: If a quotient is raised to a power, the exponent of the numerator and denominator of the quotient is the same as the power; $\left(\dfrac{2}{3}\right)^2 = \dfrac{2^2}{3^2}$.

······▶ Now you are ready for:
Exs. 32–55 on pp. 518–519

Look Back ◀─────
Describe each rule of exponents in your own words. Give an example for each rule.

9-2 Exercises and Problems

1. **Reading** Which rule of exponents involves adding exponents? subtracting exponents?

Simplify. Write each answer without negative exponents.

2. $y^2 \cdot y^5 \cdot y^{-3}$

3. $x^{-6} \cdot x^2 \cdot t^3$

4. $x^{1/2} \cdot x^{1/2} \cdot x^2$

5. $(3t^4)(9t^0)$

6. $(5r^2)(-4r^{-3})$

7. $(8b^3)(2ab)(a^{-2})$

8. $\dfrac{m^6 n^4}{mn^3}$

9. $\dfrac{d^{12} d^4}{d^8}$

10. $\dfrac{45u}{9u^5}$

11. $\dfrac{6a^{10}}{8a^2}$

12. $\dfrac{9jk^{12}}{3j^4 k^2}$

13. $\dfrac{3x^8 y^2}{x^2 x^5}$

Simplify each pair of expressions. Compare the results.

14. $4^{(2+3)}$ and $4^2 + 4^3$

15. $2^{(3 \cdot 2)}$ and $2^3 \cdot 2^2$

16. $(5 \cdot 2)^3$ and $5 \cdot 2^3$

17. $(6-4)^2$ and $6^2 - 4^2$

18. 3^{-2} and $-(3^2)$

19. $\left(\dfrac{3}{4}\right)^2$ and $\dfrac{3^2}{4}$

20. **a.** Ferhan rewrote the product $(x+4)(x-2)(x+1)$ in expanded form. Explain each step of her solution.

   b. Write the product $(y+2)(y-3)(y-5)$ in expanded form.

   c. Use either Ferhan's method or the binomial theorem and Pascal's triangle to write $(z-4)^3$ in expanded form.

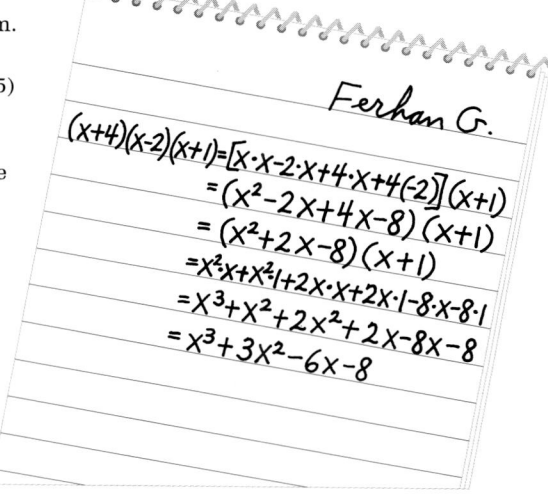

Ferhan G.

$(x+4)(x-2)(x+1) = [x \cdot x - 2 \cdot x + 4 \cdot x + 4(-2)](x+1)$
$= (x^2 - 2x + 4x - 8)(x+1)$
$= (x^2 + 2x - 8)(x+1)$
$= x^2 \cdot x + x^2 \cdot 1 + 2x \cdot x + 2x \cdot 1 - 8 \cdot x - 8 \cdot 1$
$= x^3 + x^2 + 2x^2 + 2x - 8x - 8$
$= x^3 + 3x^2 - 6x - 8$

Complete.

21. $8a^5 = 4a^2 \cdot \underline{\ ?\ }$

22. $18x^{15} = 3x^7 \cdot \underline{\ ?\ }$

23. $2a^6 = 2a \cdot \underline{\ ?\ }$

Factor completely.

24. $4x^5 - 2x^4 + 16x^2$

25. $x^4 - 2x^3 - 15x^2$

26. $6x^7 - 28x^6 + 16x^5$

27. $9p^3 q + 15p^2$

28. $48u^5 v^5 - 60u^3 v^6 w$

29. $49x^3 y - 35x^2 y^5$

9-2 Power and Quotient Rules

517

Answers to Exercises and Problems ··

1. product of powers rule; quotient of powers rule

2. y^4

3. $\dfrac{t^3}{x^4}$

4. x^3

5. $27t^4$

6. $-\dfrac{20}{r}$

7. $\dfrac{16b^4}{a}$

8. $m^5 n$

9. d^8

10. $\dfrac{5}{u^4}$

11. $\dfrac{3a^8}{4}$

12. $\dfrac{3k^{10}}{j^3}$

13. $3xy^2$

14. 1024 and 80; $4^{(2+3)} \neq 4^2 + 4^3$

15. 64 and 32; $2^{(3 \cdot 2)} \neq 2^3 \cdot 2^2$

16. 1000 and 40; $(5 \cdot 2)^3 \neq 5 \cdot 2^3$

17. 4 and 20; $(6-4)^2 \neq 6^2 - 4^2$

18. $\dfrac{1}{9}$ and -9; $3^{-2} \neq -(3^2)$

19. $\dfrac{9}{16}$ and $\dfrac{9}{4}$; $\left(\dfrac{3}{4}\right)^2 \neq \dfrac{3^2}{4}$

20. **a.** First, Ferhan multiplied the two binomials on the left by multiplying each term of the first binomial by each term of the second. Next, she simplified like terms and multiplied the resulting trinomial by the remaining binomial. She multiplied each term of the trinomial by each

term of the binomial and used the product of powers rule. Finally, she simplified the result by combining like terms.

   b. $y^3 - 6y^2 - y + 30$

   c. $z^3 - 12z^2 + 48z - 64$

21. $2a^3$

22. $6x^8$

23. a^5

24. $2x^2(2x^3 - x^2 + 8)$

25. $x^2(x-5)(x+3)$

26. $2x^5(3x-2)(x-4)$

27. $3p^2(3pq + 5)$

28. $12u^3 v^5(4u^2 - 5vw)$

29. $7x^2 y(7x - 5y^4)$

BY THE WAY...

The game of volleyball was invented in Massachusetts in 1896. Now over 150 countries belong to the International Volleyball Federation.

Volleyball In the sport of volleyball, a ball is hit over a net into another team's court. The receiving team may hit the ball no more than three times before the ball is hit back to the other team's court. The ball cannot be hit by the same player twice in a row.

30. Derek hits a volleyball almost straight up. The equation $h = 32t - 16t^2$ models the height of the ball, in feet, t seconds after he hits it. How many seconds does his teammate have to hit the ball before it hits the ground?

31. Julie dives for a volleyball and hits it toward the net. The equation $h = 24t - 16t^2$ models the height of the ball, in feet, t seconds after she hits it.

   a. Write the equation in factored form. (Make sure it is completely factored.)

   b. Suppose nothing blocks the ball's path. After how many seconds will the ball hit the ground?

   c. The top of the net is about 8 ft from the ground. Suppose Julie's shot reaches the net one second after she hits it. Does the ball go over the net?

Simplify. Write each answer without negative exponents.

32. $(2y^{-5})^4$

33. $(8k^6)^{1/3}$

34. $(m^8)(m^{-2})^4$

35. $(8y^3)(2y^2)^{-1}$

36. $(a^2b)^3$

37. $(2n^3p^5)^3$

38. $\left(\dfrac{5}{x^2}\right)^3$

39. $\left(\dfrac{d^3}{c^4}\right)^2$

40. $\left(\dfrac{a^{-2}}{b^{-3}}\right)^{-1}$

41. $\left(\dfrac{6s^2}{4t^6}\right)^2$

42. $\dfrac{x^{-2}y^{-3}}{x^5y^{-4}}$

43. $\left(\dfrac{rs^{-5}}{s^{-7}}\right)^{-2}$

Simplify each pair of expressions. Compare the results.

44. $(3x)^2$ and $3x^2$

45. $(-5x^7)^2$ and $-5(x^7)^2$

46. $\dfrac{(-6a)^2}{3}$ and $\dfrac{-(6a^2)}{3}$

47. **Writing** Explain why it makes sense to use the fact that $\dfrac{a^3}{b^3} = \left(\dfrac{a}{b}\right)^3$ to simplify $\dfrac{12^3}{4^3}$.

Ongoing **ASSESSMENT**

48. **Writing** Devin wanted to understand why the expressions $1^0, 2^0, 3^0, \ldots, a^0$ are all equal to 1.

   a. Devin used the quotient of powers rule to show that $3^0 = 1$. Explain how his work helped him understand that $3^0 = 1$.

   b. Does Devin's method work for bases other than 3? Explain why or why not.

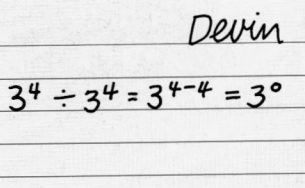

Devin

$3^4 \div 3^4 = 3^{4-4} = 3^0$

Answers to Exercises and Problems ·····

30. 2 seconds

31. a. $h = 8t(3 - 2t)$

   b. 1.5 seconds

   c. Since $h = 8$ when $t = 1$, the ball hits the top of the net and may fall on either side of the net.

32. $\dfrac{16}{y^{20}}$

33. $2k^2$

34. 1

35. $4y$

36. a^6b^3

37. $8n^9p^{15}$

38. $\dfrac{125}{x^6}$

39. $\dfrac{d^6}{c^8}$

40. $\dfrac{a^2}{b^3}$

41. $\dfrac{9s^4}{4t^{12}}$

42. $\dfrac{y}{x^7}$

43. $\dfrac{1}{r^2s^4}$

44. $9x^2$ and $3x^2$; $(3x)^2 \neq 3x^2$

45. $25x^{14}$ and $-5x^{14}$; $(-5x^7)^2 \neq -5(x^7)^2$

46. $12a^2$ and $-2a^2$; $\dfrac{(-6a)^2}{3} \neq \dfrac{-(6a^2)}{3}$

49. a. Write an equation to show how the measures in the diagram are related. *(Section 9-1)*

b. Is your equation from part (a) a rational equation?

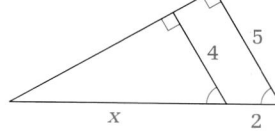

Solve each proportion. *(Toolbox Skill 17)*

50. $\dfrac{x}{8} = \dfrac{3}{4}$

51. $\dfrac{5}{y} = \dfrac{12}{31}$

52. $\dfrac{4.1}{8.2} = \dfrac{7}{t}$

53. $\dfrac{2}{3} = \dfrac{x+1}{9}$

54. Solve the quadratic equation $x^2 + x - 6 = 0$ by factoring. *(Section 4-4)*

Working on the Unit Project

As you complete Exercise 55, think about how the weather, land, trees, and buildings where you live might affect the power output from a wind machine installed there.

If you need to produce more power from a wind machine, you can install it higher up, where the wind speed is greater. The physical features of the region determine how much greater the wind speed is at greater heights.

This formula shows how wind speed increases with the height above the ground. The diagram below contains values of g.

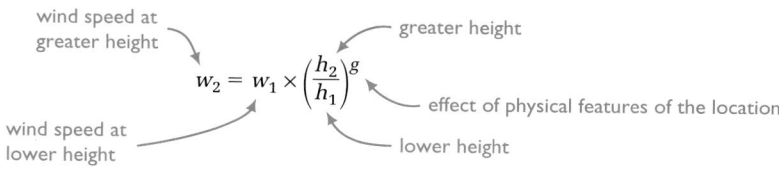

$$w_2 = w_1 \times \left(\frac{h_2}{h_1}\right)^g$$

wind speed at greater height — greater height

wind speed at lower height — lower height

effect of physical features of the location

55. Kaylie lives in a wooded area. She measures a wind speed of 10 mi/h at a height of 10 ft above the ground. What is the wind speed at the same location 50 ft above the ground?

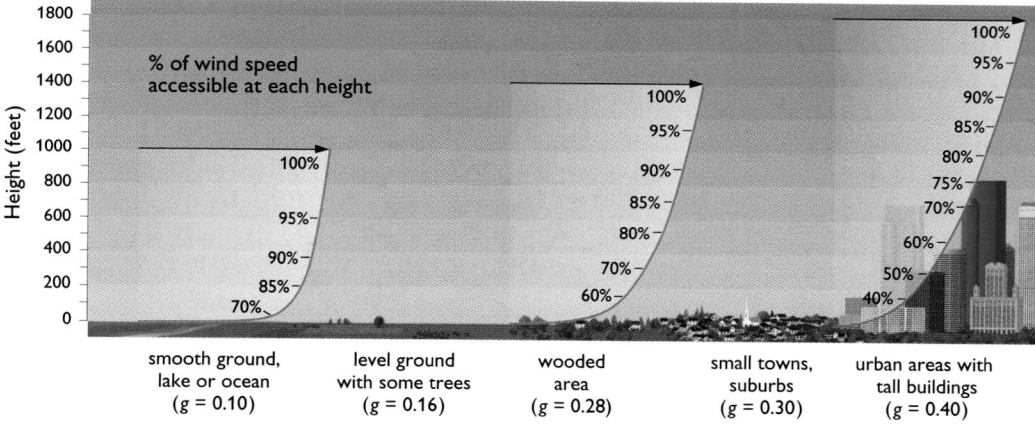

% of wind speed accessible at each height

Height (feet)

| smooth ground, lake or ocean ($g = 0.10$) | level ground with some trees ($g = 0.16$) | wooded area ($g = 0.28$) | small towns, suburbs ($g = 0.30$) | urban areas with tall buildings ($g = 0.40$) |

9-2 Power and Quotient Rules

519

Practice 70 For use with Section 9-2

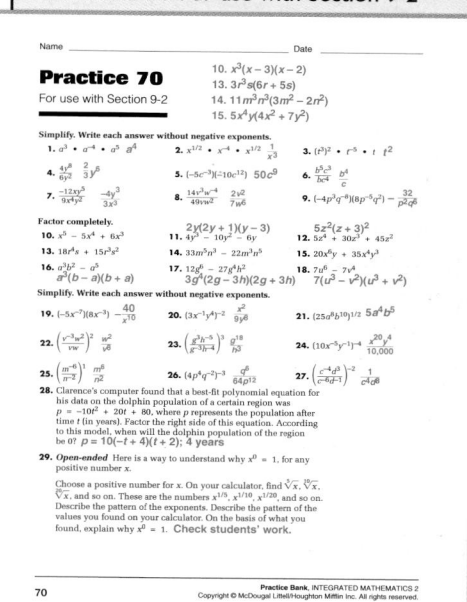

Answers to Exercises and Problems

47. Since $\dfrac{12}{4} = 3$, it is easy to simplify $\dfrac{12^3}{4^3}$ using the given rule. $\dfrac{12^3}{4^3} = \left(\dfrac{12}{4}\right)^3 = 3^3 = 27$. This is easier than finding that $12^3 = 1728$, $4^3 = 64$, and $1728 \div 64 = 27$.

48. a. Since $x \div x = 1$ for every x except 0, $3^4 \div 3^4 = 1$. Then Devin could see that $3^4 \div 3^4 = 1$ and $3^4 \div 3^4 = 3^0$, so $3^0 = 1$.

b. Devin's method works for every base except 0 because $x \div x = 1$ for every x except 0 and the quotient of powers rule is true for every base except 0.

49. a. Equations may vary.

Example: $\dfrac{x}{x+2} = \dfrac{4}{5}$

b. Yes.

50. 6

51. $\dfrac{155}{12} = 12\dfrac{11}{12}$ or about 12.9

52. 14

53. 5

54. $x = -3$ or $x = 2$

55. about 15.7 mi/h

519

PLANNING

Objectives and Strands
See pages 502A and 502B.

Spiral Learning
See page 502B.

Materials List
➤ Graph paper

Recommended Pacing
Section 9-3 is a two-day lesson.

Day 1

Pages 520–521: Opening paragraph through Sample 2, *Exercises 1–10*

Day 2

Pages 522–524: Using Common Multiples through Look Back, *Exercises 11–38*

Extra Practice
See pages 628–629.

Warm-Up Exercises
Warm-Up Transparency 9-3

Support Materials
➤ Practice 71
➤ Enrichment 63 in the Activity Bank
➤ Study Guide 9-3
➤ Problem Set 20
➤ Diagram Master 2 in the Explorations Lab Manual
➤ Quiz 9-3
➤ Test 37
➤ Alternative Assessment 3

Section 9–3 Solving Rational Equations

Against the Wind

Focus
Solve rational equations that simplify to linear or quadratic equations.

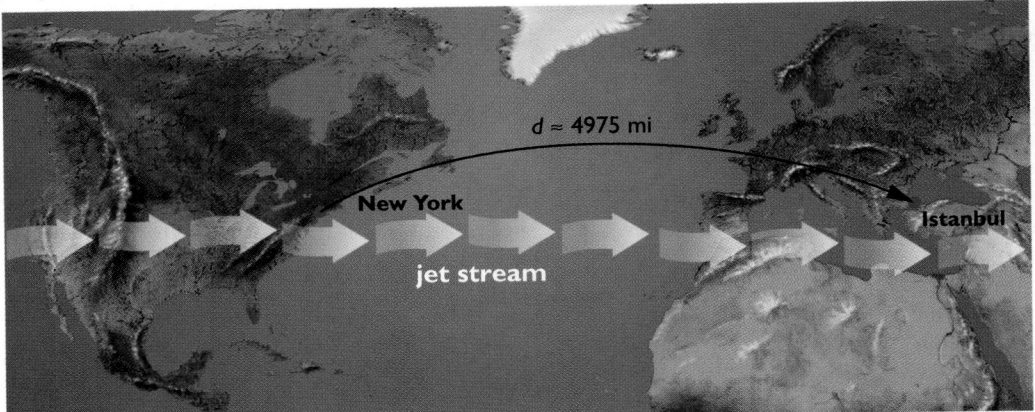

A pilot flying over the ocean may need to know the *point of no return* in an emergency. This is the point where it would take the pilot as much time to return to the starting point as to continue on to the destination. Wind affects the point of no return.

BY THE WAY...

A jet stream is a strong wind current that occurs at higher altitudes. Jet streams move from west to east everywhere except for a region around part of the equator. There the jet stream moves from east to west.

Talk it Over

1. Rose takes a flight from New York City to Istanbul, Turkey. Tashiki takes a flight from Istanbul to New York City. Whose flight is faster? Why?

2. How many miles has the plane traveled when it is half way between the two cities?

3. Do you think the halfway point is the point of no return? Why or why not?

Sample 1

A plane flying the 4975 mi from New York City to Istanbul travels at a speed of about 675 mi/h with the wind. In the other direction, the wind slows the plane down to about 525 mi/h. Find the point of no return.

Unit 9 Polynomial and Rational Functions

Answers to Talk it Over

1. Rose's; From New York City to Istanbul, the plane is flying *with* the wind. The speed of the wind increases the plane's speed. From Istanbul to New York City, the plane is flying *against* the wind. The speed of the wind decreases the plane's speed.

2. 2487.5 miles

3. No; the point of no return is the point at which the flying *times* to the two cities are the same. The halfway point is the point at which the *distances* to the two cities is the same. Because of the effects of the wind, the plane flying from New York City to Istanbul reaches the point of no return before it reaches the halfway point, and the plane flying from Istanbul to New York City reaches the point of no return after it reaches the halfway point.

Sample Response

Problem Solving Strategy: Use a formula.

The point of no return occurs where the time to fly back to New York City is equal to the time to fly on to Istanbul. Use this formula: $\text{time} = \dfrac{\text{distance}}{\text{rate}}$.

$$\underset{\substack{\text{time needed to fly back} \\ \text{to New York City}}}{} = \underset{\substack{\text{time needed to continue} \\ \text{on to Istanbul}}}{}$$

distance from starting point ⟶
rate to fly back ⟶
$$\frac{d}{525} = \frac{4975 - d}{675} \qquad \substack{\longleftarrow \text{ distance left to fly after } d \text{ miles} \\ \longleftarrow \text{ rate to fly to destination}}$$

$$675d = 525(4975 - d) \qquad \longleftarrow \text{ Use cross products.}$$

$$675d = 2{,}611{,}875 - 525d \qquad \longleftarrow \text{ Use the distributive property.}$$

$$1200d = 2{,}611{,}875$$

$$d \approx 2177$$

The point of no return is about 2177 mi from the starting point.

Sample 2

Solve the equation $\dfrac{1}{x - 4} = \dfrac{2}{x^2 - 16}$.

Sample Response

$$\frac{1}{x - 4} = \frac{2}{x^2 - 16}$$

$$x^2 - 16 = 2(x - 4) \qquad \longleftarrow \text{ Use cross products.}$$

$$x^2 - 16 = 2x - 8 \qquad \longleftarrow \text{ Use the distributive property.}$$

$$x^2 - 2x - 8 = 0 \qquad \longleftarrow \text{ Write the equation in standard form.}$$

$$(x + 2)(x - 4) = 0 \qquad \longleftarrow \text{ Factor.}$$

$$x + 2 = 0 \quad or \quad x - 4 = 0 \qquad \longleftarrow \text{ Use the zero-product property.}$$

$$x = -2 \qquad\qquad x = 4$$

Check Substitute the results in the original equation.

$$\frac{1}{-2 - 4} \overset{?}{=} \frac{2}{(-2)^2 - 16} \qquad \substack{\longleftarrow \text{ Substitute } -2 \\ \text{ for } x.}$$

$$\frac{1}{-6} \overset{?}{=} \frac{2}{-12}$$

$$\frac{1}{-6} = \frac{1}{-6} \; ✔ \qquad \substack{\longleftarrow \text{ This is a valid statement.} \\ -2 \text{ is a solution.}}$$

The solution is -2.

$$\frac{1}{4 - 4} \overset{?}{=} \frac{2}{4^2 - 16} \qquad \substack{\longleftarrow \text{ Substitute 4} \\ \text{ for } x.}$$

$$\frac{1}{0} = \frac{2}{0} \qquad \substack{\longleftarrow \text{ Division by zero is undefined.} \\ 4 \text{ is not a solution.}}$$

When a solution is not a solution of the original equation, it is called an **extraneous solution**.

┈┈▶ Now you are ready for:
Exs. 1–10 on p. 524

9-3 Solving Rational Equations

Talk it Over

Questions 1–3 prepare students for Sample 1 by having them think about the effect of wind on the speed of an airplane and about the difference between the *halfway point* and the *point of no return*.

Multicultural Note

Istanbul, Turkey's largest city, lies along the Bosporus, a strait that forms part of the water link between the Mediterranean Sea and the Black Sea. It is the only major city in the world where boundaries encompass parts of two continents (Europe and Asia). Known in prior eras as Constantinople, this city was the capital of the eastern remnant of the Roman Empire from A.D. 330 to 1453 and was the capital of the Ottoman Empire from 1453 to 1922. The city is world famous for its mosques, palaces, museums, and bazaars.

Additional Sample

S1 Suppose the wind conditions change in Sample 1 and the speed of the plane from New York City to Istanbul is 625 mi/h. In the other direction, the wind slows the plane down to 550 mi/h. Find the new point of no return. Is it closer or farther away from the halfway point than the point of no return in Sample 1? Why?

$$\frac{d}{550} = \frac{4975 - d}{625}$$

$$625d = 550(4975 - d)$$

$$1175d = 2{,}736{,}250$$

$$d \approx 2329$$

The point of no return is about 2329 mi from the starting point. The halfway point is $4975 \div 2 = 2487.5$ mi from the starting point. The new point of no return is closer to the halfway point than the point of no return in Sample 1 because the difference in speed of the plane in both directions is less than the difference in Sample 1.

521

S2 Solve the equation
$\frac{1}{x} = \frac{-2}{x^2 - 3}$.

$$\frac{1}{x} = \frac{-2}{x^2 - 3}$$

$$x^2 - 3 = -2x$$

$$x^2 + 2x - 3 = 0$$

$$(x + 3)(x - 1) = 0$$

$$x + 3 = 0 \quad \text{or} \quad x - 1 = 0$$

$$x = -3 \qquad x = 1$$

Check: $\frac{1}{-3} = \frac{-2}{6}$

$$-\frac{1}{3} = -\frac{1}{3} \checkmark$$

$$\frac{1}{1} = \frac{-2}{1 - 3}$$

$$\frac{1}{1} = \frac{1}{1} \checkmark$$

The solutions are −3 and 1.

S3 Solve.

a. $\frac{-5}{x + 2} + \frac{2}{3} = 12$

Multiply both sides of the equation by the common multiple $3(x + 2)$.

$$3(x + 2)\left(\frac{-5}{x + 2} + \frac{2}{3}\right)$$

$$= 3(x + 2)(12)$$

$$3(x + 2)\left(\frac{-5}{x + 2}\right) + 3(x + 2)\left(\frac{2}{3}\right)$$

$$= 36x + 72$$

$$-15 + 2x + 4 = 36x + 72$$

$$-83 = 34x$$

$$-2.441 = x$$

The solution is −2.441.

b. $\frac{t}{t + 1} + \frac{3}{t - 3} = \frac{7t - 9}{t^2 - 2t - 3}$

Look for a common multiple of the denominators. Factor the expression $t^2 - 2t - 3$.

$$t^2 - 2t - 3 = (t - 3)(t + 1)$$

A common multiple is $(t - 3)(t + 1)$. Multiply both sides of the equation by the common multiple.

$$(t - 3)(t + 1)\left(\frac{t}{t + 1} + \frac{3}{t - 3}\right) =$$

$$(t - 3)(t + 1)\left(\frac{7t - 9}{(t - 3)(t + 1)}\right)$$

$$(t - 3)t + (t + 1)(3) = 7t - 9$$

$$t^2 - 3t + 3t + 3 = 7t - 9$$

$$t^2 - 7t + 12 = 0$$

Factor.

$$t^2 - 7t + 12 = 0$$

$$(t - 4)(t - 3) = 0$$

$$t - 4 = 0 \text{ or } t - 3 = 0$$

$$t = 4 \qquad t = 3$$

The solution is $t = 4$. $t = 3$ is an extraneous solution.

Using Common Multiples

Some rational equations cannot be solved using cross products. You need to eliminate the denominators. You can do this by multiplying both sides of the equation by a *common multiple* of the denominators.

Sample 3

Solve.

a. $\frac{3}{5} + \frac{4}{x - 3} = 7$

b. $\frac{d}{d + 2} + \frac{2}{d - 2} = \frac{d + 6}{(d - 2)(d + 2)}$

Sample Response

a. First look for a common multiple of the denominators. A common multiple is an expression that has both denominators as factors.

$$\frac{3}{5} + \frac{4}{x - 3} = 7 \quad \longleftarrow \quad \textbf{5(x − 3)} \text{ is a common multiple.}$$

> **Watch Out!**
> A common multiple of $\frac{3}{5}$ and $\frac{4}{x - 3}$ is $5(x - 3)$, not $5x - 3$.

Then multiply both sides of the equation by this common multiple.

$$5(x - 3)\left(\frac{3}{5} + \frac{4}{x - 3}\right) = 5(x - 3)(7)$$

$$\cancel{5}(x - 3)\left(\frac{3}{\cancel{5}}\right) + 5(\cancel{x - 3})\left(\frac{4}{\cancel{x - 3}}\right) = 35x - 105 \quad \longleftarrow \quad \text{Use the distributive property.}$$

$$(x - 3)3 + 5(4) = 35x - 105 \quad \longleftarrow \quad \text{Simplify.}$$

$$3x + 11 = 35x - 105$$

$$116 = 32x$$

$$3.625 = x$$

The solution is 3.625.

b. Multiply both sides of the equation by a common multiple of the denominators: $(d - 2)(d + 2)$.

$$(d - 2)(d + 2)\left(\frac{d}{d + 2} + \frac{2}{d - 2}\right) = (d - 2)(d + 2)\left(\frac{d + 6}{(d - 2)(d + 2)}\right)$$

$$(d - 2)(\cancel{d + 2})\left(\frac{d}{\cancel{d + 2}}\right) + (\cancel{d - 2})(d + 2)\left(\frac{2}{\cancel{d - 2}}\right) = d + 6 \quad \longleftarrow \quad \text{Use the distributive property.}$$

$$(d - 2)d + (d + 2)2 = d + 6 \quad \longleftarrow \quad \text{Simplify.}$$

$$d^2 - 2d + 2d + 4 = d + 6$$

$$d^2 - d - 2 = 0$$

> **Watch Out!**
> Check both possible solutions. One solution may be extraneous.

$$(d - 2)(d + 1) = 0 \quad \longleftarrow \quad \text{Factor. Then use the zero-product property.}$$

$$d - 2 = 0 \quad \text{or} \quad d + 1 = 0$$

$$d = 2 \qquad\qquad d = -1$$

The solution is −1.

Talk it Over

4. In Sample 3, part (b), why is 2 an extraneous solution?

5. What is a common multiple of the denominators in

   the equation $4 + \dfrac{3}{y+2} = 5$?

Sample 4

Emily Johns has only six hours to make a pamphlet with eight pages of text and two pages of graphics. She knows her rate for producing graphics pages is one page per hour slower than her rate for producing text pages. At what rate will she need to make text pages?

Sample Response

Problem Solving Strategy: Use a table.

Let x = the rate in pages per hour for making text pages.

	Number of Pages	Rate (pages/hour)	Time (hours)
Text	8	x	$\dfrac{8}{x}$
Graphics	2	$x - 1$	$\dfrac{2}{x-1}$

Model the situation with an equation.

time for making text pages	+	time for making graphics pages	=	total time for making the pamphlet
$\dfrac{8}{x}$	+	$\dfrac{2}{x-1}$	=	6

$$\text{time} = \frac{\text{number of pages}}{\text{rate}}$$

Multiply both sides of the equation by a common multiple of the denominators.

$$x(x-1)\left(\frac{8}{x} + \frac{2}{x-1}\right) = x(x-1)(6)$$

$$\cancel{x}(x-1)\left(\frac{8}{\cancel{x}}\right) + x\cancel{(x-1)}\left(\frac{2}{\cancel{x-1}}\right) = 6x^2 - 6x \quad \longleftarrow \text{ Use the distributive property.}$$

$$(x-1)8 + 2x = 6x^2 - 6x \quad \longleftarrow \text{ Simplify.}$$

$$8x - 8 + 2x = 6x^2 - 6x$$

$$0 = 6x^2 - 16x + 8$$

$$0 = 2(3x-2)(x-2) \quad \longleftarrow \text{ Factor.}$$

$$3x - 2 = 0 \quad or \quad x - 2 = 0 \quad \longleftarrow \text{ Use the zero-product property.}$$

$$x = \frac{2}{3} \qquad\qquad x = 2$$

The solution $x = \dfrac{2}{3}$ makes no sense in this situation because it gives a negative pages/hour rate for making graphics pages. Emily Johns must make text pages at a rate of 2 pages/hour.

9-3 Solving Rational Equations

523

Answers to Talk it Over

4. When 2 is substituted into the original equation, it produces a fraction with a denominator of zero. Since division by zero is undefined, 2 is an extraneous solution.

5. $y + 2$

523

Now you are ready for:
Exs. 11–38 on pp. 524–526

Look Back

Give two reasons why a solution of an equation may not be a solution of the original problem.

9-3 Exercises and Problems

1. **Reading** Why is one of the solutions in Sample 2 an extraneous solution?

Solve.

2. $\dfrac{12 - x}{4x} = \dfrac{1}{12}$

3. $\dfrac{1}{x} = \dfrac{4}{x - 2}$

4. $\dfrac{3}{y + 1} = \dfrac{y}{2}$

5. $\dfrac{2a + 5}{a - 1} = \dfrac{3a}{a - 1}$

6. $\dfrac{2}{c(c - 2)} = \dfrac{1}{c - 2}$

7. $\dfrac{3}{2x - 2} = \dfrac{2x - 1}{x}$

For Exercises 8–10, use the map.

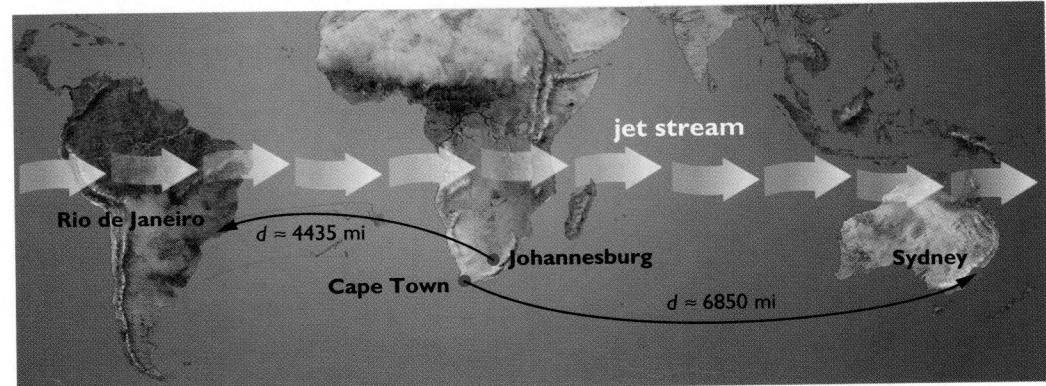

8. A plane flying from Johannesburg, South Africa, to Rio de Janeiro, Brazil, travels at a speed of about 550 mi/h. In the other direction, the wind increases the plane's speed to 650 mi/h. Find the point of no return.

9. A plane is flying from Cape Town, South Africa, to Sydney, Australia. According to the cockpit readings, its speed relative to the ground is about 590 mi/h.

   a. The plane's speed is increased by a 45 mi/h wind. How fast is the plane really going?

   b. Suppose the plane has to fly back to Cape Town. Its speed is decreased by the 45 mi/h wind. What is its actual return speed?

10. Use the facts in Exercise 9. Find the point of no return for the flight to Sydney.

Solve.

11. $2 + \dfrac{3}{x} = x$

12. $\dfrac{1}{3} + \dfrac{1}{a} = 2a$

13. $\dfrac{6}{t} - \dfrac{2}{t - 1} = 1$

14. $\dfrac{x - 1}{x} + \dfrac{9}{4x} = 6$

15. $\dfrac{x}{x - 2} + \dfrac{30}{x + 2} = 9$

16. $\dfrac{1}{x + 1} - \dfrac{1}{x + 2} = \dfrac{1}{2}$

524   **Unit 9** Polynomial and Rational Functions

Answers to Look Back

The solution may produce a fraction with a denominator of zero, or it may produce an impossible situation, such as a negative length or a negative amount of time.

Answers to Exercises and Problems

1. Substituting 4 in the original equation produces two fractions with denominators of zero. Since division by zero is undefined, 4 is not a solution of the original equation.

2. 9

3. $-\dfrac{2}{3}$

4. $-3, 2$

5. 5

6. no solution

7. 0.25, 2

8. about 2402 mi from the starting point

9. a. about 635 mi/h
   b. about 545 mi/h

10. about 3164 mi from the starting point

11. $3, -1$

17. **Reading** In Sample 4, why is $x = \frac{2}{3}$ not a solution of the problem?

18. It takes Paul Lien five hours to type ten pages of text and create five pages of graphics. His rate for typing text pages is two pages per hour faster than his rate for creating graphics pages.

 a. How many text pages can Paul type in one hour?

 b. About how long does it take Paul to type one text page?

Find the unknown dimensions.

19.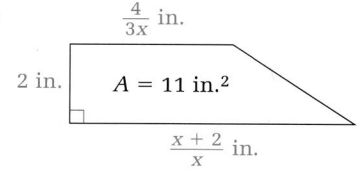

20.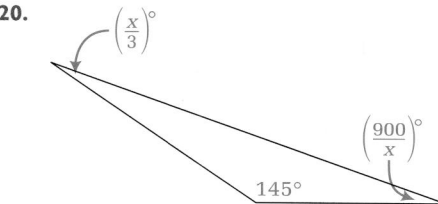

21. Jane can mow the lawn in 50 min. When she and her brother, Mike, work together, they can finish in 30 min. How long does it take Mike when he works alone?

Fuel Efficiency Use the information below for Exercises 22 and 23.

The yearly cost of fueling your car can be modeled by this equation:

$$\text{yearly fuel cost} = \frac{\text{distance traveled} \times \text{price per gallon}}{\text{car's fuel efficiency rate}}$$

22. Alice Volk drives about 10,000 mi each year. She pays an average of $1.30 per gallon of gasoline. Her yearly fuel cost is about $800. What is her car's fuel efficiency rate in miles per gallon?

23. Rob Scudder drives about 18,000 miles each year. He pays an average of $1.25 per gallon of gasoline. Rob wants to buy a new car with a better fuel efficiency rate.

 a. Write an expression to represent Rob's current yearly fuel cost.

 b. The new car Rob wants to buy travels eight more miles per gallon than his old car. Write an expression to represent his yearly fuel cost for the new car.

 c. Suppose Rob saves $400 in yearly fuel cost by buying the new car. Write and solve an equation to find the fuel efficiency rate for his old car and for his new car.

24. A marathon runner decides that any rate faster than 0.20 miles per minute can be maintained for only half of a 26.2 mile race.

 Suppose the second half of a race will be run at 0.20 miles per minute. How fast does the runner need to run the first half to complete the race in under 2.5 hours?

BY THE WAY...

The initial route of the 1908 Olympic marathon was 26 mi long. The length was increased to 26.2 mi so that the runners would finish in front of the royal box of Queen Alexandra of Great Britain. The standard marathon distance has been 26.2 mi ever since.

Error Analysis

Exs. 11–16 require that students find and use a common multiple. Remind students to multiply each term on both sides of the equation by the common multiple. Students should also be careful when using the distributive property to avoid errors such as writing $x - 3(x + 2)$ as $x - 3x + 6$ instead of as $x - 3x - 6$.

Problem Solving

For Ex. 19, students will need to recall and use the formula for finding the area of a trapezoid.

Research

For Exs. 22 and 23, you may wish to have students research information to determine the fuel efficiency of the family car(s), a school bus, or some other motor vehicle they use for transportation.

Assessment: Standard

Students should be able to describe the type of variation in Ex. 23 in words; that is, that the yearly fuel cost varies inversely as the car's fuel efficiency rate, and decide if this statement makes sense. They should use graphics calculators to investigate the yearly fuel cost for various fuel efficiency rates.

Answers to Exercises and Problems

12. $\frac{1 + \sqrt{73}}{12} \approx 0.795$, $\frac{1 - \sqrt{73}}{12} \approx -0.629$

13. 2, 3

14. $\frac{1}{4}$

15. 3, 1

16. 0, −3

17. The solution $x = \frac{2}{3}$ is an extraneous solution. It gives a negative pages/ hour rate for making graphics pages.

18. a. 4 pages/hour

 b. about 15 min

19. The bases are 4 in. long and 7 in. long.

20. 20°, 15°

21. 75 min

22. 16.25 mi/gal

23. a. $\frac{22{,}500}{x}$

 b. $\frac{22{,}500}{x + 8}$

 c. $\frac{22{,}500}{x} - 400 = \frac{22{,}500}{x + 8}$; old car: about 17.6 mi/gal; new car: about 25.6 mi/gal

24. at least 0.155 mi/min

Interdisciplinary Problems

Exs. 35–38 involve concepts of power and energy as they are used in physics. The research students do for these exercises will help them to better understand the meaning of these important physical concepts.

Working on the Unit Project

Each student in a project group should research the meanings of the terms identified in Exs. 35–37. They should write down their definitions for use in a group discussion. Ex. 38 can be worked on as a group activity.

25. Open-ended Determine the distance from your home to school. Assume you can walk at an average rate of four miles per hour. How much do you have to increase your speed so that it takes you one minute less time to walk to school?

Simplify. Write each answer without negative exponents. *(Section 9-2)*

26. $(mn^2)^3$

27. $5\left(\dfrac{a}{b}\right)^{-3}$

28. $\left(\dfrac{x^2 y^3}{x^{-4}}\right)^2$

Find the measure of each unknown side in each figure. *(Section 8-8)*

29.
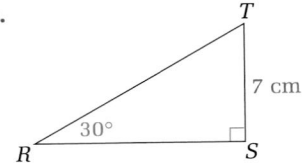

30.
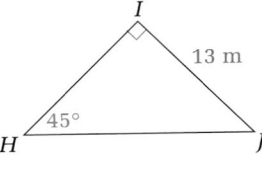

31.
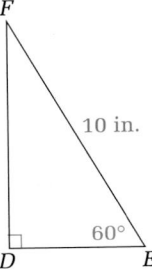

Graph each function. Find the x-intercepts. *(Section 4-1)*

32. $y = x^2 - 9$

33. $y = (x + 7)^2$

34. $y = x^2$

Working on the Unit Project

35. Research Look up the definitions of the words *power* and *energy*. Describe how they are related to one another. Can you have power without energy? Can you have energy without power?

36. Research Look up the definitions of *watt* and *kilowatt-hour*. Tell whether each is a unit of power or of energy.

37. Research Sometimes power is measured in *horsepower* (hp). What does 1 hp represent? How is horsepower related to watts?

38. Suppose an appliance has a power rating of P watts (W) and it uses E watt-hours (W · h) of electricity. The equation $P = \dfrac{E}{t}$ can be used to find the number of hours, t, that the appliance can operate. How long would a 2000 W air conditioner operate if it uses 150 W · h of electricity?

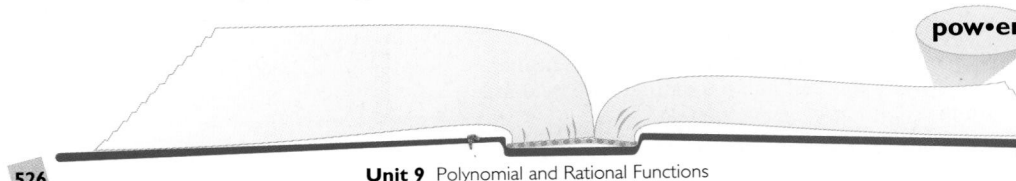

pow•er

Answers to
Exercises and Problems

25. Answers may vary. An example is given. For a distance of 3 mi from school, you would have to increase your rate by about 0.09 mi/h.

26. $m^3 n^6$

27. $\dfrac{5b^3}{a^3}$

28. $x^{12} y^6$

29. *RT*: 14 cm; *RS*: $7\sqrt{3}$ cm ≈ 12.1 cm

30. *HI*: 13 m; *HJ*: $13\sqrt{2}$ m ≈ 18.4 m

31. *DE*: 5 in.; *FD*: $5\sqrt{3}$ in. ≈ 8.7 in.

32. $x = 3$ and -3
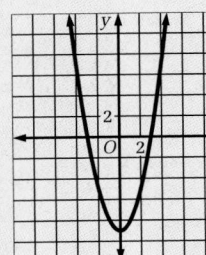

33. -7
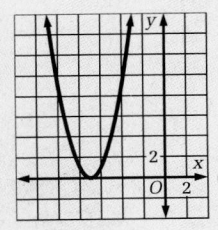

34. 0
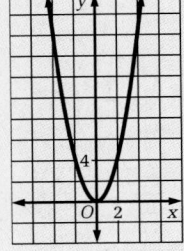

35. Power is the rate at which energy is harnessed, converted, or used. Energy is a source of power. A system can have energy without power, but if there is power, there is energy being used.

36. Kilowatt-hour is the unit of energy equivalent to that transferred or expended in one hour by one kilowatt of power. A watt is a unit of power equal to one joule per second.

37. 1 hp represents one horsepower, which is defined as 550 foot-pounds per second or 33,000 foot-pounds per minute; 1 hp = 745.7 W.

38. about 0.075 h or about 4.5 min

Quick Quiz (9-1 through 9-3)
See page 553.

1. **Writing** Explain what part exponents play in deciding whether or not an equation is a polynomial equation.

Estimated budget for buying a home		
	A	**B**
1	Down Payment	18,000
2	Realtor's Fee	6,000
3	Appraisal	250
4	Credit Report	50
5	Escrow Waiver Fee	125
6	Settlement Fees	200
7	Underwriter Fee	50
8	Document Preparation	100
9	Title Insurance	200
10	Deed and Mortgage	25
11	Total	25,000

2. Susan Duclos is planning to buy a house three years from now. She estimates she will need about $25,000 to cover a down payment and other costs. She deposits $7000 at the end of each year for three years.   9-1

   a. Write an expression for the amount of money she will have at the end of the third year.

   b. Susan wonders what yearly growth rate she must get to meet her goal. Write an equation to model the situation.

Tell whether each expression is a polynomial. Write *Yes* or *No*. Give a reason for your answer.

3. $5x^2 - 3x - 7$

   $(5x - 7)(x + 1)$

4. $3x^{1/2} - x - \frac{1}{4}$

5. $\frac{1}{2}x^3 + x$

6. $\frac{x - 1}{x^2 + 2}$

Simplify. Write each answer without negative exponents.   9-2

7. $(yz^2)(y^{-3}z)$

8. $(m^2n^{-4})^3$

9. $(-10a^{-3})(5a^2)^{-1}$

10. $\frac{d^{-3}d^7}{d^{-1}d^9}$

11. $\left(\frac{8f^3}{2f^8}\right)^2$

12. $\frac{1}{2}\left(\frac{pq}{q^{-2}}\right)^3$

Solve.   9-3

13. $\frac{2}{s + 3} - \frac{1}{s - 3} = 1$

14. $\frac{26}{r - 1} - \frac{26}{r} = 13$

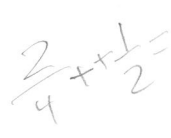

15. Several members of a hiking club contributed equally to raise $60 to pay for a club picnic. When two members were unable to go, their money was refunded and the remaining members had to pay an extra dollar each. How many members went on the hike?

9-3 Solving Rational Equations

527

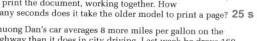
Practice 71 For use with Section 9-3

Answers to Checkpoint

1. If any term of an equation contains an exponent that is not a whole number, the equation is not a polynomial equation.

2. a. If g is the growth rate, the amount can be expressed as $7000 + 7000g + 7000g^2$.

   b. $7000 + 7000g + 7000g^2 = 25{,}000$

3. Yes; each term can be written with exponents that are whole numbers.

4. No; $3x^{1/2}$ cannot be written with a whole-number exponent.

5. Yes; each term can be written with exponents that are whole numbers.

6. No; the term cannot be written with whole-number exponents.

7. $\frac{z^3}{y^2}$

8. $\frac{m^6}{n^{12}}$

9. $\frac{-2}{a^5}$

10. $\frac{1}{d^4}$

11. $\frac{16}{f^{10}}$

12. $\frac{p^3q^9}{2}$

13. 0, 1

14. 2, −1

15. 10 members

Graphing Cubic Functions

The Third Degree

Objectives and Strands
See pages 502A and 502B.

Spiral Learning
See page 502B.

Materials List
➤ Graphics calculator or graphing software such as Plotter Plus
➤ Graph paper

Recommended Pacing
Section 9-4 is a two-day lesson.

Day 1

Pages 528–529: Exploration through Graphs of Cubic Functions, *Exercises 1–16*

Day 2

Pages 530–531: Sample 1 through Look Back, *Exercises 17–44*

Extra Practice
See pages 628–629.

Warm-Up Exercises
💡 Warm-Up Transparency 9-4

Support Materials
➤ Practice 72
➤ Enrichment 64 in the Activity Bank
➤ Study Guide 9-4
➤ Problem Set 21
➤ Diagram Masters 2, 20 in the Explorations Lab Manual
💡 Overhead Visual 9
➤ McDougal Littell Mathpack software: *Function Investigator*
➤ Function Investigator with Matrix Analyzer Activity Book: Function Investigator Activity 18
➤ Using TI-81 and TI-82 Calculators: Zeros and Factoring
➤ Using Plotter Plus: Zeros of Functions
➤ Using IBM/Mac Plotter Plus Disk: Function Plotter
➤ Quiz 9-4

Focus

Analyze graphs of polynomial functions written in factored form.

TECHNOLOGY NOTE

Be sure to set an appropriate window on your graphics calculator, especially when graphing cubic functions. You may miss some characteristics of a graph if the window is not set correctly.

EXPLORATION

(What) does the graph of a polynomial function of degree three look like?

• **Materials:** graphics calculators or graphing software
• **Work with another student.**

① Graph each quadratic function. What are the x-intercepts of each graph? How can you use the factored form of the function to predict the number of x-intercepts?

  a. $y = x^2$ **b.** $y = (x + 3)^2$ **c.** $y = (x + 3)(x - 1)$

② Graph each function listed below on a graphics calculator or using graphing software. Make a sketch of each graph. Record the number of x-intercepts for each graph. List the x-intercepts.

Function	Graph	X-intercepts	Number of X-intercepts
$y = x^3$		O	l
$y = (x+2)^3$			
$y = (x-3)(x+1)^2$			
$y = (x-3)^2(x+1)$			
$y = x(x-3)(x+2)$			
$y = (x+2)(x-1)(x-4)$			

③ If you write each function in the table in expanded form, you get a polynomial of degree 3. A polynomial function of degree 3 is called a **cubic function.**

Look for patterns in your table. How can you use the factored form of a cubic function to predict the number of x-intercepts? the behavior of the graph?

Unit 9 Polynomial and Rational Functions

Answers to Exploration

1, 2. See answers in back of book.

3. The number of distinct factors tells you the number of x-intercepts. If a factor repeats, the graph will touch the x-axis at that point and change direction.

4. Both graphs intersect the x-axis at $x = -1$ and $x = 3$.

The graph of $y = (x - 3)(x + 1)^2$ touches the axis but does not cross it at $x = -1$ and crosses the axis at $x = 3$. The graph of $y = (x - 3)^2(x + 1)$ touches the axis but does not cross it at $x = 3$ and crosses the axis at $x = -1$.

5. a. double zero at $x = 2$

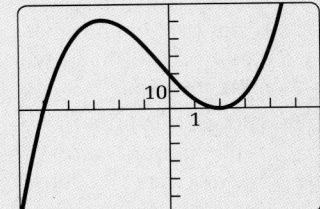

④ Compare the graphs of the functions
$y = (x - 3)(x + 1)^2$ and $y = (x - 3)^2(x + 1)$.
How are they alike? How are they different?

⑤ Suppose x is the control variable of a function and y is the dependent variable. A **zero of a function** is a value of x that makes $y = 0$. A cubic function with a squared factor has a **double zero**. A cubic function with a cubed factor has a **triple zero**.

For each function, use the chart below to help you predict when, if ever, a double zero or triple zero will occur. Test your predictions by graphing the function.

a. $y = (x - 2)(x - 2)(x + 5)$ **b.** $y = (x + 3)^3$

c. $y = (x + 1)^2(x - 2)$ **d.** $y = (x + 4)(x - 1)(x + 3)$

e. $y = (x + 1)(x - 5)^2$ **f.** $y = (x - 5)^3$

GRAPHS OF CUBIC FUNCTIONS

Function	$y = (x - 2)^3$	$y = (x - 2)^2(x + 1)$	$y = (x - 2)(x + 1)(x + 4)$
Number of x-intercepts	1	2	3
x-intercepts	2	2, −1	2, −1, −4
Zeros	2 is a triple zero.	−1 and 2 are zeros. 2 is a double zero.	2, −1, and −4 are zeros.
Graph	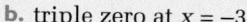		
	The graph flattens out and crosses the x-axis when $x = 2$ only.	The graph touches the x-axis at two points but does not cross it when $x = 2$.	There are no multiple zeros, so the graph crosses the x-axis at three different points.

······▶ **Now you are ready for:**
Exs. 1–16 on p. 532

9-4 Graphing Cubic Functions

529

Answers to Exploration ···

b. triple zero at $x = -3$ **c.** double zero at $x = -1$ **d.** no multiple zeros

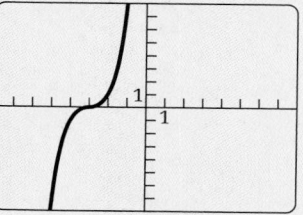   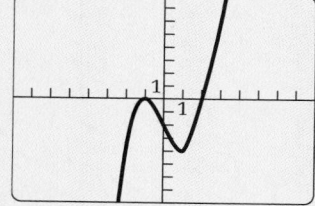   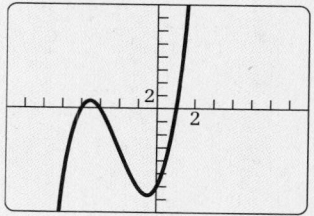

e. double zero at $x = 5$

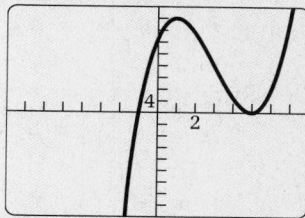

f. triple zero at $x = 5$

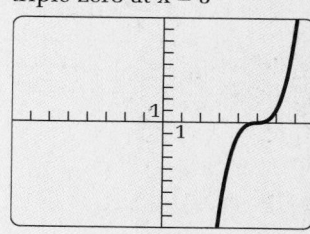

529

TEACHING

Exploration

The goal of the Exploration is to have students discover the characteristics of the graphs of cubic functions. They also use cubic equations written in factored form to predict the behavior of the graph, including the number of real number zeros (x-intercepts) of the function.

Communication: Discussion

Students can see that the concavity of the graph of a cubic equation (concave up or concave down) may change once if it has a *point of inflection*. For example, the graph of a cubic equation that has a triple zero has a point of inflection where the graph crosses the x-axis.

Using Technology

Students can use the *Function Investigator* software to do the Exploration. When students use a graphics calculator, their graphs should show all intercepts, peaks, valleys, and points of inflection. Encourage experimentation. Start with the standard graph screen. Zoom in or out until all the features mentioned above are visible. Then go to the ZOOM menu. Use ZBox (TI-82 or TI-83) or Box (TI-81) to draw a box around the portion of the graph where all the key features are found. Press ENTER to see the improved graph.

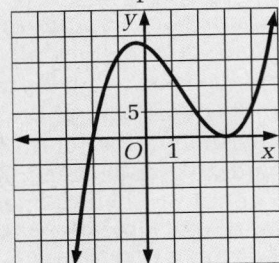
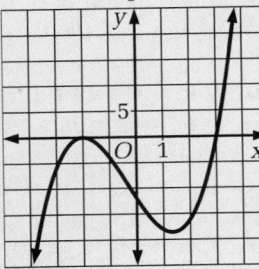
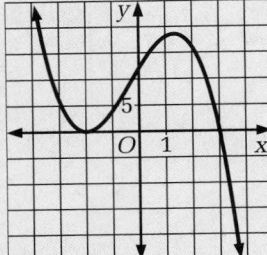
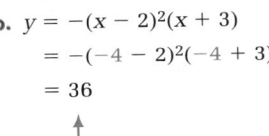

Match each function with its graph.

a. $y = (x - 2)^2(x + 3)$

b. $y = -(x - 2)^2(x + 3)$

c. $y = (x - 2)(x + 3)^2$

A.

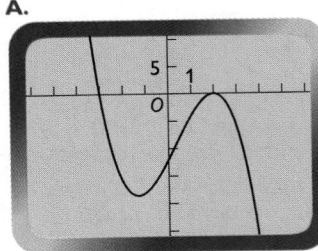

B.

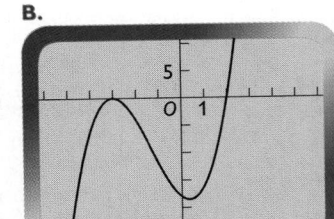

C.

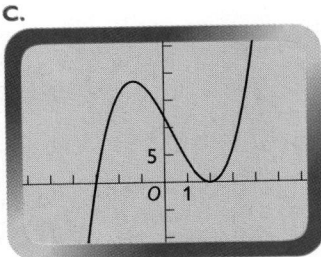

Sample Response

Problem Solving Strategy: Break the problem into parts.

Step 1 Find the x-intercepts of the graph of each function.

a. $0 = (x - 2)^2(x + 3)$
2 and −3

b. $0 = -(x - 2)^2(x + 3)$
2 and −3

c. $0 = (x - 2)(x + 3)^2$
2 and −3

In this case, all three functions cross the x-axis at $x = 2$ and at $x = -3$.

Step 2 Find any double or triple zeros.

All three functions have a squared factor, so all three functions have a double zero.

a. $0 = (x - 2)^2(x + 3)$
2 is a double zero.

b. $0 = -(x - 2)^2(x + 3)$
2 is a double zero.

c. $0 = (x - 2)(x + 3)^2$
−3 is a double zero.

The only graph that has a double zero of −3 is B.
Graph B matches function (c).

Step 3 Decide if the graph of the function starts above or below the x-axis.
Choose an x-coordinate to the left of the smallest x-intercept as a test point.

a. $y = (x - 2)^2(x + 3)$
$= (-4 - 2)^2(-4 + 3)$
$= -36$

The smallest x-intercept is −3. Substitute −4 for x in each function.

b. $y = -(x - 2)^2(x + 3)$
$= -(-4 - 2)^2(-4 + 3)$
$= 36$

The y-value of function (a) is negative. The graph starts below the x-axis.

Graph C matches function (a).

The y-value of function (b) is positive. The graph starts above the x-axis.

Graph A matches function (b).

Unit 9 Polynomial and Rational Functions

1. In Sample 1, why can you match graph B with function (c) before you complete step 3?

2. In Sample 1, the y-value of function (a) is negative when $x = -4$. How do you know that all the y-values are negative for x-values less than -3?

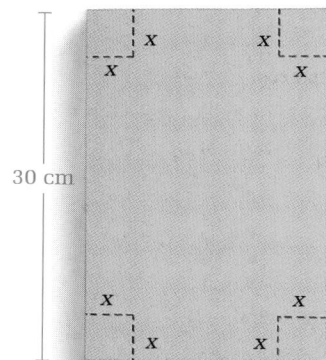

— 20 cm —

30 cm

Sample 2

A box can be made from a rectangular piece of cardboard by cutting a square off of each corner. About how much should be cut off of each corner of the cardboard shown to make a box with the largest volume?

Sample Response

Problem Solving Strategy: Use a graph.

Let x = the length of the square that is cut off of each corner. Write a function for the volume of the box in terms of x.

$$V = x(30 - 2x)(20 - 2x) \quad \longleftarrow \quad \text{Volume} = \text{length} \times \text{width} \times \text{height}$$

Graph the function.

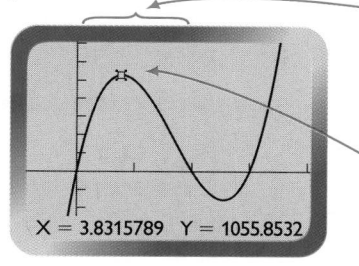

X = 3.8315789   Y = 1055.8532

You can only cut between 0 and 10 cm off of any corner. Trace the graph across this domain.

The maximum y-value represents the largest volume. It occurs when $x \approx 3.8$.

Cut a square about 3.8 cm × 3.8 cm off of each corner of the cardboard.

Look Back

What does the factored form of a cubic function tell you about its graph? What information do you need to find before you can sketch the graph of a function in factored form?

▶ Now you are ready for:
Exs. 17–44 on pp. 532–535

9-4 Graphing Cubic Functions

531

Answers to Talk it Over

1. It is the only graph that has a double zero of −3.

2. For all values of x less than −3, $x + 3$ is negative and $(x − 2)^2$ is positive. The product of a negative number and a positive number is always a negative number.

Answers to Look Back

The factored form tells you where the graph intersects the x-axis and whether there is a double or triple zero at that point. You need to know the x-intercepts and y-intercept; which points, if any, touch the x-axis but do not cross it; and whether the graph starts above or below the x-axis; the maximum and minimum points of the graph.

Reasoning

Ask students to suppose they had to sketch the graphs of the functions in Sample 1 using paper and pencil. What information would they find valuable?

Additional Sample

S2 Suppose a box is made from a 30 cm square piece of cardboard by cutting a square off at each corner. About how much should be cut off of each corner of the cardboard to make a box with the largest volume?
Let x = the length of the square that is cut off of each corner.
$V = x(30 − 2x)(30 − 2x)$
Graph the function.

Note that x must be between 0 and 15. Trace across this domain to the maximum point (5, 2000). Cut a 5 × 5 square from each corner.

Teaching Tip

The number of times a graph changes direction *can be* an indication of the degree of its function. In general, this number is one less than the degree of the function. For example, the graph of a line never changes direction and has degree one. The graph of a quadratic function changes direction once and has degree two. This is always true for linear and quadratic functions. However, it is not always true for functions of degree three or higher. The graph of a cubic function may never change direction, change direction once, or change direction twice.

Look Back

Students may need to refer to the chart on page 529 and Sample 1 on page 530 to answer these questions.

531

APPLYING

Suggested Assignment

Day 1

Standard 2–16

Extended 1–16

Day 2

Standard 17–22, 26, 30–44

Extended 17–22, 26, 30–44

Integrating the Strands

Algebra Exs. 1–36, 40–44

Functions Exs. 1–36, 40–44

Geometry Exs. 27, 28, 37–39

Discrete Mathematics
Exs. 34–36

Logic and Language Exs. 1, 17–22, 33, 43

Communication: Reading

Ex. 1 can be used to check students' understanding of the definition of a cubic function. Exs. 11–16 can be used to do the same for linear, quadratic, and cubic functions.

Answers to
Exercises and Problems

1. Expand the factored form to show that the highest power of x is 3. Answers may vary. Example: $y = x^3 - 2x^2 + 5x + 1$

2. **a.** twice
   b. $x = 0$, $x = 4$
   c. 0 and 4; 4 is a double zero.

3. **a.** once
   b. $x = -3$
   c. -3; -3 is a triple zero.

4. **a.** three times
   b. $x = -3$, $x = 1$, and $x = 5$
   c. -3, 1, and 5; no multiple zeros

5. **a.** once
   b. $x = -8$
   c. -8; -8 is a triple zero.

6. **a.** three times
   b. $x = -2$, $x = 3$, and $x = -1$
   c. -2, 3, and -1; no multiple zeros

7. **a.** twice
   b. $x = 1$ and $x = -4$
   c. 1 and -4; 1 is a double zero.

8. **a.** twice
   b. $x = -5$ and $x = 2$

532

1. **Reading** How could you verify that the functions listed in the Exploration are cubic functions? Give an example of a cubic function that is not written in factored form.

For Exercises 2–10:

a. Tell how many times the graph of each function intersects the *x*-axis.

b. List the *x*-intercepts.

c. List the zeros of the function. Tell which, if any, are double or triple zeros.

2. $y = -x(x - 4)^2$ 3. $y = (x + 3)^3$ 4. $y = (x + 3)(x - 1)(x - 5)$

5. $y = (x + 8)^3$ 6. $y = (x + 2)(x - 3)(x + 1)$ 7. $y = (x - 1)^2(x + 4)$

8. $y = (x + 5)(x - 2)(x + 5)$ 9. $y = (x - 7)(x + 4)^2$ 10. $y = x^2(x + 2)$

Classify each function as *linear*, *quadratic*, or *cubic*.

11. $y = (x - 4)^2$ 12. $y = x^3 + 2x^2 - 3x + 1$ 13. $y = 3x - 5$

14. $y = (x + 2)(x - 3)(x + 1)$ 15. $y = -3x^2 + 8x - 2$ 16. $y = 3(x + 2)$

Match each function with its graph.

17. $y = x(x - 4)^2$ 18. $y = x^2(x - 4)$ 19. $y = (x - 1)(x + 4)^2$

20. $y = (x - 1)^2(x + 4)$ 21. $y = (x + 4)^3$ 22. $y = (x - 1)(x + 4)(x + 1)$

A.
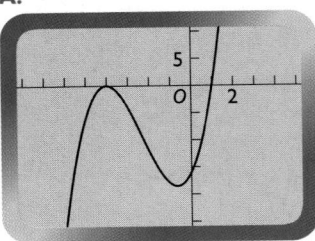

B.
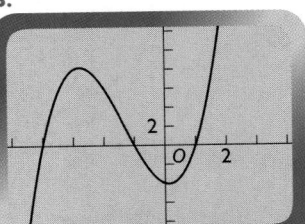

C.
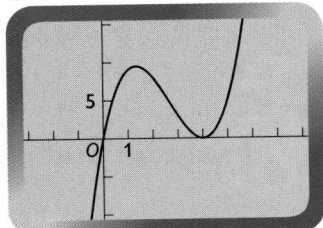

D.
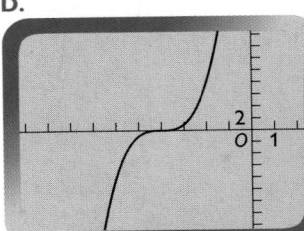

E.
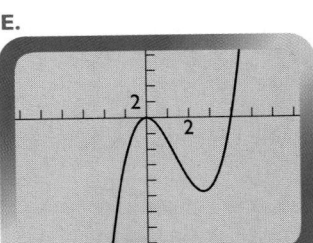

F.
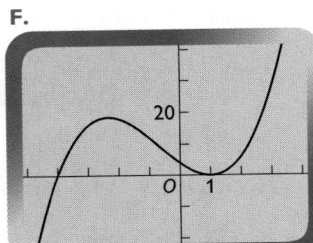

c. -5 and 2; -5 is a double zero.

9. **a.** twice
   b. $x = 7$ and $x = -4$
   c. 7 and -4; -4 is a double zero.

10. **a.** twice
    b. $x = 0$ and $x = -2$
    c. 0 and -2; 0 is a double zero.

11. quadratic   12. cubic

13. linear   14. cubic

15. quadratic   16. linear

17. C   18. E

19. A   20. F

21. D   22. B

23. The graph crosses the *x*-axis at -5, -2, and 0.

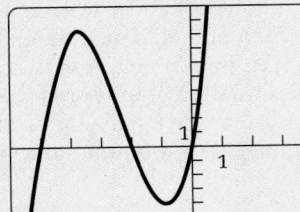

24. The graph crosses the *x*-axis at -3 and touches the *x*-axis at 3.

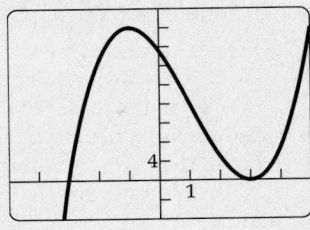

TECHNOLOGY For each function, predict the shape of its graph. Make a sketch of each prediction. Check your prediction using a graphics calculator or graphing software.

23. $y = x(x + 5)(x + 2)$ 24. $y = (x + 3)(x - 3)^2$ 25. $y = (x - 4)^3$

26. Michael and Kira each use a different method to determine whether the graph of $y = x(x - 3)(x + 12)$ starts above or below the x-axis.

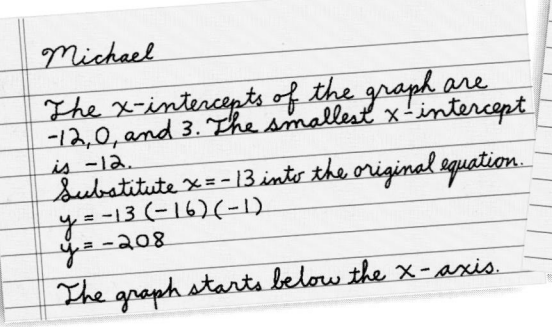

Michael

The x-intercepts of the graph are $-12, 0,$ and 3. The smallest x-intercept is -12.
Substitute $x = -13$ into the original equation.
$y = -13(-16)(-1)$
$y = -208$
The graph starts below the x-axis.

Kira

Since each factor of $y = x(x-3)(x+12)$ is negative for x-values smaller than -12, the graph starts below the x-axis.
$(negative) \times (negative) \times (negative) =$ a negative y-value.

a. Describe each person's method.

b. Which method do you think is easier? Why?

27. **Group Activity** Work with another student. You will need a graphics calculator.

a. Each of you should write down three numbers to represent the length, width, and height of a box. Multiply the three numbers to find the volume of the box.

b. Let w = the width of the box. Write expressions in terms of w for the length and height. Write a function in terms of w for the volume of the box.

c. Give your partner the volume you found in part (a) and the function you wrote in part (b). Graph the function you receive on a graphics calculator. What do the x-values represent? What do the y-values represent?

d. What part of your graph from part (c) applies to the volume of a box? Explain.

e. Use your graph to find the dimensions your partner wrote down in part (a). Check your answers with each other. Discuss any differences.

9-4 Graphing Cubic Functions   **533**

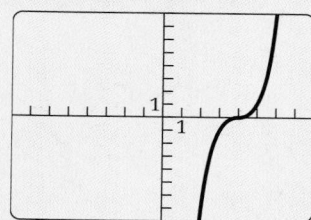
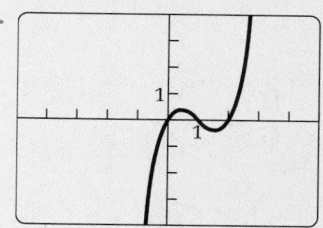

Reasoning

In Ex. 29, students explore the idea that the graph of a cubic function will always begin and end at opposite ends of the y-axis. In other words, if the graph begins below the x-axis, it will end above the x-axis; if it begins above the x-axis, it will end below the x-axis. This is true because its degree is odd. Any function with an odd degree will exhibit this behavior. Any function with an even degree will have a graph that begins and ends at the same end of the y-axis.

Communication: Drawing

Exs. 30–33 illustrate the correlation between the x-intercepts and zeros of a function to the degree of the function. Students should understand that, in general, the greatest number of possible real solutions is equal to the degree of the equation.

Answers to
Exercises and Problems

28. a.
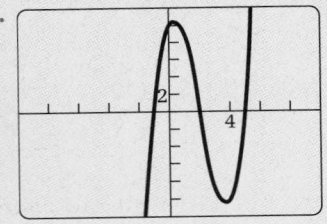

b. $x = -1$, $x = 2$, and $x = 5$

c. $V \approx 10.4$; $x \approx 0.3$

29. a.
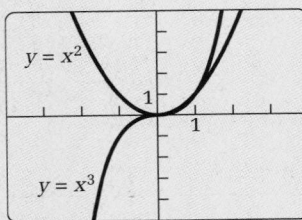

Summaries may vary. An example is given. In the first quadrant, the graphs are very similar. However, the graph of $y = x^2$ is a parabola contained within Quadrants I and II, while the graph of $y = x^3$ is an S-shaped curve contained within Quadrants I and III.

534

---

28 TECHNOLOGY The volume of a box is represented by the function $V = x^3 - 6x^2 + 3x + 10$, where x represents the length of the square that should be cut from each corner of a rectangular piece of cardboard to form the box.

   a. Use a graphics calculator to graph the function. Make a sketch of the graph.

   b. What are the x-intercepts of the graph?

   c. Use the graph to estimate the box's largest possible volume. What is the length of the square that should be cut from each corner to get the largest volume for the box?

29 TECHNOLOGY Use a graphics calculator or graphing software.

   a. Graph the functions $y = x^2$ and $y = x^3$. How are the graphs of the functions alike? How are they different?

   b. Graph each of the functions $y = x^4$, $y = x^5$, $y = x^6$, and $y = x^7$ on the same axes. Describe the similarities and differences among the graphs. Which ones are most alike?

   c. What do you think the graph of $y = x^{15}$ will look like? What about $y = x^{16}$? Graph the functions to check your predictions.

Ongoing ASSESSMENT

30. For each type of function, tell if a graph of this type can have only one x-intercept. If so, sketch a graph of that type through the x-intercept shown. If not, explain why not.

   a. linear function

   b. quadratic function

   c. cubic function

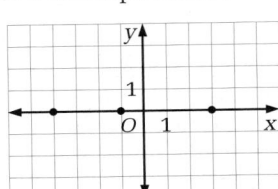

31. Repeat Exercise 30 for a graph having only the two x-intercepts shown.

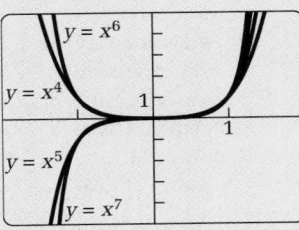

32. Repeat Exercise 30 for a graph having only the three x-intercepts shown.

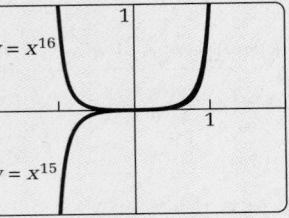

33. **Writing** How does the degree of a function relate to the number of zeros? to the possible number of x-intercepts? Explain your reasoning.

Review PREVIEW

Solve. *(Section 9-3)*

34. $\dfrac{5x + 2}{x + 7} = \dfrac{6x}{x + 7}$

35. $\dfrac{6}{t} - \dfrac{2}{t - 1} = 1$

36. $\dfrac{4}{x + 1} + \dfrac{1}{x - 2} = 2$

534   **Unit 9** Polynomial and Rational Functions

---

b.
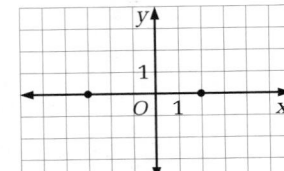

Summaries may vary. An example is given. In the first quadrant, all four graphs are very similar. The graphs of the equations with even exponents are nearly identical U-shaped curves contained within Quadrants I and II. The graphs of the functions with odd exponents are nearly identical S-shaped curves contained within Quadrants I and III.

c. The graph of $y = x^{15}$ will be an S-shaped curve contained within Quadrants I and III. The graph of $y = x^{16}$ will be a U-shaped curve contained within Quadrants I and II.

Complete each sentence so that it is a true statement. Be as specific as possible. *(Section 5-1)*

37. Every rectangle is also a _?_.

38. All _?_ are also rhombuses.

39. If a quadrilateral is a _?_, then it is also a kite.

Use the quadratic formula to find the solutions of each equation. *(Section 4-5)*

40. $-2x^2 + 5x + 3 = 0$

41. $x^2 - 3x + 3 = 0$

42. $6x^2 + 11x = 10$

 Working on the Unit Project

Less than 60% of the wind's power can actually be converted to energy. Other factors, such as turbine design, further reduce the amount of energy produced. The equation $P = 0.25s^3$ can be used to estimate the speed of the wind, s, in miles per hour, needed to generate P watts of power for a wind machine that uses 25% of the available wind power.

43. **a.** Graph the function $P = 0.25s^3$.

   b. Explain why some portions of the graph do not apply to this situation.

   c. What values of s are reasonable for this situation?

44. Estimate the wind speed needed to operate each of these items.

   a. a radio that needs 70 watts of power

   b. a clock that needs 5 watts of power

   c. an electric oven that needs about 3200 watts of power

   d. a home heating system that needs about 12,000 watts of power

The students and faculty at the Tvind School in Denmark built one of the world's largest wind turbines. The Tvind machine provides enough power to supply the school with its electrical and heating needs.

9-4 Graphing Cubic Functions

535

Answers to Exercises and Problems

30. a. Yes. Example: $y = x + 2$

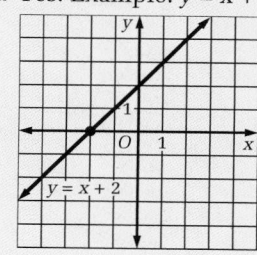

b. Yes. Example: $y = (x + 2)^2$

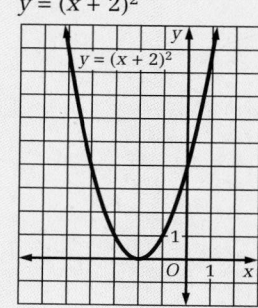

c. Yes. Example: $y = (x + 2)^3$

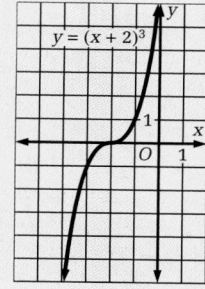

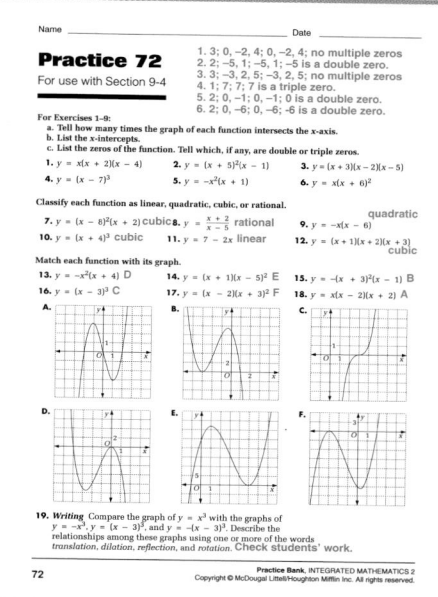
31. a. No linear function has two x-intercepts.

   b. Yes. Example: $y = (x + 3)(x - 2)$

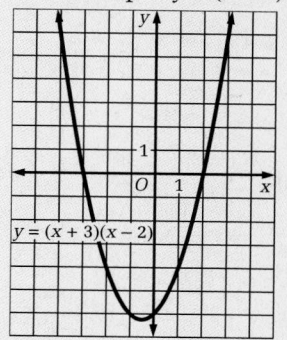

   c. Yes. Example: $y = (x - 2)^2(x + 3)$

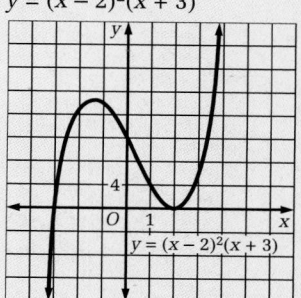

32–44. See answers at back of book.

535

Objectives and Strands
See pages 502A and 502B.

Spiral Learning
See page 502B.

Materials List
➤ Graphics calculator

Recommended Pacing
Section 9-5 is a one-day lesson.

Extra Practice
See pages 628–629.

Warm-Up Exercises
Warm-Up Transparency 9-5

Support Materials
➤ Practice 73
➤ Enrichment 65 in the Activity Bank
➤ Study Guide 9-5
➤ Problem Set 21
➤ Additional Exploration 12
Overhead Visual 9
➤ McDougal Littell Mathpack software: *Function Investigator*
➤ Using Plotter Plus: Approximating Roots of Polynomial Equations
➤ Quiz 9-5

Section 9-5

Focus
Solve cubic equations by various methods.

Solving Cubic Equations

Light the Way

Many public buildings have battery-operated emergency lights that go on automatically during a power failure. There is always a chance that an emergency light may fail to work. Because of this, most rooms contain two or more emergency lights.

BY THE WAY...

A faulty setting at an electrical plant near Niagara Falls has twice resulted in a blackout of the Northeastern United States and Ontario, Canada. The only lights seen in the normally bright city skylines were from cars or lights operating on emergency systems.

Talk it Over

1. Let p = the probability that each emergency light will work. What is the probability that a light will not work?

2. In a room with three emergency lights, what is the probability that all three lights will not work?

3. Find the complement of the probability you wrote in question 2. What does the complement represent?

4. The reliability of a set of three emergency lights is given by the equation $r = 1 - (1 - p)^3$. Expand the right side of the equation to write a polynomial function to represent the reliability of the lighting system.

536   **Unit 9** Polynomial and Rational Functions

Answers to Talk it Over

1. $1 - p$

2. $(1 - p)^3$

3. $1 - (1 - p)^3$; the probability that at least one light will work

4. $p^3 - 3p^2 + 3p$

Sample 1

Suppose a building inspector requires an emergency lighting system to be 98% reliable. How reliable does each light need to be?

Sample Response

Problem Solving Strategy: Use a graph.

Use the expanded polynomial function you wrote in question 4 on page 536.

$r = p^3 - 3p^2 + 3p$

$0.98 = p^3 - 3p^2 + 3p$ ← The system needs to be 98% reliable.

$0 = p^3 - 3p^2 + 3p - 0.98$ ← Write the equation in standard form.

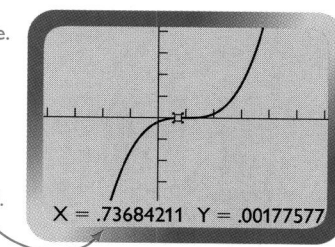

Graph the related function $y = x^3 - 3x^2 + 3x - 0.98$.
The x-intercept tells you the value of x when y is zero.

The x-intercept is about 0.74.

X = .73684211   Y = .00177577

Each light needs to be at least 74% reliable.

Sample 2

Solve $0 = p^3 - 3p^2 + 3p$.

Sample Response

$0 = p^3 - 3p^2 + 3p$

$0 = p(p^2 - 3p + 3)$ ← Factor out a p from each term.

$p = 0$ or $p^2 - 3p + 3 = 0$ ← Use the zero-product property.

$p = -\dfrac{b}{2a} \pm \dfrac{\sqrt{b^2 - 4ac}}{2a}$ ← Use the quadratic formula.

$= -\dfrac{(-3)}{2(1)} \pm \dfrac{\sqrt{(-3)^2 - 4(1)(3)}}{2(1)}$ ← Substitute **1** for a, -3 for b, and **3** for c.

$= \dfrac{3}{2} \pm \dfrac{\sqrt{-3}}{2}$

$= 1.5 \pm \dfrac{i\sqrt{3}}{2}$

$p \approx 1.5 + 0.87i$ or $p \approx 1.5 - 0.87i$

The solutions are 0, about $1.5 + 0.9i$, and about $1.5 - 0.9i$.

9-5 Solving Cubic Equations

537

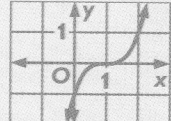

Talk it Over

5. All coordinates in an x-y *coordinate plane* are real numbers. Suppose you solved the equation in Sample 2 by graphing. Would you find all the solutions? Why or why not?

6. How can you solve the equation $x^3 + 3x^2 + 2x = 0$ without using a graph or the quadratic formula?

Look Back

How can you tell if you can use the zero-product property to solve a cubic equation?

9-5 Exercises and Problems

1. **Reading** Explain why the zero-product property could not be used to solve the equation in Sample 1.

Solve each equation without graphing.

2. $x^3 - 5x^2 + 6x = 0$

3. $x^3 + 2x^2 + 2x = 0$

4. $(x - 1)(x + 3)(3x - 1) = 0$

5. $x^3 + 3x^2 - 4x = 0$

6. $x^3 - 4x = 0$

7. $(x + 6)(x - 2)^2 = 0$

8. **Writing** Andrew solved the equation $x^3 - x^2 - 2x = 1$. Explain what is wrong with his solution.

If possible, factor and solve each equation *without graphing*. If it is not possible, write *solve by graphing*.

9. $x^3 + x + 2 = 0$

10. $x^3 + 7x^2 + 10x = 0$

11. $x^3 + 2x^2 - 3x = 1$

12. $x^3 - 2x^2 + 4x = 0$

13. $x^4 - 2x^3 - 15x^2 = 0$

14. $x^3 + x^2 = -4$

15. The equation $r = p^3 - 3p^2 + 3p$ can be used to find the reliability of a system of three lights. Micah wants to find the reliability of each light, p, when the system is 75% reliable.

   a. Write an equation in standard form to represent the situation.

   b. **Writing** Micah entered $y = x^3 - 3x^2 + 3x - 0.75$ on her graphics calculator. Explain how she can use the graph of this function to estimate p when $r = 0.75$.

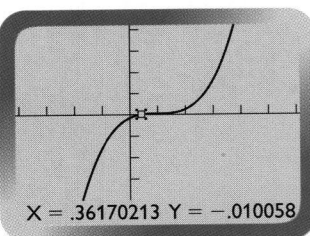

X = .36170213   Y = −.010058

You've made a serious mistake here. Let's talk! — Andrew Rose

$x^3 - x^2 - 2x = 1$
$x(x^2 - x - 2) = 1$
$x(x - 2)(x + 1) = 1$
$x = 1$ or $x - 2 = 1$ or $x + 1 = 1$
$x = 1$ or $x = 3$ or $x = 0$

Check $x = 1$:
$1^3 - 1^2 - 2(1) \stackrel{?}{=} 1$
$-2 \neq 1$

Check $x = 3$:
$3^3 - 3^2 - 6 \stackrel{?}{=} 1$
$12 \neq 1$

Check $x = 0$:
$0^3 - 0^2 - 2(0) \stackrel{?}{=} 1$
$0 \neq 1$

Unit 9 Polynomial and Rational Functions

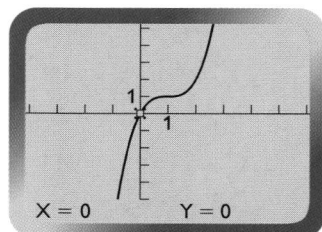

X = 0   Y = 0

16. Writing Rebecca tried to solve the equation in Sample 2 by using a graphics calculator. Describe the steps you think she followed.

17. In Sample 2 on page 506, Kia needs to find an investment that offers a yearly growth rate, g, so that $1000g^3 + 1000g^2 + 1000g = 3500$.

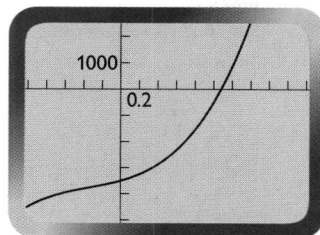

1000

0.2

a. Write an equation in standard form to represent the situation.

b. Use the graph of the related function at the right to estimate g.

18. TECHNOLOGY The yearly profits for the Zavala family restaurant can be modeled by this equation:

$$y = -0.00135x^3 + 0.0125x^2 + 412x - 12{,}225$$

The average number of customers per month is represented by x and the profit for the year is represented by y.

a. About how many customers need to visit the restaurant each month in order for the restaurant to break even (profit = 0)?

b. About how many customers does the restaurant need each month to make a $50,000 profit for the year?

19. The numbers 1, 4, 10, and 20 are called *tetrahedral numbers* because they are related to shapes called *tetrahedrons*.

1 dot

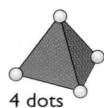
4 dots

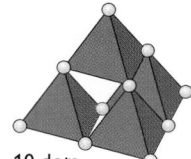
10 dots

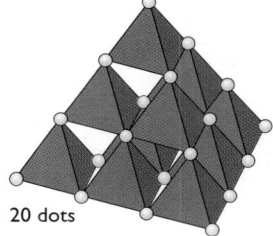
20 dots

a. Count the number of dots on the base of each group of tetrahedrons. Any face can be the base. Look for a pattern. How many dots do you think there will be on the base of the fifth tetrahedron?

b. How many dots in all do you think will be in the fifth tetrahedron?

c. The formula $t = \frac{1}{6}n^3 + \frac{1}{2}n^2 + \frac{1}{3}n$ can be used to find the nth tetrahedral number. Use the formula to check your prediction from part (b).

d. TECHNOLOGY Use a graphics calculator to decide if 100 is a tetrahedral number. If so, what is n?

9-5 Solving Cubic Equations

539

Assessment: Standard

By examining their results in Exs. 2–14, students should be able to write a generalization describing when a cubic equation can be solved by factoring or by graphing.

Integrating the Strands

Ex. 15, as well as previous work in this section on the reliability of a set of emergency lights, integrates the strands of algebra, geometry, and statistics and probability.

Research

For Ex. 19, students may want to research the uses of tetrahedrons in different areas of study. Students should first define a tetrahedron, and then research, for example, how they serve as mathematical models in other sciences such as chemistry.

Students may also be interested in researching the life of Ada Lovelace (1815–1852) who analyzed patterns to better understand how the *Difference Engine*—one of the first calculators—worked. After analyzing patterns, she was able to predict that the function for the nth tetrahedral number is a cubic.

Using Technology

In Ex. 19, n is the number of dots on the base of the tetrahedron. To solve part (d), students can use a graphics calculator. For the TI-82 or TI-83, build a table. Press $\boxed{Y=}$ and enter Y1=(1/6)X³+ (1/2)X² + (1/3)X. On the TI-82, press $\boxed{2nd}$ [TblSet] and use TblMin=1, ΔTbl=1. On the TI-83, press $\boxed{2nd}$ [TblSet] and use TblStart=1, ΔTbl=1. Press $\boxed{2nd}$ [TABLE] and examine the tetrahedral numbers displayed in the Y1-column to see if 100 is among them.

For the TI-81, graph the related equation $y = \frac{1}{6}x^3 + \frac{1}{2}x^2 + \frac{1}{3}x - 100$. Use ZOOM and TRACE to see if the x-intercept is a positive integer.

539

Answers to Exercises and Problems

1. The expression $p^3 - 3p^2 + 3p - 0.98$ cannot be written as a product of linear factors.

2. 0, 2, 3

3. $0, -1 + i, -1 - i$

4. $1, -3, \frac{1}{3}$

5. 0, −4, 1

6. 0, 2, −2

7. −6, 2

8. Andrew used a method erroneously based on the zero-product property. He assumed that if the product of two numbers is equal to one, then at least one of the numbers is one.

9. Solve by graphing.

10. 0, −5, −2

11. Solve by graphing.

12. 0, about $1 - 1.7i$, about $1 + 1.7i$

13. 0, 5, −3

14. Solve by graphing.

15. a. $0 = p^3 - 3p^2 + 3p - 0.75$

b. The x-intercept on Micah's graph is the value of p when $r = 0.75$, so she can estimate the value of the x-intercept. $p \approx 0.4$.

16–19. See answers in back of book.

Working on the Unit Project

You may wish to provide each group with a copy of the table in Ex. 28 to help them organize their work. Students can then complete Ex. 28 as a group activity.

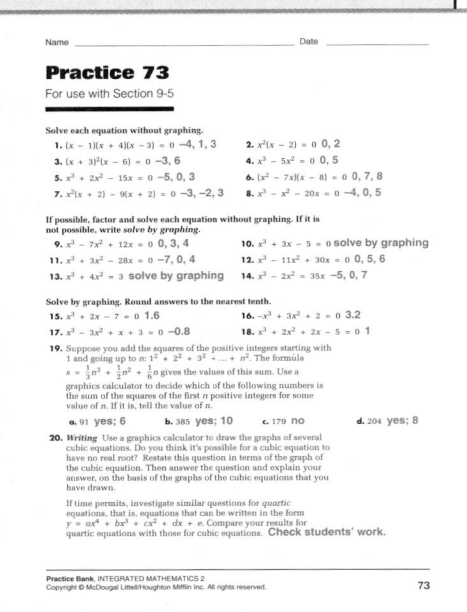
Answers to
Exercises and Problems

20. Summaries may vary. An example is given. To solve by graphing, graph the related function $y = x^3 - x^2 - 6x$ and find the x-intercepts. You can also factor the left side as $x(x - 3)(x + 2)$ and use the zero-product property.

21. −1 and −3; −3 is a double zero.

22. 0, 2, and −3; no multiple zeros

23. −5; −5 is a triple zero.

24. No; the conditional "If $(x - 1)(x + 2) = 0$, then $x = 1$" is not true since x can also be −2.

25. $t = \frac{x}{2} - 2$

26. $t = \frac{y}{2} + 2$

27. $t = 9 - \frac{x}{2}$

540

---

20. **Writing** Write a note to someone who missed class explaining how to solve the equation $x^3 - x^2 - 6x = 0$. Describe two methods, one of which uses graphing.

List the zeros of each cubic function. Tell which, if any, are double or triple zeros. (Section 9-4)

21. $y = (x + 1)(x + 3)^2$ 22. $y = x(x - 2)(x + 3)$ 23. $y = (x + 5)^3$

24. Is this statement a true biconditional? Explain why or why not. (Section 7-4)

$(x - 1)(x + 2) = 0$ if and only if $x = 1$.

Solve each equation for t. (Toolbox Skill 15)

25. $x = 2(t + 2)$ 26. $y = 2t - 4$ 27. $x = -2(t - 1) + 16$

Working on the Unit Project

The power created by some wind turbines can be modeled by the equation
$$P = 0.2s(V - s)^2$$
where s = the blade speed in feet per second,
V = the wind speed in feet per second, and
P = the power in kilowatts (kW).

28. **a.** Copy the table. Multiply each wind speed by 1.47 to convert the units from mi/h to ft/s. Then write the equation for each wind speed.

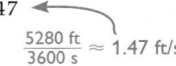
$\dfrac{5280 \text{ ft}}{3600 \text{ s}} \approx 1.47$ ft/s

Wind speed (mi/h)	Wind speed (ft/s)	Function $P = 0.2s(V - s)^2$	Maximum Power (kW)
5	7.35	$P = 0.2s(7.35 - s)^2$	?
8	?	?	?
10	?	?	?
14	?	?	?

b. Find the zeros for each function you wrote in part (a). What do they represent in this situation?

c. Graph each function in part (a). Find the maximum amount of power this type of wind machine can generate at each speed. Complete the last column of the chart.

d. Approximate the wind speed needed for this type of wind turbine to supply all the electricity for your group's typical household.

e. Do you think this type of wind turbine is a practical alternative to buying electricity from the power company in your area? Why or why not?

540   **Unit 9** Polynomial and Rational Functions

This Savonius rotor has S-shaped blades that are made with split oil drums.

---

28. **a, c.**

Wind speed (mi/h)	Wind speed (ft/s)	Function $P = 0.2s(V - s)^2$	Maximum power (kW)
5	7.35	$P = 0.2s(7.35 - s)^2$	about 11.8
8	11.76	$P = 0.2s(11.76 - s)^2$	about 48.2
10	14.7	$P = 0.2s(14.7 - s)^2$	about 94.1
14	20.58	$P = 0.2s(20.58 - s)^2$	about 258.3

b. 5 mi/h: 0 and 7.35; 8 mi/h: 0 and 11.76; 10 mi/h: 0 and 14.7; 14 mi/h: 0 and 20.58; the wind speeds at which no power is produced

c. Check students' graphs.

d. Check students' work.

e. Answers may vary.

Focus

Graph parametric equations to solve problems.

Parametric Equations

time travel

EXPLORATION

Why *does the path of a thrown ball look like a parabola?*

* **Materials: graphics calculators**
* **Work with another student.**

TECHNOLOGY NOTE

Choose parametric and simultaneous modes.

Use $0 \leq t \leq 1.2$ and increments of 0.1 for the *t*-values.

Use $0 \leq x \leq 7.6$ and increments of 0.8 for the *x*-values.

Use $-1.6 \leq y \leq 3.44$ and increments of 0.8 for the *y*-values.

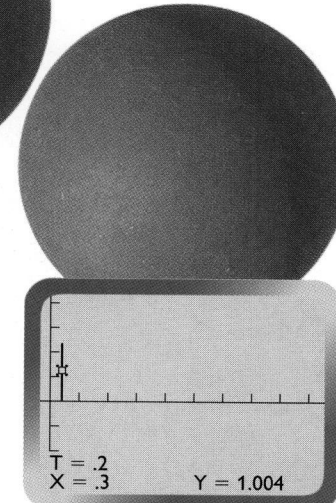

T = .2
X = .3   Y = 1.004

① To model tossing a ball straight up, graph $x_1 = 0.3$ and $y_1 = 6t - 4.9t^2$ on a graphics calculator. The *y*-values represent the height of the ball, in meters, *t* seconds after being tossed.

② Trace along the graph to see the path of the ball. Record the values for *t* and *y* in a table.

③ A ball rolling along the ground moves forward at a constant speed as long as nothing slows it down. Model rolling a ball by graphing $x_2 = 0.3 + 6t$ and $y_2 = 0.1$. Trace along the graph to see the path of the ball. Record the values for *t* and *x* in a table.

④ When a ball is tossed at an angle, two things happen:

➤ Gravity pulls the ball toward Earth.
➤ The ball moves forward at a constant speed.

Model throwing a ball at an angle by graphing $x_3 = 0.3 + 6t$ and $y_3 = 6t - 4.9t^2$. Trace along the graph to make a table of values for *t*, *x*, and *y*.

⑤ In step 4, the calculator graphs the path of the ball by using *t* to find *x* and *y*. To find *y* in terms of *x*, solve the equation $x = 0.3 + 6t$ for *t* and substitute your result into $y = 6t - 4.9t^2$. What kind of equation do you get?

⑥ Put your calculator in function mode. Graph your equation from step 5. How is this graph like the one you made in step 4? How is it different?

9-6 Parametric Equations

541

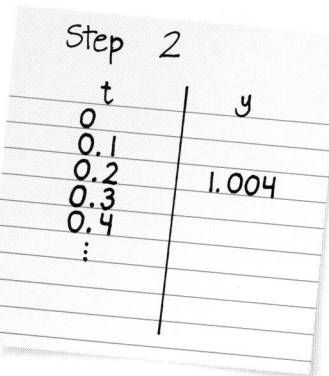

Step 2

t	y
0	
0.1	
0.2	1.004
0.3	
0.4	
...	

PLANNING

Objectives and Strands
See pages 502A and 502B.

Spiral Learning
See page 502B.

Materials List
➤ Graphics calculator

Recommended Pacing
Section 9-6 is a two-day lesson.
Day 1
Pages 541–542: Exploration through top of page 542, *Exercises 1–8*
Day 2
Pages 542–544: Sample 1 through Look Back, *Exercises 9–27*

Extra Practice
See pages 628–629.

Warm-Up Exercises
Warm-Up Transparency 9-6

Support Materials
➤ Practice 74
➤ Enrichment 66 in the Activity Bank
➤ Study Guide 9-6
➤ Problem Set 21
➤ Diagram Master 21 in the Explorations Lab Manual
➤ McDougal Littell Mathpack software: *Function Investigator*
➤ Using TI-81 and TI-82 Calculators: Shooting Baskets Using Parametric Equations
➤ Quiz 9-6
➤ Test 38

Answers to Exploration

1. Check students' graphs.

2.

t	y	t	y
0	0	0.7	1.799
0.1	0.551	0.8	1.664
0.2	1.004	0.9	1.431
0.3	1.359	1.0	1.1
0.4	1.616	1.1	0.671
0.5	1.775	1.2	0.144
0.6	1.836		

3.

t	x	t	x
0	0.3	0.7	4.5
0.1	0.9	0.8	5.1
0.2	1.5	0.9	5.7
0.3	2.1	1.0	6.3
0.4	2.7	1.1	6.9
0.5	3.3	1.2	7.5
0.6	3.9		

4. See answers in back of book.

5. quadratic

6. They are the same graph except the graph from the equation in step 5 also graphs values for *x* and *y* that cannot be used to represent or solve the problem. The graph in step 5 describes the ball's height above the ground as a function of the horizontal distance from the point where the ball was thrown.

Exploration

The goal of this Exploration is to introduce students to the concept of a parameter and how it can be used to write and graph parametric equations.

In step 1, notice that the equation for x_1 does not contain t. The ball is tossed straight up, so only its vertical position changes. In step 2, y_2 is constant because the ball does not move off the ground. You can think of $x_1 = 3$ as the horizontal distance from the origin of the person tossing the ball. Think of $y_2 = 0.1$ as the distance of the center of the ball above the ground. Discuss what interpretations make sense in step 4.

Additional Samples

S1 Adam Jones is piloting a plane that is dropping supplies to a group of campers in a remote wilderness. They have placed a target on the ground where they want the supplies to land. The path of the supplies is modeled (in meters) by these parametric equations: $x = 125t$ and $y = 110 - 4.9t^2$.

a. How far from the target should the supplies be released?

Method 1. Make a table of values for t, x, and y.

t	$x = 125t$	$y = 110 - 4.9t^2$
0	0	110
1	125	105.1
2	250	90.4
3	375	65.9
4	500	31.6
4.5	562.5	10.77
4.7	587.5	1.76

At $t = 4.7$, the supplies are only 1.76 m above the ground; about 590 m.

Method 2. Graph the parametric equation.

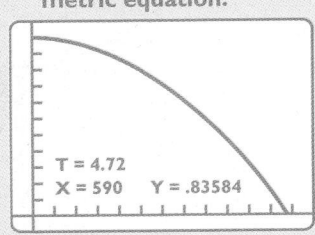

T = 4.72
X = 590   Y = .83584

Sample continued on next page.

▶ Now you are ready for:
Exs. 1–8 on pp. 544–545

The equations $x = 0.3 + 6t$ and $y = 6t - 4.9t^2$ are called **parametric equations** because both x and y are written in terms of a third value, t. The variable t is called the **parameter.**

Sample 1

A warden pilot stocks remote ponds with fish by flying overhead in his plane and dropping the fish into the pond.

The path of the fish is modeled by these parametric equations:

$$x = 120t$$

The horizontal distance from the point of release, in meters, t seconds after the fish are released.

$$y = 80 - 4.9t^2$$

The height off the ground, in meters, t seconds after the fish are released.

a. How far from the center of the pond should the fish be released in order to land in the center?

b. Write an equation for y in terms of x.

Sample Response

a. Method **1**

Make a table of values for t, x, and y. Then find the horizontal distance the fish travel before they enter the water.

t	$x = 120t$	$y = 80 - 4.9t^2$
0	0	80.0
1	120	75.1
2	240	60.4
3	360	35.9
4	480	1.6

At $t = 4$, the fish are only 1.6 m above the water.

Method **2**

Graph the parametric equations. Then trace to estimate the horizontal distance the fish travel before they enter the water.

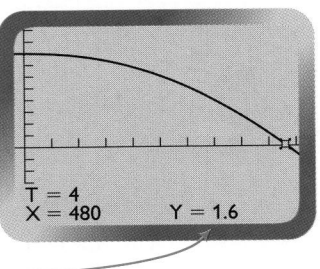

T = 4
X = 480   Y = 1.6

The fish should be released about 480 m from the center of the pond.

b. Solve $x = 120t$ for t.

$x = 120t$

$\dfrac{x}{120} = t$

Then substitute for t in the second equation.

$y = 80 - 4.9t^2$

$y = 80 - 4.9\left(\dfrac{x}{120}\right)^2$ ← Substitute $\dfrac{x}{120}$ for t in $y = 80 - 4.9t^2$.

$y = 80 - 4.9\left(\dfrac{x^2}{14,400}\right)$ ← Use the power of a quotient rule.

$y = 80 - 0.00034x^2$

Unit 9 Polynomial and Rational Functions

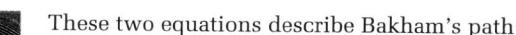
During a football game, Tony held the ball on the 50 yard line while Bakham ran toward the goal line. After waiting 3 s, Tony threw the ball to Bakham.

Let x = the number of yards from the goal line
y = the number of yards from the sideline, and
t = the number of seconds that Bakham has been running.

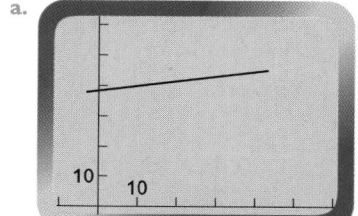

These two equations describe Bakham's path:

$$x_1 = 42 - 6t \qquad\qquad y_1 = 45 - t \qquad\qquad 0 \le t \le 7.5$$

These two equations describe the ball's path as viewed from above:

$$x_2 = 50 - 22(t - 3) \qquad y_2 = 27 + 6(t - 3) \qquad 3 \le t \le 7.5$$

a. Graph Bakham's path.

b. Graph the ball's path as viewed from above.

c. Did Bakham catch the ball? Explain your reasoning. (Assume that the ball would have been at a reasonable height to be caught.)

Sample Response

TECHNOLOGY NOTE

The range for t is $0 \le t \le 7.5$. To graph the second pair of equations for $t \ge 3$, enter $x_2 = 50 - 22(t - 3)(t \ge 3)$, and $y_2 = 27 + 6(t - 3)(t \ge 3)$.

a.
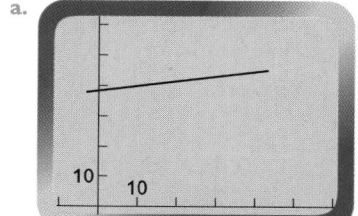

b.
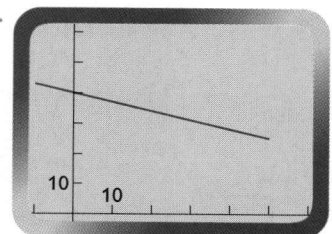

c. Bakham did not catch the ball. Both Bakham and the ball were at the point $x = 6$, $y = 39$, but not at the same time.

The ball was at the point $x = 6$, $y = 39$ 5 s after Bakham began running.

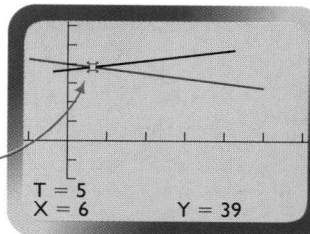

Bakham was not at the point $x = 6$, $y = 39$ until 6 s after he began running.

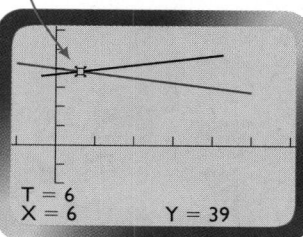

9-6 Parametric Equations

543

---

b. Write the equation for y in terms of x.

Solve $x = 125t$ for t.

$$t = \frac{x}{125}$$

Substitute t in the second equation.

$$y = 110 - 4.9t^2$$
$$= 110 - 4.9\left(\frac{x}{125}\right)^2$$
$$= 110 - 4.9\left(\frac{x^2}{15,625}\right)$$
$$= 110 - 0.0003136x^2$$

S2 During a football game, Ralph was punting for his team. He made a line-drive kick from his own 45 yard line while his teammate Jamaal ran down the field to cover the punt. It took Ralph 1.5 s to catch and punt the ball. Let x = the number of yards from the goal line, y = the number of yards from the sideline, and t = the number of seconds that Jamaal has been running. These two equations describe Jamaal's path: $x_1 = 36 - 6t$ and $y_1 = 45 - 4t$ where $0 \le t \le 6$. These two equations describe the ball's path as viewed from above: $x_2 = 45 - 30(t - 1.5)$ and $y_2 = 27 + 4(t - 1.5)$ where $1.5 \le t \le 6$.

a. Graph Jamaal's path.

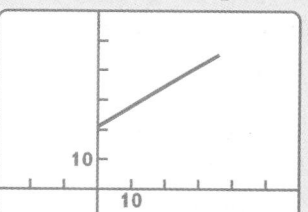

b. Graph the ball's path as viewed from above.

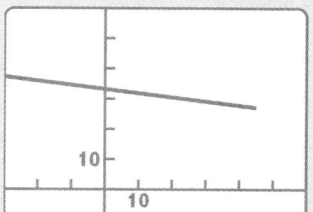

c. Does the ball hit Jamaal as he is going down the field?

No. The ball and Jamaal are at the same place at different times, as shown by the following graphs.

Sample continued on next page.

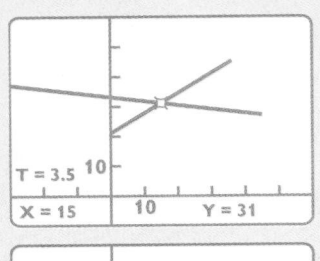

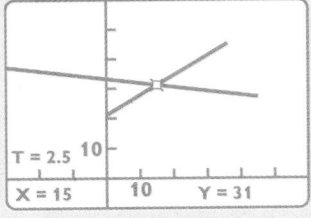

APPLYING

····▶ Now you are ready for:
Exs. 9–27 on pp. 545–548

Look Back ◀

Explain how the path of a ball can be represented by parametric equations using three variables or by a single equation using two variables.

9-6 Exercises and Problems

1. **Reading** What is the control variable and what is the dependent variable for each equation in step 4 of the Exploration?

2. Suppose the path of a ball is described by the parametric equations $x = 7t$ and $y = 4t - 4.9t^2$. These equations are graphed below. Distance is measured in meters.

   a. How high is the ball a half second after it is released?

   b. About how long after the ball is thrown does it hit the ground?

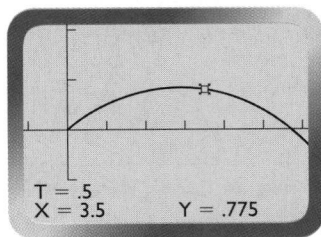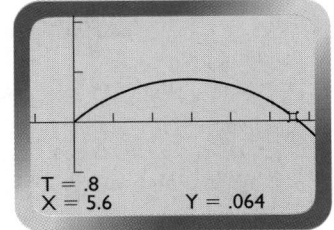

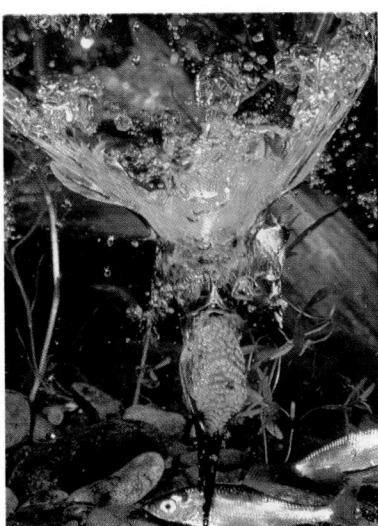

3. **Ornithology** Susan noticed that belted kingfishers pause in midair right before they dive into the water for fish. Susan modeled a bird's path on a calculator. Each interval is 1 m.

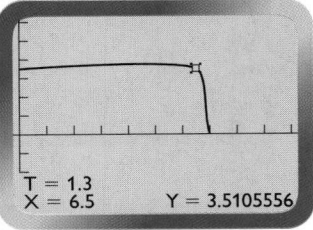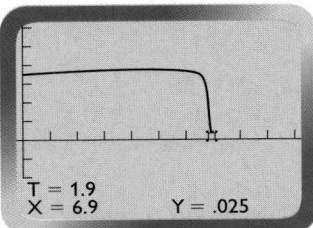

   a. According to Susan's model, how far above the water was the kingfisher when it began to dive?

   b. About how long did this bird fly before diving?

   c. When did the kingfisher enter the water?

4. **Writing** Write a note to someone who missed class. Explain what you learned from the Exploration.

Answers to Look Back ·······⋮

The path can be represented by two parametric equations that describe the horizontal distance from the point where the ball was thrown, *x*, and its height above the ground, *y*, separately as functions of time, *t*. A single equation representing the path describes the ball's height above the ground, *y*, as a function of the horizontal distance from where it was thrown, *x*.

Answers to Exercises and Problems ·················

1. In the first equation, the control variable is *t*, and the dependent variable is *x*. In the second equation, the control variable is *t*, and the dependent variable is *y*.

2. a. about 0.775 m
   b. about 0.8 s

3. a. about 3.5 m
   b. about 1.3 s
   c. about 1.9 s after beginning its flight

4. Summaries may vary. An example is given. The motion of a thrown object can be described by a pair of linear equations called parametric equations that describe the horizontal distance from the point where the object was thrown and the object's height above the ground as functions of time. The motion can also

For Exercises 5–7, write y in terms of x by following these steps:

a. Solve the first equation for t.

b. Substitute your answer to part (a) into the second equation and simplify.

5. $x = 4t - 3; y = 2t$

6. $x = 7t; y = 2t^2 - t + 4$

7. $x = 2 - t; y = \dfrac{t^2 - 1}{t}$

8. a. Graph the parametric equations $x = 1 - t$ and $y = t^3 - 1$.

b. Write an equation for y in terms of x.

9. Wildlife Conservation When a warden pilot drops fish into ponds near mountains, he must fly at a higher altitude to avoid the trees and hills.

The path of the fish can be described by the parametric equations $x = 130t$ and $y = 150 - 4.9t^2$.

a. How far from the center of the pond should the fish be released?

b. About how long are the fish in the air?

10. Football In Sample 2, Tony threw a ball to Bakham.

a. Bakham's path is described by the equations $x = 42 - 6t$ and $y = 45 - t$. How long after Bakham begins running does he cross the goal line?

b. If Tony throws the ball at $t = 3$, the ball's path as viewed from above is described by $x = 50 - 22(t - 3)$ and $y = 27 + 6(t - 3)$. How long after Tony throws the ball does it cross the goal line?

c. How long must Tony wait before throwing the ball if he wants it to cross the goal line when Bakham does? Can Bakham catch it? Why or why not?

11. You can use the parametric equations in Sample 2 to write an equation for y in terms of x. Then Bakham's path is described by $y = 38 + \dfrac{x}{6}$ and the ball's path as viewed from above is described by $y = \dfrac{447}{11} - \dfrac{3x}{11}$.

a. Graph this system of equations.

b. Can you tell from the graph whether Bakham caught the ball? Explain.

c. What does the intersection of the lines represent?

12. a. Aviation Heidi Cohen is flying a small airplane at an altitude of 14,000 ft. When she begins her landing, she descends at a rate of 14 ft/s. Write an equation to model the plane's altitude t seconds after she begins her descent.

b. Heidi is flying at a speed of 200 ft/s. She maintains this horizontal speed for most of her descent. Write an equation to describe the plane's horizontal position t seconds after she begins her descent.

c. Graph your parametric equations from parts (a) and (b).

d. About how far before the airport should Heidi begin her descent?

e. Write an equation for y in terms of x.

9-6 Parametric Equations

545

Answers to Exercises and Problems

be described by a single quadratic equation that describes the object's height above the ground as a function of the horizontal distance from the point where the object was thrown.

5. a. $t = \dfrac{x + 3}{4}$ **b.** $y = \dfrac{x + 3}{2}$

6. a. $t = \dfrac{x}{7}$

b. $y = \dfrac{2x^2}{49} - \dfrac{x}{7} + 4$

7. a. $t = 2 - x$

b. $y = \dfrac{3 - 4x + x^2}{2 - x}$

8. a.

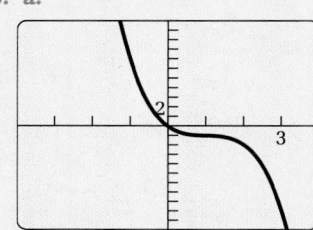

b. $y = -x^3 + 3x^2 - 3x$

9. a. about 719 meters

b. about 5.5 seconds

10–12. See answers in back of book.

Communication: Discussion

Discuss common situations for parameters and how using parametric equations when time is limited is advantageous. Students could also write one or two situations where parameters could be used to model and solve a problem.

Using Technology

If students use a TI-81, TI-82, or TI-83 for Ex. 13, suggest using $0 \le t \le 100$, Tstep=1, $0 \le x \le 3000$, $-1 \le y \le 2$. In part (c), stop from time to time as you trace. Press ▼ several times. Trace until you locate a T-value that results in no horizontal motion of the cursor when you press ▼ repeatedly.

connection to HISTORY

The Pacific Railroad was the first railroad to cross a continent. The Central Pacific Railroad Company and the Union Pacific Railroad Company laid the tracks that met at Promontory Summit, Utah.

13. a. The Central Pacific Railroad began construction in Sacramento in early January, 1863. The workers created an average of about 9 mi of track each month. Write parametric equations to model the construction of the Central Pacific Railroad.

Let x_1 = the number of miles along the track route from Sacramento to the newest end of the track.

Let t = the time, in months, after January 1, 1863.

Let $y_1 = 1$. (A horizontal line raised off the x-axis can represent the track.)

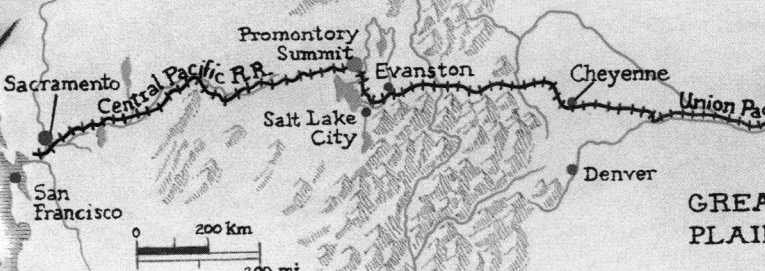

b. The Union Pacific Railroad started regular construction in Omaha 33 months after the Central Pacific Railroad. The workers then created an average of about 25 mi of track each month. Write parametric equations to model the construction of the Union Pacific Railroad.

Let x_2 = the number of miles along the track route from Sacramento to the newest end of the track.

Newest end of Union Pacific Railroad track

← 1774 mi →
Sacramento   Omaha

Let t = the time, in months, after January 1, 1863.

Let $y_2 = 1$.

c. Graph the equations you wrote in parts (a) and (b). Use TRACE to find when the two tracks met.

d. According to your graph from part (c), about how much track did each company build?

e. **Writing** What factors may have caused the building rates of the two companies to be so different?

BY THE WAY...

Just days before the two tracks were joined, the Central Pacific Railroad company set a record when it laid 10 miles of track in one day, beating the 8.5 mile record set by their rivals, the Union Pacific Railroad Company.

546   **Unit 9** Polynomial and Rational Functions

Answers to Exercises and Problems

13. a. $x_1 = 9t$; $y_1 = 1$

   b. $x_2 = 1774 - 25(t - 33)$; $y_2 = 1$

   c.

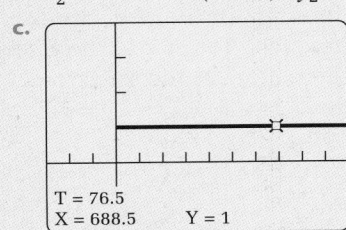

   T = 76.5
   X = 688.5   Y = 1

76.5 months after the start of the Central Pacific or May, 1869

   d. The Central Pacific laid about 688.5 miles of track and the Union Pacific laid about 1087.5 miles of track.

   e. Answers may vary. An example is given. The Central Pacific Railroad Company was laying track in the mountains,

whereas the Union Pacific Railroad Company was laying track on flat land.

14. a. $x_1 = 20t$; $y_1 = 1$

   b. $x_2 = 1774 - 40(t - 0.5)$; $y_2 = 1$

   c. about 29.5 hours later or about 7:30 P.M. the next day; The trains will meet near Promontory Station.

15. a. $y = \sin t$

   b. $x = \cos t$

   c. circle

   d. Graph the parametric equations $x = 2 \cos t$ and $y = 2 \sin t$.

16. Answers may vary. An example is given. The path of a ball thrown into the air can be represented by the parametric equations

546

14. During the 1890s, a train to Omaha leaving Sacramento at 2 P.M. would travel at an average speed of 20 mi/h. A second train heading west from Omaha at 2:30 P.M. would travel at an average speed of 40 mi/h.

  a. Write parametric equations to model the motion of the train from Sacramento. (Let x_1 = the distance in miles of the train from Sacramento, t = the number of hours after 2:00 P.M., and y_1 = 1.)

  b. Write parametric equations to model the motion of the train from Omaha. (Let x_2 = the distance in miles of the train from Sacramento, t = the number of hours after 2:00 P.M., and y_2 = 1.2.)

  c. If neither train stops along the way, when will the trains pass each other? Use the map on page 546 to estimate where the trains will be when they pass each other.

15 TECHNOLOGY Use the figure at the right.

  Let $C(x, y)$ = any point one unit away from the origin.

  Let t = the measure of the angle $\overline{OC}$ makes with the x-axis.

  a. Use the sine ratio to write an equation for y in terms of t.

  b. Use the cosine ratio to write an equation for x in terms of t.

TECHNOLOGY NOTE

Use $0 \le t \le 360$,
$-1.8 \le x \le 1.8$, and $-1.2 \le y \le 1.2$.

  c. Use a graphics calculator to graph the parametric equations from parts (a) and (b). What shape do you get?

  d. **Writing** Explain how you can use a graphics calculator to graph all points two units away from the origin.

16. **Open-ended** Think of a situation that could be modeled with parametric equations. Explain what x, y, and t represent.

Ongoing **ASSESSMENT**

17. **Writing** In Sample 2, suppose Tony waits 4 s to throw the ball instead of 3 s. The path of the ball as viewed from above can be described by the parametric equations $x_2 = 50 - 22(t - 4)$ and $y_2 = 27 + 6(t - 4)$ for $4 \le t \le 7.5$. Bakham's path is still described by the parametric equations $x_1 = 42 - 6t$ and $y_1 = 45 - t$. Can Bakham catch the ball, assuming that it is not too high or too low? Explain your reasoning.

Review **PREVIEW**

Solve. *(Section 9-5)*

18. $4x^3 - 12x^2 + 8x = 0$ **19.** $x^3 - 2x^2 = 7x$ **20.** $6x^4 + 10x^3 + 2x^2 = 0$

Simplify. *(Sections 3-5, 3-7)*

21. $\begin{bmatrix} 2 & 7 \\ -5 & 1 \end{bmatrix} + \begin{bmatrix} 3 & -3 \\ 4 & -2 \end{bmatrix}$ **22.** $2\begin{bmatrix} 3 \\ -1 \\ 0 \end{bmatrix} - \begin{bmatrix} -4 \\ 8 \\ 2 \end{bmatrix}$ **23.** $\begin{bmatrix} 1 & 1 \\ 0 & 3 \\ 2 & 9 \end{bmatrix}\begin{bmatrix} 5 & -1 & 7 \\ -2 & 1 & 0 \end{bmatrix}$

9-6 Parametric Equations

Answers to Exercises and Problems

$x = 1 + t$ and $y = 6t - t^2$. How long does it take for the ball to reach its maximum height? x represents the horizontal distance from the point where the ball was thrown as a function of time, t, and y represents the ball's height above the ground as a function of time, t.

17. Yes, he catches the ball because his path and the path of the ball intersect at $t = 6$ seconds.

18. 0, 1, 2

19. 0, $1 + 2\sqrt{2}$, $1 - 2\sqrt{2}$

20. 0, $\dfrac{-5 + \sqrt{13}}{6}$, $\dfrac{-5 - \sqrt{13}}{6}$

21. $\begin{bmatrix} 5 & 4 \\ -1 & -1 \end{bmatrix}$

22. $\begin{bmatrix} 10 \\ -10 \\ -2 \end{bmatrix}$

23. $\begin{bmatrix} 3 & 0 & 7 \\ -6 & 3 & 0 \\ -8 & 7 & 14 \end{bmatrix}$

Using Technology

If students use a TI-81, TI-82, or TI-83 for Ex. 15, suggest using Tstep=1. After they have successfully completed the exercise, you can use the situation to point out how crucial the T-settings are. Have students change the Tstep from 1 to 60. The calculator will display a regular hexagon. For Tstep = 90, the display shows a square. If you use TRACE, the cursor does not creep along the sides of the polygon but jumps from vertex to vertex. Discuss why this behavior occurs.

You may wish to discuss the effect of changing the MODE setting from Connected to Dot. Also consider what happens if you use $0 \le t \le 270$, $0 \le t \le 150$, or some other interval for the values of t.

Assessment: Open-ended

In Ex. 15, if $C(x, y)$ is any point 2 units away from the origin, ask students how this would change the parametric equations for y in terms of t and x in terms of t? How would it change the graph?

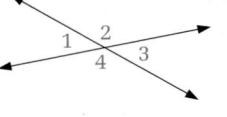

24. The measure of $\angle 1$ is 40°. What are the measures of $\angle 2$, $\angle 3$, and $\angle 4$?
(Section 7-7)

Complete each statement using *pyramid, prism, rectangles, triangles, base,* or *bases.* (Toolbox Skill 28)

25. A _?_ has one _?_. Its other faces are _?_.

26. A _?_ has two congruent _?_ . Its other faces are _?_.

Working on the Unit Project

27. Al, Ja-Wen, and Odessa did an experiment on their sports field to measure the speed of the wind. They measured the time (in seconds) that it took for a feather to fall to the ground from a height of 7 ft. They also measured the horizontal distance (in feet) that the feather traveled.

a. The three students say that the speed of the wind is the horizontal distance the feather traveled divided by the time it took to hit the ground. Explain their reasoning. What are the units of the wind speed they found?

b. The students modeled the path of the feather by the parametric equations $x = 3t$ and $y = 7 - 5t$. Graph these equations on your calculator.

c. According to this model, how long did it take the feather to reach the ground? When the feather lands, how far is it from the ladder?

d. Use your answers to part (c) to calculate the wind speed found by the students.

e. Do you think the graph in part (b) is a good model for the path of the feather? Why or why not?

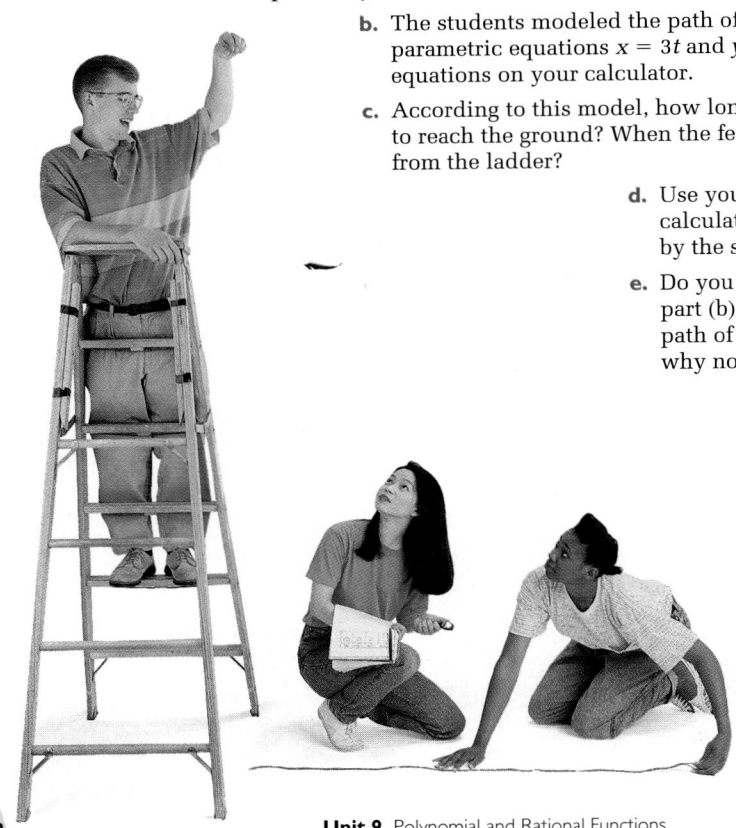

Answers to Exercises and Problems

24. $m \angle 2 = 140°$; $m \angle 3 = 40°$; $m \angle 4 = 140°$

25. pyramid; base; triangles

26. prism; bases; rectangles

27. a. If the air had been still, the feather would have dropped right down to the ladder base. The wind blows the feather some distance from the base of the ladder as it falls. Thus, the horizon-

tal displacement of the feather is $d = rt$, where r is the wind speed, so $r = \frac{d}{t}$ in ft/s.

b.

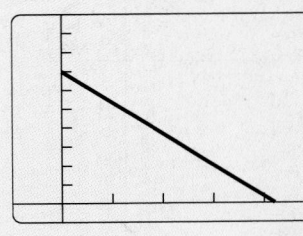

c. 1.4 s; 4.2 ft

d. 3 ft/s

e. Answers may vary. An example is given. No; the model does not take into account the vertical component of the fall and the effect of gravity. Also, a feather does not usually fall straight down but sways from side to side.

Unit Project 9

Completing the Unit Project

Now you are ready to debate the pros and cons of using wind power to generate electricity in your area. You should include these points in your debate:

➤ the amount of electricity used by a typical household in your area

➤ the effect of the weather and geography in your area on the amount of electricity that can be produced by a wind turbine

➤ the feasibility of installing a wind turbine at a great enough height to generate sufficient electricity

➤ the cost of purchasing electricity from a local power company

➤ the effect on the environment

Look Back ◄

How could you make your point of view more persuasive in the debate about wind power? What additional information could you obtain in order to strengthen your argument?

Alternative Projects

Project 1: Other Alternative Energy Sources

Research other alternative sources of energy, such as hydropower, solar power, or geothermal power. Find out how they are used in various parts of the world, including South America, Asia, Africa, and Europe.

Project 2: Using Parametric Equations

Try the experiment described in "Working on the Unit Project" Exercise 27 in Section 9-6. You may use facial tissue in place of a feather. Use the distance formula to write parametric equations for the horizontal distance x and the height y in feet after t seconds. Compare your equations with the equations in Exercise 27. Explain any differences. Use your parametric equations to write an equation for y in terms of x.

Assessment

A scoring rubric for the Unit Project can be found on pages 502 and 503 of this Teacher's Edition and also in the *Project Book*.

Quick Quiz (9-4 through 9-6)

Use the equation
$y = -2x^3 - 5x^2 + 3x$ for
Exs. 1–4.

1. Factor the equation completely. [9-4]
   $y = -x(2x - 1)(x + 3)$

2. Tell how many times the graph intersects the x-axis. [9-4] 3

3. Classify the equation as linear, quadratic or cubic. [9-4] cubic

4. Solve the equation without graphing. [9-5]
   $x = 0, x = \frac{1}{2}, x = -3$

5. Solve the equation
   $0 = p^3 - 2p^2 - 8p$. [9-5]
   $p = 0, p = 4, p = -2$

6. Using the parametric equations $x = 16 - 3(t + 2)$ and $y = 2t - 1$, write an equation for y in terms of x.
   [9-6] $y = -\frac{2}{3}x + \frac{17}{3}$

For Questions 1 and 2, model each situation with an equation. Do not solve the equation.   9-1

1. Cindra Bede has 1.75 lb cement, 7 lb gravel, and 3.25 lb sand to make concrete. She knows that 30% of the dry ingredients should be sand. How much more sand does she need?

2. Fred is planting a vegetable garden with an area of 120 ft². The length of the garden is along the side of his house. The length is 8 ft more than twice the width. Fred wants to put a fence around the other three sides. How much fence does he need?

Tell whether each expression is a polynomial. Write Yes or No. Give a reason for your answer.

3. $\frac{x - 3}{x}$

4. $3x^3 - x + 10$

5. $2x^{1/3} + 3x^{1/2}$

6. $x^{-5} + x^{-3}$

7. $\frac{x^{1/4} - 5}{2x^3 + 10}$

8. $\frac{1}{4}x^2 - 4x - 4$

Simplify. Write each answer without negative exponents.   9-2

9. $(4m^4)(3m^{-2})(2m)^2$

10. $(a^{-1}b)(ab)^{-1}$

11. $x^{-5}(2x^3y^{-5})$

12. $(rst)^6(rst)^{-3}$

13. $\frac{w^2w^{-4}w^5}{5w^{-3}}$

14. $\left(\frac{p^{-2}q^{-1}}{p^{-1}q^{-2}}\right)^3$

Solve.   9-3

15. $\frac{1}{x^2 - 4} = \frac{1}{x - 2}$

16. $\frac{z}{z - 1} + \frac{1}{z} = 1$

17. $\frac{x - 3}{x} - \frac{1}{x + 2} = -1$

18. Carbonation Bottling Company installs a new machine that can cap 100 more bottles per hour than their old machine. This new machine takes one hour less than the old machine to cap 5600 bottles.

   a. Write an equation to model the situation.

   b. Solve the equation you wrote in part (a). What is the bottling speed of the new machine?

19. **Writing** In Exercise 18, there are two possible solutions to the equation. Explain why only one of the solutions is a solution to the problem.

List the zeros of each cubic function. Tell which, if any, are double or triple zeros.   9-4

20. $y = x(x - 5)(x + 2)$

21. $y = (x + 3)^2(x - 1)$

22. $y = (x - 4)^3$

23. $y = (x - 2)(x + 6)^2$

24. **Open-ended** Write a cubic function that has a graph that crosses the x-axis at exactly two points.

Answers to Unit 9 Review and Assessment

1. $\frac{3.25 + x}{12 + x} = 0.30$

2. $w(2w + 8) = 120$; fencing required will be $4w + 8$.

3. No; $\frac{x - 3}{x}$ is a rational expression but is not a polynomial.

4. Yes; it consists only of terms with whole-number exponents.

5. No; both terms cannot be written with whole-number exponents.

6. No; both terms cannot be written with whole-number exponents.

7. No; the expression cannot be written as a monomial or a sum of monomials with whole number exponents.

8. Yes; it consists only of terms with whole-number exponents.

9. $48m^4$

10. $\frac{1}{a^2}$

11. $\frac{2}{x^2y^5}$

12. $r^3s^3t^3$

13. $\frac{w^6}{5}$

14. $\frac{q^3}{p^3}$

15. -1

16. $\frac{1}{2}$

17. $\sqrt{3}, -\sqrt{3}$

18. a. $\frac{5600}{x} - 1 = \frac{5600}{x + 100}$

    b. 800 bottles per hour

Match each function with its graph.

25. $y = (x - 7)(x - 3)(x + 1)$

26. $y = \frac{1}{2}x^3$

27. $y = x(x - 2)^2$

28. $y = -(x - 7)(x - 3)(x + 1)$

A.

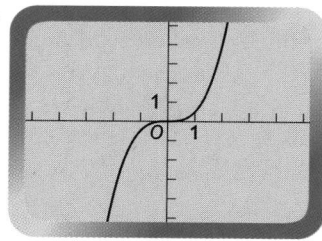

B.

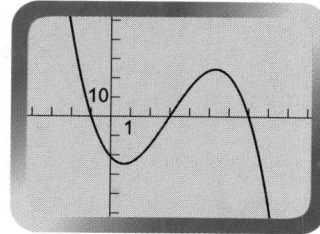

C.

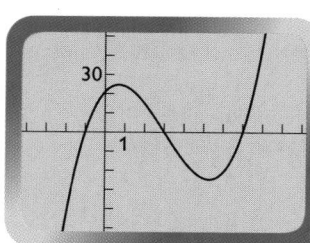

D.

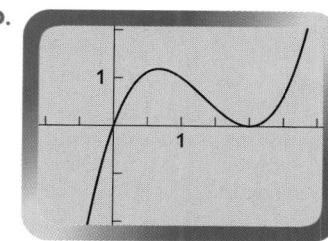

Solve.

9-5

29. $0 = x(x^2 - 4x + 1)$ **30.** $0 = (x + 3)(2x^2 + 7x - 4)$ **31.** $0 = 2x^3 - 12x^2 + 18x$

32. In three years, Al estimates he will need about $300 to update his music system. His savings account balance, s, after 3 years will be $s = 60g^3 + 60g^2 + 60g + 60$, where g is the yearly growth rate.

Use the graph of $y = 60x^3 + 60x^2 + 60x + 60 - 300$ to estimate the yearly growth rate he must get to reach his goal.

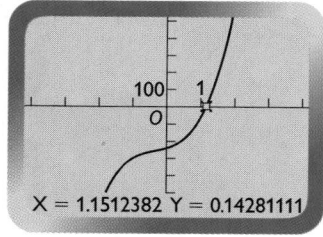

X = 1.1512382 Y = 0.14281111

Answers to Unit 9 Review and Assessment ·······································

19. The other solution, −800, does not make sense. The number of bottles capped per hour must be positive.

20. −2, 0, and 5; no multiple zeros

21. −3 and 1; −3 is a double zero.

22. 4; 4 is a triple zero.

23. −6 and 2; −6 is a double zero.

24. Answers may vary. Example: $y = x(x + 2)^2$

25. C

26. A

27. D

28. B

29. 0, $2 + \sqrt{3} \approx 3.7$, $2 - \sqrt{3} \approx 0.27$

30. $-4, -3, \frac{1}{2}$

31. 0, 3

32. about 1.2

33. A fly lands on a spider's web and tries to move across it.

Let x = the horizontal distance from the fly's landing point.

Let y = the vertical distance from the fly's landing point.

Let t = the time, in seconds, since the fly landed on the web.

The fly's path can be described by these parametric equations:

$$x = 3 - 2t \qquad y = 6 + t \qquad 0 \le t \le 10$$

The spider sees the fly after 2 s and tries to catch the fly. The spider's path can be described by these parametric equations:

$$x = -2 - t \qquad y = -4 + 3t \qquad 2 \le t \le 10$$

a. Graph the path of the fly.

b. Graph the path of the spider.

c. Where do their paths intersect?

d. Does the spider catch the fly? If so, at what time? If not, why not?

34. **Self-evaluation** Think about the application problems you have solved in this unit. Do you find it more difficult to set up an equation or to solve the equation once you have set it up? How can you improve upon your problem solving skills?

35. **Group Activity** Work with another student.

a. One person should draw separate graphs of three different cubic functions:

➤ One graph should have only one x-intercept.

➤ One should have only two x-intercepts.

➤ One should have three different x-intercepts.

The other person should write three cubic functions:

➤ One should have a triple zero.

➤ One should have a double zero.

➤ One should have no multiple zeros.

b. Trade papers. The person who receives the functions should describe the graph of each function. The person who receives the graphs should write a function for each of the graphs.

c. Exchange papers and check each other's work. Discuss and resolve any differences.

d. Switch roles and repeat parts (a)–(c) using new graphs and functions.

Unit 9 Polynomial and Rational Functions

Answers to Unit 9 Review and Assessment ·

33. a, b.

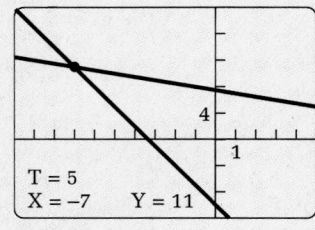

T = 5
X = -7   Y = 11

c. $(-7, 11)$

d. Yes; at $t = 5$.

34. Answers may vary.

35. a, b. Answers may vary. Examples are given.

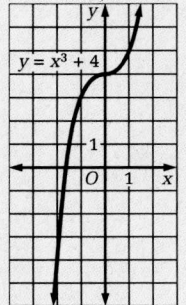

$y = x^3 + 4$

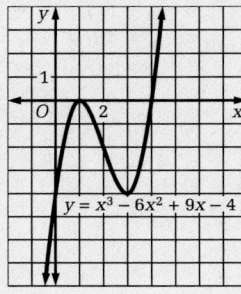

$y = x^3 - 6x^2 + 9x - 4$

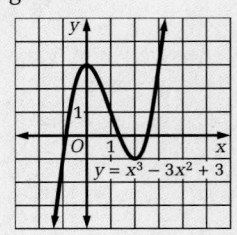

$y = x^3 - 3x^2 + 3$

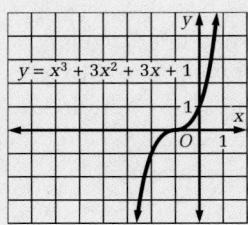

$y = x^3 + 3x^2 + 3x + 1$

IDEAS AND (FORMULAS) $= x^2$

ALGEBRA

➤ **Problem Solving** Some situations can be modeled by polynomial equations or rational equations. *(pp. 505–508)*

➤ Expressions with positive, zero, or negative exponents can be simplified by using the rules of exponents. *(pp. 513–516)*

➤ Product of Powers Rule: $a^m \cdot a^n = a^{m+n}$ *(p. 513)*

➤ Quotient of Powers Rule: $\dfrac{a^m}{a^n} = a^{m-n}$, $a \neq 0$ *(p. 513)*

➤ Power of a Power Rule: $(a^m)^n = a^{m \cdot n}$ *(p. 516)*

➤ Power of a Product Rule: $(ab)^n = a^n \cdot b^n$ *(p. 516)*

➤ Power of a Quotient Rule: $\left(\dfrac{a}{b}\right)^n = \dfrac{a^n}{b^n}$, $b \neq 0$ *(p. 516)*

➤ To factor a polynomial completely, first you need to find the greatest common factor (GCF) of all the terms. *(p. 514)*

➤ Rational equations can be solved by cross multiplying or by using common multiples of the denominators. *(pp. 521–523)*

➤ Rational equations can have extraneous solutions that do not apply to the situations the equations model. *(pp. 521–523)*

➤ You can tell if a cubic function has a double or triple zero by analyzing the factored form or by graphing the function. *(p. 529)*

➤ **Problem Solving** To solve problems involving cubic equations, you can graph a related equation and find the x-intercepts. Some cubic equations can also be solved by factoring and using the quadratic formula. *(p. 537)*

➤ The path of a moving object can be described by parametric equations expressing horizontal and vertical position in terms of time. *(pp. 541–542)*

➤ You can analyze parametric equations by making a table of values for x, y, and t or by graphing the x-y pairs. *(p. 542)*

➤ You can use substitution to write a pair of parametric equations as a single equation in terms of x and y. *(p. 542)*

Key Terms

- **polynomial** (p. 507)
- **standard form of a polynomial** (p. 507)
- **extraneous solution** (p. 521)
- **double zero** (p. 529)
- **parameter** (p. 542)

- **degree** (p. 507)
- **rational expression** (p. 508)
- **cubic function** (p. 528)
- **triple zero** (p. 529)

- **polynomial equation** (p. 507)
- **rational equation** (p. 508)
- **zero of a function** (p. 529)
- **parametric equation** (p. 542)

Unit 9 Review and Assessment

553

Quick Quiz (9-1 through 9-3)

1. Is the equation
$$-\frac{1}{4}x^2 - 6x^4 = 12y + x$$ a polynomial equation? If yes, what is its degree? If no, explain why not. [9-1]
Yes; 4.

2. Marissa wants to make a peach colored frosting for a cake. Yellow should be 75% of the number of food coloring drops in the icing. She has already added two drops of red and three drops of yellow food coloring. Marissa wonders how many more food coloring drops to add. Model the situation with an equation. [9-1]
$\frac{x+3}{x+5} = 0.75$

3. Simplify $\dfrac{16a^6bc^2}{-12a^2(b^2c)^2}$. Write your answer without negative exponents. [9-2]
$-\dfrac{4a^4}{3b^3}$

4. Factor $8m^2n^2 + 10m^4n^5 - 2m^3n^2$ completely. [9-2]
$2m^2n^2(4 + 5m^2n^3 - m)$

5. Solve $\dfrac{3}{x+2} - \dfrac{x}{x-1} = 5$. [9-3]
$x = -\frac{1}{3} \pm \dfrac{\sqrt{46}}{6}$

6. Find the unknown dimensions. [9-3]
base = 3 m, height = 5 m,
x = 2 m

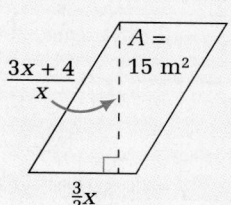

553

Answers to Unit 9 Review and Assessment

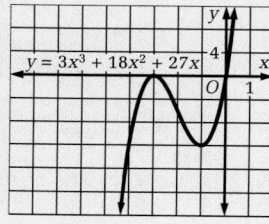

$y = 3x^3 + 18x^2 + 27x$

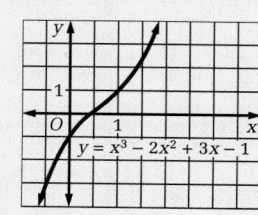

$y = x^3 - 2x^2 + 3x - 1$

35. c, d. Check students' work.

OVERVIEW

➤ **Unit 10** covers three-dimensional figures. Students explore looking at these figures from different perspectives, constructing the figures, and rotating plane figures about a line in order to develop a space figure.

➤ Work in Unit 10 includes locating points in space, drawing space figures on a three-dimensional coordinate grid, and finding distances and midpoints of space figures. Students write equations of spheres, and of circles whose centers are located at the origin and away from the origin.

➤ Designing a container is the theme of the Unit Project. Students look at cross sections and rotations in the designing of containers. They also examine the conditions they want their containers to meet, as well as the shape necessary for the container to have in order to hold the object it is to contain.

➤ Connections to geology, archaeology, seismology, agriculture, literature, computer-aided designs, mosques, and party decorations are integrated into the teaching materials and exercises.

➤ Graphics calculators are used in Section 10-6 to graph a circle. Computer software, such as Plotter Plus, can also be used in Section 10-6 to explore circles.

➤ Problem-solving strategies used in Unit 10 include using manipulatives, patterns, drawings, coordinates, tables, formulas, and technology.

Unit Objectives

Section	Objectives	NCTM Standards
10-1	• Visualize space figures.	1, 2, 4, 7
10-2	• Describe space figures that are formed by rotating plane figures around a line.	1, 2, 4, 5, 8
10-3	• Describe or draw a set of points that meet one or more conditions.	1, 2, 3, 4, 5, 8
10-4	• Describe the location of points in space using three coordinates.	1, 2, 4, 5, 8
	• Find midpoints of segments in three dimensions.	
10-5	• Find the distance between two points in three dimensions.	1, 2, 4, 5, 8
10-6	• Graph a circle and find the equation of a circle or a sphere.	1, 2, 4, 5, 8

Skills Bank To extend the curriculum and provide practice with skills, you may wish to assign the following topic from the **Skills Bank** ancillary: linear-quadratic and quadratic-quadratic systems (for use after Section 10-6).

Section	Connections to Prior and Future Concepts
10-1	**Section 10-1** introduces visualizing space figures. Students examine space figures from different perspectives, and explore methods of building models for different space figures. Cross sections of a space figure are introduced. Students were introduced to space figures in Unit 9 of Book 1, where they found volume and surface area of certain figures. Visualizing space figures is a skill used throughout the remainder of Unit 10 and in Unit 3 of Book 3.
10-2	**Section 10-2** introduces the concept of an axis of rotation. Students use a plane figure, rotating it about a line, to develop a space figure. Students explore which space figures can and cannot be found by rotating a plane figure about a line.
10-3	**Section 10-3** introduces the concept of a locus. Students explore finding a set of points that satisfy one condition or multiple conditions. Conditions are limited first to a plane, then extended to points in space that could satisfy the given conditions.
10-4	**Section 10-4** introduces graphing points on a three-dimensional coordinate system. The midpoint formula, first used in Section 5-3 of Book 2, is extended to three-dimensional coordinates. Students develop skill at graphing rectangular prisms on the three-dimensional coordinate system. Three-dimensional coordinates are discussed again in Unit 1 of Book 3.
10-5	**Section 10-5** extends the concept of the distance formula, first used in Section 5-2 of Book 2, to three dimensions.
10-6	**Section 10-6** introduces finding the equations that represent circles and spheres whose centers are at the origin. Equations of circles whose centers are not at the origin are also developed. This skill depends upon using the distance formula, presented in Section 5-2 of Book 2. Equations of circles centered at the origin play a role in developing the trigonometric functions in Unit 8 of Book 3.

Integrating the Strands

Strands	Sections
Algebra	10-1, 10-4, 10-5, 10-6
Measurement	10-2
Geometry	10-1, 10-2, 10-3, 10-4, 10-5, 10-6
Statistics and Probability	10-2, 10-5
Discrete Mathematics	10-4
Logic and Language	10-2, 10-3, 10-4, 10-6

Section Planning Guide

➤ Essential exercises and problems are indicated in boldface.
➤ Ongoing work on the Unit Project is indicated in color.
➤ Exercises and problems that require student research, group work, manipulatives, or graphing technology are indicated in the column headed "Other."

Section	Materials	Pacing	Standard Assignment	Extended Assignment	Other
10-1	stiff paper, protractor, scissors, removable tape, cardboard box	Day 1 Day 2	**6**, 7, **9–19** **20–29**, 30, 31, **40–45**, 46–48	**6**, 7, **9–19** **20–29**, 30–32, **34–45**, 46–48	1–5, 8 33, 48c
10-2	scissors, tape, long pencil	Day 1	**3–11**, **15–19**, 24–26, 27, 28	1, **3–11**, 12–14, **15–19**, 20–26, 27, 28	2
10-3		Day 1	**2–11**, **14**, **15**, 16, 19, 20, 22–27, 28, 29	1, **2–11**, 12, 13, **14**, **15**, 16–20, 22–27, 28, 29	21
10-4	cardboard box, scissors, large needle, thread, 10 buttons or paper clips, tape	Day 1	**1–6**, **8–19**, 20, 21, 25–33, 34	**1–6**, **8–19**, 20–33, 34	7
10-5	medium-size boxes, heavy paper, protractor, scissors	Day 1 Day 2	**1–6**, **9–16**, 17 **18–25**, 29–38, 39	**1–6**, 7, 8, **9–16**, 17 **18–25**, 26–38, 39	
10-6	graphics calculator	Day 1 Day 2	**1–12** **17–21**, 23, **24–27**, 29–32, 33, 34	**1–12**, 13, 15, 16 **17–21**, 22, 23, **24–27**, 28–32, 33, 34	14 29b
Review Test		**Day 1** **Day 2**	**Unit Review** **Unit Test**	**Unit Review** **Unit Test**	

Yearly Pacing	Unit 10 Total 13 days (2 for Unit Project)	Units 1–10 Total 160 days	Remaining 0 days	Total 160 days

Support Materials

➤ See **Project Book** for notes on Unit 10 Project: Design and Build a Container.
➤ UPP and disk refer to **Using Plotter Plus** booklet and **Plotter Plus** disk.
➤ TI-81/82 refers to **Using TI-81 and TI-82 Calculators** booklet.
➤ Warm-up exercises for each section are available on **Warm-Up Transparencies.**

Section	Study Guide	Practice Bank	Problem Bank	Activity Bank	Explorations Lab Manual	Assessment Book	Visuals	Technology
10-1	10-1	Practice 76	Set 22	Enrich 67	Masters 2, 22–24	Quiz 10-1		
10-2	10-2	Practice 77	Set 22	Enrich 68	Add. Expl. 13 Master 2	Quiz 10-2		
10-3	10-3	Practice 78	Set 22	Enrich 69	Master 1	Quiz 10-3 Test 41		
10-4	10-4	Practice 79	Set 23	Enrich 70	Master 7	Quiz 10-4	Folder 10	
10-5	10-5	Practice 80	Set 23	Enrich 71	Masters 7, 25	Quiz 10-5	Folder 10	
10-6	10-6	Practice 81	Set 23	Enrich 72	Add. Expl. 14 Masters 2, 7	Quiz 10-6 Test 42		TI-81/82, p. 50 UPP(disk): Circular Function Quiz
Unit 10	Unit Review	Practice 82	Unifying Problem 10	Family Involve 10		Tests 43–46		

UNIT TESTS

Form A

Spanish versions of these tests are on pages 154–157 of the **Assessment Book.**

Name _____ Date _____ Score _____

Test 43

Test on Unit 10 (Form A)

Directions: Write the answers in the spaces provided.

For Questions 1–4, use the pattern at the right.

Bottom

1. What space figure is formed when the pattern is folded up?

2. Draw the space figure formed.

3. Draw a vertical cross section of the space figure. Identify the shape.

☐ or ☐
rectangle or square

4. Draw a horizontal cross section of the space figure. Identify the shape.

☐
rectangle

For Questions 5–8, use the figure at the right.

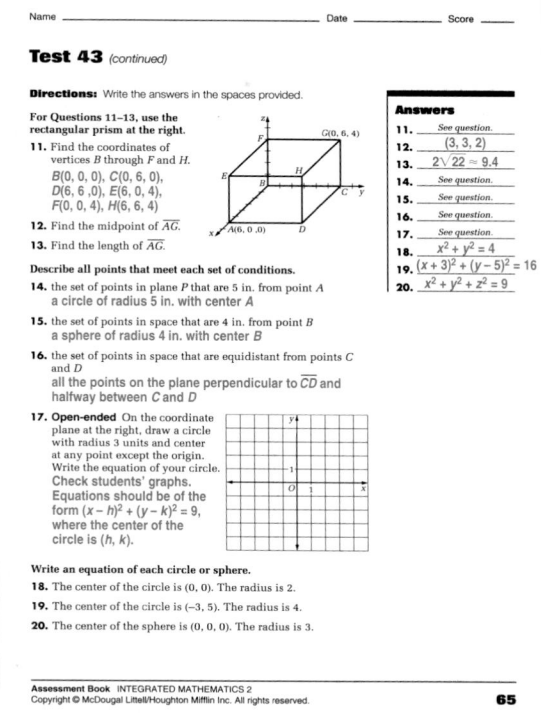

5. Describe the space figure formed when you rotate the rectangle about the x-axis. Draw the figure on the graph.
a cylinder with radius 1 and height 4

6. Find the volume of the space figure formed in Question 5.

7. Find the surface area of the space figure formed in Question 5.

8. **Writing** Imagine rotating the rectangle about the y-axis. Explain how the volume and surface area of this space figure compare to that of the space figure in Question 5.
Sample answer: The space figure is a cylinder with radius 4 and height 1. The volume is 16π, which is 4 times that of the cylinder above. The surface area is 40π, which is also 4 times that of the cylinder above.

9. Find the length of a diagonal of a rectangular prism with sides of length 4, 6, and 9.

10. Is the triangle with vertices M(2, 2, 0), N(4, 4, 4), and P(2, 0, 2) *scalene, isosceles,* or *equilateral*?

Answers
1. rectangular prism
2. See question.
3. See question.
4. See question.
5. See question.
6. 4π ≈ 12.6 units³
7. 10π ≈ 31.4 units²
8. See question.
9. √133 ≈ 11.5
10. isosceles

Name _____ Date _____ Score _____

Test 43 (continued)

Directions: Write the answers in the spaces provided.

For Questions 11–13, use the rectangular prism at the right.

11. Find the coordinates of vertices B through F and H.
B(0, 0, 0), C(0, 6, 0), D(6, 6, 0), E(6, 0, 4), F(0, 0, 4), H(6, 6, 4)

12. Find the midpoint of $\overline{AG}$.

13. Find the length of $\overline{AG}$.

Describe all points that meet each set of conditions.

14. the set of points in plane P that are 5 in. from point A
a circle of radius 5 in. with center A

15. the set of points in space that are 4 in. from point B
a sphere of radius 4 in. with center B

16. the set of points in space that are equidistant from points C and D
all the points on the plane perpendicular to $\overline{CD}$ and halfway between C and D

17. **Open-ended** On the coordinate plane at the right, draw a circle with radius 3 units and center at any point except the origin. Write the equation of your circle. Check students' graphs. Equations should be of the form $(x - h)^2 + (y - k)^2 = 9$, where the center of the circle is (h, k).

Write an equation of each circle or sphere.

18. The center of the circle is (0, 0). The radius is 2.

19. The center of the circle is (−3, 5). The radius is 4.

20. The center of the sphere is (0, 0, 0). The radius is 3.

Answers
11. See question.
12. (3, 3, 2)
13. 2√22 ≈ 9.4
14. See question.
15. See question.
16. See question.
17. See question.
18. $x^2 + y^2 = 4$
19. $(x + 3)^2 + (y − 5)^2 = 16$
20. $x^2 + y^2 + z^2 = 9$

Form B

Name _____ Date _____ Score _____

Test 44

Test on Unit 10 (Form B)

Directions: Write the answers in the spaces provided.

For Questions 1–4, use the pattern at the right.

Bottom

1. What space figure is formed when the pattern is folded up?

2. Draw the space figure formed.

3. Draw a vertical cross section of the space figure. Identify the shape.

△ isosceles triangle

4. Draw a horizontal cross section of the space figure. Identify the shape.

☐ square

For Questions 5–8, use the figure at the right.

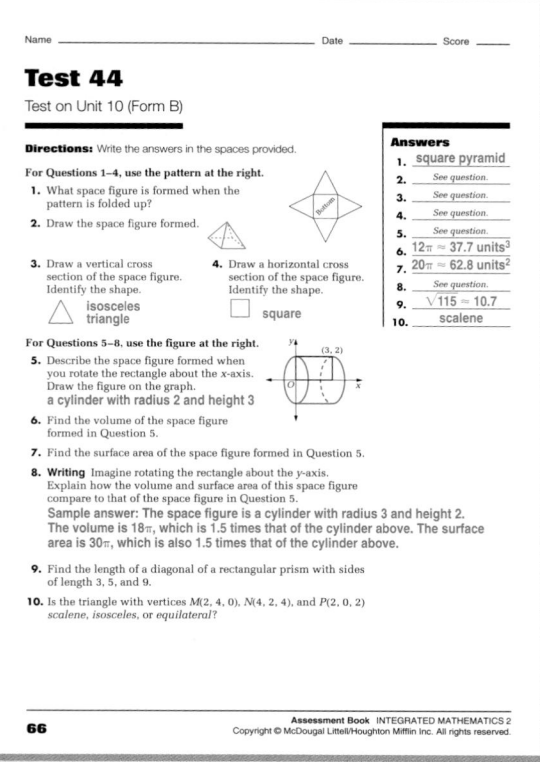

5. Describe the space figure formed when you rotate the rectangle about the x-axis. Draw the figure on the graph.
a cylinder with radius 2 and height 3

6. Find the volume of the space figure formed in Question 5.

7. Find the surface area of the space figure formed in Question 5.

8. **Writing** Imagine rotating the rectangle about the y-axis. Explain how the volume and surface area of this space figure compare to that of the space figure in Question 5.
Sample answer: The space figure is a cylinder with radius 3 and height 2. The volume is 18π, which is 1.5 times that of the cylinder above. The surface area is 30π, which is also 1.5 times that of the cylinder above.

9. Find the length of a diagonal of a rectangular prism with sides of length 3, 5, and 9.

10. Is the triangle with vertices M(2, 4, 0), N(4, 2, 4), and P(2, 0, 2) *scalene, isosceles,* or *equilateral*?

Answers
1. square pyramid
2. See question.
3. See question.
4. See question.
5. See question.
6. 12π ≈ 37.7 units³
7. 20π ≈ 62.8 units²
8. See question.
9. √115 ≈ 10.7
10. scalene

Name _____ Date _____ Score _____

Test 44 (continued)

Directions: Write the answers in the spaces provided.

For Questions 11–13, use the rectangular prism at the right.

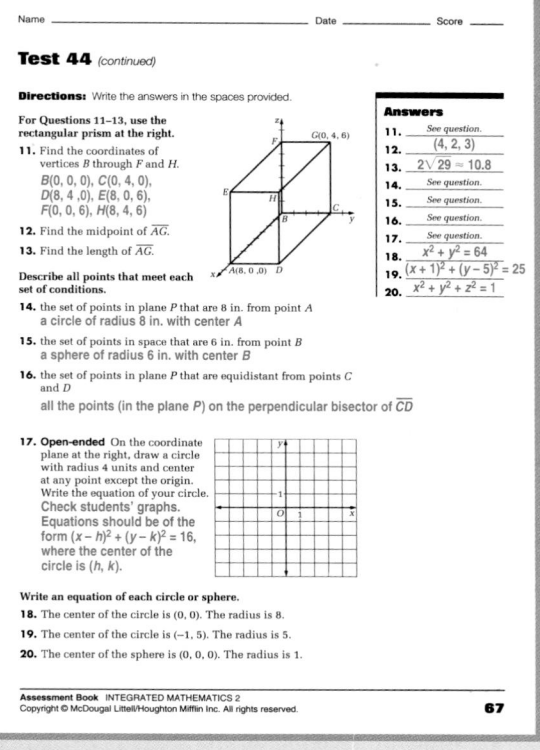

11. Find the coordinates of vertices B through F and H.
B(0, 0, 0), C(0, 4, 0), D(8, 4, 0), E(8, 0, 6), F(0, 0, 6), H(8, 4, 6)

12. Find the midpoint of $\overline{AG}$.

13. Find the length of $\overline{AG}$.

Describe all points that meet each set of conditions.

14. the set of points in plane P that are 8 in. from point A
a circle of radius 8 in. with center A

15. the set of points in space that are 6 in. from point B
a sphere of radius 6 in. with center B

16. the set of points in plane P that are equidistant from points C and D
all the points (in the plane P) on the perpendicular bisector of $\overline{CD}$

17. **Open-ended** On the coordinate plane at the right, draw a circle with radius 4 units and center at any point except the origin. Write the equation of your circle. Check students' graphs. Equations should be of the form $(x - h)^2 + (y - k)^2 = 16$, where the center of the circle is (h, k).

Write an equation of each circle or sphere.

18. The center of the circle is (0, 0). The radius is 8.

19. The center of the circle is (−1, 5). The radius is 5.

20. The center of the sphere is (0, 0, 0). The radius is 1.

Answers
11. See question.
12. (4, 2, 3)
13. 2√29 ≈ 10.8
14. See question.
15. See question.
16. See question.
17. See question.
18. $x^2 + y^2 = 64$
19. $(x + 1)^2 + (y − 5)^2 = 25$
20. $x^2 + y^2 + z^2 = 1$

OUTSIDE RESOURCES

Books/Periodicals

Eddins, Susan, Oswan Maxwell, and Floramma Stanislaus. "Geometric Transformations." *Mathematics Teacher* (March 1994): pp. 177–189.

Holden, Linda. *Thinker Tasks Critical Thinking Activities Book 3: Visual Perception.* Creative Publications, 1986.

Johnson, Christine V. *Washington MESA Packaging and the Environment.* Addison Wesley: Innovative Learning Publications, 1994.

Software

Cappo, Marge and Mike Fish. *Super Factor.* Pleasantville, NY: Sunburst, 1985. Apple and IBM.

Bretl, Thomas. *Building Perspective.* Pleasantville, NY: Sunburst, 1991. Apple, Macintosh, and IBM.

Videos

Math Works: Program 5: Geometry: Explore Geometric Shapes. Agency for Instructional Technology, 1985.

Math Works: Program 13: Geometry. (Move Objects in Space). Agency for Instructional Technology, 1985.

Mathematical Eye. Program 9. Symmetry. Journal Films, 1988.

Earth Revealed: Program 9: Earthquakes. Annenberg CPB Collection, 1992.

Futures 2. Program 6: Industrial Design. PBS, 1992.

➤ Students design and build a container to hold an object or collection of objects of their choice.

➤ Students provide a written description of the container including drawings of its three-dimensional shape.

➤ Students work together in a co-operative group and contribute to the project's success. ....●

PROJECT PLANNING

Materials List

➤ Poster board or drawing paper

➤ Construction instruments, such as glue, scissors, tape, rulers, compasses, protractors, and marker pens

Project Teams

Have students work on the project in groups of three. One way for the individuals in the group to distribute the work is as follows:

1. Researcher: provides some existing containers for the group to examine, gathers information about the material to use for the container, and coordinates the ideas for developing the container.

2. Writer/Illustrator: writes a complete description of the container, instructions for its construction, and develops a set of three-dimensional drawings that another person can use to reconstruct the container.

3. Manufacturer: creates the container, checks to make sure it will hold the object(s) for which it was designed, and insures that it will hold its shape when empty.

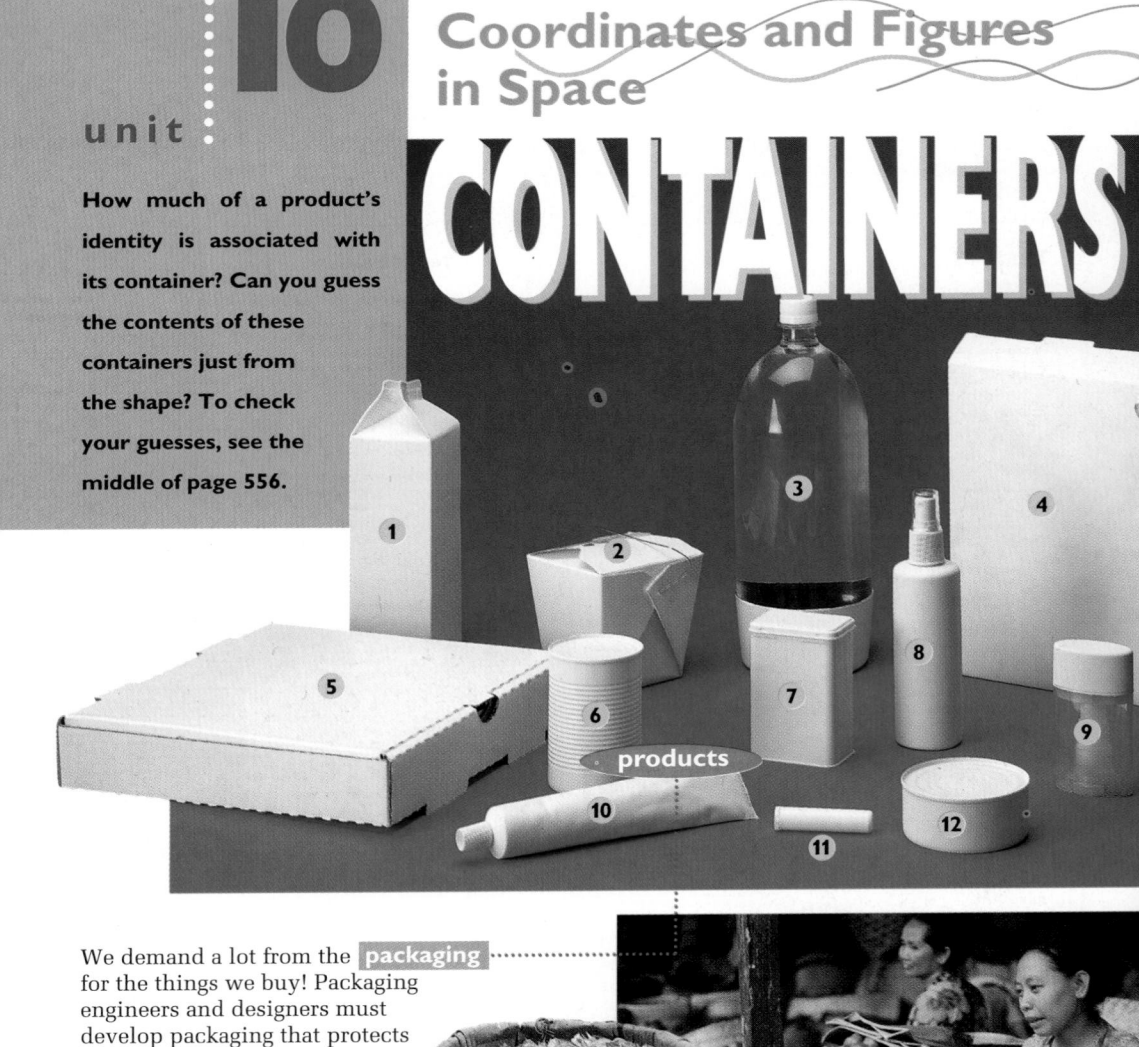

unit 10

Coordinates and Figures in Space

CONTAINERS

How much of a product's identity is associated with its container? Can you guess the contents of these containers just from the shape? To check your guesses, see the middle of page 556.

We demand a lot from the **packaging** for the things we buy! Packaging engineers and designers must develop packaging that protects products and meets our needs as consumers.

Over the ages, people throughout the world have found creative ways to make containers for carrying and storing water, food, and other materials. The beauty, strength, and **practicality** of these containers are still appreciated today.

554

▲ In Southeast Asia, bamboo is used for making baskets. Reeds and grasses are commonly used in other regions.

Suggested Rubric for Unit Project ·····························

4 Students build a container that holds an object or objects of their choice. The container keeps its shape when empty and at least one surface is flat and shaped like a polygon or circle. Students apply correctly the ideas of this unit to create a set of drawings showing its three-dimensional shape. Using the drawings, another person would be able to recon-struct the container. The written description of the container is accurate in all details.

3 Students build a container that meets most of the conditions of the project. The drawings are accurate, but the written description does not fully describe the container. The container may not always keep its shape when empty.

2 Students build a container, but it does not hold the object or objects they have chosen. The drawings do not contain enough detail for another person to reconstruct it. The written description is incomplete and not well written.

Design and Build a Container

Your project is to design and build a container to hold an object, or group of objects, of your choice. Be sure to choose something you can bring to school. When your container is finished, you should place the object in it.

Your container should keep its shape when empty. At least one surface should be flat and shaped like a polygon or a circle. Other surfaces may be curved.

Clay pots have been used for thousands of years. The earliest pottery known was found in the Near East. ➤

Provide a written description of your container as well as a set of drawings showing its three-dimensional shape. In this unit you will learn several ways to represent three-dimensional shapes on paper. Use as many of these approaches as you can to draw your container.

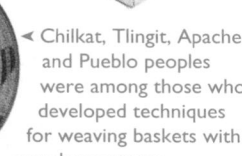

CONTAINERS OF THE WORLD

◄ Chilkat, Tlingit, Apache, and Pueblo peoples were among those who developed techniques for weaving baskets with complex patterns.

The ancient Japanese art of origami is used to make decorative boxes by paperfolding, without scissors or glue. ▼

In parts of Africa and South America, gourds have been carved out for carrying liquids and storing grain. ▼

555

Support Materials

The ***Project Book*** contains information about the following topics for use with this Unit Project.

➤ Project Description
➤ Teaching Commentary
➤ Working on the Unit Project Exercises
➤ Completing the Unit Project
➤ Assessing the Unit Project
➤ Alternative Projects
➤ Outside Resources

ADDITIONAL BACKGROUND

Multicultural Note

Indonesia is a mountainous island country in Southeast Asia. Its population in 1991 was approximately 193 million. Indonesia comprises around 17,000 islands. The island of Bali lies east of Java, the most populous island in Indonesia. Many people consider Bali one of the most beautiful places on Earth. Many Indonesians live on farms and follow traditional ways of life. To honor important personal or familial events, villagers often hold a *selametan*, or religious ceremonial feast. Rice, the staple food of Indonesia, is served at most feasts, along with curries and other spicy dishes.

Suggested Rubric for Unit Project

1 Students may or may not be successful in building a container. Their drawings do not accurately represent the three-dimensional shape of the container. The written description is inadequate. The group should be encouraged to speak with the teacher as soon as possible to review their work and to make a new start on the project.

Containers Used for Microwave Food Products

Anyone who develops a container or any special type of packaging must consider a wide variety of variables and implications. For instance, the sale of microwave-packaged foods has reached billions of dollars per year. To capture this expanding market, the manufacturing industry has devised numerous packaging innovations. This has led to concern from the FDA's Center for Food Safety and Applied Nutrition (CFSAN) that high temperature use of these materials may cause packaging components such as adhesives, polymers, paper, and paperboard, known as indirect food additives, to migrate into food at excessive levels. ....•

ALTERNATIVE PROJECTS

Project 1, page 599

Design a Birdhouse

Research the kinds of birdhouses that attract different kinds of birds. Design a birdhouse and make three-dimensional drawings showing how to construct it.

Project 2, page 599

Make a Pop-Up Book

Look at examples of pop-up books available in the children's section of local libraries or bookstores. Create a pop-up book that demonstrates some ideas about coordinates and figures in space presented in this unit.

Getting Started

For this project you should work in a group of three students. Here are some ideas to help you get started.

☞ Discuss what object or objects you may choose to package.

☞ Will you package your object as a gift? for mailing? for sale? for storage?

☞ Discuss how the properties of the object may affect the design of the container.

☞ Think about what material you will use for your container. Consider its weight, strength, flexibility, cost, and disposal. What tools will you need to cut and assemble it?

☞ Plan to meet later to discuss which kinds of drawings you can use to represent your container on paper.

> **Answers to quiz on page 554:**
> 1. milk; 2. takeout food or restaurant leftovers; 3. soda; 4. cereal; 5. pizza; 6. soup; 7. bandages; 8. hair spray; 9. deodorant; 10. toothpaste; 11. lip balm; 12. tuna or cat food

Can We Talk CONTAINERS

Working on the Unit Project

Your work in Unit 10 will help you design and build your container.

Related Exercises:

Section 10-1, Exercises 46–48
Section 10-2, Exercises 27, 28
Section 10-3, Exercises 28, 29
Section 10-4, Exercise 34
Section 10-5, Exercise 39
Section 10-6, Exercises 33–34

Alternative Projects p. 599

➤ What are some other natural containers like eggs and seed pods? How does their design suit their function?

➤ In a recent survey, 67% of people said fast-food packaging is "wasteful." What other products can you think of with wasteful packaging?

➤ Many food products are packaged in rectangular boxes. What other package shapes are common in grocery stores? Why do you think these shapes are used?

➤ Many snack foods are packaged in airtight bags that are difficult to tear open. Can you think of any other types of packaging for which protection of the contents leads to inconvenience for the consumer?

➤ In 1990 a major fast-food chain replaced its plastic foam containers with paper ones. What other changes in packaging have you noticed in recent years?

Answers to Can We Talk? ·······

➤ Answers may vary. Examples are given. An empty coconut shell, huge leaves from trees, hollowed out trunks from dead trees. In these examples, each is round or can be made round to carry liquids, like water.

➤ Answers may vary. Examples are given. Laundry detergents, some powdered drink mixes, gelatins, and lunch meals produced for sale in a grocery store.

➤ Answers may vary. Examples are given. Cylinders and cubes. These shapes have a flat bottom that sits easily on a shelf.

➤ Answers may vary. Examples are given. Packaging meats in plastic that is difficult to open, packaging jars or containers with a foil seal on the top, or making boxes that do not open or close easily.

➤ Answers may vary. Examples are given. Many places use recycled paper for their bags, there is less thick plastic being used and more paper or thin plastic. Companies are using smaller packages for the same amount of product, and companies are producing refills for their product in addition to original containers.

Figures in Space

> Focus
> Visualize space figures.

Any Way You Look at IT

One way to represent a three-dimensional figure, or **space figure,** is to draw it as you would view it from different directions. Mary Conlan's plans for the table she is building include three views.

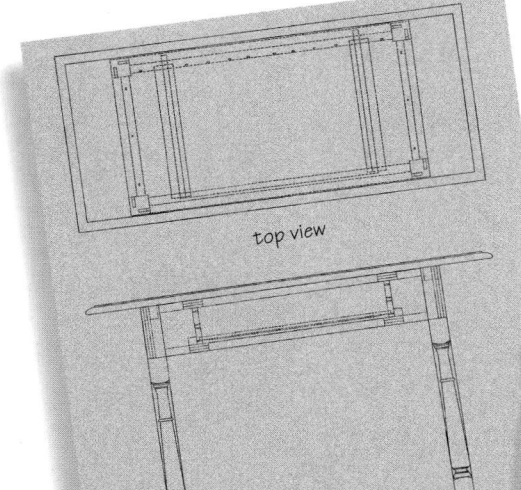

top view

front view

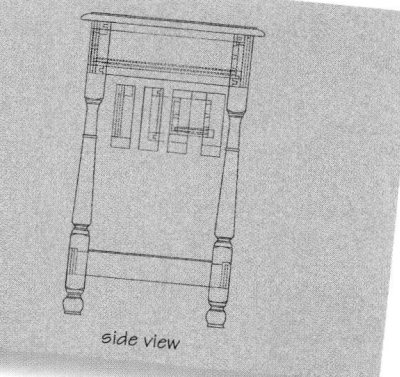

side view

Talk it Over

1. Describe Mary Conlan's table. How is it like tables you have seen? How is it different?

2. Do you think another furniture maker could build Mary Conlan's table given only the front view and the side view? Explain.

557

PLANNING

Objectives and Strands
See pages 554A and 554B.

Spiral Learning
See page 554B.

Materials List
➤ Stiff paper
➤ Ruler
➤ Protractor
➤ Scissors
➤ Removable tape
➤ Graph paper
➤ Cardboard box

Recommended Pacing
Section 10-1 is a two-day lesson.
Day 1
Pages 557–559: Opening paragraph through Exploration, *Exercises 1–19*
Day 2
Pages 559–560: Cross Sections through Look Back, *Exercises 20–48*

Extra Practice
See pages 630–631.

Warm-Up Exercises
Warm-Up Transparency 10-1

Support Materials
➤ Practice 76
➤ Enrichment 67 in the Activity Bank
➤ Study Guide 10-1
➤ Problem Set 22
➤ Diagram Masters 2, 22–24 in the Explorations Lab Manual
➤ Quiz 10-1
➤ Alternative Assessment 1

Answers to Talk it Over

1. Mary Conlan's table is rectangular, has four legs and a drawer centered lengthwise beneath the top base. Many tables are designed this way. Mary's table is different from other tables in that its legs are connected near the bottom by wooden slats, and there is also some type of structure underneath the drawer.

2. Yes; the top view only shows that the top base is rectangular. A furniture maker can see the straight edges of the top base from the front and side views and determine that the top base must be rectangular with length given in the front view and width given in the side view.

Talk it Over

Questions 1 and 2 lead students to realize that to visualize a three-dimensional object drawn on paper correctly, it is usually necessary to have multiple views of the object.

Exploration

The goal of the Exploration is to have students gain more familiarity with space figures. Students learn that a variety of prisms and pyramids can be created from the four given shapes and that different patterns may fold up to form the same space figure. Step 5 continues the line of reasoning begun in the Talk it Over questions on page 557.

Using Manipulatives

If models of the space figures shown in this section are available, you may wish to have students use them as they work this section.

558

Triangular Prism

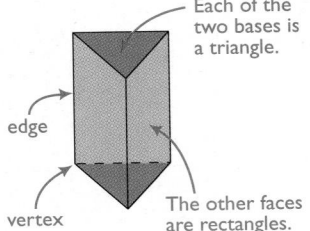

Each of the two bases is a triangle.

edge

vertex

The other faces are rectangles.

EXPLORATION

What does a space figure look like in two dimensions?

- **Materials: stiff paper, rulers, protractors, scissors, removable tape**
- **Work with another student.**

① Draw and cut out three copies of figure B and two copies of figure C.

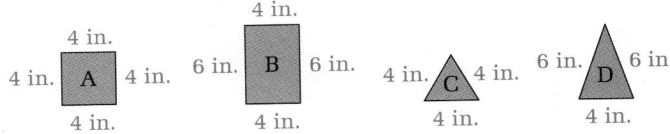

② Tape the shapes together in the pattern shown.

③ Fold your pattern as shown to build a model of a triangular prism.

④ Using any of the shapes A–D, one of you should build a pyramid. The other should build a prism different from the one in step 3. Draw a picture of your pyramid or prism.

Watch Out!
Do not take apart the prism from step 3.

Square Pyramid

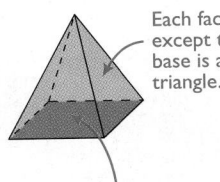

Each face except the base is a triangle.

The base is a square.

⑤ Here are top, front, and side views of the prism in step 3. Draw top, front, and side views of your pyramid or prism.

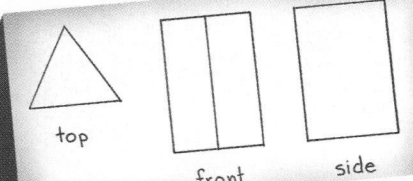

top

front   side

558   **Unit 10** Coordinates and Figures in Space

Answers to Exploration

1–8. Check students' work.

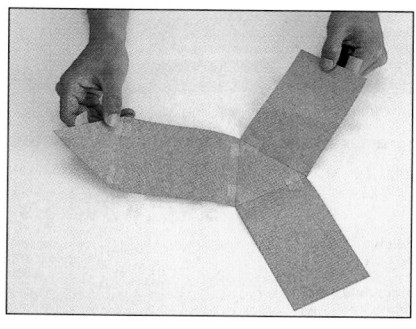

Now you are ready for:
Exs. 1–19 on pp. 560–562

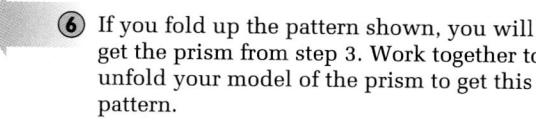

6 If you fold up the pattern shown, you will get the prism from step 3. Work together to unfold your model of the prism to get this pattern.

7 Draw two different patterns for your pyramid or prism from step 4. Draw two different patterns for your partner's pyramid or prism. Compare patterns for the same space figure.

8 Look at the figures other groups made. How many different pyramids and prisms did your class make?

Cross Sections

Imagine the shape of a slice through a loaf of bread. You just pictured a *cross section* of the loaf. A **cross section** of a space figure is the intersection of a plane and the figure.

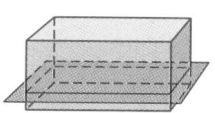

horizontal cross section

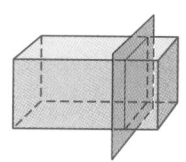

vertical cross section

Cross sections can be at any angle. Different space figures can have cross sections that are the same shape.

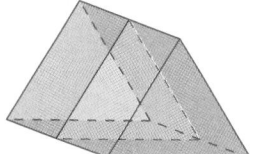
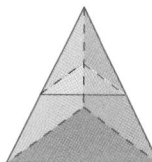
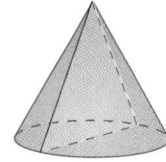
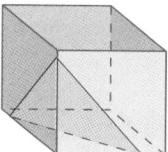

Talk it Over

3. Give an example and a counterexample of the statement "Parallel cross sections of a space figure are congruent."

4. A slice of bread shows a cross section of a loaf of bread. What are some other everyday objects whose cross sections are easily seen?

10-1 Figures in Space

559

Error Analysis

Since cross sections can be at any angle, and different space figures can have cross sections that are the same shape, students should not make the error of assuming that if cross sections are the same shape, then the space figures are the same.

Talk it Over

Questions 3 and 4 check students' understanding of the concepts associated with cross sections.

Reasoning

As an extension of Talk it Over question 3, you might wish to explore this statement with students: Parallel cross sections of a space figure are similar.

Answers to Talk it Over

3. Answers may vary. An example is given. All parallel horizontal or vertical cross sections of a cube are congruent. Counterexample: Two parallel cross sections of a sphere may be circles with different diameters.

4. Answers may vary. Examples: a page of a book, cards in a deck, coins in a pile

Draw several vertical and horizontal cross sections of a cone. Identify each shape.

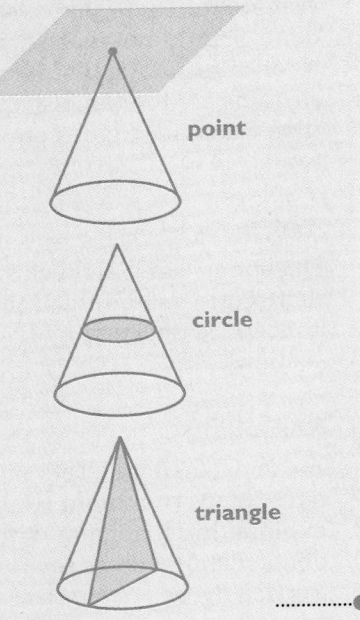

point

circle

triangle

APPLYING

Suggested Assignment

Day 1

Standard 6, 7, 9–19

Extended 6, 7, 9–19

Day 2

Standard 20–31, 40–48

Extended 20–32, 34–48

Integrating the Strands

Algebra Exs. 43, 44

Geometry Exs. 1–42, 45–48

Communication: Drawing

Many students have difficulty visualizing and drawing three-dimensional figures on paper. The use of manipulatives, drawing activities that use different viewing points, and patterns, such as in Exs. 1–8, can help students to develop their spatial perception and to understand concepts involving spatial relationships.

Sample

Draw several vertical and horizontal cross sections of a cylinder. Identify each shape.

Sample Response

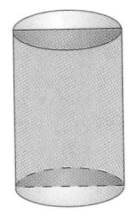 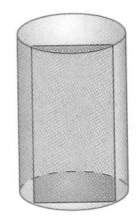 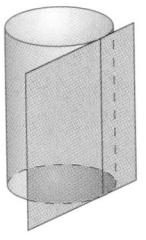 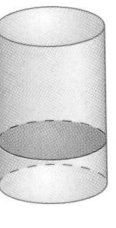 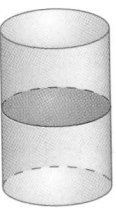

a rectangle | a smaller rectangle | a segment | a circle | another circle

---

▶ **Now you are ready for:**
Exs. 20–48 on pp. 562–564

Look Back ◀

What are some different ways that you can represent a space figure?

10-1 Exercises and Problems

Using Manipulatives Draw and cut out copies of figures A–D in the Exploration to make the patterns shown. Fold each pattern into a space figure. Describe or draw each space figure.

1.    2.   3.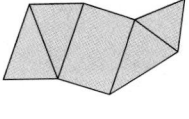

For Exercises 4 and 5, use one of your space figures from Exercises 1–3.

4. Draw a front view, side view, and top view of your space figure.

5. Draw a different pattern for your space figure.

Answers to Look Back

To represent a space figure in two dimensions, you can draw it as it would be seen from different directions. You can make a pattern, or you can show what different cross sections would look like. You can use dotted lines for edges of the figure that are hidden from your view, and you can shade surface area in the same way.

Answers to Exercises and Problems

1. triangular pyramid
2. triangular prism
3. rectangular pyramid
4, 5. Answers may vary. An example is given using the triangular prism from Exercise 2.

4.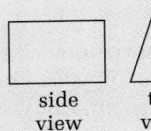

front view   side view   top view

5.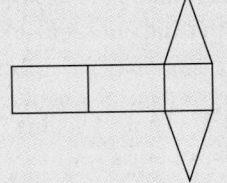

6. Here are two patterns for a cube.

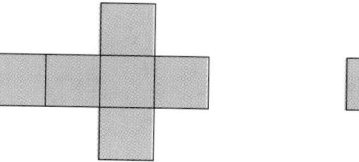

  a. Draw two other patterns that can be folded up to get a cube.

  b. Draw two patterns of six connected squares that cannot be folded up to get a cube.

7. **Open-ended** Find a simple object at school or at home that looks very different from two points of view. Describe or sketch the object from those views.

8. **Group Activity** Work with another student.

  a. Each of you should decide on a space figure. Draw a pattern for your figure.

  b. Exchange patterns with your partner. What space figure does your partner's pattern make? Draw it.

  c. Draw another pattern for the figure.

9. Four students are seated at the corners of a table, all looking at the same object. This is what they see.

Jade's view

Keiko's view

Luisa's view

Miika's view

  a. How many cubes are in the object? It may help to build the object with sugar cubes or other cubes you have at home.

  b. Describe the order of the students around the table.

connection to **SCIENCE**

Here are some general shapes that crystals in nature may imitate.

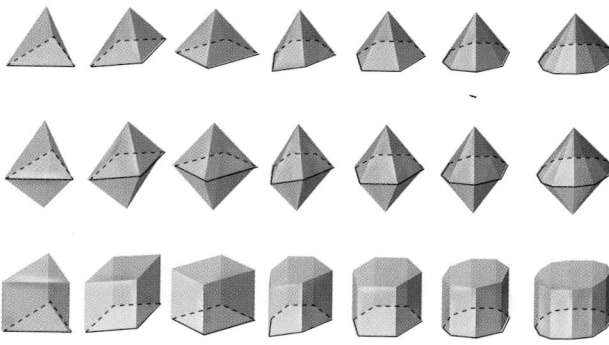

10. How many prisms are drawn?

11. How many pyramids are drawn?

12. Describe the space figures that are not prisms or pyramids.

13. How are the figures in each column similar?

10-1 Figures in Space

561

Answers to Exercises and Problems

6. Answers may vary. Examples are given.

  a.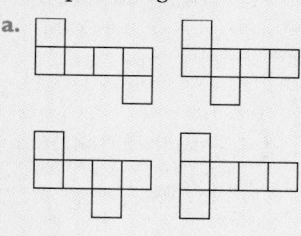

  b.

7. Answers may vary. An example is given. An unsharpened pencil looked at head-on lengthwise looks like a rectangle. Looked on head-on at the eraser, the pencil looks like a circle.

8. **a–c.** Check students' work.

9. **a.** 9 cubes

  b. Jade, Luisa, Keiko, and Miika are in order clockwise.

10. 7 prisms

11. 7 pyramids

12. Each of the other figures is like a pair of pyramids joined at the base.

13. Each column contains a pyramid, a double pyramid, and a prism made from the same base.

Cooperative Learning

Ex. 8 provides an opportunity for students to use what they have learned from the Exploration and from Exs. 1–6. If students create incorrect patterns, their partners can point out errors and help them to create correct patterns.

Research

Some students may be interested in researching crystalline shapes found in nature. These students could prepare a report for the class.

For Exercises 14–19, sketch each space figure. If not possible, give a reason.

14. a pyramid with exactly 10 faces
15. a prism with exactly 10 faces
16. a prism with exactly 10 edges
17. a pyramid with exactly 10 edges
18. a pyramid with exactly 7 vertices
19. a prism with exactly 7 vertices
20. **Reading** Can a space figure have more than one cross section?

connection to GEOLOGY

Cross sections are used by geologists. Examine the cross section of the Antarctic shown below.

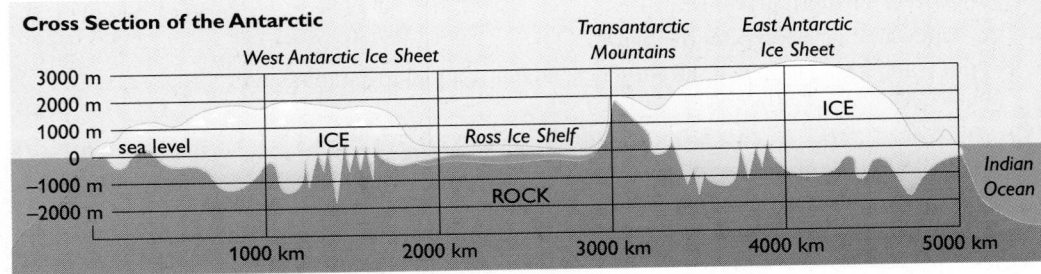

21. About how far above sea level is the highest point of this region?
22. What information does the cross section tell you that you cannot get from an ordinary map?
23. Approximately what percent of the cross-sectional area above sea level is rock?

For Exercises 24–29, sketch a vertical and horizontal cross section of each object. Identify each shape.

24. a sharpened pencil
25. a ball
26. a bowl
27. a hexagonal prism
28. a cylinder
29. a square prism

30. Name a space figure that has a hexagon as a horizontal cross section and a triangle as a vertical cross section.
31. Name a space figure that has a circle as a horizontal cross section and a triangle as a vertical cross section.
32. **Open-ended** Draw three cross sections of a cube that are not squares.

Unit 10 Coordinates and Figures in Space

Answers to Exercises and Problems

14. a pyramid whose base is a nonagon (a polygon with nine sides)

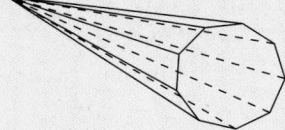

15. an octagonal prism

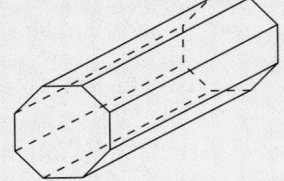

17. a pentagonal pyramid

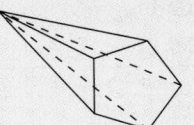

18. a hexagonal pyramid

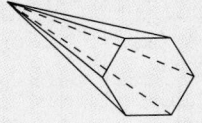

16. not possible; The number of edges of a prism must be a multiple of 3.

33. **Research** Doctors use CAT scans to get cross-sectional images of the body. In what kinds of situations is a CAT scan an especially useful medical tool?

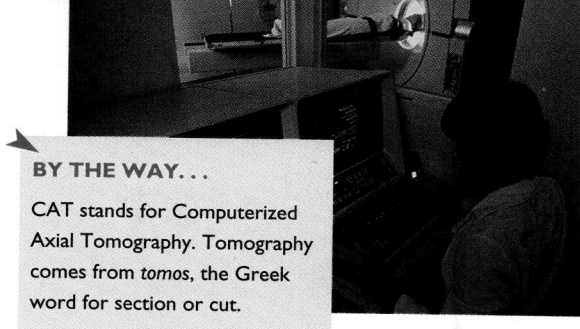

BY THE WAY...

CAT stands for Computerized Axial Tomography. Tomography comes from *tomos*, the Greek word for section or cut.

connection to **LITERATURE**

In Edwin A. Abbott's book *Flatland,* the narrator is a square who lives in a two-dimensional world inhabited by polygons. Confined to moving in a plane, he can see only the outlines of polygons, not their interiors. A sphere passes through Flatland and surprises the narrator by appearing as a circle that changes size.

FLATLAND

Stranger. You are living on a Plane. What you style Flatland is the vast level surface ... on ... the top of which you and your countrymen move about, without rising above it or falling below it.

I am not a plane Figure, but a Solid. You call me a Circle; but in reality I am not a Circle, but an infinite number of Circles, of size varying from a Point to a Circle of thirteen inches in diameter, one placed on the top of the other. When I cut through your plane as I am now doing, I make in your plane a section which you, very rightly, call a Circle...

...You cannot indeed see more than one of my sections, or Circles, at a time; for you have no power to raise your eye out of the plane of Flatland; but you can at least see that, as I rise in Space, so my sections become smaller. See now, I will rise; and the effect upon your eye will be that my Circle will become smaller and smaller till it dwindles to a point and finally vanishes.

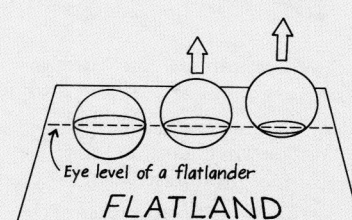

Eye level of a flatlander

FLATLAND

34. What is the radius of the sphere that speaks to the narrator in this passage?

For Exercises 35–38, suppose each space figure passes through Flatland. Describe how it might look to someone in Flatland. Draw some sketches.

35. cylinder   **36.** cone   **37.** square pyramid   **38.** cube

39. **Writing** Explain how a Flatlander could tell the difference between a sphere and a cone passing through Flatland.

10-1 Figures in Space   563

28.

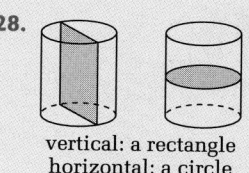

vertical: a rectangle
horizontal: a circle

29.

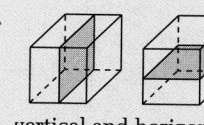

vertical and horizontal:
a rectangle

30. a hexagonal pyramid

31. a cone

32. Sketches may vary. Examples are given.

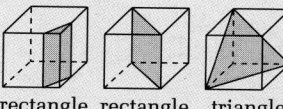

rectangle   rectangle   triangle

33. Answers may vary. Example: to find tumors and abnormal growths

34. 6.5 in.

35–39. See answers in back of book.

Answers to Exercises and Problems

19. not possible; The number of vertices of a prism must be even.

20. Yes.

21. about 3000 m

22. information about the region below the surface, such as the height of rock formations under the ice

23. Estimates may vary. Example: about 2%

24.

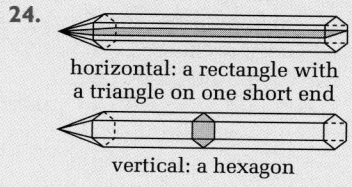

horizontal: a rectangle with a triangle on one short end

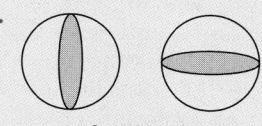

vertical: a hexagon

25.

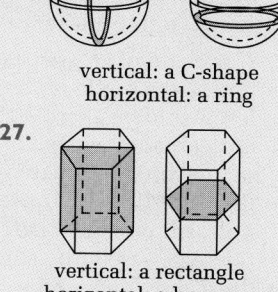

vertical and horizontal:
a circle

26.

vertical: a C-shape
horizontal: a ring

27.

vertical: a rectangle
horizontal: a hexagon

Working on the Unit Project

Students can start working on Exs. 46–48 in their project groups of three. One member of each group can be assigned the job of bringing a cardboard box to school for Ex. 47.

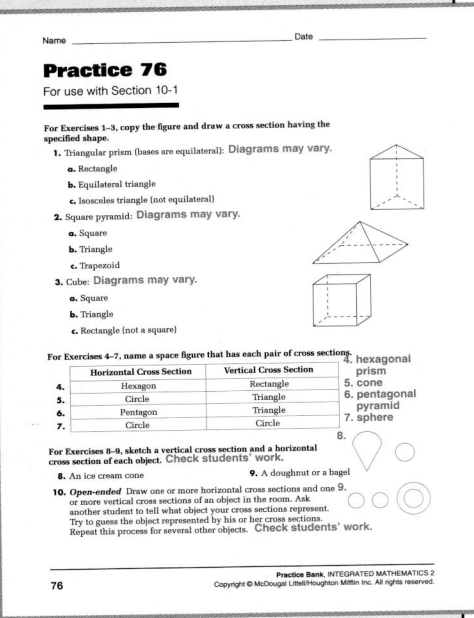
Answers to Exercises and Problems

40–42. Answers may vary. Examples are given.

40. Any vertical or horizontal cross section of a cube is a square. A horizontal cross section of a square pyramid is a square.

41. Any cross section of a sphere is a circle. A cross section of a cone may be a circle.

42. Any vertical cross section of a cone or a pyramid standing on its base is a triangle.

43.

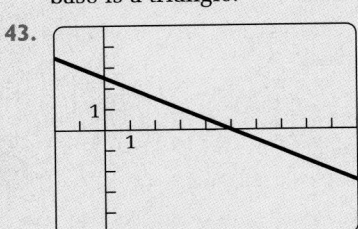

44. d

45. a. about 198 cubic in.
   b. about 66 cubic in.

Open-ended Describe or draw two space figures that have each cross section.

40. a square   41. a circle   42. a triangle

43. Graph the parametric equations. *(Section 9-6)*
$$x = 2t + 1$$
$$y = 2 - t$$

44. Choose the letter of the equation that cannot be true if y varies inversely with x. *(Section 2-3)*

   a. $x = \dfrac{7}{y}$ **b.** $xy = 7$ **c.** $y = \dfrac{7}{x}$ **d.** $y = 7x$

45. Find the volume of each space figure. *(Toolbox Skill 28)*
   a. a cylinder with height 7 in. and radius 3 in.
   b. a cone with height 7 in. and radius 3 in.

Working on the Unit Project

As you complete Exercises 46–48, think about how you can use cross sections and patterns to help you design and make your container.

46. The bottles at the right contain common household products.

   a. Identify a product each bottle might hold.

   b. Draw and describe two horizontal cross sections of each bottle.

   c. Why do you think these bottles are shaped as they are?

47. Unfold a cardboard box. Draw a pattern that may have been used to make the box.

48. **a.** Measure the height and diameter of a twelve-ounce soft drink can.

   b. List the dimensions of several possible boxes that could hold 24 twelve-ounce cans without allowing them to move. Which dimensions do you think are best? Why?

   c. **Research** What are the dimensions of boxes used by grocery stores? What are the advantages of these dimensions? Are there any disadvantages?

---

46. a. Answers may vary. Examples: household cleaner, laundry detergent, window cleaner

   b. A horizontal cross section of the bottle on the left would be a circle. A horizontal cross section of the bottle in the middle would be an ellipse, unless it passed through the region with the handle. Then it would be two circles. A horizontal cross section passing through the lid of this bottle would be a circle. A horizontal cross section of the bottle on the right would be an ellipse unless it passed through the trigger. Then it would be a trapezoid or a parallelogram. A horizontal cross section passing through the lid of this bottle would be a circle and a parallelogram.

   c. Answers may vary. An example is given. The shape of the bottle makes it easy to identify its contents. The shapes also make the bottles easy to hold for the tasks intended for them.

47, 48. See answers in back of book.

Rotations in Space

Focus
Describe space figures that are formed by rotating a plane figure around a line.

Changing the Flat

This is an unopened tissue party decoration. It is made of tissue paper sandwiched between two cardboard copies of a two-dimensional figure, or **plane figure**.

To open it, you rotate one of the cardboard ends until it joins with the other cardboard end.

When you do this, you are rotating a plane figure around a line to form a space figure. The line is called the **axis of rotation**.

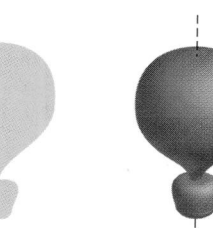

Talk it Over

1. You can think of each object below as the result of rotating a plane figure around an axis. Describe the plane figure. Where is the axis of rotation?

2. What other everyday objects can you think of as the result of rotating a plane figure around an axis?

3. Describe a horizontal and a vertical cross section of each object in question 1.

BY THE WAY...

The tin can was developed in England in 1810. However, the can opener was not invented until 1858! The first cans came with the instructions: "Cut round on the top with a chisel and hammer."

10-2 Rotations in Space

565

Answers to Talk it Over

1. For each figure, the axis is a line passing through the centers of the circles that form the top and bottom of the object. The drawings show the plane figure and the axis.

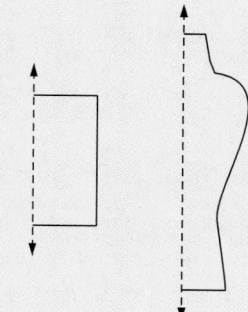

2. Answers may vary. Examples: a conical lamp shade, a ball, a glass jar, a funnel

3. For each object, a horizontal cross section is a circle. A vertical cross section has the shape of the rotated plane figure along with its reflection across the axis of rotation.

PLANNING

Objectives and Strands
See pages 554A and 554B.

Spiral Learning
See page 554B.

Materials List
➤ Paper
➤ Scissors
➤ Tape
➤ Long pencil
➤ Graph paper

Recommended Pacing
Section 10-2 is a one-day lesson.

Extra Practice
See pages 630–631.

Warm-Up Exercises
Warm-Up Transparency 10-2

Support Materials
➤ Practice 77
➤ Enrichment 68 in the Activity Bank
➤ Study Guide 10-2
➤ Problem Set 22
➤ Additional Exploration 13
➤ Diagram Master 2 in the Explorations Lab Manual
➤ Quiz 10-2
➤ Alternative Assessment 2

Talk it Over

Questions 1–3 guide students to visualize the rotation of a plane figure around an axis.

Using Manipulatives

You may wish to demonstrate the rotation in Talk it Over question 1 by using a rectangular piece of cardboard.

Additional Sample

S1 In Sample 1, suppose the figure being rotated in part (a) is a square. What would be the coordinates of points *C* and *D*? How would the space figure that is formed be affected?

C(3, 3); *D*(3, 0)
For the rotation about the *y*-axis or the *x*-axis, the space figure is a cylinder whose radius is equal to its height.

Visual Thinking

Check students' understanding of Sample 1 by asking them to create their own sketches of each rotation. Encourage them to experiment with other shapes and rotations. Ask them to explain their sketches to the class. This activity involves the visual skills of *interpretation* and *perception*.

Describe the space figure formed when you rotate each rectangle around the *y*-axis. Do the same for rotation around the *x*-axis.

a.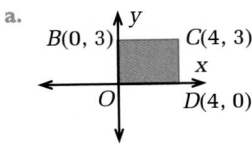

b.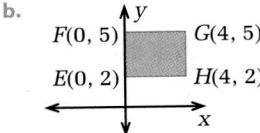

Sample Response

a. When you rotate rectangle *OBCD* around the *y*-axis, you get a cylinder. The radius is 4 and the height is 3.

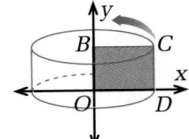 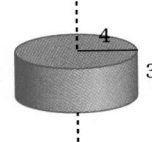

When you rotate rectangle *OBCD* around the *x*-axis, you get a cylinder. The radius is 3 and the height is 4.

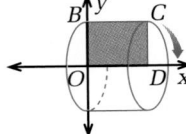 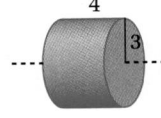

b. When you rotate rectangle *EFGH* around the *y*-axis, you get a cylinder. The radius is 4 and the height is 3.

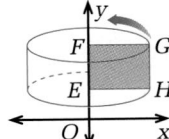 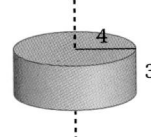

When you rotate rectangle *EFGH* around the *x*-axis, you get this ring shape. The radius of the outer cylinder is 5 and the height is 4. The radius of the inner cylinder is 2 and the height is 4.

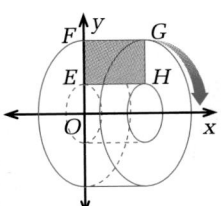 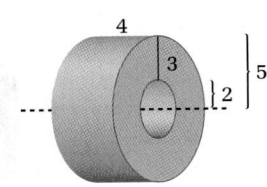

4. Explain how to find the surface area and volume of the first cylinder in Sample 1.

5. What space figure do you get if you rotate rectangle *EFGH* from Sample 1 around the line $y = 2$?

6. Describe a horizontal and a vertical cross section of each space figure in Sample 1.

Sample 2

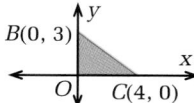

a. Describe the space figure formed when $\triangle OBC$ is rotated around the *y*-axis. Do the same for rotation around the *x*-axis.

b. Which of the two space figures has the greater volume?

Sample Response

a. When you rotate $\triangle OBC$ around the *y*-axis, you get a cone with radius 4 and height 3.

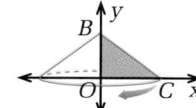 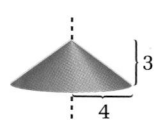

When you rotate $\triangle OBC$ around the *x*-axis, you get a cone with radius 3 and height 4.

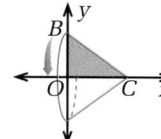 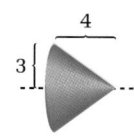

b. The formula for the volume V of a cone is $V = \frac{1}{3}\pi r^2 h$, where r is the radius and h is the height.

Cone around the *y*-axis: $V = \frac{1}{3}\pi(4)^2(3) = 16\pi$ (cubic units)

Cone around the *x*-axis: $V = \frac{1}{3}\pi(3)^2(4) = 12\pi$ (cubic units)

The cone around the *y*-axis has the greater volume.

Look Back

Name two space figures you can get by rotating a plane figure around an axis. Describe a vertical and horizontal cross section for each space figure.

For question 4, you may need to remind students that the surface area of a cylinder is equal to the areas of the two circular bases plus the area of the curved surface; that is, S.A. = $2\pi r^2 + 2\pi rh$, where r is the radius of the cylinder and h is its height. The volume of a cylinder is equal to the area of a base times the height: $V = \pi r^2 h$.

Additional Sample

S2 In Sample 2, suppose $\triangle OBC$ is an isosceles right triangle whose legs are 6 units long. Would the rotation of $\triangle OBC$ about the *y*-axis and *x*-axis still form a cone? Would the volumes of the two cones be the same or different? Why?
Yes; same; because the radius and height of the cone are equal. For each cone, $V = \frac{1}{3}\pi(6)^2 6 = 72\pi$.

Look Back

Students' responses to this Look Back should help them to connect the idea of rotating a plane figure to the idea of a cross section.

Answers to Talk it Over

4. Surface area = $2\pi r^2 + 2\pi rh = 2\pi(4)^2 + 2\pi(4)(3) = 56\pi$; Volume = $\pi r^2 h = \pi(4)^2(3) = 48\pi$

5. a cylinder with radius 3 and height 4

6. Answers may vary. Examples are given.

   a. *y*-axis: A horizontal cross section is a circle with radius 4; a vertical

cross section can be a rectangle 3 units high. *x*-axis: A horizontal cross section can be a rectangle 4 units wide; a vertical cross section can be a circle with radius 3.

   b. *y*-axis: A horizontal cross section is a circle with radius 4; a vertical

cross section can be a rectangle 3 units high. *x*-axis: A horizontal cross section is a rectangle, a pair of rectangles, or a segment 4 units long; a vertical cross section can be a ring.

Answers to Look Back

Answers may vary. Examples are given. A cone can be generated by rotating a triangle about the *y*-axis. A horizontal cross section of the cone is a circle. A vertical cross section is a triangle. A cylinder can be generated by rotating a rectangle around the *y*-axis. A horizontal cross section of the cylinder is a circle. A vertical cross section is a rectangle.

Integrating the Strands

Measurement Exs. 13, 14

Geometry Exs. 1–24, 26–28

Statistics and Probability
Ex. 25

Logic and Language Exs. 1, 14

Using Manipulatives

If any students have difficulty visualizing the space figures formed in Exs. 3–9, they can use cutouts of the shapes as in Ex. 2.

Using Technology

Encourage students to use any three-dimensional software packages that may be available to explore this topic further.

Assessment: Standard

In Ex. 13, students should be able to hypothesize that the volumes of cylinders formed by rotating a rectangle about each side are in the reverse ratio as the sides of rotation.

10-2 Exercises and Problems

1. **Reading** Suppose you rotate a plane figure around two different axes. Are the resulting two space figures necessarily the same?

2. **Using Manipulatives** You will need paper, scissors, tape, and a long pencil.

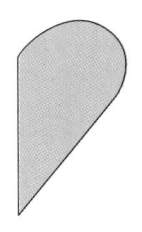

   a. Cut out a copy of the figure at the right.

   b. Tape the straight edge of the figure to the pencil as shown.

   c. Roll the pencil between your hands. If you spin the pencil quickly enough, the plane figure will blur and begin to look like a space figure. Sketch two different views of the space figure.

Describe or sketch the shape formed by rotating each figure around the indicated axis.

3.
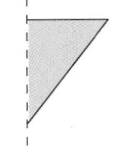

4.

5.

Describe or sketch the space figure formed by each rotation.

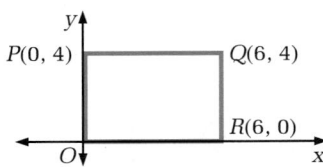

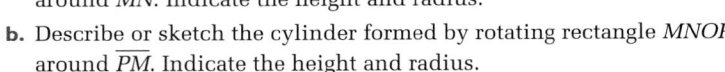

6. Rotate $OPQR$ around the y-axis.

7. Rotate $\triangle OPR$ around the y-axis.

8. Rotate $OPQR$ around the x-axis.

9. Rotate $\triangle OPR$ around the x-axis.

10. Find the volume and surface area of the space figure in Exercise 6.

11. Find the volume of the space figure in Exercise 9.

12. a. Describe or sketch the cylinder formed by rotating rectangle $MNOP$ around $\overline{MN}$. Indicate the height and radius.

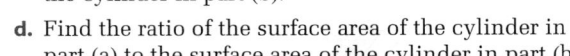

   b. Describe or sketch the cylinder formed by rotating rectangle $MNOP$ around $\overline{PM}$. Indicate the height and radius.

   c. Find the ratio of the volume of the cylinder in part (a) to the volume of the cylinder in part (b).

   d. Find the ratio of the surface area of the cylinder in part (a) to the surface area of the cylinder in part (b).

13. Repeat Exercise 12 with this rectangle.

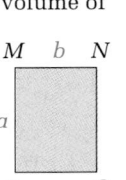

Answers to Exercises and Problems

1. No; consider Sample 1.

2. a, b. See students' work.

c.

3. cone   4. sphere

5. a figure that looks like a cone with the top cut off.

6. a cylinder with radius 6 and height 4

7. a cone with radius 6 and height 4

8. a cylinder with radius 4 and height 6

9. a cone with radius 4 and height 6

10. Volume: 144π; Surface area: 120π

11. 32π

12. a. height = 2, radius = 1

    b. height = 1, radius = 2

    c. (a) 2π; (b) 4π, ratio = 1:2

    d. (a) 6π; (b) 12π; ratio = 1:2

13. a. height = b, radius = a

    b. height = a, radius = b

    c. (a) $a^2b\pi$; (b) $ab^2\pi$; ratio = $a:b$

    d. (a) $2ab\pi + 2a^2\pi$; (b) $2ab\pi + 2b^2\pi$; ratio = $a:b$

14. the cylinder with the large radius; Since the radius is squared to find the volume and $x > y$, then $\pi x^2 y > \pi x y^2$.

15. Yes; a triangle can be rotated around an axis to form a cone.

14. Writing Which cylinder do you think has the greater volume? Explain your reasoning.

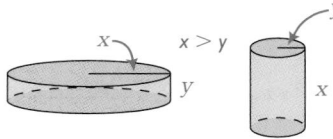

Tell whether each space figure can be formed by rotating a plane figure around an axis. Give a reason for your answer.

15. a cone   **16.** a pyramid   **17.** a sphere

Career Designers such as engineers and architects often use computer-aided design (CAD) programs in their work. Many computer 3-D graphics packages have a *surface revolution* tool. You draw a shape, and the surface revolution tool rotates it around an axis.

For Exercises 18 and 19, sketch the figure that is rotated to form the space figure. Indicate the axis of rotation.

18.    **19.**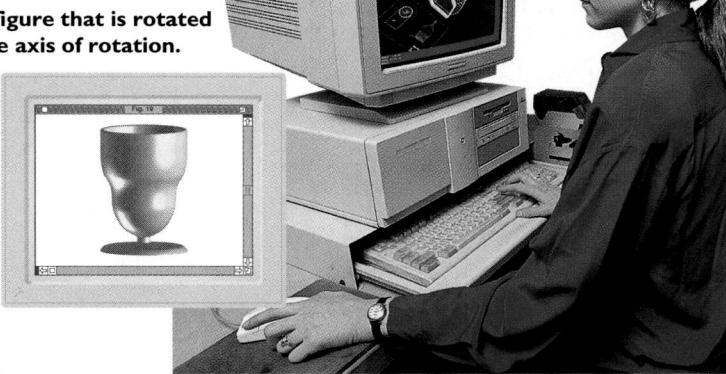

Suppose you enter each plane figure into the computer and use the surface revolution tool to rotate it around the dashed line. Describe or sketch the space figure the computer will draw.

20. 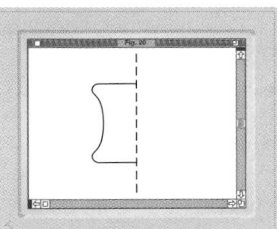   **21.** 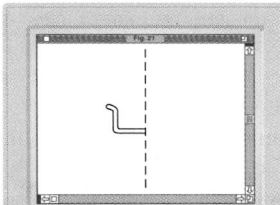   **22.**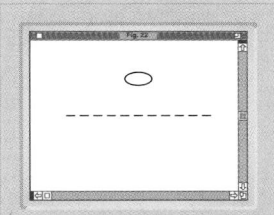

Ongoing **ASSESSMENT**

23. Open-ended Imagine an object you can design with a surface revolution tool. Draw the shape you will rotate and sketch what your finished object will look like.

10-2 Rotations in Space   **569**

 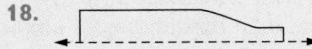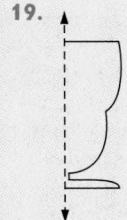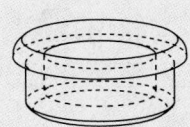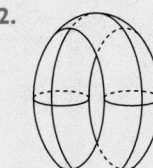

24. Draw two different views of your mathematics book. *(Section 10-1)*

25. You roll a die three times. What is the probability of rolling a "1" exactly twice? *(Section 6-8)*

26. **Given** *P* is on the perpendicular bisector of $\overline{AB}$. *(Section 8-6)*

Prove *PA = PB*

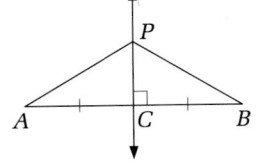

Working on the Unit Project

As you complete Exercises 27 and 28, think about how you can use rotations to help design your container.

27. Give several examples of containers that have an axis of rotation.

28. A fruit juice company designs a new can. The new can has the same height and diameter as the old can, but the bottom of the new can is indented about $\frac{5}{16}$ in.

old can new can

$\frac{5}{16}$ in.

a. On a set of axes, draw a figure that can be rotated around the *y*-axis to model the old can. On a different set of axes, draw a figure that can be rotated around the *y*-axis to model the new can.

b. Will the new can hold as much juice as the old can?

c. Why do you think the new can was designed to have the same height and diameter as the old can?

d. Give other examples of containers that appear to hold more than they actually do.

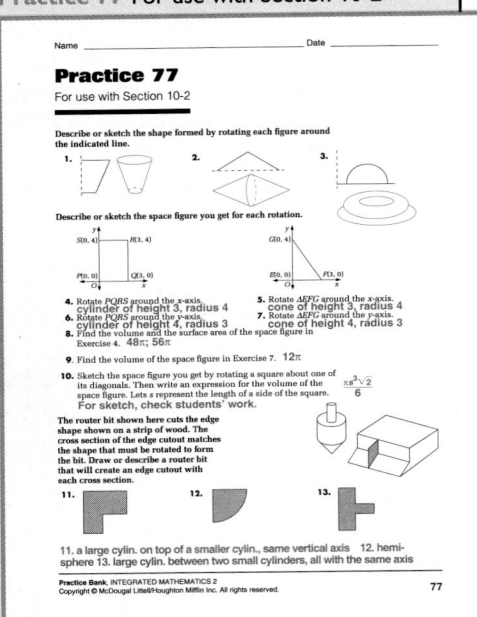
Answers to Exercises and Problems

24. Drawings may vary. Examples are given.

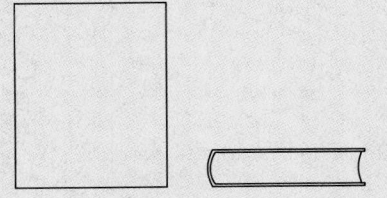

25. about 7%

26. See answers in back of book.

27. Answers may vary. Examples: any cans or bottles

28. a.

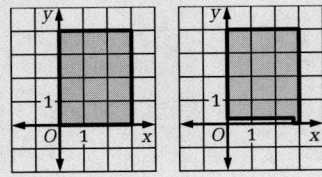

b. No.

c. The new can will appear to contain the same amount of juice as the old can so the consumers will not realize they are paying the same price for less juice unless they check the label.

d. Answers may vary. Example: a cereal box that has been redesigned so that the area of the front of the box is greater than that of the old box, but the other dimensions are altered so that the volume of the box is actually less than that of the old box.

Points That Fit Conditions

It's Around Here Somewhere

Focus

Describe or draw a set of points that meet one or more conditions.

On January 17, 1994, a large earthquake struck the western United States. The earthquake recording station at Topopah Spring, Nevada, recorded that the *epicenter* was located about 370 km away. The epicenter of a quake is the place on the surface of Earth above the focus of the quake.

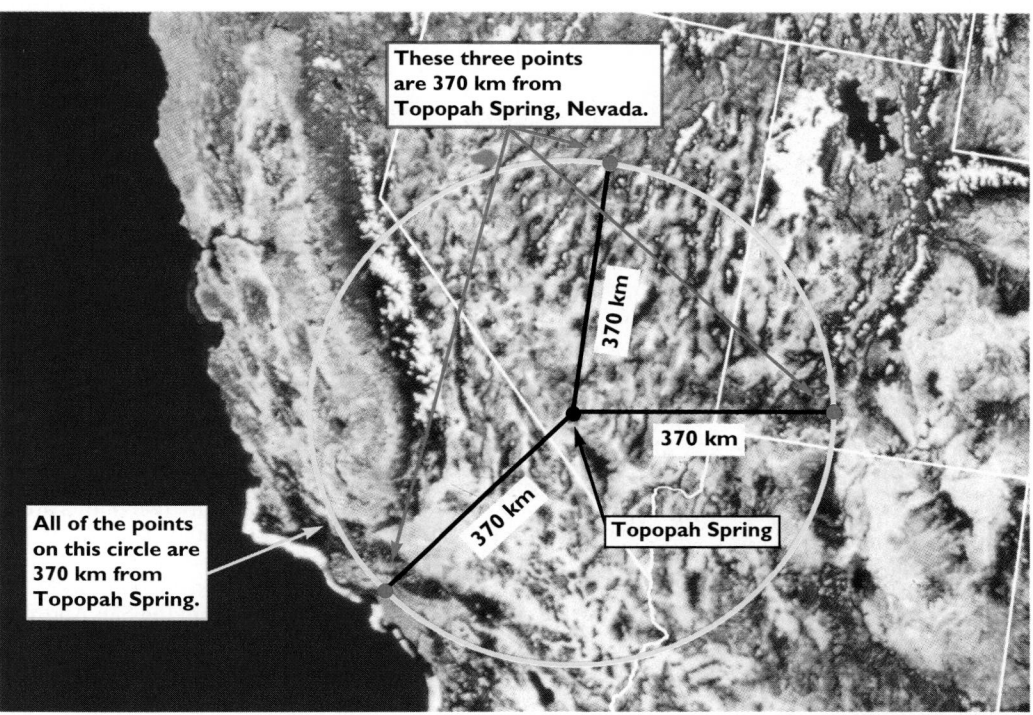

These three points are 370 km from Topopah Spring, Nevada.

370 km

370 km

370 km

Topopah Spring

All of the points on this circle are 370 km from Topopah Spring.

Earthquake stations record only the distance to the epicenter, not the direction. The location of the epicenter could be any point on a circle with radius 370 km centered at the recording station.

10-3 Points That Fit Conditions

571

PLANNING

Objectives and Strands
See pages 554A and 554B.

Spiral Learning
See page 554B.

Materials List
➤ Graph paper

Recommended Pacing
Section 10-3 is a one-day lesson.

Extra Practice
See pages 630–631.

Warm-Up Exercises
Warm-Up Transparency 10-3

Support Materials
➤ Practice 78
➤ Enrichment 69 in the Activity Bank
➤ Study Guide 10-3
➤ Problem Set 22
➤ Diagram Master 1 in the Explorations Lab Manual
➤ Quiz 10-3
➤ Test 41

Communication: Discussion

When discussing the earthquake on page 571, students need to understand that the *distance* to the epicenter is one condition that defines a circle having a radius of 370 km. If the *direction* to the epicenter were known, the second condition would locate the exact position of the epicenter.

Additional Sample

S1 Answer each question.

a. In Sample 1, would changing the distance from 5 in. to any other distance affect the general shape of the figures that are described? **No.**

b. Describe the set of points in plane *W* that are equidistant from the circumference of a circle whose radius is 10 in.
the center of the circle

c. Describe the set of points in space that are equidistant from two parallel lines *a* and *b*.
a plane that is halfway between *a* and *b*

Mathematical Procedures

Points that fit conditions determine various kinds of geometric figures. These figures may be plane figures or space figures. In geometry, the term *locus* is used to describe figures whose points fit one or more conditions.

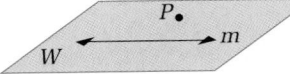

Point *P* and line *m* are in plane *W*. Describe the set of points in plane *W* and in space that meet each condition.

a. 5 in. from point *P*   **b.** 5 in. from line *m*

c. 5 in. from plane *W*

Sample Response

a. in plane *W*: a circle with radius 5 in.

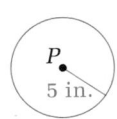

in space: a sphere with radius 5 in.

b. in plane *W*: two parallel lines each 5 in. from the given line

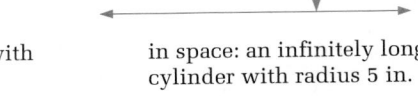

in space: an infinitely long cylinder with radius 5 in.

c. No points in plane *W* meet the condition.

in space: two parallel planes planes 5 in. from plane *W*.

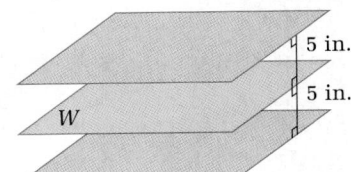

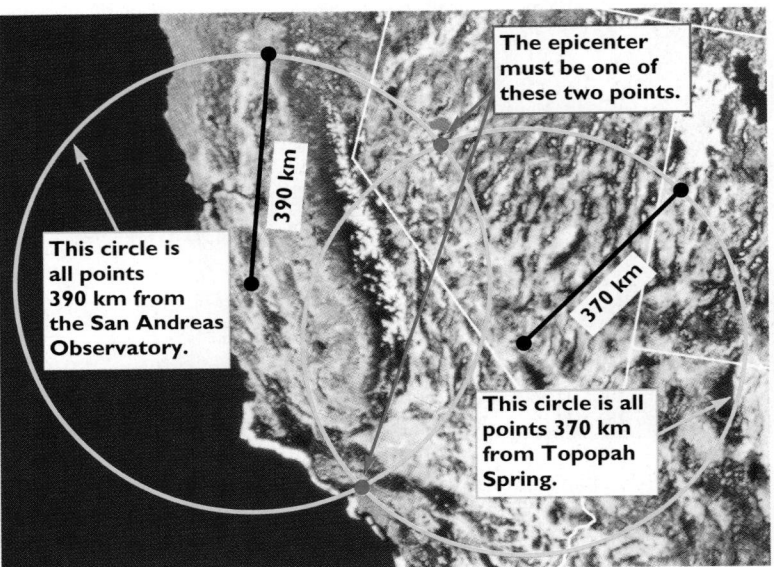

The epicenter must be one of these two points.

This circle is all points 390 km from the San Andreas Observatory.

390 km

370 km

This circle is all points 370 km from Topopah Spring.

The San Andreas Observatory recorded that the epicenter of the January 17, 1994, earthquake was located about 390 km away.

Only two points are both 370 km away from Topopah Spring and 390 km away from the San Andreas Observatory. The epicenter must be one of these two points.

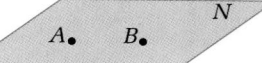

Talk it Over

1. How could you use data from a third recording station to decide which of the two points is the epicenter?

2. Do you know which of the two points was the epicenter?

Sample 2

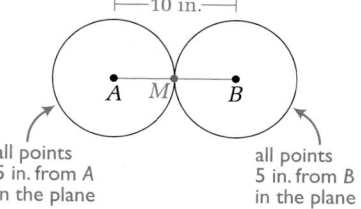

Points *A* and *B* are in plane *N*. For each condition, describe the set of points that are in plane *N* and 5 in. from both *A* and *B*.

a. *A* and *B* are 10 in. apart.

b. *A* and *B* are 8 in. apart.

c. *A* and *B* are 12 in. apart.

Sample Response

a. *M* is on both circles, so *M* is 5 in. from both *A* and *B*.

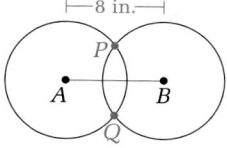

all points 5 in. from *A* in the plane

all points 5 in. from *B* in the plane

b. *P* and *Q* are 5 in. from both *A* and *B*.

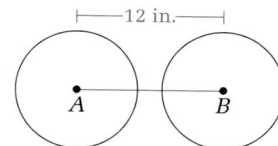

c. No points are on both circles, so no points are 5 in. from both *A* and *B*.

Talk it Over

3. In part (b) of Sample 2, explain why *P* and *Q* are on the perpendicular bisector of $\overline{AB}$.

4. If *A* and *B* are 10 in. apart, describe the set of points that are in space and 5 in. from *A* and *B*.

5. If *A* and *B* are 12 in. apart, describe the set of points that are in space and 5 in. from *A* and *B*.

BY THE WAY...

Almost two thousand years ago, earthquakes were detected in China with a device like the one at the right. Even slight tremors caused a metal ball to fall from the mouth of one of the dragons into the mouth of a metal toad. Observers could tell the direction of the earthquake by seeing which ball fell.

A modern reconstruction of Chang Heng's earthquake detector of A.D. 132.

573

Answers to Talk it Over

1. The circle determined by the third station would intersect the first two circles at one of their intersection points.

2. The 1994 earthquake was near the point in Los Angeles, California.

3. If a point is the same distance from both endpoints of a line segment, then it lies on the perpendicular bisector of the segment.

4. Point *M*, the only point on both the sphere with radius 5 in. centered at *A* and the sphere with radius 5 in. centered at *B*.

5. No points meet the condition.

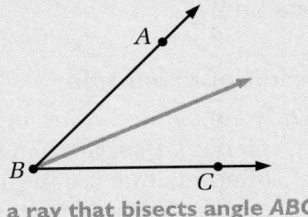
In Sample 2, point *Q* is the same distance from both *A* and *B*. It is said to be **equidistant** from *A* and *B*.

Sample 3

Points M and N are in plane R. Describe all points that are equidistant from M and N.

   a. in plane *R*   **b.** in space

Sample Response

a. In plane *R*, all the points on the perpendicular bisector of $\overline{MN}$ are equidistant from *M* and *N*.

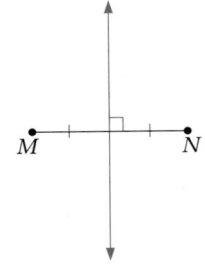

b. In space, all the points on the plane perpendicular to $\overline{MN}$ and halfway between *M* and *N* are equidistant from both points.

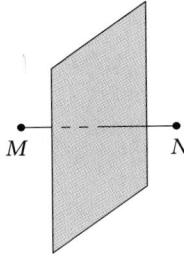

Look Back ←

Give an example of a condition that is met by a different set of points in a plane and in space.

10-3 Exercises and Problems

1. **Reading** If you want to locate the epicenter of an earthquake, why do you need more than one recording station?

2. What is the set of all points that are 1 m from the floor of the room you are in?

3. Imagine a point, *P*, on the floor of the room you are in.
   a. What is the set of all points on the floor that are 2 m from *P*?
   b. What is the set of all points in the room that are 2 m from *P*?

4. Imagine a line, $\overleftrightarrow{CD}$, down the middle of the floor of the room you are in.
   a. What is the set of all points on the floor that are 2 m from $\overleftrightarrow{CD}$?
   b. What is the set of all points in the room that are 2 m from $\overleftrightarrow{CD}$?

For Exercises 5–10, *A* and *B* are 6 cm apart in plane *S*. Describe or draw all points in plane *S* that meet each set of conditions.

5. 4 cm from both *A* and *B*

6. 2 cm from *A* and 4 cm from *B*

7. 2 cm from both *A* and *B*

8. 1 cm from *A* and 3 cm from *B*

9. 3 cm from both *A* and *B*

10. 4 cm from *A* and 5 cm from *B*

11. Describe the set of points 60 mi from the control room at the top of an airport's control tower.

12. **Writing** Suppose you are designing a track and field stadium. Why might you want to know the set of points where a shot putter's shot put can land?

13. **Writing** In a thunderstorm, if you hear thunder five seconds after you see lightning, then the lightning is about one mile away. Each second corresponds to about $\frac{1}{5}$ mi. Describe how the principle used to locate the epicenter of an earthquake can be used to locate lightning in a thunderstorm.

14. What is the set of all points equidistant from the floor and the ceiling of the room you are in?

15. Describe all points in a plane and in space that are 5 cm from a segment.

16. **Seismology** On April 18, 1993, many earthquake stations in South America recorded an earthquake. The Cocahabamba station in Bolivia is about 1200 km east and 1900 km south of the Cayambe station in Ecuador. The Cerro El Oso station in Venezuela is about 1100 km east and 1000 km north of the Cayambe station.

a. Plot the relative positions of the three recording stations on graph paper. Write a scale on your diagram.

b. The Cayambe station recorded that the epicenter of the quake was about 1300 km away. Sketch or use a compass to draw all the possible locations of the epicenter.

c. The Cocahabamba station also recorded that the epicenter was about 1300 km away. Sketch or use a compass to draw all the possible locations of the epicenter.

d. The Cerro El Oso station recorded that the epicenter was about 2500 km away. Estimate the location of the epicenter.

BY THE WAY...

There are thousands of earthquake recording stations worldwide. The IRIS Data Management Center provides data from the stations shown below.

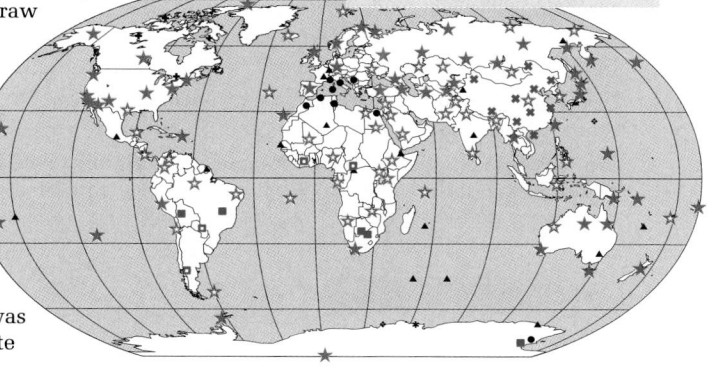

Students Acquiring English

For Ex. 16, have students acquiring English work with partners to follow the directions for the activity. Suggest that they begin by reviewing the directions together, making sure that they understand the materials needed and the order of the steps.

Assessment: Open-ended

For Ex. 16, ask students why they would need to record the finding of the Cerro El Oso station to estimate the location of the epicenter. Would it be possible that only two stations would be necessary to find the location? Draw a sketch to describe this possibility.

Answers to Exercises and Problems

10. two points found by intersecting circles, one circle with center *A* and radius 4 cm, and the second circle with center *B* and radius 5 cm

11. a dome-shaped space figure consisting of the points on a sphere with center at the control room and radius 60 mi that are on or above the intersection of the sphere and the plane of the ground (The ground is not actually a plane, nor is the control room a point.)

12. Answers may vary. For example, you would not want the shot-put area to be unrealistically small nor larger (and so more expensive) than it need be. You would also not want to position the areas for other events where athletes might be hit by the shot put.

13. Three different recording stations can determine the distance from a given lightning flash using the given formula. Then circles can be drawn with the point where all three circles intersect determining the location of the source of the lightning.

14. a plane parallel to both the floor and ceiling, halfway between them

15. in a plane: a plane figure consisting of two parallel line segments each 5 cm from the given segment with their endpoints on each side of the given segment joined by a semicircle with center at the endpoint of the given segment and radius 5 cm; in space: a capsule-shaped figure consisting of a cylinder with radius 5 cm and length that of the segment with each end of the cylinder a hemisphere with center at the endpoint of the segment and radius 5 cm

16. **a–d.** See answers in back of book.

575

For Exs. 17 and 18, you may wish to provide students with copies of the map to save class time. They can be photocopied directly from the textbook and even scaled up in size to make it easier for students to shade them or draw points.

Answers to
Exercises and Problems ············

17. See answers in back of book.

18. **a.** the points on the perpendicular bisector of the segment joining the points for Lamu and Mount Kilimanjaro

   b. Answers may vary. An example is given. about 300 km east and 50 km south of Nyahururu Falls

   c.

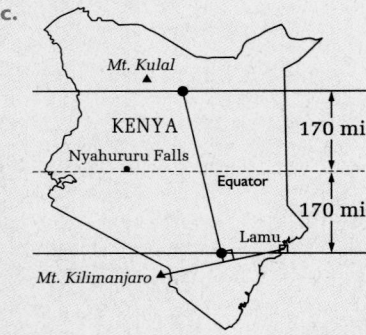

   d. No points meet the condition.

19. in a plane: a third parallel line halfway between the given lines; in space: a plane parallel to the given lines and halfway between them

20. in a plane: a single point (the center of the circle); in space: a line perpendicular to the plane of the circle that passes through the center

21. The focus of a parabola is a fixed point that is the same distance as the directrix from any point on the parabola. The directrix of a parabola is a fixed line that is the same distance as the focus from each point on the parabola. All points on the parabola are equidistant from the focus and the directrix, and the focus is not on the directrix.

576

---

connection to **SOCIAL STUDIES**

This map shows the locations of some of the mosques in the northernmost part of the town of Lamu, Kenya. Criers call from the mosques at dawn, at noon, in the afternoon, at nightfall, and after dark. The circles show how far away each crier can be heard.

17. Trace the part of Lamu Town shown.

   a. Shade the area where you can hear a crier calling from mosque *A*.

   b. With another color, shade the area where you can hear a crier calling from both mosque *A* and mosque *B*.

   c. **Open-ended** With another color, shade an area where you can hear a crier calling from each of three different mosques. Which mosques are they?

   d. With another color, shade an area where you cannot hear any criers from the mosques shown.

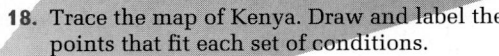

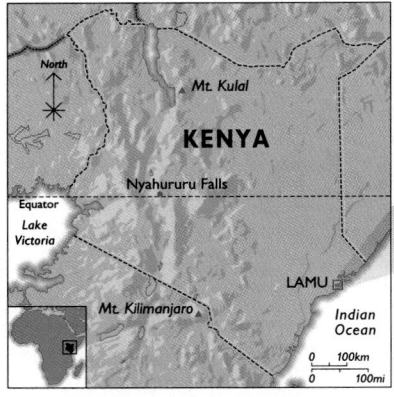

18. Trace the map of Kenya. Draw and label the points that fit each set of conditions.

   a. equidistant from Lamu and Mount Kilimanjaro

   b. equidistant from Lamu, Mount Kilimanjaro, and Mount Kulal

   c. 170 mi away from the equator and equidistant from Lamu and Mount Kilimanjaro

   d. equidistant from Lamu, Mount Kilimanjaro, Mount Kulal, and Nyahururu Falls

19. Describe the set of points in plane *F* and in space that are equidistant from two parallel lines in plane *F*.

20. Circle *D* is in plane *T*. Describe the set of points in plane *T* and in space that are equidistant from all the points on circle *D*.

21. **Research** The points on a parabola meet conditions related to the *focus* and *directrix* of the parabola. What are the focus and directrix? What conditions do the points on the parabola meet?

Ongoing **ASSESSMENT**

22. **Open-ended** For each answer, make up a problem like the ones in Samples 1, 2, or 3.

   a. Answer: a point   **b.** Answer: a line   **c.** Answer: no points

---

22. Answers may vary. Examples are given.

   a. Describe the set of points in a plane that are equidistant from three noncollinear points.

   b. Describe the set of points in a plane that are equidistant from the endpoints of a segment.

   c. Given two points *A* and *B* that are 10 cm apart, describe the set of points in a plane that are 4 cm from *A* and *B*.

23. a cone with height 2 and radius 5; $\frac{50\pi}{3}$

24. The conclusion assumes that the converse is automatically true, which may not be the case. Marya may have decided to write a let-

ter to her cousin without having first received a letter herself. Her cousin may or may not write back.

25. $\left(-1\frac{1}{2}, 2\frac{1}{2}\right)$

26. $(3, -4)$

27. $\left(-1\frac{3}{4}, 6\frac{1}{2}\right)$

28, 29. Answers may vary.

23. Describe or draw the space figure formed when you rotate △*MNO* around the *x*-axis. Find its volume. *(Section 10-2)*

24. What is wrong with the conclusion below? *(Section 1-7)*

If Marya gets a letter, then she will write a letter to her cousin. Marya writes a letter to her cousin. Conclusion: Marya got a letter.

Find the coordinates of the midpoint of the segment whose endpoints are given. *(Section 5-3)*

25. (0, 4) and (−3, 1)　　　**26.** (−2, −5) and (8, −3)　　　**27.** (0.5, 6) and (−4, 7)

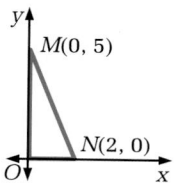

Working on the Unit Project

28. Choose an object or objects that you will design your container to hold. Describe the object or objects.

29. a. Which of the following conditions should your container meet?

easy to open, unbreakable, resealable, waterproof, lightweight

b. What other conditions should your container meet?

Working on the Unit Project

Project groups should agree on a set of objects for Ex. 28 and the conditions for Ex. 29. This information will be needed when students are ready to complete their containers.

Quick Quiz (10-1 through 10-3)

See page 601.

Unit 10　CHECKPOINT

1. Writing Describe a sphere in terms of its cross sections, as a rotation in space, and as a set of points that fit a condition.

2. Draw a pattern for a pentagonal prism.　　**10-1**

3. Draw two cross sections of a pentagonal prism.

Describe or sketch the space figure formed by rotating each plane figure around the y-axis. Indicate the height and radius.　　**10-2**

4.

y
P(0, 6)　Q(8, 6)
　　　　R(8, 0)
O　　　　　x

5.

y
L(0, 5)
　　　　N(2, 0)
O　　　　x

6. Points *A* and *B* are 6 in. apart in plane *W*. Describe all points in plane *W* that are 5 in. from *A* and *B*.　　**10-3**

7. Points *C* and *D* are 5 in. apart in plane *W*. Describe all points in plane *W* that are 2 in. from *C* and *D*.

8. Points *E* and *F* are 4 in. apart in plane *W*. Describe all points in space that are equidistant from *E* and *F*.

10-3 Points That Fit Conditions

577

Practice 78 For use with Section 10-3

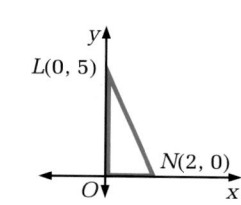

Answers to Checkpoint

1. Any cross section of a sphere is a circle with a radius no bigger than the radius of the sphere. A sphere can be produced by rotating a semicircle about its diameter. A sphere is the set of all the points in space that are a given distance from a given point.

2.

3.

4. a cylinder with radius 8 and height 6

5. a cone with radius 2 and height 5

6. two points on the perpendicular bisector of $\overline{AB}$ each 5 in. from *A* and *B*

7. No points meet the condition.

8. a plane that is perpendicular to $\overline{EF}$ and intersects $\overline{EF}$ at its midpoint

PLANNING

Objectives and Strands
See pages 554A and 554B.

Spiral Learning
See page 554B.

Materials List
➤ Cardboard box at least 10 in. × 10 in. × 10 in.
➤ Scissors
➤ Large needle
➤ Thread
➤ 10 buttons or paper clips
➤ Tape
➤ Graph paper

Recommended Pacing
Section 10-4 is a one-day lesson.

Extra Practice
See pages 630–631.

Warm-Up Exercises
Warm-Up Transparency 10-4

Support Materials
➤ Practice 79
➤ Enrichment 70 in the Activity Bank
➤ Study Guide 10-4
➤ Problem Set 23
➤ Diagram Master 7 in the Explorations Lab Manual
Overhead Visual 10
➤ Quiz 10-4

Section 10-4

Coordinates in Three Dimensions

Name That Point

Focus

Describe the location of points in space using three coordinates. Find midpoints of segments in three dimensions.

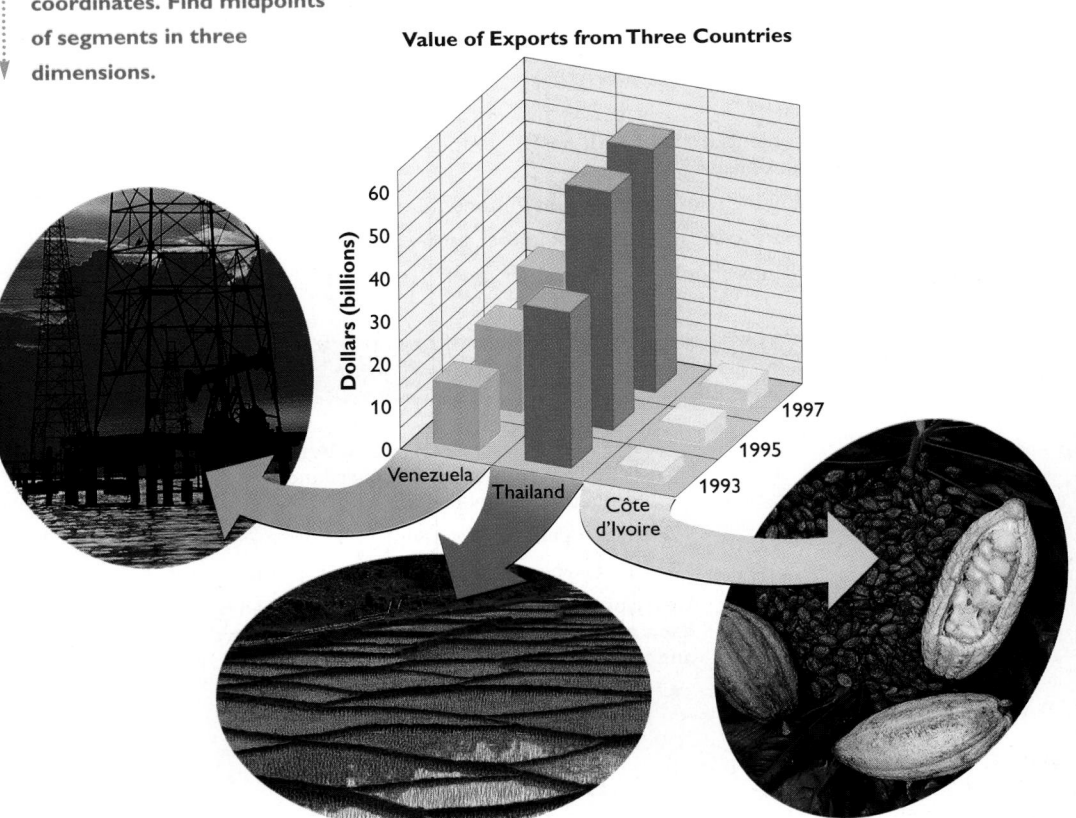

Value of Exports from Three Countries

Talk it Over

1. Which country increased its earnings from exports the most from 1993 to 1997?

2. Which country earned less than $20 billion in 1997?

3. About how much did Venezuela earn in exports in 1993?

Answers to Talk it Over

1. Thailand
2. Côte d'Ivoire
3. about $15 billion

The graph of exports is a model in three-dimensional space. To locate points in space, three coordinate axes are needed.

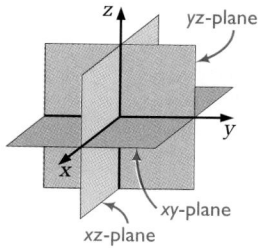

yz-plane
xz-plane
xy-plane

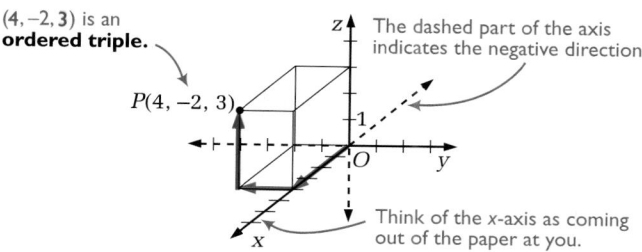

$(4, -2, 3)$ is an **ordered triple.**

$P(4, -2, 3)$

The dashed part of the axis indicates the negative direction.

Think of the x-axis as coming out of the paper at you.

To locate point $P(4, -2, 3)$, start at the origin. Move 4 units toward you on the x-axis, 2 units to the left parallel to the y-axis, and 3 units up parallel to the z-axis.

Talk it Over

4. On which axis does the point (5, 0, 0) lie?

5. Describe how you would locate the point (6, 4, −1) in three dimensions.

6. Does it matter which axis you move along first to locate a point? Explain.

Sample 1

Coordinates of vertices **D** and **F** of the rectangular prism are given. Find the coordinates of vertices **B**, **A**, and **H**.

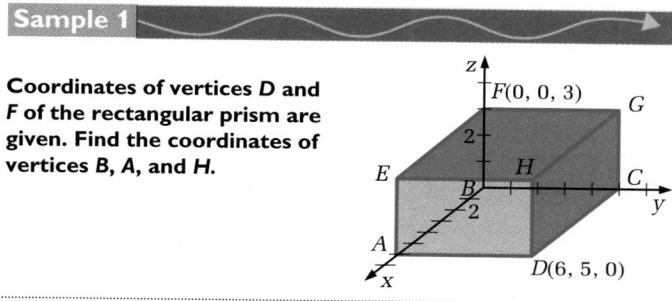

Sample Response

B is at the origin. The coordinates of B are $(0, 0, 0)$.

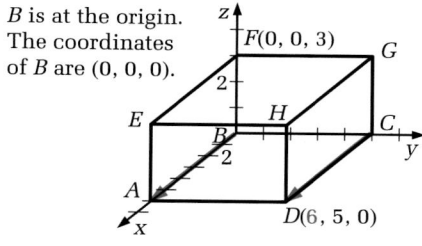

A has the same x-coordinate as point D. The coordinates of A are $(6, 0, 0)$.

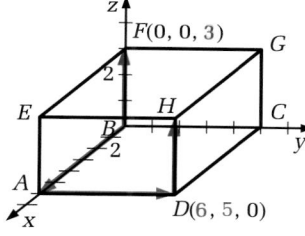

H has the same x- and y-coordinates as point D and the same z-coordinate as F. The coordinates of H are $(6, 5, 3)$.

10-4 Coordinates in Three Dimensions

579

Answers to Talk it Over

4. the x-axis

5. Start at the origin. Move 6 units toward you on the x-axis, 4 units to the right parallel to the y-axis, and −1 unit parallel to the z-axis.

6. No; the order in which you move will take you along a different path, but each path will lead you to the same point, provided you move the correct number of units along each axis as indicated by the coordinates of the ordered triple.

TEACHING

Talk it Over

Questions 1–3 prepare students to work with coordinates in three dimensions by having them work with the more familiar three-dimensional bar graph.

Multicultural Note

Venezuela is on the Caribbean coast of South America. Oil revenues make up most of its export earnings. The mining of iron ore is an important economic activity, and steel, textiles, paper are also produced. Coffee, rice, fruit, and sugar are the primary crops.

Thailand is in southeastern Asia on the Indochinese and Malayan peninsulas. Thailand is one of the largest producers of tin. It also exports rice and teak wood.

In 1985, Ivory Coast officially changed its name to Côte d'Ivoire. The country is on the southern coast of west Africa. Cote d'Ivoire is the most prosperous of the tropical African nations. The primary crops are coffee and cocoa. Mineral resources include diamonds and manganese.

Additional Sample

S1 Coordinates of vertices R and T of the rectangular prism are given. Find the coordinates of S and W.

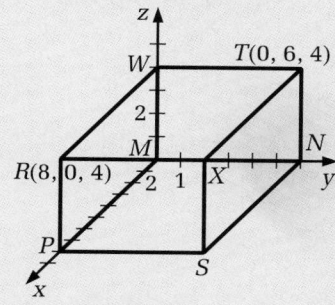

S has the same x-coordinate as point R and the same y-coordinate as point T. The coordinates of S are **(8, 6, 0)**. The coordinates of W are **(0, 0, 4)**.

579

Additional Sample

S2 Use the drawing in Sample 2 to find the coordinates of the midpoint of $\overline{AG}$.

$A(6, 0, 0)$; $G(0, 5, 3)$

Midpoint of $\overline{AG}$ is

$\left(\dfrac{6+0}{2}, \dfrac{0+5}{2}, \dfrac{0+3}{2}\right) = \left(3, \dfrac{5}{2}, \dfrac{3}{2}\right)$.

Reasoning

The fact that the midpoint of $\overline{FD}$, found in Sample 2, and the midpoint of $\overline{AG}$, found in Additional Sample S2, are the same point can be used as the basis for a discussion about whether the internal diagonals of a rectangular prism *all* have the same midpoint. Students can work some examples and make a conjecture about this.

Teaching Tip

You may need to remind some students that the *mean* of a set of numbers is their average.

Error Analysis

Students may make errors in identifying the axes associated with the coordinates of a point in three dimensions. The Look Back can be used to identify this type of error and to correct it.

Sample 2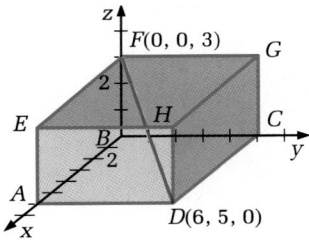

Find the coordinates of the midpoint of $\overline{FD}$.

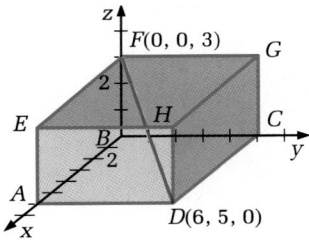

Sample Response

As in two dimensions, each of the coordinates of the midpoint of a segment is the mean of the corresponding coordinates of its endpoints.

$F(0, 0, 3)$ ← endpoints of $\overline{FD}$
$D(6, 5, 0)$ ←

$\left(\dfrac{0+6}{2}, \dfrac{0+5}{2}, \dfrac{3+0}{2}\right) = \left(3, \dfrac{5}{2}, \dfrac{3}{2}\right)$ ← midpoint of $\overline{FD}$

THE MIDPOINT FORMULA FOR THREE DIMENSIONS

The midpoint of the segment with endpoints (x_1, y_1, z_1) and (x_2, y_2, z_2) has coordinates

$$\left(\dfrac{x_1 + x_2}{2}, \dfrac{y_1 + y_2}{2}, \dfrac{z_1 + z_2}{2}\right).$$

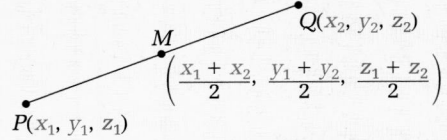

Look Back ←

Are point $F(1, 2, 3)$ and point $G(3, 2, 1)$ the same point? Explain.

Unit 10 Coordinates and Figures in Space

Answers to Look Back

No; F is at the location 1 unit along the x-axis, 2 units parallel to the y-axis, and 3 units parallel to the z-axis. G is at the location 3 units along the x-axis, 2 units parallel to the y-axis, and 1 unit parallel to the z-axis.

10-4 Exercises and Problems

1. In which year was the per capita consumption of bottled water the least?

2. Which drink lost popularity from 1985 to 1995?

3. Estimate the per capita consumption of soft drinks in 1990.

4. Do you think this graph accurately reflects your beverage consumption? Explain.

5. **Reading** What is an ordered triple?

6. Find the missing coordinates of each vertex.
   a. $O(0, 0, \underline{?})$
   b. $P(0, \underline{?}, \underline{?})$
   c. $Q(\underline{?}, 0, \underline{?})$
   d. $T(\underline{?}, \underline{?}, \underline{?})$

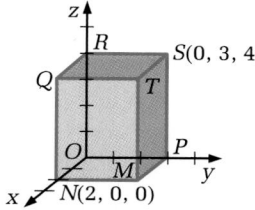

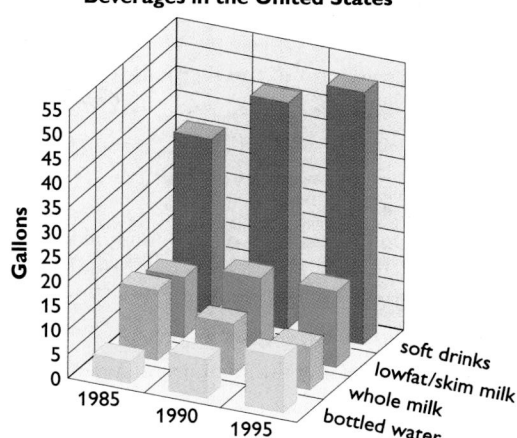

Per Capita Consumption of Beverages in the United States

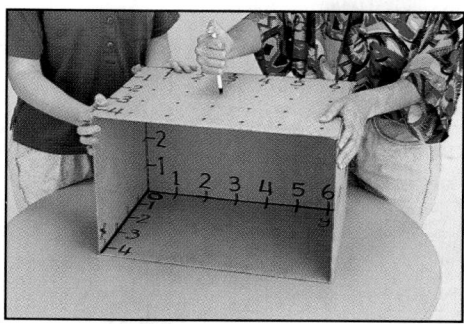

7. **Group Activity** Work with another student. You will need a cardboard box at least 10 in. × 10 in. × 10 in., scissors, a large needle, thread, at least ten buttons or paper clips, and tape.

   a. Draw and label axes on three inside edges of the box as shown. The tick marks should be about 3 in. apart.

   b. Copy the x- and y-axes on the top of the box. Mark the xy-grid with holes as shown.

   c. Cut at least ten pieces of thread about 3 in. longer than your z-axis. Tie a button or paper clip to the end of each thread.

   d. Plot the point (1, 2, 3) by putting the thread through hole (1, 2) in the top of the box. Pull the button down inside until it is level with z = 3. Put tape over the hole to keep the rest of the thread from sliding through.

   e. List and plot at least ten ordered triples for which $x + y - z = 0$. Is the point (1, 2, 3) a solution of this equation?

   f. What do you notice about the solutions of $x + y - z = 0$?

10-4 Coordinates in Three Dimensions

Answers to Exercises and Problems

1. 1985

2. whole milk

3. about 46 gallons

4. Answers may vary.

5. An ordered triple (x, y, z) is three numbers that designate the position of a point in three-dimensional space. The x-coordinate, y-coordinate, and z-coordinate give the point's distance along each axis.

6. a. $O(0, 0, 0)$
   b. $P(0, 3, 0)$
   c. $Q(2, 0, 4)$
   d. $T(2, 3, 4)$

7. a–d. Check students' work.
   e. Answers may vary. Examples: $(-1, 1, 0)$, $(5, -3, 2)$, $(2, 1, 3)$; Yes.
   f. The points lie in one plane.

581

For Exercises 8–10, use the rectangular prism at the right.

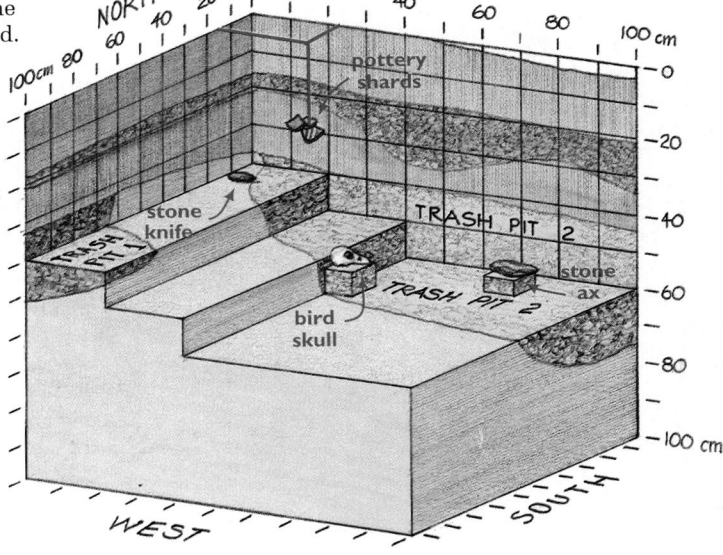

8. Find the coordinates of vertices *A* through *G*.

9. Find the volume and the surface area of the prism.

10. Find the coordinates of the midpoint of $\overline{BH}$.

Find the midpoint of the segment with the given endpoints.

11. $L(0, 0, 0)$ $P(-2, -2, -2)$

12. $R(3, 6, 9)$ $S(1, 5, 4)$

13. $W(2, 0, -3)$ $Z(4, -1, 3)$

14. $T(-1, -1, -1)$ $V(1, 1, 1)$

15. **a.** Plot and connect the vertices of quadrilateral *ABCD*:
    $A(0, 0, 0)$, $B(5, 0, 0)$, $C(5, -5, 0)$, $D(0, -5, 0)$

    b. On the same set of axes, plot quadrilateral *EFGH*:
    $E(0, 0, 5)$, $F(5, 0, 5)$, $G(5, -5, 5)$, $H(0, -5, 5)$

    c. Draw $\overline{AE}$, $\overline{BF}$, $\overline{CG}$, and $\overline{DH}$.

    d. Describe the space figure.

16. **a.** How many different ordered triples contain each of the numbers 0, 1, and 2?

    b. Plot the ordered triples from part (a).

17. What is the *y*-coordinate of all points on the *z*-axis?

18. What is the *z*-coordinate of all points in the *xy*-plane?

19. What is the *z*-coordinate of all points 3 units below the *xy*-plane?

Career Archaeologists are studying a campsite near Boston that was used from 3000 years ago to 500 years ago by the Massachuseog people and their ancestors. They used the campsite when they came to the coast in the fall to gather supplies for the winter.

Archaeologists carefully remove dirt one layer at a time and record the locations of objects that they find.

For Exercises 20–24, use the diagram.

20. What object is at about this location: 3 cm from north wall, 10 cm from east wall, and 41 cm below surface?

21. What is the location of the stone ax?

22. **Writing** How is the method of recording three-dimensional locations in archaeology different from the method used in mathematics? Describe advantages and disadvantages of each method.

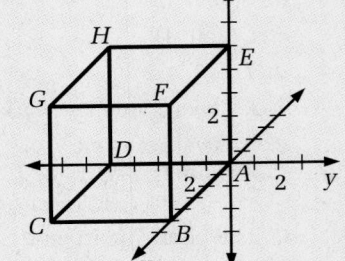

582

Unit 10 Coordinates and Figures in Space

Answers to Exercises and Problems

8. $A(2, 0, 0)$, $B(0, 0, 0)$, $C(0, 5, 0)$, $D(2, 5, 0)$, $E(2, 0, 3)$, $F(0, 0, 3)$, $G(0, 5, 3)$

9. Volume = 30 cubic units; Surface area = 62 square units

10. $\left(1, \frac{5}{2}, \frac{3}{2}\right)$

11. $(-1, -1, -1)$

12. $\left(2, \frac{11}{2}, \frac{13}{2}\right)$

13. $\left(3, -\frac{1}{2}, 0\right)$

14. $(0, 0, 0)$

15. a–c.

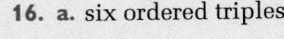

d. cube with edge = 5

16. **a.** six ordered triples

b.

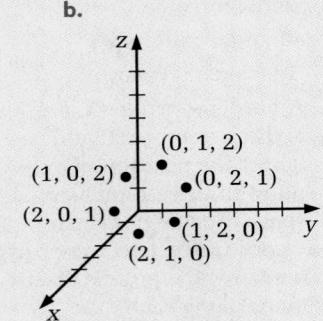

23. Which do you think was in the campsite longer, the pottery shards or the bird skull? Why?

24. **Open-ended** Why do you think archaeologists need to keep a record of the precise locations of objects?

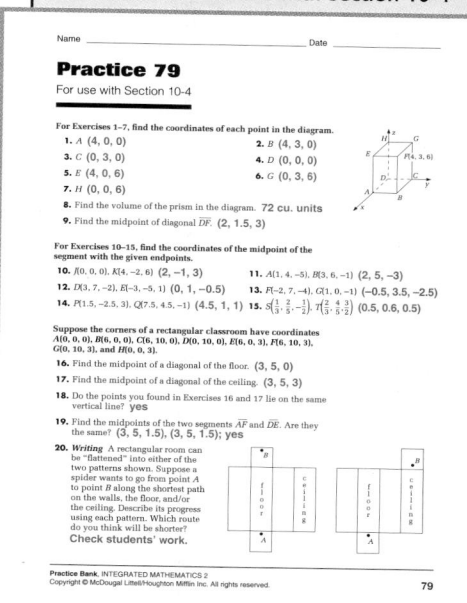

By the way...

In 1934 archaeologist Florence Hawley Ellis used data from trash mounts to help explain why people settled and later deserted Chaco Canyon, New Mexico.

Ongoing **ASSESSMENT**

25. **Open-ended** Imagine your classroom in a three-dimensional coordinate system.

  a. Where would you place the origin?

  b. What distance would you use for one unit along each axis?

  c. Estimate the coordinates of the center of the classroom.

  d. Estimate the coordinates of two other points of interest in the room.

Review **PREVIEW**

26. Describe the set of points in space that are 12 in. from a line. *(Section 10-3)*

Simplify. *(Section 3-5)*

27. $6\begin{bmatrix} 3 & 5 \\ 4 & 6 \end{bmatrix}$

28. $-1\begin{bmatrix} 15 & 9 & 14 & 7 \\ 2 & 5 & 40 & 22 \\ 0 & 1 & 30 & 35 \end{bmatrix}$

29. $[2 \ 1 \ 6 \ 20] - [4 \ 0 \ 2 \ 6]$

Find the value of the variable in each figure. *(Section 8-7)*

30.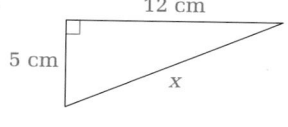

12 cm

5 cm

x

31.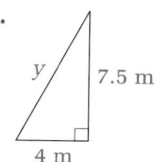

y

7.5 m

4 m

Find the distance between each pair of points. *(Section 5-2)*

32. (0, 0) and (4, 7.5)

33. (2, 3) and (6, 10.5)

 Working on the Unit Project

34. a. **Open-ended** In a three-dimensional coordinate system, plot eight points that are the vertices of a rectangular prism.

  b. Suppose the prism in part (a) is a container and you want to divide it into four congruent spaces. You can use the midpoints of the top and bottom edges to help you place cardboard dividers. Write the coordinates of these midpoints.

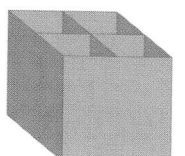

10-4 Coordinates in Three Dimensions

583

Working on the Unit Project

As students work on Ex. 34 in their project groups, you can circulate among the groups to check that they are plotting the points correctly in the three-dimensional coordinate system.

Practice 79 For use with Section 10-4

Name _____ Date _____

Practice 79
For use with Section 10-4

For Exercises 1–7, find the coordinates of each point in the diagram.

1. A (4, 0, 0) **2.** B (4, 3, 0)
3. C (0, 3, 0) **4.** D (0, 0, 0)
5. E (4, 0, 6) **6.** G (0, 3, 6)
7. H (0, 0, 6)

8. Find the volume of the prism in the diagram. 72 cu. units

9. Find the midpoint of diagonal $\overline{DF}$. (2, 1.5, 3)

For Exercises 10–15, find the coordinates of the midpoint of the segment with the given endpoints.

10. J(0, 0, 0), K(4, −2, 6) (2, −1, 3) **11.** A(1, 4, −5), B(3, 6, −1) (2, 5, −3)
12. D(3, 7, −2), E(−3, −5, 1) (0, 1, −0.5) **13.** F(−2, 7, −4), G(1, 0, −1) (−0.5, 3.5, −2.5)
14. P(1.5, −2.5, 3), Q(7.5, 4.5, −1) (4.5, 1, 1) **15.** $S\left(\frac{1}{3}, \frac{2}{3}, -\frac{1}{3}\right), T\left(\frac{2}{3}, \frac{4}{3}, \frac{3}{2}\right)$ (0.5, 0.6, 0.5)

Suppose the corners of a rectangular classroom have coordinates A(0, 0, 0), B(6, 0, 0), C(6, 10, 0), D(0, 10, 0), E(6, 0, 3), F(6, 10, 3), G(0, 10, 3), and H(0, 0, 3).

16. Find the midpoint of a diagonal of the floor. (3, 5, 0)

17. Find the midpoint of a diagonal of the ceiling. (3, 5, 3)

18. Do the points you found in Exercises 16 and 17 lie on the same vertical line? yes

19. Find the midpoints of the two segments $\overline{AF}$ and $\overline{DE}$. Are they the same? (3, 5, 1.5), (3, 5, 1.5); yes

20. **Writing** A rectangular room can be "flattened" into either of the two patterns shown. Suppose a spider wants to go from point A to point B along the shortest path on the walls, the floor, and/or the ceiling. Describe its progress using each pattern. Which route do you think will be shorter? Check students' work.

Practice Bank, INTEGRATED MATHEMATICS 2
Copyright © McDougal Littell/Houghton Mifflin Inc. All rights reserved.

79

---

27. $\begin{bmatrix} 18 & 30 \\ 24 & 36 \end{bmatrix}$

28. $\begin{bmatrix} -15 & -9 & -14 & -7 \\ -2 & -5 & -40 & -22 \\ 0 & -1 & -30 & -35 \end{bmatrix}$

29. $[-2 \ 1 \ 4 \ 14]$

30. 13 cm

31. 8.5 m

32. 8.5

33. 8.5

34. Answers may vary. Examples are given.

  a. (0, 0, 0), (2, 0, 0), (2, 2, 0), (0, 2, 0), (2, 0, 2), (2, 2, 2), (0, 2, 2), (0, 0, 2)

  b. (1, 0, 0), (0, 1, 0), (1, 2, 0), (2, 1, 0), (1, 0, 2), (0, 1, 2), (2, 1, 2), (1, 2, 2)

Answers to Exercises and Problems ····································

17. 0 **18.** 0 **19.** −3

20. stone knife

21. 70 cm from the north wall, 10 cm from the east wall, and 58 cm below the surface

22. The archaeology method adds two additional axes, those of west and south, opposite north and east. These additional axes add boundaries to the three-dimensional area and add more descriptive tools for locating objects. Too many alternatives or too much information can be cumbersome, however. The mathematics method is more simple.

23. bird skull; because it was found farther down below the surface

24. Answers may vary. An example is given. The location of objects helps archaeologists place the objects in chronological order. By doing this, they are able to formulate theories about the civilizations they have discovered.

25. **a–d.** Answers may vary.

26. an infinitely long cylinder with radius 12 in.

583

PLANNING

Objectives and Strands
See pages 554A and 554B.

Spiral Learning
See page 554B.

Materials List
➤ Medium-size boxes
➤ Heavy paper
➤ Ruler
➤ Protractor
➤ Scissors
➤ Graph paper

Recommended Pacing
Section 10-5 is a two-day lesson.

Day 1

Pages 584–586: Exploration through The Distance Formula, *Exercises 1–17*

Day 2

Pages 586–587: Talk it Over 3 through Look Back, *Exercises 18–39*

Extra Practice
See pages 630–631.

Warm-Up Exercises
💡 Warm-Up Transparency 10-5

Support Materials
➤ Practice 80
➤ Enrichment 71 in the Activity Bank
➤ Study Guide 10-5
➤ Problem Set 23
➤ Diagram Masters 7, 25 in the Explorations Lab Manual
💡 Overhead Visual 10
➤ Quiz 10-5
➤ Alternative Assessment 3

Section 10-5

The Distance Formula in Three Dimensions

Focus

Find the distance between two points in three dimensions.

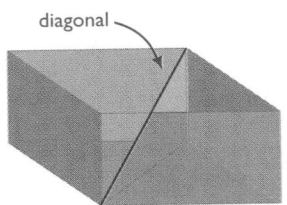

diagonal

EXPLORATION

(What) is the length of a diagonal of a box?

- **Materials: medium boxes (no larger than 14 in. × 14 in. × 14 in.), large sheets of heavy paper, rulers, protractors, scissors**
- **Work with another student.**

A **diagonal of a rectangular prism** is a segment that joins one vertex to the vertex that is farthest from it. In this Exploration you will make and measure a diagonal of a box.

① Choose a box.

② Measure and record the length and width of the inside of your box to the nearest eighth of an inch. Measure and record the height of your box.

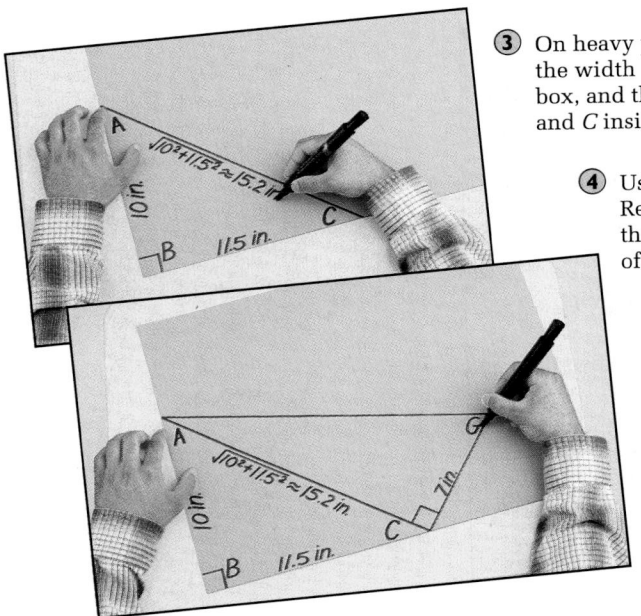

③ On heavy paper, draw right △ABC so that AB is the width of your box, BC is the length of your box, and the right angle is at B. Label points A, B, and C inside the triangle.

④ Use the Pythagorean theorem to find AC. Record the result on your drawing. This is the length of a diagonal of the bottom face of your box.

⑤ Draw right △ACG so that CG is the height of your box and the right angle is at C. Label point G inside the triangle.

⑥ Use the Pythagorean theorem to find AG. This is the length of a diagonal of your box. Measure $\overline{AG}$. Are the two numbers close? Record AG on your drawing.

584 **Unit 10** Coordinates and Figures in Space

Answers to Exploration

1–8. Answers may vary. An example is given.

1. A shoe box $5\frac{7}{8}$ in. wide, $12\frac{1}{4}$ in. long, and $3\frac{3}{8}$ in. high is used in the following examples.

2–6. Check students' work.

AB	BC	CG	AC	AG
$5\frac{7}{8}$ in.	$12\frac{1}{4}$ in.	$3\frac{3}{8}$ in.	about 13.6 in.	about 14.0 in.

6. The numbers should be close.

7, 8. Check students' work.

⑦ Cut out quadrilateral *ABCG* and fold it along the line that passes through *A* and *C*.

⑧ Fit the folded quadrilateral into your box so that △*ABC* is flat on the bottom and $\overline{AG}$ shows a diagonal of the box.

Watch Out!
A diagonal of a face of a rectangular prism is not a diagonal of the prism.

Talk it Over

1. Do all diagonals of a rectangular prism have the same length?

2. In the Exploration, suppose *x* is the width, *y* is the length, and *z* is the height of a box. Use the Pythagorean theorem to show that

$$AG = \sqrt{(\sqrt{x^2 + y^2})^2 + z^2} = \sqrt{x^2 + y^2 + z^2}.$$

LENGTH OF A DIAGONAL OF A RECTANGULAR PRISM

A rectangular prism with edges of length *x*, *y*, and *z* has a diagonal of length *d*, where

$$d = \sqrt{x^2 + y^2 + z^2}.$$

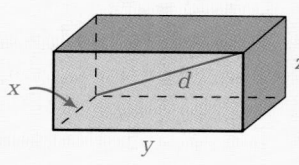

Sample 1

Find the length of a diagonal of a rectangular prism with edges of length 2 cm, 8 cm, and 5 cm.

Sample Response

Problem Solving Strategy: Use a formula.

Substitute 2 for *x*, 8 for *y*, and 5 for *z* in the formula for the length of a diagonal of a rectangular prism.

$$d = \sqrt{x^2 + y^2 + z^2} = \sqrt{2^2 + 8^2 + 5^2} = \sqrt{4 + 64 + 25} = \sqrt{93} \approx 9.64$$

The length of a diagonal is about 9.6 cm.

Answers to Talk it Over

1. Yes.

2. $\overline{AG}$ is the hypotenuse of a right triangle with legs of lengths $AC = \sqrt{x^2 + y^2}$ and $GC = z$; $AG = \sqrt{(\sqrt{x^2 + y^2})^2 + z^2} = \sqrt{x^2 + y^2 + z^2}$

TEACHING

Exploration

The goal of the Exploration is to have students make a box so they can find the length of one of its diagonals. This activity prepares students for understanding the distance formula in three dimensions, which is discussed on page 586.

Talk it Over

It is important that students understand the derivation of the formula in question 2. Students should refer to steps 4–6 of the Exploration to find the length of $\overline{AG}$.

Additional Sample

S1 Find the length of a diagonal of a rectangular prism with edges of length 3 in., 9 in., and 7 in.

Use a formula.
$$d = \sqrt{x^2 + y^2 + z^2}$$
$$= \sqrt{3^2 + 9^2 + 7^2}$$
$$= \sqrt{9 + 81 + 49}$$
$$= \sqrt{139} \approx 11.79$$

The length of a diagonal is about 11.8 in.

The Distance Formula

To find the distance from a point to the origin, imagine that the segment connecting the point and the origin is a diagonal of a rectangular prism. The distance to the origin is the length of the diagonal.

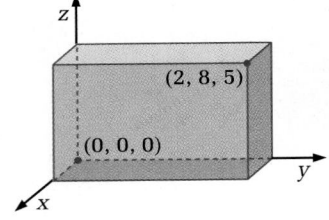

▶ Now you are ready for:
Exs. 1–17 on p. 588

Talk it Over

Suppose the prism above is translated as shown below.

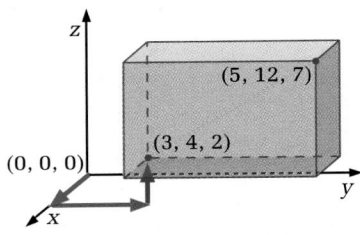

3. Do you think that translating the prism changes the length of the diagonal?

4. How can you find the lengths of the edges of the prism?

5. How can you find the length of the diagonal from (3, 4, 2) to (5, 12, 7)?

The distance between any two points in three dimensions can be found using a three-dimensional version of the distance formula.

THE DISTANCE FORMULA IN THREE DIMENSIONS

The distance, d, between the points (x_1, y_1, z_1) and (x_2, y_2, z_2) is

$$d = \sqrt{(x_2 - x_1)^2 + (y_2 - y_1)^2 + (z_2 - z_1)^2}.$$

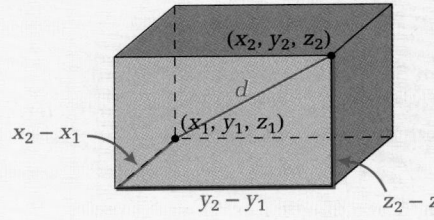

Answers to Talk it Over

3. No.

4. Subtract the x-coordinates of the endpoints of a width to find the width of the prism. Subtract the y-coordinates of a length to find the length of the prism. Subtract the z-coordinates of a height to find the height of the prism.

5. Find the change in x-coordinates, y-coordinates, and z-coordinates. Substitute these values for x, y, and z in the formula for a diagonal of a prism and simplify.

Find the distance between (3, 4, 2) and (5, 12, 7).

Sample Response

$d = \sqrt{(x_2 - x_1)^2 + (y_2 - y_1)^2 + (z_2 - z_1)^2}$ ⟵ Use the distance formula.

$= \sqrt{(5 - 3)^2 + (12 - 4)^2 + (7 - 2)^2}$ ⟵ Let $(x_1, y_1, z_1) = (3, 4, 2)$ and $(x_2, y_2, z_2) = (5, 12, 7)$.

$= \sqrt{4 + 64 + 25}$

$= \sqrt{93}$

≈ 9.64

The distance between the two points is about 9.6.

Sample 3

Tell whether the triangle formed by $P(4, 0, 0)$, $Q(0, 2, 0)$, and $R(3, 3, 5)$ is *scalene*, *isosceles*, or *equilateral*. Explain your answer.

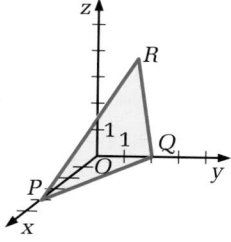

Sample Response

To classify the triangle as scalene, isosceles, or equilateral, find the lengths of the sides and compare them.

Use the distance formula to find PQ, QR, and RP.

$PQ = \sqrt{(0 - 4)^2 + (2 - 0)^2 + (0 - 0)^2} = \sqrt{16 + 4 + 0} = \sqrt{20}$

$QR = \sqrt{(3 - 0)^2 + (3 - 2)^2 + (5 - 0)^2} = \sqrt{9 + 1 + 25} = \sqrt{35}$

$RP = \sqrt{(4 - 3)^2 + (0 - 3)^2 + (0 - 5)^2} = \sqrt{1 + 9 + 25} = \sqrt{35}$

Since $QR = RP = \sqrt{35}$, the triangle is isosceles.
The triangle is not equilateral, because $PQ \neq \sqrt{35}$.

> ⋯➤ Now you are ready for:
> **Exs. 18–39 on pp. 588–590**

Look Back ⟵

How is the distance formula in three dimensions like the distance formula in two dimensions? How is it different?

Additional Samples

S2 Find the distance between (5, 3, 6) and (10, 8, 14).

Use the distance formula.
$d =$
$\sqrt{(10 - 5)^2 + (8 - 3)^2 + (14 - 6)^2}$
$= \sqrt{25 + 25 + 64}$
$= \sqrt{114} \approx 10.68$
The distance between the two points is about 10.7.

S3 Tell whether the triangle formed by $A(5, 0, 0)$, $B(0, 4, 0)$, and $C(5, 4, 6)$ is *scalene*, *isosceles*, or *equilateral*. Explain your answer.

$AB =$
$\sqrt{(0 - 5)^2 + (4 - 0)^2 + (0 - 0)^2}$
$= \sqrt{41}$

$BC =$
$\sqrt{(5 - 0)^2 + (4 - 4)^2 + (6 - 0)^2}$
$= \sqrt{61}$

$AC =$
$\sqrt{(5 - 5)^2 + (4 - 0)^2 + (6 - 0)^2}$
$= \sqrt{52}$

Since $AB \neq BC \neq AC$, the triangle is scalene. ⋯⋯⋯•

Answers to Look Back ⋯⋯⋯⋮

In both formulas, the distance is the square root of the sum of the squares of the differences of each pair of corresponding coordinates. In three dimensions, three coordinates are involved. In two dimensions, only two coordinates are involved.

587

Suggested Assignment

Day 1

Standard 1–6, 9–17

Extended 1–17

Day 2

Standard 18–25, 29–39

Extended 18–39

Integrating the Strands

Algebra Exs. 1–7, 9–34, 36–39

Geometry Exs. 1–34, 39

Statistics and Probability Ex. 35

Mathematical Procedures

The Pythagorean theorem underlies many solutions to problems involving length and distance in relation to rectangular prisms, pyramids, and cones. The theorem is used in the derivation of the distance formula, both in its two-dimensional and three-dimensional forms.

Reasoning

Many students will be able to apply the formulas given in this section. Exs. 7, 17, and 26–28 will demonstrate students' depth of understanding of the formulas.

10-5 Exercises and Problems

Use the Pythagorean theorem to calculate the lengths AC and AG in each figure to the nearest tenth.

1.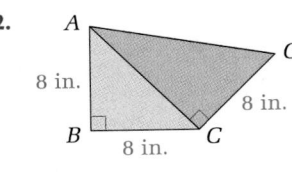

2.

3.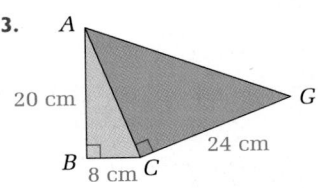

Interior dimensions are given. Find the length of a diagonal of each prism. Will the object fit inside?

4. 10.5 in.

5. 28 in.

6. 79 in.

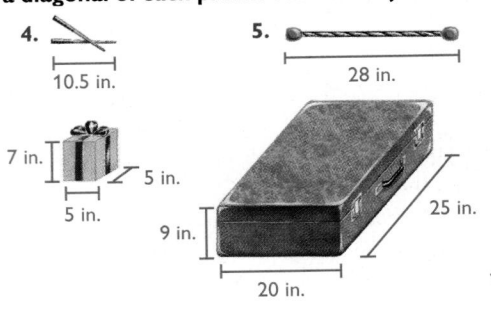 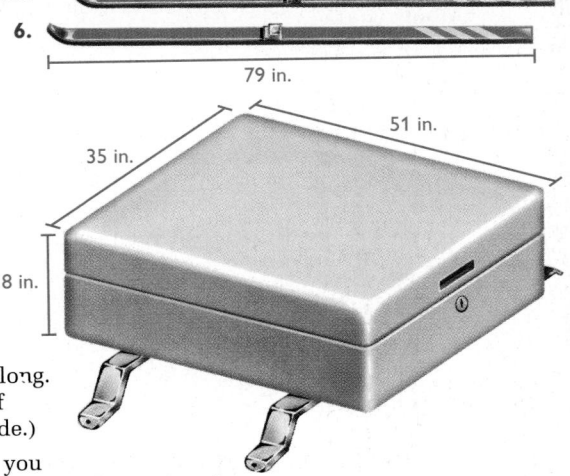

7. **Open-ended** Find dimensions for two different boxes whose diagonals are 50 cm long. (*Hint*: choose lengths for two of the sides of each box and find the length of the third side.)

8. **Reading** How can you use a prism to help you find the distance from a point to the origin in three dimensions?

Find the distance from each point to the origin.

9. (1, 1, 1)

10. (2, 2, 2)

11. (−3, 3, 3)

12. (1, 2, 3)

13. (−1, 2, −3)

14. (1, 3, 5)

15. (2, 5, 7)

16. (3, 4, 12)

17. **Open-ended** Choose a point with three nonzero coordinates and find its distance from the origin.

Find the distance between each pair of points.

18. (4, 3, 6) and (6, 6, 1)

19. (2, 3, 4) and (2, 3, 7)

20. (−7, 8, 9) and (7, 8, 9)

21. (−1, 6, −5) and (3, −2, −7)

Tell whether each triangle is *scalene*, *isosceles*, or *equilateral*. Explain.

22. $A(6, 1, 4)$, $B(4, 3, 2)$, $C(6, 4, 4)$

23. $D(0, 0, 0)$, $E(3, 4, 5)$, $F(3, 4, 0)$

24. $P(2, 3, 4)$, $Q(3, 4, 2)$, $R(4, 2, 3)$

25. $L(5, 9, 3)$, $M(1, 11, 7)$, $N(1, 5, 7)$

Open-ended Find the three-dimensional coordinates of a point that is not on any axis and is the given distance from the origin.

26. $\sqrt{3}$

27. $\sqrt{14}$

28. $\sqrt{21}$

Answers to Exercises and Problems

1. $AC = 5$; $AG = 5\sqrt{2} \approx 7.07$

2. $AC = 8\sqrt{2} \approx 11.31$; $AG = 8\sqrt{3} \approx 13.86$

3. $AC = 4\sqrt{29} \approx 21.54$; $AG = 4\sqrt{65} \approx 32.25$

4. $d = 3\sqrt{11} \approx 9.95$; No.

5. $d = \sqrt{1106} \approx 33.26$; Yes.

6. $d = 5\sqrt{116} \approx 64.42$; No.

7. Answers may vary. Examples: about 20 cm by 24 cm by 39 cm, about 25 cm by 15 cm by 41 cm

8. Place one vertex of the prism at the origin and another vertex at the given point. The distance between these vertices is the length of the diagonal of the prism.

9. $\sqrt{3} \approx 1.73$

10. $2\sqrt{3} \approx 3.46$

11. $3\sqrt{3} \approx 5.20$

12. $\sqrt{14} \approx 3.74$

13. $\sqrt{14} \approx 3.74$

14. $\sqrt{35} \approx 5.92$

15. $\sqrt{78} \approx 8.83$

16. 13

17. Answers may vary. Example: (−8, 3, 5); $\sqrt{98} \approx 9.9$

18. $\sqrt{38} \approx 6.16$

19. 3

20. 14

21. $2\sqrt{21} \approx 9.17$

22. isosceles; $AC = BC = 3$; not equilateral because $AB = 2\sqrt{3}$

23. isosceles; $EF = DF = 5$; not equilateral because $DE = 5\sqrt{2}$

Product Evaluation The table gives the ratings by the editors of a magazine on three features of camcorders. A rating of 5 is the highest rating in each category.

Ratings of Camcorders			
Camcorder	Color accuracy	Low-Light performance	Picture clarity
Brand A	4	1	4
Brand B	3	5	2
Brand C	3	5	3
Brand D	4	3	4
Brand E	4	1	3
Brand F	3	1	2

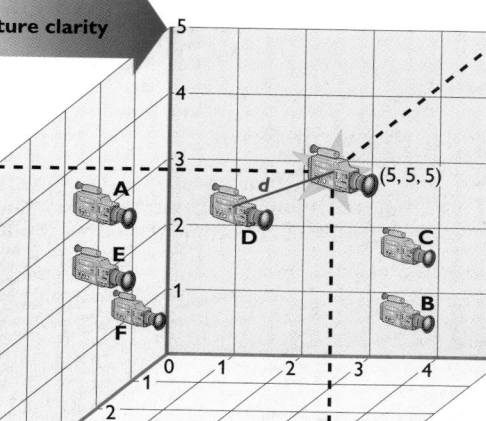

For Exercises 29–31, use the table above.

29. **a.** Rank the camcorders by simply adding the three ratings. What is one disadvantage of this method?

    b. Rank the camcorders by using the distance formula to find each camcorder's "distance" from the perfect rating of (5, 5, 5).

    c. Do the ranking methods in parts (a) and (b) give the same results? Explain which ranking method you prefer.

30. Suppose you think "picture clarity" is more important than "color accuracy" or "low-light performance." How can you modify the distance formula you use in ranking the camcorders?

31. Suppose there are five features to consider in ranking the camcorders. How can you modify the distance formula?

32. The length of a diagonal of a cube is 12 in.

    a. Find the length of each side of the cube.

    b. Find the volume and the surface area of the cube.

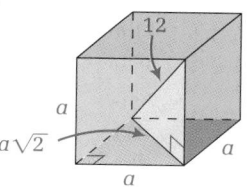

10-5 The Distance Formula in Three Dimensions

589

Answers to Exercises and Problems

24. equilateral; $PQ = QR = PR = \sqrt{6}$

25. isosceles; $LM = MN = 6$; not equilateral because $LN = 4\sqrt{3}$

26–28. Answers may vary. Examples are given.

26. (1, 1, 1)

27. (1, 2, 3)

28. (1, 2, 4)

29. **a.** Brand C and Brand D (tie), Brand B, Brand A, Brand E, Brand F; Answers may vary. An example is given. This method does not weight the ratings according to importance. For example, most people do not consider low-light performance and picture clarity equally important. A camcorder with good color accuracy, picture clarity, and poor low-light performance could score lower than one with mediocre ratings on all three.

    b. Brand D, Brand C, Brand B, Brand A, Brand E, Brand F

c. Results are similar; preferences may vary.

30. Answers may vary. An example is given. One way would be to give more weight to picture clarity by multiplying its contribution to the distance formula by 2 (or some other factor depending upon how much weight you feel it deserves).

31. Find the "distance" from the perfect rating of (5, 5, 5, 5, 5).

32. **a.** $4\sqrt{3} \approx 6.93$

    b. Volume = $192\sqrt{3} \approx 332.6$ in.³; Surface area = 288 in.²

589

33. **Writing** Describe the triangle whose vertices are (x, y, z), (y, z, x), and (z, x, y).

34. Find the midpoint of the segment with endpoints $(0, 0, 0)$ and $(10, -2, 2)$. *(Section 10-4)*

35. Suppose you toss a coin and roll a die. Find the probability of getting heads on the coin and "3" on the die, or $P(\text{H and } 3)$. *(Section 6-4)*

Tell how to translate the graph of $y = x^2$ in order to produce the graph of each function. *(Section 4-2)*

36. $y = (x - 4)^2$ 37. $y = (x + 2)^2$ 38. $y = x^2 - 7$

Working on the Unit Project

39. Steve wants to mail a rainstick to his pen pal in Hong Kong. The rainstick is 31.5 in. long. Steve finds these two rectangular boxes at home.

   a. Which box should Steve use? Why?

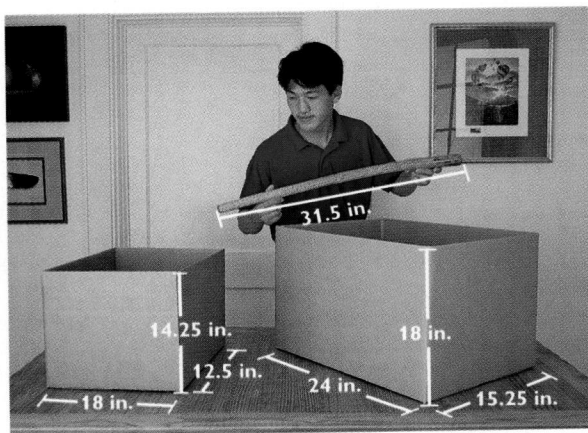

31.5 in.

14.25 in. 12.5 in. 18 in. 24 in. 15.25 in. 18 in.

BY THE WAY...

Rainsticks are made from dead cactus branches. When a rainstick is rotated, the small stones within it travel down through a formation of sharp thorns, producing a soothing, rain-like sound. People in Chile and elsewhere have used rainsticks in ceremonies since ancient times. Many musicians today use the rainstick as a percussion instrument.

   b. **Open-ended** Design a long triangular prism box that can hold the rainstick. Draw the box on a three-dimensional grid with one edge of the box on the *z*-axis. Give the coordinates of the vertices. What are the advantages of your box over the box that Steve used? What are the disadvantages?

590   Unit 10 *Coordinates and Figures in Space*

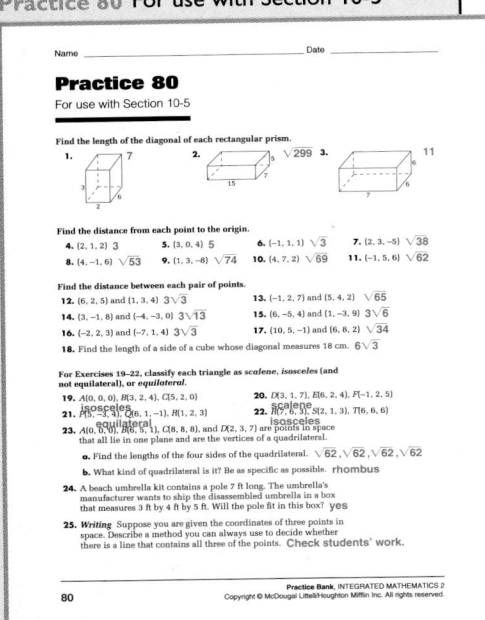
Answers to Exercises and Problems

33. It is equilateral.

34. $(5, -1, 1)$

35. $\frac{1}{12}$ or about 8.3%

36. Translate the graph 4 units to the right.

37. Translate the graph 2 units to the left.

38. Translate the graph down 7 units.

39. **a.** Steve should use the large box; the diagonal of the large box measures $\sqrt{1132.56} \approx 33.65$ in., which is long enough to fit the 31.5 in. rainstick. The diagonal of the small box is only $\sqrt{683.3} \approx 26.14$ in.

   b. Answers may vary. The box could have a base that is an equilateral triangle with sides about 3 in. long. This would make the box slightly less than 3 in. deep, which would accommodate a standard rainstick. The box would be just over 31.5 in. long. This package would have less wasted space and, depending on how it is sent, could be cheaper to ship. It would be difficult to stack or store because of its unusual shape.

Circles and Spheres

Focus
Graph a circle and find
the equation of a circle or
a sphere.

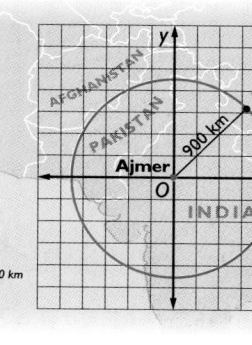

Journey
to the Center

possible location
of epicenter

(x, y)

On September 29, 1993,
a violent earthquake
shook the Ajmer record-
ing station in Rajasthan,
India. The station's
instruments showed that
the epicenter was about
900 km away.

Imagine that the Ajmer recording station is at the origin of
a coordinate system, and the epicenter is at some point
(x, y). You can use the distance formula to find an equation for all points (x, y) that are 900 km from the origin.

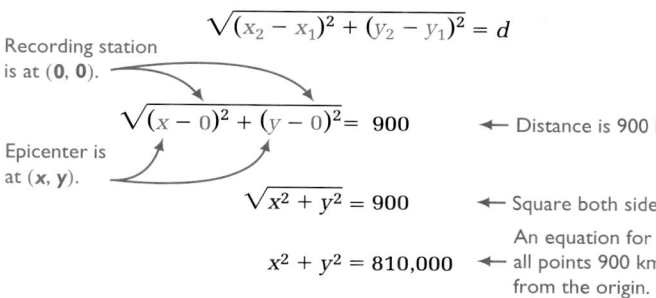

$$\sqrt{(x_2 - x_1)^2 + (y_2 - y_1)^2} = d$$

Recording station
is at $(0, 0)$.

$$\sqrt{(x - 0)^2 + (y - 0)^2} = 900 \qquad \leftarrow \text{Distance is 900 km.}$$

Epicenter is
at (x, y).

$$\sqrt{x^2 + y^2} = 900 \qquad \leftarrow \text{Square both sides.}$$

$$x^2 + y^2 = 810{,}000 \qquad \leftarrow \begin{array}{l}\text{An equation for} \\ \text{all points 900 km} \\ \text{from the origin.}\end{array}$$

Talk it Over

1. Explain why the graph of $x^2 + y^2 = 810{,}000$ is a circle.

2. How can you find an equation of a circle with center $(0, 0)$
   and radius 5?

3. Explain how you can use the three-dimensional
   distance formula to find an equation of the sphere
   with center $(0, 0, 0)$ and radius 900.

10-6 Circles and Spheres

591

Answers to Talk it Over

1. The graph is the set of
   points 900 km from the
   origin. This set of points
   defines a circle with radius
   900 km and center $(0, 0)$.

2. Use the distance formula,
   substituting 0 for x_1 and y_1
   and 5 for d. The equation
   of the circle is $x^2 + y^2 = 25$.

3. Substitute 0 for x_1, y_1, and
   z_1, and 900 for d. The
   equation of the sphere is
   $x^2 + y^2 + z^2 = 810{,}000$

PLANNING

Objectives and Strands
See pages 554A and 554B.

Spiral Learning
See page 554B.

Materials List
➤ Graph paper
➤ Graphics calculator

Recommended Pacing
Section 10-6 is a two-day lesson.
Day 1
Pages 591–593: Opening para-
graph through Sample 2, *Exercises
1–16*
Day 2
Pages 593–594: Sample 3
through Look Back, *Exercises
17–34*

Extra Practice
See pages 630–631.

Warm-Up Exercises
Warm-Up Transparency 10-6

Support Materials
➤ Practice 81
➤ Enrichment 72 in the Activity
  Bank
➤ Study Guide 10-6
➤ Problem Set 23
➤ Additional Exploration 14
➤ Diagram Masters 2, 7 in the
  Explorations Lab Manual
➤ Using TI-81 and TI-82
  Calculators: The Circle Game
➤ Using IBM Plotter Plus Disk:
  Circular Function Quiz
➤ Quiz 10-6
➤ Test 42

The real-world situation regarding an earthquake in India (page 591) is analyzed and modeled by using the distance formula in two dimensions. Students should understand that all points 900 km from the Ajmer recording station form a circle with radius 900 km. The equation for this circle, $x^2 + y^2 = 900^2$, is derived by using the distance formula.

Talk it Over

Question 3 generalizes the two-dimensional discussion of a circle to the three-dimensional equation of a sphere.

Additional Sample

S1 Graph the circle $x^2 + y^2 = 49$.

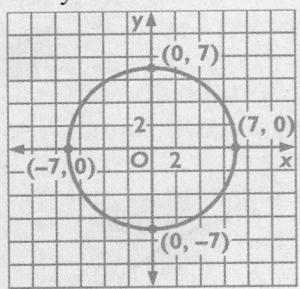

Using Technology

When you use function mode to display circles on a graphics calculator, the left and right sides of the circle will generally appear to have gaps. Discuss why this is the case.

You may wish to use the ZOOM feature to draw a box around one of the small areas where a gap occurs. When you display this portion of the graph, many of the points that seemed to be missing will be filled in.

EQUATIONS OF CIRCLES AND SPHERES CENTERED AT THE ORIGIN

The equation of a circle with center (0, 0) and radius r is $x^2 + y^2 = r^2$.

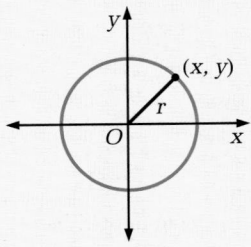

The equation of a sphere with center (0, 0, 0) and radius r is $x^2 + y^2 + z^2 = r^2$.

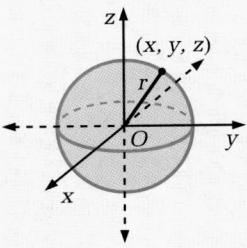

Sample 1

Graph the circle $x^2 + y^2 = 36$.

Sample Response

Method ❶ Use graph paper.

Since the equation is in the form $x^2 + y^2 = r^2$, the center is (0, 0) and $r^2 = 36$.

Therefore, $r = \sqrt{36} = 6$.
The radius is 6.

From the origin, mark a radius of 6 on the x- and y-axes. Sketch the circle.

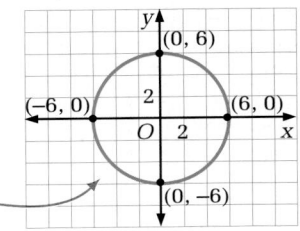

Method ❷ Use a graphics calculator.

Since $x^2 + y^2 = 36$ is not a function, graph two semicircles, each of which is a function.

$$x^2 + y^2 = 36$$
$$y^2 = 36 - x^2$$

Graph $Y_1 = \sqrt{36 - x^2}$.

Graph $Y_2 = -\sqrt{36 - x^2}$.

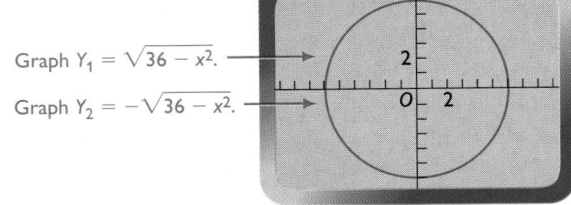

TECHNOLOGY NOTE

To make the graph appear circular, you may have to use the calculator feature that "squares" the screen. See Technology Handbook page 605.

Unit 10 Coordinates and Figures in Space

a. Find an equation of the circle. The center is at the origin.

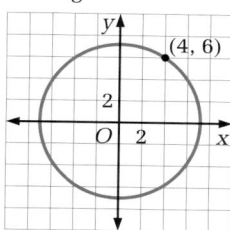
(4, 6)

b. Find an equation of the sphere. The center is at the origin.

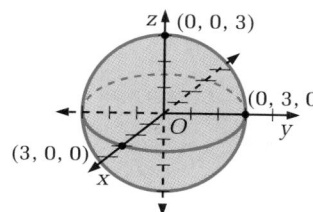
z (0, 0, 3)
(0, 3, 0)
(3, 0, 0)

Sample Response

a. The center is (0, 0). The equation is of the form $x^2 + y^2 = r^2$.

The radius, r, is the distance between the points (0, 0) and (4, 6).

$$r = \sqrt{(4-0)^2 + (6-0)^2} = \sqrt{52}$$

An equation is $x^2 + y^2 = 52$. ⟵ $r^2 = (\sqrt{52})^2 = 52$

b. The center is (0, 0, 0) and the radius is 3. The equation is of the form $x^2 + y^2 + z^2 = r^2$. Substitute 3 for r.

An equation is $x^2 + y^2 + z^2 = 9$.

┈┈► Now you are ready for:
Exs. 1–16 on pp. 594–595

The Shillong earthquake recording station in Meghalaya, India, is about 1700 km east of the Ajmer station. The instruments at Shillong showed that the epicenter was about 1800 km away. Find an equation of a circle that describes all points 1800 km from the Shillong station.

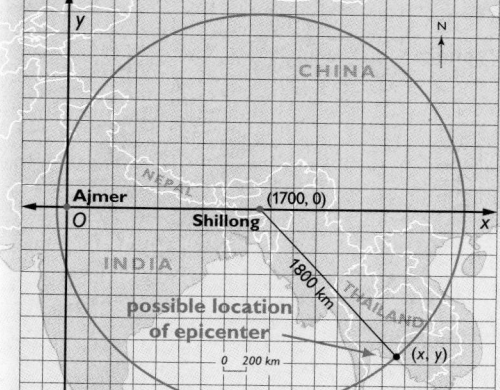
CHINA
Ajmer (1700, 0)
O Shillong X
NEPAL
INDIA
1800 km
THAILAND
possible location of epicenter
0 200 km
(x, y)
N

Sample Response

Problem Solving Strategy: Use a formula.

The distance from the Shillong station at (1700, 0) to the epicenter (x, y) is 1800. Use the distance formula.

$$\sqrt{(x_2 - x_1)^2 + (y_2 - y_1)^2} = d$$
$$\sqrt{(x - 1700)^2 + (y - 0)^2} = 1800$$
$$(x - 1700)^2 + y^2 = 3{,}240{,}000$$

An equation of the circle is
$$(x - 1700)^2 + y^2 = 3{,}240{,}000.$$

10-6 Circles and Spheres

S2 **a.** Find an equation of the circle. The center is at the origin.

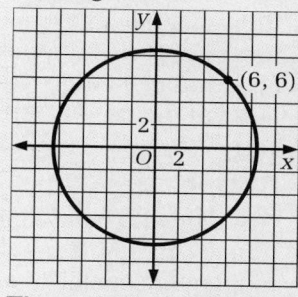
y
(6, 6)
O 2 x

The radius is the distance between the points (0, 0) and (6, 6).

$$r = \sqrt{(6-0)^2 + (6-0)^2}$$
$$= \sqrt{72}$$

An equation is $x^2 + y^2 = 72$.

b. Find an equation of the sphere. The center is at the origin.

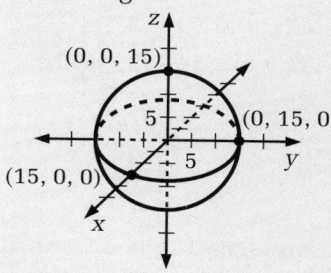
z
(0, 0, 15)
(0, 15, 0)
(15, 0, 0)
x y

The center is (0, 0, 0) and the radius is 15. An equation is $x^2 + y^2 + z^2 = 225$.

S3 In Sample 3, suppose that a third recording station is 1400 km south of the Ajmar station. The instruments of this station showed that the epicenter was about 2800 km away. Find an equation of a circle that describes all points 2800 km from this station. The distance from the third station at (0, –1400) to the epicenter (x, y) is 2800 km. Use the distance formula.

$$\sqrt{(x-0)^2 + (y+1400)^2} = 2800$$

An equation of the circle is $x^2 + (y + 1400)^2 = 7{,}840{,}000$.

Talk it Over

4. Use the map in Sample 3. The Lhasa recording station in Tibet, China, is about 400 km north of the Shillong station. The epicenter was about 2000 km from the Lhasa station.

   a. What would be the coordinates of the Lhasa recording station?

   b. What is an equation of the circle with its center at Lhasa that contains the epicenter (x, y)?

5. How can you use the equations of the circles with centers at Ajmer, Shillong, and Lhasa to find values for x and y?

EQUATIONS OF CIRCLES NOT CENTERED AT THE ORIGIN

The equation of a circle with center (h, k) and radius r is $(x - h)^2 + (y - k)^2 = r^2$.

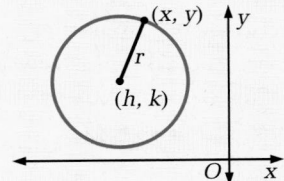

········► **Now you are ready for:**
: **Exs. 17–34 on pp. 596–598**

Look Back ◄

What information do you need to know about a circle to find its equation? What information do you need to know about a sphere to find its equation?

10-6 Exercises and Problems

For Exercises 1–7, write an equation of each circle or sphere.

1.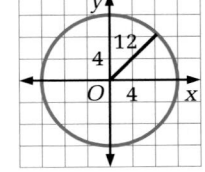

2.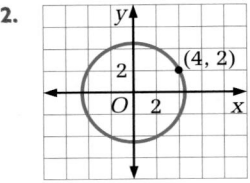

3.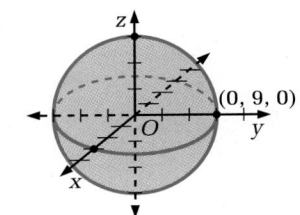

4. The center of the circle is $(0, 0)$. The radius is 2.5.

5. The center of the circle is $(0, 0)$. The endpoints of a diameter are $(5, 0)$ and $(-5, 0)$.

6. The center of the sphere is $(0, 0, 0)$. The radius is 6.

7. The center of the sphere is $(0, 0, 0)$. The radius is 4.

 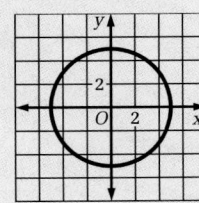

8. **Reading** Describe two methods you could use to graph the equation of a circle whose center is at the origin.

For Exercises 9–12, graph each circle.

9. $x^2 + y^2 = 25$ 10. $x^2 + y^2 = 100$ 11. $x^2 + y^2 = 15$ 12. $x^2 + y^2 = 3$

connection to **LANGUAGE ARTS**

Robin Mandel used ideas from geometry in his 1993 high school graduation speech at University School in Milwaukee, Wisconsin. Here is part of his speech.

"... Think of yourself as a point in space. Picture yourself hovering in three dimensions. Give yourself a radius, say arm's length, that you can reach out in all directions. Imagine that every time you think a new thought, or hear a different idea, or meet a new person, you reach out and touch another point. Learn about covalent chemical bonding, touch another point. Read a book about life as a teacher in rural New Mexico, touch another point. Keep reaching and accumulating points and a shape begins to emerge. In geometry, here at this very school, I learned the name of the shape defined by a set of points equidistant from a central point in all directions. It's called a sphere.

"Metaphorically speaking, then, *you* are the center point of the sphere of your life's experiences. The more points you can touch, the more complete your sphere becomes. As time goes on, you fill in the spaces of your sphere. And you have to remember to work in three dimensions and reach in all directions. Reach only one direction and you might end up a hemisphere, and those don't roll very far."

13. What is Robin trying to describe by using the idea of a sphere?
14. **Research** What is a *metaphor*? What does Robin mean by "metaphorically speaking"?
15. **Writing** Describe the sphere of your life or of the life of someone you know well. What is the radius of the sphere?
16. **Writing** Choose a different idea from the mathematics you have learned this year (such as *deductive reasoning, functions, transformations, modeling*). Write an essay about something in your life. Use the ideas and words of mathematics to help explain it.

10-6 Circles and Spheres

595

Answers to Exercises and Problems

10.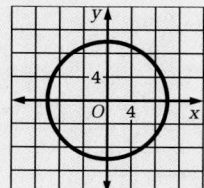

11.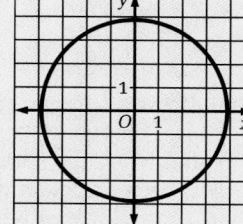

12.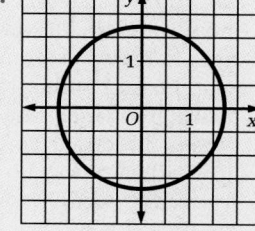

Application

Ex. 22 is an application of the mathematics of this section to agriculture. Students discover that in order to water the entire field, the spacing of the sprinklers is important.

Write an equation of each circle or sphere.

17. The center of the circle is (1, 3). The radius is 2.5.

18. The center of the circle is $(-3, -2)$. The radius is 8.

19. The center of the sphere is (0, 0, 0). The radius is 4.

Write an equation of each circle.

20.

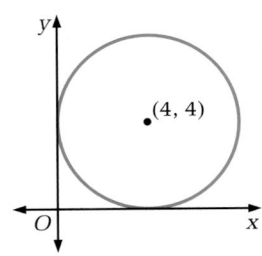

21.

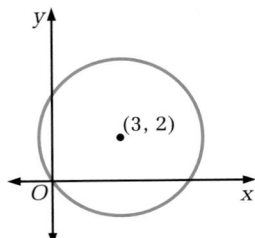

22. Agriculture A *linear irrigation system* uses many sprinklers connected to a long water pipe on wheels. The spray from each sprinkler covers a circular area. As the water pipe moves across the field, the entire field can be watered.

   a. Suppose the sprinklers spray water 20 ft and are spaced along the water pipe every 40 ft. Write equations for circles A, B, and C.

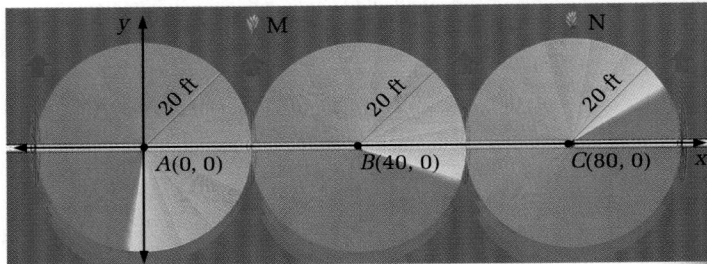

   b. Will plants M and N get the same amount of water? Explain.

   c. Suppose instead that the sprinklers are spaced along the water pipe every 35 ft. Write equations for circles D, E, and F.

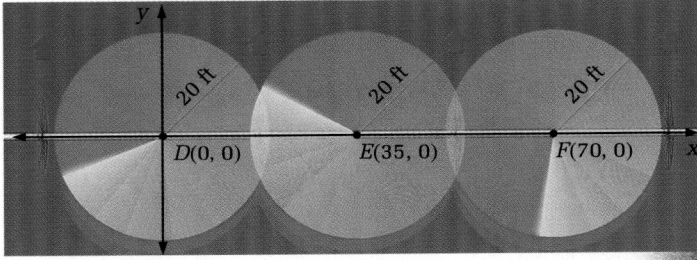

   d. Explain why a farmer might use the spacing in part (c) instead of the spacing in part (a).

Unit 10 Coordinates and Figures in Space

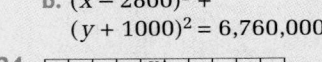
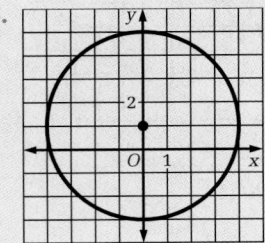

Answers to Exercises and Problems

17. $(x - 1)^2 + (y - 3)^2 = 6.25$

18. $(x + 3)^2 + (y + 2)^2 = 64$

19. $x^2 + y^2 + z^2 = 16$

20. $(x - 4)^2 + (y - 4)^2 = 16$

21. $(x - 3)^2 + (y - 2)^2 = 13$

22. a. $x^2 + y^2 = 400$;
$(x - 40)^2 + y^2 = 400$;
$(x - 80)^2 + y^2 = 400$

b. No; plant N will receive more water. Plant M lies right in between circles A and B and will only be watered when the pipe is directly overhead. Plant N will be watered repeatly from the time circle C reaches plant N until the pipe travels 40 ft, the diameter of the circle.

c. $x^2 + y^2 = 400$;
$(x - 35)^2 + y^2 = 400$;
$(x - 70)^2 + y^2 = 400$

d. The spacing in part (c) assures an overlap region when the spray from each sprinkler covers a circular area with radius 20 ft.

23. a. (2800, −1000)

b. $(x - 2800)^2 + (y + 1000)^2 = 6,760,000$

24.

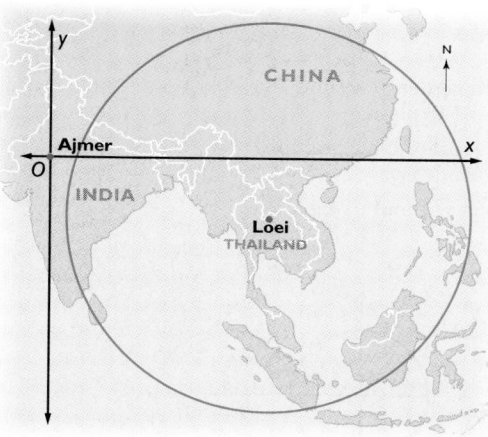

23. Seismology Use the diagram of earthquake recording stations.

    a. The Loei station in Thailand is about 2800 km east and 1000 km south of the Ajmer station. What are the coordinates of the Loei station?

    b. The epicenter of the September 29 earthquake was about 2600 km from the Loei station. Use your answer from part (a) to write an equation of the circle on which the epicenter lies.

Graph each circle.

24. $x^2 + (y - 1)^2 = 16$ **25.** $(x - 3)^2 + (y + 2)^2 = 49$

26. The equation of a circle is $(x - 8)^2 + (y + 4)^2 = 9$.

    a. Find the center and the radius of the circle.

    b. Is the point $(5, -5)$ inside or outside the circle? Use a drawing to explain.

27. The equation of a sphere is $(x - 8)^2 + (y + 4)^2 + (z - 5)^2 = 36$.

    a. Find the center and the radius of the sphere.

    b. **Open-ended** Find the coordinates of the endpoints of a diameter.

Career Investigators sometimes measure the marks tires leave on the road at the site of an accident. In some circumstances, knowing the radius of the circle on which the tire marks lie helps investigators estimate how fast a car was traveling when the tires began to slip.

28. a. The y-axis is perpendicular to the 33 m segment. Explain why the point $(16.5, r - 3.5)$ is on the circle.

    b. Substitute the coordinates $(16.5, r - 3.5)$ into the equation $x^2 + y^2 = r^2$.

    c. Solve the equation from part (b) for r to find the radius of the circle on which the tire marks lie.

    d. The equation $v = \sqrt{\mu g r}$ describes the speed of the car, where μ is the coefficient of friction (which depends on the road surface), g is the acceleration due to gravity, and r is the radius of the curve.

    Find the speed of the car in meters per second if $\mu = 0.8$, $g = 9.8$ m/s^2, and $r =$ the value you found in part (c).

(Not drawn to scale.)

10-6 Circles and Spheres

597

Answers to Exercises and Problems

25.

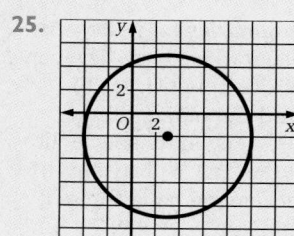

26. a. $(8, -4)$; 3

b. outside

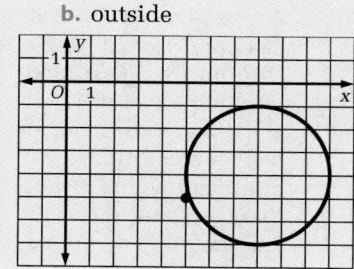

27. a. $(8, -4, 5)$; 6

b. Answers may vary. An example is given. The coordinates of the endpoints of a diameter are $(14, -4, 5)$ and $(2, -4, 5)$.

28. a. The point $(16.5, y)$ is a vertex of a rectangle whose other three coordinates are $(0, 0)$, $(16.5, 0)$, and $(0, r - 3.5)$, so $y = r - 3.5$.

b. $16.5^2 + (r - 3.5)^2 = r^2$

c. $r \approx 40.64$ m

d. about 17.85 m/s

29. **a.** Sketch the line $y = -x + 3$ and the circle with center $(0, 0)$ and radius 2. Do you think the two graphs intersect? Explain.

   b. TECHNOLOGY Graph the circle and line from part (a) on a graphics calculator. Do they intersect? Use ZOOM if necessary.

   c. How can you tell if the circle and line intersect without using a graphics calculator?

Ongoing **ASSESSMENT**

30. **Writing** Explain the steps you would take to write the equation of circle O and the equation of circle H. Then write each equation.

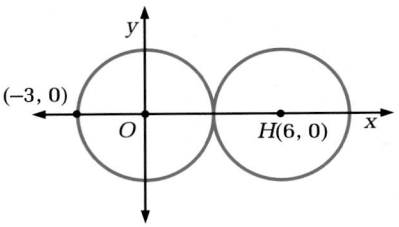

$(-3, 0)$
O
$H(6, 0)$

Review **PREVIEW**

31. The diagonal $\overline{AB}$ of a rectangular prism has endpoints $(10, 2, 3)$ and $(6, 4, 4)$. Use the distance formula to find the length of $\overline{AB}$. *(Section 10-5)*

32. Use the implication "All squares are rectangles." *(Section 7-2)*

   a. Tell whether the implication is *True* or *False*.

   b. Write the converse of the implication. Tell whether it is *True* or *False*. If it is false, give a counterexample.

Working on the Unit Project

33. Write an equation for the edge of the bottom of the cylinder.

34. If your container has a circle in its design, draw it on a coordinate grid and write an equation for it.

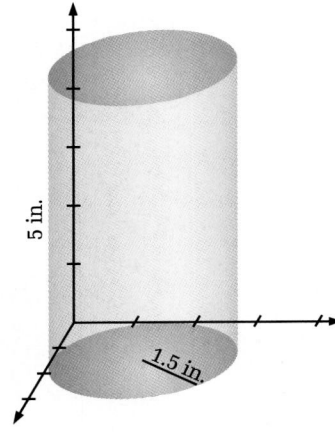

5 in.

1.5 in.

598   **Unit 10** Coordinates and Figures in Space

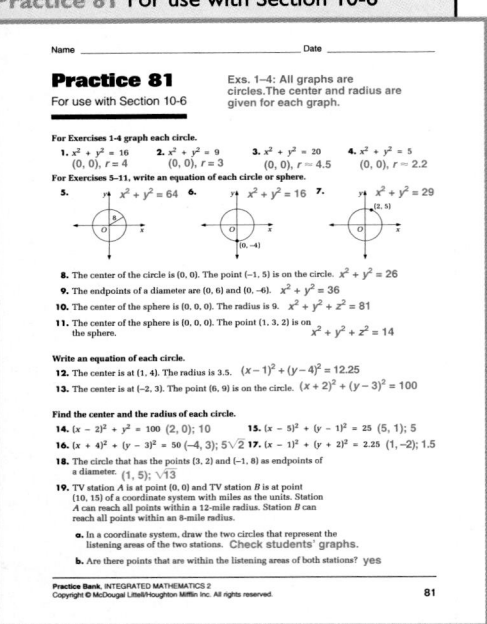

Answers to Exercises and Problems

29. **a.**

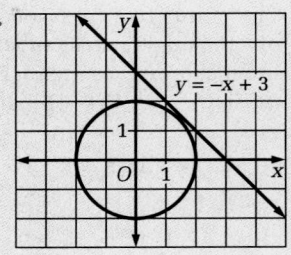

$y = -x + 3$

No; if you substitute the linear function into the circle equation and solve for x, you get a negative discriminant. Therefore, there are no real roots for the system, so there are no points of intersection.

b. They do not intersect.

c. Answers may vary. An example is given. Substituting the linear function into the circle equation and solving for x gives a negative discriminant which means there are no real roots and therefore no points of intersection.

30. Summaries may vary. An example is given. The center of circle O is $(0, 0)$. Find the radius. Since $(-3, 0)$ is on the circle, the radius is 3. Substitute in the general equation of a circle: $x^2 + y^2 = 9$. To find the equation of circle H, notice that the center is

Completing the Unit Project

Now you are ready to complete your container.

Your completed project should include these things:

➤ a container to hold an object or objects of your choice

➤ a written description of the container

➤ a set of drawings that represent the three-dimensional shape of the container in enough detail for another person to reconstruct it

Look Back

Which of the drawing techniques discussed in this unit do you think would be most useful to someone trying to reproduce your container? Why?

Alternative Projects

Project 1: Design a Birdhouse

Research the kinds of birdhouses that attract different kinds of birds. What shapes are common in birdhouses? Design a birdhouse and make drawings showing how to construct it.

Project 2: Make a Pop-up Book

Reading a book is usually a two-dimensional experience: the words lie flat on the page. But a pop-up book is three-dimensional. Look in the children's section of a bookstore to see how pop-up books work. Create a pop-up book that demonstrates some of the ideas about coordinates and figures in space that you learned in this unit.

Unit 10 Completing the Unit Project

599

Assessment

A scoring rubric for the Unit Project can be found on pages 554 and 555 of this Teacher's Edition and also in the *Project Book*.

Answers to Exercises and Problems

given and circle H intersects circle O on the x-axis. Since $y = 0$, $x = 3$ and the point $(3, 0)$ is on circle H. Then the radius is 3 and the equation of circle H is $(x - 6)^2 + y^2 = 9$.

31. $\sqrt{21} \approx 4.6$

32. **a.** True.

b. All rectangles are squares; False. Counterexamples may vary. An example is given. The rectangle with length 4 units and width 2 units is not a square.

33. $(x - 1.5)^2 + (y - 1.5)^2 = (1.5)^2$

34. Answers may vary.

Quick Quiz (10-4 through 10-6)

1. How is finding the midpoint of a segment in three dimensions like finding the midpoint of a segment in two dimensions? How is it different? [10-4]

In both cases, each coordinate of the midpoint is found by finding the mean of the corresponding coordinates of the endpoints. In three dimensions, there are three coordinates. In two dimensions, there are two coordinates.

Find the distance between each pair of points. [10-5]

2. $(6, 5, 4)$ and $(1, 1, 3)$

$\sqrt{42} \approx 6.48$

3. $(1, 5, 1)$ and $(4, 2, 2)$

$\sqrt{19} \approx 4.36$

Find the equation of each circle. [10-6]

4.

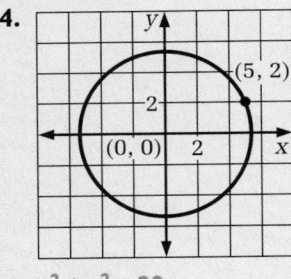

$x^2 + y^2 = 29$

5.

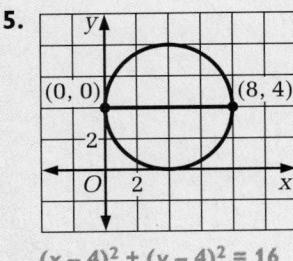

$(x - 4)^2 + (y - 4)^2 = 16$

---

1. What space figure does the pattern at the right represent?　10-1

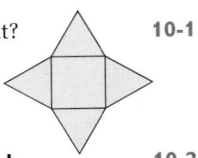

2. Draw two different views of a cylinder.

3. Name three space figures that have a circle as a horizontal cross section.

Describe or sketch the space figure formed by rotating each plane figure around the indicated line.　10-2

4.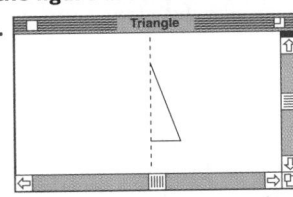

5.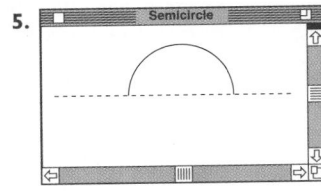

6.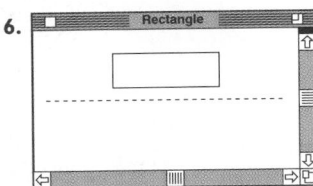

7. a. Open-ended Draw a rectangle and label its length and width. Rotate the rectangle around its longer side. Sketch the space figure formed.

　　b. Find the volume of the space figure.

8. Describe the set of points in space that are 6 cm from a point.　10-3

9. Describe the set of points in a plane that are 3 m from a line in the plane.

10. Describe the set of points in space that are equidistant from two points.

11. Writing Explain how to locate the epicenter of an earthquake if you know the distance of the epicenter from three earthquake recording stations.

12. Two vertices of the rectangular prism at the right are $E(5, 0, 4)$ and $C(0, 6, 0)$.　10-4

　　a. Find the coordinates of the other six vertices.

　　b. Find the midpoint of $\overline{EC}$.

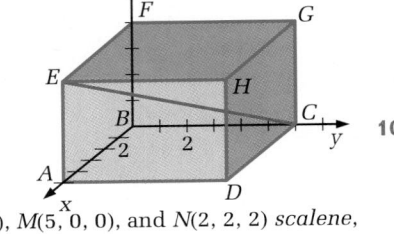

13. Find the length of a diagonal of a rectangular prism with sides of length 3, 6, and 9.　10-5

14. Is the triangle formed by $L(0, 3, 0)$, $M(5, 0, 0)$, and $N(2, 2, 2)$ *scalene*, *isosceles*, or *equilateral*? Explain.

15. Graph the circle $x^2 + y^2 = 49$.　10-6

Write an equation of each circle or sphere.

16. The center of the circle is $(2, -1)$ and the radius is 5.

17. The center of the sphere is $(0, 0, 0)$ and the radius is 6.

18. a. Self-evaluation Choose a radius and a height. Represent a cylinder with these dimensions as many ways as you can.

　　b. Group Activity Exchange one of your representations with another student. Sketch each other's cylinder.

Answers to Unit 10 Review and Assessment

1. square pyramid

2.

3. Answers may vary. Examples are given. a cylinder, a sphere, a cone

4. a cone

5. a sphere

6. a hollow cylinder

7. a. Answers may vary. An example is given.

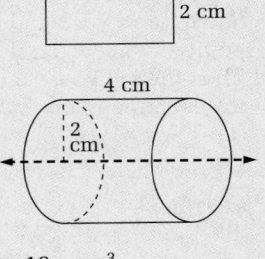

　　b. 16π cm³

IDEAS AND (FORMULAS) $=X^2$

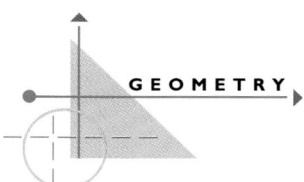

GEOMETRY

- ➤ Space figures are often represented by drawing several views. *(p. 557)*
- ➤ A pattern showing an "unfolded" space figure is another way to represent a space figure. *(p. 559)*
- ➤ Cross sections can help you visualize space figures. *(p. 559)*
- ➤ Some space figures are created by rotating a plane figure around a line called the axis of rotation. *(p. 565)*
- ➤ A circle can be considered the set of all points in a plane a given distance from a point. *(p. 571)*
- ➤ A sphere can be considered the set of all points in space a given distance from a point. *(p. 572)*
- ➤ If the set of points in a plane that meets one condition does not intersect the set of points in the same plane that meets another condition, then there are no points that meet both conditions. *(p. 573)*
- ➤ To locate points in three-dimensional space, three coordinate axes are needed. *(p. 579)*

ALGEBRA $)x^2$

$(x$

- ➤ Each of the coordinates of the midpoint of a segment is the mean of the corresponding coordinates of its endpoints. If the endpoints have coordinates (x_1, y_1, z_1) and (x_2, y_2, z_2), the midpoint has coordinates
  $$\left(\frac{x_1 + x_2}{2}, \frac{y_1 + y_2}{2}, \frac{z_1 + z_2}{2}\right). \text{ (p. 580)}$$
- ➤ The distance between the points (x_1, y_1, z_1) and (x_2, y_2, z_2) is $\sqrt{(x_2 - x_1)^2 + (y_2 - y_1)^2 + (z_2 - z_1)^2}$. *(p. 586)*
- ➤ The equation of a circle with center $(0, 0)$ and radius r is $x^2 + y^2 = r^2$. *(p. 592)*
- ➤ The equation of a sphere with center $(0, 0, 0)$ and radius r is $x^2 + y^2 + z^2 = r^2$. *(p. 592)*
- ➤ The equation of a circle with center (h, k) and radius r is $(x - h)^2 + (y - k)^2 = r^2$. *(p. 594)*

Key Terms

- **space figure** (p. 557)
- **axis of rotation** (p. 565)
- **diagonal of a rectangular prism** (p. 584)
- **cross section** (p. 559)
- **equidistant** (p. 574)
- **plane figure** (p. 565)
- **ordered triple** (p. 579)

Unit 10 Review and Assessment

601

Quick Quiz (10-1 through 10-3)

1. What is the name of the figure whose faces are rectangles and whose bases are triangles? [10-1]
   triangular prism

2. What figure is formed by a vertical cross section of a cylinder? [10-1] rectangle

3. Name two space figures you can get by rotating a rectangle around an axis. [10-2] cylinder, ring

4. Describe the set of points equidistant from the surface of a sphere. [10-3]
   the center of the sphere

Answers to Unit 10 Review and Assessment ·······

8. a sphere with radius 6 cm

9. a pair of parallel lines each 3 m from the given line

10. a plane halfway between the two points and containing the perpendicular bisector of the line segment joining the two points

11. Each station's recordings determine a circle. The

intersection of the three circles is the epicenter of the quake.

12. a. $A(5, 0, 0)$; $B(0, 0, 0)$; $D(5, 6, 0)$; $F(0, 0, 4)$; $G(0, 6, 4)$; $H(5, 6, 4)$

    b. $(2\frac{1}{2}, 3, 2)$

13. $\sqrt{126} \approx 11.22$

14. scalene; $LM = \sqrt{34}$, $MN = \sqrt{17}$, $LN = 3$

15.

16. $(x - 2)^2 + (y + 1)^2 = 25$

17. $x^2 + y^2 + z^2 = 36$

18. a. Answers may vary.
    b. Answers may vary.

Contents of Student Resources

Student Resources

Technology Handbook

Using a Graphics Calculator

This handbook introduces you to the basic features of most graphics calculators. Check your calculator's instruction manual for specific keystrokes and any details not provided here.

Performing Calculations

➤ The Keyboard

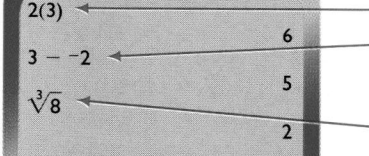

Look closely at your calculator's keyboard. Notice that most keys serve more than one purpose. Each key is labeled with its primary purpose, and labels for any secondary purposes appear somewhere near the key. You may need to press **2nd**, **SHIFT**, or **ALPHA** to use a key for a secondary purpose.

Examples of using the x^2 key:

Press x^2 to square a number.

Press **2nd** and then x^2 to take a square root.

Press **ALPHA** and then x^2 to get the letter I.

➤ The Home Screen

Your calculator has a "home screen" where you can do calculations. You can usually enter a calculation on a graphics calculator just as you would write it on a piece of paper.

Shown below are other things to remember as you enter calculations on your graphics calculator.

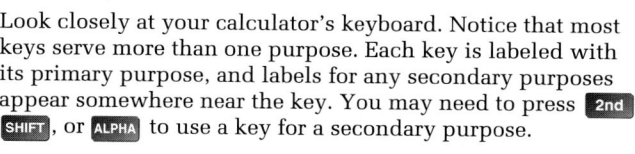

```
2(3)
              6
3 − −2
              5
³√8
              2
```

— The calculator may recognize implied multiplication.

— The calculator has a subtraction key, **−**, and a negation key, **(−)**. If you use these incorrectly, you will get an error message.

— You may need to get a cube root (or other operation that is not often used) from a **MATH** menu.

Technology Handbook

Try This

1. Use your calculator to find the value of each expression.

   a. $\sqrt[3]{64}$ b. 2^5 c. $\sin 75°$

2. Which of the following are true?

   a. $\sin 60° > \cos 30°$ b. $\tan 45° = \cos 45°$ c. $2\sin 30° = 1$

3. Find the value of each expression.

   a. $5!$ b. $\dfrac{5!}{3!}$ c. $\dfrac{5!}{(2!)(3!)}$

Displaying Graphs

➤ The Viewing Window

When you use a graphics calculator to display graphs, think of the screen as a "viewing window" that lets you look at a portion of the coordinate plane.

On many calculators, the standard viewing window uses values from -10 to 10 on both the x- and y-axes. You can adjust the viewing window by pressing the [RANGE] or [WINDOW] key and entering new values for the window variables.

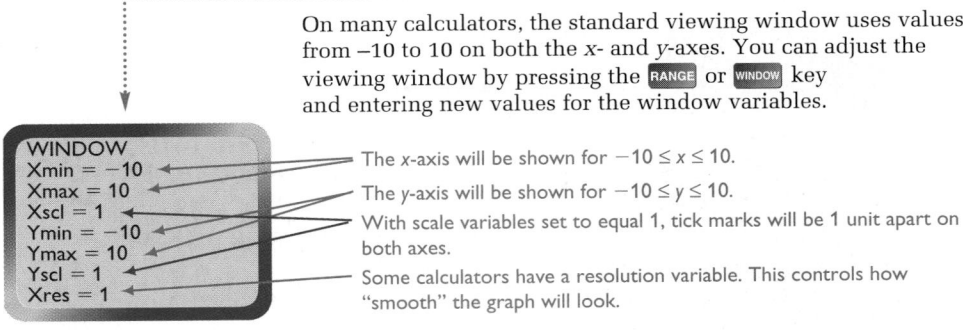

WINDOW
Xmin = -10 — The x-axis will be shown for $-10 \le x \le 10$.
Xmax = 10 — The y-axis will be shown for $-10 \le y \le 10$.
Xscl = 1 — With scale variables set to equal 1, tick marks will be 1 unit apart on both axes.
Ymin = -10
Ymax = 10
Yscl = 1 — Some calculators have a resolution variable. This controls how "smooth" the graph will look.
Xres = 1

➤ Entering and Graphing a Function

To graph a function, enter its equation in the form $y = \dots.$
If the equation does not use x and y, rewrite the equation.
Let $x =$ the control variable and $y =$ the dependent variable. Set the variables for an appropriate viewing window. The graph of $y = \frac{1}{2}x + 3$ is shown using the standard viewing window.

Use parentheses. If you enter $y = 1/2x + 3$ instead, the calculator may interpret the equation as $y = \frac{1}{2x} + 3$.

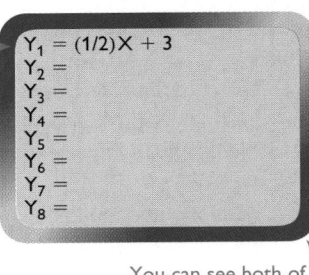

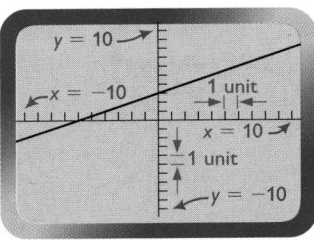

You can see both of these displays at the same time if your calculator has a split-screen mode.

Student Resources

Answers to Try This

1. a. 4
   b. 32
   c. about 0.966
2. c
3. a. 120
   b. 20
   c. 10

➤ Squaring the Screen

A "square screen" is a viewing window with equal unit spacing on the two axes. For example, the graph of $y = x$ is shown for two different windows.

Standard Viewing Window

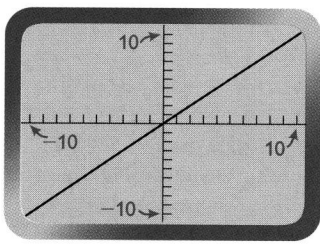

Square Screen Window

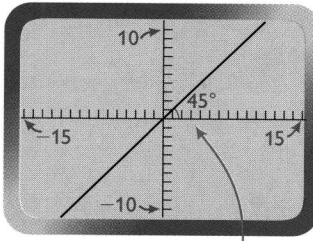

On a square screen, the line $y = x$ makes a 45° angle with the x-axis.

On many graphics calculators, the ratio of the screen's height to its width is about 2 to 3. Your calculator may have a feature that gives you a square screen. If not, choose values for the window variables that make the "length" of the y-axis about two-thirds the "length" of the x-axis:

$$(\text{Ymax} - \text{Ymin}) \approx \tfrac{2}{3}(\text{Xmax} - \text{Xmin})$$

Try This

4. Enter and graph each equation separately. Use the standard viewing window. You may need to put the equation in function form, $y = ...$, first.

   a. $y = 3x + 1$ **b.** $x + 2y = 4$ **c.** $y = |x|$ **d.** $y = \dfrac{5}{x}$

5. Find a good viewing window for the graph of $y = 65 - 3x$. Be sure your window shows where the graph crosses both axes.

6. Find a viewing window that will allow you to graph these two lines so that they appear to be perpendicular: $y = 2x + 1$ and $y = -0.5x - 2$.

Reading a Graph
➤ The TRACE Feature

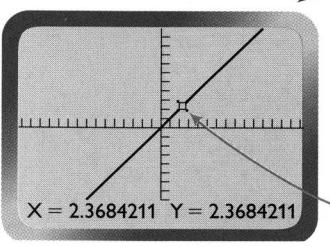

X = 2.3684211   Y = 2.3684211

After a graph is displayed, you can use the calculator's TRACE feature. When you press **TRACE**, a flashing cursor appears on the graph. The x- and y-coordinates of the cursor's location are shown at the bottom of the screen. Press the left- and right-arrow keys to move the TRACE cursor along the graph.

The TRACE cursor is at the point (2.3684211, 2.3684211) on the graph of $y = x$.

Technology Handbook

Answers to Try This

4. **a.**

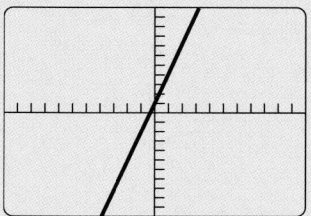

b.

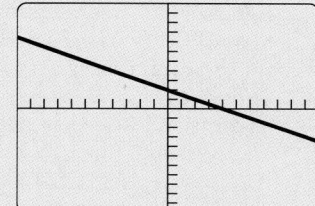

c.

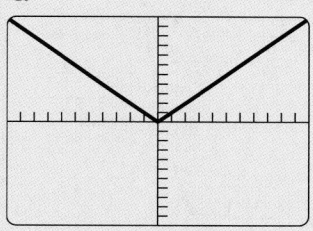

d.

5. Answers may vary. An example is given. [−5, 30] and Xscl=5 for x, [−10, 75] and YSCL=5 for y.

6. Answers may vary. An example is given. [−7.5, 7.5] and Xscl=1 for x, [−5, 5] and YSCL=1 for y.

Suppose you want to find the radius of a circular hole with an area of 20 in². The formula for the area of a circle is $A = \pi r^2$. Rewrite the equation using x and y. Graph the equation $y = \pi x^2$.

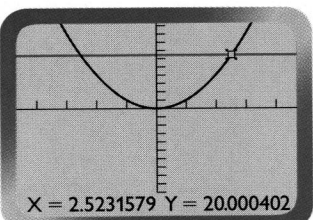

Using the TRACE key, move the cursor along the graph until the y-value is approximately equal to 20. This will give you the value of x that is the radius of the circular hole.

X = 2.5231579 Y = 20.000402

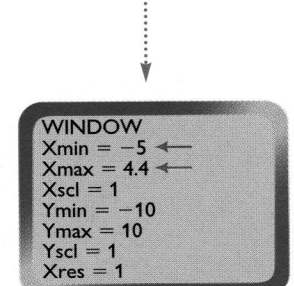

Another way to solve the problem is to graph two equations on the same screen: $y = \pi x^2$ and $y = 20$. Use TRACE to move the cursor to the intersection of the two lines to find your answer.

X = 2.5231579 Y = 20.000402

➤ **Friendly Windows**

As you press the right-arrow key while tracing a graph, you may notice that the x-coordinate increases by "unfriendly" increments.

Your calculator may allow you to control the x-increment, ΔX, directly. If not, you can control it indirectly by choosing an appropriate Xmax for a given Xmin. For example, on a TI-82 or TI-83 graphics calculator, choose Xmax so that

$$Xmax = Xmin + 94\Delta X.$$

This number depends upon the calculator you are using.

```
WINDOW
Xmin = −5   ⟵
Xmax = 4.4  ⟵
Xscl = 1
Ymin = −10
Ymax = 10
Yscl = 1
Xres = 1
```

Suppose you want ΔX to equal 0.1. If Xmin = −5, then set Xmax equal to −5 + 94(0.1), or 4.4. This gives a "friendly window" where the TRACE cursor's x-coordinate will increase by 0.1 each time you press the right-arrow key.

Try This

7. Graph the equation $y = x^2 + 2x - 1$. Choose a friendly window where $\Delta X = 0.1$. Use the TRACE feature to determine, to the nearest tenth, the x-coordinate of each of the two points where the graph crosses the x-axis.

Student Resources

Answers to Try This

7.

TI-82 or TI-83: window of [−4, 5.4] and Xscl=0.5 for x, and [−2, 2] and Yscl=0.5 for y. Graph crosses at 0.4 and −2.4.
TI-81: window of [−4, 5.5] and Xscl=0.5 for x, and [−2, 2] and Yscl=0.5 for y. Graph crosses at 0.4 and −2.4.

➤ The TABLE Feature

Instead of tracing the graph of an equation, you may wish to examine a table of values. Not all calculators have a TABLE feature. Check to see if yours does.

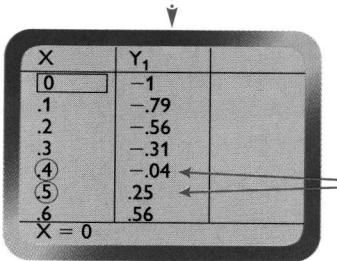

The screen shows a table of values for $y = x^2 + 2x - 1$. Here the value of x increases from a minimum of 0 in steps of 0.1. Some calculators have a table set-up feature that allows you to set the table minimum and the change in the control variable.

Notice that the y-values change sign between $x = 0.4$ and $x = 0.5$.

Taking a Closer Look at a Graph
➤ The ZOOM Feature

Suppose you are interested in the point where the graph of the equation $y = x^2 + 2x - 1$ crosses the positive x-axis. Tracing the graph shows that the x-coordinate of the point is between 0.4 and 0.5.

| Move the TRACE cursor to a point just below the x-axis. The y-coordinate of this point is negative but close to 0. | Move the TRACE cursor to a point just above the x-axis. The y-coordinate of this point is positive but close to 0. |

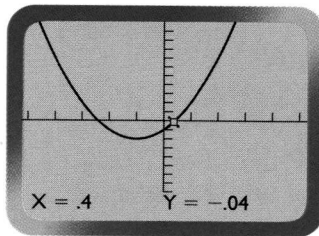

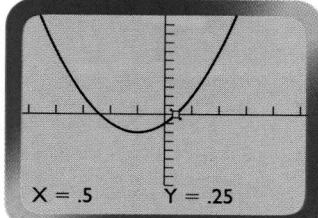

To get a closer look at the point of interest, you can use the ZOOM feature. Your calculator may have more than one way to zoom. A common way is to put a "zoom box" around the point. The calculator will then draw what's inside the box at full-screen size.

Technology Handbook

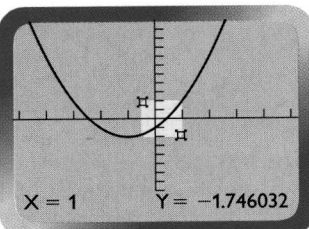

Define a "zoom box" . . .

X = 1   Y = −1.746032

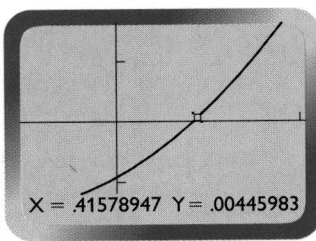

and then zoom.

X = .41578947 Y = .00445983

You create a "zoom box" by fixing first one corner and then the opposite corner of the box. (See your calculator's manual.)

Tracing reveals that the graph crosses the x-axis between $x = 0.41$ and $x = 0.42$. Repeat zooming and tracing.

On many graphics calculators you can use  and ▼ to move between graphs. This process helps you solve the system:

$$x + y = 3$$
$$x = \frac{2}{3}y - 5$$

Rewrite the equations. Enter $Y_1 = -X + 3$ and $Y_2 = \left(\frac{3}{2}\right)X + \left(\frac{15}{2}\right)$.

1 TRACE along the first line (Y_1) until you are near the intersection.

2 Press ▲.

3 Now you are on the other line.

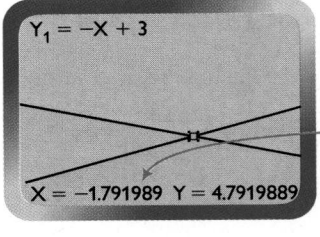

$Y_1 = -X + 3$

X = −1.791989 Y = 4.7919889

The x-coordinates are the same. The y-coordinates are close.

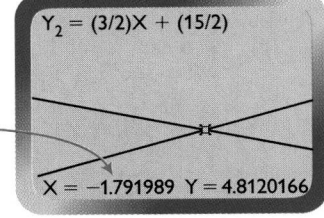

$Y_2 = (3/2)X + (15/2)$

X = −1.791989 Y = 4.8120166

You can ZOOM in and repeat the process described above until the y-coordinates are the same to the nearest tenth, hundredth, or any other decimal place. Some calculators have an intersection feature that lets you find the intersection of two graphs.

Try This

8. Try zooming in on the point where the graph of $y = x^2 + 2x - 1$ crosses the negative x-axis. Between what two values, to the nearest hundredth, does the x-coordinate of the point lie?

9. Solve this sytem by graphing: $9x + 3y = 14$
$\qquad\qquad\qquad\qquad\qquad\quad -3x + 2y = 8$

Student Resources

Answers to Try This

8. between −2.41 and −2.42

9.

Intersection
X=.14814815   Y=4.2222222

Comparing Graphs

➤ **Using a List to Graph a Family of Curves**

Some calculators allow you to enter a list as an element in an expression. The calculator can then plot a function for each value in the list and graph a family of curves.

$Y_1 = \{1, -2, 0.5\}X^2$
plots the family of functions
$y = x^2, y = -2x^2, y = 0.5x^2$.

$Y_2 = X^2 + \{-4, 5, 2\}$
plots the family of functions
$y = x^2 - 4, y = x^2 + 5, y = x^2 + 2$.

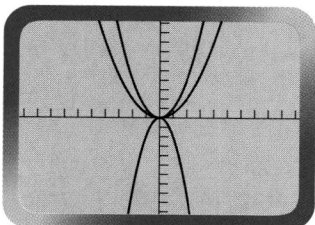 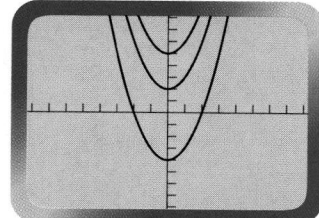

Using Matrices

➤ **Entering and Multiplying a Matrix by a Number**

Suppose you want to enter this table of sales data as a matrix on your calculator.

This Month's Sales by Age Group				
	VCRs	CD players	Faxes	Telephone answerers
Under 25	73	211	24	106
25–49	132	188	67	142
Over 49	89	55	46	98

Press the matrix function key. Select EDIT and choose matrix [A].

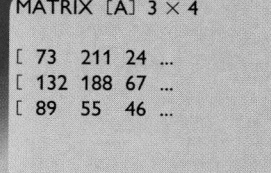

Set the dimensions. The matrix has 3 rows and 4 columns of data.

Enter the elements of the matrix $\begin{bmatrix} 73 & 211 & 24 & 106 \\ 132 & 188 & 67 & 142 \\ 89 & 55 & 46 & 98 \end{bmatrix}$.

Technology Handbook

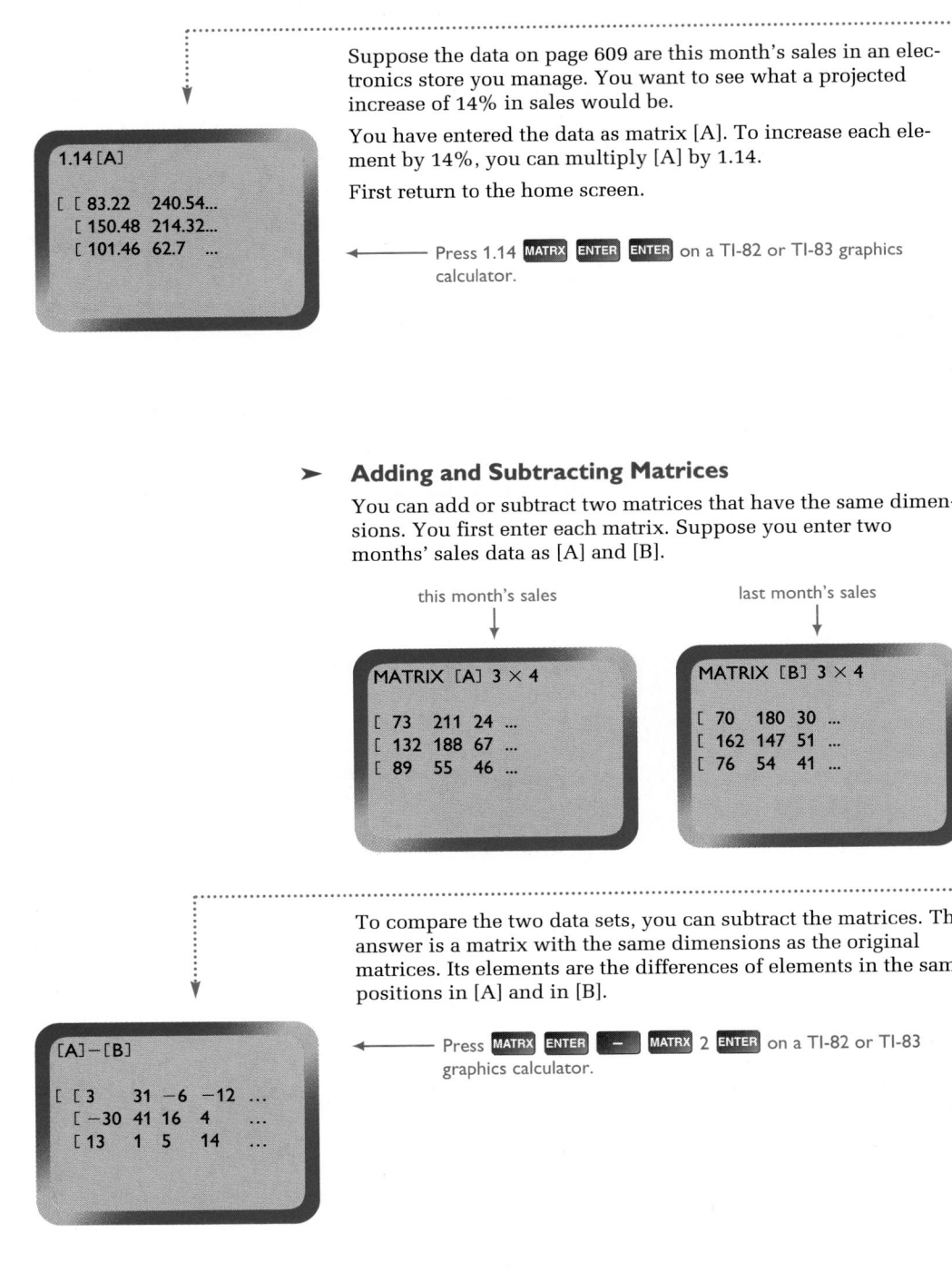

Suppose the data on page 609 are this month's sales in an electronics store you manage. You want to see what a projected increase of 14% in sales would be.

You have entered the data as matrix [A]. To increase each element by 14%, you can multiply [A] by 1.14.

First return to the home screen.

Press 1.14 **MATRX** **ENTER** **ENTER** on a TI-82 or TI-83 graphics calculator.

Adding and Subtracting Matrices

You can add or subtract two matrices that have the same dimensions. You first enter each matrix. Suppose you enter two months' sales data as [A] and [B].

To compare the two data sets, you can subtract the matrices. The answer is a matrix with the same dimensions as the original matrices. Its elements are the differences of elements in the same positions in [A] and in [B].

Press **MATRX** **ENTER** **−** **MATRX** 2 **ENTER** on a TI-82 or TI-83 graphics calculator.

Student Resources

➤ Finding the Product of Two Matrices

You can multiply two matrices when the number of columns of the first matrix is the same as the number of rows of the second matrix.

Suppose you want to find this product: $\begin{bmatrix} 9 & 4 \\ 3 & 1 \\ 2 & 8 \\ 1 & 5 \end{bmatrix} \begin{bmatrix} 4 & 2 & 0 \\ 3 & 0 & 2 \end{bmatrix}$

Enter the two matrices as [A] and [B]. Their dimensions are 4×2 and 2×3. Then find the product of the matrices.

[A] [B]

[[48 18 8]
 [15 6 2]
 [32 4 16]
 [19 2 10]]

Press **MATRX** **ENTER** **MATRX** 2 **ENTER** on a TI-82 or TI-83 graphics calculator.

➤ Finding the Inverse of a Matrix

You can use a graphics calculator to find the inverse of a matrix when the number of rows is the same as the number of columns.

Suppose you want to find the inverse of this matrix: $\begin{bmatrix} 3 & -1 \\ 4 & 0 \end{bmatrix}$

Enter the elements of the matrix as [A].

To find $[A]^{-1}$ press **MATRX** **ENTER** 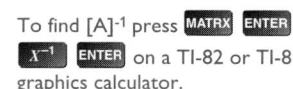 x^{-1} **ENTER** on a TI-82 or TI-83 graphics calculator.

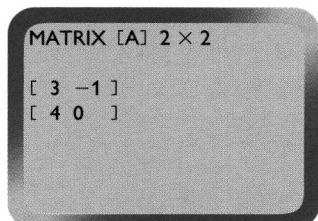

MATRIX [A] 2×2

[3 −1]
[4 0]

$[A]^{-1}$

[[0   .25]
 [−1 .75]]

Try This

Use matrices A, B, C, or D to find each answer. If a matrix does not exist, write *not defined*.

$A = \begin{bmatrix} 3 & 4 \\ 6 & 7 \end{bmatrix}$ $B = \begin{bmatrix} 5 & 11 \\ -3 & -7 \end{bmatrix}$ $C = \begin{bmatrix} 9 & 3 \\ 12 & 4 \end{bmatrix}$ $D = \begin{bmatrix} 2 & 0 & -8 & 1 \\ 5 & 7 & 3 & 9 \end{bmatrix}$

10. $A + B$ **11.** $B - C$ **12.** $2A$ **13.** AB

14. $C + D$ **15.** CD **16.** A^{-1} **17.** D^{-1}

Technology Handbook

611

Answers to Try This

10.

[A]+[B]

[[8 15]
 [3 0]]

11.

[B]−[C]

[[−4 8]
 [−15 −11]]

12.

2[A]

[[6 8]
 [12 14]]

13.

[A][B]

[[3 5]
 [9 17]]

14. not defined

15.

[C][D]

[[33 21 −63 36]
 [44 28 −84 48]]

16.

$[A]^{-1}$

[[−2.33 1.33]
 [2   −1   ]]

17. not defined

611

Working with Statistics

➤ Histograms, Line Graphs, and Box-and-Whisker Plots

Many graphics calculators can display histograms, line graphs, and sometimes even box-and-whisker plots of data that you enter. For example, the histogram below displays the data about the readers of *Galaxy*, a science magazine.

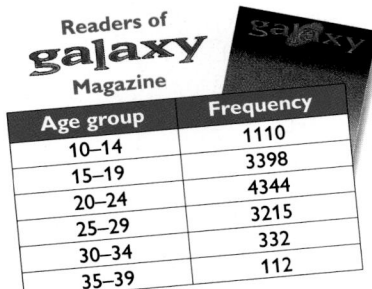

Readers of galaxy Magazine

Age group	Frequency
10–14	1110
15–19	3398
20–24	4344
25–29	3215
30–34	332
35–39	112

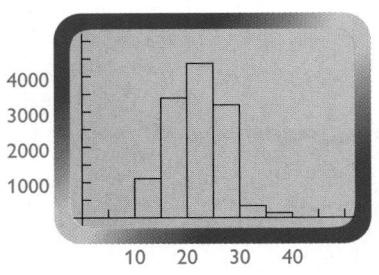

➤ Scatter Plots and Curve Fitting

Curve fitting is the process of finding an equation that describes a set of ordered pairs. Often, the first step is to graph the paired data in a scatter plot.

The scatter plot below displays the data for an Olympic event. It also shows a fitted line, called a *regression line*, that the calculator fit to the data.

Men's Winning Times in Olympic 400 m Freestyle Swimming		
Year	Years after 1960	Time (seconds)
1960	0	258.3
1964	4	252.2
1968	8	249.0
1972	12	240.27
1976	16	231.93
1980	20	231.31
1984	24	231.23
1988	28	226.95
1992	32	225.00
1996	36	227.97

The equation of the regression line is $y = 254 - 0.911x$ where x is the years after 1960 and y is the winning time.

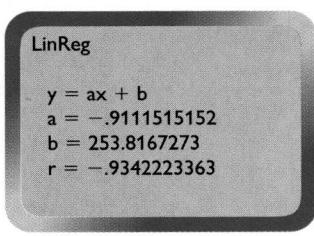

LinReg

$y = ax + b$
$a = -.9111515152$
$b = 253.8167273$
$r = -.9342223363$

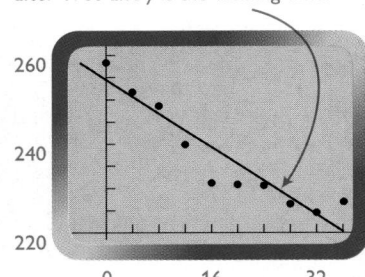

Student Resources

➤ Using a Spreadsheet

In addition to using a graphics calculator, you may want to use a computer with a spreadsheet program. A spreadsheet can help you solve a problem like this one: Suppose you want to buy a portable CD player that costs $85, including tax. You already have $11 and can save $5 per week. After how many weeks can you buy the player?

A spreadsheet is made up of cells named by a column letter and a row number, like A3 or B4. You can enter a label, a number, or a formula into a cell.

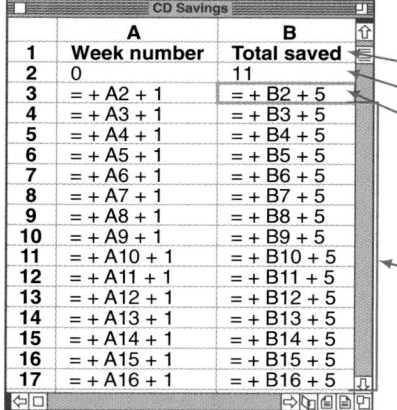

Cell B1 contains the label "Total saved."

Cell B2 contains the number 11.

Cell B3 contains the formula "=+B2+5." This formula tells the computer to take the number in cell B2, add 5 to it, and put the result in cell B3. (Likewise, the formula in cell A3 tells the computer to take the number in cell A2, add 1 to it, and put the result in cell A3.)

Instead of typing a formula into each cell individually, you can use the spreadsheet's copy and fill commands.

In this spreadsheet, the computer has replaced all the formulas with calculated values. You can have the computer draw a scatter plot with a line connecting the plotted points. As you can see, you will have enough money to buy the portable CD player after 15 weeks.

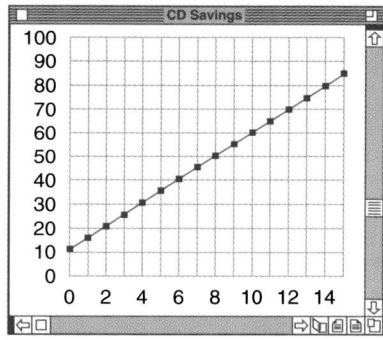

Technology Handbook

613

Extra Practice

Unit 1

In Exercises 1–4, estimate each amount. `1-1`

1. At a factory that makes compact discs, 2 out of a batch of 50 discs are found to be defective. Estimate the number of defective discs in a monthly output of 3,500 discs.

2. In a sample of wild bird food, 27 seeds out of a sample of 60 seeds are sunflower seeds. Estimate the number of sunflower seeds in a package of about 1500 seeds.

3. **a.** Roberto Rodriguez got 3 hits in 5 official trips to the plate in one baseball game. Based on this game, how many hits would he get in a season in which he has 400 official trips to the plate?

   b. Do you think this is a good method of predicting his record for the season? Why or why not?

4. Floyd Jefferson made 4 and missed 3 jump shots from outside the lane in yesterday's basketball game. Suppose he takes 56 jump shots from outside the lane in a season. Estimate the number of these he will make and the number he will miss.

5. Name a sample group from the population of all triangles. `1-1`

Use this simulation of random guessing on a test for Exercises 6–10. `1-2`

Suppose each question on a 10-question multiple-choice test has three answer-choices. A die is used to simulate random guessing on the test. Rolling a 1 or a 2 represents a correct answer. The results of six trials of rolling a die 10 times are shown.

Trial #	Numbers Rolled
First	2, 3, 5, 1, 6, 4, 2, 3, 2, 5
Second	4, 1, 2, 2, 5, 3, 6, 3, 6, 2
Third	1, 3, 4, 6, 4, 5, 3, 6, 3, 4
Fourth	3, 1, 2, 2, 5, 6, 4, 1, 3, 2
Fifth	4, 5, 3, 1, 5, 5, 2, 1, 2, 4
Sixth	5, 2, 4, 1, 6, 3, 4, 3, 3, 5

Use the table to estimate the probability of each event.

6. Exactly four questions were answered correctly.

7. Four or more questions were answered correctly.

8. Fewer than four questions were answered correctly.

9. All ten questions were answered correctly.

10. What is the mean number of questions answered correctly?

Answers to Extra Practice Unit 1

1. 140

2. 675

3. **a.** 240

   b. No. The sample size is too small.

4. 32 made; 24 missed

5. all triangle types: isosceles, scalene, equilateral, right, acute, obtuse

6. $\frac{1}{2}$

7. $\frac{2}{3}$

8. $\frac{1}{3}$

9. 0

10. about 3.3

11. systematic

12. convenience

13. cluster

14. systematic

15. random

16. No.

17. 0 times

18. Answers may vary. An example is given. Patients who go to the dentist may take better care of their teeth than the general population.

19. 48

Suppose names are to be selected from a list of magazine subscribers to receive a special offer. Classify each sample as *random, convenience, stratified random, cluster,* or *systematic.* **1-3**

11. Every fourth name in the list of subscribers is selected.

12. The first 200 names in the list are selected.

13. Subscribers having a ZIP code that begins with the digits 012 are selected.

14. The list is alphabetized, and the first 10 subscribers whose last names begin with each letter of the alphabet are selected.

15. The subscribers are numbered, the numbers are written on slips of paper, and 200 slips are drawn from a paper bag containing all the slips.

Use this dentist's survey in Exercises 16–18. **1-4**

16. Can the dentist find the median of the answers to Question 2?

17. State a possible answer to Question 1 that is not one of the multiple choices.

18. What biases might be reflected in the results of the survey?

> **DENTIST'S SURVEY**
> 1. How many times a day do you brush your teeth?
>   a. once
>   b. twice
>   c. three times
>   d. four or more times
> 2. How much time do you spend brushing on each occasion?
>   a. very little
>   b. 1 min
>   c. 2 min
>   d. a very long time

Predict the next number in each pattern. **1-5**

19. 3, 6, 12, 24, _?_

20. 1, −2, 3, −4, _?_

21. 11, 101, 1001, 10,001, _?_

22. 1, 8, 27, 64, _?_

23. Suppose you take the product of four consecutive positive integers and add 1. For example, $(1 \cdot 2 \cdot 3 \cdot 4) + 1 = 25$. Try other examples and make a conjecture about the kind of number you always get.

Use the Venn diagram, which shows how students responded to a survey about after-school activities. Tell whether each statement about the students in the survey is *True* or *False*. **1-6**

24. All the students in the glee club were involved in an indoor activity.

25. If a student attends an indoor activity, then the student is in the debating club.

26. No students are in both the glee club and the debating club.

27. If a student is on the school newspaper, then that student is also in the debating club.

28. Some students on the school newspaper are in the glee club.

> all after school activities
> indoor activities — glee club
> school newspaper — debating club

For Exercises 29–32: **1-7**

a. Tell whether or not each statement is true. If not, give a counterexample.

b. Write the converse of each statement. Tell whether or not it is true. If not, give a counterexample.

29. If $x > 2$, then $x > 5$.

30. If $a + b = a + c$, then $b = c$.

31. If it is midnight, the sun is not out.

32. If $x + y = 5$, then $xy = 6$.

Extra Practice

Answers to Extra Practice Unit 1

20. 5

21. 100,001

22. 125

23. You always get an odd perfect square.

24. True.

25. False.

26. True.

27. False.

28. False.

29. a. False; $x = 3$.
  b. If $x > 5$, then $x > 2$; the converse is true.

30. a. True.
  b. If $b = c$, then $a + b = a + c$; the converse is true.

31. a. True.
  b. If the sun is not out, then it is midnight. The converse is false. It could be cloudy or raining. and the sun would not be out, or it could be 2 A.M.

32. a. False; $x = 1$; $y = 4$.
  b. If $xy = 6$, then $x + y = 5$; the converse is false, too. Let $x = 1$ and $y = 6$.

Answers to

1. nonlinear growth

2. linear decay

3. constant

4. none of these

5. a. $-\frac{4}{3}$

   b. decreasing

6. a. $\frac{1}{3}$

   b. increasing

7. a. $\frac{3}{2}$

   b. increasing

8. a. 0

   b. constant

9. a. $-\frac{3}{2}$

   b. decreasing

10. a. 0

   b. constant

11. $y = 5x - 23$

12. $y = -\frac{3}{2}x - 5$

13. $y = \frac{4}{3}x + \frac{1}{3}$

14. $y = \frac{3}{4}x + 11$

15. $y = \frac{1}{2}x + \frac{23}{2}$

16. $y = -\frac{1}{2}x + 2$

17. a. slope $= \frac{1}{2}$; vertical intercept $= 0$

   b.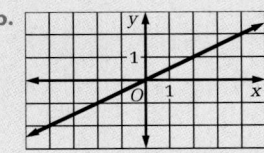

   c. increasing function

18. a. slope $= -2$; vertical intercept $= 3$

   b.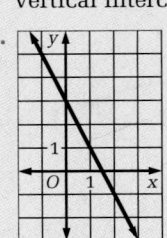

   c. decreasing function

19. a. slope $= 0$; vertical intercept $= -1.5$

   b.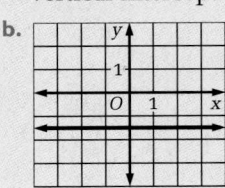

   c. constant function

Unit 2

Tell whether each graph is an example of *linear growth, nonlinear growth, linear decay, nonlinear decay, a constant,* **or** *none of these.* **2-1**

1.
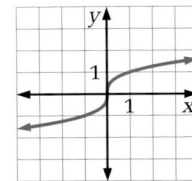

2.
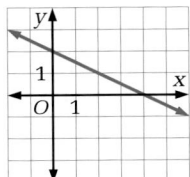

3.
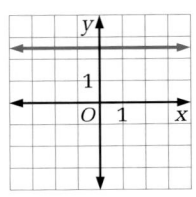

4.
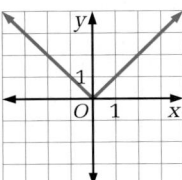

For each pair of points: **2-2**

  a. Find the slope of the line that contains the points.

  b. Describe the line as *increasing, decreasing,* or *constant.*

   5. $(0, 4)$ and $(3, 0)$ **6.** $(-5, 2)$ and $(4, 5)$ **7.** $(7, 2)$ and $(-1, -10)$

   8. $(-3, 6)$ and $(2, 6)$ **9.** $(-1, 8)$ and $(9, -7)$ **10.** $(1, -2)$ and $(6, -2)$

Write an equation for the line through each pair of points. **2-2**

  11. $(4, -3)$ and $(6, 7)$ **12.** $(0, -5)$ and $(-6, 4)$ **13.** $(2, 3)$ and $(-7, -9)$

  14. $(-8, 5)$ and $(0, 11)$ **15.** $(1, 12)$ and $(-5, 9)$ **16.** $(-8, 6)$ and $(6, -1)$

For each equation: **2-2**

  a. Identify the slope and the vertical intercept of the graph.

  b. Draw the graph.

  c. Write *increasing function, decreasing function,* or *constant function* to describe the graph.

  17. $y = \frac{1}{2}x$ **18.** $y = -2x + 3$ **19.** $y = -1.5$

  20. $y = x - 1.5$ **21.** $y = \frac{2}{3}x - 1$ **22.** $y = -\frac{5}{2}x + 4$

Find y when $x = 8$. **2-3**

  23. $xy = 24$ **24.** $x = \frac{52}{y}$ **25.** $y = \frac{7.2}{x}$

Rewrite the equation in the $y = \frac{k}{x}$ form. **2-3**

  26. $xy = -28$ **27.** $\frac{13}{y} = x$ **28.** $-xy = 12$

Student Resources

---

20. a. slope $= 1$; vertical intercept $= -1.5$

   b.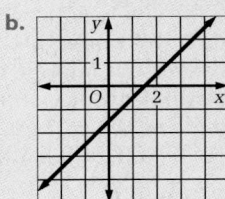

   c. increasing function

21. a. slope $= \frac{2}{3}$; vertical intercept $= -1$

   b.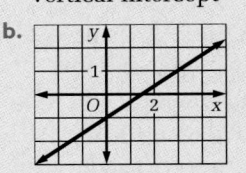

   c. increasing function

22. a. slope $= -\frac{5}{2}$; vertical intercept $= 4$

   b.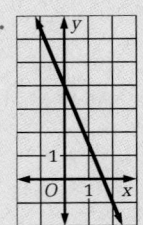

   c. decreasing function

Find the surface area and the volume of the sphere described. Leave your answer in terms of π. `2-4`

29. radius = 1.5   **30.** diameter = 9   **31.** diameter = 21

Find the radius of each sphere described. `2-4`

32. volume = 972π **33.** surface area = 484π **34.** volume = 7776π

Sphere Q has radius 15. Sphere R has radius 20. Find the ratio of each pair of measurements of the two spheres. `2-4`

35. the diameters   **36.** the surface areas   **37.** the volumes

For each equation: `2-5`

a. Find the value of y when $x = 10$.
b. Find the value of x when $y = 24$.

Round all decimal answers to the nearest tenth.

38. $y = 7x^3$ **39.** $y = \dfrac{\pi x^2}{5}$ **40.** $y = 0.008x^3$

41. $y = \dfrac{11}{25}x^2$ **42.** $y = 24{,}000x^3$ **43.** $y = \dfrac{1}{3}\pi x^2$

Evaluate each expression when $a = 64$. `2-6`

44. $(27a)^{1/3}$ **45.** $25a^{1/2}$ **46.** $(49a)^{1/2}$

47. $8a^{1/3}$ **48.** $\left(\dfrac{a}{125}\right)^{1/3}$ **49.** $\dfrac{16}{a^{1/2}}$

Rewrite each expression using fractional exponents. `2-6`

50. $15\sqrt{c}$ **51.** $\sqrt[3]{7x}$ **52.** $\sqrt[3]{\dfrac{b}{5}}$

Rewrite each expression in radical form. `2-6`

53. $(29pq)^{1/3}$ **54.** $\dfrac{y^{1/2}}{3x^{1/2}}$ **55.** $-(8v)^{1/2} \cdot \left(\dfrac{w}{2}\right)^{1/3}$

Use the equation $y = 15(2^x)$. Find the value of y for each value of x. `2-7`

56. $x = 6$ **57.** $x = 12$ **58.** $x = 15$

Use the equation $y = 16\left(\dfrac{1}{2}\right)^x$. Find the value of y for each value of x. `2-7`

59. $x = 4$ **60.** $x = 7$ **61.** $x = 10$

Extra Practice

Answers to Extra Practice Unit 2

23. $y = 3$
24. $y = 6.5$
25. $y = 0.9$
26. $y = -\dfrac{28}{x}$
27. $y = \dfrac{13}{x}$
28. $y = -\dfrac{12}{x}$
29. 9π; 4.5π
30. 81π; 121.5π

31. 441π; 1543.5π
32. 9
33. 11
34. 18
35. 3:4
36. 9:16
37. 27:64
38. a. 7000
    b. 1.5

39. a. 62.8
    b. 6.2; −6.2
40. a. 8
    b. 14.4
41. a. 44
    b. 7.4; −7.4
42. a. 24,000,000
    b. 0.1

43. a. 104.7
    b. 4.8; −4.8
44. 12
45. 200
46. 56
47. 32
48. 0.8
49. 2
50. $15c^{1/2}$
51. $7^{1/3}x^{1/3}$ or $(7x)^{1/3}$
52. $\left(\dfrac{b}{5}\right)^{1/3}$
53. $\sqrt[3]{29pq}$
54. $\dfrac{\sqrt{y}}{3\sqrt{x}}$
55. $-\sqrt{8v} \cdot \sqrt[3]{\dfrac{w}{2}}$
56. 960
57. 61,440
58. 491,520
59. 1
60. 0.125
61. 0.015625

Unit 3

Solve each system of equations by graphing. `3-1`

1. $y = x - 5$
$y = -2x - 2$

2. $y = \frac{1}{2}x + 4$
$y = 2x + 1$

3. $y = -x + 3$
$y = \frac{5}{2}x + 3$

4. $y = 2x + 3$
$y = \frac{1}{2}x$

5. $y = -3x + 8$
$y = -\frac{2}{3}x + 1$

6. $y = 0.4x - 6$
$y = -1.2x + 2$

Solve each system of equations by substitution. `3-2`

7. $b = 2a + 11$
$a + b = 5$

8. $w = \frac{1}{3}v - 5$
$\frac{2}{3}v - w = 7$

9. $2c - d = 7$
$d = 3c - 11$

10. $q = \frac{1}{2}p - 7$
$-2p - q = 2$

11. $g - 3h = -4$
$-3g + 8h = 13$

12. $x = 5y - 2$
$\frac{1}{2}x + 2y = 8$

For each system of equations: `3-3`

a. Without graphing, describe the relationship of the graphs of the equations.

b. Tell whether the system has *no solution, one solution,* or *many solutions.*
Identify the system as *consistent* or *inconsistent.*

13. $y = 5x + 2$
$y = -5x + 2$

14. $y = -2x + 5$
$y = -2x - 1$

15. $y = 3x - 7$
$-2y = -6x + 14$

16. $x - 4y = 18$
$3x - 12y = 18$

17. $2x + 3y = 12$
$2x + 3y = -12$

18. $3x - 6y = 9$
$5x - 10y = 15$

Write an equation of the line that fits each description. `3-3`

19. The line goes through $(-4, 1)$ and is parallel to the line $y = -2x + 11$.

20. The line goes through $(6, 7)$ and is perpendicular to the line $y = 3x - 4$.

21. The line goes through $(-2, 5)$ and is perpendicular to the line $x = -1$.

22. The line goes through $(-3, -8)$ and is parallel to the line $x = 5$.

Use the addition-or-subtraction method to solve each system of equations. `3-4`

23. $y + z = 5$
$2y - 3z = 15$

24. $3x - 5y = 9$
$-x + 4y = -10$

25. $4c - 3d = -5$
$5c - d = 13$

26. $4a + 2b = 12$
$7a - 4b = 21$

27. $j + 4k = 7$
$5j + 6k = -7$

28. $3p - 5q = 11$
$7p + 10q = 4$

29. $-7x + 3y = 3$
$\frac{1}{3}x + y = 9$

30. $2v - 3w = 9$
$3v - 7w = 11$

Answers to Extra Practice Unit 3

1. $(1, -4)$

2. $(2, 5)$

3. $(0, 3)$

4. $(-2, -1)$

5. $(3, -1)$

6. $(5, -4)$

7. $(-2, 7)$

8. $(6, -3)$

9. $(4, 1)$

10. $(2, -6)$

11. $(-7, -1)$

12. $(8, 2)$

13. a. lines intersecting
b. one solution; consistent

14. a. parallel lines
b. no solution; inconsistent

15. a. same line
b. many solutions; consistent

16. a. parallel lines
b. no solution; inconsistent

17. a. parallel lines
b. no solution; inconsistent

18. a. same line
b. many solutions; consistent

19. $y = -2x - 7$

20. $y = -\frac{1}{3}x + 9$

21. $y = 5$

22. $x = -3$

23. $(6, -1)$

24. $(-2, -3)$

25. $(4, 7)$

26. $(3, 0)$

27. $(-5, 3)$

28. $(2, -1)$

Simplify. `3-5`

31. $\begin{bmatrix} -2 & 1 \\ 4 & 0 \end{bmatrix} + \begin{bmatrix} 3 & -1 \\ 3 & 1 \end{bmatrix}$

32. $\begin{bmatrix} 1 & 2 \\ -5 & 4 \\ -3 & 0 \end{bmatrix} - \begin{bmatrix} 1 & 6 \\ -2 & 0 \\ 4 & 5 \end{bmatrix}$

33. $2\begin{bmatrix} 7 & 2 & 0 \\ -3 & 1 & 1 \\ 4 & 2 & -1 \end{bmatrix}$

34. $\begin{bmatrix} -1 \\ 0 \\ 2 \\ 3 \\ -4 \end{bmatrix} - 3\begin{bmatrix} 3 \\ 5 \\ 7 \\ -10 \\ 2 \end{bmatrix}$

35. $-5\begin{bmatrix} 1 & -2 & -2 \\ 0 & 3 & -1 \end{bmatrix} + 2\begin{bmatrix} 3 & 1 & 6 \\ -5 & 2 & 0 \end{bmatrix}$

Find the coordinates of the vertices of △DEF after each transformation. Write your answer as a matrix. `3-6`

36. a translation 1 unit left, 2 units up

37. a dilation with scale factor 3 and center at the origin

38. a translation 3 units right, 4 units down

39. a dilation with scale factor $\frac{1}{2}$ and center at the origin

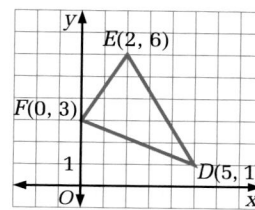

Find the product of each pair of matrices. `3-7`

40. $\begin{bmatrix} 0 & -1 & 0.25 \\ 2 & -1 & 5 \end{bmatrix}\begin{bmatrix} 3 & 0 \\ 0.5 & 4 \\ 2 & -1 \end{bmatrix}$

41. $\begin{bmatrix} 4 & 2 & -3 & 0 & 1 \\ -1 & 2 & 0 & 5 & 3 \end{bmatrix}\begin{bmatrix} 1 \\ 1 \\ -1 \\ 2 \\ 3 \end{bmatrix}$

42. $\begin{bmatrix} 3 & 0 & -3 \\ 1 & 2 & 4 \\ -1 & 2 & 0 \end{bmatrix}\begin{bmatrix} 2 & 1 \\ -2 & 3 \\ -4 & 5 \end{bmatrix}$

43. $\begin{bmatrix} 7 & 10 & -11 & -3 \end{bmatrix}\begin{bmatrix} 1 & 1 \\ 2 & -2 \\ 3 & 5 \\ -1 & 4 \end{bmatrix}$

Use a graphics calculator to find the inverse of each matrix, if it exists. Round each element to the nearest hundredth. `3-8`

44. $\begin{bmatrix} 3 & 2 \\ -1 & 1 \end{bmatrix}$

45. $\begin{bmatrix} 7 & -3 \\ -9 & 4 \end{bmatrix}$

46. $\begin{bmatrix} 2 & 3 & 0 \\ -3 & 5 & -4 \\ -1 & 1 & -1 \end{bmatrix}$

Extra Practice

Answers to Extra Practice Unit 3 ··

29. (3, 8)

30. (6, 1)

31. $\begin{bmatrix} 1 & 0 \\ 7 & 1 \end{bmatrix}$

32. $\begin{bmatrix} 0 & -4 \\ -3 & 4 \\ -7 & -5 \end{bmatrix}$

33. $\begin{bmatrix} 14 & 4 & 0 \\ -6 & 2 & 2 \\ 8 & 4 & -2 \end{bmatrix}$

34. $\begin{bmatrix} -10 \\ -15 \\ -19 \\ 33 \\ -10 \end{bmatrix}$

35. $\begin{bmatrix} 1 & 12 & 22 \\ -10 & -11 & 5 \end{bmatrix}$

36. $\begin{array}{ccc} D' & E' & F' \end{array}$
$\begin{bmatrix} 4 & 1 & -1 \\ 3 & 8 & 5 \end{bmatrix}$

37. $\begin{array}{ccc} D' & E' & F' \end{array}$
$\begin{bmatrix} 15 & 6 & 0 \\ 3 & 18 & 9 \end{bmatrix}$

38. $\begin{array}{ccc} D' & E' & F' \end{array}$
$\begin{bmatrix} 8 & 5 & 3 \\ -3 & 2 & -1 \end{bmatrix}$

39. $\begin{array}{ccc} D' & E' & F' \end{array}$
$\begin{bmatrix} 2.5 & 1 & 0 \\ 0.5 & 3 & 1.5 \end{bmatrix}$

40. $\begin{bmatrix} 0 & -4.25 \\ 15.5 & -9 \end{bmatrix}$

41. $\begin{bmatrix} 12 \\ 20 \end{bmatrix}$

42. $\begin{bmatrix} 18 & -12 \\ -18 & 27 \\ -6 & 5 \end{bmatrix}$

43. $\begin{bmatrix} -3 & -80 \end{bmatrix}$

44. $\begin{bmatrix} 0.2 & -0.4 \\ 0.2 & 0.6 \end{bmatrix}$

45. $\begin{bmatrix} 4 & 3 \\ 9 & 7 \end{bmatrix}$

46. $\begin{bmatrix} -1 & 3 & -12 \\ 1 & -2 & 8 \\ 2 & -5 & 19 \end{bmatrix}$

Unit 4

For the graph of each function, find an equation of the line of symmetry and the coordinates of the vertex. Tell whether the value of the function at the vertex is a maximum or a minimum. 4-1

1. $y = -x^2 + 4x - 7$
2. $y = 2x^2 + 4x$
3. $y = -3x^2 - 18x + 5$
4. $y = 0.125x^2 - 2x - 6$
5. $y = -0.2x^2 + 6.4x - 1$
6. $y = 0.01x^2 + 0.5x - 2$

Find the y-intercept of each function. 4-1

7. $y = 4x^2 + x - 2$
8. $y = -x^2 - 6x + 10$
9. $y = 5x^2 - 2x$

Use the graph to estimate the x-intercepts. 4-1

10. $y = \frac{2}{3}x^2 - \frac{1}{3}x - 2$
11. $y = -x^2 + 4x + 1$
12. $y = 2x^2 + 5x - 4$

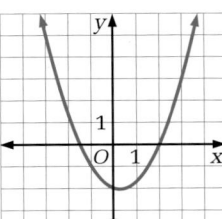
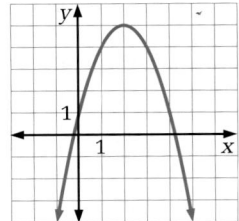
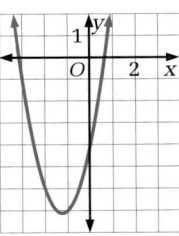

Tell how to translate the graph of $y = 0.5x^2$ in order to produce the graph of each function. 4-2

13. $y = 0.5(x + 3)^2 - 7$
14. $y = 0.5(x - 1)^2 - 4$
15. $y = 0.5(x - 6)^2 + 2$
16. $y = 0.5(x + 9)^2$

For the graph of each function: 4-2

a. Find the coordinates of the vertex.

b. Find the y-intercept.

17. $y = (x - 7)^2 - 1$
18. $y = -0.2(x + 5)^2 - 11$
19. $y = -5(x + 1)^2 + 14$
20. $y = 2.5(x + 6)^2 + 8$

Solve using algebra. 4-3

21. $4x^2 + 2 = 17$
22. $(x - 3)^2 = 15$
23. $(x + 1)^2 - 2 = 9$
24. $2(x - 3)^2 - 1 = 6$
25. $-3x^2 + 5 = -8$
26. $4(x - 5)^2 - 7 = 12$
27. $0.5(x + 4)^2 + 2 = 7$
28. $-0.25(x - 6)^2 + 3 = -14$

Answers to
Unit 4 Extra Practice

1. $x = 2$; $(2, -3)$; maximum
2. $x = -1$; $(-1, -2)$; minimum
3. $x = -3$; $(-3, 32)$; maximum
4. $x = 8$; $(8, -14)$; minimum
5. $x = 16$; $(16, 50.2)$; maximum
6. $x = -25$; $(-25, -8.25)$; minimum
7. -2
8. 10
9. 0
10. $x = -1.5, 2$
11. Estimates may vary. Examples are given. $x = -\frac{1}{3}, 4\frac{1}{3}$
12. Estimates may vary. Examples are given. $x = -3.1, 0.6$
13. 3 units left, 7 units down
14. 1 unit right, 4 units down
15. 6 units right, 2 units up
16. 9 units left
17. a. $(7, -1)$
    b. 48
18. a. $(-5, -11)$
    b. -16
19. a. $(-1, 14)$
    b. 9
20. a. $(-6, 8)$
    b. 98
21. $x = \pm\frac{\sqrt{15}}{2}$ or about 1.94, about -1.94
22. $x = \pm\sqrt{15} + 3$ or about 6.87, about -0.87
23. $x = \pm\sqrt{11} - 1$ or about -4.32, about 2.32
24. $x = \pm\sqrt{3.5} + 3$ or about 4.87, about 1.13
25. $x = \pm\sqrt{\frac{13}{3}}$ or about 2.08, about -2.08
26. $x = \pm\frac{\sqrt{19}}{2} + 5$ or about 7.18, about 2.82
27. $x = \pm\sqrt{10} - 4$ or about -7.16, about -0.84
28. $x = \pm2\sqrt{17} + 6$ or about -2.25, about 14.25
29. $(x - 7)(x + 3)$
30. $(2x - 5)(x + 8)$
31. $(3x - 7)(x - 2)$
32. $(7x + 6)(x + 2)$
33. $(5x - 3)(2x + 5)$
34. $(4x - 7)(3x + 1)$
35. $(9x + 5)(9x - 5)$
36. $(a - 12b)(a + 12b)$
37. $(2 - 7x)(2 + 7x)$
38. $(x - 6)^2$
39. $(3x + 1)^2$
40. $(5x - 2)^2$
41. $x = 11, -3$
42. $x = 2, 1.5$
43. $x = 2, -\frac{2}{3}$
44. $x = \frac{11 \pm \sqrt{93}}{2}$ or about 10.32, about 0.68
45. $x = -3 \pm \sqrt{11}$ or about 0.32, about -6.32
46. $x = 1 \pm \sqrt{15}$ or about 4.87, about -2.87

Factor. 4-4

29. $x^2 - 4x - 21$

30. $2x^2 + 11x - 40$

31. $3x^2 - 13x + 14$

32. $7x^2 + 20x + 12$

33. $10x^2 + 19x - 15$

34. $12x^2 - 17x - 7$

35. $81x^2 - 25$

36. $a^2 - 144b^2$

37. $4 - 49x^2$

38. $x^2 - 12x + 36$

39. $9x^2 + 6x + 1$

40. $25x^2 - 20x + 4$

Solve by factoring. 4-4

41. $x^2 - 8x = 33$

42. $2x^2 = 7x - 6$

43. $3x^2 - 4x + 1 = 5$

Solve using the quadratic formula. 4-5

44. $x^2 - 11x + 7 = 0$

45. $x^2 + 6x - 2 = 0$

46. $x^2 - 2x - 14 = 0$

47. $3x^2 + 8x + 2 = 0$

48. $-5x^2 + 3x + 1 = 0$

49. $2x^2 + 8x - 7 = 0$

50. $0.5x^2 + 0.25x - 4 = 0$

51. $(x - 6)^2 + 3x = 29$

52. $2(x + 3)^2 - 5 = x$

For Exercises 53–58: 4-6

a. Use the discriminant to tell whether each equation has *one solution,* *two solutions,* or *no solutions* in the set of real numbers.

b. Solve each equation that has at least one real-number solution. Graph the related quadratic function for each equation that has no real-number solutions.

53. $x^2 - x - 1 = 0$

54. $x^2 - 3x + 5 = 0$

55. $1.5x^2 + 3.5x + 2 = 0$

56. $2x^2 - 9x + 10 = 0$

57. $-x^2 + 4x - 5 = 0$

58. $2x^2 - 3x + 2 = 0$

Simplify. 4-6

59. $(6 + 4i) - (7 + 2i)$

60. $-i(-3 + 5i)$

61. $(10 + 3i)(8 - i)$

Solve, using complex numbers. 4-6

62. $x^2 + 6x + 10 = 0$

63. $x^2 - 2x + 11 = 0$

64. $-2x^2 + 6x - 7 = 0$

Solve each system by substitution. 4-7

65. $y = 2x^2 + 5$
$y = 2x^2 - 4x - 7$

66. $y = -2x^2 - x + 7$
$y = -x^2 + x - 8$

67. $y = 4x^2 + 2x + 1$
$y = 3x^2 - 2x + 1$

Solve each system by graphing. 4-7

68. $y = 0.5x^2 - 3x$
$y = -0.5x^2 + x - 4$

69. $y = x^2 - 2x - 3$
$y = -x^2 + 4x + 5$

70. $y = 2x^2 - 3$
$y = 2x^2 - 4x + 1$

Extra Practice

621

b. $x = 2.5, 2$

57. a. no solutions

b.

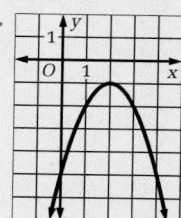

58. a. no solutions

b.

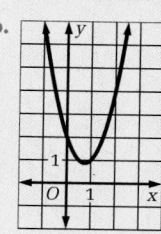

59. $-1 + 2i$

60. $5 + 3i$

61. $83 + 14i$

62. $-3 \pm i$

63. $x = 1 \pm \sqrt{10}i$ or about $1 + 3.16i$, about $1 - 3.16i$

64. $x = \dfrac{3}{2} \pm \dfrac{\sqrt{5}}{2}i$ or about $1.5 + 1.12i$, about $1.5 - 1.12i$

65. $(-3, 23)$

66. $(3, -14), (-5, -38)$

67. $(-4, 57), (0, 1)$

68. $(2, -4)$

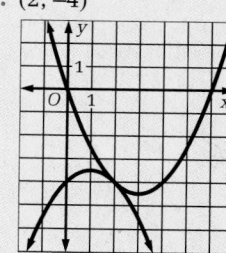

69. $(-1, 0), (4, 5)$

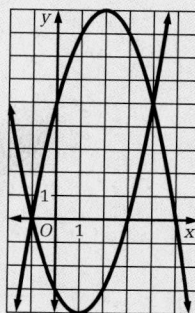

70. $(1, -1)$

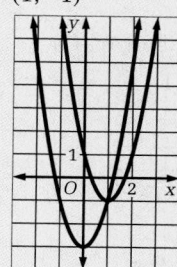

Answers to Extra Practice Unit 4

47. $x = \dfrac{-4 \pm \sqrt{10}}{3}$ or about -0.28, about -2.39

48. $x = \dfrac{3 \pm \sqrt{29}}{10}$ or about -0.24, about 0.84

49. $x = -2 \pm \dfrac{\sqrt{30}}{2}$ or about 0.74, about -4.74

50. $x = -0.25 \pm \sqrt{8.0625}$ or about 2.59, about -3.09

51. $x = \dfrac{9 \pm \sqrt{53}}{2}$ or about 8.14, about 0.86

52. $x = \dfrac{-11 \pm \sqrt{17}}{4}$ or about -1.72, about -3.78

53. a. two solutions
b. $x = \dfrac{1 \pm \sqrt{5}}{2}$ or about 1.62, about -0.62

54. a. no solutions

b.

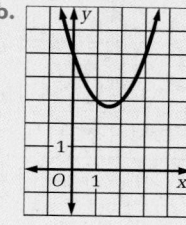

55. a. two solutions
b. $x = -1, -\dfrac{4}{3}$

56. a. two solutions

Unit 5

Tell whether each statement is *True* or *False*. If it is false, explain why. `5-1`

1. All squares are rhombuses.

2. Every parallelogram is a rectangle.

3. If a quadrilateral is a kite, then it is a rhombus.

4. A quadrilateral is rhombus only if it is a kite.

Find the distance between each pair of points. `5-2`

5. $(-3, 5)$ and $(6, -7)$ **6.** $(5, -1)$ and $(8, -9)$ **7.** $(3, 11)$ and $(-4, -2)$

8. Use the distance formula to show that quadrilateral *ABCD* with vertices $A(3, 1)$, $B(10, 2)$, $C(5, 7)$, and $D(-2, 6)$ is a rhombus. `5-2`

9. Use the distance formula to show that quadrilateral *PQRS* with vertices $P(7, 2)$, $Q(3, 5)$, $R(-1, 2)$, and $S(3, -4)$ is a kite. `5-2`

Find the coordinates of the midpoint of each segment whose endpoint coordinates are given. `5-3`

10. $(-5, 2)$ and $(7, 8)$ **11.** $(4, -2)$ and $(-7, 9)$ **12.** $(11, 4)$ and $(-3, -6)$

13. $(3.25, 2.5)$ and $(-1.25, 5.5)$ **14.** $\left(\frac{2}{3}, \frac{5}{4}\right)$ and $\left(\frac{7}{3}, \frac{3}{4}\right)$

***M* is the midpoint of $\overline{AB}$. Find the coordinates of *B*.** `5-3`

15. $A(-1, 7)$; $M(4, 2)$ **16.** $A(3, -5)$; $M(2, -1)$ **17.** $A(-1, 6)$; $M(-4, -7)$

For each transformation, tell what type of transformation is described. `5-4`

18. $(x, y) \rightarrow (5x, 5y)$ **19.** $(x, y) \rightarrow (-x, y)$ **20.** $(x, y) \rightarrow (y, -x)$

For each transformation, find the coordinates of the image of $\triangle ABC$. Sketch the original figure and the image figure on graph paper. `5-4`

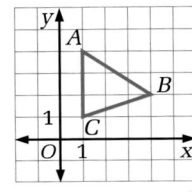

21. Shift the figure 3 units to the left and 1 unit down.

22. Reflect the figure over the *y*-axis.

23. Rotate the figure 90° counterclockwise.

24. Dilate the figure using a scale factor of 2 and using the origin as the center of dilation.

Name each missing coordinate without introducing a new variable. `5-5`

25.
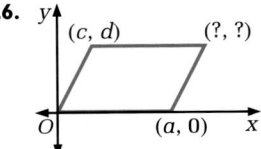

26.

27.
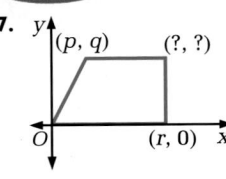

Student Resources

Answers to
Unit 5 Extra Practice

1. True.

2. False; a parallelogram may have no right angles.

3. False, a kite may not have four sides of equal measure.

4. True.

5. 15

6. $\sqrt{73}$

7. $\sqrt{218}$

8. $AB = BC = CD = DA = 5\sqrt{2}$

9. $PQ = QR = 5$; $RS = SP = 2\sqrt{13}$

10. $(1, 5)$

11. $(-1.5, 3.5)$

12. $(4, -1)$

13. $(1, 4)$

14. $(1.5, 1)$

15. $(9, -3)$

16. $(1, 3)$

17. $(-7, -20)$

18. dilation

19. reflection over the *y*-axis

20. 90° clockwise rotation or 270° counterclockwise rotation

21. $A'(-2, 3)$; $B'(1, 1)$; $C'(-2, 0)$

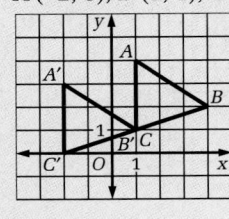

22. $A'(-1, 4)$; $B'(-4, 2)$; $C'(-1, 1)$

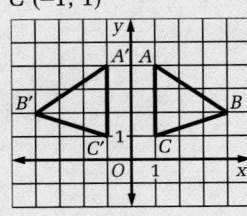

23. $A'(-4, 1)$; $B'(-2, 4)$; $C'(-1, 1)$

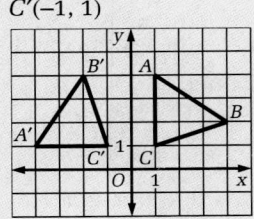

24. $A'(2, 8)$; $B'(8, 4)$; $C'(2, 2)$

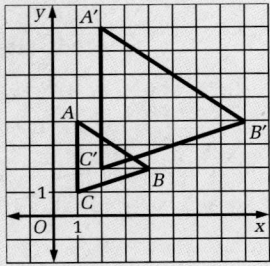

28. Quadrilateral *DEFG* has vertices *D*(0, 0), *E*(5, 0), *F*(7, 4), and *G*(2, 4). Use slopes to show that *DEFG* is a parallelogram.   `5-6`

Use the coordinates in the diagram to answer each question.   `5-6`

29. Is the figure a trapezoid? How do you know?

30. Find the coordinates of the midpoints of the diagonals. Do the diagonals have the same midpoint?

31. Find the lengths of the diagonals. Do the diagonals have the same length?

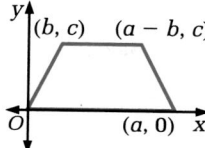

Unit 6

`6-1`

1. The math club has 7 members: 3 boys and 4 girls. One boy and one girl must be chosen to represent the school at a statewide math contest. In how many ways can the choice be made?

2. In how many ways can you form a numeral between 400 and 999 using only the digits 2, 3, 5, 6, 7, and 8 under each condition?

   a. Any digit may appear more than once.

   b. No digit may be repeated.

3. A ship has 4 different signal flags. How many different signals can be formed using from 1 to 4 of these flags placed vertically along the mast?

 `6-2`

4. A store manager has chosen 7 items to put on sale: one item each week for seven weeks. In how many different ways can the manager choose the order in which the items go on sale?

5. How many four-letter sequences of letters can be formed using the letters of each word, without repeating any letters?

   a. HOUSE   **b.** FOLDER   **c.** FACTORIES

 `6-3`

6. Suppose one card is drawn at random from a standard deck. What is the probability that the card is a heart or an ace?

7. Suppose you roll two dice. Find each probability.

   a. *P*(matching numbers)   **b.** *P*(sum is 5)   **c.** *P*(sum is 2 or 11)

8. Suppose a die is rolled and a coin is flipped. `6-4`

   a. Are these two events independent?

   b. Find the probability that the die came up 5 and the coin came up tails.

Answers to Extra Practice Unit 5 ·······················

25. (0, *b*); (*a*, 0)

26. (*a* + *c*, *d*)

27. (*r*, *q*)

28. slope of $\overline{DE}$ = slope of $\overline{FG}$ = 0; slope of $\overline{DG}$ = slope of $\overline{EF}$ = 2

29. Yes; two sides are parallel with slope = 0.

30. $\left(\dfrac{a-b}{2}, \dfrac{c}{2}\right), \left(\dfrac{a+b}{2}, \dfrac{c}{2}\right)$; No.

31. $\sqrt{(a-b)^2 + c^2}$; $\sqrt{(a-b)^2 + c^2}$; Yes.

Answers to Extra Practice Unit 6 ·······················

1. 12

2. a. 144

   b. 80

3. 64

4. 5040

5. a. 120

   b. 360

   c. 3024

6. $\dfrac{16}{52} = \dfrac{4}{13}$

7. a. $\dfrac{1}{6}$

   b. $\dfrac{1}{9}$

   c. $\dfrac{1}{12}$

8. a. Yes.

   b. $\dfrac{1}{12}$

9. Suppose the 13 diamonds from a standard deck of cards are placed face down on a table and two cards are turned over. Find each probability. **6-4**

   a. $P(\text{ace and king})$

   b. $P(\text{both face cards})$

   c. $P(\text{both are even-numbered})$

Find the value of each expression. **6-5**

10. $_5P_3$ 11. $_7C_4$ 12. $_6C_3$ 13. $_8P_2$

Rita wants to choose 4 of her 10 insect specimens to display at the science fair. **6-5**

14. In how many ways can the choice of 4 be made?

15. In how many ways can she choose 4 specimens and display them in a row in a glass-topped case?

Find each value using Pascal's triangle. **6-6**

16. $_8C_1$ 17. $_7C_2$ 18. $_5C_4$ 19. $_6C_6$

Use a row of Pascal's triangle to find the numbers of ways of answering a 6-question true-false test and getting each number of questions correct. **6-6**

20. 5   21. 2   22. 3   23. 4

At Three Corners, equal numbers of cars choose the left fork to Plainfield and the right fork to Centerville. Find the probability that, out of the next 5 cars, the given number will head toward Plainfield. **6-7**

24. 5   25. 1   26. 2   27. 3

28. For cars approaching a certain intersection in one direction, the traffic light cycles between a 55-second period of red and a 25-second period of green. Suppose you drive through this intersection in this direction at four random times during one week. **6-8**

   a. What is the probability that the light will be green exactly once?

   b. What is the probability that the light will be green exactly twice?

29. A die is rolled five times. What is the probability that a multiple of 3 comes up exactly twice? **6-8**

Use the binomial theorem to write each power of a binomial in expanded form. **6-9**

30. $(x + y)^5$ 31. $(a - 3)^4$ 32. $(10 - w)^3$ 33. $(2c + d)^6$

Answers to Extra Practice Unit 6

9. a. $\dfrac{1}{156}$

   b. $\dfrac{1}{26}$

   c. $\dfrac{5}{39}$

10. 60

11. 35

12. 20

13. 56

14. 210

15. 5040

16. 8

17. 21

18. 5

19. 1

20. 6

21. 15

22. 20

23. 15

24. $\dfrac{1}{32}$

25. $\dfrac{5}{32}$

26. $\dfrac{5}{16}$

27. $\dfrac{5}{16}$

28. a. about 0.406

    b. about 0.277

29. about 0.329

30. $x^5 + 5x^4y + 10x^3y^2 + 10x^2y^3 + 5xy^4 + y^5$

31. $a^4 - 12a^3 + 54a^2 - 108a + 81$

32. $1000 - 300w + 30w^2 - w^3$

33. $64c^6 + 192c^5d + 240c^4d^2 + 160c^3d^3 + 60c^2d^4 + 12cd^5 + d^6$

Unit 7

Graph each conjunction or disjunction on a number line. `7-1`

1. $x > -1$ and $x < 3$ **2.** $x > 2$ or $x < 1$ **3.** $x > -3$ and $x > -1$

For Exercises 4–7, use the Venn diagram showing juniors on the school newspaper staff and in the Community Service Club. Match each letter A–D with the person it represents. `7-1`

4. Chu Hua is on the newspaper staff and is not in the Community Service Club.

5. Alvin is on the newspaper staff and is in the Community Service Club.

6. Lourdes is not in the Community Service Club and is not on the newspaper staff.

7. Terumi is in the Community Service Club and is not on the newspaper staff.

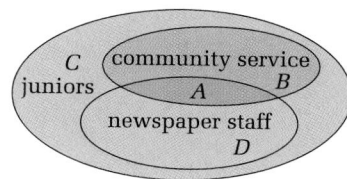

Graph each conjunction or disjunction on a coordinate plane. `7-1`

8. $y > 1$ and $y < 3$ **9.** $y < x$ or $y > 2$ **10.** $y < x + 1$ and $y > -x + 1$

For Exercises 11–13: `7-2`

a. Rewrite each implication in if-then form. Tell whether each implication is *True* or *False*. If it is false, give a counterexample.

b. Write the converse of each implication. Tell whether each converse is *True* or *False*. If it is false, give a counterexample.

11. $xy = xz$ implies that $y = z$.

12. Thanksgiving always falls on a Thursday.

13. An integer is evenly divisible by 10 only if its last digit is 0.

What conclusion can you reach when both premises are true? `7-3`

14. If you have two C's, you are not on the honor roll. Ji Sun is on the honor roll.

15. If our team plays the Tigers, we will win. If our team beats the Tigers, we will be in the semi-finals.

For Exercises 16–17, decide if each argument is *valid* or *invalid*. Explain your reasoning. `7-3`

16. If a quadrilateral is a rhombus, its diagonals are perpendicular.

The diagonals of $ABCD$ are perpendicular.

Therefore, $ABCD$ is a parallelogram.

17. If this month has 30 days, then it is not February.

This month is February.

Therefore, it does not have 30 days.

Answers to Extra Practice Unit 7 ···

1.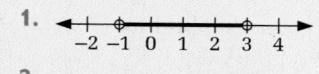

2.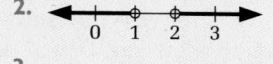

3.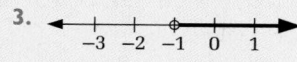

4. D

5. A

6. C

7. B

8.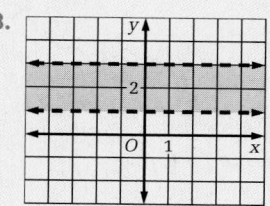

9.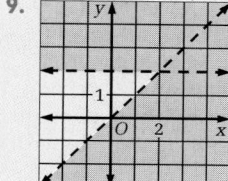

10.

11. a. If $xy = xz$, then $y = z$. False; $x = 0$, $y = 1$, $z = 2$.

   b. If $y = z$, then $xy = xz$. True.

12. a. If it is Thanksgiving, then it is Thursday. True.

   b. If it is Thursday, then it is Thanksgiving. False; Thanksgiving is only the fourth Thursday in November.

13. a. If an integer is evenly divisible by 10, then its last digit is 0. True.

   b. If an integer's last digit is 0, then it is evenly divisible by 10. True.

14. Ji Sun does not have two C's.

15. If our team plays the Tigers, then we will be in the semi-finals.

16. invalid; The final conclusion does not follow from the first two statements. $ABCD$ could be a kite.

17. valid; indirect argument

Tell whether each biconditional is *True* or *False*. Explain your reasoning. 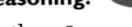 **7-4**

18. A number is greater than 3 if and only if its square is greater than 9.

19. A quadrilateral is a parallelogram if and only if all four of its sides are congruent.

20. One team wins a baseball game if and only if that team outscores the other team.

21. A substance is transparent if and only if you can see through it.

22. Copy and complete this proof. **7-5**

 Given Seattle

Prove New York

Available Flights:
Flight 102: Denver → Cincinnati
Flight 104: Cincinnati → New York
Flight 103: Seattle → Denver

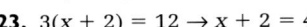

Statements	**Justifications**
1. Seattle	1. ?
2. Denver	2. ?
3. ?	3. Flight 102: Denver → Cincinnati
4. ?	4. ?

Identify the postulate used in each implication. **7-6**

23. $3(x + 2) = 12 \rightarrow x + 2 = 4$

24. If $5x - 3 = 42$, then $5x = 45$

25. If $x = 4 + y$ and $y = 7$, then $x = 11$

26. If $x^2 = 36$, then $x = \pm 6$.

27. Write a paragraph proof for the solution of the equation $2x - 5 = 17$. **7-6**

In Exercises 28 and 29, state a conclusion that can be made in one step from the given information. Give a reason. **7-7**

28. $\angle R$ and $\angle S$ are complementary and $\angle R = 33°$.

29. $\angle A$ and $\angle B$ are supplementary angles.

30. Write a flow proof: If $m \angle 2 = m \angle 3$ and $m \angle 1 = 150°$, then $m \angle 3 = 30°$. **7-7**

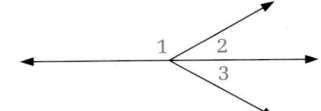

Use the diagram for Exercises 31–34. Justify each statement. **7-8**

31. $m \angle 1 = m \angle 3$

32. $m \angle 1 = m \angle 4$

33. $m \angle 3 = m \angle 4$

34. $\angle 2$ and $\angle 3$ are supplementary

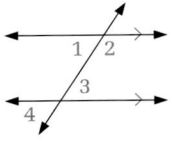

626   **Student Resources**

Answers to
Unit 7 Extra Practice ·················

18. False; if $x > 3$, then $x^2 > 9$, but $(-4)^2 > 9$ although $-4 \ngtr 3$.

19. False; if four sides are congruent, the quadrilateral is a parallelogram; but not every parallelogram has four congruent sides.

20. True; this is the definition of a win.

21. True; this is the definition of transparent.

22. *Given:* Seattle
Prove: New York

Statements	**Justifications**
1. Seattle	1. Given
2. Denver	2. Flight 103: Seattle → Denver
3. Cincinnati	3. Flight 102: Denver → Cincinnati
4. New York	4. Flight 104: Cincinnati → New York

23. Division Property of Equality

24. Addition Property of Equality

25. Substitution Property

26. Definition of square root

27. Given the equation $2x - 5 = 17$. Addition Property of Equality allows you to add 5 to both sides of the equation, leaving you with $2x = 22$. Then the Division Property of Equality allows you to divide both sides of the equation by 2, leaving you with $x = 11$.

28. $\angle S = 57°$; The sum of the measures of complementary angles equals 90°.

29. $m \angle A + m \angle B = 180°$; definition of supplementary

30. Statements

$$m \angle 1 + m \angle 2 = 180° \overset{\text{❶}}{\rightarrow} m \angle 1 = 150° \;\overset{\text{❷}}{\underset{m \angle 2 = m \angle 3}{\Big\}}}\; \overset{\text{❸}}{\rightarrow} 150° + m \angle 3 = 180° \overset{\text{❹}}{\rightarrow}$$
$$m \angle 3 = 30°$$

Justifications

1. If the sides of an angle form a straight line, then the angle is a straight angle with measure 180°.
2. Given
3. Substitution property (Steps 1 and 2)
4. Subtraction property of equality

31. If two ∥ lines are intersected by a transversal, then alternate interior ⦞ are = in measure.

32. If two ∥ lines are intersected by a transversal, then corresponding ⦞ are = in measure.

33. Vertical ⦞ are = in measure.

34. If two ∥ lines are intersected by a transversal, then co-interior ⦞ are supplementary.

626

Unit 8

Write a flow proof. 8-1

1. **Given** ∠1 and ∠2 are supplementary.

Prove $m\angle 3 = m\angle 4$

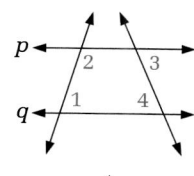

Use the given angle measures to decide whether lines *j* and *k* are parallel. 8-1

2. $m\angle 1 = 40°$; $m\angle 2 = 40°$

3. $m\angle 2 = (2x)°$; $m\angle 3 = (180 - 2x)°$

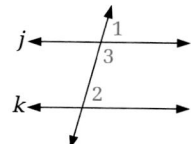

Find the measure of each angle. 8-2

4.

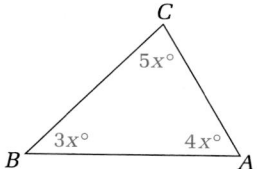

5.

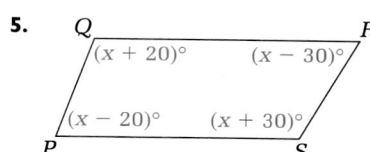

Find the measure of each side. 8-3

6. $\overline{AD}$

7. $\overline{BC}$

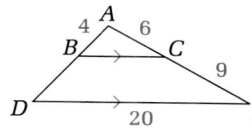

Write a paragraph proof. 8-4

8. **Given** $m\angle 1 = m\angle 4$; $m\angle 2 = m\angle 3$

Prove $\triangle DEG \cong \triangle EDF$

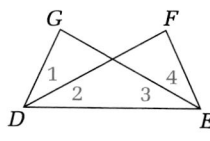

For Exercises 9–12, copy the triangles and mark any parts that are equal in measure. Identify the postulate or theorem you would use to prove that $\triangle ABC \cong \triangle DEF$. 8-5

9. $AB = DE$; $m\angle B = m\angle E$; $BC = EF$

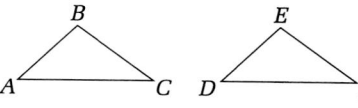

10. $m\angle A = m\angle D$; $m\angle B = m\angle E$; $m\angle C = m\angle F$

11. $m\angle A = m\angle D$; $BC = EF$; $m\angle C = m\angle F$

12. $AB = DE$; $BC = EF$; $CA = FD$

Write a two-column proof. 8-5

13. **Given** $\overline{AC}$ bisects $\overline{BD}$.
$\overline{BD}$ bisects $\overline{AC}$.

Prove $\overline{AB} \parallel \overline{CD}$

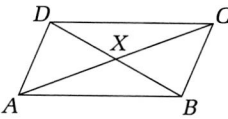

Extra Practice

627

$m\angle 1 + m\angle 2$ and $m\angle DEF = m\angle 3 + m\angle 4$. By the addition property of equality, $m\angle 1 + m\angle 2 = m\angle 3 + m\angle 4$. Then, by substitution, $m\angle EDG = m\angle DEF$. $DE = DE$ by the reflexive property. Therefore, $\triangle DEG \cong \triangle EDF$ by ASA.

9. SAS

10. not enough information

11. AAS

12. SSS

13. Given: $\overline{AC}$ bisects $\overline{BD}$.
$\overline{BD}$ bisects $\overline{AC}$.
Prove: $\overline{AB} \parallel \overline{CD}$

Statements	Justifications
1. $\overline{AC}$ bisects $\overline{BD}$; $\overline{BD}$ bisects $\overline{AC}$.	1. Given
2. $AX = CX$; $BX = DX$	2. Definition of bisector
3. $m\angle AXB = m\angle CXD$	3. Vertical ∡ are = in measure.
4. $\triangle AXB \cong \triangle CXD$	4. SAS
5. $m\angle DCX = m\angle BAX$	5. CPCTE
6. $\overline{AB} \parallel \overline{CD}$	6. If two line are intersected by a transversal and alternate interior ∡ are = in measure, then the lines are ∥.

Answers to Extra Practice Unit 8

1. ❶∠1 and ∠2 are supplementary.→❷ $p \parallel q$ →❸ $m\angle 3 = m\angle 4$

Justifications:

1. Given

2. If two lines are intersected by a transversal and co-interior ∡ are supplementary, then the lines are ∥.

3. If two ∥ lines are intersected by a transversal, then alternate interior ∡ are = in measure.

2. Yes.

3. Yes.

4. $A = 60°$; $B = 45°$; $C = 75°$

5. $m\angle P = 70°$; $m\angle Q = 110°$; $m\angle R = 60°$; $m\angle S = 120°$

6. $AD = 10$

7. $BC = 8$

8. It is given that $m\angle 1 = m\angle 4$ and $m\angle 2 = m\angle 3$. Since the measure of the whole is equal to the measure of its non-overlapping parts, $m\angle EDG =$

627

14. In $\triangle PQR$, $PQ = RQ$. The measure of $\angle Q$ is 9 less than 5 times the measure of $\angle P$. Find the measures of the three angles of the triangle.  **8-6**

Write a two-column proof. **8-6**

15. **Given** $AC = BC$; $m \angle 1 = m \angle 2$.
  Prove $AE = BD$

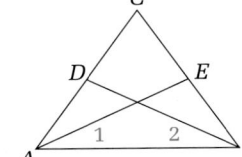

Find the measure of each unknown side. **8-7**

16. 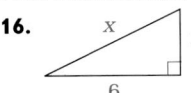   **17.** 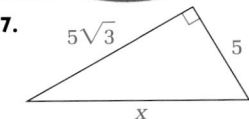   **18.**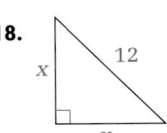

Solve each proportion. **8-7**

19. $\dfrac{6}{x} = \dfrac{4}{9}$ **20.** $\dfrac{x}{18} = \dfrac{8}{x}$ **21.** $\dfrac{2x + 3}{10} = \dfrac{x}{4}$

22. a. Find the length of the hypotenuse of $\triangle XYZ$. **8-8**
  b. Find the sine, cosine, and tangent ratios for $\angle X$ in $\triangle XYZ$.

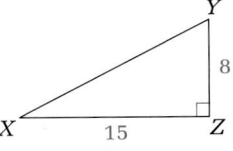

23. For parts (a)–(c), find the value of each sum. **8-8**
  a. $(\sin 30°)^2 + (\cos 30°)^2$ **b.** $(\sin 60°)^2 + (\cos 60°)^2$ **c.** $(\sin 45°)^2 + (\cos 45°)^2$
  d. Find a pattern in your answers to parts (a), (b), and (c). Make a conjecture.

Unit 9

In Exercises 1–4, write an equation to model each situation. **9-1**

1. 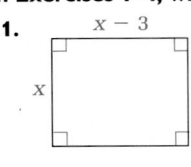   **2.** 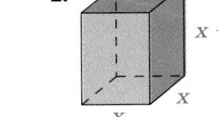   **3.**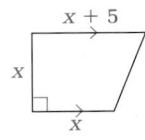

$A = 240 \text{ in.}^2$ $V = 175 \text{ in.}^3$ $A = 192 \text{ cm}^2$

4. A photographic developing solution should be 16% developer. The solution now contains 42 mL of water and 3 mL of developer. Some developer needs to be added to make a 16% solution. Let $x =$ the amount of developer to be added.

**Answers to
Unit 8 Extra Practice**

14. $m \angle P = m \angle R = 27°$;
  $m \angle Q = 126°$

15. Given: $AC = BC$; $m \angle 1 = m \angle 2$.
  Prove: $AE = BD$

Statements	Justifications
1. $AC = BC$; $m \angle 1 = m \angle 2$	1. Given
2. $AB = AB$	2. Reflexive property of equality
3. $m \angle DAB = m \angle EBA$	3. If two sides of a triangle are = in measure, then the $\angle$ opposite those sides are = in measure.
4. $\triangle DAB \cong \triangle EBA$	4. ASA
5. $AE = BD$	5. CPCTE

16. $x = 3\sqrt{5}$

17. $x = 10$

18. $x = 6\sqrt{2}$

19. $x = 13.5$

20. $x = 12$ or -12

21. $x = 6$

22. a. 17

  b. $\sin X = \dfrac{8}{17}$; $\cos X = \dfrac{15}{17}$;

  $\tan X = \dfrac{8}{15}$

23. a. 1
  b. 1
  c. 1
  d. Conjecture:
  $(\sin x)^2 + (\cos x)^2 = 1$

Factor completely. 9-2

5. $3c^3d^5 - 6c^2d^6$

6. $7x^4y^2 - 28x^2y^4$

7. $2k^3 + 2k^2 - 40k$

8. $5u^2v^2 + 30uv^3 - 80v^4$

9. $21m^3n + 33mn^4$

10. $45a - 125ab^2$

Simplify. Write each answer without negative exponents. 9-2

11. $(25x^6y^8)^{1/2}$

12. $(2p^4q^{-5})^3(p^2q)$

13. $(r^{-2}s^4)^3(r^6s^3)^{-1}$

14. $\dfrac{v^{-5}w^{-7}}{v^3w^{-2}}$

15. $\left(\dfrac{15ab^{-3}}{25a^4b^{-1}}\right)^3$

16. $\left(\dfrac{d^3e^{-5}}{2d^{-1}e^{-2}}\right)^{-4}$

Solve. 9-3

17. $\dfrac{5}{b-3} = \dfrac{6}{b}$

18. $\dfrac{1}{2w} = \dfrac{5}{w+9}$

19. $\dfrac{6}{t(t+1)} = \dfrac{2}{t+1}$

20. $\dfrac{3}{2n+5} = \dfrac{4}{n}$

21. $\dfrac{x}{x-6} = \dfrac{3}{x-8}$

22. $\dfrac{5}{p+2} + \dfrac{3}{p-2} = 4$

23. $\dfrac{r-3}{2r} + \dfrac{9}{r} = 2$

24. $3 + \dfrac{5}{a-3} = -a$

25. $\dfrac{5y}{y+4} - \dfrac{2}{y+1} = 1$

List the zeros of each function. Tell which, if any, are double or triple zeros. 9-4

26. $y = x(x-3)(x+7)$

27. $y = (x+5)^2(x-8)$

28. $y = -x^2(x-5)$

29. $y = (x+9)^3$

30. $y = x(x+10)^2$

31. $y = -x^3$

Match each graph with one of the functions A–F. 9-4

32.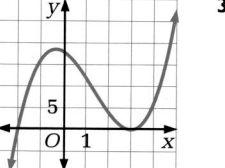

33.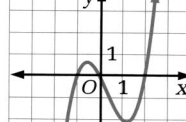

34.

35.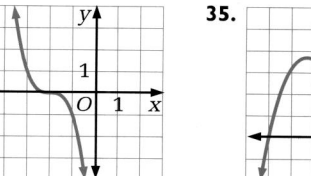

A. $y = -(x+2)^3$

B. $y = (x+2)^3$

C. $y = (x-2)^2(x+3)$

D. $y = x(x-2)(x+1)$

E. $y = (x-2)(x+3)^2$

F. $y = (x-3)^2(x+2)$

Solve each equation without graphing. 9-5

36. $(x+1)(x-6)^2 = 0$

37. $x^3 - 9x = 0$

38. $x^3 - 5x^2 - 14x = 0$

39. Use the parametric equations $x = 40t$ and $y = 7 - t^2$. 9-6

   a. Write y in terms of x by solving the first equation for t and substituting your answer into the second equation.

   b. Graph the parametric equations.

   c. Estimate the value of x for which $y = 0$.

Answers to Extra Practice Unit 9 ···············

1. $x(x-3) = 240$

2. $x^2(x+2) = 175$

3. $\dfrac{x(2x+5)}{2} = 192$

4. $\dfrac{3+x}{45+x} = 0.16$ or

   $\dfrac{42}{45+x} = 0.84$

5. $3c^2d^5(c-2d)$

6. $7x^2y^2(x-2y)(x+2y)$

7. $2k(k+5)(k-4)$

8. $5v^2(u+8v)(u-2v)$

9. $3mn(7m^2 + 11n^3)$

10. $5a(3-5b)(3+5b)$

11. $5x^3y^4$

12. $\dfrac{8p^{14}}{q^{14}}$

13. $\dfrac{s^9}{r^{12}}$

14. $\dfrac{1}{v^8w^5}$

15. $\dfrac{27}{125a^9b^6}$

16. $\dfrac{16e^{12}}{d^{16}}$

17. $b = 18$

18. $w = 1$

19. $t = 3$

20. $n = -4$

21. $x = 9, x = 2$

22. $p = 3, p = -1$

23. $r = 5$

24. $a = \pm 2$

25. $y = 2, y = -1.5$

26. $0, 3, -7$

27. -5 (double), 8

28. $5, 0$ (double)

29. -9 (triple)

30. $0, -10$ (double)

31. 0 (triple)

32. F

33. D

34. A

35. C

36. $x = -1, x = 6$

37. $x = -3, x = 0, x = 3$

38. $x = -2, 0, 7$

39. a. $y = 7 - \dfrac{x^2}{1600}$

   b.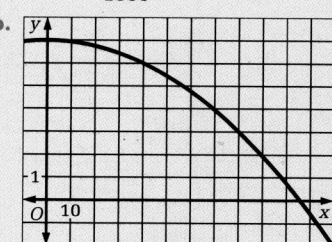

   c. $x =$ about 106

Unit 10

Draw a vertical cross section and a horizontal cross section of each space figure. `10-1`

1.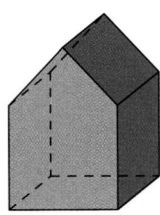

2.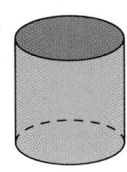

3.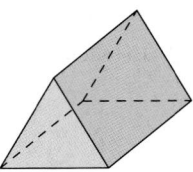

For Exercises 4–6: `10-2`

a. Describe or sketch the shape given by rotating each figure around the given axis.

b. Find the volume of the space figure.

4.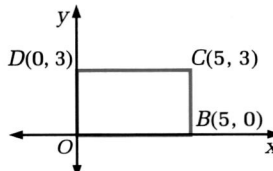

Rotate around *y*-axis

5.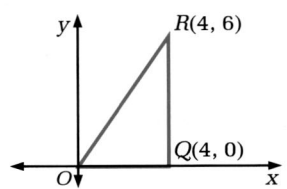

Rotate around *x*-axis

6.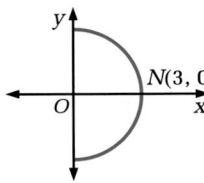

Rotate around *y*-axis

Draw the plane figure that is rotated to form each space figure. Indicate the axis of rotation. `10-2`

7.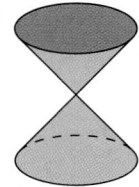

8.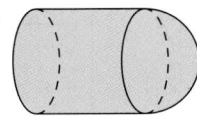

9.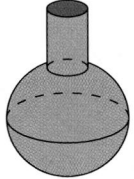

For Exercises 10–13, points *A* and *B* are 5 cm apart. Describe the set of points that fit each condition. `10-3`
a. in a plane containing *A* and *B*
b. in space

10. 2 cm from point *A*

11. equidistant from *A* and *B*

12. 3 cm from the line through *A* and *B*

13. 2.5 cm from both *A* and *B*

Answers to Extra Practice Unit 10

1.

2.

3.

4. a. cylinder of height 3 and radius 5

  b. $V = 75\pi$ units^3

5. a. cone of height 4 and radius 6

  b. $V = 48\pi$ units^3

6. a. sphere of radius 3

  b. $V = 36\pi$ units^3

7.

8.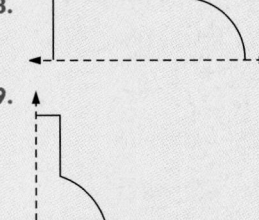

9.

With points A and B as in Exercises 10–13, describe the set of points in a plane containing A and B that fit each condition. 10-3

14. 3 cm from A and 4 cm from B

15. 2 cm from A and 1 cm from B

Give the coordinates of each point in the rectangular prism at the right. 10-4

16. B **17.** E

18. F **19.** G

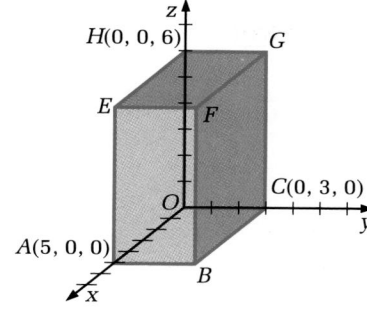

Find the midpoint of the segment with the given endpoints. 10-4

20. $(0, 0, 0), (-2, 6, 10)$

21. $(1, 3, -4), (5, -7, -2)$

22. $(-1, -8, 7), (1, 3, -4)$

Find the distance between each pair of points. 10-5

23. $(1, 4, 7)$ and $(3, -2, 4)$

24. $(5, -1, 2)$ and $(4, 3, -6)$

25. $(-1, -3, 2)$ and $(1, 11, 7)$

26. $(4, 7, -8)$ and $(1, -5, -4)$

Write an equation of each circle or sphere. 10-6

27. The center of the circle is $(0, 0)$. The points $(0, 4)$ and $(0, -4)$ are endpoints of a diameter.

28. The center of the circle is $(0, 0)$. The point $(5, 12)$ is on the circle.

29. The center of the sphere is $(0, 0, 0)$. The radius is 8.

30. The center of the sphere is $(0, 0, 0)$. The point $(7, 0, 0)$ is on the sphere.

Answers to Extra Practice Unit 10

10. a. a circle of radius 2 cm with center A

   b. a sphere of radius 2 cm with center A

11. a. all points on the line perpendicular to $\overline{AB}$ at its midpoint

   b. all points on the plane perpendicular to $\overline{AB}$ at its midpoint

12. a. two parallel lines on

either side of the line joining $\overline{AB}$, both 3 cm away from the line AB

   b. a cylinder around the line AB with a radius of 3 cm

13. a. the midpoint of $\overline{AB}$

   b. the midpoint of $\overline{AB}$

14. two points, each 3 cm from A and 4 cm from B; The points are the intersection

points of a circle with center A and radius 3 cm and a circle with center B and radius 4 cm.

15. No points meet the conditions.

16. $(5, 3, 0)$

17. $(5, 0, 6)$

18. $(5, 3, 6)$

19. $(0, 3, 6)$

20. $(-1, 3, 5)$

21. $(3, -2, -3)$

22. $(0, -2.5, 1.5)$

23. 7

24. 9

25. 15

26. 13

27. $x^2 + y^2 = 16$

28. $x^2 + y^2 = 169$

29. $x^2 + y^2 + z^2 = 64$

30. $x^2 + y^2 + z^2 = 49$

Toolbox

➤ Statistics and Probability

Data Displays and Measures

Skill 1	Using a Fitted Line

A **fitted line** is a line that passes as close to as many data points on a scatter plot as possible.

Example The table shows sales of CDs at a record store that was trying out different weekly schedules with different numbers of hours of operation. Make a scatter plot of the data. Draw a fitted line. Predict sales for a 45-hour week.

Hours of operation	54	48	60	65	40	60	48	56
CDs Sold	710	530	850	940	520	740	630	750

To predict sales for a 45-hour week, draw a vertical line from 45 on the horizontal axis to the fitted line. Then draw a horizontal line to the vertical axis. The point where the horizontal line meets the vertical axis is the prediction.

A 45-hour week should produce about 550 CD sales.

When two data sets increase together, their relationship is called a **positive correlation.** The points of a graph of the data *rise* to the right, as in the Example above. If the points of the graph of two data sets *fall* to the right, the graph shows a **negative correlation.**

1. Make a scatter plot using the data in the table below showing the use of a small beach on days with different high temperatures.

High temperature (°F)	65	72	90	85	85	72	100	95
Beach Users	20	60	120	90	110	85	150	130

2. Does your scatter plot show a *positive correlation*, a *negative correlation*, or *no correlation*?

3. Draw a fitted line for your scatter plot.

Use your fitted line to predict the number of beach users on days with each high temperature.

4. 80°F   **5.** 75°F   **6.** 105°F   **7.** 60°F

Skill 2	Using a Histogram and a Frequency Table

A **histogram** displays grouped data. Each group is defined by an interval on the horizontal axis. The height of the bar for an interval indicates the number of data items that fall in the group. This number is called a **frequency.**

Example The frequency table and the histogram show the number of supporters for candidate Kaoru Hirakawa in different age groups in her city.

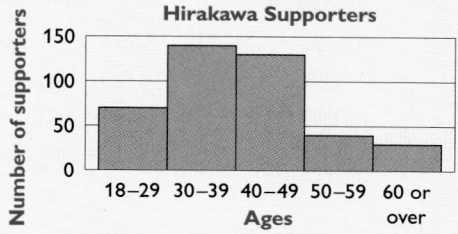

Age Group	Frequency
18–29	70
30–39	140
40–49	130
50–59	40
60 or over	30

Use the table or the histogram to answer each question.

a. How many Hirakawa supporters are between the ages of 50 and 59?

Histogram: The bar for the interval 50–59 has height 40.
Frequency table: The frequency for the age group 50–59 is 40.

There are 40 supporters between the ages of 50 and 59.

b. In which age groups does she have the greatest support and the least support?

Using the histogram, you see that the tallest bar is for the interval 30–39. She has the greatest support in this age group. The shortest bar is for the group "60 or over." She has the least support in this age group.

Toolbox

633

Answers to Skill 1

1.
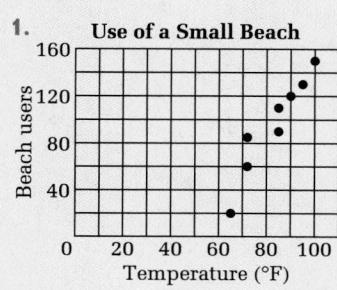

2. positive correlation

3–7. Answers may vary. Examples are given.

3.
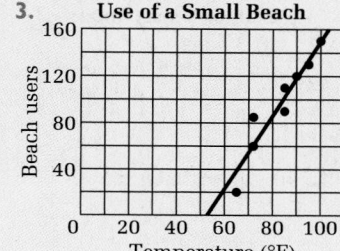

4. about 85 people

5. about 70 people

6. about 160 people

7. about 20 people

Use the histogram or the frequency table to answer each question.

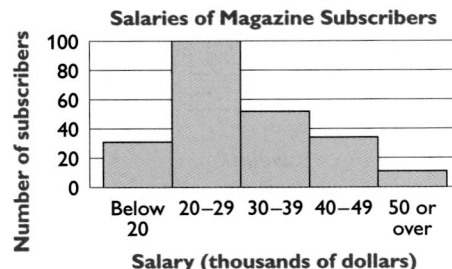

Salaries of Magazine Subscribers

Salary Range (thousand $)	Number of subscribers
Below 20	30
20–29	100
30–39	52
40–49	34
50 or over	11

How many subscribers make each salary?

1. Below $20,000   **2.** Between $20,000 and $29,000   **3.** $50,000 or over

4. Which salary range has the most subscribers? the least?

Skill 3   Making a Stem-and-Leaf Plot

A **stem-and-leaf plot** displays every data item but also groups the data by intervals, like a histogram.

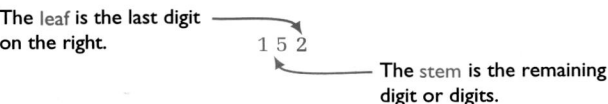

The leaf is the last digit on the right.

1 5 2

The stem is the remaining digit or digits.

Example Make a stem-and-leaf plot from the table below that shows the daily protein intake of health club members for one day.

Protein Consumed (grams)

63	68	69	82	84
43	84	87	70	72
52	75	71	68	44
56	57	63	76	64

Protein Consumed (grams)

```
4 | 3 4
5 | 2 6 7
6 | 3 3 4 8 8 9
7 | 0 1 2 5 6
8 | 2 4 4 7
```

This row displays the numbers 63, 63, 64, 68, 68, 69.

1. In the Example, what data items do the numbers in the fourth row of the stem-and-leaf plot represent?

2. Make a stem-and-leaf plot of the data in the table at the right, showing times of runners in a 10 km road race.

3. In your stem-and-leaf plot, which interval contains the most data items? Which interval contains the fewest?

Finishing Times (minutes)

52	34	45	63	71
45	41	32	50	62
52	44	43	51	46
51	66	65	66	58

Answers to Skill 2 · · · · · · · · · · · · ·

1. 30

2. 100

3. 11

4. $20,000–$29,000;
$50,000 or over

Answers to Skill 3 · · · · · · · · · · · · ·

1. the numbers 70, 71, 72, 75, 76

2. **Finishing Times (minutes)**
```
3 | 2 4
4 | 1 3 4 5 5 6
5 | 0 1 1 2 2 8
6 | 2 3 5 6 6
7 | 1
```

3. 40–49 and 50–59; 70–79

mean: The sum of the data in a data set divided by the number of items.	median: The middle number or the mean of the two middle numbers in a data set when the data are arranged in order.
mode: The data item, or items, appearing most often. There may be more than one mode or no mode.	range: The difference between the smallest and largest data items.

 **Examples**   The following high temperatures were recorded on days in March:

42, 38, 56, 56, 60, 40, 65, 45, 48, 42, 56.

Find the mean, the median, the mode, and the range of the data.

Mean: There are 11 temperatures. Add the numbers. Divide the sum by 11.

$$\frac{42 + 38 + 56 + 56 + 60 + 40 + 65 + 45 + 48 + 42 + 56}{11} = 49.8$$

To the nearest tenth, the mean is 49.8.

Median: List the numbers in order. Find the middle number.

38 40 42 42 45 48 56 56 56 60 65

The median is 48.

Mode: Since 56 appears three times, and no other number appears more than twice, 56 is the mode.

Range: The smallest number is 38. The largest is 65. Subtract to find the range.

$$65 - 38 = 27$$

The range is 27.

Use the table at the right showing protein per serving of some foods.

1. Find the mean of the data.
2. Find the median of the data.
3. Find the mode of the data.
4. Find the range of the data.

Protein per serving (g)					
24	36	42	10	32	24
10	18	16	18	12	30

Answers to Skill 4

1. about 22.7
2. 21
3. 10, 18, and 24
4. 32

A **box-and-whisker plot** shows the median and range of data.

Example   Make a box-and-whisker plot of these scores:
68, 78, 93, 79, 72, 88, 44, 79, 75, 82, 71, 89, 75, 88, 73, 80, 66, 100, 75, 92.

Step 1 Write the scores in order from lowest to highest.

Step 2 Find the median, the *extremes,* and the *quartiles* of the ordered data set.

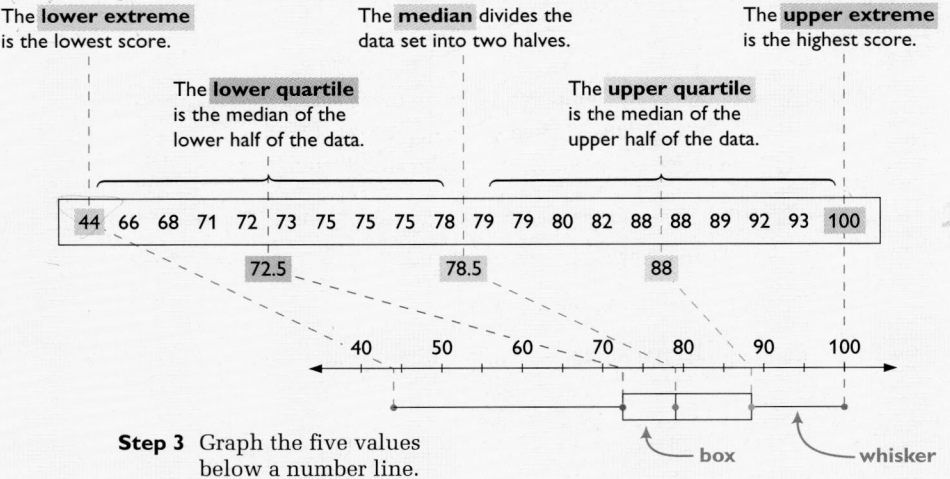

The **lower extreme** is the lowest score.

The **median** divides the data set into two halves.

The **upper extreme** is the highest score.

The **lower quartile** is the median of the lower half of the data.

The **upper quartile** is the median of the upper half of the data.

44 66 68 71 72 | 73 75 75 75 78 | 79 79 80 82 88 | 88 89 92 93 100

72.5   78.5   88

40   50   60   70   80   90   100

Step 3 Graph the five values below a number line.

box   whisker

Step 4 Draw a box from the lower quartile to the upper quartile.
Draw a vertical line through the median.

Step 5 Draw line segments, or whiskers, from the box to the extremes.

You can see from the box-and-whisker plot that:

• About half the data are above 78.5.   • No data are below 44 or above 100.

• About 25% of the data are above 88.   • About 25% of the data are below 72.5.

---

1. Make a box-and-whisker plot of the data shown in the table at the right.

2. For what number is it true that about 25% of the data fall above the number?

3. For what number is it true that about 25% of the data fall below the number?

Fuel Economy (mi/gal)				
34	28	36	38	28
30	40	38	26	22
32	34	32	44	42
48	20	22	26	30

Student Resources

Answers to Skill 5

1.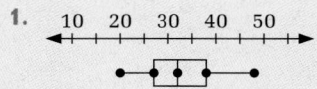
   10 20 30 40 50

2. 38

3. 27

Probability

To describe how likely an event is, you use a number on a scale from 0 to 1. This number is called the **probability** of the event.

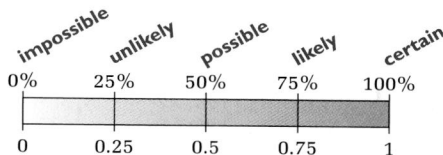

Probability that is based on the result of an experiment is called **experimental probability**. An **event** consists of one **outcome** or a group of outcomes of the experiment.

The experimental probability of an event E is the ratio:

$$P(E) = \frac{\text{number of times the event } E \text{ happened}}{\text{number of times the experiment was done}}$$

Example   Janelle Franklin had 21 hits in her first 62 official at-bats for her high school softball team. What is the probability that she will get a hit?

The event E is "getting a hit."

$$P(E) = \frac{\text{hits}}{\text{at-bats}} = \frac{21}{62} \approx 0.339$$

The experimental probability of her getting a hit is about 0.34, or 34%.

Example   Suppose Janelle has 20 more at-bats. How many hits can she expect?

Multiply the experimental probability by the number of future at-bats.

$(0.339)(20) = 6.78$

She can expect about 7 more hits.

The table shows how many of each different size of a particular style of sweatshirt were sold at one store last month. Find the probability that a sweatshirt sold will be each size.

Size	Number Sold
Extra Small	12
Small	15
Medium	32
Large	44
Extra Large	14

1. Large

2. Medium

3. Extra Small

4. Extra Large

5. Suppose 150 sweatshirts are sold next year. How many will be Extra Large?

Toolbox

Answers to Skill 6

1. about 38%

2. about 27%

3. about 10%

4. about 12%

5. 18 sweatshirts

When all outcomes of an experiment are equally likely, you can find the **theoretical probability** of an event without performing any trials of the experiment. The theoretical probability $P(E)$ is found by counting the ways the experiment can turn out.

$$P(E) = \frac{\text{number of favorable outcomes}}{\text{number of possible outcomes}}$$

← "Favorable" means included in the event E.

Example   A spinner like the one shown at the right is spun. What is the probability that the spinner ends up pointing at a number greater than 3?

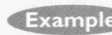

The event E is that a number greater than 3 will come up.
There are five possible outcomes: 1, 2, 3, 4, or 5 comes up.
There are two favorable outcomes: 4 or 5 comes up.

$P(\text{number greater than 3}) = \frac{2}{5} = 0.4$

The theoretical probability is $\frac{2}{5}$, or 0.4, or 40%.

A standard deck of playing cards has 52 cards, with 13 cards in each of four suits: clubs, spades, diamonds, and hearts. Face cards are jacks, queens, and kings.

Example   Suppose you pick a card at random from the 13 hearts of a standard deck. What is the probability that it is a face card?

There are 13 possible outcomes:

There are 3 favorable outcomes:

$P(\text{face card}) = \frac{3}{13} \approx 0.23$, or about 23%

Use the spinner above. Find each probability.

1. The pointer lands on 5.
2. The pointer lands on an odd number.
3. The pointer does not land on 1.
4. The pointer lands on a number less than 6.

A card is chosen at random from the 13 hearts of a standard deck. Find each probability.

5. $P(\text{ace of hearts})$
6. $P(\text{queen or king of hearts})$
7. $P(2, 3, \text{ or } 4 \text{ of hearts})$
8. $P(\text{not a face card})$
9. $P(\text{a diamond})$
10. $P(\text{not a diamond})$

Answers to Skill 7

1. 20%
2. 60%
3. 80%
4. 100%
5. about 8%
6. about 15%
7. about 23%
8. about 77%
9. 0
10. 100%

Geometric probability is probability based on areas and lengths.

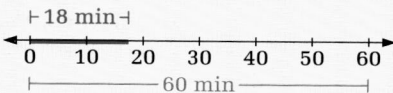 Suppose in a one-hour TV program, 18 minutes are taken up by commercials. You tune in at a random time. What is the probability that you will tune in on a commercial?

Step 1 Model the situation with a number line. Use minutes as units.

```
      ⊢ 18 min ⊣
  ◄─┼──┼──┼──┼──┼──┼──►
    0  10 20 30 40 50 60
    ⊢───────── 60 min ─────────⊣
```

Step 2 Find the ratio of the length of the segment modeling commercial time to the length of the segment modeling total time.

$$P(\text{tuning in on a commercial}) = \frac{\text{commercial time}}{\text{total time}}$$

$$= \frac{18}{60} = \frac{3}{10}, \text{ or } 0.3, \text{ or } 30\%$$

If you can model the outcomes of an experiment by points in a plane, you can use geometric probability.

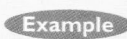 In a game, Trúc Ha hits a baseball over the park fence toward the wall of the house shown. Each window measures 2.5 ft by 4.5 ft. What is the probability that her hit will break a window?

The area of the four windows is $4(2.5)(4.5) = 45$ (ft²).

The wall area is $(20)(30) = 600$ (ft²).

$$P(\text{breaking a window}) = \frac{\text{area of 4 windows}}{\text{wall area}}$$

$$= \frac{45}{600} = \frac{3}{40}, \text{ or } 0.075, \text{ or } 7.5\%$$

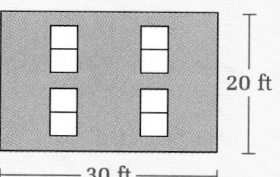

1. In any 10-minute interval, a bus comes to the Eucalyptus Street stop and waits for 1.5 min. Suppose you arrive at the stop at a random time. What is the probability that a bus is waiting?

Find the probability that a point chosen at random in each figure is in the shaded region.

2.
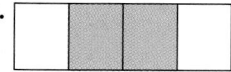

3.
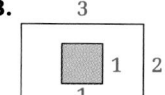

4.
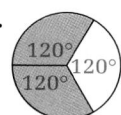

Toolbox

Answers to Skill 8 ················

1. 15%
2. 50%
3. about 17%
4. about 67%

➤Algebra and Graphing

Algebraic Expressions

Skill 9	Using Order of Operations

People who work with mathematics follow a special **order of operations** so that they will agree on the value of a numerical expression. To simplify expressions such as $48 + (12 - 8)^2 \div 8$, you must carry out operations in the following order.

Parentheses ⟵ Simplify inside parentheses.

Exponents ⟵ Then calculate any powers.

Multiplication and Division ⟵ Then do these as they appear from left to right.

Addition and Subtraction ⟵ Then do these as they appear from left to right.

Example Simplify $48 + (12 - 8)^2 \div 8$.

$$48 + (12 - 8)^2 \div 8 = 48 + 4^2 \div 8 \quad \longleftarrow \text{Simplify inside parentheses first.}$$
$$= 48 + 16 \div 8 \quad \longleftarrow 4^2 \text{ means } 4 \cdot 4.$$
$$= 48 + 2 \quad \longleftarrow \text{Do division next.}$$
$$= 50 \quad \longleftarrow \text{Do addition last.}$$

Example Evaluate $7x^2 - 3x + 5$ when $x = -2$.

$$7x^2 - 3x + 5 = 7(-2)^2 - 3(-2) + 5 \quad \longleftarrow \text{Substitute } -2 \text{ for } x.$$
$$= 7 \cdot 4 - 3(-2) + 5 \quad \longleftarrow (-2)^2 \text{ means } (-2)(-2).$$
$$= 28 - (-6) + 5 \quad \longleftarrow \text{Do multiplication next.}$$
$$= 28 + 6 + 5 \quad \longleftarrow \text{To subtract } -6, \text{ add its opposite.}$$
$$= 39 \quad \longleftarrow \text{Do addition last.}$$

Simplify each expression.

1. $12 \div 2^2 + 9$
2. $(13 - 5)^2 + 6 \div 2$
3. $4 + 5(7 - 9)$
4. $6 + 2^5 - 3 \cdot 5$
5. $7^2 - 4 \cdot 8 + 26 \div 13$
6. $(10 - 7)^4 + (5 - 1)^2 \div 8$

Evaluate each expression when $x = 3$.

7. $x^2 - 7x + 12$
8. $4x^3 - 5x + 1$
9. $15 - 4x^2$
10. $-2x^2 + 6x - 4$
11. $2x^5 - 4(x - 1)$
12. $(x - 5)^3 - 4(x + 1)^2$

Evaluate each expression when $a = -10$ and $b = 2$.

13. $3(a + b)$
14. $-a - b^2$
15. $-a^2 b$
16. $-4a^2 + b^2$
17. $-4(a^2 + b^2)$
18. $-4(a + b)^2$

Student Resources

Answers to Skill 9 ·······················

1. 12
2. 67
3. −6
4. 23
5. 19
6. 83
7. 0
8. 94
9. −21
10. −4
11. 478
12. −72
13. −24
14. 6
15. −200
16. −396
17. −416
18. −256

You can simplify expressions like $3(x + 2)$ using the distributive property.

Distributive Property For all numbers a, b, and c,
$$a(b + c) = ab + ac \text{ and } a(b - c) = ab - ac.$$

Example $3(x + 2) = 3 \cdot x + 3 \cdot 2$
$$= 3x + 6$$

Example $5(a - 7) = 5 \cdot a - 5 \cdot 7$
$$= 5a - 35$$

To simplify some expressions, you use the fact that $-a = -1a$. Read $-a$ as "the opposite of a."

Example $-(y - 5) = -1(y - 5)$
$$= (-1)y - (-1)(5) \quad \longleftarrow \text{ Use the distributive property.}$$
$$= -y - (-5)$$
$$= -y + 5$$

Example $9 - 2(x + 4) = 9 - (2x + 2 \cdot 4) \quad \longleftarrow \text{ Use the distributive property.}$
$$= 9 - (2x + 8)$$
$$= 9 - 2x - 8 \quad \longleftarrow \quad -1(2x + 8)$$
$$= -2x + 1$$

When you add expressions, each expression is a **term** of the sum. Terms with the same variables and powers are called **like terms**. You use the distributive property in reverse to **combine like terms**.

Example $2x^2 + 4xy - 5x^2 + 7xy = (2x^2 - 5x^2) + (4xy + 7xy) \quad \longleftarrow \text{ Group like terms.}$
$$= (2 - 5)x^2 + (4 + 7)xy \quad \longleftarrow \text{ Use the distributive property.}$$
$$= -3x^2 + 11xy$$

Simplify.

1. $3(x + 4) - 5$

2. $-2(y - 7) + 3$

3. $4n - (3n + 5m)$

4. $5(-k + 3) - 2(k - 4)$

5. $4x^2 + 3x - x^2$

6. $4xy + 3yz - 7xy$

7. $-a^2 + ab - 5a^2$

8. $-2hk + 4k^2 - k^2 + 5hk$

9. $3 + 9x^3 - 10 - 2x^3$

Toolbox   641

Answers to Skill 10

1. $3x + 7$

2. $-2y + 17$

3. $n - 5m$

4. $-7k + 23$

5. $3x^2 + 3x$

6. $-3xy + 3yz$

7. $-6a^2 + ab$

8. $3k^2 + 3hk$

9. $7x^3 - 7$

You can use the distributive property to expand a product.

Example $3x(x + 2) = 3x \cdot x + 3x \cdot 2$

$= 3x^2 + 6x$

Example $-2x(x - 5) = (-2x)x - (-2x)5$

$= -2x^2 - (-10x)$

$= -2x^2 + 10x$

Example $(x + 4)(x - 3) = (x + 4)x - (x + 4)3$ ← Use the distributive property.

$= x^2 + 4x - (3x + 12)$ ← Use the distributive property again.

$= x^2 + 4x - 3x - 12$

$= x^2 + x - 12$

Expand each product.

1. $x(2x + 3)$

2. $-4x(x - 5)$

3. $7a(-2a + 6)$

4. $(x + 5)(x - 9)$

5. $(y - 6)(y - 2)$

6. $(x - 3)(-x + 10)$

7. $(2x + 1)(x - 7)$

8. $(-3n + 7)(n + 5)$

9. $(4x - 2)(x - 5)$

10. $(3x - 4)(2x - 11)$

11. $(2x + 1)(7x - 8)$

12. $(-3k + 2)(-5k + 4)$

To simplify the square root of an integer, you first find the largest perfect-square factor of the integer. Then use the fact that for all nonnegative numbers a and b,

$\sqrt{}$ is the radical symbol. $\sqrt{ab} = \sqrt{a} \cdot \sqrt{b}$.

Example $\sqrt{18} = \sqrt{9 \cdot 2}$ ← 9 is the largest perfect-square factor of 18. Write 18 as 9 · 2.

$= \sqrt{9} \cdot \sqrt{2}$ ← Use the fact that $\sqrt{ab} = \sqrt{a} \cdot \sqrt{b}$.

$= 3\sqrt{2}$ ← Write $\sqrt{9}$ as 3.

Note: It would *not* have been helpful to write $\sqrt{18}$ as $\sqrt{6 \cdot 3}$, because neither 6 nor 3 is a perfect square.

Answers to Skill 11 ⋯⋯⋯⋯⋯⋯⋯⋯⋯⋯⋯⋯⋯⋯⋯⋯⋯⋯⋯⋯

1. $2x^2 + 3x$

2. $-4x^2 + 20x$

3. $-14a^2 + 42a$

4. $x^2 - 4x - 45$

5. $y^2 - 8y + 12$

6. $-x^2 + 13x - 30$

7. $2x^2 - 13x - 7$

8. $-3n^2 - 8n + 35$

9. $4x^2 - 22x + 10$

10. $6x^2 - 41x + 44$

11. $14x^2 - 9x - 8$

12. $15k^2 - 22k + 8$

To simplify a product of radical factors, you use the fact that for all nonnegative numbers a and b,

$$\sqrt{a} \cdot \sqrt{b} = \sqrt{ab}.$$

Example $5\sqrt{3} \cdot \sqrt{2} = 5\sqrt{3 \cdot 2}$ ← Use the fact that $\sqrt{a} \cdot \sqrt{b} = \sqrt{ab}$.

$\qquad\qquad\qquad = 5\sqrt{6}$

Example $4\sqrt{5} \cdot 2\sqrt{15} = 4 \cdot 2 \cdot \sqrt{5} \cdot \sqrt{15}$ ← Group radical terms.

$\qquad\qquad\qquad = 8\sqrt{5 \cdot 15}$ ← Use the fact that $\sqrt{a} \cdot \sqrt{b} = \sqrt{ab}$.

$\qquad\qquad\qquad = 8\sqrt{75}$ ← Simplify.

$\qquad\qquad\qquad = 8\sqrt{25 \cdot 3}$ ← 25 is the largest perfect square factor of 75.

$\qquad\qquad\qquad = 8\sqrt{25} \cdot \sqrt{3}$ ← Use the fact that $\sqrt{ab} = \sqrt{a} \cdot \sqrt{b}$.

$\qquad\qquad\qquad = 8 \cdot 5\sqrt{3}$ ← Write $\sqrt{25}$ as 5.

$\qquad\qquad\qquad = 40\sqrt{3}$

Simplify.

1. $\sqrt{45}$ **2.** $\sqrt{300}$ **3.** $\sqrt{76}$ **4.** $5\sqrt{12}$ **5.** $12\sqrt{125}$

6. $\sqrt{6} \cdot \sqrt{7}$ **7.** $3\sqrt{5} \cdot \sqrt{2}$ **8.** $4.2\sqrt{11} \cdot \sqrt{3}$ **9.** $8\sqrt{2} \cdot 3\sqrt{3}$

10. $\sqrt{6} \cdot \sqrt{6}$ **11.** $\left(3\sqrt{3}\right)^2$ **12.** $2\sqrt{6} \cdot 3\sqrt{2}$ **13.** $4\sqrt{5} \cdot 3\sqrt{10}$

Solving Equations and Inequalities

Skill 13   Solving Linear Equations

You can solve some equations by *undoing* operations. Your goal is to get the variable alone on one side of the equation.

Example Solve $\frac{x}{2} + 7 = 40$.

$\qquad \frac{x}{2} + 7 - 7 = 40 - 7$ ← Undo addition of 7. Subtract 7 from both sides.

$\qquad\qquad \frac{x}{2} = 33$

$\qquad\qquad 2 \cdot \frac{x}{2} = 2 \cdot 33$ ← Undo division by 2. Multiply both sides by 2.

$\qquad\qquad x = 66$

Toolbox

Answers to Skill 12

1. $3\sqrt{5}$ **8.** $4.2\sqrt{33}$

2. $10\sqrt{3}$ **9.** $24\sqrt{6}$

3. $2\sqrt{19}$ **10.** 6

4. $10\sqrt{3}$ **11.** 27

5. $60\sqrt{5}$ **12.** $12\sqrt{3}$

6. $\sqrt{42}$ **13.** $60\sqrt{2}$

7. $3\sqrt{10}$

Example Solve $\dfrac{n-5}{3} = -11$.

$$3 \cdot \dfrac{n-5}{3} = 3(-11) \qquad \longleftarrow \text{ Multiply both sides by 3.}$$

$$n - 5 = -33$$

$$n - 5 + 5 = -33 + 5 \qquad \longleftarrow \text{ Add 5 to both sides.}$$

$$n = -28$$

When the variable appears on both sides of an equation, you will need to get the variable terms on the same side.

Example Solve $7x = 3(x + 1)$.

$$7x = 3x + 3 \qquad\qquad \longleftarrow \text{ Use the distributive property.}$$

$$7x - 3x = 3x + 3 - 3x \qquad \longleftarrow \text{ Subtract } 3x \text{ to get the variable terms on one side.}$$

$$4x = 3 \qquad\qquad \longleftarrow \text{ Combine like terms.}$$

$$x = \dfrac{3}{4}, \text{ or } 0.75 \qquad \longleftarrow \text{ Divide both sides by 4.}$$

Example Solve $\dfrac{2}{3}x = 4x - 10$.

$$\dfrac{2}{3}x - 4x = 4x - 10 - 4x \qquad \longleftarrow \text{ Subtract } 4x \text{ from both sides.}$$

$$\dfrac{2}{3}x - 4x = -10$$

$$\dfrac{3}{2}\left(\dfrac{2}{3}x - 4x\right) = \dfrac{3}{2}(-10) \qquad \longleftarrow \text{ Multiply both sides by } \dfrac{3}{2}, \text{ the reciprocal of } \dfrac{2}{3}.$$

$$x - 6x = -15 \qquad\qquad \longleftarrow \text{ Use the distributive property.}$$

$$-5x = -15 \qquad\qquad \longleftarrow \text{ Combine like terms.}$$

$$x = 3 \qquad\qquad\quad \longleftarrow \text{ Divide both sides by } -5.$$

Solve each equation.

1. $\dfrac{x}{6} = 12$

2. $\dfrac{n}{2} + 5 = 8$

3. $\dfrac{3}{4}x - 11 = 4$

4. $\dfrac{x+5}{3} = 10$

5. $\dfrac{x-7}{2} = 2$

6. $\dfrac{n-15}{2} = -5$

7. $\dfrac{w}{10} - 3.2 = 5.4$

8. $\dfrac{x-7}{2} + 4 = 2$

9. $3x = 2x - 5$

10. $-2x + 35 = 3x$

11. $\dfrac{x-7}{2} + 4 = 2x$

12. $5(x - 8) = 2x + 8$

13. $\dfrac{x}{3} - 5 = -4x$

14. $\dfrac{2}{3}n - 7 = n$

15. $\dfrac{2x+1}{5} = x$

644   **Student Resources**

Answers to Skill 13 ··

1. $x = 72$

2. $n = 6$

3. $x = 20$

4. $x = 25$

5. $x = 11$

6. $n = 5$

7. $w = 86$

8. $x = 3$

9. $x = -5$

10. $x = 7$

11. $x = \dfrac{1}{3}$

12. $x = 16$

13. $x = \dfrac{15}{13}$

14. $n = -21$

15. $x = \dfrac{1}{3}$

To solve an inequality, you can use the same "undoing" operations that you used to solve equations.

Example Solve and graph the inequality $2x - 3 < 5$. 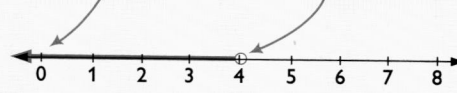 Read "is less than."

$$2x - 3 < 5$$

$$2x - 3 + 3 < 5 + 3 \qquad \longleftarrow \text{Undo subtraction of 3. Add 3 to both sides.}$$

$$2x < 8$$

$$\frac{2x}{2} < \frac{8}{2} \qquad \longleftarrow \text{Undo multiplication by 2. Divide both sides by 2.}$$

$$x < 4$$

Draw a ray to the left to include all points less than 4.   Use an open circle to show that 4 is not included.

An inequality is reversed when you multiply or divide by the same negative number on both sides of an inequality.

Example Solve and graph the inequality $-2(x + 1) \le 8$. 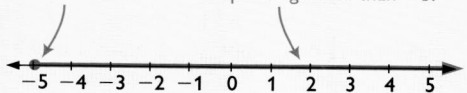 Read "is less than or equal to."

$$-2(x + 1) \le 8$$

$$\frac{-2(x + 1)}{-2} \ge \frac{8}{-2} \qquad \longleftarrow \begin{array}{l}\text{When you divide both sides by } -2, \\ \text{reverse the inequality symbol. Read} \\ \text{"}\ge\text{" as "is greater than or equal to."}\end{array}$$

$$x + 1 \ge -4$$

$$x + 1 - 1 \ge -4 - 1 \qquad \longleftarrow \text{Subtract 1 from both sides.}$$

$$x \ge -5$$

Use a closed circle to show that -5 is included.   Draw a ray to the right to include all points greater than -5.

Solve and graph each inequality.

1. $x + 3 < 7$ **2.** $2 - x \le 4$ **3.** $-3x < 15$

4. $2(x - 1) \ge -6$ **5.** $10 > -5(x + 2)$ **6.** $-2x + 7 \le 5$

7. $4 - 3x > -2$ **8.** $5(4 - x) \ge 20$ **9.** $x > 3x + 8$

Toolbox   645

Answers to Skill 14

1. $x < 4$

2. $x \ge -2$

3. $x > -5$

4. $x \ge -2$
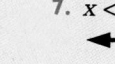

5. $x > -4$
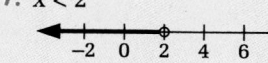

6. $x \ge 1$

7. $x < 2$

8. $x \le 0$
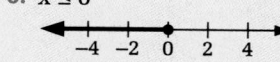

9. $x < -4$
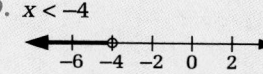

Solving a formula or an equation for a variable means rewriting the formula or equation to get the variable alone on one side.

> **Example** Solve the formula $A = lw$ for w.
>
> $$A = lw$$
>
> $$\frac{A}{l} = \frac{lw}{l}$$ ⟵ Undo multiplication by l. Divide both sides by l.
>
> $$\frac{A}{l} = w$$

> **Example** Solve the equation $3x + 2y = 10$ for y.
>
> $$3x + 2y = 10$$
>
> $$3x + 2y - 3x = 10 - 3x$$ ⟵ Undo addition of $3x$. Subtract $3x$ from both sides.
>
> $$2y = 10 - 3x$$
>
> $$\frac{1}{2} \cdot 2y = \frac{1}{2}(10 - 3x)$$ ⟵ Multiply both sides by the reciprocal of 2.
>
> $$y = 5 - \frac{3}{2}x$$ ⟵ Use the distributive property.

Solve each equation for the variable shown in red.

1. $A = \frac{1}{2}bh$ **2.** $C = 2\pi r$ **3.** $A = \frac{1}{2}(a + b)$ **4.** $2x + y = 13$

5. $5x + 2y = 8$ **6.** $m = (n - 2)180$ **7.** $2x + y = 13$ **8.** $y = mx + b$

You can "undo" the squaring of a variable in an equation by taking the square root of both sides. Remember that every positive number has both a positive and a negative square root. The symbol $\sqrt{3}$ means "the *positive* square root of 3."

> **Example** Solve $x^2 = 14$.
>
> $$x^2 = 14$$ Take the square root of both sides.
>
> $$x = \pm\sqrt{14}$$ ⟵ Use "$\pm$" to show that 14 has both a positive and a negative square root.
>
> $$x \approx \pm 3.74$$

Answers to Skill 15

1. $h = \frac{2A}{b}$

2. $r = \frac{C}{2\pi}$

3. $b = 2A - a$

4. $y = 13 - 2x$

5. $y = 4 - \frac{5}{2}x$

6. $n = \frac{m}{180} + 2$

7. $x = \frac{13}{2} - \frac{y}{2}$

8. $x = \frac{y - b}{m}$

Example Solve $x^2 + 16 = 81$.

$x^2 + 16 - 16 = 81 - 16$ ← Undo addition of 16. Subtract 16 from both sides.

$x^2 = 65$

$x = \pm\sqrt{65}$ ← Take the square root of both sides.

$x \approx \pm 8.06$ ← 65 [INV] [x^2]

You can undo the cubing of a variable in an equation by taking the cube root of both sides. Remember that a positive number has a positive cube root, and a negative number has a negative cube root. There is no "$\pm$" in the solution.

Example Solve $x^3 = 27$.

$x = \sqrt[3]{27}$ ← Take the cube root of both sides.

$x = 3$ ← 27 [INV] [y^x] 3 [=]

Solve.

1. $x^2 = 49$

2. $x^2 = 19$

3. $x^3 = 8$

4. $x^3 = 64$

5. $x^3 = -125$

6. $x^2 + 25 = 36$

7. $x^2 - 16 = 81$

8. $49 - x^2 = 25$

Skill 17   Solving Proportions

You can solve some proportions by "undoing." If the variable is in the numerator of one of the equal fractions, you can use multiplication to undo the division.

Example Solve the proportion $\frac{x}{14} = \frac{8}{35}$.

$\frac{x}{14} = \frac{8}{35}$

$14 \cdot \frac{x}{14} = 14 \cdot \frac{8}{35}$ ← Multiply both sides by 14.

$x = \frac{16}{5}$ ← Simplify.

$x = 3.2$

Toolbox 647

You can solve any proportion by using the fact that the two cross products are equal.

Proportion: $\frac{a}{b} = \frac{c}{d}$ Cross products: $ad = bc$

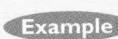 **Example** Solve the proportion $\frac{15}{x} = \frac{20}{21}$.

$$\frac{15}{x} = \frac{20}{21}$$

$15 \cdot 21 = x \cdot 20$ ⟵ Set the two cross products equal.

$315 = 20x$ ⟵ Simplify.

$\frac{315}{20} = \frac{20x}{20}$ ⟵ Divide both sides by 20.

$15.75 = x$ ⟵ Simplify.

Solve each proportion.

1. $\frac{x}{12} = \frac{13}{10}$
2. $\frac{18}{25} = \frac{z}{15}$
3. $\frac{y}{8} = \frac{14}{20}$
4. $\frac{24}{x} = \frac{15}{7}$

5. $\frac{28}{w} = \frac{16}{9}$
6. $\frac{11}{8} = \frac{5}{y}$
7. $\frac{17}{40} = \frac{q}{24}$
8. $\frac{12}{19} = \frac{33}{n}$

Skill 18   Using the Zero-Product Property

Zero-Product Property If a product of factors is zero, one or more of the factors must be zero.

 **Example** Solve the equation $(20 - x)(30 - 5x) = 0$.

$20 - x = 0$	or	$30 - 5x = 0$

⟵ At least one of the two factors must be 0.

$20 - x + x = 0 + x$ $30 - 5x + 5x = 0 + 5x$

$20 = x$ $30 = 5x$

$\frac{30}{5} = \frac{5x}{5}$

The solutions are 20 and 6. $6 = x$

Solve each equation.

1. $x(x + 10) = 0$
2. $2x(4 - x) = 0$
3. $-4x(x - 3) = 0$

4. $(x + 1)(x + 6) = 0$
5. $(x + 4)(x - 7) = 0$
6. $(2x - 1)(2x + 6) = 0$

 648   **Student Resources**

Answers to Skill 17 ············

1. $x = 15.6$

2. $z = 10.8$

3. $y = 5.6$

4. $x = 11.2$

5. $w = 15.75$

6. $y = \frac{40}{11} \approx 3.64$

7. $q = 10.2$

8. $n = 52.25$

Answers to Skill 18 ············

1. $0, -10$

2. $0, 4$

3. $0, 3$

4. $-1, -6$

5. $-4, 7$

6. $\frac{1}{2}, -3$

Graphs, Equations, and Inequalities

Skill 19   Recognizing Functions

A **function** is a relationship in which each value of the **control variable** determines exactly one value of the **dependent variable.**

Vertical Line Test: A graph with the control variable on the horizontal axis represents a function if no vertical line meets the graph in more than one place.

Example   To tell whether each graph is a function, imagine drawing vertical lines through it.

No two points on the graph lie on the same vertical line. →

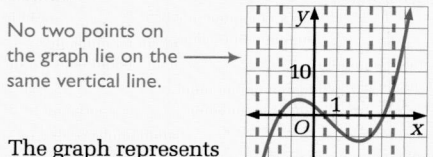

The graph represents a function.

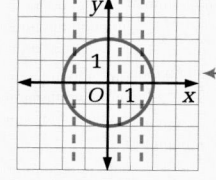

Two points lie on the same vertical line.

The graph does not represent a function.

Tell whether each graph represents a function when _x_ is the control variable.

1.

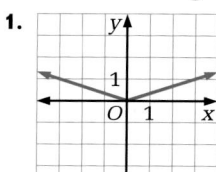

2.

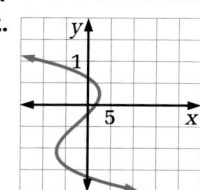

3.

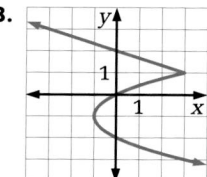

4.

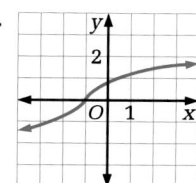

Skill 20   Making a Table of Values to Graph

Example   Make a table of values and graph the function $y = 2x + 1$.

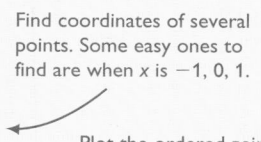

y = 2x + 1		
x	**y**	**(x, y)**
−2	−3	(−2, −3)
−1	−1	(−1, −1)
0	1	(0, 1)
1	3	(1, 3)

Find coordinates of several points. Some easy ones to find are when x is −1, 0, 1.

Plot the ordered pairs. Connect them.

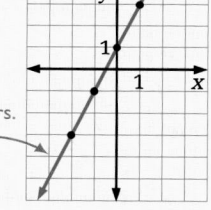

Answers to Skill 19

1. Yes.
2. No.
3. No.
4. Yes.

1.

y = x – 3		
x	**y**	**(x, y)**
–3	–6	(–3, –6)
–2	–5	(–2, –5)
–1	–4	(–1, –4)
0	–3	(0, –3)
1	–2	(1, –2)
2	–1	(2, –1)
3	0	(3, 0)

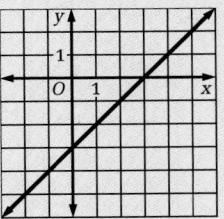

2.

y = 3x – 4		
x	**y**	**(x, y)**
–3	–13	(–3, –13)
–2	–10	(–2, –10)
–1	–7	(–1, –7)
0	–4	(0, –4)
1	–1	(1, –1)
2	2	(2, 2)
3	5	(3, 5)

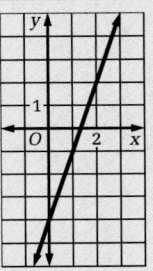

3.

y = –2x + 3		
x	**y**	**(x, y)**
–1	5	(–1, 5)
0	3	(0, 3)
1	1	(1, 1)
2	–1	(2, –1)
3	–3	(3, –3)

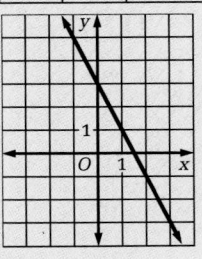

Example Make a table of values and graph the function $y = x^2 - 3$.

$y = x^2 - 3$		
x	**y**	**(x, y)**
–3	6	(–3, 6)
–1	–2	(–1, –2)
0	–3	(0, –3)
1	–2	(1, –2)
3	6	(3, 6)

Choose enough values to see the shape of the graph.

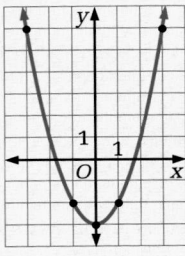

Make a table of values for each function and graph the function.

1. $y = x - 3$

2. $y = 3x - 4$

3. $y = -2x + 3$

4. $y = \frac{1}{2}x + 1$

5. $y = |x|$

6. $y = x^2 + 1$

7. $y = 2x^2 - 5$

8. $y = \frac{1}{x}$

Skill 21 **Finding Slope**

The **slope** of a line is the ratio of *rise* to *run*.

Example Find the slope of $\overline{AB}$.

slope $= \frac{\text{rise}}{\text{run}} = \frac{4.8}{9.6} = 0.5$

The slope is 0.5.

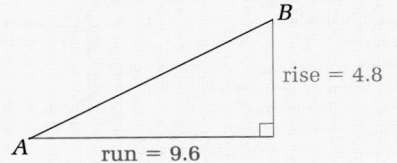

You can find the slope of a line in a coordinate system if you know two points on the line.

Example You can find the slope of the line shown using the points $(-2, 1)$ and $(3, 4)$.

vertical change

Subtract the y-coordinates.

slope $= \frac{\text{rise}}{\text{run}} = \frac{4 - 1}{3 - (-2)} = \frac{3}{5} = 0.6$

horizontal change

Subtract the x-coordinates in the same order.

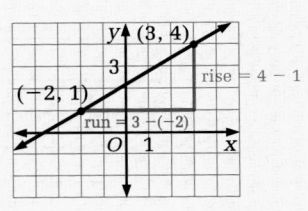

The slope of the line is 0.6.

Student Resources

4.

$y = \frac{1}{2}x + 1$		
x	**y**	**(x, y)**
–3	$-\frac{1}{2}$	$\left(-3, -\frac{1}{2}\right)$
–2	0	(–2, 0)
–1	$\frac{1}{2}$	$\left(-1, \frac{1}{2}\right)$
0	1	(0, 1)
1	$1\frac{1}{2}$	$\left(1, 1\frac{1}{2}\right)$
2	2	(2, 2)

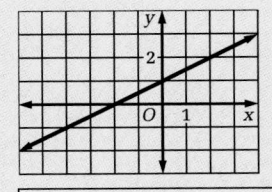

5.

$y = |x|$		
x	**y**	**(x, y)**
–3	3	(–3, 3)
–2	2	(–2, 2)
–1	1	(–1, 1)
0	0	(0, 0)
1	1	(1, 1)
2	2	(2, 2)

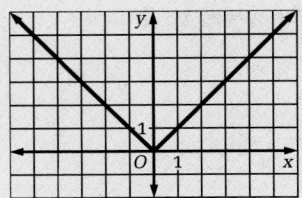

The **slope of a horizontal line** is 0. The **slope of a vertical line** is undefined. A **negative slope** indicates that the line is "downhill" from left to right.

 Find the slope of the line $y = 3$.

Two points on this line are (0, 3) and (4, 3).

slope $= \dfrac{3 - 3}{4 - 0} = \dfrac{0}{4}$, or 0

The slope is 0. (The line is horizontal.)

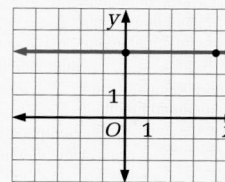

Find the slope of each line.

1.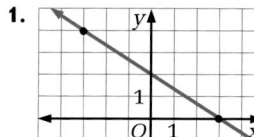

2. the line through $(1, -4)$ and $(3, 7)$

3. the line through $(-6, 2)$ and $(4, -2)$

4. the line through $(5, 0)$ and $(5, 5)$

Skill 22   Modeling Direct Variation

When the ratio of two variable quantities is a constant k, their relationship is called a **direct variation.** You can model a direct variation with an equation of the form $\dfrac{y}{x} = k$, or $y = kx$.

One quantity **varies directly with** another quantity.

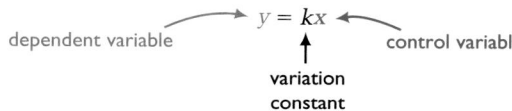

dependent variable $y = kx$ control variable

variation constant

 The pressure on an underwater object varies directly with the depth of the object below the surface. Suppose the pressure on an object at a depth of 50 ft is 21.7 lbs/in.² Find the pressure on an object at a depth of 85 ft.

Method ❶ Use a proportion. The ratio depth : pressure is constant.

depth $\longrightarrow$
pressure $\longrightarrow$ $\dfrac{50}{21.7} = \dfrac{85}{y}$

$50y = (21.7)(85)$ $\longleftarrow$ Set the cross products equal.

$y = \dfrac{(21.7)(85)}{50} = 36.89$

Continued on next page.

Toolbox

651

Answers to Skill 20

6.

$y = x^2 + 1$		
x	y	(x, y)
-3	10	$(-3, 10)$
-2	5	$(-2, 5)$
-1	2	$(-1, 2)$
0	1	$(0, 1)$
1	2	$(1, 2)$
2	5	$(2, 5)$
x	y	(x, y)

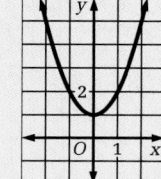

7, 8. See answers in side-column at the right.

Answers to Skill 21

1. $-\dfrac{2}{3}$

2. $\dfrac{11}{2}$

3. $-\dfrac{2}{5}$

4. undefined

7.

$y = 2x^2 - 5$		
x	y	(x, y)
-3	13	$(-3, 13)$
-2	3	$(-2, 3)$
-1	-3	$(-1, -3)$
0	-5	$(0, -5)$
1	-3	$(1, -3)$
2	3	$(2, 3)$

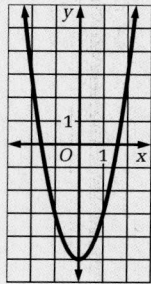

8.

$y = \dfrac{1}{x}$		
x	y	(x, y)
-4	$-\dfrac{1}{4}$	$\left(-4, -\dfrac{1}{4}\right)$
-3	$-\dfrac{1}{3}$	$\left(-3, -\dfrac{1}{3}\right)$
-2	$-\dfrac{1}{2}$	$\left(-2, -\dfrac{1}{2}\right)$
-1	-1	$(-1, -1)$
$-\dfrac{1}{2}$	-2	$\left(-\dfrac{1}{2}, -2\right)$
0	—	—
$\dfrac{1}{2}$	2	$\left(\dfrac{1}{2}, 2\right)$
1	1	$(1, 1)$
2	$\dfrac{1}{2}$	$\left(2, \dfrac{1}{2}\right)$
3	$\dfrac{1}{3}$	$\left(3, \dfrac{1}{3}\right)$
4	$\dfrac{1}{4}$	$\left(4, \dfrac{1}{4}\right)$

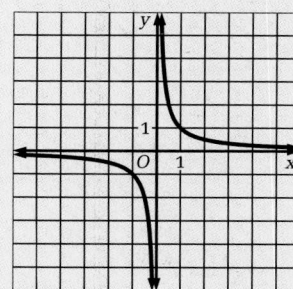

Method ❷ Use the equation $y = kx$.

Step 1 First find the variation constant.

Let $x =$ the depth (ft) and $y =$ the pressure (lbs/in.^{2}).

$y = kx$ ⟵ Write the general form of the equation.

$21.7 = k \cdot 50$ ⟵ Substitute **50** for **x** and **21.7** for **y**.

$k = \dfrac{21.7}{50} = 0.434$ ⟵ Solve for k, the variation constant.

Step 2 $y = kx$ ⟵ Write the general form of the equation.

$y = (0.434)(85)$ ⟵ Substitute 0.434 for k and 85 for x.

$y = 36.89$

The pressure is 36.89 lbs/in.^{2}

---

1. The distance a car travels at a constant speed varies directly with time. Suppose the car goes 92 miles in 2 h. How far would it go in 3.5 h?

2. The bounce height of a rubber ball varies directly with the drop height. A ball dropped from a height of 6.5 ft bounces to a height of 5.2 ft. How high will the ball bounce if dropped from 5.5 ft?

Skill 23   Using $y = mx + b$

One form of the equation of a line is **slope-intercept form:**

$$y = mx + b$$

slope ⟶   ⟵ vertical intercept

Example Find the slope and the vertical intercept of the line $y = \dfrac{2}{3}x - 5$.

The line is in the form $y = mx + b$. Therefore, the slope is $\dfrac{2}{3}$, and the vertical intercept is -5.

Example Write an equation for the line shown at the right.

Step 1 Use $(-3, 4)$ and $(3, 0)$ to find the slope m.

$$m = \frac{0 - 4}{3 - (-3)} = \frac{-4}{6} = -\frac{2}{3}$$

Step 2 The graph crosses the vertical axis at $(0, 2)$, so $b = 2$.

Step 3 Substitute the values in $y = mx + b$: $y = -\dfrac{2}{3}x + 2$.

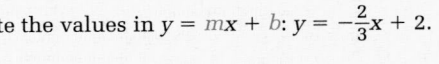

Answers to Skill 22

1. 161 mi

2. 4.4 ft

Find the slope and the vertical intercept of each line.

1. $y = 3x - 4$ **2.** $y = -2.5x + 11.2$ **3.** $y = 6 - 7x$ **4.** $y = 4x$

Write an equation of each line in the form $y = mx + b$.

5.

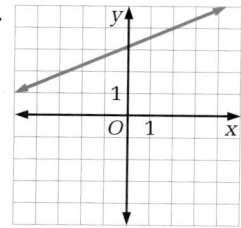

6.

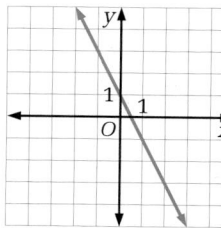

7.

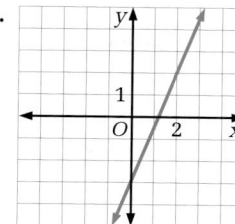

Skill 24   Using Intercepts to Graph

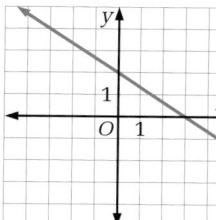

The **horizontal intercept** of a graph is the x-coordinate of the point where the graph crosses the x-axis. The **vertical intercept** is the y-coordinate of the point where the graph crosses the y-axis.

The graph at the left crosses the horizontal axis at $(3, 0)$ and the vertical axis at $(0, 2)$.

The horizontal intercept of the graph is 3.

The vertical intercept of the graph is 2.

If you know the equation of a line, one way to graph the line is to use the intercepts.

Example   Use the intercepts to graph the line $2x - 5y = 15$.

To find the vertical intercept, substitute 0 for x:

$$2x - 5y = 15$$
$$2(0) - 5y = 15$$
$$-5y = 15$$
$$y = -3$$

To find the horizontal intercept, substitute 0 for y:

$$2x - 5y = 15$$
$$2x - 5(0) = 15$$
$$2x = 15$$
$$x = 7.5$$

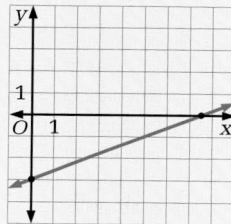

Plot the points $(0, -3)$ and $(7.5, 0)$.
Connect the points.

Toolbox

Answers to Skill 23

1. slope = 3;
vertical intercept = −4

2. slope = $-\frac{5}{2}$ or −2.5;

vertical intercept = $\frac{56}{5}$
or 11.2

3. slope = −7;
vertical intercept = 6

4. slope = 4;
vertical intercept = 0

5. $y = \frac{1}{2}x + 3$

6. $y = -2x + 1$

7. $y = \frac{5}{2}x - 3$

1. vertical intercept = 6;
horizontal intercept = 2

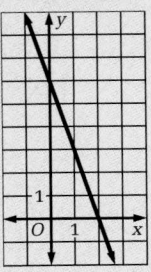

2. vertical intercept = −5;
horizontal intercept = 2

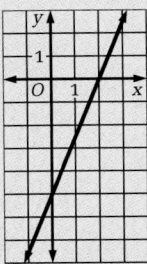

3. vertical intercept = 3;
horizontal intercept = −3

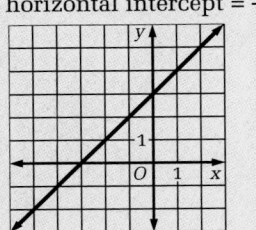

4. vertical intercept = −8;
horizontal intercept = 2

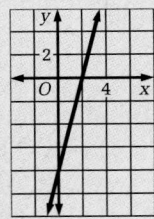

5. vertical intercept = −3;
horizontal intercept = $\frac{3}{2}$

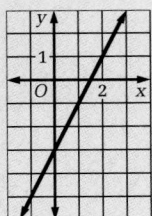

6. vertical intercept = 5;
horizontal intercept = 2

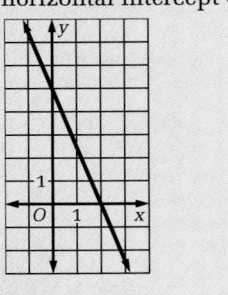

Use the vertical and horizontal intercepts to graph each equation.

1. $3x + y = 6$

2. $5x - 2y = 10$

3. $-3x + 3y = 9$

4. $4x = y + 8$

5. $y = 2x - 3$

6. $y = -2.5x + 5$

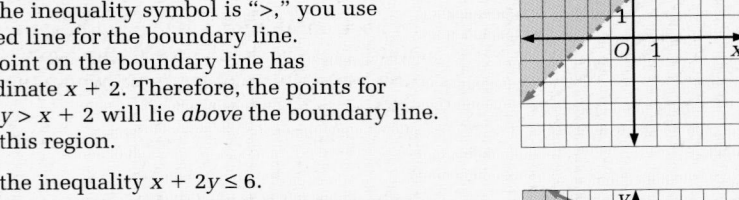

Skill 25 Graphing an Inequality in Two Variables

To graph a **linear inequality** in two variables, such as $y > x + 2$, you shade a region on a coordinate plane whose edge is a line. The edge is called a **boundary line**. The shaded part of the graph of a linear inequality is the **solution region**.

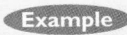 **Example** Graph the inequality $y > x + 2$.

First graph the boundary line: $y = x + 2$.
Since the inequality symbol is ">," you use a dashed line for the boundary line.
Each point on the boundary line has y-coordinate $x + 2$. Therefore, the points for which $y > x + 2$ will lie *above* the boundary line. Shade this region.

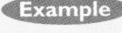 **Example** Graph the inequality $x + 2y \leq 6$.

First rewrite the inequality in slope-intercept form.

$$x + 2y \leq 6$$
$$x + 2y - x \leq 6 - x \quad \leftarrow \text{ Subtract } x \text{ from both sides.}$$
$$2y \leq 6 - x$$
$$\tfrac{1}{2} \cdot 2y \leq \tfrac{1}{2}(6 - x) \quad \leftarrow \text{ Multiply both sides by } \tfrac{1}{2}.$$
$$y \leq 3 - \tfrac{1}{2}x$$

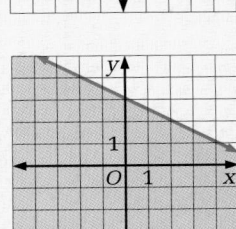

Graph the boundary line $y = 3 - \frac{1}{2}x$.

Since the symbol in the inequality is "≤," the boundary line is a solid line.

Each point on the boundary line has y-coordinate $3 - \frac{1}{2}x$. Therefore, the solution region lies *below* and includes the boundary line. Shade this region.

Graph each inequality.

1. $y > -x + 3$

2. $y \leq 2x - 4$

3. $y < \frac{1}{2}x + 1$

4. $2x + 3y \geq 6$

5. $x - 3y > 3$

6. $3x + 2y \leq 9$

Student Resources

1.

$y = -x + 3$		
x	**y**	**(x, y)**
0	3	(0, 3)
3	0	(3, 0)

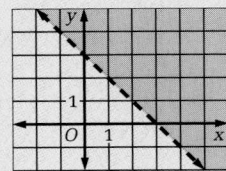

2.

$y = 2x - 4$		
x	**y**	**(x, y)**
0	−4	(0, −4)
2	0	(2, 0)

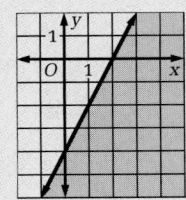

3.

$y = \frac{1}{2}x + 1$		
x	**y**	**(x, y)**
0	1	(0, 1)
−2	0	(−2, 0)

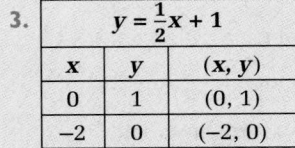
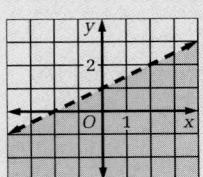

➤Geometry and Measurement

Formulas and Relationships

An angle whose measure is 90° is called a **right angle.** An angle whose measure is 180° is called a **straight angle.**

Two angles whose measures add up to 90° are **complementary.**
Two angles whose measures add up to 180° are **supplementary.**

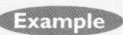 A mark like this indicates a right angle.

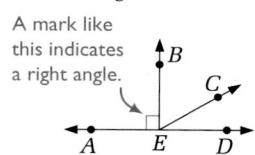

∠AEB is a right angle.
∠BEC and ∠CED are complementary.

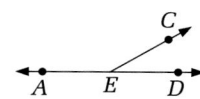

∠AED is a straight angle.
∠AEC and ∠CED are supplementary.

Example Find the unknown angle measure in the figure.

The sum of the measures of the angles of a triangle is 180°.

$x + 40 + 30 = 180$

$x = 180 - 70$

$\quad = 110$

The unknown angle measure is 110°.

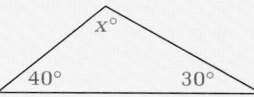

Example Find the unknown angle measures in the figure.

Vertical angles are equal in measure.

∠AOD and ∠BOC are vertical angles, so $y = 55$.

∠AOB and ∠BOC are supplementary, so $x = 180 - 55 = 125$.

The angle measures are 125° and 55°.

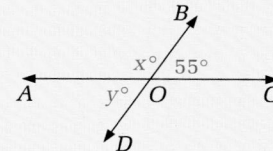

Find each unknown angle measure.

1.

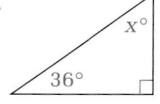

2.

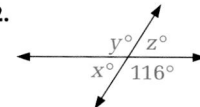

3.

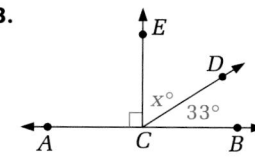

Toolbox

655

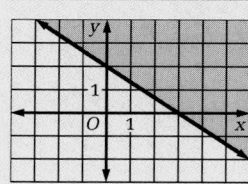
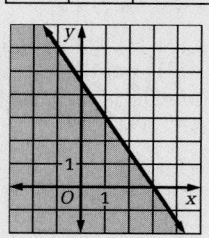

Certain marks in a geometry diagram indicate special relationships between lines, segments, and angles.

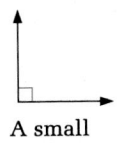 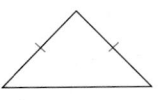 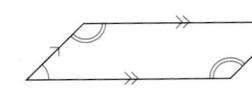

| A small square indicates a right angle. | Tick marks indicate sides that are equal in measure. | Arcs indicate angles that are equal in measure. | Arrowheads indicate parallel lines or segments. |

Example List all the relationships indicated by marks in the figure.

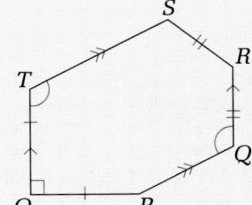

Angles   Since ∠*TOP* is marked with a small square,
∠*TOP* is a right angle.

Since ∠*T* and ∠*Q* both have one arc,
∠*T* and ∠*Q* are equal in measure.

Sides   Since sides *TO* and *OP* both have one tick
mark, side *TO* ≅ side *OP*.

Since sides *SR* and *RQ* both have two tick
marks, side *SR* ≅ side *RQ*.

Since sides *RQ* and *TO* both have one arrowhead,
side *RQ* is parallel to side *TO*.

Since sides *PQ* and *ST* both have two arrowheads,
side *PQ* is parallel to side *ST*.

List all the relationships indicated by marks in each figure.

1.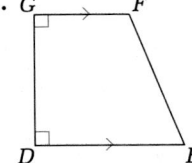

2.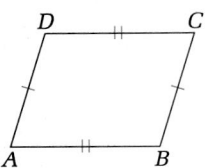

3.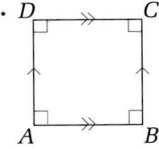

4.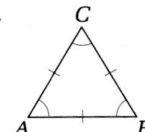

5.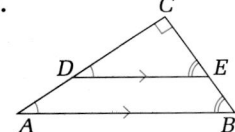

6.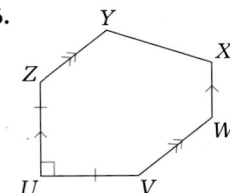

Student Resources

Answers to Skill 27 ···

1. ∠*G* and ∠*D* are right
angles. Side *GF* is parallel
to side *DE*.

2. Side *AB* ≅ side *DC*. Side
AD ≅ side *BC*.

3. All angles are right angles.
Side *AD* is parallel to side
BC. Side *DC* is parallel to
side *AB*.

4. Side *AB* ≅ side *BC* ≅ side
AC. ∠*A*, ∠*B*, and ∠*C* are
equal in measure.

5. Side *AB* is parallel to side
DE. ∠*A* is equal in measure to ∠*CDE*. ∠*B* is equal
in measure to ∠*CED*. ∠*C* is
a right angle.

6. ∠*ZUV* is a right angle.
Side *ZY* is parallel to side
VW. Side *ZU* is parallel to
side *WX*. Side *UZ* ≅ side
UV.

In formulas from geometry:

A = area   S.A. = surface area V = volume

Parallelogram	**Triangle**	**Trapezoid**
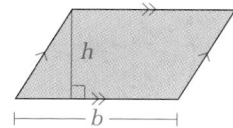	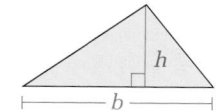	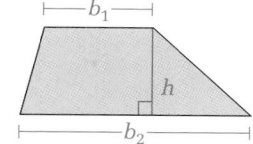
A = base $\times$ height $A = bh$	$A = \frac{1}{2} \times$ base $\times$ height $A = \frac{1}{2}bh$	$A = \frac{1}{2} \times$ sum of bases $\times$ height $A = \frac{1}{2}(b_1 + b_2)h$
Circle	**Sector**	**Prism**
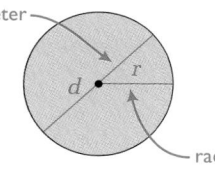	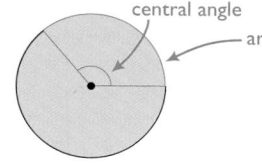	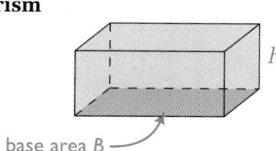
Circumference of a circle: $C = 2\pi r$ $C = \pi d$ $A = \pi r^2$	$\dfrac{\text{arc length}}{\text{circumference}} = \dfrac{\text{central} \angle}{360°}$ $\dfrac{\text{area of sector}}{\text{area of circle}} = \dfrac{\text{central} \angle}{360°}$	S.A. = areas of two bases + areas of faces V = area of base $\times$ height of prism
Cylinder	**Pyramid**	**Cone**
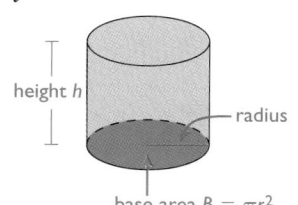	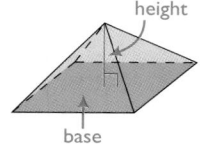	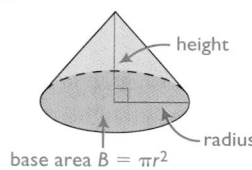
S.A. = areas of two bases + area of curved surface S.A. $= 2\pi r^2 + 2\pi rh$ V = area of base $\times$ height $V = Bh = \pi r^2 h$	S.A. = area of base + areas of faces $V = \frac{1}{3} \times$ area of base $\times$ height $V = \frac{1}{3}Bh$	$V = \frac{1}{3} \times$ area of base $\times$ height $V = \frac{1}{3}Bh = \frac{1}{3}\pi r^2 h$

Example Find the area of the trapezoid shown.

$$A = \frac{1}{2}(b_1 + b_2)h \quad \longleftarrow \quad \text{Write the formula for the area of a trapezoid.}$$

$$A = \frac{1}{2}(21 + 33)13 \quad \longleftarrow \quad \text{Substitute } \mathbf{21} \text{ for } b_1, \mathbf{33} \text{ for } b_2, \text{ and } \mathbf{13} \text{ for } h.$$

$$= \frac{1}{2}(54)13 = 351$$

The area is 351 cm². $\quad \longleftarrow \quad$ cm × cm = cm²

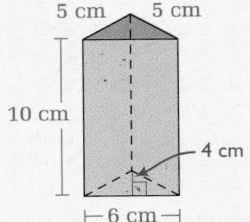

Example Use the the triangular prism shown.

Find: **a.** the volume   **b.** the surface area

a. Volume of a prism = area of base × height of prism.

Step 1 Find the area of the triangular base of the prism.

$$B = \frac{1}{2}bh \quad \longleftarrow \quad \text{Write the formula for the area of a triangle.}$$

$$= \frac{1}{2}(6)(4) \quad \longleftarrow \quad \text{Substitute } \mathbf{6} \text{ for } b \text{ and } \mathbf{4} \text{ for } h.$$

$$= 12$$

Step 2 Find the volume of the prism.

$$V = Bh \quad \longleftarrow \quad \text{Write the formula for the volume of a prism.}$$

$$= 12 \cdot 10 \quad \longleftarrow \quad \text{Substitute } \mathbf{12} \text{ for } B \text{ and } \mathbf{10} \text{ for } h.$$

$$= 120$$

The volume of the prism is 120 cm³. $\quad \longleftarrow \quad$ cm × cm × cm = cm³

b. Surface area of a prism = area of two bases + area of three faces

$$\text{S.A.} = \overbrace{12 + 12} + \overbrace{6 \cdot 10 + 5 \cdot 10 + 5 \cdot 10}$$

$$= 184$$

The surface area is 184 cm².

Find the area of each figure.

1. a parallelogram of height 10 ft with a base of length 16 ft

2. a trapezoid of height 3 in. with bases of length 5 in. and 8 in.

3. a sector with central angle 40° and radius 9 in.

Find the surface area of each space figure.

4. a rectangular prism with dimensions 18 in., 12 in., and 4.5 in.

5. a cylinder of height 20 cm and with a base of radius 5 cm

Find the volume of each space figure.

6. a triangular prism whose height is 8 cm and whose base area is 25 cm²

7. a cylinder of height 8.5 m and with a base of radius 2 m

8. a pyramid of height 12 in., whose base is a square with sides of length 10 in.

Answers to Skill 28

1. 160 ft²

2. 19.5 in.²

3. 9π in.² ≈ 28.274 in.²

4. 702 in.²

5. 250π cm² ≈ 785.4 cm²

6. 200 cm³

7. 34π m³ ≈ 106.8 m³

8. 400 in.³

Trigonometry

Skill 29 Finding Sine, Cosine, and Tangent Ratios

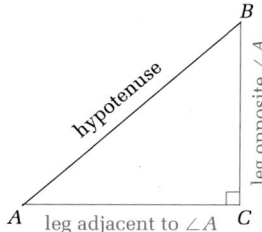

Suppose $\angle A$ is one of the acute angles of a right triangle. The **trigonometric ratios** for $\angle A$ are ratios of the measures of the sides of the triangle.

Sine of $\angle A$ $\sin A = \dfrac{\text{leg opposite } \angle A}{\text{hypotenuse}} = \dfrac{BC}{AB}$

Cosine of $\angle A$ $\cos A = \dfrac{\text{leg adjacent to } \angle A}{\text{hypotenuse}} = \dfrac{AC}{AB}$

Tangent of $\angle A$ $\tan A = \dfrac{\text{leg opposite } \angle A}{\text{leg adjacent to } \angle A} = \dfrac{BC}{AC}$

Example Write each trigonometric ratio as a fraction and as a decimal rounded to the nearest hundredth.

- **a.** $\sin P$
- **b.** $\cos P$
- **c.** $\tan P$
- **d.** $\sin Q$
- **e.** $\cos Q$
- **f.** $\tan Q$

a. $\sin P = \dfrac{\text{leg opposite } \angle P}{\text{hypotenuse}} = \dfrac{15}{17} \approx 0.88$

b. $\cos P = \dfrac{\text{leg adjacent to } \angle P}{\text{hypotenuse}} = \dfrac{8}{17} \approx 0.47$

c. $\tan P = \dfrac{\text{leg opposite } \angle P}{\text{leg adjacent to } \angle P} = \dfrac{15}{8} \approx 1.88$

d. $\sin Q = \dfrac{\text{leg opposite } \angle Q}{\text{hypotenuse}} = \dfrac{8}{17} \approx 0.47$

e. $\cos Q = \dfrac{\text{leg adjacent to } \angle Q}{\text{hypotenuse}} = \dfrac{15}{17} \approx 0.88$

f. $\tan Q = \dfrac{\text{leg opposite } \angle Q}{\text{leg adjacent to } \angle Q} = \dfrac{8}{15} \approx 0.53$

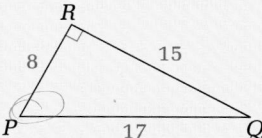

Use the triangle at the right. Find the value of each trigonometric ratio.

- **1.** $\sin A$
- **2.** $\cos A$
- **3.** $\tan A$
- **4.** $\sin B$
- **5.** $\cos B$
- **6.** $\tan B$

Draw and label a right triangle that fits each description.

7. $\triangle ABC$ with $\sin A = \dfrac{\text{leg opposite } \angle A}{\text{hypotenuse}} = \dfrac{3}{5}$

8. $\triangle XYZ$ with $\cos X = \dfrac{\text{leg adjacent to } \angle X}{\text{hypotenuse}} = \dfrac{5}{13}$

Toolbox

659

Answers to Skill 29

1. $\dfrac{4}{8.5} \approx 0.47$

2. $\dfrac{7.5}{8.5} \approx 0.88$

3. $\dfrac{4}{7.5} \approx 0.53$

4. $\dfrac{7.5}{8.5} \approx 0.88$

5. $\dfrac{4}{8.5} \approx 0.47$

6. $\dfrac{7.5}{4} = 1.875$

7.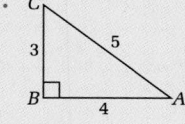

8.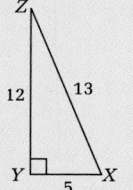

You can use the trigonometric ratios to find missing lengths in right triangles. The ratios are programmed into scientific calculators. There is a table of trigonometric ratios on page 668.

Example Find the missing length in the triangle at the right.

Since x is the measure of the leg opposite $\angle A$, and 24 is the measure of the hypotenuse of the right triangle, you use the sine ratio.

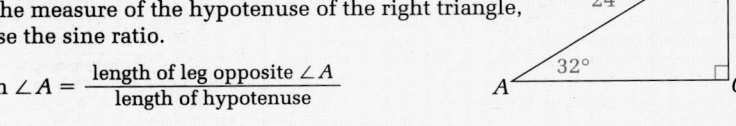

$$\sin \angle A = \frac{\text{length of leg opposite } \angle A}{\text{length of hypotenuse}}$$

$$\sin 32° = \frac{x}{24}$$

$$0.5299 \approx \frac{x}{24} \quad \longleftarrow \text{Make sure your calculator is in degree mode. Use the } \boxed{\text{sin}} \text{ key.}$$

$$0.5299 \cdot 24 \approx \frac{x}{24} \cdot 24 \quad \longleftarrow \text{Multiply both sides by 24.}$$

$$12.7 \approx x$$

Example Find the missing length in the triangle at the right.

Use the tangent ratio.

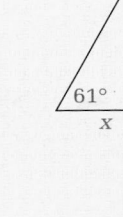

$$\tan 61° = \frac{49}{x}$$

$$1.804 \approx \frac{49}{x} \quad \longleftarrow \text{Use the } \boxed{\text{tan}} \text{ key on your calculator.}$$

$$1.804 \cdot x \approx \frac{49}{x} \cdot x \quad \longleftarrow \text{Multiply both sides by } x.$$

$$1.804x \approx 49$$

$$\frac{1.804x}{1.804} \approx \frac{49}{1.804} \quad \longleftarrow \text{Divide both sides by 1.804.}$$

$$x \approx \frac{49}{1.804} \approx 27.2$$

Find each missing length.

1.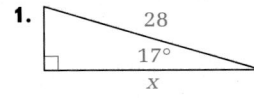

2.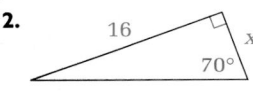

3.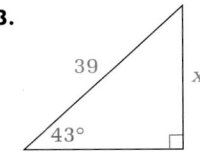

Student Resources

Answers to Skill 30

1. $x \approx 26.8$

2. $x \approx 5.8$

3. $x \approx 26.6$

The Pythagorean Theorem

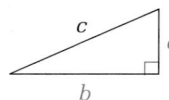

The Pythagorean Theorem In any right triangle with legs of length a and b and hypotenuse of length c,

$$a^2 + b^2 = c^2.$$

Example Find the missing length in the triangle at the right.

$c^2 = 6.4^2 + 12^2$ ← Use the Pythagorean theorem: $c^2 = a^2 + b^2$

$c^2 = 40.96 + 144$

$c^2 = 184.96$

$c = \sqrt{184.96}$ ← Find the positive square root.

$c = 13.6$

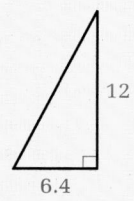

12

6.4

Find the missing length in the right triangle with legs a and b and hypotenuse c.

1. $a = 5, b = 12, c = ?$ **2.** $a = 10, c = 14.5, b = ?$ **3.** $b = 24, c = 75, a = ?$

If the lengths of the sides of a triangle satisfy the relationship $a^2 + b^2 = c^2$, the triangle is a right triangle with hypotenuse c.

Example Is the triangle with sides of the given lengths a right triangle?

   a. 15, 20, 25   **b.** 8, 10, 13

If the triangle is a right triangle, the longest side must be the hypotenuse.

a. $a^2 + b^2 \overset{?}{=} c^2$ **b.** $a^2 + b^2 \overset{?}{=} c^2$

    $15^2 + 20^2 \overset{?}{=} 25^2$ $8^2 + 10^2 \overset{?}{=} 13^2$

    $225 + 400 \overset{?}{=} 625$ $64 + 100 \overset{?}{=} 169$

        $625 = 625$ ✔ $164 \neq 169$

The triangle is a right triangle.   The triangle is not a right triangle.

Tell whether a triangle with sides of the given lengths is a right triangle.

1. 6, 8, 10   **2.** 2.1, 2.8, 3.5   **3.** 2.5, 6, 6.5   **4.** 10, 17.5, 20

Toolbox

661

Answers to Skill 31

1. 13
2. 10.5
3. about 71.1

Answers to Skill 32

1. Yes.
2. Yes.
3. Yes.
4. No.

Transformations

Skill 33 | Translating a Figure

A **translation** of a plane figure slides the figure without changing its size or shape and without turning it. Each point of the figure moves the same distance and in the same direction.

Example Translate △*ABC* 4 units to the right and 1 unit down.

Step 1 Translate each vertex 4 units to the right and 1 unit down:

$A(-4, 4) \rightarrow A'(0, 3)$

$B(-1, 2) \rightarrow B'(3, 1)$

$C(-2, -1) \rightarrow C'(2, -2)$

Each translated vertex is labeled with a prime (').

Step 2 Connect the vertices. The translated triangle is △*A'B'C'*.

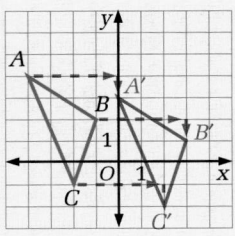

Draw each translation of △*DEF*.

1. 3 units to the left.   2. 2 units down

3. 2 units to the right and up 3 units

4. 4 units to the left and down 1 unit

5. 1 unit to the right and down 4 units

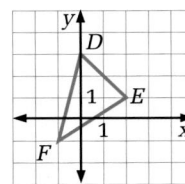

Skill 34 | Rotating a Figure

A **rotation** moves each point of a figure through a circular arc about a common point, called the **center of rotation.** Each point of the figure is rotated by the same number of degrees.

Example Rotate △*ABC* 90° counterclockwise about the origin.

Imagine that △*ABC* is a paper triangle fixed to a stick, $\overline{OC}$. Suppose you press down on the stick at the center of rotation *O* and rotate the stick through a quarter of a circle (90°) counterclockwise. The rotated triangle is △*A'B'C'*.

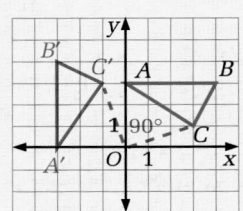

Student Resources

Answers to Skill 33

1.

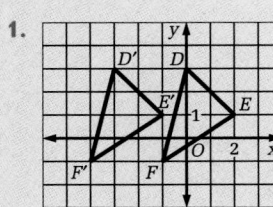

2.

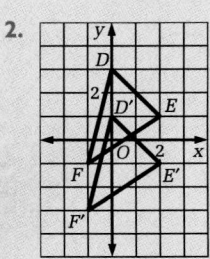

3.

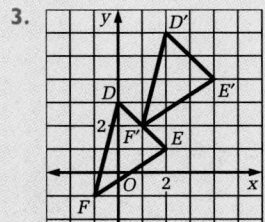

4.

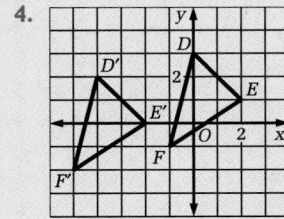

5.

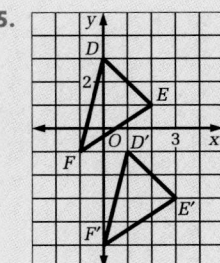

It is easier to draw a rotation on polar graph paper.

Example Rotate △*DEF* 60° counterclockwise about the origin.

Step 1 Move each vertex along its circle six lines in the counterclockwise direction. (From one line to the next is 10°, and 6 · 10° is 60°.) Label the new points *D'*, *E'*, *F'*.

Step 2 Connect the vertices. The rotated triangle is △*D'E'F'*.

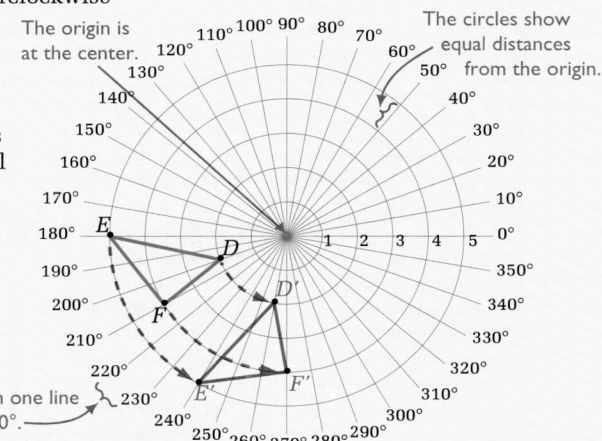

The origin is at the center.

The circles show equal distances from the origin.

A rotation from one line to the next is 10°.

Draw each rotation of △*PQR* about the origin.

1. 90° counterclockwise
2. 90° clockwise
3. 180° clockwise
4. 270° counterclockwise

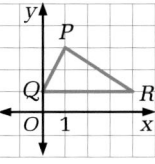

Skill 35   Dilating a Figure

A **dilation** transforms a figure into a similar figure. The ratio of any length in the transformed figure to the corresponding length in the original figure is the **scale factor**.

Example Draw a dilation of △*ABC*, with center *P*, in which the scale factor is 3.

Step 1 Draw rays from *P* through the vertices of △*ABC*.

Step 2 Measure the distance from *P* to each vertex of the original triangle along these rays. Mark points *A'*, *B'*, and *C'* on these rays that are 3 times as far from *P* as the corresponding vertex of the original figure.

Step 3 Connect the vertices. The dilated triangle is △*A'B'C'*.

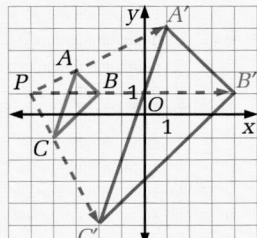

Toolbox

663

1.

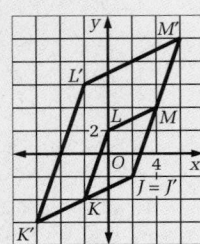

2.

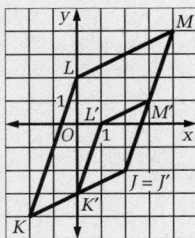

3.

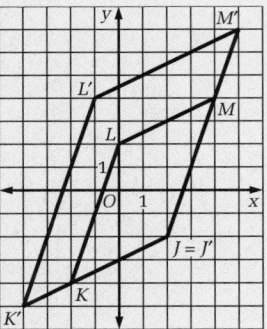

4.

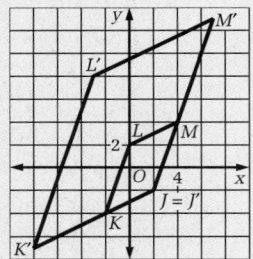

Draw a dilation of the parallelogram *JKLM* with each scale factor and with center *J*.

1. scale factor 2

2. scale factor $\frac{1}{2}$

3. scale factor $\frac{3}{2}$

4. scale factor $\frac{5}{2}$

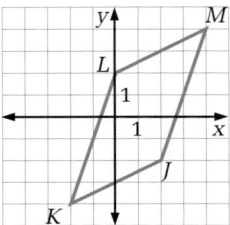

Skill 36	Reflecting a Figure

A **reflection** is a flip over a line. The line is called the **line of reflection.** The reflected figure is congruent to the original figure, but its orientation is reversed.

Example Draw the reflection of △*ABC* over the *x*-axis.

Label the vertices with primes.

Point A is 3 units above the *x*-axis.

Point A′ is 3 units below the *x*-axis.

Notice in the sample that a reflection has these properties:

➤ Each segment connecting a vertex of the original figure with its corresponding vertex in the reflected figure is cut in half by the line of reflection, in this case, the *x*-axis.

➤ The vertices of the original figure in *clockwise* order correspond to the vertices of the reflected figure in counterclockwise order.

Draw a reflection of △*DEF* over each line.

1. the *x*-axis

2. the *y*-axis

3. the line *x* = 1

4. the line *y* = −1

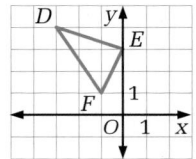

Student Resources

1.

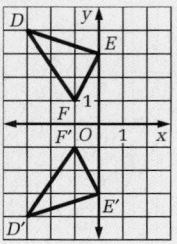

2.

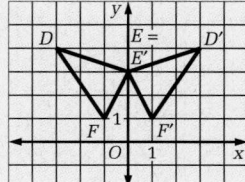

3.

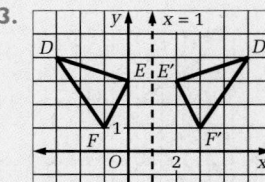

4.

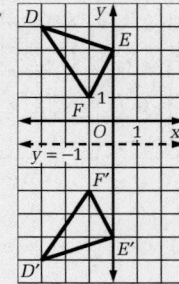

Table of Measures

Time

60 seconds (s) = 1 minute (min)
60 minutes = 1 hour (h)
24 hours = 1 day
7 days = 1 week
4 weeks (approx.) = 1 month

$\left.\begin{array}{l}365 \text{ days} \\ 52 \text{ weeks (approx.)} \\ 12 \text{ months}\end{array}\right\}$ = 1 year

10 years = 1 decade
100 years = 1 century

Metric

Length

10 millimeters (mm) = 1 centimeter (cm)

$\left.\begin{array}{l}100 \text{ cm} \\ 1000 \text{ mm}\end{array}\right\}$ = 1 meter (m)

1000 m = 1 kilometer (km)

Area

100 square millimeters = 1 square centimeter
(mm²)   (cm²)
10,000 cm² = 1 square meter (m²)
10,000 m² = 1 hectare (ha)

Volume

1000 cubic millimeters = 1 cubic centimeter
(mm³)   (cm³)
1,000,000 cm³ = 1 cubic meter (m³)

Liquid Capacity

1000 milliliters (mL) = 1 liter (L)
1000 L = 1 kiloliter (kL)

Mass

1000 milligrams (mg) = 1 gram (g)
1000 g = 1 kilogram (kg)
1000 kg = 1 metric ton (t)

Temperature   Degrees Celsius (°C)

0°C = freezing point
of water
37°C = normal body
temperature
100°C = boiling point
of water

United States Customary

Length

12 inches (in.) = 1 foot (ft)

$\left.\begin{array}{l}36 \text{ in.} \\ 3 \text{ ft}\end{array}\right\}$ = 1 yard (yd)

$\left.\begin{array}{l}5280 \text{ ft} \\ 1760 \text{ yd}\end{array}\right\}$ = 1 mile (mi)

Area

144 square inches (in.²) = 1 square foot (ft²)
9 ft² = 1 square yard (yd²)

$\left.\begin{array}{l}43{,}560 \text{ ft}^2 \\ 4840 \text{ yd}^2\end{array}\right\}$ = 1 acre (A)

Volume

1728 cubic inches (in.³) = 1 cubic foot (ft³)
27 ft³ = 1 cubic yard (yd³)

Liquid Capacity

8 fluid ounces (fl oz) = 1 cup (c)
2 c = 1 pint (pt)
2 pt = 1 quart (qt)
4 qt = 1 gallon (gal)

Weight

16 ounces (oz) = 1 pound (lb)
2000 lb = 1 ton (t)

Temperature   Degrees Fahrenheit (°F)

32°F = freezing point
of water
98.6°F = normal body
temperature
212°F = boiling point
of water

Tables

Table of Symbols

Symbol		Page	Symbol		Page
$=$	equals, is equal to	5	$x^{1/3}$	cube root of x	100
$\dfrac{1}{a}$	reciprocal of a	8	$\overline{AB}$	segment AB	112
$P(E)$	probability of event E	8	$A \rightarrow A'$	point A goes to point A' after a transformation	160
$>$	is greater than	15	A^{-1}	inverse of matrix A	174
$<$	is less than	15	$\cos A$	cosine of $\angle A$	192
$\geq$	is greater than or equal to	15	$\pm$	plus-or-minus sign	200
$\leq$	is less than or equal to	15	i	$\sqrt{-1}$	225
a^n	nth power of a	15	$\cong$	congruent, is congruent to	243
$-a$	opposite of a	15	AB	the length of $\overline{AB}$	251
$°$	degree(s)	33	$!$	factorial	304
$|a|$	absolute value of a	34	$_nP_r$	permutation	304
$\cdot$	$\times$ (times)	35	$_nC_r$	combination	329
$\neq$	is not equal to	43	$p \rightarrow q$	p implies q, or if p, then q	373
$\triangle ABC$	triangle ABC	43	$\therefore$	therefore	380
π	pi, a number approximately equal to 3.14	65	$p \leftrightarrow q$	p if and only if q	387
(x, y)	ordered pair	68	$m \angle A$	measure of angle A	408
m	slope	68	$\|$	is parallel to	417
k	variation constant	70	$\measuredangle$	angles	418
$\overleftrightarrow{AB}$	line AB	73	$\perp$	is perpendicular to	434
$\tan A$	tangent of $\angle A$	73	$a : b$	ratio of a to b	444
$\approx$	is approximately equal to	85	$\sim$	similar, is similar to	449
$\sqrt[3]{a}$	cube root of a	86	$\triangle$	triangles	460
$\sqrt{a}$	nonnegative square root of a	93	$\overrightarrow{AB}$	ray AB	468
a^{-n}	$\dfrac{1}{a^n}, a \neq 0$	99	$\sin A$	sine of $\angle A$	491
$x^{1/2}$	square root of x	100	(x, y, z)	ordered triple	579

Table of Squares and Square Roots

No.	Square	Sq. Root	No.	Square	Sq. Root	No.	Square	Sq. Root
1	1	1.000	51	2,601	7.141	101	10,201	10.050
2	4	1.414	52	2,704	7.211	102	10,404	10.100
3	9	1.732	53	2,809	7.280	103	10,609	10.149
4	16	2.000	54	2,916	7.348	104	10,816	10.198
5	25	2.236	55	3,025	7.416	105	11,025	10.247
6	36	2.449	56	3,136	7.483	106	11,236	10.296
7	49	2.646	57	3,249	7.550	107	11,449	10.344
8	64	2.828	58	3,364	7.616	108	11,664	10.392
9	81	3.000	59	3,481	7.681	109	11,881	10.440
10	100	3.162	60	3,600	7.746	110	12,100	10.488
11	121	3.317	61	3,721	7.810	111	12,321	10.536
12	144	3.464	62	3,844	7.874	112	12,544	10.583
13	169	3.606	63	3,969	7.937	113	12,769	10.630
14	196	3.742	64	4,096	8.000	114	12,996	10.677
15	225	3.873	65	4,225	8.062	115	13,225	10.724
16	256	4.000	66	4,356	8.124	116	13,456	10.770
17	289	4.123	67	4,489	8.185	117	13,689	10.817
18	324	4.243	68	4,624	8.246	118	13,924	10.863
19	361	4.359	69	4,761	8.307	119	14,161	10.909
20	400	4.472	70	4,900	8.367	120	14,400	10.954
21	441	4.583	71	5,041	8.426	121	14,641	11.000
22	484	4.690	72	5,184	8.485	122	14,884	11.045
23	529	4.796	73	5,329	8.544	123	15,129	11.091
24	576	4.899	74	5,476	8.602	124	15,376	11.136
25	625	5.000	75	5,625	8.660	125	15,625	11.180
26	676	5.099	76	5,776	8.718	126	15,876	11.225
27	729	5.196	77	5,929	8.775	127	16,129	11.269
28	784	5.292	78	6,084	8.832	128	16,384	11.314
29	841	5.385	79	6,241	8.888	129	16,641	11.358
30	900	5.477	80	6,400	8.944	130	16,900	11.402
31	961	5.568	81	6,561	9.000	131	17,161	11.446
32	1,024	5.657	82	6,724	9.055	132	17,424	11.489
33	1,089	5.745	83	6,889	9.110	133	17,689	11.533
34	1,156	5.831	84	7,056	9.165	134	17,956	11.576
35	1,225	5.916	85	7,225	9.220	135	18,225	11.619
36	1,296	6.000	86	7,396	9.274	136	18,496	11.662
37	1,369	6.083	87	7,569	9.327	137	18,769	11.705
38	1,444	6.164	88	7,744	9.381	138	19,044	11.747
39	1,521	6.245	89	7,921	9.434	139	19,321	11.790
40	1,600	6.325	90	8,100	9.487	140	19,600	11.832
41	1,681	6.403	91	8,281	9.539	141	19,881	11.874
42	1,764	6.481	92	8,464	9.592	142	20,164	11.916
43	1,849	6.557	93	8,649	9.644	143	20,449	11.958
44	1,936	6.633	94	8,836	9.695	144	20,736	12.000
45	2,025	6.708	95	9,025	9.747	145	21,025	12.042
46	2,116	6.782	96	9,216	9.798	146	21,316	12.083
47	2,209	6.856	97	9,409	9.849	147	21,609	12.124
48	2,304	6.928	98	9,604	9.899	148	21,904	12.166
49	2,401	7.000	99	9,801	9.950	149	22,201	12.207
50	2,500	7.071	100	10,000	10.000	150	22,500	12.247

Tables

Table of Trigonometric Ratios

Angle	Sine	Cosine	Tangent	Angle	Sine	Cosine	Tangent
1°	.0175	.9998	.0175	46°	.7193	.6947	1.0355
2°	.0349	.9994	.0349	47°	.7314	.6820	1.0724
3°	.0523	.9986	.0524	48°	.7431	.6691	1.1106
4°	.0698	.9976	.0699	49°	.7547	.6561	1.1504
5°	.0872	.9962	.0875	50°	.7660	.6428	1.1918
6°	.1045	.9945	.1051	51°	.7771	.6293	1.2349
7°	.1219	.9925	.1228	52°	.7880	.6157	1.2799
8°	.1392	.9903	.1405	53°	.7986	.6018	1.3270
9°	.1564	.9877	.1584	54°	.8090	.5878	1.3764
10°	.1736	.9848	.1763	55°	.8192	.5736	1.4281
11°	.1908	.9816	.1944	56°	.8290	.5592	1.4826
12°	.2079	.9781	.2126	57°	.8387	.5446	1.5399
13°	.2250	.9744	.2309	58°	.8480	.5299	1.6003
14°	.2419	.9703	.2493	59°	.8572	.5150	1.6643
15°	.2588	.9659	.2679	60°	.8660	.5000	1.7321
16°	.2756	.9613	.2867	61°	.8746	.4848	1.8040
17°	.2924	.9563	.3057	62°	.8829	.4695	1.8807
18°	.3090	.9511	.3249	63°	.8910	.4540	1.9626
19°	.3256	.9455	.3443	64°	.8988	.4384	2.0503
20°	.3420	.9397	.3640	65°	.9063	.4226	2.1445
21°	.3584	.9336	.3839	66°	.9135	.4067	2.2460
22°	.3746	.9272	.4040	67°	.9205	.3907	2.3559
23°	.3907	.9205	.4245	68°	.9272	.3746	2.4751
24°	.4067	.9135	.4452	69°	.9336	.3584	2.6051
25°	.4226	.9063	.4663	70°	.9397	.3420	2.7475
26°	.4384	.8988	.4877	71°	.9455	.3256	2.9042
27°	.4540	.8910	.5095	72°	.9511	.3090	3.0777
28°	.4695	.8829	.5317	73°	.9563	.2924	3.2709
29°	.4848	.8746	.5543	74°	.9613	.2756	3.4874
30°	.5000	.8660	.5774	75°	.9659	.2588	3.7321
31°	.5150	.8572	.6009	76°	.9703	.2419	4.0108
32°	.5299	.8480	.6249	77°	.9744	.2250	4.3315
33°	.5446	.8387	.6494	78°	.9781	.2079	4.7046
34°	.5592	.8290	.6745	79°	.9816	.1908	5.1446
35°	.5736	.8192	.7002	80°	.9848	.1736	5.6713
36°	.5878	.8090	.7265	81°	.9877	.1564	6.3138
37°	.6018	.7986	.7536	82°	.9903	.1392	7.1154
38°	.6157	.7880	.7813	83°	.9925	.1219	8.1443
39°	.6293	.7771	.8098	84°	.9945	.1045	9.5144
40°	.6428	.7660	.8391	85°	.9962	.0872	11.4301
41°	.6561	.7547	.8693	86°	.9976	.0698	14.3007
42°	.6691	.7431	.9004	87°	.9986	.0523	19.0811
43°	.6820	.7314	.9325	88°	.9994	.0349	28.6363
44°	.6947	.7193	.9657	89°	.9998	.0175	57.2900
45°	.7071	.7071	1.0000				

Postulates and Theorems

Postulates of Algebra

Postulate 1   **Addition Property of Equality** If the same number is added to equal numbers, then the sums are equal. *(p. 402)*

$$a = b \rightarrow a + c = b + c$$

Postulate 2   **Subtraction Property of Equality** If the same number is subtracted from equal numbers, then the differences are equal. *(p. 402)*

$$a = b \rightarrow a - c = b - c$$

Postulate 3   **Multiplication Property of Equality** If equal numbers are multiplied by the same number, then the products are equal. *(p. 402)*

$$a = b \rightarrow ac = bc$$

Postulate 4   **Division Property of Equality** If equal numbers are divided by the same nonzero number, then the quotients are equal. *(p. 402)*

$$a = b \text{ and } c \neq 0 \rightarrow \frac{a}{c} = \frac{b}{c}$$

Postulate 5   **Reflexive Property of Equality** A number is equal to itself. *(p. 402)*

$$a = a$$

Postulate 6   **Substitution Property** If values are equal, then one value may be substituted for the other. *(p. 402)*

$$a = b \rightarrow a \text{ may be substituted for } b.$$

Postulate 7   **Distributive Property** An expression of the form $a(b + c)$ is equivalent to $ab + ac$. *(p. 402)*

$$a(b + c) = ab + ac$$

Postulates and Theorems of Geometry

Angles

Theorem 7.1   If two angles are supplements of the same angle, then they are equal in measure. *(p. 409)*

Theorem 7.2   If two angles are complements of the same angle, then they are equal in measure. *(p. 409)*

Postulate 8   If the sides of an angle form a straight line, then the angle is a straight angle with measure 180°. *(p. 410)*

Postulates and Theorems of Geometry (cont.)

Postulate 9   For any segment or angle, the measure of the whole is equal to the sum of the measures of its non-overlapping parts. *(p. 410)*

Theorem 7.3   Vertical angles are equal in measure. *(p. 411)*

Theorem 8.5   The sum of the measures of the angles of a triangle is 180°. *(p. 440)*

Theorem 8.8   An exterior angle of a triangle is equal in measure to the sum of the measures of its two remote interior angles. *(p. 443)*

Theorem 8.12   If two sides of a triangle are equal in measure, then the angles opposite those sides are equal in measure. *(p. 473)*

Theorem 8.13   If two angles of a triangle are equal in measure, then the sides opposite those angles are equal in measure. *(p. 473)*

Theorem 8.14   If a triangle is equilateral, then it is also equiangular, with three 60° angles. *(p. 474)*

Theorem 8.15   If a triangle is equiangular, then it is also equilateral. *(p. 474)*

Parallel Lines

Postulate 10   If two parallel lines are intersected by a transversal, then corresponding angles are equal in measure. *(p. 416)*

Theorem 7.4   If two parallel lines are intersected by a transversal, then alternate interior angles are equal in measure. *(p. 417)*

Theorem 7.5   If two parallel lines are intersected by a transversal, then co-interior angles are supplementary. *(p. 417)*

Postulate 11   If two lines are intersected by a transversal and corresponding angles are equal in measure, then the lines are parallel. *(p. 431)*

Theorem 8.1   If two lines are intersected by a transversal and alternate interior angles are equal in measure, then the lines are parallel. *(p. 433)*

Theorem 8.2   If two lines are intersected by a transversal and co-interior angles are supplementary, then the lines are parallel. *(p. 433)*

Theorem 8.3   If two lines are perpendicular to the same transversal, then they are parallel. *(p. 434)*

Theorem 8.4   If a transversal is perpendicular to one of two parallel lines, then it is perpendicular to the other one also. *(p. 434)*

Postulate 12   Through a point not on a given line, there is one and only one line parallel to the given line. *(p. 439)*

Similar and Congruent Triangles

Postulate 13 If two angles of one triangle are equal in measure to two angles of another triangle, then the two triangles are similar. (AA Similarity) *(p. 450)*

Theorem 8.9 If a line is drawn from a point on one side of a triangle parallel to another side, then it forms a triangle similar to the original triangle. *(p. 452)*

Theorem 8.10 If two angles and the included side of one triangle are equal in measure to the corresponding angles and side of another triangle, then the triangles are congruent. (ASA) *(p. 459)*

Theorem 8.11 If two angles and a non-included side of one triangle are equal in measure to the corresponding angles and side of another triangle, then the triangles are congruent. (AAS) *(p. 459)*

Postulate 14 If two sides and the included angle of one triangle are equal in measure to the corresponding sides and angle of another triangle, then the triangles are congruent. (SAS) *(p. 466)*

Postulate 15 If three sides of one triangle are equal in measure to the corresponding sides of another triangle, then the triangles are congruent. (SSS) *(p. 466)*

Theorem 8.17 If the altitude is drawn to the hypotenuse of a right triangle, then the two triangles formed are similar to the original triangle and to each other. *(p. 482)*

Quadrilaterals

In a parallelogram, the diagonals have the same midpoint. *(p. 282)*

In a kite, the diagonals are perpendicular to each other. *(p. 282)*

In a rectangle, the diagonals are equal in measure. *(p. 282)*

In a parallelogram, opposite sides are equal in measure. *(p. 282)*

In a triangle, a segment that connects the midpoints of two sides is parallel to the third side and half as long. *(p. 283)*

Theorem 7.6 If a quadrilateral is a parallelogram, then consecutive angles are supplementary. *(p. 419)*

Theorem 7.7 If a quadrilateral is a parallelogram, then opposite angles are equal in measure. *(p. 419)*

Theorem 8.6   The sum of the measures of the angles of a quadrilateral is 360°. *(p. 441)*

Theorem 8.7   If both pairs of opposite angles of a quadrilateral are equal in measure, then the quadrilateral is a parallelogram. *(p. 441)*

Right Triangles

Theorem 8.18   In any right triangle, the square of the length of the hypotenuse is equal to the sum of the squares of the lengths of the legs. *(p. 482)*

Theorem 8.19   If the altitude is drawn to the hypotenuse of a right triangle, then the measure of the altitude is the geometric mean between the measures of the parts of the hypotenuse. *(p. 484)*

Lines

Theorem 8.16   If a point is the same distance from both endpoints of a segment, then it lies on the perpendicular bisector of the segment. *(p. 475)*

A-1 Applying Geometry Formulas

For use after Section 5-6

You can find the areas of composite figures and regular polygons by breaking them into smaller parts. Then you can use familiar area formulas (see page 657).

(see page 657)

Focus

Focus

Apply geometry formulas to composite figures, sectors, and space figures.

Talk it Over

1. Find the area of the figure at the right.

2. Describe another way to break up the figure. Tell what formulas you would use to find the area.

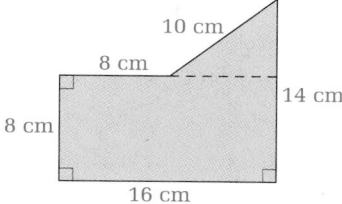

Working with Sectors

You can use what you know about sectors and circles to find an arc length and the area of a sector (see page 657).

(see page 657)

Sample

A jewelry designer wants to put a gold wire border on an arc of a circular pin. About what length of wire is needed?

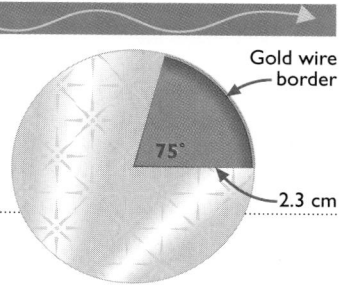

Gold wire border

75°

2.3 cm

Sample Response

Set up and solve a proportion: $\dfrac{\text{arc length}}{\text{circumference}} = \dfrac{\text{central} \angle}{360°}$

Let x = arc length.

Circumference = $2\pi(2.3) \approx 14.45$

$$\frac{x}{14.45} \approx \frac{75}{360}$$

The measure of the central angle is 75°.

$$x \approx 3.01$$

About 3 cm of wire is needed.

Talk it Over

3. The jewelry designer wants part of the pin to be turquoise, as shown above. What is the area of this part of the pin?

Appendix 1

673

Answers to Talk it Over

1. $A = 152$ cm²

2. Answers may vary. For example, you can use the area formulas for a trapezoid and a square.

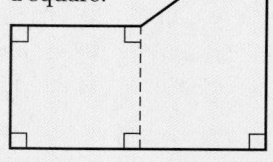

3. Use the formula $\dfrac{\text{area of sector}}{\text{area of circle}} = \dfrac{\text{central} \angle}{360°}$. The area of the turquoise part of the pin is about 3.5 cm².

4. Descriptions may vary. An example is given. Both the surface area and the volume increase more quickly than the edge length because their respective formulas involve squaring and cubing the edge length.

Edge length	Volume	Surface area
1	1	6
2	8	24
3	27	54
⋮	⋮	⋮
s	s^3	$6s^2$

Changing Dimensions of Space Figures

You can use area and volume formulas to explore the effects of changing various dimensions of space figures. (See pages 85 and 657.)

Cube Measurements

Edge length	Volume	Surface area
1	1	6
2	?	?
3	?	?
s	?	?

Talk it Over

4. Copy and complete the table. Compare how the volume and the surface area of the cube change as the edge length increases.

A-1 Exercises and Problems

Find the area of the shaded part of each figure.

1.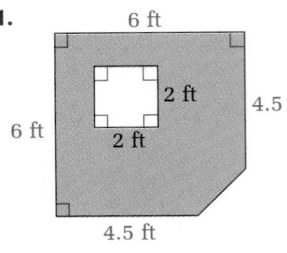
6 ft / 6 ft / 2 ft / 2 ft / 4.5 ft / 4.5 ft

2.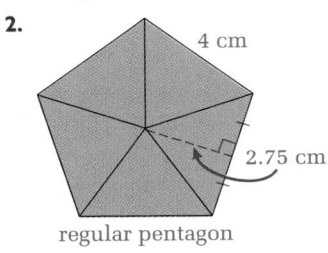
4 cm / 2.75 cm
regular pentagon

3.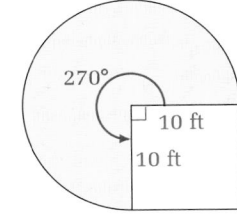
270° / 10 ft / 10 ft

Large Slice
9 in.

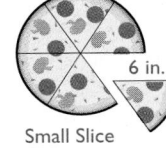
Small Slice
6 in.

4. Marie Li wants to put a string of lights around the outside edge of a balcony with the dimensions of the shaded part of the figure in Exercise 3. About how long a string of lights does she need?

5. At Luca's Pizza, you can buy a large slice for $1.35 or a small slice for $1.00. Compare the areas of the slices shown. Which is a better deal? Explain.

6. Describe at least two different methods for finding the area of a regular hexagon. Include sketches with your descriptions. For each method, tell what dimensions you need to know.

7. A small globe has a 12 in. diameter. A large globe has an 18 in. diameter. Drew assumes that the volume of the large globe is 1.5 times the volume of the small globe. Why might Drew make this assumption? Is he correct? Explain.

8. **a.** A manufacturer decides to decrease the height of a can by 10% so that it will hold 10% less. Will this work?

   b. Will the surface area of the new can be 10% smaller than the surface area of the original can? Explain.

8.9 cm
10.8 cm

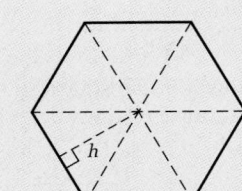

Circle Relationships

For use after Section 8-6

In Section 1-5 you made some conjectures about geometric figures based on several observations. Many properties of circles can be discovered by using inductive reasoning.

> **Sample**

> ┈┈┈┈┈┈┈┈┈**Focus**
>
> **Make and test conjectures**
> **about chords and angles.**

Jake drew a circle and marked two points, *A* and *B*. He then drew several angles through points *A* and *B* with vertex *X* also on the circle.

Jake measured each angle and then conjectured that all angles formed in this way have the same measure. Test Jake's conjecture.

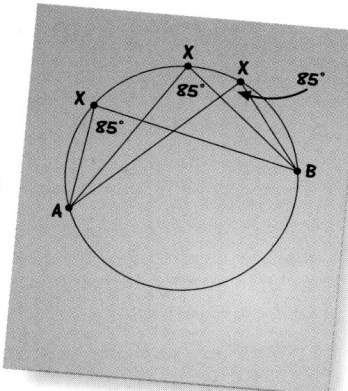

Sample Response

Repeat Jake's procedure on a different circle, using different points.

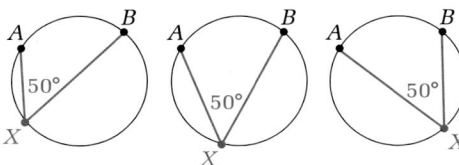

Sometimes *m∠AXB* = 50°.

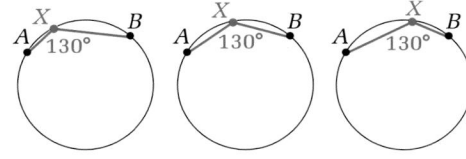

Sometimes *m∠AXB* = 130°.

Jake's conjecture is false. The angles do not always have the same measure.

> **Talk it Over**
>
> 1. Lucy notices that the two angle measures in the Sample add up to 180°. Make and test a conjecture based on Lucy's observation.
>
> 2. Explain why a test of a conjecture is not the same as a proof.

Appendix 2

675

Answers to Talk it Over

1. Answers may vary. An example is given. Any two angles passing through two points on a circle with their vertices on the circle are either equal or are supplementary angles. You can test this conjecture by drawing and measuring more examples.

2. When you test a conjecture, you might not test the case that turns out to be an exception. Once you prove a conjecture using logic, postulates, definitions, given information, or proven theorems as justification, it is not possible to find a counterexample.

Answers to Exercises and Problems

1. a–c. The perpendicular bisectors of two chords drawn on the same circle intersect at the center of the circle. Answers should show that this conjecture has been tested for various examples.

2. a–d. The midpoints of two chords of equal length drawn on the same circle are the same distance from the center of the circle. Answers should show that this conjecture has been tested for various examples.

A-2 Exercises and Problems

A *chord* is a line segment that connects two points on a circle. In Exercises 1–4, you will explore some properties of chords.

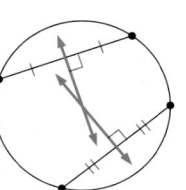

1. **a.** Draw a circle with a radius of about 5 cm. Then draw two chords that do not intersect.

   b. Construct the perpendicular bisector of each chord. Make the bisectors long enough to intersect.

   c. Make and test a conjecture about the intersection point of the perpendicular bisectors of two chords.

2. **a.** Draw a circle with a radius of about 5 cm. Then draw two chords of equal length that do not intersect.

   b. Use your results from Exercise 1 to find the center of the circle.

   c. Measure the distance from the midpoint of each chord to the center of the circle.

   d. Make and test a conjecture about the distance from the center of a circle to chords of equal length.

3. Use your results from Exercise 1 to devise a method for finding the center of a circular object, such as a jar lid or a plate. Carry out your plan by finding the centers of two or three objects. Evaluate how well your plan worked.

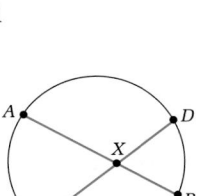

4 TECHNOLOGY Use geometric drawing software.

   a. Draw a circle with a radius between 3 cm and 6 cm. Then draw two chords that intersect each other. Label the chords as shown.

   b. Measure and record the lengths of $\overline{AX}$, $\overline{BX}$, $\overline{CX}$, and $\overline{DX}$.

   c. Find the products $AX \cdot BX$ and $CX \cdot DX$. Make and test a conjecture about these products.

5. Janine drew $\triangle PQR$ with its vertices on a circle as shown. Two of the vertices are endpoints of a diameter of the circle. She conjectured that all triangles drawn in this way are right triangles.

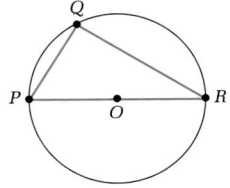

   a. Test Janine's conjecture.

   b. Janine drew line segment OQ and marked the diagram as shown. How does she know that $\triangle POQ$ and $\triangle ROQ$ are isosceles triangles?

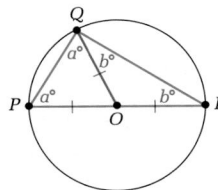

   c. How can Janine prove that $\triangle PQR$ is a right triangle? (*Hint:* Use what you know about the sum of the angles of $\triangle PQR$.)

Answers to Exercises and Problems

3. Answers may vary. Methods should make use of the fact that the perpendicular bisectors of chords drawn on the same circle intersect at the center of the circle.

4. **a–c.** The products $AX \cdot BX$ and $CX \cdot DX$ are equal. Answers should show that this conjecture has been tested for various examples.

5. **a.** Answers should show that Janine's conjecture has been tested for various examples.

   b. $\overline{OP}$, $\overline{OQ}$, and $\overline{OR}$ are all radii of the circle, so they have the same length. $\triangle POQ$ has two sides equal, and $\triangle ROQ$ has two sides equal, so they are both isosceles.

   c. The sum of the angles of $\triangle PQR = 180°$, so $a° + a° + b° + b° = 2(a° + b°) = 180°$. Thus, $a° + b°$ must equal $90°$. Since $m\angle PQR = a° + b°$, it is a right angle, and $\triangle PQR$ is a right triangle.

Glossary

absolute value (p. 34) The distance that a number is from zero on a number line. An absolute value is a positive number or zero.
$$|-3| = 3 \quad |0| = 0 \quad |3| = 3$$

alternate interior angles (p. 416) Two interior angles on opposite sides of a transversal.

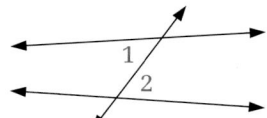

Angles 1 and 2 are alternate interior angles.

altitude of a triangle (p. 481) A segment drawn from a vertex perpendicular to the line containing the opposite side.

altitude
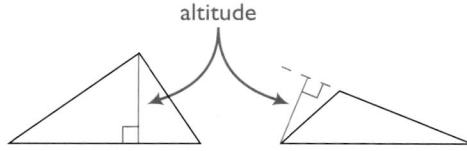

angle bisector (p. 468) A ray that begins at the vertex and divides the angle into two angles equal in measure.

angle bisector
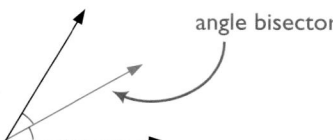

axis of rotation (p. 565) The line around which a plane figure is rotated to make a space figure.

biased sample (p. 17) A sample that over-represents or under-represents part of the population.

biconditional (p. 386) The conjunction of a true conditional and its true converse, usually written using the phrase "if and only if."

binomial (p. 351) An expression that can be written as the sum of two monomials.

binomial experiment (p. 339) An experiment with a fixed number of independent trials. For each trial there are two mutually exclusive, independent outcomes, success and failure. Each trial has the same $P(\text{success})$, and $P(\text{success}) + P(\text{failure}) = 1$.

binomial theorem (p. 353) If n is a positive integer, then $(a + b)^n$ is
$(_nC_0)a^n b^0 + (_nC_1)a^{n-1}b^1 + (_nC_2)a^{n-2}b^2 + \dots + (_nC_{n-2})a^2 b^{n-2} + (_nC_{n-1})a^1 b^{n-1} + (_nC_n)a^0 b^n$
where the coefficients $(_nC_r)$ are combinations found in the nth row of Pascal's triangle. *See also* Pascal's triangle.

boundary line (p. 654) A line that is the edge of a region of a graph of a linear inequality on a coordinate plane.

box-and-whisker plot (p. 636) A method for displaying the median, quartiles, and extremes of a data set.

center of dilation (p. 159) The point where lines drawn from corresponding points on the original figure and its image meet. *See also* dilation.

chain rule (p. 380) A rule of logic which states: If p is true, then q is true. If q is true, then r is true. Therefore, if p is true, then r is true.

cluster sample (p. 17) A sample that consists of items in a particular group.

coefficient (p. 352) A number multiplied by a variable in a term of an expression.

co-interior angles (p. 416) Two interior angles on the same side of a transversal.

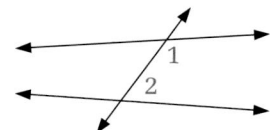

Angles 1 and 2 are co-interior angles.

combination (p. 329) A selection made from a group of items when order is not important. The number of ways to select r items from a group of n items is found in row n, diagonal r, of Pascal's triangle.

complementary angles (p. 655) Two angles whose measures have the sum 90°.

Glossary

complementary events (p. 312) Two mutually exclusive events that together include all possibilities.

complex number (p. 225) A number of the form $a + bi$, where a and b are real numbers, and i is the imaginary unit $\sqrt{-1}$.

compound events (p. 320) Events made up of two or more events that can happen either at the same time or one after the other.

conclusion of an implication (p. 373) The *then* part of an *if-then* statement. *See also* implication.

conclusion of a logical argument (p. 380) A statement resulting from the premises of a logical argument.

conditional (p. 373) An *if-then* statement. *See also* implication.

congruent (p. 244) Having the same size and shape.

congruent triangles (p. 449) Two triangles whose vertices can be matched up so that corresponding parts (angles and sides) are equal in measure.

conjecture (p. 31) A statement, opinion, or conclusion based on observation.

conjunction (p. 367) Two statements connected by *and*. A conjunction is true when both statements are true.

consecutive angles (p. 419) In a polygon, two angles that share a side.

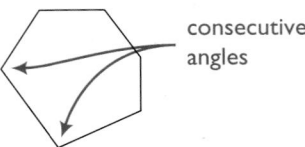

consecutive angles

consecutive sides (p. 244) In a polygon, two sides that share a vertex.

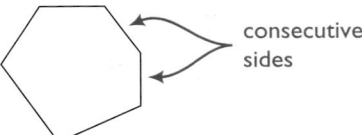

consecutive sides

consistent system (p. 136) A system of equations that has one or more solutions.

constant graph (p. 61) The graph of the function $y = c$ where c is any number.

convenience sample (p. 17) A sample that is chosen to make it easy to gather data.

converse (p. 39) A statement obtained by interchanging the *if* and *then* parts of an *if-then* statement.

corresponding angles (p. 416) Two angles in corresponding positions relative to two lines and their transversal.

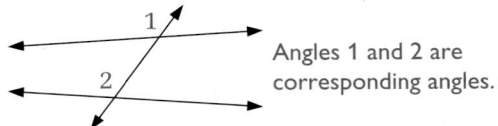

Angles 1 and 2 are corresponding angles.

counterexample (p. 33) An example that shows that a statement is not always true.

cross section (p. 559) The intersection of a plane and a space figure.

cubic function (p. 528) A polynomial function of degree three.

database (p. 365) An organized listing of information.

decay graph (p. 61) The graph of a decreasing function.

deductive reasoning (p. 38) Using facts, definitions, logic, and accepted rules and properties to reach conclusions.

degree of a polynomial (p. 507) The largest exponent of a polynomial.

dependent events (p. 320) A sequence of events where one event affects another event.

diagonal (p. 281) A segment joining two nonconsecutive vertices of a polygon.

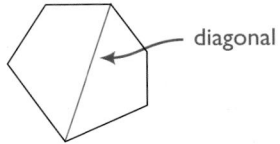

diagonal

diameter of a sphere (p. 85) A segment that joins two points on the surface of the sphere and passes through the center. Also, the length of such a segment.

dilation (p. 159) A transformation that results in a reduction or an enlargement of a figure. Lines drawn through the corresponding points on the original figure and its image meet at a point called the *center of dilation*.

dimensions of a matrix (p. 151) The number of rows and columns of a matrix. *See also* matrix.

direct argument (p. 380) A rule of logic that states: If p is true, then q is true. p is true. Therefore, q is true.

direct variation (p. 70) A linear function of the form $y = kx$, $k \neq 0$, where k is the *variation constant*.

direct variation with the cube (p. 94) A function of the form $y = kx^3$, $k \neq 0$, where y varies directly with x^3, and k is the *variation constant*.

direct variation with the square (p. 92) A function of the form $y = kx^2$, $k \neq 0$, where y varies directly with x^2, and k is the *variation constant*. The graph of this function is a *parabola*.

discriminant (p. 222) The expression under the radical sign of the quadratic formula, $b^2 - 4ac$. *See also* quadratic formula.

disjunction (p. 367) Two statements connected by *or*. A disjunction is true when at least one of the statements is true.

domain (p. 62) All the values of the control variable of a function. *See also* function.

double zero (p. 529) When a cubic function has a squared factor, the function has a double zero. At one point where $y = 0$, the graph of the function will just touch the x-axis but will not cross it. *See also* zero.

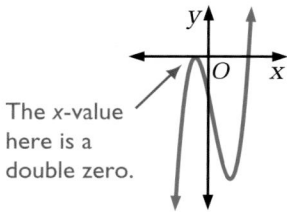

The x-value here is a double zero.

doubling period (p. 106) The amount of time it takes for a quantity to double.

element of a matrix (p. 151) Each entry in a matrix. *See also* matrix.

equiangular triangle (p. 474) A triangle in which all angles are equal in measure.

equidistant (p. 574) At the same distance.

event (p. 296) A set of outcomes. *See also* outcome.

expanded form (p. 351) When an expression is written as a sum, it is in expanded form.

experimental probability (p. 637) In an experiment, the ratio of the number of times an event occurs to the number of times the experiment is performed.

exponential decay (p. 108) A decreasing exponential function. An example is the function $y = a\left(\frac{1}{2}\right)^x$, $a \neq 0$, used to model halving.

exponential form (p. 100) When an expression is written as a power or a product of powers, it is in exponential form.

exponential function (p. 107) A function of the form $y = ab^x$, where $a > 0$, $b > 0$, and $b \neq 1$.

exponential growth (p. 107) An increasing exponential function. An example is the function $y = a \cdot 2^x$, $a \neq 0$, used to model doubling.

exterior angle (pp. 33, 442) An angle formed by extending a side of a polygon.

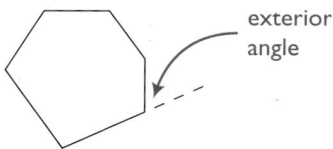

exterior angle

extraneous solution (p. 521) A solution of a simplified equation that is not a solution of the original equation.

factored form (p. 351) When an expression is written as a product of its factors, it is in factored form.

factorial (p. 304) The symbol ! after a positive integer. It means the product of all the positive integers from 1 to that number.

$$7! = 7 \cdot 6 \cdot 5 \cdot 4 \cdot 3 \cdot 2 \cdot 1$$

$(0! = 1$ by definition.$)$

fitted line (p. 632) A line that passes as close to as many data points on a scatter plot as possible.

flow proof (p. 396) A proof written as a diagram using arrows to show the connections between statements. Numbers written over the arrows refer to a numbered list of the justifications for the statements.

frequency (p. 633) The number of times an event or data item occurs within an interval.

frequency table (p. 633) A table that displays the exact number of data items in an interval.

function (p. 60) A relationship where there is only one value of the dependent variable for each value of the control variable. All the values of the control variable are known as the *domain*. All the values of the dependent variable over the domain are known as the *range*.

geometric mean (p. 483) If a, b, and x are positive numbers, and $\frac{a}{x} = \frac{x}{b}$, then x is the geometric mean between a and b.

geometric probability (p. 639) Probability based on areas and lengths.

growth graph (p. 61) The graph of an increasing function.

half-life (p. 108) The amount of time it takes for a quantity to divide in half.

Glossary

horizontal intercept (p. 122) The *x*-coordinate of the point where a graph intersects the *x*-axis. Also called *x*-intercept.

hyperbola (p. 77) The graph of a function of the form $y = \frac{k}{x}$, $x \neq 0$ and $k \neq 0$. *See also* inverse variation.

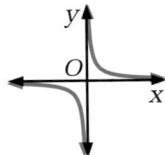

hypothesis (p. 373) The *if* part of an *if-then* statement. *See also* implication.

image (p. 159) The result of a transformation.

imaginary unit (p. 225) The number *i* such that $i = \sqrt{-1}$ and $i^2 = -1$.

implication (p. 373) A statement with an *if* part and a *then* part. The *if* part is the *hypothesis* and the *then* part is the *conclusion*. Also called a *conditional*.

inconsistent system (p. 136) A system of equations that has no solutions.

independent events (p. 320) A sequence of events where one event does not affect another event.

indirect argument (p. 380) A rule of logic which states: If *p* is true, then *q* is true. *q* is not true. Therefore, *p* is not true.

inductive reasoning (p. 31) A method of reasoning in which a conjecture is made based on several observations.

invalid argument (p. 381) An argument that does not use rules of logic.

inverse matrices (p. 174) Two 2×2 matrices whose product is the matrix $\begin{bmatrix} 1 & 0 \\ 0 & 1 \end{bmatrix}$. The symbol A^{-1} is used to represent the inverse of matrix *A*.

inverse variation (pp. 76, 77) A function of the form $xy = k$, or $y = \frac{k}{x}$, $x \neq 0$ and $k \neq 0$, where *y* varies inversely with *x*, and *k* is the *variation constant*. The graph of this function is a *hyperbola*.

isosceles triangle (p. 473) A triangle with two sides equal in measure.

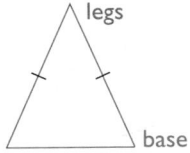

kite (p. 244) A quadrilateral with two pairs of consecutive sides equal in measure. These pairs do not have a side in common.

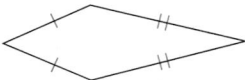

linear graph (p. 60) The graph of a linear function.

linear inequality (p. 654) An inequality whose graph on a coordinate plane is bounded by a line called a *boundary line*.

linear system (p. 121) Two or more linear equations stating relationships between the same variable quantities.

mathematical model (p. 67) An equation, table, graph, function, or inequality that represents a real-life situation.

matrix (p. 151) An arrangement of numbers, called *elements*, in rows and columns.

matrix equation (p. 175) An equation with a matrix term.

mean (p. 635) In a data set, the sum of the data divided by the number of items.

median (p. 635) In a data set, the middle number or the average of the two middle numbers when the data are arranged in numerical order.

midpoint (p. 259) The point halfway between the endpoints of a segment.

mode (p. 635) The most frequently occurring item, or items, in a data set.

monomial (p. 206) A number, a variable, or the product of a number and one or more variables.

mutually exclusive events (p. 311) Two events that cannot happen at the same time.

negation (p. 367) A statement involving *not*.

odds against (p. 314) The ratio of unfavorable outcomes to favorable outcomes of an event. The outcomes must be equally likely.

odds in favor (p. 314) The ratio of favorable outcomes to unfavorable outcomes of an event. The outcomes must be equally likely.

order of operations (p. 640) A set of rules that states the order in which you simplify an expression.

***or* rule** (p. 380) A rule of logic which states: *p* is true or *q* is true. *p* is not true. Therefore, *q* is true.

ordered triple (p. 579) The ordered group of three numbers, (*x*, *y*, *z*), associated with each point in a three-dimensional coordinate system.

Student Resources

outcome (p. 296) One possible result. When each outcome of an event has the same chance of happening, the outcomes are *equally likely*. A set of outcomes is an *event*.

parabola (pp. 92, 187) The graph of $y = ax^2 + bx + c$, $a \neq 0$. The point where the curve turns is either the highest point or the lowest point and is called the *vertex*. *See also* direct variation with the square.

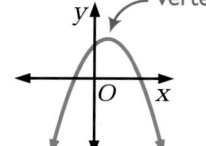 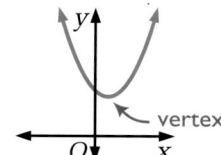

paragraph proof (p. 396) A proof whose statements and justifications are written in paragraph form.

parallelogram (p. 245) A quadrilateral with two pairs of parallel sides.

parametric equations (p. 542) Equations where two variables are expressed in terms of a third variable. This third variable is called the *parameter*.

Pascal's triangle (p. 334) A triangular arrangement of numbers. The number in row n, diagonal r, is the combination $_nC_r$. When you expand $(a + b)^n$, the coefficients are the numbers in row n. *See also* binomial theorem.

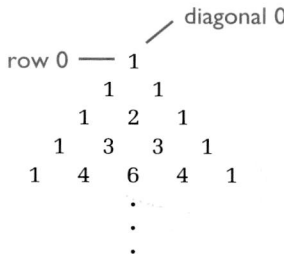

permutation (p. 304) The arrangement of any number of items in a definite order.

perpendicular bisector (p. 475) A line, ray, or segment that bisects a segment and is perpendicular to it.

plane (p. 559) A flat surface that extends without ending and has no thickness.

plane figure (p. 565) A two-dimensional figure.

polynomial (p. 507) An expression that can be written as a monomial or a sum of monomials. The monomials are called the *terms* of the polynomial.

polynomial equation (p. 507) An equation that can be written with a polynomial as one side and 0 as the other side.

population (p. 3) An entire group.

postulate (p. 402) A statement assumed to be true without proof.

premise (p. 380) A given statement in an argument. The resulting statement is called the *conclusion*.

probability tree diagram (p. 346) A tree diagram with the probability of each branch written on that branch.

pure imaginary number (p. 225) A number of the form bi, where i is the imaginary unit $\sqrt{-1}$ and b is any real number except zero.

Pythagorean theorem (p. 661) If the length of the hypotenuse of a right triangle is c and the lengths of the legs are a and b, then $c^2 = a^2 + b^2$.

quadratic equation (p. 201) Any equation that can be written in the form $0 = ax^2 + bx + c$, $a \neq 0$.

quadratic formula (p. 215) The formula
$$x = -\frac{b}{2a} \pm \frac{\sqrt{b^2 - 4ac}}{2a}, \text{ for the solutions of the}$$
equation $0 = ax^2 + bx + c$, $a \neq 0$.

quadratic function (p. 187) Any function that can be written in the form $y = ax^2 + bx + c$, $a \neq 0$.

quadratic system (p. 231) Two or more quadratic functions in the same variables.

quadrilateral (p. 245) A polygon with four sides.

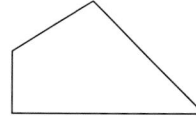

radical form (p. 100) When an expression is written using the symbol $\sqrt{\ }$, it is in radical form.

radius of a sphere (p. 85) A segment from the center of a sphere to its surface. Also, the length of such a segment.

random sample (p. 17) A sample in which each member of the population has an equally likely chance of being selected, and the members of the sample are chosen independently

range of a data set (p. 635) The difference between the extremes in a data set.

range of a function (p. 62) All the values of the dependent variable over the domain. *See also* function.

rational equation (p. 508) An equation with only rational expressions on both sides.

rational expression (p. 508) An expression that can be written as the quotient of two polynomials.

real number (p. 225) A complex number of the form $a + bi$, where a is either a rational or irrational number and $b = 0$.

reciprocals (p. 174) Two numbers whose product is 1.

rectangle (p. 245) A quadrilateral with four right angles.

reflection (p. 266) A transformation involving flipping a figure over a line called *the line of reflection*.

remote interior angles (p. 442) In a triangle, the two angles that are not at the vertex where an exterior angle has been drawn.

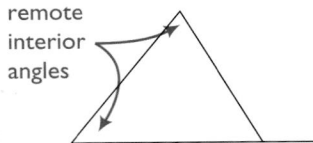

rhombus (p. 244) A quadrilateral with four sides of equal measure.

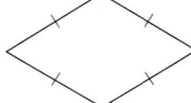

right angle (p. 655) An angle whose measure is 90°.

rotation (p. 267) A transformation involving turning a figure clockwise or counterclockwise around a point called *the center of rotation*.

sample (p. 3) A subset of the population on which a study or an experiment is being done.

sample space (p. 320) A set of all possible outcomes.

scalar multiplication (p. 152) Multiplication of a matrix by a number. The product matrix is the result of multiplying each element by the number.

scale factor (p. 159) The ratio of a length on an image to the corresponding length on the original figure of a dilation.

segment bisector (p. 468) A ray, line, or segment that divides a segment into two parts of equal measure.

similar triangles (p. 449) Two triangles whose vertices can be matched up so that corresponding angles are equal and corresponding sides are in proportion.

simulation (p. 10) Using an experiment based on a real-life situation to answer a question.

slope (p. 68) The measure of the steepness of a line given by the ratio of rise to run for any two points on the line.

slope-intercept form (p. 68) A linear equation written in the form $y = mx + b$, where m represents the slope and b represents the vertical intercept.

solution of a system of equations (p. 122) An ordered pair whose coordinates make all equations of the system true.

solution region (p. 124) The graph of the points that make all the inequalities of a system of inequalities true.

space figure (p. 557) A three-dimensional figure.

sphere (pp. 84, 592) The set of points in space that are equidistant from a point.

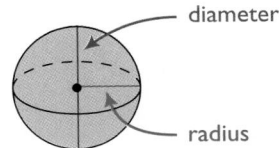

square (p. 245) A quadrilateral with four right angles and four sides of equal measure.

square root (p. 403) One of two equal factors of a number.

standard form of a quadratic function (p. 187) A quadratic function written in the form $y = ax^2 + bx + c$, $a \neq 0$.

standard form of a quadratic equation (p. 201) A quadratic equation written in the form $0 = ax^2 + bx + c$, $a \neq 0$.

standard form of a polynomial (p. 507) A polynomial written so that the term with the highest exponent is first, the term with the second highest exponent is second, and so on.

standard position (p. 275) The position of a polygon on a coordinate plane such that one vertex is at the origin and one side is on the *x*-axis. This placement makes calculations of slope and length easier.

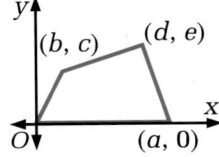

Student Resources

stem-and-leaf plot (p. 634) A display of data where each number is represented by a *stem* and a *leaf.*

straight angle (p. 655) An angle whose measure is 180°.

stratified random sample (p. 17) A sample chosen by dividing a population into subgroups with each population member in only one subgroup, and then selecting members randomly from each subgroup.

supplementary angles (p. 655) Two angles whose measures have the sum 180°.

systematic sample (p. 17) A sample chosen by using an ordered list of a population and then selecting members systematically from the list.

system of equations (p. 121) Two or more equations that state relationships between the same variable quantities.

system of inequalities (p. 124) Two or more inequalities that state relationships between the same variable quantities.

theorem (p. 408) A statement that is proven.

theoretical probability (p. 638) When all outcomes of an experiment are equally likely, the probability of an event is the ratio of favorable outcomes to the number of possible outcomes.

transformation (p. 159) A change in size or position made to a figure.

translation (pp. 161, 267) A transformation that moves each point of a figure the same distance in the same direction.

transversal (p. 416) A line that intersects two lines in the same plane at two different points.

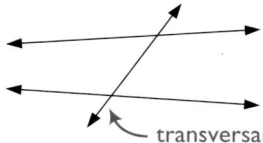

transversal

trapezoid (p. 245) A quadrilateral with one pair of parallel sides.

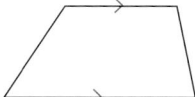

tree diagram (pp. 11, 296) A diagram that links items in different categories in all possible ways.

trial (p. 10) One run of an experiment.

trigonometric ratios (p. 659) The *sine, cosine,* and *tangent ratios* of an angle.

trinomial (p. 206) An expression that can be written as the sum of three monomials.

triple zero (p. 529) When a cubic function has a cubed factor, the function has a triple zero. The graph will flatten out and cross the *x*-axis one time only. *See also* zero.

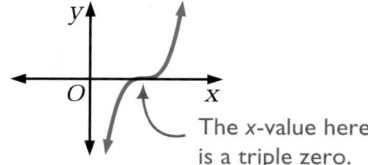

The *x*-value here is a triple zero.

two-column proof (p. 396) A proof written in two columns. Statements are listed in one column and justifications are listed in the other column.

valid argument (p. 380) An argument that uses rules of logic.

variation constant (p. 70) The nonzero constant *k* in a direct variation. *See also* direct variation.

Venn diagram (p. 38) A diagram used to show relationships between groups.

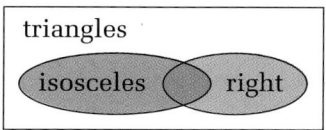

vertex of a parabola (p. 188) The maximum or minimum point of a parabola. *See also* parabola.

vertical angles (p. 410) Two angles formed by intersecting lines and facing in opposite directions.

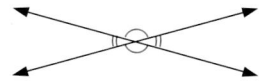

vertical intercept (p. 68) The *y*-coordinate of a point where a graph intersects with the *y*-axis. Also called *y*-intercept.

x-intercept (p. 189) The *x*-coordinate of a point where a graph intersects the *x*-axis (where *y* = 0). Also called a *horizontal intercept.*

y-intercept (p. 189) The *y*-coordinate of a point where a graph intersects the *y*-axis (where *x* = 0). Also called a *vertical intercept.*

zero of a function (p. 529) A value of the control variable of a function that makes the dependent variable equal 0.

zero-product property (p. 209) When a product of factors is zero, one or the more of the factors must be zero. If *ab* = 0, then *a* = 0 or *b* = 0.

Index

Student Resources

Student Resources

Student Resources

Index

Credits

DESIGN

Book Design: Two Twelve Associates, Inc.
Cover Design: McDougal Littell Design Department
Electronic Technical Art: American Composition & Graphics, Inc.

ACKNOWLEDGMENTS

20 From *The Crystal Desert*, by David G. Campbell. Boston: Houghton Mifflin Company, 1992. **50** From *The Phantom Tollbooth*, by Norton Juster. New York: Bullseye Books published by Alfred A. Knopf, Inc., 1961. **89** From *Journey to the Centre of the Earth*, by Jules Verne, translated by Robert Baldick. New York: Penguin Books, 1984. **220** From "An Aerial Reconnaissance" in *The Real Münchhausen*, retold by Angelita von Münchhausen, illustrated by Harry Carter. Copyright © 1960 by Angelita von Münchhausen. Copyright by Devin-Adair, Publishers, Inc., Old Greenwich, Connecticut, 06870. All rights reserved. **247** From *Our Town*, by Thorton Wilder. New York: HarperCollins, Publishers, 1957. **333** "The Old Method" by Chu Shih-Chieh. Originally appeared in a Chinese book entitled *Precious Mirror of the Four Elements* around A.D. 1303. **342** From *Rosencrantz & Guildenstern Are Dead* by Tom Stoppard. New York: Gove Press, Inc., 1967. **369** Source of data: Museum of Fine Arts, Boston, Massachusetts **378** From *The Andromeda Strain*, by Michael Crichton. New York: Dell Publishing, 1969. **383** From "A Case of Identity," by Arthur Conan Doyle. Originally appeared in Arthur Conan Doyle's *The Adventures of Sherlock Holmes*, published in 1892 by George Newnes, Limited. First U.S. edition also published in 1892. **446** "Cuadrados Y Angulos," from *De El Duce Daño*, by Alfonsina Storni. Buenos Aires: Sociedad Editora Latino America, 1988. **562** Adapted from *Global Atlas* published by Gage Educational Publishing Company. **563** From *Flatland, a Romance of Many Dimensions*, by Edwin A. Abbott. Originally published in 1884 by Seeley & Company, Ltd., London. **595** From "Time and Space," by Robin Mandel. Originally appeared in USM Today, published by the University School of Milwaukee, Summer 1993. **576** Adapted from "Figure 23: Sound Analysis" from *The Relationship Between Culture and Urban Forms in a Swahili Town* by Seyed Mohamed Maulana, a thesis submitted in 1988 to the University of Washington, Seattle, Washington.

STOCK PHOTOGRAPHY

vii Superstock; **ix** Peabody Essex Museum of Salem, MA. Photo by Mark Sexton.; **xi** © 1977 Robert Caputo/Aurora (t); Sabah Collection, Kuwait National Museum, Courtesy Aramco Services Co. (b); Photo by Oskar Prochnow, from *Formenkunst der Natur: Bildtafeln und Einfuhring,* published by Ernst Wasmuth Verlag, © 1934 (m); **xii** Glenn Dean/Renard Represents; **xiii** © Steve Nelson (b); Warren Morgen/Westlight (t); **xxvi** Coco McCoy/Rainbow (bl); ©

Earth Scenes/Mickey Gibson (br); Anthropology Dept., University of Arizona (tl); Pierre Mion/National Geographic Society (tr); **1** Richard Pasley/Stock Boston (t); © Alice Billings (bl); Mandana MacPherson/Used Rubber U.S.A. (br); Courtesy: Deja Shoes (m); **2** Patricia J. Bruno/Positive Images (b); **3** Wide World Photos; **5** Stamp Design © 1993 United States Postal Service, photo Wide World Photos; **6** Courtesy Michigan Biotechnology Institute; photo by Leavenworth Photography, Lansing, MI. (b); **7** National Archives (l); View of Thieving Lane, Now Bow Street, pub. 1807 (print) Royal Academy of Art Library, London/The Bridgeman Art Library (b); **10** Glenn Dean/Renard Represents; **12** The Bettmann Archive; **14** © Barrie Rokeach; **15** Dan McCoy/Rainbow; **20** © Earth Scenes/Doug Allan; **21** Philip Habib/Tony Stone Images/Chicago Inc.; **23** Warren Morgen/Westlight; **25** Superstock; **27** Copyright © 1993 NBA Properties, Inc. All rights reserved.; **28** Peter Menzel/Stock Boston; Bob Daemmrich/The Image Works; Stuart Franklin/Magnum Photos; Bryan Peterson/The Stock Market; **30** Charles Gupton/Stock Boston; **31** Bob Daemmrich (r); **36** Covent Garden: with St. Paul's Church by Nebot, Balthasar (fl. 1730–c.65), Guildhall Art Gallery, Corporation of London/The Bridgeman Art Library (l); E.W. Gilbert, "Pioneer Maps of Health and Disease in England," Geographical Journal, 124 (1958), 172–183. (r); **42** © Howard M. Paul; **48** L. Villota/The Stock Market; **53** Bob Daemmrich/Stock Boston; **56** © Arthur M. Greene (t); **56–57** Rod Planck/Photo Researchers, Inc. (b); **57** Gayle Dana/Desert Research Institute (bl); © Boyd Norton (br); **58** © Peter Essick; Courtesy Dept. of Parks and Recreation, California State Park System. (l); **59** Smithsonian Institution (bl); © David Jensen (mr); **62** Walter Hodges/Allstock; **65** Fotopic Int'l/Stock Imagery; **67** Charles Gupton/Stock Boston; **69** Bob Daemmrich/The Image Works; **73** © Nordic Track, the world's best aerobic exerciser. (tm); **74** Liane Enkelis/ Mono Lake Committee (br); Georg Gerster/Comstock; **78** © 1990 Robert A. Tyrrell; **80** M.P. Kahl/Photo Researchers, Inc. (br); © Animals Animals/Geoff Kidd (br); **81** Courtesy Casio Inc. (mr); Mark Burnett/ Stock Boston (tl); **83** Bob Daemmrich/Stock Boston; **85** John Biever/Sports Illustrated; **86** © 1992 Mickey Pfleger; **87** Superstock; **88** From *Tents, Architecture of the Nomads* by Torvald Faegre, Bantam Doubleday Dell (br); David Rosenberg/Allstock (m); David Hiser/Tony Stone Images/Chicago Inc. (t); **93** © Steve Powell/Allsport (br); © Duomo 1991 (l); **94** Glen Allison/Tony Stone Images/Chicago Inc.; **96** Nick Gunderson/Allstock; **97** RKO (Courtesy Kobal Collection); **98** Comstock; **100** Photo reprinted courtesy of Texas Instruments, Inc. All Rights Reserved.; **101** Togo International (m); **103** John Lund/Tony Stone Images/Chicago Inc.; **104** © Larry Ford; **106** Michael Mu Po Shum/Tony Stone Images; **107** From *The Craft of the Japanese Sword* by Leon and Hiroko Kapp and Yoshinda Yoshihara. Photographed by Tom Kishida.

Credits

Levi Strauss & Co. Archives (br); © Earth Scenes/Holt Studios (bl); Courtesy of Wham-O (br); **429** © Michael Freeman (bl); Wm N. Fish/U.S. First (r & t); **430** U.S. Dept. of the Interior, National Park Service, Edison National Historic Site.; **435** © David Pelly; **436** Drawing by Oscar Niemeyer, copyright © Fundacao Oscar Niemeyer, Rio de Janeiro; **437** Courtesy of the Queens Borough Public Library (t); Photo courtesy of the Collection of Winifred Latimer Norman and the Queens Borough Public Library. (t); **438** Spencer Jones/FPG International (b); Courtesy Vogue. Copyright © 1926 (renewed 1954) by the Conde Nast Publications, Inc. (t); **439** The Science Museum, London, England. From the book Flying Machine published by Alfred A. Knopf, Inc., 1990.; **445** Detail from a studio art quilt, Thinking of Winter. © Carol H. Gersen 1984 Photo Credit: David Caras; **446** Nemesio Antúnez, New York, New York 10008, 1967. Oil on canvas, 22 x 24". Courtesy Courturier Gallery, Stamford, CT and Los Angeles, CA.; **448** Illustration © 1988 by David Macaulay from *The Way Things Work*. Reprinted by permission of Houghton Mifflin Company. All rights reserved.; **449** Don & Pat Valenti/Tony Stone Images/Chicago Inc.; **453** © Margaret Courtney-Clarke; **454** Scala/Art Resource; **455** Robert Semeniuk/The Stock Market; **456** Sabah Collection, Kuwait National Museum. Courtesy Aramco Services Co. (t); **460** © M. Courtney-Clarke; **465** © David Muench; **466** Vince Streano/Tony Stone Images/Chicago Inc. (l); © Gary Braasch (r); **469** Tony Craddock/Photo Researchers, Inc.; **471** Tom Bean/The Stock Market; **472** Photo by Oskar Prochnow, from *Formenkunst der Nature: Bildrafeln und Einfuhring*, published by Ernst Wasmuth Verlag, © 1934.; (c) 1977 Robert Caputo/Aurora (t); **473** Frank Viola/Comstock; **476** © Animals Animals/Fred Whitehead; **479** James D. Nations/D. Donne Bryant Stock; **480** David Austen/Tony Stone Images/Chicago Inc.; **485** Dennis Hallinan/FPG International; © Alec Duncan (r); **486** Scala/Art Resource; **488** © Tony Freeman/Photo Edit; **489** Bertram Frauenknecht/Verlag Bertram Frauenknecht; **493** David C. Bitters/The Picture Cube (tr); © 1993 Alex Maclean/ Landslides (bl); Frank Siteman/Stock Boston (br); Superstock (tl); Bryan F. Peterson/The Stock Market (r); Peabody Essex Museum Salem, MA. Photo by Mark Sexton. (l); **498** © Robert & Linda Mitchell (r); © M. Courtney-Clarke (l); **502** Nathan Bilow/Allsport (l & t); Hans Brox/Scan-Foto (r & t); **502–503** Bruce Berman/The Stock Market (b); **503** Sovfoto/Eastfoto; © Paul Agoglia; **504** Peter Menzel/Stock Boston; **505** © Ernest H. Robl; **509** Stan Musilek/Gump's By Mail; **514** Vic Bider/ProFiles West; **515** © Dan Paul; **518** © Tony Duffy/Allsport; **525** Allsport; **535** Tvindkraft; **536** Richard Howard/Black Star; **540** Arthur Tress/Photo Researchers, Inc.; **542** Bill Cross/Maine Dept. of Inland Fisheries; **543** © Alex Maclean/Landslides; **544** Heintges/Allstock; **545** Tom Bean/The Stock Market (bl); © Alex Maclean/Landslides (r); **546** Southern Pacific Lines (r); NPS/Golden Spike National Historic Site (r); Tom Hardin/Golden Spike Nat. Hist. Site (br); **550** Edward L. Miller/Stock Boston; **552** Camerique/EP Jones (tl); **554** Doranne Jacobson (b); **555** Terry E. Eiler/Stock Boston (tl); Chad Slattery/Tony Stone Images/Chicago Inc. (inset); Jeff Isaac Greenberg/Photo Researchers, Inc. (inset); Jacques Jengoux/Tony Stone Images/Chicago Inc. (inset); Ian Murphy/Tony Stone Images/Chicago Inc. (br); D. Weiss © 1992 (bl); Michael Newman/Photo Edit (inset); Stephen R.

Swinburne/Stock Boston (tr); **557** Courtesy Mary Conlan (m & r); **561** Dan McCoy/Rainbow; **563** Terry Qing/FPG International; **565** David Ball/The Stock Market (br); Smithsonian Institution (bl); **569** Dan McCoy/Rainbow; **571** U.S. Geological Survey/Science Photo Library/Photo Researchers, Inc.; **572** U.S. Geological Survey/Science Photo Library/Photo Researchers, Inc.; **573** Natural History Museum, London; **575** David Madison/Duomo (tl); U.S. Geological Society (br); **576** © Boyd Norton; **578** Superstock (tl); Wendy Stone/Odyssey/Chicago (bl); Jack Fields/Photo Researchers, Inc. (br); **583** Florence Hawley Ellis Archive; **589** © Kenji Kerins; **595** © Jane Barclay Mandel; **596** David Schultz/Tony Stone Images/Chicago Inc.; **597** Jim Pickerell/FPG International

ASSIGNMENT PHOTOGRAPHERS
Kindra Clineff **xxvi** (t), **xv**, **16, 40, 41, 75, 84, 121, 127, 131, 137** (tl), **141, 144, 173, 180, 186** (r), **242, 243** (t), **256** (t,r), **280, 287, 297, 298, 306, 327, 329, 330, 331, 332, 358, 362, 367** (l), **367** (r), **383, 415, 420, 423, 424** (3rd from top), **428** (t), **456** (l), **456** (bl), **470, 492, 497, 508, 510, 523, 531, 539, 551, 561, 564, 565** (tm), **565** (tl), **565** (bl)   Jeffrey Dunn **557** (bl)   Steve Greenberg **vii, 266**   Richard Haynes **v, viii, x, xiv, xv, 2** (t), **4, 6** (t), **9, 19, 29, 31, 41, 45, 52, 91, 105, 113, 115, 126** (bl), **135, 137, 164, 165, 174, 178, 193, 206, 240, 243** (b), **254, 264, 267, 288–289, 294, 295, 302, 305, 316, 334** (l), **338** (l), **364, 379, 406, 421, 431, 433, 442, 464, 481, 506, 529, 533, 548, 552** (br), **558, 559, 581** (b), **581** (m), **584, 585, 590**   Ken Karp **292** (t)   Ken O'Donoghue **603**   Tony Scarpetta **150, 362** (t), **554** (t), **555** (m), **599**   Nancy Sheehan **viii, xv, 197, 221, 235**   Tracey Wheeler **v, 471, 549, 556**

ILLUSTRATIONS
Arnold Bombay **129, 131**   Jana Brenning **259, 262**   Dan Collins **428** (t)   Chris Costello **184, 400, 405** (b), **428** (m), **444** (tr), **486, 502**   Steve Cowden **413, 455** (t), **488, 496, 511**   Christine Czernota **xv, 52, 180** (r), **198, 204, 218** (m), **229, 235, 236, 287, 358, 563** (mr), **599**   DLF Group **56, 57, 59** (t), **111, 247, 374, 422, 506, 576, 591, 593, 597** (t), **597** (b)   Bob Doucet **479**   Nancy Chandler Edwards **11, 32, 35, 132, 146, 149, 172, 254, 261, 274** (b), **388, 405** (t), **444, 517, 518, 528, 533, 538**   Glasgow & Associates **263**   Robert Hynes **199**   Piotr Kaczmareck **248, 394, 444** (tl), **513, 519, 520, 524, 561, 596, 597**   Photo manipulations by Piotr Kaczmareck **505**   Joe Klim **240–241, 256** (m), **274** (t), **285, 286, 461, 480, 588**   Ellen Kuzdro **546**   Andrew Myer **35, 50, 119** (t), **128, 253, 272**   Steve Patricia **582** (br)   Deborah Perugi **119** (b), **456** (b), **465, 499**   Neil Pinchin **24, 38** (b), **47** (t), **49** (t), **51, 60, 61, 62, 63, 83, 89, 134, 140, 277, 328, 372, 399, 578, 581** (tr), **589, 673** (b), **674** (br), **675** (t)   Photo manipulations by Lisa Rahon **235, 379, 381, 386, 391, 392, 433, 435, 449, 465, 476, 489, 514, 541**   Patrice Rossi **494**   Krystyna Stasiak **43**   Rod Thomas **379**   George Ulrich **213** (t), **234** (bm)

TYPOGRAPHIC TITLES
Frank Loose Design **3, 9, 16, 23, 31, 38, 45, 59, 67, 75, 84, 91, 99, 105, 121, 129, 135, 142, 151, 159, 165, 174, 187, 193, 199, 206, 214, 222, 230, 243, 251, 259, 266, 274, 280, 295, 302, 310, 319, 328, 333, 338, 345, 351, 365, 373, 379, 386, 394, 401, 408, 415, 431, 439, 449, 458, 466, 472, 481, 489, 505, 513, 520, 528, 536, 541, 557, 565, 571, 578, 584, 591**

Selected Answers

Unit 1

Pages 3–5 Talk it Over

1. Answers may vary. An example is given. People may have expressed no preference for either design or wanted both issued as stamps. **2.** about 75%; about 25% **3.** Answers may vary. An example is given. Yes; both indicate that the young Elvis stamp is preferred by most people. **4.** Answers may vary. **5–7.** Answers may vary. Examples are given. **5.** They are easy to compile and compare. **6.** b; A larger sample can more accurately reflect the diversity in the student body. **7.** (1) Can the information you are looking for be found by asking a yes-no or multiple-choice question? (2) How should you word the survey questions? (3) How should you interpret the results? (4) What size sample group would give you reasonable results? (5) How should you choose your sample group?

Pages 6–8 Exercises and Problems

1. about 0.45% **3.** a sample **5. a.** Answers may vary. Two examples are given. Choose one response to complete each question. (1) I would be willing to pay an average percent of increase of $?$ for recycled paper products. (a) 0% (b) 3% (c) 6% (d) 9% (2) Which percent shows how much more you would be willing to pay for a product made from recycled plastic packaging? (a) 2% or less (b) 4% (c) 6% (d) 8% **b.** No. My questions would give results for only two products, not all four. **7.** about 7200 people **9.** about 45 chicks **18.** 2 **19.** $-\frac{1}{2}$

20. -24 **21.**

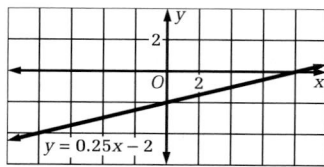

x	y
-8	-4
-4	-3
0	-2
4	-1
8	0

slope = 0.25; x-intercept = 8; y-intercept = -2

$y = 0.25x - 2$

22. $\frac{1}{6}$ **23.** $\frac{1}{2}$ **24.** $\frac{1}{3}$ **25.** 0

Pages 10–12 Talk it Over

1. Answers may vary, but should be reasonably close to 0.8. **2. a.** Yes; guessing on a true-false question involves two outcomes with equal probabilities, as does tossing a coin. **b.** No; spinning the spinner involves two outcomes with unequal probabilities. **c.** Yes; the possible outcomes (an even number or an odd number) have equal probabilities. **3.** less accurate **4.** There are only two possibilities: the light will be red or the light will not be red. The sum of the two probabilities is 1. $P(\text{red}) + P(\text{not red}) = 1$, so $P(\text{not red}) = 1 - P(\text{red}) = 1 - \frac{1}{3} = \frac{2}{3}$. **5.** No; you simply need an event with the same probability of getting a red light at the first traffic light. You could use any two numbers between 1 and 6.

Pages 12–15 Exercises and Problems

1. 25 trials; 100 trials; The greater the number of trials, the more accurate the results. **3. a.** Estimates may vary; about 60%. **b.** about 12 **c.** Answers may vary. **d.** Answers may vary. An example is given. No. A sample of 20 is quite small. **5.** No; that is much too small a sample. **7, 9.** Answers may vary. Answers are based on the results from Ex. 6. **7.** 0.4 **9.** 0.6 **13. a.** Answers may vary. Examples are given. Make a spinner and divide it into fourths. Mark $\frac{1}{4}$ "park close" and the other $\frac{3}{4}$ "park far." Then do trials to estimate the average time. **b.** about 1 out of 4 times **17.** about 113 mysteries **18.** $-5x + 5y + 7$ **19.** $12a^2 + 8b - 4ab$ **20.** $9n - 5mn$

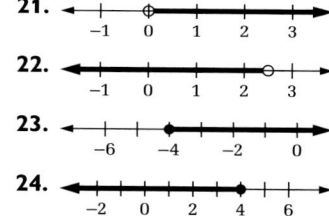

21.

22.

23.

24.

Page 18 Talk it Over

1. people in town who watch sports on TV but who did not attend the game or people who neither watch sports on TV nor attended the game. **2. a.** stratified random sample or cluster sample; Yes. Only one school and one classroom are represented, not all students from all grades in all schools. **b.** It would be better and less likely to be biased. There is the underlying assumption that all the food in all the buildings is identical. The method offers a better cross-section of the population. However, the use of the cafeteria must be equally distributed among the entire student population of the district. **3.** The school or the class may be all male or the sports director could have chosen all males by chance. **4–6.** Answers may vary. Examples are given. **4.** Make a list of the social security numbers of all the members of the population, and then select every 50th number. **5.** Ask the first 20 people exiting a movie theater what they thought of the movie. **6.** Ask the people in a corner of a restaurant to evaluate the food they ate for their meal.

Pages 20–22 Exercises and Problems
1. a. Answers may vary. Examples: random, convenience, stratified random, cluster, systematic
b. Descriptions may vary. An example is given. All of the methods involve choosing some smaller group to represent a larger group. The methods vary in how the members of the sample are related. The members may not be connected in any way or they may be connected by inclination or location, for example.
3. a. cluster **b.** teenagers who do not read the magazine **7.** Answers may vary. An example is given. He may choose several locations, collect samples from each, and compare the number of healthy amphipods to the total number. **9.** Answers may vary. An example is given. The sample is a convenience sample. Whether the sample is a random sample depends on how the lunch schedule is arranged at the school. The first 50 students may all be the same age or may all be in the same class. Also, teachers may also use the cafeteria and they would not be represented.
11, 13. For each type of sample, an example of a method for choosing the sample from a 250-word glossary is described. **11.** Open to a page. Choose the first 13 words on the page. **13.** Choose every tenth word. **15.** Answers may vary. An example is given. Assign each word in the glossary a number from 1 to n, where n is the number of words. Print each number on a piece of paper, mix the papers together in a bowl, and draw out 13 of them. Use the corresponding words in your sample. **19. a.** −1, 1
b. $\frac{2}{11} \approx 0.18$ **23.** Answers may vary. An example is given. Make a spinner divided into 8 sections. Shade one section for "below poverty level" and leave the other sections unshaded. Spin 50 times to approximate about 6 people below the poverty level.
24. $-72m^2$ **25.** $-30wxy$ **26.** $7x - 6$ **27.** between 6700 and 7300 people

Pages 23–24 Talk it Over
1–4. Answers may vary. Examples are given.
1. Both ask the same question. Both have an apparent built-in bias. The first raises the issue of personal civil rights, which might influence a positive response. The second raises the issue of public safety in a negative manner, perhaps influencing a negative response. **2.** Because of the issues raised in the answer to question 1, more "yes" answers might be expected to the first survey, more "no" answers to the second. **3.** Answers may vary. **4.** The survey should raise no issues other than the question at hand: "Should the city permit in-line skating on the sidewalk?" **5.** The choices in the box on the left are less precise. The phrases "some" and "not very many" have no exact meaning. **6. a.** Yes; No; No.
b. Yes; Yes; Yes.

Pages 26–29 Exercises and Problems
1. Answers may vary. It is reasonable to say that none of the questions is worded in such a way as to influence a response. **3, 5.** Answers may vary. Examples are given. **3.** Other questions might cover availability of sports programs, clubs, social activities, school facilities, availability and quality of food services, grading practices, or interaction between students and teachers. Questions: (5) How do you feel about the time allowed for each class period? (a) too long (b) never enough time (c) just right (d) occasionally not enough time (6) How do you feel about school lunches? (a) would like more variety of foods (b) usually can find something I like (c) always find something I like (d) never eat school lunches (7) How many extracurricular activities do you participate in? (a) 0 (b) 1 (c) 2 (d) 3 or more (8) How many sports activities do you participate in? (a) 0 (b) 1 (c) 2 (d) 3 or more **5.** The sample may be biased (that is, it was not randomly selected). Those interpreting the results may decide to ignore input from those in the sample who are in their first year at the school. The answers to Question 4 might be grouped into "satisfied" (those who selected "a") and "dissatisfied" (those who selected any other choice). **7.** Answers may vary. An example is given. If the question suggests a response conveying dissatisfaction, you may be more likely to get that response. For example, "Do you think the school requires too much homework?" would be biased. **9, 11, 13.** Answers may vary. Examples are given. **9.** People who choose not to participate may have strong positive or negative opinions. Why not eliminate those choosing not to respond from the sample, rather than assigning them a response they did not make? How large a group was surveyed? **11.** The sample is fairly small, considering results from at most 5000 viewers in a nation of 250 million people, most of whom watch television at some time. How were the 10,000 people selected?

Integrated Mathematics

What sort of information is collected in the diaries and how is it used? **13.** The graph does not give an accurate picture of team salaries. Three of the salaries under $1,000,000 are actually under $500,000. The graph would give a truer picture if the intervals were $0–$500,000, $500,001–$1,000,000, and so on. **18.** a cluster sample **19.** 13 m **20.** 16 in. **21.** 15 cm **22.** 0.5; 1.75 **23.** 0

Page 30 Checkpoint

1. Answers may vary. An example is given. A random sample chosen from the student population could be surveyed. Questions might include, "How often do you eat in the cafeteria? Would you buy this food if it were offered? Would having this food available make you more likely to use the cafeteria?" **2.** about 190 students **3.** Answers may vary. Examples are given. Use a spinner with $\frac{2}{3}$ representing "at least 60" and $\frac{1}{3}$ representing "under 60." Use a die. If 1 or 2 is rolled, let that represent "under 60." If 3, 4, 5, or 6 is rolled, let that represent "at least 60." **4.** random **5.** cluster **6. a.** Both parts of both questions give information that may influence the answers. **b.** Which shape is more appealing? (a) circular (b) rectangular; Which shape tastes better? (a) circular (b) rectangular

Pages 32–34 Talk it Over

1, 2. Answers and explanations may vary. Examples are given. **1.** No; there are infinitely many odd numbers, and there is no way to test every possible pair of them to check that all the sums are even. **2.** It is odd; the sum of two odd numbers is even, and when you add one more odd number to this even sum the result will be odd. **3, 4.** Answers may vary. Examples are given. **3.** No; the property you are testing might be unique to regular polygons. Also, if you test only regular polygons, your conjecture would apply only to them. **4.** No; for example, you already know the sum of the measures of the interior angles of a triangle is 180°. **5.** one **6.** You should test acute, obtuse, and scalene triangles. You may also test right, isosceles, and equilateral triangles, so long as you do not consider them exclusively. **7.** The inequality is false; any number $x \geq 0$ provides a counterexample.

Pages 34–37 Exercises and Problems

3. Answers may vary. An example is given. A reasonable conjecture is that everyone called to the principal's office has been given some good news, so Shing should not be worried. **5. a–e.** Answers may vary. Examples are given. **a.** Marvin might conjecture that driving a red car increases your chances of getting a speeding ticket. **b.** No; they issue many tickets to all different types of cars. **c.** He could observe a stretch of highway for a given period of time and record how many tickets are issued in general and how many to red cars. **d.** He may have been driving more, enjoying his new car. He may also have been showing off his new car, or feeling a sense of adventure that made him behave less responsibly. **e.** Some people might associate red cars with sportiness and speed. Others might see no connection. **7.** Beginning with the third number, each number in the pattern is the sum of the two previous numbers. The next number is 21. **9.** Beginning with the second row, the digits of the square of an n-digit number with all of its digits 1 are the counting numbers in increasing order up to n, then in decreasing order back down to 1. The next row is $1111 \cdot 1111 = 1234321$. **11, 13.** Each conjecture is based on inductive reasoning. **11.** The product of two odd numbers is odd. **13.** If a triangle has its vertices on a circle and one side of the triangle is a diameter of the circle, the angle opposite the diameter is a right angle. **15.** False; any number $x \leq 0$ is a counterexample. **17.** True. **21.** 11 **23.** Based on the conjecture given, Dr. Snow might have increased access to clean water either by temporarily bringing water into the area or by extending the water-pumping system. **26.** Parents who work regular daytime jobs would be underrepresented. **27.** control variable: length of the test; dependent variable: amount of paper used **28.** control variable: number of people for whom she is fixing breakfast; dependent variable: number of eggs used **29.** 2 **30.** 5

Pages 39–40 Talk it Over

1. True. **2.** True. **3.** False. **4.** True. **5.** False. **6.** All students who are not wearing a sweater are not wearing a blue sweater. **7.** Every student who is not wearing a sweater is not wearing a blue sweater. **8.** Statements 4 and 5 are converses of each other. **9. a.** $2a + 4b + 6 = 2(a + 2b + 3)$; Any integer that is the product of 2 and another integer is even. **b.** $2a + 4b + 7 = (2a + 4b + 6) + 1$; $2a + 4b + 6$ was shown to be even in part (a) and any integer that is 1 more than an even integer is odd.

Pages 41–44 Exercises and Problems

3. True. **5.** False. **7.** True. **9.** True. **11.** Answers may vary. All students who work at a job watch TV. Some students who work at a job watch movies. No students who work at a job do volunteer work. **15.** Open the person's airway and breathe slowly for the person if necessary. **17.** Rachel is older than Hector (or Hector is younger than Rachel). **19.** If the base angles of a triangle are equal in measure, then the sides opposite the base angles are equal in measure. **21. a.** No. **b.** Yes; $2x$ is even because any integer that is the product of 2 and another integer is

even.   **c.** Yes; $2x + 1$ is odd, because $2x$ is even and any integer that is 1 more than an even integer is odd. **23.** physical education class will be held indoors **25.** $\triangle PQR$ is not isosceles   **27.** $5x - 7 \leq -17$ **29.** quadrilateral $MNOP$ is a rectangle   **31.** Answer is based on the following facts. Any even number can be written as $2m$ for some integer m, and any odd number can be written as $2n + 1$ for some integer n. Also, any integer that is the product of 2 and another integer is even, and any integer that is 1 more than an even integer is odd. Let $2x + 1$ and $2y + 1$ be two odd numbers. Then $(2x + 1)(2y + 1) = 4xy + 2x + 2y + 1 = 2(2xy + x + y) + 1$, which is odd.   **33.** Methods may vary. An example is given. Draw two intersecting lines and number the angles 1–4 in order so that $\angle 1$ and $\angle 3$ are vertical angles. $\angle 1$ and $\angle 2$ together form a straight angle, so $\angle 1 + \angle 2 = 180°$. But $\angle 2$ and $\angle 3$ together form a straight angle, so $\angle 2 + \angle 3 = 180°$, also. Then $\angle 1 + \angle 2 = \angle 2 + \angle 3$, and $\angle 1 = \angle 3$.
37. Answers may vary. An example is given. I think the inequality is true for all x. I will test some numbers.

x	$-x$	x^2	$-x \overset{?}{\leq} x^2$	
2	-2	4	$-2 \leq 4$	✓
0	0	0	$0 \leq 0$	✓
-2	2	4	$2 \leq 4$	✓
$-\dfrac{1}{2}$	$\dfrac{1}{2}$	$\dfrac{1}{4}$	$\dfrac{1}{2} \leq \dfrac{1}{4}$	No.

The inequality is not true for $x = -\dfrac{1}{2}$, so it is not true for all x.   **38.** cube; 600 in.^{2} **39.** triangular prism; 108 cm^2 **40.** cylinder; 96π in.^{2} **41. a.** slope = 2; vertical intercept = -1 **b.** $y = 2x - 1$ **42. a.** slope = -1; vertical intercept = 0   **b.** $y = -x$ **43. a.** Slope is undefined; there is no vertical intercept.   **b.** $x = 3$

Pages 45–47 Talk it Over
1. Selbst getan ist wohl getan; Quien mucho abarca, poco aprieta.   **2.** "It" refers to Earth. Recycling helps preserve the natural resources of Earth.   **3.** No. The converse is "If you get another one free, then you buy two of something." The free item is conditional upon the purchase of the first two.   **4.** Answers may vary. An example is given. If I live in California, then I live in San Fancisco. Converse: If I live in San Francisco, then I live in California.   **5.** $0 = 0$ **6. a.** Gavin's prediction is more likely to be correct. The slope of the income line is less than the slope of the expenses line. If things continue as they are now, expenses will surpass income in about 2 years. **b.** 1994; 2000 **c.** The reasonable answer is "Gavin's."

3. a. False; $|-3| > 0$ for $n = -3$. **b.** If $n > 0$, then $|n| > 0$ for all n. **c.** True.   **5. a.** True. **b.** If a triangle is isosceles, then two sides of the triangle are congruent. **c.** True.   **7. a.** True. **b.** If a figure has four equal sides, then it is a square. **c.** False; it could be an octagon or a rhombus.   **9.** No; they might have lost Friday's game but other teams who had to win may also have lost, or been eliminated in some other way.

28.

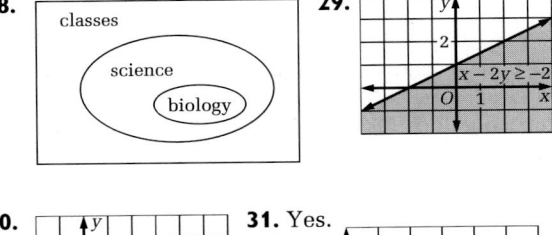

29.

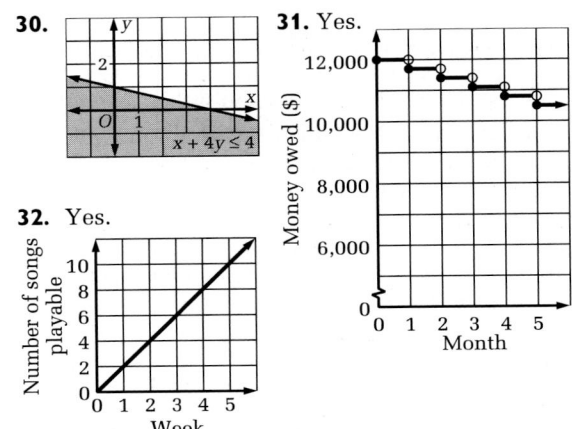

30.

31. Yes.

32. Yes.

Pages 53–54 Unit 1 Review and Assessment
1. A survey is less expensive and requires less planning than a census.   **2.** about 1440   **3.** about 90 min; Use a spinner divided into quarters. Each quarter represents a student from each class.   **4.** No.   **5.** Yes.
6. No.   **7.** Yes.   **8.** Answers may vary. An example is given. A cluster sample consists of items in a group such as a neighborhood or household. Since the members of the group are not chosen independently of each other, they may share opinions and experiences to a greater extent than members of a random sample. This certainly might influence the results.
9. Answers may vary. Examples are given. The manager is limiting the sample to those at home when the calls are made. Also, the audience includes many people outside that age group. Even if the manager has some reason to limit responses to those in that group, he or she has no way of knowing if a person giving a response is actually between 35 and 49.
10. Answers may vary. Examples are given. How was the sample chosen? How was the survey worded? What were the actual responses?

11. No; it will bisect the base only if the triangle is isosceles. A counterexample is given.

12. Yes. Let $4m$ and $4n$ be two different numbers that are both multiples of 4. Then $4m + 4n = 4(m + n)$, which is a multiple of 4. **13. a.** Answers may vary. An example is given. No; it is reasonable to assume that more than two students, or only one student, will get off at some bus stop. **b.** This would make her prediction more reasonable, since a brother and sister are likely to get off at the same stop. **14.** Let $2m$ and $2n$ be any two even numbers. Then $2m + 2n = 2(m + n)$, which is even, since any integer that is the product of 2 and an integer is even. **15.** False. **16.** True. **17.** False. **18.** None of the students in the Freshmen Singers is in the chorus. **19–21.** Counterexamples may vary. **19. a.** Most likely answer: True. **b.** If you sit in the front row at a movie, you arrived after most people. **c.** False; you may simply like to sit close to the screen. **20. a.** True. **b.** If two lines are perpendicular, they intersect to form right angles. **c.** True. **21. a.** False; $\frac{2}{3}$ is a rational number and $\frac{2}{3} = \frac{1}{\frac{1}{2} + 1}$; $\frac{1}{2}$ is not an integer. **b.** If x is an integer, then $\frac{1}{x + 1}$ is a rational number. **c.** False; -1 is an integer and $\frac{1}{-1 + 1} = \frac{1}{0}$ is not a rational number, it is undefined. **22.** Answers may vary. An example is given. A triangle can have at most one right angle. (The sum of the measures of the angles of a triangle is 180°. If a triangle contained two right angles, the sum of the three angle measures would have to be $90° + 90° + x = 180° + x$, which would be greater than 180°.)

Unit 2

Pages 59–62 Talk it Over

1. Answers may vary. An example is given. The path is downhill and bumpy at first, then downhill and straight until it becomes flat and straight. The graph then turns uphill and bumpy until it then becomes uphill and straight at the end. **2.** Answers may vary. An example is given. The graph is nonlinear decreasing from point A to point B, then linear decreasing from point B to point C. **3. a.** D and E or E and F **b.** B and C, C and D, or E and F **c.** E and F **4. a.** A; B, C, D **b.** C; none; A **c.** A; B, C, D **5.** The checkout time during the first week in July remained constant. **6.** Answers may vary. An example is given. Yes. By looking at the water level change from September to October for the years 1983, 1984, 1985, and 1986,

you can make a reasonable estimate of the water level for October 1987. **7.** about 67 g **8.** Yes. The steepness of the graph can tell you how fast the temperature is changing at each depth. **9.** Answers may vary. An example is given. The graph is linear and decreasing from a depth of 0 to 10 meters, constant from a depth of 10 to 13 meters, and nonlinear and decreasing from 13 to 40 meters. **10.** Answers may vary. An example is given. Yes; no two points lie on the same vertical line (vertical-line test). **11.** 1987; 2000 **12.** $100,000; $1,400,000

Pages 63–66 Exercises and Problems

3. nonlinear and increasing **5.** linear and increasing on the interval from 10 to 20; constant on the interval from 20 to 25; linear and increasing on the interval from 25 to 35; constant on the interval from 35 to 40; linear and increasing on the interval from 40 to 50; constant on the interval from 50 to 55; nonlinear and increasing on the interval from 55 to 75; constant on the interval from 75 to 80; nonlinear and increasing on the interval from 80 to 100 **7.** No; a constant graph is a horizontal line and its slope is 0. The graph of $x = 4$ is a vertical line and its slope is undefined. **9.** It would be reasonable to advise her to invest because according to the graph in Ex. 3, the use of cellular telephones has increased throughout the 1990s. **11.** No; according to the graph in Ex. 5, the temperature can feel hotter or cooler, depending on the relative humidity. **13.** linear growth **15.** nonlinear decay **19. a.** circumference of a circle

b.
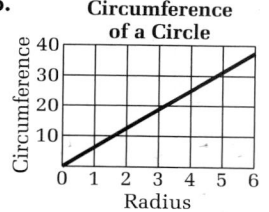
Circumference of a Circle

c. linear and increasing **d.** a growth graph because the circumference increases as the radius increases **e.** No; No; because the radius and the circumference cannot be negative.

21. a.
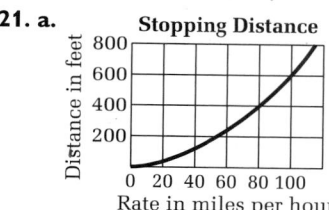
Stopping Distance

b. nonlinear and increasing **c.** a growth graph because stopping distance increases with increasing speed **d.** For every speed, there is one stopping distance and the graph passes the vertical-line test. **e.** domain: $0 \le s \le 110$; range: $0 \le d \le 715$ **26.** The survey did not claim that three out of four doctors recommend the medication, only that three out of four doctors who use it recommend it. Gabriel did not consider that the sample was biased.

27.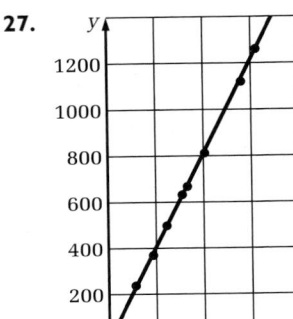

28. True. **29.** False.

b. 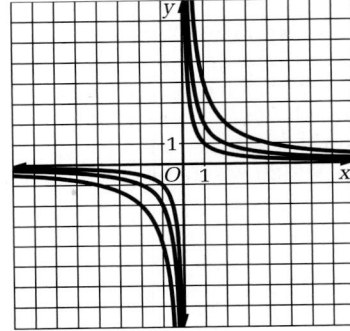   **c.** decreasing

27. A and D   **34.** linear growth   **35.** nonlinear decay
36. constant   **37.** 48   **38.** −14   **39.** −25   **40.** $l = \dfrac{A}{w}$

41. $h = \dfrac{V}{B}$ **42.** $r = \dfrac{D}{t}$

Pages 67–70 Talk it Over

1. Maximum heart rate declines with age.   **2.** −0.8a is always a negative number since a must be positive, so at any age −0.8a + 176 is less than 176.
3. a. Answers may vary. An example is given.
$0 \le a \le 80$ **b.** Based upon the domain given in question 3(a), $112 \le h \le 176$.   **4. a.** decreases by 8
b. linear   **c.** decreasing   **d.** decay graph; As a increases, h decreases.   **5.** Direct variation is a linear function with y-intercept $b = 0$.   **6.** 4   **7.** 0   **8.** The graph would not be as steep. It would rise 3 units for every positive 1 increase in x.   **9.** The graph would have the same slope, but would be shifted up 2.5 units.

Pages 70–74 Exercises and Problems

1. 176 beats/min   **3.** 0; constant   **5.** 3; increasing
7. 0; constant   **9.** $y = 3x - 2$ **11.** $y = -2x + 5$
13. $y = \dfrac{2}{3}x - 9$ **15.** c; $58.32   **17.** $m = \dfrac{d - 0}{c - c} = \dfrac{d}{0} =$

undefined   **21. a.** slope = 7; vertical intercept = 0

b. 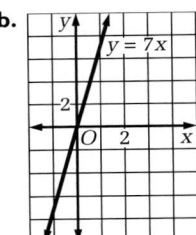   **c.** increasing

23. a. slope = 1; vertical intercept = 3.7
b. 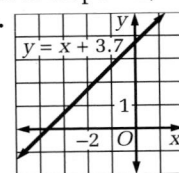   **c.** increasing

25. a. slope = $-\dfrac{3}{5}$; vertical intercept = 2

Pages 76–77 Talk it Over

1. a curve; The points on the scatter plot indicate a curve would fit to connect the points.   **2.** Answers may vary. An example is given. The graph of an inverse variation is a curve and the graph of a direct variation is a line. In an inverse variation, the products of corresponding x- and y-values are constant. In a direct variation, the quotients are constant.   **3.** the first quadrant   **4.** the third quadrant   **5.** For every ordered pair (x, y) for which $xy = 12$, it is also true that $(-x)(-y) = 12$. So, for every point of the graph in the first quadrant, there is a corresponding point in the third quadrant.   **6.** Divide both sides of the equation $xy = k$ by x.   **7.** The graph of $xy = -k$ is the image of $xy = k$ reflected over the vertical axis.
8. The smaller the value of k, the closer the curve lies to the axes. When k is larger, the curve lies farther out and its ends approach the axes more slowly.

Pages 79–82 Exercises and Problems

1. quadrant I   **3. a.** Only one pair of dimensions is given for each pair of numbers; that is, a box w glasses wide and l glasses long is identical to one l glasses wide and w glasses long.

b. If x is the width and y is the length, the equation $xy = 48$ relates the width and length of each box.

width	length
1	48
2	24
3	16
6	8

5. No; $xy \neq$ constant.
9. $y = -\dfrac{7}{x}$ **11.** 12   **13.** $\dfrac{1}{2}$

15. a. The total needed for rent each month is $600. The more students sharing the apartment, the less each must pay. An equation would be share of rent $r = \frac{600}{s}$, where s is the number of students sharing the apartment. **b.** 5   **17.** 90 beats per second   **19. a.** Let x be the rate of travel (in mph) and y the time it takes to get to the lake (in hours); $y = \frac{12}{x}$.

b.

Method of travel	x	y
backpacking	3	4
cross-country skiing	4	3
bicycling	10	1.2
car: slow & scenic	25	0.48
car: moderate	45	0.27
car: speed limit	55	0.22

c. Answers may vary. An example is given. $3 \leq x \leq 55$; The methods of travel given are the only feasible ones and the given rates are reasonable.   **24.** b and d

25. 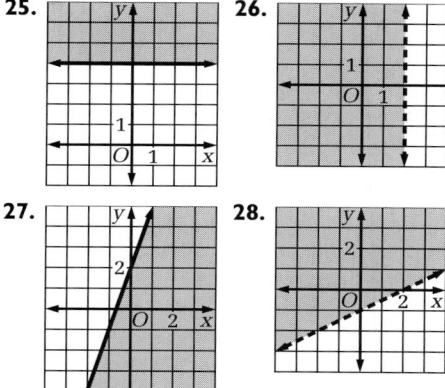 **26.**

27. **28.**

29. S.A. = 248 cm²; V = 240 cm³   **30.** $V \approx 804.25$ m³
31. S.A. ≈ 70.69 ft²; $V \approx 42.41$ ft³

Page 83 Checkpoint
1. Answers may vary. An example is given. The graph represents the amount of money in a student's bank account over a series of months. The first drop is in August as the student buys back-to-school supplies and clothing. Then the amount in the account stays low as the student has no job for a few months and cuts back on expenditures. In December and January, the student gets a job at the mall during peak Christmas shopping and inventory times. He puts all money earned in the bank anticipating a big ski vacation in late winter.   **2.** time; heart rate   **3.** $0 \leq t \leq 80$; $70 \leq h \leq 105$ **4.** Over the interval $0 \leq t \leq 15$, the graph is nonlinear increasing. Over the interval

$15 \leq t \leq 35$, the graph is constant. Over the interval $35 \leq t \leq 55$, the graph is linear decreasing. And over the interval $55 \leq t \leq 80$, the graph is constant.   **5. a.** 8
b. −3   **c.** $y = 8x - 3$ **d.** 1.25   **6. a.** $y = \frac{10}{x}$
b. 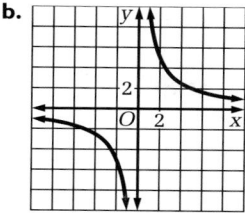   **c.** The graph is a hyperbola.
d. 4   **e.** 1.25

Pages 84–86 Talk it Over
1. Answers may vary. Examples are given. (1) Peel the orange carefully with the peeler, trying to make rectangular, triangular, or square pieces. Lay the pieces out and measure the area of each piece using the ruler. Add the areas to find the total surface area. (2) Wrap the string around the orange so that the entire surface is covered. Then arrange the string to form a rectangular region and calculate its area. (3) Wrap the orange with aluminum foil, cutting away the overlap. Unwrap the foil and use the ruler to measure the area of the foil that covered the orange. Find the area of this foil to find the surface area of the orange.
2. Answers may vary. Examples are given. (1) Cut six curved pieces off the orange so that you have a cube on the inside plus the six curved pieces. Measure the volume of the cube and estimate the volume of the six curved pieces. (2) Cut the orange into sections and carefully arrange the sections into a prism-like shape and find its volume.   **3.** Answers may vary. An example is given. Use the string to find the circumference, $C = 2\pi r$. Divide the circumference by 2π to find r.   **4.** $V = 2\pi r^3$; The sphere fills $\frac{2}{3}$ of the cylinder.   **5.** Surface area is two-dimensional and so is measured in square units. Volume is three-dimensional and so is measured in cubic units.
6. Answers may vary.   **7.** Diameter $d = 2r$, so use the formula S.A. $= 4\pi r^2 = 4\pi\left(\frac{d}{2}\right)^2 = \pi d^2$.   **8. a.** Substitute 1810 for S.A. in the equation S.A. $= 4\pi r^2$. Using 12.57 as an estimate for 4π, divide both sides of the equation by 12.57 to get $143.99 \approx r^2$. Take the square root of 143.99 to estimate $r \approx 12.0$ cm.   **b.** Answers may vary. An example is given. Sample 2 uses volume to find r and involves calculating a cube root. This problem uses surface area to find r and involves calculating a square root.
9. Yes. Using $d = 2r$, $\frac{(d_1)^2}{(d_2)^2} = \frac{(2r_1)^2}{(2r_2)^2} = \frac{4(r_1)^2}{4(r_2)^2} = \frac{(r_1)^2}{(r_2)^2}$.

10. Yes. Using $d = 2r$, $\frac{(d_1)^3}{(d_2)^3} = \frac{(2r_1)^3}{(2r_2)^3} = \frac{8(r_1)^3}{8(r_2)^3} = \frac{(r_1)^3}{(r_2)^3}$.

Pages 87–90 Exercises and Problems

3. S.A. = 64π ft²; $V = \frac{256\pi}{3}$ ft³ **5.** S.A. = 400π mi²;

$V = \frac{4000\pi}{3}$ mi³

	Type of Ball	Diameter (cm)	Radius (cm)	Surface Area (cm²)	Volume (cm³)
7.	soccer ball	22.0	11.0	1520.5	5575.3
9.	tennis ball	6.5	3.25	132.7	143.8
11.	table tennis ball	3.7	1.85	43.0	26.5

13. 3 cm **15.** 5 m **21.** Answers may vary. An example is given. The inner core since the crust is just a very thin layer and the core is a fairly large sphere **23.** about 7 billion km³ **25.** about 612 billion km³ **27.** about 17 billion km³ **29. a.** about $\frac{125.65}{1}$ or 125.65:1 **b.** about $\frac{1408.48}{1}$ or 1408.48:1 **34.** c and d **35.** $\frac{1}{4} = 0.25$ **36.** $\frac{3}{8} = 0.375$ **37.** $\frac{3}{8} = 0.375$ **38.** Yes; variation constant 196. **39.** No. **40.** Yes; variation constant 13. **41.** No.

Pages 92–94 Talk it Over
1. Changing the sign of k reflects the graph of $y = kx^2$ over the horizontal or x-axis. When k is positive, the graph is a parabola that opens up; when k is negative, the graph is a parabola that opens down. **2.** As k increases, the parabola becomes "narrower" or closer to the vertical or y-axis. Check students' graphs.
3. Changing the sign of k reflects the graph of $y = kx^3$ over the vertical or y-axis. **4.** As k increases, the curve becomes "narrower" or closer to the vertical or y-axis. Check students' graphs.

Pages 96–98 Exercises and Problems
1. When k is positive, the graph is in quadrants I and II; when k is negative, the graph is in quadrants III and IV.

3. Answers may vary. An example is given.

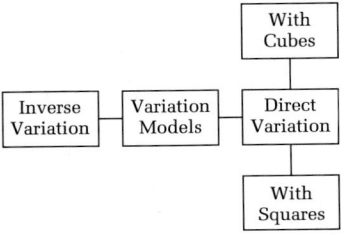

5. about 1.1; about −1.1 **7.** about 1.6; about −1.6

9. $E = ks^2$ **11.** 98 in.² **15.** about 1.5 **17.** about 1.6
19. about 23.6 mi/h **21.** It is decreased to $\frac{1}{8}$ of the power generated by the original wind speed.
23. a. It is multiplied by 8. **b.** It is divided by 8.
26. S.A. $\approx$ 615.8 cm²; $V \approx$ 1436.8 cm³
27. S.A. $\approx$ 45.4 in.²; $V \approx$ 28.7 in.³
28. S.A. $\approx$ 48,305.1 cm²; $V \approx$ 998,306.0 cm³ **29.** 8
30. 12 **31.** 25 **32.** 23.4 **33.** 108 **34.** 972

Page 101 Talk it Over
1. 9 **2.** 3 **3.** −2 **4.** $a \cdot b^{1/2} = 36$; $(ab)^{1/2} = 12$; The values are different since in the first equation a is not raised to the $\frac{1}{2}$ power. **5.** $\sqrt{5x}$ **6.** $4n^{1/3}$

Pages 102–104 Exercises and Problems
1. when $x = 0$ **3.** $\frac{5}{u^5}$ **5.** $\frac{12}{m^2n^4}$ **7.** $4v^2$ **9.** $\frac{15p^4}{n^5}$
13. 8 **15.** −3 **17.** $-2x^{1/3}$ **19.** $s^{1/2}t^{1/3}$ **21.** $7(8x)^{1/2}$
23. $\left(\frac{s}{2}\right)^{1/2}$ **25.** $-6\sqrt[3]{w}$ **27.** $\sqrt{\frac{4}{r}}$ **35.** $A = kx^2$
36. $V = kr^3$ **37.** inductive **38.** deductive **39.** 144
40. 1920 **41.** 5625 **42.** 186,624

Pages 107–108 Talk it Over
1. a. 25,000 m³ **b.** $n = -1$; $V = 25,000$ m³
c. 12,500 m³; the volume of the landfill 6 years before the newspaper report **2. a.** nonlinear; growth
b. present volume of the landfill **c.** No; if the graph were to intersect the horizontal axis, it would be at $V = 0$. Although at some point the actual volume of the landfill was zero, the value of the function $50,000(2^n)$ is never zero. **d.** Answers may vary. An example is given. The part of the graph that models the volume of the landfill is the portion for a few doubling periods before and after the year the report was written, that is, −3 or $-2 \le n \le 2$ or 3. Past doubling probably occurred only a few times. At some time in the future, the landfill will be completely filled up. Trash will be disposed of in some other manner. **3.** The area of the original piece in the data in Table 1 was 625.625 in.². After n tears, the area is $A = 625.625\left(\frac{1}{2}\right)^n$ in.². **4. a.** No; the dimensions of each sheet would get smaller and smaller but would never reach zero. **b.** The graph of the function never intersects the horizontal axis.

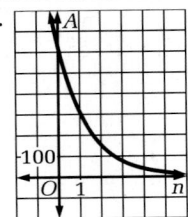

1. a. Let n be the number of tears and p the number of pieces; $p = 2n$.

b.

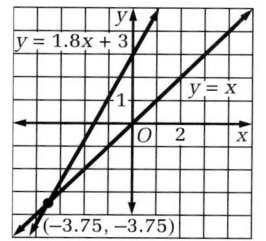

3. 3.2 million m³; This is one-fourth of the volume if the doubling period is three years.   **5.** 1,856
7. 60,817,408   **9.** No; the graph intersects the horizontal axis.   **17. a.** Let x be the number of 1600-year half-lives that have passed and y be the amount in grams of radium present; $y = 120\left(\frac{1}{2}\right)^x$.   **b.** about 7336 years

19. a. Let x be the number of 18-year doubling periods and y be the population; $y = 329{,}000(2^x)$.   **b.** 2070
c. Answers may vary. An example is given. No; it is not likely that the country's resources could indefinitely support a population that doubles every eighteen years.   **22.** $\frac{36}{x^4}$ **23.** $\frac{7}{x^4y^6}$ **24.** 1   **25.** 3   **26.** 0

27. $-\frac{1}{2}$ **28.** undefined   **29.** right triangle

30. rectangle   **31.** trapezoid   **32.** parallelogram

1. dependent variable: freshman enrollment; control variable: years   **2.** domain: 1993–2000; range: about 392,000–425,000   **3.** The graph is drawn in linear segments. It is decreasing from 1993 to 1995; increasing from 1995 to 1997; and decreasing from 1997 to 2000.   **4. a.** 3   **b.** 5   **c.** $y = 3x + 5$ **d.** 3   **e.** Let x represent the number of CD's ordered and y represent the total cost. Then $3x$ would be the cost for the CD's plus \$5 handling charge to arrive at the equation $y = 3x + 5$.   **5.** Explanations may vary. An example is given. direct variation; Each of the quotients $\frac{y}{x}$ is approximately equal to 1.1.   **6.** Explanations may vary. An example is given. inverse variation; Each of the products xy is approximately equal to 12.26.

7. a. $y = \frac{144}{x}$ **b.** 7.2   **8.** about 113.1 in.³   **9. a.** 9 : 25
b. 36 ft²   **10.** direct variation with the square
11. about 15 km/h   **12.** about 0.576 g/cm²   **13.** $\frac{x^9}{y}$
14. g^2 **15.** $-\frac{20r}{t^3}$ **16.** $\frac{1}{64}$ **17.** 33.3 km/h
18. Descriptions may vary. 2An example is given. The graph of an exponential function with base 2 gets closer and closer to the horizontal axis but does not intersect it, yet it does intersect the vertical axis. As the value of the control variable increases, the value of the dependent value increases without bound.
19. a. 5,000 g   **b.** about 17 days   **c.** Let x be the number of 5-day half-lives that have passed and y be the amount (in grams) of the substance present; $y = 5000\left(\frac{1}{2}\right)^n$.   **d.** 5.29×10^{-19} g

Unit 3

1.

Cost of Membership

	FitnessPLUS	Bodyworks
5 months	350	400
10 months	650	575

2. FitnessPLUS costs less for 5 months; Bodyworks costs less for 10 months.   **3.** FitnessPLUS: slope = 60, y-intercept = 50; Bodyworks: slope = 35, y-intercept = 225. The y-intercepts represent the initiation fee to join, and the slope represents the monthly dues or the rate at which the total cost is increasing.
4. FitnessPLUS: \$470; Bodyworks: \$470. After seven months, the costs have averaged out. However, you will be paying \$25 more each month forever at FitnessPLUS.   **5.** The x-coordinate is the number of months. The y-coordinate is the cost.   **6.** Bodyworks; For every value of $n > 7$, the graph of the Bodyworks function is under the graph of the FitnessPLUS function, and therefore is less expensive since the y-axis represents the cost.   **7.** From the graph, $n \approx 8.5$; $(n, c) \approx (8.5, 45)$.   **8.** No. Since you cannot rent a locker for a portion of a month, you need to see only between which two months the solution lies.   **9.** The maximum amount spent will be the cost of lunch and dinner and will be less than or equal to \$50 (but no more than \$50). The cost of the lunch and dinner is positive or zero for each.   **10.** (10, 40), (20, 10), (0, 30), (30, 0), (−10, −10), and (−20, 10), for $l + d \le$ 50; (10, 40), (0, 30), (20, 10), (30, 0), and (50, 30), for $l \ge 0$; (30, 0), (−20, 10), (20, 10), (0, 30), (10, 40), and (50, 30), for $d \ge 0$.   **11.** (10, 40), (0, 30), (30, 0), and (20, 10); The region is the triangle portion of the graph bounded by the equation $l + d = 50$, the l-axis, and the d-axis.

1. The solution of a system of equations is the ordered pair(s) for which both equations are true. The solution is the point of intersection of the graphs of the equations.   **3.** about (−2, 4.5)
5. (−3.75, −3.75)   **7.** (−5, 3)

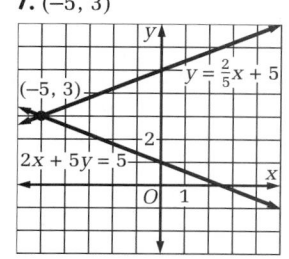

13. a. $c = 120 + 50n$ **b.** greatest slope: FitnessPLUS, where $c = 50 + 60n$; greatest intercept: Bodyworks, where $c = 225 + 35n$

Selected Answers

9

c.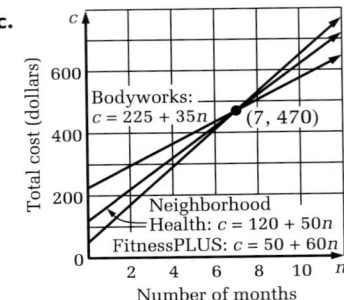

d. FitnessPLUS is cheapest for three months. At seven months, all plans have the same cost. The graph supports these answers since the line for Fitness-PLUS cost is below the other two lines at three months. All three graphs intersect at (7, 470), so all three plans cost $470 for seven months.

15.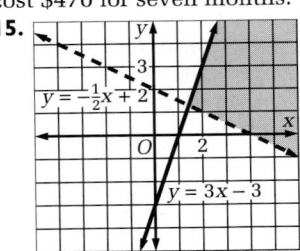

17.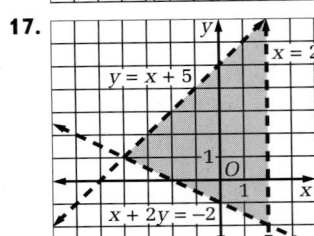

21. trapezoid

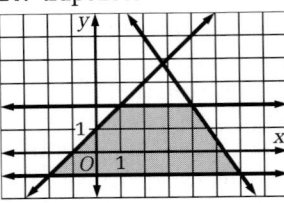

23. rectangle

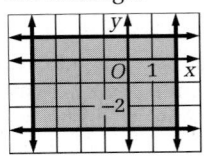

25. $y = 100\left(\frac{1}{2}\right)^n$, where n = the number of 1600-year half-lives. **26.** $(8x)^{1/2}$ **27.** $-5t^{1/3}$ **28.** $(7m)^{1/3}$
29. $m = 7.5$ **30.** $a = -12$ **31.** $n = \frac{15}{7}$

Pages 129–130 Talk it Over
1. The cost to use one electronic bulb is the initial cost ($24) plus $.01/day for electricity. The total cost is $c = 24 + 0.01x$, where x = number of days used. The cost to use the equivalent in 100-watt bulbs is the cost of twenty bulbs at $.75 each ($15) plus $.04/day for electricity. The total cost is $c = 15 + 0.04x$, where x = number of days used.

2. about 301 days; At that point, the graphs of the two equations intersect and from there on the electronic bulb costs less in total cost. **3.** No. It is a very close estimate, but although these two coordinates are on the graph of $y = 24 + 0.01x$, they are not *exactly* on the graph of $y = 15 + 0.04x$. The exact intersection point cannot be read all the time. **4.** $x = 300$ days, as compared to 301 days solving by graphing and using TRACE **5.** $y = 27$ **6.** $x - 2y = -11$ gives $-1 - 2(5) = -1 - 10 = -11$ ✓; $x + y = 4$ gives $-1 + 5 = 4$ ✓.
7. Graphing both equations on one set of axes, you

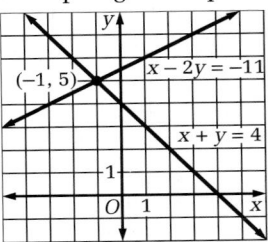

find the graphs intersect at $(-1, 5)$, so $(-1, 5)$ is the solution of the system.

Pages 132–134 Exercises and Problems
1. a. 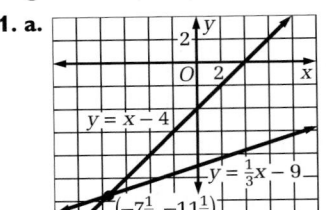 **b.** $\left(-7\frac{1}{2}, -11\frac{1}{2}\right)$

3. (3, 8) **5.** (0, −1) **7.** (0, −3) **9. a.** Melissa solved for x in the first equation and substituted that expression into the second equation to solve for y. Bjorn solved the second equation for y and substituted that expression into the first equation to solve for x.
b. Yes. After solving for the first variable and then substituting into the original equation to solve for the second variable, both will get the same result. They just did it in different orders. **c.** Answers may vary. An example is given. Melissa's method is easier for this system of equations. At different times, different methods are easier. It depends upon the equations as to which way is easiest. **11.** $7\frac{1}{2}$ years **13.** 112 general admission tickets; 207 student tickets
15. (104, 28)

20.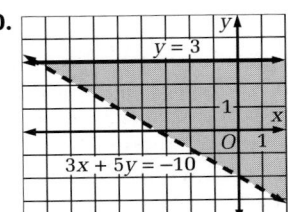

21. $-3x^2 + 4x$
22. $x^2 - 3x - 54$
23. $-5x^2 + 50x$
24. $6x^2 - 5x - 56$
25. $\frac{1}{4}$ **26.** 0 **27.** 3
28. undefined

1. $-\frac{1}{5}$; $\frac{4}{3}$ 2. 0; undefined; No, because the slope of a vertical line is undefined.   3. The slope in the sample graph appears to be $\frac{1}{2}$ $\left(\frac{\text{rise}}{\text{run}} = \frac{2}{4}\right)$ and the y-intercept 2, so $\frac{1}{2}$ and 2 are reasonable values for m and b.   4. The slope will be the same, -2; substitute -6 for x, -1 for y, and -2 for m in the equation $y = mx + b$, so $-1 = (-2)(-6) + b$ and $b = -13$. The equation is $y = -2x - 13$.   5. $x = 4$

Pages 139–141 Exercises and Problems

3. **a.** parallel lines   **b.** no solution, inconsistent
5. **a.** intersecting lines   **b.** one solution, consistent
7. **a.** slopes: $\overline{AB} = -\frac{1}{8}$; $\overline{BC} = 3$; $\overline{CD} = -\frac{1}{8}$; $\overline{AD} = 3$
b. It is a parallelogram because opposite sides are parallel. It is not a rectangle because the slopes are not negative reciprocals of each other, and it is not a rhombus because the sides are not all the same length.   **9.** parallel   **11.** intersects   **17.** $-\frac{1}{3}$
19. $y = -4x - 10$ 21. $y = 2$ 23. $y = 3x + 12$
25. In both procedures, you use the slope-intercept form of an equation and substitute the slope of the line whose equation you are trying to find and the coordinates of the given point. Also, in both cases, you find the slope of the line from the slope of the given line. However, if you are finding an equation of a parallel line, you use the slope of the given line. If you are finding an equation of a perpendicular line, you use the negative reciprocal of the slope of the given line.   27. a rectangle since there are two pairs of parallel sides and two pairs of perpendicular sides
29. **a.** $m = 1$ **b.** $y = x + 1$; $y = x - 1$ **c.** no solution
31. $(20, -10)$ 32. $(2, -5)$ 33. $\left(\frac{1}{2}, 3\right)$ 34. No; if $x = -1$, then -1 is not less than -2.   35. $y = \frac{3}{2}$ 36. $x = 4$
37. $n = -\frac{3}{5}$

Pages 142–147 Talk it Over
1. The first column of rods (red, black, red) represent the numbers 4, -3, 11. The second column (black, red, black) represent -5, 2, -12.   2. red: positive; black: negative   3. Each column of the diagram represents an equation with the variables in the same position. Each equation is written in vertical form rather than in horizontal form; the Chinese method does not explicitly use variables.   4. because the coefficients of none of the variables is 1   5. $(-2, -1)$
6. The substitution method uses more steps than the addition-or-subtraction method. Answers may vary. An example is given. The addition-or-subtraction method is easier because it requires fewer steps.

7. In the first step, the scales remain balanced because equal amounts were added to each side. In the second step, the scales remain balanced because nothing was added or subtracted, just simplified.
8. The only difference is that you would add to eliminate the x-terms instead of subtracting. The result would be $1.6y = 29$ or $y = 18.125$.   9. If you want to eliminate y, multiply both sides of the first equation by 7.3 and subtract to eliminate the y-terms.
10. Multiply both sides of the first equation by 2 or by 3.   11. They are alike in that both last lines do not involve a variable. They are different in that one is true and the other is false. A false statement implies the system is inconsistent (parallel lines) and has no solution (or it is not true for any value of x).
12–14. Answers may vary. Examples are given.
12. substitution; One equation is already solved for c.
13. graphing; Both equations are in slope-intercept form.   14. subtraction; This will eliminate the x-term so that you can solve for y first.   15. They are the same line. The result, $-14 = -14$, is true for all values of c and d.

Pages 147–149 Exercises and Problems
3. $(8, -1)$ 5. $\left(-\frac{33}{5}, -7\right)$ 7. $(-6, -19)$ 9. $(1, 4)$
13. $x = 147°$, $y = 33°$ 15. 9 in., 17 in., 17 in.
19. $(-2, -4)$ 21. $(-5, 2)$ 23. **a.** t represents the number of tapes that are bought; c represents the number of CDs that are bought. The line labeled $6t + 12c = 200$ represents Cherub Records; the line labeled $8t + 10c = 200$ represents Flower's Music.
b. $(11, 11)$ **c.** $\left(11\frac{1}{9}, 11\frac{1}{9}\right)$ **d.** For $0 \le t \le 11$, it is cheaper to buy at Flower's Music. For $12 \le t \le 33$, you get more for your money at Cherub Records.
e. Answers may vary. An example is given. Graphing is visual and gives a better overall picture. The addition-or-subtraction method is more cumbersome.
25. addition-or-subtraction; It is easier to multiply both equations by a number than to solve one or both of the equations for a variable.   27. graphing; Both equations are in slope-intercept form and the lines are perpendicular.   29. no solution   31. $(1, 2)$
34. $y = -2x - 4$ 35. about 0.55   36. about 0.20
37. about 0.26

Page 150 Checkpoint
1. one solution; Putting the second equation in slope-intercept form, $m = -\frac{1}{2}$. Since the two slopes are different, the lines intersect and there is one solution.
2. **a.** Let $c = $ costs and $t = $ tons of waste. Then the system of equations is $c = 400t$
$$c = 350 + 80t.$$

Selected Answers

11

b.

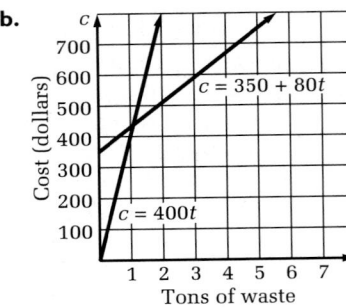

c. Direct disposal is cheaper for one ton of cardboard waste. Using a compactor is cheaper for two tons of cardboard waste. The point when the costs are equal is at slightly more than one ton of waste.

3.

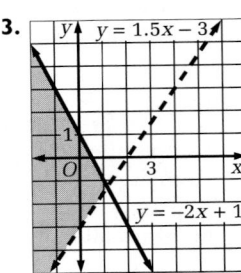

4. $\left(\frac{1}{2}, \frac{1}{2}\right)$ **5.** (225, 236)
6. $y = -3x + 11$ **7.** $y = \frac{1}{3}x + \frac{2}{3}$
8. (1, 1) **9.** infinitely many solutions **10.** (5, 16)
11. substitution, because one equation is already solved for y; The solution is (−3, 15).

6. $J'(-7, 7), K'(-3, 7), L'(-3, 2), M'(-6, 2)$
7.

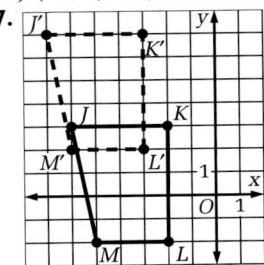

Pages 152–155 Talk it Over
1. row 2, column 1 **2.** the price of shrimp kurma
3. 4 × 2 **4. a.** 1.04 is the same as 100% + 4% when you multiply by the price. **b.** 3 × 2 **5.** 65 **6.** 2 × 4; 2 × 4 **7.** Yes. You are multiplying each entry by a single number, or scalar, not another matrix. **8.** 652
9. a. how many more CDs and tapes were sold in February than in January **b.** Negative numbers mean the music store sold less in those categories in February than in January.

Pages 155–158 Exercises and Problems
1. 12 elements **3.** 3 × 5 **5.** 1 × 4
15. $\begin{bmatrix} 1.1 & -7.5 \\ -1.9 & 1.3 \\ -1.0 & 6.7 \end{bmatrix}$ **17.** $\begin{bmatrix} 14 \\ 26 \\ 51 \end{bmatrix}$ **25.** $\left(-4, -\frac{23}{4}\right)$

26. no solution **27.** $\left(-\frac{1}{3}, \frac{1}{3}\right)$ **28.** (4, −2) **29.** $\frac{d^4}{9c^5}$

30. m^3n^4 **31.** $\frac{-18b^2}{a^3}$ **32.** $\frac{9}{x^3}$ **33.** translation

34. dilation

Pages 159–162 Talk it Over
1. the point in the upper right corner, where all the lines meet **2.** $\frac{2}{1}$ **3.** The coordinates are twice as large. **4.** $\begin{bmatrix} -3 \\ 8 \end{bmatrix}$ **5. a.** The first row represents the x-coordinate of each vertex in the polygon. The second row represents the y-coordinate of each vertex in the polygon. The four columns represent the four vertices, P, Q, R, and S. **b.** $\begin{bmatrix} 1 & 5 & 5 \\ -2 & -2 & 1 \end{bmatrix}$

Pages 162–164 Exercises and Problems
3. d **5.** $\begin{bmatrix} 4 & 12 & 4 \\ 12 & 2 & 6 \end{bmatrix}$ **7.** $\begin{bmatrix} \frac{2}{3} & 2 & \frac{2}{3} \\ 2 & \frac{1}{3} & 1 \end{bmatrix}$ **9.** $\begin{bmatrix} 1 & 3 & 2 & 0 \\ 5 & 2 & -1 & 0 \end{bmatrix}$

11. $\begin{bmatrix} -2 & 1 & -2 \\ 3 & 3 & -1 \end{bmatrix}$ **13.** dilation with center at the origin and scale factor 3 **15.** dilation with center at the origin and scale factor $\frac{1}{2}$ **20.** Both are 2 × 4.

21. a. $\begin{bmatrix} 74 & 61 & 34 & 61 \\ 213 & 130 & 210 & 205 \end{bmatrix}$ **b.** 34

22. a. $\begin{bmatrix} 112 & 196 & 210 & 119 \\ 441 & 140 & 280 & 35 \end{bmatrix}$ **b.** 140 **23.** $y = \frac{16}{3} - \frac{4}{3}x$

24. $x = \frac{5}{2}y - \frac{21}{2}$ **25.** $y = \frac{39}{4} - \frac{1}{4}x$

Pages 165–169 Talk it Over
1. $520 **2.** I multiplied the amount of carnations sold by the price of carnations, the amount of irises sold by the price of irises, and the amount of roses sold by the price of roses. Then the products were added together. **3.** $156 income from the sale of carnations, $204 income from the sale of irises, $160 income from the sale of roses, and $520 total income from all sales **4.** [−17] **5.** No. If you multiply a 3 × 1 matrix by a 1 × 5 matrix, for example, you will have a 3 × 5 matrix, not a single number.
6. Selections may vary. An example is given. Row 2 of L, column 3 of $R = -3 \cdot 6 + 4 \cdot 4 = -18 + 16 = -2$, which is in row 2, column 3 of P. ✓ **7.** Yes. In order for each row to be multiplied by a corresponding column and put in its proper place in the product matrix, the column number in the first matrix must match the row number in the second matrix. **8.** She was trying to multiply a 4 × 1 matrix by a 2 × 4 matrix. The number of columns of matrix A is not equal to the number of rows of matrix B.
9. $AB = \begin{bmatrix} -18 & 3 \\ -30 & 2 \end{bmatrix}$; $BA = \begin{bmatrix} 2 & 2 \\ -45 & -18 \end{bmatrix}$;

$AC = \begin{bmatrix} 29 & 10 \\ 50 & 19 \end{bmatrix}$; $CA = \begin{bmatrix} 29 & 10 \\ 50 & 19 \end{bmatrix}$; $BC = \begin{bmatrix} -28 & 22 \\ -45 & -63 \end{bmatrix}$;

$CB = \begin{bmatrix} -48 & 23 \\ -30 & -43 \end{bmatrix}$ **10.** Yes. The result is dependent upon the order of matrices in multiplication. From question 9 above, $AB \neq BA$, $BC \neq CB$.

Pages 170–173 Exercises and Problems
3. $[-4]$ **5.** The number of columns of the first matrix (3) does not match with the number of rows of the second matrix (2). **11.** $AB = [7.45 \quad -0.99]$
13. $\begin{bmatrix} -6 \\ 40 \\ 20 \end{bmatrix}$ **17.** Yes; 1×3. **20.** $P'(0, 3)$, $Q'(3, 3)$, $R'(3, 0)$ **21.** $\frac{1}{4}a + 3b$ **22.** $-12m + 12n$
23. $-12y^2 + 6y$ **24.** $(-11, -58)$ **25.** infinitely many solutions **26.** $(-2, 1)$

Pages 175–176 Talk it Over
1. $AA^{-1} = \begin{bmatrix} -8 & 1 \\ -6 & 2 \end{bmatrix}\begin{bmatrix} -0.2 & 0.1 \\ -0.6 & 0.8 \end{bmatrix} = \begin{bmatrix} 1 & 0 \\ 0 & 1 \end{bmatrix}$ ✓;
$A^{-1}A = \begin{bmatrix} -0.2 & 0.1 \\ -0.6 & 0.8 \end{bmatrix}\begin{bmatrix} -8 & 1 \\ -6 & 2 \end{bmatrix} = \begin{bmatrix} 1 & 0 \\ 0 & 1 \end{bmatrix}$ ✓
2. $\begin{bmatrix} 0.1875 & 0.125 \\ -0.0625 & -0.375 \end{bmatrix}$ **3.** C^{-1} does not exist.
4. $\begin{bmatrix} -8 & 1 \\ -6 & 2 \end{bmatrix}\begin{bmatrix} x \\ y \end{bmatrix} = \begin{bmatrix} -8x + y \\ -6x + 2y \end{bmatrix}$ using matrix multiplication. **5.** Multiply both sides by the inverse matrix of $\begin{bmatrix} -8 & 1 \\ -6 & 2 \end{bmatrix}$.
6. $\begin{bmatrix} -0.2 & 0.1 \\ -0.6 & 0.8 \end{bmatrix}\begin{bmatrix} -8 & 1 \\ -6 & 2 \end{bmatrix}\begin{bmatrix} x \\ y \end{bmatrix} = \begin{bmatrix} -0.2 & 0.1 \\ -0.6 & 0.8 \end{bmatrix}\begin{bmatrix} 10 \\ 16 \end{bmatrix}$;
$\begin{bmatrix} x \\ y \end{bmatrix} = \begin{bmatrix} -0.4 \\ 6.8 \end{bmatrix}$; The solution is $(-0.4, 6.8)$.
7. $(-8)(-0.4) + 6.8 = 10$ ✓ and $(-6)(-0.4) + (2)(6.8) = 16$ ✓

Pages 177–179 Exercises and Problems
1. $\begin{bmatrix} -3 & 9 \\ -6 & 4 \end{bmatrix}$ **18.** $\begin{bmatrix} 11 \\ 168 \end{bmatrix}$ **19.** $[63 \quad -88]$ **20.** $\begin{bmatrix} 0 & 0 \\ -55 & 33 \end{bmatrix}$
21. If you are in Port Moresby, then you are south of the equator. **22.** 42 **23.** 14 **24.** 14 **25.** $16\frac{4}{9}$

Pages 181–182 Unit 3 Review and Assessment
1. a. $c = 93 + 42h$
$c = 225$
b.
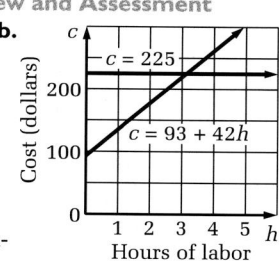
c. ABC Auto Repair is cheaper if repairs take 2 hours. Bob's Auto Shop is cheaper if the repairs take 4 hours. The graph shows a "break-even point" at slightly more than three hours.

2.
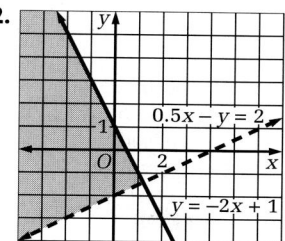
3. $2050 **4.** B and C because they are the same line (C is just twice B) **5.** A and C or A and B will be inconsistent. A and C both have $8x - 2y$ in common but different constants c when written in the form $ax + by = c$. So A and C are parallel lines and the system is inconsistent. If you multiply equation B by two, you obtain an equivalent equation to that of C, so A and B are also inconsistent. **6.** $y = -3x + 11$ **7.** infinitely many solutions **8.** $(3, -1)$ **9.** $(2, 13)$
10. Answers may vary. An example is given.
$\begin{bmatrix} 1.75 & 1.25 & 2.00 & 1.50 & 1.50 \\ 0 & 2.00 & 1.50 & 0 & 0 \\ 1.25 & 2.00 & 1.50 & 1.50 & 1.50 \end{bmatrix}$
11. a. $\begin{bmatrix} 2.40 & 3.00 & 4.00 \\ 7.00 & 8.00 & 10.00 \\ 8.00 & 8.00 & 10.00 \end{bmatrix}$; $\begin{bmatrix} 9.60 & 12.00 & 16.00 \\ 28.00 & 32.00 & 40.00 \\ 32.00 & 32.00 & 40.00 \end{bmatrix}$
b. $\begin{bmatrix} 9.60 & 12.00 & 16.00 \\ 28.00 & 32.00 & 40.00 \\ 32.00 & 32.00 & 40.00 \end{bmatrix}$ ✓. They are the same.
12. $\begin{bmatrix} -1 & 1 & \frac{7}{3} \\ -1 & \frac{2}{3} & -\frac{1}{3} \end{bmatrix}$ **13.** $\begin{bmatrix} -4 & 2 & 6 \\ -5 & 0 & -3 \end{bmatrix}$ **14.** $BA = \begin{bmatrix} 62 & 0 \\ -2 & 10 \\ -11 & 24 \end{bmatrix}$

15.
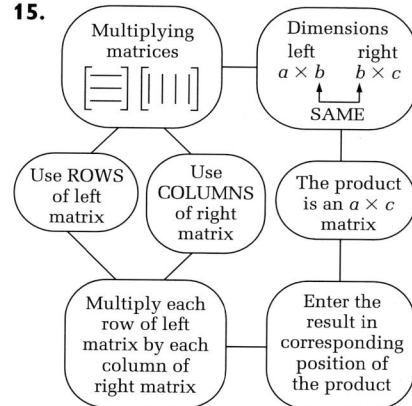

The map shows how to set up two matrices in order to multiply them. It also shows how to do the multiplication and the dimensions of the product.
16. about $(4.59, 0.412)$

Selected Answers

Page 187 Talk it Over

1.
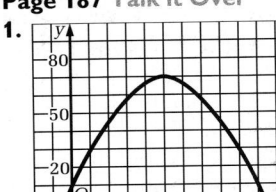

a. (0, 10) **b.** 70 ft
c. Estimates may vary.
Example: ≈208 ft

2. The graph still passes through (0, 10) but opens up instead of down and is shifted to the left.

Pages 190–192 Exercises and Problems
5. C **7.** D **9.** up **11.** $x = \frac{3}{2}$ **13.** $x = 1$ **15.** $(-2, -1)$;
minimum **17.** Choice of parabola may vary. All parabolas are given.

$y = -2x^2 + 12x - 14$ $y = x^2 + 4x + 3$

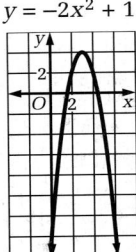   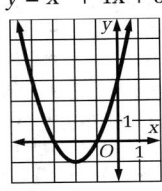

$y = -0.25x^2 - 0.5x + 2.5$

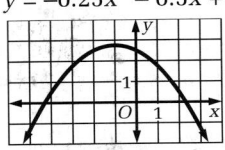

21. -3 **23.** -2 **25, 27.** Estimates may vary. Exact values are given. **25.** 0 and 4; $\frac{1}{2}(0^2) - 2(0) = 0$;

$\frac{1}{2}(4^2) - 2(4) = 0$ **27.** -4 and 5;

$0.2(-4)^2 - 0.2(-4) - 4 = 0$; $0.2(5)^2 - 0.2(5) - 4 = 0$

30. $\begin{bmatrix} 3 & 2 \\ 4 & -1 \end{bmatrix} \begin{bmatrix} x \\ y \end{bmatrix} = \begin{bmatrix} 5 \\ 3 \end{bmatrix}$ **31.** $\begin{bmatrix} 4 & -2 \\ -3 & 5 \end{bmatrix} \begin{bmatrix} x \\ y \end{bmatrix} = \begin{bmatrix} 8 \\ -6 \end{bmatrix}$

32. $\begin{bmatrix} -3 & 1 \\ 2 & 1 \end{bmatrix} \begin{bmatrix} x \\ y \end{bmatrix} = \begin{bmatrix} -4 \\ 21 \end{bmatrix}$ **33.** $r \approx 4$ cm

34. $y = x^2 + 4$ **35.** $y = (x - 4)^2$ **36.** $y = (x + 4)^2$

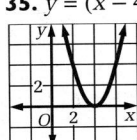   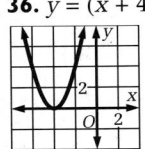

Pages 194–196 Talk it Over
1. Yes. **2.** No. **3.** Yes. **4.** Answers may vary. An example is given. You can tell if the graph has the same shape or position as a parabola with a simpler equation. You can determine the coordinates of the

vertex and tell whether the parabola opens up or down. **5.** (0, 0); (0, 3); The vertex is translated 3 units up. **6.** In equation (a), the vertex is translated down 2 units; in equation (b), the vertex is translated 4 units to the left; in equation (c), the vertex is translated 1 unit to the right and 3 units up. **7.** Yes. Explanations may vary An example is given. According to the order of operations, the power should be simplified first. Then the expression can be multiplied by 3. If you distribute the 3 first and then simplify the power, you actually multiply each term by 3^2 or 9. **8.** The equations have the same graph; they are equivalent equations.

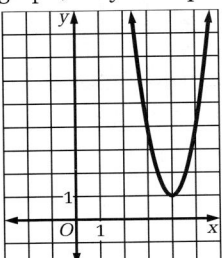

Pages 196–198 Exercises and Problems
1. the graph in step 8, $y = (x - 7)^2 + 4$
3. $y = 5(x + 8)^2$, $y = \frac{2}{3}(x + 1)^2$, $y = 0.01(x - 3)^2$,
$y = 12(x - 5)^2$ **5.** Move the graph 2 units to the right and 3 units up. **7.** Move the graph 2 units to the left and 5 units up. **9.** $y = \frac{1}{3}(x + 4)^2 - 3$ **13.** $(-6, 0)$; 36
15. (5, 2); 27 **17.** (1, 11); 16 **22.** $(-6, -23)$;
minimum **23.** $\left(-\frac{1}{5}, \frac{19}{5}\right)$; minimum **24.** (3, 10);
maximum

25.
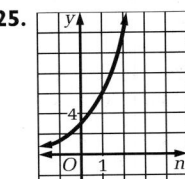

Since the equation $y = 3(2n)$ is an exponential function with base 2, its graph represents exponential growth.

26. 13 and -13 **27.** 28 and -28 **28.** 8 and -8

Pages 200–202 Talk it Over
1. The number represented by the variable is a speed. A negative value would not make sense. **2.** Yes; the solution set of an equation is not changed when both sides of the equation are divided by the same non-zero number. **3.** Yes; $\frac{2\pi}{9.8}$ is a constant coefficient for
C^2. **4.** The x-intercepts are the solutions of the equation. **5.** Both processes involve undoing. In Sample 1, since you are looking for a wavelength, you find only the positive square root. In Method 1 of Sample 2, since you do not know that the value you are looking

for is positive, you find both square roots.
6. Check by substituting both values for x in the original equation.   **7.** Check by graphing the related equation $y = 2(x + 5)^2 - 22$ and finding the x-intercepts.

Pages 203–205 Exercises and Problems
3. -2 **5. a.** 3   **b.** $x = 3$ **c.** $y = -x^2 + 6x - 5$ **d.** $x = -\frac{-6}{2} = 3$
e. The equation of the line of symmetry found from the graph and the equation found from the formula are the same, $x = 3$; and the mean of the solutions is also 3.   **7.** $x \approx 57.58$ **9.** 40 and -40 **11.** 7 and -7 **13.** about 1.7, about -1.7; $\pm\sqrt{3}$ **15.** about 4.9, about -2.9; $1 \pm \sqrt{15}$ **17.** 2, -8 **19.** $3 \pm \sqrt{30}$; about 8.5, about -2.5 **21.** 6, -2 **23.** $-23 \pm \sqrt{122}$; about -12, about -34 **32.** $(0, -1)$ **33.** $(-15, 0)$
34. $(2, 11)$ **35.** False. For example, Sarah might be in some other classroom, the cafeteria, or a hallway.
36. $x^2 - 2x - 15$ **37.** $2y^2 - 20y + 32$
38. $36z^2 - 42z - 18$

Pages 207–209 Talk it Over
1. $(2x - 3)(x - 1)$ **2. a.** 1 and -3 or -1 and 3
b. $(2x + 1)(x - 3)$ **3. a.** 2   **b.** $2(2x^2 + 5x + 3)$
c. $2(2x + 3)(x + 1)$ **4.** b   **5.** Substitute -1 and 1.25 for x in the original equation.   **6.** about -1 and about 1.25   **7.** The x-intercepts of the graph of $y = 4x^2 - x - 5$ are the solutions of the equation $4x^2 - x - 5 = 0$.

Pages 210–212 Exercises and Problems
5. $(2x - 1)(x - 3)$ **7.** $(7n + 3)(n + 2)$
9. $(3x + 1)(4x - 3)$ **11.** $(4z + 1)(6z - 5)$
13. $3(x - 1)(2x - 7)$ **15.** $2(6d - 5)(d - 2)$ **21.** $(x - 7)^2$
23. $(x + 4)(x - 4)$ **25.** $(x - 5y)(x + 5y)$ **27.** $-1, \frac{1}{3}$
29. 1   **31.** $\frac{3}{2}, -\frac{1}{2}$ **33.** B   **35.** A   **39.** 3, -3
40. $5 \pm \sqrt{5}$; about 7.2, about 2.8   **41.** 1, -5
42. Let t be the time in hours and r be the rate in miles per hour; $rt = 150$ or $t = \frac{150}{r}$.   **43.** 3 h
44. a. $6x$ and 90   **b.** 15

Page 213 Checkpoint
1. No; there are some trinomials that cannot be factored. For example, $2x^2 + 3x + 5$ cannot be factored, so $2x^2 + 3x + 5 = 0$ cannot be solved by factoring.
2. $(1, 4)$; minimum   **3.** $\left(\frac{1}{2}, \frac{1}{4}\right)$; maximum   **4.** 1 unit to the right, 5 units up   **5.** 2 units to the left   **6.** $\pm 2\sqrt{2}$; about 2.8, about -2.8 **7.** $-6 \pm \sqrt{11}$; about -2.7, about -9.3 **8.** 13, 3   **9.** 9, $\frac{4}{3}$ **10.** $\frac{5}{3}, -\frac{5}{3}$ **11.** -3

Pages 214–216 Talk it Over
1. $\frac{1}{x} = \frac{x}{x + 1}$ **2.** $x + 1 = x^2$; No. To solve the equation

$x^2 - x - 1 = 0$ by factoring, you consider the factors of the first term and the third term. The only possible factoring is $(x + 1)(x - 1)$, which does not produce the correct middle term.   **3.** the numbers x for which $x + 1 = x^2$

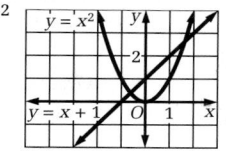

4. about -0.6 and about 1.6; The positive value is close to the golden ratio.
5. about -0.6 and about 1.6

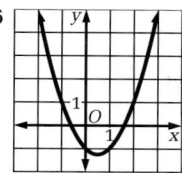

6. The x-coordinates of the points of intersection are the x-intercepts of $y = x^2 - x - 1$.   **7.** $a = 3$, $b = -2$, $c = 5$ **8.** There is no x-term so $b = 0$.   **9. a.** When -1.72 is substituted for t in the original equation, the resulting statement is true.   **b.** Since t represents a time, its value must be nonnegative.   **c.** A valid mathematical solution must make sense in real terms in order to be a valid solution for a situation.
10. about $(0.15, 17.11)$; The vertex represents the maximum height the cliff diver reaches. The first coordinate indicates the time at which he reaches his maximum height above the water and the second coordinate indicates that height.

Pages 217–221 Exercises and Problems
5. $-7, -2$ **7.** 9, 3   **9.** $-1, -\frac{2}{3}$

11. Ex. 5: $x^2 + 9x + 14 = 0$; $(x + 7)(x + 2) = 0$; $x = -7$ or $x = -2$
Ex. 6: $x^2 + 7x + 12 = 0$; $(x + 3)(x + 4) = 0$; $x = -3$ or $x = -4$
Ex. 7: $z^2 - 12z + 27 = 0$; $(z - 9)(z - 3) = 0$; $z = 9$ or $z = 3$
Ex. 8: $2n^2 + 9n + 4 = 0$; $(2n + 1)(n + 4) = 0$; $n = -\frac{1}{2}$ or $n = -4$
Ex. 9: $3x^2 + 5x + 2 = 0$; $(3x + 2)(x + 1) = 0$; $x = -\frac{2}{3}$ or $x = -1$
Ex. 10: $2x^2 + x - 3 = 0$; $(2x + 3)(x - 1) = 0$; $x = -\frac{3}{2}$ or $x = 1$

13. about -3.1, about 8.1   **17.** $-3 + \sqrt{5}$, $-3 - \sqrt{5}$
19. $-5 + \sqrt{10}$, $-5 - \sqrt{10}$ **25.** about 1.4, about -0.24

27. $-1, \frac{1}{4}$ **29.** about -3.3, about 1.3

31. about −2.6, about 2.6   **33.** about 2.3, about 0.7
35. about 0.2, about −3.5   **45.** $(x − 3)(x − 2)$
46. $(2x + 3)(x + 4)$ **47.** $(3x − 8)(x + 1)$ **48.** systematic
49. $2x^2 − 3x$ **50.** $−5xy + 5x + 2y − 2$
51. $28k^2 + 55k − 18$

Page 227 Talk it Over
1. none   **2.** infinitely many; Every point on the graph represents an ordered pair of real numbers that is a solution of the equation.

Pages 227–229 Exercises and Problems
3. zero   **5.** negative   **7. a.** one solution **b, c.** 3
9. a. two solutions **b, c.** −1, −1.5
11. a, b. no solutions   **c.**

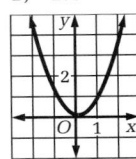

13. a, b. no solutions **c.**

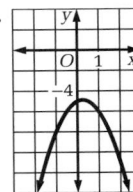

15. a. $k = 6$, $k = −6$ **b.** $k > 6$ or $k < −6$ **c.** $−6 < k < 6$
21. $0.5i$ **23.** $i\sqrt{83}$ or about $9.1i$ **25.** $6i$ **27.** $21 − 84i$
29. $−13 + 11i$ **31.** $78 − 36i$ **33.** 116   **35.** 1   **37.** i
39. about 0.5, about 0.2   **41.** −5   **43.** about $−0.5 + 0.3i$, about $−0.5 − 0.3i$ **46, 47.** Solution methods may vary. Examples are given.   **46.** undoing; about −2.8, about −7.2   **47.** factoring; −1.5   **48.** the quadratic formula; about 0.9, about −1.3   **49.** 32 students
50. $(−3, 6)$ **51.** infinitely many solutions   **52.** $(1, −2)$

Page 231 Talk it Over
1. Yes; the arcs intersect over the middle of the river and 110 ft is halfway across.   **2.** Since x is the first coordinate of the point of intersection, you will get the same value for y from either equation.
3. $−0.006(110)^2 + 1.44(110) − 16.4 =$
$−72.6 + 158.4 − 16.4 = 69.4$ ✓
4. The solution should be about $(110, 69.4)$.

Pages 233–235 Exercises and Problems
3. $(2, 1)$, $(−2, 1)$ **5.** no real solutions   **7.** $(−3, −3)$, $(3, −3)$ **9.** $(3, 3)$
11. Sketches may vary. An example is given.

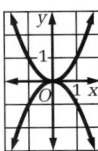

13, 15. Estimates may vary. Examples are given.
13. $(0.4, 2.3)$

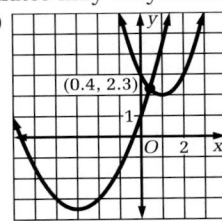

15. $(0, 0)$, $(12.5, 106.3)$

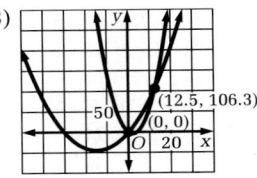

17. $\left(\sqrt{\dfrac{d − b}{a − c}}, \dfrac{ad − bc}{a − c}\right), \left(−\sqrt{\dfrac{d − b}{a − c}}, \dfrac{ad − bc}{a − c}\right)$; $a ≠ c$
23. two solutions   **24.** two solutions
25. no solutions   **26.** $(−10, 12)$
27. Area = 42 in.²   **28.** Area = 13.5 m²

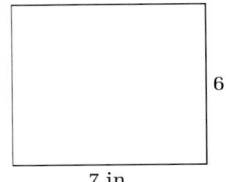

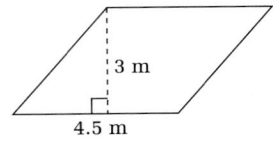

29. Area = 16 cm²

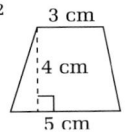

Pages 237–238 Unit 4 Review and Assessment
1. $(0, 0)$; 0   **2.** $(0, 4)$; 4   **3.** $(−6, −8)$; 10   **4.** Answers may vary. Example: $y = −x^2 − 6x − 9$ **5.** $(3, −16)$; down   **6.** $(1, 1)$; down   **7. a, b.** Answers may vary. Examples are given. **a.** $y = −x^2 + 6x − 5$
[or $y = −(x − 3)^2 + 4$] **b.** $y = −\dfrac{1}{2}x^2 + 3x − \dfrac{1}{2}$
[or $y = −\dfrac{1}{2}(x − 3)^2 + 4$] **c.** No; parabolas that are translations of each other have the same shape.
8. C   **9.** A   **10.** D   **11.** B   **12.** 4

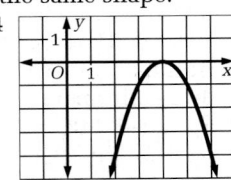

13. about 1.4, about −1.4

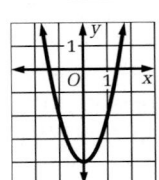

Integrated Mathematics

14. about 3.5, about −5.5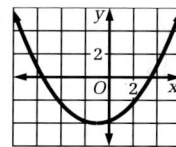

15. about 2.4, about −2.4 **16.** 10, −20 **17.** about 4.6, about −0.6 **18.** $(2x + 5)(x − 4)$ **19.** $(2n − 9)(2n + 9)$

20. $(4x − 3)^2$ **21.** $\frac{2}{3}$, 1 **22.** about −0.5, about −2.5

23. 1, −2.5 **24.** about 0.4, about 3.6 **25.** one solution **26.** two solutions **27.** no solutions
28. $24 + 12i$ **29.** $−4 − 58i$ **30.** $56 + 34i$ **31.** about $0.5 + 0.76i$, about $0.5 − 0.76i$ **32.** about −0.3, about −11.7 **33.** about $−0.1 + 0.9i$, about $−0.1 − 0.9i$
34. $(1.5, 5.25)$ **35.** $(0, 1)$, $(6, 79)$ **36.** about $(−0.9, −1.5)$, about $(0.9, −1.5)$

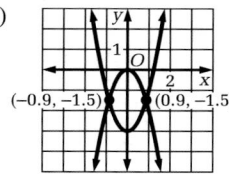

37. about $(−3.9, 3.8)$, about $(1.7, 0.7)$

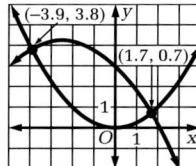

Unit 5

Page 245 Talk it Over
1. Tyler must have assumed that a quadrilateral belongs to the family of quadrilaterals linked to it below. **2.** Yes; they satisfy the definition of a parallelogram.

Pages 246–250 Exercises and Problems
1. b **3.** True. **5.** True. **7.** False. **9.** No; the figure does not have two pairs of consecutive sides congruent. **11.** No; the figure does not have two pairs of consecutive sides congruent. **29.** quadrilateral
31. rectangle; rhombus **33.** parallelogram
35. a. 33.75 ft^2 **b.** 140 m^2; Yes. **c.** the family of trapezoids: trapezoids, isosceles trapezoids; the family of parallelograms: rhombuses, rectangles, squares
37. about $(−2.148, −0.308)$; about $(2.148, −0.308)$
38. no solution **39.** $(0, 2)$ **40.** $y = 2x − 4$ **41.** $x = −2$
42. $y = 4$ **43.** 25 cm

Pages 252–254 Talk it Over
1. Answers may vary. Let $O = P_1$ and $C = P_2$. Then $x_1 = 0$, $x_2 = 6$, $y_1 = 0$, and $y_2 = 8$. **2.** No; both

changes are squared. **3.** Since $x_2 − x_1 = −(x_1 − x_2)$, $(x_2 − x_1)^2 = [−(x_1 − x_2)]^2 = (x_1 − x_2)^2$. Similarly, $(y_2 − y_1)^2 = (y_1 − y_2)^2$. **4.** 0 **5.** Subtract the y-coordinates. **6.** 6 **7.** 6 **8.** Answers may vary. An example is given. $AB = \sqrt{(−3 − 3)^2 + (4 − 1)^2} = \sqrt{36 + 9} = \sqrt{45} = 3\sqrt{5}$; $BC = \sqrt{(3 − 6)^2 + (1 − (−5))^2} = \sqrt{9 + 36} = \sqrt{45} = 3\sqrt{5}$; $CD = \sqrt{(6 − 0)^2 + (−5 − (−2))^2} = \sqrt{36 + 9} = \sqrt{45} = 3\sqrt{5}$; $DA = \sqrt{(0 − (−3))^2 + (−2 − 4)^2} = \sqrt{9 + 36} = \sqrt{45} = 3\sqrt{5}$; since the four sides are equal in measure, $ABCD$ is a rhombus. **9.** Answers may vary. An example is given. Show that each pair of consecutive sides is perpendicular.

Pages 255–258 Exercises and Problems
3. the lower line **7.** $\sqrt{85} \approx 9.22$ **9.** 3 **11.** 5
13. $\sqrt{29} \approx 5.4$ **17.** slope of $\overline{VU}$ = slope of $\overline{WT}$ = 0; slope of $\overline{VW}$ = slope of $\overline{UT} = \frac{4}{3}$; $\overline{VU} \parallel \overline{WT}$ and $\overline{VW} \parallel \overline{UT}$ so $TUVW$ is a parallelogram. **19.** $LM = LK = KJ = JM = 5$; $\overline{LK}$ and $\overline{MJ}$ have 0 slope and $\overline{LM}$ and $\overline{KJ}$ have undefined slope, so $\overline{LK} \perp \overline{LM}$, $\overline{LK} \perp \overline{KJ}$, $\overline{MJ} \perp \overline{LM}$, and $\overline{MJ} \perp \overline{KJ}$. $JKLM$ has four congruent sides and four right angles, so $JKLM$ is a square. **21.** Two pairs of consecutive sides are congruent. **23.** All sides are congruent and consecutive sides are perpendicular.
27. a. Measurements and answers may vary. The four sides of the figure are very close in length.
b. $JM = KL = \sqrt{52} \approx 7.2$; $JK = ML = \sqrt{53} \approx 7.3$; $JKLM$ is not a rhombus because all four sides are not congruent. **c.** slope of $\overline{JM}$ = slope of $\overline{KL} = \frac{3}{2}$; slope of $\overline{JK}$ = slope of $\overline{ML} = \frac{2}{7}$; $\overline{JM} \parallel \overline{KL}$ and $\overline{JK} \parallel \overline{ML}$, so $JKLM$ is a parallelogram. **d.** Answers may vary. An example is given. Drawings may be deceptive; segments that appear to be congruent may not be and may be so close that even measuring will not establish the truth. For example, in a drawing, two segments that are 32.8 mm and 32.7 mm long will certainly appear to be congruent and could not be measured accurately with a ruler. **29. a.** trapezoid
b. $AB = 8$; $BC \approx 5.1$; $CD = 4$; $AD \approx 5.8$ **c.** 30 square units **d.** about 22.9 **31.** False; if all four sides of a kite are not congruent, the kite is not a parallelogram.
32. True. **33.** y is divided by 4. **34.** y is doubled.
35. y is divided by 8. **36.** about 12.8°F **37.** 5.7
38. about 82.9

Page 259 Talk it Over
1. about $(15, 5)$ **2.** 14; The average of 3 and 25 is 14.
3. 5; The average of 7 and 3 is 5. **4.** $(14, 5)$

Pages 261–264 Exercises and Problems

3. $\left(2\frac{1}{2}, -3\frac{1}{2}\right)$ **5.** $(-1, 5)$ **7.** $\left(-2\frac{1}{2}, 5\right)$ **9.** $(1.65, 1.975)$

11. $D(4, 10)$ **13.** $D(6, 2)$

15. $PQ = \sqrt{(18 - 2)^2 + (14 - 4)^2} = \sqrt{256 + 100} = 2\sqrt{89}$; $PM = \sqrt{(10 - 2)^2 + (9 - 4)^2} = \sqrt{64 + 25} = \sqrt{89}$

25. $3\sqrt{5} \approx 6.71$ **26.** $8\sqrt{2} \approx 11.31$ **27.** 13 **28.** 4, −4
29. $5 \pm 2\sqrt{15}$; about 12.75, about −2.75 **30.** $x = -2 \pm \sqrt{15}$; about 1.87, about −5.87 **31.** dilation;
$O(0, 0)$; $B'(0, 4)$; $C'(6, 6)$; $D'(4, 0)$ **32.** translation;
$A'(1, -6)$; $B'(3, -2)$; $C'(5, -2)$; $D'(5, -4)$ **33.** rotation;
$O(0, 0)$; $B'(-3, 2)$; $C'(-3, 4)$; $D'(-1, 4)$ **34.** reflection;
$A'(-1, 1)$; $B'(-1, 3)$; $C'(-3, 3)$; $D'(-3, 0)$

Page 265 Checkpoint
1. two pairs of parallel sides; four right angles; four congruent sides; four congruent sides and four right angles; You would find the slope of a segment to determine if sides are parallel or if they meet at right angles. You would use the distance formula to show that the lengths of the sides are equal in measure.
2. a. slope of $\overline{AB}$ = slope of $\overline{DC} = \frac{2}{11}$; slope of $\overline{AD}$ =

slope of $\overline{BC} = -\frac{5}{3}$ **b.** $ABCD$ is a parallelogram since it has two pairs of parallel sides. $ABCD$ is not a rectangle since the slopes of adjacent sides are not negative reciprocals. It is not a rhombus since it does not have four congruent sides. **3. a.** slope of $\overline{WX}$ = slope of $\overline{ZY}$ = 5; slope of $\overline{XY}$ = slope of $\overline{WZ} = -\frac{1}{5}$

b. $WX = XY = YZ = WZ = \sqrt{26}$ **c.** $WXYZ$ is a square, since it is both a rectangle and a rhombus.
4. a. $2\sqrt{37} \approx 12.17$ **b.** $(-1, -1)$ **5. a.** $\sqrt{193} \approx 13.89$
b. $(-0.5, 6)$ **6. a.** $\sqrt{401} \approx 20.02$ **b.** $(2, -5.5)$ **7. a.** 5
b. $(4.5, -3)$ **8.** $(-8, -3)$ **9.** $(4, 1)$ **10.** $(7, -9)$
11. $(-2, 8)$

Pages 267–269 Talk it Over
1. $P'(6, 1)$, $Q'(5, 3)$, $R'(3, 4)$, $S'(1, -1)$ **2.** $AB = \sqrt{17}$;
$A'B' = \sqrt{17}$; No; No. **3.** No; Yes. **4.** Yes. No; the slope of $\overline{AB}$ is positive and the slope of $\overline{A'B'}$ is negative. **5.** Yes; $\overline{BC}$ is another side in the same triangle. Therefore, it will be affected in the same manner as other sides of the triangle by a transformation.

Pages 270–273 Exercises and Problems
1. rotation of 90°, 180°, 270° **7. a.** a translation 5 units to the right, 3 units down **b.** To get the coordinates of the image of $\triangle QRS$, add 5 to the original x-coordinate and subtract 3 from the original

y-coordinate. $(x, y) \rightarrow (x + 5, y - 3)$ **9.** translation 2 units to the right, 5 units down

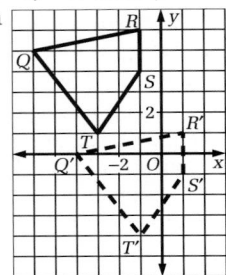

11. dilation with a scale factor of 3

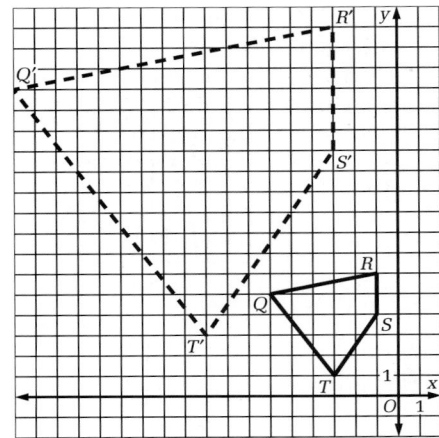

13. translation 4 units to the right

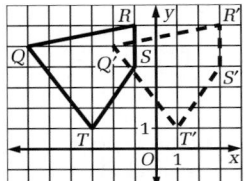

17. D **19.** C **21.** B

23.

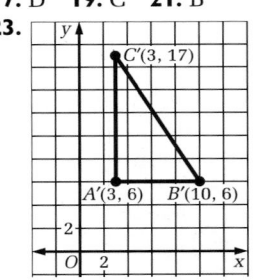

25.

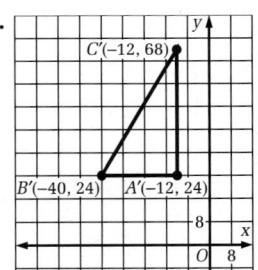

27.

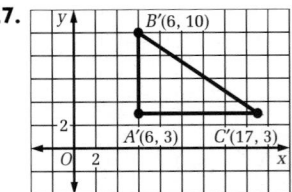

29. a. $\frac{11}{7}$ **b.** $-\frac{11}{7}; \frac{11}{7}; \frac{11}{7}; \frac{11}{7}; -\frac{7}{11}$ **c.** translation and dilation (Exs. 24–26); reflection (Ex. 23) and rotation (Ex. 27) **d.** Yes; translations, dilations preserve the orientation of the original image; reflections and most rotations do not preserve the orientation of the original image. All rotations of $180n$, where n is an integer, will produce images, any of whose sides will have slope equal to the slope of the corresponding side in the original image. **37.** $(50, -50)$ **38.** $(4, 3)$ **39.** $(-1.5, 2)$ **40. a.** $\frac{3}{49}$ or about 0.061 **b.** 6, –6 **41.** $AB = \sqrt{20} \approx 4.5$, $BC = 4$, $CD = \sqrt{32} \approx 5.7$, $AD = 10$

Pages 274–276 Talk it Over
1. 576.6 mi **2.** You will be able to read the miles traveled directly from the trip odometer.
3. a. Grace's; The arithmetic is simpler because more zeros are involved. **b.** No. **4.** $a = 4$, $b = 2$, $c = 3$
5. $a = 9$, $b = 2$, $c = 5$, $d = 6$, $e = 10$
6. one variable
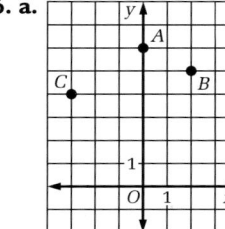

Pages 277–279 Exercises and Problems
9. a **11.** 0 **13.** 0 **15. a.** There are two possible answers: translate the triangle three units to the right or reflect the triangle over the y-axis.
b. translation: $J'(0, 0)$, $O'(3, 0)$, $L'(1, 3)$; reflection: $J'(3, 0)$, $O'(0, 0)$, $L'(2, 3)$ **17. a.** Translate the polygon one unit right and three units up. **b.** $L'(0, 0)$, $M'(3, 0)$, $N'(3, 2)$, $K'(0, 2)$ **19.** $(-3a, 2a)$ **21.** $-a$
27. $A'(-1, -2)$, $B'(-3, 1)$, $C'(-2, 2)$ **28.** $A'(0, -3)$, $B'(2, 0)$, $C'(1, 1)$ **29.** $5i$ **30.** $i\sqrt{30}$ **31.** $24 + 6i$
32. $12 - 5i$ **33.** False; for example, when $x = \frac{1}{2}$, $\frac{1}{\frac{1}{2}} = 2$ which is greater than $\frac{1}{2}$.

Pages 282–283 Talk it Over
1. parallelograms, rectangles, rhombuses, squares
2. squares, kites, rhombuses **3.** rectangles, squares
4. parallelograms, rectangles, rhombuses, squares
5. three segments; Yes.

Pages 284–286 Exercises and Problems
1. The midpoint of $\overline{OV}$ is $\left(\frac{0 + 12}{2}, \frac{0 + 5}{2}\right) = \left(6, 2\frac{1}{2}\right)$.
The midpoint of $\overline{UW}$ is $\left(\frac{10 + 2}{2}, \frac{0 + 5}{2}\right) = \left(6, 2\frac{1}{2}\right)$.

3. Ex. 2; Ex. 1 merely provides an example, while Ex. 2 constitutes a proof for the general case.
5. a. midpoint of $\overline{OR} = \left(\frac{a + 0}{2}, \frac{a + 0}{2}\right) = \left(\frac{a}{2}, \frac{a}{2}\right)$;
midpoint of $\overline{QS} = \left(\frac{0 + a}{2}, \frac{a + 0}{2}\right) = \left(\frac{a}{2}, \frac{a}{2}\right)$
b. slope of $\overline{OR} = \frac{a - 0}{a - 0} = 1$; slope of $\overline{QS} = \frac{a - 0}{0 - a} = \frac{a}{-a} = -1$; Since the slope of $\overline{OR}$ is the negative reciprocal of the slope of $\overline{QS}$, $\overline{OR} \perp \overline{QS}$. **c.** $OR = a\sqrt{2}$ and $QS = a\sqrt{2}$, so the diagonals have the same length. **9. a.** $P(a, 2c)$; $Q(2a, c)$; $R(a, 0)$; $S(0, c)$
b. rhombus **c.** $PQ = \sqrt{(2a - a)^2 + (c - 2c)^2} = \sqrt{a^2 + c^2}$; $QR = \sqrt{(2a - a)^2 + (c - 0)^2} = \sqrt{a^2 + c^2}$; $SR = \sqrt{(a - 0)^2 + (0 - c)^2} = \sqrt{a^2 + c^2}$; $PS = \sqrt{(a - 0)^2 + (2c - c)^2} = \sqrt{a^2 + c^2}$; all four sides are equal in measure and the opposite sides are parallel, so $PQRS$ is a rhombus. **17.** $(a, 0)$ **18.** $(a, 0)$
19. $(a + b, c)$ **20.** Carlos is taller than Ben.
21. If Julie enters the race, then she will get a prize.
22. $\frac{1}{80}$ **23.** $\frac{79}{80}$

Pages 288–289 Unit 5 Review and Assessment
1. True. **2.** True. **3.** True. **4.** True.
5.

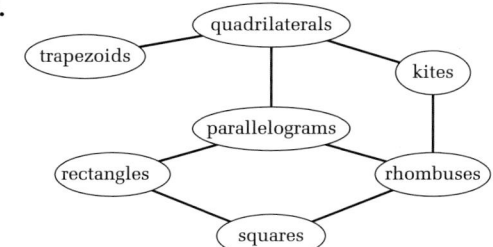

6. a.
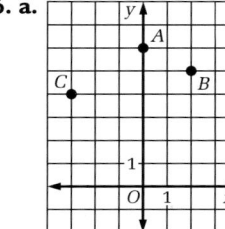
b. C **c.** A **7.** The Pythagorean theorem tells how to find the square of the distance between the two endpoints of a hypotenuse of a right triangle: $(\text{distance})^2 = (\text{change in } x)^2 + (\text{change in } y)^2$. Taking the same square root of both sides gives the distance formula: distance = $\sqrt{(\text{change in } x)^2 + (\text{change in } y)^2}$.
8. $FG = \sqrt{(-3 - 0)^2 + (0 - 2)^2} = \sqrt{13}$;
$HG = \sqrt{(-3 - 0)^2 + (0 - (-2))^2} = \sqrt{13}$;
$FJ = \sqrt{(2 - 0)^2 + (0 - 2)^2} = \sqrt{8}$;
$HJ = \sqrt{(2 - 0)^2 + (0 - (-2))^2} = \sqrt{8}$; Since $FGHJ$ has two pairs of adjacent congruent sides, $FGHJ$ is a kite.

9. slope of $\overline{MN} = \dfrac{3-5}{-1-(-5)} = -\dfrac{1}{2}$; slope of $\overline{PO} = \dfrac{2-0}{-4-0} =$ $-\dfrac{1}{2}$; slope of $\overline{MP} = \dfrac{5-2}{-5-(-4)} = -3$; slope of $\overline{NO} =$ $\dfrac{3-0}{-1-0} = -3$; slope of $\overline{MN}$ = slope of $\overline{PO}$ so $\overline{MN} \parallel \overline{PO}$; slope of $\overline{MP}$ = slope of $\overline{NO}$ so $\overline{MP} \parallel \overline{NO}$; since $MNOP$ has two pairs of parallel sides, $MNOP$ is a parallelogram. **10. a.** $(3, -1)$ **b.** $(-12, -13)$

11. Answers may vary. An example is given. Suppose the coordinates (1980, 1020) and (1990, 980) represent two points on a fitted line that describes your school's enrollment from 1980 to the present. You can use the midpoint formula to estimate your school's enrollment in 1985:
$\left(\dfrac{1980 + 1990}{2}, \dfrac{1020 + 980}{2}\right)$ = (1985, 1000); your school's enrollment was about 1000 in 1985.

12. 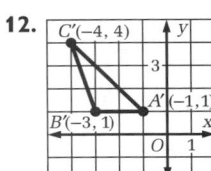 **13.**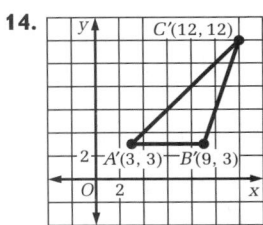

14.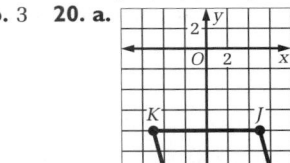

15. Ex. 12; Exs. 12 and 13 **16.** Check students' sketches. **a.** The image is a reflection over the y-axis. **b.** The image is a 180° rotation. **17.** No; a reflection over the x-axis maps (x, y) to $(x, -y)$. A 90° clockwise rotation maps (x, y) to $(y, -x)$. **18.** 10 **19. a.** 6 or 0 **b.** 3 **20. a.**

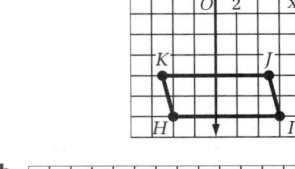

b.

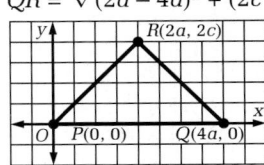 **c.** parallelogram

21. $OR = \sqrt{(2a-0)^2 + (2c-0)^2} = 2\sqrt{a^2 + c^2}$; $QR = \sqrt{(2a-4a)^2 + (2c-0)^2} = 2\sqrt{a^2 + c^2}$

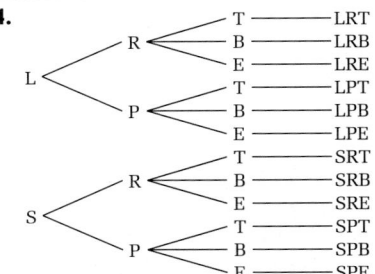

Unit 6

Pages 295–298 Talk it Over
1–3. Answers may vary. Examples are given.
1. a. Items to consider include the purpose of the trip, the weather, any special occasions to be attended, and so on. **b.** Draw a tree diagram with one column of branches for the shirts and one for the shorts or the jeans. **2.** Draw a tree diagram with one column of branches for the first color and one for the second. **3.** Both involve choosing a combination of items from a list of several items. There are more possible choices in question 2. Also, in question 2, the choices from the second category depend on the choice for the first.

4.

```
                    T ——————— LRT    The meals are
           R <      B ——————— LRB    the same; the
                    E ——————— LRE    parts of the meal
     L <            T ——————— LPT    are listed in a
           P <      B ——————— LPB    different order.
                    E ——————— LPE
                    T ——————— SRT
           R <      B ——————— SRB
                    E ——————— SRE
     S <            T ——————— SPT
           P <      B ——————— SPB
                    E ——————— SPE
```

5. Answers may vary. An example is given. You could make a chart with three columns, one for each choice. List one main dish in the first column, first row and one side dish in the second column, first row. Then list one drink choice in the third column, first row. Then with the same entries in the first two columns of the second row, list the next drink choice in the third column, second row. Proceed until all possible choices are listed. There will be twelve rows in the table. **6. a.** 4 choices **b.** 6 choices
7. Answers may vary. An example is given. Without making a table, you may be able to think of the outcomes as ordered pairs with six different first coordinates and six different second coordinates.
8. 5 outcomes **9.** 3 outcomes **10.** 18 outcomes
11. In Sample 1, exactly one item is chosen from each category. In Sample 3, you do not have to choose an item from each category. **12.** 15 accessory combinations

Pages 299–301 Exercises and Problems
1. 10 outcomes **3.** 9 outcomes **5.** white corded with built-in answering machine, white corded with

speakerphone, white cordless with built-in answering machine, white cordless with speakerphone, gray corded with built-in answering machine, gray corded with speakerphone, gray cordless with built-in answering machine, gray cordless with speakerphone, black corded with built-in answering machine, black corded with speakerphone, black cordless with built-in answering machine, black cordless with speakerphone   **7.** 8 ways (Let "H" indicate heads, and "T" tails, and the three letters indicate the position of the nickel, dime, and quarter in order from left to right. The possible outcomes are HHH, HHT, HTH, HTT, THH, THT, TTH, TTT.)   **9.** There are 36 possible results.   **11.** 16 ways   **21.** False.   **22.** True.

23. $\dfrac{50a^5}{b^2}$ **24.** $\dfrac{25x^4}{y^3}$ **25.** $\dfrac{36}{n^6}$

26.

Number of half-lives	Amount present (g)
0	600
1	300
2	150
3	75

Since the half-life is 8 days, there will be 100 g left after 16 days and before 24 days.   **27.** 6   **28.** 60
29. 3   **30.** −0.25

Pages 303–305 Talk it Over
1. a. 30 arrangements   **b.** Answers may vary. English examples: at, as; French examples: et, es
2. a. 120 arrangements   **b.** Answers may vary. English examples: rat, ate, sat; Spanish examples: ésa, ser
3. the number of arrangements when 8 are arranged 5 at a time   **4.** $(8 - 5)! = 3! = 6$ **5.** $_8P_5 = \dfrac{8!}{(8 - 5)!} = \dfrac{8!}{3!} =$
$8 \cdot 7 \cdot 6 \cdot 5 \cdot 4 = 6720$ **6.** There are four choices for the first letter, three for the second, and two for the third. By the multiplication counting principle, the number of arrangements is $4 \cdot 3 \cdot 2 = 24$. Using the permutations formula, $_4P_3 = \dfrac{4!}{(4 - 3)!} = \dfrac{4!}{1!} =$
$4 \cdot 3 \cdot 2 \cdot 1 = 24$. Both methods produce the same result.

Pages 306–309 Exercises and Problems
1. 9 factorial; $9 \cdot 8 \cdot 7 \cdot 6 \cdot 5 \cdot 4 \cdot 3 \cdot 2 \cdot 1 = 362,880$
3. 40,320 ways   **5. a.** 120 arrangements   **b.** 720 arrangements   **c.** Answers may vary. Examples are given. molds; models, seldom   **7.** 2   **9.** 5040
17. 6720   **19.** 5040   **21.** 120   **23.** 24   **25.** 24
27. 720   **32.** Lani, Eve, Derek, Peter; Lani, Eve, Peter, Derek; Lani, Derek, Eve, Peter; Lani, Derek, Peter, Eve; Lani, Peter, Derek, Eve, Lani, Peter, Eve, Derek; Eve, Lani, Derek, Peter; Eve, Lani, Peter, Derek; Eve, Derek, Lani, Peter; Eve, Derek, Peter, Lani; Eve, Peter, Derek, Lani; Eve, Peter, Lani, Derek; Derek, Eve, Lani,

Peter; Derek, Eve, Peter, Lani; Derek, Lani, Eve, Peter; Derek, Lani, Peter, Eve; Derek, Peter, Eve, Lani; Derek, Peter, Lani, Eve; Peter, Derek, Eve, Lani; Peter, Derek, Lani, Eve; Peter, Eve, Derek, Lani; Peter, Eve, Lani, Derek; Peter, Lani, Derek, Eve; Peter, Lani, Eve, Derek   **33.** $(2x + 3)(x - 2)$ **34.** $(3x - 5)(3x + 5)$
35. $(5x + 2)^2$ **36–39.** Answers may vary. Examples are given.   **36.** 0%; The sun rises every day.
37. 100%; I usually have cereal for breakfast.
38. 10%; Most of the ground is snow-covered now.
39. 50%; In New England, it is possible to have snow in December.

Pages 310–315 Talk it Over
1. 4   **2.** 26   **3.** 2   **4.** 12   **5.** 2 of diamonds, 2 of hearts   **6.** Jeannine's clue indicates her card is both a 2 and red; Chris's indicates his is one or the other. His will be harder to guess because his clue describes many more cards. Also, it is not clear if he means his card is not both.   **7.** No; each card has only one label.   **8.** No; there are three cards that are both spades and face cards.   **9. a.** 13; 39   **b.** Yes; a card cannot be a heart and not a heart at the same time.
c. 1   **10.** The events "no two people in a group of five people have the same birthday" and "at least two people in a group of five have the same birthday" are complementary. The probability that at least two of the five people have the same birthday is about $100\% - 97\%$ or 3%.   **11.** Find the probability that no two people in the group of six have the same birth date, and then subtract that probability from 1.
12. a, b. Answers may vary. For a class of 25 people, the probability that at least two people have the same birthday is about 57%.   **13.** $119:1$ **14.** about 99%
15. $6:19; 19:6$

Pages 315–318 Exercises and Problems
3. about 17% **5.** about 67% **7.** about 67%
9. rolling a 6 and rolling a prime   **11.** 25%
13. 98% **23. a.** $\dfrac{1}{24}$ or about 4.17% **b.** $1:23$
c. $\dfrac{1}{12}$ **25.** 75% **27.** 50% **29.** $35:1$ **41.** 120; 720
42. $9i$ **43.** $60i$ **44.** $34 + 22i$ **45.** $-3 + 15i$

46.

slacks color	yellow sweater	black sweater
blue	blue slacks, yellow sweater	blue slacks, black sweater
green	green slacks, yellow sweater	green slacks, black sweater

Pages 319–323 Talk it Over
1. Divide the number of entries the team has by the total number of entries.   **2.** about 0.152; about 0.015
3. dependent   **4.** dependent   **5.** independent
6. independent   **7.** In Sample 3, the list of possible

choices changes after the first choice. In Sample 2, the list does not change. In Sample 3, since songs do not repeat, the song chosen first is no longer a possible choice. There are only 49 possible choices remaining. **8. a.** independent; The choice of the first song has no effect on the choice of the second. **b.** 0.052

Pages 323–326 Exercises and Problems
1. about 0.016 **3.** about 0.063

5. a.

+	1	2	3	3
1	2	3	4	4
2	3	4	5	5
3	4	5	6	6
3	4	5	6	6

b. 2, 3, 4, 5, 6 **c.** 4; 0.3125 **d.** 0.25 **e.** The probability of an even sum is greater. P(even sum) = 0.625; P(odd sum) = 0.375 **15. a.** 0.09 **b.** about 0.067
17. about 0.000004 **19.** about 0.002 **25. a.** 0.4
b. 2:3 **26.** $P = \dfrac{I}{rt}$ **27.** $x = \dfrac{y+40}{3}$ **28.** $y = \dfrac{p-mx}{n}$
29. a. the number of arrangements when 9 are arranged 2 at a time **b.** 72

Page 327 Checkpoint 1
1. First, determine how many sums are possible when two dice are rolled. Next, determine the probability of getting a total of 6 and the probability of getting a total of 9. Finally, multiply the two probabilities. **2. a.** JOHN, JONH, JHON, JHNO, JNOH, JNHO, OJHN, OJNH, OHJN, OHNJ, ONJH, ONHJ, HOJN, HONJ, HJON, HJNO, HNJO, HNOJ, NOJH, NOHJ, NJOH, NJHO, NHJO, NHOJ **b.** Answers may vary. An example is given. No; it may not be a good idea, since his four-letter name is an obvious choice and there are only 24 permutations. With three chances to guess the code, a thief would have a 12.5% chance of doing so. **3.** 5040 **4.** 1320 **5.** P(vowel) ≈ 0.429; P(consonant) ≈ 0.571 **6.** The events are mutually exclusive since none of the letters is both a vowel and a consonant. The events are complementary since they are mutually exclusive and together they include all the possibilities. **7.** 4:3 **8.** about 0.028
9. about 0.005

Pages 328–330 Talk it Over
1. Answers may vary. An example is given. The cones in the first column show all the ways the first three flavors can be arranged. The second column shows the ways the first two and the fourth can be combined, and so on. **2.** 60 cones
3. $_5P_3 = \dfrac{5!}{(5-3)!} = \dfrac{5!}{2!} = \dfrac{120}{2} = 60$ **4.** 6; $_3P_3$

5. 10 dishes **6.** $\dfrac{1}{6}$ **7.** 15 pairs **8.** 30 ways
9. combinations; permutations

Pages 330–332 Exercises and Problems
1. the number of permutations of 7 items arranged 4 at a time **3.** the number of permutations of 8 items arranged 5 at a time **5.** $_8C_5$; 120 times; For every combination of 5 items, there are 120 arrangements of the 5 items. **7.** 1 **9.** 15 **11.** 84 **13.** 1680
17. combinations; 20 sets **25.** about 0.086 **26.** 90 ft^2
27. 4320 mm^2 **28.** 21 **29.** 405 **30.** 65,536x

Pages 333–335 Talk it Over
1. A line drawn through the center of the top circle and perpendicular to the opposite side of the triangle is an axis of symmetry. **2.** Summaries may vary. An example is given. The first and last symbols in each row are the same. The other symbols appear to be made by adding the number of marks on the two circles above a given symbol. **3.** 6 **4.** 10
5. $_4C_3 = \dfrac{4!}{3!1!} = \dfrac{24}{6} = 4$ **6.** $_4C_0 + {}_4C_1 + {}_4C_2 + {}_4C_3 = \dfrac{4!}{0!4!} + \dfrac{4!}{1!3!} + \dfrac{4!}{2!2!} + \dfrac{4!}{3!1!} = 1 + 4 + 6 + 4 = 15$

Pages 336–337 Exercises and Problems
1. a. one **b.** Given the first sixteen rows of Pascal's triangle, find the number in row 15, diagonal 5. Remember that the first row and diagonal are row 0 and diagonal 0. **c.** 1024 **5.** 10 **7.** 6 **9.** 7 **11.** 1
13. $n = 4, r = 2; n = 6, r = 1; n = 6, r = 5$ **15.** 3 ways
17. 1 way **19.** 20 combinations
24. $_{120}C_2 = \dfrac{120!}{2!118!} = \dfrac{120 \cdot 119}{2!} = 7140$

25. slope: 4; vertical intercept: 0; increasing
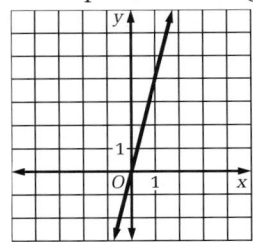

26. slope: −2; vertical intercept: 3; decreasing
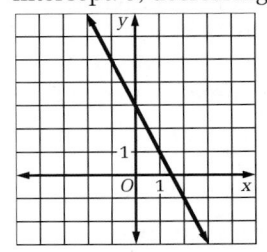

27. slope: 0; vertical intercept: −3; constant
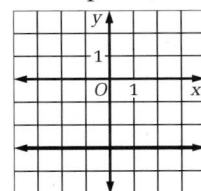

28.
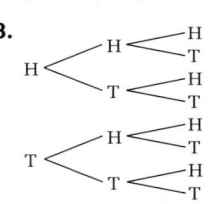

Page 340 Talk it Over

1. a. Answers may vary. I prefer Pascal's triangle, since it involves less work than making a diagram and it is not necessary to know what the actual out comes are. **b.** $_4C_2 = \frac{4!}{2!2!} = \frac{24}{2 \cdot 2} = 6$ **2.** 0.25

3. 0.3125 **4.** about 0.23

Pages 341–344 Exercises and Problems

3. 0.375 **5.** 0.3125 **7.** 0.3125 **18.** 15 ways
19. $Q'(-1, 0)$; $R'(1, 0)$; $S'(1, -4)$; $T'(-3, -3)$
20. $Q'(2, 4)$; $R'(6, 4)$; $S'(6, -4)$; $T'(-2, -2)$
21. a. about 0.167 **b.** 0.5 **c.** No; the events can happen at the same time since five is a prime number.

Page 344 Checkpoint

1. Find the number in row 5, diagonal 4. (5)
2. a. 126 groups **b.** 120 ways **3.** 1 3 3 1; Answers may vary. An example is given. The first and fourth numbers are 1. To find the second number, add the first and second numbers of row 2. To find the third number, add the second and third numbers of row 2.
4. $_4C_2$; 6 **5.** 0.125 **6.** 0.15625

Pages 346–347 Talk it Over

1. The probability of being left-handed is 0.1 and the probability of being right-handed is 0.9.
2. $_3C_2 = \frac{3!}{(3-2)!2!} = \frac{3 \cdot 2 \cdot 1}{1 \cdot 2 \cdot 1} = 3$ **3.** Answers may vary. An example is given. The number of left-handed students may be 0, 1, 2, or 3. Using the reasoning described, the probabilities would be 0 students: 0.729; 1 student: 0.081; 2 students: 0.009; 3 students: 0.001. The sum of those probabilities is only 0.82.
4. There is only one outcome for "no left-handed students" and $P(RRR) = 0.729$. Then P(at least one left-handed student) $= 1 - 0.729 = 0.271$. This method involves less computation and therefore less room for error than the other method. **5.** 0.028
6. about 0.167 **7.** about 0.833
8.

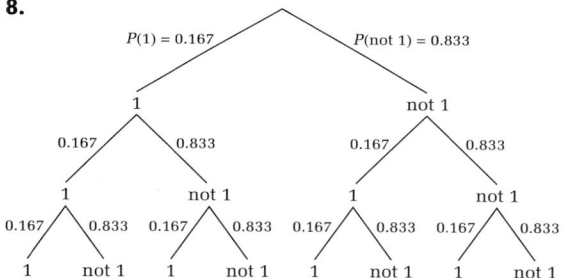

9. No; there are eight possible outcomes with varying probabilities. For example, $P(111) \approx 0.005$ and P(no 1's) ≈ 0.578.

Pages 347–350 Exercises and Problems

3. about 0.016 **5.** 0.15625 **7. a.** There are a limited number of trials. The two possible outcomes ("1" and "not 1") are mutually exclusive and $P(1) + P(\text{not } 1) = 1$. The trials are independent.
b. Solution method may vary. An example is given. Use the tree diagram shown in the answer for Talk it Over question 8. Since "rolling at least one 1" and "rolling no 1's" are complementary, find P(no 1's). The only favorable outcome is NNN with probability $\left(\frac{5}{6}\right)^3 \approx 0.579$. Then P(at least one 1) ≈ 0.421.
19. 0.3125 **20, 21.** Answers may vary. Examples are given. **20.** $(-2.7, 3.6)$ and $(0.7, 0.3)$ **21.** $(-0.5, 1)$ and $(0.5, 1)$ **22.** $V = 3a \cdot 3a \cdot 6a = 54a^3$
23. $V = 15x \cdot 10x \cdot 2y = 300x^2y$

Pages 351–354 Talk it Over

1. Both models have length $a + b$ and width $a + b$. The area of the figure on the left is $(a + b)^2$. The total area of the figures on the right is $a^2 + 2ab + b^2$.
2. $(a + b)(a + b) = (a + b)(a) + (a + b)(b) = a(a) + b(a) + a(b) + b(b) = a^2 + 2ab + b^2$ **3.** Each gold prism has a square base with side length equal to a, and a height equal to b, so the volume is $a \cdot a \cdot b = a^2b$.
4. Each green prism has a square base with side length equal to b, and a height equal to a, so the volume is $b \cdot b \cdot a = b^2a$. **5.** Answers may vary. Example: $(a + b)(a + b)(a + b) = (a + b)[(a + b)(a + b)] = (a + b)(a^2 + 2ab + b^2) = a(a^2 + 2ab + b^2) + b(a^2 + 2ab + b^2) = a(a^2) + a(2ab) + a(b^2) + b(a^2) + b(2ab) + b(b^2) = a^3 + 2a^2b + ab^2 + a^2b + 2ab^2 + b^3 = a^3 + 3a^2b + 3ab^2 + b^3$ **6.** The coefficients of $(a + b)n$ are the numbers in row n of Pascal's triangle.
7. The exponents of the a variables in $(a + b)n$ are decreasing consecutive integers from n to 0. The exponents of the b variables in $(a + b)n$ are increasing consecutive integers from 0 to n. **8.** Yes.
9. $1a^3b^0 + 3a^2b^1 + 3a^1b^2 + 1a^0b^3$ **10. a.** 7 terms
b. $a^6 + 6a^5b + 15a^4b^2 + 20a^3b^3 + 15a^2b^4 + 6ab^5 + b^6$
11. $n + 1$ **12.** The second term of the binomial is a constant, not a variable, so the coefficients of Pascal's triangle are multiplied by the constant raised to the correct power. **13.** Even powers of negative numbers are always positive. **14.** because even and odd powers of negative numbers alternate signs

Pages 354–357 Exercises and Problems

1. $x^2 + 6x + 9$ **3. a.** $m^3 + 6m^2 + 12m + 8$ **b.** There is one block with volume m^3 and one with volume 8. There are three blocks with volume $2m^2$ and three with volume $4m$. **5.** $c^3 + 3c^2d + 3cd^2 + d^3$
7. $x^5 + 5x^4y + 10x^3y^2 + 10x^2y^3 + 5xy^4 + y^5$
9. $x^3 + 6x^2 + 12x + 8$ **11.** $y^4 - 8y^3 + 24y^2 - 32y + 16$
13. $x^3 + 9x^2 + 27x + 27$ **15.** $a^{10} + 10a^9 + 45a^8 + 120a^7 + 210a^6 + 252a^5 + 210a^4 + 120a^3 + 45a^2 + 10a + 1$ **17.** Yes; each term of the expansion has the

form $_6C_rp^{(6-r)}q^r$. **19.** No; each term of the expansion has the form $_3C_rp^{(3-r)}(2q)^r$. When these terms are simplified, the coefficient of each term except the first is multiplied by a power of 2. **26.** about 0.001

27. slope of $\overline{AB} = \frac{1+1}{2+3} = \frac{2}{5}$ and slope of $\overline{CD} = \frac{-1+3}{7-2} = \frac{2}{5}$; slope of $\overline{AD} = \frac{-3+1}{2+3} = -\frac{2}{5}$ and slope of $\overline{BC} = \frac{-1-1}{7-2} = -\frac{2}{5}$; $AB = \sqrt{(2+3)^2 + (1+1)^2} = \sqrt{29}$;

$BC = \sqrt{(7-2)^2 + (-1-1)^2} = \sqrt{29}$;

$CD = \sqrt{(7-2)^2 + (-1+3)^2} = \sqrt{29}$;

$AD = \sqrt{(2+3)^2 + (-3+1)^2} = \sqrt{29}$; Since $ABCD$ has two pairs of parallel sides and all four sides have the same measure, $ABCD$ is a rhombus. **28.** True. **29.** False. **30.** True. **31.** True.

Pages 359–360 Unit 6 Review and Assessment

1.

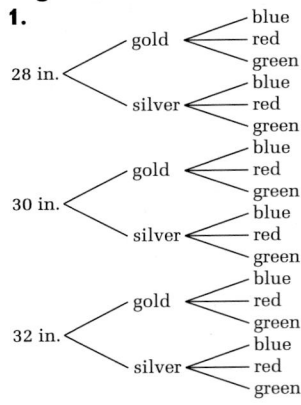

2. 6,084,000 plates **3.** 2,948,400 plates **4.** $_{15}P_{10} = 10,897,286,400$ **5.** about 0.333 **6.** about 0.833 **7.** about 0.667 **8.** 1:2 **9.** 3:1 **10.** about 0.037 **11.** about 0.018 **12.** 495 **13.** $_5P_3 = 60$; $_5C_3 = 10$; $_5C_3 = \frac{_5P_3}{_3P_3}$ **14.** 1, 4, 6, 4, 1; $_4C_0, _4C_1, _4C_2, _4C_3, _4C_4$ **15.** The number in row n, diagonal r of Pascal's triangle is equal to the number of combinations of n items selected r at a time. **16.** 0.3125 **17.** Answers may vary. An example is given. For the event "a baby is born," $P(\text{boy}) = P(\text{girl})$. If twelve babies are born at a local hospital on one day, what is the probability that at least half of them are boys? **18.** 0.3456 **19.** 0.4752 **20.** $x^4 + 8x^3 + 24x^2 + 32x + 16$ **21.** $x^5 - 15x^4 + 90x^3 - 270x^2 + 405x - 243$ **22.** $x^3 + 3x^2y + 3xy^2 + y^3$ **23.** $r^3 - 3r^2s + 3rs^2 - s^3$

Pages 366–367 Talk it Over

1. stock clerk at Food Stuff or Shop-All, ice cream server at Lunch Bag; Jean wants a job as a shop clerk *or* to work at Northmall *or* both. **2.** none; The only job that is for 20 or more hours per week pays less than $6.50. **3.** inclusive *or* **4.** exclusive *or*

Pages 369–372 Exercises and Problems

3. Jackie Winsor, The lure of Italy, On Kawara **5.** Y **7.** Z **13.** I'm outside. **15.** If the inclusive *or* is being used, the conclusion is not justified because it is possible to eat pizza while at a ball game. The conclusion would be justified only if the exclusive *or* were being used. **17.** Yes. **19.** Yes. **21.** C **23.** A

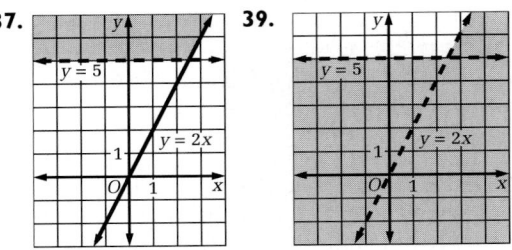

31, 33. Answers may vary. Examples are given.
31. $5 \le x \le 9$ **33.** $x > 5$ or $x < 7$ **35.** B

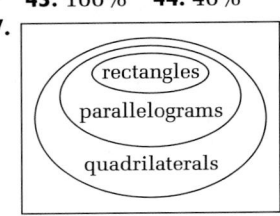

42. $x^3 + 9x^2 + 27x + 27$ **43.** 100% **44.** 40%
45. 40% **46.** 60% **47.**

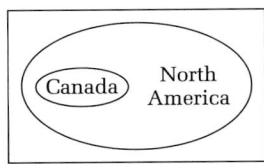

Pages 374–375 Talk it Over
1. If I am in Canada, then I am in North America.

2. a. True. **b.** If $x = 4$, then $x + 5 = 9$. **c.** True.
3. If an animal is a chinchilla, then it is a rodent.

Integrated Mathematics

4.

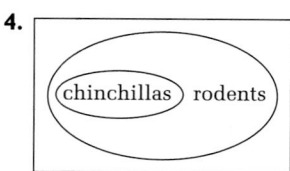

5. No. **6.** Yes.

Pages 375–378 Exercises and Problems
1. the "if" part **3.** $q \rightarrow p$ **5. a.** p: a figure is a square; q: a figure is a rhombus. **b.** The fact that a figure is a square implies that it is a rhombus.

c.

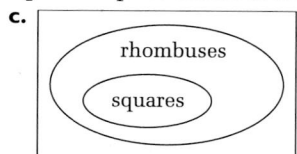

7. a. p: a figure is a cylinder; q: the formula for its volume is $V = Bh$. **b.** A figure is a cylinder only if the formula for its volume is $V = Bh$.

c.

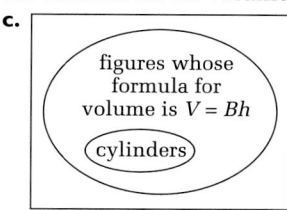

9. a. If a figure is a rectangle, then it is a parallelogram. True. **b.** If a figure is a parallelogram, then it is a rectangle. False; a rhombus is also a parallelogram. **11. a.** If today is Valentine's Day, then this month is February. True. **b.** If this month is February, then today is Valentine's Day. False; it could be February 1 instead of February 14. **13. a.** If Cleo is a golden retriever, then Cleo is a dog. True. **b.** If Cleo is a dog, then Cleo is a golden retriever. False; Cleo could be an Irish setter. **26.**

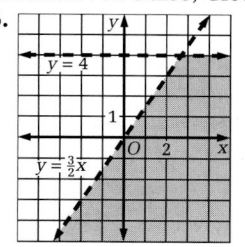

27. False. **28.** False. **29.** True.

30. a. $\begin{bmatrix} 1.69 & 2.29 & 3.89 \\ 1.75 & 2.49 & 4.19 \\ 2.19 & 2.79 & 4.99 \end{bmatrix}$ **b.** $\begin{bmatrix} 1.81 & 2.45 & 4.16 \\ 1.87 & 2.66 & 4.48 \\ 2.34 & 2.99 & 5.34 \end{bmatrix}$

31. Answers may vary. Examples are given. Leonardo Da Vinci was an artist and a scientist. Rodin was a sculptor or Marie Curie was a scientist. Diego Rivera was not a scientist.

Pages 380–382 Talk it Over
1. *or* rule **2.** chain rule **3.** direct argument
4. No; it has the form $p \rightarrow q$ and $p \rightarrow r$, $\therefore q \rightarrow r$, which is not a valid argument. **5.** Yes; it is an indirect argument.

Pages 382–384 Exercises and Problems
1. therefore q **3.** $\triangle ABC$ is not isosceles.
5. $P(A) \neq 0$. **7.** Kerry has the right to vote. **9.** valid; indirect argument **11.** invalid; It has the form $p \rightarrow q$; q; $\therefore p$, which is not a valid argument. **23. a.** If an angle is obtuse, then it measures between 90° and 180°. True. **b.** If an angle measures between 90° and 180°, then it is an obtuse angle. True. **24. a.** If $x = 5$, then $x < 8$. True. **b.** If $x < 8$, then $x = 5$. False; for example, x might be $3\frac{1}{2}$. **25. a.** If you are in California, then you are in a state bordering the Pacific Ocean. True. **b.** If you are in a state bordering the Pacific Ocean, then you are in California. False; you might be in Oregon, for example. **26.** 25%
27. 12.5% **28.** 25%

Page 385 Checkpoint
1. Answers may vary. An example is given. If you apply to the program, then you will get accepted. If you get accepted, you will be trained to fly on the space shuttle. If you fly on the space shuttle, you may get to walk in space. Therefore, if you apply to the program, you may get to walk in space.

2. **3.**

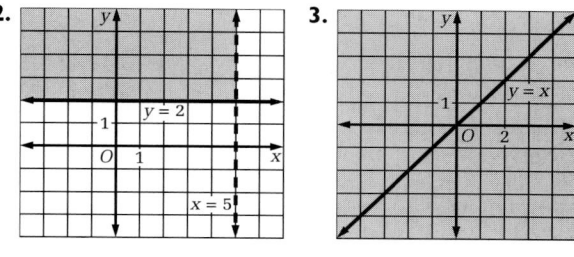

4. $13 < x < 55$;

5. If Corey is a high school student, then he is a teenager. **6.** If a number is a multiple of 4, then it is also a multiple of 2. **7.** If a matrix has 4 columns and 3 rows, then the dimensions of the matrix are 3×4. **8.** Jana scored higher than 85. **9.** valid; direct argument

Pages 386–389 Talk it Over
1. All the talking heads are using different names for the same thing. **2.** The sandwich usually consists of sandwich meats with lettuce, tomato, and dressing, and may also have onions, peppers, and other vegetables. **3. a.** hypothesis: A point is the midpoint of a segment. conclusion: The point is the same distance from each endpoint of the segment. **b.** hypothesis:

Selected Answers

A point on a segment is the same distance from each endpoint. conclusion: The point is the midpoint of the segment.   **4.** A point on a segment is the midpoint of the segment if and only if the point is the same distance from each endpoint.   **5. a.** If a quadrilateral is a rectangle, then it is a parallelogram. If a quadrilateral is a parallelogram, then it is a rectangle. **b.** False; it is not true that if a quadrilateral is a parallelogram, then it is a rectangle.   **6.** The statement is true, but it is not biconditional.   **7.** Wording may vary. An example is given. A figure is a rhombus if and only if it has four congruent sides.

Pages 389–393 Exercises and Problems
1. Answers may vary. Examples are given. If p, then q and if q, then p; $p \rightarrow q$ and $q \rightarrow p$; or $p \leftrightarrow q$.
3. Biconditionals may be written $p \leftrightarrow q$ or $q \leftrightarrow p$. One order is given. $5x = 20$, if and only if $x = 4$.
5. a. Yes. **b.** Yes **c.** $\frac{x}{2} = 7$ if and only if $x = 14$.
7. a. Yes. **b.** No. **c.** not possible   **9.** False; both conditionals are not true.   **11.** True; the two conditionals "If a figure is a parallelogram with four right angles, then it is a rectangle" and "If a figure is a rectangle, then it is a parallelogram with four right angles" are both true.
13.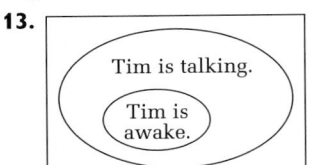
15.

> Tim is talking.
>> Tim is awake.

> Sandy is tired.
> Sandy yawns.

17. A triangle is *scalene* if and only if it has three sides that are not equal in measure.   **19.** No; the conditional "If an angle is obtuse, then the measure of the angle is 150°" is not true.   **21.** Yes; the conditionals "If two lines are perpendicular, they intersect to form a right angle" and "If two lines intersect to form a right angle, then the lines are perpendicular" are both true.   **23.** If a figure is a square, then it is a rectangle with four congruent sides. If a figure is a rectangle with four congruent sides, then the figure is a square.   **29.** valid   **31.** valid   **36.** valid   **37.** invalid
38. 6   **39.** 7.07 to the nearest hundredth   **40.** $84\sqrt{2}$
41. Fran is taller than Abby.   **42.** $x = 6$

Pages 394–396 Talk it Over
1. a. Flight 101 from Bombay to Buenos Aires
b. Bombay is the departure point.
2.

City	Flight
Bombay	Departure point
Calcutta	Flight 201: Bombay → Calcutta
Mexico City	Flight 203: Calcutta → Mexico City

3.

City	Flight
Mexico City	Departure point
Calcutta	Flight 204: Mexico City → Calcutta
Bombay	Flight 202: Calcutta → Bombay

4. *Given:* Buenos Aires
Prove: Buenos Aires to Calcutta
Statements (Justifications):
1. Buenos Aires (Given)
2. Mexico City (Flight 106: Buenos Aires → Mexico City)
3. Calcutta (Flight 204: Mexico City → Calcutta)
5. Yes; Yes. There are often many ways to prove a statement just as there can be many ways to solve a problem.
6. *Given:* Rio de Janeiro
Prove: Tokyo
Statements (Justifications):
1. Rio de Janeiro (Given)
2. New York City (Flight 102: Rio de Janeiro → New York City)
3. Tokyo (Flight 103: New York City → Tokyo)
7. It is possible to fly from Rio de Janeiro to Tokyo. You can take Flight 102 from Rio de Janeiro to New York City. Then you can take Flight 103 from New York City to Tokyo.
8. Statements
Rio de Janeiro $\xrightarrow{\ ❶\ }$ New York City $\xrightarrow{\ ❷\ }$ Tokyo
Justifications
❶ Flight 102   ❷ Flight 103

Pages 397–399 Exercises and Problems
3.

City	Flight
Calcutta	Departure point
Bombay	Flight 202: Calcutta → Bombay
Buenos Aires	Flight 101: Bombay → Buenos Aires

5. It is impossible to go from Tokyo to New York City because Euclid Airlines does not have any flights out of Tokyo.   **7.** direct argument
9. Statements Cairo $\xrightarrow{\ ❶\ }$ Bombay $\xrightarrow{\ ❷\ }$ Calcutta
Justifications ❶ Flight 104   ❷ Flight 201
18. Yes. If a quadrilateral is a rhombus, then it has four congruent sides. If a quadrilateral has four congruent sides, then it is a rhombus.   **19.** No. If a quadrilateral is a rhombus, then the quadrilateral is a square. If a quadrilateral is a square, then the quadrilateral is a rhombus. If a quadrilateral is a rhombus, it is not necessarily a square.   **20.** (−7, 14)   **21.** $n = 43$
22. $x = 4$ **23.** $a = 2$

Integrated Mathematics

1. The colonists meant that these truths do not require a proof or explanation.   **2.** the statements
3. the conclusion

Pages 404–407 Exercises and Problems

1. Subtraction property of equality   **3.** Definition of square root   **5.** It means that these truths, like a postulate, do not require a proof or explanation.
7. *Given:* $x^2 + 8 = 24$; $x > 0$
Prove: $x = 4$
Statements (Justifications):
1. $x^2 + 8 = 24$ (Given)
2. $x^2 = 16$ (Subtraction property of equality)
3. $x = 4$ or $x = -4$ (Definition of square root)
4. $x > 0$ (Given)
5. $x = 4$ (*Or* rule)
9. a. *Given:* $4x^2 + 6 = 330$; $x > 0$
Prove: $x = 9$
Statements (Justifications):
1. $4x^2 + 6 = 330$ (Given)
2. $4x^2 = 324$ (Subtraction property of equality)
3. $x^2 = 81$ (Division property of equality)
4. $x = 9$ or $x = -9$ (Definition of square root)
5. $x > 0$ (Given)
6. $x = 9$ (*Or* rule)
b. Statements
$$4x^2 + 6 = 330 \overset{❶}{\to} 4x^2 = 324 \overset{❷}{\to} x^2 = 81 \overset{❸}{\to}$$
$$x = 9 \text{ or } x = -9, x > 0 \overset{❹}{\to} x = 9$$

Justifications ❶ Subtraction property of equality ❷ Division property of equality ❸ Definition of square root; given ❹ *Or* rule   **c.** If $4x^2 + 6 = 330$, use the subtraction property of equality to subtract 6 from both sides: $4x^2 = 324$. Then use the division property of equality to divide both sides by 4: $x^2 = 81$. Then use the definition of square root: $x = 9$ or $x = -9$. Since $x > 0$, $x = 9$.   **13. a.** Answers may vary. An example is given. There are two inequality postulates because when you multiply an inequality by a positive number the inequality sign stays the same, but when you multiply an inequality by a negative number, the inequality sign is reversed. For example, for the inequality $2 < 5$, when both sides are multiplied by 3, then $6 < 15$. But when both sides are multiplied by -3, then $-6 > -15$.   **b.** If $a < b$ and $c > 0$, then $\frac{a}{c} < \frac{b}{c}$.
If $a < b$ and $c < 0$, then $\frac{a}{c} > \frac{b}{c}$.   **20.** Two-column proof: The *given* and the *prove* are stated. The premises are listed in the left column, and the justifications are listed in the right column. The final step in the proof is the *prove*. Flow proof: The statements are written from left to right with arrows between the steps. The arrows are numbered, and the justifications for each step are listed below the statements. Paragraph proof: The *given* and the *prove* statements

are written first. Then the procedure and the justification for each step is described in paragraph form.
21. Answers may vary. An example is given. Arturo's results may not be based on a random sample. The people he sees are not randomly selected; they just happen to pass the place where Arturo is.   **22.** No. A figure is a parallelogram if and only if the figure is a quadrilateral with two pairs of parallel sides.
23. No; a figure is a kite if and only if it has two pairs of consecutive sides congruent.

Page 407 Checkpoint

1. Answers may vary. An example is given. I need to plan ahead before I write a proof so that I can get from the premises to the conclusion in a straightforward, logical fashion.   **2.** A figure is a quadrilateral if and only if it is a rectangle with parallel sides.
3. No; any four-sided figure is a quadrilateral, not just rectangles.   **4.** valid; it is an indirect argument.
5. flow proof   **6.** conclusion
7. *Given:* $7x - 3 = 25$
Prove: $x = 4$
Statements (Justifications):
1. $7x - 3 = 25$ (Given)
2. $7x = 28$ (Addition property of equality)
3. $x = 4$ (Division property of equality)

Pages 408–409 Talk it Over

1. Two angles are complementary if and only if the sum of their measures equals $90°$. Two angles are supplementary if and only if the sum of their measures equals $180°$.   **2. a.** The two supplements also have the same measure.   **b.** If two angles are equal in measure, then their supplements are also equal in measure. No; an infinite number of cases cannot be tested. Yes.
3. Statements
$$\angle 1 \text{ is supplementary to } \angle 2. \overset{❶}{\to} m\angle 1 + m\angle 2 = 180° \overset{❷}{\Big\}\to}$$
$$\angle 3 \text{ is supplementary to } \angle 2. \overset{❶}{\to} m\angle 3 + m\angle 2 = 180°$$
$$m\angle 1 + m\angle 2 = m\angle 3 + m\angle 2 \overset{❸}{\to} m\angle 1 = m\angle 3$$

Justifications ❶ Definition of supplementary angles ❷ Substitution property ❸ Subtraction property of equality
4. *Given:* $\angle 1$ is complementary to $\angle 2$; $\angle 3$ is complementary to $\angle 2$. *Prove:* $m\angle 1 = m\angle 3$

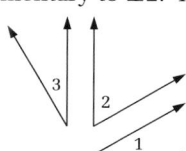 If two angles are complementary, then their sum is equal to $90°$. Therefore, $m\angle 1 + m\angle 2 = 90°$ and $m\angle 2 + m\angle 3 = 90°$. Since the sums both equal $90°$, you can say $m\angle 1 + m\angle 2 = m\angle 2 + m\angle 3$ by the substitution property. Then you can use the subtraction property of equality to subtract $m\angle 2$ from both sides of the equation. Therefore, $m\angle 1 = m\angle 3$.

Selected Answers

Pages 412–414 Exercises and Problems

1. definition   **3.** definition, postulate, theorem
5. $m \angle Q + m \angle R = 180°$; definition of supplementary angles   **7.** $m \angle H = m \angle J$; If two angles are supplements of the same angle, then they are equal in measure.   **9. a.** Yes.   **b.** The sides of the new figure are all diagonals of congruent squares. These diagonals are all congruent.
11. *Given:* $\angle 1$ and $\angle 2$ are complementary.
$$m \angle 1 = 75°$$
Prove: $m \angle 2 = 15°$
Statements
$\angle 1$ and $\angle 2$ are complementary. ❶ →
$\left. \begin{array}{l} m \angle 1 + m \angle 2 = 90° \\ m \angle 1 = 75° \end{array} \right\} $ ❷ → $75° + m \angle 2 = 90°$ ❸ →
$m \angle 2 = 15°$
Justifications ❶ Definition of complementary ∡
❷ Substitution property ❸ Subtraction property of equality   **13.** postulate
15. Proof forms may vary. A two-column proof is given.
Statements (Justifications):
1. $\angle ABC$ is a straight angle. (Given)
2. $m \angle ABC = 180°$ (If the sides of an angle form a straight line, then the angle is a straight angle with measure 180°.)
3. $m \angle ABF + m \angle FBE + m \angle EBD + m \angle DBC = m \angle ABC$ (For any angle, the measure of the whole is equal to the sum of the measures of its non-overlapping parts.)
4. $m \angle ABF + m \angle FBE + m \angle EBD + m \angle DBC = 180°$ (Substitution property [Steps 2 and 3])
5. $m \angle ABF = m \angle FBE$; $m \angle EBD = m \angle DBC$ (Given)
6. $2(m \angle FBE) + 2(m \angle EBD) = 180°$ (Substitution property [Steps 4 and 5])
7. $m \angle FBE + m \angle EBD = 90°$ (Division property of equality)
8. $m \angle FBE + m \angle EBD = m \angle FBD$ (For any angle, the measure of the whole is equal to the sum of the measures of its non-overlapping parts.)
9. $m \angle FBD = 90°$ (Substitution property [Steps 7 and 8])
10. $\angle FBD$ is a right angle. (Definition of right angle)
19. *Given:* $2(x + 7) = 3x$
Prove: $x = 14$
Statements (Justifications):
1. $2(x + 7) = 3x$ (Given)
2. $2x + 14 = 3x$ (Distributive property)
3. $14 = x$ (Subtraction property of equality)
20. one solution   **21.** many solutions   **22.** no solutions   **23.** rhombus, rectangle, square

Pages 416–419 Talk it Over

1. $\angle 3$ and $\angle 5$, $\angle 4$ and $\angle 6$ **2.** $\angle 1$ and $\angle 5$, $\angle 4$ and $\angle 8$, $\angle 2$ and $\angle 6$, $\angle 3$ and $\angle 7$ **3.** $\angle 4$ and $\angle 5$, $\angle 3$ and $\angle 6$ **4.** Corresponding angles are equal in measure. The angle measuring 70° and $\angle 1$ are corresponding

angles. Therefore, $m \angle 1 = 70°$.   **5.** Because $m \angle 1 = 70°$ (from question 4) and alternate interior angles are equal in measure, $m \angle 2 = m \angle 1 = 70°$.   **6.** $m \angle 2 = 70°$ (from question 5). Since co-interior angles are supplementary, $m \angle 2 + m \angle 3 = 180°$. By the substitution property, $70° + m \angle 3 = 180°$. Using the subtraction property of equality, $m \angle 3 = 110°$.
7. *Given:* parallelogram $ABCD$
Prove: $m \angle 1 = m \angle 3$
Plan: $\angle 1$ and $\angle 3$ are both supplementary to $\angle 2$ (Theorem 7.6). Thus, they are equal (Theorem 7.1).

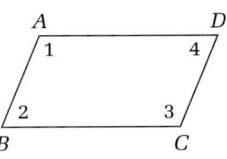

Pages 419–422 Exercises and Problems

1. $\angle 1$ and $\angle 3$, $\angle 2$ and $\angle 4$, $\angle 5$ and $\angle 7$, $\angle 6$ and $\angle 8$
3. $\angle 2$ and $\angle 3$, $\angle 6$ and $\angle 7$ **5.** co-exterior angles
7. a. alternate interior angles   **b.** Their measures are equal.   **c.** If two parallel lines are intersected by a transversal, then alternate interior angles are equal in measure.   **9.** 7.2°
13. *Given:* Lines l and m are parallel and are intersected by line t. *Prove:* $\angle 1$ and $\angle 2$ are supplementary.

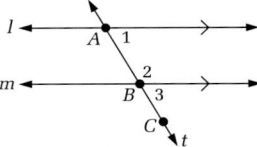

Statements (Justifications):
1. $l \parallel m$ (Given)
2. $m \angle 3 = m \angle 1$ (If two $\parallel$ lines are intersected by a transversal, then corresponding ∡ are = in measure.)
3. l, m, and t are lines. (Given)
4. $m \angle ABC = 180°$ (If the sides of an angle form a straight line, then the angle is a straight angle with measure 180°.)
5. $m \angle 2 + m \angle 3 = m \angle ABC$ (For any angle, the measure of the whole is equal to the sum of the measures of its non-overlapping parts.)
6. $m \angle 2 + m \angle 3 = 180°$ (Substitution property [Steps 4 and 5])
7. $m \angle 1 + m \angle 2 = 180°$ (Substitution property [Steps 2 and 6])
8. $\angle 1$ and $\angle 2$ are supplementary. (Definition of supplementary angles)
15. a. supplementary   **b.** equal in measure
17. *Given:* Lines j and k are parallel. Lines m and n are parallel. *Prove:* $m \angle 1 = m \angle 3$
Statements

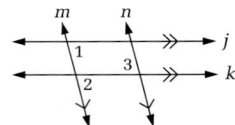

$j \parallel k$ ❶ → $m \angle 1 = m \angle 2$ $\left. \begin{array}{l} \\ \\ \end{array} \right\}$ ❸ → $m \angle 1 = m \angle 3$
$m \parallel n$ ❷ → $m \angle 2 = m \angle 3$

Justifications ❶ If two $\parallel$ lines are intersected by a transversal, then corresponding ∡ are equal in measure. ❷ If $\parallel$ lines are intersected by a transversal, then alternate interior ∡ are = in measure.
❸ Substitution property

28

Integrated Mathematics

19. $m \angle T = 57°$; $m \angle S = 123°$; $m \angle R = 57°$
22. $m \angle 2 = 140°$; $m \angle 3 = 40°$; $m \angle 4 = 140°$
23. $\sqrt{5}, -\sqrt{5}$ **24.** $-2, 6$ **25.** $1, 5$ **26.** If an animal is a bird, then it has feathers.

Pages 424–425 Unit 7 Review and Assessment
1. baseball, lacrosse ball **2.** baseball, lacrosse ball, tennis ball, basketball, soccer ball, volleyball
3. $6.4 < x < 24$

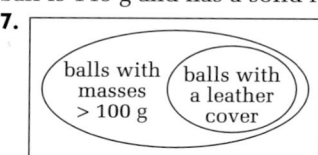

4. Ex. 1; Ex. 2 **5.** True. **6.** If a ball has a mass over 100 g , then it has a leather cover. False; the lacrosse ball is 143 g and has a solid rubber cover.
7.

```
┌─────────────────────────────┐
│  ╭─────────╮╭──────────╮     │
│  │balls with││balls with│    │
│  │ masses   ││a leather │    │
│  │ > 100 g  ││  cover   │    │
│  ╰─────────╯╰──────────╯     │
└─────────────────────────────┘
```

8. valid; indirect argument **9.** invalid; assumes exclusive *or* **10.** Answers may vary. An example is given. Premise: If I go to school, then I will take the history exam. If I take the history exam, then I will pass it. Conclusion: If I go to school, then I will pass the history exam. **11.** $x^2 = 36 \to x = 6$; $x = 6 \to$ $x^2 = 36$; If the square of a number is 36, then the number is 6; if a number is 6, then its square is 36.
12. False; $x^2 = 36 \leftrightarrow x = 6$ or $x = -6$. **13.** A biconditional is true when both of its conditionals are true.
14. a. It is possible to fly from Cairo to Mexico City. From Cairo you can fly to Bombay because Flight 104 goes from Cairo to Bombay. From Bombay you can fly to Calcutta because Flight 201 goes from Bombay to Calcutta. From Calcutta you can fly to Mexico City because Flight 203 goes from Calcutta to Mexico City.
b. Statements (Justifications):
1. Cairo (Given)
2. Bombay (Flight 104: Cairo → Bombay)
3. Calcutta (Flight 201: Bombay → Calcutta)
4. Mexico City (Flight 203: Calcutta → Mexico City)
c. chain rule
15. a. *Given:* $3a^2 - 5 = 43$; $a > 0$ *Prove:* $a = 4$
Statements

$3a^2 - 5 = 43 \overset{❶}{\to} 3a^2 = 48 \overset{❷}{\to} a^2 = 16 \overset{❸}{\to}$

$\left. \begin{array}{l} a = 4 \text{ or } a = -4 \text{❹} \\ a > 0 \end{array} \right\} \overset{}{\to} a = 4$

Justifications ❶ Addition property of equality **❷** Division property of equality **❸** Definition of square root **❹** *Or* rule

b. *Given:* $3a^2 - 5 = 43$; $a > 0$
Prove: $a = 4$
Statements (Justifications):
1. $3a^2 - 5 = 43$ (Given)
2. $3a^2 = 48$ (Addition property of equality)
3. $a^2 = 16$ (Division property of equality)
4. $a = 4$ or $a = -4$ (Definition of square root)

5. $a > 0$ (Given)
6. $a = 4$ (*Or* rule [Steps 4 and 5])
16. Statements (Justifications):
1. $\angle 1$ and $\angle 2$ are vertical ⦨. (Given)
2. $m \angle 1 = m \angle 2$ (Vertical ⦨ are = in measure.)
3. $\angle 1$ is supplementary to $\angle 2$. (Given)
4. $m \angle 1 + m \angle 2 = 180°$ (Definition of supplementary angles)
5. $m \angle 1 + m \angle 1 = 180°$ (Substitution property [Steps 2 and 4])
6. $2(m \angle 1) = 180°$ (Combine like terms.)
7. $m \angle 1 = 90°$ (Division property of equality)
8. $m \angle 2 = 90°$ (Substitution property [Steps 2 and 7])
9. $\angle 1$ and $\angle 2$ are right angles. (Definition of right angles)
17. Postulates are statements that are assumed to be true; definitions are biconditionals that give necessary and sufficient conditions for clarification; theorems are statements that are proved using previously proved theorems, definitions, and postulates.
18. *Given:* Lines j and k are parallel. Lines l and n are parallel.
Prove: $m \angle 1 = m \angle 3$
Statements (Justifications):

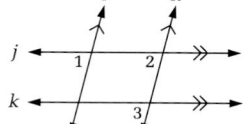

1. $l \parallel n$ (Given)
2. $m \angle 1 = m \angle 2$ (If two $\parallel$ lines are intersected by a transversal, then corresponding ⦨ are = in measure.)
3. $j \parallel k$ (Given)
4. $m \angle 2 = m \angle 3$ (If two $\parallel$ lines are intersected by a transversal, then corresponding ⦨ are = in measure.)
5. $m \angle 1 = m \angle 3$ (Substitution property [Steps 2 and 4])
19. a. 58°; $\angle 2$ and $\angle 1$ form a straight line and so are supplementary angles. **b.** 58°; $\angle 3$ and $\angle 1$ form a straight line and so are supplementary angles.
c. 122°; $\angle 4$ and $\angle 1$ are alternate interior angles.
d. 122°; $\angle 5$ and $\angle 1$ are corresponding angles.

Unit 8

Page 432 Talk it Over
1. $\angle BAC$ and the angle adjacent to $\angle DCA$
2. a. If two parallel lines are intersected by a transversal, then corresponding angles are equal in measure.
b. Yes. **3. a.** If two lines are intersected by a transversal and alternate interior angles are equal in measure, then the lines are parallel. **b.** If two lines are intersected by a transversal and co-interior angles are supplementary, then the lines are parallel.

Pages 435–438 Exercises and Problems
3. Theorem 8.2; If two lines are intersected by a transversal and co-interior ⦨ are supplementary, then the lines are $\parallel$. **5.** Theorem 8.2; If two lines are intersect-

ed by a transversal and co-interior ∠s are supplementary, then the lines are ∥. **7.** Theorem 8.1; If two lines are intersected by a transversal and alternate interior ∠s are = in measure, then the lines are ∥.
9. No. **11.** No. **13.** *Given:* $\overleftrightarrow{MQ} \parallel \overline{SR}$; $m\angle 1 = m\angle 2$
Prove: $m\angle 3 = m\angle 4$
Statements

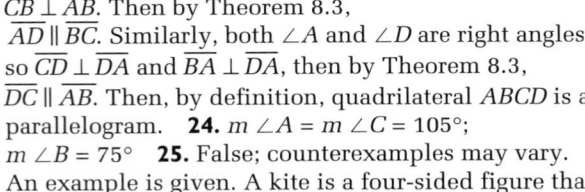

Justifications ❶ If two ∥ lines are intersected by a transversal, then alternate interior ∠s are = in measure. ❷ Substitution property
15. a. *Given:* Transversal *t* intersects lines *k* and *l*.
$k \parallel l$, $t \perp l$
Prove: $t \perp k$
Statements (Justifications):
1. $k \parallel l$ (Given)
2. $m\angle 1 = m\angle 2$ (If two ∥ lines are intersected by a transversal, then corresponding ∠s are = in measure.)
3. $t \perp l$ (Given)
4. $m\angle 2 = 90°$ (Definition of perpendicular lines)
5. $m\angle 1 = 90°$ (Substitution property [Steps 2 and 4])
6. $t \perp k$ (Definition of perpendicular lines)
b. It is given that lines *k* and *l* are parallel lines. Therefore, $m\angle 1 = m\angle 2$ since if two ∥ lines are intersected by a transversal, then corresponding ∠s are = in measure. It is also given that line $t \perp l$, so $m\angle 2 = 90°$ by the definition of perpendicular lines. Substitute $m\angle 1$ for $m\angle 2$ in the equation $m\angle 2 = 90°$, and $m\angle 1 = 90°$. By definition of perpendicular lines, $t \perp k$.
19. *Given:* $\overline{GH} \perp \overline{HJ}$; $m\angle KJH = 90°$
Prove: $\overline{GH} \parallel \overline{KJ}$
Statements (Justifications):
1. $GH \perp \overline{HJ}$; $m\angle KJH = 90°$ (Given)
2. $KJ \perp \overline{HJ}$ (Definition of ⊥ lines)
3. $GH \parallel \overline{KJ}$ (If two lines are ⊥ to the same transversal, then they are ∥.)
21. *Given:* Quadrilateral *ABCD*; ∠*A*, ∠*B*, ∠*C*, and ∠*D* are right angles. *Prove:* Quadrilateral *ABCD* is a parallelogram. Since ∠*A* and ∠*B* are right angles, $\overline{DA} \perp \overline{AB}$ and $\overline{CB} \perp \overline{AB}$. Then by Theorem 8.3, $\overline{AD} \parallel \overline{BC}$. Similarly, both ∠*A* and ∠*D* are right angles, so $\overline{CD} \perp \overline{DA}$ and $\overline{BA} \perp \overline{DA}$, then by Theorem 8.3, $\overline{DC} \parallel \overline{AB}$. Then, by definition, quadrilateral *ABCD* is a parallelogram. **24.** $m\angle A = m\angle C = 105°$; $m\angle B = 75°$ **25.** False; counterexamples may vary. An example is given. A kite is a four-sided figure that is not a parallelogram. **26.** True. **27.** $x = 20$

1. a. Check students' work. **b.** Yes. **c.** No.
2. a. $x + 2x + (x + 10) = 180°$ **b.** 42.5°
c. $m\angle B = 42.5°$, $m\angle A = 85°$; $m\angle C = 52.5°$
3. a. $(x + 60) + x + 2x + x = 360°$ **b.** $m\angle R = 120°$, $m\angle S = 60°$; $m\angle T = 120°$, $m\angle U = 60°$ **c.** Both pairs of opposite angles are equal in measure. By Theorem 8.7, *RSTU* is a parallelogram. **4.** Answers may vary. An example is given. The angles are remote to, that is distant from, ∠*CAD*. **5.** ∠*Q* and ∠*R* **6.** ∠*Q* and ∠*R*
7. Yes. If the angle adjacent to the exterior angle is obtuse, then the exterior angle must be acute because the two angles form a straight angle which measures 180°.

3. $c° = 55°$ **5.** $a° = 60°$, $b° = 50°$ **7.** $w° = 35°$, $x° = 120°$, $y° = 35°$ **13. a.** $m\angle A = 90°$, $m\angle B = 90°$, $m\angle C = 90°$, $m\angle D = 90°$ **b.** rectangle
15. a. $m\angle A = 60°$, $m\angle B = 120°$, $m\angle C = 90°$, $m\angle D = 90°$ **b.** trapezoid
17. *Given:* *JKLM* is a quadrilateral.
$m\angle J = m\angle L$, $m\angle K = m\angle M$
Prove: *JKLM* is a parallelogram.
Statements (Justifications):
1. *JKLM* is a quadrilateral. (Given)
2. $m\angle J + m\angle K + m\angle L + m\angle M = 360°$ (The sum of the measures of the ∠s of a quadrilateral is 360°.)
3. $m\angle J = m\angle L$, $m\angle K = m\angle M$ (Given)
4. $m\angle J + m\angle M + m\angle J + m\angle M = 360°$ (Substitution property [Steps 2 and 3])
5. $2(m\angle J + m\angle M) = 360°$ (Distributive property)
6. $m\angle J + m\angle M = 180°$ (Division property of equality)
7. ∠*J* and ∠*M* are supplementary angles. (Definition of supplementary angles)
8. $\overline{JK} \parallel \overline{ML}$ (If two lines are intersected by a transversal and co-interior ∠s are supplementary, then the lines are ∥.)
9. $m\angle J + m\angle K = 180°$ (Substitution property [Steps 3 and 6])
10. ∠*J* and ∠*K* are supplementary angles. (Definition of supplementary angles)
11. $\overline{JM} \parallel \overline{KL}$ (If two lines are intersected by a transversal and co-interior ∠s are supplementary, then the lines are ∥.)
12. *JKLM* is a parallelogram. (Definition of parallelogram)
27. ∠2 and ∠3 **29.** ∠1 and ∠3 **31.** $x° = 30°$, $y° = 120°$ **33.** $x° = 110°$, $y° = 40°$, $z° = 70°$, $w° = 40°$
37. No. **38.** No. **39.** Yes. **40.** Yes. **41.** $x = 7$, $y = -5$ **42.** Multiply $8 \cdot x$ and $5 \cdot 12$ to get the equation $8x = 60$. Divide both sides by 8 to obtain $x = 7.5$
43. $AF = DE$

Integrated Mathematics

1. a. $\angle A$ **b.** $\overline{DC}$ **c.** $m\angle B = m\angle E$; $m\angle C = m\angle C$; $m\angle A = m\angle D$; $AB = DE$; $AC = DC$; $BC = EC$; Since three pairs of sides are equal in measure and three pairs of angles are equal in measure, $\triangle ABC \cong \triangle DEC$ by definition.   **d.** $\triangle ECD$ **2. a.** Yes.   **b.** $\dfrac{DC}{FH} = \dfrac{5}{4}$; $\dfrac{EC}{GH} = \dfrac{5}{4}$; $\dfrac{DE}{FG} = \dfrac{5}{4}$; They are all equal.   **c.** $m\angle D = m\angle F$; $m\angle E = m\angle G$; $m\angle C = m\angle H$; $\dfrac{DC}{FH} = \dfrac{EC}{GH} = \dfrac{DE}{FG}$; Since three pairs of angles are equal in measure and three pairs of sides are in proportion, $\triangle DEC \sim \triangle FGH$ by definition.

Pages 453–455 Exercises and Problems

1. $\angle A$ and $\angle D$; $\angle B$ and $\angle E$; $\angle C$ and $\angle F$
3. $\angle B = 70°$, $\angle C = 75°$, $\angle D = 35°$, $\angle F = 75°$
5. Angles of both triangles are 59°, 60°, and 61°.
7. $\triangle ABC$, $\triangle DEF$
9. *Given:* $\overline{AB} \parallel \overline{DE}$
Prove: $\triangle ABC \sim \triangle EDC$
Since $\overline{AB} \parallel \overline{DE}$, $m\angle A = m\angle E$ and $m\angle B = m\angle D$ because if two parallel lines are intersected by a transversal, then alternate interior angles are equal in measure. Then $\triangle ABC \sim \triangle EDC$ by the AA Similarity Postulate.
11. $\dfrac{8}{16} = \dfrac{12}{b}$; $b = 24$ **13.** $\dfrac{RV}{RT} = \dfrac{RU}{RS} = \dfrac{VU}{TS}$
15. *Given:* $\overline{BC} \parallel \overline{DE}$
Prove: $\dfrac{AB}{BD} = \dfrac{AC}{CE}$
Statements (Justifications):
 1. $\overline{BC} \parallel \overline{DE}$ (Given)
 2. $m\angle ABC = m\angle ADE$ (If two $\parallel$ lines are intersected by a transversal, then corresponding $\angle$s are = in measure.)
 3. $m\angle A = m\angle A$ (Reflexive property of equality)
 4. $\triangle ABC \sim \triangle ADE$ (AA Similarity)
 5. $\dfrac{AB}{AD} = \dfrac{AC}{AE}$ (Corresponding sides of similar triangles are in proportion.)
 6. $AD = AB + BD$; $AE = AC + CE$ (For any segment, the measure of the whole is equal to the sum of the measures of its non-overlapping parts.)
 7. $\dfrac{AB}{AB + BD} = \dfrac{AC}{AC + CE}$ (Substitution property [Steps 5 and 6])
 8. $AB(AC + CE) = AC(AB + BD)$ (Multiplication property of equality)
 9. $AB \cdot AC + AB \cdot CE = AB \cdot AC + AC \cdot BD$ (Distributive property)
 10. $AB \cdot CE = AC \cdot BD$ (Subtraction property of equality)
 11. $\dfrac{AB}{BD} = \dfrac{AC}{CE}$ (Division property of equality)

21. a. I: $a° = 70°$; II: $b° = 50°$, $c° = 50°$; III: $d° = 80°$, $e° = 50°$; IV: $f° = 60°$; V: $g° = 110°$; VI: $h° = 50°$, $k° = 80°$ **b.** $\dfrac{1}{6}$ since $\triangle I$ is similar only to itself and not to any of the other 5 triangles.   **23.** $m\angle 1 = 53°$, $m\angle 2 = 37°$, $m\angle 3 = 53°$, $m\angle 4 = 53°$, $m\angle 5 = 37°$

24. Product is not defined.   **25.** $\begin{bmatrix} 1 & 2 & 3 \\ 2 & 5 & 6 \end{bmatrix} \begin{bmatrix} 1 \\ 2 \\ 3 \end{bmatrix} = \begin{bmatrix} 14 \\ 30 \end{bmatrix}$
26. a. $(3, -1)$ **b.** 10 units

1. Answers may vary. Examples are given. The sum of the measures of the angles of a triangle is 180°. Any exterior angle of a triangle is equal in measure to the sum of the measures of its two remote interior angles. If two angles of one triangle are equal in measure to two angles of another triangle, then the two triangles are similar.
2. Format and approach of proof may vary. An example is given.
Given: $m\angle 1 = 80°$;
$m\angle 2 = 100°$
Prove: $k \parallel l$

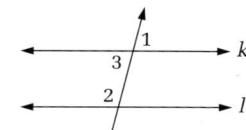

Statements (Justifications):
 1. $m\angle 1 = 80°$; $m\angle 2 = 100°$ (Given)
 2. $m\angle 1 + m\angle 2 = 180°$ (Addition property of equality)
 3. $\angle 1$ and $\angle 3$ are vertical angles. (Definition of vertical angles)
 4. $m\angle 1 = m\angle 3$ (Vertical $\angle$s are = in measure.)
 5. $m\angle 2 + m\angle 3 = 180°$ (Substitution property [Steps 2 and 4])
 6. $\angle 2$ and $\angle 3$ are supplementary. (Definition of supplementary angles)
 7. $k \parallel l$ (If two lines are intersected by a transversal and co-interior $\angle$s are supplementary, then the lines are $\parallel$.)

3. If a transversal is perpendicular to one of two parallel lines, then it is perpendicular to the other. (Theorem 8.4)   **4. a.** $x° = 50°$ **b.** $x° = 62°$ **c.** $x° = 65°$
5. There is not enough information given to prove that the triangles are similar or that they are not similar. $m\angle A \neq m\angle D$, so $\triangle ABC \not\sim \triangle DEF$, but it is possible that $\angle C = 71°$ and $\angle F = 70°$. Then $\triangle ABC \sim \triangle FED$ would be true.   **6. a.** $\triangle GHI$ and $\triangle JLK$
b. $\angle G$ and $\angle J$; $\angle H$ and $\angle L$; $\angle I$ and $\angle K$ **c.** $\overline{GH}$ and $\overline{JL}$; $\overline{GI}$ and $\overline{JK}$; $\overline{HI}$ and $\overline{LK}$ **d.** $\dfrac{GI}{JK} = \dfrac{GH}{JL} = \dfrac{HI}{LK}$ **7.** $x = 6$

1. $\overline{BC}$ **2.** ASA: angle-side-angle; AAS: angle-angle-side   **3.** The plan of the proof would be exactly the same. The proofs would differ only in that the sides used in Steps 5 and 6 would be the sides included between the congruent angles. If Theorem 8.11 were already proven, you would only need to show that the two triangles are similar and so the third pair of angles are equal in measure. Then you would have two angles and a non-included side all congruent, and you could use Theorem 8.11.   **4.** Nadine would need to know that two pairs of angles are congruent and that a pair of non-included sides are congruent.

Pages 462–465 Exercises and Problems

1.

Sides	Included Angle
$\overline{XY}$ and $\overline{YZ}$	$\angle Y$
$\overline{YZ}$ and $\overline{ZX}$	$\angle Z$
$\overline{ZX}$ and $\overline{XY}$	$\angle X$

3. 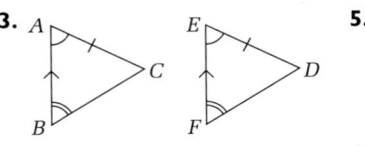   **5.** b

7. *Given: m $\angle TUW$ = m $\angle VUW$; $\overline{UW} \perp \overline{TV}$*
Prove: $\triangle TUW \cong \triangle VUW$
Statements (Justifications):
1. m $\angle TUW$ = m $\angle VUW$ (Given)
2. $UW = UW$ (Reflexive property of equality)
3. $\overline{UW} \perp \overline{TV}$ (Given)
4. m $\angle UWT$ = 90°; m $\angle UWV$ = 90° (Definition of $\perp$ lines)
5. m $\angle UWT$ = m $\angle UWV$ (Substitution property [Step 4])
6. $\triangle TUW \cong \triangle VUW$ (ASA)
11. a. $\triangle DEA \cong \triangle BEC$ **b.** $\triangle DAC \cong \triangle BCA$
13. *Given: $\overline{AC} \perp \overline{CB}$; $\overline{DB} \perp \overline{BC}$; m $\angle 1$ = m $\angle 2$*
Prove: AC = DB
Statements (Justifications):
1. $\overline{AC} \perp \overline{CB}$; $\overline{DB} \perp \overline{BC}$ (Given)
2. m $\angle ACB$ = 90°; m $\angle DBC$ = 90° (Definition of $\perp$ lines)
3. m $\angle ACB$ = m $\angle DBC$ (Substitution property [Step 2])
4. m $\angle 1$ = m $\angle 2$ (Given)
5. $BC = BC$ (Reflexive property of equality)
6. $\triangle ABC \cong \triangle DCB$ (ASA)
7. $AC = DB$ (CPCTE)
15. $x°$ = 10°   **18.** $\triangle GEF \sim \triangle DEC$ by the AA Similarity Postulate (vertical angles at E, and $\angle EGF$ and $\angle EDC$ being alternate interior angles).
$\triangle GEF \sim \triangle BCF$ by the Overlapping Similar Triangles Theorem ($\overline{GE} \parallel \overline{BC}$ because $GDBC$ is a parallelogram); $\triangle BCF \sim \triangle DEC$ by the AA Similarity Postulate (opposite angles B and D in the parallelogram and $\angle BCF$ and $\angle DEC$ being alternate interior angles).
19. obtuse   **20.** Whole and Parts Postulate: For any segment, the measure of the whole is equal to the sum of the measures of its non-overlapping parts.

Page 468 Talk it Over
1. BC = EF   **2.** BC = EF and AC = DF
3. m $\angle A$ = m $\angle D$ **4.** m $\angle C$ = m $\angle F$

Pages 469–471 Exercises and Problems
1. Yes; SSS.   **3.** Yes; ASA.   **5.** AAS
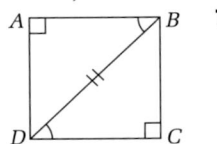   **7.** SAS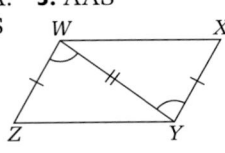

9. Using ASA: AC, m $\angle C$, m $\angle A$; AB, m $\angle A$, m $\angle B$; BC, m $\angle B$, m $\angle C$
Using SSS: AB, BC, AC
Using SAS: AC, AB, m $\angle A$; AB, BC, m $\angle B$; BC, AC, m $\angle C$
Using AAS: m $\angle A$, m $\angle B$, AC; m $\angle A$, m $\angle B$, BC; m $\angle B$, m $\angle C$, AB; m $\angle B$, m $\angle C$, AC; m $\angle A$, m $\angle C$, AB; m $\angle A$, m $\angle C$, BC
11. $x°$ = 45°
16. *Given: $\overline{RS} \parallel \overline{VT}$; RW = TW*   *Prove: RS = TV*
Statements (Justifications):
1. $\overline{RS} \parallel \overline{VT}$ (Given)
2. m $\angle RSV$ = m $\angle SVT$; m $\angle SRT$ = m $\angle VTR$ (If two $\parallel$ lines are intersected by a transversal, then alternate interior $\angle$ are = in measure.)
3. $RW = TW$ (Given)
4. $\triangle RSW \cong \triangle TVW$ (AAS)
5. $RS = TV$ (CPCTE)
17. 24   **18.**

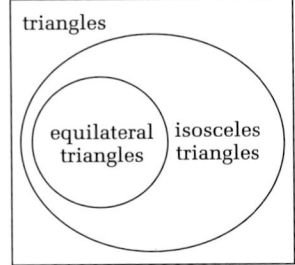

Pages 472–475 Talk it Over
1. $\overline{CB}$ **2.** $\angle B$ **3.** $\overline{AB}$ **4.** SAS   **5.** They are corresponding parts of congruent triangles.   **6.** They are equal in measure.   **7.** 30°; The triangle is equilateral and therefore equiangular having three 60° angles. Since m $\angle ABD$ = m $\angle CBD$, both would be $\frac{1}{2}$(60°) = 30°.   **8.** 24 cm   **9.** A rhombus has four sides of equal measure. Thus, D is the same distance from A as from C (since $AD = DC$), and B is the same distance from A as from C (since $AB = BC$). Both B and D lie on the $\perp$ bisector of $\overline{AC}$ (Theorem 8.16), so $\overleftrightarrow{BD}$ is the perpendicular bisector of $\overline{AC}$.   **10.** m $\angle BAD$ = m $\angle BCD$;

$m \angle ADC = m \angle ABC$; $m \angle ABD = m \angle CBD$;
$m \angle ADB = m \angle CDB$; $m \angle ABD = m \angle CDB$;
$m \angle ADB = m \angle CBD$; $m \angle ACD = m \angle BAC$;
$m \angle DAC = m \angle BCA$; $m \angle ACD = m \angle BCA$;
$m \angle DAC = m \angle BAC$

Pages 476–479 Exercises and Problems
1. $\triangle ABD$; $m \angle A = m \angle BDA$ **3.** $\triangle IJL$; $m \angle I =$
$m \angle ILJ = m \angle LJK$ **5.** $x° = 70°$ **7.** $x = 8$ **11.** $m \angle A =$
$m \angle ABC = 50°$; $m \angle ACB = 80°$; $m \angle BCD = 100°$;
$m \angle CBD = m \angle D = 40°$ **13.** 72°, 72°, 36°
15. Given: $m \angle G = m \angle H$
Prove: $GI = HI$
Statements (Justifications):
1. $m \angle G = m \angle H$ (Given)
2. Draw the angle bisector $\overrightarrow{IJ}$ as a
   helping line. Then $m \angle GIJ =$
   $m \angle HIJ$. (Definition of angle bisector)
3. $IJ = IJ$ (Reflexive property of equality)
4. $\triangle GIJ \cong \triangle HIJ$ (AAS)
5. $GI = HI$ (CPCTE)

19. a. 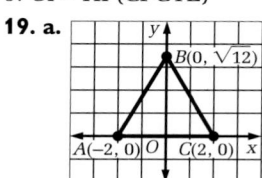 **b.** Using the distance formula gives $AB = 4$, $BC = 4$,
and $AC = 4$. Since $AB =$
$BC = AC = 4$, $\triangle ABC$ is
equilateral. Then $\triangle ABC$ is
equiangular as well be-
cause if a triangle is equi-
lateral, then it is equiangular, with three 60° angles.
21. Given: $RP = RQ$
Prove: R lies on the perpendicular bisector of $\overline{PQ}$.
Statements (Justifications):
1. $RP = RQ$ (Given)
2. Draw a line from R passing through the midpoint
   M of $\overline{PQ}$ so that $PM = QM$. (Definition of midpoint)
3. $\overleftrightarrow{RM}$ bisects $\overline{PQ}$. (Definition of a segment bisector)
4. $RM = RM$ (Reflexive property of equality)
5. $\triangle PRM \cong \triangle QRM$ (SSS)
6. $m \angle 1 = m \angle 2$ (CPCTE)
7. $m \angle 1 + m \angle 2 = m \angle PMQ$ (For any angle, the measure of the whole is equal to the sum of the measures of its non-overlapping parts.)
8. $m \angle PMQ = 180°$ (If the sides of an angle form a
   straight line, then the angle is a straight angle
   with measure 180°.)
9. $m \angle 1 + m \angle 2 = 180°$ (Substitution property
   [Steps 7 and 8])
10. $m \angle 1 + m \angle 1 = 180°$ (Substitution property
    [Steps 6 and 9])
11. $2(m \angle 1) = 180°$ (Distributive property)
12. $m \angle 1 = 90°$ (Division property of equality)
13. $\overleftrightarrow{RM} \perp \overline{PQ}$ (Definition of perpendicular)

14. $\overleftrightarrow{RM}$ is the perpendicular bisector of $\overline{PQ}$. R lies on
the perpendicular bisector of $\overline{PQ}$. (Definition of
perpendicular bisector [Steps 3 and 13])

23. a. 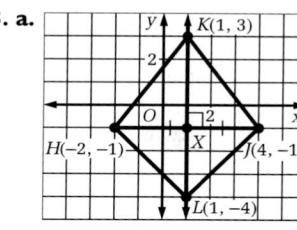 **b.** Using the distance formula, $HK =$
$JK = 5$ and $HL = JL =$
$3\sqrt{2}$. Thus K is the
same distance from
H as from J, and L is
the same distance
from H as from J. By
Theorem 8.16, both
K and L lie on the $\perp$ bisector of $\overline{HJ}$, so $\overleftrightarrow{KL}$ is the $\perp$
bisector of $\overline{HJ}$. **25.** Since $\angle ADC$ and $\angle BDC$ are right
angles, $DA = DB$, and $DC = DC$, you know $\triangle ADC \cong$
$\triangle BDC$ by SAS. **28.** Yes; SAS. **29.** $(x - 7)(x + 12)$
30. $x = 24$ **31.** 30 square units

Page 480 Checkpoint
1. Summaries may vary. An example is given.
I would determine which sides and/or angles I knew
to be equal in measure and how they were related.
If I had two sides and an included angle, I would use
SAS. If I had two angles and an included side,
I would use ASA. If the side was not included,
I would use AAS. If I had three sides, I would use
SSS. **2.** The triangles are congruent by ASA, so
$x = 7$, $y = 8$, and $z° = 50°$ **3.** $\triangle ABC$ and $\triangle EDF$; SSS
4. $\triangle GHI$ and $\triangle JKL$; SAS **5.** $m \angle N = m \angle Q$, $m \angle O =$
$m \angle R$, or $MN = PQ$ **6.** $\triangle STU$ is isosceles since
$ST = TU$.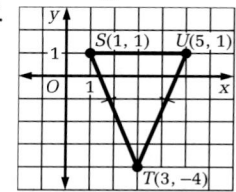

7. $m \angle A = m \angle C = 46°$; $m \angle B = 88°$

Pages 482–483 Talk it Over
1. a. RS **b.** QR **2.** $\triangle MXN \sim \triangle MYX \sim \triangle XYN$
3. c **4.** b **5.** $b + c$

Pages 485–488 Exercises and Problems
1.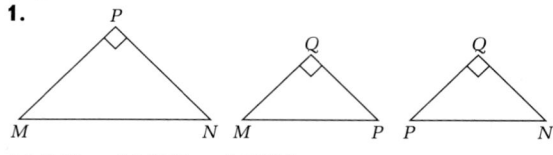

$\triangle MNP \sim \triangle MPQ \sim \triangle PNQ$
3. Sketch both triangles separately. Mark all angles
that are equal in measure.

5. *Given:* △*ABC* with right ∠*C*; $\overline{CD}$ is the altitude to the hypotenuse.   *Prove:* $a^2 + b^2 = c^2$

Statements (Justifications):
1. △*ABC* with right ∠*C*; $\overline{CD}$ is the altitude to the hypotenuse. (Given)
2. △*ABC* ~ △*CBD*; △*ABC* ~ △*ACD* (If the altitude is drawn to the hypotenuse of a right triangle, then the two triangles formed are similar to the original triangle and to each other.)
3. $\frac{c}{a} = \frac{a}{e}; \frac{c}{b} = \frac{b}{f}$ (Definition of similar triangles; corresponding sides are in proportion.)
4. $ce = a^2; cf = b^2$ (Multiplication property of equality)
5. $ce + cf = a^2 + b^2$ (Addition property of equality)
6. $c(e + f) = a^2 + b^2$ (Distributive property)
7. $e + f = c$ (For any segment, the measure of the whole is equal to the sum of the measures of its non-overlapping parts.)
8. $c(c) = a^2 + b^2$ (Substitution property [Steps 6 and 7])
9. $c^2 = a^2 + b^2$ (Definition of exponents)
7. $4\sqrt{2} \approx 5.7$ **11.** $x = 6$ or $x = -6$ **13.** 12   **15.** 8
17. 48   **21.** $x = 6$ **23.** $x = 2, y = 2\sqrt{2} \approx 2.8$
25. $AC = 30$ **27. a.** $AC = 5$ **b.** $m \angle ABD = 60°$;
$m \angle ABC = 30°$ **c.** $BC = 5\sqrt{3} \approx 8.7$ **28.** 24
29.

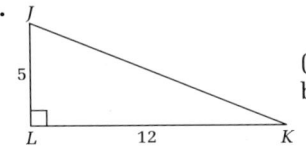

(Either ∠*L* or ∠*J* can be the right angle.)

Pages 489–491 Talk it Over
1. $m \angle A = m \angle B = 45°$ **2.** because the angles of an isosceles right triangle always have measures of 45°, 45° and 90°   **3.** $12\sqrt{2}$ cm   **4.** $8\sqrt{2} \approx 11.3$ cm
5. Yes; the sum of the angle measures is 180°, so $m \angle N = 45°$. If two angles of a triangle are equal in measure, then the sides opposite those angles are equal in measure. △*MNO* has two sides equal in measure, so it is isosceles by definition.   **6.** $MO = NO \approx 7.1$

Pages 493–496 Exercises and Problems
1. $QR = 10; PR = 10\sqrt{3}$ **3.** $EG = 5; EF = 5\sqrt{2}$
5. 173.2 ft   **7.** 127.3 ft   **9.** b   **11.** $SV = 2; VT = 2\sqrt{3}$
13. $KL = 4\sqrt{2}; KN = 11$ **19.** $x° = 60°$ **21.** $z° = 45°$
23. $x = 6\sqrt{2} \approx 8.5$ **25.** $w° = 45°$ **27.** $z \approx 12.9$
29. $\sin \angle MNO = \frac{4}{5} = 0.8; \cos \angle MNO = \frac{3}{5} = 0.6$;
$\tan \angle MNO = \frac{4}{3} \approx 1.33$ **31. a.** $\sin 60° = \cos 30° = \frac{\sqrt{3}}{2}$
b. $\sin 30° = \cos 60° = \frac{1}{2}$ **c.** $\tan 60° = \sqrt{3}$;
$\tan 30° = \frac{1}{\sqrt{3}}$ **d.** If ∠*A* and ∠*B* are complementary,
then $\sin A = \cos B$ and $\tan A = \frac{1}{\tan B}$.

In △*ABC* with right ∠*C*, let $x° = m \angle A$ and
$(90 - x)° = m \angle B$. Then $\sin x° = \sin A = \frac{BC}{AB}$,
$\cos (90 - x)° = \cos B = \frac{BC}{AB}$, $\tan x° = \frac{BC}{AC}$,
$\tan (90 - x)° = \frac{AC}{BC} = \frac{1}{\frac{BC}{AC}} = \frac{1}{\tan x°}$.

33. △*EHR* ~ △*HJR* ~ △*EJH*   **34.** $OC = \sqrt{7^2 + 5^2} = \sqrt{49 + 25} = \sqrt{74}$; $BD = \sqrt{(10 - 3)^2 + (0 - 5)^2} = \sqrt{7^2 + (-5)^2} = \sqrt{49 + 25} = \sqrt{74}$ **35.** $h \approx 2.10$ cm
36. $x = 5.6$ yd   **37.** $z = 8$ in.

Pages 498–499 Unit 8 Review and Assessment
1. *Given:* $\overrightarrow{AB} \parallel \overrightarrow{FC}$; ∠*B* and ∠*F* are right angles.
Prove: $\overrightarrow{FE} \parallel \overrightarrow{CD}$
Statements (Justifications):
1. $\overrightarrow{AB} \parallel \overrightarrow{FC}$ (Given)
2. $m \angle B = m \angle FCD$ (If two ∥ lines are intersected by a transversal, then corresponding ⩜ are = in measure.)
3. ∠*B* is a right angle. (Given)
4. $m \angle B = 90°$ (Definition of a right angle)
5. $m \angle FCD = 90°$ (Substitution property [Steps 2 and 4])
6. ∠*FCD* is a right angle. (Definition of a right angle)
7. $\overrightarrow{FC} \perp \overrightarrow{CD}$ (Definition of perpendicular lines)
8. ∠*F* is a right angle. (Given)
9. $FC \perp \overrightarrow{FE}$ (Definition of perpendicular lines)
10. $\overrightarrow{FE} \parallel \overrightarrow{CD}$ (If two lines are ⊥ to the same transversal, then they are ∥.)
2. 148°   **3.** Yes. If both pairs of opposite angles of a quadrilateral are = in measure, the quadrilateral is a parallelogram.   **4.** $m \angle 1 = 120°$
5. *Given:* $\overline{AB} \parallel \overline{DC}$ *Prove:* △*AEB* ~ △*CED*
Statements (Justifications):
1. $\overline{AB} \parallel \overline{CD}$ (Given)
2. $m \angle BAE = m \angle DCE$ (If two ∥ lines are intersected by a transversal, then alternate interior ⩜ are = in measure.)
3. $m \angle AEB = m \angle CED$ (Vertical ⩜ are = in measure.)
4. △*AEB* ~ △*CED* (AA Similarity)
6. $x = 20, y = 25$
7. *Given:* $m\angle 1 = m \angle 2; BD = DF$
Prove: *D* is the midpoint of $\overline{CE}$.
Statements (Justifications):
1. $m \angle 1 = m \angle 2$ (Given)
2. $\overline{AC} \parallel \overline{EG}$ (If two lines are intersected by a transversal and alternate interior ⩜ are = in measure, then the lines are ∥.)
3. $m \angle BCD = m \angle FED$ (If two lines are intersected by a transversal, then alternate interior ⩜ are = in measure.)
4. ∠*BDC* and ∠*FDE* are vertical angles. (Definition of vertical angles)
5. $m \angle BDC = m \angle FDE$ (Vertical ⩜ are = in measure.)

6. $BD = DF$ (Given)
7. $\triangle BDC \cong \triangle FDE$ (AAS)
8. $ED = CD$ (CPCTE)
9. D is the midpoint of $\overline{CE}$. (Definition of midpoint)
8. Answers may vary. Examples are given. bridges, roofs, swing sets, tripods, braces under a folding table, geodesic domes, trusses in houses, stepladders
9. *Given:* B is the midpoint of $\overline{AE}$, $\overline{FC}$, and $\overline{GD}$.
Prove: $\triangle ABG \cong \triangle EBD$
Statements (Justifications):
1. B is the midpoint of $\overline{AE}$, $\overline{FC}$, and $\overline{GD}$. (Given)
2. $AB = BE$; $GB = BD$ (Definition of midpoint)
3. $\angle ABG$ and $\angle EBD$ are vertical angles. (Definition of vertical angles)
4. $m \angle ABG = m \angle EBD$ (Vertical $\angle$s are = in measure.)
5. $\triangle ABG \cong \triangle EBD$ (SAS)
10. agree; A triangle can have at most one right or obtuse angle since the sum of the measures of the angles is 180°. Therefore, two angles of a triangle must be acute, and in an isosceles triangle, these are the base angles since they are equal in measure.
11. 35°, 35°, 110° **12. a.**

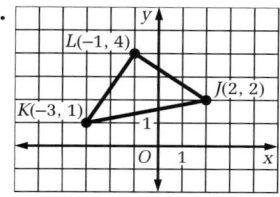

b. $JL = \sqrt{(2-(-1))^2 + (2-4)^2} = \sqrt{9+4} = \sqrt{13}$;
$KL = \sqrt{(-3-(-1))^2 + (1-4)^2} = \sqrt{4+9} = \sqrt{13}$. Since sides JL and KL are equal in measure, $\triangle JKL$ is isosceles. **13.** Since point B is the same distance from points A and C, and D is the midpoint of $\overleftrightarrow{AC}$, $\overline{BD}$ is the perpendicular bisector of $\overline{AC}$ by Theorem 8.16.
14. 20 **15. a.** $\triangle HKJ \sim \triangle HLK \sim \triangle KLJ$ **b.** $8\sqrt{5} \approx 17.9$
c. about 26.8 **16.** $AB = 7\sqrt{2}$; $\sin A = \cos A = \dfrac{1}{\sqrt{2}}$;
$\tan A = 1$ **17.** $BC = 4$; $AC = 4\sqrt{3}$; $\sin A = \dfrac{1}{2}$;
$\cos A = \dfrac{\sqrt{3}}{2}$; $\tan A = \dfrac{1}{\sqrt{3}}$ **18.** $x = 5\sqrt{3} \approx 8.7$
19. $x \approx 26.5$

Unit 9

Pages 505–507 Talk it Over
1. First simplify 468^2 and 468.125^2, then subtract 468^2 from both sides of the equation. Undo the squaring on each side to find the positive square root.
2. It is useful because it simplifies the situation so that it can be easily modeled by using the Pythagorean theorem. The answer will only be an approximation, however, because a buckled railroad track is actually curved. **3.** None of the five expressions is a polynomial because each contains a term that is not a monomial. None of the following can be

written with a whole-number exponent: $1000g^{-3}$, $1000g^{-2}$, $1000g^{-1}$, $\pi r^{1/2}$, $3\left(\dfrac{1}{b}\right)$, $\dfrac{y}{y+1}$, $\dfrac{4x^2}{y}$, $\dfrac{3x}{y}$. **4.** Yes; $2(x+3)$ is a polynomial because it can be written as a monomial or a sum of monomials with exponents that are whole numbers: $2(x+3) = 2x + 6$. **5. a.** 4 **b.** $-\pi x^4 + \sqrt{2}x^3 + 30$ **c.** zero

Pages 509–512 Exercises and Problems
3. $\pi x^2(x+3) = 200\pi$ or $x^2(x+3) = 200$

5. $\dfrac{x}{x+3} = \dfrac{4}{x+2}$

7. $\dfrac{50,015}{2} = 25,007.5$

$\dfrac{50,000}{2} = 25,000$

$\longleftarrow$ 500 m = 50,000 cm $\longrightarrow$

$25,000^2 + d^2 = 25,007.5^2$
13. -5 **15.** Yes. **17.** Yes; each term can be written with exponents that are whole numbers. **19.** Yes; each term can be written with exponents that are whole numbers. **21.** No; $3x^{1/2}$ cannot be written as a polynomial. **23. a.** Yes. **b.** Yes; all linear equations can be written in the form $ax + by + c = 0$, which is a polynomial equation for all values of a, b, and c.
25. $\dfrac{2}{7}$ or about 0.29 **30. a.** $MN = 2\sqrt{2}$; $NO = 4$;
$MP = 2$; $PO = 2\sqrt{3}$; $MO = 2 + 2\sqrt{3}$ **b.** $\sin PNO = \dfrac{\sqrt{3}}{2} \approx 0.8660$; $\cos PNO = 0.5$; $\tan PNO = \sqrt{3} \approx 1.732$
31. $-4i - 1$ **32.** -10 **33.** 5 **34.** $\dfrac{1}{n^4}$ **35.** $x^{1/2}$
36. 1; 1; 1

Pages 513–516 Talk it Over
1. a. 5 **b.** 6; The exponent of the product is the sum of the exponents of the quotient. **2.** x^{18} **3. a.** 2 **b.** 2; -2 **c.** 0; The exponent of the quotient is the difference of the exponents of the numerator and denominator.
4. x^4 **5.** $3x^3$ **6.** $4xy^2$ **7.** 5 **8.** No; he should factor $x^2 - 2x - 15$ as the product of two binomials, $x - 5$ and $x + 3$. **9. a.** 3; 3 **b.** 2; 2; The exponents of the numerator and denominator of the quotient on the right are both the same as the exponent of the quotient on the left. **10.** $\dfrac{a^4}{b^4}$ **11. a.** 2; 2; 2; 6
b. 5; 5; 10; The exponent on the right is the product of the exponents on the left. **12.** a^{14} **13. a.** 2; 2
b. 4; 4; $16x^4$; The exponent of each factor on the right is the same as the exponent of the product on the left.
14. $a^3 b^3$ **15.** $3^{1/2} \cdot 3^{1/2} = 3^{(1/2 + 1/2)} = 3^1 = 3$
16. $\left(x^{1/3}\right)^3 = x^{(1/3)(3)} = x^1 = x$; The cube root of x is the number whose cube is x. Since $\left(x^{1/3}\right)^3 = x$, $x^{1/3}$ is the cube root of x.

Selected Answers

Pages 517–519 Exercises and Problems

1. product of powers rule; quotient of powers rule
3. $\dfrac{t^3}{x^4}$ **5.** $27t^4$ **7.** $\dfrac{16b^4}{a}$ **9.** d^8 **11.** $\dfrac{3a^8}{4}$ **13.** $3xy^2$
15. 64 and 32; $2^{(3\cdot2)} \neq 2^3 \cdot 2^2$ **17.** 4 and 20;
$(6-4)^2 \neq 6^2 - 4^2$ **19.** $\dfrac{9}{16}$ and $\dfrac{9}{4}$; $\left(\dfrac{3}{4}\right)^2 \neq \dfrac{3^2}{4}$ **21.** $2a^3$
23. a^5 **25.** $x^2(x-5)(x+3)$ **27.** $3p^2(3pq+5)$
29. $7x^2y(7x - 5y^4)$ **49. a.** Equations may vary.
Example: $\dfrac{x}{x+2} = \dfrac{4}{5}$ **b.** Yes. **50.** 6 **51.** $\dfrac{155}{12} = 12\dfrac{11}{12}$ or
about 12.9 **52.** 14 **53.** 5 **54.** $x = -3$ or $x = 2$

Pages 520–523 Talk it Over

1. Rose's; From New York City to Istanbul, the plane is flying *with* the wind. The speed of the wind increases the plane's speed. From Istanbul to New York City, the plane is flying *against* the wind. The speed of the wind decreases the plane's speed.
2. 2487.5 miles **3.** No; the point of no return is the point at which the flying *times* to the two cities are the same. The halfway point is the point at which the *distances* to the two cities is the same. Because of the effects of the wind, the plane flying from New York City to Istanbul reaches the point of no return before it reaches the halfway point, and the plane flying from Istanbul to New York reaches the point of no return after it reaches the halfway point. **4.** When 2 is substituted into the original equation, it produces a fraction with a denominator of zero. Since division by zero is undefined, 2 is an extraneous solution.
5. $y + 2$

Pages 524–526 Exercises and Problems

1. Substituting 4 in the original equation produces two fractions with denominators of zero. Since division by zero is undefined, 4 is not a solution of the original equation. **3.** $-\dfrac{2}{3}$ **5.** 5 **7.** 0.25, 2
9. a. about 635 mi/h **b.** about 545 mi/h **11.** 3, −1
13. 2, 3 **15.** 3, 1 **19.** The bases are 4 in. long and 7 in. long. **21.** 75 min **26.** m^3n^6 **27.** $\dfrac{5b^3}{a^3}$
28. $x^{12}y^6$ **29.** RT: 14 cm; RS: $7\sqrt{3}$ cm $\approx$ 12.1 cm
30. HI: 13 m; HJ: $13\sqrt{2}$ m $\approx$ 18.4 m **31.** DE: 5 in.;
FD: $5\sqrt{3}$ in. $\approx$ 8.7 in.
32. $x = 3$ and -3 **33.** −7

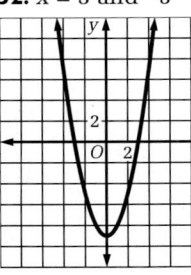 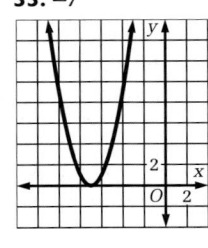

34. 0

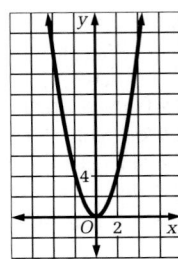

Page 527 Checkpoint
1. If any term of an equation contains an exponent that is not a whole number, the equation is not a polynomial equation. **2. a.** If g is the growth rate, the amount can be expressed as $7000 + 7000g + 7000g^2$. **b.** $7000 + 7000g + 7000g^2 = 25{,}000$ **3.** Yes; each term can be written with exponents that are whole numbers. **4.** No; $3x^{1/2}$ cannot be written with a whole-number exponent. **5.** Yes; each term can be written with exponents that are whole numbers.
6. No; the term cannot be written with whole-number exponents. **7.** $\dfrac{z^3}{y^2}$ **8.** $\dfrac{m^6}{n^{12}}$ **9.** $\dfrac{-2}{a^5}$ **10.** $\dfrac{1}{d^4}$
11. $\dfrac{16}{f^{10}}$ **12.** $\dfrac{p^3q^9}{2}$ **13.** 0, 1 **14.** 2, −1
15. 10 members

Page 531 Talk it Over
1. It is the only graph that has a double zero of −3.
2. For all values of x less than −3, $x + 3$ is negative and $(x - 2)^2$ is positive. The product of a negative number and a positive number is always a negative number.

Pages 532–535 Exercises and Problems
3. a. once **b.** $x = -3$ **c.** −3; −3 is a triple zero.
5. a. once **b.** $x = -8$ **c.** −8; −8 is a triple zero.
7. a. twice **b.** $x = 1$ and $x = -4$ **c.** 1 and −4; 1 is a double zero. **9. a.** twice **b.** $x = 7$ and $x = -4$ **c.** 7 and −4; −4 is a double zero. **11.** quadratic **13.** linear
15. quadratic **17.** C **19.** A **21.** D **34.** 2 **35.** 3, 2
36. $\dfrac{1}{2}$, 3 **37.** parallelogram **38.** squares
39. rhombus **40.** 3, $-\dfrac{1}{2}$ **41.** $\dfrac{3+\sqrt{3}i}{2}$, $\dfrac{3-\sqrt{3}i}{2}$
42. $\dfrac{2}{3}$, $-\dfrac{5}{2}$

Page 536–538 Talk it Over
1. $1 - p$ **2.** $(1 - p)^3$ **3.** $1 - (1 - p)^3$; the probability that at least one light will work **4.** $p^3 - 3p^2 + 3p$
5. No; two of the solutions, $1.5 + \dfrac{i\sqrt{3}}{2}$ and $1.5 - \dfrac{i\sqrt{3}}{2}$, are not real numbers. **6.** You could solve this equation by factoring and using the zero-product property.

Integrated Mathematics

1. The expression $p^3 - 3p^2 + 3p - 0.98$ cannot be written as a product of linear factors. **3.** $0, -1 + i,$ $-1 - i$ **5.** $0, -4, 1$ **7.** $-6, 2$ **9.** Solve by graphing. **11.** Solve by graphing. **13.** $0, 5, -3$ **21.** -1 and -3; -3 is a double zero. **22.** $0, 2,$ and -3; no multiple zeros **23.** -5; -5 is a triple zero. **24.** No; the conditional "If $(x - 1)(x + 2) = 0$, then $x = 1$" is not true since x can also be -2. **25.** $t = \frac{x}{2} - 2$ **26.** $t = \frac{y}{2} + 2$ **27.** $t = 9 - \frac{x}{2}$

Pages 544–548 Exercises and Problems

1. In the first equation, the control variable is t, and the dependent variable is x. In the second equation, the control variable is t, and the dependent variable is y. **3. a.** about 3.5 m **b.** about 1.3 s **c.** about 1.9 s after beginning its flight **5. a.** $t = \frac{x + 3}{4}$ **b.** $y = \frac{x + 3}{2}$

7. a. $t = 2 - x$ **b.** $y = \frac{3 - 4x + x^2}{2 - x}$ **9. a.** about 719 meters **b.** about 5.5 seconds

11. a. 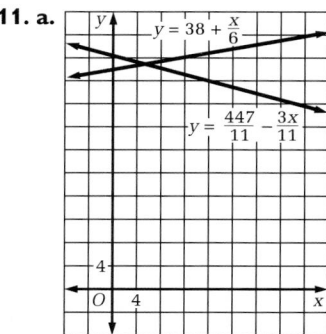 **b.** No. At (6, 39), Bakham has been running 6 s and the ball reaches this point in 5 s. Time is not indicated here. **c.** the point at which Bakham's path and the ball's path cross

13. a. $x_1 = 9t$; $y_1 = 1$ **b.** $x_2 = 1774 - 25(t - 33)$; $y_2 = 1$

c. 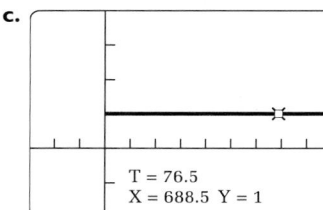 76.5 months after the start of the Central Pacific or May, 1869 **d.** The Central Pacific laid about 688.5 miles of track and the Union Pacific laid about 1087.5 miles of track. **e.** Answers may vary. An example is given. The Central Pacific Railroad Company was laying track in the mountains, whereas the Union Pacific Railroad Company was laying track on flat land. **18.** $0, 1, 2$ **19.** $0, 1 + 2\sqrt{2}, 1 - 2\sqrt{2}$ **20.** $0, \frac{-5 + \sqrt{13}}{6}, \frac{-5 - \sqrt{13}}{6}$

21. $\begin{bmatrix} 5 & 4 \\ -1 & -1 \end{bmatrix}$ **22.** $\begin{bmatrix} 10 \\ -10 \\ -2 \end{bmatrix}$ **23.** $\begin{bmatrix} 3 & 0 & 7 \\ -6 & 3 & 0 \\ -8 & 7 & 14 \end{bmatrix}$

24. $m \angle 2 = 140°$; $m \angle 3 = 40°$; $m \angle 4 = 140°$ **25.** pyramid; base; triangles **26.** prism; bases; rectangles

Pages 550–552 Unit 9 Review and Assessment

1. $\frac{3.25 + x}{12 + x} = 0.30$ **2.** $w(2w + 8) = 120$; fencing required will be $4w + 8$. **3.** No; $\frac{x - 3}{x}$ is a rational expression but is not a polynomial. **4.** Yes; it consists only of terms with whole-number exponents. **5.** No; both terms cannot be written with whole-number exponents. **6.** No; both terms cannot be written with whole-number exponents. **7.** No; the expression cannot be written as a monomial or a sum of monomials with whole number exponents. **8.** Yes; it consists only of terms with whole-number exponents.

9. $48m^4$ **10.** $\frac{1}{a^2}$ **11.** $\frac{2}{x^2 y^5}$ **12.** $r^3 s^3 t^3$ **13.** $\frac{w^6}{5}$ **14.** $\frac{q^3}{p^3}$ **15.** -1 **16.** $\frac{1}{2}$ **17.** $\sqrt{3}, -\sqrt{3}$

18. a. $\frac{5600}{x} - 1 = \frac{5600}{x + 100}$ **b.** 800 bottles per hour **19.** The other solution, -800, does not make sense. The number of bottles capped per hour must be positive. **20.** $-2, 0,$ and 5; no multiple zeros **21.** -3 and 1; -3 is a double zero. **22.** 4; 4 is a triple zero. **23.** -6 and 2; -6 is a double zero. **24.** Answers may vary. Example: $y = x(x + 2)^2$ **25.** C **26.** A **27.** D **28.** B **29.** $0, 2 + \sqrt{3} \approx 3.7, 2 - \sqrt{3} \approx 0.27$ **30.** $-4,$ $-3, \frac{1}{2}$ **31.** $0, 3$ **32.** about 1.2

33. a, b. 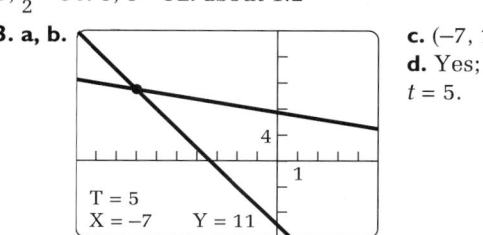 **c.** $(-7, 11)$ **d.** Yes; at $t = 5$.

Unit 10

Pages 557–559 Talk it Over
1. Mary Conlan's table is rectangular, has four legs and a drawer centered lengthwise beneath the top base. Many tables are designed this way. Mary's table is different from other tables in that its legs are connected near the bottom by wooden slats, and there is also some type of structure underneath the drawer. **2.** Yes; the top view only shows that the top base is rectangular. A furniture maker can see the straight edges of the top base from the front and side views and determine that the top base must be rectangular with length given in the front view and width given in the side view. **3.** Answers may vary. An example is given. All parallel horizontal or vertical cross sections of a cube are congruent. Counterexample: Two parallel cross sections of a sphere may be circles with different diameters. **4.** Answers may vary. Examples: a page of a book, cards in a deck, coins in a pile

9. a. 9 cubes **b.** Jade, Luisa, Keiko, and Miika are in order clockwise.   **11.** 7 pyramids   **13.** Each column contains a pyramid, a double pyramid, and a prism made from the same base.

15. an octagonal prism   **17.** a pentagonal pyramid

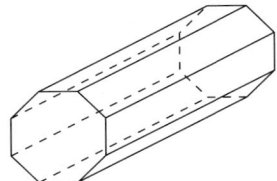 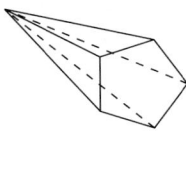

19. not possible; The number of vertices of a prism must be even.   **21.** about 3000 m
23. Estimates may vary. Example: about 2%
25. 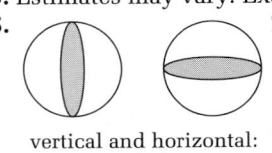   **27.**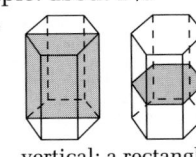

vertical and horizontal:
a circle

vertical: a rectangle
horizontal: a hexagon

29. 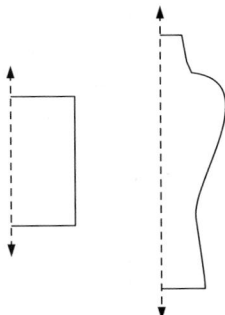   **43.**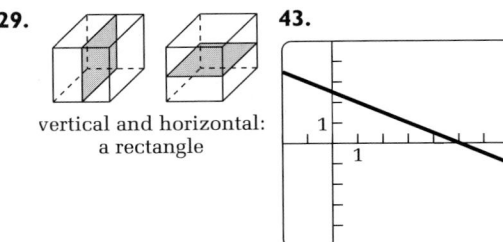

vertical and horizontal:
a rectangle

44. d   **45. a.** about 198 cubic in.
b. about 66 cubic in.

1. For each figure, the axis is a line passing through the centers of the circles that form the top and bottom of the object. The drawings show the plane figure and the axis.

2. Answers may vary. Examples: a conical lamp shade, a ball, a glass jar, a funnel   **3.** For each object, a horizontal cross section is a circle. A vertical cross section has the shape of the rotated plane figure along with its reflection across the axis of rotation.

4. Surface area $= 2\pi r^2 + 2\pi rh = 2\pi(4)^2 + 2\pi(4)(3) = 56\pi$; Volume $= \pi r^2 h = \pi(4)^2(3) = 48\pi$ **5.** a cylinder with radius 3 and height 4   **6.** Answers may vary. Examples are given. **a.** y-axis: A horizontal cross section is a circle with radius 4; a vertical cross section can be a rectangle 3 units high. x-axis: A horizontal cross section can be a rectangle 4 units wide; a vertical cross section can be a circle with radius 3. **b.** y-axis: A horizontal cross section is a circle with radius 4; a vertical cross section can be a rectangle 3 units high. x-axis: A horizontal cross section is a rectangle, a pair of rectangles or a segment 4 units long; a vertical cross section can be a ring.

3. cone   **5.** a figure that looks like a cone with the top cut off.   **7.** a cone with radius 6 and height 4
9. a cone with radius 4 and height 6   **11.** 32π
15. Yes; a triangle can be rotated around an axis to form a cone.   **17.** Yes; a semicircle can be rotated around an axis to form a sphere.
19.   **24.** Drawings may vary. Examples are given.

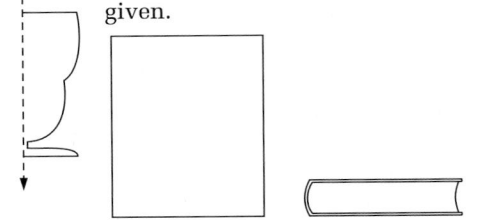

25. about 7%
26. Statements (Justifications):
1. P is on the perpendicular bisector of $\overline{AB}$. (Given)
2. $\triangle PCA$ and $\triangle PCB$ are right triangles. (Definitions of right $\triangle$s and perpendicular bisector)
3. $PC = PC$ (Reflexive)
4. $AC = BC$ (Definition of a bisector)
5. $\triangle PCA$ is congruent to $\triangle PCB$. (SAS)
6. $PA = PB$ (CPCTE)

1. The circle determined by the third station would intersect the first two circles at one of their intersection points.   **2.** The 1994 earthquake was near the point in Los Angeles, California.   **3.** If a point is the same distance from both endpoints of a line segment, then it lies on the perpendicular bisector of the segment.   **4.** point M, the only point on both the sphere with radius 5 in. centered at A and the sphere with radius 5 in. centered at B.   **5.** No points meet the condition.

3. a. a circle with center P and radius 2 m
b. a hemisphere with center P and radius 2 m

5. two points on the perpendicular bisector of $\overline{AB}$, each 4 inches from A and B **7.** No points meet the condition.   **9.** the midpoint of $\overline{AB}$ **11.** a dome-shaped space figure consisting of the points on a sphere with center at the control room and radius 60 mi that are on or above the intersection of the sphere and the plane of the ground (The ground is not actually a plane, nor is the control room a point.)   **15.** in a plane: a plane figure consisting of two parallel line segments each 5 cm from the given segment with their endpoints on each side of the given segment joined by a semicircle with center at the endpoint of the given segment and radius 5 cm; in space: a capsule-shaped figure consisting of a cylinder with radius 5 cm and length that of the segment with each end of the cylinder a hemisphere with center at the endpoint of the segment and radius 5 cm   **23.** a cone with height 2 and radius 5; $\frac{50\pi}{3}$ **24.** The conclusion assumes that the converse is automatically true, which may not be the case. Marya may have decided to write a letter to her cousin without having first received a letter herself. Her cousin may or may not write back.   **25.** $\left(-1\frac{1}{2}, 2\frac{1}{2}\right)$ **26.** $(3, -4)$ **27.** $\left(-1\frac{3}{4}, 6\frac{1}{2}\right)$

Page 577 Checkpoint
1. Any cross section of a sphere is a circle with a radius no bigger than the radius of the sphere. A sphere can be produced by rotating a semicircle about its diameter. A sphere is the set of all the points in space that are a given distance from a given point.

2.   **3.**

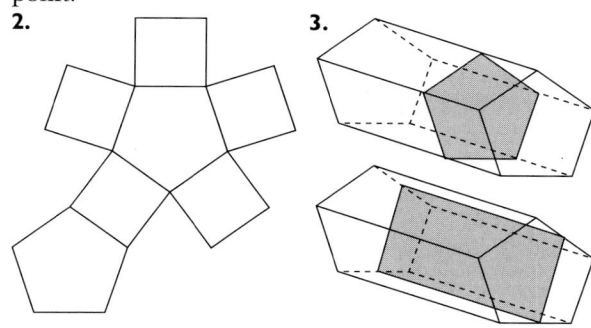

4. a cylinder with radius 8 and height 6   **5.** a cone with radius 2 and height 5   **6.** two points on the perpendicular bisector of $\overline{AB}$ each 5 in. from A and B **7.** No points meet the condition.   **8.** a plane that is perpendicular to $\overline{EF}$ and intersects $\overline{EF}$ at its midpoint

Pages 578–579 Talk it Over
1. Thailand   **2.** Côte d'Ivoire   **3.** about $15 billion
4. the x-axis   **5.** Start at the origin. Move 6 units toward you on the x-axis, 4 units to the right parallel to the y-axis, and -1 unit parallel to the z-axis.
6. No; the order in which you move will take you along a different path, but each path will lead you to the same point, provided you move the correct number of units along each axis as indicated by the coordinates of the ordered triple.

Pages 581–583 Exercises and Problems
1. 1985   **3.** about 46 gallons   **5.** An ordered triple (x, y, z) is three numbers that designate the position of a point in three-dimensional space. The x-coordinate, y-coordinate, and z-coordinate give the point's distance along each axis.   **9.** Volume = 30 cubic units; Surface area = 62 square units   **11.** $(-1, -1, -1)$
13. $\left(3, -\frac{1}{2}, 0\right)$
15. a–c.

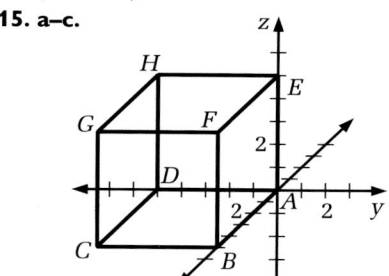

d. cube with edge = 5

17. 0   **19.** -3 **26.** an infinitely long cylinder with radius 12 in.
27. $\begin{bmatrix} 18 & 30 \\ 24 & 36 \end{bmatrix}$ **28.** $\begin{bmatrix} -15 & -9 & -14 & -7 \\ -2 & -5 & -40 & -22 \\ 0 & -1 & -30 & -35 \end{bmatrix}$
29. $[-2 \ 1 \ 4 \ 14]$ **30.** 13 cm   **31.** 8.5 m   **32.** 8.5
33. 8.5

Pages 585–586 Talk it Over
1. Yes.   **2.** $\overline{AG}$ is the hypotenuse of a right triangle with legs of lengths $AC = \sqrt{x^2 + y^2}$ and $GC = z$; $AG = \sqrt{(\sqrt{x^2 + y^2})^2 + z^2} = \sqrt{x^2 + y^2 + z^2}$ **3.** No.
4. Subtract the x-coordinates of the endpoints of a width to find the width of the prism. Subtract the y-coordinates of a length to find the length of the prism. Subtract the z-coordinates of a height to find the height of the prism.   **5.** Find the change in x-coordinates, y-coordinates, and z-coordinates. Substitute these values for x, y, and z in the formula for a diagonal of a prism and simplify.

Pages 588–590 Exercises and Problems
1. $AC = 5$; $AG = 5\sqrt{2} \approx 7.07$ **3.** $AC = 4\sqrt{29} \approx 21.54$; $AG = 4\sqrt{65} \approx 32.25$ **5.** $d = \sqrt{1106} \approx 33.26$; Yes.
9. $\sqrt{3} \approx 1.73$ **11.** $3\sqrt{3} \approx 5.20$ **13.** $\sqrt{14} \approx 3.74$
15. $\sqrt{78} \approx 8.83$ **19.** 3   **21.** $2\sqrt{21} \approx 9.17$
23. isosceles; $EF = DF = 5$; not equilateral because $DE = 5\sqrt{2}$ **25.** isosceles; $LM = MN = 6$; not equilateral because $LN = 4\sqrt{3}$ **34.** $(5, -1, 1)$ **35.** $\frac{1}{12}$ or about 8.3%   **36.** Translate the graph 4 units to the right.
37. Translate the graph 2 units to the left.
38. Translate the graph down 7 units.

Pages 591–594 Talk it Over

1. The graph is the set of points 900 km from the origin. This set of points defines a circle with radius 900 km and center $(0, 0)$.   **2.** Use the distance formula, substituting 0 for x_1 and y_1 and 5 for d. The equation of the circle is $x^2 + y^2 = 25$.   **3.** Substitute 0 for x_1, y_1, and z_1, and 900 for d. The equation of the sphere is $x^2 + y^2 + z^2 = 810,000$ **4. a.** $(1700, 400)$ **b.** $(x - 1700)^2 + (y - 400)^2 = 4,000,000$ **5.** Answers may vary. An example is given. Solve a system of two of the equations using substitution or addition-or-subtraction. For example, you could subtract the Shillong equation from the Lhasa equation and solve the resulting equation for y. You could verify your results by solving another system of two equations.

Pages 594–598 Exercises and Problems

1. $x^2 + y^2 = 144$ **3.** $x^2 + y^2 + z^2 = 81$ **5.** $x^2 + y^2 = 25$
7. $x^2 + y^2 + z^2 = 16$

9. 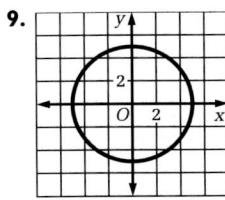   **11.**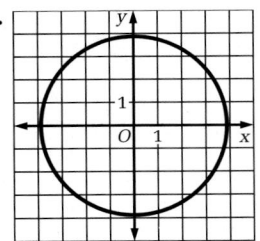

17. $(x - 1)^2 + (y - 3)^2 = 6.25$ **19.** $x^2 + y^2 + z^2 = 16$
21. $(x - 3)^2 + (y - 2)^2 = 13$

25.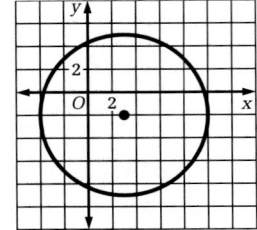

27. a. $(8, -4, 5)$; 6   **31.** $\sqrt{21} \approx 4.6$ **32. a.** True.
b. All rectangles are squares; False. Counterexamples may vary. An example is given. The rectangle with length 4 units and width 2 units is not a square.

Page 600 Unit 10 Review and Assessment

1. square pyramid
2.

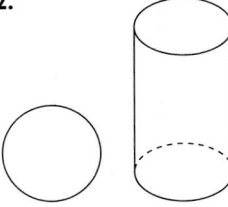

3. Answers may vary. Examples are given. a cylinder, a sphere, a cone   **4.** a cone   **5.** a sphere   **6.** a hollow cylinder   **7. a.** Answers may vary. An example is given.

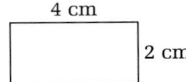

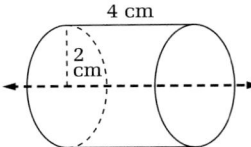

b. 16π cm^3 **8.** a sphere with radius 6 cm   **9.** a pair of parallel lines each 3 m from the given line
10. a plane halfway between the two points and containing the perpendicular bisector of the line segment joining the two points   **11.** Each stations' recordings determine a circle. The intersection of the three circles is the epicenter of the quake.   **12. a.** $A(5, 0, 0)$; $B(0, 0, 0)$; $D(5, 6, 0)$; $F(0, 0, 4)$; $G(0, 6, 4)$; $H(5, 6, 4)$
b. $(2\frac{1}{2}, 3, 2)$ **13.** $\sqrt{126} \approx 11.22$ **14.** scalene;

$LM = \sqrt{34}$, $MN = \sqrt{17}$, $LN = 3$

15.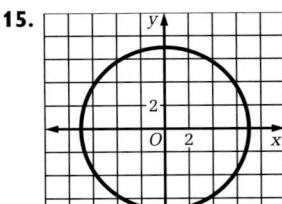

16. $(x - 2)^2 + (y + 1)^2 = 25$ **17.** $x^2 + y^2 + z^2 = 36$

Technology Handbook

Page 604 Try This
1. a. 4 **b.** 32 **c.** about 0.966   **2.** c   **3. a.** 120 **b.** 20
c. 10

Page 605 Try This
4. a.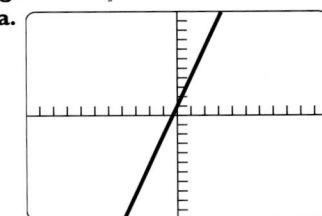

b.

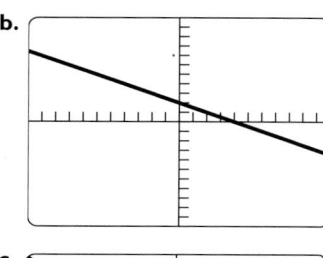

c.

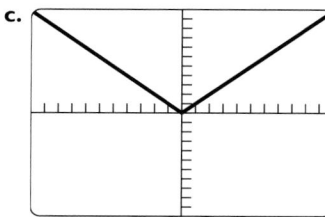

d.

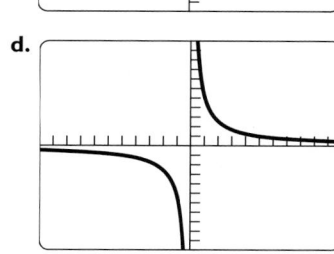

5. Answers may vary. An example is given. [−5, 30] and Xscl=5 for *x*, [−10, 75] and Yscl=5 for *y*.
6. Answers may vary. An example is given. [−7.5, 7.5] and Xscl=1 for *x*, [−5, 5] and Yscl=1 for *y*.

Page 606 Try This

7.

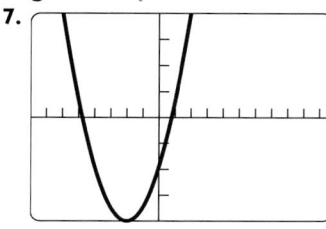

TI-82: window of [−4, 5.4] and Xscl=0.5 for *x*, and [−2, 2] and Yscl=0.5 for *y*. Graph crosses at 0.4 and −2.4. TI-81: window of [−4, 5.5] and Xscl=0.5 for *x*, and [−2, 2] and Yscl=0.5 for *y*. Graph crosses at 0.4 and −2.4.

Page 608 Try This

8. between −2.41 and −2.42

9.

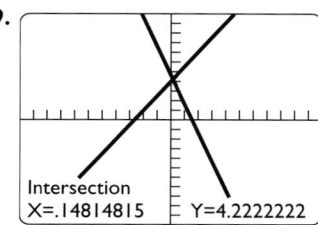

Intersection
X=.14814815   Y=4.2222222

Page 611 Try This

10.

```
[A]+[B]
        [[8 15]
         [3 0 ]]
```

11.

```
[B]−[C]
        [[−4    8  ]
         [−15 −11]]
```

12.

```
2[A]
        [[6    8 ]
         [12  14]]
```

13.

```
[A][B]
        [[3   5 ]
         [9  17]]
```

14. not defined

15.

```
[C][D]
[[33  21  −63  36]
 [44  28  −84  48]]
```

16.

```
[A]⁻¹
        [[−2.33  1.33 ]
         [2         −1   ]]
```

17. not defined

Pages 614–615 Extra Practice Unit 1
1. 140 **3. a.** 240 **b.** No. The sample size is too small. **5.** all triangle types: isosceles, scalene, equilateral, right, acute, obtuse **7.** $\frac{2}{3}$ **9.** 0 **11.** systematic
13. cluster **15.** random **17.** 0 times **19.** 48
21. 100,001 **23.** You always get an odd perfect square. **25.** False. **27.** False. **29. a.** False; $x = 3$.
b. If $x > 5$, then $x > 2$; the converse is true.
31. a. True. **b.** If the sun is not out, then it is midnight. The converse is false. It could be cloudy or raining and the sun would not be out, or it could be 2 A.M.

Pages 616–617 Extra Practice Unit 2
1. nonlinear growth **3.** constant **5. a.** $-\frac{4}{3}$
b. decreasing **7. a.** $\frac{3}{2}$ **b.** increasing **9. a.** $-\frac{3}{2}$
b. decreasing **11.** $y = 5x - 23$ **13.** $y = \frac{4}{3}x + \frac{1}{3}$
15. $y = \frac{1}{2}x + \frac{23}{2}$ **17. a.** slope $= \frac{1}{2}$;
vertical intercept $= 0$
b. 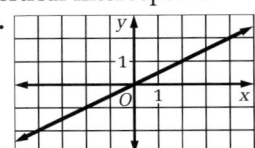 **c.** increasing function

19. a. slope $= 0$; vertical intercept $= -1.5$
b. 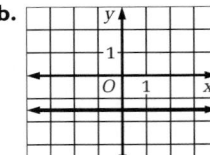 **c.** constant function

21. a. slope $= \frac{2}{3}$; vertical intercept $= -1$
b. 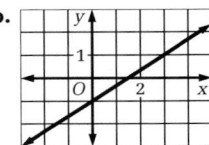 **c.** increasing function

23. $y = 3$ **25.** $y = 0.9$
27. $y = \frac{13}{x}$ **29.** 9π; 4.5π **31.** 441π; 1543.5π **33.** 11
35. 3:4 **37.** 27:64 **39. a.** 62.8 **b.** 6.2; −6.2
41. a. 44 **b.** 7.4; −7.4 **43. a.** 104.7 **b.** 4.8; −4.8
45. 200 **47.** 32 **49.** 2 **51.** $7^{1/3}x^{1/3}$ or $(7x)^{1/3}$
53. $\sqrt[3]{29pq}$ **55.** $-\sqrt{8v} \cdot \sqrt[3]{\frac{w}{2}}$ **57.** 61,440
59. 1 **61.** 0.015625

Pages 618–619 Extra Practice Unit 3
1. $(1, -4)$ **3.** $(0, 3)$ **5.** $(3, -1)$ **7.** $(-2, 7)$ **9.** $(4, 1)$
11. $(-7, -1)$ **13. a.** lines intersecting **b.** one solution; consistent **15. a.** same line **b.** many solutions; consistent **17. a.** parallel lines **b.** no solution; inconsistent **19.** $y = -2x - 7$ **21.** $y = 5$ **23.** $(6, -1)$
25. $(4, 7)$ **27.** $(-5, 3)$ **29.** $(3, 8)$ **31.** $\begin{bmatrix} 1 & 0 \\ 7 & 1 \end{bmatrix}$
33. $\begin{bmatrix} 14 & 4 & 0 \\ -6 & 2 & 2 \\ 8 & 4 & -2 \end{bmatrix}$ **35.** $\begin{bmatrix} 1 & 12 & 22 \\ -10 & -11 & 5 \end{bmatrix}$
37. $\begin{array}{ccc} D' & E' & F' \end{array}$ $\begin{bmatrix} 15 & 6 & 0 \\ 3 & 18 & 9 \end{bmatrix}$ **39.** $\begin{array}{ccc} D' & E' & F' \end{array}$ $\begin{bmatrix} 2.5 & 1 & 0 \\ 0.5 & 3 & 1.5 \end{bmatrix}$
41. $\begin{bmatrix} 12 \\ 20 \end{bmatrix}$ **43.** $[-3 \ \ -80]$ **45.** $\begin{bmatrix} 4 & 3 \\ 9 & 7 \end{bmatrix}$

Pages 620–621 Extra Practice Unit 4
1. $x = 2$; $(2, -3)$; maximum **3.** $x = -3$; $(-3, 32)$; maximum **5.** $x = 16$; $(16, 50.2)$; maximum **7.** −2
9. 0 **11.** Estimates may vary. Examples are given.
$x = -\frac{1}{3}, 4\frac{1}{3}$ **13.** 3 units left, 7 units down
15. 6 units right, 2 units up **17. a.** $(7, -1)$ **b.** 48
19. a. $(-1, 14)$ **b.** 9 **21.** $x = \pm\frac{\sqrt{15}}{2}$ or about 1.94,
about −1.94 **23.** $x = \pm\sqrt{11} - 1$ or about −4.32, about
2.32 **25.** $x = \pm\sqrt{\frac{13}{3}}$ or about 2.08, about −2.08
27. $x = \pm\sqrt{10} - 4$ or about −7.16, about −0.84
29. $(x - 7)(x + 3)$ **31.** $(3x - 7)(x - 2)$
33. $(5x - 3)(2x + 5)$ **35.** $(9x + 5)(9x - 5)$
37. $(2 - 7x)(2 + 7x)$ **39.** $(3x + 1)^2$ **41.** $x = 11, -3$
43. $x = 2, -\frac{2}{3}$ **45.** $x = -3 \pm \sqrt{11}$ or about 0.32, about
−6.32 **47.** $x = \frac{-4 \pm \sqrt{10}}{3}$ or about −0.28, about −2.39
49. $x = -2 \pm \frac{\sqrt{30}}{2}$ or about 0.74, about −4.74
51. $x = \frac{9 \pm \sqrt{53}}{2}$ or about 8.14, about 0.86 **53. a.** two
solutions **b.** $x = \frac{1 \pm \sqrt{5}}{2}$ or about 1.62, about −0.62
55. a. two solutions **b.** $x = -1, -\frac{4}{3}$
57. a. no solutions
b.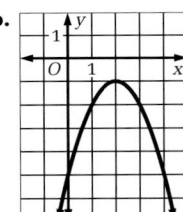
59. $-1 + 2i$ **61.** $83 + 14i$ **63.** $x = 1 \pm \sqrt{10}i$ or about
$1 + 3.16i$, about $1 - 3.16i$ **65.** $(-3, 23)$ **67.** $(-4, 57)$,
$(0, 1)$

Integrated Mathematics

69. $(-1, 0)$, $(4, 5)$

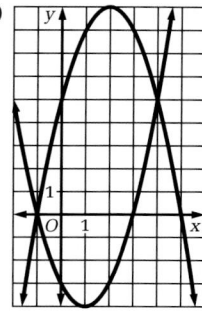

Pages 622–623 Extra Practice Unit 5

1. True.   **3.** False, a kite may not have four sides of equal measure.   **5.** 15   **7.** $\sqrt{218}$ **9.** $PQ = QR = 5$; $RS = SP = 2\sqrt{13}$ **11.** $(-1.5, 3.5)$ **13.** $(1, 4)$
15. $(9, -3)$ **17.** $(-7, -20)$ **19.** reflection over the y-axis

21. $A'(-2, 3)$; $B'(1, 1)$; $C'(-2, 0)$

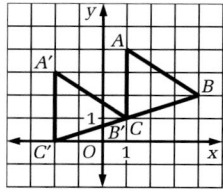

23. $A'(-4, 1)$; $B'(-2, 4)$; $C'(-1, 1)$

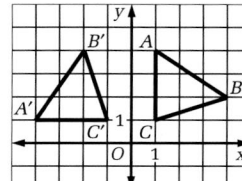

25. $(0, b)$; $(a, 0)$ **27.** (r, q) **29.** Yes; two sides are parallel with slope = 0.   **31.** $\sqrt{(a-b)^2 + c^2}$; $\sqrt{(a-b)^2 + c^2}$; Yes.

Pages 623–624 Extra Practice Unit 6

1. 12   **3.** 64   **5. a.** 120   **b.** 360   **c.** 3024   **7. a.** $\frac{1}{6}$
b. $\frac{1}{9}$ **c.** $\frac{1}{12}$ **9. a.** $\frac{1}{156}$ **b.** $\frac{1}{26}$ **c.** $\frac{5}{39}$ **11.** 35   **13.** 56
15. 5040   **17.** 21   **19.** 1   **21.** 15   **23.** 15   **25.** $\frac{5}{32}$
27. $\frac{5}{16}$ **29.** about 0.329   **31.** $a^4 - 12a^3 + 54a^2 - 108a + 81$
33. $64c^6 + 192c^5d + 240c^4d^2 + 160c^3d^3 + 60c^2d^4 + 12cd^5 + d^6$

Pages 625–626 Extra Practice Unit 7

1.

3.

5. A   **7.** B   **9.**

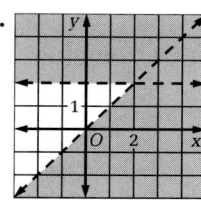

11. a. If $xy = xz$, then $y = z$. False; $x = 0$, $y = 1$, $z = 2$.
b. If $y = z$, then $xy = xz$. True.   **13. a.** If an integer is evenly divisible by 10, then its last digit is 0. True.
b. If an integer's last digit is 0, then it is evenly divisible by 10. True.   **15.** If our team plays the Tigers, then we will be in the semi-finals.   **17.** valid; indirect argument   **19.** False; if four sides are congruent, the quadrilateral is a parallelogram; but not every parallelogram has four congruent sides.   **21.** True; this is the definition of transparent.   **23.** Division Property of Equality   **25.** Substitution Property
27. Given the equation $2x - 5 = 17$. Addition Property of Equality allows you to add 5 to both sides of the equation, leaving you with $2x = 22$. Then the Division Property of Equality allows you to divide both sides of the equation by 2, leaving you with $x = 11$.   **29.** $m \angle A + m \angle B = 180°$; definition of supplementary   **31.** If two ∥ lines are intersected by a transversal, then alternate interior ∠s are = in measure.   **33.** Vertical ∠s are = in measure.

Pages 627–628 Extra Practice Unit 8

1. ❶$\angle 1$ and $\angle 2$ are supplementary. ❷$\rightarrow$ $p \parallel q$ ❸$\rightarrow$ $m \angle 3 = m \angle 4$

Justifications: ❶ Given ❷ If two lines are intersected by a transversal and co-interior ∠s are supplementary, then the lines are ∥. ❸ If two ∥ lines are intersected by a transversal, then alternate interior ∠s are = in measure.
3. Yes.   **5.** $m \angle P = 70°$; $m \angle Q = 110°$; $m \angle R = 60°$; $m \angle S = 120°$ **7.** $BC = 8$ **9.** SAS   **11.** AAS
13. *Given:* $\overline{AC}$ bisects $\overline{BD}$. $\overline{BD}$ bisects $\overline{AC}$.
Prove: $\overline{AB} \parallel \overline{CD}$
Statements (Justifications):
1. $\overline{AC}$ bisects $\overline{BD}$; $\overline{BD}$ bisects $\overline{AC}$. (Given)
2. $AX = CX$; $BX = DX$ (Definition of bisector)
3. $m \angle AXB = m \angle CXD$ (Vertical ∠s are = in measure.
4. $\triangle AXB \cong \triangle CXD$ (SAS)
5. $m \angle DCX = m \angle BAX$ (CPCTE)
6. $\overline{AB} \parallel \overline{CD}$ (If two lines are intersected by a transversal and alternate interior ∠s are = in measure, then the lines are ∥.)
15. *Given:* $AC = BC$; $m \angle 1 = m \angle 2$.
Prove: $AE = BD$
Statements (Justifications):
1. $AC = BC$; $m \angle 1 = m \angle 2$ (Given)
2. $AB = AB$ (Reflexive property of equality)

Selected Answers

3. $m \angle DAB = m \angle EBA$ (If two sides of a triangle are = in measure, then the ∠ opposite those sides are = in measure.)
4. $\triangle DAB \cong \triangle EBA$ (ASA)
5. $AE = BD$ (CPCTE)
17. $x = 10$ 19. $x = 13.5$ 21. $x = 6$ 23. a. 1 b. 1 c. 1
d. conjecture: $(\sin x)^2 + (\cos x)^2 = 1$

Pages 628–629 Extra Practice Unit 9

1. $x(x - 3) = 240$ 3. $\frac{x(2x + 5)}{2} = 192$

5. $3c^2 d^5(c - 2d)$ 7. $2k(k + 5)(k - 4)$

9. $3mn(7m^2 + 11n^3)$ 11. $5x^3 y^4$ 13. $\frac{s^9}{r^{12}}$ 15. $\frac{27}{125a^9 b^6}$

17. $b = 18$ 19. $t = 3$ 21. $x = 9, x = 2$ 23. $r = 5$
25. $y = 2, y = -1.5$ 27. -5 (double), 8   29. -9 (triple)
31. 0 (triple)   33. D   35. C   37. $x = -3, x = 0, x = 3$

39. a. $y = 7 - \frac{x^2}{1600}$ b.
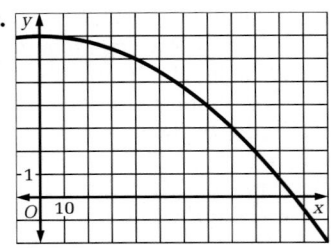
c. x = about 106

Pages 630–631 Extra Practice Unit 10
1.
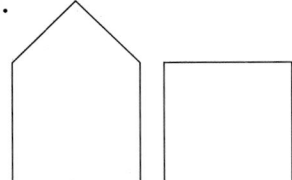

3.

5. a. cone of height 4 and radius 6
   b. $V = 48\pi$ units^3

7.   9.
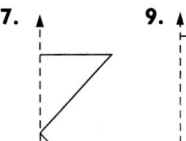
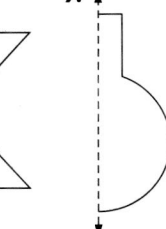

11. a. all points on the line perpendicular to $\overline{AB}$ at its midpoint b. all points on the plane perpendicular to $\overline{AB}$ at its midpoint   13. a. the midpoint of $\overline{AB}$ b. the

midpoint of $\overline{AB}$ 15. No points meet the conditions.
17. (5, 0, 6)   19. (0, 3, 6)   21. (3, −2, −3)   23. 7
25. 15   27. $x^2 + y^2 = 16$ 29. $x^2 + y^2 + z^2 = 64$

Toolbox Skills

Pages 632–633 Skill 1
1.
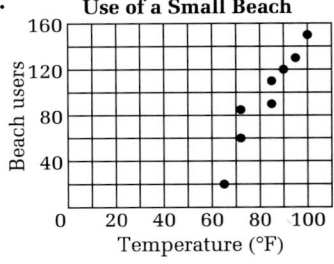

2. positive correlation
3–7. Answers may vary. Examples are given.
3.
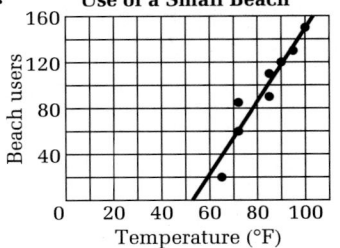

4. about 85 people   5. about 70 people
6. about 160 people   7. about 20 people

Pages 633–634 Skill 2
1. 30   2. 100   3. 11   4. $20,000–$29,000; $50,000 or over

Page 634 Skill 3
1. the numbers 70, 71, 72, 75, 76

2. **Finishing Times (minutes)**

```
3 | 2 4
4 | 1 3 4 5 5 6
5 | 0 1 1 2 2 8
6 | 2 3 5 6 6
7 | 1
```

3. 40–49 and 50–59; 70–79

Page 635 Skill 4
1. about 22.7   2. 21   3. 10, 18, and 24   4. 32

Page 636 Skill 5
1.   10   20   30   40   50   2. 38   3. 27
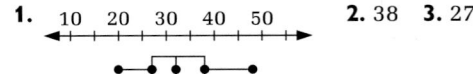

Integrated Mathematics

Page 637 Skill 6
1. about 38%   **2.** about 27%   **3.** about 10%
4. about 12%   **5.** about 18 sweatshirts

Page 638 Skill 7
1. 20%   **2.** 60%   **3.** 80%   **4.** 100%   **5.** about 8%
6. about 15%   **7.** about 23%   **8.** about 77%   **9.** 0
10. 100%

Page 639 Skill 8
1. 15%   **2.** 50%   **3.** about 17%   **4.** about 67%

Page 640 Skill 9
1. 12   **2.** 67   **3.** −6   **4.** 23   **5.** 19   **6.** 83   **7.** 0   **8.** 94
9. −21   **10.** −4   **11.** 478   **12.** −72   **13.** −24   **14.** 6
15. −200   **16.** −396   **17.** −416   **18.** −256

Page 641 Skill 10
1. $3x + 7$ **2.** $-2y + 17$ **3.** $n - 5m$ **4.** $-7k + 23$
5. $3x^2 + 3x$ **6.** $-3xy + 3yz$ **7.** $-6a^2 + ab$
8. $3k^2 + 3hk$ **9.** $7x^3 - 7$

Page 642 Skill 11
1. $2x^2 + 3x$ **2.** $-4x^2 + 20x$ **3.** $-14a^2 + 42a$
4. $x^2 - 4x - 45$ **5.** $y^2 - 8y + 12$ **6.** $-x^2 + 13x - 30$
7. $2x^2 - 13x - 7$ **8.** $-3n^2 - 8n + 35$ **9.** $4x^2 - 22x + 10$
10. $6x^2 - 41x + 44$ **11.** $14x^2 - 9x - 8$
12. $15k^2 - 22k + 8$

Pages 642–643 Skill 12
1. $3\sqrt{5}$ **2.** $10\sqrt{3}$ **3.** $2\sqrt{19}$ **4.** $10\sqrt{3}$ **5.** $60\sqrt{5}$
6. $\sqrt{42}$ **7.** $3\sqrt{10}$ **8.** $4.2\sqrt{33}$ **9.** $24\sqrt{6}$ **10.** 6
11. 27   **12.** $12\sqrt{3}$ **13.** $60\sqrt{2}$

Pages 643–644 Skill 13
1. $x = 72$ **2.** $n = 6$ **3.** $x = 20$ **4.** $x = 25$ **5.** $x = 11$
6. $n = 5$ **7.** $w = 86$ **8.** $x = 3$ **9.** $x = -5$ **10.** $x = 7$
11. $x = \frac{1}{3}$ **12.** $x = 16$ **13.** $x = \frac{15}{13}$ **14.** $n = -21$
15. $x = \frac{1}{3}$

Page 645 Skill 14
1. $x < 4$
2. $x \geq -2$
3. $x > -5$
4. $x \geq -2$
5. $x > -4$

6. $x \geq 1$
7. $x < 2$
8. $x \leq 0$
9. $x < -4$

Page 646 Skill 15
1. $h = \frac{2A}{b}$ **2.** $r = \frac{C}{2\pi}$ **3.** $b = 2A - a$ **4.** $y = 13 - 2x$
5. $y = 4 - \frac{5}{2}x$ **6.** $n = \frac{m}{180} + 2$ **7.** $x = \frac{13}{2} - \frac{y}{2}$
8. $x = \frac{y - b}{m}$

Pages 646–647 Skill 16
1. $x = \pm 7$ **2.** $x \approx \pm 4.36$ **3.** $x = 2$ **4.** $x = 4$
5. $x = -5$ **6.** $x \approx \pm 3.32$ **7.** $x \approx \pm 9.85$ **8.** $x \approx \pm 4.90$

Pages 647–648 Skill 17
1. $x = 15.6$ **2.** $z = 10.8$ **3.** $y = 5.6$ **4.** $x = 11.2$
5. $w = 15.75$ **6.** $y = \frac{40}{11} \approx 3.64$ **7.** $q = 10.2$
8. $n = 52.25$

Page 648 Skill 18
1. $0, -10$ **2.** $0, 4$ **3.** $0, 3$ **4.** $-1, -6$ **5.** $-4, 7$
6. $\frac{1}{2}, -3$

Page 649 Skill 19
1. Yes.   **2.** No.   **3.** No.   **4.** Yes.

Pages 649–650 Skill 20
1.

$y = x - 3$		
x	y	(x, y)
−3	−6	(−3, −6)
−2	−5	(−2, −5)
−1	−4	(−1, −4)
0	−3	(0, −3)
1	−2	(1, −2)
2	−1	(2, −1)
3	0	(3, 0)

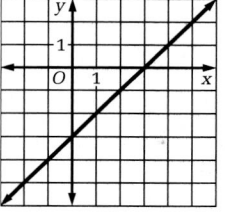

Selected Answers

2.

$y = 3x - 4$		
x	y	(x, y)
−3	−13	(−3, −13)
−2	−10	(−2, −10)
−1	−7	(−1, −7)
0	−4	(0, −4)
1	−1	(1, −1)
2	2	(2, 2)
3	5	(3, 5)

3.

$y = -2x + 3$		
x	y	(x, y)
−1	5	(−1, 5)
0	3	(0, 3)
1	1	(1, 1)
2	−1	(2, −1)
3	−3	(3, −3)

4.

$y = \frac{1}{2}x + 1$		
x	y	(x, y)
−3	$-\frac{1}{2}$	$\left(-3, -\frac{1}{2}\right)$
−2	0	(−2, 0)
−1	$\frac{1}{2}$	$\left(-1, \frac{1}{2}\right)$
0	1	(0, 1)
1	$1\frac{1}{2}$	$\left(1, 1\frac{1}{2}\right)$
2	2	(2, 2)

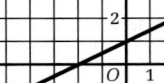

5.

$y = |x|$		
x	y	(x, y)
−3	3	(−3, 3)
−2	2	(−2, 2)
−1	1	(−1, 1)
0	0	(0, 0)
1	1	(1, 1)
2	2	(2, 2)

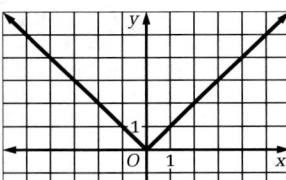

6.

$y = x^2 + 1$		
x	y	(x, y)
−3	10	(−3, 10)
−2	5	(−2, 5)
−1	2	(−1, 2)
0	1	(0, 1)
1	2	(1, 2)
2	5	(2, 5)
x	y	(x, y)

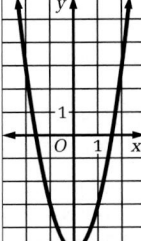

7.

$y = 2x^2 - 5$		
x	y	(x, y)
−3	13	(−3, 13)
−2	3	(−2, 3)
−1	−3	(−1, −3)
0	−5	(0, −5)
1	−3	(1, −3)
2	3	(2, 3)

8.

$y = \frac{1}{x}$		
x	y	(x, y)
−4	$-\frac{1}{4}$	$\left(-4, -\frac{1}{4}\right)$
−3	$-\frac{1}{3}$	$\left(-3, -\frac{1}{3}\right)$
−2	$-\frac{1}{2}$	$\left(-2, -\frac{1}{2}\right)$
−1	−1	(−1, −1)
$-\frac{1}{2}$	−2	$\left(-\frac{1}{2}, -2\right)$
0	—	—
$\frac{1}{2}$	2	$\left(\frac{1}{2}, 2\right)$
1	1	(1, 1)
2	$\frac{1}{2}$	$\left(2, \frac{1}{2}\right)$
3	$\frac{1}{3}$	$\left(3, \frac{1}{3}\right)$
4	$\frac{1}{4}$	$\left(4, \frac{1}{4}\right)$

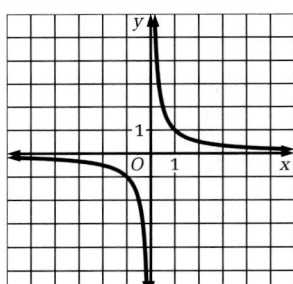

Integrated Mathematics

Pages 650–651 Skill 21

1. $-\frac{2}{3}$ **2.** $\frac{11}{2}$ **3.** $-\frac{2}{5}$ **4.** undefined

Pages 651–652 Skill 22

1. 161 mi **2.** 4.4 ft

Pages 652–653 Skill 23

1. slope = 3; vertical intercept = –4 **2.** slope = $-\frac{5}{2}$ or
–2.5; vertical intercept = $\frac{56}{5}$ or 11.2 **3.** slope = –7;
vertical intercept = 6 **4.** slope = 4; vertical
intercept = 0 **5.** $y = \frac{1}{2}x + 3$ **6.** $y = -2x + 1$

7. $y = \frac{5}{2}x - 3$

Pages 653–654 Skill 24

1. vertical intercept = 6;
horizontal intercept = 2

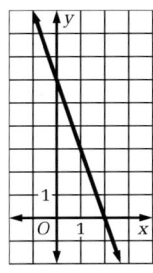

2. vertical intercept = –5;
horizontal intercept = 2

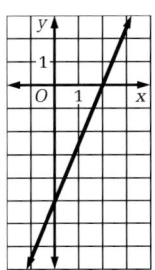

3. vertical intercept = 3;
horizontal intercept = –3

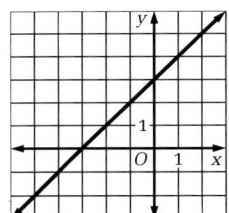

4. vertical intercept = –8;
horizontal intercept = 2

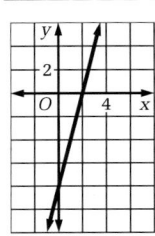

5. vertical intercept = –3;
horizontal intercept = $\frac{3}{2}$

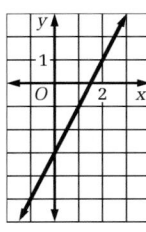

6. vertical intercept = 5;
horizontal intercept = 2

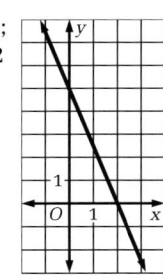

Page 654 Skill 25

1.

$y = -x + 3$		
x	**y**	**(x, y)**
0	3	(0, 3)
3	0	(3, 0)

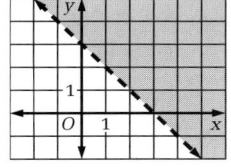

2.

$y = 2x - 4$		
x	**y**	**(x, y)**
0	–4	(0, –4)
2	0	(2, 0)

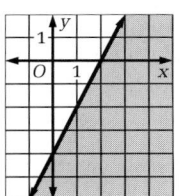

3.

$y = \frac{1}{2}x + 1$		
x	**y**	**(x, y)**
0	1	(0, 1)
–2	0	(–2, 0)

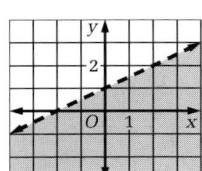

4.

$2x + 3y = 6$		
x	**y**	**(x, y)**
0	2	(0, 2)
3	0	(3, 0)

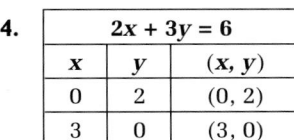

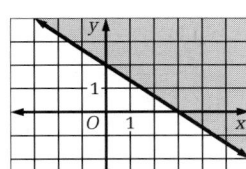

Selected Answers

5.

x − 3y = 3		
x	**y**	**(x, y)**
0	−1	(0, −1)
3	0	(3, 0)

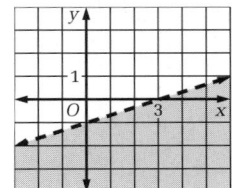

6.

3x + 2y = 9		
x	**y**	**(x, y)**
0	4.5	(0, 4.5)
3	0	(3, 0)

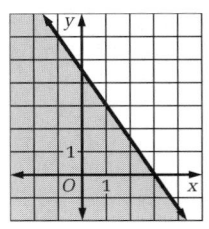

Page 655 Skill 26
1. 54°   **2.** $x° = 64°$, $y° = 116°$, $z° = 64°$ **3.** 57°

Page 656 Skill 27
1. $\angle G$ and $\angle D$ are right angles. Side GF is parallel to side DE.   **2.** Side $AB \cong$ side DC. Side $AD \cong$ side BC.
3. All angles are right angles. Side AD is parallel to side BC. Side DC is parallel to side AB.
4. Side $AB \cong$ side $BC \cong$ side AC. $\angle A$, $\angle B$, and $\angle C$ are equal in measure.   **5.** Side AB is parallel to side DE. $\angle A$ is equal in measure to $\angle CDE$. $\angle B$ is equal in measure to $\angle CED$. $\angle C$ is a right angle.   **6.** $\angle ZUV$ is a right angle. Side ZY is parallel to side VW. Side ZU is parallel to side WX. Side $UZ \cong$ side UV.

Pages 657–658 Skill 28
1. 160 ft^2 **2.** 19.5 in.^{2} **3.** 9π in.$^2 \approx 28.274$ in.^{2}
4. 702 in.^{2} **5.** 250π cm$^2 \approx 785.4$ cm^2
6. 200 cm^3 **7.** 34π m$^3 \approx 106.8$ m^3 **8.** 400 in.^{3}

Page 659 Skill 29
1. $\frac{4}{8.5} \approx 0.47$ **2.** $\frac{7.5}{8.5} \approx 0.88$ **3.** $\frac{4}{7.5} \approx 0.53$

4. $\frac{7.5}{8.5} \approx 0.88$ **5.** $\frac{4}{8.5} \approx 0.47$ **6.** $\frac{7.5}{4} = 1.875$

7. 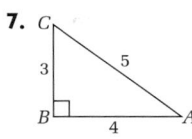   **8.**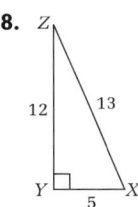

Page 660 Skill 30
1. $x \approx 26.8$ **2.** $x \approx 5.8$ **3.** $x \approx 26.6$

Page 661 Skill 31
1. 13   **2.** 10.5   **3.** about 71.1

Page 661 Skill 32
1. Yes.   **2.** Yes.   **3.** Yes.   **4.** No.

Page 662 Skill 33
1. 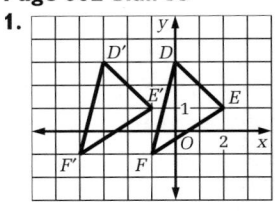   **2.**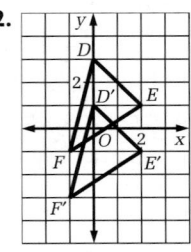

3. **4.**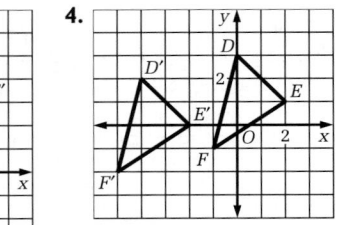

5.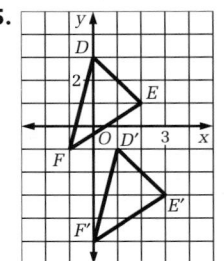

Pages 662–663 Skill 34
1. 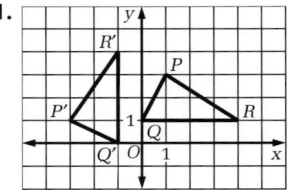   **2.**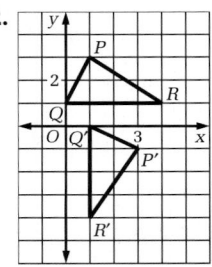

Integrated Mathematics

3.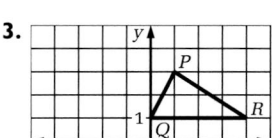

4.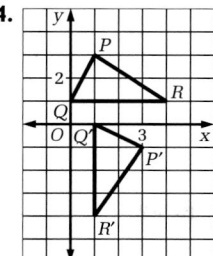

Pages 663–664 Skill 35

1.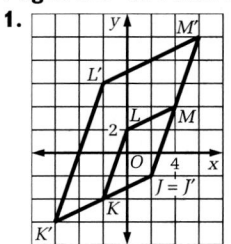

2.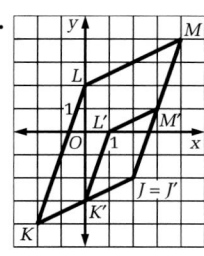

3.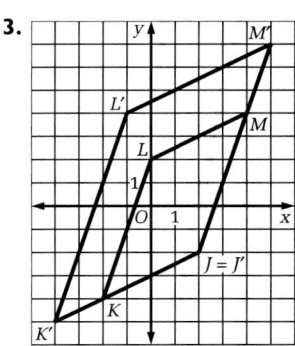

4.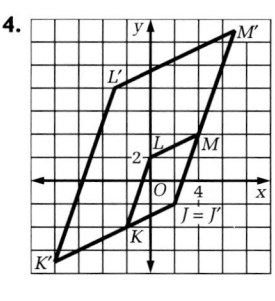

Page 664 Skill 36

1.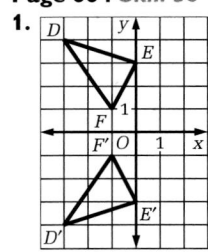

2.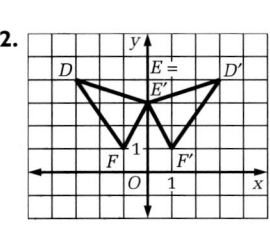

3.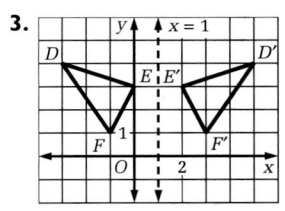

4.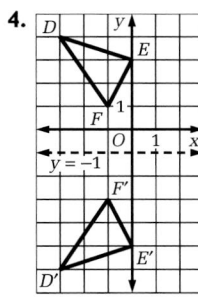

Appendix 1

Pages 673, 674 Talk it Over

1. $A = 152$ cm^2 **2.** Answers may vary. For example, you can use the area formulas for a trapezoid and a square. **3.** Use the formula $\frac{\text{sector area}}{\text{area of circle}} = \frac{\text{central } \angle}{360°}$. The area of the turquoise part of the pin is about 3.5 cm^2. **4.** Descriptions may vary. An example is given. Both the surface area and the volume increase more quickly than the edge length because their respective formulas involve squaring and cubing the edge length.

Edge length	Volume	Surface area
1	1	6
2	8	24
3	27	54
⋮	⋮	⋮
s	s^3	$6s^2$

Page 674 Exercises and Problems

1. 30.875 ft^2 **3.** about 235.5 ft^2 **4.** about 47.1 ft **7.** Drew might make this assumption because the diameter of the large globe is 1.5 times the diameter of the small globe. He is mistaken, however, because finding the volume of a sphere involves cubing its diameter. The volume of the large globe is $(1.5)^3$, or 3.375 times the volume of the small globe.

Appendix 2

Page 675 Talk it Over

1. Answers may vary. An example is given. Any two angles passing through two points on a circle with their vertices on the circle are either equal or are supplementary angles. You can test this conjecture by drawing and measuring more examples. **2.** When you test a conjecture, you might not test the case that turns out to be an exception. Once you prove a conjecture using logic, postulates, definitions, given information, or proven theorems as justification, it is not possible to find a counterexample.

Page 676 Exercises and Problems

1, 4. Answers should show that conjectures have been tested for various examples. **1. a–c.** The perpendicular bisectors of two chords on the same circle intersect at the center of the circle. **4. a–c.** The products $AX \cdot BX$ and $CX \cdot DX$ are equal.

Additional Answers

Unit 1

Page 8 Exercises and Problems
22. $\frac{1}{6}$ **23.** $\frac{1}{2}$ **24.** $\frac{1}{3}$ **25.** 0
26. Answers may vary. Sample questions are given. Answer "Yes" or "No." (1) I would be willing to recycle if I had to deliver materials to a recycling center. (2) I would be willing to recycle if materials were collected. (3) I would be willing to pay more for items packaged in recycled paper. (4) I would be willing to purchase reusable cloth shopping bags instead of using disposable paper bags. (5) I reuse materials whenever possible.

Page 21 Exercises and Problems
17. a. The ordered pairs are given for the extensions shown. (76, 79), (5, 17), (97, 50), (53, 24), (14, 66), (7, 23), (31, 39), (22, 25), (11, 21), (19, 3), (94, 93), (2, 51), (84, 58), (44, 72), (78, 70), (15, 23), (82, 62), (22, 74), (89, 70), (19, 63)
b. The graph shown is for the phone extensions given in the exercise.

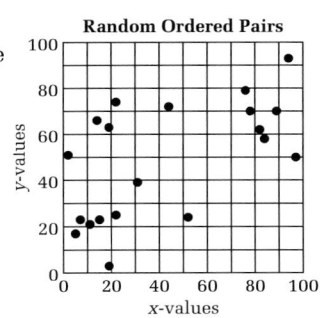

c. a positive correlation; A graphing calculator computes a correlation coefficient of 0.586. It is reasonable to expect that there would be no correlation since the phone numbers were chosen at random.
d. Descriptions may vary. An example is given. It would be reasonable to expect the graph to show no correlation, with the points widely scattered.

Page 35 Exercises and Problems
5. a–e. Answers may vary. Examples are given. **a.** Marvin might conjecture that driving a red car increases your chances of getting a speeding ticket. **b.** No; they issue many tickets to all different types of cars. **c.** He could observe a stretch of highway for a given period of time and record how many tickets are issued in general and how many to red cars. **d.** He may have been driving more, enjoying his new car. He may also have been showing off his new car, or feeling a sense of adventure that made him behave less responsibly. **e.** Some people might associate red cars with sportiness and speed. Others might see no connection. **6.** Each number in the pattern is three times the previous number. The next number is 324.
7. Beginning with the third number, each number in the pattern is the sum of the two previous numbers. The next number is 21. **8.** The sum of the first n odd numbers is n^2. The next row is $1 + 3 + 5 + 7 = 4^2$.
9. Beginning with the second row, the digits of the square of an n-digit number with all of its digits 1 are the counting numbers in increasing order up to n, then in decreasing order back down to 1. The next row is $1111 \cdot 1111 = 1234321$. **10. a.** The student should have tested quadrilaterals with no special properties, that is, quadri-

laterals that are not parallelograms or isosceles trapezoids.
b. Answers may vary. For example, when using inductive reasoning, test the most general cases so that you do not introduce special properties that influence the results.

Pages 37 Exercises and Problems
24. a. 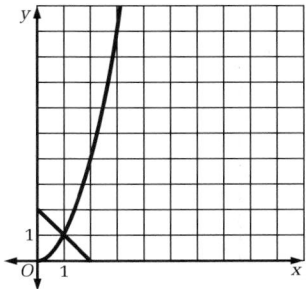 **b.** The graph of $y = -x + 2$ is a line; the graph of $y = x^2$ is a parabola.
c. Yes; at $(-2, 4)$ and $(1, 1)$.
d. Only the first-quadrant portion of the graph can be seen.

e. They might conjecture that the graphs intersect at only one point, $(1, 1)$.

Page 41 Exercises and Problems
10. Answers may vary. Examples are given. (4) If a student watches TV, then the student works at a job. False. (5) If a student does volunteer work, then the student watches TV. True. (6) Every student who watches TV watches movies. False. (7) Some students who do volunteer work watch movies. True. (8) Some students who work at a job do volunteer work. False. (9) All students who do not do volunteer work do not watch TV. False. **11.** Answers may vary. All students who work at a job watch TV. Some students who work at a job watch movies. No students who work at a job do volunteer work.

12.
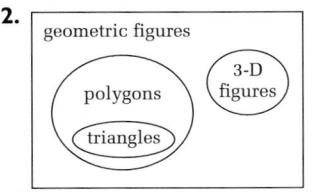

Page 42 Exercises and Problems
13. a.
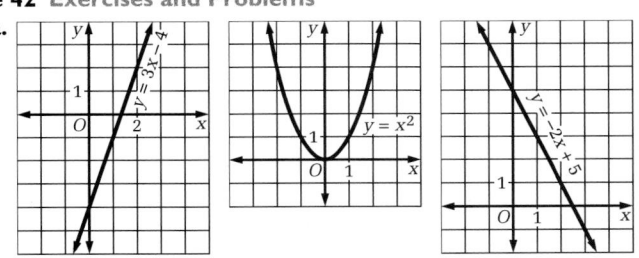

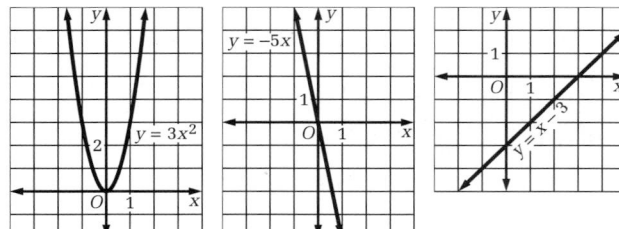

b, c. Answers may vary. Examples are given.

b. There are two main types of equations, equations of lines and equations of parabolas. Some of the equations of lines have a positive slope, some have a negative slope.

c. If a line has a positive slope, it does not have a negative slope. If a graph is a line with a positive slope, then it is not a parabola.

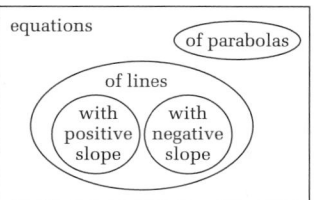

Page 49 Exercises and Problems

18. Answers may vary. Examples are given. Where did you get your statistics? Why does the graph include only lung cancer deaths? What would the graph on the left look like for the years 1960–1985?

19. When the computer got to I = 3, it tried to let X = $\frac{3}{3-3}$ = $\frac{3}{0}$, which is invalid.

Unit 2

Page 66 Exercises and Problems
28. True. **29.** False.

30. a.

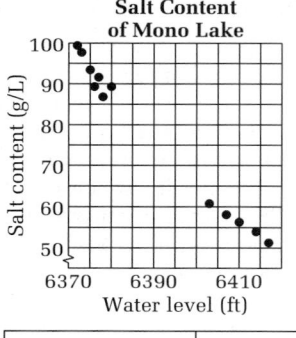

b. The graph is nonlinear and decreasing except over the intervals 6376–6377 and 6378–6380, where it is increasing.

31. a.

Water level (ft)	Percent of salt by weight
6417	5.13
6414	5.40
6410	5.63
6407	5.81
6403	6.02
6380	8.93
6378	8.68
6377	9.16
6376	8.93
6375	9.34
6373	9.77
6372	9.94

b.

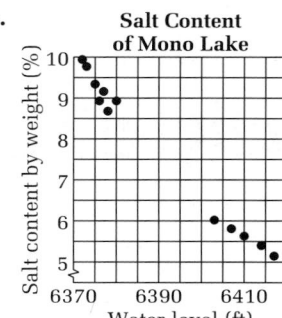

c. The graph is identical to the one in Ex. 30 (a) except for the labels on the vertical axis.

Page 72 Exercises and Problems
20. a. slope = 2; vertical intercept = –3 **b.**
c. increasing

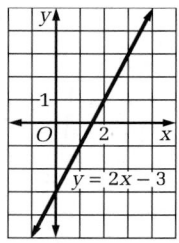

21. a. slope = 7; vertical intercept = 0 **b.**
c. increasing

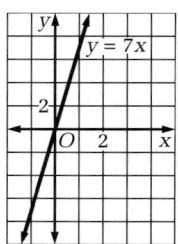

22. a. slope = –5; vertical intercept = –4 **b.**
c. decreasing

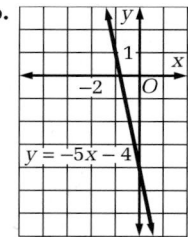

23. a. slope = 1; vertical intercept = 3.7 **b.**
c. increasing

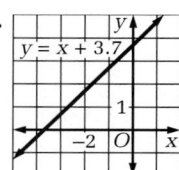

24. a. slope = 0; vertical intercept = –4.2 **b.**
c. constant

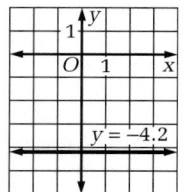

25. a. slope = $-\frac{3}{5}$; vertical intercept = 2 **b.**
c. decreasing

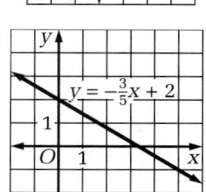

Page 75 Exploration

2.

width	length
4	9
9	4
6	6
3	12
12	3
2	18
18	2
1	36
36	1

3.

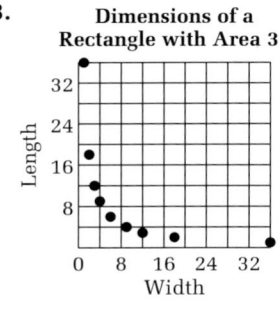

Dimensions of a
Rectangle with Area 36

Page 91 Exploration

2.

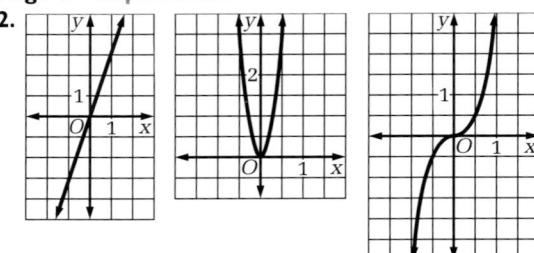

3. a. linear; nonlinear; nonlinear **b.** growth graph; none; growth graph
c. Yes; Yes; Yes. **d.** Yes; Yes; Yes.

Page 103 Exercises and Problems

31. Answers may vary. An example is given. Pendulum-based clocks
are not very portable. A spring-based wristwatch is more feasible than
one run by a pendulum and a quartz crystal makes for more accurate
time-keeping. **32.** about 23 mi/h

33. a.

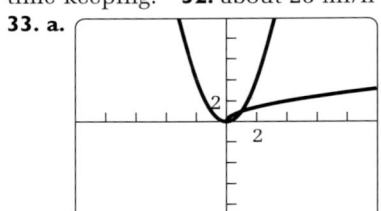
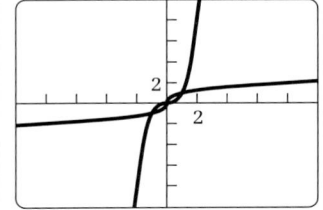

b. Answers may vary. An example is given. All four graphs are
curves; all four pass through the origin. The graphs of $y = x^2$ and
$y = x^{1/2}$ are alike in that neither graph has points below the horizontal
axis. The graph of $y = x^2$ is entirely within quadrants I and II (whether
x is positive, negative, or zero, y is positive), while the graph of
$y = x^{1/2}$ is entirely within quadrant I (x and y are both always nonnegative). On the graphs of $y = x^3$, you can see that as x increases (or
decreases), y increases (or decreases) rapidly, while on the graph of
$y = x^{1/3}$, y increases (or decreases) slowly. **c.** Answers may vary. An
example is given. In the first quadrant, the graphs look very similar.
The graph of $y = x^{1/2}$ is limited to quadrant I, while the graph of
$y = x^{1/3}$ appears in quadrant III as well. **d.** Yes; if $0 < x < 1$, $x^{1/2} > x^2$.
e. Yes; if $x < -1$ or $0 < x < 1$, $x^{1/3} > x^3$.

Page 105 Exploration

3. Answers may vary. An example is given. n tears would result in 2^n
pieces. Ten tears (which is not physically possible) would result in
1024 pieces. **4.** Answers may vary. An example is given. The height
of the final stack in the example was about $\frac{3}{16}$ in. or 0.1875 in. If it
had been possible to make four more tears, the stack would have been
about 3 in. high.

Page 111 Exercises and Problems

19. a. Let x be the number of 18-year doubling periods and y be the
population; $y = 329{,}000(2^x)$. **b.** 2070 **c.** Answers may vary. An
example is given. No; it is not likely that the country's resources
could indefinitely support a population that doubles every eighteen
years.

Unit 3

Page 126 Exercises and Problems

5. $(-3.75, -3.75)$

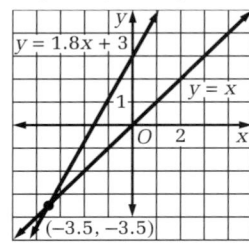

6. $(0.2, -0.8)$

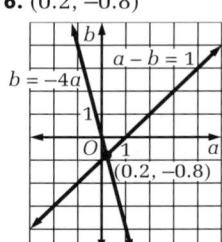

7. $(-5, 3)$

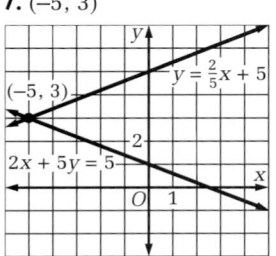

8. $(3.2, 2.6)$

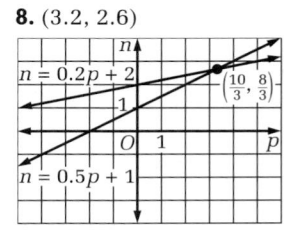

9. 31 times; If you ride the subway thirty or less than thirty times, the
cost of buying a bus pass and paying for single rides on the subway is
less expensive than the combo pass. At 31 rides/month, the combo
pass is less expensive. The point of intersection is about
$(30.6, 46)$. **10. a.** $c = 46$; $c = 27 + 0.6r$

b.

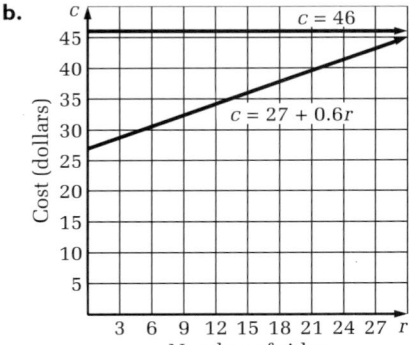

Cost (dollars)

Number of rides

c. No. For twenty rides at $.60
each ($12) plus a subway pass
($27), she will pay $39,
whereas a combo pass is $46.
The graph supports this since
the graph of subway pass/bus
rides is below the combo pass
graph.

Page 127 Exercises and Problems

13. d. FitnessPLUS is cheapest for three months. At seven months, all
plans have the same cost. The graph supports these answers since the
line for FitnessPLUS cost is below the other two lines at three
months. All three graphs intersect at $(7, 470)$, so all three plans cost
$470 for seven months.

14. a. $(0, 4)$ **b.** No; $y = x^2 + 4$ is not a linear
equation.

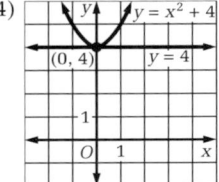

15.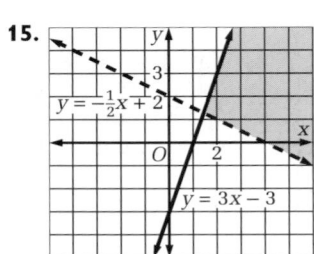

$y = -\frac{1}{2}x + 2$

$y = 3x - 3$

16.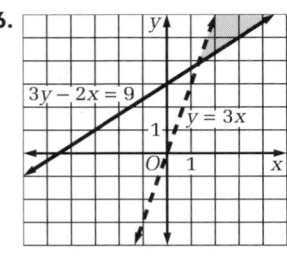

$3y - 2x = 9$

$y = 3x$

17.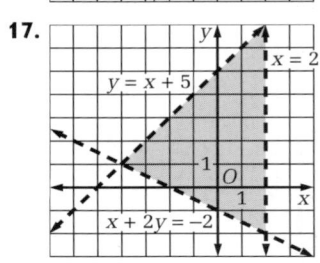

$x = 2$

$y = x + 5$

$x + 2y = -2$

18.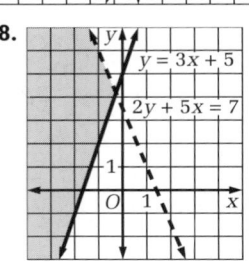

$y = 3x + 5$

$2y + 5x = 7$

19. a. $x = 3$, $y = -2$, $x = -4$, $y = \frac{2}{7}x + \frac{15}{7}$ **b.** $x \le 3$, $y \ge -2$, $x \ge -4$, $y \le \frac{2}{7}x + \frac{15}{7}$ **c.** Choices may vary. An example is given. $(0, 0)$; $0 \le 3$ ✓, $0 \ge -2$ ✓, $0 \ge -4$ ✓, $0 \le 2$ ✓

20. triangle   **21.** trapezoid   **22.** square

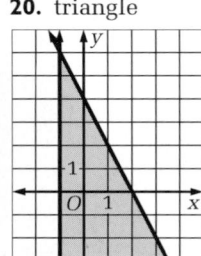   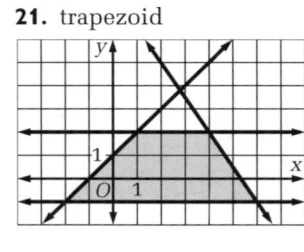   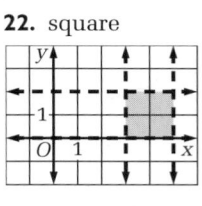

23. rectangle

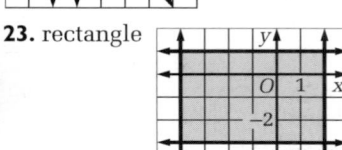

Page 132 Exercises and Problems

1. a.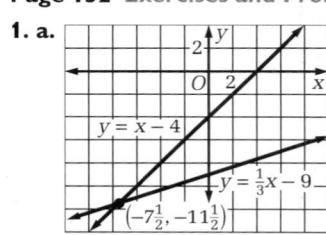

$y = x - 4$

$y = \frac{1}{3}x - 9$

$\left(-7\frac{1}{2}, -11\frac{1}{2}\right)$

b. $\left(-7\frac{1}{2}, -11\frac{1}{2}\right)$

Page 135 Exploration

3. a. Answers may vary. An example is given. $y = -x$.

b.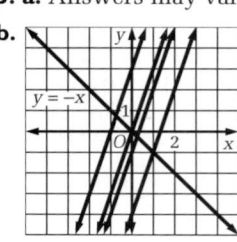

$y = -x$

Yes; the graph of $y = -x$ does intersect all of the other lines.

4. a. Yes. **b.** Yes. **c.** No.

5.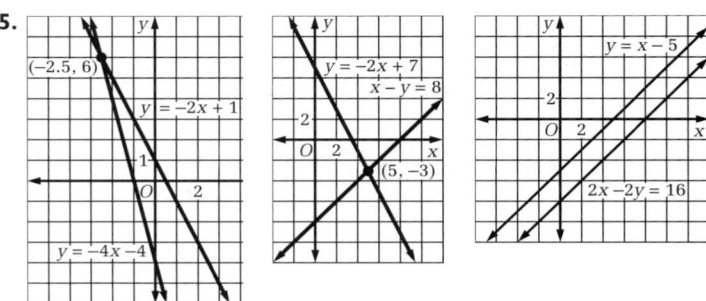

$(-2.5, 6)$

$y = -2x + 1$

$y = -4x - 4$

$y = -2x + 7$

$x - y = 8$

$(5, -3)$

$y = x - 5$

$2x - 2y = 16$

Page 139 Exercises and Problems

7. a. slopes: $\overline{AB} = -\frac{1}{8}$; $\overline{BC} = 3$; $\overline{CD} = -\frac{1}{8}$; $\overline{AD} = 3$ **b.** It is a parallelogram because opposite sides are parallel. It is not a rectangle because the slopes are not negative reciprocals of each other, and it is not a rhombus because the sides are not all the same length.

8. a.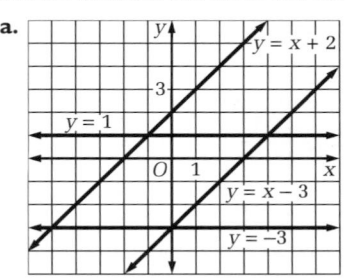

$y = x + 2$

$y = 1$

$y = x - 3$

$y = -3$

b. It is a parallelogram because opposite sides are parallel since the slopes are the same.
c. area $= bh = 5 \cdot 4 = 20$ square units

Page 157 Exercises and Problems

19. a.

	rock/pop	jazz	classical	other
CDs	2082	143	327	423
tapes	865	64	149	167

b. No; he only increased three categories by 7%: rock/pop CDs, other CDs, and classical tapes.

c.

	rock/pop	jazz	classical	other
CDs	5832	413	979	1204
tapes	2547	188	395	489

Page 181 Unit 3 Review and Assessment

11. a. $\begin{bmatrix} 2.40 & 3.00 & 4.00 \\ 7.00 & 8.00 & 10.00 \\ 8.00 & 8.00 & 10.00 \end{bmatrix}$; $\begin{bmatrix} 9.60 & 12.00 & 16.00 \\ 28.00 & 32.00 & 40.00 \\ 32.00 & 32.00 & 40.00 \end{bmatrix}$

b. $\begin{bmatrix} 9.60 & 12.00 & 16.00 \\ 28.00 & 32.00 & 40.00 \\ 32.00 & 32.00 & 40.00 \end{bmatrix}$ ✓ They are the same.

Unit 4

Page 191 Exercises and Problems

24–27. Estimates may vary. Exact values are given. **24.** 3 and -1; $-\frac{1}{3}(3^2) + \frac{2}{3}(3) + 1 = 0$; $-\frac{1}{3}((-1)^2) + \frac{2}{3}(-1) + 1 = 0$

25. 0 and 4; $\frac{1}{2}(0^2) - 2(0) = 0$; $\frac{1}{2}(4^2) - 2(4) = 0$ **26.** -5 and -1; $-(-5)^2 - 6(-5) - 5 = 0$; $-(-1)^2 - 6(-1) - 5 = 0$ **27.** -4 and 5; $0.2(-4)^2 - 0.2(-4) - 4 = 0$; $0.2(5)^2 - 0.2(5) - 4 = 0$ **28. a–c.** Answers may vary. Examples are given. **a.** a y-intercept of 10 and the same line of symmetry, $x = 100$ **b.** a y-intercept of 10 and the same line of symmetry, $x = -100$ **c.** the y-intercept, $(0, 10)$

Page 193 Exploration

2. The innermost parabola is the graph of $y = x^2$; the outermost parabola is the graph of $y = \frac{1}{10}x^2$.

Descriptions may vary. An example is given. For coefficients of x^2 between 0 and 1, the parabola becomes more shallow and wider.

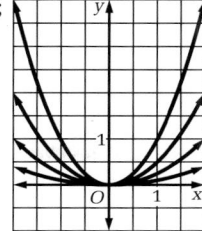

4. The parabola with the highest vertex is the graph of $y = 5x^2 + 3$. The parabola with the lowest vertex is the graph of $y = 5x^2 - 3$. When you add 3 to $5x^2$, the graph of $y = 5x^2$ translates up 3 units. When you subtract 3 from $5x^2$, the graph of $y = 5x^2$ translates down 3 units.

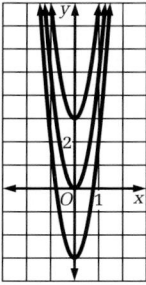

5. Answers may vary. An example is given. The graph of $y = 5x^2 - 7$ is the graph of $y = 5x^2$ translated down 7 units.

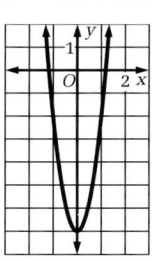

6. a. The graph of $y = 2x^2$ is translated 2 units to the left.

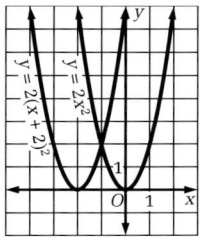

b. The graph of $y = 2x^2$ is translated 3 units to the right.

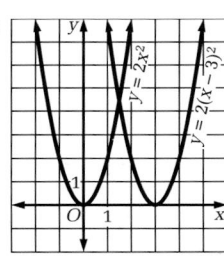

c. The graph of $y = 2x^2$ is translated 6 units to the right.

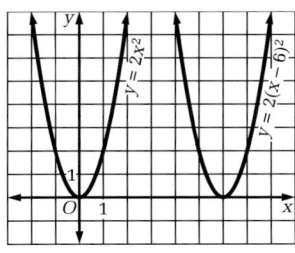

7. Answers may vary. An example is given. Each equation is in the form $y = 2(x + k)^2$. The graph of each equation is the graph of $y = 2x^2$ translated to the right or left. If k is positive, the graph is translated k units to the left. If k is negative, the graph is translated k units to the right.

8. Answers may vary. An example is given. The graph of $y = (x - 7)^2 + 4$ is the graph of $y = x^2$ translated 7 units to the right and 4 units up.

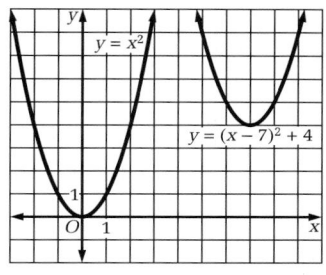

9. Answers may vary. An example is given. The graph of $y = 2(x + 3)^2 - 1$ is the graph of $y = x^2$ made narrower by a factor of 2, then the graph of $y = 2x^2$ is translated 3 units to the left and 1 unit down.

Page 197 Exercises and Problems

10. Answers may vary. An example is given.

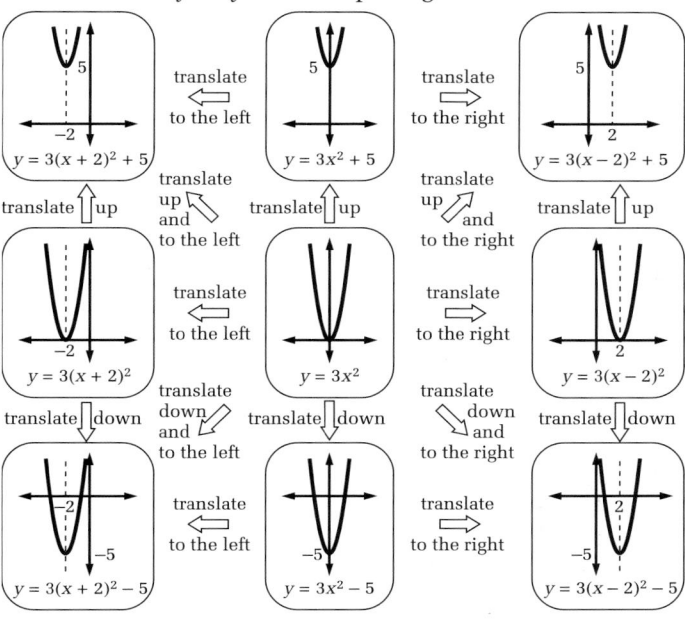

13. (−6, 0); 36 **14.** (−3, −4); 5 **15.** (5, 2); 27 **16.** (−4, −18); 14
17. (1, 11); 16 **18.** (2, 9); −7 **19. a.**
b. all real numbers $x > 0$

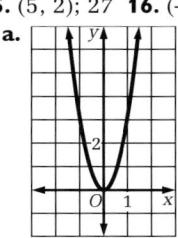

Page 205 Exercises and Problems

39. Answers may vary. Examples and explanations are given, based upon the results given for Ex. 29 in Section 4-2.

39. a. $\sqrt{800}$, or about 28.3 ft/s; found by using the equation $y = \frac{-16}{v^2(\cos A)^2}x^2 + (\tan A)x$, where $A = 45°$, $x = 25$ ft, and $y = 0$ ft

b. $y = \frac{-1}{25}x^2 + x$; by simplifying $y = \frac{-16}{(\sqrt{800})^2(\cos 45°)^2}x^2 + (\tan 45°)x$

c. 6.25 ft; by substituting the x-coordinate of the vertex into $y = \frac{-1}{25}x^2 + x$ to find the y-coordinate; $x = \frac{-b}{2a} = \frac{-1}{2\left(\frac{-1}{25}\right)} = 12.5$;

$y = \frac{-1}{25}(12.5)^2 + 12.5 = 6.25$

Page 210 Exercises and Problems

3. c.

Possible factors	Middle term
$(6m + 1)(m - 4)$	$-23m$
$(6m - 4)(m + 1)$	$2m$
$(6m - 1)(m + 4)$	$23m$
$(6m + 4)(m - 1)$	$-2m$
$(6m + 2)(m - 2)$	$-10m$
$(6m - 2)(m + 2)$	$10m$
$(3m + 1)(2m - 4)$	$-10m$
$(3m - 4)(2m + 1)$	$\mathbf{-5m}$
$(3m - 1)(2m + 4)$	$10m$
$(3m + 4)(2m - 1)$	$5m$
$(3m + 2)(2m - 2)$	$-2m$
$(3m - 2)(2m + 2)$	$2m$

The correct middle term is $-5m$.

Page 234 Exercises and Problems

15. $(0, 0)$, $(12.5, 106.3)$ **16.** $(-0.6, -3.1)$, $(0.8, 2.8)$

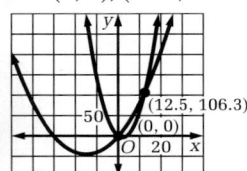 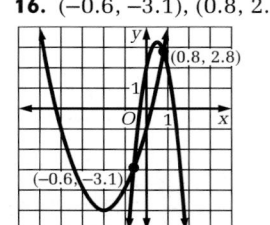

17. $\left(\sqrt{\dfrac{d - b}{a - c}}, \dfrac{ad - bc}{a - c}\right)$, $\left(-\sqrt{\dfrac{d - b}{a - c}}, \dfrac{ad - bc}{a - c}\right)$; $a \neq c$

18. $(0, 0)$, $\left(\dfrac{d - b}{a - c}, \dfrac{(d - b)(ad - bc)}{(a - c)^2}\right)$; $a \neq c$ **19. a.** $(24.5, 9.5)$, $(55.5, -21.5)$

b. $(55.5, -21.5)$ **c.** $(20.0, 10.0)$ **20.** The path would not be as high or as far. The new high point is lowered to 8.9 ft; $(43.5, -9.5)$. **21.** Answers may vary. An example is given. I would prefer the one with less friction because you slide higher and farther.

Unit 5

Page 247 Exercises and Problems

14.

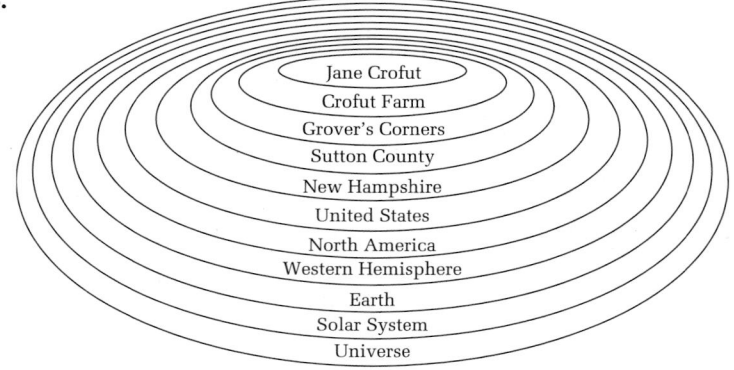

Page 258 Exercises and Problems
39. a. Results may vary. **b.** Answers may vary. The list should include a pair of dice. It may also include graph paper for displaying the target point and points rolled by the players. To calculate distances, players may need paper and pencil or a calculator. If a player's point has the same x-coordinate as the target point, the distance between the points can be found by subtracting the absolute values of the two y-coordinates. If a player's point has the same y-coordinate as the target point, the distance between the points can be found by subtracting the absolute values of the two x-coordinates. Otherwise, a

player uses the distance formula to determine how far his or her point is from the target point. **c.** Answers may vary. An example is given. Using two different-colored dice would be helpful. The directions should also indicate what happens in the case of a tie. For example, if any players' points are the same distance from the target point, those players should roll again as many times as necessary to determine a winner. **d.** Answers may vary. An example is given. Suggestions form part (c) should be incorporated.

Pages 266 and 267 Exploration
1, 3–5. See table below. **2.** *Flip horizontal* is a reflection over the x-axis; *flip vertical* is a reflection over the y-axis. **3.** See table below. x-axis reflection: The x-coordinates are the same and each y-coordinate of $A'B'C'D'$ is the opposite of the corresponding y-coordinate of $ABCD$. y-axis reflection: Each x-coordinate of $A'B'C'D'$ is the opposite of the corresponding x-coordinate of $ABCD$ and y-coordinates are the same. **4.** Image 2; Image 3; Image 1; See table below. 180° rotation: Each x-coordinate of $A'B'C'D'$ is the opposite of the corresponding x-coordinate of $ABCD$ and each y-coordinate of $A'B'C'D'$ is the opposite of the corresponding y-coordinate of $ABCD$. 270° counterclockwise rotation: Each x-coordinate of $A'B'C'D'$ is the same as the y-coordinate of the corresponding point on $ABCD$ and each y-coordinate of $A'B'C'D'$ is the opposite of the x-coordinate of the corresponding point on $ABCD$. 90° counterclockwise rotation: Each x-coordinate of $A'B'C'D'$ is the opposite of the y-coordinate of the corresponding point on $ABCD$ and each y-coordinate of $A'B'C'D'$ is the same as the x-coordinate of the corresponding point on $ABCD$. **5.** See table below. horizontal translation: Each x-coordinate of $A'B'C'D'$ is six less than the corresponding x-coordinate of $ABCD$ and the corresponding y-coordinates are the same. vertical translation: The corresponding x-coordinates are the same and each y-coordinate of $A'B'C'D'$ is six less than the corresponding y-coordinate of $ABCD$. combined horizontal and vertical translation: Each x-coordinate of $A'B'C'D'$ is six less than the corresponding x-coordinate of $ABCD$ and each y-coordinate of $A'B'C'D'$ is six less than the corresponding y-coordinate of $ABCD$.

1, 3–5.

Transformations	Coordinates of Points			
original	$A(0, 6)$	$B(2, 4)$	$C(4, 4)$	$D(2, 2)$
x-axis reflection	$A'(0, -6)$	$B'(2, -4)$	$C'(4, -4)$	$D'(2, -2)$
y-axis reflection	$A'(0, 6)$	$B'(-2, 4)$	$C'(-4, 4)$	$D'(-2, 2)$
180° rotation	$A'(0, -6)$	$B'(-2, -4)$	$C'(-4, -4)$	$D'(-2, -2)$
270° counterclockwise	$A'(6, 0)$	$B'(4, -2)$	$C'(4, -4)$	$D'(2, -2)$
90° counterclockwise	$A'(-6, 0)$	$B'(-4, 2)$	$C'(-4, 4)$	$D'(-2, 2)$
horizontal translation	$A'(-6, 6)$	$B'(-4., 4)$	$C'(-2, 4)$	$D'(-4, 2)$
vertical translation	$A'(0, 0)$	$B'(2, -2)$	$C'(4, -2)$	$D'(2, -4)$
horz/vert translation	$A'(-6, 0)$	$B'(-4, -2)$	$C'(-2, -2)$	$D'(-4, -4)$

6. x-axis reflection: $(x, y) \to (x, -y)$; y-axis reflection: $(x, y) \to (-x, y)$; 180° rotation: $(x, y) \to (-x, -y)$; 270° counterclockwise rotation: $(x, y) \to (y, -x)$; 90° counterclockwise rotation: $(x, y) \to (-y, x)$; horizontal translation a units left: $(x, y) \to (x - a, y)$; vertical translation a units down: $(x, y) \to (x, y - a)$; combined horizontal and vertical translation a units left and a units down: $(x, y) \to (x - a, y - a)$

Page 271 Exercises and Problems
11. dilation with a scale factor 3

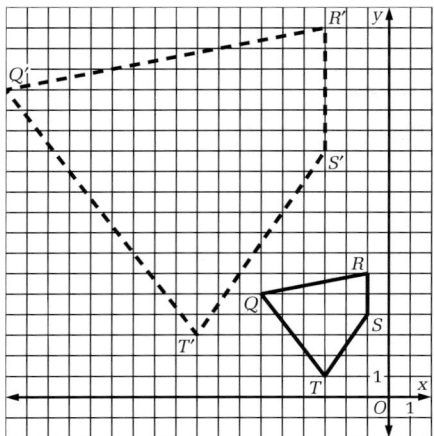

12. reflection over the x-axis

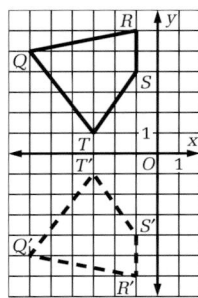

Page 272 Exercises and Problems
23.

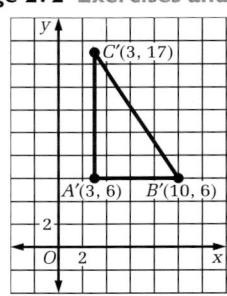

24.

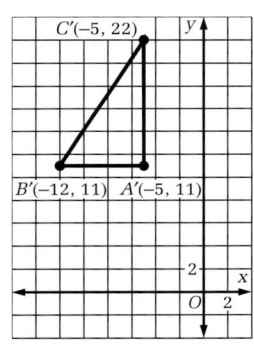

25.

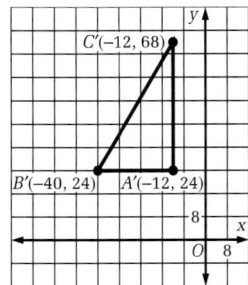

26.

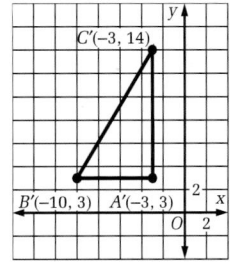

27.

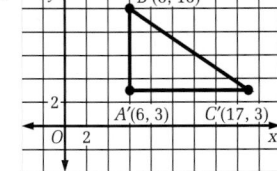

28. a. $\sqrt{170}$ **b.** $\sqrt{170}$; $\sqrt{170}$; $4\sqrt{170}$; $\sqrt{170}$; $\sqrt{170}$ **c.** reflection, rotation, and translation (Exs. 23, 24, 26, and 27); dilation (Ex. 25)
d. Yes; reflections, rotations, and transformations create images that are congruent to the original image. Dilations create images that are similar to the original image, so any corresponding sides of an original image and a dilated image will be in proportion and not necessarily equal in measure. **29. a.** $\dfrac{11}{7}$ **b.** $-\dfrac{11}{7}$; $\dfrac{11}{7}$; $\dfrac{11}{7}$; $\dfrac{11}{7}$; $-\dfrac{7}{11}$ **c.** translation

and dilation (Exs. 24–26); reflection (Ex. 23) and rotation (Ex. 27)
d. Yes; translations, dilations preserve the orientation of the original image; reflections and most rotations do not preserve the orientation of the original image. All rotations of $180n$, where n is an integer, will produce images, any of whose sides will have slope equal to the slope of the corresponding side in the original image.

Page 273 Exercises and Problems
43. a–c. Have a player roll a die twice and designate the first and second rolls as x and y. Use the patterns found in the table in the Exploration to base the moves on the given coordinates. **44.** Draw a square board. Draw the diagonals. Draw a pattern on one of the triangles produced and reflect it repeatedly over the four segments produced.

Page 277 Exercises and Problems
4.

Tahiti Time				
USA Time Zone	Pacific	Mountain	Central	Eastern
	+ 2	+ 3	+ 4	+ 5

Page 278 Exercises and Problems
22. a. They are equal. **b.** slope of $\overline{OE} = \dfrac{0-0}{a-0} = \dfrac{c-e}{b-d}$ = slope of $\overline{GF}$
$$\frac{0}{a} = \frac{c-e}{b-d}$$
$$0 = c - e$$
$$e = c$$
c. slope of $\overline{OG} = \dfrac{c}{b} = \dfrac{e}{d-a}$ = slope of $\overline{EF}$
$$\frac{c}{b} = \frac{e}{d-a}$$
$$c(d-a) = be$$
$$cd - ca = be$$
$$cd = be + ca$$
Since $e = c$, $cd = bc + ca = c(b+a)$.
So, $d = b + a$.
d. three

Page 279 Exercises and Problems
26.

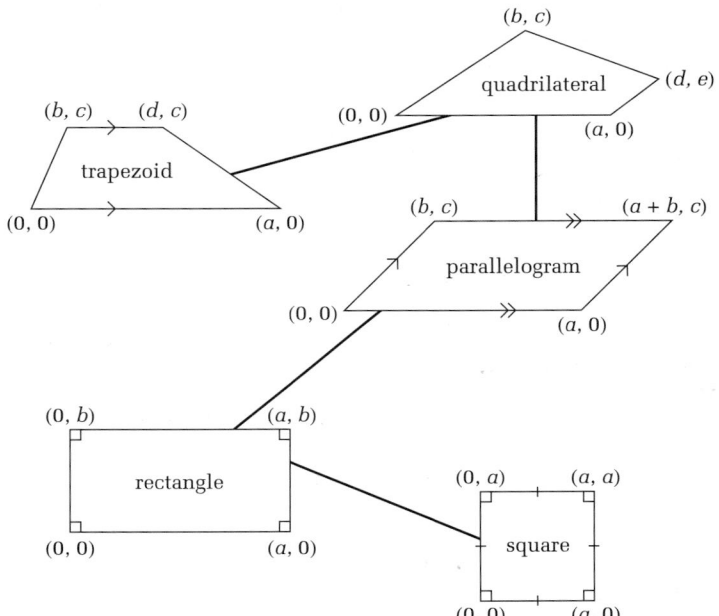

A-7

Answers may vary. Examples are given. Points on lines parallel to the x-axis have the same y-coordinate; points on lines parallel to the y-axis have the same x-coordinate; the more parallel and congruent sides a quadrilateral has, the fewer variables are necessary to name the coordinates of its vertices.

Page 285 Exercises and Problems
13. $OL = \sqrt{(a+b)^2 + (c-0)^2} = \sqrt{(a+b)^2 + c^2}$;
$MK = \sqrt{(a-b)^2 + (0-c)^2} = \sqrt{(a-b)^2 + c^2}$; since $OL = MK$,
$\sqrt{(a+b)^2 + c^2} = \sqrt{(a-b)^2 + c^2}$; by squaring both sides, $(a+b)^2 + c^2 = (a-b)^2 + c^2$; then $a^2 + 2ab + b^2 + c^2 = a^2 - 2ab + b^2 + c^2$; $2ab = -2ab$; $4ab = 0$; $a = 0$ or $b = 0$. Since $a \neq 0$, $b = 0$. Then the coordinates of the parallelogram can be written $(0, 0)$, $(a, 0)$, (a, c), and $(0, c)$ and $OKLM$ is a rectangle.

Page 286 Exercises and Problems
16. a, b. Drawings and conjectures may vary. An example is given.

a. 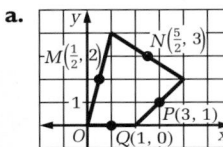 **b.** 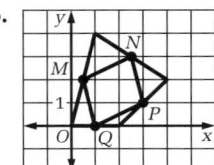 $MNPQ$ is a parallelogram.

c. $MN = \sqrt{(b+d-b)^2 + (c+e-c)^2} = \sqrt{d^2 + e^2}$;
$QP = \sqrt{(a+d-a)^2 + (e-0)^2} = \sqrt{d^2 + e^2}$; $MQ = \sqrt{(b-a)^2 + (c-0)^2} = \sqrt{(b-a)^2 + c^2}$; $NP = \sqrt{(b+d-a-d)^2 + (c+e-e)^2} = \sqrt{(b-a)^2 + c^2}$;
slope of $\overline{MN} = \frac{c+e-c}{b+d-b} = \frac{e}{d}$; slope of $\overline{QP} = \frac{e-0}{a+d-a} = \frac{e}{d}$;
slope of $\overline{MQ} = \frac{c-0}{b-a} = \frac{c}{b-a}$; slope of $\overline{NP} = \frac{c+e-e}{b+d-a-d} = \frac{c}{b-a}$; $MN = QP$ and $MQ = NP$; slope of $\overline{MN}$ = slope of $\overline{QP}$ so $\overline{MN} \parallel \overline{QP}$; slope of $\overline{MQ}$ = slope of $\overline{NP}$ so $\overline{MQ} \parallel \overline{NP}$; $MNPQ$ is a parallelogram.

Unit 6

Page 299 Exercises and Problems
6. Answers may vary. An example is given. One day in the school cafeteria, the main dish choices are chicken teriyaki and beef stroganoff. Students must also choose one side dish from each of the following groups: rice or potato; fruit, salad, or vegetable. How many different complete meals are there? **7.** 8 ways (Let "H" indicate heads, and "T" tails, and the three letters indicate the position of the nickel, dime, and quarter in order from left to right. The possible outcomes are HHH, HHT, HTH, HTT, THH, THT, TTH, TTT.) **8.** 11 different sums (2, 3, 4, 5, 6, 7, 8, 9, 10, 11, and 12) **9.** There are 36 possible results. **10.** Answers may vary. An example is given. Both exercises involve rolling a pair of dice and counting the number of dots on each top face. In Ex. 8, it is the sum of the dots on the top faces that is considered, so there are only 11 different results. In Ex. 9, the number of dots on one face indicates one set of choices, the number on the other indicates another set of choices, so there are 36 possible results. The order in which the dots on the top faces are considered makes a difference in Ex. 9 but not in Ex. 8.

Page 336 Exercises and Problems
2. a.
```
            1
          1   1
        1   2   1
      1   3   3   1
    1   4   6   4   1
  1   5  10  10   5   1
 1   6  15  20  15   6   1
1   7  21  35  35  21   7   1
1  8  28  56  70  56  28   8   1
1  9  36  84 126 126  84  36   9   1
```
b. In row 2, only 2 is surrounded by 6 numbers. Their product is 9. In rows 3–8, an example is given. Row 3 (using 3), the product is 144; Row 4 (using 4), the product is 900; Row 5 (using 5), the product is 3600; Row 6 (using 20), the product is 27,562,500; Row 7 (using 21), the product is 34,574,400; Row 8

(using 28), the product is 199,148,544. **c.** Each product is a perfect square.

Page 337 Exercises and Problems
23. Answers may vary. An example is given. Choose row 7. There are seven senior players on a team. Two captains are to be chosen from among the seniors. How many ways can the captains be chosen? The answer is the number in row 7, diagonal 2: $_7C_2 = 21$.
24. $_{120}C_2 = \frac{120!}{2!118!} = \frac{120 \cdot 119}{2!} = 7140$
25. slope: 4; vertical intercept: 0; increasing
26. slope: −2; vertical intercept: 3; decreasing

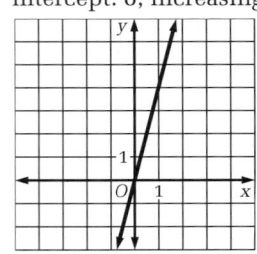 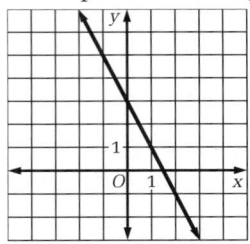

27. slope: 0; vertical intercept: −3; constant
28.

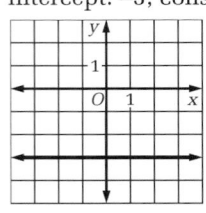 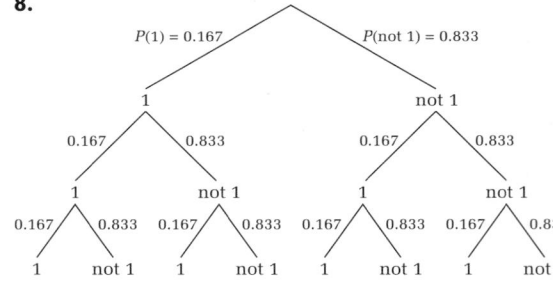

29. Extend the triangle to include 24 rows. The answer to Ex. 31 is the number in row 10, diagonal 2 (45). The answer to Ex. 32 is the number in row 23, diagonal 2 (253).

Page 346 and 347 Talk it Over
4. There is only one outcome for "no left-handed students" and $P(RRR) = 0.729$. Then P(at least one left-handed student) = $1 - 0.729 = 0.271$. This method involves less computation and therefore less room for error than the other method. **5.** 0.028 **6.** about 0.167 **7.** about 0.833
8.

9. No; there are eight possible outcomes with varying probabilities. For example, $P(111) \approx 0.005$ and P(no 1's) ≈ 0.578.

Page 355 Exercises and Problems
22. a. The coefficients of each power of 10 in the expansion for 9^n, written as $(10 - 1)^n$, are taken from row n of Pascal's triangle, but the signs alternate so that the coefficient of 10^n is positive, while the coefficient of 10^{n-1} is negative. **b.** $10^6 + 6(10^5)(-1) + 15(10^4)(-1)^2 + 20(10^3)(-1)^3 + 15(10^2)(-1)^4 + 6(10)(-1)^5 + (-1)^6$

```
   1000000
  − 600000
  + 150000
  −  20000
  +   1500
  −     60
  +      1
```
$9^6 = 531441$

A-8

c. The number pattern is derived by expanding $(10 - 1)^n$. The expanded form of $(10 + 1)^n$ has terms that are the numbers of row n of Pascal's triangle times powers of ten. The signs alternate between + and − because alternating terms have odd and even powers of −1 as factors.

Unit 7

Page 370 Exercises and Problems

12. a.

	Acute	Right	Obtuse
Scalene	E	G	F
Isosceles	A, D	B	C
Equilateral	A	—	—

b. C **c.** A, D, C, B, F

Page 375 Look Back

Six equivalent implications are given. They are all true. If a figure is an equilateral triangle, then it is an isosceles triangle. All equilateral triangles are isosceles triangles. Every equilateral triangle is an isosceles triangle. The set of equilateral triangles is a subset of the set of isosceles triangles. The fact that a figure is an equilateral triangle implies that it is an isosceles triangle. A figure is an equilateral triangle only if it is an isosceles triangle.

Six versions of the converse are given They are all false. If a figure is an isosceles triangle, then it is an equilateral triangle. All isosceles triangles are equilateral triangles. Every isosceles triangle is an equilateral triangle. The set of isosceles triangles is a subset of the set of equilateral triangles. The fact that a figure is an isosceles triangle implies that it is an equilateral triangle. A figure is an isosceles triangle only if it is an equilateral triangle.

Page 375 Exercises and Problems

6. a. p: it is Saturday; q: it is a day of the weekend. **b.** Every Saturday is a day of the weekend. **c.**

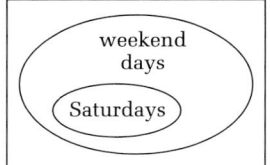

7. a. p: a figure is a cylinder; q: the formula for its volume is $V = Bh$.
b. A figure is a cylinder only if the formula for its volume is $V = Bh$.
c.

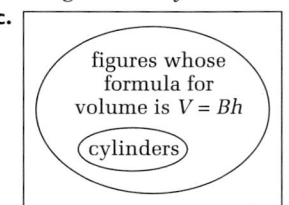

Page 396 Talk it Over
8. Statements
Rio de Janeiro $\overset{\text{❶}}{\rightarrow}$ New York City $\overset{\text{❷}}{\rightarrow}$ Tokyo
Justifications
❶ Flight 102
❷ Flight 103

Page 398 Exercises and Problems
13. a. 1, 7, 49, 343, 2401, 16807, 117649, 823543, 5764801, 40353607
b. The unit's digits in the numbers repeat in the order 1, 7, 9, 3, 1, 7, 9, 3, 1, 7, ... **13. c.** From parts (a) and (b), the unit's digits repeat in groups of 4, so when the exponent of 7 is divided by 4, if the remainder is 0, the unit's digit is 1. If the remainder is 1, the unit's digit is 7.

If the remainder is 2, the unit's digit is 9. If the remainder is 3, the unit's digits is 3. The unit's digit in all subsequent groups of four powers of 7 will be generated by multiplying $7 \cdot 1$, $7 \cdot 7$, $7 \cdot 9$, and $7 \cdot 3$. These products in turn will generate numbers whose unit's digits repeat in the order 7, 9, 3, 1. **d.** 1; When 100 is divided by 4, the number is 0, so the unit's digit of 7^{100} is 1.

Page 399 Exercises and Problems
17. Answers may vary. An example is given using each form of proof.

two-column proof:

Given: Cairo
Prove: Buenos Aires

Statements	Justifications
1. Cairo	1. Given
2. Bombay	2. Flight 104: Cairo → Bombay
3. Buenos Aires	3. Flight 101: Bombay → Buenos Aires

paragraph proof:

It is possible to fly from Cairo to Buenos Aires. From Cairo you can take Flight 104 to Bombay. From Bombay you can take Flight 101 to Buenos Aires.

flow proof:

Statements
Cairo $\overset{\text{❶}}{\rightarrow}$ Bombay $\overset{\text{❷}}{\rightarrow}$ Buenos Aires
Justfications
❶ Flight 104
❷ Flight 101

Page 405 Exercises and Problems
9 a. *Given:* $4x^2 + 6 = 330$
          $x > 0$
     Prove: $x = 9$

Statements	Justifications
1. $4x^2 + 6 = 330$	1. Given
2. $4x^2 = 324$	2. Subtraction property of equality
3. $x^2 = 81$	3. Division property of equality
4. $x = 9$ or $x = -9$	4. Definition of square root
5. $x > 0$	5. Given
6. $x = 9$	6. *Or* rule

b. Statements
$4x^2 + 6 = 330 \overset{\text{❶}}{\rightarrow} 4x^2 = 324 \overset{\text{❷}}{\rightarrow} x^2 = 81 \overset{\text{❸}}{\rightarrow} x = 9$ or $x = -9$, $x > 0 \overset{\text{❹}}{\rightarrow} x = 9$
Justifications
❶ Subtraction property of equality
❷ Division property of equality
❸ Definition of square root; Given
❹ *Or* rule

c. If $4x^2 + 6 = 330$, use the subtraction property of equality to subtract 6 from both sides: $4x^2 = 324$. Then use the division property of equality to divide both sides by 4: $x^2 = 81$. Then use the definition of square root: $x = 9$ or $x = -9$. Since $x > 0$, $x = 9$.

Page 406 Exercises and Problems
19. Answers may vary. An example is given using both forms.

Given: $5(2 + n) = 3(n + 6)$
Prove: $n = 4$

Statements
$5(2 + n) = 3(n + 6) \overset{\text{❶}}{\rightarrow} 10 + 5n = 3n + 18 \overset{\text{❷}}{\rightarrow} 10 + 2n = 18 \overset{\text{❸}}{\rightarrow} 2n = 8 \overset{\text{❹}}{\rightarrow}$
$n = 4$

Justifications

❶ Distributive property
❷ Subtraction property of equality
❸ Subtraction property of equality
❹ Division property of equality

Statements	Justifications
1. $5(2 + n) = 3(n + 6)$	1. Given
2. $10 + 5n = 3n + 18$	2. Distributive property
3. $10 + 2n = 18$	3. Subtraction property of equality
4. $2n = 8$	4. Subtraction property of equality
5. $n = 4$	5. Division property of equality

Page 407 Checkpoint

7. *Given:* $7x - 3 = 25$
  Prove: $x = 4$

Statements	Justifications
1. $7x - 3 = 25$	1. Given
2. $7x = 28$	2. Addition property of equality
3. $x = 4$	3. Division property of equality

Page 413 Exercises and Problems

10. *Given:* $\overrightarrow{PA}$ and $\overrightarrow{PC}$ form a straight angle.
   $m \angle 1 = 100°$

   Prove: $m \angle 2 = 80°$

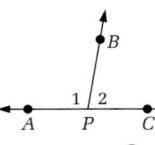

Statements

$\overrightarrow{PA}$ and $\overrightarrow{PC}$ form a straight angle. ❶→ $m \angle APC = 180°$ ❷→

$m \angle APC = m \angle 1 + m \angle 2$ ❸→ $m \angle 1 + m \angle 2 = 180°$ ❹ ⎱
$\qquad\qquad\qquad\qquad\qquad\qquad\qquad\qquad m \angle 1 = 100°$ ⎰

$100° + m \angle 2 = 180°$ ❺→ $m \angle 2 = 80°$

Justifications

❶ If the sides of an angle form a straight line, then the angle is a straight angle with measure 180°.

❷ For any angle, the measure of the whole is equal to the sum of the measures of its non-overlapping parts.

❸ Substitution property

❹ Substitution property

❺ Subtraction property of equality

11. *Given:* $\angle 1$ and $\angle 2$ are complementary.
   $m \angle 1 = 75°$
   Prove: $m \angle 2 = 15°$

Statements

$\angle 1$ and $\angle 2$ are complementary. ❶→ $m \angle 1 + m \angle 2 = 90°$ ❷ ⎱
$\qquad\qquad\qquad\qquad\qquad\qquad\qquad\qquad m \angle 1 = 75°$ ⎰

$75° + m \angle 2 = 90°$ ❸→ $m \angle 2 = 15°$

Justifications

❶ Definition of complementary ∠
❷ Substitution property
❸ Subtraction property of equality

---

15. Proof forms may vary. A two-column proof is given.

Statements	Justifications
1. $\angle ABC$ is a straight angle.	1. Given
2. $m \angle ABC = 180°$	2. If the sides of an angle form a straight line, then the angle is a straight angle with measure 180°.
3. $m \angle ABF + m \angle FBE + m \angle EBD + m \angle DBC = m \angle ABC$	3. For any angle, the measure of the whole is equal to the sum of the measures of its non-overlapping parts.
4. $m \angle ABF + m \angle FBE + m \angle EBD + m \angle DBC = 180°$	4. Substitution property (Steps 2 and 3)
5. $m \angle ABF = m \angle FBE$; $m \angle EBD = m \angle DBC$	5. Given
6. $2(m \angle FBE) + 2(m \angle EBD) = 180°$	6. Substitution property (Steps 4 and 5)
7. $m \angle FBE + m \angle EBD = 90°$	7. Division property of equality
8. $m \angle FBE + m\angle EBD = m \angle FBD$	8. For any angle, the measure of the whole is equal to the sum of the measures of its non-overlapping parts.
9. $m \angle FBD = 90°$	9. Substitution property (Steps 7 and 8)
10. $\angle FBD$ is a right angle.	10. Definition of right angle

Page 414 Exercises and Problems

18. a. Answers may vary. An example is given. A two-column proof is shown.
b. *Given:* $\angle 1$ and $\angle 2$ are supplementary.
     $\angle 1$ and $\angle 3$ are vertical angles.
   Prove: $\angle 2$ and $\angle 3$ are supplementary.

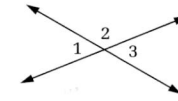

Statements	Justifications
1. $\angle 1$ and $\angle 2$ are supplementary.	1. Given
2. $m \angle 1 + m \angle 2 = 180°$	2. Definition of supplementary ∠
3. $\angle 1$ and $\angle 3$ are vertical angles.	3. Given
4. $m \angle 1 = m \angle 3$	4. Vertical ∠ are = in measure.
5. $m \angle 3 + m \angle 2 = 180°$	5. Substitution property (Steps 2 and 4)
6. $\angle 2$ and $\angle 3$ are supplementary.	6. Definition of supplementary ∠

Page 420 Exercises and Problems

13. *Given:* Lines l and m are parallel and are intersected by line t.

   Prove: $\angle 1$ and $\angle 2$ are supplementary.

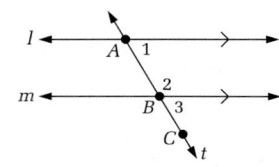

Statements	Justifications
1. $l \parallel m$	1. Given
2. $m \angle 3 = m \angle 1$	2. If two ∥ lines are intersected by a transversal, then corresponding ∠ are = in measure.
3. l, m, and t are lines.	3. Given
4. $m \angle ABC = 180°$	4. If the sides of an angle form a straight line, then the angle is a straight angle with measure 180°.
5. $m \angle 2 + m \angle 3 = m \angle ABC$	5. For any angle, the measure of the whole is equal to the sum of the measures of its non-overlapping parts.
6. $m \angle 2 + m \angle 3 = 180°$	6. Substitution property (Steps 4 and 5)
7. $m \angle 1 + m \angle 2 = 180°$	7. Substitution property (Steps 2 and 6)
8. $\angle 1$ and $\angle 2$ are supplementary.	8. Definition of supplementary angles

16.

Statements	Justifications
1. $\angle 1$ and $\angle 2$ are vertical $\angle$s.	1. Given
2. $m \angle 1 = m \angle 2$	2. Vertical $\angle$s are = in measure.
3. $\angle 1$ is supplementary to $\angle 2$.	3. Given
4. $m \angle 1 + m \angle 2 = 180°$	4. Definition of supplementary angles
5. $m \angle 1 + m \angle 1 = 180°$	5. Substitution property (Steps 2 and 4)
6. $2(m \angle 1) = 180°$	6. Combine like terms.
7. $m \angle 1 = 90°$	7. Division property of equality
8. $m \angle 2 = 90°$	8. Substitution property (Steps 2 and 7)
9. $\angle 1$ and $\angle 2$ are right angles.	9. Definition of right angles

17. Postulates are statements that are assumed to be true; definitions are biconditionals that give necessary and sufficient conditions for clarification; theorems are statements that are proved using previously proved theorems, definitions, and postulates.

21. a–c. Answers may vary. A two-column proof is given for each theorem.

a. *Given:* $9x - 10 = -1$
  Prove: $x = 1$

Statements	Justifications
1. $9x - 10 = -1$	1. Given
2. $9x = 9$	2. Addition property of equality
3. $x = 1$	3. Division property of equality

b. *Given:* $\angle V$ and $\angle W$ are supplementary.
      $m \angle V = 75°$

  Prove: $m \angle W = 105°$

Statements	Justifications
1. $\angle V$ and $\angle W$ are supplementary.	1. Given
2. $m \angle V + m \angle W = 180°$	2. Definition of supplementary $\angle$s
3. $m \angle V = 75°$	3. Given
4. $75° + m \angle W = 180°$	4. Substitution property (Steps 2 and 3)
5. $m \angle W = 105°$	5. Subtraction property of equality

c. *Given:* Lines l and k are parallel.
      Line n is a transversal.
  Prove: $m \angle 1 = m \angle 3$

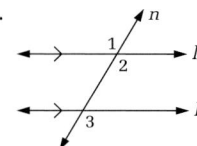

Statements	Justifications
1. $\angle 1$ and $\angle 2$ are vertical $\angle$s.	1. Definition of vertical $\angle$s
2. $m \angle 1 = m \angle 2$	2. Vertical $\angle$s are = in measure.
3. Lines l and m are parallel.	3. Given
4. $m \angle 2 = m \angle 3$	4. If two ‖ lines are intersected by a transversal, then corresponding $\angle$s are = in measure.
5. $m \angle 1 = m \angle 3$	5. Substitution property (Steps 2 and 4)

d. Answers may vary. An example is given. The two-column method is easiest to follow.

Unit 8

15. a. *Given:* Transversal t intersects lines k and l. $k \parallel l$, $t \perp l$
Prove: $t \perp k$
Statements
1. $k \parallel l$
2. $m \angle 1 = m \angle 2$

3. $t \perp l$
4. $m \angle 2 = 90°$
5. $m \angle 1 = 90°$
6. $t \perp k$
Justifications
1. Given
2. If two ‖ lines are intersected by a transversal, then corresponding $\angle$s are = in measure.
3. Given
4. Definition of perpendicular lines
5. Substitution property (Steps 2 and 4)
6. Definition of perpendicular lines
b. It is given that lines k and l are parallel lines. Therefore, $m \angle 1 = m \angle 2$ since if two ‖ lines are intersected by a transversal, then corresponding $\angle$s are = in measure. It is also given that line $t \perp l$, so $m \angle 2 = 90°$ by the definition of perpendicular lines. Substitute $m \angle 1$ for $m \angle 2$ in the equation $m \angle 2 = 90°$, and $m \angle 1 = 90°$. By definition of perpendicular lines, $t \perp k$.   **16.** The T-square can be considered a transversal to the left and right edges of the paper and the line drawn along the "other leg." Since both of these lines are perpendicular to the transversal, they are parallel to each other since Theorem 8.3 states if two lines are $\perp$ to the same transversal, then they are ‖.

21. *Given:* Quadrilateral $ABCD$; $\angle A$, $\angle B$, $\angle C$, and $\angle D$ are all right angles.

Prove: Quadrilateral $ABCD$ is a parallelogram.

Since $\angle A$ and $\angle B$ are right angles, $\overline{DA} \perp \overline{AB}$ and $\overline{CB} \perp \overline{AB}$. Then by Theorem 8.3, $\overline{AD} \parallel \overline{BC}$. Similarly, both $\angle A$ and $\angle D$ are right angles, so $\overline{CD} \perp \overline{DA}$ and $\overline{BA} \perp \overline{DA}$, then by Theorem 8.3, $\overline{DC} \parallel \overline{AB}$. Then, by definition, quadrilateral $ABCD$ is a parallelogram.

22. No; without the additional restriction that the quadrilateral is a parallelogram, at least three of the angles must be right angles to prove that the quadrilateral is a rectangle. Examples of quadrilaterals with one right angle and two right angles are given.

23. Answers may vary. An example is given. If two lines are intersected by a transversal and alternate exterior angles are equal in measure, then the lines are parallel.
Given: $m \angle 1 = m \angle 2$
Prove: $a \parallel b$
Statements

$\angle 1$ and $\angle 3$ are vertical $\angle$s.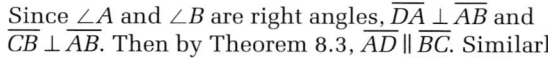

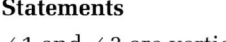
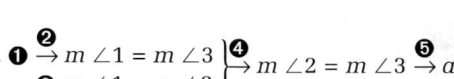

Justifications
❶ Definition of vertical angles
❷ Vertical $\angle$s are = in measure.
❸ Given
❹ Substitution property (Steps 2 and 3)
❺ If two lines are intersected by a transversal and corresponding $\angle$s are = in measure, then the lines are ‖.

24. $m \angle A = m \angle C = 105°$; $m \angle B = 75°$ **25.** False; counterexamples may vary. An example is given. A kite is a four-sided figure that is not a parallelogram.   **26.** True.   **27.** $x = 20$ **28. a.** Check that corresponding angles or alternate interior angles are equal in measure. Just one property needs to be checked, but it probably would be a good idea to use another property as verification.   **b.** The clips are parallel in any position.   **c.** Answers may vary. An example is given. The rulers are parallel, so pairs of alternate interior angles must be equal in measure.

Page 447 Exercises and Problems

34. *Given:* $\triangle ABC$ with exterior $\angle 4$
   Prove: $m\angle 4 = m\angle 1 + m\angle 2$

Statements

$m\angle BCD \overset{\mathbf{❶}}{=} 180°$ $\Big\vert\overset{\mathbf{❸}}{\rightarrow}$ $\quad m\angle 3 + m\angle 4 = 180°$ $\Big\vert\overset{\mathbf{❺}}{\rightarrow}$

$m\angle BCD \overset{\mathbf{❷}}{=} m\angle 3 + m\angle 4$ $\Big\vert$ $\quad m\angle 1 + m\angle 2 + m\angle 3 \overset{\mathbf{❹}}{=} 180°$ $\Big\vert$

$m\angle 3 + m\angle 4 = m\angle 1 + m\angle 2 + m\angle 3 \overset{\mathbf{❻}}{\rightarrow} m\angle 4 = m\angle 1 + m\angle 2$

Justifications

❶ If the sides of an angle form a straight line, then the angle is a straight angle with measure 180°.
❷ For any angle, the measure of the whole is equal to the sum of the measures of its non-overlapping parts.
❸ Substitution property (Steps 1 and 2)
❹ The sum of the measures of the $\angle\!s$ of a triangle is 180°.
❺ Substitution property (Steps 3 and 4)
❻ Subtraction property of equality

Page 477 Exercises and Problems

19. a.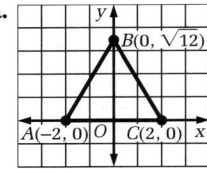
b. Using the distance formula gives $AB = 4$, $BC = 4$, and $AC = 4$. Since $AB = BC = AC = 4$, $\triangle ABC$ is equilateral. Then $\triangle ABC$ is equiangular as well because if a triangle is equilateral, then it is equiangular, with three 60° angles.

Page 480 Checkpoint

1. Summaries may vary. An example is given. I would determine which sides and/or angles I knew to be equal in measure and how they were related. If I had two sides and an included angle, I would use SAS. If I had two angles and an included side, I would use ASA. If the side was not included, I would use AAS. If I had three sides, I would use SSS.   **2.** The triangles are congruent by ASA, so $x = 7$, $y = 8$, and $z° = 50°$ **3.** $\triangle ABC$ and $\triangle EDF$; SSS   **4.** $\triangle GHI$ and $\triangle JKL$; SAS   **5.** $m\angle N = m\angle Q$, $m\angle O = m\angle R$, or $MN = PQ$
6. $\triangle STU$ is isosceles since $ST = TU$.
7. $m\angle A = m\angle C = 46°$; $m\angle B = 88°$

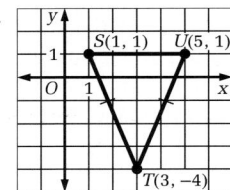

 Unit 9

Page 528 Exploration

1. a. The x-intercept is 0.
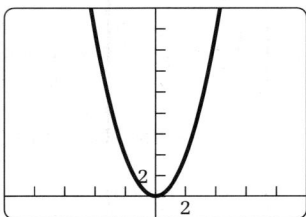

b. The x-intercept is -3.
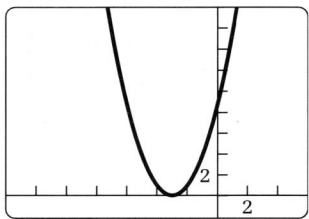

c. The x-intercepts are -3 and 1; The number of x-intercepts is the number of distinct factors.

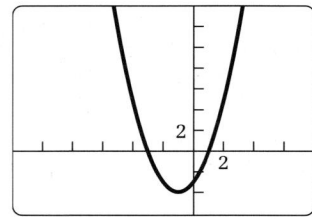

2. $y = x^3$
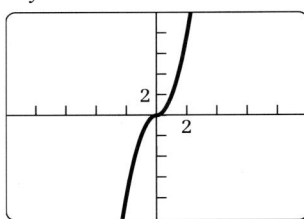

$y = (x + 2)^3$
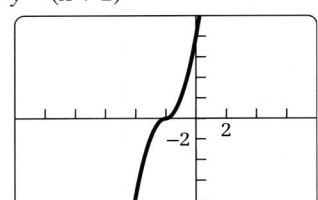

$y = (x - 3)(x + 1)^2$
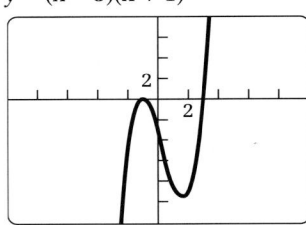

$y = (x - 3)^2(x + 1)$
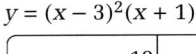
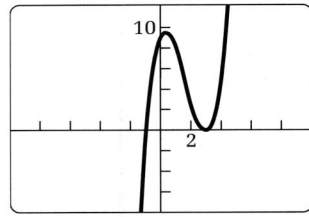

$y = x(x - 3)(x + 2)$
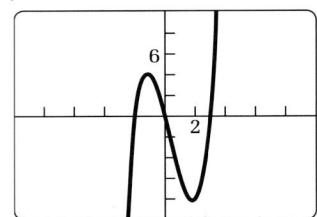

$y = (x + 2)(x - 1)(x - 4)$
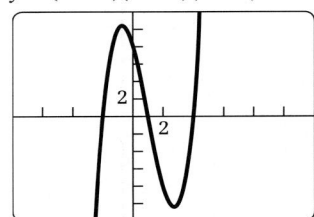

Function	x-intercepts	Number of x-intercepts
$y = x^3$	0	1
$y = (x + 2)^3$	-2	1
$y = (x - 3)(x + 1)^2$	$-1, 3$	2
$y = (x - 3)^2(x + 1)$	$-1, 3$	2
$y = x(x - 3)(x + 2)$	$0, 3, -2$	3
$y = (x + 2)(x - 1)(x - 4)$	$-2, 1, 4$	3

Page 534 and 535 Exercises and Problems

32. a. No linear function has three x-intercepts.   **b.** No quadratic function has three x-intercepts.
c. Yes. Example: $y = (x + 4)(x + 1)(x - 3)$
33. The degree of the function represents the maximum number of zeros possible, and the maximum number of x-intercepts.

34. 2   **35.** 3, 2   **36.** $\frac{1}{2}$, 3

37. parallelogram   **38.** squares

39. rhombus   **40.** 3, $-\frac{1}{2}$

41. $\dfrac{3 + \sqrt{3}i}{2}$, $\dfrac{3 - \sqrt{3}i}{2}$ **42.** $\dfrac{2}{3}$, $-\dfrac{5}{2}$

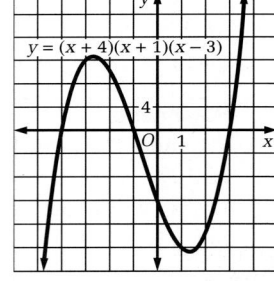

43. a.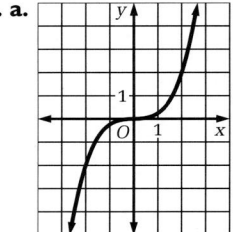
b. s and P must both be positive; there are limits to the wind's speed.   **c.** Answers may vary. Examples are given. The wind's speed must be greater than or equal to zero. Extremely high winds might damage the equipment. A reasonable upper limit might be $s < 75$ (hurricane-force winds). So $0 \le s < 75$ is a reasonable domain.
44. a. about 6.5 mi/h   **b.** about 2.7 mi/h   **c.** about 23.4 mi/h   **d.** about 36.3 mi/h

Page 539 Exercises and Problems

16. Answers may vary. An example is given. She entered $x^3 - 3x^2 + 3x$ on the Y= screen, then she pressed GRAPH to view the graph of the function. Rebecca found the x-intercept, 0.   **17. a.** $0 = 1000g^3 + 1000g^2 + 1000g - 3500$ **b.** about 1.1 **18. a.** about 30 **b.** about 165 or about 457 **19. a.** The number of dots on the base of the nth tetrahedron is equal to n plus the number of dots on the base of the $(n - 1)$th tetrahedron; 15 dots **b.** 35 dots **c.** $t = \left(\frac{1}{6}\right)5^3 + \left(\frac{1}{2}\right)5^2 + \left(\frac{1}{3}\right)5 = \frac{125}{6} + \frac{25}{2} + \frac{5}{3} = 35$ **d.** 100 is not a tetrahedral number.

Page 541 Exploration

4.

t	x	y	t	x	y
0	0.3	0	0.7	4.5	1.799
0.1	0.9	0.551	0.8	5.1	1.664
0.2	1.5	1.004	0.9	5.7	1.432
0.3	2.1	1.359	1.0	6.3	1.1
0.4	2.7	1.616	1.1	6.9	0.671
0.5	3.3	1.775	1.2	7.5	0.144
0.6	3.9	1.836			

Page 545 Exercises and Problems

10. a. 7 seconds **b.** about 5.3 seconds **c.** about 1.7 seconds; No, Bakham cannot catch the ball because it is about 2.8 yards to his left or right.

11. a.

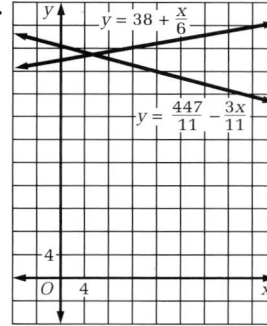

b. No. At (6, 39), Bakham has been running 6 s and the ball reaches this point in 5 s. Time is not indicated here. **c.** the point at which Bakham's path and the ball's path cross

12. Let t be the time in seconds after Heidi has begun her descent.
a. $y = 14,000 - 14t$ **b.** $x = 200t$ **c.**

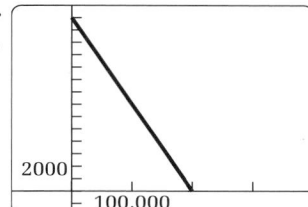

d. about 200,000 ft (about 38 mi)
e. $y = 14,000 - \frac{7x}{100}$

Unit 10

Page 563 Exercises and Problems

35–38. Sketches may vary. Examples are given.

35. a circle   **36.** a circle   **37.** a square   **38.** a square

        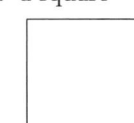

39. Answers may vary. An example is given. A sphere passing through Flatland into the space above would first appear as a point on Flatland, then as an infinite number of circles of increasing size until the diameter of the circle was equal in measure to the diameter of the sphere. Then the circles would become smaller and smaller until the

sphere appeared again as a point and, finally, disappeared. A cone, with its base parallel to Flatland, and entering Flatland with its vertex, would also first appear as a point. The cone would then appear as an infinite number of circles of increasing size until the diameter of the circle was equal in measure to the diameter of the base of the cone. At this point, the cone would disappear from Flatland. A cone could also appear as a series of triangles of increasing size if the altitude of the cone was parallel to Flatland or if the altitude of the cone formed an acute angle with Flatland as it passed through Flatland.

Page 564 Exercises and Problems

47. Drawings may vary. An example is given. Dashed lines show folds.   **48. a.** A twelve-ounce soft drink can is about $2\frac{1}{2}$ in. in diameter and about $4\frac{3}{4}$ in. high.   **b.** The case should be just over $4\frac{3}{4}$ in. high. It could have dimensions $2\frac{1}{2}$ in. by 60 in., 5 in. by 30 in., 7.5 in. by 20 in., or 10 in. by 15 in. Answers may vary.   **c.** The size most commonly used is 10 in. by 15 in. Answers may vary. For example, a box of cans that holds 6 rows of 4 cans is easier to carry than a box that holds 1 row of 24 cans.

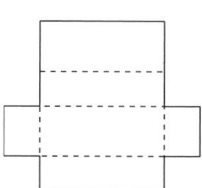

Page 570 Exercises and Problems

26.

Statements	Justifications
1. P is on the perpendicular bisector of $\overline{AB}$.	1. Given
2. $\triangle PCA$ and $\triangle PCB$ are right triangles.	2. Definitions of right $\triangle$s and perpendicular bisector
3. $PC = PC$	3. Reflexive
4. $AC = BC$	4. Definition of a bisector
5. $\triangle PCA$ is congruent to $\triangle PCB$.	5. SAS
6. $PA = PB$	6. CPCTE

Page 575 Exercises and Problems

16. a.

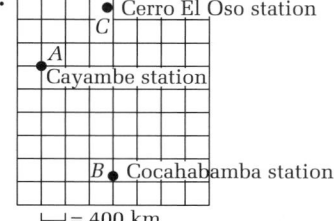

b–d.

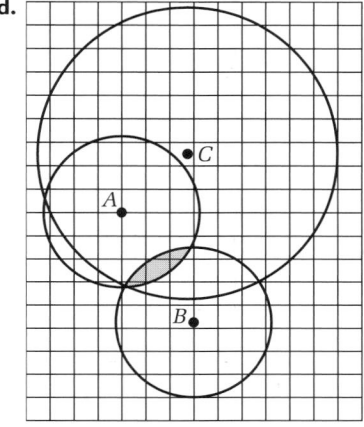

Descriptions may vary. The epicenter is in the shaded region, approximately 1000 km south and 600 km east of Cayambe station in Ecuador.

A-13

17. a.

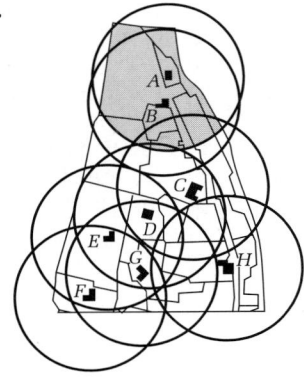

b.

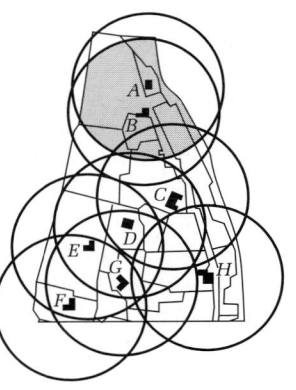

c. Answers may vary. The shaded area at the top of the map represents the area where criers from mosques A, B, and C can be heard. The shaded area at the bottom of the map represents the area where criers from mosques E, F, and G can be heard.

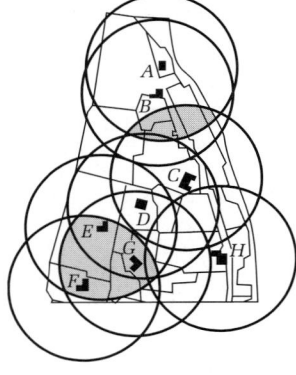

d.

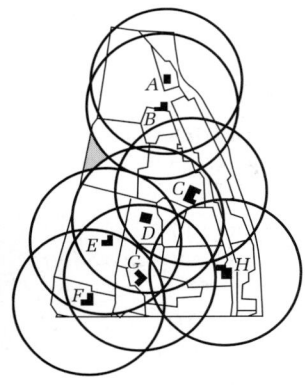